THE COMPLETE
garden flower book

THE COMPLETE
garden flower book

How to grow over 600 of the best performing varieties

bay books

CONTENTS

Perennials 6

Growing perennials 8

A-Z perennials 22

Roses 112

Growing roses 114

Annuals .118

Growing annuals 120

A-Z annuals 128

Bulbs 218

Growing bulbs 220

A-Z bulbs 236

Clematis .324

Growing clematis 326

Shrubs 330

Growing shrubs 332

A-Z shrubs 338

Herbs 420

Growing herbs 422

A-Z herbs 426

Cacti 462

Growing cacti 464

A-Z cacti 472

Succulents 486

Growing succulents 488

A-Z succulents 494

Bromeliads 548

Growing bromeliads 550

A-Z bromeliads 556

Hedges 566

Growing hedges 568

A-Z hedges 578

Groundcover 604

A-Z groundcover 611

Palms 648

Growing palms 650

A-Z palms 658

Climbers 670

Growing climbers 672

A-Z climbers 692

Cottage Gardens 724

Creating a cottage garden 726

Creating a fragrant garden 742

Patio gardens 746

Balcony gardens 750

Cottage containers 752

Cut flowers 756

Plants for cutting 759

Flower crafts 760

Drying flowers 762

Bath bags 765

Pot pourris 766

Plants for pots 770

Hanging baskets 784

Windowboxes 790

Index 796

Climate map 800

Growing
Perennials

GROWING PERENNIALS

Many of the loveliest and best-loved flowering plants are perennials. Like annuals, perennials provide a colorful display, but they have the advantage that they don't need to be changed at least twice a year. Perennials are easy-care plants which have a major place in low-maintenance gardens.

Perennials remain alive for a number of years, unlike annuals which usually last only one season, and biennials which grow and flower through a second season or year. Perennials form a variable group in terms of their size and foliage, flower shape, style, and color. In fact, there is a perennial to suit almost every climate, aspect, and soil, and some can even be grown in containers. Perennials can also be planted among shrubs, to form a background for bulbs or annuals, or in their own separate areas. Perennial borders make lively, exciting features.

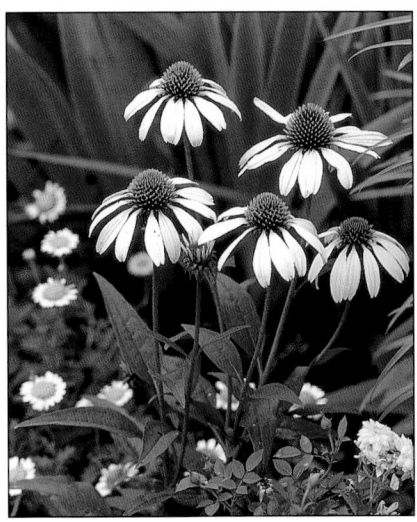

ABOVE: The white form of the purple coneflower showing its attractive, recurved petals.

LEFT: A tender, bright pink argyranthemum, and scabious, in the foreground add perennial interest to this colorful, mixed border featuring soft hues offset by green.

PERENNIALS COMBINE with annuals to form a free-flowing, rich, colorful border, a highlight of mid-summer in this gorgeous cottage garden. A pink shrub rose is flanked by two varieties of aster, while deep blue delphiniums add scale and height at the back.

EVERGREEN OR HERBACEOUS?

Some perennials are evergreen but many are herbaceous. Most herbaceous perennials grow rapidly during spring and summer to flower during the summer and the fall. After flowering they gradually die back to the crown or fleshy roots, and they remain dormant during cold winters. Since most of the hardy herbaceous perennials come from climates with very severe, cold winters, they die down naturally in the fall. In warmer areas, where they do not become completely dormant and some growth continues year round, the plants do not live as long. However, it is simple to renew these perennials as division is easy, and most increase rapidly. In time, a few can even become invasive.

PLANTING PERENNIALS

Soil preparation

Because perennials are long-term plants and because they are close planted, good soil preparation is essential. Although some perennials, such as astilbes and hostas, enjoy damp soil, many prefer well-drained conditions. If you are planting any of the latter group, check your drainage before planting. Dig some holes in the bed, fill them with water and see how long

PERENNIALS FOR SUN AND SHADE

SUNNY BORDERS

- Agapanthus
- Delphinium
- Diascia
- Eryngium
- Gypsophila
- Helenium

- Hemerocallis
- Miscanthus
- Oenothera
- Papaver
- Sedum
- Stachys

SHADY BORDERS

- *Alchemilla mollis*
- Aquilegia
- Bergenia
- Candelabra primula
- Digitalis
- Epimedium

- *Gunnera manicata*
- Helleborus
- Hosta
- Polygonatum
- Primula
- Pulmonaria
- Rodgersia (dappled)

PURE WHITE shasta daisies light up the summer garden, putting on a strong display from early summer to early fall.

it takes to drain away. If there is still water in the holes 12 hours later, you will need to improve the drainage by installing a system of sub-soil drains.

If the soil is very heavy clay, which remains wet but not waterlogged for a long time, you should dig in some gypsum, about 10.5oz per sq yd. Digging in large quantities of decayed manure or compost a few weeks before planting will also improve clay soils, and it is a must in sandy soils that have poor moisture and nutrient retention.

Thorough weeding of the area is essential, too, as it is difficult to remove weeds in densely planted beds. Remove the weeds you can see, dig or fork over the area again, water, and wait for the next lot of weeds to emerge. You may need to repeat this step if the area has been neglected for any length of time. Hand weeding or spraying with glyphosate should eliminate most weeds, but you will need to be persistent to control oxalis, bindweed and ground elder. This sounds like a lot of work when you are eager to plant out your garden, but it will be worth the wait and the effort in the long run.

Planting perennials from containers

Garden centers and nurseries will stock some perennials, especially when they are in flower. These can be planted in your yard like any other container-grown plant. When the plant is removed from its pot, loosen the rootball a little so that the roots can extend into the surrounding soil. It is essential that the planting hole is about twice the width of the container and approximately the same depth. The soil level around the plant should be exactly the same as it was in the container. Give a thorough soaking after planting. Also apply a deep mulch to the soil around the plant.

Planting bare-rooted perennials

There are also nurseries that specialize in perennials. These nurseries usually advertise in popular gardening magazines, have detailed catalogs with thorough plant descriptions, and sell by mail-order. Plants are delivered during their dormant season, which for the majority is from late fall through the

A HIGH STONE WALL marks the boundary of this meadow garden filled with golden fern-leaf yarrow, daisies, and purple loosestrife.

THESE GOLDEN-YELLOW, green-tipped spikes of a red hot poker cultivar provide a strong focus in this pastel border.

THE TALL, VERTICAL CLUMP of pink dahlias and the midnight blue spires of delphinium provide a colorful mix. They form a bright imaginative backdrop for the rich mix of annuals and perennials edging this beautiful garden bed, clearly illustrating the versatility of perennials.

winter. Plants are mailed, bare-rooted, or in small pots, having been carefully packed and labelled. On arrival, they should be planted at once. However, if the ground is frozen, or you are not ready to plant them, either unpack and water them (if necessary), and store in a bright, cool, frost-free place, or "heel in" as a temporary measure. To do this, dig a trench large enough to contain the plant roots in a sheltered part of your yard. Finally, lay the plants on their sides, cover the roots with soil, and lightly water them.

When planting bare-rooted plants, again make sure the hole is at least twice the width of the rootball, and deep enough to take the roots without kinking them. If some roots are very long, trim them cleanly with pruning shears. Hold the plant in the hole in one hand and fill the hole, poking soil between the roots. Sometimes you can make a slight mound in the center of the hole so that the roots can be spread out over it, keeping the crown high. Make sure the crown of the plant is not buried: if necessary, lift the plant and push more soil in around the roots.

Water thoroughly immediately after planting if the soil is dry, but until the plants have developed plenty of shoot growth they will not require too much watering. The area around the plants should be mulched. If the soil has been well prepared, feeding at this time is not necessary but you may give a very light sprinkling of general fertilizer if you wish.

CARE OF PERENNIALS

Perennial plantings in areas that have been well prepared need little maintenance. You must deadhead through the flowering season to prolong blooming, and cut back or tidy up after flowering. Established perennials will only need watering in prolonged dry spells, and feeding in spring as growth commences. When they become too crowded they are divided between fall and late winter, or early spring. This may be only necessary every three or four years. For details, see plant entries in the A-Z section.

Watering
Never give perennials a light watering because it will encourage surface rooting at the expense of a deep, root system. The plants need big, strong roots to sustain several years of growth, and benefit most from being given a deep, regular watering. On sandy soils choose such perennials as sedum, oenothera, and dianthus that tolerate dry conditions. A deep mulch around the plants will help conserve moisture, as will adding quantities of organic matter to the soil as the mulch breaks down.

Feeding
Perennials should not need a lot of feeding. Apply an all-purpose plant food as growth begins; if the soil has been well prepared this should be enough for the whole growing season. If your soil is very poor though, you may like to use a slow-release granular fertilizer to feed plants through the growing season, or to apply a second helping of plant food as the flower buds start to appear. A mulch of decayed manure or compost around the plants serves two functions. It improves the soil condition, and also supplies small amounts of nutrients to the plants.

Keep the entire area free of weeds until the plants cover the ground. This will ensure that any fertilizer you apply will feed your perennials and not any unwanted weeds. Avoid high nitrogen fertilizers as they tend to promote leaf growth at the expense of flowers. Rose food is ideal.

THE PENSTEMONS AND SALVIAS in the foreground make a gorgeous foil for the stiff, upright growth of Russell lupins.

Cutting flowers and deadheading
A number of perennials make very good cut flowers, and many are grown for the cut flower trade. The various daisies, chrysanthemums, Russell lupins, delphiniums, pinks, and Peruvian lilies are just a few of the perennials that are commercially grown. Regularly picking the flowers will help to ensure a long succession of bloom. If the flowers are not removed they will mature, most setting seed so that the flowering cycle will finish abruptly as the plant decides its reproductive work is over. If you do not want to take cut flowers, remember to deadhead regularly.

Exceptions to this rule are plants such as cardoon and globe thistle that have decorative seedheads. Some gardeners prefer to leave them on the plant. Many remain attractive even when dry, and they can add interest to the garden in late fall and winter, especially when covered in frost or snow.

AFTER FLOWERING

After the flowering season is over, perennials can be cut back almost to the ground. If you live in an area prone to heavy frosts, some of the more tender perennials will then need to have the crown of the plant covered. A thick layer of straw, or fall leaves, held in place by a few sticks in windy sites, will protect them from winter damage.

Alternatively, you could leave some stems sticking out of the ground to create extra, interesting shapes over winter. Grasses are especially invaluable. They are at their best when covered with frost or snow, or when helping to cast a web of shadows from the low winter sun. The birds also benefit from the seedheads.

THE BRIGHT, HOT COLORS of orange and yellow feature in this very effective planting, which shows up so impressively against the cool green of the lawn. The large clump of red hot pokers and a generous drift of deep apricot-orange geum are especially notable.

INCREASING YOUR STOCK OF PERENNIALS

Division

Clumps of perennials are divided either when they become congested, or when you want to plant sections elsewhere in the garden. In general, most perennials need dividing about every three or four years, possibly longer. Division is done after flowering or while the plants are dormant.

If you want some pieces to plant elsewhere you can sever a section with a knife, or put a spade through the clump, and lift away what you want. This might lose some of the peripheral pieces but the process is quick and simple. Otherwise, dig up the whole clump, shake off the excess soil, and pull the clump apart or cut it into sections. Replant the sections immediately, trimming off very long roots. Remember that the outer growths are the youngest to be saved, and that the center of the plant may have died, in which case it can be discarded. You may need to divide very large, heavy clumps by pushing two garden forks, back to back, into the center to prize it apart. A sharp spade may also be used but this needs a lot of force and will, of course, result in the loss of some sections of plant. This may not be of any consequence with vigorous perennials.

If you are unable to replant at once or have pieces to give away, wrap them in damp newspaper or hessian and keep in a shaded, sheltered spot, giving time to decide where to plant them. "Heeling in," as described on the previous page, is another way to store plants temporarily, and they are less likely to dry out. They can, of course, be potted up in a good quality potting mix.

Taking cuttings

Many perennial plants can be grown from cuttings and a number, including geraniums and diascias, are among the easiest plants to strike. Others that will grow readily from cuttings include penstemons and sedums.

Make a mix of two or three parts of coarse sand and one of peat, or peat substitute compost. Put the prepared mix in clean pots, preferably no larger than 4in across. A pot of this size will take a good number of cuttings. They should not be forced to sit in soil that remains wet when watered, which would rot the roots.

Take tip cuttings of unflowered shoots, no more than 2–4in long. Cut, do not tear, pieces from the parent plant. Take the cuttings early in the morning, placing the pieces in a clean plastic bag, and quickly put in a cool, shady place. Trim the cuttings by removing the lower leaves, allowing just a very few to remain on top. Cleanly cut the base of the cutting below a node (leaf junction). Another aid to rooting is to "wound" the cutting by carefully scraping about ³/₈in of the outer bark or stem cover at the base of the stem. Hormone rooting powders can also be used but are not usually necessary with most perennials.

Use a clean stick or pencil to make a hole in the compost. Put the cutting in the hole and carefully firm the surrounding mix. Once all your cuttings are in the pot you can water them thoroughly and put the pot in a warm, sheltered place out of direct sun. In warm months geraniums and daisies may be well rooted after three weeks, but many plants can take a considerable time. Check regularly to see if the cuttings need water but do not keep them wet or, as explained they will rot.

DIVIDING A CLUMP

Step 1: Use a garden fork to lift the whole perennial clump from the soil.

Step 2: Separate matted clumps by inserting two garden forks, back to back, firmly into the clump.

Step 3: First press the fork handles together, and then force them apart to split the clump in two. Repeat until the clumps are the size you want.

Step 4: Use pruning shears to cut off dead, rotten or damaged roots. The clumps will now be ready for replanting.

STRIKING A CUTTING

Step 1: Take a cutting just below a leaf node or joint. Use a sharp knife or pruning shears so that the cutting is not bruised. Trim it if necessary.

Step 2: Make a hole in the compost with your finger and insert the cutting into it. Firm the soil gently around it. If you are placing more than one cutting in the pot, plant them around the edge, giving them plenty of space.

Step 3: Water the cuttings in well, but take care not to dislodge them. Make sure the water is draining away well as the cuttings will rot if the soil remains wet.

Step 4: To make a humid atmosphere and keep the soil and cuttings moist, make a frame of sticks or wire tall enough to cover the cuttings. Place a polythene bag over the frame, and stand the pot out of direct sunlight.

A ROMANTIC GARDEN PATH is bordered by old-fashioned favorites, including perennial daisies and scented pinks.

Taking root cuttings

A number of plants, including perennials such as sea lavender, romneya, and perennial phlox, can be grown from root cuttings. As the plant will be disturbed when the cuttings are taken, this task is best done in winter.

• Remove the soil from around the base of the plant until you reach the roots. Trace them back until they are $\frac{1}{8}$–$\frac{3}{16}$in thick, and cut off some cleanly with a sharp knife or pruning shears. Immediately place them in a plastic bag so they do not dry out.

• Wash the soil from the roots and cut them into 1–2in lengths. If you intend to plant them vertically you will need to know which way is up; cut all the tops straight across and the bottoms at an angle.

• Place the cuttings vertically in a container, or lay them in horizontally and cover with about $\frac{3}{16}$in of John Innes No.1. Water thoroughly and check regularly to see whether further watering is needed.

• Once good shoots have appeared, your new plants can be potted up individually into small pots or planted into the ground. It is important to keep the cuttings moist, but if you saturate the compost the roots will rot.

WHAT CAN GO WRONG?

Perennials can be attacked by a number of insect pests and diseases, and problems that occur on specific plants will be discussed in the individual plant entries. Slugs and snails are among the worst pests for herbaceous perennials since they can destroy newly emerging growth as it appears in spring. If each successive burst of leaves is destroyed, the plant will eventually give up. You must search for and destroy these pests, perhaps picking them off by hand, or using bait or beer traps.

Overwatering or poorly drained heavy soils can also damage or kill perennials, especially if they are too wet during their dormant period when there is no foliage to transpire moisture from the plant. Waterlogged soils also provide ideal conditions for the growth and spread of various soil-borne, root-rotting fungi. A few plants, such as astilbe and hosta, actually enjoy damp or boggy ground, but most enjoy conditions with good drainage.

Yellow leaves

• Plants may have been overwatered or they may be too dry. You are actually more likely to overwater a perennial in a pot than in a border. They may also need feeding if this has not been done for some time. Try a light application of fertilizer; in warm weather there should be an improvement within two to three weeks. Toward the end of the growing season you can expect to see some leaves yellowing as they finish their useful life. Do not worry if a few leaves, especially down towards the ground, become brown or yellow during the active spring period.

Curled or distorted leaves

• Keep a regular check against aphids. They can be a terrible problem. They are small, sap-sucking insects that may be black, brown, green, or clear. They cluster thickly on the new growth of plants, sucking out the sap. This may cause curling or distortion of leaves, and flowers may fail to open if the sap has been sucked from the buds or they, too,

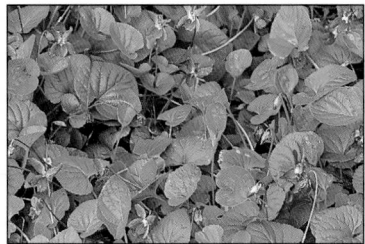

A HEALTHY display of violets.

may be distorted. Close inspection usually reveals these tiny insects; they can be squashed and wiped off the stems, hosed off or sprayed with insecticidal soap or pyrethrum-based sprays. Aphids need to be controlled as they also transmit virus diseases from plant to plant.

Silvery mottling on foliage

• Silver markings or discoloration of foliage may be the first sign of thrip attack. These tiny insects attack plant tissue and suck the sap. Unlike most sap-sucking insects they attack the top, not the under leaf. There are several different types that cause plant damage. They are readily recognizable, usually having black bodies and wings edged with hairs. Apart from the physical damage, some thrips are also responsible for transmitting virus diseases from plant to plant. Since many thrips use weeds as hosts it is important to keep them out of your beds and borders. If thrips are causing damage, make sure that the plants are not stressed through lack of water. When spraying, use an appropriate contact or systemic insecticide.

Curled and browned flowers

• Check plants for thrips because they can attack pale-colored flowers. For their control, see "Silvery mottling on foliage."

TAKING ROOT CUTTINGS

Step 1: To take root cuttings from most perennials, trace the roots back and cut out a section some ⅛–³⁄₁₆in thick.

Step 2: Wash any soil from the roots and cut them into sections 1–2in long. Mark the top of each so you know which way up to plant them.

Step 3: Place the root cuttings vertically in a container, making sure that they are the right way up. Water them in thoroughly.

Alternatively, if plants have thin roots, take cuttings in the same way but lay them horizontally and cover with a thin layer of compost.

Holes in leaves or on leaf edges
• If your plants have chewed edges or large areas of leaf missing, check for snails. They are the most likely culprits. Pick the snails off and destroy them, or use a bait if you do not have a pet.
• If there is no sign of snails, start looking for caterpillars. Chewing insects such as caterpillars can do a great deal of damage in quite a short time because they can be such voracious feeders. They can be well camouflaged, lying along leaf margins or hiding under leaves. Try first to find and destroy them, but if the damage continues, dust the plants with derris.

Mottled leaves
• Leaf mottling may be the result of mite damage. Mites are not true insects, having eight legs like other members of the arachnid family. Mites are sap suckers, and foliage attacked by mites appears mottled and discolored. With the aid of a magnifying glass the tiny creatures and their clear circular eggs can sometimes be seen on the underside of leaves. If severe mite attacks go unnoticed initially, there may be fine webbing on the underside of foliage too. Sometimes with light attacks hosing under the leaves every two to three days is enough to reduce their population to an acceptable, non-

damaging level. Mites are much worse in warm, dry weather or on plants that may be sheltered by the overhanging eaves of a house. Make sure that plants are well watered and well nourished. If mite numbers do reach unacceptable levels, clearly getting out of hand, you may need to spray with an appropriate insecticide. Many general, broad spectrum insecticides are useless against mites.

Gray/white powder on leaves
• This is probably caused by the common fungal disease, powdery mildew. In humid areas this disease is a constant problem. For plants that are very susceptible to powdery mildew, much work is being done to breed plant-resistant varieties. Meanwhile, it may be necessary to spray with a fungicide such as carbendazim or copper oxychloride or, alternatively, you can dust the plants with sulfur. If you have any

A VIBRANT show of argyranthemums.

kind of problem with powdery mildew, avoid watering the plants late in the day so that you do not increase the humidity around them overnight.

Black or dark spots on leaves
• There are many strains of fungal leaf spots that can attack a wide range of plants. If only a few leaves are affected, remove and destroy them. Avoid watering late in the day and, where possible, avoid splashing the foliage which will spread the fungal spores. Many fungal leaf spots respond well to simple fungicides such as copper oxychloride, but there are other effective fungicides available to the home gardener.

Yellow spots on top of leaves
• Yellow spots on the upper side of leaves that have blisters, or pustules on the underside, are likely to be some form of rust. There is an enormous number of rust strains, and they can attack a wide range of plants and perennials, including chrysanthemums. It is a good idea to remove the worst affected leaves immediately, and to avoid overhead watering which quickly splashes the spores around, increasing contamination. Copper oxychloride will control some rusts, though you may find you need to use a more specific fungicide.

PLANNING A PERENNIAL GARDEN

Many perennials have a long flowering period, and well-planned beds of perennials can display a succession of flowers over many months. This does, however, take a good deal of planning and usually some trial and error.

If you are planting a large area, it's best to design it on paper first, so that you can place the tallest plants at the back or in the center of the bed, also giving you time to devise your color scheme. You can experiment by using a variety of plants, all with flowers in one color or shades of one color, or you may opt for a planting of bright contrasts. Whatever scheme you choose, allow for plenty of plants to create a full, rich scene. A well-planted perennial border or garden is close-planted, so that every bit of soil is covered, providing foliage and floral interest throughout the season.

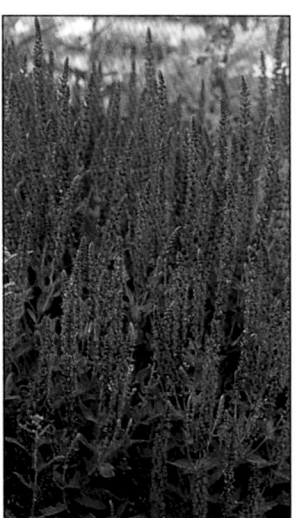

ABOVE: These rich purple spikes belong to the spectacular Salvia "Ostfriesland," *a cultivar of* Salvia nemorosa.

LEFT: True perennials, such as purple Liatris spicata, *and the yellow daisies of* Coreopsis verticillata, *mix well with annual red strawflowers and* Dahlia "Bishop of Llandaff."

THE LUSH GREEN SCENE, composed of hostas, candelabra primulas, and other shade-tolerant perennials, in a fern-filled woodland garden on the mild west coast of Scotland. Such a scene can easily be reduced and modified for the borders in a shaded city yard.

USING PERENNIALS

Perennials are among the most versatile of plants, and the vast majority of gardeners use them in conjunction with permanent plantings of shrubs, annuals, and bulbs. They are plants that require far less work and maintenance than annuals, while still giving a great deal of seasonal color and interest. In fact many low-growing perennials, such as penstemon, lamb's ears, pinks, and bergenia, make excellent border plantings, while taller growers, such as phlox and *Acanthus mollis*, can be planted among shrubs. Long-flowering plants, such as achillea and corydalis, can be used to give color between seasonal annual displays. They also give interest to a garden bed where bulbs have finished flowering and are in the process of dying down.

PERENNIAL BORDERS

Traditionally, perennials have often been close planted in a border. To get an idea of how a well-grown perennial border should look, visit the great public gardens. Gardeners have been refining the art of perennial borders for a very long time, and both first-time and experienced gardeners will find plenty of new, imaginative ideas in these schemes. Specialist nurseries often have special exhibit beds where you can also see how well various perennials combine.

FORMAL GARDENS

It is difficult for a perennial garden to look really formal, but many of the best perennial schemes have been informally planted within a formal framework. Some are enclosed within walls, while many are contained within low, formally trimmed hedges. The garden beds are laid out in strict geometric style, resembling an ornate piece of embroidery when viewed from above, their angular shapes defined by tightly pruned hedges, often of box or lavender. Sometimes the garden beds are also defined by close-mown paths of grass.

Probably the closest one can get to a formal perennial scheme is by creating a mirror-planting effect. Each part of the design mirrors the next, and the sections are divided by paths of grass, brick, gravel, or stone. For a mirror planting to be successful, the whole of the area must be in full sunlight, otherwise there is absolutely no chance of growth rates and flowering times being the same, or as near as one can get to that, given that you are dealing with living plant material.

PLANT ARRANGEMENT

Perennials come in many shapes and sizes, which is a great advantage when planning a garden. If your perennial garden is to be sited against a picket or wall you might decide to place the tallest growers at the back. This both forms a backbone and gives you the space to stand back and fully appreciate them. So, for example, the long tall spears of delphiniums generally stand behind their lower-growing neighbors. If you are designing an island bed, the tall plants are traditionally placed in the center for a formal effect, or slightly off-center so it does not look quite so inflexibly schematic. Smaller plants radiate out, down toward the front of the border, giving a graduated, tiered effect. But such arrangements are not strictly necessary. You might prefer, instead, to give a more informal look by gently mixing heights, creating undulations. When doing this, the most important point to remember is that no plant should be hidden by its neighbor, or cast in total shade, and that all should be visible from some vantage point so that you can appreciate their color and shape.

A number of plants, such as mulleins and red hot pokers, give very strong vertical accents that contrast well with lower, more variably shaped plants. And striking foliage plants, such as cardoon and *Melianthus major*, are grown more for their strong structural shape than for their flowers. (Note that the latter is tender for the first two years, but once it has a shrubby base it can be left outside all-year around in milder areas, provided it is given some frost protection.) These big plants must be sited carefully and probably not used to excess. A contrast in leaf color, shape, and texture will also add considerable interest to the perennial garden. If you have the luxury of being able to create a very large or long perennial border, you will need to think about repeating some of the shapes and colors to tie the planting together. The other great advantage of growing perennials is that you can move them around when they are dormant, or semi-dormant, if you are not totally satisfied with their appearance or performance. They allow you to modify the design.

Everyone would love to have a yard that is in full flower for months at a time. Planning to ensure a succession of blooms over many months is the hard part of designing a garden. Even if you consult the best reference books by the best writers, reliable local nurseries, and experienced friends, you will find that plants behave differently in different situations; in the end, what counts is personal experience. Prior research is essential, providing vital guidance, and it is worth walking around your neighborhood to see exactly which plants are being grown successfully.

USING COLOR

Color is, of course, a most important consideration. If you are making a large perennial garden it is a good idea to put your planting suggestions on paper, even using colored pencils or paints to help you see how the colors work together. You do not need to be an artist—rough shapes or blobs of color will do. You would not want or expect to have all the plants in flower at the one time, but you need to think about overlapping flowering times.

If you want a cool-looking yard you could restrict yourself to white, blue, cream, or pale pink flowers, with some silver foliage plants as accents. Red, yellow, and orange flowering plants will give you a hot and vibrant look. Sometimes the addition of an area of very strong color lifts the yard out of the ordinary. Some very famous long perennial borders cover a wide color range, starting with very soft pastel colors, ending with strong, hot colors. Another idea is to position clumps of the same plant at intervals along a border, as the repetition will add to the effect of the design. Even if you have only a small space to work with, you will find the repetition gives more form to the garden.

BLUE LUPINS and white poppies provide a cool contrast with the bright reds and yellows in the extensive borders behind.

PERENNIALS FOR ALL SEASONS

At every season of the year there is some perennial plant in flower. Winter brings the delicate and subtle beauty of the winter or Lenten rose (*Helleborus* spp.), and also bergenia in mild areas. Spring brings a succession of flowers in both mild and cold districts. Columbines, armeria, Solomon's seal, candelabra primula, geum, pinks, and heuchera are just a few of the beautiful spring-flowering perennials. Summer brings bergamot, achillea, platycodon, and rudbeckias, some of which flower well into the fall. Fall perennials include chrysanthemums, favored for their garden display and cut flowers, while red hot pokers, sedum, and asters provide color and interest at a time when annuals are either being pulled out or planted for the next season. These fall-flowering perennials, along with some fall-flowering bulbs such as colchicums and nerines, will carry your yard beautifully into winter.

Perennials also generally combine well with spring bulbs. While the perennials are still dormant, or are just beginning to put on new growth, the bulbs produce flowers, providing a combination of foliage and blooms. Then, when the bulbs have finished performing and the foliage is beginning to look untidy and start dying, the perennials begin to take over, becoming the dominant garden feature.

ACANTHUS MOLLIS
Bear's breeches

LITTLE FLOWERS in purple and white open along tall spikes above the foliage.

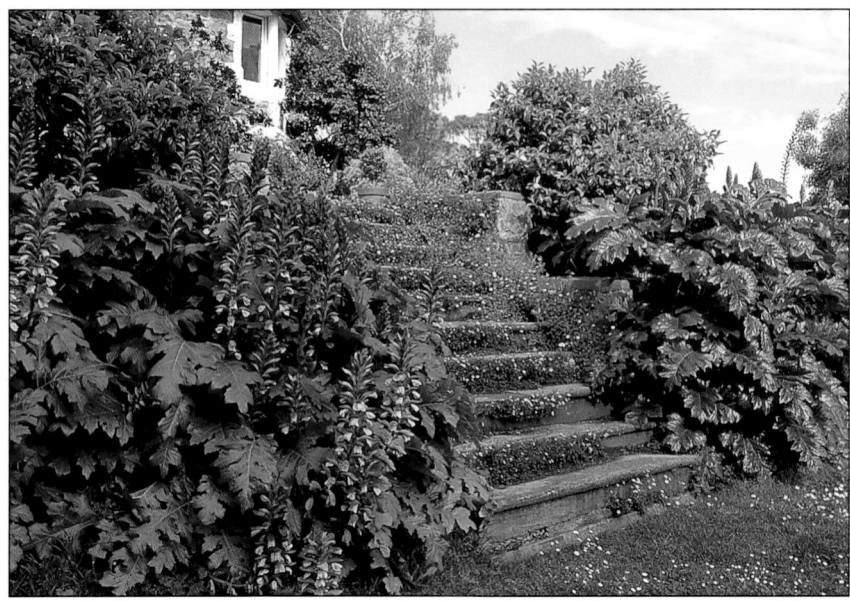

THE BEAR'S BREECHES in this Scottish garden are thriving in the open. The masses of handsome foliage suit a large yard where you can stand back and see the plants in perspective.

FEATURES

HERBACEOUS

Also known as bear's breeches, this handsome foliage plant grows from 28 to 39in high, and can make a clump close to 39in wide. The dark, glossy leaves provided the inspiration and model for the decoration on Corinthian columns. This striking feature plant is at its best when mass-planted, although one generous clump can be extremely effective in quite a small area. It enjoys full sunlight, but also tolerates shade. The stiff flower spikes of purple-and-white flowers appear among the foliage from the spring into summer. It can be quite a vigorous grower, although it dies back after flowering. It can multiply quickly once established, but is rarely troublesome.

ACANTHUS AT A GLANCE

A. mollis is a vigorous Mediterranean perennial liking dry, stoney ground. Hardy to 5°F (zone 7), with bold, shapely foliage.

Jan	/	Recommended Varieties
Feb	sow 🌱	
Mar	divide ✋	*Acanthus mollis* "Fielding Gold"
Apr	transplant ✋	*A.m.* "Hollard's Gold"
May	flowering 🌸	*A.m.* Latifolius Group
Jun	flowering 🌸	
July	/	Companion Plants
Aug	/	*Bergenia* x "Ballawley"
Sept	/	Forsythia
Oct	divide 🌱	Gypsophila
Nov	/	*Syringa vulgaris*
Dec	/	

CONDITIONS

Aspect It flowers best in full sun, but also grows in light shade.

Site Needs well-drained soil that contains plenty of organic matter to aid water retention. Give plants a deep layer of mulch with compost in the spring, and then a second application in mid-summer, if necessary.

GROWING METHOD

Propagation Grows from seed sown in spring, or divide clumps in the spring or fall. Plant new divisions 12–16in apart. Young plants must be given ample water in dry weather during the spring and summer. After flowering, cut back on the watering.

Feeding Apply a complete plant food as growth starts during the spring.

Problems Since slugs and snails can cause a lot of damage to young growth, badly disfiguring it, take precautions. No other problems are known.

FLOWERING

Season The tall spikes of purple-and-white flowers appear in late spring and summer.

Cutting It is possible to use this as a cut flower; the dried spikes make good indoor decoration.

AFTER FLOWERING

Requirements Protect young plants with straw over winter. Cut off the flowering stems once faded.

ACHILLEA
Yarrow

LONG-FLOWERING and not as invasive as the species, the new hybrid achilleas will give great pleasure for months.

ACHILLEA IS ALSO KNOWN as soldier's woundwort, nosebleed, and sanguinary, which reflects its value in herbal medicine.

FEATURES

HERBACEOUS

Yarrow are vigorous perennials offering heights from 2in to 4ft. The species has flattish heads of white flowers and feathery foliage, but cultivars have flowers in a lovely range of shades, including yellow, pink, apricot, and crimson. Flowers are long-lasting. Yarrow is quick and easy to establish, and may need to be controlled; however, the runners are quite easy to pull out. Some of the cultivars are less invasive than the species.
A. filipendulina has flat heads of bright yellow flowers that last all summer. Selected forms have deep or pale yellow blooms. Best planted in large drifts, yarrow is ideal for the back of borders or among annuals.

ACHILLEA AT A GLANCE

Mainly deciduous perennials grown for their attractive, daisy-like summer and fall flowers. Hardy to 5°F (zone 7).

Jan	/	Recommended Varieties
Feb	sow	*Achillea* "Coronation Gold"
Mar	sow	*Achillea filipendulina*
Apr	transplant	"Cloth of Gold"
May	divide	*A. f.* "Gold Plate"
Jun	flowering	*A.* x *lewisii* "King Edward"
July	flowering	*A. millefolium*
Aug	flowering	"Cerise Queen"
Sept	flowering	*A. m.* "Lilac Beauty"
Oct	/	*A. m.* "White Queen"
Nov	/	*A.* "Moonshine"
Dec	/	*A. tomentosa*

CONDITIONS

Aspect   Needs full sunlight for the best results, but will tolerate some shade for part of the day.
Site   Any well-drained soil is suitable.

GROWING METHOD

Propagation   Grows easily if established clumps are lifted and divided in the spring. Plant the vigorous new divisions 8–12in apart, and discard the old ones. New, young plants need regular watering in prolonged dry spells, but once established achillea is remarkably drought-tolerant, and needs only an occasional deep drink.
Feeding   Apply a complete plant food as growth commences in the spring.
Problems   No specific pest or disease problems are known to attack achillea.

FLOWERING

Season   The long flowering period lasts throughout the summer into early fall. Regular removal of the spent, fading flower stems will significantly prolong blooming.
Cutting   The flowers are good for cutting because they have a reasonably long vase life. Take handfuls of cut flowers for the vase as soon as the heads are fully open. Also excellent for drying.

AFTER FLOWERING

Requirements   Cut off any spent flower stalks that remain on the plant in late fall.

AGAPANTHUS
African blue lily

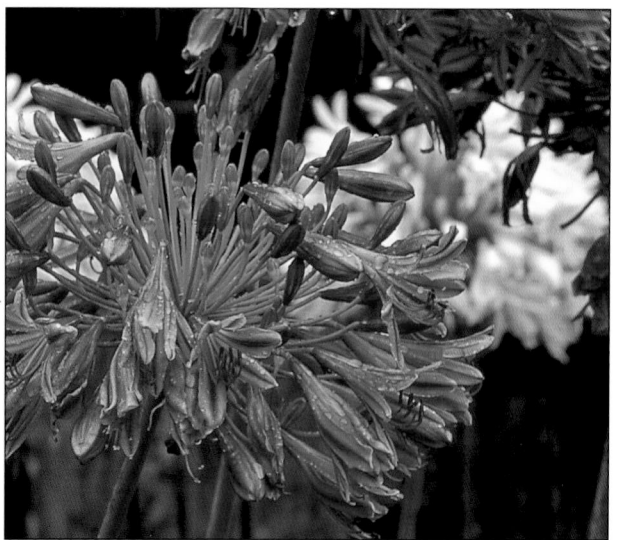

THE BLUE AND WHITE flowering heads of agapanthus are composed of numerous flowers. They make a striking feature.

THIS DENSE PLANTING of agapanthus needs little attention and rewards the gardener with its wonderful summer flowers.

FEATURES

SUMMER AUTUMN WINTER SPRING

HERBACEOUS

Agapanthus has dark green, strap-shaped leaves that grow to about 20in long. It produces rounded heads of blue or white flowers on top of stems 39in or more tall, but even without the flowers it makes a great foliage accent. It is hardy in moderate areas, but in colder regions needs winter protection. The Headbourne hybrids are particularly hardy. It can be grown in containers, and looks excellent in eye-catching tubs. Several attractive dwarf forms have foliage that rarely exceed 8in.

CONDITIONS

Aspect   Tolerates some shade, but the flowering will be poor. Full sunlight is ideal.

AGAPANTHUS AT A GLANCE	
A vigorous perennial, forming bold, eye-catching flowering clumps, from southern Africa. Many hardy to 23°F (zone 9).	
Jan /	Recommended Varieties
Feb sow	
Mar sow	*Agapanthus africanus*
Apr divide	*A. a.* "Albus"
May transplant	*A. caulescens*
Jun /	"Lilliput"
July flowering	"Loch Hope"
Aug flowering	"Peter Pan"
Sept flowering	*A. praecox* "Variegatus"
Oct /	
Nov /	
Dec /	

Site   Grows in almost any soil, but well-drained ground with organic matter is perfect. In colder yards, grow near a south-facing wall.

GROWING METHOD

Propagation   Divide clumps in the spring, ensuring that each division has a crown and a good batch of healthy roots. The latter can be shortened and some outer leaves removed, if necessary. Plant approximately 10in apart. Also grows from seed sown in the spring. It needs regular watering to establish, but once settled it can cope with long, dry periods. However, for the best growth and flowering, do not let new, young plants dry out.

Feeding   Apply complete plant food in the early spring. Potted plants will perform better with an application of slow-release granules, or a monthly liquid feed, carefully following the manufacturer's recommended rate.

Problems   There are no particular problems, but clumps will harbor groups of snails. Pick off.

FLOWERING

Season   Blooms appear in mid- to late summer, depending on the conditions.

Cutting   Agapanthus can be used as a cut flower if the stems are plunged into boiling water for 15 seconds immediately after cutting.

AFTER FLOWERING

Requirements   No pruning needed, other than cutting off spent flower stems and dead leaves. Protect crowns over winter with a thick mulch of straw or dry leaves.

ALCHEMILLA MOLLIS
Lady's mantle

LONG USED as a folk medicine to help heal wounds and gynecological problems, lady's mantle is today usually grown for its decorative value and ability to self-seed. The pure lime-green flowers brighten the yard, making a marvellous contrast against the wide, lobed leaves.

FEATURES

HERBACEOUS

This is a quick-growing herbaceous perennial mostly used as a border plant to edge paths and beds. An abundant self-seeder, it is good for suppressing weeds, filling any free spaces, often popping up in cracks in paths. Growing anywhere between 8 and 16in high, one plant may spread to 11–16in. The rounded, slightly hairy leaves overlap one another, and the plant produces trusses of bright lime-green flowers through summer. It provides a lovely contrast with other, stronger colors. The leaves tend to trap raindrops or dew, adding to the effect.

ALCHEMILLA AT A GLANCE

A. mollis is a hardy perennial grown for its prolific self-seeding and attractive lime-green foliage. Hardy to 5°F (zone 7).

		Companion Plants
Jan	/	
Feb	sow	Delphinium
Mar	sow	Dicentra
Apr	transplant	Eremurus
May	transplant	Eucomis
Jun	flowering	Euonymus
July	flowering	Geranium
Aug	flowering	Gladiolus
Sept	flowering	Lupin
Oct	divide	Rose
Nov	/	
Dec	/	

CONDITIONS

Aspect   Thrives in full sun, although it tolerates a degree of light shade.

Site   Needs well-drained soil that has a high organic content.

GROWING METHOD

Propagation   Self-sown seedlings can be easily transplanted to other positions. Clumps can be divided in the spring or fall with the divisions spaced 8–10in apart. Newly planted specimens may need watering, but mature plants tolerate dry periods. Justifiably known as a great survivor and spreader.

Feeding   Apply a complete plant food as the new growth begins.

Problems   No specific problems are known.

FLOWERING

Season   Masses of lime-green flowers appear from late spring through the summer.

Cutting   A great favorite with flower arrangements.

AFTER FLOWERING

Requirements   If you do not want plants to self-seed, trim spent flowers as soon as they fade. Once flowering has finished and growth begins to die down, the plants can be cut back hard with shears, or even a trimmer if you want to be ruthless.

ALSTROEMERIA
Peruvian Lily

ALSO KNOWN AS THE LILY of the Incas, the Peruvian lily can be placed in a mixed perennial border as here, or planted between shrubs. Bold groupings are best. Gardeners can choose from a colorful range of species and cultivars, but may be unable to obtain some of the varieties sold by florists.

FEATURES

HERBACEOUS

The Peruvian lily is grown commercially on a large scale, since the flowers are long lasting when cut. In the garden it is a herbaceous perennial with flower spikes growing mostly 12–24in high, although there are dwarf forms and very tall ones. The flowers are beautifully marked with streaks and spots of color, contrasting with a wide range of base colors of cream, yellow, orange, pink, and red. If conditions are suitable, these plants spread by means of fleshy rhizomes (roots) to form large clumps. Also excellent when grown in pots.

ALSTROEMERIA AT A GLANCE

A hardy perennial surviving 14°F (zone 8). Grown for their excellent showy flowers—many make unbeatable cut flowers.

		Recommended Varieties
Jan	/	
Feb	/	*Alstroemeria ligtu* hybrids
Mar	/	"Orange Gem"
Apr	sow	"Orange Glory"
May	/	"Princess Mira" (and all
Jun	transplant	"Princess" varieties)
July	flowering	"Solent Crest"
Aug	flowering	"Solent Rose"
Sept	flowering	"Stamoli"
Oct	divide	"Strapripur"
Nov	/	"Staroko"
Dec	/	"Stasilva"

CONDITIONS

Aspect   Needs full sunlight and shelter to thrive, especially in colder areas. Also requires shelter from strong wind. Makes an excellent potted greenhouse plant.

Site   Must have very free-draining soil containing plenty of decayed organic matter.

GROWING METHOD

Propagation   Many grow readily from seed sown in the spring, but division of established clumps is easiest; spring is generally considered the best time. Bare-root plants can be hard to establish; pot-grown plants, available in the summer, are better. Plant the roots 2in deep and about 6in apart. In a prolonged dry period, water the bedded plants regularly in the spring and summer, but restrict watering after flowering.

Feeding   Apply slow-release granular fertilizer in spring.

Problems   No specific problems are known.

FLOWERING

Season   Most species and their cultivars flower from the spring into summer, some into fall.

Cutting   This is a first-class cut flower.

AFTER FLOWERING

Requirements Cut off spent flower stems at ground level. Protect crowns with straw during cold winters.

ANEMONE X HYBRIDA
Windflower (Anemone x hybrida, syn. A. hupehensis var. japonica)

ELEGANT SIMPLICITY is the best way to describe the form of the Japanese anemone with its white, yellow, and green color scheme.

RELIABLE IN BLOOM year after year, the Japanese anemone is an attractive garden addition that softens stiff, geometric schemes.

FEATURES

HERBACEOUS

Also known as the Japanese windflower, this herbaceous perennial is one of the great joys of the fall garden. The leaves are three-lobed, somewhat maple-like, and the single or double flowers are carried on stems up to 39in high. Flowers may be single or double-colored white, pale, or deep pink. Once established, they spread into large clumps quite rapidly, traveling by underground stems, and also self-seeding. Some consider them invasive, but plants can be easily dug out and a mass-planting in full bloom is a real delight. Grow where they can remain undisturbed for some years. Site at the back of a shady bed or in dappled sunlight under trees.

ANEMONE AT A GLANCE

This is a free-flowering, quick-spreading herbaceous perennial with lovely, pale pink flowers. Hardy to 5°F (zone 7).

		Recommended Varieties
Jan	/	
Feb	/	*Anemone x hybrida*
Mar	divide	"Honorine Jobert"
Apr	transplant	A. x h. "Konigin Charlotte"
May	/	A. x h. "Luise Uhink"
Jun	/	A. x h. "Margarete"
July	/	A. x h. "Pamina"
Aug	flowering	A. x h. "Richard Ahrends"
Sept	flowering	
Oct	sow	
Nov	/	
Dec	/	

CONDITIONS

Aspect Prefers shade or semi-shade with shelter from strong winds.
Site Grows best in well-drained soil that contains plenty of organic matter.

GROWING METHOD

Propagation Increase from root cuttings in the winter, or divide established clumps in early spring, ensuring that each division has a thick set of roots. This vigorous plant can sometimes be tricky to divide and transplant. Replant the new, vigorous younger growths from the outside of the clump, generally about 12in apart. New young plants require ample watering in prolonged dry spells during the growing season.
Feeding Fertilizing is not essential, but a complete plant food can be applied in the spring.
Problems No specific problems are known.

FLOWERING

Season Flowers appear prolifically from late summer through the fall months.
Cutting Though they seem perfect for cut-flower displays, the flowers do not last that well.

AFTER FLOWERING

Requirements Cut back spent flower stems to ground level once they begin to fade, and cut the plant right back to the ground in late fall.

AQUILEGIA
Columbine

WIDELY CONTRASTING COLORS successfully combine in the flowers of this modern, long-spurred hybrid columbine.

AN OPEN WOODLAND SETTING is ideal for columbines, letting them freely self-seed forming, bold, distinctive groups.

FEATURES

HERBACEOUS

These old-fashioned favorites, also called granny's bonnets, give a fine display in the garden and make decorative cut flowers. The foliage is often blue-green, and the flowers come in single colors—white, pink, crimson, yellow, and blue—and combinations of pastel and brighter shades. There are also excellent black and whites ("Magpie"). The older forms have short-spurred flowers that resemble old-fashioned bonnets, especially "Nora Barlow," a good double which is a mix of red, pink, and green. Modern hybrids are long spurred, and available in many single colors and bicolors. Plants may be 16–28in high. Columbines are not long lived but are easily seed grown. Ideal for the dappled garden, grow them under deciduous trees and in borders.

AQUILEGIA AT A GLANCE

A clump-forming perennial, happy in semi-shade, perfect for the cottage garden where it freely self-seeds. Hardy to 5°F (zone 7).

		Recommended Varieties
Jan	/	
Feb	/	*Aquilegia bertolonii*
Mar	sow	*A. canadensis*
Apr	transplant	*A. flabellata*
May	flowering	*A. f.* var. *pumila*
Jun	flowering	*A. f.* var. *f. alba*
July	/	"Henson Harebell"
Aug	/	"Magpie"
Sept	divide	Music series
Oct	sow	*A. vulgaris* "Nora Barlow"
Nov	/	
Dec	/	

CONDITIONS

Aspect   Prefers semi-shade, and thrives in woodland gardens, but full sun is not a problem.
Site   Needs well-drained soil that contains plenty of organic matter.

GROWING METHOD

Propagation   Clumps are actually quite hard to divide, but it can be done, the fall being the best time. Columbine also grows from seed sown in early spring, or in the fall. Self-sown plants are hardy, but note that they may not always be true to type. Space plants about 12in apart. New young plants must not be allowed to dry out in prolonged dry spells in the spring and summer months. Keep a careful watch.
Feeding   Apply complete plant food in the spring as the new growth begins to emerge.
Problems   No particular pest or disease problems are known for this plant.

FLOWERING

Season   There is a long flowering period from mid-spring to mid-summer.
Cutting   Flower stems can be cut for the vase, and they make an attractive display, but the garden show lasts considerably longer.

AFTER FLOWERING

Requirements Spent flower stems can either be removed or left on the plants enabling the seeds to mature. Cut back the old growth to ground level as it dies off.

ARMERIA MARITIMA
Sea thrift

EACH FLOWERHEAD resembles a tiny posy, which is why thrift makes a fine cut flower, alone or in a composition with other flowers.

POOR STONY GROUND, which resembles thrift's natural habitat, provides ideal conditions for growing this plant.

FEATURES

EVERGREEN

Also known as sea thrift, this evergreen perennial grows in little grassy mounds 2–5in high. It occurs naturally in northern Europe and around the Mediterranean, often in very exposed situations, including cliff tops. The rounded flowerheads are carried above the foliage on stems 6–12in high. Flowers vary in color in the species and may be white, pink, or almost red, and there are a number of named cultivars available. Thrift can be used as a groundcover or edging plant, or can be planted in rockeries, on dry walls, or in poor soil where few other plants will survive. It also makes a good container plant.

ARMERIA AT A GLANCE

A. maritima is an attractive evergreen, clump-forming perennial which colonizes inhospitable areas. Hardy to 0°F (zone 7).

Jan	/	
Feb	/	
Mar	division	
Apr	/	
May	transplant	
Jun	flowering	
July	flowering	
Aug	flowering	
Sept	/	
Oct	/	
Nov	/	
Dec	/	

Recommended Varieties

Armeria maritima "Alba"
A. m. "Corsica"
A. m. "Launcheana"
A. m. "Ruby Glow"
A. m. "Splendens"
A. m. "Vindictive"

CONDITIONS

Aspect   Needs full sun all day. Thrift tolerates dry, windy conditions and salt spray, and is an excellent choice for coastal gardens.

Site   Grows in any kind of soil so long as it is very well drained. Adding sharp sand will improve the drainage.

GROWING METHOD

Propagation   Divide established clumps in the spring and replant about 6–8in apart. The species can be grown from seed sown in the spring, or from semi-ripe cuttings taken in the summer

Feeding   Give a light dressing of complete fertilizer in early spring.

Problems   Thrift has a tendency to rot if soils are in any way too heavy, poorly drained, or overwatered. In humid weather and in sheltered positions it may also be susceptible to the fungal disease which is called rust. Use a fungicide to attack the problem.

FLOWERING

Season   Thrift has a long flowering period through spring and summer, provided the plants are deadheaded regularly.

Cutting   Makes a good cut flower.

AFTER FLOWERING

Requirements   Regularly remove spent flower stems to give a prolonged flowering period.

ASTER
Michaelmas daisy

RICH MAUVE *flowers virtually obscure the foliage on a mature plant.*

THE ATTRACTIVE *Aster ericoides, which has produced many excellent cultivars.*

ONE OF *the best of the reds is the low-growing "Winston Churchill."*

FEATURES

HERBACEOUS

There is a wide variety of asters, and all of them flower in late summer and the fall. The most commonly grown is *A. novi-belgii*, which has a range of cultivars from dwarf forms 10in high to tall varieties reaching 39in. Flowers are blue, violet, pink, red, or white, and all are good for cutting. *A. ericoides* has very small leaves and produces stems of white flowers up to 39in high. *A.* x *frikartii* grows about 30in tall and has violet-blue flowers. All of these plants are extremely easy to grow and tolerate a wide range of conditions. They multiply readily. Taller varieties need staking.

ASTER AT A GLANCE

Hardy perennials creating large clumps, giving strong fall color in most situations. Hardy to 5°F (zone 7).

Jan	/	**Recommended Varieties**
Feb	sow	
Mar	sow	*Aster alpinus*
Apr	divide	*A. amellus* "Framfieldii"
May	transplant	*A. a.* "Jacqueline
Jun	/	Genebrier"
July	flowering	"Coombe Fishacre"
Aug	flowering	*A. ericoides* "Golden Spray"
Sept	flowering	*A.* x *frikartii* "Monch"
Oct	divide	*A. novae-angliae*
Nov	/	*A. novi-belgii* "Audrey"
Dec	/	

CONDITIONS

Aspect   Grows best in full sun. Tolerates light shade, but blooming may not be so prolific and growth will be less compact.

Site   Add well-rotted organic matter to the soil. Feed and water well to counter disease.

GROWING METHOD

Propagation   Divide clumps in late winter. These plants are prolific growers—one plant will multiply itself tenfold in a season. Replant divisions 8in apart. The best results are from regular watering during the spring and summer, especially in long, dry periods.

Feeding   Apply complete plant food in early spring.

Problems   Powdery mildew can be a major problem, especially with varieties of *A. novi-belgii*. Mildew-resistant varieties include *A.* x *frikartii* and varieties of *A. amellus*.

FLOWERING

Season   The long flowering display lasts from late summer into the fall.

Cutting   Cut flowers last very well if given a frequent change of water.

AFTER FLOWERING

Requirements   Cut off spent flower stems close to ground level after blooming. Plants will gradually die back, but should not need more close attention until new growth appears in the next spring.

ASTILBE HYBRIDS
Astilbe

SOFT AND FEATHERY, *the pale pink plumes on this astilbe will provide a long display of bright flowers and fern-like foliage.*

UPRIGHT SIDE BRANCHES *are an unusual feature of this deep pink astilbe cultivar. They give an eye-catching, stiff appearance.*

FEATURES

HERBACEOUS

These perennial hybrids revel in moist soil and light shade, although they can be grown in an open, sunny position if well watered. The shiny, compound leaves are quite attractive, with astilbe also bearing tall plumes of soft flowers 20in or more tall, in shades of pink, red, mauve, or white. They look best when mass-planted, and are ideal for surrounding ponds, or naturalizing in a wild garden. They can be used as cut flowers, but they are probably best left in the yard where their big, theatrical effect can be enjoyed for much longer. They can quickly flag in a heat wave; water at the first sign of wilting.

ASTILBE AT A GLANCE

A rhizomatous perennial that enjoys damp soil. Striking, tall flowerheads can reach 4ft tall. Hardy to 5°F (zone 7).

Jan	/	**Recommended Varieties**
Feb	sow	*Astilbe x arendsii*
Mar	divide	"Brautschleier"
Apr	transplant	A. x *a*."Bronce Elegans"
May	flowering	A. x *a*."Fanal"
Jun	flowering	A. x *a.* "Irrlicht"
July	flowering	A. x *a* "Snowdrift"
Aug	flowering	A. x *crispa* "Perkeo"
Sept	flowering	"Rheinland"
Oct	/	*A. simplicifolia*
Nov	divide	"Sprite"
Dec	/	

CONDITIONS

Aspect These are versatile plants, performing equally well in bright sunlight and dappled shade.

Site The ideal soil is rich in organic matter and retains plenty of moisture. Regular, heavy applications of mulch are essential.

GROWING METHOD

Propagation Divide clumps in late fall, ensuring that each division has a crown and a decent set of roots. Plant at 8–10in spacings. New, young plants need plenty of water in prolonged dry spells in the spring and summer months. Do not let them dry out.

Feeding Apply a general fertilizer as growth starts in the spring, and repeat 6–8 weeks later.

Problems No specific problems are known.

FLOWERING

Season Flowers from late spring through the summer. The flower display is longer lasting in a cooler summer.

Cutting Flowers can be cut for indoor decoration.

AFTER FLOWERING

Requirements Spent flowerheads will turn a pleasant rich brown color, and are quite attractive through the winter months. They add considerable interest to the yard. Do not cut back spent flower stems to ground level until the following spring.

ASTRANTIA MAJOR
Masterwort

ASTRANTIA MAJOR *"HADSPEN BLOOD" is a striking, vibrant red, more of an eye-catcher than the species, which is much whiter. Both can be used to link and soften more permanent shrubby features, or as part of a free-flowing, flowery display for late spring and early summer.*

FEATURES

HERBACEOUS

Also known as masterwort, *Astrantia major* is a "must-have" for the "cottage garden," a clump-forming perennial that produces delightful sprays of green or pink, sometimes reddish flowers, surrounded by green-veined white bracts. A native of central Europe, it grows about 24in tall, forming clumps 18in wide. Flowering in early and mid-summer, it can be left to colonize areas of dappled shade, though it also enjoys full sunlight. There are some excellent cultivars, including the new "Hadspen Blood," a striking blood red, "Shaggy" with long bracts, and "Sunningdale Variegated," with pale pink bracts and yellow/ cream leaves. Best in large clumps.

ASTRANTIA AT A GLANCE

A. major is a clump-forming perennial grown for its abundant, attractive flowers. Excellent cultivars. Hardy to 0°F (zones 6–7).

		Recommended Varieties
Jan	/	
Feb	/	*Astrantia major alba*
Mar	divide	*A. m.* "Claret"
Apr	divide	*A. m.* "Hadspen Blood"
May	transplant	*A. m. involucrata* "Shaggy"
Jun	flowering	*A. m. rosea*
July	flowering	*A. m. rubra*
Aug	sowing	*A. m.* "Sunningdale
Sept	/	Variegated"
Oct	/	
Nov	/	
Dec	/	

CONDITIONS

Aspect Thrives in either dappled shade or a more open, sunny position.

Soil Likes compost-rich, moist, fertile soil, though it will tolerate drier conditions. Woodland gardens and streamsides are ideal.

GROWING METHOD

Propagation Can either be grown from seed sown in late summer, once ripe, or by division in the spring. Plant out at least 18in apart, or closer for an immediate covering. Do not let young plants begin to dry out in a prolonged dry spring or summer spell. The variants do not require such moist conditions, and will tolerate drier soil.

Feeding Lay a mulch around the plants in the spring. This has two advantages: it enriches the soil and also prevents moisture loss.

Problems Slugs can be a major problem, attacking the stems and foliage. Pick off when seen. Powdery mildew can also strike; spray against attacks.

FLOWERING

Season The one flowering spell is in early and mid-summer.

Cutting Makes good cut flowers, which can be used to soften a stiff, structural arrangement, or as part of a more flowery display.

AFTER FLOWERING

Requirements Cut down the spent flower stems, and tidy up the foliage.

AURINIA SAXATILIS
Golden dust

A SHARP, ATTRACTIVE CONTRAST, with the bright yellow flowers of golden dust against clusters of green, spoon-shape foliage.

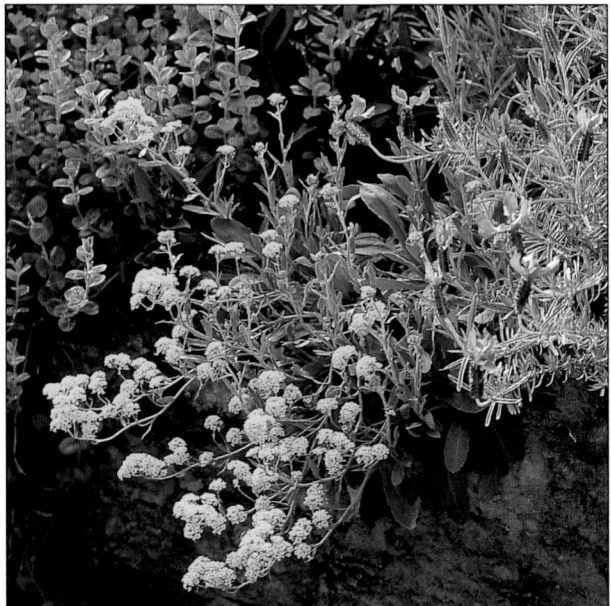

YELLOW AND BLUE always make a lively color combination, as this wonderful planting of golden dust and Italian lavender proves.

FEATURES

EVERGREEN

This is a little, rounded, evergreen perennial that can grow from 4 to 12in high, forming a mound up to 16–20in across. In the species the flowers are a clear yellow, but the various cultivars produce flowers in white, cream, lemon, or rich gold. Since its natural habitat is rocky, mountainous country, it is ideal for a rock garden, for dry, sloping ground, or for edging garden beds, provided the drainage is excellent. It is also ideally suited to troughs and the edges of large pots, perhaps containing a shrub. Although golden dust is a perennial, some gardeners grow it as part of an annual spring display.

AURINIA AT A GLANCE

A. saxatilis is an evergreen, hardy perennial that forms thick clumps topped by yellow flowers. Hardy to 0°F (zone 6–7).

Jan	/	Recommended Varieties
Feb	/	
Mar	transplant	*Aurinia saxatilis* "Citrina"
Apr	/	A. s. "Compacta"
May	flowering	A. s. "Dudley Nevill"
Jun	flowering	A. s. "Goldkugel"
July	/	A. s. "Silver Queen"
Aug	/	
Sept	/	Companion Plants
Oct	sow	*Aurinia corymbosa*
Nov	/	Aubrieta
Dec	/	

CONDITIONS

Aspect   Needs an open position in full sunlight.
Site   Soil must contain plenty of chalk, sand, or grit, and be free-draining but not rich.

GROWING METHOD

Propagation   Grows readily from seed sown in the fall. Cultivars can be grown from tip cuttings taken in late spring and early summer. Space the plants about 4in apart, giving them plenty of growing room. Aurinia is sold among the alpines at garden centers.
Feeding   Small amounts only of complete plant food may be given in early spring as a boost, but feeding is not essential.
Problems   No specific problems are known besides poor drainage. Overwatering pot-grown specimens can quickly rot and kill the plants.

FLOWERING

Season   Flowers appear from mid- to late spring, the flowers completely covering the plant and hiding the foliage.
Cutting   The flowers are not suitable for picking.

AFTER FLOWERING

Requirements   It is probably easiest to shear radically over the whole plant with clippers, unless you are waiting for the seed to ripen. Shearing the plants also helps to keep a compact, neatly rounded shape.

BERGENIA
Elephant's ears

THE WELL-DEFINED, SOLID SHAPE of bergenias makes them ideal edging plants, as this neat row beside a path demonstrates. Bergenias have other advantages, too, in that they flower in the shade and from late winter onward, both features that are not common among perennials.

FEATURES

EVERGREEN

An excellent evergreen, groundcover plant, it is also known as elephant's ears, because of the large, rounded leaves approximately 8–12in long. They are often leathery and glossy, generally green, many turning reddish in the fall. The flowers are held on short stems, from mid-spring to early summer, some, such as "Morgenrote," repeat-flowering in cool conditions. The color range is invariably shades of pink, with some white forms. Bergenia is not a fussy plant, and enjoys a wide range of conditions, from bright sun to shade, and from moist to dry ground. Long-living and easy to propagate, it can colonize areas beneath trees, edge paths, or front a border.

BERGENIA AT A GLANCE

A versatile evergreen with large, ornamental foliage that thrives in a range of conditions. Hardy to 0°F (zones 6–7).

Jan	/	Recommended Varieties
Feb	flowering	
Mar	flowering	*Bergenia* "Abendglut"
Apr	flowering	B. "Baby Doll"
May	flowering	B. "Bressingham Salmon"
Jun	/	B. "Bressingham White"
July	/	B. *cordifolia* "Purpurea"
Aug	/	B. "Morgenrote"
Sept	/	B. *purpurescens*
Oct	divide	B. "Silberlicht"
Nov	divide	
Dec	/	

CONDITIONS

Aspect — Grows in either full sunlight or shady areas, but avoid extremes of the latter.
Site — Likes well-composted, moist soil with good drainage, but it will also tolerate much poorer conditions that bring out a richer winter leaf color. Provide a late fall mulch.

GROWING METHOD

Propagation — Grows from seed sown in spring, producing hybrids, or divide in the spring or fall every five years to rejuvenate a declining plant. Plant up to 24in apart, depending on the variety, or closer for immediate coverage.
Feeding — Feed generously in early spring with a complete plant food, especially on poorer ground, and give a generous layer of mulch later in the fall.
Problems — Slugs and snails can be a major problem to the new, young foliage, ruining its shapely appearance. Pick off, or treat with chemicals. Spray with a fungicide if leaf spot occurs.

FLOWERING

Season — The flowers appear from late winter or early spring, depending on the variety, for a few weeks.
Cutting — Though the flowers are useful in cut flower arrangements, the foliage, especially when red in winter, makes a particularly attractive foil.

AFTER FLOWERING

Requirements Remove the spent flower stems and foliage.

CAMPANULA
Bellflower

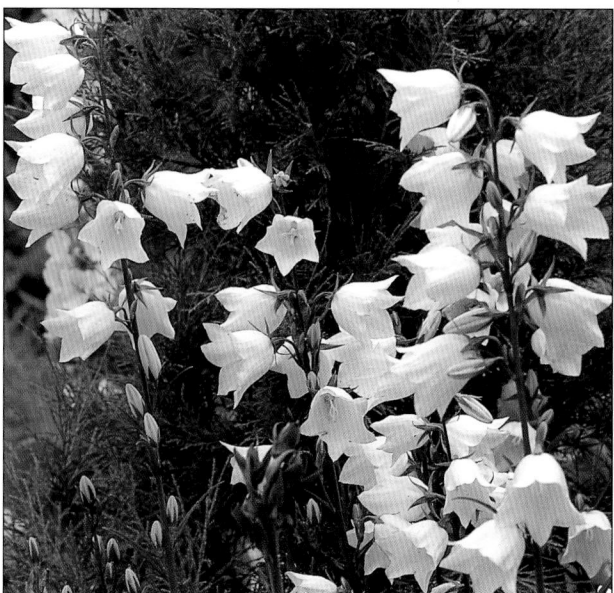

CAMPANULA PERSICIFOLIA ALBA makes a valuable addition to a white border, flowering prolifically in early and mid-summer.

CAMPANULAS ARE THE MAINSTAY of the cottage or woodland garden, freely spreading, adding plenty of color and charm.

FEATURES

HERBACEOUS

Also known as the bellflower, campanula contains about 300 species of annuals, biennials, and perennials. Generally easy to grow in either full sunlight or dappled shade, on walls, banks, and in borders, it has a wide range of flowers, from the tubular to the saucer-shaped. They also vary considerably in height, from the low, 3in-high spreaders, like *C. betulifolia,* to the 5ft-tall *C. lactiflora.* The former are excellent at the front of a border, the latter need staking at the rear. There are many excellent forms: *C. glomerata* "Superba" is a vigorous grower, reaching 24 x 24in, while *C. burghaltii* produces pale lavender tubular bells around the same time.

CAMPANULA AT A GLANCE

A near 300-strong genus, thriving in a wide variety of conditions, grown for their abundant flowers. Hardy to 5°F (zone 7).

Jan	/	Recommended Varieties
Feb	/	
Mar	sow	*Campanula arvatica*
Apr	transplant	**C. carpatica**
May	flowering	*C. garganica*
Jun	flowering	*C. latiloba*
July	flowering	*C. medium*
Aug	flowering	*C. persicifolia*
Sept	flowering	*C. thyrsoides*
Oct	divide	*C. trachelium*
Nov	/	
Dec	/	

CONDITIONS

Aspect Campanula thrive in both sunny yards and those with dappled shade.

Site There are three broad types of campanula, each requiring different conditions: well-drained, fertile soil for border plants; moist, fast-draining ground for the rock garden species; and a gritty scree bed for the alpines that dislike being wet over winter.

GROWING METHOD

Propagation Grow the species from seed in spring in a cold frame, or from cuttings, and sow alpines in a frame in the fall. Varieties must be propagated by spring cuttings, or spring or fall division if they are to grow true to the parent.

Feeding Apply a complete plant food in the spring, especially on poorer soils, or plenty of dug-in, organic material.

Problems Slugs and snails are the major problem, and if not kept under control they can ruin a border display. In some areas *C. persicifolia* is prone to rust.

FLOWERING

Season The long-lasting flowers appear from midwinter to the spring.

Cutting Makes an excellent display of cut flowers, especially the taller plants.

AFTER FLOWERING

Requirements Cut back to the ground in late fall.

CENTRANTHUS RUBER
Red valerian

TRUSSES of rich crimson and softer pink valerian provide months of bright color in the yard, rivalling the display of annuals.

RED VALERIAN flourishing in the conditions that suit it best—the fence provides shelter, and the raised bed warmth and good drainage.

FEATURES

HERBACEOUS

This evergreen perennial is very easy to grow, but it often exceeds its allotted space by self-seeding (seedlings are easy to pull out). It has a long flowering period and can survive in poor, dry soil. It generally reaches 16in tall, but in good soil tops 28in. Flowers are a deep pink to red, and there is a white form, too. Ideal for a low-maintenance yard, it is often planted in mixed borders for its long display. It is also grown in large rock gardens and on dry, fast-draining slopes. Self-sown plants can be found in almost no soil on rocky outcrops, and thrive in chalky ground.

CENTRANTHUS AT A GLANCE

C. ruber is a hardy, herbaceous perennial, a favorite in "cottage gardens" with tall, red summer flowers. Hardy to 10°F (zones 7–8).

		Companion Plants
Jan	/	
Feb	sow 🌱	*Argyranthemum foeniculaceum*
Mar	sow 🌱	*A. frutescens*
Apr	transplant 🌱	Cytisus
May	transplant 🌱	*Geranium robertianum*
Jun	flowering ❀	*Hedera colchica* "Dentata
July	flowering ❀	Variegata"
Aug	flowering ❀	*Helleborus orientalis*
Sept	flowering ❀	Stipa
Oct	/	Yucca
Nov	/	
Dec	/	

CONDITIONS

Aspect Likes full sunlight all day.
Soil Needs very well-drained soil, but it need not be particularly rich.

GROWING METHOD

Propagation Grows readily from tip cuttings taken in late spring and summer, or from seed sown in the spring. Space the plants 8in apart.
Feeding Fertilizer is generally not necessary, but you may give a little complete plant food in the spring, as new growth begins. Needs regular watering to establish, after which plants are extremely drought-tolerant.
Problems No specific problems are known.

FLOWERING

Season The very long flowering period extends from the spring until early fall, especially if plants are cut back after each flowering flush to encourage plenty of new buds.
Cutting Does not make a good cut flower.

AFTER FLOWERING

Requirements No attention is needed, beyond removing the spent flower stems. This has a double advantage: it keeps the plant looking neat, and prevents abundant self-seeding.

CHRYSANTHEMUM HYBRIDS
Dendranthema

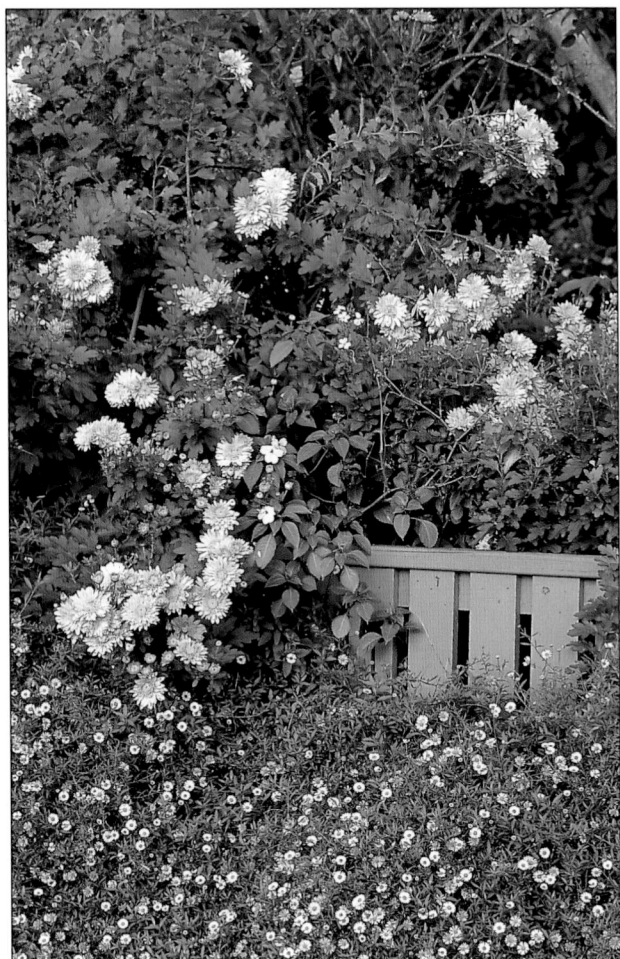

CASCADING OVER the fence onto the massed erigeron below, this wonderful garden chrysanthemum gives a prolific display.

THE QUILLED PETALS are characteristic of this open "spider" style of chrysanthemum, as is the shading of color.

HYBRID CHRYSANTHEMUMS are justifiably highly popular in the cut flower trade, and are available for most of the year.

FEATURES

HERBACEOUS

Chrysanthemums probably originated in China, but were introduced into Japan a very long time ago. A big favorite in garden and florists' displays, they are the highlight of the late summer and fall border. They are also widely used as a long-lasting cut flower. Chrysanthemums have been renamed and moved to the genus *Dendranthema*, though the name has yet to catch on. Four kinds to look out for include: the Korean (e.g. "Yellow Starlet"), which give a long flowering performance but dislike excessive winter wet (store inside in severe conditions); the thigh-high, dwarf, bushy pompons ("Mei Kyo") with a sea of rounded flowers; the clump-forming rubellums (named hybrids of *C. rubellum*) which are hardiest, have a woody base, but again dislike extreme damp; and the sprays ("Pennine") which are grown both for the border and cutting.

Color The color range is wide, covering white, cream, yellow, many shades of pink and lilac, burgundy, pale apricot, and deep mahogany.

Types There are many forms of chrysanthemums, and they have been classified by specialist societies and nurseries according to floral type. Some of the types are decorative, anemone centered, spider, pompon, single, exhibition, and Korean spray. There is virtually a shape for every taste.

Staking Many of the taller varieties need staking, which needs to be carefully thought out if the display is to avoid looking too structured. One reliable, traditional method is to insert bamboo canes at intervals around and through the planting, and thread twine from cane to cane in a criss-cross fashion, perhaps 20–24in above the ground.

CONDITIONS

Aspect Grows best in full sun with protection from strong winds.

Site Needs well-drained soil that has been heavily enriched with organic matter before planting. Plants should also be mulched with decayed compost or manure.

THIS UNUSUAL chrysanthemum has the central petals incurved like those of the Korean spray, while the outer ones are widespread.

THE RUSSET COLORS of these flowers seem appropriate to their fall flowering season, when the leaves are turning.

GROWING METHOD

Propagation In spring lift and divide the new suckering growth so that each new plant has its own roots and shoots. Cuttings of the new growth can be taken. Space plants 16in apart.

Feeding Once the plants are well established you can fertilize them every four to six weeks with a soluble liquid fertilizer.

Problems • You can spot chrysanthemum leaf miners by the wavy white or brown lines in the foliage. Furthermore, hold up the leaf to the light and you might see the pupa or grub. Control by immediately removing the affected leaves and crushing the grubs, or better still by regular spraying with a systemic insecticide.

• Chrysanthemum eelworm is evident by browning, drying leaves. Immediately destroy all infected plants. There is no available remedy.

• A number of fungal diseases can attack these plants, including leaf spot, powdery mildew, rust, and white rust. Avoid overhead watering or watering late in the day, and ensure that residue from previous plantings is cleared away. You may need to spray with a registered fungicide. White rust is a particularly serious disease, and affected plants are probably best removed and destroyed.

• Watch for aphids clustering on new growth. Pick them off by hand, wash them off, or use an insecticidal spray.

FLOWERING

Season Flowering time is mid to late fall. The exciting new race of Yoder or cushion chrysanthemums from America are dwarf, hardy, free-flowering (starting in late summer), and perfect for the front of the border. Those to look out for include "Lynn," "Robin," and "Radiant Lynn."

Cutting Cut flowers will last two to three weeks with frequent water changes, as long as the foliage is removed from the parts of the stems that are under water.

AFTER FLOWERING

Requirements Once flowering has finished, cut off plants 5–6in above the ground.

CHRYSANTHEMUM AT A GLANCE

Chrysanthemums are the colorful mainstay of the the end-of-season border. The hardy forms will tolerate 5°F (zone 7).

		Recommended Varieties
Jan	/	
Feb	sow	"Anna Marie"
Mar	sow	"Bronze Elegance"
Apr	divide	"Cappa"
May	transplant	"Faust"
Jun	/	"Lord Butler"
July	/	"Mrs Jessie Cooper"
Aug	flowering	"Poppet"
Sept	flowering	"Salmon Fairie"
Oct	/	
Nov	/	
Dec	/	

CONVALLARIA
Lily-of-the-valley

LILY-OF-THE-VALLEY makes a vivid display because of the strong contrast between the shapely oval leaves and the small, bright white flowers. It can be left to naturalize in woodland conditions, or allowed to spread through a shady border. Though invasive, it is quite easily controlled.

FEATURES

HERBACEOUS

Lily-of-the-valley is a one-species (sometimes considered three) genus, featuring the bell-shaped, fragrant *Convallaria majalis*. A native of Europe, it grows in woods and meadows, and produces 8in-tall stems of nodding white flowers shortly after the foliage has unfurled. Given the correct conditions—specifically, a cool, moist area—it can spread extremely quickly by means of underground shoots, but it is easily controlled. There are several attractive forms, "Albostriata" having cream striped foliage, and "Fortin's Giant" has flowers up to ½in across. Lily-of-the-valley is essential in a woodland area, or in a damp shady spot where little else of note will grow.

CONVALLARIA AT A GLANCE

Basically a one-species genus with wonderful, waxy, scented spring flowers. Hardy to 5°F (zone 7). Good cultivars available.

		Companion Plants
Jan	/	
Feb	/	Bergenia
Mar	/	*Euphorbia robbiae*
Apr	transplant 🌱	Galanthus
May	flowering 🌼	Primula
Jun	/	Pulmonaria
July	/	Rodgersia
Aug	sow	
Sept	division 🌼	
Oct	division 🌼	
Nov	/	
Dec	/	

CONDITIONS

Aspect   Shade is essential.
Site   The soil must be damp, rich, and leafy. For an impressive, vigorous display, apply a thick mulch of leaf mold around the clumps of plants every fall.

GROWING METHOD

Propagation   When the seed is ripe, remove the fleshy covering, and raise in a cold frame. Alternatively, divide the rhizomes in the fall. A 6in piece will provide approximately six new plants. The success rate is generally high. Make sure that young plants are not allowed to dry out. Mulch them to guarantee against moisture loss.
Feeding   Every other year, apply a scattering of complete fertilizer in the spring.
Problems   *Botrytis* can be a problem, but is rarely anything to worry about.

FLOWERING

Season   One brief display in late spring.
Cutting   Lily-of-the-valley makes excellent cut flowers, providing a striking spring display, while emitting a gentle sweet scent. They can also be lifted and grown indoors in a pot to flower the following spring. When finished, replace in the garden.

AFTER FLOWERING

Requirements   Remove the spent flower stems, but leave the foliage intact to provide the energy for next year's display.

COREOPSIS
Coreopsis

COREOPSIS ARE *wonderful plants which can quickly colonize a space, say between shrubs, producing striking, bright yellow flowers.*

THIS DOUBLE-FLOWERED FORM *of golden coreopsis provides many weeks of marvelous color throughout the summer.*

FEATURES

HERBACEOUS

Perennial coreopsis carries a profusion of bright yellow daisy-like flowers over a long period, generally through summer into the fall, though some do flower in spring. Regular deadheading will ensure a long display. *C. lanceolata*, known as calliopsis, has become naturalized in many parts of the world. The strong-growing *C. grandiflora* may grow 24–36in high, with *C.verticillata* about 8in shorter. There are several species worth trying, some with dwarf form or flowers displaying a dark eye. The foliage is variable too. The plants are easy to grow. Plant in bold clumps in a mixed border.

COREOPSIS AT A GLANCE

A genus with well over 100 species that make a big contribution to the summer and early fall display. Hardy to 5°F (zone 7).

Jan	/	Recommended Varieties
Feb	/	
Mar	/	*Coreopsis auriculata*
		"Schnittgold"
Apr	sow	*C.* "Goldfink"
May	divide	*C. grandiflora* "Early Sunrise"
Jun	flowering	*C. g.* "Mayfield Giant"
July	flowering	"Sunray"
Aug	flowering	*C. verticillata*
Sept	flowering	*C. v.* "Grandiflora"
Oct	/	*C. v.* "Zagreb"
Nov	/	
Dec	/	

CONDITIONS

Aspect   Prefers an open, sunny position right through the day, with little shade.

Site   Performs best in well-drained soil enriched with organic matter, but it will grow in poor soils too. Over-rich soil may produce a profusion of foliage with poor flowering.

GROWING METHOD

Propagation   Grows most easily from divisions of existing clumps lifted in the spring. Space new plants at about 12in intervals. Species can be grown from seed sown in mid-spring. Since cultivars of *C. grandiflora* can be ephemeral, sow seed for continuity.

Feeding   Apply complete plant food as growth begins in the spring. However, no further feeding should be needed.

Problems   No pest or disease problems are known.

FLOWERING

Season   The long flowering period extends through summer and the fall. *C.* "Early Sunrise," *C.lanceolata*, and "Sunray" flower in their first year from an early sowing.

Cutting   Flowers can be cut for indoor decoration.

AFTER FLOWERING

Requirements   Cut off spent flower stems and tidy up the foliage as it dies back. In mild, frost-free winters, coreopsis may not totally die back.

CORYDALIS
Corydalis

THE FOLIAGE and flowers of Corydalis ochroleuca are dainty and highly decorative. It looks good in walls and ornamental pots.

THE BLUE SPECIES and forms of corydalis are highly prized. This is Corydalis flexuosa, with long, upcurving spurs on its flowers.

FEATURES

HERBACEOUS

Pretty, fern-like foliage and tubular, spurred flowers are characteristic of the 300 or so species of corydalis. Only a small number of species are grown in cultivation, and they mainly flower in shades of yellow or blue, but there are some in pink or crimson. Some of the brilliant blues make a distinctive feature, and a recent cultivar with electric blue flowers, known as *C. flexuosa* "China Blue," is now widely available. It mixes well with *C. solida* "George Baker," salmon-pink, and *C. ochroleuca,* white. Heights vary from 6 to 24in. Many corydalis are excellent rock garden plants, while others are suitable for mixed borders or planting under deciduous trees. Many varieties may be available only from specialist nurseries that grow alpine plants.

CORYDALIS AT A GLANCE

A large group of annuals, biennials, and perennials, growing in a wide range of moist and dry conditions. Hardy to 5°F (zone 7).

Jan	/	
Feb	/	Recommended Varieties
Mar	/	*Corydalis cashmeriana*
Apr	divide	*C. cava*
May	transplant	*C. cheilanthifolia*
Jun	flowering	*C. elata*
July	flowering	*C.lutea*
Aug	flowering	*C.sempervirens*
Sept	divide	*C. solida*
Oct	sow	*C. s.* "Beth Evans"
Nov	/	*C. s. f. transsylvanica*
Dec	/	*C. s. f.* "George Baker"

CONDITIONS

Aspect   The preferred aspect varies with the species. Some tolerate an open, sunny position, while others need degrees of dappled sunlight. Species grown in "hot spots" should be given plenty of shade.

Site   Needs very well-drained soil that is able to retain some moisture in the summer.

GROWING METHOD

Propagation   Grows from seed sown as soon as it is ripe, in the fall. The seed is ripe when the small elongated capsules, which form after the flowers have fallen, turn brown and dry. Some species can be divided, while others produce tubers from which offsets can be taken. Plant at 4–6in intervals. New young plants need regular watering in prolonged, dry weather during the spring and summer months.

Feeding   Apply a sprinkling of slow-release fertilizer when growth commences in the spring.

Problems   There are no specific pest or disease problems.

FLOWERING

Season   Most species flower in the spring, or from spring into summer. *C. flexuosa* dies down in the summer.

Cutting   The flowers are unsuitable for cutting.

AFTER FLOWERING

Requirements   Remove spent flower stems, unless you are waiting for seed to set. Tidy up the foliage as it dies back.

CYNARA CARDUNCULUS
Cardoon

CARDOON LOOKS similar to a Scotch thistle. Its purple flowers can be left to dry, and then used for a striking indoor arrangement.

THE SILVERY LEAVES of cardoon are distinctive, large, and shapely, and a big clump forms a geometric, sculptural feature.

FEATURES

HERBACEOUS

A close relative of the globe artichoke, the cardoon is generally grown for its arching, 39in-long, silver-gray foliage. Growing up to 78in tall and almost 78in wide, it is a terrific accent plant for the back of a border, or it can be combined with low-growing green plants in an open position. Both the color and form stand out against most other plants. The purple, thistle-like flowers develop in the summer, and the dried heads left on the plant make a decorative fall feature. Cardoon is edible, being grown for the tasty, fleshy base of each leaf. It is difficult to place in a small yard, since you need room to stand back and appreciate its startling form.

CYNARA AT A GLANCE

C. cardunculus is a clump-forming perennial grown for its long, striking foliage and purple flowers. Hardy to 0°F (zones 6–7).

		Companion Plants
Jan	/	
Feb	/	Brugmansia
Mar	sow ✍	Centranthus
Apr	divide ✍	Echinops
May	transplant ✍	Geranium
Jun	flowering ✿	Miscanthus
July	flowering ✿	Rose
Aug	flowering ✿	Salvia
Sept	flowering ✿	Yucca
Oct	/	
Nov	/	
Dec	/	

CONDITIONS

Aspect Needs full sun all day for best results. Also requires shelter from strong, leaf-tearing winds.
Soil Needs rich, well-drained soil. Before planting, dig in large amounts of manure or compost.

GROWING METHOD

Propagation Propagate in late spring, or grow from seed. Position plants at least 4ft apart. Seed-grown plants vary in quality, and do not normally reach maturity in their first year. During the growing season, regular, deep watering is essential for new, young plants in prolonged dry spells.
Feeding Apply a complete plant food as growth commences in the spring, and repeat in mid-summer. When cardoon is grown as a vegetable it is given a weekly liquid feed.
Problems Beware of the sharp points on the flowerheads.

FLOWERING

Season The purple, thistle-like flowers appear during summer on stems 6½–10ft high.
Cutting If the flowers are allowed to dry on the plant, they can be cut and used as part of a big, bold indoor decoration.

AFTER FLOWERING

Requirements Once the flowers have lost their decorative value, cut off the whole stem low down. As the plant starts to die off and look untidy, cut it back just above the ground.

DELPHINIUM
Delphinium

DOZENS OF *individual flowers make up the striking spires of the delphinium. Blue shades, from pale to purple, predominate.*

THESE STAKED DELPHINIUMS, *growing in the shelter of a house, should remain stately and upright through the flowering season.*

FEATURES

HERBACEOUS

Tall, handsome, and stately, delphiniums make an outstanding feature in perennial borders. Growing 39–78in high, the long-lasting spires of blooms, originally were in a rich blue only, but now offer shades of pink, lavender, white, and red. Delphiniums should be mass-planted at the back of a border for the best effect, but they can also be placed as accent plants at intervals across a border. They mix well with climbers like clematis. Tall-growing varieties may need staking unless they are in a very sheltered spot. Colors can be mixed, but the best effect comes from massing plants of the same color.

DELPHINIUM AT A GLANCE

A hardy annual, biennial, and perennial, it is grown for its striking, vertical spires, thick with flowers. Hardy to 5°F (zone 7).

Jan	/	Recommended Varieties
Feb	sow 🖐	
Mar	sow 🖐	*Delphinium* "Bruce"
Apr	transplant 🖐	"Cassius"
May	transplant 🖐	"Emily Hawkins"
Jun	flowering 🌸	"Lord Butler"
July	flowering 🌸	"Our Deb"
Aug	flowering 🌸	"Rosemary Brock"
Sept	/	"Sandpiper"
Oct	divide 🖐	"Sungleam"
Nov	/	"Walton Gemstone"
Dec	/	

CONDITIONS

Aspect   Needs full sun and shelter from strong winds, and staking if it is not well sheltered.
Soil   Needs well-drained soil enriched with copious amounts of decayed manure or compost before planting. Water regularly and mulch.

GROWING METHOD

Propagation   Divide established clumps in the fall, ensuring each division has a crown and its own roots. Place them about 12in apart. Grows from seed sown in the spring, but the results are variable. Take 3in basal cuttings in mid-spring.
Feeding   Apply complete plant food once growth begins in the spring, and each month until flowering.
Problems   Watch for aphids on new growth, and hose off or spray with pyrethrum or insecticidal soap. In humid conditions a bad attack of powdery mildew may need to be tackled by spraying with a fungicide. Beware of slugs.

FLOWERING

Season   Blooms for a long season through early and late summer.
Cutting   Flowers make a good display, and can be dried.

AFTER FLOWERING

Requirements Remove the flower stems when the main blooms fade and small spikes may flower in late summer and early fall.

DIANTHUS CARYOPHYLLUS
Wild carnation

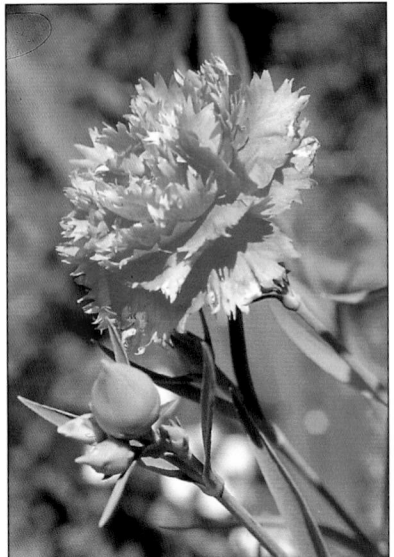

FRINGED PINK FLOWERS and silver-gray buds and stems make this a classic.

UPWARD-ANGLED CANES are one way of making sure that top-heavy blooms do not tumble onto a path. The other, more discrete method is to employ a series of small twiggy sticks.

FEATURES

EVERGREEN

Carnations are very popular, both as cut flowers and as a garden subject. Flowers are carried singly or in groups on stems 12–20in high, although florists' carnations may be taller. *Dianthus caryophyllus* from the Mediterranean, a woody perennial with elegant stiff stems, bears richly scented, purple-pink flowers that grow taller than the average, reaching 32in under perfect conditions. It has given rise to several excellent series. The Floristan Series comes in a wide color range, and makes good cut flowers, the Knight Series is shorter and bushier, and includes yellow, white, and orange blooms, and the Lilliput Series, shorter still at 8in, includes a rich scarlet.

DIANTHUS AT A GLANCE

D. caryophyllus is a colorful woody perennial, part of the large dianthus family of over 300 species. Hardy to 5°F (zone 7).

Jan	/	Companion Plants
Feb	/	Campanula
Mar	sow	Cistus
Apr	/	Crepis
May	transplant	Eryngium
Jun	flowering	Helianthemum
July	flowering	Portulaca
Aug	flowering	Sedum
Sept	/	Tulip
Oct	/	
Nov	/	
Dec	sow	

CONDITIONS

Aspect   Needs full sunlight all day. Protect from very strong winds.

Soil   Needs very well-drained soil, with plenty of additional, well-decayed organic matter. Unless the soil is alkaline, apply a light dressing of lime before each planting.

GROWING METHOD

Propagation   Grows easily from cuttings taken at almost any time. Use leafy side shoots and strip off all but the top leaves. Roots form in 3–5 weeks. Set newly rooted plants 8in apart. Water regularly to establish, then occasionally in dry weather. Carnations tolerate dry conditions well.

Feeding   Little fertilizer is needed if the soil contains plenty of organic matter, but you may give a complete feed twice, in the spring and again in mid-summer.

Problems   Carnation rust, a fungal disease, is common in warm, humid conditions. Grayish spots appear on leaves or stems, and the foliage may curl and yellow. Take prompt action by immediately spraying with a fungicide. Remove caterpillars when seen.

FLOWERING

Season   The crop of flowers appears in the summer, but it can be forced for other times. Remove any excess buds to produce good-sized, main blooms.

Cutting   An excellent cut flower. Recut stems between nodes (joints) to aid water uptake.

DIANTHUS CULTIVARS
Pinks

DIANTHUS CULTIVARS make reliable, popular edging plants with bright colors and, in many cases, a rich, pervasive scent.

ONE OF THE BEST pinks for the garden, or as a cut flower, "Doris" is vigorous, long-flowering, and sweetly scented. A "must-have."

FEATURES

EVERGREEN

Pinks are crosses of *D. caryophyllus* (wild carnation) and *D. plumarius* (cottage pink). Allwood Brothers nursery in West Sussex, England, has bred an enormous range of cultivars that are free-flowering, given the correct conditions. The gray-green foliage grows in a tufted mat and flowering stems are 4–12in tall. Most flowers are heavily scented and may be single or bicolored, some with a clear margin of contrasting color. Most are white, pink, red, deep crimson, or salmon, with cultivars ideally suited for the rock garden.

CONDITIONS

Aspect   Needs full sunlight all day, and protection from strong winds.

Site   Needs very free-draining soil, enriched with

DIANTHUS AT A GLANCE

The cultivars include perennials in a wide color range, many richly scented. Generally hardy to 5°F (zone 7).

Jan	/	Recommended Varieties
Feb	/	
Mar	sow	*Dianthus alpinus*
Apr	transplant	"Bovey Belle"
May	transplant	"Devon Glow"
Jun	flowering	*D. deltoides*
July	flowering	"La Bourboule"
Aug	flowering	"Monica Wyatt"
Sept	/	"Sam Barlow"
Oct	sow	"Whitehill"
Nov	/	"Widecombe Fair"
Dec	/	

additional decayed organic matter, well ahead of planting. Use a soil-testing kit to determine whether your soil is acid—if so, add quantities of lime according to the manufacturer's instructions. Beware of exceeding the recommended rate—it will simply do more harm than good.

GROWING METHOD

Propagation Grows easily from cuttings taken in late summer and the fall. Start fresh plants every three or four years to keep vigorous, compact growth. Space the plant approximately 6–12in apart, depending on the variety. Water until the plants are well established.

Feeding   Apply complete plant food in the early spring, when active spring growth begins.

Problems   Aphids and slugs are the two major problems. The former can be tackled by a regular spraying program with, for example, malathion. The latter can be seen late at night or early in the morning. Either treat chemically, or pick off by hand and drown.

FLOWERING

Season   Some pinks only flower during the spring, others have a long flowering period from the spring to early fall.

Cutting Pinks make excellent cut flowers, providing indoor decoration and scent.

AFTER FLOWERING

Requirements Cut off any spent flower stems to the ground as they fade. No other pruning action is necessary.

DIASCIA
Twinspur

ONE OF THE MOST USEFUL garden plants, twinspur produces flowers throughout the growing season, from the spring to fall, and at 12in tall, it makes the perfect front-of-border filler, tolerating a sunny position, and one with a degree of shade. Despite a short lifespan, it is easily propagated.

FEATURES

Twinspur has an extremely long flowering season, lasting from the spring until the first frosts. Though there is a large number of forms available, ranging from "Lilac Mist" to "Salmon Supreme," the color range is quite limited, essentially only including shades of pink. Diascia requires moist, rich soil, but over-feeding results in fewer flowers. The height ranges from 6 to 12in, which means the taller plants can be given free reign to burst through their neighbors, adding to the display. "Salmon Supreme" is an attractive low-spreader, being

6in high. *D. vigilis* is twice as tall, hardier, and even more free-flowering.

DIASCIA AT A GLANCE

A near 50-strong genus of annuals and perennials, with a pink color and a long flowering season. Hardy to 23°F (zone 9).

		Recommended Varieties
Jan	/	
Feb	sow 🖑	
Mar	divide 🖑	*Diascia barberae* "Ruby Field"
Apr	transplant 🖑	*D.* "Dark Eyes"
May	flowering 🌿	*D.* "Hector's Hardy"
Jun	flowering 🌿	*D. integerrima*
July	flowering 🌿	*D.* "Lilac Mist"
Aug	flowering 🌿	*D.* "Rupert Lambert"
Sept	flowering 🌿	*D. vigilis*
Oct	/	
Nov	/	
Dec	/	

CONDITIONS

Aspect   Enjoys full sun; though it tolerates some shade, it will not flower as long or as prolifically.

Soil   Moisture-retentive, well-drained ground.

GROWING METHOD

Propagation   This is essential, since diascias are short-lived, but propagation is easily managed. Success rates are high by all methods, though cuttings are particularly easy. Either sow the seed when ripe or in the following spring, take cuttings during the growing season, or divide in the spring. Since young plants might die in severe winters, keep indoor cuttings as possible replacements.

Feeding   Mulch well in the spring to enrich the soil.

Problems   Slugs and snails are the main enemies. Pick them off or use a chemical treatment.

FLOWERING

Season   An unusually long season from the spring, beyond the end of summer, to the first frosts.

Cutting   Diascias cut well, and although they do not last particularly long in water, replacements are quickly available from the parent plant.

AFTER FLOWERING

Requirements   Cut ruthlessly to the ground after flowering to promote a second flush of flowers.

DICENTRA SPECTABILIS
Bleeding heart

THE ARCHING STEMS of this bleeding heart carry masses of bright pink, heart-shaped flowers resembling tiny lockets.

THE BLEEDING HEART is well worth growing for its foliage alone, since the delicate, fern-like leaves are very decorative.

FEATURES

HERBACEOUS

With fern-like foliage and curving stems bearing pretty pink-and-white, heart-shaped flowers, bleeding heart is an all-time favorite perennial. It appeals to children and adults alike. There is a cultivar, "Alba," which has pure white flowers. Another species less commonly grown is *D. formosa*, which has very ferny foliage, but its flowers are not so completely heart-shaped. Bleeding heart can be grown in a mixed border or in the filtered shade of trees. Plants may reach 16–24in tall in good conditions, and form a clump approximately 20in wide.

DICENTRA AT A GLANCE

D. spectabilis is a clump-forming perennial, with arching stems and decorative deep pink flowers. Hardy to 0°F (zones 6–7).

		Recommended Varieties
Jan	/	
Feb	/	
Mar	sow	*D.* "Adrian Bloom"
Apr	transplant	"Bountiful"
May	transplant	*D. cucularia*
Jun	flowering	*D. f. alba*
July	flowering	"Langtrees"
Aug	/	"Ruby Slippers"
Sept	/	*D. macrantha*
Oct	division	*D. spectabilis*
Nov	sow	*D. s.* "Alba"
Dec	/	"Stuart Boothman"

CONDITIONS

Aspect   Dicentra grows best in filtered sunlight. Strong, hot, drying winds make it shrivel up. A sheltered position protects against late frosts.

Site   Needs well-drained soil rich in organic matter. Dig in copious quantities of decayed manure or compost several weeks before planting.

GROWING METHOD

Propagation   Divide large established clumps in the fall, and plant divisions 10–12in apart. Also grows from seed sown in the spring or fall. Needs regular, deep watering during dry periods in the spring and summer.

Feeding   Apply a sprinkling of a complete plant food whenever growth begins in the spring.

Problems   There are no specific pest or disease problems known for this plant.

FLOWERING

Season   Blooms for several weeks during late spring and early summer.

Cutting   Flowers are not suitable for cutting.

AFTER FLOWERING

Requirements   Cut out spent flower stems. As the foliage yellows and dies off, cut it off just above the ground.

DIGITALIS
Foxglove

A SUPERB DISPLAY of Digitalis grandiflora, *the yellow foxglove, which sends up 39in-high spires. It is an excellent choice for gaps toward the rear of the border, although you may have to weed out some seedlings that spread beyond the main clump.*

FEATURES

HERBACEOUS

Foxgloves are essentials for the "cottage garden," self-seeding in unexpected places, with their tall spires of often richly colored flowers. They grow in most soils and situations, from the shady to the sunny, and dryish to damp, although performance is variable at these extremes. They also make a large group of biennials and perennials ranging in height from 24in to 6½ft. The common foxglove (*D. purpurea*) can be grown as a perennial, but its lifespan is short, and the biennial is generally the preferred option. The color range includes red, yellow, white, and pink with the early summer Fox Hybrids. *D. grandiflora* has the largest flowers.

DIGITALIS AT A GLANCE

Foxgloves are grown for their tall spires of attractive, tubular flowers, usually in soft hues. Hardy to 5°F (zone 7).

		Recommended Varieties
Jan	/	
Feb	/	*Digitalis ferruginea*
Mar	sow	*D. grandiflora*
Apr	transplant	*D. lanata*
May	transplant	*D. parviflora*
Jun	flowering	*D. purpurea*
July	flowering	*D. p.* Excelsior Group
Aug	/	
Sept	/	
Oct	/	
Nov	/	
Dec	/	

CONDITIONS

Aspect   Dappled shade for part of the day is ideal, but it is not absolutely essential. Foxgloves are undemanding plants, and will grow in a wide range of yards.

Site   The soil conditions can vary, but humus-rich ground gives the best results.

GROWING METHOD

Propagation   Sow seed of new varieties in containers within a cold frame during the late spring. Space seedlings up to 18in apart. If you already have some plants, seeding is not necessary, since the foxglove is a prolific self-seeder. Dig up a new plant and transplant to where it is required. Water in well, and do not let it dry out.

Feeding   Provide a complete feed in the spring. In particularly dry soil, provide a protective spring mulch.

Problems   Leaf spot and powdery mildew can strike. Spraying is the best treatment.

FLOWERING

Season   Flowers appear in early and mid-summer.

Cutting   While they make good cut flowers, handle with extreme caution. The foliage can irritate the skin, and all parts are poisonous.

AFTER FLOWERING

Requirements   Leave just a few stems to seed where the foxgloves look good, mixing well with other plants, otherwise deadhead to avoid masses of invasive seedlings.

ECHINACEA PURPUREA
Purple coneflower

BOLDER THAN *many perennials, coneflowers are sometimes slow to appear in the spring but they are definitely worth the wait.*

THIS FINE STAND *of bright purple coneflowers adds a striking touch to this scheme. The flowers fade as they age, but petals don't fall.*

FEATURES

HERBACEOUS

Native to the prairie States of America, the coneflower is a hardy, drought-resistant plant. Its dark, cone-shaped center is surrounded by rich pink ray petals, and there are cultivars available in shades of pink-purple and white. They make excellent cut flowers. Coneflowers often grow over 39in tall, and are a great addition to a perennial border because they bloom over a long period, from mid-summer into the fall, when many other plants have finished. Echinacea should be mass-planted to get the best effect. Excellent varieties include *E. purpurea* Bressingham Hybrids, "Magnus," and "White Swan."

ECHINACEA AT A GLANCE

E. purpurea is an attractive, daisy-like perennial with purple flowers, ideal for naturalizing or borders. Hardy to 5°F (zone 7).

Jan	/	Companion Plants
Feb	sow	Allium
Mar	sow	Delphinium
Apr	transplant	Geranium
May	transplant	Gladiolus
Jun	/	Iris
July	flowering	Lavandula
Aug	flowering	Rosemary
Sept	flowering	Yucca
Oct	divide	Delphinium
Nov	/	Rose
Dec	/	

CONDITIONS

Aspect   Prefers full sunlight all day. Although it is tolerant of windy conditions, the blooms will have a better appearance if the plants are sheltered from strong winds.

Site   Needs well-drained, rich soil. Poor or sandy soils can be improved by digging in large quantities of compost or manure before planting.

GROWING METHOD

Propagation   Divide existing clumps in the early spring or fall, and replant divisions 8–10in apart. It can be grown from seeds sown in early spring, which may produce color variations. Echinacea needs regular watering to establish itself in prolonged dry spells, but occasional deep soakings in dry weather are enough, as it tolerates dry conditions well.

Feeding   Apply complete plant food in early spring and again in mid-summer.

Problems   No specific problems are known.

FLOWERING

Season   There is a long flowering period from late summer into the fall.

Cutting   Cut flowers for the vase when they are fully open, but before the petals separate.

AFTER FLOWERING

Requirements   Remove spent flower stems. The whole plant can be cut back to ground level in winter.

ECHINOPS
Globe thistle

THESE METALLIC BLUE globe thistles form an elegant picture against a stone wall.

EARLY MORNING LIGHT accentuates the rounded, slightly spiky heads of these globe thistle flowers, planted here in a bold drift in a countryside yard.

FEATURES

HERBACEOUS

This plant's very distinctive appearance makes a good accent in a mixed planting. Taller species need to be placed at the rear of a border, but others can be planted in bold groups through the bed. Most have foliage that is stiff, prickly, and finely divided, with silvery stems growing from 12in to 6½ft tall. Some of the species have foliage that has fine white hairs on the underside. The flowerheads are usually white or metallic blue, and are highly prized for their decorative value when cut and dried. The most commonly grown is *E. ritro* and its cultivars, some of which have deep blue flowers. *E. sphaerocephalus* has pale gray-to-silvery flowers.

ECHINOPS AT A GLANCE

A group of annuals, biennials, and perennials grown for their geometric shapes and blue flowers. Hardy to 23–50°F (zones 9–11).

Jan	divide	
Feb	divide	Recommended Varieties
Mar	sow	*Echinops bannaticus* "Blue Globe"
Apr	/	*E. b.* "Taplow Blue"
May	transplant	*E. ritro ruthenicus*
Jun	/	*E. r.* "Veitch's Blue"
July	flowering	
Aug	flowering	Companion Plants
Sept	flowering	Buddleja
Oct	divide	Kniphofia
Nov	divide	Perovskia
Dec	divide	

CONDITIONS

Aspect Prefers full sunlight all day.
Site Soil must be very well drained but need not be rich. The globe thistle can be grown in poor, gravel-like, or sandy soils.

GROWING METHOD

Propagation It can either be grown from seed, from division of existing clumps, or from root cuttings. All propagation is done from the fall to winter. Plant out about 16in apart and water regularly to establish. Although drought-tolerant, this plant benefits from occasional deep watering during prolonged dry spring and summer periods.
Feeding Apply a complete plant food or poultry manure in early spring.
Problems There are no known pest or disease problems, but plants will rot on sticky clay or poorly drained soil.

FLOWERING

Season Each species or variety will flower for approximately two months.
Cutting Flowerheads required for drying should be cut before the blooms are fully open.

AFTER FLOWERING

Requirements Cut off any remaining spent flowerheads, unless you want the seed to ripen. As the plant dies down, clean away dead foliage, wearing gloves to protect yourself against the foliage.

EPIMEDIUM
Barrenwort / Bishop's miter

NEW GROWTH on the bishop's miter bears attractive bronze or pink shadings, but the older foliage is plain green.

A DENSE CARPET of bishop's miter makes wonderful groundcover under a grove of shapely Japanese maples.

FEATURES

HERBACEOUS

EVERGREEN

This low-growing perennial is grown more for its attractive foliage than its flowers, although the blooms are quite attractive. The shape resembles a bishop's miter, giving rise to its common name. Many species have small, starry flowers in white, cream, or yellow, although there are pale and rose-pink varieties, too. This is a woodland plant that makes a good groundcover or filler for shady parts of the yard. Some die down completely in winter, while others remain evergreen. Plants are rarely more than 12in tall. Combine it with plants such as Solomon's seal, primrose, or lenten rose, which enjoy similar woodland-type conditions.

EPIMEDIUM AT A GLANCE

An evergreen, deciduous perennial making excellent groundcover in shady situations. Small flowers. Hardy to 5°F (zone 7).

		Recommended Varieties
Jan	/	
Feb	sow	*Epimedium cantabrigiense*
Mar	/	*E. grandiflorum*
Apr	transplant	*E. g.* "Nanum"
May	flowering	*E. g.* "Rose Queen"
Jun	/	*E. perralderianum*
July	/	*E. pinnatum colchicum*
Aug	/	*E. x rubrum*
Sept	sow	*E. x versicolor* "Sulphureum"
Oct	divide	
Nov	/	
Dec	/	

CONDITIONS

Aspect   Epimedium needs dappled shade and protection from strong winds.

Site   Requires well-drained soil, heavily enriched with organic matter. Regular mulching is beneficial to retain moisture.

GROWING METHOD

Propagation   Clumps can be divided in the fall, although with some varieties this is not easy. Pull apart or cut away sections of plant, keeping both roots and a bud or shoot on each piece. Plant 6–8in apart. Some species seed readily. Keep young plants well watered until they are well established.

Feeding   Apply a slow-release fertilizer in the spring.

Problems   Snails may attack soft new growth when it appears, so take precautions.

FLOWERING

Season   The small flowers appear in spring, along with the leaves. But shear off the foliage of all varieties in winter, even when green (except *E. perralderianum*), to prevent the flowers being obscured. Fresh leaves will quickly follow.

Cutting   Flowers can be cut for the vase and last quite well in water.

AFTER FLOWERING

Requirements   Spent flower stems can be clipped off. Old, dead foliage should be tidied up and removed by the end of the fall.

ERYNGIUM
Sea holly

AN OUTSTANDING PLANT for the Mediterranean-style garden is Eryngium maritimum. *It has strong architectural features with a stiff, branching habit, and mid- to late summer flowers. It can be grown in the border, or better still, in a gravel bed to highlight the shape.*

FEATURES

HERBACEOUS

EVERGREEN

Sea holly is a 230-species strong genus, with annuals, biennials, and perennials. Although they are related to cow parsley, they bear no resemblance, being grown for their marvellous, attractive, spiky appearance, blue flowers (though some are white or green), and ability to thrive in poor, rocky, sunny ground. Heights can vary considerably, from *E. alpinum*, 28in tall, which as its name suggests grows in the Alps, to *E. eburneum* from South America, which can reach 5ft, and *E. pandanifolium*, which is much taller at 10ft. One of the most attractive is the Moroccan *E. variifolium*, which has rounded, white-veined foliage setting off the pale blue flowers. It is

also more manageable at 14in high—good for the front of a border.

CONDITIONS

Aspect   Grow in full sunlight, well out of the shade.
Site   There are two types of sea holly, with different growing needs. Most prefer fast-draining, fertile ground (e.g. *E. alpinum* and *E. bourgatii*), and some (e.g. *E. eburneum*) poor stony ground, out of the winter wet.

GROWING METHOD

Propagation   Sow the seed when ripe; alternatively, take root cuttings in late winter, or divide in the spring.
Feeding   Only for the first kind of sea holly, which benefits from a spring feed and some well-rotted manure. Good drainage is important.
Problems   Slugs and snails are the main problem when sea holly is grown in the border, damaging the new, young leaves. Promptly remove when seen, or use a chemical treatment.

FLOWERING

Season   The earliest sea hollies begin flowering in early summer, while others last from mid- to early or mid-fall in dry weather.
Cutting   Sea holly makes an invaluable cut flower. They also make exceptional dried arrangements, combining with other architectural plants and softer, flowery ones.

AFTER FLOWERING

Requirements   Cut back the spent flowering stems to the ground.

ERYNGIUM AT A GLANCE

Annuals, and deciduous/evergreen perennials grown for their shape. Hardiness varies from 13°F (zone 8) to 0°F (zones 6–7).

Month		Recommended Varieties
Jan	/	
Feb	sow	*Eryngium alpinum*
Mar	division	*E. a.* "Blue Star"
Apr	transplant	*E. bourgatii*
May	transplant	*E. b.* "Oxford Blue"
Jun	flowering	*E. giganteum*
July	flowering	*E. x oliverianum*
Aug	flowering	*E. x tripartitum*
Sept	flowering	
Oct	sow	
Nov	/	
Dec	/	

EUPHORBIA
Spurge

THE HIGHLY VERSATILE spurge tolerates a wide range of conditions. One of its chief attractions is its striking bracts.

A MIXED BORDER showing the value of propagating your own euphorbia. Strong shapes, flowing clumps, it even thrives in the shade.

FEATURES

HERBACEOUS

EVERGREEN

A large group of important shrubs, annuals, biennials, perennials, and subshrubs, ranging from tree-like succulents to structural clumps for the border. The latter spurges, evergreen and deciduous, grow in a wide range of conditions, from shade to sun, and tend to be quite sturdy, many leaning at 45° if not standing upright. Many of the evergreens benefit from being cut back to produce vigorous new spring growth. For example *E. characias* yields stems covered in small, stiff, outward-pointing leaves and yellow-green flowers. A big clump makes a bold, striking feature. *E. griffithii* "Fireglow," deciduous, is about half as high and produces early summer orange-red terminal bracts. It spreads to form a large colony. And *E. schillingii*, a recent find in Nepal by plant hunter Tony Schilling, flowers in late summer and has yellow bracts.

CONDITIONS

Aspect	Depending on your choice of plant, spurges like full sunlight or light shade.
Soil	This can vary from light, fast-draining soil to damp, moist ground, rich with leaf mold.

GROWING METHOD

Propagation	Sow the seed when ripe, or the following spring. Alternatively, divide perennials in the spring, or take spring cuttings.
Feeding	Spurges that require rich soil can be given a scattering of complete plant food and mulched in the spring. Those that require fast-draining ground need only be fed.
Problems	Aphids can be a problem in a bad year; spray at the first sign of an attack.

FLOWERING

Season	Flowers appear in the spring or summer.
Cutting	While the stem structure of most spurges makes them theoretically good as cut flowers, note that the milky sap can badly irritate the skin; if any part of the plant is ingested, severe discomfort results. Wear gloves and goggles.

AFTER FLOWERING

Requirements	Cut back the brownish or lackluster stems in the fall to promote fresh new growth.

EUPHORBIA AT A GLANCE

A genus of some 2,000 species. The border kind tend to be grown for their structure. Frost-tender to hardy 0°F (zones 6–7).

		Recommended Varieties
Jan	/	
Feb	/	*Euphorbia amygdaloides var. robbiae*
Mar	divide	
Apr	transplant	*E. characias*
May	flowering	*E. characias wulfenii*
Jun	flowering	*E. griffithii* "Dixter"
July	flowering	*E. myrsinites*
Aug	flowering	*E. palustris*
Sept	flowering	*E. polychroma*
Oct	sow	
Nov	/	
Dec	/	

GERANIUM
Cranesbill

THE FOLIAGE *on this clump-forming, North American* Geranium macrorrhizum *is as attractive as its pink-white or pink flowers. The leaves are scented and quickly form a dense carpet.*

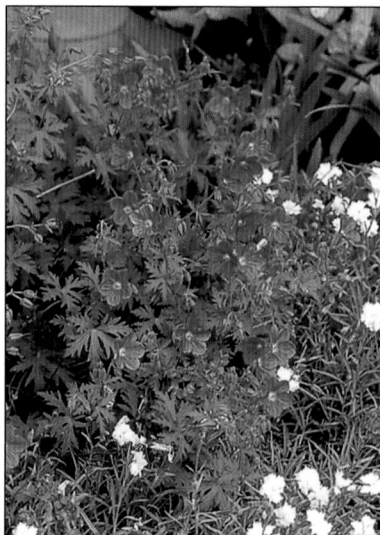

GERANIUM PRATENSE, *with its deep violet flowers that bloom over a long period.*

FEATURES

HERBACEOUS

EVERGREEN

There are a great many perennial species of the true, hardy geranium, and many are reliable, long-flowering plants. Most cranesbill geraniums (not to be confused with tender, pot-plant pelargoniums) are easy to grow and are ideal in perennial borders, as edging plants, or as an infill between shrubs. Some species self-sow freely, but unwanted seedlings are easily removed. Cranesbills range from about 6 to 39in tall. Most have attractive, deeply divided leaves, and the flowers cover a range of shades, mostly in violet, blue, pink, rose, and cerise. Species worth seeking out include *G. endressii* and its cultivars, especially "Wargrave Pink," *G. pratense*, *G. psilostemon*, *G. himalayense*, and *G. sanguineum*. A variety of *G. sanguineum*, "Lancastriense," is a dwarf-growing type that can be used as groundcover.

GERANIUM AT A GLANCE

A genus of some 300 annuals, biennials, and perennials grown for their big flowering clumps. Most are hardy to 5°F (zone 7).

Jan	/	Recommended Varieties
Feb	sow 🖐	
Mar	sow 🖐	*Geranium himalayense*
Apr	divide 🖐	"Gravetye"
May	transplant 🖐	"Johnson's Blue"
Jun	flowering 🌿	*G.* x *oxonianum* "Wargrave Pink"
July	flowering 🌿	*G. palmatum*
Aug	flowering 🌿	*G. pratense* "Mrs Kendall Clark"
Sept	flowering 🌿	*G. psilostemon*
Oct	sow 🖐	
Nov	/	
Dec	/	

CONDITIONS

Aspect — Most like sunlight; others prefer shade.

Site — Needs open, well-drained soil, but it need not be rich. Very acid ground should be limed before planting; use a soil-testing kit to ascertain the quantity required.

GROWING METHOD

Propagation — Most cranesbills are easily grown from seed sown in the fall, but note that the results will be variable. They can also be grown from cuttings taken in the growing season. Established clumps can be lifted and divided in the spring. The exact spacing depends on the variety, but it is usually within the range of 8–16in. Established plants tolerate dry conditions and rarely need watering, except in prolonged droughts.

Feeding — Apply a little complete plant food when growth starts in the spring.

Problems — No specific pest or disease problems are known for these plants.

FLOWERING

Season — Cranesbills flower through the spring, into late summer.

Cutting — Flowers do not cut well.

AFTER FLOWERING

Requirements — Remove spent flower stems, unless you want the plants to seed. Some pruning may be needed through the growing season if growth becomes too rampant. Prune to maintain shape.

GEUM CHILOENSE

Avens

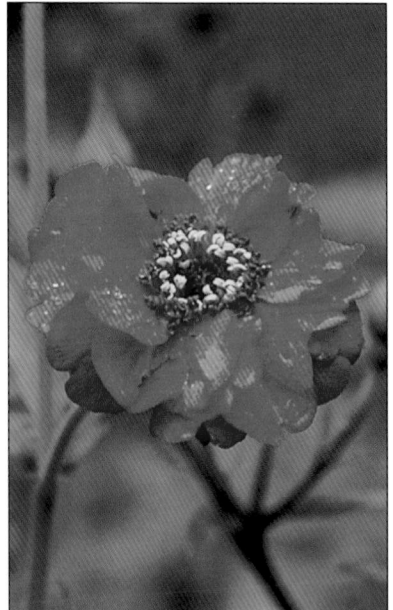

THE BRIGHT RED double geum "Mrs J Bradshaw," a justifiably popular perennial.

LIKE MOST PERENNIALS, geums look best when planted together in large numbers. Here a mass of deep red flowers looks wonderful against a background of green foliage.

FEATURES

HERBACEOUS

Although there are many species of geum, the two most commonly grown are cultivars. "Lady Stratheden" has double yellow flowers, and "Mrs J Bradshaw" bright scarlet double flowers. Flowers appear on stems 12–20in tall high that emerge from large rosettes of slightly hairy, lobed compound leaves. Foliage is generally evergreen, but may be herbaceous in some areas. Geums can be planted as accent plants, preferably in groups, in the wild garden or near the front of a mixed border. While flowers are not very suitable for cutting, they give a long, vibrant display in the yard if they are regularly deadheaded.

GEUM AT A GLANCE

A brightly colored perennial, essential for the spring border, with plenty of attractive cultivars. All hardy to 0°F (zones 6–7).

Jan	/	Recommended Varieties
Feb	sow 🖎	
Mar	divide 🖎	"Borisii"
Apr	transplant 🖎	"Fire Opal"
May	flowering 🌺	"Lady Stratheden"
Jun	flowering 🌺	*G. montanum*
July	/	"Mrs J Bradshaw"
Aug	/	*G. rivale*
Sept	/	*G. urbanum*
Oct	divide 🖎	
Nov	/	
Dec	/	

CONDITIONS

Aspect   Prefers full sunlight, but it can also be grown successfully in dappled shade.

Site   Needs well-drained soil. Plants will benefit from the addition of plenty of decayed manure or compost before planting.

GROWING METHOD

Propagation   Clumps can be divided in the spring or fall. Cut back foliage to reduce moisture loss while divisions re-establish. It also grows from seed sown in spring, but plants may not be true to type. Plant about 10–12in apart. Since most popular varieties tend to be short-lived, propagate often for a regular supply.

Feeding   Apply complete plant food in early spring and again in mid-summer.

Problems   No particular problems are known.

FLOWERING

Season   There is a long flowering display, through late spring and mid-summer. Young vigorous plants will keep going to the fall.

Cutting   Regular cutting (or deadheading) is essential to prolong the display.

AFTER FLOWERING

Requirements   None, apart from the removal of spent flower stems and any dead foliage that may accumulate under the rosette.

GUNNERA MANICATA
Gunnera

THE HUGE, *theatrical, eye-catching leaves of* Gunnera manicata.

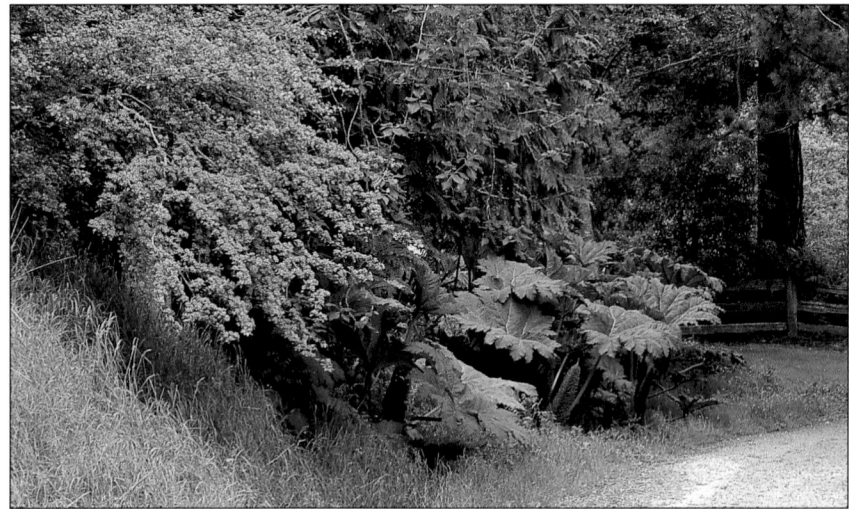

DAMP GROUND *at the bottom of this steep bank allows the clump of gunnera to thrive in its favorite conditions. The attractive pink-flowering shrub beside it is a hawthorn (*Crataegus *species).*

FEATURES

HERBACEOUS

This is not a plant for small yards. Growing to 8½ft high, clumps grow 10–13ft wide. The huge rhubarb-like leaves can be well over 42in in diameter, and are supported by long, stout, hairy stems. This is a magnificent feature plant from Africa, Australasia, and South America. It needs a damp or wet yard area, beside a pond or stream, or to the edge of a lawn. In summer it produces a dramatic tall spike of greenish flowers, often completely concealed by the foliage, but this plant is grown for the impact of its giant, architectural foliage. It is herbaceous, dying right back to the ground in winter. This is not a difficult plant to grow in the correct conditions, but it must be carefully sited. It needs space to grow, and gardeners need space to stand back and admire it.

GUNNERA AT A GLANCE

One of the largest, most spectacular perennials, it produces huge, often lobed, leaves. Spectacular flower spike. Hardy to 5°F (zone 7).

		Recommended Varieties
Jan	/	
Feb	/	*Gunnera arenaria*
Mar	/	*G. flavida* (groundcover)
Apr	transplant 🌿	*G. hamiltonii*
May	transplant 🌿	*G. magellanica*
Jun	/	(groundcover)
July	flowering 🌼	*G. manicata*
Aug	/	*G. prorepens*
Sept	sow 🌱	*G. tinctoria*
Oct	/	
Nov	/	
Dec	/	

CONDITIONS

Aspect Grows both in semi-shade and sunlight in cool, damp areas.

Site Likes a rich, moist soil. Dig plenty of organic matter into the ground before planting, and mulch crowns heavily with decayed compost or manure for protection.

GROWING METHOD

Propagation Divide small clumps in the spring, replanting them no less than 6½ft apart. Cuttings can be taken from new growth, too. Pot them up and nurture them until they are well rooted. Plants can be raised from seed, but this is slow and difficult. Keep moist throughout the spring and summer.

Feeding Apply pelleted poultry manure as new growth commences in the early spring to give the plant a boost. Add a fresh mulch of rotted manure at the same time.

Problems No specific pest or disease problems are known for gunnera.

FLOWERING

Season Heavy spikes of greenish flowers are produced in early summer.

Fruits The inflorescence is followed by fleshy red-green fruits, which can be ornamental.

AFTER FLOWERING

Requirements As the weather becomes cold in the fall and leaves begin to brown, cut off the foliage and cover the crown of the plant with a thick layer of straw. Use a large leaf as a hat to keep it dry.

GYPSOPHILA PANICULATA

Baby's breath

THE WONDERFUL, MASSED DISPLAY OF Gypsophila paniculata *"Pink Star" in full bloom. The rippling, airy mound of flowers justifiably led to its common name, baby's breath. It makes a stunning sight in its native habitats, spreading across the sandy steppes of the Far East and eastern Europe.*

FEATURES

HERBACEOUS

Baby's breath is an eye-catching border perennial that grows to 4ft high, and produces a summer flower display that looks like a puffy aerial cloud. The flowers appear in mid- and late summer, and are white on the species, though there are gently colored cultivars. "Compacta Plena" is soft pink, "Flamingo" is lilac-pink, and "Rosenschleier" pale pink. The latter is also quite short, at 1ft tall, and is worth repeat-planting in a long border. "Bristol Fairy" has the advantage of large, white flowers, ½in across, but it is not as vigorous as the rest and is relatively short-

lived, needing to be propagated every few years. *G. paniculata* mixes well with contrasting, vertical plants.

CONDITIONS

Aspect	Full sunlight is required for it to thrive.
Site	Free-draining soil is essential, since the plant's native habitat is sandy steppes and stony sites in eastern Europe, Central Asia, and China.

GROWING METHOD

Propagation	Sow seed in a cold frame in spring, or in pots in a gently heated greenhouse in winter. Species can be propagated by root cuttings, again in late winter. Though adult plants tolerate some dryness, the young plants must not be allowed to dry out. Water regularly in the growing season. Plant out in its final position, since it dislikes disturbance.
Feeding	A scattering of complete plant food in the spring.
Problems	Generally problem-free.

FLOWERING

Season	The one flowering period is mid- and late summer; an unmissable sight.
Cutting	Makes excellent cut flowers—the light sprays of white-to-pink flowers add considerably to any arrangement, formal or flowery.

AFTER FLOWERING

Requirements	Cut back to ground level in the fall.

GYPSOPHILA AT A GLANCE

A striking, tallish herbaceous perennial that gives an impactful, flowery mid-summer display. Hardy to 0°F (zones 6–7).

Jan	/	Companion Plants
Feb	/	
Mar	sow 👈	*Agapanthus africanus*
Apr	transplant 👈	*Geranium himalayense*
May	/	*Iris* "Magic Man"
Jun	/	*Osteospermum* "Whirligig"
July	flowering ✤	*Salvia cacaliifolia*
Aug	flowering ✤	*Silene coeli-rosa*
Sept	/	*Solanum crispum*
Oct	/	
Nov	/	
Dec	/	

HELENIUM AUTUMNALE
Sneezeweed

STILL ONE OF THE BEST and most popular cultivars of sneeze-weed, "Moerheim Beauty" has been a favorite since the 1930s.

ORANGE AND TAWNY COLORS are a feature of sneezeweed, a reliable perennial that brightens the fall garden.

FEATURES

HERBACEOUS

As its Latin name suggests, this herbaceous perennial flowers from late summer to mid-fall. The straight species has bright golden, daisy-like flowers with dark centers, but many of the most popular cultivars have flowers in rich tones of orange-red or copper-red. "Butterpat," "Moerheim Beauty," and "Waldtraut," are among the most popular varieties. Sneezeweed can grow 39–60in or more high, eventually forming large clumps over 20in across. Flowers cut well, but the plant is probably more valuable for its contribution to the fall garden. Place at the back of a perennial border or among shrubs. Easy to grow.

HELENIUM AT A GLANCE

A group of annuals, biennials and perennials. Grown for their prolific, bright flowering display. Hardy to 5°F (zone 7).

		Recommended Varieties
Jan	/	
Feb	sow 🖐	
Mar	sow 🖐	"Butterpat"
Apr	transplant 🖐	"Chipperfield Orange"
May	transplant 🖐	"Crimson Beauty"
Jun	/	"Moerheim Beauty"
July	flowering ✿	"Rotgold"
Aug	flowering ✿	"The Bishop"
Sept	flowering ✿	
Oct	/	
Nov	/	
Dec	/	

CONDITIONS

Aspect Needs to be grown in full sun right through the day. Avoid shade.

Site Needs a moisture-retentive soil heavily enriched with organic matter. It will not thrive in dry soil. Mulch around clumps to help keep soil moist.

GROWING METHOD

Propagation Established clumps can be lifted and divided about every three years. Discard the oldest central sections and replant the divisions about 12in apart in spring or fall. Give new young plants a regular watering right through the growing season.

Feeding Apply complete plant food as new growth commences in spring.

Problems Sneezeweed is generally free from problems, although slugs and snails can damage newly emerging growth in damp weather.

FLOWERING

Season The flowering season starts in mid-summer and continues into the fall.

Cutting Flowers cut well for indoor decoration.

AFTER FLOWERING

Requirements Spent flower stems should be removed. As the plant dies down, cut off and remove dead foliage. It can be chopped and left on the ground as a mulch. With flowers blooming into the fall, the foliage remains in good condition until attacked by frost.

HELLEBORUS
Lenten rose

PRETTY SHADINGS *of color are shown on the Lenten rose. Seedlings often produce unexpected colors, which can be maintained if the plants are then propagated by division.*

NATIVE *to Corsica and Sardinia, this is the green-flowered* Helleborus argutifolius.

FEATURES

EVERGREEN

Various species of hellebores are known as the Christmas or Lenten rose because of their flowering times—mid-winter or early spring. *H. niger*, which has pure white flowers with green centers, can be difficult to grow to perfection; *H. argutifolius* (syn. *H. corsicus*) and H. *orientalis* are more resilient. *H. argutifolius* has lovely lime-green flowers and spiny-toothed leaf margins, while *H. orientalis* is more variable and may have white, green, pink, or mottled flowers. Cultivars include a deep crimson variety. These perennials are mostly evergreen and are best planted under deciduous trees, where they can remain undisturbed. Some are fairly short-lived, but they tend to self-seed freely so that numbers readily increase, creating an impressive sight.

HELLEBORUS AT A GLANCE

A free-spreading, attractively flowering perennial in a wide range of colors. Excellent in woodland. Hardy to 23–59°F (zones 9–11).

Jan	flowering 🌿	Recommended Varieties
Feb	flowering 🌿	
Mar	flowering 🌿	*Helleborus argutifolius* (syn.
Apr	divide ✍	H. *corsicus*)
May	transplant ✍	H. *foetidus*
Jun	/	H. *lividus*
July	/	H. *niger*
Aug	/	H. x *nigercors*
Sept	/	H. *orientalis* Cultivars
Oct	/	H. x *sternii* Blackthorn
Nov	/	Group
Dec	/	H. *viridis*

CONDITIONS

Aspect   Prefers dappled sunlight under trees, or in other partially shaded spots.
Site   Soil must be well enriched with organic matter, and able to retain moisture. Excellent in winter containers.

GROWING METHOD

Propagation   Divide clumps in the spring or summer, directly after flowering, replanting the divisions about 8–12in apart. Seed can be sown when ripe, but seedlings will take about three years to flower. Seedlings often produce interesting shades. Recently planted hellebores need plenty of water in prolonged, dry spells in the spring and summer.
Feeding   Apply a little complete plant food in the spring. Mulch each spring with manure or compost to aid moisture retention.
Problems   Leaf blotch can disfigure and weaken plants. Spray with a fungicide. Beware aphids, particularly after flowering. Slugs attack the flowers and foliage.

FLOWERING

Season   From mid-winter to early spring.
Cutting   Lenten roses provide attractive cut flowers at the time of year when supply is short.

AFTER FLOWERING

Requirements   Prune off the dead flower stems and any dead leaves. Do not disturb.

HEMEROCALLIS
Daylily

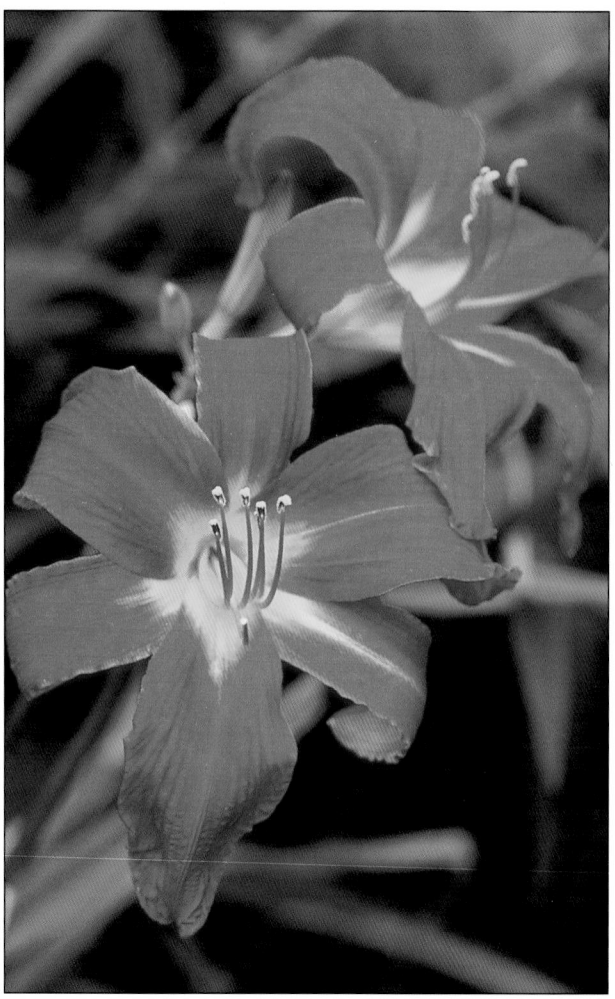

MAHOGANY RED is one of the many strong colors available in the huge range of daylily cultivars now available from specialist growers.

THE MASS PLANTING of this creamy yellow daylily increases its impact. Blooms will appear one after the other for many weeks.

FEATURES

HERBACEOUS

EVERGREEN

Easily grown in a wide range of conditions, the daylily is a trouble-free plant with single or double flowers. As its name suggests, individual flowers last only one day, but they are produced over a long period. They come in a wide range of colors, the main ones being shades of yellow, orange, red, magenta, and purple. There is an enormous number of exciting, attractive hybrids available from specialist growers. The clumps of grassy foliage may be from 10–39in high; some are evergreen while others die down in winter. While straight species are not as readily available as the hybrids, they are important in hybridizing new varieties and several species are worth seeking out. They include *H. altissima* from China, which has pale yellow fragrant flowers on stems 5ft or so high, and *H. lilio-asphodelus*, which has pale yellow fragrant flowers above leaves 22in high.

Categories Daylilies have been divided into five categories which list them according to flower type. The divisions are circular, double, spider-shaped, star-shaped, and triangular. Most are single; hot weather can produce extra petals and stamens.

Dwarf forms The number of dwarf forms available is steadily increasing and they may be better suited to today's smaller gardens. Those with a reliable reflowering habit can also be successfully grown in pots. Use a good quality potting mix and crowd three plants into a 8in pot for good effect. "Little Grapette," "Little Gypsy Vagabond," "Penny's Worth," and "Stella d'Oro" are good ones to try, all growing about 12 x 18in.

Uses Mass plantings of dwarf or tall forms create the best effect. Daylilies are not plants that should be dotted about in the garden. Use large numbers of either the one variety or use varieties of similar color; it is clearly preferable to planting a mixture of types or colors. In a mixed border they give a very pleasing effect as the foliage is very full.

"BURNING DAYLIGHT," one of the top daylilies, blooms prolifically in sun or semi-shade.

MANY OF the finest daylily cultivars are in creamy yellow or orange tones, not surprisingly as these are the colors of many of the species.

CONDITIONS

Aspect Grows best in full sun but tolerates semi-shade. Can be mass planted on banks or sloping ground as the roots are very efficient soil binders.

Site Grows in any type of soil, wet or dry, but to get maximum growth from the newer hybrids the soil should be enriched with manure or compost before planting.

HEMEROCALLIS AT A GLANCE

A genus of semi-, evergreen, and herbaceous perennials; 30,000 cultivars that give a long summer show. Hardy to 5°F (zone 7).

		Recommended Varieties
Jan	/	
Feb	sow	"Burning Daylight"
Mar	sow	"Cartwheels"
Apr	transplant	"Golden Chimes"
May	transplant	"Neyron Rose"
Jun	flowering	"Pink Damask"
July	flowering	"Red Precious"
Aug	flowering	"Stafford"
Sept	flowering	"Whichford"
Oct	divide	"Zara"
Nov	/	
Dec	/	

GROWING METHOD

Propagation Divide established clumps in spring or fall. Cut back foliage before or straight after division. Spacing may be from 6–12in, depending on variety.
New plants need regular watering to establish. Once established, plants are very drought tolerant, but better sized blooms can be expected if deep waterings are given every week or two.

Feeding Grows without supplementary fertilizer, but an application of complete plant food in early spring encourages stronger, more vigorous growth.

Problems Daylilies growing in very soggy ground tend to survive quite well but produce few flowers. Otherwise no problems.

FLOWERING

Season Depending on variety, plants may be in bloom any time from late spring until the fall. Most flowers only last one day.

Cutting Single flowers can be cut for the vase. Attractive and well worth using.

AFTER FLOWERING

Requirements Cut off any spent flower stems. Herbaceous types that die down in the fall can have their foliage cut back too.

HEUCHERA SANGUINEA
Coral flower

DAINTY LITTLE PINK FLOWERS are massed above the attractive foliage, making the North American coral flower an excellent choice for the front of a border or a garden bed. Here they are planted to provide an excellent foil for the abundant blooms of white roses behind.

FEATURES

EVERGREEN

This perennial forms a low rosette of lobed leaves that make a neat plant for edging, or for mass-planting at the front of the border. The foliage is evergreen. Established plantings produce a striking display of blooms. The flower stems, which stand above the foliage, are from 12 to 18in tall. The species has red flowers; cultivars are available with pink, white, or deeper crimson blooms. Note the superb foliage varieties ("Palace Purple"—chocolate-colored; "Pewter Moon"—gray; and "Snow Storm"—white flecked). New American varieties include "Pewter Veil."

HEUCHERA AT A GLANCE

H. sanguinea is a red-flowering, summer perennial forming low, wide clumps, 6 x 12in. Hardy to 5°F (zone 7).

		Recommended Plants
Jan	/	
Feb	sow	*Heuchera americana*
Mar	sow	"Chocolate Ruffles"
Apr	divide	*H. cylindrica*
May	transplant	"Green Ivory"
Jun	flowering	"Helen Dillon"
July	flowering	"Persian Carpet"
Aug	flowering	"Pewter Moon"
Sept	/	"Rachel"
Oct	divide	"Red Spangles"
Nov	/	"Scintillation"
Dec	/	

CONDITIONS

Aspect   Prefers full sun but tolerates light shade.
Site   Needs very well-drained, open-textured soil. Permanently wet soil will kill this plant.

GROWING METHOD

Propagation   Clumps can be divided in the spring or in the fall, but ensure that each division has its own set of healthy roots. It can also be grown from seed sown in the spring; cuttings will also root quite freely. Plant at approximately 8–10in intervals for a good effect.
Feeding   Apply a complete plant food when growth commences in the spring.
Problems   Vine weevil grubs may devour roots and stems. Destroy the infected clump, and use severed shoots as cuttings.

FLOWERING

Season   It flowers well through most of the summer, with a few spikes hanging on until the early fall.
Cutting   Flowers do not last well as cut blooms.

AFTER FLOWERING

Requirements   Promptly remove any spent flower stems once they begin to look untidy. Apart from the removal of any dead leaves, this is all that is necessary.

HOSTA
Plantain lily

LEAVES PATTERNED VARIOUSLY in lime-green and blue make this Hosta *"Frances Williams" an outstanding garden feature. Here it lights up a dull area under a tree, the little available light being reflected outward by the lime-green. In shady areas where few flowers bloom, it is a real bonus.*

FEATURES

HERBACEOUS

Also known as the plantain lily, this herbaceous perennial is grown for its attractive, decorative foliage. It is long-lived, and foliage may be tiny or up to 18in wide and 36in high. There are hundreds of cultivars with leaves that may be light or dark green, chartreuse or yellow, gray-green or blue. Many are variegated. Leaf texture also varies: it can be smooth or shiny, matt or powdery, puckered or corrugated. Hostas are excellent at forming big, bold clumps that keep down the weeds, but until they emerge in late spring some weeding will be necessary; they also benefit from heavy mulching. Hostas look best mass-planted near water features, or when allowed to multiply in shady areas under trees.

Variegations Cultivars with cream, white, or yellow variegations will brighten a shady part of the yard, and so long as the tree or shrub canopy is high enough to let sufficient light reach the hostas, they will maintain their variegation. Likewise, plants with sharp chartreuse or acid-lime-colored foliage can be used to give a lift to shady areas. Types can be mixed to create a wealth of different effects.

Flowers The bell-shape flowers, mostly in mauve shades, appear in the summer and are held high above the foliage. Some species, such as *H. plantaginea* and its cultivar "Grandiflora," produce pure white, lightly fragrant flowers. However, few gardeners plant hostas just for the flowers; the leaves alone are good enough.

HOSTA AT A GLANCE

A mainly clump-forming perennial from the Far East. Grow in pots or the garden for the foliage. Hardy to 0°F (zones 6–7).

Month	Activity	Recommended Varieties
Jan	/	
Feb	/	"Aureomarginata"
Mar	sow	"Blue Angel"
Apr	divide	"Francee"
May	transplant	"Frances Williams"
Jun	flowering	"Golden Tiara"
July	flowering	"Love Pat"
Aug	divide	*H. lancifolia*
Sept	flowering	"Shade Fanfare"
Oct	/	"Wide Brim"
Nov	/	
Dec	/	

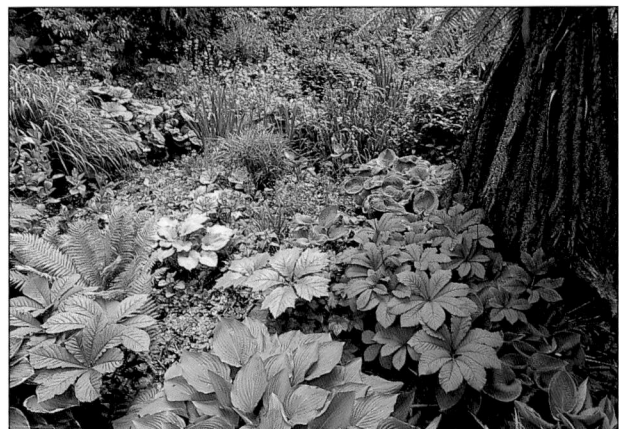

PURE WHITE FLOWERS appear on some species of hosta, such as Hosta plantaginea *and some of its cultivars.*

HOSTAS, RODGERSIAS, and ferns revel in the light shade and constant damp soil prevalent in woodlands.

Companions   Since hostas do not come into leaf early in the spring, the early-flowering bulbs, such as snowdrops and snowflakes, or early perennials, such as corydalis, can be planted among them. They make a bright, successful show.

CONDITIONS

Aspect   Most hostas grow in full sunlight if well watered. They thrive in shade or dappled light. Blue-leaved forms can be the hardest of all to place because they turn green with either too much sun or too heavy shade. Yellow or gold forms are best with direct sunlight in the early morning or late in the afternoon.

Site   Needs rich, moisture-retentive soil. Large amounts of decayed manure or compost should be dug into the ground before planting. Mulch plants after planting. Superb in tubs, getting bigger and better each year.

GROWING METHOD

Propagation   Divide the fleshy underground rhizomes in early spring. Most hostas are best divided every four to five years. Plant the dwarf cultivars 6in

apart, the larger ones at intervals of 36in. Several species can be raised from seed, though they may not be true to type.

Feeding   Apply pelletted poultry manure in the spring.

Problems   Slugs and snails can be a major problem. Pick off snails, and avoid watering in the evening. Place slug pellets or sharp sand around the leaves.

FLOWERING

Season   Flowers are produced in the summer. The color range varies from white to purple.

Cutting   Hosta provides cut flowers; the foliage is also attractive.

AFTER FLOWERING

Requirements   Cut off any spent flower stems in the spring. Continue watering the plants until the foliage begins to die down, and then tidy up the clumps, which can look unsightly. Mulch the area with supplies of compost or manure. Some hostas (*sieboldiana*) produce good fall tints. The seedheads can be left on for winter decoration.

KNIPHOFIA
Red hot poker

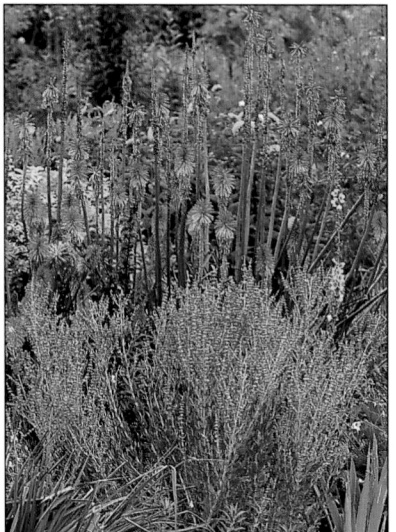

FLAME-COLORED pokers and soft purple perovskia both tolerate dry conditions.

THE COLORS in this generous planting of red hot pokers reflect both the yellow achillea behind and the red plants in the foreground. The abundant grassy foliage provides a valuable contrast.

FEATURES

EVERGREEN

These evergreen perennials, also known as torch lilies, make great feature plants, with their bright flower spikes in cream, orange, red, yellow, and many shadings of these colors. Flower stems stand high above the grassy foliage, which may be anywhere from 24in to 6½ft tall. Even out of flower, the distinctive foliage makes red hot poker a good accent plant. Since clumps should remain undisturbed for many years, plant red hot pokers in their final position.

CONDITIONS

Aspect Needs full sunlight all day. A valuable plant because it tolerates a wide range of exposed windy or coastal areas.

KNIPHOFIA AT A GLANCE

A genus of some 70 species of evergreen and deciduous perennials, grown for their flowering spires. Hardy to 5°F (zone 7).

Jan	/	Recommended Varieties
Feb	/	
Mar	sow	"Bees Sunset"
Apr	divide	"Brimstone"
May	transplant	"Buttercup"
Jun	flowering	*K. caulescens*
July	flowering	"Little Maid"
Aug	flowering	"Royal Standard"
Sept	flowering	"Samuel's Sensation"
Oct	flowering	"Sunningdale Yellow"
Nov	/	*K. triangularis*
Dec	/	

Site Needs well-drained soil. Although it tolerates poorer soils, especially sandy ones, you will get better results if the soil is enriched with manure or compost.

GROWING METHOD

Propagation Well-established clumps can be divided in late spring. Foliage on new divisions must be reduced by half to allow successful root regrowth to take place. The smaller-growing forms can be planted at 20in spacings, but the large growers may need up to 30in or more. Needs regular watering to establish in prolonged dry spells, after which it is very drought-tolerant.

Feeding Grows without supplementary fertilizer, but complete plant food applied in the spring should noticeably increase the quantity and quality of the flowers.

Problems No specific problems are known.

FLOWERING

Season Flowering times can vary slightly with species and cultivar. Generally, red hot pokers flower in late summer and early fall.

Cutting The flowers last well when cut if the stems are scalded for approximately 10 seconds. They make an invaluable tall, stiff background for a display of smaller, flowery cuttings.

AFTER FLOWERING

Requirements Spent flower stalks should be promptly cut off. Any dead leaves should be pulled away to give the clump a clean look. Protect the crown with straw or leaves in cold areas.

LEUCANTHEMUM
Shasta daisy

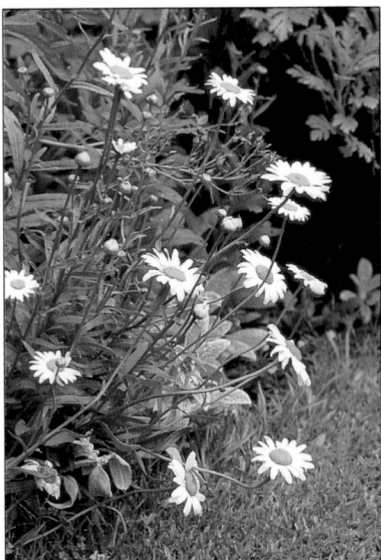

LONG-STEMMED shasta daisies are an ideal component of flower arrangements.

A CONTINUOUS PLANTING of shasta daisies fills this awkward narrow space between a path and a low brick wall. The cheerful white flowers appear throughout the summer.

FEATURES

HERBACEOUS

Leucanthemum x *superbum* (Shasta daisy) looks wonderful when planted in a mixed border, where the large white flowers mix with more brightly colored flowers. Despite being easy to grow and multiplying rapidly, the daisies do not become a menace. Flower stalks can grow 24–36in tall, while the dark green leaves are only 4–6in high. Shasta daisies make striking cut flowers, livening up any arrangement. There are a number of named cultivars, some, such as "Esther Read," "Wirral Supreme," and "Cobham Gold," with double flowers. (Despite its name, the flowers on "Cobham Gold" are cream, not gold.) "Everest" is probably the largest of the single cultivars, though it is rarely available.

LEUCANTHEMUM AT A GLANCE

L. x *superbum* is a vigorous, clump-forming perennial with many attractive cultivars, mainly in white. Hardy to 23°F (zone 9).

Jan	/	Recommended Varieties
Feb	/	
Mar	divide	*Leucanthemum* x *superbum*
Apr	transplant	"Aglaia"
May	transplant	"Alaska"
Jun	flowering	"Bishopstone"
July	flowering	"Cobham Gold"
Aug	flowering	"Horace Read"
Sept	flowering	"Phyllis Smith"
Oct	divide	"Snowcap"
Nov	/	
Dec	/	

CONDITIONS

Aspect   Prefers full sunlight all day and wind protection.

Site   The soil should be well drained, and improved by the addition of decayed compost or manure.

GROWING METHOD

Propagation   Divide the clumps in early spring or late summer, replanting only the younger, vigorous, outer growths, each with its own set of roots and shoots. Plant the divisions approximately 10in apart. Cuttings of young, short shoots can also be taken in early spring.

Feeding   Apply complete plant food as growth begins in the spring. Liquid fertilizer applied in late spring should help produce better blooms.

Problems   The main problems are aphids, slugs, earwigs, and chrysanthemum eelworm. The first can be tackled with a proprietary spray, and the second and third by traps (saucers filled with beer, and inverted flower pots filled with straw placed on bamboo canes). In the case of eelworm, evident from browning/blackening, drying foliage from the base upward, the whole plant must be destroyed.

FLOWERING

Season   Flowering is all summer long.

Cutting   Cut flowers regularly for indoor decoration, which will also prolong the garden display.

AFTER FLOWERING

Requirements   Cut back spent flower stems to the ground.

LIGULARIA
Ligularia

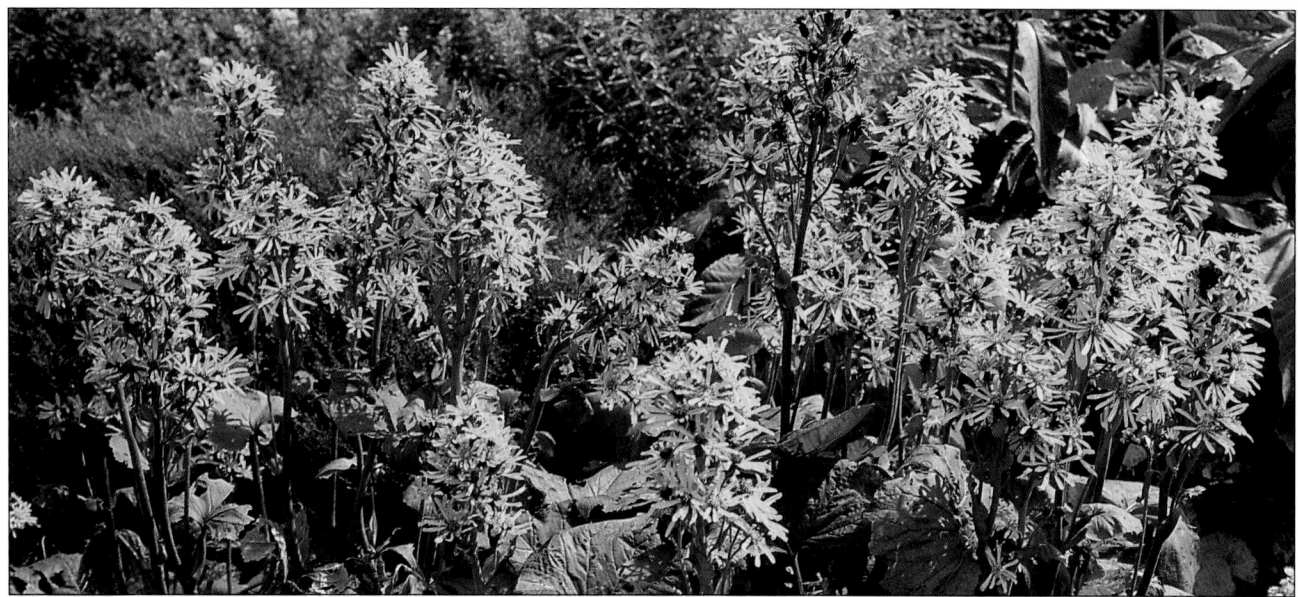

A MARVELLOUS ligularia display—spikes of bright yellow, eye-catching flowers. No matter what size your border, there is a suitable ligularia. They vary from the medium to tall, at 6ft high. Big groupings invariably succeed much better than a few individual flowers.

FEATURES

HERBACEOUS

Ligularia, with its bright yellow daisies, has four key advantages. It mainly flowers in mid- and late summer, and tolerates dappled shade, making it invaluable for the border. It often has interesting, well-displayed foliage; it can be shaped like a kidney, a five-pointed star, or be oval, held on tallish stems. The fourth advantage is that these are tall plants, adding height to schemes, being from 36in to 6ft tall. They can be used in small groups to punctuate arrangements of smaller plants, or form an impressive massed display. The flowers are yellow or orange. *L. dentata* "Othello" has purple-tinged leaves with a red underside, and "Desdemona" has brownish-green leaves, similarly colored beneath. With room for only one ligularia, "The Rocket" offers height,

yellow flowers, black stems, and interesting, big-toothed foliage.

CONDITIONS

Aspect   Tolerates full sun and some light shade. Also requires shelter from cutting winds.

Site   The soil must be moist—ligularias grow well beside ponds and streams—for a big performance. If the soil begins to dry out to any degree, the plants quickly show signs of distress by wilting.

GROWING METHOD

Propagation   Increase the species by sowing seed or division in the spring or fall. Cultivars can only be raised by division. Make sure that the emerging new growth is well-watered, and never allowed to dry out. Set out from 24in to 4ft apart.

Feeding   Border plants need plenty of well-rotted manure or compost, and a deep mulch to guard against moisture loss.

Problems   Slugs and snails can be a major problem, especially as the leaves emerge. Pick off or treat chemically.

FLOWERING

Season   Generally from late summer into the fall, but some flower in mid-summer, and *L. stenocephala* in early summer.

Cutting   It is not advisable to strip the plants of their impressive flowering stems, especially when you only have room for a few plants.

AFTER FLOWERING

Requirements   Cut back to the ground.

LIGULARIA AT A GLANCE

A genus of 150 species of perennials grown for their tall flower spikes and large, architectural foliage. Hardy to 0°F (zones 6–7).

Jan	/	Recommended Varieties
Feb	sow	
Mar	sow	*Ligularia dentata*
Apr	transplant	*L. d.* "Desdemona"
May	transplant	*L. d.* "Othello"
Jun	/	"Gregynog Gold"
July	flowering	*L. przewalskii*
Aug	flowering	"The Rocket"
Sept	/	*L. wilsoniana*
Oct	divide	
Nov	/	
Dec	/	

LIMONIUM LATIFOLIUM
Sea lavender

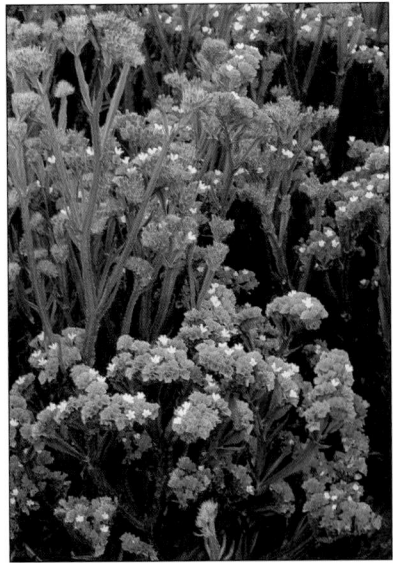

THE MOST FAMILIAR *annual statice is* Limonium sinuatum *"Blue Peter."*

SEA LAVENDER *has broad, slightly fleshy leaves, and flowers for several months. It is equally successful as part of a free-flowing design or, as shown, as a segregated, eye-catching feature.*

FEATURES

EVERGREEN

HERBACEOUS

Limonium latifolium (sea lavender) is a perennial type of statice often grown for its tall, finely branched stems of tiny white and pale lavender flowers, which are widely used both in fresh and dried floral arrangements. Flower stems may be over 20in high, and the cultivar "Violetta" has deep violet flowers. The plant forms a basal rosette of broad, rounded, slightly fleshy leaves growing around 10in high. Clumps may ultimately spread 18in or more wide. This is a good plant for rockeries because it is quite drought tolerant. Sea lavender is native to parts of south-east and central Europe, thriving in dry summers and cold winters.

LIMONIUM AT A GLANCE

L. latifolium is a perennial grown in windy coastal areas for its abundant, late summer flowers. Hardy to 0°F (zones 6–7).

		Companion Plants
Jan	/	
Feb	/	Eremurus
Mar	divide	Escallonia
Apr	transplant	Linum
May	/	Kniphofia
Jun	/	Olearia
July	/	Perovskia
Aug	flowering	Scabiosa
Sept	flowering	
Oct	sow	
Nov	/	
Dec	/	

CONDITIONS

Aspect   Prefers full sun all day, and tolerates exposed windy or coastal sites.

Site   The soil must be very well drained, but need not be rich. In fact, sea lavender tolerates very poor soil.

GROWING METHOD

Propagation   Grows from seed sown as soon as it is ripe, when the flowers have dried and turned brown, or from root cuttings taken in spring. New plantings should be spaced about 10–12in apart. Water regularly to establish new plants, and then give an occasional deep soaking during prolonged dry spring and summer weather.

Feeding   Does not need feeding, but a little complete plant food may be applied in early spring, giving a decent boost.

Problems   Heavy, poorly drained soils or overwatering may cause the plant to rot and collapse.

FLOWERING

Season   Sea lavender flowers in late summer, when its spikelets of lavender flowers with white calyces begin to appear.

Cutting   Flowers can be cut for drying when most of the flowers on the stem have fully opened.

AFTER FLOWERING

Requirements   Cut off any remaining flower stems when they are past their best.

LIRIOPE MUSCARI
Lilyturf

STRIKING FLOWER SPIKES in deep violet add to the attraction of this variegated form of liriope.

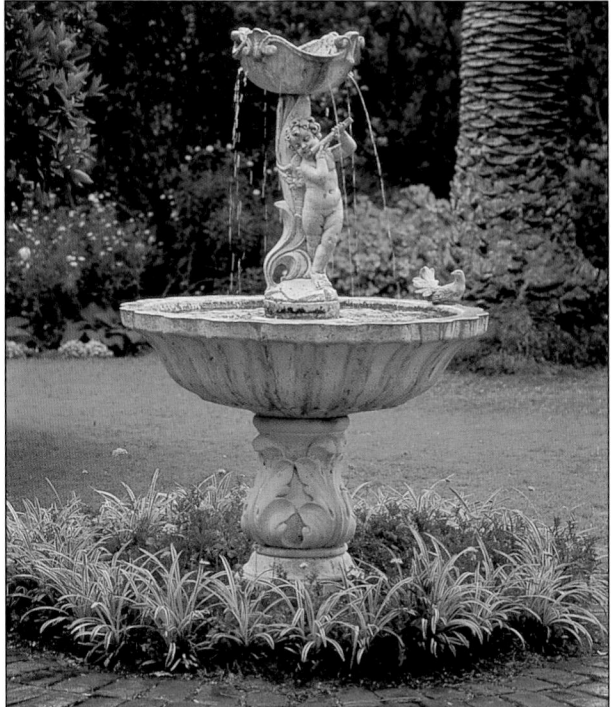

AMONG ITS MANY USES, liriope makes an excellent edging for garden beds. Here it accentuates the circular form of the fountain.

FEATURES

HERBACEOUS

This plant, known as lilyturf, is sometimes confused with *Ophiopogon jaburan* which is called white lilyturf. The two are similar but *Ophiopogon* has white flowers. Liriope grows in early summer about 12–14in high. The species has dark green leaves, but there are variegated forms as well. A spike of deep violet flowers stands well above the leaves. A tough and useful Far Eastern plant for the garden, especially as it flowers in the fall.

LIRIOPE AT A GLANCE

L. muscari is a stout perennial ideal for difficult places, which also provides good ground cover. Hardy to 0°F(zones 6–7).

		Recommended Varieties
Jan	/	
Feb	/	*Liriope muscari* "Big Blue"
Mar	sow	*L. m.* "Gold Banded"
Apr	divide	*L. m.* "Majestic"
May	transplant	*L. m.* "Monroe White"
Jun	/	
July	/	Companion Plants
Aug	/	Dicentra
Sept	flowering	Dryopteris
Oct	flowering	*Euphorbia robbiae*
Nov	flowering	Polypodium
Dec	/	Ribes
		Vinca major and *minor*

CONDITIONS

Aspect   Will grow in shade or dappled sunlight, but flowers best in full sun.

Site   Tolerates most soils but acid is preferred; grows best in well-drained soil enriched with plenty of organic matter.

GROWING METHOD

Propagation   The easiest method of increase is to lift and divide the clumps in the spring. Replant the divisions approximately 3–4in apart. Water young plants regularly during prolonged dry spring and summer weather. Plants tolerate drought but prefer some regular water.

Feeding   Apply complete plant food in the spring.

Problems   No specific problems are known.

FLOWERING

Season   The flowering begins in the early fall, and continues until the end of the season.

Cutting   Lasts quite well in water.

AFTER FLOWERING

Requirements   Cut off spent flowerheads once the flowers have dropped. As growth dies down toward winter, cut it off cleanly.

LOBELIA CARDINALIS
Cardinal flower

THIS LOBELIA is also known as cardinal flower, an apt description, since the tall spikes of flowers are the same scarlet as a cardinal's robes.

IN ITS NATURAL HABITAT in North America this lobelia grows on wet meadows and river banks. It thrives on plenty of moisture.

FEATURES

SUMMER AUTUMN WINTER SPRING
HERBACEOUS

To most people, lobelia is a small edging plant with bright blue flowers. There are, however, about 400 species of lobelia, many of them perennials. This herbaceous species with bright scarlet flowers is also known as the cardinal flower and grows to about 36in tall. With its dark green leaves and bright flowers, it really stands out—it is sometimes used as a feature plant. It can also be used in a mixed border or mass-planted among shrubs, so long as the ground retains plenty of moisture.

LOBELIA AT A GLANCE

L. cardinalis is a clump-forming, short-lived perennial, grown for its striking, vivid red flowers. Hardy to 5°F (zone 7).

Jan	/	Recommended Varieties
Feb	/	
Mar	sow 🖑	*Lobelia* "Cherry Ripe"
Apr	divide 🖑	"Dark Crusader"
May	transplant 🖑	"Kompliment Scharlach"
Jun	/	"Queen Victoria"
July	flowering ❀	*L. siphilitica*
Aug	flowering ❀	*L. tupa*
Sept	flowering ❀	
Oct	/	
Nov	/	
Dec	/	

CONDITIONS

Aspect Grows in full sunlight or semi-shade.
Site Needs rich and moisture-retentive soil, as these plants are not tolerant of drought. A streamside setting is ideal.

GROWING METHOD

Propagation Plants are usually divided every two or three years, in the spring. Plant the divisions about 12in apart. Lobelia must be kept moist and well watered while it is in active growth, especially during prolonged dry spells in the spring and summer.
Feeding Apply a complete plant food, and a mulch of compost or manure in the spring.
Problems Slugs and snails will attack the flower spikes. Put down slug pellets or beer traps.

FLOWERING

Season There is a long flowering period through the summer and fall period when the brilliant scarlet blooms appear.
Cutting Flowers are not suitable for cutting.

AFTER FLOWERING

Requirements Cut off spent flower stems. The dark-leaved hybrids ("Cherry Ripe") are not fully hardy and need a thick, protective winter mulch.

LUPINUS POLYPHYLLUS
Lupins

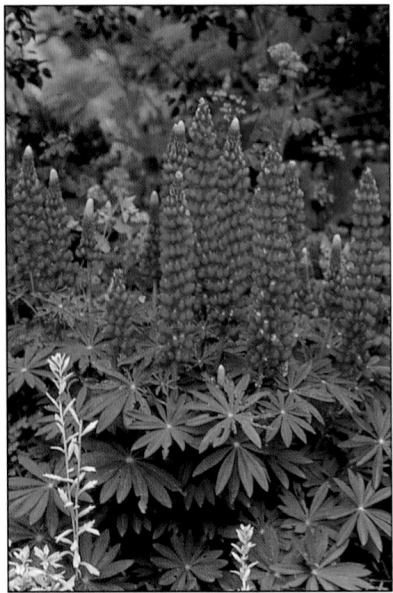

RUSSELL LUPINS are noteworthy for
their rich colors, including this pinky-red.

LUPINS ARE traditional favorites for perennial borders, where they provide vertical interest.
Here they are growing among oriental poppies, campion, and gray-leaved germander.

FEATURES

HERBACEOUS

This herbaceous perennial lupin is generally
known as the Russell lupin, named after the
hybridizer who began developing many fine
strains of this plant early this century. It
produces tall, densely packed spires of blooms
in myriad colors. Growing well over 42in tall,
these are plants for a massed display. They
flower in early to mid-summer and can look
unsightly after flowering; placed at the rear of
a border the problem is solved. Although they
can be cut for indoor use they give much more
value in the yard, with several spikes per plant.
The only irritation is that plants can be short-
lived, and should therefore be divided
regularly.

LUPINUS AT A GLANCE

L. polyphyllus is an attractive, summer-flowering perennial with
striking vertical spires of purple flowers. Hardy to 5°F (zone 7).

Jan	/	Recommended Varieties
Feb	/	
Mar	sow 👆	Band of Noble Series
Apr	transplant 👆	"Esmerelder"
May	transplant 👆	"Helen Sharman"
Jun	flowering 🌸	"Kayleigh Ann Savage"
July	flowering 🌸	"Olive Tolley"
Aug	/	"Pope John Paul"
Sept	/	"The Page"
Oct	sow	"The Chatelaine"
Nov	/	
Dec	/	

CONDITIONS

Aspect   Grows in full sunlight or semi-shade, but it
does need wind protection.

Site   Soil need not be rich—moderate fertility will
suffice—but it must be well drained. Light,
slightly sandy, acidic soil is ideal.

GROWING METHOD

Propagation   Division of these plants may be difficult. Many
strains come true from seed, which should be
soaked in warm water before planting in the
spring or fall. Cuttings can be taken from new
shoots emerging from the crown in early
spring. Set plants approximately 12–16in
apart. Give ample water to young plants to
help them establish.

Feeding   Needs little fertilizer, as lupins fix nitrogen in
nodules on their roots. High potash fertilizer
may be applied as buds begin to form.

Problems   Powdery mildew may be a problem in humid
conditions; if necessary, spray with a fungicide.
Control lupin aphids with an appropriate
spray. Virus may cause stunting and
discoloration. Destroy affected plants.

FLOWERING

Season   Early and mid-summer.

Cutting   Flowers may be cut for the vase.

AFTER FLOWERING

Requirements   Cut off the spent flower stems before they
manage to set seed. This will encourage
smaller spikes to follow.

LYCHNIS CORONARIA
Rose campion

THE DISTINCTIVE ARRANGEMENT of petals on Lychnis chalcedonica *has given rise to its common name, Maltese cross. The bright red flowers show up well against white or blue flowers.*

TRUE CAMPION, Lychnis coronaria, *has abundant, bright cerise flowers.*

FEATURES

SUMMER AUTUMN WINTER SPRING

HERBACEOUS

Rosettes of soft, silver-gray foliage make *Lychnis coronaria* a very useful plant in the garden, and they contrast with the deep cerise or magenta flowers that appear on stems 12–16in high. There is also a white-flowered form. Easily grown in a sunny, well-drained position, rose campion tends to be short-lived, but it self-seeds prolifically to provide a fresh supply. It can be grown as a border plant or as part of a mixed perennial display. *L. flos-jovis* is another species where silvery foliage effectively combines with purple-red blooms. Another popular species of lychnis is the Maltese cross, *L. chalcedonica*, which has mid-green leaves and produces a rounded head of bright scarlet flowers. Pink and white forms, and a double, "Flore Plena," are also available.

LYCHNIS AT A GLANCE

L. coronaria is a flowery, short-lived purple-red perennial that gives a prolific late summer display. Hardy to 5°F (zone 7).

		Recommended Varieties
Jan	/	
Feb	/	*Lychnis alpina*
Mar	sow	*L. chalcedonica*
Apr	division	*L. coronaria* Alba Group
May	transplant	*L. c.* Atrosanguinea Group
Jun	/	*L. flos-cuculi*
July	flowering	*L. viscaria* subsp.
Aug	flowering	"Splendens Plena"
Sept	flowering	*L. yunnanensis*
Oct	sow	
Nov	/	
Dec	/	

CONDITIONS

Aspect Grows best in full sunlight, but it tolerates shade for part of the day.

Site Needs very well-drained soil, but the soil need not be especially rich.

GROWING METHOD

Propagation Tends to self-seed. These plants may show variation from the parent plant. Divide clumps in spring, discard the oldest, lackluster sections, and space the new vigorous ones about 8in apart. There are some beautiful strains to be raised from seed, with mixtures of white, deep violet, carmine, and rose-pink flowers, and a pastel eye.

Feeding Needs little fertilizer. A little complete plant food may be given in early spring.

Problems No pest or disease problems are known, but overwatering or prolonged summer rain in heavy ground may cause rotting.

FLOWERING

Season Flowers in mid- to late summer, but it is well worth the wait, with a big showy display that maintains interest in the border at a time when many other plants are flagging.

Cutting Flowers are unsuitable for cutting.

AFTER FLOWERING

Requirements If you do not want plants to self-seed, deadhead with vigilance as the flowers fade. This should also prolong blooming. Completely spent stems should be cut off as low to the ground as possible.

LYSIMACHIA PUNCTATA
Loosestrife

A STRONG, MASSED DISPLAY of loosestrife. Individually unremarkable, a clump makes a splendid feature beside a pond or stream.

FEATURES

EVERGREEN

HERBACEOUS

Loosestrife, which is widely naturalized in Europe and northeast North America, has stalks of bright yellow flowers in summer. It thrives in damp, boggy ground and can easily become invasive. The flowering stems reach 3ft high, bearing slightly coarse foliage. Other species offer white flowers on stiff, blue-green stems (*L. ephemerum*), while *L. nummularia* "Aurea" is a complete contrast. It grows 2in high, but spreads indefinitely, with evergreen, bright yellow leaves and summer flowers in a matching color. With room for only one, try *L. clethroides*, which has attractive white flowers (36 x 24in). The new variegated form, *L. p.* "Alexander" is a great success.

LYSIMACHIA AT A GLANCE

L. punctata is an erect, herbaceous perennial grown for its yellow flowers and ability to colonize damp areas. Hardy to 0°F (zones 6–7).

		Recommended Varieties
Jan	/	
Feb	/	*Lysimachia atropurpurea*
Mar	/	*L. ciliata*
Apr	divide	*L. clethroides*
May	/	*L. minoricensis*
Jun	flowering	*L. nummularia* "Aurea"
July	flowering	*L. thyrsiflora*
Aug	flowering	*L. vulgaris*
Sept	/	
Oct	divide	
Nov	/	
Dec	/	

CONDITIONS

Aspect Loosestrife tolerates both full sun and light, dappled shade, but growing in the former gives by far the best results.

Site Moist ground is essential. Add plenty of organic matter to border plants, and mulch well to guard against moisture loss.

GROWING METHOD

Propagation Seed can be difficult. The most reliable method is by spring or fall division.

Feeding Humus-rich ground produces the best display. Fork plenty of well-rotted manure and compost around the plants in the spring.

Problems Colonies of slugs and snails can be a major problem, attacking and disfiguring the new, emerging foliage. Either pick off by hand or treat chemically. Plants grown in areas cut by strong winds may need to be staked.

FLOWERING

Season Flowers appear in the summer, their timing depending on your chosen variety.

Cutting They make unremarkable cut flowers, given the enormous competition in summer, but are nonetheless very useful when bulking out large displays with their flowering spires.

AFTER FLOWERING

Requirements Cut back the old, spent flowering stems down to the ground.

MACLEAYA CORDATA
Plume poppy

THE PLUME POPPY starts inauspiciously, but quickly puts out tall, white summer flowers, making it an indispensable feature plant. It is a key ingredient for the rear of the border, where its lobed, olive-green foliage makes a lovely background for smaller plants. The plume poppy does not need staking.

FEATURES

SUMMER AUTUMN WINTER SPRING

HERBACEOUS

The plume poppy is an essential plant for the rear of the border, tall, graceful, and showy. Growing 8ft tall, it sports long, thin stems with mid- and late summer panicles of pale white flowers. "Flamingo" has pinkish flowers. The large, lobed foliage is equally attractive. With more room in the border, *M. microcarpa* can be grown. It is slightly invasive and has pink flowers, while "Kelway's Coral Plume" produces coral-pink flowers opening from pure pink buds. The plume poppy's natural habitat is Chinese and Japanese meadows, where it makes large impressive colonies, spreading quickly through the damp soil by underground rhizomes and flowering all summer long.

MACLEAYA AT A GLANCE

M. cordata is a rhizomatous perennial with gray-green foliage, grown for its tall flower spikes. Hardy to 0°F (zones 6–7).

Jan	/	**Companion Plants**
Feb	/	
Mar	/	Clematis Gypsophila
Apr	division	Hibiscus
May	/	Miscanthus
Jun	/	Lobelia
July	flowering	Osteospermum
Aug	flowering	Rose
Sept	/	Salvia
Oct	division	
Nov	/	
Dec	/	

CONDITIONS

Aspect Macleaya likes full sun and light shade, although the former produces a longer, better display. Avoid dark areas and open, windy sites; shelter is required.

Site Light, well-drained soil is ideal.

GROWING METHOD

Propagation The quickest, easiest results are either by making spring or fall divisions, or by separating lengths of rhizome when the plant is dormant. Make sure each has its own root system. Water new plants well, and space out at 3ft intervals.

Feeding Provide moderate applications of compost and well-rotted manure in the spring as a mulch.

Problems Colonies of slugs can be a severe problem, badly attacking the new, vigorous growth. Either pick off by hand or treat accordingly with chemicals.

FLOWERING

Season Flowers appear in mid- and late summer, on long, thin stems, producing an airy display.

Cutting Macleaya make very attractive cut flowers, requiring a regular change of water, their airy panicles adding considerably to both formal and flowery arrangements.

AFTER FLOWERING

Requirements Cut back old growth to the ground.

MECONOPSIS
Himalayan blue poppy

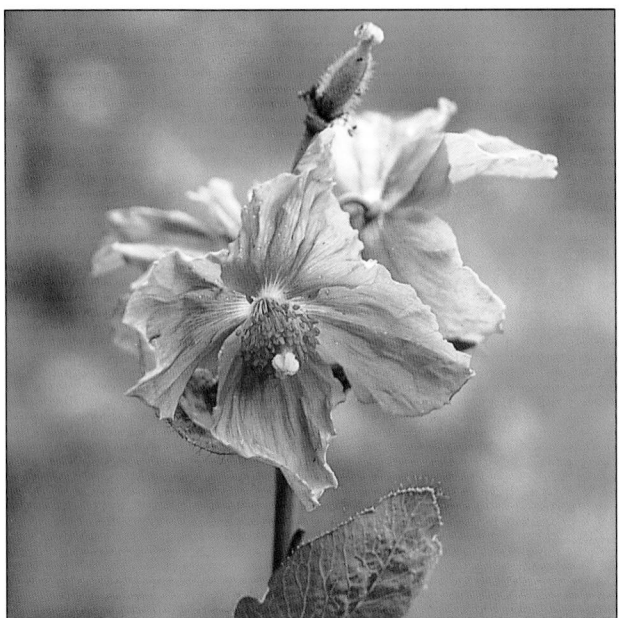

NO OTHER blue flower has quite the same startlingly clear color as the amazing blue poppy, a true delight whenever it can be grown.

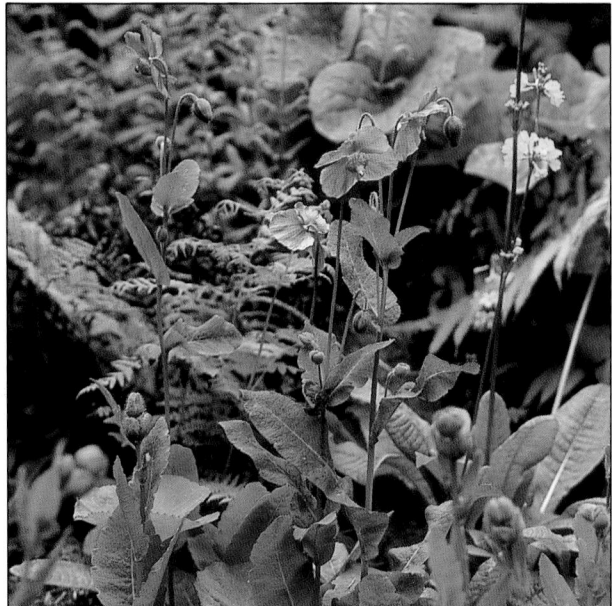

WOODLAND CONDITIONS where the soil never dries out are essential for the Himalayan or Tibetan blue poppy.

FEATURES

HERBACEOUS

Meconopsis betonicifolia is the beautiful blue poppy everyone loves. There is probably no other plant that produces such an intense sky-blue flower. Its natural habitat is very high altitude alpine meadows in China. Plants do not flower the first year, and they die down in winter, growing and blooming in the second year. If meconopsis is prevented from blooming the first time it sets buds, it is more likely to become perennial. Growing to almost 6½ft in its native habitat, in cultivation it is more likely to be 20–28in tall. Looks best when grown as part of a massed display, or threaded through a border.

MECONOPSIS AT A GLANCE

M. betonicifolia is a deciduous perennial, making a strong show, with blue or white early summer flowers. Hardy to 0°F (zones 6–7).

Jan	/	Recommended Varieties
Feb	/	
Mar	sow	*Meconopsis cambrica*
Apr	transplant	*M. betonicifolia*
May	transplant	*M. grandis*
Jun	flowering	*M. napaulensis*
July	flowering	*M. quintuplinervia*
Aug	flowering	*M. x sheldonii*
Sept	flowering	*M. x s.* "Slieve Donard"
Oct	sow	*M. superba*
Nov	/	
Dec	/	

CONDITIONS

Aspect   Needs partial, dappled shade; also provide some protection from strong, cutting, drying winds.

Site   Needs well-drained soil that is rich in organic matter. In colder regions it grows best in acid soil.

GROWING METHOD

Propagation   Grows from fresh ripe seed sown in the fall, or in spring. Give winter seedlings frost protection in a greenhouse, but beware of damping off, and plant out in late spring or early summer. Initially, water well. Do not waterlog or the crowns will rot.

Feeding   Apply a little general fertilizer in the spring.

Problems   Overwet soil, especially during winter, will rot the crown. Downy mildew may be a problem in some seasons. Spray plants with a fungicide at the first sign of an attack.

FLOWERING

Season   Abundant flowers begin appearing at the start of summer.

Cutting   While they make extremely good cut flowers, they do not last long.

AFTER FLOWERING

Requirements   Remove spent flower stems, unless you are waiting for seed to ripen. Once growth dies down, cut it off at ground level.

MELIANTHUS MAJOR
Honey bush

NECTAR-RICH, these dark red flowers are very attractive to insects. The foliage too is unusual, with its distinctive color and form.

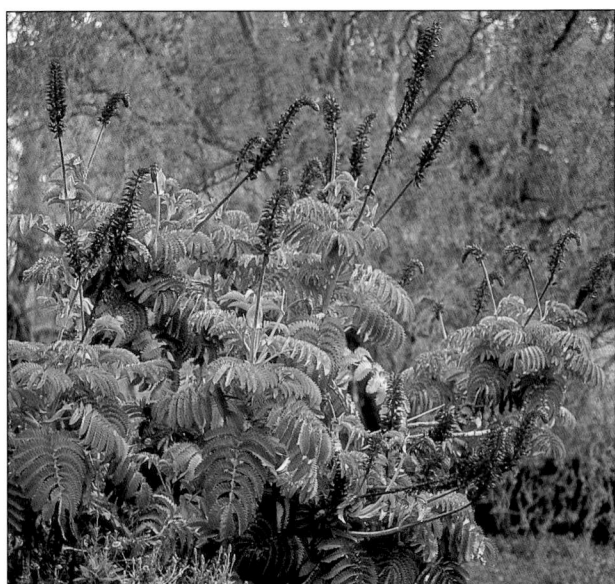

THE BLUE-GREEN FOLIAGE of honey flower is a feature in itself. Only in a large yard will you appreciate the full effect.

FEATURES

EVERGREEN

This very striking evergreen plant, with its unusual blue-green foliage, really stands out. It is grown as a feature in a mixed border or as a focal point in an annual or perennial display. In a large yard it could be repeat-planted to tie together various arrangements. Honey bush can grow to 6ft in height, and it spreads by suckers, forming a large clump if left undivided. The dark mahogany-red flowers contain copious quantities of nectar, attractive to bees. Although native to South Africa, and initially tender here, after two years the base becomes woody and it can survive outside if given good frost protection in mild areas. It can also be grown in a large pot.

MELIANTHUS AT A GLANCE

M. major is a tender, southern African plant with wonderful, architectural foliage. It is damaged below 41°F (zone 11).

		Companion Plants
Jan	/	
Feb	/	Canna
Mar	sow	Choisya
Apr	divide	*Hosta* "Krossa Regal"
May	transplant	Philadelphus
Jun	flowering	Pinus
July	flowering	Pseudopanax
Aug	flowering	Salvia
Sept	/	
Oct	/	
Nov	/	
Dec	/	

CONDITIONS

Aspect Needs full sun all day (i.e. a south-facing wall).
Site Soil must be well drained but it need not be specially rich—in fact over-rich soils will produce good foliage effects but poor flowering. However, the outstanding architectural foliage is the main reason for growing this striking plant.

GROWING METHOD

Propagation Grows from seed sown in the spring or from division of suckers from an existing plant, also in spring. Plant at least 39in apart. For best growth, give deep watering every week or two in hot, dry spells during the growing season. It will, however, tolerate drought well.
Feeding Apply a complete plant food in the spring.
Problems Red spider mites may strike. Use an appropriate insecticide.

FLOWERING

Season Dark crimson flowers may appear in late summer or earlier on long stems that survive the winter.
Cutting Flowers are probably best left on the plant, as they do not smell particularly pleasant.

AFTER FLOWERING

Requirements Cut off the spent flower stems, unless you are waiting for seed to set and ripen. Protect the base and roots with straw or bracken against frost. The older and woodier the plant, the better its chance of survival.

MIMULUS
Monkey flower

THE MONKEY FLOWER is an indispensable part of the cottage garden. It forms bright clumps, spreads within reason, never becoming invasive, and gives a long flowering season from spring to summer. It is ideal for a site near a pond, its shapes reflecting gently in the water.

FEATURES

HERBACEOUS

The genus has 150 species, and while they are classified as annuals, perennials and shrubs of varying degrees of hardiness, from the gardener's viewpoint most are grown as the first. *M. cardinalis,* scarlet monkey flower, however, is an attractive, reliable perennial. It grows 3ft high, producing vertical stems with eye-catching, tubular scarlet flowers in summer. Clumps usually spread 24in. In the wild, from western North America down to Mexico, it is pollinated by hummingbirds. *M. luteus,* monkey musk, has yellow flowers with a red throat, and self-seeds freely through the garden. *M. guttatus* has attractive, funnel-shape yellow flowers.

MIMULUS AT A GLANCE

Mimulus contains many ideal, damp garden plants, creating colonies with bright flowers. Several hardy to 5°F (zone 7).

		Recommended Varieties
Jan	/	
Feb	/	*Mimulus aurantiacus*
Mar	divide	Calypso hybrids
Apr	transplant	*M. cardinalis*
May	flowering	*M. c* "Whitecroft Scarlet"
Jun	flowering	"Highland Red"
July	flowering	*M. lewisii*
Aug	flowering	*M. ringens*
Sept	/	
Oct	sow	
Nov	/	
Dec	/	

CONDITIONS

Aspect Mimulus thrive in either full sun or light shade.

Site Provide rich, moist soil. In their natural habitat many mimulus grow alongside streams and ponds. They are ideal for the bog garden or a running stream. However, *M. cardinalis* will tolerate drier ground.

GROWING METHOD

Propagation Divide in spring, setting out vigorous new clumps up to 3ft apart. Softwood cuttings can be taken in the early part of summer, while semi-ripe, slightly hardier ones can be taken after mid-summer. Sow seed in spring or fall.

Feeding Add plenty of well-rotted manure and compost, and a spring mulch to preserve moisture loss.

Problems Slugs and snails can be a major problem, devouring tender new growth. Either pick them off by hand, trap and remove, or treat with a chemical.

FLOWERING

Season The flowers appear from late spring to summer.

Cutting Mimulus make good cut flowers, though they do not tend to last long. Regular, fresh supplies will be needed.

AFTER FLOWERING

Requirements Cut back to ground level in late fall, and remove the dead foliage which can prove a haven to slugs and snails.

MISCANTHUS SINENSIS
Miscanthus

FINE STRIPES in cream and green make "Variegatus" a popular form of miscanthus.

ZEBRA GRASS is the common name given to "Zebrinus," with its yellow-spotted horizontal markings. Ornamental grasses can provide useful contrast in the perennial garden.

FEATURES

SUMMER AUTUMN WINTER SPRING

HERBACEOUS

This is a group of large, ornamental, herbaceous perennial grasses. The plain green species is not often grown as the many cultivars with striped or banded foliage are much more decorative. Cultivars range in height from about 32in to 6½ft. Clumps spread from short, thick rhizomes and become very wide after a few years if not divided. Commonly grown cultivars include "Zebrinus" with distinct, horizontal gold banding, and "Variegatus" with long cream or white stripes, while other varieties such as "Silberfeder," "Morning Light" and var. *purpurascens* are worth seeking out. All produce pale, creamy beige feathery plumes of flowers in late summer, and fall, often accompanied by good fall color. The tall growers look good crested with frost.

MISCANTHUS AT A GLANCE

M. sinensis is a deciduous, large perennial, growing 6ft x 6ft. Produces blue-green foliage. Hardy to 0°F (zones 6–7).

Jan	/	Recommended Varieties
Feb	sow	"Ferne Osten"
Mar	sow	"Flamingo"
Apr	transplant	"Gracillimus"
May	divide	"Kleine Fontane"
Jun	/	"Kleine Silberspinne"
July	/	"Morning Light"
Aug	flowering	"Strictus"
Sept	flowering	"Undine"
Oct	flowering	
Nov	/	
Dec	/	

CONDITIONS

Aspect Grows best in full sun, but tolerates shade for part of the day.

Site Prefers a soil that has been heavily enriched with organic matter to aid moisture retention. Avoid any damp or boggy ground. Good drainage really is essential for a massed, architectural display.

GROWING METHOD

Propagation Clumps can be lifted and divided in spring. This can require considerable muscle and effort because the roots are extremely tenacious. Replant the divisions approximately 12in apart, or closer if you want quicker, immediate coverage. Water well until established.

Feeding Complete plant food can be applied in the spring, when new growth begins, but it is not essential if the soil contains plenty of manure or compost.

Problems No specific pest or disease problems are known to attack this plant.

FLOWERING

Season Flowering plumes appear well above the foliage in the fall.

Cutting Plumes can be cut and dried like pampas grass.

AFTER FLOWERING

Requirements Once foliage starts to die off and become unsightly, cut it off at ground level. If the foliage is left uncut to provide winter shapes and outlines, especially when frosted, it must be cut back by early spring.

MONARDA DIDYMA
Bergamot

THE HOT-PINK FLOWERS *on this bergamot are easy to place in the yard. They combine well with blue or white schemes.*

FOR COLOR *over a long period, this brilliant red variety of bergamot, "Cambridge Scarlet," is hard to beat. It requires little care.*

FEATURES

HERBACEOUS

This aromatic herbaceous perennial is also known as bee balm and Oswego tea. The name "bee balm" refers to its nectar-rich flowers, which are very attractive to bees, and "Oswego tea" to its use by the Oswego Indians and early colonists of North America as a tea substitute. Growing approximately 36in tall, bergamot flowers from mid- to late summer. The heads of tubular flowers are red, pink, white, or purple, with some outstandingly named cultivars, including "Cambridge Scarlet" and "Croftway Pink." It is easy to grow—being a member of the mint family, its roots spread vigorously. It makes a lively addition to a mixed planting for its bright scarlet or pink flowers.

MONARDA AT A GLANCE

M. didyma is a clump-forming perennial with lance-shape leaves, and bright, late summer flowers. Hardy to 0°F (zones 6–7).

		Recommended Varieties
Jan	/	
Feb	sow	"Aquarius"
Mar	sow	"Beauty of Cobham"
Apr	transplant	"Cambridge Scarlet"
May	transplant	"Croftway Pink"
Jun	/	"Fishes"
July	flowering	"Mahogany"
Aug	flowering	"Prarienacht"
Sept	/	"Sagittarius"
Oct	sow	"Scorpion"
Nov	/	
Dec	/	

CONDITIONS

Aspect Grows in either full sunlight or semi-shade, but flowering will be best in the open.

Site Needs well-drained soil that is made moisture-retentive by the addition of large amounts of decayed organic matter.

GROWING METHOD

Propagation Lift and divide clumps in the spring before new growth begins. Replant the young, vigorous outer growths 8–12in apart. Plants usually need dividing every two or three years. Bergamot may be also be grown from seed sown in the early spring or fall, but this does not develop true to type. It needs regular, deep watering through prolonged dry spells in the heat of summer.

Feeding If the soil is well supplied with humus, but a little fertilizer is needed. Apply some complete plant food in the spring.

Problems Since snails love to eat the new growth as it appears, take precautions. Mildew can be a problem at times. You may need a fungicide spray or it might become severe. Remove all dead and diseased leaves.

FLOWERING

Season Flowers in mid- and late summer.

Cutting Makes a decent cut flower. Use the scented leaves in a pot pourri.

AFTER FLOWERING

Requirements Prune off spent flower stems. Cut plants back to ground level once growth begins to die off.

OENOTHERA
Evening primrose

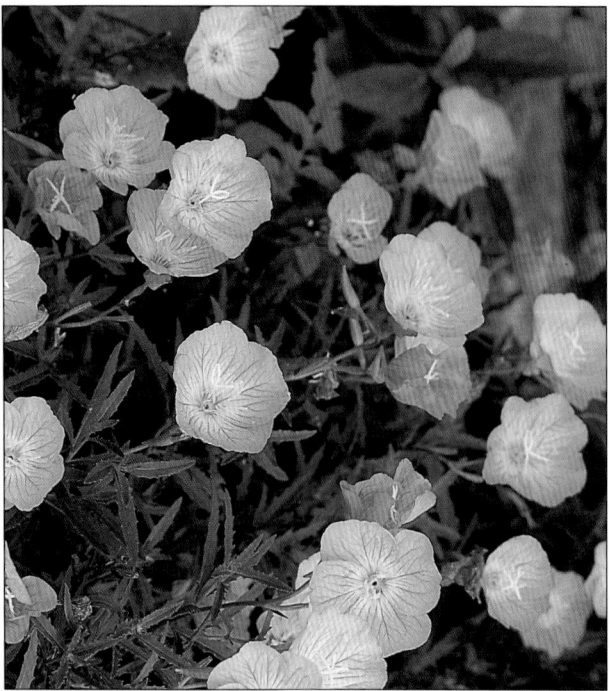

THOUGH EVENING PRIMROSE is thought of as yellow, the flowers of Oenothera speciosa "Rosea" are pink-and-white, with yellow.

O. SPECIOSA "ROSEA" is doubly attractive because it grows 12in high, mixes well with argyranthemum, and forms large clumps.

FEATURES

HERBACEOUS

Evening primrose is an essential plant for formal and cottage-style yards. While each flower (white, yellow, or pink, depending on the variety) opens and fades fast, barely lasting 24 hours, there is an abundance of new buds developing through the summer and early fall. The plant has two extra advantages. Often fragrant, and often tall, it can make an eye-catching addition to the border. *O. biennis*, the traditional favorite, is actually an annual or biennial. *O. fruticosa*, a biennial or perennial, has two fine forms, "Fyrverkeri" ("Fireworks"),

which has red buds opening to yellow flowers and purple-tinged leaves, and subsp. *glauca*, with yellow flowers and purple leaves.

CONDITIONS

Aspect Grow in an open, sunny position.
Site Moderately rich soil will suffice, although evening primrose can self-seed and appear in even the stoniest ground.

GROWING METHOD

Propagation Sow seed or divide in early spring, or take cuttings of non-flowering shoots. Keep in a frost-free place in winter, plant out in spring.
Feeding Not necessary, although moderate quantities of manure will suffice in especially poor soil.
Problems Slugs tend to be the main problem, attacking tender new growth. Pick off or treat with chemicals. The sturdy kinds of evening primrose are free-standing, but others (*O. macrocarpa*) may require support.

FLOWERING

Season Lasts from late spring to late summer, with flowers tending to open in early evening, when they release their scent.
Cutting Short-lived but attractive flowers.

AFTER FLOWERING

Requirements Collect seed when ripe, if required, and then cut spent stems to the ground.

OENOTHERA AT A GLANCE

A genus of mainly annuals and biennials, with excellent perennials. Scented and yellow flowering, they are hardy to 5°F (zone 7).

Jan	/	Recommended Varieties
Feb	sow	
Mar	divide	*Oenothera biennis*
Apr	transplant	*O. fruticosa*
May	flowering	*O. f.* "Fyrverkeri"
Jun	flowering	*O. f.* subsp. *glauca*
July	flowering	*O. macrocarpa*
Aug	flowering	*O. speciosa* "Rosea"
Sept	/	*O. stricta* "Sulphurea"
Oct	/	
Nov	/	
Dec	/	

PAEONIA
Paeony species and cultivars

GLORIOUS COLOR *and perfume combine in this extensive planting of peony cultivars to produce a spectacular result.*

THIS HALF-OPENED *peony flower gives a hint of delights to come, with a touch of white against the bright pink.*

FLUTED PETALS *give extra interest to this single white peony. The large mass of central stamens adds a touch of color.*

FEATURES

HERBACEOUS

Beautiful to look at and fragrant, too, peonies are among the aristocrats of the plant world, and although there are only 33 wild species, there are many hundreds of cultivars. Peonies were prized by the Chinese for many hundreds of years, and by the early 18th century they had developed the garden peonies from which the forms of *P. lactiflora* (often referred to as Chinese peonies) are generally descended. Peonies were first introduced into Europe at the end of the 18th century. Peonies are divided into two groups: the tree peonies, which are shrubby and derived from *P. suffruticosa*, and the herbaceous peonies, of which the cultivars of *P. lactiflora* are most commonly grown. Although the name "tree peony" is used, this is an exaggeration—they rarely grow more than 6½ft tall. Herbaceous peonies grow about 39in high and wide. Plants are long-lived.

Flowers　Flowers may be single or double and come in every shade of pink, red, purple, white, and cream, many with a delicious light perfume. Some flowers have a large central boss of golden stamens, and some have fringed or crimped edges on the petals. Among the categories of flowers recognized are: small, 2–4in across; medium, 4–6in across; large, 6–8in across; and very large, over 8in across. Tree peonies are generally 2–12in. Other categories have been developed in the United States where a great deal of hybridizing is practiced.

CONDITIONS

Aspect　Needs full sunlight or semi-shade, with protection from strong winds.

Site　Soil must be well drained, but heavily enriched with manure or compost. Dig it over deeply to allow the free spread of roots.

THE ATTRACTIVE FOLIAGE greatly adds to the value of peonies and often emerges with lovely rich red and bronze tints.

THE VERY POPULAR double cultivar "Rubra Plena" is a rich crimson anemone-centered peony that looks very like a camellia.

GROWING METHOD

Propagation Divide plants in the spring or fall, taking care not to break the brittle roots. Each division must have roots and dormant growth buds. Crowns should be replanted 1in below the surface, and spaced about 20in apart. Plants can be raised from seed but they will take four to five years to reach flowering size, and only the species will be true to type. Peony seeds generally need two periods of chilling with a warm period between, and care should be taken not to disturb the seeds during this time. Most seeds germinate during the second spring after sowing.

Feeding Apply a general fertilizer in early spring. At the same time, mulch but avoid the crown.

PAEONIA AT A GLANCE

A genus of over 30 species of clump-forming perennials and sub-shrubs, often with highly scented flowers. Hardy to 5°F (zone 7).

Month	Activity	Recommended Varieties
Jan	/	
Feb	/	*P. cambessedesii*
Mar	/	"Defender"
Apr	divide	*P. lactiflora* "Bowl of
May	transplant	Beauty"
Jun	flowering	*P. l.* "Festiva Maxima"
July	/	*P. l.* "Sarah Bernhardt"
Aug	/	*P. mlokosewitschii*
Sept	/	*P. obovata*
Oct	sow	
Nov	sow	
Dec	sow	

Problems Botrytis or gray mold is the main problem with peonies. It can cause rotting of stems and leaf bases. Destroy affected foliage, improve drainage and air circulation, and spray with a fungicide. Replace the top layer of soil carefully around the plants.

FLOWERING

Season The flowering period is invariably in early summer. Some peonies bloom for only a short time, but the flowers on other types are much longer lasting.

Cutting Cut flowers for indoor use when the blooms are opening. Peonies are excellent cut flowers, which will last longer if kept in a cool part of the home and given frequent water changes.

AFTER FLOWERING

Requirements Remove spent flower stems, but allow the foliage to die down naturally before trimming it back. Some varieties produce lovely fall color. Do not cut down the flowering stems of varieties such as *P. mlokosewitschii* that produce handsome berries.

HINT

Disturbance Peonies may flower poorly, if at all, in the first year after planting, but this should improve year by year. Generally speaking, peonies are best left undisturbed; even 50-year-old clumps can be seen flowering profusely. It may be wiser to increase your stock by buying young container-grown plants than split a precious specimen.

PAPAVER ORIENTALE
Oriental poppy

THIS FRINGED red flower indicates the wide range of colors within P. orientale. *No border should be without one.*

THE STRIKING SHAPE of Papaver orientale. *Note the straight, slightly furry stem with, here, pink flowers and a black basal mark.*

FEATURES

HERBACEOUS

The oriental poppy is a clump-forming perennial with a variety of different forms, and colors ranging from soft hues to sharp red. They all bear the hallmarks of the species *P. orientalis* from northeast Turkey and Iran, which has a large cupped bowl of a flower with paper-thin petals. Growing up to 36in tall, with a similar spread, they self-seed freely, creating attractive colonies. They look the part in both wild or natural gardens, and large mixed borders. "Black and White" is a striking contrast of white petals and a black mark at its base. "Cedric Morris" is soft pink with a black base. "Indian Chief" is reddish-brown.

PAPAVER AT A GLANCE

P. orientalis is a perennial with 12in-long leaves, and big, cupped flowers in a range of colors. Hardy to 0°F (zones 6–7).

		Recommended Varieties
Jan	/	
Feb	/	*Papaver orientale* "Allegro"
Mar	/	*P. o.* "Beauty of Livermere"
Apr	division ✋	*P. o.* "Black and White"
May	flowering ✋	*P. o.* Goliath Group
Jun	flowering ✋	*P. o.* "Mrs Perry"
July	flowering ✋	*P. o.* "Patty's Plum"
Aug	/	*P. o.* "Perry's White"
Sept	/	*P. o.* "Picotee"
Oct	sow ✋	*P. o.* "Turkish Delight"
Nov	/	
Dec	/	

CONDITIONS

Aspect   Provide full sunlight, the conditions it receives in its natural habitat.

Site   Rich soil and good drainage bring out the best in these plants.

GROWING METHOD

Propagation   Since they self-seed freely, propagation may not be necessary. Slicing off sections of root in late fall or early winter will provide abundant new plants. The success rate is invariably high. Alternatively, divide clumps in the spring, or sow seed in pots in the fall in a cold frame. Plant out the following spring, 9in apart.

Feeding   Add plenty of rich, friable compost in spring to add fertility to poor soils. This also improves the drainage, which needs to be quite good.

Problems   Fungal wilt and downy mildew can be problems; spray at the first sign.

FLOWERING

Season   The flowers appear from late spring to mid-summer.

Cutting   Poppies do not make good cut flowers.

AFTER FLOWERING

Requirements   When the flowers have died down, severely cut back the foliage to the ground. This will produce a second showing of attractive summer leaves.

PENSTEMON
Beard tongue

MANY MONTHS *of fine bloom can be expected from this fine red cultivar—well into the fall, if it is regularly deadheaded.*

A GENEROUS PLANTING *of these attractive white cultivars makes a perfect surround for this small ornamental fountain.*

FEATURES

SUMMER AUTUMN WINTER SPRING

EVERGREEN

This very large group of perennials consists of 250 species and countless cultivars, all originating in a wide variety of habitats in the southern and western United States. Their tubular or funnel-shaped flowers come in a range of shades of pink, red, purple, lavender, blue, and white, some with a contrasting throat. There is a large range of cultivars in many of these shades. Collections of young rooted cuttings can also be bought. Penstemons have a long flowering period, through the summer to mid-fall, especially if the spent blooms are regularly cut, but many plants can be short-lived. Take cuttings regularly. The various species and hybrids grow anything from 4 to 24in tall.

PENSTEMON AT A GLANCE

A large genus of perennials grown for their late-season flower display. Hardiness varies from the frost-tender to 5°F (zones 10–7).

		Recommended Varieties
Jan	/	
Feb	sow	"Alice Hindley"
Mar	sow	"Beech Park"
Apr	transplant	"Chester Scarlet"
May	transplant	"Evelyn"
Jun	flowering	"Garnet"
July	flowering	"Margery Fish"
Aug	flowering	"Osprey"
Sept	flowering	"Pennington Gem"
Oct	flowering	"Rubicundus"
Nov	/	
Dec	/	

CONDITIONS

Aspect Grows best in full sunlight with some protection from strong, cutting winds. Since most varieties are not fully hardy, warmth and shelter are essential.

Site Needs very open and well-drained soil.

GROWING METHOD

Propagation They grow well from cuttings taken in mid-summer, then overwintered in a greenhouse frame. A wide range of penstemons can be grown from seed, which is widely available. They need a cold period before germination; sow in the fall or refrigerate the seed for three weeks before sowing in the spring.

Feeding Apply a general fertilizer as new growth commences in the spring.

Problems No specific pest or disease problems, but root rot may occur on sticky clay soil.

FLOWERING

Season Most have a fairly long flowering period, from the summer to mid-fall. However, many can only be seen as true perennials in milder parts of the country, being killed by winter frosts; raise new stock to replace any losses. "Garnet" is the hardiest.

Cutting This is not a satisfactory cut flower.

AFTER FLOWERING

Requirements Either cut entirely to the ground, or leave some stems as frost protection. Protect clumps with a mulch of straw or bracken.

PHLOX PANICULATA
Perennial phlox

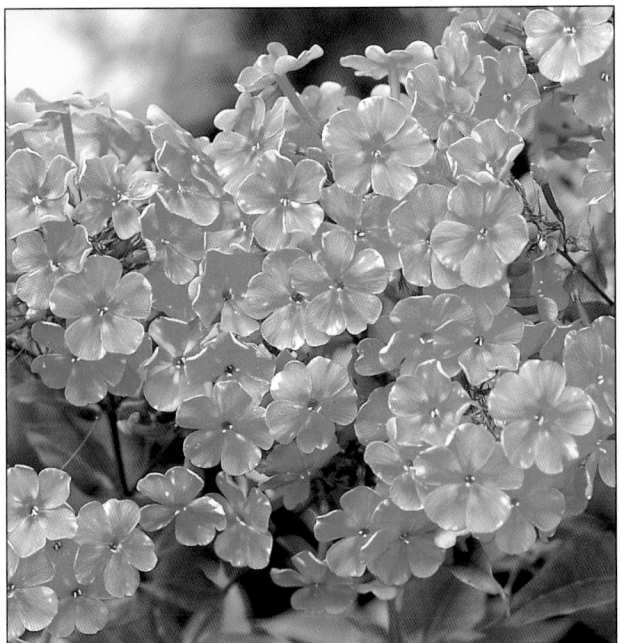

THE ATTRACTIVE, *individual flowers on the heads of perennial phlox last right through the season, making it essential in any border.*

A GREAT STANDBY *for the summer yard, perennial phlox fills the whole of the back of this border with two shades of pink.*

FEATURES

HERBACEOUS

Easy to grow and producing a summer-long display of flowers, perennial phlox has a place in any perennial collection. Plants may grow from 16 to 36in tall, and the clumps spread rapidly; position new plantings 12in apart. The large heads of flowers, some with a contrasting eye, come in shades of red, pink, orange, mauve, purple, and white. This plant looks best mass-planted, either in solid blocks of one color or in mixed colors. Also note the highly popular, new variegated cultivars. With mixed plantings, ensure that the taller forms do not obscure the shorter ones.

PHLOX AT A GLANCE

P. paniculata is an erect, herbaceous perennial with scented flowers, and many excellent cultivars. Hardy to 5°F (zone 7).

Jan	/	Recommended Varieties
Feb	sow	
Mar	sow	*Phlox paniculata* "Alba Grandiflora"
Apr	transplant	*P. p.* "Blue Ice"
May	transplant	*P. p.* "Bumble's Delight"
Jun		*P. p.* "Eventide"
July	flowering	*P. p.* "Le Mahdi"
Aug	flowering	*P. p.* "Prince of Orange"
Sept	flowering	*P. p.* "Prospero"
Oct	divide	*P. p.* "White Admiral"
Nov	/	
Dec	/	

CONDITIONS

Aspect   Prefers full sunlight with some protection from strong wind.
Site   Needs a well-drained soil enriched with organic matter.

GROWING METHOD

Propagation   Divide clumps in the fall every three or four years, making sure that each division has a crown and a good set of roots. Replant only the younger, vigorous outer growths, discarding the rest. Plants propagated from root cuttings will be free of eelworm.
Feeding   Apply a complete plant food in spring and mulch well with rotted manure or compost, but do not cover the crowns.
Problems   Powdery mildew can be a problem. Spray with a fungicide. Phlox eelworm causes leaves to shrivel, and shrubs distort. Plants must be destroyed.

FLOWERING

Season   From the summer into early fall.
Cutting   It makes a good cut flower.

AFTER FLOWERING

Requirements Remove spent flower stems as they fade. In late fall, cut off any remaining growth. Give the plants a thorough tidy-up for the winter.

PHYSOSTEGIA VIRGINIANA
Obedient plant

THE SHORT SPIKES of flowers are attached to the obedient plant by a joint, so they can be rearranged as you please.

OBEDIENT PLANT looks best in large plantings. It is well worth devoting yard space to it, since the flowers last for several months.

FEATURES

HERBACEOUS

This is an easy-care, fast-growing perennial. Since it spreads by stolons (runners) and seed, large clumps can develop in one season. Excess plants are quite easily removed. The dark green leaves are only 4–6in long, but flowering stems bring the height up to 4ft. The flowers in the species are pinky-mauve, but there are cultivars with flowers in various shades of pink, red, and white. It looks best when planted in large drifts in a border, or among shrubs. The common name refers to the fact that flowers remain fixed the way they are turned. It is also sometimes known as "false dragon's head."

PHYSOSTEGIA AT A GLANCE

P. virginiana is a spreading, tall perennial with purple or lilac-tinged flowers lasting into the fall. Hardy to 32°F (zone 10).

Jan	/	Recommended Varieties
Feb	/	
Mar	divide	*Physostegia virginiana* "Alba"
Apr	transplant	P. v. "Crown of Snow"
May	transplant	P. v. "Red Beauty"
Jun	/	P. v. "Summer Snow"
July	flowering	P. v. "Vivid"
Aug	flowering	P. v. subsp. *speciosa*
Sept	flowering	"Bouquet Rose"
Oct	sow	
Nov	/	
Dec	/	

CONDITIONS

Aspect Grows well in both full sunlight and semi-shade. However, some form of protection from strong winds is desirable. The taller varieties may need staking.

Site Tolerates a wide range of soils, but the best results occur when it's grown in well-drained soil, rich in organic matter.

GROWING METHOD

Propagation Divide old clumps in the spring, planting new divisions in groups for the best effect. The oldest sections can be discarded. Because of its vigorous habit, you need to divide it every couple of years. Physostegia tolerates dry periods well, but you must water young plants regularly until they are established.

Feeding Apply a complete plant food in spring. Mulch with decayed organic matter at the same time.

Problems No specific problems are known.

FLOWERING

Season Flowers appear from mid- to late summer into the fall.

Cutting Frequent cutting of blooms should produce a second flush of flowers. Scald-cut the stems to prolong their vase life.

AFTER FLOWERING

Requirements Remove spent flower stems and tidy up growth as it dies down.

PLATYCODON
Balloon flower

THE BUDS of platycodon swell into a balloon shape, hence the common name, then pop open to reveal these beautiful flowers.

THIS WELL-ESTABLISHED CLUMP of balloon flower is supported by stakes guaranteeing height, as well as color.

FEATURES

HERBACEOUS

Also known as Chinese bellflower, this herbaceous perennial grows approximately 20in high, slightly taller in perfect conditions. It has a shortish flowering period in late summer, and the open, bell-shape flowers come in a range of blue shades, but also in white and pale pink. Flowers last well when cut. There are several named cultivars available, including double and semi-double examples. Since clumps are compact and spread slowly, they are best planted where they can remain undisturbed for some years. The new growth appears in late spring; mark its position to avoid hauling it out as a weed.

PLATYCODON AT A GLANCE

P. grandiflorus is a one-specie genus grown for its beautiful purple-blue flowers. Several fine cultivars. Hardy to 5°F (zone 7).

Jan	/	Companion Plants
Feb	/	Aster
Mar	sow	Clematis
Apr	divide	Dahlia
May	transplant	Fuchsia
Jun	/	Osteospermum
July	/	Phygelius
Aug	flowering	*Rhodochiton atrosanguineus*
Sept	flowering	Rose
Oct	/	
Nov	/	
Dec	/	

CONDITIONS

Aspect Grows in sun or dappled sunlight.
Site Grows best in a well-drained soil enriched with plenty of organic matter.

GROWING METHOD

Propagation Seed is the best means of propagation; sow in the spring. Young shoots can be taken as cuttings, and the double forms must be grown from cuttings. Also, clumps can be lifted and divided in the spring; replant the divisions approximately 8–10in apart. Give newly bedded plants a regular watering during prolonged dry spells in the spring and summer.

Feeding Apply a complete plant food when new growth begins to appear in the spring.

Problems Slugs can be a major problem devouring new growth. Either pick off by hand or treat chemically.

FLOWERING

Season A relatively short display, which is more than compensated for by the nature of the exquisite flowers.

Cutting Flowers can be cut for the vase.

AFTER FLOWERING

Requirements Cut all spent flower stems right back to the ground, and then the whole plant as the growth dies off.

POLYGONATUM
Solomon's seal

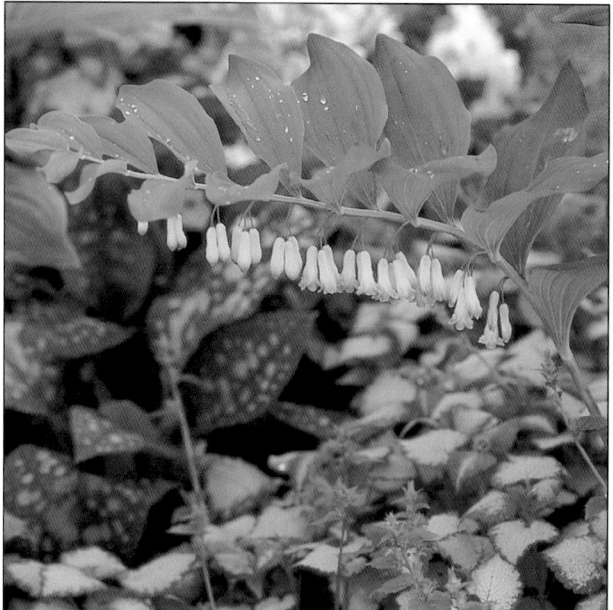

A HORIZONTAL STEM of pretty white Solomon's seal flowers is suspended above a groundcover of lungwort and dead nettle.

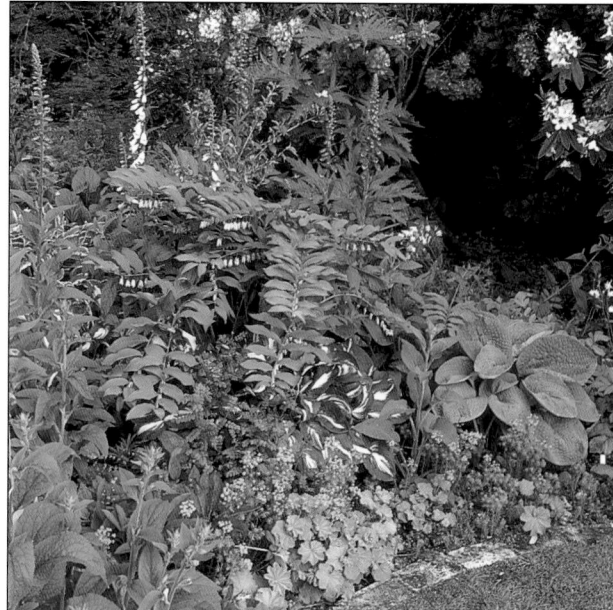

SOLOMON'S SEAL grows tall in the dappled shade of this yard, where it is teamed with hostas, lady's mantle, and foxgloves.

FEATURES

HERBACEOUS

This lovely herbaceous perennial is ideal for naturalizing in the dappled shade of a yard. The plant has a graceful, arching habit with stems 24–36in long. The finely veined foliage tends to stand up on the stem, while the tubular white bell flowers hang down. It grows from a creeping rhizome and will spread to form a colony of plants, given the correct conditions. If space is no problem, plant several to start your display, letting them form large colonies. A number of other species are grown, some, such as *P. odoratum*, with scented flowers; "Flore Pleno" has double flowers. There are two variegated, eye-catching forms.

POLYGONATUM AT A GLANCE

P. x hybridum (multiflorum) is a rhizomatous perennial with green-tipped white flowers and black fruit. Hardy to 0°F (zones 6–7).

Jan	/	
Feb	/	Recommended Varieties
Mar	divide	
Apr	transplant	*P. biflorum*
May	flowering	*P. falcatum*
Jun	/	*P. f.* "Variegatum"
July	/	*P. hookeri*
Aug	/	*P. odoratum* "Flore Pleno"
Sept	/	*P. verticillatum*
Oct	sow	
Nov	/	
Dec	/	

CONDITIONS

Aspect Needs a sheltered spot in part or full shade.
Site The soil should drain well but be heavily enriched with organic matter to retain some moisture at all times. The plants benefit from an early spring mulch.

GROWING METHOD

Propagation Established clumps can be divided in early spring; new divisions should be positioned 8–10in apart. This plant is best left undisturbed for several years, if possible. Young plants need to be watered regularly during the growing season; do not let them dry out.
Feeding Apply complete plant food as new growth commences in the spring.
Problems Plants can be severely devastated by attacks of sawfly larvae, which reduce them to skeletons. Either treat with a spray, or pick off the caterpillars.

FLOWERING

Season Flowers appear in late spring.
Cutting Flowers can be cut for indoor decoration. They last fairly well and make a good display.

AFTER FLOWERING

Requirements Do not cut down the flower stems or you will end up weakening the plant, and consequently losing the attractive, yellow fall tints.

POTENTILLA
Cinquefoil

A SMART RED AND WHITE MIX of cinquefoil with annual heartsease, or Viola tricolor, *growing through it.*

DESPITE THE SMALL FLOWERS, these bright little plants are difficult to overlook in any perennial yard.

FEATURES

HERBACEOUS

There are over 500 species of cinquefoil, including annuals, perennials, and small shrubs. All have the characteristic five-lobed leaf, and the single or double flowers may be white or in shades of yellow, red, or pink. Cinquefoil belongs to the rose family, and the foliage can be attractive, even when plants are not in flower. They may be from 2–20in or more high. The short types make good edging plants, while the taller ones can be used successfully in a mixed planting. Since flower stems tend to flop over, they may need light support. Many red cinquefoils are hybrids of *P. atrosanguinea*, while some yellows derive from *P. argyrophylla* and *P. recta*. Some cinquefoils tend to self-seed.

POTENTILLA AT A GLANCE

A 500-species genus, mainly of herbaceous perennials and shrubs. An excellent color range. Hardy to 0°F (zones 6–7).

		Recommended Varieties
Jan	/	
Feb	/	*Potentilla cuneata*
Mar	sow	"Gibson's Scarlet"
Apr	transplant	*P. megalantha*
May	transplant	*P. nepalensis* "Miss
Jun	flowering	Willmott"
July	flowering	"William Rollison"
Aug	flowering	
Sept	flowering	
Oct	sow	
Nov	/	
Dec	/	

CONDITIONS

Aspect While it needs full sunshine, cinquefoil will also tolerate some dappled shade.

Site Needs well-drained soil enriched with some organic matter.

GROWING METHOD

Propagation Species and single-flowered varieties grow from both seed and cuttings. Sow the seed in early to mid-spring. The hybrid doubles must be grown from divisions taken during the spring or fall, or you can use spring cuttings. The plant spacing depends on ultimate size, and may be anywhere from 6 to 16in.

Feeding Apply a complete plant food as new growth commences in the spring.

Problems Since these plants can easily flower themselves to death, propagate regularly to ensure you always have a good supply.

FLOWERING

Season Flowers may begin in late spring in warm spells, but the main flowering period is during the summer months. Give the plant a light trim in early spring to force plenty of new growth and buds.

Cutting Flowers do not last well when cut.

AFTER FLOWERING

Requirements Cut off spent flower stems at ground level, and tidy up the plants as the growth dies off. In milder areas the foliage may hang on.

PRIMULA VULGARIS
Primrose

A CARPET OF PALE YELLOW PRIMROSES is one of the finest ways to announce the arrival of spring in the yard. Given a cool, sheltered spot, they will thrive and multiply year by year, even if they receive little attention.

FEATURES

HERBACEOUS

This is the true primrose of European woodlands. The species generally has soft, pale yellow flowers tucked in among the leaves on very short stalks, although white or pale pink forms are occasionally found. Cultivars come in a huge range of colors, with single or double flowers, some on short stalks, others on quite tall ones. Primroses look their best when mass-planted under deciduous trees, or in drifts at the front of a lightly shaded bed or border. They can also be grown well in pots. Plants grow from about 4 to 6in high, with flowering stems about the same height.

PRIMULA AT A GLANCE

P. vulgaris is an evergreen or semi-evergreen with scented, spring, generally pale yellow flowers. Hardy to 5°F (zone 7).

Jan	/	
Feb	sow 👈	Recommended Varieties
Mar	flowering 🌸	"Ken Dearman"
Apr	flowering 🌸	"Miss Indigo"
May	flowering 🌸	*Primula vulgaris* "Lilacina Plena"
Jun	/	
July	/	P. v. subsp. *sibthorpii*
Aug	/	"Wanda"
Sept	sow 👈	
Oct	divide 👈	
Nov	/	
Dec	/	

CONDITIONS

Aspect   Prefers to grow in semi-shade, and must have protection from the summer sun.
Site   Grows best in a medium-to-heavy moisture-retentive soil, heavily enriched with organic matter. Mulch around the plants in spring.

GROWING METHOD

Propagation   Lift and divide the crowns after flowering, in late fall, and replant about 4–6in apart. Sow your plant's own seed when ripe (from late spring to early fall); sow bought seed in early spring. Do not let young plants dry out.
Feeding   Little fertilizer is needed if the soil is well enriched with plenty of humus, but a little general fertilizer in early spring gives an extra boost.
Problems   Generally trouble-free.

FLOWERING

Season   Flowering usually lasts for several weeks during the spring. Deadheading prolongs the blooming. Massed displays look best.
Cutting   Makes a fine small bouquet, mixed with a range of other early spring miniatures.

AFTER FLOWERING

Requirements   In suitable conditions, plants may self-seed. Remove dead leaves around the plant base.

PRIMULA SPECIES
Candelabra primulas

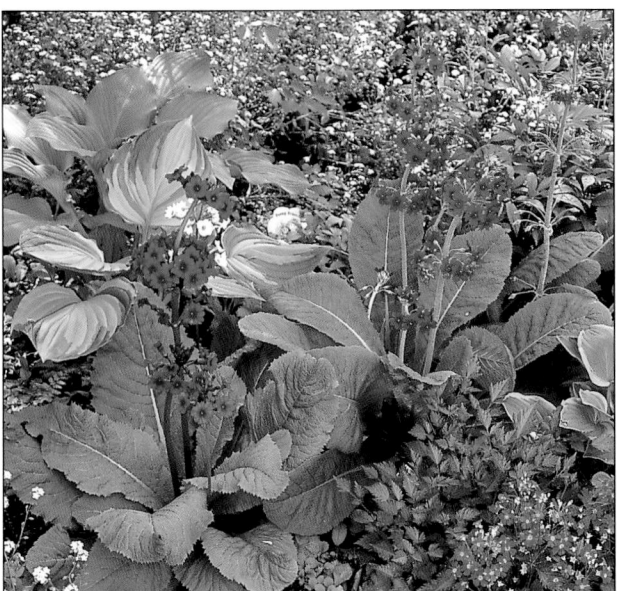

PRIMULA PULVERULENTA *happily combine here with hostas, both enjoying the damp conditions of a bog garden.*

THE CHARACTERISTIC TIERS of flowers are well displayed in this healthy clump of white perennial primulas.

FEATURES

HERBACEOUS

EVERGREEN

Candelabra primulas, which produce their flowers in distinct whorls or tiers up the stems, form one group among the several hundred species of primula. Most are herbaceous, but *P. helodoxa*, which has clear yellow flowers, is evergreen. Other species in this group include *P. aurantiaca*, *P. bulleyana*, *P. japonica*, and *P. pulverulenta*. Flowers may be white, or in shades of yellow, orange, pink, red, or purple. Plant heights vary from 24 to 39in. These are plants that need to be placed in large groups for maximum impact. They need damp soil, often being planted around ponds and water features. Given the right conditions, these plants give a great show every year.

PRIMULA AT A GLANCE

Candelabra primulas are deciduous or semi-evergreen, flower on tall stems, and brighten up damp areas. Hardy to 5°F (zone 7).

		Recommended Varieties
Jan	/	
Feb	sow 🖐	*Primula beesiana*
Mar	sow 🖐	*P. bulleyana*
Apr	flowering 🌸	"Inverewe"
May	flowering 🌸	*P. japonica*
Jun	/	Pagoda Hybrids
July	/	*P. japonica*
Aug	/	*P. pulverulenta*
Sept	sow 🖐	
Oct	divide 🖐	
Nov	/	
Dec	/	

CONDITIONS

Aspect Candelabra primulas thrive in dappled shade.
Site Needs deep, moisture-retentive soil that is heavily enriched with organic matter, but it clearly dislikes being waterlogged over the winter months.

GROWING METHOD

Propagation Lift and divide the crowns after flowering, in late fall, and replant about 4–6in apart. Sow your plant's own seed when ripe (from late spring to early fall); sow bought seed in early spring. Do not let young plants dry out.
Feeding Little fertilizer is needed if the soil is well enriched with plenty of humus, but a scattering of general fertilizer in early spring gives an extra boost.
Problems Generally trouble-free.

FLOWERING

Season This charming, essential primula flowers during the spring.
Cutting Flowers probably last a few days in the vase, and they add considerable charm to any arrangement, but the massed garden display is more rewarding.

AFTER FLOWERING

Requirements Spent flower stems can be cut off, unless you are waiting for seed to set. In good conditions many of the species will self-seed.

PULMONARIA
Lungwort

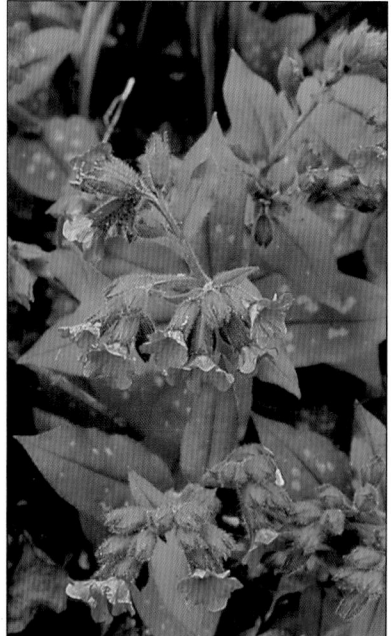

FLOWERING PULMONARIA are an essential feature of the spring yard.

THE SPOTTED FOLIAGE of lungwort makes dense and attractive groundcover under trees. It is a reliable grower, so long as it gets regular water in the spring and summer.

FEATURES

HERBACEOUS

EVERGREEN

Lungwort is well suited to planting under trees, between shrubs, or at the front of a shady border. The abundant flowers appear before the leaves have fully developed, and are mostly in shades of blue, pink, and white. The foliage is very handsome, often silver-spotted, and if sheared over after flowering, produces a second, fresh mound of leaves. The whole plant is rarely more than 10–12in high, and when established is very decorative, even out of flower. The plant gets its common name from the similarity between a spotted leaf and a diseased lung.

PULMONARIA AT A GLANCE

A genus of 14 species of deciduous and evergreen perennials.
A flowering spreader for damp shade. Hardy to 0°F (zones 6–7).

Jan	/	Recommended Varieties
Feb	/	
Mar	flowering	*Pulmonaria angustifolia*
Apr	flowering	*P. a.* "Munstead Blue"
May	flowering	*P. longifolia* "Bertram Anderson"
Jun	divide	*P. officinalis* Cambridge Blue Group
July	/	*P. o.* "Sissinghurst White"
Aug	/	*P. rubra*
Sept	/	*P. saccharata* Argentea Group
Oct	divide	
Nov	/	
Dec	/	

CONDITIONS

Aspect Grows best in light shade, or in borders that are shady during the hottest part of the day. The leaves quickly wilt under a hot sun.

Site The soil should be heavily enriched with decayed organic matter, but it also needs to drain quite well.

GROWING METHOD

Propagation Grows from ripe seed, or by division of clumps, either after flowering or in the fall. Replant divisions approximately 6in apart. Better still, let plants freely hybridize. Young and established plants need moist soil during the growing season.

Feeding Apply a little complete fertilizer in early spring and mulch well.

Problems No specific problems are known.

FLOWERING

Season Lungworts flower in the spring.

Cutting Flowers last quite well in a vase.

AFTER FLOWERING

Requirements Spent flowers can be cut off if you do not want seeding to occur. After the flowers have finished, the foliage can be cut back to produce new fresh growth for the summer. Otherwise, little attention is required until the fall, when the foliage can be tidied as it fades.

PULSATILLA VULGARIS
Pasque flower

FOLK MEDICINE makes use of the pasque flower, but it should be treated with caution, since it can be fatal if used incorrectly.

LIGHT FROST here coats buds of the pasque flower, showing up its silky hairs. They will be more obvious on the seedheads.

FEATURES

HERBACEOUS

The soft purple flowers appear before the leaves on this small, spring-flowering perennial. The whole plant is covered with silky hairs, giving it a delicate appearance that belies its hardy nature. After the petals have fallen, a decorative seedhead forms. The finely divided leaves grow from 4 to 6in long, while the flowers may be on stems 4–12in tall. Pasque flower should be planted in groups or drifts to get the best effect. There are now pink, white, and red forms available. Since the leaves and flowers may cause skin irritation, wear gloves when handling if you have sensitive skin.

PULSATILLA AT A GLANCE

P. vulgaris is an attractive, clump-forming perennial, with bell-like, silky flowers in shades of purple. Hardy to 0°F (zones 6–7).

Month	Activity	Recommended Varieties
Jan	/	
Feb	/	*Pulsatilla alpina subsp.*
Mar	/	*apiifolia*
Apr	flowering	*P. halleri*
May	flowering	*P. halleri subsp. slavica*
Jun	flowering	*P. vernalis*
July	sow	*P. vulgaris*
Aug	sow	*P. v.* "Eva Constance"
Sept	/	*P. v.* var. *rubra*
Oct	divide	
Nov	/	
Dec	/	

CONDITIONS

Aspect   Prefers full sun but tolerates semi-shade.
Site   Needs very well-drained, gritty soil, rich in organic matter. They thrive on lime.

GROWING METHOD

Propagation   Divide existing clumps after the foliage has died down, and then replant the divisions approximately 6–8in apart. Named varieties must be divided, but the species can also be grown from seed sown as soon as it is ripe in July. Overwinter the seedlings in a greenhouse or frame. Pot up when the new leaves begin to show in the spring.

Feeding   Apply a little general fertilizer when growth commences in the spring.

Problems   No specific pest or disease problems are known for this plant.

FLOWERING

Season   Flowers appear in the spring and early summer, generally before the leaves. They last well and the display is prolonged by the pretty, silky seedheads.

Cutting   The flowers are unsuitable for cutting, but the seedheads add to an attractive display.

AFTER FLOWERING

Requirements   Plants should be left alone until the seedheads have faded or fallen. Cut off spent stems, and trim off the foliage as the plant dies.

RANUNCULUS
Buttercup

A STRONG, vivid display of ranunculus showing how they can enliven a border. By mixing two or three different varieties you will certainly get extra impact. However, since some types of ranunculus can rapidly multiply and spread, you must take great care when selecting a particular variety.

FEATURES

EVERGREEN

HERBACEOUS

Buttercups basically divide into the invasive and the less-so. Take care which you chose for the border. The genus contains about 400 species of annuals, biennials, and perennials, with a wide range of demands, which vary from free-draining alpine slopes to ponds.

R. ficaria, lesser celandine, is a woodland type with early spring, yellow flowers that can become a weed. There are several cultivars; "Brazen Hussy" has dark brown foliage and yellow flowers, while "Salmon's White" is cream with a blue tint on the reverse.

R. aconitifolius "Flore Pleno," fair maids of France, likes full sun and has white, long-lasting flowers. And *R. flammula,* lesser spearwort, is a marginal aquatic for early summer with yellow flowers.

RANUNCULUS AT A GLANCE

A large genus of over 400 species with many annuals, biennials, and perennials, hardy to 5°F (zone 7) for all kinds of garden.

		Recommended Varieties
Jan	/	
Feb	/	*Ranunculus aconitifolius*
Mar	sow	"Flore Pleno"
Apr	transplant	*R. calandrinioides*
May	flowering	*R. ficaria* "Brazen Hussy"
Jun	flowering	*R. f.* "Picton's Double"
July	flowering	*R. f.* "Salmon's White"
Aug	/	*R. flammula*
Sept	/	*R. gramineus*
Oct	divide	*R. montanus* "Molten Gold"
Nov	/	
Dec	/	

CONDITIONS

Aspect It tolerates a wide range of conditions from medium to dappled shade, to full sun. When buying a ranunculus do carefully check its specific needs.

Site This too varies considerably from moist, rich soil, to fertile, free-draining ground, to gritty, fast-draining soil for the alpine types, to ponds and pond margins for the aquatics.

GROWING METHOD

Propagation Divide in the spring or fall, or sow fresh, ripe seed in the fall.

Feeding This depends entirely on the natural habitat and growing needs of the plant. Border perennials need reasonable applications of well-rotted manure in the spring, as new growth appears, while the woodland types need plenty of leafy compost dug in around the clumps.

Problems Slugs and snails are a particular nuisance; pick off or use chemical treatment.

FLOWERING

Season From late spring to mid-summer, depending on the chosen variety.

Cutting All ranunculus make excellent cut flowers, being especially useful in spring before the main flush of garden flowers.

AFTER FLOWERING

Requirements Cut back all spent stems.

RODGERSIA
Rodgersia

NO GARDEN IS COMPLETE without rodgersia. They can be grown apart from other plants, perhaps surrounded by gravel, highlighting the shapely, distinctive leaves, which on R. pinnata *grow 10in long. Or grow them in a mixed border, where they add strength and structure.*

FEATURES

HERBACEOUS

A six-species genus with particularly interesting foliage, and flowers, ideal for the border or shady woodland garden. The three most commonly grown types are *R. aesculifolia, R. pinnata,* and *R. podophylla* (the last two having handsome, bronze new foliage). All form big, bold clumps in the right conditions. The first has crinkled leaves like those of a horse-chestnut, up to 10in long, with tall panicles of creamy white flowers; height 6½ft. *R. pinnata* "Superba," 4ft, has purple-bronze foliage and white, pink, or red flowers. And *R. podophylla,* 5ft, with creamy green flowers, also has horse-chestnut-type leaves, reddish in the fall.

RODGERSIA AT A GLANCE

These tall, clump-forming perennials add structure to any damp-ish garden. Whitish summer flowers; hardy to 0°F (zone 7).

		Recommended Varieties
Jan	/	
Feb	/	*Rodgersia aesculifolia*
Mar	sow 🖐	*R. pinnata*
Apr	dvide 🖐	*R. p.* "Elegans"
May	transplant 🖐	*R. p.* "Superba"
Jun	/	*R. podophylla*
July	flowering 🌸	*R. sambucifolia*
Aug	flowering 🌸	
Sept	/	
Oct	/	
Nov	/	
Dec	/	

CONDITIONS

Aspect   Rodgersia, from the mountaineous Far East, like full sun or partial shade. They thrive in both conditions.

Site   Grow in rich, damp ground; they grow by streams in the wild, and also in woodland settings.

GROWING METHOD

Propagation   Either divide, which is the easiest method, or grow from seed in the spring, raising the plants in a cold frame. Water the new young plants well, and do not let them dry out in prolonged, dry spells. They quickly wilt and lose energy, and their performance is badly affected.

Feeding   Add plenty of well-rotted manure or compost to the soil. The shadier the conditions, the less rich the soil need be.

Problems   Vine weevil grubs can demolish the roots of container-grown perennials. While slugs rarely attack the new emerging growth, when they do strike they can ruin a potentially impressive display with tall, astilbe-like flowers. Pick off any offenders or treat with a chemical.

FLOWERING

Season   Flowers appear in mid- and late summer, and in early summer in the case of *R. sambucifolia.*

Cutting   Rodgersia make good cut flowers, helping create an impressive display.

AFTER FLOWERING

Requirements Cut the spent stems to the ground, and promptly remove all debris.

ROMNEYA COULTERI
Californian tree poppy

CRIMPED WHITE PETALS *around a mass of golden stamens make the matilija poppy as effective in close-up as in a group.*

THE BLUE-GREEN FOLIAGE *and splendid white flowers of the matilija poppy make an eye-catching display in the garden.*

FEATURES

EVERGREEN

Also known as the matilija poppy, this lovely perennial is not always easy to accommodate. It is native to the canyons and dry riverbeds in parts of California where there is generally rain only in winter, and where summers are hot and dry. When conditions are suitable, this plant can spread via underground roots. The large, white, summer flowers have beautiful crinkled petals that look like silk. Plants grow from 3 to 6½ft tall, and the blue-green foliage is deeply cut and attractive. Place these perennials in groups among shrubs or mixed perennials. Most plants available are likely to be hybrids of the standard species and *R. coulteri* var. *trichocalyx.*

ROMNEYA AT A GLANCE

This is a deciduous sub-shrub with gray-green leaves and highly attractive white summer flowers. Hardy to 0°F (zones 6–7).

Month	Activity	Companion Plants
Jan	/	
Feb	/	
Mar	sow	Ceanothus
Apr	division	Clematis
May	transplant	Delphinium
Jun	flowering	Helenium
July	flowering	Hemerocallis
Aug	flowering	Pelargonium
Sept	/	Pennisetum
Oct	/	Philadelphus
Nov	/	
Dec	/	

CONDITIONS

Aspect Romneya needs bright, full sunlight all day.
Site Needs well-drained, preferably sandy or gravelly loam; avoid thick, heavy, wet clay. They can be tricky and slow to establish, but thereafter thrive, given the correct conditions.

GROWING METHOD

Propagation Grows from seed sown in the spring, but it is easiest propagated from root cuttings or suckers growing away from the main plant in spring. Wait until plants are very well established before attempting to disturb the roots— something they do not react well to. Position plants approximately 16in apart. Water regularly in the spring, when the foliage is growing and buds are appearing; thereafter, water occasionally in prolonged, dry spells.
Feeding Give a little complete plant food in early spring.
Problems Poor drainage can kill Californian tree poppies. Can become invasive.

FLOWERING

Season Right through the summer.
Cutting Like all poppies they make lovely cut flowers. Scald or burn the stems before arranging.

AFTER FLOWERING

Requirements Cut off spent flowers. As the plant flowers on new growth, it is best to cut it down to the ground in winter. Protect the crown with straw or bracken in cold areas.

RUDBECKIA
Coneflower

THE DAISY-LIKE *flower shape of the coneflower, a bright color, and a central dark marking. It looks best in a bold group display.*

A VALUABLE, *forceful, late summer display from a mass planting of coneflowers, especially useful when many borders are starting to fade.*

FEATURES

HERBACEOUS

The coneflower rewards a bright, sunny position with a bold display of daisy-like flowers. The genus consists of annuals, biennials, and perennials, with some traditional garden favorites. *R. fulgida*, Black-eyed Susan, grows 36 x 18in, producing yellow-orange flowers at the end of summer, into the fall. "Goldsturm" has bigger flowers but only grows two-thirds as tall. For a powerful, vigorous display at the back of the border, try *R. lacinata*. It has thin, wiry stems, lemon-yellow flowers, and puts on a mid-summer to mid-fall display that can reach 8ft high, while its spread is relatively contained at just 3ft.

RUDBECKIA AT A GLANCE

A near 20-species genus with annuals, biennials, and perennials, often with striking, yellowish flowers. Hardy to 0°F (zones 6–7).

Jan	/	Recommended Varieties
Feb	/	"Goldquelle"
Mar	sow	"Herbstonne"
Apr	divide	*Rudbeckia fulgida* var. *deamii*
May	transplant	*R. f.* var. *sullivantii*
Jun	/	"Goldsturm"
July	flowering	*R. laciniata*
Aug	flowering	*R. maxima*
Sept	flowering	
Oct	flowering	
Nov	divide	
Dec	/	

CONDITIONS

Aspect A bright, open sunny position is essential. Avoid shady areas. The plant's natural habitat is North American meadows and big, open woods.

Site Do not plant in over-dry, Mediterranean-style yards. The soil must remain heavy and lightly damp. In the wild *R. fulgida* grows in marshy valleys.

GROWING METHOD

Propagation Either divide in the spring or fall, or sow seeds in the spring in a cold frame. Do not let the new, young plants dry out.

Feeding Fertility must be quite high. Dig large quantities of well-rotted manure and compost into poor soil.

Problems Slugs can be a major problem. Keep watch, and pick them off by hand or treat chemically. A potentially good flowering display can be quickly ruined if they take control.

FLOWERING

Season A long flowering season from the summer to late fall.

Cutting Rudbeckia make good cut flowers, adding height and color to any arrangement. They are especially useful, having a dark-colored central disk (black, brown, or green) in the center of the flower.

AFTER FLOWERING

Requirements Cut back to the ground, although some stems can be left to provide interesting shapes over winter, especially when frosted.

SALVIA
Sage

SALVIA X SYLVESTRIS "MAINACHT" ("MAY NIGHT") is a wonderful, clumpy perennial that sends up spires of rich blue flowers. It can be guaranteed to soften even the most rigid landscaped yard, flowering in early and mid-summer. "Blauhugel" ("Blue Mound") is very similar.

FEATURES

HERBACEOUS

EVERGREEN

Salvias are a huge plant group of over 700 species, comprising shrubs, herbaceous perennials, and annuals. Most people associate salvias with red or purple flowers, but there are also species with cream, yellow, white, blue, and pink flowers. Many have highly aromatic foliage, with scents ranging from the delicious to the outright unpleasant: the foliage of pineapple sage, *S. elegans* (syn. *S. rutilans*) has a delicious perfume, while the bog sage (*S. uliginosa*) smells rather unpleasant. Most salvias are extremely easy to grow and once established need little attention, beyond occasional deep watering in hot weather and some cutting back after flowering. The tall salvias are ideal for the rear of the border or as fillers between shrubs. There are many others of varying heights that are suitable as edging plants or for planting among annuals, bulbs, and other perennials. *Salvia* x *sylvestris* "Mainacht" ("May Night"), shown above, is an exceptionally good border perennial, but if it is unavailable there are plenty of fine alternatives, including "Rose Queen."
Common sage, *S. officinalis*, is a highly popular salvia. It has gray, wrinkly foliage and flowers that are usually pale violet. The one problem is that, in certain conditions, it spreads like a weed. Coming from the Mediterranean, it demands sharp drainage and dislikes a soaking wet summer.

Others For spring–summer flowers in a range of colors, from cream to lilac and blue, try *S. sclarea*. It is perfectly hardy, and grows up to 3ft high. *S. bulleyana* is equally easy, and grows approximately 16in–3ft high. It has yellow flowers with a brownish lower lip appearing from the middle to the end of summer, and is also fully hardy, coming from western China. For an early summer–fall flower show, use *S. forsskaolii* from the Black Sea coast. It grows 3ft tall high, and bears white flowers with lips in violet and faint yellow. Alternatively, try *S.* x *superba*. It has violet flowers from mid-summer to the fall, and reaches the same height. For mild areas where you can grow half-hardy plants, there are plenty more salvias, including *S. microphylla*, and the bog sage, *S. uliginosa*. The former has rich green leaves and magenta flowers at the end of summer to early fall. Bog sage has bright blue flowers with a touch of white, and blooms from late summer to the fall. Both reach 3ft high.

CONDITIONS

Aspect Provide full sunlight, perhaps in a scree bed, and, in the case of half-hardy plants, a position against a south-facing wall.

Site Any well-drained soil is suitable. Mulching with decayed manure in the early spring improves the soil condition.

SALVIA SCLAREA VAR. TURKESTANICA *can be grown as a perennial or biennial. It produces wonderful pink stems of pinky-white flowers, and is perfectly hardy.*

THE ELECTRIC BLUE *Salvia transsylvanica contrasting with a "Star Gazer" lily.*

GROWING METHOD

Propagation Salvias grow from seed that has been sown in the spring, or from cuttings that have been taken in late summer through to the fall. Many species can also be propagated from rooted divisions of an established clump. Simply lift such a clump and you will find numerous pieces with both roots and shoots. The divisions are best taken in the spring months. Set each division approximately 10in apart. Salvias need regular watering to establish. Once established, plants can be drought-tolerant.

Feeding A complete plant food or pelleted poultry manure can be applied in the spring, in poor soil, as the new growth commences. However, note that too much fertilizer will be counter-

productive, merely resulting in all foliage and very few flowers.

Problems The worst problems tend to occur when you provide a certain species with the wrong conditions. Carefully check the notes invariably supplied with plants when buying from a garden center or specialist nursery. As a general rule, avoid damp ground and any shady areas.

FLOWERING

Season Many salvias have a very long flowering period, extending into the fall before being cut down by frost.

Cutting None of the salvias mentioned makes a particularly good cut flower, but their long, dependable flowering season makes them a great asset in any part of the yard.

AFTER FLOWERING

Requirements Borderline, half-hardy species will need plenty of protection in cold areas over winter. Provide a thick, protective layer of straw or bracken, held in place with sticks. As a precaution against any losses, keep a stock of new, young plants. The tender salvias must be kept indoors in winter, in a frost-free place. Plants can be tip-pruned after each flowering flush to promote further blooming. In late fall plants can be cut back to just above ground level. If you do not want to lift and divide a clump you can wait until new growth starts in the spring, and simply divide any growth that is becoming too crowded. A number of perennial salvias are extremely vigorous, but they can be kept in control by pulling out the new plants or the running roots when they are getting invasive.

SALVIA AT A GLANCE

A large genus with fine perennials. The color range is mainly blue. Hardy plants to 0°F (zones 6–7); half-hardy 23°F (zone 9).

Jan	/	Recommended Varieties
Feb	/	
Mar	sow	*Salvia argentea*
Apr	divide	*S. bulleyana*
May	transplant	*S. forsskaolii*
Jun	flowering	*S. involucrata* (half-hardy)
July	flowering	*S. microphylla* (half-hardy)
Aug	flowering	*S. patens* (half-hardy)
Sept	flowering	*S. sclarea*
Oct	flowering	*S.* x *superba*
Nov	/	*S. uliginosa* (half-hardy)
Dec	/	

SCABIOSA
Scabious

SCABIOSA CAUCASICA "CLIVE GREAVES" is a wonderful laven-der blue and looks especially impressive when planted in thick clusters.

SCABIOUS ARE VERSATILE PLANTS. They make a wonderful addition to most yards, whether schematic or cottage-style.

FEATURES

HERBACEOUS

Scabious is a vital ingredient of cottage-style, flowery gardens, rock gardens, and mixed borders. From hot, dry, stony sites, mainly in the Mediterranean, it provides pale hues in blue, pink, yellow, or white. The flowers are held above long, thin stems, many attracting bees and butterflies. Heights generally range from 12 to 36in. There are plenty of interesting choices, and top of the list are the dwarf forms "Butterfly Blue" and "Pink Mist," both relatively new and proving extremely popular. On the plus side, they flower for six months; the down side is they are short-lived. Take cuttings to maintain the display.

SCABIOSA AT A GLANCE	
A genus of annuals, biennials, and perennials, providing abundant soft colors. Good for romantic displays. Hardy to 0°F (zones 6–7).	
Jan	/
Feb	/
Mar	sow
Apr	divide
May	transplant
Jun	flowering
July	flowering
Aug	flowering
Sept	flowering
Oct	sow
Nov	/
Dec	/

Recommended Varieties

Scabiosa caucasica
"Clive Greaves"
S. c. "Miss Willmott"
"Chile Black"
S. columbaria var. *ochroleuca*
S. lucida
"Pink Mist"

CONDITIONS

Aspect	Full sunlight is essential.
Site	Dryish, free-draining soil is important, so that the roots are not plunged in soaking wet ground over the winter months. The soil must also veer from the neutral toward the slightly alkaline.

GROWING METHOD

Propagation	Scabious is not long-lived, and begins to lose its vigor and impact after three years. It is therefore vital to replenish the garden with spring divisions, or to sow fresh, ripe seed in pots in a cold frame to maintain a good supply.
Feeding	Do not over-feed the soil, which will be counter-productive, producing leaf growth at the expense of flowers. Very poor soils, however, may need some additions of compost in the early spring.
Problems	Spray at the first sign of powdery mildew.

FLOWERING

Season	The flowers appear right through the summer, in some cases not until mid-summer, often into early fall.
Cutting	Scabious make excellent sprays of cut flowers, and are indispensable for indoor arrangements, either adding to flowery schemes or softening more rigid, structured ones.

AFTER FLOWERING

Requirements	Cut all spent stems down to the ground.

SEDUM SPECTABILE
Ice plant

DENSE FLOWERHEADS of Sedum spectabile *"Brilliant" provide a rich source of nectar, attracting butterflies and other insects.*

BILLOWING HEADS of sedum add color to the fall yard. Here they edge a mixed border, with white beard tongue behind.

FEATURES

HERBACEOUS

One of over 600 species of succulent sedums, spectabile is unusual because it is frequently used in perennial plantings where many succulents look out of place. It has fleshy, soft green leaves on stems that can reach 24in tall. Similar varieties are available with purple and variegated leaves. Since the new growth appears at the base of older stems, dividing plants is easy. The large heads of flowers are a soft mauve-pink in the species, but there are cultivars with colors ranging from bright hot pinks to rosy red, and the brick red of "Herbstfreude" ("Autumn Joy"). The plants flower from late summer into the fall. This is an easy-care plant that accepts a wide range of conditions.

SEDUM AT A GLANCE

S. spectabile is a clump-forming, late season perennial with pink flowers. Many excellent forms. Hardy to 5°F (zone 7).

Jan	/	Recommended Varieties
Feb	/	
Mar	/	*Sedum alboroseum*
Apr	divide 🐝	"Mediovariegatum"
May	/	*S. cauticola*
Jun	/	"Herbstfreude" ("Autumn
July	/	Joy")
Aug	flowering 🍂	"Ruby Glow"
Sept	flowering 🍂	*S. spectabile* "Brilliant"
Oct	divide 🐝	*S. telephium maximum*
Nov	sow 🖐	"Atropurpureum"
Dec	/	

CONDITIONS

Aspect	Prefers full sun, but tolerates some light shade for part of the day.
Site	While it can grow in a sandy, well-drained soil, it will tolerate a heavier soil, which gives it an advantage over other sedums.

GROWING METHOD

Propagation	Clumps of plants are easily pulled apart or sliced apart with a spade in the spring or late fall. The divisions are best replanted at approximately 6–8in intervals. Division gives very high success rates. It is also possible to propagate sedum by striking from stem cuttings. Water regularly to establish new young plants.
Feeding	Slow-release fertilizer can be applied in the spring, as new growth commences. Avoid overfeeding, because this may result in plenty of sappy leaf growth at the expense of a display of flowers.
Problems	Plants in containers may rot at the base if overwatered. Vine weevil grubs may devour both bases and roots with devastating effect.

FLOWERING

Season	The late, highly rewarding display occurs at the end of summer, running through the fall.
Cutting	A long-lasting cut flower.

AFTER FLOWERING

Requirements Leave the skeletal flowerheads over winter to provide attractive, burnished tints.

SISYRINCHIUM
Sisyrinchium

SISYRINCHIUM IDAHOENSE "ALBUM" *is a clump-forming white flower that at 5in tall is ideal for edging borders.*

SISYRINCHIUM MACROCARPON *is 30in tall, has eye-catching vertical foliage, and gentle yellow flowers in early summer.*

FEATURES

EVERGREEN

This is a star plant for the border, with spires of pale yellow flowers over summer, 36in high, and iris-like, strap-shaped foliage. The only problem is that it can self-seed too much for the liking of some, although with vigilance the seedlings are easily removed. The genus also offers blue, mauve, and white flowers. *S. idahoense* is a lovely violet-blue, with a yellow throat, growing 12in high, while *S. graminoides* is slightly taller at 20in, with a deeper blue flower, although it self-seeds more prolifically. For a dwarfish, low-growing white, try "Pole Star," good for the rock garden, where it can best be seen and appreciated. It grows to just 1 x 2½in, and is perfectly hardy.

SISYRINCHIUM AT A GLANCE

S. striatum is an evergreen perennial with spires of pale yellow flowers and long, stiff, pointed leaves. Hardy to 5°F (zone 7).

Jan	/	Recommended Varieties
Feb	/	
Mar	sow	*Sisyrinchium angustifolium*
Apr	transplant	"Biscutella"
May	/	"Californian Skies"
Jun	flowering	*S. californicum*
July	flowering	"E. K. Balls"
Aug	/	*S. idahoense*
Sept	divide	*S. macrocarpon*
Oct	/	"Quaint and Queer"
Nov	/	*S. striatum* "Aunt May"
Dec	/	

CONDITIONS

Aspect Full sun is required, well away from the shade.
Site Relatively poor soil is adequate, but free-draining ground is essential. Do not let the plants stand out in damp, wet soil over the winter months.

GROWING METHOD

Propagation Divide in late summer to guarantee a supply of vigorous plants, since mature ones become quite lackluster after three years. Alternatively, sow seed in the spring. To prevent any established plants from self-seeding, cut off the flowers the moment they begin to fade.
Feeding Some enriching with well-rotted manure or compost will provide a boost to poor areas of ground. High levels of fertility, however, are not necessary.
Problems Generally trouble-free.

FLOWERING

Season Flowers in early and mid-summer.
Cutting They make unusual, striking cut flowers, adding smart verticals to any arrangement, forming a basic structure. Use both flowering stems and foliage.

AFTER FLOWERING

Requirements Cut back the flowering stems to the ground, either promptly to prevent large-scale self-seeding, or later to increase numbers, especially when established plants are past their best.

SOLIDAGO

Golden rod

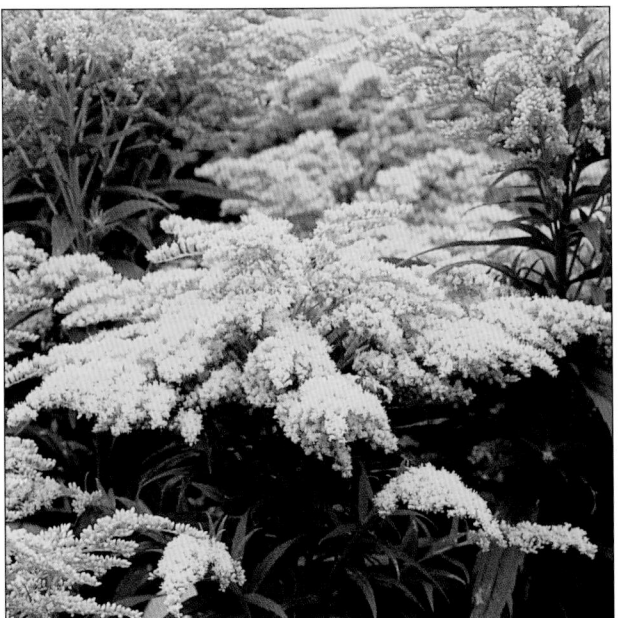

THE HIGHLY DISTINCTIVE sight of golden rod: a bright spray of yellow flowers, and long, thin, dark green leaves.

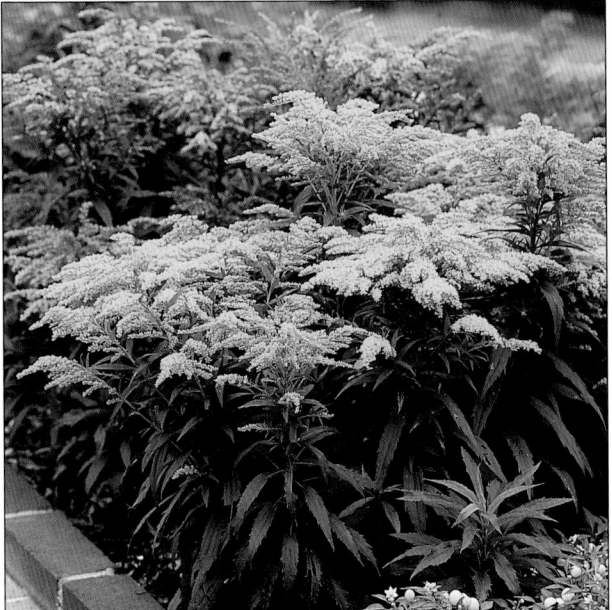

A PERFECT EXAMPLE OF HOW an invasive plant, such as golden rod, can be reined in and controlled by hard landscaping.

FEATURES

HERBACEOUS

Golden rod forms large colonies of sometimes quite tall yellow plants, reaching 6ft high. The small flowers in themselves are nothing special, but they appear in such profusion that they make quite an impact. There are plenty of varieties to choose from. The key differences are more to do with height than color. "Crown of Rays" grows to 24in high, and as its name suggests has bright yellow flowers. "Goldenmosa" is almost as bright and grows slightly taller, and has yellow-green foliage. But if you need a golden rod for the rear of the border, especially one where the soil is quite poor, the best choice is "Golden Wings." It can reach 6ft tall, topping smaller plants

with its late summer and early fall show. The best choice of golden rod for growing at the front of the border is the 8in-high "Queenie" or *S. virgaurea minuta*.

CONDITIONS

Aspect	Grow in full sunlight in the border. Avoid borders that are in the shade.
Site	Free-draining soil, preferably quite sandy or gritty, is ideal.

GROWING METHOD

Propagation	Golden rod self-seeds, but to be sure of getting new plants that are true to type, spring or fall division invariably give successful results.
Feeding	High soil fertility is not in any way essential. Very poor ground can be improved in the spring, however, by digging in some quantities of well-rotted manure.
Problems	Powdery mildew can strike quite severely; treat with a fungicide at the first sight of an attack. Repeat sprayings are necessary to control major outbreaks.

FLOWERING

Season	Generally mid- to late summer, though sometimes slightly before and after.
Cutting	Not the best cut flowers—there are better alternatives—but they effectively bulk up any arrangement.

AFTER FLOWERING

Requirements	Cut back spent flower stems.

SOLIDAGO AT A GLANCE

Varieties of golden rod create mainly big, bold, clumps of bright yellow flowers. Can be invasive. Hardy to 0°F (zones 6–7).

Jan	/	Recommended Varieties
Feb	/	
Mar	/	*Solidago cutleri*
Apr	divide	*S. flexicaulis* "Variegata"
May	transplant	"Golden Baby"
Jun	/	"Goldenmosa"
July	flowering	"Queenie"
Aug	flowering	*S. virgaurea minuta*
Sept	/	
Oct	/	
Nov	/	
Dec	/	

STACHYS BYZANTINA
Lamb's ears

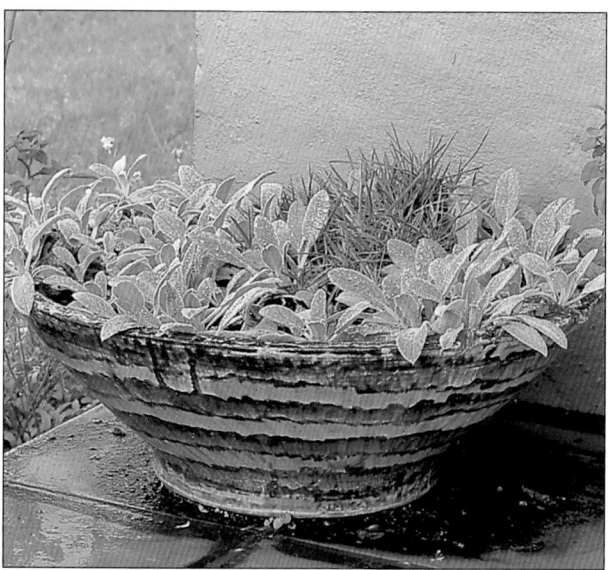

SINCE LAMB'S EARS, or lamb's tails, needs good drainage, grow it in an attractive container if your soil is relentlessly heavy and damp.

MORE TRADITIONAL is this planting, where lamb's ears edge a garden bed. The plants will multiply rapidly, given the right situation.

FEATURES

HERBACEOUS

Lamb's ears is a low-growing, evergreen perennial most often used as an edging plant. It could also be used to edge rose beds, but wherever it is planted it must have excellent drainage and full exposure to the sun. The leaves are densely covered with hairs, giving them a white, or pale gray, woolly appearance, hence its common name. It produces pink-purple flowers on spikes that stand above the foliage, but they are not especially attractive; it is grown for its foliage, not the flowers (*S. macrantha* "Robusta" and *S. officinalis* are the exceptions). "Cotton Boll" has woolly flowers good for dried flower arrangements if they are cut when fully open. Plants grow 6–8in tall, but spread a good distance.

STACHYS AT A GLANCE

S. byzantina is a valuable garden plant, noted for its front-of-the border color and soft, silky foliage. Hardy to 0°F (zones 6–7).

Jan	/	Recommended Varieties
Feb	/	
Mar	sow	*S. coccinea*
Apr	divide	*Stachys byzantina* "Big Ears"
May	transplant	*S. b.* "Cotton Boll"
Jun	flowering	*S. b.* "Primrose Heron"
July	flowering	*S. macrantha*
Aug	flowering	*S. m.* "Robusta"
Sept	flowering	*S. officinalis*
Oct	divide	
Nov	/	
Dec	/	

CONDITIONS

Aspect   Full sunlight is essential all day for the plants to thrive and perform well.

Site   Needs very fast-draining soil. It grows well in poor, sandy, or gravelly soil. Avoid thick, wet, heavy clay at all costs.

GROWING METHOD

Propagation   Grows readily from cuttings that are taken in the spring or fall. The new divisions must be planted out approximately 8in apart. Water new plants regularly. Once they are established, they need only be watered very occasionally.

Feeding   Grows without supplementary fertilizer, but a little complete plant food can be applied in the early spring.

Problems   There are no specific problems, but container plants will quickly fail if they are overwatered, and border plants rot if waterlogged.

FLOWERING

Season   Flowers are produced in the summer, sometimes into the fall, but the tactile gray foliage is by far the chief attraction.

Cutting   Use the foliage in an arrangement; the flower spikes can be cut and dried for later use.

AFTER FLOWERING

Requirements   Cut spent flower stems at the base. Trailing growth can be shortened at any time, but plants may need to be cut back hard in the early spring.

STOKESIA LAEVIS
Stokes' aster

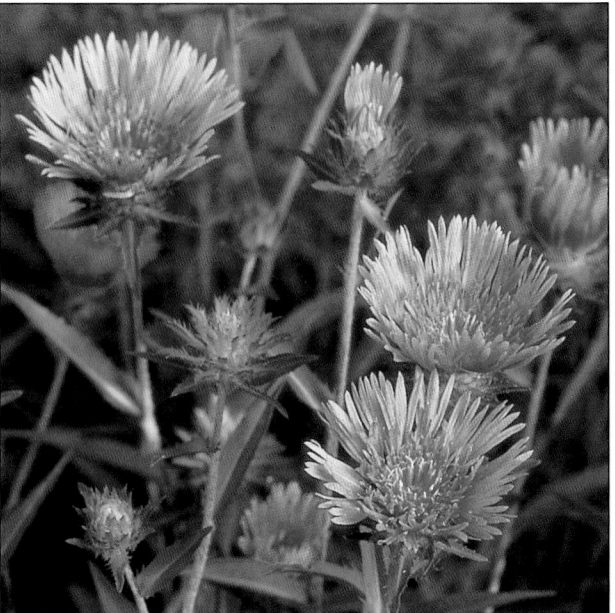

THE FLOWERING HEADS of Stokes' aster are quite complex, made up from many "petals" (more properly bracts or ray florets).

IT IS HARD to understand why the pretty Stokes' aster should go out of fashion, but it is certainly grown less often than before.

FEATURES

HERBACEOUS

Stokes' aster is an easily grown plant that provides great decorative value throughout its long flowering period from mid-summer to early fall. It makes excellent cut flowers, too. Flower stems 12–20in tall rise from a cluster of dark green basal leaves. Although this plant is completely herbaceous in cold areas, the basal growth remains evergreen in mild winters. Its flowers are reminiscent of large cornflowers or asters, and come in shades of blue, white, and mauve. This plant can look outstanding in mass plantings, but is equally at home in a mixed border, or when grown in wooden tubs or pots.

STOKESIA AT A GLANCE

S. laevis is an evergreen, perennial, sprawling plant with large, purple, flat, late summer flowers. Hardy to 5°F (zone 7).

Jan	/	Companion Plants
Feb	sow 🌱	Aster
Mar	divide 🌿	Box
Apr	transplant 🌿	Dahlia
May	transplant 🌿	Fuchsia
Jun	/	Miscanthus
July	/	Penstemon
Aug	flowering 🌼	Potentilla
Sept	flowering 🌼	Stipa
Oct	flowering 🌼	
Nov	divide 🌿	
Dec	/	

CONDITIONS

Aspect   While Stokes' aster prefers full sunlight, it barely tolerates dappled shade. Provide a shelter to protect from strong winds.

Site   Needs well-drained soil enriched with compost or manure.

GROWING METHOD

Propagation   Divide established clumps in the spring or fall, replanting divisions approximately 10in apart. The plant can also be grown from root cuttings taken in the early spring, and from fall seed. It tolerates dry periods, but looks best if given an occasional deep watering during prolonged, dry spells. Provide young plants with twiggy support.

Feeding   Apply some complete plant food in the spring.

Problems   Poorly drained, heavy soils induce root or crown rot, which kills plants.

FLOWERING

Season   The long flowering period is from late summer into the fall.

Cutting   Cut flowers regularly for the vase. This both gives a good ornamental display and prolongs the garden show, inducing plenty of new flower buds.

AFTER FLOWERING

Requirements   Prune all spent flower stems. As the growth dies back, promptly clear away all of the dead foliage.

THALICTRUM
Meadow rue

THE FLUFFY PINK FLOWERS of meadow rue do not last long, but the pretty foliage persists well until the fall.

FINER FOLIAGE, smaller starry flowers and very full growth are features of the related Thalictrum delavayi *and its cultivars.*

FEATURES

HERBACEOUS

Thalictrum aquilegiifolium is easy and quick to grow, a herbaceous perennial reaching about 42in tall. The rather fern-like, blue-green foliage is attractively lobed, and the flowers are mauve-pink in dense, fluffy heads. While the floral display does not last long, the foliage adds months of charm. Meadow rue can be planted in mixed borders or in light shade under trees. There are a number of cultivars, including a white form and one with violet blooms. Also try *T. delavayi* (syn. *T. dipterocarpum*) and its cultivars "Album" and "Hewitt's Double." This has finer foliage and the pink-mauve flowers are star shaped.

THALICTRUM AT A GLANCE

T. aquilegiifolium is a clump-forming, rhizomatous perennial with gorgeous sprays of purple flowers. Hardy to 5°F (zone 7).

Jan	/	Recommended Varieties
Feb	/	
Mar	divide	*Thalictrum aquilegiifolium* var. *album*
Apr	transplant	*T. a.* "Thundercloud"
May	/	*T. delavayi*
Jun	flowering	*T. flavum* subsp. *glaucum*
July	flowering	*T. kiusianum*
Aug	/	*T. minus*
Sept	/	*T. rochebruneanum*
Oct	sow	
Nov	/	
Dec	/	

CONDITIONS

Aspect Grow in either light shade, or in a border with morning sun followed by plenty of afternoon shade.

Soil Likes well-drained soil that has been enriched with organic matter.

GROWING METHOD

Propagation Grows from seed sown in the spring or fall, or by divisions of a clump made in spring. Plant the new divisions approximately 10–12in apart. Do not let the young plants dry out—give regular, deep waterings through dry springs and summers.

Feeding As growth begins in the spring, apply complete plant food and mulch around the plants with well-decayed manure or compost.

Problems No specific pest or disease problems are known to attack this plant. Generally trouble-free. Note that growth begins late in spring, so avoid damaging new growth while weeding.

FLOWERING

Season Flowers appear during early summer, depending on temperatures.

Cutting Both the foliage and flowers can be cut for the vase.

AFTER FLOWERING

Requirements Cut off any spent flower stems, unless you want to save seed. When the plants die down in the fall, cut off the foliage at ground level.

TIARELLA
Foam flower

THE FOAM FLOWER *produces both a fine early summer bloom display, and often burnt-red-colored fall foliage.*

GIVEN A FREE RUN, Tiarella polyphylla *produces a large, spreading clump with wonderful spires of white flowers.*

FEATURES

HERBACEOUS

Tiarella trifoliata is a North American clump-forming rhizomatous perennial, making excellent groundcover in light shade. From late spring to mid-summer it produces light airy sprays of white flowers, on 12in-long panicles, held above the foliage. A more invasive plant is *T. cordifolia*, foam flower, from east North America, where it grows in mountainside woods, forming extensive colonies, remorselessly spreading by underground stolons. *T. wherryi*, also from North America, is more compact and less invasive—the better choice for a smaller, shady area. Its natural habitat is shady ravines and rocky woods. The white flowers are tinged pink. "Bronze Beauty"

is a popular choice, benefiting from contrasting white flowers and bronze-red foliage.

CONDITIONS

Aspect	Thrives in both dappled and darkish shade, which is its natural habitat.
Site	It tolerates a wide range of soils, but naturally prefers rich, fertile ground, damp but definitely not boggy.

GROWING METHOD

Propagation	Division is the simplest method, although ripe seed can also be sown. Sow in pots in the fall in a cold frame, and keep young plants well watered. Do not let them dry out.
Feeding	The ground needs to be quite rich. Fork in leaf mold and compost in the early spring, and again in the fall, between plants.
Problems	Slugs can strike, but given the situation, out of the way in the shade, and the plant's vigor, it is rarely a major problem. Treat with slug pellets if matters get out of hand.

HARVESTING

Season	A profusion of white flowers appear from late spring to mid-summer.
Cutting	There are better choices for airy white sprays in the summer, but nonetheless they make good cut flowers.

AFTER FLOWERING

Requirements	Cut back to the ground.

TIARELLA AT A GLANCE

T. trifoliata is a North American white perennial, ideal for spreading quickly through shady sites. Hardy to 5°F (zone 7).

Jan	/	Recommended Varieties
Feb	/	
Mar	sow	*Tiarella cordifolia*
Apr	divide	"Elizabeth Oliver"
May	flowering	*T. polyphylla*
Jun	flowering	*T. p.* pink
July	flowering	*T. wherryi*
Aug	/	*T. w.* "Bronze Beauty"
Sept	sow	
Oct	/	
Nov	/	
Dec	/	

TRADESCANTIA
Tradescantia / spiderwort

SPIDERWORT FLOWERS look like small purple irises but each lasts only a day. The surrounding buds are waiting their turn to open.

DENSE PLANTINGS of spiderwort produce plenty of flowers that thrive in filtered sunlight, ideal for a mixed or herbaceous border.

FEATURES

HERBACEOUS

This North American herbaceous perennial is a spreading plant with tapering, strap-like leaves and showy, triangular flowers in rich purple, rose-pink, or white. The flowers generally last only one day but they appear in succession over a long period. There are several named cultivars available. Spiderwort grows from 12 to 24in high, and is multi-stemmed. It is easy to grow in the correct conditions and can make a tall groundcover in filtered sunlight under trees. In a mild winter it may not die down completely.

TRADESCANTIA AT A GLANCE

T. virginiana is a purple, repeat-flowerer in a genus of largely tender indoor plants. Ideal for the border. Hardy to 5°F (zone 7).

		Recommended Varieties
Jan	/	
Feb	/	*Tradescantia* x *andersoniana*
Mar	divide	"Bilberry Ice"
Apr	/	*T.* x *a.* "Isis"
May	/	*T.* x *a.* "Osprey"
Jun	flowering	*T.* x *a.* "Purple Dome"
July	flowering	*T.* x *a.* "Red Cloud"
Aug	flowering	*T.* x *a.* "Zwanenburg Blue"
Sept	flowering	
Oct	divide	
Nov	divide	
Dec	/	

CONDITIONS

Aspect It requires full sunlight or partial shade.
Site It grows best in soil that is well drained, but is also heavily enriched with plenty of decayed, organic matter.

GROWING METHOD

Propagation Clumps can be lifted and divided in the spring and fall. The species can be grown from seed sown in the fall. It is occasionally self-sown. New plantings should be approximately 12–18in apart, depending on how rapidly you need cover. Needs regular watering during a prolonged, dry growing period.
Feeding Apply a complete plant food when growth starts in the spring.
Problems No specific problems are known.

FLOWERING

Season The long succession of flowers starts in early summer and continues through to mid-fall.
Cutting The buds continue to open when cut.

AFTER FLOWERING

Requirements Growth starts to yellow and die back after flowering. Clean away dead foliage, and tidy up for the winter.

TRILLIUM
Wake robin

THE WAKE ROBIN is the perfect plant for a moist shady area, whether it be light or deep shade. The plants are quickly identified by their three leaves, three calyces, and three petals.

FEATURES

HERBACEOUS

Trilliums are deciduous perennials that make excellent groundcover in partial or full shade, with spring and early summer flowers. The color range includes white, maroon, pink, yellow, bronze-green, and red-purple. *T. grandiflorum*, the North American wake robin, has 3in-long white flowers and veined petals. It is long-lived and easy to grow, requiring little attention. *T. sessile* "Rubrum" has claret petals and attractively mottled foliage. Several clones bear this name and there is little to choose between them. At the front of a shady, slightly acidic border, try *T. rivale*. It grows 6in tall and wide, has pointed ovate petals, white or pale pink, with purple speckling toward the base. *T. luteum* has scented yellowish flowers and mottled, pale and dark leaves. It grows 16in tall, spreading by almost the same amount.

CONDITIONS

Aspect   Mottled or deep shade is required. Avoid open areas with full sunlight.

Site   The soil should be the acid side of neutral, although some trilliums will tolerate low levels of alkalinity.

GROWING METHOD

Propagation   Preferably divide the rhizomes when dormant, ensuring each section has one strong growing point. Note that they are slow to establish. It is quite possible to sow ripe, late summer seed in a cold frame, but the 5–7 years to flower is prohibitively long.

Feeding   The soil needs to be rich, with plenty of well-rotted leaf mold and compost, being damp and free-draining. Where necessary, provide a thick mulch every spring and fall.

Problems   Both slugs and snails feed on the tender new foliage. Pick off by hand when this becomes a problem, or use a chemical treatment.

FLOWERING

Season   The flowers appear in spring and summer.

Cutting   They make attractive cut flowers, especially *T. grandiflorum*, with its near diamond-shaped white flowers.

AFTER FLOWERING

Requirements   Cut spent stems to the ground.

TRILLIUM AT A GLANCE

A 30-species strong genus with rhizomatous perennials, excellent for flowering ground cover in shade. Hardy to 5°F (zone 7).

Month		Recommended Varieties
Jan	/	
Feb	/	
Mar	/	
Apr	transplant	*Trillium cernuum*
May	flowering	*T. chloropetalum*
Jun	flowering	*T. cuneatum*
July	/	*T. erectum*
Aug	/	*T. grandiflorum*
Sept	sow	*T. g. flore-pleno*
Oct	divide	*T. luteum*
Nov	/	*T. rivale*
Dec	/	*T. viride*

VERBASCUM
Mullein

MULLEINS ARE FAMED *for their striking shape and bright flowers, but as seen here they can blend with the gentlest design.*

MULLEINS HAVE *few equals as accent plants, since they are tough and adaptable, capable of tolerating many climates and conditions.*

FEATURES

EVERGREEN

HERBACEOUS

'Not all mulleins are reliably perennial—some are best treated as biennials and replaced after two years. However, most are easy to raise. They are grown for their large rosettes of foliage, often silver or gray, from which emerges a tall, striking spike of flowers up to 6ft high. They make eye-catching accent plants in any sunny part of the yard. The various species and their cultivars have flowers in a range of colors, including white and gentler shades of yellow, pink, and purple. The common mullein, *V. thapsus*, also known as Aaron's rod, freely self-seeds. Mullein has a long folk history, first as a candle, then as a medical treatment.

VERBASCUM AT A GLANCE

A 360-species genus, famed for its dramatic, colored spires in summer. Heights 12in–6ft. Hardy to 5°F (zone 7).

		Recommended Varieties
Jan	/	
Feb	/	*Verbascum bombyciferum*
Mar	/	*V. chaixii* "Album"
Apr	sow	*V. c.* "Cotswold Beauty"
May	transplant	*V. c.* "Gainsborough"
Jun	flowering	*V. dumulosum*
July	flowering	"Golden Wings"
Aug	flowering	"Helen Johnson"
Sept	sow	"Letitia"
Oct	/	*V. phoeniceum*
Nov	/	
Dec	/	

CONDITIONS

Aspect	Grows best in full sunlight all day.
Site	Grows in any kind of well-drained soil, even poor and alkaline ones.

GROWING METHOD

Propagation	Grows from seed sown as soon as it is ripe, or from root cuttings taken in late fall or winter. The seed forms on the spike after the flowers have fallen, and is ripe when it has changed color, becoming brown or black. Sow in pots in a cold frame in either the spring or fall. Plants of the larger mullein species need to be planted out approximately 39in apart.
Feeding	Apply a complete plant food in early spring, when new growth commences.
Problems	No specific problems are known.

FLOWERING

Season	Mullein produces flowers right through the summer, but its amazing spire of a stem remains a big architectural feature long after the flowers have finished.
Cutting	A nipped-off section of the flowering spire considerably adds to a formal, architectural display.

AFTER FLOWERING

Requirements	Cut off the spent flower spike, unless you want seed to set.

VIOLA ODORATA
English violet

DESPITE the range of cultivars available, the violet species is still a big favorite.

VIOLETS PROVIDE great groundcover under deciduous trees or in other shaded, sheltered spots. They do, however, need high levels of sunlight to put on a good flowering display.

FEATURES

EVERGREEN

Violets have been in cultivation since ancient times, and were highly valued by the ancient Greeks. In Victorian period an enormous number of varieties was grown, including a wide range of the double Parma violets. The violet's sweet fragrance and elegant flowers make them big favorites with gardeners and florists alike. The plants have a creeping habit, spreading up to 12in, and are rarely more than 6–8in tall. There are cultivars with single or double flowers in purple, pink, white, or bicolors, but the deep purple is probably the best loved. There are other violet species to grow in the garden, from the summer-flowering *V. cornuta*, fine under hybrid tea roses, to the spring/summer *V. sororia* and its form, "Freckles."

VIOLA AT A GLANCE

V. odorata is a rhizomatous, semi-evergreen perennial with blue or white flowers. A good self-seeder. Hardy to 0°F (zone 6–7).

Jan	/	Recommended Varieties
Feb	/	
Mar	flowering 🌱	*Viola cornuta*
Apr	flowering 🌱	*V. c.* Alba Group
May	flowering 🌱	*V. c.* Lilacina Group
Jun	/	*V. c.* "Minor"
July	/	*V. odorata* "Alba"
Aug	/	*V. o.* "Rosea"
Sept	divide 🖐	*V. sororia* "Freckles"
Oct	/	*V. s.* "Priceana"
Nov	/	
Dec	/	

CONDITIONS

Aspect   It needs either shade, or light dappled sunshine.

Site   For the best results it needs well-drained, moisture-retentive soil, heavily enriched with organic matter.

GROWING METHOD

Propagation   Clumps can be lifted and divided, or runners can be dug up and replanted every couple of years, in the spring or fall. Set out at 8in spacings, with the plant crowns kept just above soil level. Violets self-seed, too. Keep young plants well watered during the first growing season.

Feeding   Apply complete plant food in spring after flowering ceases.

Problems   Slugs and snails can be a major nuisance, devouring tasty new growth. Pick off by hand, or treat chemically.

FLOWERING

Season   Violets flower from late winter into early spring.

Cutting   Scalding the stems of cut violets before arranging them will certainly increase their vase life.

AFTER FLOWERING

Requirements   No special treatment is needed, but excess runners can be removed during the growing season if they are invasive. This has the added benefit of channeling vigor back to the main crown.

Growing Roses

GROWING ROSES

A favorite of many, roses, with their single, semi-double or fully double flowers, and their bicolored, multicolored, striped or "hand-painted" blooms, are often richly scented and deck bushy stems.

FEATURES

Plant roses to color beds, borders, patio pots, hanging baskets and rocky yards. Position them so that they form a canopy over pergolas, obelisks, arches, trees, walls and fences.

There are seven distinct groups of roses:

Large-flowered roses (hybrid tea):
These form shapely double blooms on long stems and are good for cutting. They are usually grown as bushes to 3ft high. Choice varieties are soft peachy-pink "Scent-Sation," golden-yellow "Lions International," and white "Polar Star."

Cluster-Flowered (floribunda)
Sumptuous heads adorn stems from 2–3ft. Plant tangerine-orange "Razzle Dazzle," sparkling yellow "Charter 700," and scarlet "Invincible" to fringe a path or driveway.

English roses
They combine the scent and cupped- or rosette-shaped flower of an old-fashioned rose with the color range and repeat-flowering qualities of a cluster flowered variety. Forming plants from 3–6ft, newcomers include warm-pink "Anne Boleyn," yellow and spray-flowered "Blythe Spirit," and scarlet "Falstaff."

Miniature and patio
Small cluster-flowered roses that reach 15–24in—they flower all summer and spill from patio pots. Look out for peachy-apricot "Sweet Dream" and vermilion "Top Marks."

Shrub roses
Some varieties treat us to a succession of flowers, others to a billowing surge of bloom in mid-summer. Outstanding varieties included repeat-flowering, creamy white "Sally Holmes," and single pink and white "Ballerina."

Carpeters
Also known as ground-cover roses — they spread and suppress weeds — the famed County Series yields a spectacular display of flush upon flush of blossom. Riveting are single, scarlet and golden-centerd "Hampshire" and semi-double, bright yellow "Gwent."

LEFT: The shape of rose flowers vary considerably, from high and split-centered, globular, open cup-shaped and quartered to flat, rosette and pompon. Most are grafted onto rootstocks in order to charge them with vigor.

Climbers and ramblers
Thrusting skywards to cloak walls, fences, arches, pergolas and trees with a welter of blossom, climbers, such as honey-colored "Penny Lane," delight us with a succession of perfumed blooms.
Ramblers (including cream "Bobbie James") usually flower once in a midsummer.

CONDITIONS

Aspect	Roses need bright sunlight to excel. Some, such as "Canary Bird" and "Flower Carpet" also flower magnificently in light shade.
Site	Though a few kinds thrive in light sandy or stony soils, most benefit from humus-rich loam. Drainage must be good.

GROWING METHOD

Planting	Garden-center bushes can be planted throughout the year, provided the soil is "open." Mail-order plants are delivered bare rooted and dispatched from November to March.
Feeding	Sprinkle a high-potash and magnesium rich granular fertilizer over the root area in April and prick it into the surface. Follow with a 3in mulch. Repeat feeding in June.
Dead heading	Nip off faded blooms at the "knuckle" to channel energy into new flowering shoots.
Propagation	Take 9in cuttings of ramblers, climbers, miniatures and vigorous cluster-flowered varieties from the fully mature middle part of a pencil-thick side shoot in September. Remove all but two leaves at the top. Make a horizontal cut below the bottom bud and a sloping cut above the top bud. Nip off thorns. Insert cuttings 6in deep in a straight-backed trench lined with sharp sand. Firm soil around them. Roots will form within eight weeks.
Pruning	Prune with pruning shears from March to early April. *Large Flowered and Cluster Flowered bushes and standards:* Shorten main stems by half their height, cutting to a bud. Reduce side shoots to two buds. to two buds. *Miniature and shrub roses:* Shorten dead and broken stems to live wood. *Climbers:* Cut back flowered shoots to within 3in of the main stem. *Ramblers:* Prune in September. Remove flowered shoots at ground level and replace with current-year stems.
Problems	Control black spot, mildew and rust disease, together with greenfly and other sap-sucking insects, by spraying with a pesticide containing pirimicarb, bupirimate and triforine. Wearing gloves, remove the suckers, which are more thorny, with paler green leaves than varietal shoots. Twist them from the stock.

Sceptered Isle

Raised by David Austin Roses, "Sceptered Isle" is an English Rose whose cupped and perfumed soft pink blooms grow freely above the foliage on stems to 3ft. Blooming continuously from early summer to mid-fall, it needs full sun to form a stocky bush. Dead-head regularly.
Create an arresting feature by inter-planting it with silver- and fern-leaved Artemisia "Powis Castle." Grown as a standard, it rewards you with a large head of blossom which makes a stunning focal point in a bed or border.

SCEPTERED ISLE AT A GLANCE

Must have full sunlight in order to thrive and bloom freely. Fully hardy to frost hardy.

Month	Activity	Month	Activity
JAN	rest		deadheading
FEB	rest	OCT	light pruning
MAR	planting, pruning	NOV	planting
APR	feeding	DEC	rest
MAY	mulching		
JUN	flowering		OTHER ENGLISH ROSES:
JULY	flowering, deadheading		"The Countryman"
AUG	flowering, deadheading		"Port Meirion"
			"Barbara Austin"
SEPT	flowering,		"Dr Herbert Gray"

Graham Thomas

A glorious English Rose, "Graham Thomas," (named after the famed rosarian and writer), sports unusually rich golden yellow flowers. This color is missing from old-fashioned roses from which the variety was born. Forming a rounded bush to 4ft high and across, its branches elegantly arch. Interestingly, it can also be trained as a climber to 6–8ft. If you plant it to cover a wall, set the root system at least 15in from the brickwork to avoid moisture being sucked from the root area. Fan-train shoots as low as possible to trigger an abundance of blossom.

GRAHAM THOMAS AT A GLANCE

Flowers best when grown in full sunlight. Fully hardy to frost hardy.

Month	Activity	Month	Activity
JAN	rest	SEPT	flowering, deadheading
FEB	rest	OCT	light pruning
MAR	planting, pruning	NOV	planting
APR	feeding	DEC	rest
MAY	mulching		
JUN	flowering, deadheading		
JULY	flowering, feeding		
AUG	flowering, deadheading		

FELICIA

FLOWER CARPET

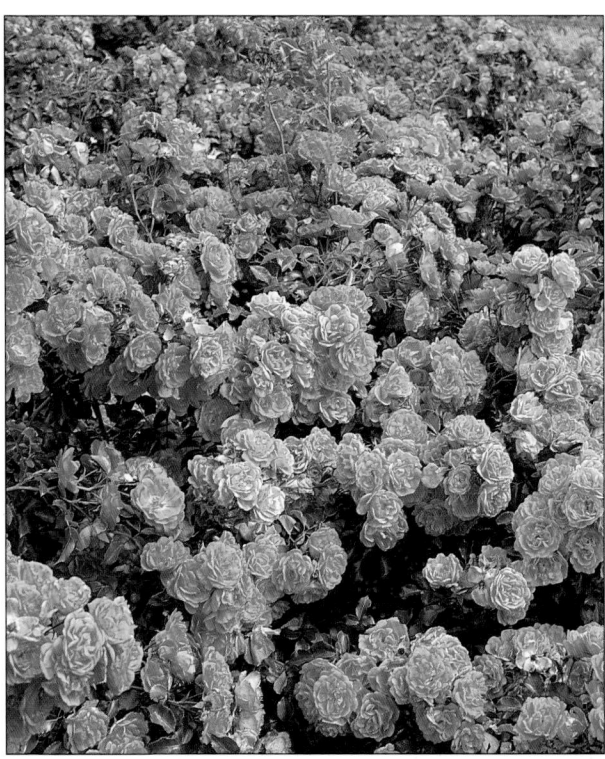

A prized Hybrid Musk — the family bears large trusses of bloom in early summer and intermittently later—"Felicia" is a joy. Yielding aromatically fragrant silver-pink blooms amid dark green leaves on sturdy shoots to 5ft long, it's very healthy and seldom suffers from pests and diseases. If there's room, encourage it to flower bounteously by pegging down shoots so they radiate from the center of the bush. Alternatively, set "Felicia" to cover a trellis-clad sunny wall or fence.

Spreading enthusiastically to 4ft "Flower Carpet," which grows to 2ft high, treats us to an almost non-stop parade of huge trusses of semi-double bright pink flowers from June to November. Unlike many varieties, it romps in light shade and flowers as well there as in full sun. Its shining, glossy leaves appear to be fully resistant to black spot, mildew and rust.

It is even more alluring when trained as a standard. It's such a profuse performer that flower-bowed branches are liable to snap, so support them with strings tied to a cane fastened to the main stem. Its cousins, "White Flower Carpet" and "Sunshine," a new yellow form, are equally healthy and spirited.

FELICIA MOON AT A GLANCE

Performs best when grown in full sunlight. Fully hardy to frost hardy.

JAN	rest	SEPT	flowering, deadheading
FEB	rest	OCT	light pruning
MAR	planting, pruning	NOV	planting
APR	feeding	DEC	rest
MAY	mulching		
JUN	flowering, deadheading		
JULY	flowering, feeding		
AUG	flowering, deadheading		

OTHER HYBRID MUSKS:

"Pax"

"Penelope"

"Camelia"

"Francesca"

FLOWER CARPET AT A GLANCE

Flowers freely in full sunlight or light shade. Fully hardy to frost hardy.

JAN	rest	SEPT	flowering, deadheading
FEB	rest	OCT	light pruning
MAR	planting, light pruning	NOV	planting
APR	feeding	DEC	rest
MAY	mulching		
JUN	flowering, deadheading		
JULY	flowering, feeding		
AUG	flowering, deadheading		

OTHER FLOWER CARPET FORMS:

"White Flower Carpet"

"Sunshine"

Growing Annuals

GROWING ANNUALS

Annuals are perhaps the easiest plants you will ever grow. Yet their ease of growth in no way detracts from their ability to provide color in the yard, in some cases virtually all year around. Whether your yard is large, small, or you work within the confines of just a small courtyard, annuals are the plants for you.

Miracles are happening in our gardens every day, but perhaps the greatest "miracle" in which we can take part is growing plants from seeds. Nothing is quite as amazing, or as humbling, as seeing a fully grown plant, that started life as a tiny seed, burst into flower and create a riot of color just a few months after it was sown. Some annuals need no more care than simply scattering the seeds over the surface of the ground and "raking" them in using your fingertips; others only demand that they are sown to the correct depth and then given space to grow as they develop. By their very nature, many annuals produce brilliant results, even in the poorest of soils. So get some seed catalogs, visit the local garden center, and start performing your own gardening miracles with the easiest plants on earth!

LEFT: Annuals like these purple violas and white-flowered lobularia (alyssum) can be sown directly into the soil where you want them to flower, in criss-crossing patterns as here.

ABOVE: Rudbeckia or coneflower is available in a wide range of sizes, and provides valuable color in late summer.

MANY ANNUALS THRIVE in some of the most inhospitable parts of the yard. These portulacas, or sun flowers, are perfectly at home growing on a rock garden with very little soil for their roots—and are just as suited to light, sandy soils and make good summer bedding plants.

WHAT ARE ANNUALS?

Virtually all annuals are raised by sowing seeds, either in the early spring under cover (in a heated greenhouse, conservatory, or on the kitchen windowsill), or directly into prepared soil outdoors. Some annuals are so adaptable that you only need sow them once—from then onward these so-called "self-seeders" regularly drop seeds into the soil which then "come up," or germinate, of their own accord. In many ways, these "hardy annuals" do a better job of sowing than we do, finding just the right spot for perfect growth, often in places we might never dream of sowing seeds, such as in cracks in the sidewalk and in the gravel of driveways.

At the other extreme are annuals that need to be started into growth long before the warmer days of spring arrive outdoors. The so-called "half-hardy" annuals are those plants that are damaged by frosts, but perform brilliantly during the summer months. For these you must be able to provide suitable growing conditions, especially at sowing time, when temperature is all-important for getting the seeds to come up. In some cases, such as with ricinus, the castor oil plant, it is grown as a half-hardy annual, even though it is by nature a shrub, which in its native habitat would, like the shrubs in our gardens, eventually form a large plant. Petunias are another example of a half-hardy annual that is really a perennial plant, and quite capable of surviving the winter if potted-up and kept protected in a cold but frost-free place over winter. It helps to understand what the terms mean when growing annuals, since you will come across them all the time in catalogs and on the back of seed packets.

HARDY ANNUALS

The easiest of all annuals to grow, sow hardy annuals exactly where you want the plants to flower. Many hardy annuals do not like root disturbance, so bear this in mind.

They are given their ideal planting distances by gradually "thinning out" as the young plants grow—all this means is carefully removing a few plants every few weeks in the spring, to give those left behind more room to develop. By early summer this thinning should be complete, and plants can be left to produce flowers. Hardy annuals are not affected by low temperatures, and many, like calendula, the pot marigold, are sown and germinate outdoors in September, for strong plants with earlier flowers the following spring. Most self-seeders belong to this group.

HALF-HARDY ANNUALS

As already mentioned, these plants are not able to withstand frost or freezing temperatures and must be raised from seed every season, often starting in late winter and very early spring. Many half-hardy annuals are actually perennials—plants that keep growing year after year, but which are better suited to our needs when grown as strong, young plants every season. Half-hardy annuals are only planted (or moved outdoors if grown in containers) when spring frosts are finished. The exact timing of this depends on the area you garden in, but this book gives sowing/planting times for average conditions. At the other end of the season, the first fall frosts will flatten most half-hardy annuals, and they can be removed for composting.

HARDY BIENNIALS

A biennial is simply a plant that straddles two growing seasons before it produces its show of flowers or foliage. A good example is cheiranthus, or wallflower, which is sown outdoors in early summer. The young leafy plants are grown on, then lifted and planted in October where you want the flowers to grow the following spring. Think of hardy biennials as annuals with a foot in two seasons—instead of producing their flowers or leaves all within what we think of as "summer," they get going in one season, spend the winter building up speed, then go all-out for flowering the next spring and summer. Biennials are especially useful for filling any gaps between late spring and early summer, and many, such as Sweet William, are easy and worthwhile plants for cut flowers.

BUYING SEEDS

Growing from seed is addictive—once you have sampled one seed catalog, you will certainly want more. You can buy annual seeds by sending for them via post or a home delivery service, by visiting garden centers or the gardening section of hardware stores, or, increasingly, by buying them with your other shopping at the supermarket.

The choice will always be greater in catalogs, but the more limited range that you may find in garden centers can actually be more helpful. The seed packets are guaranteed to be colorful, giving encouragement to the beginner. Some mail order seed companies pack their products in plain, information-only packets—this is no reflection on the quality of the seeds, but they do lack inspiration! Bright, colorful packets are a great help when planning a color-themed display with annuals, so do not be afraid to play around with a handful of packets until you get a good balance or contrast of colors just to your liking.

If you do buy seeds from garden centers and similar outlets, always avoid any packets that are faded, yellow, and have obviously been exposed to the sun, as the results are likely to be disappointing.

SEED PACKETS

Remember that seeds are alive, and need looking after to keep them in tiptop condition until sowing. Inside most seed packets you will find another, smaller packet made of foil. Seeds are sealed inside this inner packet in a kind of suspended animation that preserves them until the foil seal is broken. This is when the normal ageing process of the seed begins. Where this type of storage is not vital for success, seeds are simply found sealed within the outer paper packet. Foil packets should not be opened until the time of sowing, for best results. On most packets the inspiration on the front is backed by full growing instructions on the reverse. The better packets give sowing times, expected flowering period, and alternative sowing times in the fall. Keep seed packets after sowing—along with catalogs, they build up into an invaluable library that you can refer to as and when necessary. Always keep seeds in a cool, dry, frost-free place.

YOUNG PLANTS

Many half-hardy annuals included in this book can also be bought in the spring and summer as "young plants," and this is stated, where relevant, in the "features" paragraph for each of the 90 annuals covered. The term "young plant" covers anything from ready-germinated trays of small seedlings to a large plant, perhaps in flower, growing in a 3½in pot that you can find for sale in garden centers. Buying young plants simply means that a lot of the work in raising the plants from seed has been done for you by the grower—which has advantages and disadvantages. Young plants are a great help if you do not have facilities for raising seeds or enough space, and they are often delivered ready to go directly into containers. The range compared to the number of varieties available from seed is limited, although this is always improving. You pay for convenience: seed-raising is usually cheaper than buying in young plants.

WHAT CAN GO WRONG?

Yellow leaves
● Seedlings are being grown too cold in the early stages, or plants may have been planted outdoors too early.
● Plants may need feeding—water thoroughly with an all-purpose liquid or soluble plant food, wetting the leaves at the same time to act as a foliar feed.

Curled or distorted leaves
● Look for clusters of aphids attacking flower buds and the youngest leaves at the shoot tips. Rub them off with your fingers or use a spray containing permethrin.
● Drift from weedkillers can cause this problem, so take great care if you are treating a lawn for weeds using a hormone-based weedkiller. Avoid days when there is any breeze, and keep well away from bedding displays.

Holes and silvery trails on/in leaves
● Slugs and snails will eat most annual plants and are a particular threat in late spring and early summer, especially after rain, when the air is warm and moist. They leave silver slime trails on the soil and on plants where they have been feeding. Chemical slug pellets can be scattered sparingly among plants, or an unbroken ring of sharp grit 2in wide can be used as a physical deterrent on smaller areas. Another option is to check plants at night and pick off slugs and snails while they feed, dropping them into salty water.

White "powder" on leaves
● Powdery mildew affects many annuals, but usually not until late summer. This disease is not a serious threat and treatment is not needed.

Seedlings indoors suddenly collapse
● "Damping off" disease can attack annual seedlings, and is a particular problem if the compost becomes too wet. Always use clean pots for sowing and fresh compost. If it does attack, water lightly with a copper-based fungicide and resow to play safe.

Leaf edges chewed
● Various caterpillars will attack annuals and can soon strip leaves bare. Pick them off by hand or use a spray containing permethrin, wetting both sides of the leaves with a strong jet from a sprayer.

Plants cut off at ground level
● Cutworms can sever newly planted bedding plants outdoors, causing a sudden wilting and yellowing of plants under attack. Search around in the soil and the greenish-brown caterpillars are easily found and destroyed.

Creamy-white grubs eating roots
● Vine weevil grubs can cause severe damage to container plants. Never re-use old compost, and if you find grubs, treat all pots with biological control or a chemical based on phenols as a drench.

ORANGE MARIGOLDS, red and orange nasturtiums, asters, and brown-coned rudbeckia intermingle to form a color-coordinated annual border.

One of the wisest approaches is to decide carefully just what you feel you can achieve with your existing facilities. If your propagator (somewhere that plants are raised from seeds in the early stages) is just the kitchen windowsill, buying half-hardy annuals as young plants may be the best option. These small plug plants are delivered in mid-spring and can be potted up and grown on placed on the windowsill, or even next to the glass in an unheated conservatory. This eliminates the often tricky job of germinating the seeds to begin with, but means you can still grow the plants you really want. And of course, there is nothing to stop you sowing hardy annuals directly into the soil outdoors at the correct time.

If you are more restricted, say to just a small courtyard or balcony, young plants may be the whole solution—larger plants are delivered (or can be bought) in late spring and early summer, and these can be planted directly into containers and hanging baskets without growing on. Even then there is nothing to stop you scattering a few seeds of malcolmia, Virginian stock, in the top of your courtyard pots for some quick and scented flowers!

Most seed catalogs and specialist young plant suppliers carry extensive and informative sections on young plants, and they are well worth getting. Pay particular attention to "last order dates"—these are the cut-off points for placing your order for young plants and many start to appear as early as January and February.

ANNUALS IN CONTAINERS
A container in the broadest gardening sense is anything capable of holding compost and supporting plant growth—this could be anything from a 3½in-diameter plastic plant pot to a large terracotta trough or tub. Whatever you use, it must have some form of drainage, and this is usually through holes in the base. Molded plastic containers often have no preformed holes, so you must drill these before planting up. Waterlogged compost kills plant roots and the whole plant will soon die.

For most uses, a good "multipurpose" compost serves all of an annual plant's needs—from sowing to growing on, and finally being planted up. Most multipurpose composts are based on peat, with plant nutrients and other materials, such as water-storing granules and "wetters" (allowing dried-out compost to be re-wetted), already added. An increasing number of composts available are based on recycled materials, and the coir-based ones are improving constantly. A few specific plants prefer a soil-based compost, such as the "John Innes" types, both for sowing and growing—details of these are given under "growing method" sections of this book, where relevant. Always buy fresh bags of compost in spring, avoiding any that are over-heavy and wet, or split, with green algae growing in them, or faded and past their use-by date.

There is no reason why hardy annuals cannot be used for container growing—the fact that many are usually sown directly into the soil is not a problem. Simply sow them in small pots or multi-cell trays (plastic trays where the area is divided into individual units or "cells") at the same times as recommended for outdoor sowing, and plant into your containers during the spring. Where appropriate under each plant entry, varieties suited to containers are given—these are usually dwarf versions of taller varieties, and the range is increasing all the time. Half-hardy annuals offer great scope for container growing, for the reasons already discussed.

SOWING ANNUALS

Annual seeds are sown indoors or outdoors. Those sown outdoors are the easiest—they need no extra warmth or heat, just sow them in a patch of well-prepared ground and thin them out to give space as they grow. Sowing depth will depend on the size of the seed, but it is essential to work the soil using a rake (or your fingers in a small area) so it is fine and crumbly to at least 1in deep.

Seed can then be simply scattered over the soil and raked in, or sown in seed drills—these are simply grooves made in the soil with the head of a rake, the edge of a piece of wood, a length of bamboo cane, or even the side of your hand. Whichever you use, just press the edge into the soil to make a groove of the correct depth. Then sprinkle the seeds thinly along the drill, by rubbing them between your finger and thumb. Once finished, soil is moved back over the seeds with a rake or by lightly brushing the flat of your hand over the sown area. Take care not to disturb the sown seeds, and label with the variety and date sown. If you are sowing a large area with a variety of hardy annuals, or planning a mixture of hardy and half-hardy varieties, mark the sown patches with boundaries of light-colored sand—a traditional but still effective way of seeing just where you have been! By sowing in short drills within these marked areas it is easy to tell the annuals from the weeds, because they come up in rows.

Indoors, half-hardy annuals are sown ideally in a heated propagator with temperature control, and this piece of equipment is virtually essential when raising plants like pelargoniums (bedding geraniums) and begonias, both of which need high, constant temperatures. Otherwise, a brightly lit windowsill in a warm kitchen will work miracles—many half-hardy annuals are very undemanding once they have come up, and if not kept over-wet will grow steadily, even in quite cool conditions.

Narrow "windowsill propagators" are available that have a heated base and allow you to move pots on and off as seedlings appear—these are invaluable if you plan to do a lot of seed-raising. For all the plants in this book, a 3½in-diameter pot is sufficient for the germination of an average packet of half-hardy annual seeds. If you raise half-hardy annuals, remember that they will not be able to go out until after the last spring frosts. You can sow many plants later than the ideal times—this book describes the optimum sowing times unless otherwise stated—and plan for a later display of flowers, with the advantage of them being easier to raise and care for a little later in the spring season.

SOIL PREPARATION

All that annuals need to grow well is soil that has had plenty of "organic matter" added before sowing or planting, and this is best done by digging it in thoroughly the previous fall or in early spring. Suppliers of manure take some tracking down these days, so using home-made compost (or leaf mold) is a better option.

Whatever you use, it must be dark, well-rotted, and thoroughly broken down. Organic matter is vital for improving the soil's ability to hold onto moisture at the height of summer, and also supplies some plant foods. To take proper care of feeding, scatter pelleted poultry manure over the area 2–3 weeks before sowing/planting and rake it in. This should provide ample nutrients for the rest of the summer.

THINNING OUT

"Thinning out" or "thinning" means allowing sufficient room for plants to develop fully. This is most important with hardy annuals—as young seedlings grow larger, some are gradually removed to leave room for those left behind. Make sure you put your fingers on the soil when pulling plants out, or there is a risk the plants you leave behind will be uprooted. Water well after thinning, to settle seedlings back in. Thinning can start when plants are just 1in tall and is usually finished by early summer. Fall-sown annuals should be thinned in the spring, in case some plants are lost during the winter months.

GROWING ON

Once seedlings have been transplanted (moved) to either individual pots or cell trays, they are "grown on." This stage lasts until they are finally hardened off before planting outdoors or in pots. During growing on, make sure plants do not dry out, spread them out (if pot-grown) as they develop, and keep a look out for pests and diseases. Some plants (like thunbergia, Black-eyed Susan) benefit from being potted on when their roots fill the pot.

HARDENING OFF

Toughening plants raised indoors ready for outdoor conditions is vital if they are not to suffer a growth check when you put them out. Few of us have (or have the room for) the traditional "cold frame," which was the classic way of hardening off. These days we can make use of garden fleece, which is much easier, and just as effective. From mid-May onward, plants can be stood outside on warm days, in a sunny spot. For the first week, bring them in at night, then leave them out, but covered with fleece at night. Gradually, unless frost is forecast, the fleece can be left off even at night, but replaced during frosty spells. By early June, plants will be hardened off and ready to plant.

PLANTING

Whether you are planting in beds or containers, water the pots/trays the previous night to soak the roots. Planting can be done with a trowel—or even by hand in light soils. Using your hands is certainly the best way of planting up containers and hanging baskets. Never plant the base of plants deeper than they were growing originally. Firm well, and water. Keep labels with the plants for future reference, and note the planting date on the label, too.

WATERING

Lack of water causes many hardy annuals to flower and then quickly die. When the soil feels dry, enough water should be given so that it gets down to the roots—the soil should feel moist at least 6in down. Use a trowel and check that this is happening. Containers need much more care, since they rely solely on you for their water. Choosing a compost that contains water-storing crystals provides the best insurance. Do not overwater early on or roots may rot, but check them at least every other day and never allow them to dry out.

FEEDING

By mixing slow-release fertilizer granules with the compost before planting, you can take care of feeding for the whole season—you just need to water the plants. Outdoors, bedding displays will benefit from liquid feeding every 2–4 weeks. Many hardy annuals need no extra feeding and actually thrive on poor, hungry soils.

USING ANNUALS IN YOUR GARDEN

With annuals, the sky really is the limit. You can choose to grow just hardy or half-hardy annuals, a mixture of both, or you can be more adventurous and put them to work for you in a wide range of yard situations. Or, of course, you could just leave them to do their own thing!

Once you have annuals in your yard, you will never want to be without them. Self-seeding annuals, like limnanthes and nigella, will want to do their own thing and grow where they fall, while others such as lavatera and ricinus are put to much better use by carefully planning where they will grow. You can find a spot for annuals in every yard, and sometimes they can even help you out of a tight corner! What better plants could you ask for?

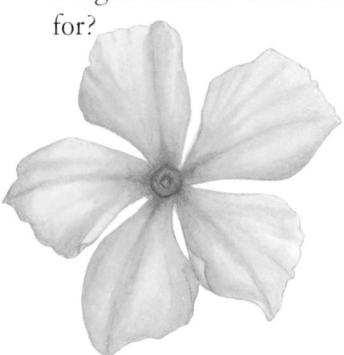

ABOVE: The delicately veined flower of agrostemma, the corncockle, an easily grown hardy annual that is sown outdoors in spring where you want it to flower.

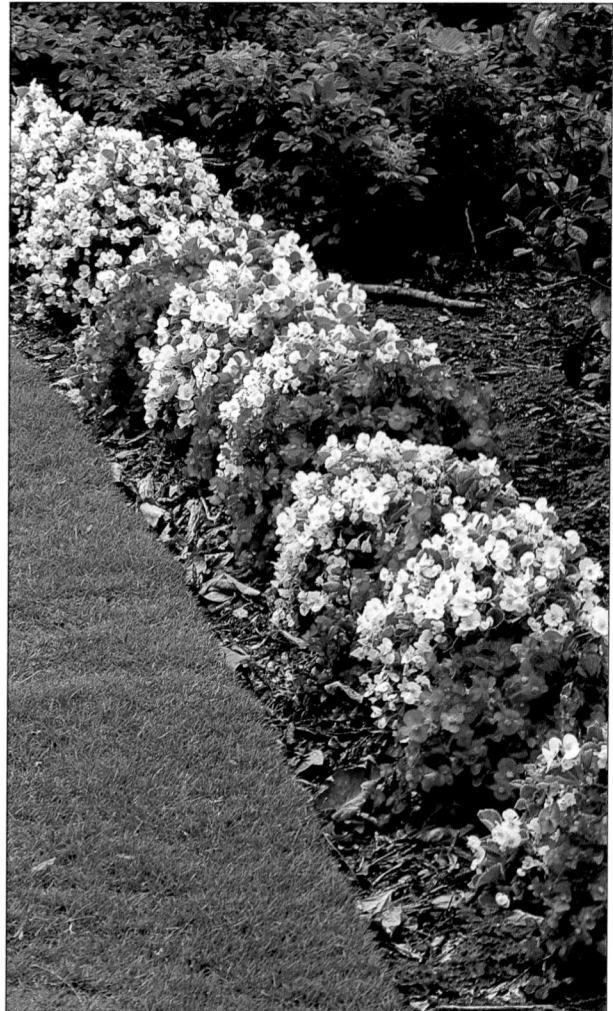

AS EDGING PLANTS these Begonia semperflorens *are a good choice. Being of even height, they are good for growing in line.*

BEDDING SCHEMES

We see annuals used in bedding schemes almost every day of our lives, on traffic islands, in public parks, and in each other's yards. The "scheme" part of the phrase comes from the fact that many of these impressive colorful displays are pre-planned, and in many ways made-to-measure. If that is the effect you are after, you must do your homework. The structure of a basic bedding scheme is quite simple—you have tall plants in the center of the bed, and the shortest plants around the edge. In between are plants in a range of sizes and with varying growth habits, which fill the space between the tallest and the shortest. Bedding schemes can be as simple, or as elaborate, as you choose. The key points to remember are to decide which plants are going where, how many you need, and of course, whether they are suited to being grown together.

HARDY ANNUAL SCHEMES

Creating a show using just hardy annuals is both very easy and tremendous fun. The sheer range of hardy annual varieties is enormous and it is easy to be spoiled for choice. You can go out and sow an entire bed with hardy annuals at one go, then sit back and wait for the seedlings to come up. Then all you need to do is keep down annual weeds (all perennial weeds should be removed before sowing), thin out every few weeks until early summer, push in twiggy supports for taller, straggly plants, and enjoy the show.

THIS SUMMER BEDDING SCHEME features zinnias in the center of the bed (with variegated tradescantia creeping through) then scarlet salvias, dropping down to the pink fluffy heads of ageratum, the floss flower, below.

The best effect is from bold groups of color, so sow in patches at least 2ft across. Sow roughly circular areas as a foolproof guide, although interweaving shapes can create some dramatic effects, with different plants merging as they grow into each other. Take a tip from the traditions of the past and mark out the sown areas with sand, just so you know what is where, and label each patch, or mark the varieties clearly on a sketch plan, if you have one. Using just hardy annuals means there is no need for heating early in the season, and no crisis when growing space runs short. Many hardy annuals can also be sown in the fall, usually September, to grow through the winter and then give an early performance the following spring.

CARE-FREE HARDY ANNUALS
What could be better than a plant you only buy once, but will then always have many of? It sounds too good to be true, but that is just what you get with a great many hardy annuals—the self-seeders that arrive in a packet and then spread to all their favorite spots. We have to thank the origins of many of these plants for their valuable qualities. Agrostemma (corncockle), for example, was once a common weed of cornfields, and many other care-free annuals like it thrive on the poorest and hungriest of soils. These plants will tell you where they prefer growing by seeding themselves there, and they will need no more attention, other than being pulled out when they get too

dominant or invasive in areas set aside for more carefully planned activities. Calendula, centaurea, eschscholzia, papaver, and tropaeolum are all good examples of care-free annuals.

BORDER FILLERS
With the sudden loss of a favorite plant, your dreams of a "perfect" border can soon evaporate, and this is where annuals can get you out of a tight spot. Any spare patch of ground can be sown, or planted, with annuals, which will grow quickly to fill any gaps. You might even scatter seeds among perennial plants and let them get on with things. Lunaria (honesty), is quite at home growing among spring-flowering perennial euphorbias; the purple lunaria flowers make a good contrast with the pale yellow-green euphorbias. For a touch of the tropical, ricinus, the castor oil plant, is unbeatable, with its large, exotic-looking leaves in a range of colors. Sunflowers (helianthus) are always a good choice for some instant color when it's needed, and the newer dwarf varieties like "Pacino" are easy to grow in pots for planting out whenever their bright flowers are needed to perk up flagging borders.

ABUTILON
Flowering maple

ABUTILON has a distinct exotic look, with its hanging, bell-like flowers that are either single or bicolored, as seen here.

BEING A SHRUB, abutilon can be kept from year to year in a frost-free greenhouse and planted outdoors in mixed borders in the summer.

FEATURES

A deciduous tender shrub that is easy to raise from seed sown in the spring, with maple-like leaves and showy, hanging, bell-shaped flowers in a wide range of colors. Plants make bushy growth, and are useful in summer bedding schemes and for courtyard containers sited in a warm spot, but they must be protected from frost. Abutilon can be kept in a conservatory or frost-free greenhouse in the winter and will flower throughout spring and summer. Plants grow to 2–3ft tall. Varieties such as *Abutilon pictum* "Thompsonii," with variegated leaves, are available from garden centers as young plants in the spring; these can be potted up, grown on, and then planted outdoors after the last frosts.

ABUTILON AT A GLANCE

A deciduous shrub grown as a summer bedding and container plant, with bell-like flowers. Frost hardy to 23°F (zone 9).

Jan	/	
Feb	sow	Recommended Varieties
Mar	pot up	**Abutilon hybrids:**
Apr	pot on	"Large Flowered Mixed"
May	harden off/plant	"Mixed Colors"
Jun	flowering	
July	flowering	
Aug	flowering	
Sept	flowering	
Oct	/	
Nov	/	
Dec	/	

CONDITIONS

Aspect Grow in full sunlight in borders or on a south-facing courtyard. In southern areas, plants grown against a south-facing wall in well-drained soil will often survive mild winters outdoors without protection.

Site Mix plenty of rotted manure/compost into soil before planting, and use multipurpose compost in containers. Soil should be well-drained but moisture-retentive for best results.

GROWING METHOD

Sowing In February, sow in 3½in-diameter pots, cover seed with its own depth of multipurpose compost, and keep at 70°F in light. Seedlings appear over 1–2 months, so check regularly. When plants are 2in tall, pot up into 3½in pots and grow on. Plant out in early June after the last frosts.

Feeding Apply liquid feed weekly. Mix slow-release fertilizer granules with container compost.

Problems Use sprays containing pirimicarb for aphids, malathion for mealy bugs, and bifenthrin for red spider mite, or, on plants growing in conservatories, use natural predators.

FLOWERING

Season Flowers appear all summer outdoors, and some may appear year-around on indoor plants and those grown in southerly, mild areas, especially near the coast.

Cutting Not suitable.

General Plants can be potted up before frosts and kept indoors. Increase favorites by taking cuttings in spring, rooting them on a windowsill or in a heated propagator.

AGERATUM
Floss flower

AGERATUM FLOWERS are carried on neat-growing plants and are good for "cooling down" other plants with bright flowers.

MODERN VARIETIES of ageratum for bedding produce masses of flowers which gradually rise above the leaves as they open.

FEATURES

Ageratum, a half-hardy annual, has fluffy long-lived flowers in blue, pink, white and bicolors such as blue-white. Use dwarf varieties for edging, as they grow up to 6in. Tall varieties are used in borders and for cutting, growing to 2½ft. Use for bedding/containers. Available as young plants.

CONDITIONS

Aspect   Needs full sun and a sheltered position.

AGERATUM AT A GLANCE

A half-hardy annual grown for its fluffy flowers, ideal for edging, bedding, containers, and cutting. Frost hardy to 32°F (zone 10).

Jan	/	RECOMMENDED VARIETIES
Feb	sow	
Mar	sow	*Ageratum houstonianum:*
Apr	grow on	**For bedding**
May	plant	"Adriatic"
Jun	flowering	"Bavaria"
July	flowering	"Blue Champion"
Aug	flowering	"Blue Mink"
Sept	flowering	"Pink Powderpuffs"
Oct	/	"White Blue"
Nov	/	"Capri"
Dec	/	"White Hawaii"
		For cutting
		"Blue Horizon"

Site   Prefers well-drained soil enriched with rotted manure or compost well ahead of planting. In containers use multipurpose compost and ensure that there is good drainage.

GROWING METHOD

Sowing   Sow seeds in 3½in pots in February/March and just cover, and keep at 70°F. Seedlings appear after a week and can be moved to cell trays of multipurpose compost when two leaves are developed. Harden off and plant outside after frosts, spacing tall varieties 12–16in apart, dwarf varieties 4–6in apart.

Feeding   Apply liquid feed fortnightly to maintain strong growth, or mix slow-release fertilizer with compost before planting up.

Problems   Ageratum can suffer from root rot so grow in well-drained containers on heavy clay soils, and avoid getting the compost too wet.

FLOWERING

Season   Flowers appear all summer until the first frosts. Regular dead-heading, especially after heavy rain, will prolong flowering and often encourage a second "flush" of color.

Cutting   Tall varieties are suitable for cutting.

AFTER FLOWERING

General   Remove plants when past their best, usually after the first sharp frosts of fall.

AGROSTEMMA
Corncockle

SOFT PINK "Milas" is one of the best known of the corncockle varieties. Pink and white varieties are also available.

GROW AGROSTEMMA in bold clumps in borders where the tall lanky, swaying plants help to give each other support.

FEATURES

A very easily grown hardy annual for use in cottage gardens and borders where it self-seeds year after year. Plants are tall, growing 2–3ft tall, and carry pink, purple, or white trumpet-like blooms. The seeds are poisonous. Commonly known as corncockle.

CONDITIONS

Aspect   Grow in full sun.

AGROSTEMMA AT A GLANCE

A tall hardy annual grown for its pink, purple, or white flowers which are ideal for cottage borders. Frost hardy to 5°F (zone 7).

Jan	/	Recommended Varieties
Feb	/	
Mar	sow	*Agrostemma githago:*
Apr	thin out	"Milas"
May	flowering	"Ocean Pearl"
Jun	flowering	"Purple Queen"
July	flowering	"Rose of Heaven"
Aug	flowering	
Sept	flowering	
Oct	sow	
Nov	/	
Dec	/	

Site

Succeeds on well-drained and even light, sandy soils that are quite "hungry" (it used to grow as a weed in cornfields). Excessive feeding may actually reduce the number of flowers.

GROWING METHOD

Sowing   Sow outdoors from March onward when the soil is warming up, in patches or drills ½in deep where you want the plants to flower. Thin seedlings so they are eventually 6–12in apart. Do not transplant. Can also be sown in pots in the fall, overwintered in a sheltered spot then potted up in spring for flowers in early summer.

Feeding   Extra feeding is unnecessary, but water occasionally but thoroughly in dry spells.

Problems   Agrostemma is a floppy plant and twiggy supports can be useful.

FLOWERING

Season   Summer onward, but earlier flowers are produced by sowing in the fall.

Cutting   Short-lived as a cut flower, and rather floppy.

AFTER FLOWERING

General   Dead-heading throughout summer will keep flowers coming but always leave a few to ripen and set seeds. Plants will self-sow and germinate the following spring. Alternatively, collect seedheads in paper bags and store.

ALCEA
Hollybock

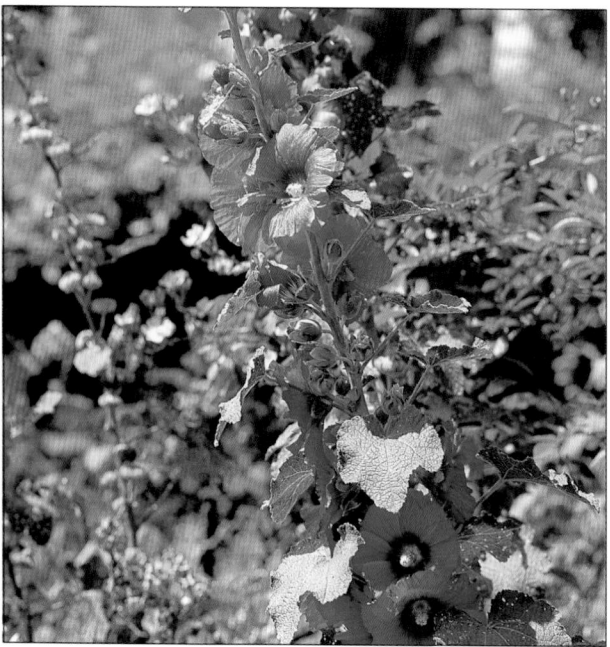

FLOWERS OF ALCEA come in a wide range of colors and are carried along the entire length of the tall leafy stems.

THE TALL STEMS of hollyhocks tend to lean over as they mature, so support them at the base with short lengths of bamboo cane.

FEATURES

Alcea is also known as althaea, and is the familiar "hollyhock" found in cottage borders. Flowers are single or double in a range of colors, and carried on stems which can be up to 8ft tall depending on variety. Tall varieties are best at the back of borders. Alcea is grown as an annual sown in spring, or as a biennial sown in summer. Spring-sown plants suffer less with rust disease. Fully hardy.

CONDITIONS

Aspect   Needs full sun.
Site   Plants can often be found growing in cracks

ALCEA AT A GLANCE

A hardy biennial grown as an annual or biennial for its tall spikes of flowers suited to cottage gardens. Frost hardy to 5°F (zone 7).

Jan	/	Recommended Varieties
Feb	sow	*Alcea rosea:*
Mar	grow on	**Single flowered**
Apr	sow outdoors	"Nigra"
May	plant	"Single Mixed"
Jun	flowers/sow	**Double flowered**
July	flowering	"Chater's Double Mixed"
Aug	flowering	"Majorette Mixed"
Sept	flowers/plant	"Peaches 'n' Dreams"
Oct	/	"Powder Puffs Mixed"
Nov	/	"Summer Carnival
Dec	/	Mixed"

between paving slabs and in walls but the tallest spikes are produced by adding generous amounts of rotted manure or compost to the soil before planting. Soil must have good drainage. In windy spots stake tall varieties.

GROWING METHOD

Sowing
To grow as an annual sow seed in 3½in pots of multipurpose compost in February. Just cover the seeds and keep at 68°F. Seedlings appear in about two weeks and can be transplanted to individual 3½in pots of compost. Grow on and plant in May after hardening off. Seeds can also be sown outdoors in April. To grow as biennials, sow seed in midsummer but germinate outdoors in a shaded spot. Plant in September.

Feeding
A monthly liquid feed encourages growth.
Problems
Rust disease spoils the look of and weakens growth and is worse in wet summers. Control is difficult but for a few plants pick off leaves and try a spray containing mancozeb.

FLOWERING

Season
Early spring-sown plants grow rapidly and flower from early summer. Those planted in fall will overwinter in the ground and flower in early summer the following season.
Cutting
Striking as cut flowers—take them when there are plenty of flowerbuds still to open.

AFTER FLOWERING

General
Leave a few spikes to set self-sown seeds, but remove dead plants to reduce rust problems.

AMARANTHUS

Love-lies-bleeding

SOME AMARANTHUS produce masses of copper-crimson leaves in summer and red flower spikes. They make good pot plants.

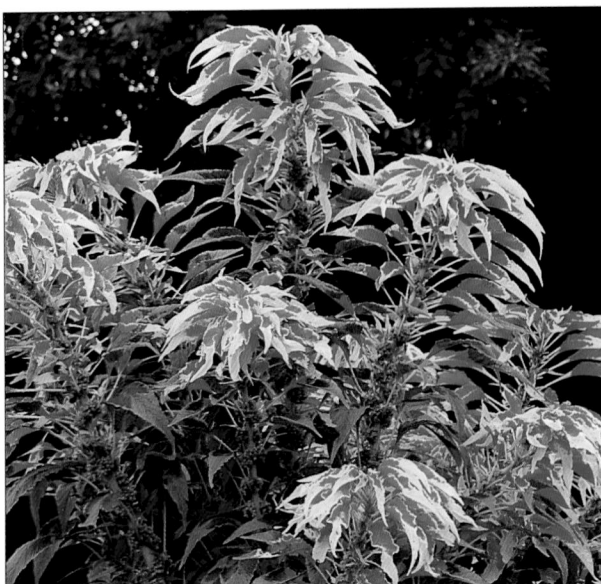

"JOSEPH'S COAT," 2ft tall, has striking gold-and-crimson upper leaves and green-yellow lower leaves marked with brown.

FEATURES

Amaranthus is grown for its colorful, exotic-looking foliage and its spiky, erect or drooping tassels of blood-red, green, golden-brown, purple, or multi-colored flowers up to 18in long. Leaves can be red, bronze, yellow, brown, or green, depending on the variety grown. Size ranges from 15in to 4ft tall. Use plants as potted plants, in courtyard containers, and as dramatic centerpieces in summer bedding displays. Superb when used cut for fresh or dried flower arrangements indoors.

CONDITIONS

Aspect Full sun and shelter is essential for success.
Site Soil should be well-drained, with plenty of rotted compost or manure added. Varieties of *Amaranthus caudatus* will also succeed on thin, dry soils. Use multipurpose compost in containers and pots. In northern areas grow in 8–10in diameter pots in the greenhouse or conservatory. Tall-growing varieties may need staking.

GROWING METHOD

Sowing Sow seeds in March at 70°F in 3½in-diameter pots of multipurpose compost, just covering the seed. Seeds germinate in 7–14 days or sooner, and should be transplanted into cell trays or 3½in-diameter pots of multipurpose compost. Plant outside after the last frosts in late May/early June, 1–3ft apart, and water.
Feeding Feed weekly from early summer onward with general-purpose liquid feed. In containers, mix slow-release fertilizer with compost before planting, and also feed every two weeks with half-strength liquid feed.
Problems Aphids can feed on the colorful leaves and build up into large colonies, unless caught early. Use a spray containing permethrin.

FLOWERING

Season Foliage is colorful from early summer onward, and is joined by flowerheads and then colorful seedheads later on.
Cutting Varieties grown for their flowers can be cut and used fresh, while seedheads can be left to develop, then cut and dried for indoor use.

AFTER FLOWERING

General Remove plants when past their best.

AMARANTHUS AT A GLANCE

A half-hardy annual grown for its leaves and flowers for bedding, containers, and for drying. Frost hardy to 32°F (zone 10).

Month	Activity	Recommended Varieties
Jan	/	
Feb	/	*Amaranthus caudatus:*
Mar	sow	"Green Thumb"
Apr	transplant	"Viridis"
May	transplant	*Amaranthus cruentus:*
Jun	flowering	"Golden Giant"
July	flowering	"Split Personality"
Aug	flowering	"Ruby Slippers"
Sept	flowering	*Amaranthus hybridus:*
Oct	flowering	"Intense Purple"
Nov	/	*Amaranthus tricolor:*
Dec	/	"Aurora Yellow"
		"Joseph's Coat"

ANTIRRHINUM
Snapdragon

OLDER VARIETIES of snapdragon like this have flowers that "snap" when squeezed. This trick is not found in newer types.

DWARF VARIETIES reaching just 6in are colorful for bed edges and have bushy growth without the need for pinching out.

FEATURES

Antirrhinums fall into three groups: tall varieties up to 4ft for cutting; intermediates for bedding, 18in; dwarf varieties for edging/containers, 12in. Color range is wide, and includes bicolors and doubles. Flowers of older varieties open when squeezed at the sides, hence the name "snapdragon." Grow as a half-hardy annual. Available as young plants.

CONDITIONS

Aspect Must be in full sunlight all day.
Site Soil must be very well-drained but have plenty

ANTIRRHINUM AT A GLANCE

A half-hardy annual grown for tubular flowers, used for containers, bedding displays, and cutting. Frost hardy to 32°F (zone 10).

Jan	/	Recommended Varieties
Feb	sow	
Mar	sow	*Antirrhinum majus:*
Apr	grow on	**For containers**
May	plant	"Lipstick Silver"
		"Magic Carpet Mixed"
Jun	flowering	"Tom Thumb Mixed"
July	flowering	**For bedding**
Aug	flowering	"Brighton Rock Mixed"
Sept	flowering	"Corona Mixed"
		"Sonnet Mixed"
Oct	/	**For cutting**
Nov	/	"Liberty Mixed"
Dec	/	

of rotted compost or manure dug in before planting. In containers, use multipurpose compost and ensure good, free drainage.

GROWING METHOD

Sowing Sow in February/March and barely cover the very fine seed. Use 3½in pots of multipurpose compost and keep in light at 64°F. Seedlings appear after a week and can be transplanted to cell trays when two young leaves have developed. Plant outside after hardening off, following the last frosts, 6–18in apart, depending upon the variety. Those grown for bedding purposes should have the growing tip pinched out when 6in tall to encourage bushy growth.

Feeding Liquid-feed plants in beds with a handheld feeder fortnightly. Mix slow-release fertilizer with container compost before planting up.

Problems Seedlings are prone to "damping off," so water the pots with a copper-based fungicide. Plants suffer with rust disease. Grow a resistant variety such as "Monarch Mixed" or use a spray containing penconazole at regular intervals.

FLOWERING

Season Flowers appear all summer and should be removed as they fade to keep buds coming.

Cutting Tall varieties are excellent as cut spikes.

AFTER FLOWERING

General Pull plants up when they are over.

ARCTOTIS
African daisy

AFRICAN DAISIES should be pinched out when they are 5in tall to encourage branching and masses of summer flowers.

WHEN PLANTED in groups of 3–6 plants, arctotis will form spreading clumps in sunny, south-facing borders and on banks.

FEATURES

African daisy is a perennial grown as a half-hardy annual for its flowers in shades of pink, red, yellow, gold, white, and even blue, often with darker center. Plants reach 18in in height and have attractive silvery leaves. Use in bedding or as a container plant. Flowers are good for cutting.

CONDITIONS

Aspect   Must have full sun all day long for the flowers to stay open and give the best display, so

ARCTOTIS AT A GLANCE	
A half-hardy annual grown for its flowers, used in bedding, containers and as a cut flower. Frost hardy to 32°F (zone 10) .	

Month		Recommended Varieties
Jan	/	
Feb	sow	*Arctotis hybrida:*
Mar	sow	"Harlequin"
Apr	transplant	"Special Hybrids Mixed"
May	transplant	"Treasure Chest"
Jun	flowering	"T&M Hybrids"
July	flowering	*Arctotis hirsuta*
Aug	flowering	
Sept	flowering	*Arctotis venusta*
Oct	/	
Nov	/	
Dec	/	

Site   choose a south-facing border, patio or bank. Soil must be well-drained but moisture-retentive, so work in rotted compost before planting. In containers use multipurpose compost and ensure drainage by adding a 2in layer of gravel or polystyrene chunks.

GROWING METHOD

Sowing   Sow in February/March in small pots of multipurpose compost, just covering the seed, and keep at 64°F. Seedlings appear in 2–3 weeks and are transplanted individually into 3½in pots. Grow on, harden off at the end of May before planting after frosts, spacing plants 12–18in apart.

Feeding   Extra feeding is rarely necessary but container-grown plants benefit from liquid feed every two weeks. Avoid getting the compost too wet, especially in cooler, wet spells.

Problems   Grows poorly on heavy, badly drained soils. Plants in containers must receive full sun.

FLOWERING

Season   Flowers from early summer onwards.
Cutting   A useful but short-lived cut flower.

AFTER FLOWERING

General   Pot up before frosts and keep dry and frost-free over winter. Take and root cuttings in spring.

BEGONIA

Begonia

FOR BEDDING DISPLAYS *in partial shade few plants can equal the mixed varieties of* Begonia semperflorens, *seen here.*

IN CONTAINERS *begonias give a show from early summer, and you can choose dark-leaved types for specific color schemes.*

FEATURES

Excellent for bedding and containers, begonias have fleshy green or bronze leaves and flowers in many colors, and are grown as half-hardy annuals. "Fibrous" rooted varieties of *Begonia semperflorens* grow up to 8in, have many small flowers and do well in shaded spots. "Tuberous" rooted types reach 10in tall with fewer but larger flowers up to 4in across. Trailing varieties are also available for hanging baskets, reaching 1–2ft. Flowers are in mixed or single colors. A wide range of all types are available as young plants.

CONDITIONS

Aspect   Will succeed best in partial shade with at least

Site   some protection from direct hot sun. Soil should be very well prepared with plenty of rotted manure or compost mixed in. Begonias produce masses of fine feeding roots. Plants do not like very heavy clay soils that stay wet for long periods, so grow in containers if necessary, using multipurpose compost when potting up in spring.

GROWING METHOD

Sowing   Sow January/February. Seed is as fine as dust, so mix with a little dry silver sand and sow on the surface of 3½in pots of seed compost based on peat or coir. Stand the pot in tepid water until the compost looks moist. Keep at 70°F in a heated propagator in a light spot, and carefully transplant seedlings to cell trays when they have produced several tiny leaves. Seed raising is a challenge so consider growing from young plants. Plant outdoors after the last frosts in early June, 6–8in apart depending on variety.

Feeding   Water regularly in dry spells and liquid feed bedding displays every 2–3 weeks, or mix slow-release fertilizer with compost first.

Problems   Overwatering causes root rot and death. Remove faded flowers, especially in wet spells.

FLOWERING

Season   Flowers from early summer until frost.
Cutting   Not suitable as a cut flower.

AFTER FLOWERING

General   Varieties that form round tubers can be potted up in the fall, dried off and then grown again the following spring.

BEGONIA AT A GLANCE

A half-hardy annual grown for its flowers and green/bronze foliage, useful for bedding/containers. Frost hardy to 32°F (zone 10).

Jan	sow	Recommended Varieties
Feb	sow	*Begonia semperflorens:*
Mar	transplant	"Ambassador Mixed"
Apr	grow on	"Cocktail Mixed"
May	harden off	"Pink Sundae"
Jun	flowering	**Tuberous varieties**
July	flowering	"Non-Stop Mixed"
Aug	flowering	"Non-Stop Appleblossom"
Sept	flowering	"Pin-Up"
Oct	/	**Trailing varieties**
Nov	/	"Illumination Mixed"
Dec	/	"Show Angels Mixed"

BELLIS
Daisy

VARIETIES OF BELLIS *differ greatly. Some have small flowers with yellow centers, or the whole flower is a mass of fine petals.*

AFTER THE SPRING SHOW *is over bellis can be replanted on rock gardens where it will grow as a perennial in spreading clumps.*

FEATURES

All varieties of bellis are related to garden daisies, and are perennials grown as hardy biennials. Use in spring bedding and containers, with bulbs like tulips. Plants are spreading, 4–8in high, with white, pink, red, or bicolored double or "eyed" flowers. Petals can be tubular, or fine and needle-like. Available as young plants.

CONDITIONS

Aspect   Needs a sunny, warm spot to encourage early

BELLIS AT A GLANCE		
A perennial grown as a biennial for spring bedding displays and used with bulbs in yard containers. Frost hardy to 5°F (zone 7).		
Jan	/	Recommended Varieties
Feb	flowering	*Bellis perennis:*
Mar	flowering	**Small flowers**
Apr	flowering	"Carpet Mixed"
May	flowers/sow	"Medici Mixed"
		"Pomponette Mixed"
Jun	sow	"Pomponette Pink"
July	grow on	"Buttons"
Aug	grow on	**Large flowers**
Sept	grow on	"Blush"
Oct	plant	"Giant Flowered Mixed"
Nov	/	"Goliath Mixed"
Dec	/	"Habanera Mixed"

flowers when grown for spring displays.

Site   Most soils are suitable, but adding well-rotted manure or compost before planting increases plant vigor and flower size. In containers, use multipurpose compost and make sure the container is very free-draining.

GROWING METHOD

Sowing   Sow seed outdoors in May/June in fine soil in drills ½in deep. Keep well-watered and when plants are large enough, space small clumps out in rows, 4–6in apart. Alternatively, pot up into 3½in pots. Grow on during the summer, then water, lift carefully, and plant out in beds or containers in the fall, spacing 6–8in apart.

Feeding   Liquid feed can be given every 2–3 weeks in the spring when growth starts, but avoid feeding in winter, and take special care not to overwater containers or plants will rot off.

Problems   Bellis is trouble-free.

FLOWERING

Season   Flowers appear from early spring into the summer. Removal of faded flowers helps prolong flowering and reduces self-seeding.

Cutting   Can be used in small spring posies.

AFTER FLOWERING

General   Plants are removed to make way for summer bedding and can either be discarded or replanted and left to grow as perennials.

BRACHYSCOME
Swan river daisy

SWAN RIVER DAISIES produce mounds of small, daisy-like flowers in profusion throughout the summer months.

FOR MIXED SHADES and "eyes" of different colors, choose an up-to-date variety of Brachyscome iberidifolia *such as "Bravo Mixed."*

FEATURES

Brachyscome is covered in mounds of daisy flowers, and is good in beds and in hanging baskets and courtyard containers. It makes an effective edging plant, where it can develop unhindered without being crowded out by more vigorous plants. Leaves are light green and feathery, with a delicate appearance. Plants grow 9in tall with a similar spread. Choose single colors or mixtures. Brachyscome can be planted in May before the last frosts, and will tolerate short dry spells. A half-hardy annual, also seen as "brachycome."

CONDITIONS

Aspect   Choose a south-facing position in full sunlight.

BRACHYSCOME AT A GLANCE		
A half-hardy annual grown for its daisy-like flowers, useful for bedding, baskets, and containers. Frost hardy to 32°F (zone 10)		
Jan	/	Recommended Varieties
Feb	/	
Mar	sow	*Brachyscome iberidifolia:*
Apr	sow/transplant	"Blue Star"
May	plant outdoors	"Bravo Mixed"
Jun	flowering	"Mixed"
July	flowering	"Purple Splendor"
Aug	flowering	"White Splendor"
Sept	flowering	
Oct	/	
Nov	/	
Dec	/	

Site   Choose a warm, sheltered spot away from wind. Brachyscome likes rich, well-drained soil, with plenty of rotted compost or manure added. Use multipurpose potting compost in containers.

GROWING METHOD

Sowing   Sow in March and April in 3½in diameter pots, just covering the seeds, and germinate at 64°F. Seedlings emerge within three weeks. Transplant into cell trays of multipurpose compost, and plant out in beds, 9–12in apart.

Feeding   Liquid-feed each week outdoors. Add slow-release fertilizer granules to container compost, and also liquid-feed every two weeks in the summer. Avoid overwatering, especially in dull, wet spells, or plants may rot off.

Problems   Support floppy plants with small twigs. Avoid planting among large, vigorous container plants that will swamp low growers and cast them in shade at the height of summer. Control slugs with pellets or set slug traps in bedding displays.

FLOWERING

Season   Flowers appear all summer and are faintly scented—this is best appreciated by growing them at nose height in hanging baskets, flower bags, and windowboxes.

Cutting   Not suitable.

AFTER FLOWERING

General   Remove when flowers are over and add to the compost heap or bin.

BRASSICA
Ornamental cabbage and kale

ORNAMENTAL KALES help pack a punch in the yard during the fall, with their bright leaves that deepen in color when the temperature falls below 50°F. Plants grown in containers should be kept in a sheltered spot during spells of severe winter weather.

FEATURES

Ornamental cabbages and kales are grown for colorful fall and winter foliage, growing 12–18in tall and wide. Use for bedding or large pots. Leaf color is pink, rose, or white, and improves with temperatures below 50°F. Damage is caused by severe frost. Available as young plants.

CONDITIONS

Aspect   Needs full sunlight to develop good color.

BRASSICA AT A GLANCE		
A hardy annual grown for its brightly colored leaves that last from the fall until spring. Frost hardy to 5°F (zone 7).		
Jan	leaves	Recommended Varieties
Feb	leaves	**Cabbages**
Mar	leaves	"Delight Mixed"
Apr	leaves	"Northern Lights"
May	leaves	"Ornamental Mixed"
Jun	sow	"Tokyo Mixed"
July	sow	
Aug	grow-on	**Kales**
Sept	plant	"Nagoya Mixed"
Oct	leaves	"Red & White Peacock"
Nov	leaves	"Red Chidori"
Dec	leaves	

Site

Enrich soil with rotted compost or manure ahead of planting. Adding lime will improve results in acid soils. Avoid places exposed to driving winter winds. Plant up containers using multipurpose compost, making sure pots and tubs are free-draining.

GROWING METHOD

Sowing   Seed is sown in June/July in 3½in pots of multipurpose compost and kept out of the sun. Large seedlings appear after a week and are transplanted to individual 3½in pots. Grow these on outdoors, watering frequently, and then plant out in beds or in containers in the early fall where the display is required.

Feeding   Give a high-potash liquid feed fortnightly throughout the summer months. Tomato food is suitable and encourages leaf color.

Problems   Cabbage caterpillars will also attack ornamental varieties and kales. Pick off by hand or use a spray containing permethrin.

FLOWERING

Season   Plants are at their best in the fall and early winter. Any surviving the winter will produce tall clusters of yellow flowers during spring.

Cutting   Whole heads makes a striking, unusual element in winter flower arrangements.

AFTER FLOWERING

General   Remove in the spring or if killed by frosts.

BROWALLIA
Bush violet

BROWALLIA FLOWERS have an almost crystalline texture when lit by the sun. They appear in masses on rounded plants, and at the height of summer can almost completely hide the leaves. Seen here are the varieties "Blue Troll" and "White Troll."

FEATURES

Browallia takes its common name from its violet-blue flowers, which have a pale "eye." White flowered varieties and mixtures are available. Plants grow up to 12in and are suitable for containers and baskets, and in warmer areas, bedding. Varieties of *Browallia speciosa* are grown as half-hardy annuals and can also be used as indoor potted plants.

CONDITIONS

Aspect   Needs a warm, sheltered spot in sunlight.

BROWALLIA AT A GLANCE

A half-hardy annual grown for its blue, white, or pink flowers, useful for bedding/container planting. Frost hardy to 32°F (zone 10).

Jan	/	Recommended Varieties
Feb	sow	
Mar	sow	*Browallia speciosa:*
Apr	grow on	**Blue flowers**
May	plant	"Blue Troll"
Jun	flowering	"Blue Bells"
July	flowering	"Starlight Blue"
Aug	flowering	
Sept	flowering	**White flowers**
Oct	/	"White Troll"
Nov	/	
Dec	/	**Blue/pink/white flowers**
		"Jingle Bells"

Site   Browallia does not tolerate poor drainage, and on heavy soils should only be grown as a container plant, using multipurpose compost. Otherwise, mix in well-rotted compost or manure several weeks before planting out.

GROWING METHOD

Sowing   For summer bedding, sow the seed on the surface of 3½in pots of multipurpose compost in February/March. Keep at 64°F and do not let the surface dry out. Seedlings appear in 2–3 weeks and should be transplanted to individual cell trays or 3in pots. Harden off at the end of May and plant in early June. For flowering potted plants, seed can be sown in the same way until June.

Feeding   Give plants a liquid feed fortnightly or, in containers and windowboxes, mix slow-release fertilizer with the compost first.

Problems   Aphids sometimes attack the soft leaves, so use a spray containing permethrin if they appear.

FLOWERING

Season   Flowers appear from early summer onward and continue until the first frosts. Take off faded flowers regularly to encourage buds.

Cutting   Not suitable as a cut flower.

AFTER FLOWERING

General   Plants die when frosts arrive. Potted plants indoors can be kept alive indefinitely.

CALCEOLARIA
Slipper flower

THE HOT COLORS OF THE "SUNSET" strain of calceolaria excel outdoors and combine well with marigolds.

FEATURES

Only a few varieties of calceolaria are suitable for outdoors; these are different to the indoor pot type. By nature shrubs, they are grown from seed each year as hardy annuals and are useful for bedding and containers. None grow more than 16in tall and wide.

CONDITIONS

Aspect   Needs full sun or part shade.

CALCEOLARIA AT A GLANCE

A half-hardy annual, calceolaria is used for bedding and containers, with bright flowers. Frost hardy to 32°F (zone 10).

Jan	sow 🖐	**Recommended Varieties**
Feb	sow 🖐	*Calceolaria hybrids:*
Mar	transplant 🖐	"Little Sweeties Mixed"
Apr	grow on 🖐	"Midas"
May	harden off 🖐	"Sunshine"
Jun	flowering 🌸	"Sunset Mixed"
July	flowering 🌸	
Aug	flowering 🌸	
Sept	flowering 🌸	
Oct	/	
Nov	/	
Dec	/	

Site

Slipper flowers thrive in moist soil where their roots stay as cool as possible. Mix in well-rotted compost or manure before planting and use a peat- or coir-based multipurpose compost for filling containers.

GROWING METHOD

Sowing   The fine seed can be sown on the surface of peat- or coir-based multipurpose compost in a 3½in pot, January–March, at a temperature of 64°F. Keep in a bright place. Seedlings appear in 2–3 weeks and can be transplanted to cell trays, then hardened off and planted after frosts, 6–12in apart, or used with other plants in containers.

Feeding   Liquid feed every 3–4 weeks or mix slow-release fertilizer with compost before planting.

Problems   Slugs will eat the leaves of young plants in wet spells during early summer. Protect plants with a barrier of grit or eggshell or scatter slug pellets sparingly around plants.

FLOWERING

Season   Plants will flower from early summer until frosts. Take off dead flowers weekly.

Cutting   A few stems can be taken but avoid damaging the overall shape and appearance of the plant.

AFTER FLOWERING

General   Remove plants in fall when finished.

CALENDULA
Pot marigold

MIXED VARIETIES of calendula offer a wide color range, most commonly shades of orange and yellow, as seen here.

CALENDULA is a bushy plant producing masses of summer flowers —the edible petals can be scattered on summer salads.

FEATURES

Also known as English marigold, calendula is a fast-growing, hardy annual with daisy-type flowers in shades of yellow, orange, red, pinkish, and even green. Flowers can be fully double, while others have a distinct darker "eye." The edible petals can be used in salads. Perfect for a "cottage garden" bed or border, and very easy to grow, the large curled seeds are sown straight into the soil outdoors. Plant size ranges from 12 to 28in tall and wide.

CONDITIONS

Aspect Needs full sunlight to succeed.
Site Does well even in poor soil, which can increase the number of flowers. Add rotted organic matter to the soil ahead of planting time to improve results. Calendula does not do well on heavy, badly drained soils, so grow in containers under these conditions.

GROWING METHOD

Sowing March to May or August/September are the sowing periods. Sow the large seeds direct into finely raked moist soil where you want plants to flower, in drills ½in deep, and cover. Thin out as seedlings grow so that plants are eventually spaced 10–12in apart. Fall-sown plants flower earlier the following year. If flowers for cutting are required, sow seed thinly in long rows.
Feeding Liquid feed once a month to encourage larger blooms. Use a feed high in potash to encourage flowers rather than leafy growth—tomato fertilizers are a good choice.
Problems The leaves are prone to attack by aphids, causing twisting and damage. Use a spray containing permethrin, but avoid eating flowers. Powdery mildew can affect leaves in late summer, but is not worth treating—pick off the worst affected leaves and compost them.

FLOWERING

Season Flowers appear in late spring on plants sown the previous fall, and from early summer on spring-sown plants. Removal of faded blooms will keep up a succession of flowers.
Cutting Good as a cut flower—cutting helps to keep flowers coming. Cut when flowers are well formed but before petals open too far.

AFTER FLOWERING

General Pull up after flowering. Will self-seed if a few heads are left to ripen fully and shed seeds.

CALENDULA AT A GLANCE

A hardy annual for growing in beds and borders and a useful cut flower in many shades. Frost hardy to 5°F (zone 7).

		Recommended Varieties
Jan	/	*Calendula officinalis:*
Feb	/	"Art Shades Mixed"
Mar	sow	"Fiesta Gitana Mixed"
Apr	sow	"Greenheart Orange"
May	thin out	"Kablouna Lemon Cream"
Jun	flowering	"Kablouna Mixed"
July	flowering	"Orange King"
Aug	flowers/sow	"Pacific Beauty"
Sept	flowers/sow	"Pink Surprise"
Oct	/	"Princess Mixed"
Nov	/	"Radio"
Dec	/	"Touch of Red Mixed"

CALLISTEPHUS
China aster

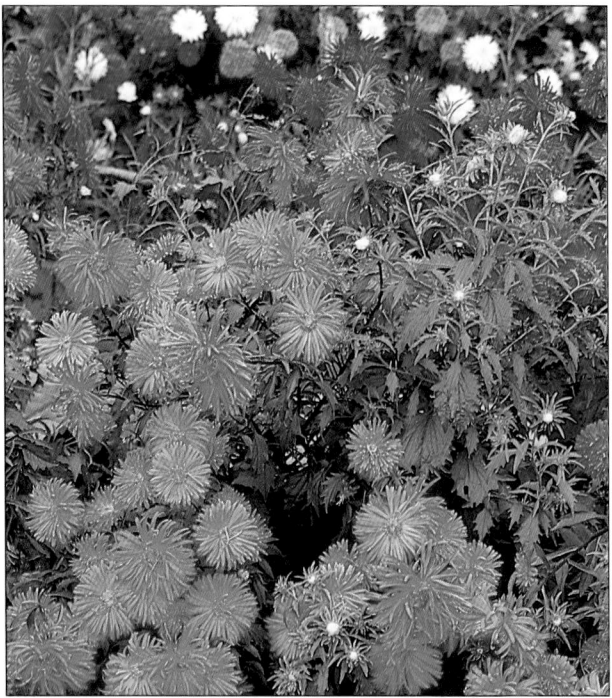

CHINA ASTERS, with their large, showy, and often double flowers, can be used as summer bedding plants for massed displays.

AS A CUT FLOWER, callistephus is unrivalled for producing long-lasting blooms in late summer when other flowers are past their best.

FEATURES

China asters are half-hardy annuals and are not to be confused with the perennial asters or Michaelmas daisies. Grow as bedding, as cut flowers, and in large pots. Flowers come in a wide range, from narrow, quill-like petals to bicolors, and also single shades. Size ranges from 8 to 36in tall, depending on the variety. Available as young plants.

CONDITIONS

Aspect   Must have a warm spot in full sunlight all day.

CALLISTEPHUS AT A GLANCE	
A half-hardy annual grown for its flowers, used in bedding, container,s and as a cut flower. Frost hardy to 32°F (zone 10).	
Jan /	Recommended Varieties
Feb /	*Callistephus chinensis:*
Mar sow	"Apricot Giant"
Apr sow	"Dwarf Comet Mixed"
May plant	"Matsumoto Mixed"
Jun flowering	"Moraketa"
July flowering	"Milady Mixed"
Aug flowering	"Ostrich Plume Mixed"
Sept flowering	"Red Ribbon"
Oct flowering	"Teisa Stars Mixed"
Nov /	
Dec /	

Site   Plants need well-drained soil with added organic matter, such as rotted manure or compost, dug in before planting. If grown in containers, use multipurpose compost mixed with slow-release fertilizer granules.

GROWING METHOD

Sowing   Sow in March/April in 3½in pots of compost and keep at 61°F. Seedlings appear after a week and can be transplanted to cell trays and grown on. Planted in late May, plants are not damaged by the last frosts. Seed can also be sown direct into the ground in late April and May. Plant 8–24in apart.

Feeding   Water regularly and give plants in containers a general liquid feed every two weeks. In beds, feed when you water with a handheld feeder.

Problems   Aphids cause the leaves to distort, which can affect flowering. Use a spray containing dimethoate. If plants suddenly collapse and die, they are suffering from aster wilt and should be removed with the soil around their roots and put in the trashcan. Avoid growing asters in that spot and try "resistant" varieties.

FLOWERING

Season   Early summer to early fall.
Cutting   An excellent and long-lasting cut flower.

AFTER FLOWERING

General   Remove plants after flowering and compost any that do not show signs of wilt disease.

CAMPANULA
Canterbury bells

THE BELL-LIKE flowers of Campanula medium *give it its common name of Canterbury bells. It is seen here growing with ageratum.*

WHEN CANTERBURY BELLS display this characteristic "saucer" behind the cup-shaped bloom, they simply ooze charm.

FEATURES

Canterbury bells are best in massed plantings in mixed borders and are good for cutting. Dwarf varieties can be used for bedding and in containers. The large, bell-like single or double flowers are blue, pink, mauve, or white, on stems 2–3ft high, rising from large clumps. Usually grown as a hardy biennial, the dwarf variety "Chelsea Pink" is grown as an annual, flowering three months after sowing in February. Stake tall plants.

CONDITIONS

Aspect   Grow in an open spot in full sunlight.

CAMPANULA AT A GLANCE

A hardy biennial grown for bedding and for tall flower spikes that are ideal for cutting. Frost hardy to 5°F (zone 7).

Jan	/	Recommended Varieties
Feb	/	
Mar	/	*Campanula medium:*
Apr	sow 🖐	**Tall varieties**
May	sow 🖐	"Calycanthema Mixed"
		"Cup and Saucer Mixed"
Jun	flowers/sow 🖐🖐	"Rosea"
July	flowering 🖐	"Single Mixed"
Aug	flowering 🖐	
Sept	flowering 🖐	**Shorter/dwarf varieties**
Oct	plant 🖐	"Bella Series"
		"Bells of Holland"
Nov	/	"Chelsea Pink"
Dec	/	"Russian Pink"

Site

Plenty of well-rotted manure or compost dug into the soil produces strong growth. Requires good drainage but the soil should retain moisture and not dry out completely. In containers, use multipurpose compost.

GROWING METHOD

Sowing   Sow the fine seed from April to June outdoors, or in small pots of multipurpose compost. Just cover the seed. Either transplant seedlings to 12in apart or pot up individually into 3½in pots. Grow on through the summer and plant during the fall in groups of 3–5, spacing plants 12in apart. Flowers will appear the following summer.

Feeding   Give a monthly liquid feed, starting a few weeks after transplanting or potting up, and make sure potted plants do not dry out. Scatter a general granular fertilizer over beds in spring to keep growth strong and encourage flowers.

Problems   Slugs will eat the crowns of plants in early summer, especially after rain, so scatter slug pellets or use a physical barrier, like grit.

FLOWERING

Season   Flower spikes appear from early summer onward. A second "flush" of flowers is possible if all stems are cut to the ground when faded.

Cutting   Campanula are good cut flowers, so grow extra plants of a tall variety in rows just for cutting.

AFTER FLOWERING

General   Remove plants after the flowering season and add them to the compost heap or bin.

CATHARANTHUS
Madagascar periwinkle

THE FAMILIAR FLOWERS of Catharanthus roseus *look similar to those of its close relative, the hardy vinca.*

FOR BEDDING DISPLAYS, catharanthus is available in mixed colors that often contain flowers with darker "eyes," as seen here.

FEATURES

Varieties of *Catharanthus roseus* have pink/rose, mauve, or white flowers, often with a deeper center. These plants quickly spread, growing to 10–16in, and are suitable for massed bedding displays or pots indoors. Grow as a half-hardy annual.

CONDITIONS

Aspect   Needs full sunlight to succeed outdoors.

CATHARANTHUS AT A GLANCE

A half-hardy annual grown for its bright flowers and ideal for use in containers on a warm sunny yard. Frost hardy to 32°F (zone 10).

Jan	/	Recommended Varieties
Feb	/	
Mar	sow	*Catharanthus roseus:*
Apr	transplant	"Apricot Delight"
May	harden off/plant	"Pacifica Red"
Jun	flowering	"Peppermint Cooler"
July	flowering	"Pretty In… Mixed"
Aug	flowering	"Tropicana Mixed"
Sept	flowering	"Terrace Vermillion"
Oct	/	
Nov	/	
Dec	/	

Site   Needs good drainage, but enrich the soil with well-rotted manure or compost before planting. For containers, use multipurpose compost mixed with extra slow-release fertilizer before planting up.

GROWING METHOD

Sowing   Sow seed in March/April in 3½in pots of multipurpose compost and lightly cover. Keep at 64°F in a light spot and transplant seedlings when they are 1in tall, into cell trays. Keep in a warm greenhouse or warm spot indoors and do not get the compost too wet. Harden off in late May and plant 8–12in apart in their final positions or use in containers.

Feeding   In bedding displays, apply a liquid plant food monthly to keep plants growing vigorously throughout the summer months.

Problems   Overwatering and wet soil/compost can lead to rotting. If red spider mite attacks the leaves, use a spray containing bifenthrin.

FLOWERING

Season   Flowers appear throughout the summer.
Cutting   Not suitable for cutting.

AFTER FLOWERING

General   Remove plants after the first fall frosts and use for composting.

CELOSIA
Prince of Wales' feathers

THE FEATHERY FLOWERS of celosia are made up of masses of smaller flowers, and have a distinctive, plume-like shape.

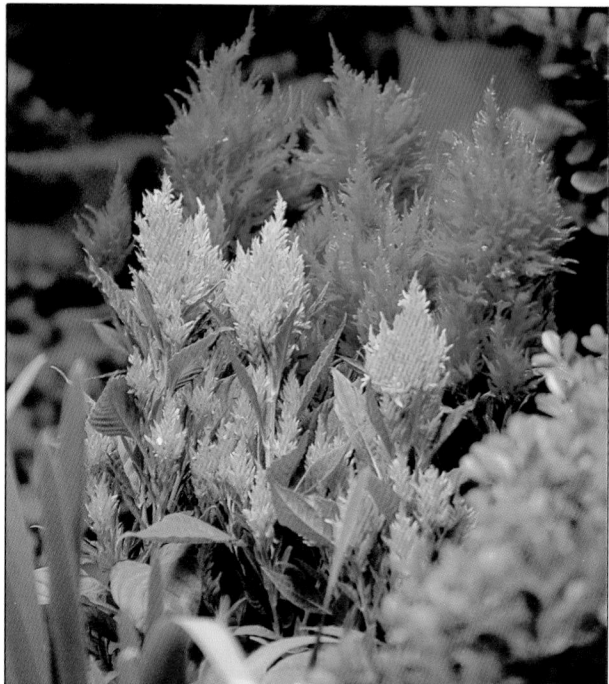

THE BRILLIANT PLUMES of cockscomb always look best in patio pots and containers when planted together in groups of 4–6 plants.

FEATURES

Also known as Prince of Wales' feathers, celosia, or cockscomb has plume-like or crested flowers (shown left) ranging in color from deep crimson to scarlet, orange, and yellow. Tall forms grow to 30in, the dwarf forms to 10–12in. Grow it as a half-hardy annual and use in bedding or as a striking plant for containers. Good for cutting.

CONDITIONS

Aspect   Must have a sunny, warm spot to do well.

CELOSIA AT A GLANCE

A half-hardy annual grown for its feathery, plume-like flowerheads in a range of colors. Frost hardy to 32°F (zone 10).

Jan	/	Recommended Varieties
Feb	sow	
Mar	sow	**Plumed**
Apr	pot on	*Celosia argentea:*
May	harden off/plant	"Kimono Mixed"
		"Dwarf Geisha"
Jun	flowering	"Century Mixed"
July	flowering	"New Look"
Aug	flowering	*Celosia spicata:*
Sept	flowering	"Flamingo Feather"
Oct	/	**Crested**
Nov	/	*Celosia cristata:*
Dec	/	"Jewel Box Mixed"

Site   Needs well-drained soil that has been enriched with well-rotted manure or compost. Good soil preparation is essential to ensure strong plants and large flowerheads. Plant up containers using multipurpose compost

GROWING METHOD

Sowing   Celosias dislike having their roots disturbed so sow 2–3 seeds per cell in a multi-cell tray using multipurpose compost, in February/March. Keep at 64°F and when the seedlings appear after 2–3 weeks, remove all but the strongest. Carefully pot the young plants on into 3½in pots, then harden off for two weeks before planting after the last frosts. Plant without damaging the roots, 6–12in apart, and water.

Feeding   Feed bedding monthly with liquid feed. Mix slow-release fertilizer with the compost before planting up containers.

Problems   Wet, cold soil/compost can cause rotting of the roots, so avoid heavy soils and grow in pots.

FLOWERING

Season   Flowers appear throughout summer.

Cutting   May be used as a cut flower for unusual indoor decoration. Cut some plumes and hang them upside down in a dry, airy place for later use in dried flower arrangements.

AFTER FLOWERING

General   Remove plants after the first frosts of fall.

CENTAUREA

Cornflower

CORNFLOWERS should have pale, fading flowers removed regularly. For indoor use, cut the stems when the buds are still closed.

GROWN IN GROUPS like this, cornflowers will support each other quite naturally. In windy spots, push twigs in between plants.

FEATURES

Cornflower, *Centaurea cyanus*, is one of the easiest hardy annuals to grow and can be used in bedding, containers, and for cut flowers. Other than blue, there are mixtures available and single colors such as the "Florence" types in red, pink, and white, reaching 14in tall. Taller varieties like "Blue Diadem" are best for cutting. Regular removal of dead flowers is essential to prolong flowering and to stop plants from becoming shabby.

CENTAUREA AT A GLANCE

A hardy annual grown for its "cottage garden"-style flowers in various colors, useful for cutting. Frost hardy to 5°F (zone 7).

		Recommended Varieties
Jan	/	
Feb	/	*Centaurea cyanus*:
Mar	sow 🖐	**Short varieties**
Apr	thin out 🖐	"Florence Blue"
May	flowering 🌸	"Florence Mixed"
Jun	flowering 🌸	"Florence Pink"
July	flowering 🌸	"Florence Red"
Aug	flowering 🌸	"Florence White"
Sept	flowers/sow 🌸🖐	"Midget Mixed"
Oct	/	**Tall varieties**
Nov	/	"Blue Diadem"
Dec	/	"Black Ball"

CONDITIONS

Aspect   Needs full sunlight all day.
Site   Must have very well-drained soil, but no special soil preparation is necessary. Staking is necessary when grown in windy situations, but the plants are self-supporting when they are planted in groups. For container growing, use multipurpose compost.

GROWING METHOD

Sowing   Sow seed in the spring where plants are to flower in short rows ½in deep and approximately 12in apart. Thin out so the plants are finally 3–6in apart. This can also be done in late September for stronger plants and earlier flowers, but leave thinning out until the following spring. Can also be sown in pots and transplanted to cell trays for plants to use in courtyard containers.
Feeding   Extra feeding is usually unnecessary.
Problems   White mildew affects leaves but is not serious.

FLOWERING

Season   Summer until early fall.
Cutting   Cut before the petals open too far.

AFTER FLOWERING

General   Remove plants once flowering is finished. Plants self-seed if they are left in the ground.

CHEIRANTHUS
Wallflower

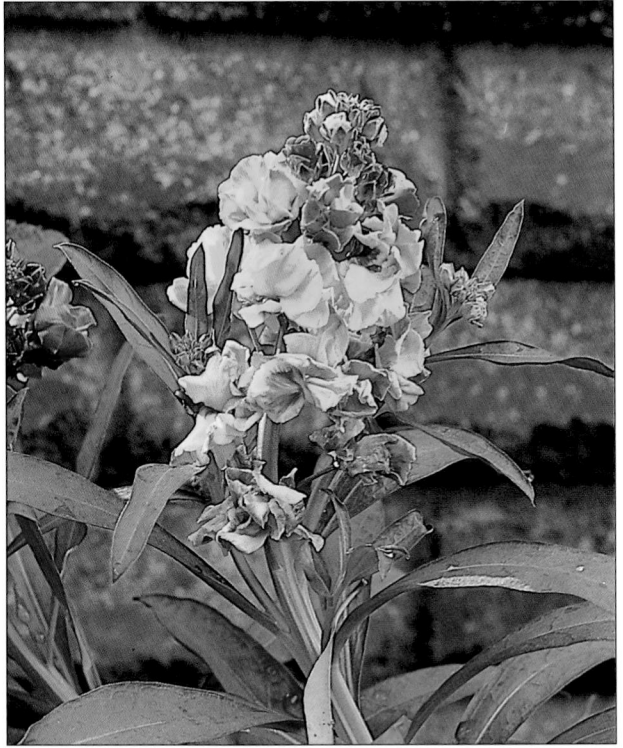

THE INTENSE COLORS of wallflowers are only matched by their strong, lingering scent that is best on warm, still days.

"IVORY WHITE" is a useful single-colored variety of Cheiranthus cheiri *for bedding schemes that are color-themed.*

FEATURES

Wallflowers have fragrant flowers of yellow, brown, cream, red, and orange and are grown for their sweet spring scent. These hardy biennials grow between 8 and 18in, depending on the variety, and are available as mixed or single colors. Plants are used for bedding but may also be used in courtyard containers, where they can be moved near doors and windows when in bloom. Ready-grown plants can be bought in early fall.

CHEIRANTHUS AT A GLANCE

With its bright flowers and strong scent, this biennial is useful for spring bedding and for containers. Frost hardy to 5°F (zone 7).

Jan	/	Recommended Varieties
Feb	flowering	
Mar	flowering	*Cheiranthus cheiri:*
		Tall
Apr	flowering	"Blood Red"
May	sow	"Cloth of Gold"
Jun	sow	"Harlequin"
		Medium
July	thin out	"My Fair Lady Mixed"
Aug	grow on	"Vulcan Improved"
Sept	grow on	**Dwarf**
Oct	plant	"Prince Mixed"
Nov	/	"Tom Thumb Mixed"
Dec	/	

CONDITIONS

Aspect Grow in full sunlight for the best scent.
Site Must have very well-drained soil. Add lime before planting to reduce the effect of clubroot disease. Use multipurpose compost in containers and windowboxes. Avoid places exposed to winter winds and move containers to shelter during severe winter weather.

GROWING METHOD

Sowing Sow May/June outdoors in rows 12in apart and ½in deep. As plants grow, thin them to 12in apart, and pinch when 3in tall to make growth bushy. Can also be sown in pots and transplanted into 3½in pots. Plant in October in beds or containers. When lifting plants, keep as much soil on the roots as possible.
Feeding Give a liquid feed monthly during summer.
Problems Avoid growing in soil known to be infected with clubroot disease, or raise plants in pots using multipurpose compost.

FLOWERING

Season Late winter through to the spring.
Cutting Cut stems last well in water.

AFTER FLOWERING

General Remove plants in late spring after flowering.

CLEOME
Spider flower

SPIDER FLOWERS are available as single colors or mixed. The popular "Color Fountains Mixed" is seen here in a summer border.

THE EXOTIC FEEL that cleome adds to the yard can be used to best effect on a warm courtyard where their scent lingers in still air.

FEATURES

The spider-like flowers of *Cleome spinosa*, in pink, white, or rose, have narrow petals with long stamens. They appear all summer up and down the length of the stem. These large half-hardy annuals grow to 5ft tall with a single stem, and with lobed leaves. Plant at the back of borders or use them as central "dot" plants in large tubs for an "exotic" feel. Look out for the thorny stems and pungent leaves.

CONDITIONS

Aspect   Needs full sunlight and a sheltered position to achieve maximum height during the summer.

CLEOME AT A GLANCE

A half-hardy annual grown for its exotic flowers and ideal as a centerpiece for bedding/containers. Frost hardy to 32°F (zone 10).

Jan	/	Recommended Varieties
Feb	sow 🌱	
Mar	sow 🌱	*Cleome spinosa:*
Apr	grow on 🌱	**Mixed colors**
May	harden off/plant 🌱	"Color Fountain Mixed"
Jun	flowering 🌸	
July	flowering 🌸	**Single colors**
Aug	flowering 🌸	"Cherry Queen"
Sept	flowering 🌸	"Helen Campbell"
Oct	/	"Pink Queen"
Nov	/	"Violet Queen"
Dec	/	

Site

Needs good drainage but tolerates a wide range of soils. For best results, improve soil by digging in rotted manure or compost, and use multipurpose compost with slow-release fertilizer added when planting containers. Stems are generally strong enough that they can be grow without extra support.

GROWING METHOD

Sowing   Sow seeds in 3½in pots of multipurpose compost in February/March and keep at 64°F. Seedlings appear after two weeks and are transplanted to 3½in pots, grown on in a warm greenhouse or conservatory. Pot on into 5in containers in early May, and harden off before planting after the last frosts.

Feeding   Feed plants in beds fortnightly with liquid feed from a handheld applicator. Don't allow the compost in containers to become over-wet.

Problems   Aphids attack young plants and cause twisted growth. Check under the leaves regularly and use a spray with permethrin if necessary, making sure the spray gets under the leaves.

FLOWERING

Season   The long flowering period extends throughout summer and well into mild falls. The long thin seed pods give it a real "spidery" look.

Cutting   Useful as a cut flower, but watch the spines.

AFTER FLOWERING

General   Remove plants after flowering, but wear gloves for protection, since the stems are spiny.

CONSOLIDA
Larkspur

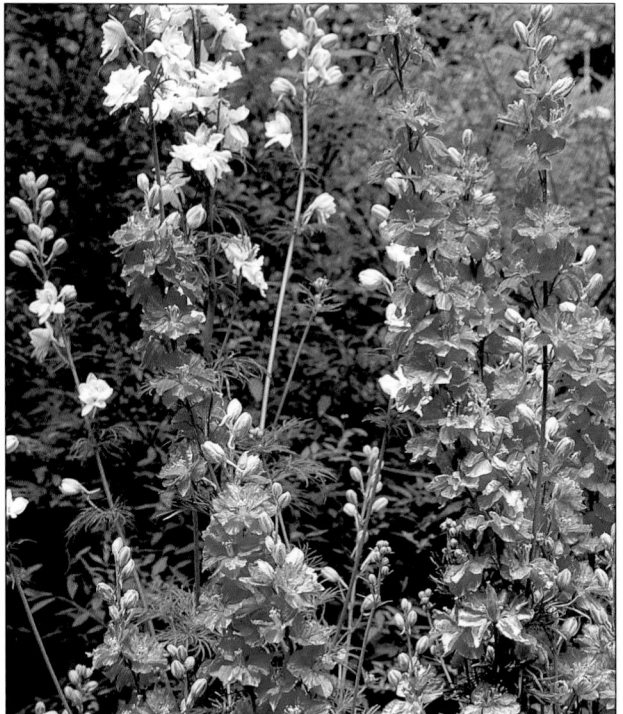

LARKSPUR IS DOUBLY useful as a cut flower, because the spikes can be dried and used for dried flower arrangements.

FINELY DIVIDED LEAVES are characteristic of Consolida ajacis, while flowers can be single, as here, or double, in various colors.

FEATURES

Consolida ajacis, larkspur, is related to delphinium but is not as tall and is grown as a hardy annual. Ideal for a "cottage garden" border, larkspur grows up to 3ft tall and has spikes of pink, white, red, blue, and violet single or double flowers, with finely cut leaves. Good for cutting. Seeds are poisonous.

CONDITIONS

Aspect   Grow in a sunny, open spot.

CONSOLIDA AT A GLANCE

A hardy annual grown for its spikes of bright flowers that are useful for borders and cutting. Frost hardy to 5°F (zone 7).

		Recommended Varieties
Jan	/	
Feb	/	*Consolida ajacis:*
Mar	sow	**Tall, for cutting**
Apr	thin out	"Earl Grey"
May	thin/flowers	"Frosted Skies"
Jun	flowering	"Giant Imperial Mixed"
July	flowering	"Hyacinth Flowered Mixed"
Aug	flowering	
Sept	flowers/sow	**Short, for bedding**
Oct	/	"Dwarf Hyacinth Flowered Mixed"
Nov	/	"Dwarf Rocket Mixed"
Dec	/	

Site

Soil can be enriched with manure or compost well ahead of planting, but it must be well-drained. Plants will also grow well on thin and hungry soils. Plants should support each other as they grow and not need artificial support. Use taller varieties at the rear of borders.

GROWING METHOD

Sowing   Sow direct where the plants are to grow for best results, in short rows ½in deep, in either March or September. Expect seedlings to appear in 2–3 weeks. Thin plants out as they grow so they are eventually 3–6in apart, depending on the variety.

Feeding   Extra feeding is not necessary.

Problems   Slugs eat young seedlings so scatter slug pellets around plants or protect them with a 2in wide barrier of sharp grit.

FLOWERING

Season   Flowers appear from spring onward on fall-sown plants, June onward from spring sowings. Removing faded flower spikes will encourage more flowers.

Cutting   An excellent cut flower. Cut long stems and scald ends before soaking in cool water.

AFTER FLOWERING

General   Leave a few plants to die down naturally and self-seed into the soil, otherwise pull up when finished and use for composting.

COREOPSIS
Coreopsis

COREOPSIS ARE wonderful plants which can quickly colonize a space, say between shrubs, producing striking, bright yellow flowers.

THIS DOUBLE-FLOWERED FORM of golden coreopsis provides many weeks of marvellous color throughout the summer.

FEATURES

Perennial coreopsis carries a profusion of bright yellow daisy-like flowers over a long period, generally through summer into the fall, though some do flower in spring. Regular deadheading will ensure a long display. *C. lanceolata*, known as calliopsis, has become naturalized in many parts of the world. The strong-growing *C. grandiflora* may grow 24–36in high, with *C.verticillata* about 8in shorter. There are several species worth trying, some with dwarf form or flowers displaying a dark eye. The foliage is variable too. The plants are easy to grow. Plant in bold clumps in a mixed border.

COREOPSIS AT A GLANCE

A genus with well over 100 species that make a big contribution to the summer and early fall display. Hardy to 5°F (zone 7).

Jan	/	Recommended Varieties
Feb	/	
Mar	/	*Coreopsis auriculata*
		"Schnittgold"
Apr	sow 🕮	*C.* "Goldfink"
May	divide 🕮	*C. grandiflora* "Early Sunrise"
Jun	flowering 🌸	*C. g.* "Mayfield Giant"
		"Sunray"
July	flowering 🌸	*C. verticillata*
Aug	flowering 🌸	*C. v.* "Grandiflora"
Sept	flowering 🌸	*C. v.* "Zagreb"
Oct	/	
Nov	/	
Dec	/	

CONDITIONS

Aspect Prefers an open, sunny position right through the day, with little shade.

Site Performs best in well-drained soil enriched with organic matter, but it will grow in poor soils too. Over-rich soil may produce a profusion of foliage with poor flowering.

GROWING METHOD

Propagation Grows most easily from divisions of existing clumps lifted in the spring. Space new plants at about 12in intervals. Species can be grown from seed sown in mid-spring. Since cultivars of *C. grandiflora* can be ephemeral, sow seed for continuity.

Feeding Apply complete plant food as growth begins in the spring. However, no further feeding should be needed.

Problems No pest or disease problems are known.

FLOWERING

Season The long flowering period extends through summer and the fall. *C.* "Early Sunrise," *C.lanceolata*, and "Sunray" flower in their first year from an early sowing.

Cutting Flowers can be cut for indoor decoration.

AFTER FLOWERING

Requirements Cut off spent flower stems and tidy up the foliage as it dies back. In mild, frost-free winters, coreopsis may not totally die back.

COSMOS
Cosmos

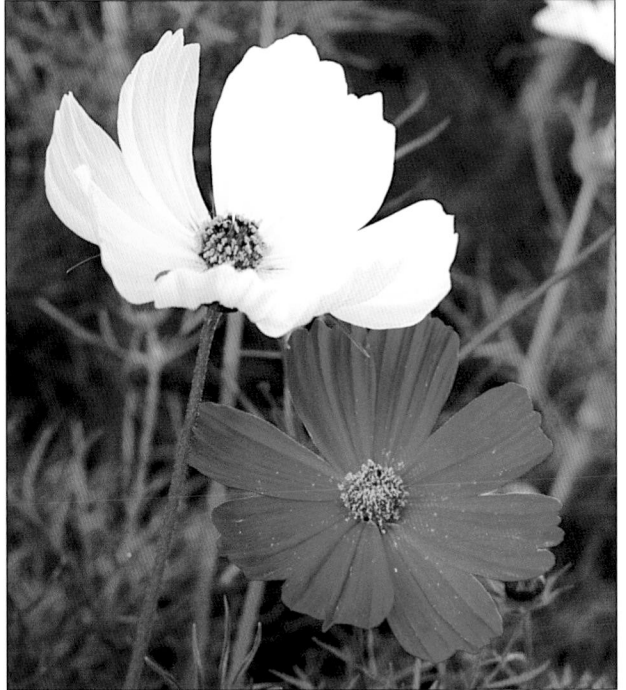

"SENSATION MIXED" is a tall-growing (3ft) cosmos with single flowers of red, pink, white, and shades in between.

DURING THE SUMMER, varieties of Cosmos bipinnatus *grown in borders form masses of feathery leaves topped by flowers.*

FEATURES

Cosmos, with their finely cut, feathery foliage and large daisy-type flowers grow up to 5ft tall, but shorter varieties are available and can be used in containers. Varieties of *Cosmos bipinnatus* have red, pink, purple, or white flowers, while yellow, orange, and scarlet are available in varieties of *Cosmos sulphureus*. Cosmos is grown as either a hardy or a half-hardy annual, and is an excellent choice for a cottage yard-style border. "Seashells" has tubular "fluted" petals, and the taller varieties such as "Sensation Mixed" are good for cutting.

COSMOS AT A GLANCE

A hardy or half-hardy annual grown for its large daisy-like flowers. For borders, pots, and cutting. Frost hardy to 32°F (zone 10).

Jan	/	**Recommended Varieties**
Feb	/	
Mar	sow	*Cosmos bipinnatus:*
		"Daydream"
Apr	sow/transplant	"Gazebo"
May	sow/plant	"Picotee"
Jun	flowering	"Seashells/Sea Shells"
July	flowering	"Sensation Mixed"
		"Sonata Mixed"
Aug	flowering	*Cosmos favorureus:*
Sept	flowering	"Ladybird Mixed"
Oct	/	"Ladybird Scarlet"
Nov	/	"Sunny Red"
Dec	/	

CONDITIONS

Aspect Needs full sunlight to flourish.
Site Well-drained soil is essential for success, and good results are guaranteed on light and slightly hungry soils. Pea sticks or twiggy shoots may be needed for support in exposed spots. Any multipurpose compost will give good results in courtyard pots and containers.

GROWING METHOD

Sowing Raise plants by sowing in March at 61°F. Sow the long thin seeds in 3½in pots of multipurpose compost, then transplant to cell trays and grow on. Harden off at the end of May before planting after frosts, or sow in April/May directly into the ground where the plants are to grow. Final spacing between plants should be 6–18in, depending on the variety grown.
Feeding Generally not necessary.
Problems Slugs will eat young seedlings outdoors, so protect with slug pellets.

FLOWERING

Season Flowers appear from the early summer onward.
Cutting The taller varieties are ideal as cut flowers. Ensure regular removal of faded flowers.

AFTER FLOWERING

General Pull up plants when frosted, but leaving a few to die off will ensure some self-sown seedlings.

DAHLIA
Bedding dahlia

BEDDING DAHLIAS *are usually available in mixed colors. By planting time you can usually separate plants by flower color.*

"DOUBLE DELIGHT MIXED" is a popular bedding variety ideally suited for growing in courtyard containers, reaching 18in tall.

FEATURES

Seed-raised bedding dahlias are close cousins of the "border" dahlia grown from tubers. A wide range is available, the dwarfer types growing only 12in tall. Flower color is varied and some, like "Redskin," also have bronze leaves. Grow as half-hardy annuals, and use for bedding displays, courtyard containers, and even windowboxes. Choose from single, double, or decorative "collarette" flowers. Widely available as young plants.

CONDITIONS

Aspect   Bedding dahlias need full sunlight all day.
Site   Dig in large amounts of decayed manure or

DAHLIA AT A GLANCE

A half-hardy annual grown for its pretty flowers and an ideal summer bedding or container plant. Frost hardy to 32°F (zone 10).

Jan	/	Recommended Varieties
Feb	sow 🖐	*Dahlia hybrids:*
Mar	sow 🖐	**Taller varieties**
Apr	transplant/grow 🖐	"Collarette Dandy"
May	harden off/plant 🖐	"Coltness Hybrids Mixed"
Jun	flowering 🌿	"Pompon Mixed"
July	flowering 🌿	**Shorter varieties**
Aug	flowering 🌿	"Diablo Mixed"
Sept	flowering 🌿	"Dwarf Double Delight"
Oct	flowering 🌿	"Dwarf Amore"
Nov	/	"Figaro Mixed"
Dec	/	"Redskin"

---

compost at least two or three weeks before planting. Soil must be well-drained but moisture-retentive. For containers, use multipurpose compost with added slow-release fertilizer granules to keep growth strong through the summer months.

GROWING METHOD

Sowing   Sow seed February/March in 3½in pots and just cover. Water and keep at 61°F in a light spot. Transplant seedlings when large enough to handle into individual 3½in pots and grow on. Harden off at the end of May and plant in early June, when all frosts are over, spacing plants 6–12in apart.

Feeding   Water and liquid-feed once a week, depending on the soil and weather conditions. Continue watering regularly throughout the season.

Problems   Dahlia leaves are eaten by slugs, so protect them with slug pellets. Flowers may be chewed by earwigs—to catch them, fill upturned pots with straw and support these on canes among the flowers. Powdery mildew can affect leaves in the late summer but is not serious.

FLOWERING

Season   The main show is from midsummer onward, lasting well into fall until the first frosts.

Cutting   Taller varieties of bedding dahlias make useful and long-lived cut flowers.

AFTER FLOWERING

General   Remove plants when the leaves turn black and collapse. Fleshy tubers of favorite plants can be stored dry and frost-free over the winter.

DELPHINIUM
Annual delphinium

"PACIFIC GIANTS MIXED" is a popular variety of delphinium and comes in a range of colors as well as the blue seen here.

ANNUAL DELPHINIUMS can be used as "gap fillers" in mixed borders, and can be left to grow as a permanent feature if required.

FEATURES

Certain varieties of delphinium can be grown from seed and treated as half-hardy annuals, even though they are by nature perennials. The flower spikes of up to 5ft are perfect for giving height to summer bedding schemes and are attractive for cutting. Favorite plants can be moved to a permanent position in the fall. Seeds and plants are poisonous.

CONDITIONS

Aspect Best in full sun.

DELPHINIUM AT A GLANCE

A perennial treated as a half-hardy annual and grown for its tall spikes of flowers in summer. Frost hardy to 5°F. (zone 7)

Jan	/	Recommended Varieties
Feb	/	**Delphinium hybrids:**
Mar	sow	"Connecticut Yankees"
Apr	transplant	"Dreaming Spires"
May	grow/plant	"Dwarf Pacific Mixed"
Jun	flowering	"Dwarf Magic Fountains Mixed"
July	flowering	"Pacific Giants Mixed"
Aug	flowering	
Sept	flowering	*Delphinium grandiflorum:*
Oct	/	"Blue Butterfly"
Nov	/	"Sky Blue"
Dec	/	

Site Delphiniums need shelter from strong winds, and well-drained, moist soil enriched with rotted organic matter before planting. Plants may need support with twiggy sticks or short canes when growing strongly.

GROWING METHOD

Sowing Sow in pots of multipurpose compost in March at 60°F, just covering the seeds. Move seedlings into cell trays and grow on in a cold frame or sheltered spot outdoors before planting in May where you want flowers, which appear from midsummer onward.

Feeding Keep well-watered after planting and liquid feed every 2–3 weeks using a hand-held feeder.

Problems Slugs can decimate young plants in spring so scatter slug pellets or protect with a 2in wide band of sharp grit.

FLOWERING

Season Flowers appear from midsummer onward.

Cutting For best results cut when the lowest flowers on the spike are fully open and the top buds are starting to show color.

AFTER FLOWERING

General If you want to keep certain plants, cut off the foliage as it browns, label them clearly, and then lift and replant when they are fully dormant in the late fall or very early the following spring.

DIANTHUS BARBATUS

Sweet William

THE IMPACT OF SWEET WILLIAMS comes from their massed heads of small flowers, which often have attractive "picotee" edges.

STRONG SCENT is a characteristic of Dianthus barbatus *varieties and makes this an ideal plant for cutting in bunches in early summer.*

FEATURES

Sweet Williams are varieties of *Dianthus barbatus* and have flowers in pink, white, red, burgundy, and bicolors, on large rounded heads. Individual flowers often have darker central "eyes." Plants have clumping growth up to 18in, while dwarf forms grow to just 6in. The flowers appear from the spring into early summer and are scented and ideal for cutting. They are easily grown from seed as a hardy biennial, and useful for bedding schemes and as blocks of spring color in mixed borders. Some less common varieties, like "Sooty," have dark, almost black flowers.

DIANTHUS AT A GLANCE

A summer-sown biennial grown for its large heads of scented flowers in spring and early summer. Frost hardy to 5°F (zone 7).

Jan	/	Recommended Varieties
Feb	/	
Mar	/	*Dianthus barbatus:*
Apr	flowering	**Tall varieties**
May	flowers/sow	"Auricula-Eyed Mixed"
		"Forerunner Mixed"
Jun	flowers/sow	"Gemstones"
July	flowering	"Harlequin"
		"Monarch Mixed"
Aug	grow on	**Dwarf varieties**
Sept	grow on	"Dwarf Mixed"
Oct	plant	"Indian Carpet Mixed"
Nov	/	
Dec	/	

CONDITIONS

Aspect Grow Sweet Williams in full sunlight.

Site Needs well-drained soil that has been limed before planting, and has had plenty of rotted compost mixed in several weeks before.

GROWING METHOD

Sowing Sow the fine seed in rows outdoors, ½in deep and just cover, in May/June. Transplant the seedlings so they are in rows 6in apart and pinch out the growing tips to make them bushy. Water regularly throughout the summer months, and then lift and plant into their flowering positions in October, keeping the roots intact. For cut flowers only, the plants can be left growing in rows.

Feeding Liquid-feed monthly during the summer.

Problems Poor drainage during winter can kill plants. If leaves are attacked by rust disease, try a spray containing the fungicide penconazole.

FLOWERING

Season Flowers appear from late spring to early summer, and it is possible to get a second "flush" if all the stalks are cut hard back after the first flowers have faded.

Cutting An excellent cut flower, and ideal for making into a small, rounded bouquet.

AFTER FLOWERING

General Pull plants up when they are past their best, or leave some to develop into bigger clumps.

DIANTHUS CHINENSIS
Chinese pink

AS CONTAINER PLANTS, Chinese pinks are perfect as tidy edging plants, all growing to the same height. They are also valuable as colorful fillers and effectively bridge the gap between taller plants in the center of large tubs and trailing plants falling over the edges.

FEATURES

Growing 8–12in high, varieties of *Dianthus chinensis* are suitable for massed planting, edging garden beds, or for use in troughs or pots. Chinese pink is grown as a half-hardy annual, although it is fully hardy outdoors. Flower are red, pink, or white, with only slight scent. Available as young plants.

CONDITIONS

Aspect   Needs full sunlight to flower at its best.

DIANTHUS AT A GLANCE		
A hardy annual grown for its small brightly colored pink-type flowers, used in bedding/pots. Frost hardy to 5°F (zone 7).		
Jan	/	Recommended Varieties
Feb	/	
Mar	sow	*Dianthus chinensis:*
Apr	transplant	"Baby Doll Mixed"
May	harden off/plant	"Black & White Minstrels"
Jun	flowering	"Double Gaiety Mixed"
July	flowering	"Princess Mixed"
Aug	flowering	"Raspberry Parfait"
Sept	flowering	"Snowfire"
Oct	/	"Strawberry Parfait"
Nov	/	"T&M Frosty Mixed"
Dec	/	

Site   Needs well-drained soil, but dig in plenty of well-rotted manure or compost when preparing beds. Lime can be added to the soil before planting and raked in. Containers must have very good drainage.

GROWING METHOD

Sowing   Sow seeds in 3½in pots of multipurpose compost in March, just cover, and keep at 60°F in a light place. When seedlings are 1in tall, transplant to cell trays and grow on with some protection (a cold frame is suitable). Harden off at the end of May and plant out in beds or containers.

Feeding   Do not overwater—a good weekly watering should be sufficient—and add liquid feed every 2–3 weeks. Plants in containers need no extra feeding if slow-release fertilizer is added.

Problems   Overwatering will cause yellowing of the leaves and rotting off at soil/compost level.

FLOWERING

Season   Plants come into flower from early summer onward and will continue until the fall if dead flowerheads are removed regularly.

Cutting   Taller varieties can be used as cut flowers, but choose a variety known for its scent such as "Double Gaiety Mixed."

AFTER FLOWERING

General   Remove plants when finished and compost.

DIGITALIS
Foxglove

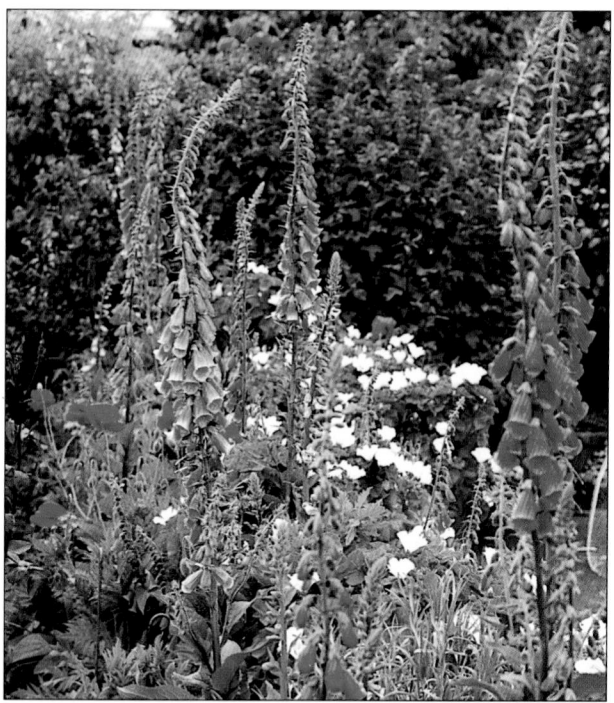

FOXGLOVES are perfect for cottage-style borders and make good companions for the red poppies and white lavatera.

WHITE FOXGLOVES are useful for a specific color scheme—this is a white-flowered plant of the "Excelsior Hybrids".

FEATURES

Varieties of *Digitalis purpurea* grow up to 6ft tall with spikes of tubular pink, white, magenta, cream, or purple flowers, each with a spotted lip. Plant in groups in borders or in a partly-shaded spot under trees. All parts of the plant are poisonous, including the seeds. Grow as a hardy biennial, although the variety "Foxy" can be treated as an annual and sown in spring.

CONDITIONS

Aspect   Succeeds in part or dappled shade, or in sun.

DIGITALIS AT A GLANCE

A hardy biennial grown for tall spikes of flowers appearing in early summer. Useful for shade. Frost hardy to 5°F (zone 7).

		Recommended Varieties
Jan	/	
Feb	/	
Mar	/	*Digitalis purpurea:*
Apr	sow	"Alba"
May	sow/transplant	"Excelsior Hybrids"
Jun	sow/flowers	"Foxy Mixed"
July	flowering	"Giant Spotted Mixed"
Aug	grow	"Glittering Prizes Mixed"
Sept	grow	"Selected Mixed"
Oct	plant	"Suttons Apricot"
Nov	/	
Dec	/	

Site   Soil needs to be free-draining and enriched with organic matter well ahead of planting—use rotted compost or manure in generous amounts. Staking is necessary when plants are grown in a position exposed to winds.

GROWING METHOD

Sowing   Sow the very small seed in a 3½in pot and barely cover, from April–June. Keep outside in a coldframe or sheltered spot, and transplant seedlings individually to 3½in pots. Grow on through the summer, potting on into 5in pots when roots fill the smaller pots. Plant out in October where you want the plants to flower. The variety "Foxy" can be sown in February in warmth and planted in May for flowers the same summer. Treat as a half-hardy annual.

Feeding   Feed fortnightly with liquid feed while plants are in pots and do not allow to dry out. Water in spring during dry spells as growth begins.

Problems   No special problems affect foxgloves.

FLOWERING

Season   Flowers appear in early summer.
Cutting   Not particularly good as a cut flower.

AFTER FLOWERING

General   Once stems have flowered, cut them off just above the leaves and plants may then produce several shorter flowering stems. Leave a few spikes to set seed pods which will self-seed.

DOROTHEANTHUS
Mesembryanthemum or Livingstone daisy

LIVINGSTONE DAISIES set beds alight with color on bright sunny days when the flowers open fully. Planted 6in apart they soon knit together to create a tapestry of color, and look especially at home when creeping among pieces of stone on a sunny rock garden.

FEATURES

Mesembryanthemum, also known as Livingstone daisy, is ideal for planting on dry, sunny banks, on rock gardens, and in pots of free-draining compost. It has a spreading habit, but is only 6in tall at most. The fleshy leaves have a crystalline texture with bright, daisy-like flowers in many shades. Grow as a half-hardy annual. All varieties of *Dorotheanthus bellidiformis* have the habit of closing their flowers in dull and wet spells of weather, opening again in bright sunshine.

DOROTHEANTHUS AT A GLANCE

A half-hardy, spreading annual grown for its daisy-like flowers that open fully in sunshine. Frost hardy to 32°F (zone 10).

Jan	/	**Recommended Varieties**
Feb	/	*Dorotheanthus bellidiformis:*
Mar	sow	"Gelato Pink"
Apr	sow/transplant	"Harlequin Mixed"
May	plant/harden off	"Lunette" ("Yellow Ice")
Jun	flowering	"Magic Carpet Mixed"
July	flowering	"Sparkles"
Aug	flowering	
Sept	flowering	
Oct	/	
Nov	/	
Dec	/	

CONDITIONS

Aspect   Needs full direct sun all day and will perform even better on a south-facing sloping bank.

Site   Needs very well drained soil, with no special soil preparation necessary, since plants grow better on light, sandy, and hungry soils. If grown in containers, used soil-based compost and mix with fifty percent grit for good drainage.

GROWING METHOD

Sowing   Sow seed in a 3½in pot of soil-based seed compost in March and barely cover. Keep at 64°F in a light place. When seedlings are large enough, transplant to cell trays of soil-based potting compost and grow on. Harden off at the end of May for two weeks and plant after the last frosts 6in apart.

Feeding   Extra feeding is unnecessary and produces leaves at the expense of flowers. Take care not to overwater in beds or pots, else plants will rot.

Problems   Slugs will attack the fleshy young leaves so scatter slug pellets after planting out.

FLOWERING

Season   Flowers appear from midsummer onward. Remove faded flowers to encourage more.

Cutting   Not suitable for cutting.

AFTER FLOWERING

General   Pull up and compost when finished.

ESCHSCHOLZIA
California poppy

FALL SOWING of eschscholzia will produce early spring flowers around the same time as this bright green Euphorbia polychroma.

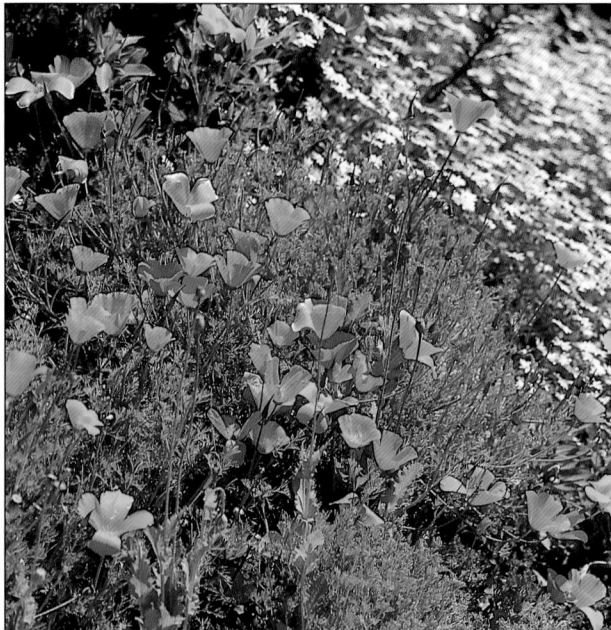

DRY, HOT, SUN-BAKED banks are perfect for California poppies, where conditions are very like those of their native State.

FEATURES

The bright flowers and finely divided blue-green foliage of the California poppy are best in large drifts, although it grows well even in cracks in paving slabs and in gravel, and thrives on dry soils in full sun. Varieties of *Eschscholzia californica* have flowers in yellow, cream, pink/beige, apricot, and scarlet. They grow 12in tall and wide. Grow as a hardy annual, sowing where plants are to flower. Very easy to grow and quickly self-seeds.

CONDITIONS

Aspect   Eschscholzia thrives in hot, sun-baked spots where other annuals struggle to grow. Must have full sunlight and likes it hot.

Site   Poor, light soil often gives the best results, so long as drainage is good. No special soil preparation is necessary, and avoid adding compost or manure, which encourages leafy growth at the expense of flowers.

GROWING METHOD

Sowing   Sow in March or September outdoors where the plants are to flower, since it dislikes being transplanted. Spread seed thinly in short drills ½in deep and cover. Thin out the seedlings as they grow to allow 3–6in between plants. Water thoroughly after thinning to settle plants back in.

Feeding   Except in spells of drought, watering is not necessary, and extra feed is not required.

Problems   No particular problems.

FLOWERING

Season   Long flowering period through the spring and summer months if faded flowers are removed.

Cutting   Use as a cut flower, although flowers close at night. Cut long stems and place in water immediately to just below the flower buds.

AFTER FLOWERING

General   Often self-seeds, so seedlings can be expected the following season. These will appear in cracks in the sidewalk, along paths and drives, and in gravel, where they are perfectly at home in dry, poor soil conditions.

ESCHSCHOLZIA AT A GLANCE

A hardy annual grown for its bright poppy-like flowers and ideal for light, dry soils and along paths. Frost hardy to 5°F (zone 7).

Jan	/	Recommended Varieties
Feb	/	
Mar	sow	*Eschscholzia californica:*
Apr	thin out	"Apricot Bush"
May	thin out	"Apricot Chiffon"
Jun	flowering	"Apricot Flambeau"
July	flowering	"Dalli"
Aug	flowering	"Mission Bells Mixed"
Sept	flowers/sow	"Prima Ballerina"
Oct	/	"Rose Bush"
Nov	/	"Thai Silk Mixed"
Dec	/	*Eschscholzia lobbii:*
		"Moonlight"

EUPHORBIA

Snow-on-the-mountain

THE COLOR of snow-on-the-mountain comes from its white-edged leaves; this becomes more intense near the tops of the plants.

WHEN GROWN IN POTS, Euphorbia marginata can be planted in mixed borders in groups of 3–5 plants for cool splashes of color.

FEATURES

Commonly known as snow-on-the-mountain, *Euphorbia marginata* is grown for its attractive leaves. The flowers are insignificant, but the leaves have an edging of white. Plants grow 2–3ft tall and are used in annual or mixed borders. Grow as a hardy annual. The milky sap is poisonous.

CONDITIONS

Aspect   Needs to be grown in the open in full sun.

EUPHORBIA AT A GLANCE

A hardy annual grown for its attractive leaves, which are streaked and edged with white. Frost hardy to 23°F (zone 9).

Jan	/	Recommended Varieties
Feb	/	
Mar	sow 🖐	*Euphorbia marginata:*
Apr	thin out 🖐	"Summer Icicle"
May	thin out 🖐	
Jun	flowering 🌿	
July	flowering 🌿	
Aug	flowering 🌿	
Sept	flowering 🌿	
Oct	/	
Nov	/	
Dec	/	

Site   Does not tolerate poor drainage and succeeds best in light and slightly hungry soils—sandy soils give good results. Add very well-rotted organic matter before planting to help retain soil moisture.

GROWING METHOD

Sowing   Sow seed during March direct into the ground, where plants are to grow, which avoids root disturbance as they develop. Make short drills ½in deep and scatter seed thinly, then cover. Plants are gradually thinned out so that final spacing is 6–12in by early summer. In exposed yards, short twigs can be used as supports. Alternatively, sow in pots in a cold frame and transplant to cell trays, planting out in May.

Feeding   Grows well without extra feeding.

Problems   Trouble-free.

FLOWERING

Season   From early summer onward.

Cutting   Foliage may be used in arrangements but stems must be burnt or scalded to stop the milky sap bleeding. Wear gloves to avoid getting the irritant sap on skin.

AFTER FLOWERING

General   Remove plants in late summer and fall when they are past their best, but leave a few to die down and self-seed into the soil.

GAZANIA
Gazania

GAZANIA *flowers often have striking darker markings toward their centers.*

IN MILD COASTAL YARDS *it is worth leaving gazanias out during the winter months, since they often survive unharmed and will give an early show of flowers in the following spring.*

FEATURES

Gazanias come in an amazing range of brilliant colors, from pastel pinks to cream, strong reds, and mahogany. Modern varieties with striped petals are very eye-catching. All have contrasting "eyes" to their flowers. Gazanias are grown as half-hardy annuals from spring-sown seeds and used in beds and courtyard pots. Flowers tend to close up in dull weather, but newer varieties like "Daybreak Bright Orange" stay open for longer. They grow up to 12in tall and wide and thrive in coastal yards.

CONDITIONS

Aspect For the flowers to open reliably, gazanias must be grown where they get roasting sun all day.

GAZANIA AT A GLANCE

A half-hardy annual grown for its bright flowers that open fully in sun. Use in beds and containers. Frost hardy to 23°F (zone 9).

Jan	/	Recommended Varieties
Feb	/	
Mar	sow	*Gazania rigens:*
Apr	transplant	"Chansonette"
May	harden off/plant	"Chansonette Pink Shades"
Jun	flowering	"Daybreak Bright Orange"
July	flowering	"Daybreak Red Stripe"
Aug	flowering	"Harlequin Hybrids"
Sept	flowering	"Mini Star Mixed"
Oct	/	"Sundance Mixed"
Nov	/	"Talent"
Dec	/	

Site Needs well-drained soil that is not too rich or leafy growth is the result. Light sandy soils give the best results. If growing in courtyard containers, choose clay pots or troughs and use a soil-based compost with extra sharp grit mixed in to ensure good drainage at all times.

GROWING METHOD

Sowing Seed is sown in March at 68°F in a heated propagator, in 3½in pots. Just cover the seeds and keep in a light place. Seedlings appear in 1–2 weeks and can be transplanted into cell trays, when large enough. Grow on in a greenhouse or conservatory, then harden off and plant in late May, spacing plants 12in apart. In mixed containers, make sure they are not shaded out by other plants growing nearby.

Feeding Only water gazanias when the soil or compost is dry, and stand courtyard pots undercover during prolonged spells of summer rain.

Problems No real problems, but slugs may attack leaves in wet weather, so protect with slug pellets.

FLOWERING

Season The flowering period lasts throughout summer if dead flowers and their stalks are removed.

Cutting Flowers are not suitable for cutting.

AFTER FLOWERING

General Favorite plants can be lifted, potted up, and kept dry in a frost-free greenhouse over winter. Cuttings can be taken in the spring and new plants grown on for planting out.

GODETIA
Godetia

FOR A RAINBOW of summer color, sow a mixed variety of godetia that includes shades of rose, pink, and white flowers.

AT ITS PEAK, godetia is smothered in masses of bright flowers with large petals that have a texture similar to crepe paper.

FEATURES

Godetia is available in a wide range of varieties and many colors. This hardy annual can be spring- or fall-sown, the latter giving earlier flowers on bigger plants. Size ranges from 8 to 36in; the taller varieties are ideal for cutting. Don't labor over godetia—the best flowers are produced on slightly hungry, dry soils.

GODETIA AT A GLANCE

Grown for its bright single or double flowers, this hardy annual can be spring- or fall-sown. Frost hardy to 5°F (zone 7).

		Recommended Varieties
Jan	/	
Feb	/	*Godetia hybrids:*
Mar	sow	**Tall varieties**
Apr	sow	"Duke of York"
May	thin out	"Grace Mixed"
Jun	flowering	"Schamini Carmine"
July	flowering	"Sybil Sherwood"
Aug	flowering	**Dwarf varieties**
Sept	flowers/sow	"Charivari"
Oct	/	"Lilac Pixie"
Nov	/	"Precious Gems"
Dec	/	"Salmon Princess"

CONDITIONS

Aspect	Needs an open position in full sunlight.
Site	Needs perfect drainage, but not rich soil.

GROWING METHOD

Sowing	Sow where plants are to grow, just covering the seeds in shallow drills 6in apart during March/April, or during September. Thin out seedlings until they are 6–12in apart, depending on the variety. Do not thin fall-sown plants until the following spring, to allow for winter losses.
Feeding	Not needed, or excessive leafy growth results.
Problems	Overwatering quickly causes root rot, followed by collapse and death of plants.

FLOWERING

Season	Flowers appear from May onward on plants sown the previous fall. Spring-sown plants start flowering from June.
Cutting	An excellent cut flower, especially if the taller varieties such as "Schamini Carmine" and "Grace Mixed" are grown in rows.

AFTER FLOWERING

General	Remove plants when flowering is over. A few can be left to self-seed onto the soil.

GOMPHRENA
Globe amaranth

"STRAWBERRY FIELDS" is a large-growing variety of gomphrena with red flowers 2in across, on stems 30in tall.

GLOBE AMARANTH makes a good edging for paths—choose one of the lower-growing varieties such as "Gemini Mixed" at 2ft.

FEATURES

Also commonly known as bachelor's buttons, gomphrena is a half-hardy annual growing 12–30in tall, depending on the variety. Its rounded heads of purple, pink, white, red, and mauve flowers are used in bedding displays and for cutting and drying. "Strawberry Fields" has bright red flowers.

GOMPHRENA AT A GLANCE

A half-hardy annual grown for its clover-like flowerheads, used in bedding and for cutting. Frost hardy to 32°F (zone 10).

Jan	/	Recommended Varieties
Feb	/	
Mar	sow	**Gomphrena globosa:**
Apr	transplant	"Buddy"
May	harden off/plant	"Full Series"
Jun	flowering	"Gemini Mixed"
July	flowering	"Globe Amaranth"
Aug	flowering	"Qis Mixed"
Sept	flowering	
Oct	/	**Gomphrena hybrid:**
Nov	/	"Strawberry Fields"
Dec	/	

CONDITIONS

Aspect	Must have a sunny spot.
Site	Needs well-drained soil enriched with rotted manure or compost.

GROWING METHOD

Sowing	Sow in March in 3½in pots of multipurpose compost, just covering the seeds (soaking for a few days before helps germination). Keep at 64°F in a warm, dark place such as an airing cupboard and check regularly—seedlings appear in approximately two weeks. Transplant into cell trays, grow on under cover, harden off in late May, and plant out after frosts, 10–12in apart.
Feeding	Give an all-purpose liquid feed monthly.
Problems	No special problems affect gomphrena.

FLOWERING

Season	Flowers appear from midsummer to fall.
Cutting	Used fresh as a cut flower, but can also be dried in late summer by hanging upside-down in a warm, dry, airy place.

AFTER FLOWERING

General	Pull up in the fall and use for composting.

GYPSOPHILA
Baby's breath

CLOUDS OF SMALL FLOWERS are produced on annual gypsophila all summer if a few seeds are sown at two-week intervals from April until early June. For cut flowers, grow plants in a spare corner because they look bare once you begin to regularly remove stems.

FEATURES

Hardy annual varieties of *Gypsophila elegans* grow up to 2ft tall and wide, with many-divided stems bearing small, dainty pink, white, or rose flowers. It is widely used in flower arranging and as a "foil" for other plants in summer bedding schemes. The dwarf-growing *Gypsophila muralis* "Garden Bride," at 6in, is ideal for baskets and containers.

CONDITIONS

Aspect Grow gypsophila in full sunlight.
Site Rotted compost or manure should be dug in

before planting, for strong plants and better flowers, but the soil must also be well-drained. Varieties grown in baskets and containers will succeed in any multipurpose compost.

GROWING METHOD

Sowing Seeds can go directly into the ground, where plants will grow and flower. Sow in short drills ½in deep in April, then thin to finally leave plants 4–6in apart to give each other support and allow room to grow. September sowing produces stronger plants with earlier flowers the following spring—do not thin out until after winter.

Feeding Feeding is not generally necessary if the soil has been well prepared beforehand. In dry spells, give the soil a thorough soaking, and do not let containers dry out.

Problems Gypsophila is trouble-free, but young plants are prone to rotting off in heavy soils.

FLOWERING

Season Flowers appear from June onward on spring-sown plants, several weeks earlier on those sown the previous fall.

Cutting Excellent when cut and an ideal "filler" to marry together other flowers in a wide range of floral arrangements.

AFTER FLOWERING

General Pull up plants and use for composting.

GYPSOPHILA AT A GLANCE

Gypsophila is a hardy annual grown for tall, much-branching stems of flowers, for beds/cutting. Frost hardy to 5°F (zone 7).

		Recommended Varieties
Jan	/	
Feb	/	
Mar	/	**Gypsophila elegans:**
Apr	sow	"Bright Rose"
May	thin out	"Color Blend"
Jun	flowering	"Covent Garden"
July	flowering	"Kermesina"
Aug	flowering	"Monarch White"
Sept	flowers/sow	"Rosea"
Oct	/	"Snow Fountain"
Nov	/	"White Elephant"
Dec	/	**Gypsophila muralis:**
		"Garden Bride"

HELIANTHUS
Sunflower

SUNFLOWERS have a central "disc" which eventually becomes the fat seedhead in fall and makes useful food for the birds.

"PACINO" is a modern variety of Helianthus annuus, small enough to be used in patio pots, growing to only 18in tall.

FEATURES

Sunflowers range in height from 18in up to 15ft depending on the variety grown. They can be used in bedding, in patio containers, as cut flowers, or can be grown as traditional "giants" to several feet tall. Plants produce single or multi-flowered heads and the color range is enormous. "Teddy Bear" has furry, double flowers. Annual sunflowers are fully hardy and flower from mid-summer onward. Certain varieties such as "Prado Sun & Fire" have been bred to be pollen-free and these are ideal for use as indoor cut flowers. Seedheads left in the yard in the fall provide food for birds.

CONDITIONS

Aspect   Must have an open position in full sun.

HELIANTHUS AT A GLANCE

A hardy annual grown for its large flowers on both dwarf and tall plants; some are ideal for cutting. Frost hardy to 5°F (zone 7).

		Recommended Varieties
Jan	/	
Feb	/	*Helianthus annuus:*
Mar	sow	**Tall varieties**
Apr	thin out	"Italian White"
		"Pastiche"
May	support	"Velvet Queen"
Jun	flowering	**For containers**
July	flowering	"Big Smile"
Aug	flowering	"Pacino"
Sept	flowering	**Double flowers**
Oct	/	"Orange Sun"
Nov	/	"Sungold Double"
Dec	/	"Teddy Bear"

Site   Tolerates most soil conditions but soil enriched with plenty of manure or compost makes growth both rapid and vigorous, producing the largest flowerheads. Plants grown in groups in borders tend to support each other, but in exposed spots tie tall varieties to a cane. Use multipurpose compost mixed with slow-release fertilizer for planting up patio containers and windowboxes.

GROWING METHOD

Sowing   Seeds are large and easy to handle—sow three seeds outdoors where plants are to grow in March, removing all but the strongest when 6in tall. Can also be sown three seeds to a 3½in pot of compost and treated in the same way. Pot-grown plants can be kept outdoors and planted when the roots fill the pot. Spacing depends on the variety grown.

Feeding   Extra feeding is not usually needed but keep plants well watered in long dry spells.

Problems   Slugs and snails can attack young plants cutting them off at ground level, so protect with slug pellets or a barrier of sharp grit.

FLOWERING

Season   Throughout summer and early fall.

Cutting   A very good cut flower but use a heavy vase or add some weight to the bottom of it to prevent it toppling over. Pollen-free varieties should be grown if allergies are a known problem.

AFTER FLOWERING

General   Leave the seedheads as bird food during fall and winter, and then dig out the extensive roots. Sunflower roots can help break-up and loosen heavy, compacted soils.

HELICHRYSUM
Strawflower

FOR DRYING cut helichrysum before the flowers reach this stage, while the petals are still curved inward (bottom right).

PAPER DAISIES ARE APT to be rather leggy, but the range of flower colors can be stunning, as shown here.

FEATURES

Varieties of strawflower come from *Helichrysum bracteatum*, with plants growing 6–24in tall. They are among the easiest annuals to grow for dried flowers, with double blooms in many colors, and petals that feel straw-like. Dwarf varieties make long-lasting container plants. A half-hardy annual.

CONDITIONS

Aspect   Must have a warm spot in full sun.

HELICHRYSUM AT A GLANCE

A half-hardy annual grown for its long-lasting dried flowers, and also used in bedding and containers. Frost hardy to 32°F (zone10).

Month	Activity	Recommended Varieties
Jan	/	
Feb	/	*Helichrysum bracteatum:*
Mar	sow	**Tall varieties**
Apr	transplant/grow	"Drakkar Pastel Mixed"
May	harden off/plant	"Monstrosum Double Mixed"
Jun	flowering	"Pastel Mixed"
July	flowering	"Swiss Giants"
Aug	flowering	**Dwarf varieties**
Sept	flowers/cutting	"Bright Bikini"
Oct	flowers/cutting	"Chico Mixed"
Nov	/	"Hot Bikini"
Dec	/	

Site   Needs very well-drained soil that has been enriched with rotted compost or manure. If growing in containers use multipurpose compost and add slow-release fertilizer. Tall varieties will need staking as they develop.

GROWING METHOD

Sowing   Sow seeds in March in 3½in pots of multipurpose compost and germinate at 64°F. Transplant seedlings to cell trays when large enough and grow on, then harden off at the end of May, and plant 6–24in apart depending on the variety. Seed can also be sown direct into short drills in the soil during May and the young plants gradually thinned to the planting distances above. In containers pack 2–3 plants together in groups to get a good block of flower color.

Feeding   Helichrysum grows well without extra feeding, but water container-grown plants regularly.

Problems   By late summer the leaves are often attacked by mildew, but it is not worth treating.

FLOWERING

Season   Flowers appear from early to midsummer.

Cutting   Pick the flowers when the petals are still incurved. Hang the bunches upside down in a dry, airy place to dry out. Long-lasting.

AFTER FLOWERING

General   Cut what you want and then pull up.

HELIPTERUM
Everlasting daisy

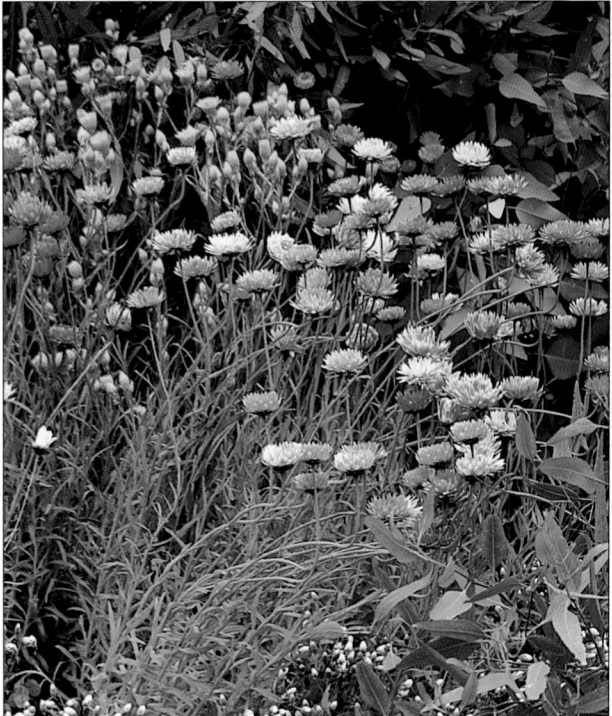

WHEN PLANTS REACH this stage of growth the entire plant can be harvested and hung up to dry. Individual stems are then cut off.

THINNING PLANTS to 6–12in apart helps them support each other. The flowers have a distinct rustle in a breeze.

FEATURES

The papery flowers of everlasting daisies come mainly in pinks and white. They grow 12–18in tall, and can be used in bedding or cut for dried flower arrangements. In catalogs they are also found listed under acrolinium and rhodanthe. Hardy annual.

CONDITIONS

Aspect   These Australian natives need full sun.
Site   Helipterum must have perfectly drained soil

HELIPTERUM AT A GLANCE

A half-hardy annual grown for its pinkish, "papery" flowers that are good for cutting and drying. Frost hardy to 32°F (zone 10).

Jan	/	Recommended Varieties
Feb	/	
Mar	/	**Helipterum hybrids:**
Apr	sow	"Bonny"
May	sow/thin	"Double Mixed"
Jun	flowering	"Goliath"
July	flowering	"Pierrot"
Aug	flowers/cutting	"Special Mixed"
Sept	flowers/cutting	
Oct	/	
Nov	/	
Dec	/	

and does not require special preparation—the best results are obtained on thin and hungry soils that mimic the plant's natural growing conditions. Sheltered hot-spots are best.

GROWING METHOD

Sowing   Sow seeds direct into the soil in short drills ½in deep and 6in apart in April and May. Thin the seedlings as they grow, so plants are eventually 6–12in apart by early summer. Water only during long dry spells, but this is not necessary when flower buds begin to appear.
Feeding   Do not feed.
Problems   Plants fail on heavy, wet soils that are slow to warm up in spring, so try growing them in raised beds which have better drainage.

FLOWERING

Season   Although the plants flower for only a brief spell the effect is long-lasting because of their "everlasting" nature.
Cutting   Ideal as cut, dried flower. For the best results cut off whole plants when most of the flowers are still just opening out, and hang upside down in a dry, airy place.

AFTER FLOWERING

General   Plants sometimes self-seed. Any plants not lifted for drying are pulled up in fall and added to the compost heap.

IBERIS
Candytuft

CANDYTUFT is available in a wide range of colorful mixtures. Each 2in-wide "flower" is actually a mass of smaller flowers.

ALL SORTS OF COLORS appear in varieties of Iberis umbellata, *including white as seen here. The flowers have a sweet fragrance.*

FEATURES

Very decorative plants that grow no more than 12in tall, varieties of *Iberis umbellata,* a hardy annual, have sweet-scented flowers in white, pink, mauve, red, and purple. They produce good results even in poor soils and quickly self-seed so you get new plants springing up every year, which are at home growing in-between paving and in gravel drives. The best plants with the most flowers come from sowing in early spring.

CONDITIONS

Aspect
Site   Iberis prefers an open spot in full sun. Although it is happy in poor soil, adding rotted manure or compost before planting will help keep moisture in and reduce the need for extra watering during summer.

IBERIS AT A GLANCE

Iberis is a hardy annual grown for its heads of bright, scented flowers which are used in bedding. Frost hardy to 5°F (zone 7).

Jan	/	Recommended Varieties
Feb	/	
Mar	sow 🖎	**Iberis umbellata:**
Apr	sow 🖎	"Dwarf Fairy Mixed"
May	thin out 🖎	"Fantasia Mixed"
Jun	flowering 🌼	"Flash Mixed"
July	flowering 🌼	"Spangles"
Aug	flowering 🌼	
Sept	sow 🖎	
Oct	/	
Nov	/	
Dec	/	

GROWING METHOD

Sowing   Seed is sown outdoors in March/April where the plants are to flower. Mark out circular patches of ground with sand and make short parallel drills ½in deep inside the circle, spaced 6in apart. Sow the seeds thinly in these drills and cover with fine, raked soil. Seedlings appear in 2–3 weeks and should be thinned out so they are eventually 3–6in apart by early summer. Can also be sown in September for earlier flowers.

Feeding   Extra feeding is not necessary. Watering in early summer will stop plants flowering prematurely before they achieve a good size.

Problems   Being relatives of brassicas like cabbage, they can suffer from clubroot disease. Treatment is not worthwhile, but to continue to enjoy candytuft where clubroot is present, sow a pinch of seed in 3½in pots of multi-purpose compost in early spring and plant out clumps in early summer. Disease-free roots will support the plants and let them flower.

FLOWERING

Season   Flowers will appear from early summer.
Cutting   Good cut flower. Flowers that are well-formed but not over-mature should last well if picked early in the day and immediately plunged into water to soak before arranging.

AFTER FLOWERING

General   Plants can be cut down after flowering, given a good soak with liquid feed, and they will usually produce a second "flush" of flowerheads several weeks later. Candytuft self-seeds very easily so leave a few plants to die away naturally and scatter their seeds. Seed can also be collected for sowing the following spring.

IMPATIENS

Busy lizzie

VIGOROUS AND LARGE-FLOWERED, "Accent Mixed" will carpet the ground in borders or fill containers in sun or shade.

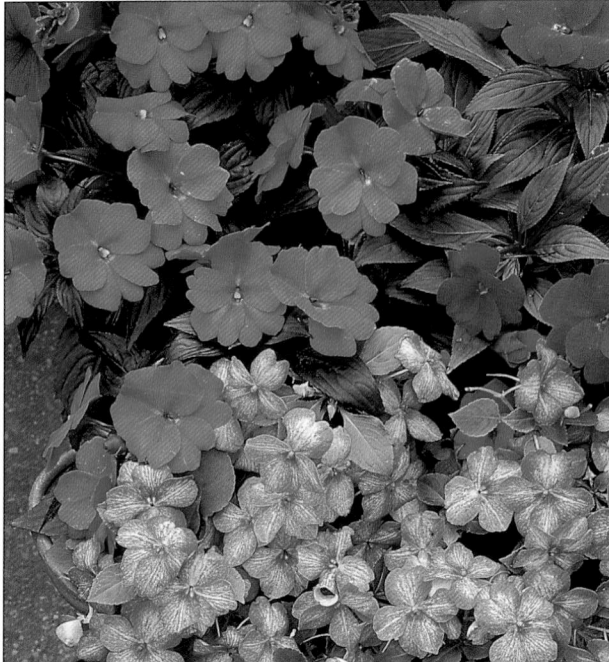

NEW GUINEA busy lizzies can be successfully combined with smaller flowered varieties like this delightful "Mosaic Lilac."

FEATURES

Impatiens perform well in sun or shade and a huge range is available. Use in bedding, tubs, windowboxes, hanging baskets, and flower bags. As well as busy lizzies, there are also the larger "New Guinea" types (12in), and the "balsams," with bushy growth (10in). Busy lizzies grow from 6–12in tall and wide depending on variety. All impatiens are half-hardy annuals, and raising from seed requires some care. Widely available as young plants by mail order, they can also be bought ready-grown in spring. Flowers can be single or double in mixed or various colors.

IMPATIENS AT A GLANCE

A half-hardy annual grown for its flowers for bedding, containers, and hanging planters. Frost hardy to 32°F (zone 10).

		Recommended Varieties
Jan	/	
Feb	sow	**Busy lizzies:**
Mar	sow	"Accent Mixed"
Apr	grow on	"Bruno"
May	harden/plant	"Mosaic Rose"
Jun	flowering	"Super Elfin Mixed"
July	flowering	**New Guinea impatiens:**
Aug	flowering	"Firelake Mixed"
Sept	flowering	"Spectra"
Oct	flowering	"Tango"
Nov	/	**Impatiens balsamifera:**
Dec	/	"Tom Thumb Mixed"

CONDITIONS

Aspect   Will succeed in full sun or moderate shade.

Site   Soil should have rotted manure or compost mixed in before planting, and should be well-drained. Avoid planting in windy spots. In containers and baskets use multipurpose compost with slow-release fertilizer added.

GROWING METHOD

Sowing   In late February/March sow seeds onto a fine layer of vermiculite in 3½in pots of seed compost. Tap to settle but do not cover. Seal in a clear plastic bag or put in a heated propagator, in a bright place at 70–75°F. Seedlings appear in 2–3 weeks and are transplanted to cell trays when 1in tall. Grow on, then harden off and plant out after frosts, 6–12in apart.

Feeding   Apply liquid feed weekly to beds or containers using a hand-held feeder.

Problems   Damping off disease attacks seedlings. Use clean pots, fresh compost, and treat with a copper-based fungicide if seedlings collapse.

FLOWERING

Season   Flowers appear on young plants before planting and then throughout summer. Take off dead flowers to keep new ones coming.

Cutting   Not suitable as a cut flower.

AFTER FLOWERING

General   Remove when plants are past their best.

IPOMOEA
Morning glory

"HEAVENLY BLUE" morning glory never looks better than when scrambling through a host plant like this apple.

FEATURES

Look under ipomoea or morning glory in seed catalogs to find varieties of this stunning climber. Most familiar is sky-blue flowered "Heavenly Blue," others are red, pink, white, mauve, chocolate, one is striped, and "Murasaki Jishi" is double-flowered. Average height is 10–12ft. Plants will climb fences and other plants. For patios grow 3–4 plants in a 12in pot up a wigwam of 5ft canes. A half-hardy annual with flowers mostly 3in across. Seeds are poisonous.

IPOMOEA AT A GLANCE

A half-hardy annual climber grown for its trumpet-shaped flowers that open in the morning. Frost hardy to 32°F (zone 10).

		Recommended Varieties
Jan	/	
Feb	/	Ipomoea hybrids:
Mar	/	"Cardinal"
Apr	sow	"Chocolate"
May	grow on	"Early Call Mixed"
Jun	plant	"Flying Saucers"
July	flowering	"Grandpa Otts"
Aug	flowering	"Heavenly Blue"
Sept	flowering	"Mini Sky-Blue"
Oct	/	"Murasaki Jishi"
Nov	/	"Platycodon Flowered
Dec	/	White"

CONDITIONS

Aspect Must have full sun all day.
Site Mix rotted compost with soil before planting. In containers use multipurpose compost with slow-release fertilizer added. All ipomoeas must have shelter from wind, and must have support for their twining stems.

GROWING METHOD

Sowing Soak the seeds in warm water the night before sowing, then sow one to a 3½in pot, 1in deep, in April. Keep in a temperature of at least 70°F and put in bright light when the big pink seedlings come up 1–2 weeks later. Keep warm and grow on, potting on into 5in pots when the roots fill the pot. Support shoots with short stakes. Gradually harden-off in late May, planting out or into containers in early June.
Feeding Feed monthly with a high-potash tomato food.
Problems Seedlings will turn yellow if they are kept too cold in the early stages. Red spider mite feeds on leaves—use a spray containing bifenthrin.

FLOWERING

Season Summer.
Cutting Unsuitable for cutting.

AFTER FLOWERING

General Use for composting when finished.

KOCHIA
Summer cypress

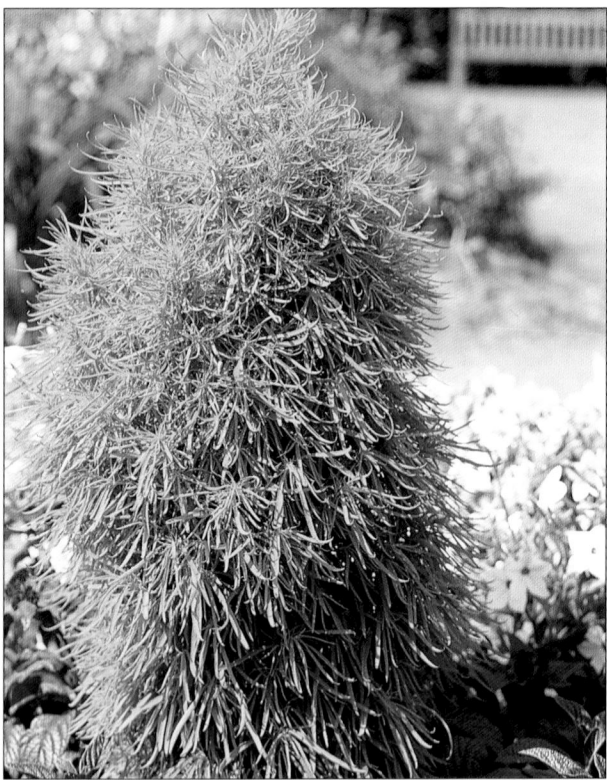

SUMMER CYPRESS is so-called because it resembles a dwarf conifer in color and shape. In early fall plants turn bright red.

KOCHIA MAKES a bold plant for the focus of a bedding display— seen here with pink nicotianas and silver-leaved senecio.

FEATURES

Summer cypress is a bushy half-hardy foliage annual that grows up to 3ft high with soft, light-green feathery foliage forming an upright cone- or dome-shape. "Trichophylla" has narrow leaves and looks similar to a dwarf conifer in summer, turning to a fiery bronze red in fall, hence its other common name of burning bush. Grow in groups of 2–3 or singly as the centerpiece of a bedding scheme.

KOCHIA AT A GLANCE

A half-hardy annual grown for its light-green leaves on bushy plants which turn red in fall. Frost hardy to 32°F (zone 10).

Jan	/	**Recommended Varieties**
Feb	sow 🌱	
Mar	sow 🌱	**Kochia scoparia:**
Apr	grow on 🌱	"Trichophylla"
May	harden off/plant 🌱	
Jun	leaves 🍃	**For all-green leaves**
July	leaves 🍃	"Evergreen"
Aug	leaves 🍃	
Sept	leaves 🍃	
Oct	leaves 🍃	
Nov	/	
Dec	/	

CONDITIONS

Aspect   Needs full sun to get the best leaf color.
Site   Grows on most soils but must be well-drained. Add manure/compost before planting.

GROWING METHOD

Sowing   Sow February/March on the surface of a 3½in pot of moist multipurpose compost but do not cover. Keep at 61°F in a bright spot, and expect seedlings in 2–3 weeks. When large enough, transplant to 3½in pots of multipurpose compost and grow on, hardening off in late May and planting outdoors after the last frosts. Space plants at least 2ft apart to allow room for development. They can also be planted in rows as a temporary and unusual summer "hedge."

Feeding   Water thoroughly in early summer for 2–3 weeks after planting. Extra feeding is not essential to get good results.

Problems   No particular problems.

FLOWERING

Season   Not grown for flowers but leaves.
Cutting   Unsuitable for cutting.

AFTER FLOWERING

General   Pull up and compost in fall.

LATHYRUS
Sweet pea

SWEET PEAS are perhaps the easiest and most rewarding of cut flowers you can grow. Choose a variety known for its fragrance.

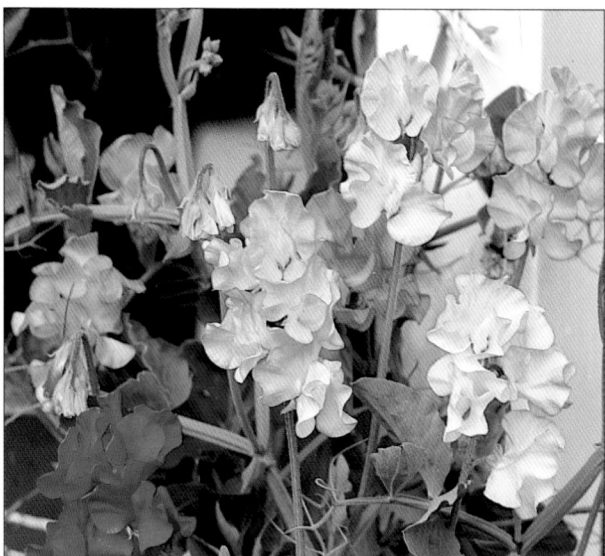

CLIMBING VARIETIES of Lathyrus odoratus make useful "living screens" in summer with the added benefits of color and scent.

FEATURES

Varieties of *Lathyrus odoratus*, or sweet pea, occupy several pages in seed catalogs, but there are two basic groups—the tall climbers reaching 6–8ft, used as cut flowers and for screening, and dwarf "patio" varieties reaching up to 3ft which are used in bedding, baskets, and containers. Not all sweet peas have good scent, so check before buying seeds, and choose a fragrant mixed variety for a range of flower colors, which can be white, pink, red, mauve, orange, or blue, as well as many with picotee and other patterns. Sweet peas are easily-grown hardy annuals.

CONDITIONS

Aspect   Grow in full sun.

LATHYRUS AT A GLANCE

A hardy annual climber producing often strongly-scented flowers which are ideal for cutting. Frost hardy to 5°F (zone 7).

Jan	/	Recommended Varieties
Feb	/	
Mar	sow 🌱	Lathyrus odoratus:
Apr	grow on 🌱	Tall, fragrant varieties
May	plant 🌱	"Bouquet Mixed"
Jun	flowering 🌸	"Great Expectations"
July	flowering 🌸	"Old Fashioned Mixed"
Aug	flowering 🌸	"Old Spice Mixed"
Sept	flowering 🌸	Dwarf/patio varieties
Oct	sow 🌱	"Explorer"
Nov	/	"Fantasia Mixed"
Dec	/	"Jet-Set Mixed"
		"Knee-High"

Site   Needs well-drained soil packed with organic matter. Add compost or rotted manure the fall before sowing or planting. Climbing varieties need canes, bean netting, fences, or other supports to grow through. Use multipurpose compost for planting up baskets and patio containers.

GROWING METHOD

Sowing   Seeds can be sown individually in 3½in pots in February/March and germinated in a coldframe, cold porch, or even outdoors in a spot sheltered from rain. Nick or file the tough seed coat until a pale "spot" appears, then sow 1in-deep in soil-based seed compost. Pinch out the growing tips when plants are 3in tall to encourage sideshoots to grow. Grow outside, then plant out in May, 12in apart for climbers, and 6–12in apart for patio varieties used in baskets and containers.

Feeding   Plants benefit from a monthly feed with liquid tomato food. Water thoroughly in dry spells.

Problems   Mice will dig young seedlings up so set traps. Powdery mildew can attack leaves in the summer—use a spray containing sulfur.

FLOWERING

Season   Seed can also be sown in October, and plants overwintered for flowers from early summer. Spring-sown plants flower from June.

Cutting   Cut when the first few flowers on the stalk are opening and stand up to their necks in water.

AFTER FLOWERING

General   Cut off at ground level in fall so the nitrogen-rich roots rot down in the soil.

LAVATERA
Annual mallow

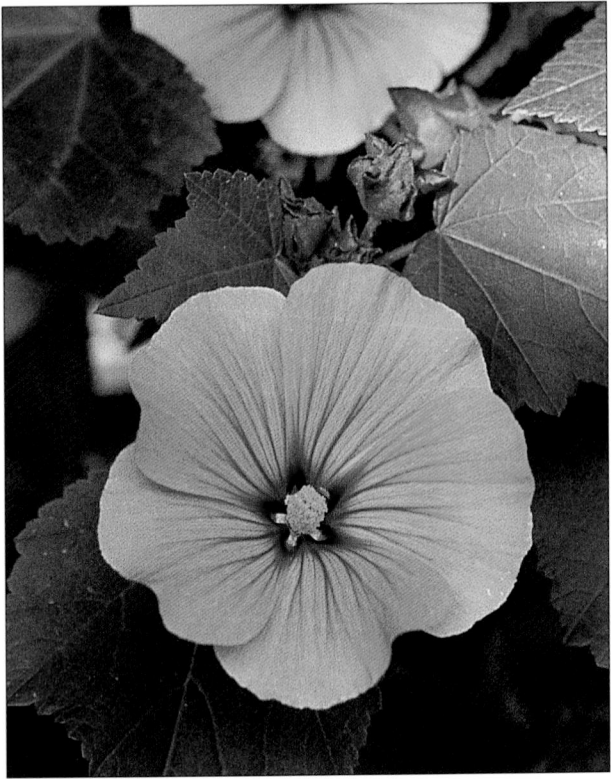

"SILVER CUP" is one of the most popular varieties of annual mallow, with rose-pink flowers up to 5in across.

IN MIXED BORDERS annual mallow can be sown direct into open patches of soil, for mounds of color from mid to late summer.

FEATURES

White, rose, pink, and red flowers with a silky sheen are characteristic of annual mallow. Plants grow between 2–4ft depending on variety, and bloom continuously from mid-June onward. Use them as the centerpiece in summer bedding schemes or grow in large blocks in annual borders. An easily-grown hardy annual that is also useful as a cut flower.

LAVATERA AT A GLANCE

A hardy annual grown for its large, colorful summer flowers on bushy plants 2–4ft tall. Frost hardy to 5°F (zone 7).

		Recommended Varieties
Jan	/	
Feb	/	**Lavatera trimestris:**
Mar	sow	"Beauty Mixed"
Apr	sow/thin out	"Dwarf White Cherub"
May	sow/thin out	"Loveliness"
Jun	flowering	"Mont Blanc"
July	flowering	"Mont Rose"
Aug	flowering	"Parade Mixed"
Sept	flowering	"Pink Beauty"
Oct	/	"Ruby Regis"
Nov	/	"Silver Cup"
Dec	/	

CONDITIONS

Aspect   Must have full sun all day.
Site   Lavatera needs good drainage but not rich soil —plants flower better if the ground is hungry, making them good plants for light sandy soils. They do well in seaside gardens.

GROWING METHOD

Sowing   Seed is sown outdoors March–May, and earlier sowings mean earlier flowers. Mark out circles 2ft or more across, then sow seed in short drills ½in deep. When seedlings appear thin them out gradually so they are 1–2ft apart by early summer. Growing this way creates a roughly circular block of color, which can be used as the centerpiece of a bedding scheme using annuals.

Feeding   Feeding is not necessary. Water thoroughly in early summer during long dry spells.

Problems   Sometimes killed suddenly by soil fungal diseases–grow in a new spot the next season.

FLOWERING

Season   Summer.
Cutting   Grow a few plants just for cut stems.

AFTER FLOWERING

General   Leave a few plants to self-seed, then pull up.

LIMNANTHES
Poached egg flower

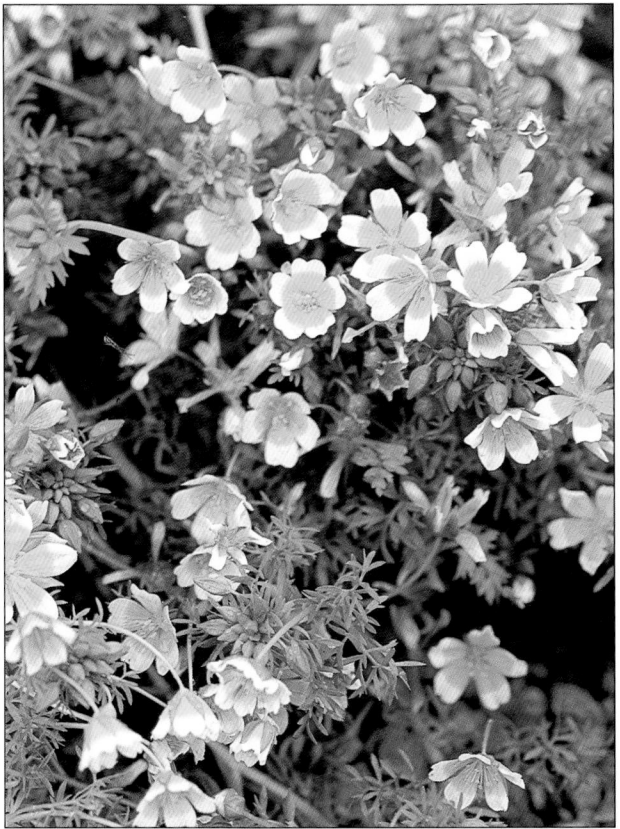

POACHED EGG FLOWER has 1in-wide flowers like tiny eggs in early summer, and attractive, divided, fern-like leaves.

THE SEEDS OF LIMNANTHES go everywhere after flowering and seem to enjoy spreading along path edges in particular.

FEATURES

Limnanthes douglasii has cup-shaped white flowers with bright yellow centers, which explains its common name of poached egg flower. Plants grow to 6–9in in height and have a spreading habit. A hardy annual, it self-seeds very easily and keeps on coming. Grow in annual beds, along path edges and among other plants in borders.

LIMNANTHES AT A GLANCE

A hardy annual that quickly self-seeds, producing masses of yellow/white flowers in summer. Frost hardy to 5°F (zone 7).

Jan	/	Recommended Varieties
Feb	/	
Mar	sow	*Limnanthes douglasii*
Apr	sow/thin	
May	sow/thin	
Jun	flowering	
July	flowering	
Aug	/	
Sept	sow	
Oct	/	
Nov	/	
Dec	/	

CONDITIONS

Aspect   Prefers full sun and an open situation.
Site   Needs moisture-retentive soil with rotted organic matter mixed in well ahead of sowing.

GROWING METHOD

Sowing   Spring or fall are the sowing times. Sow from March to May or in September. Either sow seed in short drills ½in deep or mark areas of soil, scatter the seed over the surface, and rake in. Seedlings appear after 1–2 weeks and should be thinned out so they are about 3–6in apart, although this is not too critical. If sowing in fall do not thin until spring in case of winter losses.
Feeding   Feeding is not necessary, but water thoroughly in dry spells during early summer.
Problems   No special problems.

FLOWERING

Season   Overwintered plants flower from late spring depending on the weather, and are very attractive to bees and beneficial garden insects.
Cutting   Not suitable for cutting.

AFTER FLOWERING

General   Pull plants up as soon as they are over.

LIMONIUM
Statice

LONG AFTER the small pale flowers have faded the colorful papery bracts are still going strong, and they keep their color when dried.

"PURPLE MONARCH" is a classic strain of statice for cutting and drying. It grows to 24in.

FEATURES

Annual varieties of *Limonium sinuatum* grow up to 3ft tall and have peculiar winged stems. The actual flowers are small, but statice is grown for its papery bracts of purple, white, pink, apricot, yellow, rose, or blue, which persist all summer, and can be used as a cut and dried flower. A half-hardy annual that is used solely for cutting, or in the case of the short varieties as a bedding/container plant.

CONDITIONS

Aspect   Grow in full sun in an open position.

LIMONIUM AT A GLANCE	
A half-hardy annual grown for its heads of brightly colored bracts used for bedding and drying. Frost hardy to 23°F (zone 9).	
Jan /	Recommended Varieties
Feb sow	
Mar sow/transplant	*Limonium sinuatum:*
Apr grow on	**Tall varieties**
May grow on/harden	"Art Shades Mixed"
Jun plant/grow	"Forever Mixed"
July flowering	"Forever Moonlight"
Aug flowers/cutting	"Sunburst Mixed"
Sept flowers/cutting	"Sunset Mixed"
Oct /	**Short varieties**
Nov /	"Biedermeier Mixed"
Dec /	"Petite Bouquet"

Site
Must have very well-drained soil, and is quite happy in sandy, light soils that are on the "hungry" side. If growing dwarf varieties for containers use multipurpose compost. Statice does exceedingly well in seaside gardens.

GROWING METHOD

Sowing   Sow seed in February/March in a 3½in pot of multipurpose compost and keep at 64°F. Transplant to cell trays, grow on, then harden off in late May and plant after the last frosts 6–18in apart. If growing for cut flowers, seed can be sown outdoors in rows from early May, ½in deep and thinned to similar spacings.

Feeding   Does not need regular feeding, but water well if dry straight after planting out.

Problems   Plants may rot on heavy, wet soils, and powdery mildew can attack the leaves in late summer, but this is rarely serious.

FLOWERING

Season   Long flowering period throughout summer.

Cutting   Ideal cut flower. Can be used fresh, or cut and dried by hanging bunches upside down in a dry airy place. Cut when the flowerheads are showing maximum color. Dried flowers retain their color well over a long period.

AFTER FLOWERING

General   Pull plants up and compost when all the flowers have been cut or have gone over.

LINARIA
Toadflax

WHEN SOWN IN BOLD PATCHES varieties of Linaria maroccana *soon knit together to produce a tapestry of color if one of the mixtures such as* "Fairy Bouquet" *is grown. Clumps can also be carefully lifted and planted into patio pots in late spring and early summer.*

FEATURES

Linaria is commonly known as toadflax and has dainty little flowers like tiny snapdragons in a wide color range including white, cream, yellow, red, blue, and pink. Plants grow 9–24in and are good massed in drifts in annual borders, or used as fillers in mixed border plantings. Most annual toadflax are varieties of *Linaria maroccana*. A hardy annual that can be sown direct outdoors.

LINARIA AT A GLANCE

A hardy annual grown for its spikes of pretty flowers like small snapdragons appearing in summer. Frost hardy to 5°F (zone 7).

Jan	/	Recommended Varieties
Feb	/	
Mar	sow 🖑	*Linaria anticaria*
Apr	sow/thin out 🖑	
May	sow/thin out 🖑	*Linaria maroccana:*
Jun	thin/flowers 🖑 🌸	"Fairy Bouquet"
July	flowering 🌸	"Fantasia Blue"
Aug	flowering 🌸	"Fantasia Mixed"
		"Fantasia Pink"
Sept	flowering 🌸	"Northern Lights"
Oct	/	
Nov	/	*Linaria reticulata:*
Dec	/	"Crown Jewels"

CONDITIONS

Aspect   Needs a warm, sunny spot.
Site   Well-drained soil enriched with manure or compost ahead of planting is essential. Very good plants can be grown on light, sandy soils.

GROWING METHOD

Sowing   Seeds are best sown in short drills ½in deep March–May. Mark the sowing areas with a ring of light-colored sand and label if sowing more than one annual in the same bed. The seedlings will appear in rows and can be told from nearby weed seedlings quite easily. Thin the seedlings out so they are finally 4–6in apart by early summer. Alternatively, leave them to grow as small clumps of 4–6 plants every 12in or so.
Feeding   Feeding is rarely needed but water well after the final thinning if the soil is dry.
Problems   No special problems.

FLOWERING

Season   Flowers appear early to mid summer.
Cutting   Not usually used for cutting.

AFTER FLOWERING

General   Leave a few plants to die down and self-seed. Others can be pulled up and composted.

LOBELIA
Lobelia

LOBELIA FLOWERS *are tubular with a large lower "lip" divided into three rounded lobes. Dark flowers have pale throats.*

IN THIS HANGING BASKET *lobelias mingle with begonias and brachyscome, and bright red nasturtiums creep up from below.*

FEATURES

Choose the bushier "edging" varieties for bedding schemes and the "trailers" for hanging baskets, flower bags, and containers. Flower color ranges from white through pink, mauve and white to blue, and striking two-toned varieties like "Riviera Blue Splash" are also available. Edgers grow 4–6in tall, trailers up to 18in long when well-fed, and plants have a similar spread. Varieties of *Lobelia erinus* are available as single or mixed colors, and modern coated seed makes sowing much easier. A range of varieties are available as young plants by mail order. Half-hardy.

LOBELIA AT A GLANCE

A half-hardy annual used as an edging plant or a trailing plant for baskets, with many small flowers. Frost hardy to 32ºF (zone 10).

Jan	sow	Recommended Varieties
Feb	sow/transplant	
Mar	sow/transplant	*Lobelia erinus:*
Apr	grow on	**Edging varieties**
May	harden off/plant	"Cambridge Blue"
Jun	flowering	"Crystal Palace"
July	flowering	"Mrs Clibran Improved"
Aug	flowering	"Riviera Lilac"
Sept	flowering	**Trailing varieties**
Oct	/	"Cascade Mixed"
Nov	/	"Fountains Mixed"
Dec	/	"Regatta Mixed"
		"String of Pearls Mixed"

CONDITIONS

Aspect   Flowers best when grown in full sun.

Site   Enrich soil with rotted compost or manure before planting. Drainage must be good, but lobelia must also have adequate moisture all through the season. For baskets and containers use multipurpose compost and add slow-release fertilizer granules before planting up.

GROWING METHOD

Sowing   Sow January–March in a 3½in pot of multipurpose compost. Sow the tiny seeds evenly over the surface but do not cover, and put in a well-lit spot at 64ºF. When the seedlings form a green "mat," carefully tease them apart into small clumps of 4–6, and transplant each clump to one unit of a multi-cell tray. Grow on, harden off in late May and plant after frosts.

Feeding   Feed fortnightly with high-potash liquid feed, and never allow the plants to dry out.

Problems   Trouble-free, but if seedlings keel over in spring water with copper-based fungicide.

FLOWERING

Season   Flowers appear from June onward.

Cutting   Not suitable for cutting.

AFTER FLOWERING

General   Go over plants with shears when they look untidy and water with liquid feed—this encourages more flowers. Compost in fall.

LOBULARIA
Alyssum

ALYSSUM IS COMPACT and this makes it the ideal edging plant to fill in between other summer bedders. Flowers smell of honey.

"CARPET OF SNOW" is used here in a bed to create living lines and patterns around slightly taller plants like these violas.

FEATURES

Lobularia maritima, alyssum, has masses of tiny flowers in various colors in round heads; white, pink, lavender, and purple. All varieties smell sweetly of honey, although you need to get up close. None grow more than 6in high, making alyssum ideal as an edging plant, but it is also useful for planting in pots, troughs, and hanging baskets.

CONDITIONS

Aspect   Grow alyssum in a spot receiving full sun.
Site   Must have well-drained soil and adding rotted

LOBULARIA AT A GLANCE

A low-growing hardy annual for edging summer bedding schemes, with honey-scented flowers. Frost hardy to 5°F (zone 7).

		Recommended Varieties
Jan	/	
Feb	sow	*Lobularia maritima :*
Mar	sow/transplant	"Aphrodite"
Apr	sow/grow on	"Creamery"
May	sow/harden off	"Easter Basket Mixed"
Jun	flowering	"Easter Bonnet"
July	flowering	"Golf Mixed"
Aug	flowering	"Golf Rose"
Sept	flowering	"Little Dorrit"
Oct	/	"Rosie O'Day"
Nov	/	"Snow Carpet"
Dec	/	"Snow Crystals"

organic matter helps retain soil moisture. For baskets and patio containers plant using multipurpose potting compost.

GROWING METHOD

Sowing   Alyssum grown for bedding and containers is best raised in early spring. Sow a whole packet of seeds in February/March in a 3½in pot of multipurpose compost, and just cover. When seedlings are ½in tall split up into small clumps of 4–6 seedlings and transplant each to individual units of a multi-cell tray. This is especially useful to get a good spread of different flower colors when growing a mixed variety. Grow on and harden off in late May before planting out. Seeds can also be sown direct into the soil in an annual border during April/May ½in deep.
Feeding   Extra feeding is unnecessary.
Problems   Look out for slugs—they will attack newly-planted alyssum, especially after rain.

FLOWERING

Season   Flowers often appear before planting and until late summer—clip them over with shears and water well to encourage a second flush.
Cutting   Not suitable as a cut flower.

AFTER FLOWERING

General   Seeds will self-sow very easily, and come up the following spring. Compost when finished.

LUNARIA
Honesty

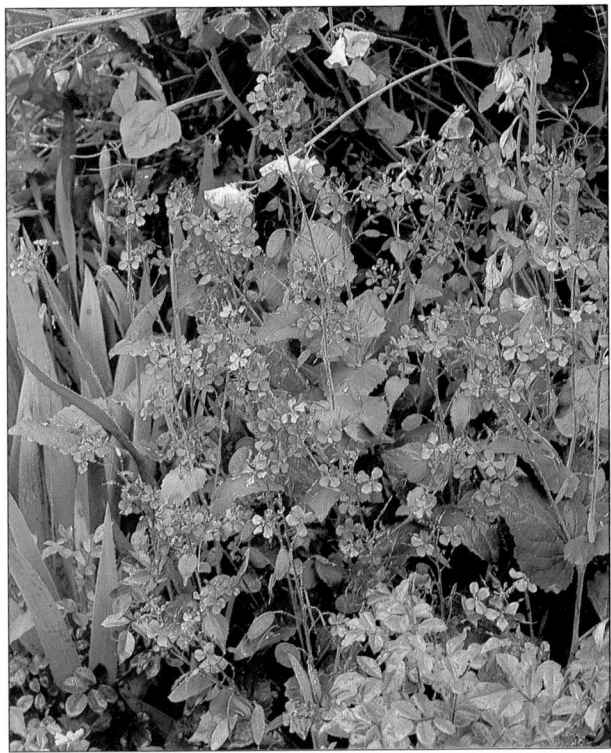

THE SEEDHEADS *of* Lunaria annua *are sought after for dried flower arrangements. Here they are still in the green stages of growth.*

"ALBA VARIEGATA" has leaves splashed with creamy-white and also white flowers. It adds easy and quick color to spring borders.

FEATURES

Honesty, *Lunaria annua*, a hardy biennial is also known as the money plant because of its large circular, smooth, silvery seedheads that resemble coins. It grows up to 3ft tall and is a plant that is best left to do its own thing, self-seeding very quickly, and thriving under dry hedges where most plants will not grow, and will seed into mixed borders. Flowers are purple or white and appear in early spring, and variegated varieties are available.

LUNARIA AT A GLANCE

A hardy biennial grown for its pretty purple/white flowers followed by large silvery seedheads. Frost hardy to 5°F (zone 7).

Jan	/	Recommended Varieties
Feb	/	
Mar	sow/flowers	*Lunaria annua:*
Apr	thin/flowers	"Fine Mixed"
May	thin/flowers	"Mixed"
Jun	flowering	
July	/	**Variegated leaves**
Aug	/	"Variegata"
Sept	/	
Oct	/	**White flowers**
Nov	/	"Alba Variegata"
Dec	/	

CONDITIONS

Aspect Succeeds in sun or the shade cast by hedges and large shrubs.
Site Thriving in poor soils, plants grow larger still if they are sown into soil that has been improved with rotted manure or compost, and produce the best seedheads for drying.

GROWING METHOD

Sowing Mark out patches using sand and sow the large seeds 1in deep in short drills, with 2–3in between each seed in March. Seedlings are quick to appear and can be thinned or left to develop as they are. Next spring look out for seedlings and move them when small to where you want plants to grow.
Feeding Needs no extra feeding or watering.

FLOWERING

Season Flowers from early spring to early summer.
Cutting Can be cut for flowers but some must be left to set seed if you want the large, silvery heads.

AFTER FLOWERING

General Cut when the seedheads are mature and dry, on a warm day, and hang upside-down in a dry, airy place until you can carefully remove the outer skin of the pod. Leave a few plants to die down naturally and self-seed.

LUPINUS
Annual lupin

SHORTER AND SQUATTER than their perennial cousins, annual lupins can create a sea of color when sown in large drifts like this. As the flowers fade the spikes should be removed completely with pruning shears to divert energy into new flowers rather than seed pods.

FEATURES

By growing annual lupins from seed you can enjoy the features of their perennial relatives without giving up too much space in the yard. Annual lupins are smaller, growing between 1–3ft tall, but have very colorful spikes in mixed shades and also striking single colors such as the blue-flowered *Lupinus texensis*. Hardy annuals. Seeds and plants are poisonous if eaten.

LUPINUS AT A GLANCE

A hardy annual grown for its spikes of colorful and spicey-scented flowers during summer. Frost hardy to 5°F (zone 7).

Jan	/	**Recommended Varieties**
Feb	/	
Mar	/	**Lupinus hybrids:**
Apr	sow 🌱	"Biancaneve"
May	thin out 🌱	"New White"
Jun	flowering 🌸	"Pink Javelin"
July	flowering 🌸	"Pixie Delight"
Aug	flowering 🌸	"Sunrise"
Sept	flowering 🌸	**Yellow flowers**
Oct	/	*Lupinus luteus*
Nov	/	**Blue flowers**
Dec	/	*Lupinus texensis*
		Lupinus varius

CONDITIONS

Aspect   Needs full sun.
Site   Well-drained, light soil is best for annual lupins, but mix in rotted manure or compost.

GROWING METHOD

Sowing   The large seeds can go straight into the ground in April, but to ensure germination the tough seed coat must be nicked with a sharp knife or rubbed down with a file until the pale inside just shows. Next, soak the seeds on wet tissue paper and sow when they have swollen up, 3–6in apart and 2in deep, where you want plants to grow. Thin seedlings to 6in apart when well established. To grow in pots do the same, sowing one seed to a 3½in pot, then plant out.

Feeding   Lupins need no extra feeding.
Problems   Fat green lupin aphids can kill entire plants, so use a spray containing permethrin.

FLOWERING

Season   Flowers appear from midsummer.
Cutting   Cut when some buds at the base of the flower spike are fully open.

AFTER FLOWERING

General   Cut off to leave the nitrogen-rich roots to rot in the ground, and compost the tops.

MALCOLMIA
Virginian stock

PINK IS JUST *one of the colors found in Virginian stocks. Expect reds, yellows, and whites from a variety like "Fine Mixed."*

JUST FOUR WEEKS *after sowing plants will be in flower.* Malcolmia maritima *thrives in the thin light soils of seaside gardens.*

FEATURES

Keep a packet of Virginian stock, *Malcolmia maritima* seed to hand at all times and sow a pinch of seeds every two weeks in gaps and under windows—plants will flower just a month later. They grow 6–8in high with small, single, four-petalled, sweetly scented flowers in red, mauve, pink, yellow, and white from June–September. They can also be sown into patio tubs. Hardy annual.

MALCOLMIA AT A GLANCE

Hardy annual grown for its pink, red, yellow, or white flowers. Flowers a month after sowing. Frost hardy to 5°F (zone 7).

Jan	/	Recommended Varieties
Feb	/	*Malcolmia maritima:*
Mar	sow 🖐	"Fine Mixed"
Apr	sow/flowers 🖐 🐾	"Mixed"
May	sow/flowers 🖐 🐾	
Jun	sow/flowers 🖐 🐾	
July	sow/flowers 🖐 🐾	
Aug	sow/flowers 🖐 🐾	
Sept	sow/flowers 🖐 🐾	
Oct	sow 🖐	
Nov	/	
Dec	/	

CONDITIONS

Aspect — Prefers full sun but tolerates some shade.
Site — Will grow on most soils but needs good drainage to do well.

GROWING METHOD

Sowing — Seed can be scattered in small patches 12in across on the soil where you want flowers, and mixed in using your fingertips, or it is simply scattered along the cracks in paths and driveways, from March onward, and repeated every few weeks all through the summer. Mark sown areas in borders with a label or circle of light-colored sand. Seedlings soon come up and there is no need to bother with thinning. For early flowers the following spring sow in October.

Feeding — Not necessary.
Problems — Trouble-free.

FLOWERING

Season — Expect flowers all summer long with repeat sowings.
Cutting — Unsuitable as a cut flower.

AFTER FLOWERING

General — Pull up as soon as the plants are over, and resow. Self-sown seedlings soon appear.

MATTHIOLA
Brompton stock

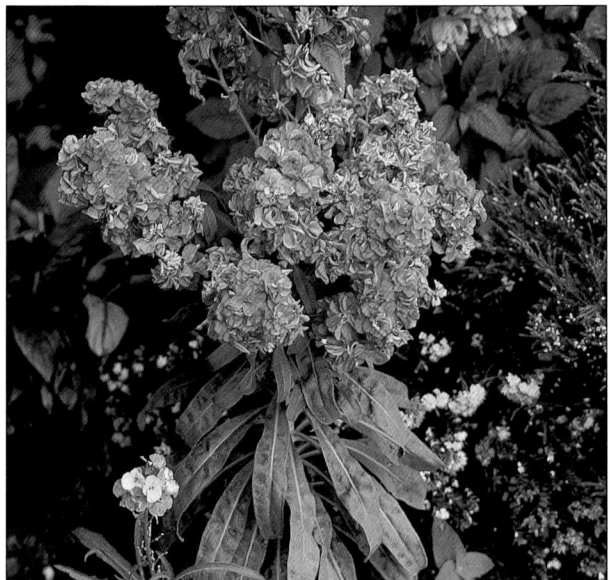

WHEN BEDDED-OUT in spring Brompton stocks provide an early splash of color and fill the air with scent on warm days.

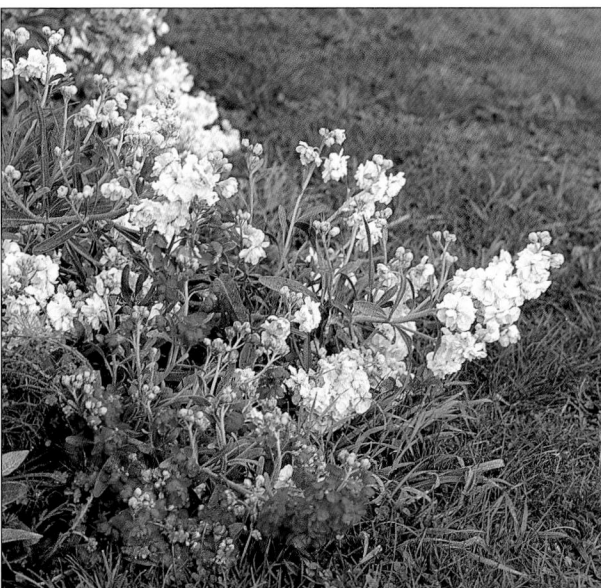

FLOWER COLOR varies, and it should be possible to see the color in the flower buds before you plant, ensuring an even display.

FEATURES

The sweetly scented flowers of Brompton stocks are held above the gray-green leaves on plants up to 18in tall. There is a full range of pastel colors with some stronger purples, crimson and magenta as well; the flowers are double. Derived from *Matthiola incana*, Brompton stocks are beautiful in massed spring plantings, giving off a delicious strong fragrance. They are grown as biennials.

CONDITIONS

Aspect   Need full sun and a sheltered position.

Site   Must have well-drained soil. Incorporate rotted manure or compost into the soil a few weeks before planting. Tall varieties will need short stakes to prevent their flowers flopping.

MATTHIOLA AT A GLANCE

A hardy biennial sown in summer for strongly-scented pink flowers the following spring. Frost hardy to 5°F (zone 7).

Jan	grow on 🖙	Recommended Varieties
Feb	plant 🖙	*Matthiola incana:*
Mar	plant 🖙	"Brompton Mixed"
Apr	flowering ❀	"Brompton Dwarf Mixed"
May	flowering ❀	"Spring Flowering Mixed"
Jun	sow 🖙	
July	sow/transplant 🖙	
Aug	transplant 🖙	
Sept	grow on 🖙	
Oct	grow on 🖙	
Nov	grow on 🖙	
Dec	grow on 🖙	

GROWING METHOD

Sowing   June/July is the time to sow seed, in a 3½in pot of multipurpose compost. When the seedlings are large enough, transplant one seedling to a 3½in pot of multipurpose compost, water well and grow on. Later, pot on into 5in pots. When the first frosts arrive take the young plants into a coldframe, cold greenhouse or porch, standing them outside during mild spells all through the winter months. Keep on the dry side and only water when they wilt. Plant out from February onward when the soil is workable, or pot on into large pots and grow in a cool conservatory or porch with canes for support.

Feeding   Do not feed until 2–3 weeks before planting out, then give a general purpose liquid feed.

Problems   Cabbage butterflies will lay eggs on the young plants in late summer and the caterpillars can strip leaves, so use a spray containing permethrin, or pick them off by hand.

FLOWERING

Season   Brompton stocks will fill beds and borders with color and scent during April and May, weather permitting. They perform best in calm, mild spells with plenty of sunshine. While most plants will have double flowers, there may be singles that can be put to one side, planted separately, and used for cutting.

Cutting   A good cut flower. Scald stems after picking and change vase water every couple of days.

AFTER FLOWERING

General   Dig plants up when the show is over and prepare the ground for summer bedding plants. Add to the compost heap/bin.

MIMULUS
Monkey flower

MONKEY FLOWERS have blooms that are face-like and marked with intricate patterns and spotting. They are good for shade.

PLANT MIMULUS along the edges of a path. Monkey flowers will bloom in just nine weeks.

FEATURES

Mimulus or monkey flower is grown as a half-hardy annual and is useful for summer bedding and containers, with bright flowers in a range of colors, mainly red and orange, on plants 12–18in tall and wide. It is very useful for growing in shaded and wet spots.

CONDITIONS

Aspect   Will grow in sun or shade.

MIMULUS AT A GLANCE	
Grown as a half-hardy annual for bedding, windowboxes, and hanging baskets. Colorful flowers. Frost hardy to 5°F (zone 7).	
Jan /	Recommended Varieties
Feb sow	**Mimulus hybrids:**
Mar sow/transplant	"Calypso"
Apr grow on	"Extra Choice Mixed"
May grow on/harden	"Magic Ivory"
Jun flowering	"Magic Pastels Mixed"
July flowering	"Malibu"
Aug flowering	"Malibu Orange"
Sept flowering	"Malibu Sunshine"
Oct /	"Queen's Prize Mixed"
Nov /	"Sparkles"
Dec /	"Viva"

Site   Needs moist soil so dig in plenty of rotted organic matter well-ahead of planting. Use a peat- or coir-based multipurpose compost for growing mimulus in containers. Add slow-release fertilizer granules when planting.

GROWING METHOD

Sowing   Sow in 3½in pots in February/March, barely covering the fine seed. Keep at 54°F in bright light and expect seedlings after about two weeks. When large enough transplant to cell trays and grow on until the end of May, then harden off and plant from mid-May onward, 6–12in apart, or in groups of 2–3 in troughs and pots.

Feeding   Feed monthly with liquid feed and ensure that containers never dry out or flowering will be reduced and plants damaged.

Problems   If slugs attack plants growing in shaded areas protect with slug pellets or scatter sharp grit to make a physical barrier. Container-grown plants suffer in excessive heat so move them to a position where they are out of midday sun.

FLOWERING

Season   Summer, from June onward.
Cutting   Not suitable for cutting.

AFTER FLOWERING

General   Pull up and compost when finished.

MOLUCCELLA
Bells of Ireland

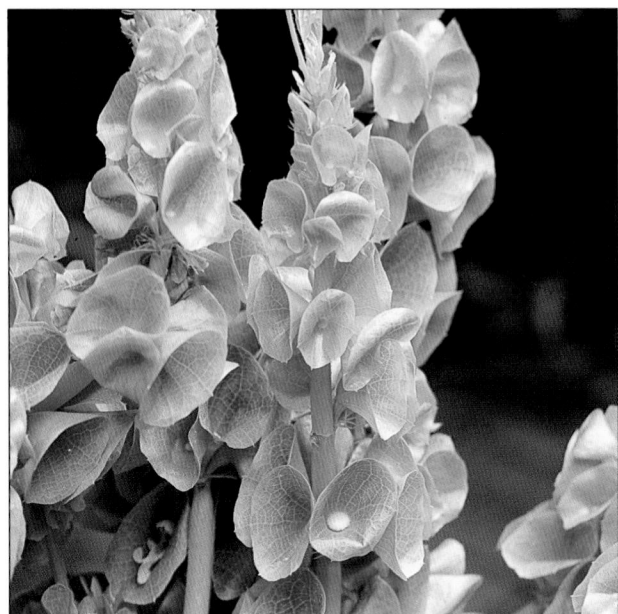

THE FLOWERS OF Moluccella laevis *are actually small, pale, and found in the center of each of the showier bell-like bracts.*

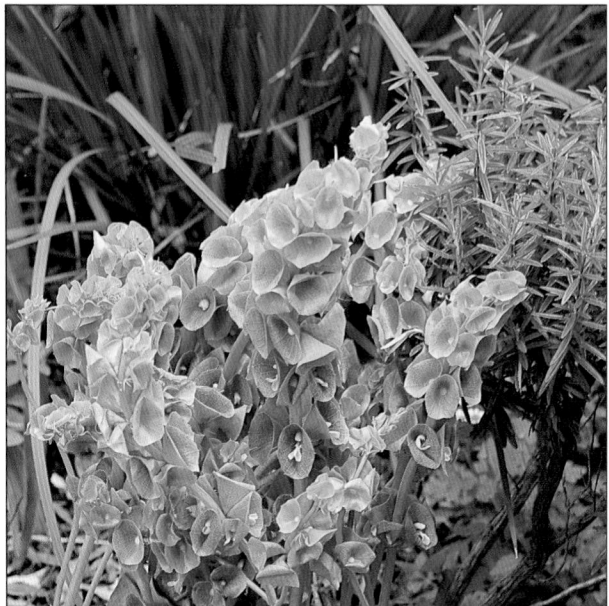

MOLUCCELLA *is ideal for use in mixed borders to add a welcome touch of vivid green. Sow in patches 2ft across.*

FEATURES

A half-hardy annual, also known as shell flower, moluccella is very lightly scented, and produces 2–3ft tall spikes in summer. It has small flowers surrounded by the more obvious and showy bell- or shell-like apple-green bracts. You can grow moluccella in flower beds and mixed borders, but its main value is as a cut flower, either fresh or dried. It is long-lasting when dried in late summer, the green spikes gradually fade from green to pale brown through fall and into winter.

CONDITIONS

Aspect   Needs an open spot in full sun.

MOLUCCELLA AT A GLANCE

A half-hardy annual grown for its tall spikes of green bracts that are used for drying. Frost hardy to 32°F (zone 10).

Month	Activity		Recommended Varieties
Jan	/		
Feb	sow 🖐		*Moluccella laevis*
Mar	sow 🖐		
Apr	transplant/grow 🖐		
May	plant/sow 🖐		
Jun	flowering 🌿		
July	flowering 🌿		
Aug	flowering 🌿		
Sept	flowers/cutting 🌿		
Oct	/		
Nov	/		
Dec	/		

Site   Must have good drainage, and working rotted manure or compost into the ground before sowing or planting helps. Avoid exposed, windy spots or the tall stems may be flattened.

GROWING METHOD

Sowing   Either sow seed in 3½in pots of multipurpose compost in February/March at 64°F, or sow directly in the soil where they are to grow in late April and May. Gradually thin out so plants are spaced 12–16in apart. Plants raised under cover are hardened off before being planted.

Feeding   If organic matter has already been added to the soil, extra feeding is not necessary, but keep plants well-watered during long dry spells.

Problems   Seeds can sometimes be slow and difficult to germinate, so put them in the bottom of a refrigerator for two weeks before you sow, to "chill" them, then sow in pots as described above and expect seedlings in 2–3 weeks.

FLOWERING

Season   Even after the actual flowers have faded the green bracts go on providing color and interest until they are cut for drying.

Cutting   Ideal as a cut flower, used fresh or dried. Cut when flowers are well-formed. Leaves can be removed to display the green bracts better. The stems dry to a light brown color.

AFTER FLOWERING

General   Remove roots when stems have been harvested, but leave a few behind to develop on the plant and finally shed seeds, which will self-sow.

MYOSOTIS
Forget-me-not

FORGET-ME-NOTS flower from early spring after growing slowly during the winter months. Flowers often have yellow "eyes."

"MONTE CARLO" early double tulips rising up through a haze of forget-me-nots is a springtime classic that is seldom bettered.

FEATURES

Forget-me-nots are useful spring bedding plants, producing swathes of pink, blue, or white flowers from April onward. They go well with bulbs like tulips which push up through the myosotis flowers. Grow as a hardy biennial and use shorter varieties such as "Blue Ball," reaching 6in, in winter and spring patio containers. None grow more than 12in tall, and these are the ideal choice for spring bedding displays. Available by mail order in fall as ready-grown young plants.

MYOSOTIS AT A GLANCE

A hardy biennial grown for its small flowers which appear in masses from early spring. Frost hardy to 5°F (zone 7).

		Recommended Varieties
Jan	/	
Feb	/	*Myosotis sylvatica:*
Mar	/	"Blue Ball"
Apr	flowering	"Carmine King"
May	flowers/sow	"Compindi"
Jun	sow	"Indigo"
July	grow on	"Light Blue"
Aug	grow on	"Music"
Sept	grow on	"Rosylva"
Oct	plant	"Royal Blue"
Nov	/	"Spring Symphony Mxd"
Dec	/	"Victoria Mixed"

CONDITIONS

Aspect Full or dappled sunlight is suitable.

Site Responds well to soil with plenty of rotted compost or manure mixed in that holds plenty of moisture. When planting containers in fall ensure good drainage and use a multipurpose compost.

GROWING METHOD

Sowing Seed is sown direct into the ground May–July, in drills ½in deep. Thin seedlings as they develop so plants are eventually 3–6in apart, keep weed free and water copiously in dry spells. Plant into their flowering positions/containers in October and water to settle in.

Feeding Do not feed after planting in fall, but scatter a general granular fertilizer around plants in spring as they show signs of growth.

Problems Powdery mildew can affect leaves but this is generally not worth treating.

FLOWERING

Season From late winter to early summer.

Cutting Not suitable for cutting.

AFTER FLOWERING

General Remove plants to make way for summer bedding, but if you leave a few to die down they will self-sow into the soil.

NEMESIA
Nemesia

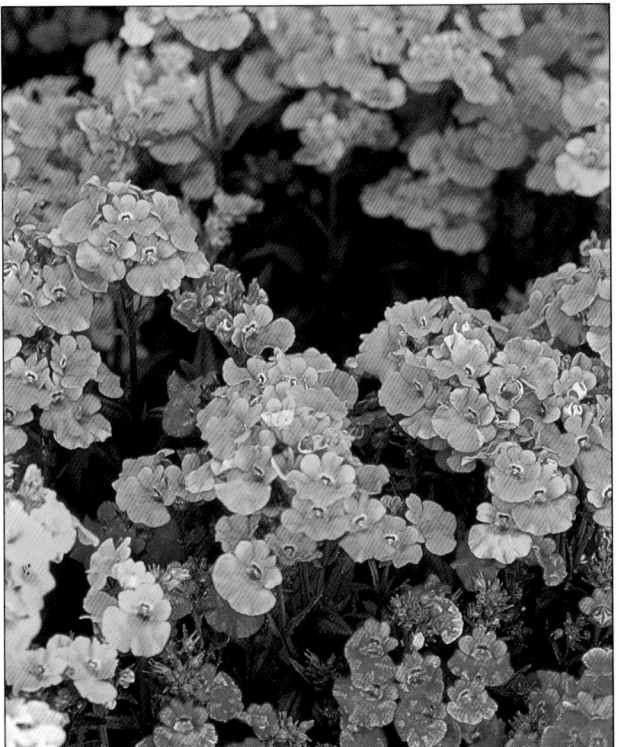

THE TWO-LIPPED FLOWERS of nemesias come in an array of colors and they all have patterns deep in the flower's "throat."

NEMESIAS CARRY THEIR flowers in large, almost flat heads with individual flowers pointing off in all directions.

FEATURES

No varieties of *Nemesia strumosa* grow more than 12in high making them ideal for beds and containers. Grown as a half-hardy annual, flowers can be single colors or bright and varied mixtures. Good as edging for troughs and windowboxes. Very easy to grow.

CONDITIONS

Aspect   Must have full sun to grow successfully.

NEMESIA AT A GLANCE

A half-hardy annual grown for its pretty lipped flowers, used for bedding and patio containers. Frost hardy to 32°F (zone 10).

Jan	/	Recommended Varieties
Feb	/	
Mar	sow	*Nemesia strumosa:*
Apr	sow/transplant	**Mixed colors**
May	harden off/plant	"Carnival Mixed"
Jun	flowering	"Pastel Mixed"
July	flowering	"Sparklers"
Aug	flowering	"Tapestry"
Sept	flowering	**Single colors**
Oct	/	"Blue Gem"
Nov	/	"Fire King"
Dec	/	"KLM"
		"National Ensign"

Site   In containers use multipurpose compost with slow-release fertilizer mixed well in. Soil with plenty of organic matter dug in well-ahead of planting gives good results, and must be well-drained.

GROWING METHOD

Sowing   Raise plants by sowing in small pots of soil-based seed compost starting in March/April (and repeating every few weeks for a succession of flowers), just covering the seeds. Keep at 60°F in a light place, and transplant to cell trays when seedlings are large enough to handle. Grow on and harden off in late May before planting after the last frosts, 6–12in apart. In containers make sure they are not swamped.

Feeding   Give a liquid feed to plants grown as bedding every two weeks, with a hand-held feeder. Regular watering in dry spells is vital.

Problems   Plants may rot off in heavy, wet soils.

FLOWERING

Season   For more flowerheads, pinch out growing tips of plants when they are 4in high.

Cutting   Not suited to cutting.

AFTER FLOWERING

General   Pull plants up when finished—this is quite often as they have a short flowering period.

NEMOPHILA
Baby blue eyes

NEMOPHILA MENZIESII *flowers are a brilliant sky-blue with a distinctive paler "eye," carried over bright green feathery leaves.*

NEMOPHILA *can be grown with other hardy annuals such as limnanthes, the poached egg flower, for a striking color combination.*

FEATURES

Nemophila is an easy annual sown in fall or spring. Flowers are sky-blue, white, or black/white. Plants grow to 8in high, with feathery leaves and a carpeting habit. Use them in borders, on rockeries, and around the edge of containers and windowboxes.

CONDITIONS

Aspect   Needs full sun or part shade to succeed.

NEMOPHILA AT A GLANCE

A hardy spreading annual grown for its flowers for beds, rockeries and container edges. Frost hardy to 5°F (zone 7).

Jan	/	Recommended Varieties
Feb	/	
Mar	/	*Nemophila menziesii:*
		(Also listed as *N. insignis*)
Apr	sow 🖐	"Baby Blue Eyes"
May	flowers/sow 🌱🖐	"Penny Black"
		"Snowstorm"
Jun	flowering 🌱	
July	flowering 🌱	*Nemophila maculata:*
Aug	flowering 🌱	"Five Spot"
Sept	flowers/sow 🌱🖐	
Oct	/	
Nov	/	
Dec	/	

Site   Needs well-drained soil, but mix in well-rotted organic matter before sowing to retain moisture. Nemophila will thrive in most multipurpose composts used in containers.

GROWING METHOD

Sowing   Sow seeds straight into the soil in fall or spring, in drills ½in deep. Seeds sown in fall will produce young plants that survive the winter and flower earlier. Gradually thin plants out so they are 3–6in apart as flowers appear.

Feeding   On well-prepared soil feeding is unnecessary, although large beds can be fed monthly with a general liquid feed applied through a hand-held feeder. Keep plants watered in dry spells or they may quickly die off.

Problems   Aphids can attack the soft leaves, so use a spray containing permethrin.

FLOWERING

Season   On fall-sown plants flowers appear from early spring to the first frosts, but appear slightly later on spring-sown plants.

Cutting   Not suitable for use as a cut flower.

AFTER FLOWERING

General   Leave plants to set seed and die back before removing—nemophila self-seeds and plants will appear on their own each spring.

NICOTIANA
Tobacco plant

"DOMINO SALMON PINK" is a popular variety of nicotiana because of its striking color and sheer flower power. Here in a bedding display it covers the ground and produces tubular, salmon-pink flowers non-stop through the summer. It is also useful for containers.

FEATURES

Not grown for tobacco but for their tubular flowers. Choose from dwarf modern varieties growing 1ft tall with upward-facing flowers, for bedding and containers, to *Nicotiana sylvestris* at 5ft for large borders—plant it behind other plants and especially against a dark evergreen background so that the large leaves as well as the flowers are shown off to best effect. Some release scent in the evening, so plant near doors and windows, or grow a few in large tubs that can be moved into the house or conservatory on a warm summer evening. Flowers can be pink to lime-green. A half-hardy annual. Widely available as young plants in a good selection of varieties.

NICOTIANA AT A GLANCE

A half-hardy annual grown for it colorful and often scented flowers, used in bedding/containers. Frost hardy to 32°F (zone 10).

Jan	/	Recommended Varieties
Feb	/	
Mar	sow 👌	*Nicotiana sanderae:*
Apr	transplant/grow on 👌	"Domino Mixed"
		"Domino Salmon Pink"
May	harden off/plant 👌	"Havana Appleblossom"
		"Hippy Mixed"
Jun	flowering	"Lime Green"
July	flowering	"Merlin Peach"
Aug	flowering	
Sept	flowering	*Nicotiana langsdorfii*
Oct	/	
Nov	/	*Nicotiana sylvestris*
Dec	/	

CONDITIONS

Aspect Full sun or light shade. The flowers stay open longer in sun.

Site Grow in well-drained, moisture-retentive soil with rotted manure/compost mixed in. For container growing use multipurpose compost.

GROWING METHOD

Sowing Use 3½in diameter pots of multipurpose compost, sow the fine seed on the surface in March, but do not cover, and keep in a light place at 70°F. Tiny seedlings emerge within three weeks. Transplant to cell trays of multipurpose compost or into 3½in diameter pots when each young plant has developed 3–4 small leaves. Grow on and harden off in late May, then plant after the last frosts in your area, 12–18in apart depending on the variety grown.

Feeding Liquid feed weekly outdoors. Add slow-release fertilizer granules to container compost before planting.

Problems Use a spray containing pirimicarb for aphids. Destroy plants attacked by virus, showing any puckered and mottled leaves

FLOWERING

Season Flowers all summer. Nip off dead flowers.
Cutting Not suitable.

AFTER FLOWERING

General Remove plants after first frosts. It is possible to collect seed from *Nicotiana sylvestris* that can then be sown the following spring.

NIGELLA
Love-in-a-mist

"MISS JEKYLL" with semi-double blue flowers is a reliable variety of Nigella damascena. *Each flower has a feathery "collar."*

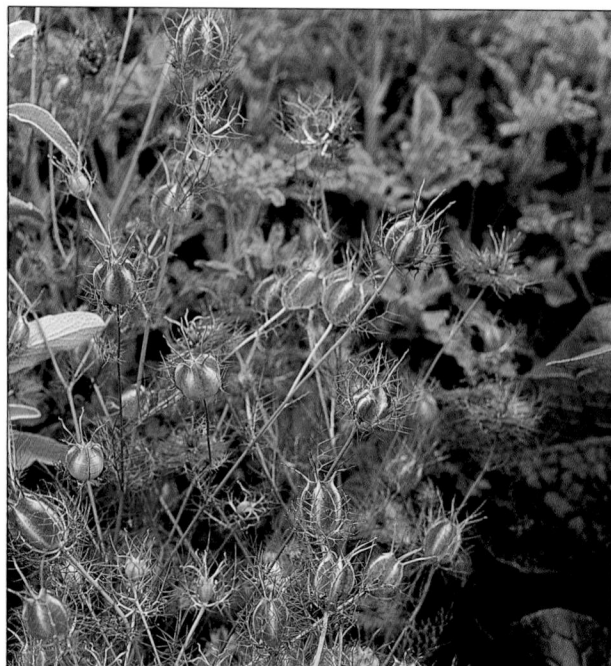

AFTER THE FLOWERS come the curiously attractive seedheads that give the plant its other common name, devil-in-a-bush.

FEATURES

Love-in-a-mist has fine, feathery leaves, with a fringe of foliage surrounding and slightly veiling each of the flowers, hence its common name. When the spiky seed pods appear it is also called devil-in-a-bush. Flowers are blue, pale and deep pink, white, or purple. Nigella grows 18in tall and is good for big drifts in beds or for cutting. Hardy annual. The variety "Transformer" has novel seed pods.

CONDITIONS

Aspect   Give it a sunny spot in an open position.

NIGELLA AT A GLANCE

A hardy annual grown for its flowers and its attractive, inflated seed pods which can be dried. Frost hardy to 5°F (zone 7).

Jan	/	Recommended Varieties
Feb	/	
Mar	sow 🌱	*Nigella damascena:*
Apr	flowers/thin 🌱🌱	"Dwarf Moody Blue"
May	flowering 🌼	"Miss Jekyll"
Jun	flowering 🌼	"Miss Jekyll Alba"
July	flowering 🌼	"Mulberry Rose"
Aug	flowering 🌼	"Oxford Blue"
Sept	flowers/sow 🌼🌱	"Persian Jewels"
Oct	/	"Shorty Blue"
Nov	/	*Nigella orientalis:*
Dec	/	"Transformer"

Site   Needs good drainage but isn't too fussy about soils—rotted organic matter may be dug in ahead of planting, but this is not essential, and good results can be had on quite thin, poor soils as long as it is grown in full sun.

GROWING METHOD

Sowing   Sow in March or September, in short drills ½in deep. Thin plants as they grow so there is about 6–8in between them as they begin to produce flower buds. Leave thinning of fall-sown plants until spring in case there are winter losses. Plants can also be raised in cell trays, sowing 2–3 seeds per tray and removing all but the strongest seedling—nigella does not like disturbance.

Feeding   Does not need extra feeding during summer.
Problems   Plants are trouble free.

FLOWERING

Season   Fall-sown plants flower from late spring, spring-sown from early summer.
Cutting   Delightful cut flower. Remove foliage from lower part of stalk to prolong flower life.

AFTER FLOWERING

General   The inflated seed pods that form are useful in dried flower arrangements. Pick stems after pods have dried on the plant and hang upside-down in a warm, airy place. Nigella self-seeds prolifically and will produce masses of seedlings the following spring. Dead plants can be pulled up and composted.

OSTEOSPERMUM
Osteospermum

OSTEOSPERMUM flowers are at their best in full sun in an open situation.

CREATE A CARPET OF OSTEOSPERMUM BEDDING in early summer that will continue to flower in flushes until the first frosts. Remember to propagate fresh plants each year.

FEATURES

Many varieties of osteospermum can be bought in spring as young plants, but others can be grown from seed and treated as half-hardy annuals. Growing from seed is a cost-effective way of raising large numbers of plants quickly. Favorite plants can be potted-up in fall and kept in a well-lit frost-free place over winter, then increased by cuttings in spring. In mild areas plants will often survive the winter outdoors and carry on producing a few flowers except in severe spells. In some catalogs it is listed as dimorphotheca. Plants can grow 12–30in tall.

CONDITIONS

Aspect   Must have full, baking sun for best results.

OSTEOSPERMUM AT A GLANCE

A hardy/half-hardy annual grown for its brightly-colored daisy-like flowers that appear all summer. Frost hardy to 23°F (zone 9).

Jan	/	Recommended Varieties
Feb	/	Osteospermum hybrids:
Mar	sow	"Gaiety"
Apr	sow/transplant	"Giant Mixed"
May	harden off/plant	"Glistening White"
Jun	flowering	"Ink Spot"
July	flowering	"Potpourri"
Aug	flowering	"Salmon Queen"
Sept	flowering	"Starshine"
Oct	flowering	"Tetra Pole Star"
Nov	/	
Dec	/	

Site

Is not fussy about soil but it must be very well-drained. A sheltered spot with the sun beating down all day is ideal. Plants also perform well in containers and these should be sited in full sun facing south if possible. Use multipurpose compost.

GROWING METHOD

Sowing   March/April is the time to sow, sowing seed thinly in 3½in diameter pots of soil-based seed compost, and just covering. Germinate at 64°F in a bright spot. Seedlings are transplanted to cell trays or individual 3½in pots when large enough to handle. Harden off for two weeks and start planting from mid-May onward.

Feeding   Water well to establish and then water only in long spells of hot, dry weather. Extra feeding is unnecessary, but container-grown plants will benefit from occasional liquid feeds given for the benefit of other plants.

Problems   Aphids can attack the leaves, flower stalks and buds so choose a spray containing permethrin and wet both sides of the leaves.

FLOWERING

Season   Flowers appear from early summer onward with a peak later on when temperatures reach their highest.

Cutting   Flowers are unsuitable for cutting.

AFTER FLOWERING

General   After the main flowering give plants an overall clipping to tidy them up and maintain compact growth. Lift and pot favorite plants and keep frost-free over winter.

PAPAVER NUDICAULE
Iceland poppy

ICELAND POPPY has petals with the texture of crepe paper and a velvety sheen. The center of the flower is a mass of yellow stamens.

THEIR TALL STEMS mean the flowers of Papaver nudicaule waft gently in the breeze, and look good like this, massed in bedding.

FEATURES

Varieties of *Papaver nudicaule* are available in a wide range of colors and range from 10–30in tall depending on variety. They can be treated as either half-hardy annuals or hardy biennials sown in summer or fall. Tall varieties are used for cutting. Plants sown early flower from April onward.

CONDITIONS

Aspect — Can be grown in cool and warm areas.
Site — Poppies need well-drained but moisture-retentive soil with plenty of rotted organic

matter added ahead of planting or sowing.

GROWING METHOD

Sowing — Sow seed outdoors April-June or in September. Scatter the seed thinly along shallow drills ½in deep, and rake over with fine soil. Thin out when seedlings are 2in high, so that the spacing is ultimately at about 6–12in intervals by October. Do not disturb the fine roots when thinning out, and always water when finished to settle plants back in. Thin fall-sown poppies in spring in case of winter losses. For earlier flowers sow in pots at 60°F in February and grow in cell-trays, planting in late May.

Feeding — Extra feeding not needed.

Problems — Fall-sown plants may rot off in heavy soils, so sow in cell trays and keep dry in a coldframe over winter, planting out in spring.

FLOWERING

Season — Flowers appear during early summer and should be picked off as they fade.

Cutting — Excellent cut flower. Pick when buds are just opening. Singe stem ends before arranging.

AFTER FLOWERING

General — Leave a few plants to self-seed, but otherwise pull up after the flowers are finished.

PAPAVER AT A GLANCE

A hardy biennial (or half-hardy annual) grown for its large showy flowers that appear in summer. Frost hardy to 5°F (zone 7).

Jan	/	Recommended Varieties
Feb	/	*Papaver nudicaule:*
Mar	/	**Biennials**
Apr	sow	"Large Flowered Special
May	flowers/sow	Mixture"
Jun	flowers/sow	"Meadow Pastels"
July	flowering	"Red Sails"
Aug	flowering	"Wonderland Mixed"
Sept	flowers/sow	
Oct	plant	**Half-hardy annuals**
Nov	/	"Summer Breeze"
Dec	/	

PAPAVER RHOEAS
Shirley poppy

THE UNOPENED BUDS of Shirley poppies gradually rise up from among the leaves before bursting open as the petals unfurl.

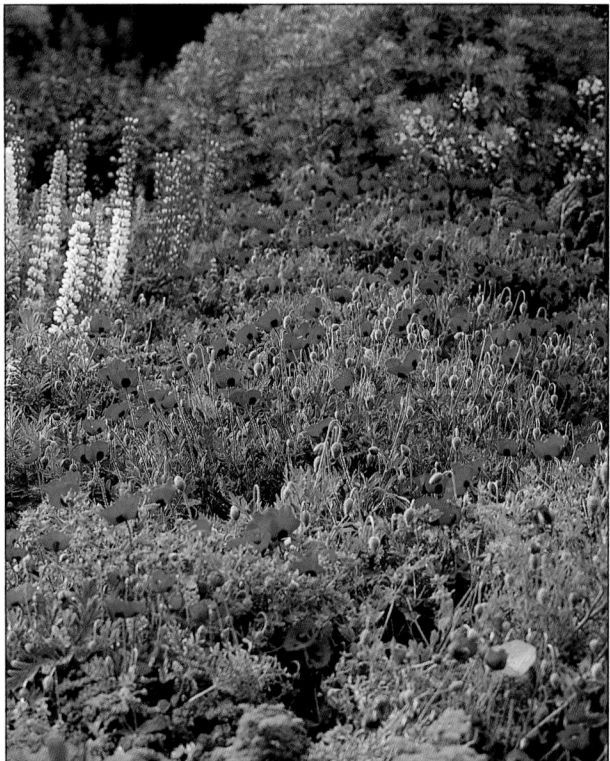

WHEN ALLOWED TO self-seed, poppies will come up among other plants. Unwanted plants are very easily pulled out.

FEATURES

Shirley poppies, varieties of *Papaver rhoeas*, generally grow to about 2ft high, have a very delicate appearance, and come in a wide range of colors including pastels. There are single or double varieties and they look effective in large drifts, but can also be sown in patches 1–2ft across and used as fillers in mixed borders. Each flower can be 3in across. A hardy annual.

PAPAVER AT A GLANCE

Shirley poppies are hardy annuals sown in spring or fall and grown for their large flowers. Frost hardy to 5°F (zone 7).

Jan	/	Recommended Varieties
Feb	/	*Papaver rhoeas:*
Mar	sow	"Angels Choir Mixed"
Apr	sow/thin	"Angel Wings Mixed"
May	flowers/sow	"Mother of Pearl"
Jun	flowering	"Selected Single Mixed"
July	flowering	"Shirley Double Mixed"
Aug	flowering	"Shirley Single Mixed"
Sept	flowers/sow	
Oct	/	
Nov	/	
Dec	/	

CONDITIONS

Aspect	Avoid any shade and grow in full sun.
Site	Must have very well-drained soil. Rotted compost or manure should be added to the soil a few weeks before sowing.

GROWING METHOD

Sowing	The fine seed can either be scattered on the soil and simply raked in, and the area marked with a circle of sand, or it can be sown in short ⅛in deep drills. March–May and September are the sowing times. Gradually thin out the seedlings until they are 12in apart, but avoid transplanting as they dislike disturbance. If sowing in fall leave thinning until the following spring in case of winter losses.
Feeding	Extra summer feeding is not required, but water thoroughly should plants start to wilt.
Problems	Trouble-free.

FLOWERING

Season	Fall-sown plants flower from late spring onward, while spring-sown flower in summer.
Cutting	Suitable as a cut flower if stems are scalded before arranging.

AFTER FLOWERING

General	Leave a few plants to die down and self-seed.

PELARGONIUM
Bedding geranium

DARK ZONED LEAVES and an enticing range of single and two-tone flower colors are characteristic of "Avanti Mixed."

YOU MAY BE SURPRISED to see an ivy-leaved geranium as good as "Summertime Lilac" coming true from seed.

FEATURES

Better known as geraniums, seed-raised pelargoniums are available with large bright flowerheads for bedding, and also as trailing "ivy-leaved" types. Seeds are sown January/February and need warmth to succeed, so consider buying them as young plants delivered ready-grown in spring. Varieties for bedding and patio containers grow no more than 1ft, while ivy-leaved types can spread and trail up to 2ft. Flowers may be single colors or mixtures—the new "ripple" varieties are eye-catching. Plant 1–2ft apart. All are half-hardy annuals.

PELARGONIUM AT A GLANCE

Half-hardy annuals grown for their flowers and also the attractive ivy-like foliage of some varieties. Frost hardy to 32°F (zone 10).

Jan	sow	*Recommended Varieties*
Feb	sow	
Mar	transplant	**Pelargonium hybrids:**
Apr	pot on	**For bedding**
May	harden off/plant	"Avanti Mixed"
Jun	flowering	"Raspberry Ripple"
July	flowering	"Ripple Mixed"
Aug	flowering	"Sensation Mixed"
Sept	flowering	"Stardust Mixed"
Oct	/	"Video Mixed"
Nov	/	**Ivy-leaved varieties**
Dec	/	"Summertime Lilac"
		"Summer Showers"

CONDITIONS

Aspect   Must be grown in full sun.
Site   Well-prepared soil with rotted compost or manure mixed in gives best results. Soil must be well-drained, and when planting up containers use multipurpose compost with slow-release fertilizer mixed in. Bedding geraniums do well in terracotta containers.

GROWING METHOD

Sowing   Sow January/February in a heated propagator in a guaranteed temperature of 64°F. Seedlings appear in 2–3 weeks and can be transplanted to 3in pots or cell trays of multipurpose compost. Plants must have good light and a temperature of 61–64°F to grow well. Pot on into 4–5in diameter pots, harden off in late May, and plant out after the last frosts.

Feeding   Liquid feed bedding plants every 2–3 weeks.
Problems   Heavy wet soils can lead to rotting of the stems, so grow in containers. Snap off faded flowerheads to avoid gray mold.

FLOWERING

Season   Flowers appear from early summer onward.
Cutting   Not suitable.

AFTER FLOWERING

General   Pull up and compost. Favorite plants can be kept dry and frost-free over winter.

PETUNIA
Petunia

"FANTASY MIXED" is the latest in a new range of "milliflora" petunias with 1in flowers, ideal for containers and baskets.

MULTIFLORA PETUNIAS such as "Summer Morn Mixed" have 2in flowers and are suited to large patio tubs and bedding.

FEATURES

Petunias come in a wide range of different types depending on whether they are raised from seed or bought as young plants. Most petunias are perennials grown as half-hardy annuals. Seed-raised varieties fall into the following groups: Millifloras—small flowers 1in across on compact mounds, for containers and hanging baskets; Multifloras—plenty of 2in-wide flowers on bushy plants. For bedding and patio containers, with good weather resistance; Floribundas—intermediate in size between multifloras and grandifloras with 3in flowers; Grandifloras—large trumpet-like 5in flowers that can bruise in heavy rain and are best for containers in a sheltered position. These all grow 9–12in tall and can spread up to 2ft, and are also available as double-flowered varieties. Plant 9–12in apart. Flower color varies from single shades to striped, picotee, and other variations. Many seed-raised varieties are also widely available as young plants. An increasing number of petunias are only available as young plants, setting no seed. These are suited to container growing, and include many large double-flowered "patio" varieties such as "Able Mabel" and the vigorous Surfinias which can trail to 4–5ft—see page 194.

PETUNIA AT A GLANCE

A half-hardy annual grown for all-round use in summer bedding, hanging baskets and containers. Frost hardy to 5°F (zone 7).

Jan	sow	*Recommended Varieties*
Feb	sow	*Petunia hybrida:*
Mar	sow/transplant	**Millifloras**
Apr	pot on/grow on	"Fantasy Mixed"
May	harden off/plant	**Multifloras**
Jun	flowering	"Celebrity Bunting"
July	flowering	"Summer Morn Mixed"
Aug	flowering	**Floribundas**
Sept	flowering	"Mirage Mixed"
Oct	/	"Niagara Mixture"
Nov	/	**Grandifloras**
Dec	/	"Daddy Mixed"
		"Lavender Storm"

CONDITIONS

Aspect Choose a sunny, south-facing situation for petunias in beds and containers.

Site Avoid spots exposed to wind (which damages the flowers). Light, free-draining soil with rotted compost/manure mixed in is best.

PETUNIA "ABLE MABEL" is the first of a revolutionary new type of double-flowered "patio" petunia available only as young plants.

In containers use multipurpose compost.

GROWING METHOD

Sowing Sowing can take place January–March where a temperature of 70°F is possible. Sow onto the level surface of a 3½in pot of multipurpose compost, but do not cover seeds, and keep in the light. Seedlings will appear inside two weeks, and should be transplanted to cell trays of multipurpose compost when large enough. Pot on into 3½in diameter pots, grow-on and harden off before planting out in early June.

Feeding Give a weekly liquid feed with a high-potash fertilizer to encourage flowers. Mix slow-release fertilizer granules with container compost.

Problems Slugs eat leaves in wet weather–use pellets or slug traps. Plants with mottled, crinkled leaves affected by virus should be destroyed.

FLOWERING

Season Flowers appear all summer. Pick off dead flowers regularly.

Cutting Not suitable.

AFTER FLOWERING

General Remove when flowers end.

FOR A TOUCH OF the patriotic, "Celebrity Bunting" is a stunning multiflora variety with blend of red, white, and blue flowers.

PHLOX
Annual phlox

"TWINKLE MIXED" is a striking variety of annual phlox growing about 6in tall with star-like flowers in various shades.

THE FLOWERS OF *annual phlox open at their peak to make rounded heads of color that can completely fill summer containers.*

FEATURES

Annual phlox are versatile plants that can be used for bedding, containers, and as unique cut flowers. They are half-hardy annuals, growing between 4–18in tall depending on the variety –taller are better for cutting. Flower color ranges from the blue of "Bobby Sox" to the varied shades of "Tapestry" which is also scented. Several varieties are now available as young plants by mail order. Flowers are long-lived and plants are easy to care for.

PHLOX AT A GLANCE

A half-hardy annual grown for its heads of colorful flowers, for bedding, containers, and for cutting. Frost hardy to 23°F (zone 9).

		Recommended Varieties
Jan	/	
Feb	sow 🖐	*Phlox drummondii:*
Mar	sow/transplant 🖐	"African Sunset"
Apr	grow on 🖐	"Bobby Sox"
May	harden off/plant 🖐	"Bright Eyes"
Jun	flowering 🌼	"Brilliant"
July	flowering 🌼	"Cecily Old & New Shades"
Aug	flowering 🌼	"Double Chanel"
Sept	flowering 🌼	"Phlox of Sheep"
Oct	/	"Tapestry"
Nov	/	"Tutti-Frutti"
Dec	/	"Twinkle Mixed"

CONDITIONS

Aspect — Needs full sun.
Site — Needs well-drained soil with manure or compost mixed in to improve moisture holding. Phlox grow well in multipurpose compost used to fill summer containers.

GROWING METHOD

Sowing — Sow seed in February/March in 3½in pots of multipurpose compost, keep at 64°F, and expect seedlings in 1–3 weeks. Transplant to cell trays or 3½in pots, pinch out the tips when 3in high, and grow on until late May, then harden off and plant after the last frosts in your area.
Feeding — Add slow-release fertilizer granules to compost before planting containers, which should be sufficient. Plants in beds can be given a liquid feed every 2–3 weeks in summer.
Problems — Plants will struggle on heavy soils in a cold spring so delay planting until warmer weather.

FLOWERING

Season — Flowers appear all summer until frosts.
Cutting — Tall varieties are good for cutting and some like "Tapestry" have a strong, sweet scent.

AFTER FLOWERING

General — Pull up after flowering and compost them.

PORTULACA
Sun plant

DOUBLE-FLOWERED *mixed varieties of portulaca come in a wide range of colors, but attractive single colors are also available.*

SUN PLANTS *can survive the winter in mild seaside gardens, and thrive in the well-drained soil of rockeries.*

FEATURES

Commonly known as sun plant, portulaca grows 6in high with a spreading habit and succulent leaves. The 2in flowers open in sun, although modern varieties open even on dull days. It thrives in poor, dry soils and is easily ruined by too much coddling. A half-hardy annual, for beds, pots, and rockeries.

CONDITIONS

Aspect   A hot, sunny position gives the best plants.

PORTULACA AT A GLANCE

Portulaca is a half-hardy annual grown for summer flowers, and gives good results even on thin soils. Frost hardy to 32°F (zone 10).

		Recommended Varieties
Jan	/	
Feb	/	*Portulaca grandiflora:*
Mar	sow	"Cloudbeater Mixed"
Apr	sow	"Double Mixed"
May	harden off/plant	"Kariba Mixed"
Jun	flowering	"Patio Gems"
July	flowering	"Sundance"
Aug	flowering	"Sundial Mango"
Sept	flowering	"Sundial Mixed"
Oct	/	"Sundial Peppermint"
Nov	/	"Swanlake"
Dec	/	

Site   Unless soil is very well-drained plants are prone to rotting. Otherwise plants grow and flower well even where the soil is quite poor—particularly in seaside gardens—as they are adapted to live on little water. Grow them on their own in patio containers, using soil-based potting compost mixed fifty-fifty with sharp grit. Do not feed, and water only when plants start to wilt. Place pots in blazing sunshine.

GROWING METHOD

Sowing   Sow seeds in March/April in 3½in pots of soil-based seed compost and germinate at 64°F in good light. Keep the seedlings on the dry side and transplant to cell trays of soil-based compost with grit added. Grow on, harden off in late May, and plant after frosts, watering in well, then only when plants wilt.

Feeding   Feeding portulaca is not necessary.

Problems   Seedlings will "damp off" if the compost is kept too wet. If they do fall over, water the pots lightly with a copper-based fungicide.

FLOWERING

Season   Flowers appear throughout summer and into early fall.

Cutting   Not suitable.

AFTER FLOWERING

General   Pull plants up after the first fall frosts and add their fleshy remains to the compost heap.

PRIMULA
Polyanthus

*NOT AN F1 HYBRID STRAIN, but "Giant Superb Mixed"
polyanthus are tough, large-flowered, and full of character.*

*F1 "CRESCENDO MIXED" exhibit the clearer, more uniform colors
of a highly bred strain, but seed is more expensive.*

FEATURES

Polyanthus, a hybrid type of primula, is
perfect in patio pots or mass-planted in the
garden for a stunning spring display. Its very
brightly-colored flowers up to 2in across, on
stems 6–12in tall, rise from neat clumps of
bright green, crinkled leaves. A hardy
perennial, it is grown as a hardy biennial for
spring bedding and containers. Widely
available as young plants.

CONDITIONS

Aspect   Grows in full sun or light shade under trees.
Site   Needs well-drained soil but with plenty of

PRIMULA AT A GLANCE

A hardy biennial grown for its bright spring flowers for use in
bedding and containers. Frost hardy to 5°F (zone 7).

		Recommended Varieties
Jan	/	
Feb	flowering	**Primula hybrids:**
Mar	flowers/sow	"Crescendo Mixed"
Apr	flowers/sow	"Dobies Superb Mixed"
May	flowers/sow	"Giant Superb Mixed"
Jun	sow/grow	"Gold Lace"
July	sow/grow	"Harlequin Mixed"
Aug	grow	"Heritage Mixed"
Sept	grow	"Large Flowered Mixed"
Oct	plant	"Pacific Giants Mixed"
Nov	/	"Spring Rainbow Mixed"
Dec	/	"Unwins Superb Mixed"

organic matter mixed in to help retain
moisture—plants do not like to be bone dry at
any stage while growing. For containers use
multipurpose compost with gravel or chunks
of styrofoam put in the base.

GROWING METHOD

Sowing   Polyanthus seed can be tricky to germinate,
and the most important rule is not to keep it
too warm. Sow in 3½in pots of peat-based seed
compost from March–July, barely cover, then
stand outside in a covered, shaded spot out of
the sun. Seedlings will appear 2–3 weeks later.
Transplant to cell trays or 3½in pots of peat-
based potting compost, and pot on into 5in
pots when roots are well-developed. Grow
during the summer in a shaded spot and do
not let them dry out. Plant out in October
where flowers are required the following
spring, in beds or containers with bulbs and
other plants.

Feeding   Feed fortnightly with liquid feed in summer.
Problems   Slugs can devour leaves so use slug pellets.
Never bury the crowns or plants may rot.

FLOWERING

Season   Flowers appear earlier in mild winters and
carry on throughout spring.
Cutting   Charming in spring posies.

AFTER FLOWERING

General   Polyanthus taken from spring displays can be
planted in borders where they will form large
clumps and flower regularly every spring.

RANUNCULUS
Persian buttercup

DOUBLE FLOWERS are characteristic of Ranunculus asiaticus *varieties, and are all clear and bright as in this yellow-flowered plant.*

YOU CAN PLANT ranunculus in beds in spring when the worst of the winter is over, where they will give a bright show of color.

FEATURES

Hardy varieties of *Ranunculus asiaticus* are sown in late summer and fall for flowers during winter and spring. Seed-raised plants reach about 8–10in tall. Flowers are double. Young plants are sometimes offered in spring catalogs for delivery in late summer/fall ready for potting up. Add them to your spring containers as they come into flower—they will grow happily in a cold greenhouse or porch.

RANUNCULUS AT A GLANCE

A half-hardy annual grown for its large, double, buttercup-like flowers that appear in spring. Frost hardy to 23°F (zone 9).

Jan	grow 🌱	Recommended Varieties
Feb	grow 🌱	
Mar	flowering 🌸	Ranunculus hybrids:
Apr	flowering 🌸	"Bloomingdale Mixture"
May	flowering 🌸	
Jun	/	
July	/	
Aug	sow 🌱	
Sept	sow/transplant 🌱	
Oct	sow/grow 🌱	
Nov	grow 🌱	
Dec	grow 🌱	

CONDITIONS

Aspect   Give as much sun as possible, and move containers into shelter during stormy or very frosty weather to stop damage to the flowers.

Site   Use a multipurpose compost for potting up and potting on, and for filling containers if you are creating an "instant" display as the plants come into flower from early spring.

GROWING METHOD

Sowing   Sow seed August–October in 3½in pots of peat-based compost, just covering the seeds. Stand outdoors in shade and keep moist—if they get too hot the seeds will not come up. When seedlings appear, bring them into full light and transplant when large enough into 4in pots. Grow outdoors until frosts start, then move under protection at night and out during the day. A cool porch is useful. In winter keep plants dry under cover.

Feeding   Feeding is not usually required.

Problems   No special problems.

FLOWERING

Season   Late winter and throughout spring.

Cutting   Cut when the buds are just unfurling.

AFTER FLOWERING

General   Plants will survive most winters in a sheltered spot and can be planted out in borders.

RESEDA
Mignonette

MIGNONETTE FLOWERS individually are insignificant, but the strong sweet fragrance is striking and well worth the effort of sowing.

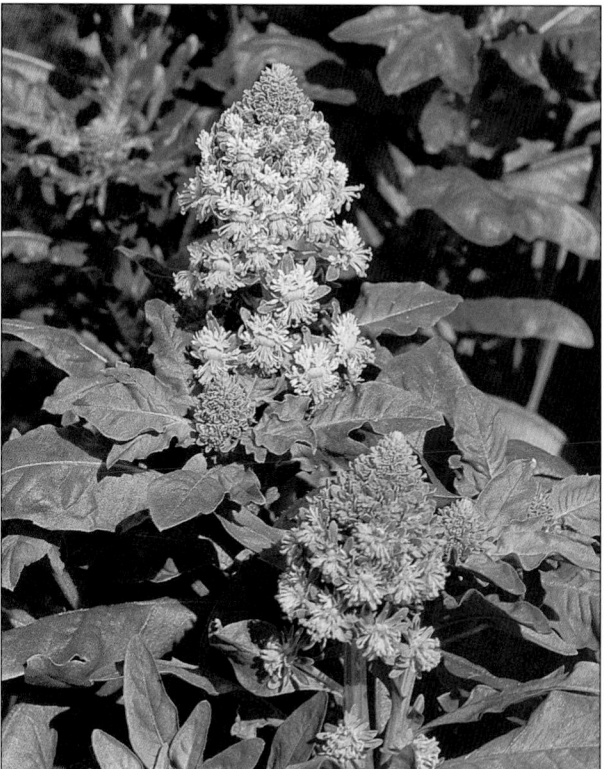

THE FLOWERHEADS of Reseda odorata branch out as they develop. Sow along path edges so the fragrance can be enjoyed.

FEATURES

Mignonette has greenish, pink, red, yellow, or coppery flowers and grows to 12in. It is not particularly striking but is grown mainly for its strong, fruity fragrance–grow it near doors, windows, in patio pots, and near sitting areas to appreciate the qualities of this easily- grown hardy annual. It makes a good addition to cottage-style borders.

RESEDA AT A GLANCE

An easily grown hardy annual grown for its highly fragrant spikes of summer flowers. Frost hardy to 5°F (zone 7).

Jan	/	Recommended Varieties
Feb	/	*Reseda odorata:*
Mar	sow	"Crown Mixture"
Apr	sow/thin out	"Fragrant Beauty"
May	thin out	"Machet"
Jun	flowering	"Sweet Scented"
July	flowering	
Aug	flowering	
Sept	flowers/sow	
Oct	sow	
Nov	/	
Dec	/	

CONDITIONS

Aspect   Needs full sun.
Site   Needs well-drained soil—dig in organic matter and add lime to acid soils.

GROWING METHOD

Sowing   Seed is sown directly into the ground in short drills ½in deep, 6in apart. Thin seedlings to 6in apart. Sowing can take place in March/April or September/October. Fall-sown plants need protecting with cloches during cold spells, and should not be thinned until spring. For pots, sow a pinch of seeds in each unit of a cell tray and thin to 2–3 seedlings, grow on and plant up when ready—reseda does not like root disturbance.
Feeding   Extra feeding is not usually necessary
Problems   Free of troubles.

FLOWERING

Season   Flowers appear from late spring on fall-sown plants, later on spring-sown.
Cutting   Cut when just a few flowers are opening. Dried flowers retain their fragrance.

AFTER FLOWERING

General   Pull plants up when they are past their best, but leave a few to produce seeds and self-sow.

RICINUS
Castor oil plant

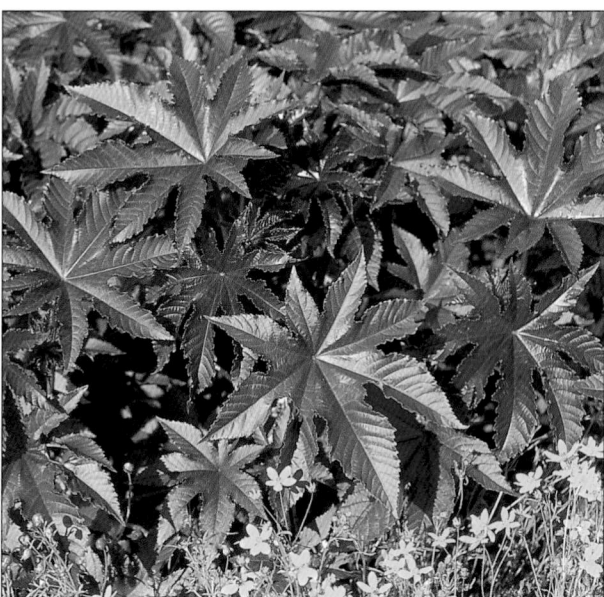

THE VARIETY "IMPALA" is an excellent choice if you want bold, dark leaves for a dramatic show, growing 4ft tall.

BY MIDSUMMER the leaves of ricinus will have formed a dense canopy when grown in beds and planted 2–3ft apart.

FEATURES

A striking and memorable plant grown for its large, lobed, exotic-looking leaves, which are used for bedding, borders, and large tubs and containers. The often brightly-colored summer flowers are followed by spiny seed clusters. By nature an evergreen shrub, ricinus is fast growing and plants are raised fresh from seed each year—in long hot summers they can reach 6ft by 3ft tall and wide. Annual flowering climbers like thunbergia or ipomoea will climb its stems, their bright orange/blue flowers contrasting with the often deeply colored ricinus foliage. All parts of the plant are poisonous, especially the seeds. Treat as a half-hardy annual and scrap plants at the end of the summer.

RICINUS AT A GLANCE

A half-hardy annual with large, exotic leaves in a range of colors, and prized as bold bedder. Frost hardy to 32°F (zone 10).

Jan	/	**Recommended Varieties**
Feb	/	*Ricinus communis:*
Mar	sow	"Carmencita"
Apr	pot on	"Carmencita Pink"
May	harden/plant	"Impala"
Jun	leaves	"Gibbsonii"
July	leaves	"Red Spire"
Aug	leaves	"Zanzibarensis"
Sept	leaves	
Oct	/	
Nov	/	
Dec	/	

CONDITIONS

Aspect   Must have full sun. In northern areas choose a sheltered, south-facing spot.

Site   Soil should be well-drained with plenty of rotted compost or manure dug in. Use loam-based or multipurpose potting compost in containers. In windy spots, stake plants.

GROWING METHOD

Sowing   Soak the hard seeds overnight in warm water, then sow individually in 3½in diameter pots of soil-based compost, 2in deep in March, and keep at 70°F. Seedlings appear within three weeks. Pot on into 5in diameter pots when 6in tall. In beds plant 3–6ft apart after the last frosts.

Feeding   Apply liquid feed weekly from early summer, or mix slow-release fertilizer with the potting compost before planting.

Problems   Red spider mite attacks leaves. Wetting the leaves thoroughly every day can help, or use a spray containing bifenthrin.

FLOWERING

Season   The large leaves keep coming all summer long and are joined later by clusters of flowers that rise up above them.

Cutting   Leaves are useful for flower arranging, but avoid getting the sap on skin.

AFTER FLOWERING

General   Plants are usually killed by the first frosts of fall. Ripe seeds can be saved for sowing again the following spring.

RUDBECKIA
Coneflower

RUDBECKIA "RUSTIC DWARFS" is one of the best seed-raised foms. It produces a range of flower colors, yellow through to red, with dark firey centers or cones. Rudbeckia is also known as black-eyed Susan.

FEATURES

Rudbeckia or coneflower is one of the easiest and most versatile of all annuals. Try tiny "Toto" at just 8in in patio containers, or, where space allows, "Indian Summer" at 3ft. There are intermediate varieties in many shades, and some have an unusual and striking green center or "cone." Half-hardy.

CONDITIONS

Aspect   Rudbeckias need full sun to succeed.
Site   Soil must be well-drained but have rotted compost or manure worked in before planting out. For container growing use multipurpose compost with slow-release fertilizer mixed in.

RUDBECKIA AT A GLANCE

Grown for its large, showy flowers, rudbeckia grows well in bedding/containers and is half-hardy. Frost hardy to 5°F (zone 7).

Jan	/	Recommended Varieties
Feb	sow 🌱	*Rudbeckia hirta:*
Mar	sow/transplant 🌱	**Tall varieties**
Apr	grow on 🌱	"Goldilocks"
May	harden off/plant 🌱	"Indian Summer"
		"Marmalade"
Jun	flowering 🌼	"Rustic Dwarfs"
July	flowering 🌼	**Short varieties**
Aug	flowering 🌼	"Becky Mixed"
Sept	flowering 🌼	"Sonora"
Oct	flowering 🌼	"Toto"
Nov	/	**Green cone/center**
Dec	/	"Irish Eyes"

GROWING METHOD

Sowing   Sow February/March in pots of multipurpose compost and keep at 64°F. Seedlings appear in 1–2 weeks and are fast growing, soon ready for transplanting into cell trays or 3½in pots. Pot larger varieties on into 5in pots when roots fill the pots, and grow outdoors from mid-May, covering with garden fleece at night if frosty. Plant 6–24in apart after the last frosts.

Feeding   Rudbeckias are strong growers and need little extra feeding in the soil, but give container plants a fortnightly liquid feed unless fertilizer granules are mixed with the compost first.

Problems   Slugs can attack after planting so protect with slug pellets or a barrier of sharp grit.

FLOWERING

Season   Summer is the peak period for flowering and regular removal of faded heads should ensure some color right up to the first fall frosts.

Cutting   Good for cutting because of its strong stems. "Sonora" is especially good, and "Indian Summer" has flowers up to 8in across.

AFTER FLOWERING

General   Pull plants up and use for compost when they have been knocked down by frosts.

SALPIGLOSSIS
Salpiglossis

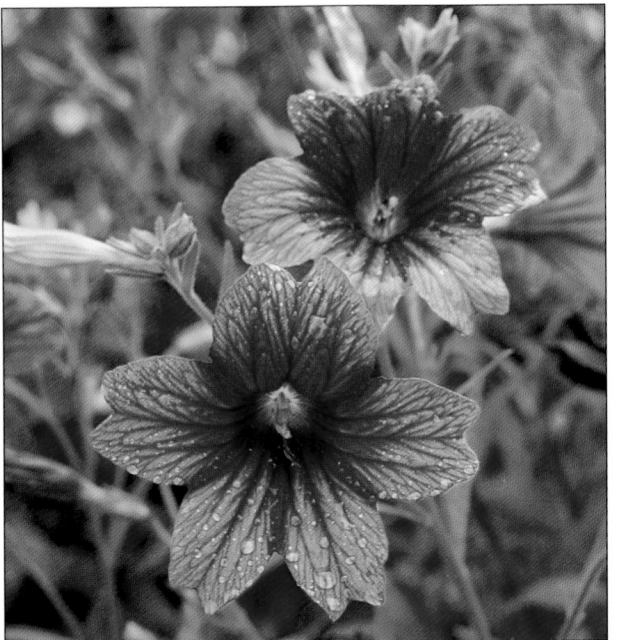

PETAL VEINING in salpiglossis is intricate and gives rise to the common name of painted tongue. Many different colors are available.

THE EXOTIC LOOK can be had by growing mixed salpiglossis in large bold drifts. Choose a variety like "Casino" at just 18in.

FEATURES

Salpiglossis blooms are trumpet-shaped and come in a range of colors, all with patterned veins. They must have shelter and warmth to do well, so for guaranteed success use them in containers on sunny patios or in south-facing beds protected from the wind. Choose mixed colors or try dark brown "Chocolate Pot," striking "Kew Blue" or even the blue/yellow mix Chili Blue." Half-hardy, growing up to 2ft. Available as young plants.

CONDITIONS

Aspect Must be in full sun and protected from wind.

SALPIGLOSSIS AT A GLANCE	
Half-hardy annual grown for its exotic flowers but needing a sheltered spot in the yard to do well. Frost hardy to 32°F (zone 10).	
Jan /	Recommended Varieties
Feb sow	*Salpiglossis sinuata:*
Mar transplant/sow	"Batik"
Apr grow on	"Bolero"
May harden off/plant	"Carnival"
Jun flowering	"Casino"
July flowering	"Chili Blue"
	"Chocolate Pot"
Aug flowering	"Chocolate Royale"
Sept flowering	"Festival Mixed"
Oct /	"Flamenco Mixed"
Nov /	"Kew Blue"
Dec /	"Triumph Mixed"

Site

Drainage must be good or plants will rot— prepare soil by digging in plenty of rotted manure or compost well before planting. Use multipurpose compost in containers and make sure there is a 2in layer of gravel in the base to guarantee good drainage. Support plants with twigs or short canes as they get taller and begin to flower.

GROWING METHOD

Sowing Sow in a 3½in pot in February/March and just cover the fine seed. Keep at a temperature of 75°F in a light place, and when seedlings are large enough transplant to cell trays or 3½in pots. Grow on and then harden off in late May before planting after frosts in early June. Plants are quite brittle so handle carefully.

Feeding Little additional feeding should be needed for plants in bedding displays, but containers can be liquid-fed every two weeks if slow-release fertilizer is not used; otherwise just water well.

Problems The flowers are very prone to bruising and damage by wind and heavy rain, so pick off casualties after unsettled spells to avoid an attack by gray mold which can cause rotting.

FLOWERING

Season Flowers appear throughout the summer.

Cutting Weak-stemmed as a cut flower.

AFTER FLOWERING

General Pull up after fall frosts and compost.

SALVIA
Scarlet sage

IF BRIGHT RED hurts your eyes, try one of the newer mixed salvia varieties containing more subtle shades of mauve, pink, and salmon.

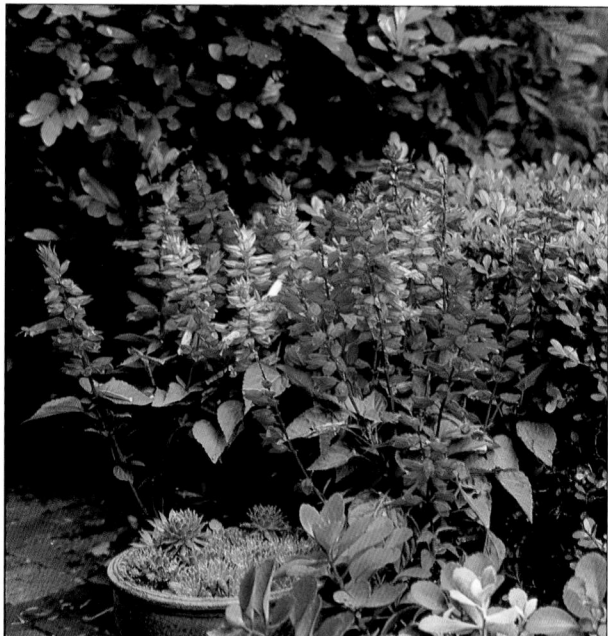

TO APPRECIATE SALVIAS to the full, grow them in wide, low pans on the patio and keep fed and watered throughout the summer.

FEATURES

Salvia splendens or scarlet sage is used in bold groups in bedding and is also a useful container plant. Most varieties grow to 1ft with similar spread, but giants like "Rambo" with red flowers reach 2ft. Flowers are long and tubular, in spikes, and colors other than the typical vibrant red include pink, mauve, salmon, pastel shades, and even bicolors such as "Salsa Bicolor Mixed," with white tipped blooms. Choose single colors or mixtures. Grown as a half-hardy annual but is in fact a perennial plant. Several varieties are usually available as young plants by mail order.

SALVIA AT A GLANCE

A half-hardy annual grown for its often bright flowers which are useful for bedding and pots. Frost hardy to 32°F (zone 10).

Jan	/	Recommended Varieties
Feb	sow 🖐	
Mar	sow/transplant 🖐	*Salvia splendens:*
Apr	grow on 🖐	"Blaze of Fire"
May	harden off/plant 🖐	"Firecracker"
Jun	flowering	"Orange Zest"
July	flowering	"Phoenix Mixed"
Aug	flowering	"Phoenix Purple"
Sept	flowering	"Rambo"
Oct	/	"Red Arrow"
Nov	/	"Scarlet King"
Dec	/	"Scarlet O'Hara"
		"Sizzler Burgundy"
		"Sizzler Mixed"

CONDITIONS

Aspect Plant salvias in a warm spot in full sun.
Site Tolerates a wide range of soils but drainage must be very good or plants may rot. Mix in well-rotted compost or manure before planting and use multipurpose compost for filling patio pots and windowboxes. Make sure plastic containers have drainage holes, and drill some if necessary, then put in 2in of gravel.

GROWING METHOD

Sowing February/March is the time to sow salvias, using 3½in pots of multipurpose compost. Lightly cover seeds and keep in a bright spot such as a windowsill at 64°F; expect seedlings in 2–3 weeks. Transplant into cell trays or 4in pots, grow on, harden off in late May before planting 6–12in apart.
Feeding Liquid feed plants in beds monthly. Mix slow-release fertilizer with compost at planting.
Problems Heavy wet soils can cause root rots, and slugs and snails will eat leaves of young plants in damp and wet spells. Use slug pellets.

FLOWERING

Season Cut faded spikes right back and plants will often produce a succession of flowers right into the late summer months.
Cutting Not suitable.

AFTER FLOWERING

General Dig out when over and compost.

SCABIOSA
Sweet scabious

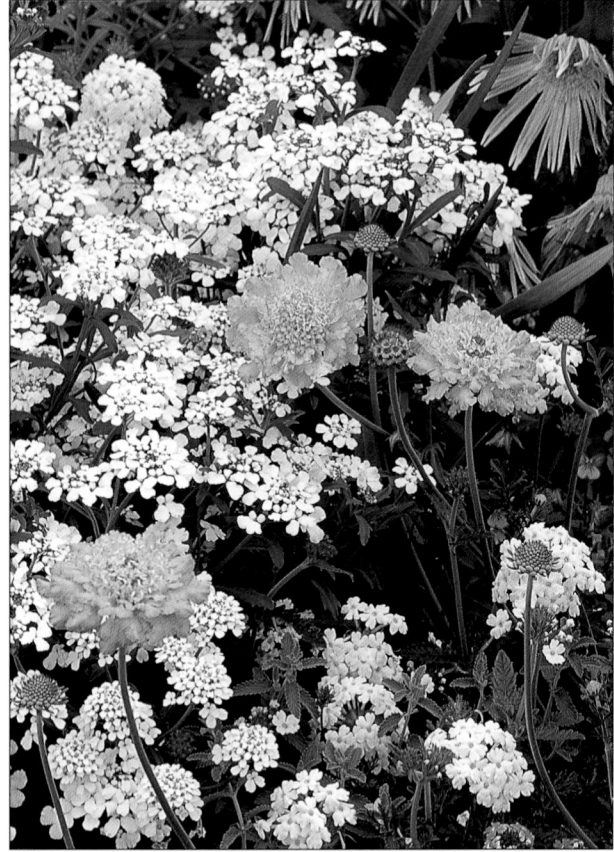

FOR A COTTAGE GARDEN feel, make sure you include pink scabious heads with other plants such as this white candytuft.

AS A BORDER FILLER sweet scabious is very useful and can be sown in any gaps during March and April for flowers from June.

FEATURES

Also known as pincushion flower, varieties of *Scabiosa atropurpurea* are easily-grown hardy annuals. The rounded flowerheads come in shades of blue, mauve, purple, pink, white, or crimson. Growing to 12–20in with tall, wire-like stems, scabious is best used for growing in big patches and for use as a filler in between other plants in a mixed or cottage-garden style border. A related variety, "Paper Moon," is grown for its spherical heads of dry bracts that follow the flowers.

CONDITIONS

Aspect   Prefers full sun and protection from wind.
Site   Well-drained soil is best—prepare ground by digging in organic matter well in advance.

GROWING METHOD

Sowing   Sow outdoors March/April where plants are to flower, in short drills ½in deep. Thin plants to 6–12in apart by early summer, and keep weed-free.
Feeding   Extra feeding in summer is not needed.
Problems   No particular problems.

FLOWERING

Season   Flowers appear from mid- to late summer.
Cutting   Excellent and long-lasting cut flower.

AFTER FLOWERING

General   Pull plants up when they are over.

SCABIOSA AT A GLANCE

An easily-grown hardy annual with rounded flowerheads that are useful in borders and for cutting. Frost hardy to 5°F (zone 7).

Jan	/	Recommended Varieties
Feb	/	*Scabiosa atropurpurea:*
Mar	sow	"Ace of Spades"
Apr	sow/thin out	"Border Hybrids"
May	thin out	"Dobies Giant Hybrids"
Jun	flowers/thin out	"Double Mixed"
July	flowering	"Dwarf Double Mixed"
Aug	flowering	"Tall Double"
Sept	flowering	
Oct	/	*Scabiosa stellata:*
Nov	/	"Paper Moon"/"Ping Pong"/"Drum Stick"
Dec	/	

SCHIZANTHUS
Poor man's orchid

THE EXOTIC APPEAL *of schizanthus earns it the common name of poor man's orchid. Each flower has a network of darker veining.*

THE FINELY DIVIDED *leaves are the perfect foil for the large heads of flowers. Varieties like "Pierrot" are distinctly dome-shaped.*

FEATURES

Also known as butterfly flower, schizanthus is stunning when used in bedding or in large pots and troughs. It has fern-like foliage and brilliantly colored, trumpet-shaped flowers in rich tones of pink, purple, magenta, pastels, or white. The flower throats are intricately patterned. Only the dwarf varieties reaching 8–12in are worth growing outdoors, and they must have shelter from strong winds and the hot midday sun. Schizanthus is a half-hardy annual and very sensitive to even slight frost.

SCHIZANTHUS AT A GLANCE

A half-hardy annual grown in containers on patios or in south-facing borders for summer flowers. Frost hardy to 32°F (zone 10).

Jan	/	Recommended Varieties
Feb	/	
Mar	sow	*Schizanthus pinnatus:*
Apr	transplant	"Angel Wings Mixed"
May	harden off	"Disco"
Jun	plant/flowers	"My Lovely"
July	flowering	"Pierrot"
Aug	flowering	"Star Parade"
Sept	flowering	
Oct	/	
Nov	/	
Dec	/	

CONDITIONS

Aspect Must be sheltered and have full sun.
Site Well-drained soil that has been enriched before planting with rotted manure or compost produces strong plants. Peat- or coir-based potting compost guarantees good results when containers are used.

GROWING METHOD

Sowing Seeds are sown in March at 61°F in small pots of peat- or coir-based seed compost, and seedlings appear after 1–2 weeks. Transplant to cell trays or 3½in pots, grow through spring and plant after hardening off, in early June. Space plants 6–12in apart. Pinch out growing tips when 4in high to make bushy plants.
Feeding Liquid feed monthly, and water containers regularly—if slow-release fertilizer is added to the compost extra feeding is not necessary.
Problems No special problems.

FLOWERING

Season Flowers reach a peak in mid to late summer and keep coming if faded stems are removed.
Cutting Not usually used as a cut flower.

AFTER FLOWERING

General The soft leafy plants soon break down when put on the compost heap.

SENECIO

Dusty miller

A WHITE WOOLLY LAYER covering the otherwise green leaves gives Senecio cineraria *its attractive silvery-gray appearance.*

OVERWINTERED PLANTS will keep on growing the following season, get larger, and also produce heads of bright yellow flowers.

FEATURES

Grown for its attractive silver-gray foliage, *Senecio cineraria* is often found listed under "cineraria" in seed catalogs. Use in bedding schemes and as a foliage container plant. Plants grow up to 12in tall and wide in summer, but if left outdoors over winter can be twice that if the yellow flowerheads are allowed to develop. Usually grown as a half-hardy annual, senecio is naturally an evergreen, eventually developing a tough woody base.

SENECIO AT A GLANCE

Prized for its silver-gray leaves and grown as a foliage bedding plant and for using in containers. Frost hardy to 23°F (zone 9).

Jan	/	Recommended Varieties
Feb	sow 🖐	
Mar	sow 🖐	*Senecio cineraria:*
Apr	transplant 🖐	**Fine, divided leaves**
May	harden off/plant 🖐	"Dwarf Silver"
Jun	leaves 🍃	"Silver Dust"
July	leaves 🍃	
Aug	leaves 🍃	**Rounded leaves**
Sept	leaves 🍃	"Cirrus"
Oct	leaves 🍃	
Nov	/	
Dec	/	

CONDITIONS

Aspect   Must have full sun.
Site   Well-drained soil is needed, but plants do well in light, sandy soils, especially in seaside gardens. Use multipurpose compost in pots.

GROWING METHOD

Sowing   Start plants in February/March at 68°F, by sowing seed in a small pot of compost and just covering. Expect seedlings after 1–2 weeks and keep in good light. Keep compost slightly on the dry side to avoid "damping off." Transplant to cell trays or 3½in pots, grow on, then harden off at the end of April and plant in May, 12in apart.

Feeding   Planted containers need liquid feed every two weeks, and regular watering. Plants stand dry spells outside but water them if they wilt.

Problems   If seedlings collapse, give a light watering with a copper-based fungicide.

FLOWERING

Season   The silvery leaves are attractive all summer.
Cutting   Foliage can be used in arrangements.

AFTER FLOWERING

General   Pull up and compost in fall. In many areas plants will survive the winter if left and produce bigger clumps of leaves and flowers.

SOLENOSTEMON
Coleus or flame nettle

"BLACK DRAGON" is a modern variety of coleus with black-edged, pinkish-red leaves, and is useful for specific color themes.

LEAF COLOR is apparent from an early age with solenostemon, making it possible to group the different colors when planting.

FEATURES

Look under "coleus" in seed catalogs for a wide range of varieties of this striking foliage plant. A half-hardy annual, solenostemon is a valuable bedding and container plant with large multicolored leaves that add a certain "tropical" and eccentric element to summer gardens. As well as mixtures, dark-leaved varieties like "Black Dragon" can be put to use in color-themed displays. Size range is 8–18in depending on variety, and it is important to remove all flowerheads as they appear or the plant will stop producing leaves. Varieties are available as young plants.

CONDITIONS

Aspect   Flame nettles need full sun to really thrive and also need shelter from persistent winds.
Site   Well-drained soil that has had plenty of rotted

manure or compost mixed in before planting produces strong plants with good color. Where they are grown in patio containers use multipurpose compost with slow-release fertilizer granules added at planting time.

GROWING METHOD

Sowing   March is the time to sow seed, in 3½in pots of multipurpose compost, just scattering the seed on the surface—don't cover. Keep at 75°F where they get bright light. Seedlings grow slowly but when they are large enough, transplant to 3½in pots or large cell trays. Pinch out the growing tip when plants are 3in tall to encourage bushy growth and the maximum number of leaves. Harden off in late May and plant after frosts, 6–12in apart.
Feeding   Liquid feeding every two weeks during summer maintains vigorous leaf growth. If slow-release fertilizer has been used, feed only monthly with half-strength liquid feed.
Problems   Slugs and snails attack young plants, so protect with slug pellets or a barrier of sharp grit around each plant.

FLOWERING

Season   All flowers should be removed as soon as they appear to encourage maximum leaf growth. Plants generally stay colorful until frosts.
Cutting   Not suitable.

AFTER FLOWERING

General   Favorite plants can be lifted and potted up in fall, and kept dry over winter in a frost-free greenhouse or cool room. Take cuttings from these plants in spring.

SOLENOSTEMON AT A GLANCE

A half-hardy annual grown for its brightly-colored leaves which are used in bedding and for patio pots. Frost hardy to 32°F (zone 10).

		Recommended Varieties
Jan	/	
Feb	/	*Solenostemon scutellarioides:*
Mar	sow	"Black Dragon"
Apr	transplant	"Camelot Mixed"
May	harden off/plant	"Dragon Sunset & Volcano, Mixed"
Jun	leaves	"Fairway"
July	leaves	"Flame Dancers"
Aug	leaves	"Magic Lace"
Sept	leaves	"Salmon Lace"
Oct	/	"Top Crown"
Nov	/	"Wizard Mixed"
Dec	/	

TAGETES
Marigold

THESE SINGLE-FLOWERED French marigolds are much daintier than their loud cousins with larger double flowers.

SINGLE FLOWER COLORS are useful in color-themed displays and this double-flowered French marigold would go well with blues.

FEATURES

The marigold "family" is made up of African and French types, and tagetes. All are easily grown half-hardy annuals and their flowers are among some of the loudest available—bright oranges, reds, yellows, and bronzes that set borders and containers alight. Plant size varies from 6in dwarfs to 3ft giants, and there are unusual flower colors such as "Vanilla" and even bright stripey-petalled varieties such as "Mr Majestic." Use them for bold bedding or as reliable patio container plants. Flowers can be single, semi or fully double and up to 3in across. Many varieties are also available as young plants.

TAGETES AT A GLANCE

A half-hardy annual grown for its bright flowers which are ideal for bedding and patio pots/troughs. Frost hardy to 32°F (zone 10).

		Recommended Varieties
Jan	/	
Feb	sow 🖎	**African marigolds**
Mar	sow 🖎	"Inca Mixed"
Apr	sow/transplant 🖎	"Shaggy Maggy"
May	harden off/plant 🖎	"Vanilla"
Jun	flowering 🌼	**French marigolds**
July	flowering 🌼	"Boy O'Boy Mixed"
Aug	flowering 🌼	"Mischief Mixed"
Sept	flowering 🌼	"Mr Majestic"
Oct	/	*Tagetes tenuifolia:*
Nov	/	"Lemon Gem"
Dec	/	"Red Gem"

CONDITIONS

Aspect   Must have a sunny position.
Site   Marigolds are not too fussy about soils, but mixing in rotted compost before planting helps keep soil moist. For container growing use multipurpose compost with slow-release fertilizer granules mixed well in. Tall varieties of African marigold need shelter from wind.

GROWING METHOD

Sowing   All marigolds can be sown February–April, but a May sowing on a windowsill will also be successful as they are fast growers and soon catch up. Just cover the large seeds with compost and keep at 70°F. Seedlings will appear in a week and can be transplanted to cell trays. Grow on, harden off in late May and plant after frosts. Nip off any flower buds that appear before and two weeks after planting.
Feeding   Fortnightly liquid feeding keeps plants in beds going strong. Keep containers well watered.
Problems   Slugs and snails can strip plants overnight so protect with slug pellets in wet/warm spells.

FLOWERING

Season   Early sowings produce earlier flowers and vice-versa. Late sowings provide handy color in late summer and if grown in pots, plants can be used to revive flagging summer containers.
Cutting   African marigolds are useful for cutting.

AFTER FLOWERING

General   Pull plants up when finished and compost.

THUNBERGIA
Black-eyed Susan

BLACK-EYED SUSAN is one of the brightest and showiest of all the annual climbers, and readily entwines the stems of other plants. It hates having its roots disturbed so sow seeds straight into small pots, and pot 2–3 plants on together when necessary. Plant out after frosts.

FEATURES

The flowers of thunbergia can be orange, yellow, or white, and sometimes the black eye is missing altogether. Grow as a half-hardy annual for indoors and out. Outdoors, grow up wigwams of 5ft canes, either in borders, or large tubs for a moveable display of color. In hanging baskets thunbergia soon entwines the chains, making an effective camouflage. In patio tubs train plants up through other tall annuals like ricinus and sunflowers, or plant them around the base of outdoor plants in early summer. In colder areas grow plants in the conservatory or porch to guarantee a good show of flowers. Seed pods tend to set very easily which reduces the ability of the plant to keep flowering, so nip these off regularly.

THUNBERGIA AT A GLANCE

A half-hardy annual climber flowering in summer for patio containers, baskets, and bedding. Frost hardy to 32°F (zone 10).

Jan	/	Recommended Varieties
Feb	/	
Mar	sow 🖐	*Thunbergia alata:*
Apr	pot on/grow on 🖐	"Susie Mixed"
May	harden/plant out 🖐	
Jun	flowers 🌸	
July	flowers 🌸	
Aug	flowers 🌸	
Sept	flowers 🌸	
Oct	/	
Nov	/	
Dec	/	

CONDITIONS

Aspect   A south-facing spot in full sun is essential. In conservatories direct hot sun should be avoided or the leaves may be scorched.

Site   In containers use multipurpose compost with slow-release fertilizer added. Well-drained, moisture retentive soil, with rotted manure or compost is needed outdoors.

GROWING METHOD

Sowing   Soak seeds overnight then sow three to a 3½in diameter pot in March. Germinate at 64°F. Germination is erratic and seedlings may take a month to emerge. A small wigwam of canes will support the shoots. Grow several plants on in large pots during May, then harden off and plant after the last frosts. They dislike root disturbance.

Feeding   Liquid feed once a week in summer.

Problems   Red spider mite attacks leaves. Wet the leaves daily or use a spray containing pirimiphos-methyl. Indoors use the predator phytoseiulus. Whitefly will feed on the leaves and cause sticky "honeydew." Use a spray containing permethrin or the natural encarsia indoors.

FLOWERING

Season   Flowers appear all summer and the flowering period is extended when plants are grown under some form of protection.

Cutting   Not suitable.

AFTER FLOWERING

General   Nip off faded flowers. Remove outdoor plants after frosts and add to the compost heap.

TITHONIA
Mexican sunflower

THE DAHLIA-LIKE FLOWERS of tithonia have an "exotic" feel to them and each one can be up to 3in across, on strong stems.

THE HEART-SHAPED LEAVES of Mexican sunflower are an added bonus, and each flower also has a distinct swollen "neck."

FEATURES

Tithonia, as its common name suggests, comes from warmer areas, so does well when there is plenty of sun. Grow as a half-hardy annual. "Fiesta del Sol" is just 1ft tall, while "Torch" can reach 4ft. Flowers are large, exotic-looking and dahlia-like, red-orange, and have a distinct swollen "neck."

CONDITIONS

Aspect   Must have full sun or plants will suffer.

TITHONIA AT A GLANCE		
A half-hardy annual grown for its large orange flowers on strong stems. Use in bedding and pots. Frost hardy to 32°F (zone 10).		
Jan	/	Recommended Varieties
Feb	sow	*Tithonia rotundifolia:*
Mar	sow	**Tall varieties**
Apr	sow/transplant	"Goldfinger"
May	harden off/plant	"Torch"
Jun	flowering	
July	flowering	**Short varieties**
Aug	flowering	"Fiesta del Sol"
Sept	flowering	
Oct	/	
Nov	/	
Dec	/	

Site

Not fussy about soil, but needs good drainage. Plant in a fairly sheltered spot away from cold driving winds. Tithonia has a tendency to go pale and yellow when growing conditions are poor. Grow plants in containers if the soil is heavy, using multipurpose compost.

GROWING METHOD

Sowing   Sow seeds February to April in 3½in pots of multipurpose compost, just covering them, and germinate at 64°F in a warm place or heated propagator. Transplant to individual 3½in pots or large cell trays and grow on. Harden off for 2–3 weeks and plant in early summer when the soil warms up. If seedlings or young plants turn yellow they are being kept too cold. Can also be sown outdoors in early June where plants are to flower.

Feeding   Feed container-grown plants twice a month with liquid feed.

Problems   Slugs may attack the leaves after early summer rains so protect with slug pellets.

FLOWERING

Season   Flowers appear from midsummer and later sowings continue to give color into fall.

Cutting   Suitable for use as a cut flower.

AFTER FLOWERING

General   Pull up after flowering. May self-seed.

TORENIA
Wishbone flower

WISHBONE FLOWER gets its common name from the dark markings found on the lower lip of the flowers of some varieties.

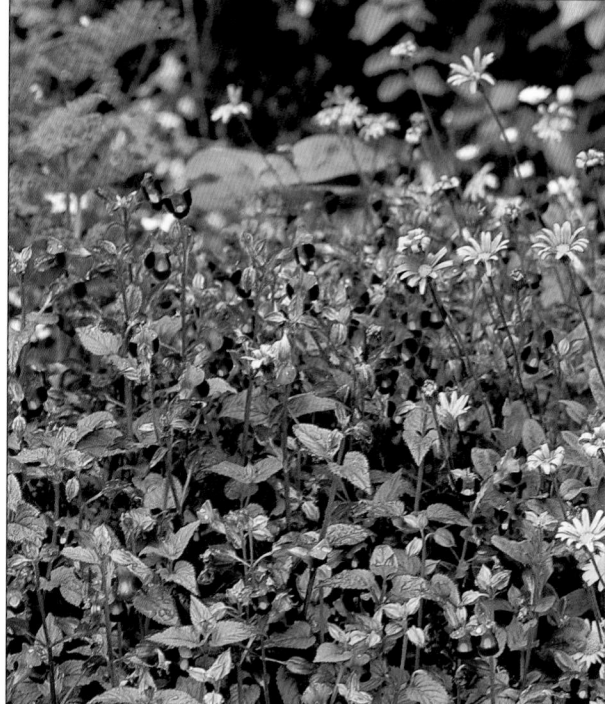

SHELTER IS ESSENTIAL for success with torenia, which can also be potted up and grown on as a flowering plant for indoors.

FEATURES

Wishbone flower needs to be in the "front row" of a summer bedding scheme, or used around the edge of pots and troughs. The variety "Susie Wong" has bright yellow flowers with black throats, and a spreading habit making it ideal for baskets. Half-hardy annuals, torenias grow no more than 1ft in height.

CONDITIONS

Aspect   Choose a sheltered spot with sun.

TORENIA AT A GLANCE

A low growing half-hardy annual grown for its colorful lipped flowers, for edging in beds and pots. Frost hardy to 32°F (zone 10).

		Recommended Varieties
Jan	/	
Feb	/	*Torenia fournieri:*
Mar	sow	"Clown Mixed"
Apr	sow/transplant	"Susie Wong"
May	grow/harden off	
Jun	plant/flowers	
July	flowering	
Aug	flowering	
Sept	flowering	
Oct	/	
Nov	/	
Dec	/	

Site

Dig in rotted manure or compost a few weeks ahead of planting out, or use multipurpose compost for container growing. Soil and compost used must be free-draining. Avoid planting where winds are persistent.

GROWING METHOD

Sowing   Sow the very small seeds in pots or trays in March/April, barely cover and keep at 64°F in a well-lit place. When large enough the seedlings can be transplanted to cell trays and grown on until late May, then hardened off and planted well after the last frosts, 6in apart, or in groups in patio pots. Plant five plants to a 16in diameter hanging basket, four around the sides and one in the center. "Susie Wong" will creep in and out of other plants.

Feeding   Feed regularly every 2–3 weeks with a balanced liquid plant food.

Problems   Trouble free.

FLOWERING

Season   Throughout summer.

Cutting   Not used as a cut flower.

AFTER FLOWERING

General   Pull or dig out the plants when flowering has stopped. They will sometimes self-seed, and they will then produce seedlings in the following year.

TROPAEOLUM
Nasturtium

"MOONLIGHT" is a climbing variety of nasturtium reaching 6ft with soft yellow flowers against light green leaves.

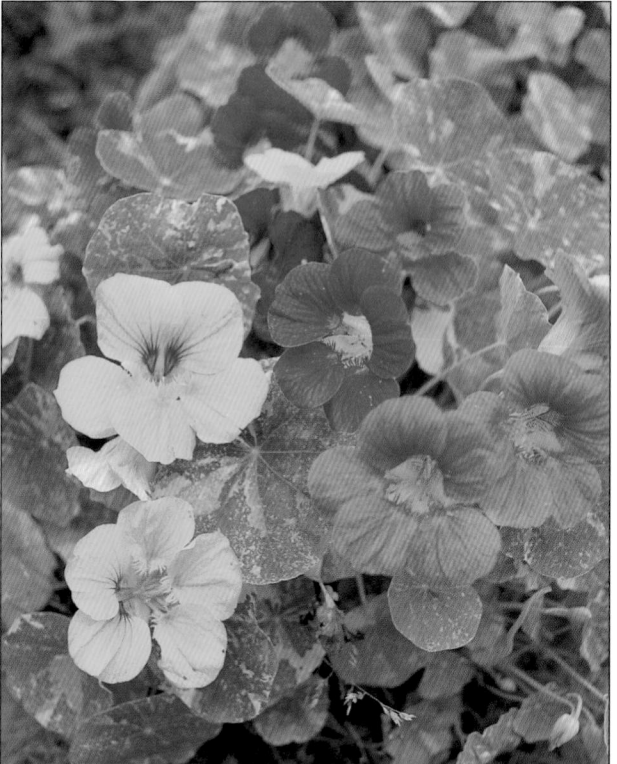

FOR DOUBLE VALUE grow "Alaska Mixed" with light green leaves speckled with creamy-white, plus red and yellow flowers.

FEATURES

With big seeds and quick growth, tropaeolum, better known as nasturtium, is one of the easiest of all hardy annuals to grow. Plants just 9in tall are perfect for bedding and patio planters, while others will scramble up throughout a dull hedge. The color range is huge, and single and mixed colors are available. For pretty leaves too, grow "Alaska Mixed," which is speckled with white.

TROPAEOLUM AT A GLANCE

A hardy annual grown for its colorful flowers and often variegated leaves. For beds and containers. Frost hardy to 32°F (zone 10).

Jan	/	Recommended Varieties
Feb	sow	
Mar	sow	*Tropaeolum majus:*
		Tall climbers
Apr	transplant	"Climbing Mixed"
May	transplant	"Jewel of Africa"
		Short, mixed colors
Jun	flowering	"Alaska Mixed"
July	flowering	"Gleam Mixed"
Aug	flowering	"Tip Top Mixed"
Sept	flowering	**Single colors**
Oct	/	"Empress of India"
Nov	/	"Gleaming Mahogany"
Dec	/	"Moonlight"

CONDITIONS

Aspect Needs full sun.
Site Poor, thin soil gives excellent results when grown under hedges or in bedding displays.

GROWING METHOD

Sowing Simply push the large seeds 1–2in into the soil in April, in groups of 3–5 where plants are to flower. Fleshy seedlings appear 2–3 weeks later and they can all be left to develop and form a large clump. If needed for containers, sow three seeds to a 3½in pot at the same time and keep warm until seedlings appear, then keep outdoors.

Feeding Feeding encourages leaves at the expense of flowers, although if other plants are growing in a container or basket, some extra feeding is unavoidable. Don't feed plants growing in soil.

Problems Aphids and caterpillars feed under the leaves, so check regularly and squash if seen.

FLOWERING

Season Flowering is all summer long.
Cutting Not used cut, but flowers and the peppery leaves can be used raw in summer salads.

AFTER FLOWERING

General Pull up and compost. Self-seeds very easily.

VERBENA
Verbena

SOFTER PASTEL SHADES can be found in modern varieties of verbena—these are just a few flowers of the variety "Romance Pastels."

"PEACHES & CREAM" has a unique color that makes it a real winner, at 8in, for patio containers and hanging baskets.

FEATURES

Most verbenas grow 6–12in tall and are prized for their heads of bright flowers. Mixtures or single shades like "Peaches & Cream" are used for planting containers or for bedding. Raise from seed—although this is tricky—or grow them from mail order plants. Most trailing verbenas are not seed raised but bought as ready-grown plants from garden centers and mail order catalogs in spring.

VERBENA AT A GLANCE

A half-hardy annual used in bedding and containers. Masses of bright flowers appear during summer. Frost hardy to 32°F (zone 10).

		Recommended Varieties
Jan	/	
Feb	/	*Verbena hybrida:*
Mar	sow	**Mixed colors**
Apr	transplant	"Crown Jewels"
May	grow/harden off	"Novalis Mixed"
Jun	flowering	"Raspberry Crush"
July	flowering	"Romance Pastels"
Aug	flowering	**Single colors**
Sept	flowering	"Adonis Blue"
Oct	/	"Apple Blossom"
Nov	/	"Peaches & Cream"
Dec	/	**Spreading/trailing**
		"Misty"

CONDITIONS

Aspect   Needs full sun for best results.
Site   Use multipurpose compost in containers, and mix rotted compost with soil outdoors.

GROWING METHOD

Sowing   To succeed with verbena seed, sow on the surface of peat-based seed compost in March and cover the seeds with a thin layer of fine vermiculite. Water and keep at 70°F. Seedlings appear 2–3 weeks later, and should be kept slightly on the dry side. When large enough, transplant seedlings to cell trays or individual 3in pots, and grow on. Plant after hardening off in late spring/early summer.
Feeding   Feed monthly with balanced liquid feed.
Problems   Powdery mildew can attack leaves—use a spray containing sulfur at the first signs.

FLOWERING

Season   Flowers appear all summer.
Cutting   Not used for cutting.

AFTER FLOWERING

General   Pull up when finished and use for compost.

VIOLA CORNUTA
Viola

DIMINUITIVE *"Bambini" violas are guaranteed to steal your heart with their inquisitive whiskery faces.*

FOR A TOUCH OF DRAMA *try combining the moody "Blackjack" with a clear yellow variety in a hanging basket.*

FEATURES

Violas are smaller than pansies but they are no less prolific, and what they lack in size they make up for in sheer character. Most are varieties of *Viola cornuta*, and all are quite hardy, being sown in spring or summer. Grow single colors, mixtures like "Bambini," or trailing yellow "Sunbeam" for hanging baskets. Violas grow to around 6in, making bushy little plants for bedding or containers. Try planting them in cottage style wicker baskets. Available as young plants.

VIOLA AT A GLANCE

A hardy annual grown for its pretty little pansy flowers which appear on branching plants. Frost hardy to 5°F (zone 7).

Jan	/	
Feb	sow 🌱	Recommended Varieties
Mar	sow 🌱	**Viola hybrids:**
Apr	sow/flower 🌱🌸	"Bambini Mixed"
May	sow/flower 🌱🌸	"Blackjack"
Jun	sow/flower 🌱🌸	"Blue Moon"
July	sow/flower 🌱🌸	"Cuty"
Aug	grow on/flowers 🌸	"Juliette Mixed"
Sept	grow on/flowers 🌸	"Midnight Runner"
Oct	plant 🌱	"Princess Mixed"
Nov	/	"Sorbet Yesterday, Today & Tomorrow"
Dec	/	"Sunbeam"

CONDITIONS

Aspect Grows well in sun or dappled, light shade.
Site Soil does not need to be over prepared, but must be well-drained. For container growing use multipurpose compost.

GROWING METHOD

Sowing Sow from February under cover for flowers the same summer, or outside May–July for flowers the following spring. Either way, sow in a 3½in pot of multipurpose compost and barely cover seeds. In early spring keep at 60°F and transplant seedlings when large enough to cell trays, grow, harden off, and plant in late May. When summer sowing, stand the pot outside in shade to germinate then treat seedlings the same, planting out in October where you want the plants to flower.

Feeding Extra feeding is not usually necessary.
Problems Use slug pellets if the leaves are attacked.

FLOWERING

Season Spring-sown plants flower during summer, summer-sown the following spring/summer.
Cutting The delicate cut stems of "Queen Charlotte" are sometimes used for making scented posies.

AFTER FLOWERING

General Plants often carry on as short-lived perennials, and also self-seed freely.

VIOLA TRICOLOR
Wild pansy

EACH FLOWER of wild pansy is like a tiny whiskered "face" and individual plants all vary from each other very slightly.

ONE PLANT left in the ground to mature through the summer will shed hundreds of seeds which will germinate the next spring.

FEATURES

Viola tricolor is the wild pansy, also known commonly as heartsease or Johnny-jump-up. It is usually grown as a hardy annual but can also be treated as a biennial. Much daintier than its relatives the pansies, these plants are at home in cottage-style beds and as pot edging. A few single colored varieties are available, such as the unusual "Bowles' Black," having black flowers with a small central yellow "eye".

VIOLA AT A GLANCE

A hardy annual grown for its pretty little pansy flowers which appear on branching plants. Frost hardy to 5°F. (zone 7)

Jan	/	Recommended Varieties
Feb	sow	
Mar	sow	*Viola tricolor*
Apr	sow/flower	**Single colors:**
May	sow/flower	**Blue**
Jun	sow/flower	"Prince Henry"
July	sow/flower	**Yellow**
Aug	grow on/flowers	"Prince John"
Sept	grow on/flowers	
Oct	plant	
Nov	/	
Dec	/	

CONDITIONS

Aspect
Site — Grows well in sun or dappled, light shade. Soil does not need to be over prepared, but must be well-drained. Multipurpose compost is best for growing *Viola tricolor* in containers.

GROWING METHOD

Sowing — Sow from February under cover for flowers the same summer, or outside May–July for flowers the following spring. Either way, sow in a 3½in pot of multipurpose compost and barely cover seeds. In early spring keep at 60°F and transplant seedlings when large enough to cell trays, grow, harden off, and plant in late May. When summer sowing, stand the pot outside in shade to germinate, treat seedlings the same, and plant in October.

Feeding — Extra feeding is not usually necessary.

Problems — Use slug pellets if the leaves are attacked.

FLOWERING

Season — Spring-sown plants flower during summer, summer-sown the following spring/summer.

Cutting — Not suitable for cutting.

AFTER FLOWERING

General — Pull plants up and compost, or leave a few to shed seeds. They will sometimes grow as perennials and last for several years.

VIOLA WITTROCKIANA
Pansy

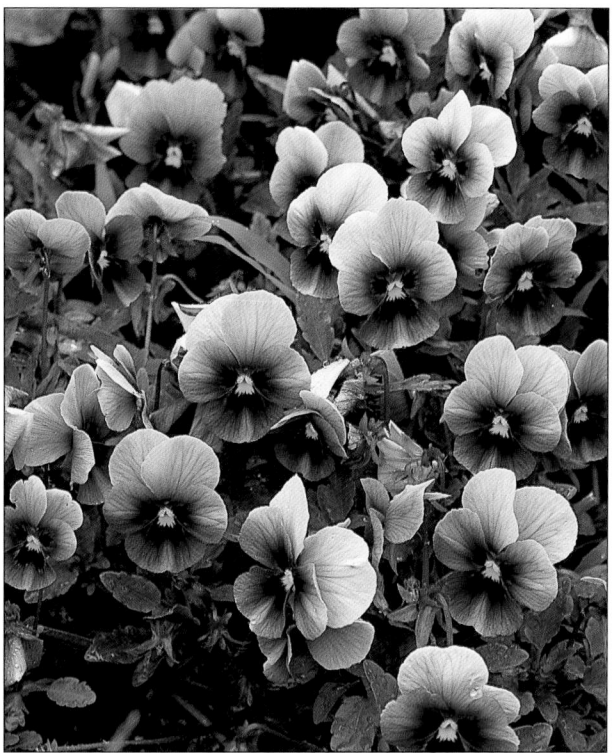

PANSY FLOWERS have "faces" that tend to face the sun, especially in early spring. Use them in patio pots with bulbs like tulips.

"JOLLY JOKER" is a unique and prolific variety of summer-flowering pansy with orange and rich royal purple two-tone flowers.

FEATURES

Pansies are hardy and will flower almost all year around. There are two groups, summer flowering, and fall/winter flowering. None grow more than 8in tall. Flowers are like large flat "faces" up to 3in across. Colors vary enormously from single, pastel shades to striking bicolors, and are available in mixtures or as single colors. Many varieties are available as young plants by mail order. Most are varieties of *Viola wittrockiana*.

VIOLA AT A GLANCE

Hardy and grown either as an annual or a biennial for flowers in summer and fall/winter. Frost hardy to 5°F (zone 7).

Jan	/	
Feb	sow	
Mar	sow	
Apr	sow/flower	
May	sow/flower	
Jun	sow/flower	
July	sow/flower	
Aug	grow on/flowers	
Sept	grow on/flowers	
Oct	plant	
Nov	/	
Dec	/	

Recommended Varieties

Viola wittrockiana:

Summer flowers
  "Antique Shades"
  "Padparadja"
  "Romeo & Juliet"
  "Watercolors"

Fall/winter flowers
  "Homefires"
  "Ultima Pastel Mixed"
  "Universal Mixed"
  "Velour Mixed"

CONDITIONS

Aspect   Fall/winter pansies need full sun. Summer flowering varieties like dappled shade.

Site   Add plenty of manure to the soil. Winter pansies need excellent drainage. Use multipurpose compost for containers.

GROWING METHOD

Sowing   Sow from February under cover for flowers the same summer, or outside May–July for flowers the following spring. Either way, sow in a 3½in pot of multipurpose compost and barely cover seeds. In early spring keep at 60°F and transplant seedlings when large enough to cell trays, grow, harden off, and plant in late May. When summer-sowing, stand the pot outside in shade to germinate then treat seedlings the same, planting out in October where you want the plants to flower.

Feeding   Liquid feed summer plants every two weeks.

Problems   Spray with permethrin if aphids attack.

FLOWERING

Season   Spring-sown plants flower in summer, fall-sown from October onward.

Cutting   Pansies last a few days in water.

AFTER FLOWERING

General   Pull up and compost when finished.

ZINNIA
Zinnia

ZINNIA FLOWERS tend to come as doubles but plants sometimes appear that are single like this. Zinnias are good bee plants.

IF PINCHED WHEN YOUNG zinnias make bushy, branching plants that fill gaps in mixed borders quickly. Take dead flowers off.

FEATURES

There is a zinnia for every garden. Dwarf varieties at 6in tall are suited to beds and containers, while "Dahlia-Flowered Mixed" has big heads on stems 2ft high, and is useful for mixed borders. Modern varieties have fully double flowers, and some like "Zebra Mixed" are stripey. "Starbright Mixed" is an unusual variety with masses of small orange and gold flowers. Red, yellow, pink, scarlet, orange, lavender, purple, white, and even green are typical flower colors. Half-hardy annual.

ZINNIA AT A GLANCE

A half-hardy annual grown for its bright flowers in a wide range of colors, for bedding and cutting. Frost hardy to 32°F (zone 10).

Jan	/	Recommended Varieties
Feb	/	
Mar	/	**Zinnia hybrids:**
Apr	/	**Tall varieties**
May	sow	"Allsorts"
Jun	thin out	"Dahlia-Flowered Mixed"
July	flowering	"Zebra Mixed"
Aug	flowering	**Short varieties**
Sept	flowering	"Belvedere"
Oct	flowering	"Fairyland"
Nov	/	"Persian Carpet Mixed"
Dec	/	"Starbright Mixed"
		"Thumbelina"

CONDITIONS

Aspect Zinnias enjoy heat and need sun and shelter.
Site Must have well-drained soil, previously improved with rotted organic matter. For containers use multipurpose compost.

GROWING METHOD

Sowing Although half-hardy, zinnias grow best when sown direct where they are to flower, in short drills ½in deep. Do this in May and cover seedlings with a piece of garden fleece on frosty nights. Thin out seedlings so the young plants are eventually 6–24in apart, depending on their final size. To grow dwarf varieties in containers sow 2–3 seeds to a 3in pot at the same time, leave just the strongest, grow on, and plant when ready, not disturbing the roots.
Feeding Extra feeding is usually not necessary.
Problems Powdery mildew can be a problem, so avoid planting too close—sulfur sprays can help. Stem rots cause plants to collapse suddenly.

FLOWERING

Season Flowers appear from midsummer onward.
Cutting Very good cut flower. "Envy Double" is a striking plant with double green flowers.

AFTER FLOWERING

General Pull up in fall and compost.

Growing
Bulbs

GROWING BULBS

Bulbs are the easiest of plants to grow—probably no other plant group gives as much variety and pleasure to the gardener with so little effort. Even people without yards can enjoy bulbs as there are so many that make excellent container plants.

Most people think of bulbs as an essential part of spring, but spring is by no means their only season—there are bulbs that flower through the summer, fall, and even through the depths of the winter. They are usually very easy to look after, and many types will go on giving pleasure for years with the minimum of attention.

ABOVE: These parrot tulips just breaking from their buds already show the typical ruffled petals and color streaking.

LEFT: Deepest blue hyacinths make a wonderful foil for the bright yellow tulips in this landscape planting.

BULBS, CORMS, TUBERS, AND RHIZOMES

What most people know as bulbs covers a whole range of plants with some kind of underground storage organ that allows their survival over their dormant season, which may be winter or summer. They include true bulbs and plants with corms, tubers, and rhizomes.
• True bulbs are made up of a bud enclosed by modified leaves or fleshy scales from which roots and shoots emerge. The shoots grow out of the pointed top and the roots from the other end. Most, such as onions, daffodils, and hyacinths, have an outer papery cover or tunic: lilies, which are bulbs, too, have a bulb of swollen leaf bases but lack the protective tunic.
• Corms are bulb-like structures formed by the enlargement

of an underground stem base. They do not have the "rings" of true bulbs, but stems grow out of the top and roots from the base in the same way. Freesias, gladioli, and crocuses all grow from corms.
• Tubers are swollen underground parts of roots or stems. Dahlias grow from buds at the ends of tubers.
• Rhizomes may grow underground or along the soil surface. They are fleshy, tuberous roots with new growth emerging from the end. Some irises grow from rhizomes (other irises are bulbs). Some bulbous plants described as having rhizomes or tubers appear to have little more than a small crown from which the roots emerge.

For convenience, all the above groups are discussed throughout this book as bulbs.

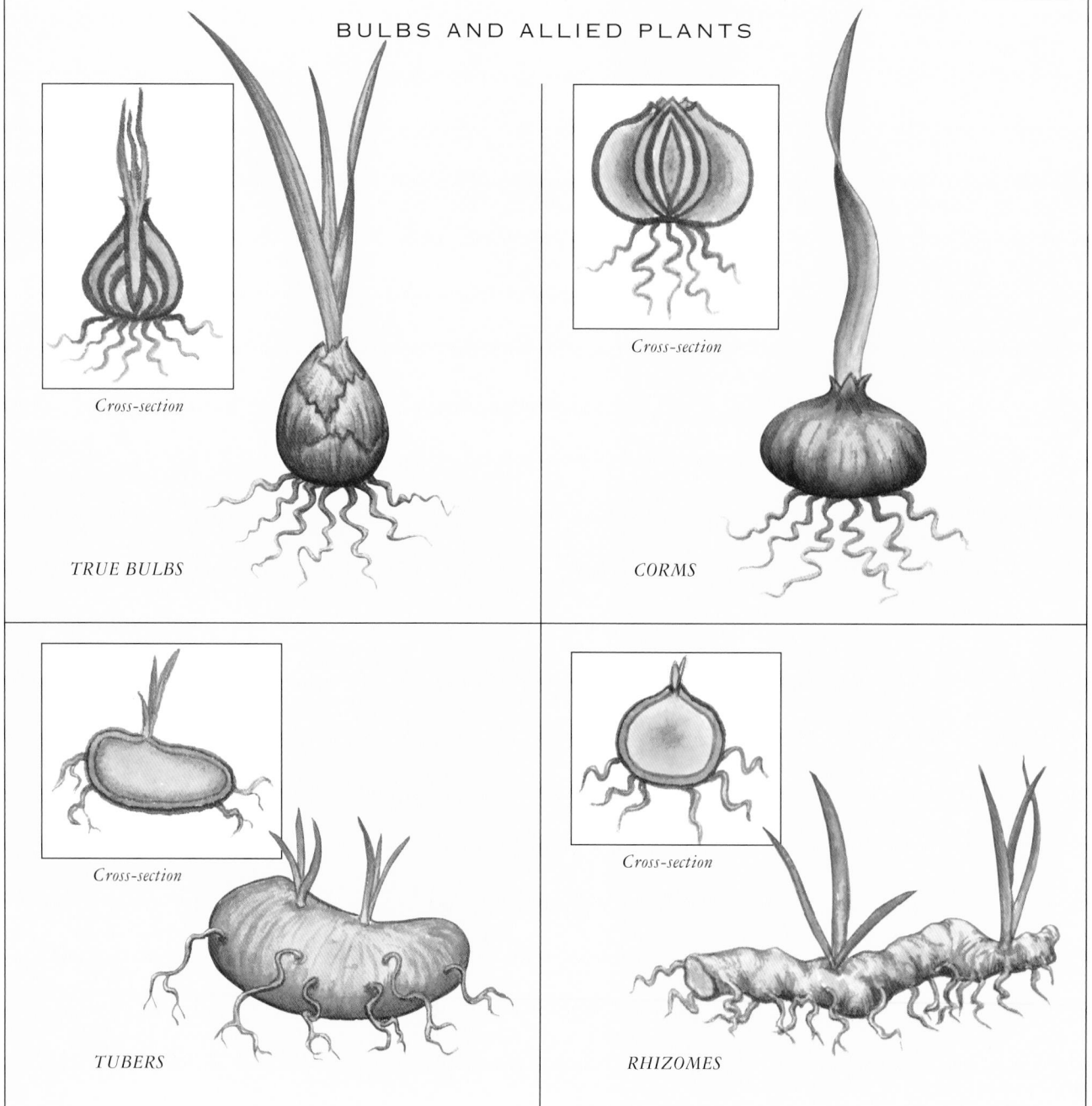

BULBS AND ALLIED PLANTS

Cross-section

Cross-section

TRUE BULBS

CORMS

Cross-section

Cross-section

TUBERS

RHIZOMES

TENDER BULBS

Indoors or out?

Some bulbs are not suitable for growing outdoors, and must be grown in a greenhouse or conservatory, or in the home, to produce good results. In many cases, bulbs can be started into growth under protection and brought outside later in the season when the weather has warmed up: when grown in containers, these look good on patios or even positioned amongst other flowering plants in borders so that the container is hidden. Other bulbs, however, need to be grown under protection throughout their lives, as their flowers would be spoiled outdoors.

Which bulbs must be considered tender enough for indoor cultivation often depends on the area in which you live, and the situation of your own garden. Species that can be grown successfully outside in mild areas would often fail in cold, exposed gardens, but even in mild regions a garden may be exposed to cold, windy weather that makes it unsuitable for the more tender plants.

Experience is often the only way to gain an accurate picture of which plants are hardy enough for your conditions, but when growing dubiously hardy bulbs, always play safe and overwinter one or two specimens under cover in case an unexpectedly cold winter destroys your outdoor stock. Protect slightly tender bulbs by heaping straw, dry leaves, or bracken over the planting site once the foliage has died down in the fall: this helps to prevent frost penetrating to the bulbs below ground. Deep planting is also recommended for extra protection.

The table below gives a guide to the plants that need indoor conditions, and those that are risky outdoors in all but the most favored areas of the country. It is often adequate to bring tender bulbs under cover for the winter only: the information under each bulb entry gives further details.

THE TUBEROUS ROOTS of dahlias can be left in the ground in some areas, but are better lifted and stored in a frost-free place.

TENDER BULBS

BULBS FOR THE HOUSE, GREENHOUSE, OR CONSERVATORY ONLY

- Achimenes
- Clivia
- Gloriosa
- Hippeastrum
- Lachenalia
- Sinningia

BULBS NEEDING PROTECTION OR OVERWINTERING UNDER COVER IN COLD AREAS

- Agapanthus
- Amaryllis
- Canna
- Crinum
- Cyrtanthus
- Dierama
- Eremurus
- Eucomis
- Gladiolus callianthus
- Hedychium
- Hymenocallis
- Ixia
- Nerine
- Polianthes
- Romulea
- Schizostylis
- Sparaxis
- Sprekelia
- Tigridia
- Tritonia
- Zantedeschia
- Zephyranthes

AGAPANTHUS PLANTS are suitable for leaving outdoors over winter in warmer areas of the country only.

STRONGLY CONTRASTING white and rich crimson tulips are mass planted under a silver birch tree in this lovely garden. The tulip planting is brilliantly set off by the wide, sweeping border of purple Virginian stock.

CHOOSING BULBS

What do you want from your plants?

There are so many bulbs, in such a range of colors, sizes, and forms, that it is all too easy to get carried away when buying them. Their appeal is instantaneous: here they are, ready packaged, just needing to be popped into the soil—and within a short time, with no further effort, you can expect to be enjoying the brilliant flowers pictured on the display units at garden centers.

Perhaps one of their greatest virtues is that the bulk of bulbs appear for sale at just the time when summer is finally drawing to a close. The summer flowers are nearly over, trees will soon be shedding their leaves, and the days growing shorter and more gloomy; the cold, wet, miserable weeks of winter stretch out ahead. No wonder we are so pleased to see the arrival of bulbs, with their promise of the spring to come!

But in order to achieve the best possible results from your bulbs, you should plan for them more carefully. Consider the type of garden in which they are to be grown; whether it is mild and sheltered or cold and exposed. Where in the garden are the bulbs to grow? Is there space on a rock garden or in a border? Do you have an area of lawn where bulbs could be naturalized, and if so, are you prepared for the grass to be

untidy while the bulb foliage is dying down? Do you want all your bulbs to flower in spring, or would a longer flowering season be more appropriate? Do you want bulbs in pots for growing on the patio, or varieties that will flower out of season to brighten up the home in the middle of winter? If you have a good idea of what you want from your bulbs *before* you go out to buy them, it could save you making some expensive mistakes.

Choose for color

Consider the color schemes of your bulb planting as you would any other item, either inside your home or outside it. Do you want strong contrasts in color, gradations of a single color, or colors that complement each other? Do you want to create a bright, warm, active look or do you want to give a cooler, calmer impression? Warm, active colors are red, yellow, orange, and bright pink, while blue, lavender, white, cream, pale pink, and pale yellow are cooler colors.

Blue and white spring-flowering bulbs include spring star flower, grape hyacinth, bluebell, and hyacinth, all of which would team well with white or cream daffodils. Some of the brightest bulbs in the "hot" color range are ranunculus and harlequin flowers (sparaxis). Both these are more commonly available in mixed colors but sometimes you can find a supplier who is able to sell them as single colors. Anemones also come in strong colors and these too can be purchased in single colors. Greater impact is generally achieved by planting blocks of single colors rather than mixtures. Try bulbs in blocks of red, orange, and yellow for a tremendous impact, or if you want a quieter look, plant groups of two shades of pink and white.

Many bulbous plants, such as daffodils, come in a wide range of varieties but a fairly limited color range: they also look their best if planted in groups of one variety. Corn lily is another good example. Although there is a wide color range available, and corn lilies can be purchased in mixtures, these flowers look best if planted in blocks of one color. They can, of course, be planted as mixtures, especially in an informal garden setting, but in nature they would be more likely to grow in blocks of one color.

Consider flowering time
Some gardeners prefer one huge display over three or four weeks in spring while others may find more interest in spreading the season over several months of the year. For instance, with crocus alone, different varieties provide blooms from late fall right through to mid-spring. There is some form of bulbous plant to give a display in every month of the year if that is what you require.

It can be hard to give precise information on exactly when different species will be in bloom, as the time can vary from one district to another and even from one garden to another because of variation in microclimates. However, if you spend some time noting the times when bulbs flower in your garden, in future seasons you will be able to plan to have a succession of bulbs in flower during many months of the year.

BUYING BULBS

There are several different ways in which you can buy bulbs. Most garden centers, and several other stores, sell bulbs in perforated plastic bags backed by a card giving planting details, along with a picture of the bulb in flower. Bulbs are also available in small netting sacks with attached pictures and growing instructions. Most garden centers and nurseries sell bulbs in bulk in the main planting season, and you can make your own selection from large bins. Another option is to send away for catalogs from bulb-growing nurseries and order bulbs by mail—these growers advertise in popular gardening magazines. The range of bulbs available from specialist nurseries is generally very much more extensive than what is on offer at your local garden center. Mail order is a good option if you want some of the more unusual varieties, and if you want to order a lot of bulbs as it can be a good deal cheaper, though you need to take postal charges into account. When planning to buy by mail order, remember that you need to order well in advance of the planting date; if you leave it until bulbs are starting to appear in stores, the specialist suppliers are likely to have sold out of many of the less common varieties. Once you are on the mailing list of mail order suppliers, they will send you their catalogues in plenty of time in future years.

When buying bulbs at a garden center, try to buy them as soon as possible after they have been delivered, as they tend to deteriorate in the warm conditions, and will soon become bruised as other buyers sort through them to make their choice. Select plump, firm, well-rounded bulbs and make sure there are no soft spots or patches of mould. Especially avoid buying any bulbs that are starting to shoot and showing signs

HYACINTH BULBS will be on sale from early fall. Select yours early to be sure of getting the best available.

GOLDEN DAFFODILS planted in sweeping drifts beneath a fine magnolia tree show to advantage against an old stone wall.

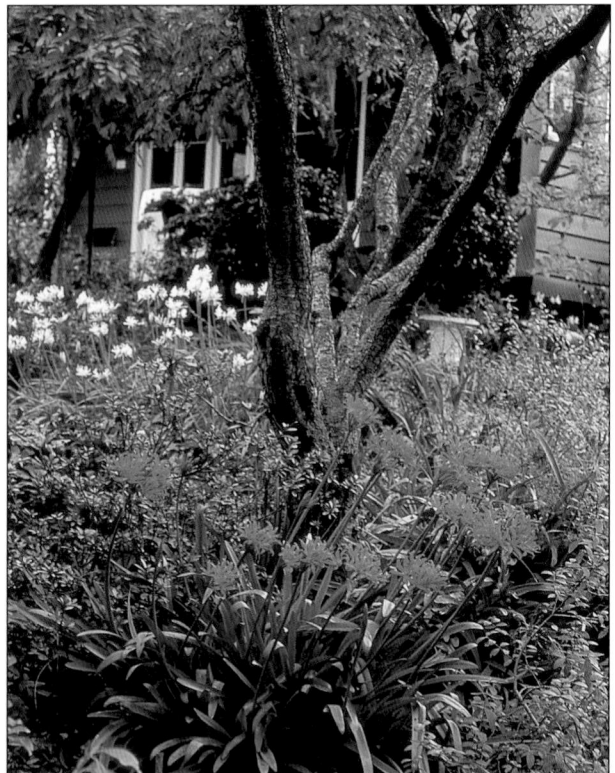

GROUPS OF BRIGHT PINK, fall-flowering nerines provide showy splashes of color as summer flowers fade.

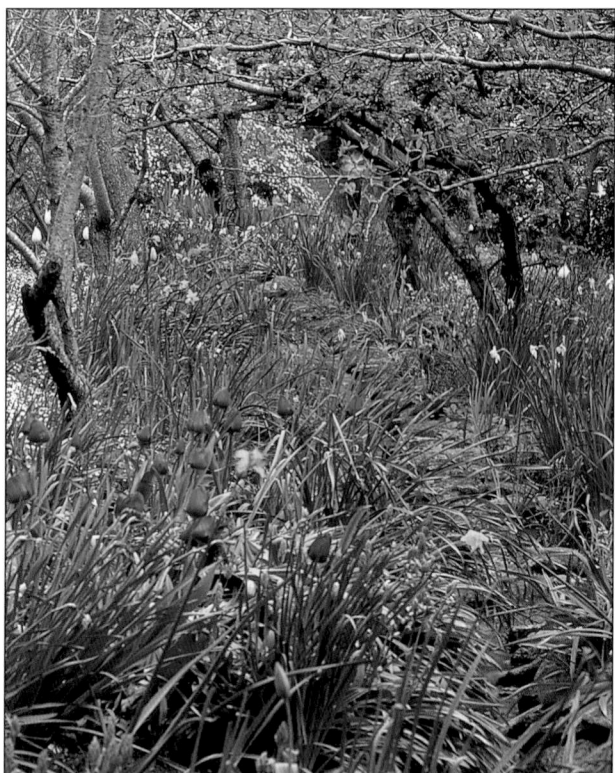

BLUEBELLS, TULIPS, and daffodils are here planted informally in a lovely woodland setting beside a tiny stream.

of growth. Unless there is just the tiniest shoot appearing and you know you can plant the bulbs at once, these bulbs will be a bad buy as they will not thrive. Some chain stores and supermarkets sell bulbs and continue to display them long after they should have been planted out or discarded. If you see long pale shoots emerging from bulbs definitely don't buy them. These bulbs have been stored for too long in poor conditions. They are badly stressed and have used up a great deal of their stored reserves of energy and growing capacity so that they may fail completely or do very poorly. Try to make your selection early in the season so that you have a choice of the best on offer.

Bulbs are best planted as soon as possible once you get them home, but if you are forced to delay planting for a short while, store the bulbs in paper bags or nets—not plastic bags—and keep them in a cool, dry, airy place. If the weather is very warm, the crisper drawer of a refrigerator can be a good place to keep bulbs in good condition, but do not put them in the main part of the refrigerator as this will dry them out.

PLANTING BULBS

Choosing a site

For the majority of bulbs, choose an open planting site where they will receive sun for at least half a day. There are a few bulbs that will grow well in shade but most like at least some sun. Even woodland species such as bluebell and wood anemone grow as understorey plants in deciduous woodlands and so receive some sun during their early growing and flowering period, before the trees are fully in leaf.

The vast majority of bulbs need well-drained soil or they will rot. If there is any doubt about the drainage, plant bulbs

in raised beds or mix sharp sand or grit with the soil in the planting area. Bulbs like a fairly rich, fertile soil. At least a month before planting, incorporate a generous amount of well-rotted manure or garden compost into the planting area.

Positioning the bulbs

Your bulbs will look more natural if you plant them in clumps or groups, not in straight lines. The depth depends on the size of the bulb but it is usually two or three times its diameter (see diagram on page 11). Details of planting depths are given in the individual entries for each bulb, and refer to the depth of soil above the tip of the bulb. Spacing between bulbs is also dependent on size. Larger bulbs are usually set out about 3in apart and smaller ones 1–2in apart, but they can be crowded together for effect.

Be sure to plant the bulbs the right way up. Usually the pointed part points upwards, but there are exceptions to this rule: ranunculus and anemone have the claws or points facing down into the soil and some lilies and crown imperials are sometimes planted on their sides to avoid moisture collecting between the scales, which can lead to rotting.

In dry conditions, bulbs may need to be watered in after planting, but it is usually not necessary to water again at least until leaf shoots have appeared.

Planting under trees

Mass planting of bulbs that flower through winter and early spring under deciduous trees can turn what might otherwise be a somewhat dull area of the garden into a lovely feature. Although it is sometimes difficult to dig and plant in these areas as the soil is hard and full of matted roots, the result can be well worth the effort. The leaves that fall from the trees in fall break down into leafmould which provides ideal growing conditions for the bulbs.

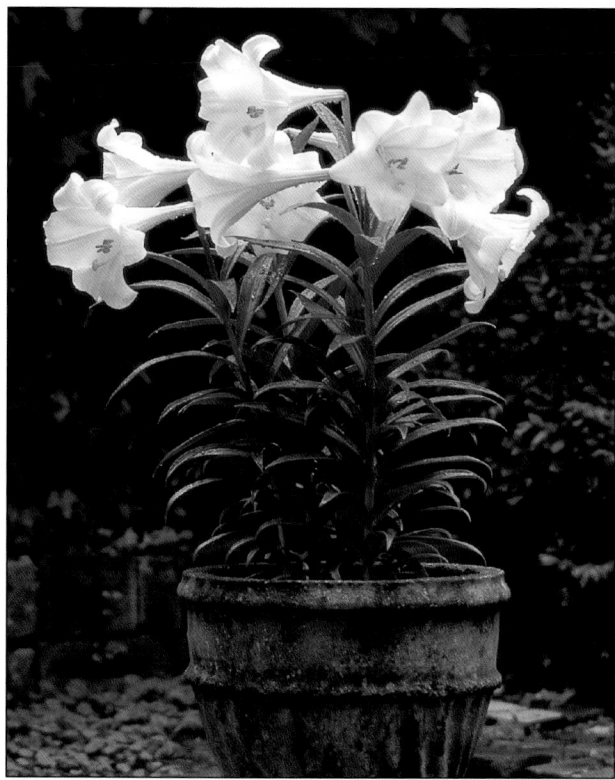

MAJESTIC WHITE LILIES grown in a large ceramic container make a stunning decoration for a courtyard.

INCREASING YOUR STOCK OF BULBS

Left to themselves, many bulbs will multiply of their own accord, but there are a number of ways in which you can help the process along.

Separation

Many bulbs produce offsets or bulblets that can be gently broken away from the mother bulb when the bulbs are lifted, and planted separately. Most first-year bulblets will reach flowering size in two or three years if they are planted separately, but some are slower to flower. When separating clumps of dahlia tubers, make sure each tuber has an "eye" attached or it will not sprout and flower.

PROPAGATING DAHLIAS

bud

DAHLIAS are propagated by dividing the tuber clump, but only tubers with a bud or "eye" at the top will grow.

THREE WAYS TO PROPAGATE LILIES

1. DETACHING SCALES

THE LILY BULB consists of lots of scales. Remove the outer scales.

PUSH the individual scales, right way up, into a box of moist peat.

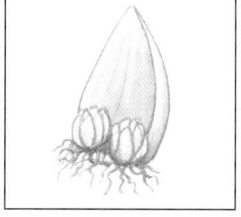

BULBLETS will appear at the base of each scale.

POT UP the scales when the new bulblets appear.

2. DETACHING AERIAL BULBILS

BULBILS grow in the leaf axis of some species. Collect them and pot them up.

3. DETACHING BULBLETS

OFFSETS on the base of some lilies can be detached and planted out.

LIFTING BULBS

1. PUT A FEW STAKES around the edge of the clump so that you know where to dig when the leaves have died down.

2. AFTER THE LEAVES have died down, use a spade to outline the area of the clump.

3. LIFT THE CLUMP UP with a fork and shake off as much soil as possible.

4. SEPARATE THE BULBS from the clump, clean them and then store them in a dry, airy place or replant them.

Scoring and scooping

Cut a V-shape into the base plate of a mature bulb at planting time, taking care not to damage the growth bud of the bulb. This should result in many small offsets being produced by the end of the growing season. Or score through the basal plate of the bulb at right angles with a sharp knife to produce the same result. Depending on species these small offsets should produce bulbs of flowering size in two to four years.

With a sharp-sided teaspoon or curved knife, you can scoop out the entire basal plate and bulblets will form around the rim of the scooped out area. Wear gloves if you are treating hyacinths as the sap can sometimes irritate the skin.

Lilies

These techniques are not suitable for lilies, which are propagated by other methods (see page 13).
• A mature lily bulb is composed of numerous individual scales. The individual scales can be carefully removed and planted upright in a coarse, free-draining mixture such as three parts coarse washed sand and one part peatmoss or peat substitute. The scales should produce bulblets at their bases.

• Some lilies produce aerial bulbils in the axis of the leaf and these can be collected as they are about to fall. Potted into pots or trays they should produce leaves by the following spring and reach flowering size in two or three years.
• Other lilies produce bulblets just below the soil surface, around the base of the stem. If these are carefully dug out from among the roots they can be potted up and will form flowering plants in two or three years.

CARING FOR GROWING BULBS

Once planted, bulbs need little maintenance. Once the plants are actively growing, the soil should be kept moist, but never soggy. Bulbs do not usually need feeding before they flower. They are fed after blooming, when they are storing food for the following season's growth. Special instructions for feeding and watering are included in the entries for individual plants where appropriate.

AFTER FLOWERING

• After flowers have finished, cut off the spent flower stems but do not cut back the foliage. If you cut off the leaves before they have died down naturally, the bulb will not have the reserves to grow and flower the following season.

• After flowering, feed the plants with a liquid or granular balanced fertilizer and continue to water in dry conditions until the leaves begin to die off naturally. This may take about two or three months.

• If bulbs have been planted in clumps, you may be able to plant annuals between the clumps, using either seed or seedlings. Quick growers such as Virginian stock will provide a pretty distraction from the dying bulb foliage. You could also put in summer-flowering annuals or perennials that will be ready to take over the display once the bulbs have truly died down. Or you can, of course, purchase some "potted color"—annuals that are already in bloom.

• Bulbs do not usually need to be lifted every season. Most are left in the ground and lifted only every two or three years, or in a number of cases only every four or five years. Many bulbs flower well when they are crowded and then it is only necessary to lift and divide clumps when the flower numbers or quality drop off.

• Take care when you lift bulbs that you do not cut or

TALL WHITE RANUNCULUS dominate this white border, formed of plants with contrasting shapes, textures, and sizes.

A CARPET OF COLOR has been created in this garden bed by combining white tulips with violas and anemones in a range of colors. To achieve such a pleasing effect, careful planning before planting is necessary.

TALL BEARDED IRIS make an elegant border for this attractive garden path. Irises come in a rich array of colors.

ZEPHYR LILY, with its starry white flowers and deep green glossy foliage, makes an ideal edging plant. Here it grows with portulacas.

damage them—it is easy to slice into them with a spade or spear them with a fork. Discard damaged, soft, or rotted bulbs immediately. Place the sound bulbs to dry in a cool, airy spot, brush off excess soil and then store them in nets, old stockings, or in single layers in cardboard boxes. Ideally, bulbs should be stored so that they do not touch each other: they can be kept separate with shredded paper or something similar.

• Because lilies have no protective outer sheath on their bulbs, they must be lifted, the clumps divided if necessary, and the bulbs replanted at once. They can be stored for short periods in damp sphagnum moss but take care that they don't dry out.

• Some bulbous plants, such as freesias, produce quite a lot of seed if the spent flower stems are not cut off. You can collect these seeds when they are ripe or allow them to self-sow. Seedlings may take two to five years to reach flowering size, depending on the type of bulb, and they will probably not be true to type. The results can, however, be interesting as you never know quite what to expect. Particularly good seedlings should be marked at flowering time so that the bulbs can be propagated at the end of the season.

MAKING THE MOST OF BULBS IN THE GARDEN

You may wish to plant groups of bulbs under deciduous trees or in other permanent places in the garden but there are many other options. Bulbs mix well with many herbaceous perennials as the new growth of the perennials tends to camouflage the not-so-attractive foliage of the bulbs as it yellows and dies off. Bulbs in this situation can usually be left in the ground for several years before they need to be lifted and divided.

Many bulbs can be treated like annuals for a seasonal display, then lifted, and stored for use the following season. This, of course, creates more work but the results can be well worth the effort, allowing you to create different displays each year. You can have a delightful show of bulbs on their own but consider the possibility of planting bulbs and spring bedding plants together for a really stunning spring display. As well as forming an attractive association, the bedding plants help to mask the dying foliage of the bulbs, which must be left to die down naturally if the bulbs are to flower well next season. Hardy annuals sown in the fall will also serve the same purpose. Plant your bulbs and bedding plants at the same time, placing a bulb between each of the plants. For best effect, planting should be quite dense. You can experiment with color combinations or opt for tried and tested associations such as yellow lily-flowered tulips and blue forget-me-nots.

• An early-flowering bedding plant such as white primula could be interplanted with cream or yellow narcissi, or deep blue anemones for a vivid contrast.

• White, yellow-centerd primulas would team well with blue *Anemone blanda* and the dwarf narcissus "Tête-à-Tête."

• Other spring-flowering plants to combine with bulbs include polyanthus, wallflowers, and forget-me-nots.

Dwarf bulbs are ideal for growing on a rockery, usually providing color and interest before the other alpine plants come into their own. Suitable bulbs include alliums, chionodoxa, crocus, cyclamen, iris, muscari, narcissus, oxalis, and rhodohypoxis, among others.

IF YOU WANT show quality tuberous begonias, grow them under cover. Here they grow in a conservatory, where they can also be placed on raised benches so the flowers are more easily admired.

NATURALIZING BULBS IN GRASS

Bulbs naturalized in grass make a very attractive feature in gardens. However, you need to remember that the bulb foliage must be allowed to die down naturally if the bulbs are to perform well in future years, and that means that the grass cannot be mown for several weeks after the bulbs have finished flowering. This can look rather untidy, so a position for naturalized bulbs needs to be chosen with some care. Popular sites are the perimeters of lawns or under deciduous trees. In a small garden with a limited area of lawn used for many purposes, naturalizing in turf may not be a practical idea.

Choose bulbs that will flower at an appropriate period; early spring is convenient because the grass can then be mown from late spring onward. Some summer-flowering bulbs are good in a wildflower meadow, and autumn-flowering bulbs such as colchicum also grow well in grass. You can either lift a square of turf, plant a group of bulbs, and replace the cut turf, or you can plant larger bulbs individually, using a trowel or bulb-planting tool to cut a hole in the turf. Place the bulb in the bottom of the hole and replace the plug of soil and turf. Give a good watering after planting, both to settle the bulbs and to help the turf re-establish.

After the bulbs have bloomed, give the plants an application of balanced fertilizer and water the area regularly if conditions are dry. Once the bulb foliage has yellowed and died off mowing can be resumed—this usually takes some six weeks after flowering.

MINIATURE PINK NERINES and other small bulbous plants grow between paving stones where they benefit from the sharp drainage.

GROWING BULBS IN CONTAINERS

Many bulbs make lovely container plants. Pots full of bulbs are ideal for balcony gardens and patios, and for instant color, pots of bulbs in bud or in flower can be plunged into garden beds throughout the growing season.

Use a good quality potting compost, and make sure the base of the container is crocked for good drainage. Plant the bulbs at the same depth as you would in the soil, crowding them into the container for a good flowering display. Keep the compost moist at all times; regular watering will be needed.

Growing bulbs indoors

"Prepared" bulbs are specially treated to flower early—often in time for Christmas. Plant them in a shallow pot or bowl of moist potting compost and put them in a cold place such as a garden shed, keeping them dark by placing them in a black plastic bag. Leave them for 8–12 weeks; when shoots begin to appear, move them into a bright, cool room. Once flower buds begin to show color, move the bulbs to their flowering position in the home.

The bunch-flowered narcissus "Paperwhite" is unusual in that it doesn't need a cold, dark period after planting; bulbs can be left on a cool, light

Continued on page 234

A POT OF JACOBEAN LILIES can be brought to the fore when they flower.

POTTING NARCISSI FOR INDOOR USE

1. CHOOSE A POT at least twice as tall as the bulbs.

2. HALF FILL the pot with a good soil-less potting compost.

3. POSITION THE BULBS with their tops level with the top of the pot and a small gap between each and around the edge of the pot.

4. COVER THE BULBS with the compost and gently firm it down. Water, drain and place in a cold—40°F—position in total darkness. A cold, dark period of 8–12 weeks is necessary.

5. WHEN SHOOTS appear, move the pot into a bright, cool position at about 50°F.

6. WHEN BUDS appear, move the pot into its flowering position, still in bright light.

WHAT CAN GO WRONG?

There are relatively few pest and disease problems that regularly beset the home gardener growing bulbs. Bulbs that fail to come up at all have usually been planted too deep or have rotted through disease or waterlogging, especially in clay based soils. Yellowing foliage early in the growing season may also be caused by waterlogging. More serious pests of bulbs are often associated with storage conditions and it is wise to examine bulbs for damage, decay or insect pests such as aphids before planting. Diseases specific to certain bulbs are mentioned in the text under individual entries.

Failure to flower
This may be due to a number of reasons, including:
- natural offsets are not sufficiently mature to flower.
- foliage has been cut off prematurely the previous season.
- insufficient sunlight or lack of water while the foliage is still green.
- congestion of bulbs.
- "blindness"—a condition that occurs especially with daffodils and tulips. The flower bud forms but gives up trying to continue on to bloom. It may be due to incorrect storage temperature, lack of chilling or fluctuating temperatures as the flower bud emerges from the bulb.

Leaf scorch
- This fungal disease affects bulbs of daffodils and narcissi, and others including hippeastrum, crinum and belladonna lilies. It is worse in wet seasons, and occurs at the top of the bulb scales so that emerging leaves are infected. The leaf tips are reddish and scorched, and later on brown spots appear further down the leaf. Eventually the tissue around these damaged areas goes yellow. Remove and destroy the worst affected leaves and spray with a suitable fungicide if symptoms persist.

Bulb rots
- These may be caused by a number of bacteria or fungi, and lead to rotting and decay of the bulbs either in store or in the ground. They are made worse by poor drainage and overwet soil conditions. Damaged bulbs are particularly prone to infection, so take care when handling or lifting bulbs and discard damaged ones.

Grey mould (botrytis species)
- Grey mould attacks an enormous range of plants. It may manifest itself initially by spotting on leaves or stems, followed by breakdown of the tissue and the typical furry grey growth. Poor air circulation, overcrowding, overwatering and cool, humid weather conditions are favorable to its spread. Improve growing conditions and spray if necessary with a suitable fungicide.

Bulb flies
- Bulb flies lay their eggs in the soil near the bulb neck; the maggots tunnel into the bulb to feed. Affected plants produce sparse, yellow foliage and fail to flower. If you are not lifting the bulbs in the fall, pull soil up round their necks to fill the holes left by the leaves dying down.

Thrips
- Gladioli are very susceptible to attack by thrips, or thunderflies. These tiny winged insects cause silver streaking and flecking of both foliage and flowers; in a bad attack, the display can be ruined. The pest is worst in hot, dry conditions. Affected plants can be sprayed with a contact insecticide. Thrips overwinter on the corms, so after an attack, dust the corms with HCH dust after lifting and again before planting out in spring.

Lily beetle
- These small, scarlet beetles can be a serious pest of lilies and other plants such as fritillaries. Both larvae and adults feed on the leaves and stems of plants, often causing considerable damage. They are quite conspicuous and should be picked off by hand and destroyed whenever they are noticed; bad infestations can be sprayed with a contact insecticide. Beetles overwinter on weeds and plant debris, so clean up round the planting area in the fall.

Aphids
- These may attack a range of bulbous plants and should be sprayed or hosed off as they can carry virus diseases. A bad infestation disfigures flowers and foliage.

MULTI-COLORED RANUNCULUS and anemone are crowded together to produce this bright springtime scene.

Continued from page 232

windowsill directly after planting and flowers will appear in about six weeks. Plant mid-November for Christmas blooms.

Normally, non-prepared bulbs will flower at their normal period. They should be planted and left out in a sheltered position in the garden in their containers until flower buds are showing, when they can be brought into the house.

After flowering

If after flowering the whole plant and bulb are planted out into the garden, there is some chance of the bulb flowering the following year. Bulbs that stay in their pots until they have died down will in most cases not reflower the following year. When the foliage on these bulbs has died down, lift the bulbs, store them and replant them in the garden at the right time the following season. They may not flower that year but should do so the next. They are not suitable for growing as indoor-flowering plants again.

BULBS AS CUT FLOWERS

Many bulbous plants produce flowers that are ideal for cutting for the house. Most are best picked before they are fully open. For longer vase life, change the water daily or add a few drops of household bleach, or a proprietary cut flower food to the water.

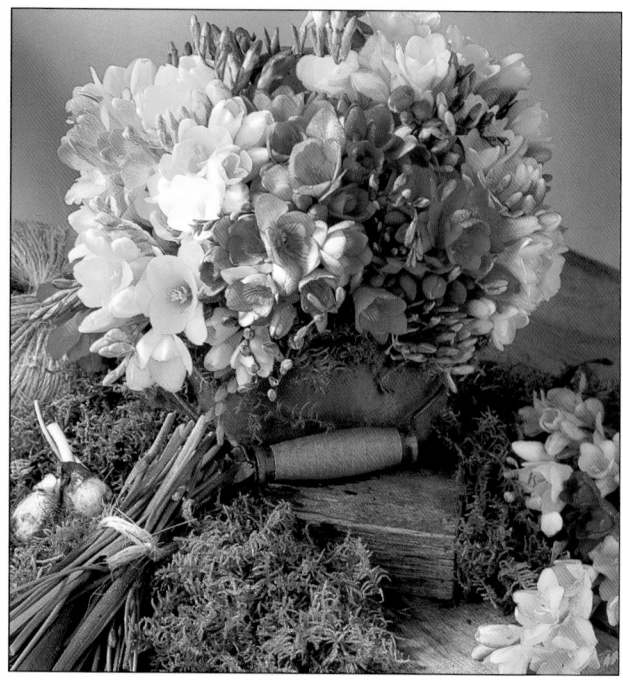

FRAGRANT FREESIAS come in a glorious range of colors to epitomize the joy of the spring garden.

THIS RUSTIC BASKET of choice hyacinth blooms could not fail to lift the spirits, appearing as they do just when winter draws to a close.

TULIPS MAKE ideal cut flowers and several colorful bunches are here shown to perfection against the terracotta of the containers.

ACHIMENES
Hot water plant

HOT CERISE PINK *flowers decorate this pretty little plant throughout summer. Hot water plants come in a range of colors.*

THE LARGE, *delicate purple-blue flowers of* Achimenes *"Paul Arnold" help to make this one of the most popular varieties.*

FEATURES

Achimenes are easy to grow and undemanding; they are raised from small rhizomes that look a little like miniature fir cones. Leaves are toothed, elongated, and slightly furry in texture, and the colorful, trumpet-shaped flowers are carried in profusion on short stems above the foliage. The plants often assume a semi-trailing habit, making them good for growing in a basket, or in a raised pot where the stems can cascade.

Flowers are available in a wide range of shades including cream, pink, red, purple, and blue; some varieties have attractively veined throats. Although individual flowers are quite short lived, they are quickly replaced by a profusion of others throughout the season. The plants grow to about 10in.

ACHIMENES AT A GLANCE

A colorful house and greenhouse plant, flowering throughout the summer. Minimum temperature 50°F (zone 11).

Jan	/	
Feb	plant 👌	Recommended Varieties
Mar	plant 👌	"Little Beauty"
Apr	/	"Paul Arnold"
May	/	"Peach Blossom"
Jun	flowering 🌺	"Queen of Sheba"
July	flowering 🌺	
Aug	flowering 🌺	
Sept	flowering 🌺	
Oct	/	
Nov	/	
Dec	/	

CONDITIONS

Aspect   Bright light is necessary, but not direct sun, which may scorch the foliage and flowers.

Site   House plant, preferring cool to moderately warm conditions without marked temperature fluctuations. Use soil-less potting compost, based on peat or peat substitute.

GROWING METHOD

Planting   Bury the rhizomes shallowly—about ⅜in deep—in a pot of moist compost, spacing them about ½in apart, in early spring. Keep the pot in a warm room.

Feeding   Feed with a high potash liquid fertilizer every 10 days or so from when the flower buds appear. Keep the compost just moist when the rhizomes start to grow, increasing the watering slightly as flowers start to form, but ensure the compost is never saturated. Tepid water is preferred, hence their common name. Stop watering when the flowers have faded.

Problems   No specific problems, though aphids may attack the new growth.

FLOWERING

Season   Flowers profusely throughout the summer.

Cutting   Flowers are not suitable for cutting.

AFTER FLOWERING

Requirements   Stop watering once the flowers have faded and allow the plants to dry off. Remove the dead top growth and keep the rhizomes in the pot of dry compost over winter in a frost-free place. The following spring, tip them out, pot them up carefully in fresh compost, and water to start them into growth again.

AGAPANTHUS
African lily

THE BLUE AND WHITE *flowering heads of agapanthus are each composed of numerous individual flowers.*

THIS DENSE PLANTING *of agapanthus needs little attention and yet rewards the gardener with its wonderful summer flowers.*

FEATURES

Usually sold as perennials, agapanthus have showy heads of bright blue, trumpet-shaped flowers. Their foliage is deep green and strap shaped, forming a rosette; the stout flowering stems arise from the center in mid-summer. Several species are available, but they all like a sheltered spot—in cold gardens, they can be grown under cover in a greenhouse, being moved outside in warm summer weather. "Headbourne Hybrids" are the most widely available; flowers may be several shades of blue, or white. They are deciduous, reasonably hardy, and grow from 2–4ft. *Agapanthus umbellatus* (*A. africanus*) is evergreen with purple-blue flowers, but most plants under this name are in reality *A. campanulatus*, a deciduous species with blue or white flowers to 3ft.

AGAPANTHUS AT A GLANCE

Stately plants with eye-catching, rounded heads of blue flowers. Best in warmer gardens.

Jan	/	
Feb	/	Recommended Varieties
Mar	/	"Headbourne Hybrids"
Apr	plant 🌱	"Bressingham Blue"
May	plant 🌱	
Jun	/	
July	flowering 🌼	
Aug	flowering 🌼	
Sept	flowering 🌼	
Oct	/	
Nov	/	
Dec	/	

CONDITIONS

Aspect — A sheltered position in full sun is required.

Site — Usually best grown in tubs or large pots on a sunny patio. Suitable for reasonably sheltered gardens only: can be grown in a conservatory or greenhouse in cold areas. Plants need free-draining soil with plenty of organic matter such as well-rotted garden compost. In containers, use loam-based potting compost with extra organic matter added.

GROWING METHOD

Planting — Plant the fleshy roots 4–6in deep in late spring. Take care not to let the roots dry out before planting.

Feeding — Apply a high potash liquid fertilizer occasionally during the growing season; container-grown plants should be fed every 14 days. Keep the soil moist but never waterlogged through the growing season; do not let plants in pots dry out at any time.

Problems — Plants may fail to perform well in exposed gardens, otherwise they are generally trouble free.

FLOWERING

Season — Flowers from mid to late summer.

Cutting — Stems may be cut when the lowest flowers on the globe-shaped head are opened, but they are better enjoyed on the plant.

AFTER FLOWERING

Requirements — Allow the leaves of deciduous varieties to die down and cover the crowns with a layer of straw to protect them during the winter months. In cold areas, move the plants under cover until spring.

ALLIUM
Ornamental onion

LARGE ROUNDED HEADS are typical of alliums and the star-burst effect of this one looks stunning in the yard.

THE PURPLE-PINK FLOWERS of Allium oreophilum *(also known as* A. ostrowskianum) *brighten up the early summer garden.*

FEATURES

There are a large number of *Allium* species, including edible onions, garlic, and chives as well as many ornamental plants. Typically, they produce rounded heads of flowers, often in rosy purple shades, but there are also yellow- and white-flowered species. Some are small-growing and suitable for the rock garden, while others make excellent plants for the middle or back of borders. *A. giganteum* produces its eye-catching heads of mauve-pink, starry flowers on stems 3ft or more high, while *A. moly* grows to only 8in and has loose clusters of golden yellow blooms. Many alliums make excellent cut flowers. They are usually long lasting in water, and the dried inflorescence that remains after the blooms have fallen can be used successfully in dried arrangements, too.

ALLIUM AT A GLANCE

Versatile and varied bulbs with usually rounded heads of starry flowers in spring and early summer.

		Recommended species
Jan	/	
Feb	/	*Allium albopilosum*
Mar	/	A. *beesianum*
Apr	flowering	A. *caeruleum*
May	flowering	A. *giganteum*
Jun	flowering	A. *karataviense*
July	flowering	A. *moly* "Jeannine"
Aug	/	A. *neopolitanum*
Sept	plant	A. *oreophilum*
Oct	plant	A. *schubertii*
Nov	/	A. *siculum*
Dec	/	

CONDITIONS

Aspect Best in full sun but will tolerate light shade.
Site Alliums in borders should be positioned where other plants will help to hide their often untidy foliage. Smaller species are suitable for rock gardens. The soil must be well-drained and should contain plenty of well-decayed manure or compost. Add a dressing of lime to acid soils before planting.

GROWING METHOD

Planting Plant in fall. Planting depth varies according to the size of the bulb: cover bulbs with soil to three times their height.
Feeding Apply a high potash liquid fertilizer as buds form. Water during dry spells, but never allow the soil to become sodden. After flowering, stop watering altogether.
Problems Plants may suffer from the fungal disease rust, causing orange pustules on the foliage: destroy affected specimens. Feeding with high potash fertilizer may increase resistance to attacks.

FLOWERING

Season Flowers in late spring and summer.
Cutting Cut alliums when about half the flowers are fully open.

AFTER FLOWERING

Requirements Foliage starts to die down before blooming is complete. Cut off the spent flower stems if required. Overcrowded clumps can be divided in fall, replanting immediately.

ALSTROEMERIA
Peruvian lily

THE FLOWERS *of alstroemeria are very delicately marked when viewed close-up, and have an almost orchid-like appearance.*

SUMMER BORDERS *are brightened by these colorful, long-lasting flowers that are also excellent for cutting for the home.*

FEATURES

These exotic-looking plants are prolific flowerers and can be spectacular in borders. The open-faced flowers are carried in clusters at the top of 3ft stems; the sword-like foliage is dark green. The plants may take a year to become established and produce flowers, but when they have settled in, flowering is profuse. Container-grown plants become established more quickly. The color range includes yellow, cream, orange, red, salmon, and pink. The Princess series contains dwarf varieties that represent a major breeding breakthrough. Alstroemerias are from South America and are not always reliably hardy; Ligtu hybrids are among the hardiest types.

ALSTROEMERIA AT A GLANCE

When established, these plants produce a profusion of colorful, attractively marked summer flowers on tall stems.

Jan	/	Recommended Varieties
Feb	/	
Mar	plant 🖐	Ligtu hybrids
Apr	plant 🖐	Princess series
May	/	
Jun	flowering 🐾	
July	flowering 🐾	
Aug	flowering 🐾	
Sept	/	
Oct	/	
Nov	/	
Dec	/	

CONDITIONS

Aspect Full sun or partial shade.
Site Alstroemerias do well in a sheltered border and are very effective mixed with herbaceous perennials. They require free-draining soil.

GROWING METHOD

Planting Plant the fleshy tubers 6in deep in spring, as soon as you obtain them. Handle them carefully, as they are usually brittle and break easily. Do not let them dry out before planting. You can also obtain alstroemerias as container-grown plants in summer.
Feeding Add a balanced granular fertilizer to the soil before planting. Water plants in very dry conditions, but never allow the soil to become waterlogged.
Problems Plants may fail to flower in their first season after planting. When established, however, they can be very invasive, and should be planted where their spread can be kept in check. Slugs find them attractive, and should be controlled with slug pellets where necessary.

FLOWERING

Season Flowers in midsummer.
Cutting Alstroemerias last very well in water, and should be cut as the buds start to open.

AFTER FLOWERING

Requirements Remove dead heads. When the foliage has died down, protect the crowns with a mulch of dry straw or leaves through the winter. Crowded clumps can be split in spring.

AMARYLLIS BELLADONNA
Belladonna lily

THESE TALL FLOWER STEMS appear before the leaves, which is why belladonna lilies are also known as "naked ladies."

BRIGHT PINK BELLADONNA LILIES brighten the late summer and fall garden. The foliage here is from a clump of daylilies.

FEATURES

This beautiful South African bulb produces its multiple and sweetly perfumed blooms on sturdy purple-green stems 24in or more high. The funnel-shaped flowers may be various shades of pink or white and the flowering stem appears before the leaves, giving the plant its alternative common name of naked lady. This bulb is a great asset in the garden as the flowering period is fall, while the glossy strap-like leaves look good throughout winter and early spring. It makes an excellent cut flower. Best flowering comes from clumps that are left undisturbed for several years.

AMARYLLIS AT A GLANCE

A tall plant producing its stems of fragrant, funnel-shaped flowers in fall. Needs a warm, sheltered, sunny position.

		Recommended Varieties
Jan	/	
Feb	/	"Johannesburg"
Mar	/	"Kimberley"
Apr	/	"Major"
May	/	
Jun	plant 🌿	
July	plant 🌿	
Aug	/	
Sept	flowering 🌸	
Oct	flowering 🌸	
Nov	/	
Dec	/	

CONDITIONS

Aspect Prefers a warm, sheltered spot in full sun—the bulbs need a good summer baking to produce the best flowers.

Site A good plant for a flower bed under a south-facing wall. *Amaryllis belladonna* can also be grown in containers, planting the large bulbs singly in 8in pots. Well-drained soil is required: poor soil is tolerated but best results are achieved by digging in decayed organic matter a month or more before planting.

GROWING METHOD

Planting Plant bulbs with their necks just at ground level and 8–12in apart in early to mid-summer.

Feeding Apply a balanced fertilizer after flowering, as the leaves appear. Water in dry periods while the plant is in growth.

Problems It is rarely troubled by any problems.

FLOWERING

Season Flowers in very late summer and fall.

Cutting A good cut flower for large arrangements.

AFTER FLOWERING

Requirements Remove spent flower stems. Protect the crowns with a mulch of peat over winter. Leave bulbs undisturbed for several years. If lifting and dividing, do so in early summer.

ANEMONE
Windflower

THE DARK CENTERS, deep blue or black, of Anemone coronaria make a stunning contrast to the rich colors of the petals.

THIS MIXED PLANTING of Anemone coronaria shows some of the range of color and form available from this lovely plant.

FEATURES

Anemones, also known as windflowers, form a large and versatile group of plants, the most commonly grown species being *A. coronaria*, *A. blanda* and *A. nemorosa. Anemone coronaria* grows from a hard little tuber, *A. blanda* from hard tuberous roots, and *A. nemorosa* from very brittle, creeping rhizomes. The flowers are often very colorful, and can be daisy-like with lots of petals, or cup-shaped, rather like poppies. Anemones flower in spring; *A. coronaria* will also flower in summer, depending on the planting time. They are excellent for cutting.

ANEMONE AT A GLANCE

Low-growing, hardy plants which form a colorful carpet of spring or summer flowers.

Jan	/	
Feb	flowering 🌱	Recommended Varieties
Mar	flower 🌱/plant 🐚 *	*Anemone blanda:*
Apr	flower 🌱/plant 🐚 *	"Atrocaerulea"
May	/	"White Splendor"
Jun	flowering 🌱	"Radar"
July	flowering 🌱	*Anemone coronaria:*
Aug	flowering 🌱	"Mona Lisa"
Sept	plant 🐚**	"Mister Fokker"
Oct	plant 🐚**	*Anemone nemorosa:*
Nov	/	"Alba Plena"
Dec	/	"Purity"
		"Robinsoniana"
		"Vestal"

* summer flowering   **spring flowering

TYPES

A. coronaria Reaching 6–8in high, *A. coronaria* is available in a lovely range of clear colors including red, white, blue, violet, cerise, and pink, all with a black to deep navy blue center. The most popular strains are "de Caen," with single poppy-like flowers, and "St Brigid," with semi-double to double flowers. There are many named cultivars in both these strains. They can be planted in single blocks of color or mixed at random, and they can be grown in containers as well as making an excellent garden display.

A. blanda This native of Greece and Turkey bears daisy-like flowers, usually in shades of blue, although white and pink forms are available. One of spring's early bloomers, its flowers are carried on stems some 6–10in high above ferny, divided leaves. A variety of cultivars is available now and some of these are grown as potted plants. This species seeds readily and can be naturalized under trees.

A. nemorosa The wood anemone, *A. nemorosa*, likes a cool, moist climate and is often grown massed under deciduous trees, imitating its natural habitat. Here, its starry, white (sometimes lavender blue), single flowers, with their central boss of golden stamens, make a glorious showing in late spring and into early summer. The wood anemone's mid-green foliage is deeply cut. Growth may be from 4–8in high. This species increases rapidly where it finds the growing conditions suitable, and plants will eventually increase to carpet the ground.

THE BRIGHT, DAISY-LIKE flowers of Anemone blanda brighten up the garden in late winter or very early spring.

WOODLAND ANEMONE (Anemone nemorosa) makes a pretty groundcover in a cool, moist climate, where it naturalizes readily.

CONDITIONS

Aspect
All anemones prefer some protection from strong wind. *A. coronaria* is best in full sun, while *A. nemorosa* prefers to be grown in dappled sunlight or with morning sun and afternoon shade. *A. blanda* comes from exposed sites in mountainous districts and so will tolerate full sun or part shade.

Site
A. blanda and *A. nemorosa* grow well under deciduous trees, or on a rock garden, while *A. coronaria* provides bright color toward the front of beds and borders. Soil must be well drained or tubers and roots will rot. All anemone species prefer a soil rich in organic matter although *A. blanda* is happy to grow in quite poor soils as long as drainage is good. Plenty of well-decayed compost or manure should be dug into the ground about a month before planting the bulbs.

GROWING METHOD

Planting
Plant tubers of *A. coronaria* 2in deep and 4–6in apart in September and October for spring flowers, or in March and April to bloom in summer. *A. blanda* and *A. nemorosa* should be planted 2–3in deep and 4in apart in early fall. Take care not to damage brittle roots; soaking the tubers or rhizomes overnight before planting will help them to get established quickly. After planting, mulch soil with bark chips or leafmold.

Feeding
A balanced fertilizer can be applied after flowering, but feeding is not usually necessary in reasonably fertile soils.

Water in after planting if the soil is dry, and ensure the soil is kept moist but not waterlogged when the flower buds start to form.

Problems
Mosaic virus can cause distortion and mottling of the leaves and eventual death of plants. Control aphids, which spread the virus.

FLOWERING

Season
A. coronaria will bloom from late winter until mid-spring, or in mid-summer, depending on planting time. *A. blanda* flowers in early spring while *A. nemorosa* flowers later in spring and into early summer.

Cutting
A. coronaria makes an excellent cut flower. Cut rather than pull flowers from the plant. The flowers of *A. blanda* and *A. nemorosa* may last a few days in the vase but these anemones make a much better showing in the ground. Leaving the flowers on the plants allows seed to form to increase your stock.

AFTER FLOWERING

Requirements
If dry, continue to water plants until the foliage dies down. Cut off spent flowerheads unless you require seeds to form. Tubers of *A. coronaria* can be lifted, cleaned, and stored in a dry, airy place until the following fall, or left in the ground as long as drainage is good. The other species are best left in the ground to form large colonies. Lift, divide, and replant in fall if required.

ANOMATHECA
Syn. *Lapeirousia laxa*

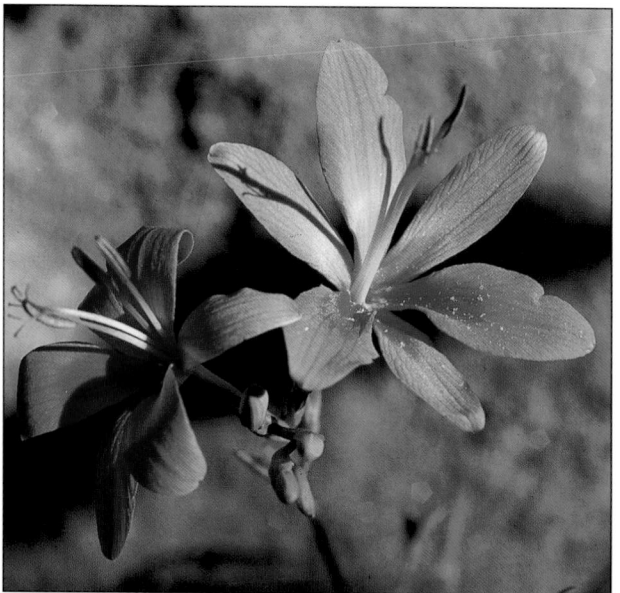

THE OPEN-FACED, trumpet-shaped flowers resemble those of freesias, and are carried on slender spikes above the foliage.

THESE PLANTS may well be quite small, but the bright color of the flowers really stands out in the garden, even when seen from a distance.

FEATURES

Occasionally known as scarlet freesia, this pretty little plant is trouble-free and most rewarding in the garden. It multiplies readily from seed sown in spring. The trumpet-shaped flowers are pale scarlet with darker markings. They appear in mid-summer and are followed by seed pods which split open to expose red seeds. The slightly stiff, ribbed, sword-shaped leaves grow about 6–8in high while the flowers are held on spikes which extend well above the foliage. There is a pure white cultivar, "Alba," but this is not nearly as vigorous as the species. *Anomatheca viridis* has unusual green flowers and is normally grown as an indoor plant, flowering in early spring.

ANOMATHECA AT A GLANCE

A graceful, pretty bulb with sprays of trumpet-shaped flowers. Reasonably hardy in most areas.

		Recommended Varieties
Jan	/	
Feb	/	
Mar	/	*Anomatheca laxa:*
Apr	plant 🖑	"Alba"
May	/	"Joan Evans"
Jun	/	
July	flowering	*Anomatheca viridis*
Aug	flowering	
Sept	flowering	
Oct	/	
Nov	/	
Dec	/	

CONDITIONS

Aspect   Grows happily in full sun or partial shade.
Site   This bulb is very useful for the front of borders, or for growing in pots for the patio or in the house or conservatory. Ideally, soil should be well drained but it need not be rich.

GROWING METHOD

Planting   Plant corms about 2in deep and 4in apart in spring.
Feeding   Supplementary feeding is generally not needed, but on poor soils a balanced fertilizer can be applied after planting. Plants in containers should be given a liquid feed every 14 days throughout the growing season. In very dry springs, water occasionally once plants have started into growth.
Problems   No specific pest or disease problems are known for this plant.

FLOWERING

Season   Flowers generally appear in mid-summer.
Cutting   This is not a good choice as a cut flower.

AFTER FLOWERING

Requirements   Cut off faded flower stems immediately after flowering if you do not want seed to set. In warm gardens the corms can be left in the ground, but in cooler areas they are better lifted in the fall and stored for replanting next spring.

BEGONIA
Begonia

EXQUISITE FORM and beautiful color shadings make this tuberous begonia a show stopper. It's worth the effort to produce blooms like this.

THE LARGE, many-petalled flowers of some begonia hybrids are reminiscent of camellias. This variety is "Roy Hartley."

FEATURES

Tuberous begonias result from the breeding and selection of several South American species and many are grown by specialists for exhibition. *Begonia tuberhybrida* is the most commonly grown type; the hybrid "Non-Stop" strain is particularly popular for its prolonged flowering. Begonias make excellent house plants, but can also be grown in containers on patios or in beds outdoors; pendulous varieties are especially suitable for hanging baskets. Flowers can take many forms, including single or double, camellia-flowered, or carnation-flowered—some are very simple while others are heavily ruffled. Flowers appear in threes, with the large, central male flower being the showpiece; the small female flowers are usually removed as they develop. The color range includes many shades of red, pink, yellow, cream, and white, with some bicolors. Plants grow some 10–18in high.

BEGONIA AT A GLANCE

Very large, showy flowers are carried throughout the summer. Plants are frost-tender.

Jan	/	Recommended Varieties
Feb	/	"Billie Langdon"
Mar	plant 🐾 (under cover)	"Can-Can"
Apr	plant 🐾 (under cover)	"Fairylight"
May	plant 🐾 (under cover)	"Orange Cascade"
Jun	plant 🐾 (outside)	"Roy Hartley"
July	flowering 🌸	"Sugar Candy"
Aug	flowering 🌸	
Sept	flowering 🌸	
Oct	/	
Nov	/	
Dec	/	

CONDITIONS

Aspect   Begonias prefer dappled sun or light shade, and need shelter from wind.

Site   Grow the plants in the house or conservatory, or in pots or flowerbeds outdoors when all risk of frost has passed. Soil should be rich and moisture-retentive, with plenty of organic matter such as well-rotted garden compost.

GROWING METHOD

Planting   Dormant tubers can be started off in pots of moist peat or compost under cover in spring, pressing the tuber into the soil with the dished side up. Spray the top of the tuber once only with a fine mist of water, and keep the compost just moist. Pot-grown plants can also be bought in leaf later in the spring. Plant out when all risk of frost is over, 9–12in apart.

Feeding   Apply high potash liquid fertilizer every 14 days throughout the growing period. Keep the plants moist at all times, but do not allow the soil to become waterlogged.

Problems   Powdery mildew may be a problem, especially in hot, dry weather. If this occurs, try to improve air circulation around the plants and use a suitable fungicide if necessary.

FLOWERING

Season   From early summer right through to fall.

Cutting   Flowers are unsuitable for cutting.

AFTER FLOWERING

Requirements   Lift tubers as the stems die down in fall. Store them in dry peat in a cool, frost-free place until the following spring.

CAMASSIA
Quamash

THE INTENSE BLUE flower spikes of Camassia leichtlinii *make a striking group among other border plants. A moisture-retentive soil is needed for best results—regular watering is likely to be necessary if the weather is dry. Camassias can cope with heavier soil conditions than many other bulbs.*

FEATURES

The botanical name of this plant is derived from that given to it by Native Americans, who grew the bulbs for food. It is relatively unusual among bulbous plants in preferring moist, heavy soils. The tall, graceful flower stems carry dense spires of starry blue flowers. *Camassia leichtlinii* is very reliable, with 3ft flowering stems: *C. quamash (C. esculenta)* is a little shorter and has flowers varying from white, through pale blue to deep purple. *C. cusickii* produces its 4ft pale lavender flower spikes in late spring.

CAMASSIA AT A GLANCE

Tall, stately spikes of blue, starry flowers provide valuable color in the perennial border in early summer.

Jan	/	Recommended Varieties
Feb	/	*Camassia cusickii*
Mar	/	
Apr	/	*Camassia leichtlinii:*
May	flowering 🌸	"Electra"
Jun	flowering 🌸	"Blue Danube"
July	flowering 🌸	"Semiplena"
Aug	flowering 🌸	
Sept	plant ✋	*Camassia quamash*
Oct	plant ✋	
Nov	/	
Dec	/	

CONDITIONS

Aspect Full sun or light, dappled shade will suit these bulbs.

Site Camassias make excellent border plants, valuable for early summer color. A moisture-retentive, fertile soil is preferred, though they will also grow adequately in free-draining conditions.

GROWING METHOD

Planting Plant the bulbs in early to mid-fall, 3–4in deep. Space them about 6in apart.

Feeding Feeding is not usually necessary, but an application of a balanced, granular fertilizer can be made in spring, especially on poor soils. Water thoroughly in dry conditions and on free-draining soil.

Problems Camassias are usually trouble free.

FLOWERING

Season Flowers from late spring through early summer.

Cutting Stems can be cut as the lowest buds on the spike begin to open.

AFTER FLOWERING

Requirements Cut down the flowering spikes when the flowers have faded. Do not disturb the bulbs until they become overcrowded, when they can be lifted and divided in fall.

CANNA
Indian shot

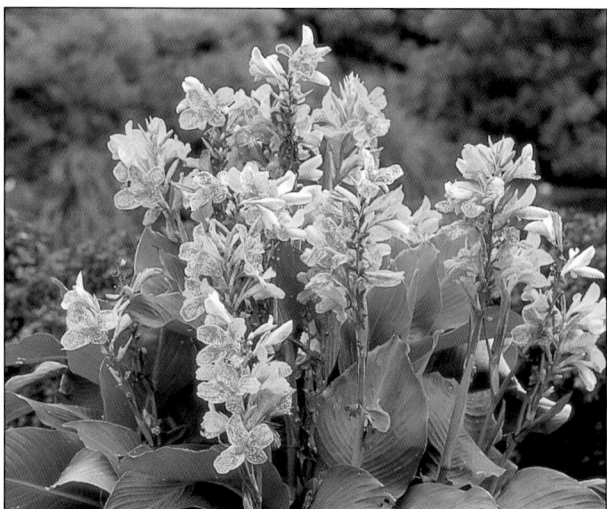

THE APRICOT-ORANGE FLOWERS of these cannas will contribute a rich, flamboyant color to the garden for many months.

THE COLOR of these scarlet cannas is highlighted by the darker green, slightly bronzed foliage that surrounds them.

FEATURES

Canna is an exotic-looking plant with bold, brilliantly colored flowers carried on tall stems, up to 4ft, above large, paddle-shaped leaves. The large blooms form an impressive spike; colors available are mainly shades of yellow, orange, and red. Sometimes the flowers are bi-colored, or spotted, streaked, or splashed with a contrasting shade. The foliage is also attractive, and in some varieties is tinged with bronze or purple. There are a number of varieties with attractively variegated foliage, which has yellow or pink veins.

Cannas are not hardy and must be protected from frost. *Canna indica* is the best known species, but most varieties generally available are hybrids, often sold as *Canna hybrida*. A wide range of named varieties is available from specialist suppliers.

CANNA AT A GLANCE

An impressive, exotic-looking plant with tall stems of brightly colored flowers and lush, attractive foliage.

Jan	/	Recommended Varieties
Feb	/	
Mar	plant (indoors)	"Durban"
Apr	plant (indoors)	"Lucifer"
May	plant (outdoors)	"Oiseau de Feu" ("Firebird")
Jun	plant (outdoors)	"Picasso"
July	flowering	"Wyoming"
Aug	flowering	
Sept	flowering	
Oct	/	
Nov	/	
Dec	/	

CONDITIONS

Aspect These plants must have an open but sheltered position in full sun.

Site Cannas make an impressive focal point in a bedding display, in mixed or herbaceous borders, or grow well in tubs and large containers. Soil should be free draining but rich in organic matter. In cold areas, the plants are best grown in a greenhouse or conservatory.

GROWING METHOD

Planting Set the rhizomes about 3in deep in fertile soil in late spring, once the risk of frosts is over. Better plants will be obtained by starting the rhizomes off in pots in a frost-free greenhouse in April, and planting them outide in early summer, once all risk of frost is over and the weather is suitably warm.

Feeding Give an occasional high potash liquid feed as the flower buds develop. Keep the soil moist at all times but make sure that it is never waterlogged.

Problems No specific problems are generally experienced.

FLOWERING

Season Flowers in mid to late summer, until the first frosts.

Cutting Flowers are not suitable for cutting—they are best enjoyed on the plants.

AFTER FLOWERING

Requirements Lift and dry the rhizomes in early fall, before the first frosts. Store them in a cool, frost-free place in just-moist peat or sand through the winter. If kept bone dry, the rhizomes will shrivel.

CHIONODOXA
Glory of the snow

"PINK GIANT," a variety of Chionodoxa siehei, *has relatively large blooms in a pale, purplish-pink shade.*

THE BRIGHT BLUE flowers of chionodoxa, with their prominent central white eye, make a cheerful sight in the early spring months.

FEATURES

This dainty little bulb is ideal for rock gardens or raised beds, with its mass of open, star-shaped blue flowers with white centers. They are carried on short spikes of up to a dozen or so flowers per spike. The strap-shaped leaves form loose, rather untidy rosettes.
Chionodoxa luciliae (C. gigantea) grows to 4in tall with clear blue, white-eyed flowers some 1½in or more across. *Chionodoxa siehei,* which used to be known as *C. luciliae,* and is sometimes listed as *C. forbesii,* reaches 4–10in, with slightly smaller flowers that are available in pale blue, white, or purplish-pink forms. The flowers have a distinct white eye and a central boss of stamens, tipped with gold. *C. sardensis* has flowers of a striking gentian blue

with a tiny white center that is almost unnoticeable.

CONDITIONS

Aspect Full sun or dappled shade is suitable, though they grow best in an open, sunny position.
Site Chionodoxa is suitable for window boxes, rock gardens, raised beds, the front of borders, or naturalized in grass. Soil should be free-draining, but otherwise these bulbs are not fussy about their growing conditions.

GROWING METHOD

Planting Plant the bulbs in groups about 3in deep and 3in apart in early fall.
Feeding A balanced granular fertilizer can be sprinkled over the soil surface in spring, but plants usually grow well without supplementary feeding, except in very poor, thin soils. Watering is necessary only in very dry conditions.
Problems Apart from occasional slug damage, plants are generally trouble-free.

FLOWERING

Season Chionodoxa flowers in early spring, sometimes appearing as the snow is thawing to live up to its common name.
Cutting Flowers can be cut when they begin to open. They are valuable for cutting when few other flowers are available in the garden.

AFTER FLOWERING

Requirements Lift and divide overcrowded plants when the foliage dies down in early summer after flowering, otherwise little attention is needed.

CHIONODOXA AT A GLANCE

A low-growing bulb producing plenty of bright blue flowers in early spring.

Month	Activity
Jan	/
Feb	flowering
Mar	flowering
Apr	flowering
May	/
Jun	/
July	/
Aug	/
Sept	plant
Oct	/
Nov	/
Dec	/

Recommended Varieties

Chionodoxa siehei:
"Alba"
"Pink Giant"
"Rosea"

CLIVIA MINIATA
Kaffir lily

CLIVIAS MAKE SHOWY *and colorful house plants, and will bloom for many years if they are given a winter rest.*

THE PALE *creamy yellow flowers of* Clivia miniata citrina *make this unusual plant worth seeking out.*

FEATURES

This evergreen forms a striking house or conservatory plant, with long, deep green, strap-shaped leaves that overlap at the base rather like a leek. In spring or summer, a stout stem pushes between the leaf bases and grows to about 18in, carrying a head of 20 or so bright orange, bell-shaped flowers. These are marked with yellow in the throat and have prominent golden anthers.

Selected hybrids have larger flowers in various rich orange shades: a beautiful yellow-flowered variety, *C. miniata citrina*, has been developed but to date these plants are scarce and expensive, as are cultivars with cream-striped foliage.

CLIVIA AT A GLANCE

A striking house plant with large heads of orange, bell-shaped flowers on stout stems. Minimum temperature 50°F (zone 11).

Jan	/	Recommended Varieties
Feb	flowering	
Mar	flowering	*Clivia miniata citrina*
Apr	flowering	"Striata"
May	transplant	
Jun	/	
July	/	
Aug	/	
Sept	/	
Oct	/	
Nov	/	
Dec	/	

CONDITIONS

Aspect   Clivia prefers a reasonably bright position in the home, but not one in direct sun, which will scorch the foliage. Provide shading in a greenhouse or conservatory.

Site   Grow as a room plant while it is flowering; during the summer the container can be placed in a sheltered position outdoors. Use a loam-based or soil-less potting compost.

GROWING METHOD

Planting   Clivias are usually bought as house plants in growth.

Feeding   Give a high potash liquid feed every two or three weeks from early spring through the summer. Keep the compost thoroughly moist from spring to fall, then keep the plant cool and water it very sparingly in winter.

Problems   Mealy bugs can appear as fluffy white blobs between the leaf bases; use a systemic insecticide to control them.

FLOWERING

Season   Flowers may be carried any time between late winter and early summer.

Cutting   Not suitable for cutting.

AFTER FLOWERING

Requirements   Remove spent flower stalks. Repot only when essential; crowded plants tend to flower more reliably.

COLCHICUM AUTUMNALE
Fall crocus, meadow saffron

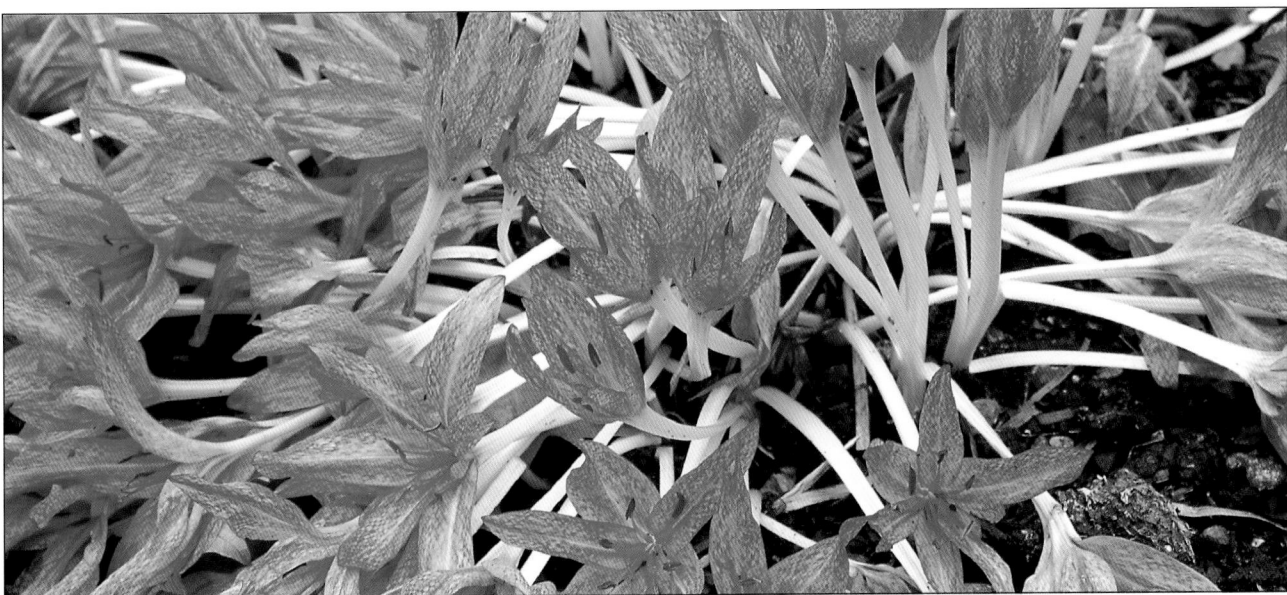

THE DELICATE COLOR and form of meadow saffron flowers are particularly prominent, as they appear long before the leaves. They are very welcome as they appear in fall when the yard is often looking rather untidy and faded after its summer exuberance.

FEATURES

This is another beautiful plant to brighten and lift the garden in fall. It is unusual in that the 6–9in-high flowers emerge directly from the neck of the corm, the leaves not appearing until months later, in spring. Although the flowers look similar to crocuses, the plants are not related. Up to a dozen rose pink to pale lilac, goblet-shaped flowers emerge from each corm. There is a pure white form, "Alba," and a glorious double form known as "Waterlily," that has a profusion of rose-lilac petals. Always plant in quite large groups for the best effect.

This easy-care bulb gives great rewards. It has a long history of use in herbal medicine but all parts of the plant are poisonous.

COLCHICUM AT A GLANCE

A crocus-like plant valuable for its fall flowers held on delicate stems.

		Recommended Varieties
Jan	/	
Feb	/	
Mar	/	"Alboplenum"
Apr	/	"Album"
May	/	"Pleniflorum"
Jun	/	"The Giant"
July	plant	"Waterlily"
Aug	plant	
Sept	flowering	
Oct	flowering	
Nov	flowering	
Dec	/	

CONDITIONS

Aspect Colchicum grows in full sun or very light shade.

Site Suitable for rock gardens, borders, or for naturalizing in grassed areas or in light shade under trees. For best results grow this plant in well-drained soil to which organic matter has been added.

GROWING METHOD

Planting Corms should be planted in late summer, 3in deep and 4–6in apart, in groups. Established clumps are best divided at this time, too.

Feeding Apply a generous mulch of decayed organic matter in winter. Further feeding is not usually necessary. Water in dry spells when the leaves appear in spring, and throughout their growing period.

Problems No specific pest or disease problems are common for this plant.

FLOWERING

Season Flowers spring out of the ground in fall.

Cutting Cut flowers for the vase when the goblet shape is fully formed but before it opens out. Flowers last about a week in the vase.

AFTER FLOWERING

Requirements Spent flowers may be cut off or left on the ground. Dead foliage may need tidying up at the end of the season.

CONVALLARIA MAJALIS
Lily-of-the-valley

LONG A FAVORITE *with spring brides, fragrant lily-of-the-valley is an easy and rewarding bulb to grow.*

IDEAL FOR EDGING *a shady garden, these beautiful plants are also completely reliable, increasing, and flowering every year.*

FEATURES

This is a tough little plant with a dainty appearance that belies its ease of growth. It is ideal for naturalizing in shady spots in the yard and also under trees where it can grow undisturbed. The dainty little white bell flowers are borne in spring; they are delightfully scented and last well in the vase. Flower stems may be 8–10in high, just topping the broadish, furled leaves that clasp the flower stems in pairs. There are several named cultivars but the straight species is by far the most popular. Previously used in folk medicine, the plant is now known to contain several poisonous substances although research continues on its potential medical use. The fleshy rhizomes with their growth shoots are known as "pips."

CONVALLARIA AT A GLANCE

A low-growing plant with very fragrant, dainty white bells on arching stems in late spring. Ideal for light shade.

Jan	/	Recommended Varieties
Feb	/	
Mar	/	"Albostriata"
Apr	flowering	"Fortin's Giant"
May	flowering	"Flore Pleno"
Jun	/	"Prolificans"
July	/	*Convallaria majalis rosea*
Aug	/	
Sept	/	
Oct	plant	
Nov	plant	
Dec	plant	

CONDITIONS

Aspect   Prefers to grow in partial shade; ideal under deciduous trees.

Site   A good ground cover plant; also suitable for mixed beds and borders. Soil should be free-draining but moisture-retentive, containing large amounts of decayed organic matter.

GROWING METHOD

Planting   The pips are planted in late fall about 1in deep and 4in apart. Congested clumps can be divided in fall or winter.

Feeding   In early winter apply a generous mulch of decayed manure or compost, or pile on the decaying leaves of deciduous trees. Keep soil moist throughout the growing season, giving a thorough soaking when necessary.

Problems   Few problems are encountered but poor drainage may rot the root system.

FLOWERING

Season   Flowers appear from mid-spring.

Cutting   This lovely cut flower perfumes a whole room. Pull the stems from the plant. It is traditional to use the foliage to wrap around the bunch.

AFTER FLOWERING

Requirements   If possible, leave the plants undisturbed for several years. If clumps are extremely dense and flowering poor, lift and divide sections during fall or early winter.

CRINUM
Swamp lily

LIGHT PERFUME is an added reason to grow these pretty pink crinums. They are a good choice for a sheltered border.

VERY TALL STEMS carry the white flowers of Crinum x powellii *well-clear of the leaves so that the blooms are always well-displayed.*

FEATURES

There are more than 100 species of crinum, but *C.* x *powellii* and the more tender *C. moorei* are the two most commonly grown. Both bear large, scented, lily-like flowers in pale pink or white on stems up to 3ft high; plants have long, strap-shaped, light-green leaves. The flowers appear from middle to late summer and sometimes into fall.

The bulbs can grow very large indeed, up to 6in or more across, and can be very weighty. In time very large clumps are formed and they require considerable physical effort to lift and divide. Crinums need a sheltered position to do well. In cool areas they can also be grown quite successfully in containers that can be moved under cover in fall.

CRINUM AT A GLANCE

Large, scented, lily-like flowers in late summer and fall. This plant needs a sheltered, sunny position to thrive.

		Recommended Varieties
Jan	/	
Feb	/	*Crinum* x *powellii:*
Mar	/	"Album"
Apr	plant 🖐	"Roseum"
May	plant 🖐	
Jun	/	*Crinum moorei*
July	/	
Aug	flowering 🌤	*Crinum bulbispermum:*
Sept	flowering 🌤	"Album"
Oct	/	
Nov	/	
Dec	/	

CONDITIONS

Aspect   Grow crinum in a sunny, south-facing, sheltered position. *C. moorei* is best grown in a pot in a conservatory.

Site   Suitable for borders or as a specimen plant in a container on a patio or similar. Soil must be free-draining but moisture-retentive.

GROWING METHOD

Planting   Plant in spring, which is also the best time to divide existing clumps. *C.* x *powellii* should have the neck of the bulb above soil level, while *C. moorei* should be planted with the nose of the bulb at the level of the soil.

Feeding   Balanced fertilizer may be applied as new growth starts in spring. Keep the soil moist while the plants are in growth. Water plants in containers regularly.

Problems   Not generally susceptible to disease or pests but snails love to eat the foliage and flowers.

FLOWERING

Season   Flowers appear during summer and into the fall months.

Cutting   It is possible to cut blooms for the house but they last longer on the plant.

AFTER FLOWERING

Requirements   Cut off the flowering stalk when the flowers are over. Protect the crowns with a mulch of peat over winter, or move plants under cover. Disturb established plants as little as possible.

CROCOSMIA
Montbretia

THE VIBRANT COLOR of crocosmia flowers gives great decorative value but is matched by vigorous growth that may need to be controlled.

THE CLEAR, GOLDEN YELLOW flowers of "Citronella" make a pleasant change from the intense orange-reds of other varieties.

FEATURES

Also known as montbretia, some types of crocosmia are extremely vigorous and can become invasive in warm areas. It will often survive in old, neglected yards where virtually everything else has disappeared. The foliage is slender, sword-shaped, and upright or slightly arching. The flowers are carried on double-sided spikes that also arch gracefully, reaching some 2–3ft tall. Most types have eye-catching bright reddish-orange flowers that open progressively from the base of the spike. In cold areas, plants should be protected with a mulch of dry leaves over winter, and should be planted in a reasonably sheltered position.

CROCOSMIA AT A GLANCE

A vigorous plant with sword-shaped leaves and brightly colored spikes of flowers through the summer.

Jan	/	Recommended Varieties
Feb	/	
Mar	plant 🌱	"Bressingham Blaze"
Apr	plant 🌱	"Canary Bird"
May	/	"Citronella"
Jun	/	"Emily McKenzie"
July	flowering 🌸	"Jackanapes"
Aug	flowering 🌸	"Lucifer"
Sept	flowering 🌸	"Solfaterre"
Oct	/	
Nov	/	
Dec	/	

CONDITIONS

Aspect Grows best in a fully open, sunny position.
Site Good in beds or borders in well-drained soil.

GROWING METHOD

Planting Plant corms in spring, 3in deep and about 6in apart. Pot-grown specimens can be planted throughout the spring and summer, even when in flower. It usually becomes necessary to thin out clumps every few years.
Feeding A balanced fertilizer can be applied in early summer, but feeding is not generally necessary.
Problems There are no pests or diseases that commonly attack crocosmia.

FLOWERING

Season There is a long flowering period all through summer. Congested clumps often seem to produce more blooms.
Cutting Flowers are not suitable for cutting and are better appreciated in the garden.

AFTER FLOWERING

Requirements Cut off spent flower stems as soon as the blooms have faded to avoid seed setting and plants spreading. When the leaves have died down, protect the corms with a mulch of straw or dry leaves in all but very warm, sheltered yards.

CROCUS
Crocus

SAFFRON CROCUS (Crocus sativus) *displays branched bright orange stigmas, the source of saffron, the costly spice used in cooking.*

CROCUS CHRYSANTHUS "ARD SCHENK"—one of the most popular species—pushes up white goblet-shaped flowers in spring.

FEATURES

There are more than 80 species of crocus, mainly late winter and spring flowering, but there are some fall bloomers, too. Crocus are among the earliest flowers to appear in spring, often pushing their flowers up through the snow. In some species flowers appear some weeks before the leaves. Crocus are mostly native to the countries around the Mediterranean Sea where they usually grow at high altitudes. They do, however, extend as far east as Afghanistan.

Appearance   Crocus foliage is short, rather sparse, and looks like a broad-leaf grass. The gorgeous little goblet-shaped flowers are borne on short stems 2–5in high. Most are blue, violet, white, yellow, or cream but some species have pink flowers. Many have deeper colored stripes or feathering on the petals.

Uses   Although unsuitable for cutting, these little bulbous plants are one of the greatest delights of the yard. They are often mass-planted in garden beds, especially at the front of borders. They can be naturalized in lawns or grouped together under deciduous trees. Crocuses are excellent plants for rock gardens and they make good container plants, being especially suitable for winter and early spring window-boxes. The floral display of some individual species in the yard can be short, but by growing a selection of species you can enjoy these charming flowers over an extended period, from early fall right through to late spring.

POPULAR SPECIES

Spring   Some of the most popular spring-flowering species are *C. biflorus*, *C. chrysanthus*, *C. flavus*, *C. minimus*, *C. tommasinianus* and *C. vernus*. Cultivars of a number of these species are available, with the many and varied cultivars of *C. chrysanthus* being especially popular, although each of these species have their admirers. *C. ancyrensis* is particularly early flowering, appearing in January and February.

Autumn   Fall-flowering species include *C. kotschyanus*, *C. niveus*, *C. laevigatus*, *C. longiflorus*, *C. nudiflorus*, *C. sativus* (the saffron crocus), *C. serotinus* (also known as *C. salzmannii*) and *C. speciosus*. *Crocus sativus* is well known as the source of the costliest of all herbs and spices. Native to temperate Eurasia and widely grown in Mediterranean regions, saffron crocus needs a very specific climate to flourish and is an extremely labor-intensive crop to harvest. Saffron comes only from the stigmas of the flowers and 75,000 flowers are needed to make up a pound of pure saffron.

CONDITIONS

Aspect   Prefers an open, sunny position but may be grown in light shade.

Site   Good for rock gardens, raised beds, the fronts of borders or naturalized in grass. Soil must be well-drained, preferably containing plenty of well-rotted organic matter.

FALL-BLOOMING Crocus serotinus *here displays its beautiful pale lilac flowers and stiff, grass-like foliage. All crocus look best when planted like* *this, in a random fashion that mimics their natural growth.*

GROWING METHOD

Planting Plant new corms about 2in deep and 2–4in apart. Spring-flowering varieties should be planted in fall, from September to November, while fall-flowering species should be planted in July and August. The corms of some species become quite large over time; lift and plant them further apart as it becomes necessary.

Feeding Apply a light dressing of balanced fertilizer after flowering, particularly in poor soil conditions. Watering is necessary only if conditions are very dry: however, fall-flowering types are likely to need watering after planting in summer.

Problems Few problems are encountered when crocuses are grown in the right aspect and soil. However, birds can sometimes damage flowers. Some birds, particularly sparrows, seem to be attracted by the shape or color of flowers and can peck them to pieces. If this occurs you will have to place a frame covered in wire netting over the plants.

FLOWERING

Season Flowering depends on the species; some varieties begin flowering in late winter to very early spring, others slightly later in spring. Fall-flowering species flower between September and early December, and may overlap with the earliest of the winter-flowering species growing against a warm wall.

Cutting Crocuses are not good cut flowers although they may last a few days in the vase.

AFTER FLOWERING

Requirements It is essential not to remove crocus leaves before they have yellowed as they are important in building up the corms and, therefore, next season's flowering potential. Plantings may need lifting and dividing every 3–4 years, but they can be left until corms start to push their way to the surface.

CROCUS AT A GLANCE

Low-growing bulbs valuable for their early spring flowers in a range of colors. Good for containers.

		Recommended Varieties
Jan	flowering*	*Crocus chrysanthus:*
Feb	flowering*	"Cream Beauty"
Mar	flowering*	"Ladykiller"
Apr	flowering*	"Snow Bunting"
May	/	*Crocus tommasinianus:*
Jun	/	"Ruby Giant"
July	plant**	*Crocus vernus:*
Aug	plant**	"Little Dorrit"
Sept	**/ *	"Queen of the Blues"
Oct	**/ *	"Vanguard"
Nov	**/ *	
Dec	flowering **	

* spring flowering species   ** fall flowering species

CYCLAMEN
Cyclamen

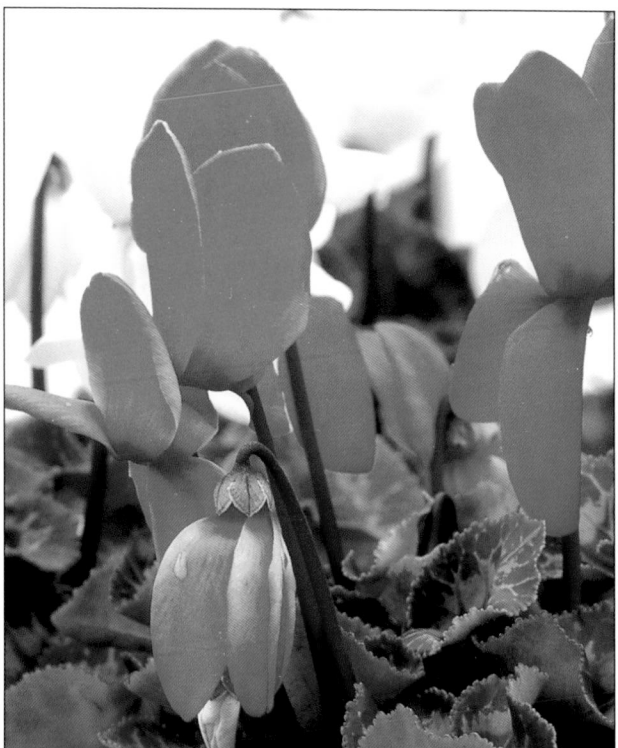

GORGEOUS UPSWEPT PETALS and a range of glorious colors ensure the lasting popularity of florist's cyclamen as house plants.

NEAPOLITAN CYCLAMEN (Cyclamen hederifolium) *provides weeks of flowers and many months of decorative foliage.*

FEATURES

Cyclamen form an enchanting group of plants admired for their attractive, mostly marbled foliage and distinctive flowers with swept back, slightly twisted petals. Some, such as the florists' cyclamen, have large showy flowers, while many of the species have small flowers growing only 3–4in high. Some cyclamen flower in fall or winter, while others flower in late winter and spring. Native to parts of Europe and countries around the Mediterranean, all share a similar need to be kept rather dry during their dormant period. Plants growing in good conditions can remain undisturbed for many years. The original tubers will increase greatly in size and many new plants will come from self-sown seed.

Uses
The smaller varieties make a great show when planted in masses or drifts. The floral display is quite long-lasting and even out of flower the marbled leaves make a good groundcover for many months of the year. Cyclamen can be grown in light shade under trees, in rock gardens, and in containers.
Potted plants of *C. persicum* hybrids in bloom make excellent house plants and are available from late summer right through the winter. The flowers may be delicately scented. In warm rooms in the home it can be difficult to keep these plants in good condition, and they are sometimes best considered as short-term floral decoration.

TYPES

Florists'
Florists' cyclamen (*C. persicum*) is usually seen as a flowering potted plant for indoor use, and many hybrids are available, including very fragrant miniature types. The beautifully marbled foliage and spectacular flowers make this a very showy plant. The flowers with their swept back petals come in every shade of pink and red, purple, cerise, white, and bicolors, and there are some fancy frilled or ruffled kinds. This species came originally from the eastern Mediterranean but many of the modern hybrids grown bear little resemblance to the original species.

Garden
The most easily-grown garden cyclamen is the Neapolitan cyclamen (*C. hederifolium*) which flowers during fall. It can be grown more successfully in warmer areas than most of the other species. *C. hederifolium* has beautifully marbled foliage about 3–4in high, with the small, clear pink flowers held above the leaves. There is also a pure white form of this species. *C. coum* flowers from late winter into spring and has larger, very deep pink flowers on short stems. Again, there is a white form of this species available. *C. repandum*, another spring bloomer, has probably the largest flowers of all the species cyclamens but none of these have flowers that are the size of the florists' cyclamen. The foliage on *C. repandum* is noted for its reddish undersides.

THESE CYCLAMEN COUM are thriving in an alpine-type sink garden: when they are allowed to self-seed, they soon form dense colonies. The marbled leaves are attractive, as well as the dainty, pale pink and purple flowers with their upswept petals.

CONDITIONS

Aspect   The ideal situation for hardy cyclamen is beneath deciduous trees where there is some winter sun but dappled sunlight for the rest of the year. In the home, florists' cyclamen need a cool, bright position.

Site   Hardy cyclamen can be grown on rock gardens, under trees and shrubs, and in borders. The soil must be well-drained with a high organic content. Indoors, choose a bright, cool windowsill or a conservatory.

GROWING METHOD

Planting   The flattened tubers (often wrongly referred to as corms) should be planted with their tops just below the soil surface. Plant in late summer and early fall at about 6in intervals. Pot-grown seedlings are easier to establish than dry tubers, and can be obtained from garden centers and specialist nurseries.

Feeding   If soil is poor, a sprinkling of balanced fertilizer can be given when growth begins and again after flowering. Florists' cyclamen should be given high potash liquid fertilizer every 14 days from when the flower buds appear until flowering is over. Water carefully from the base to avoid splashing the top of the tuber; never leave the pots standing in water.

Problems   Florists' cyclamen grown indoors often succumb to overwatering, drying out, and a dry, overwarm atmosphere. Vine weevils are attracted to the tubers and may cause the sudden collapse of the plant: use a soil insecticide if they are caught in time.

CYCLAMEN AT A GLANCE

Characteristic, upswept petals on a mound-forming plant with attractive marbled foliage. Suitable for outdoors or as pot plants.

Jan	flowering	Recommended Varieties
Feb	flowering	
Mar	flowering	*Cyclamen cilicium album*
Apr	flowering	*Cyclamen coum album*
May	/	*Cyclamen hederifolium*
Jun	/	"Bowles' Apollo"
July	plant	"Silver Cloud"
Aug	plant	*Cyclamen libanoticum*
Sept	flowering	*Cyclamen pseudibericum*
Oct	flowering	*Cyclamen purpurascens*
Nov	flowering	*Cyclamen repandum*
Dec	flowering	*Cyclamen persicum:* many
		hybrids available

FLOWERING

Season   *C. persicum* flowers through winter into spring. *C. hederifolium* has a long flowering period in fall, while *C. coum* and *C. repandum* flower betwen late winter and spring.

Cutting   Pull flowers from the plant with a rolling motion and cut off the thin base of the stalk.

AFTER FLOWERING

Requirements   Outdoors, leave spent flowering stems to set seed and do not disturb tubers. After flowering, allow pot plants to die down and keep dry over summer. Start into growth again in August.

CYRTANTHUS ELATUS
Vallota, Scarborough lily

SCARLET FLOWERS with a flared, trumpet-like shape make Scarborough lily a most striking plant.

IN WARM AREAS Scarborough lily can be grown outdoors, but it is more reliable as a pot plant for the conservatory or greenhouse.

FEATURES

Still more commonly known under its earlier botanical name of *Vallota*, this old favorite should be more widely grown. Four or more brilliant scarlet, open trumpet-shaped blooms are held on a sturdy stem some 18in tall among dark green, strappy leaves. The plant originates from South Africa, and unfortunately, is not hardy enough to try outdoors except in the most favored, warmest areas of the country. However, it makes a good pot plant for a cool greenhouse or conservatory, or it can be grown indoors on a sunny windowsill. During the summer, the pots can be taken outside to decorate the patio. The Scarborough lily is not difficult to cultivate, and deserves to be more popular.

CYRTANTHUS AT A GLANCE

A tender bulb with large, trumpet-shaped flowers in summer—an excellent house or greenhouse plant. Min 45°F (zone 11).

Jan	/	Recommended Varieties
Feb	/	"Pink Diamond"
Mar	/	
Apr	/	
May	/	
Jun	plant 🖐	
July	flowering 🌸	
Aug	flowering 🌸	
Sept	flowering 🌸	
Oct	/	
Nov	/	
Dec	/	

CONDITIONS

Aspect	Grows best in a bright, sunny position.
Site	Must be grown as a house or greenhouse plant in all but the very warmest areas of the country.

GROWING METHOD

Planting	Plant bulbs in summer with the tip of the bulb just at or above soil level. Set one bulb in a 5in pot.
Feeding	Apply liquid fertilizer every 14 days as soon as growth appears. Keep the plant well-watered throughout the spring and summer, but reduce watering after flowering.
Problems	No specific pest or disease problems are known for this plant.

FLOWERING

Season	Flowers usually appear in midsummer.
Cutting	Flowers will last well when cut but probably give better decorative value if they are left on the plant.

AFTER FLOWERING

Requirements	Cut off the spent flower stems. Reduce watering and allow the compost to dry out completely between late winter and mid-spring. Do not repot for several years as the plants flower best when the pot is crowded. Offsets are produced freely, and some of these may be removed to pot up and grow on to flowering size in two or three years.

DAHLIA
Dahlia

THE RICH PINK of this freshly opened dahlia will gradually lighten to a delicate pale pink as the flower ages.

BICOLORED DAHLIAS have always had a strong following, whether in small, neat forms or dinner-plate sized blooms.

FEATURES

Dahlias come in many different flower forms and in a huge range of colors. Flower sizes range from tiny pompoms less than 2in across to huge blooms 12in or more wide, and they may be single, double, or semi-double. Most home gardeners are content to have a beautiful garden display but there are many enthusiasts who grow dahlias for showing.

Dahlias are grouped into different classes according to the shape and form of their flowers, and classes include single, anemone-flowered, collerette, waterlily, decorative, ball, pompon, cactus, and semi-cactus. There is also a miscellaneous group for any other type not covered by these classes. Plants can be anywhere from 12in to nearly 5ft high. They have a long flowering season from mid to late summer right through the fall. An ever-increasing range of bedding dahlias can be grown from seed; they form tubers which can be lifted and stored in the normal way in fall. Bedding varieties can also be bought as growing plants in spring.

CONDITIONS

Aspect   Dahlias prefer full sun all day with protection from strong wind. The taller varieties need staking.

Site   Dahlias are especially suitable for the herbaceous or mixed border, where they provide very welcome late summer color, but they can also be grown as bedding plants or the smaller varieties can be grown in containers. Soil must be well-drained and heavily enriched with manure or compost. Dahlias give best results in rich soil and are heavy feeders.

GROWING METHOD

Planting   The tuberous roots should be planted 4–6in deep with the neck containing the sprouting eyes pointing up, in middle to late spring. Spacing between plants depends on variety— set small growers about 12in apart, very large growers 30–40in apart. The stakes and labels should be put in at planting time to avoid damaging tubers later.

Dahlia tubers can also be potted up in moist compost in a warm greenhouse in early spring, and cuttings taken of the shoots that arise from the tubers. These can be potted up individually and planted out in the yard when the risk of frost has passed. This is a good way to increase your stock of a particularly prized variety.

Feeding   When flowering has begun, feed dahlias monthly with balanced fertilizer, or apply a high potash liquid feed every 14 days from when the flower buds begin to form. Applying a mulch of well-rotted garden compost will also help to retain soil moisture. Water well after planting tubers if the soil is dry, but further watering is usually unnecessary until after growth begins. During the growing and flowering season, it is important to make sure the plants never go short of water.

Problems   Dahlias are affected by a number of viruses, notably dahlia mosaic virus, which causes

THIS SHRUB-LIKE DAHLIA with its clear, scarlet flowers will give many months of color in the garden if dead blooms are regularly removed. Dahlias prefer a sunny corner of the yard where they are protected from the wind.

yellowing foliage and sometimes stunted plants. It is transmitted by aphids. Spotted wilt virus causes spots and rings on leaves; it is carried by thrips and affects a range of plants. Watch for thrips and aphids early in the season and spray if necessary. Snails love dahlia foliage and flowers so take care to control them. They will climb up into the plant and stay there: if plants are being damaged, search for snails on and under the leaves and destroy them, or use slug bait, making sure it is positioned out of the reach of pets and wildlife. Earwigs can also damage blooms, feeding mainly at night and causing ragged holes in petals or distorted blooms. During the day they can be trapped in upturned pots stuffed with straw positioned on stakes among the plants.

FLOWERING

Season	The long flowering period lasts from midsummer to the first frosts. Deadhead the plants regularly to prolong blooming.
Cutting	Cut flowers early in the day, remove lower leaves, and scald stems for 10–15 seconds before arranging them. They are very long lasting in a vase.

AFTER FLOWERING

Requirements Tubers may survive in the ground for several years if the soil is well-drained, but in heavy soils and in cold areas, they are better lifted in late fall. Cut off the stem 6–8in above ground, dig up the clump carefully, and shake off excess soil. Stand upside-down to drain moisture from the stem, then store in a cool, airy place such as a garden shed, lightly covered with sand, soil, or peat, for replanting next spring. Tubers can be divided, but make sure that each section has a portion of stem with a visible bud or "eye"—the tuberous root portion on its own cannot grow.

DAHLIAS AT A GLANCE

Spectacular flowering plants giving four months of bloom. Perfect for cutting, showing, or garden decoration.

Jan	/	Recommended Varieties
Feb	/	"Bishop of Llandaff"
Mar	/	"Daleko Jupiter"
Apr	plant	"Firebird"
May	plant	"Glorie van Heemstede"
Jun	/	"Grenidor Pastelle"
July	flowering	"Hamari Gold"
Aug	flowering	"Jescot Julie"
Sept	flowering	"Kenora Fireball"
Oct	flowering	"Wootton Cupid"
Nov	/	
Dec	/	

DIERAMA PULCHERRIMUM
Fairy fishing rods, wandflower

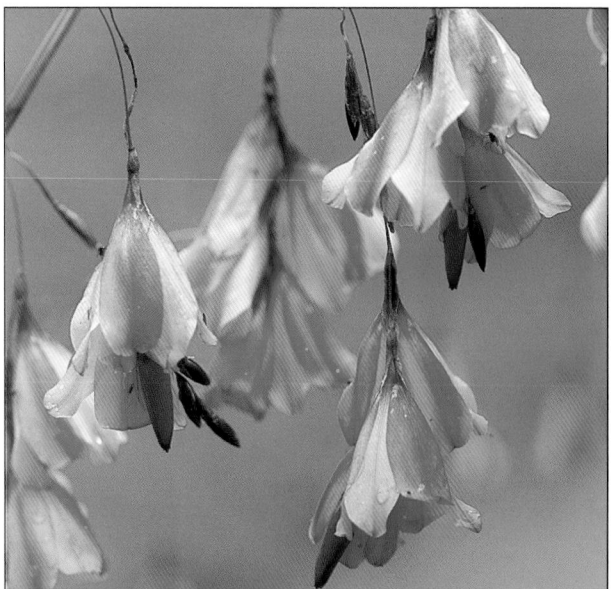

SILKY FLOWERS in two shades of pink are suspended from the fine stems of this lovely South African plant.

AN ESTABLISHED CLUMP of fairy fishing rods produces many flowering stems. It is easy to see how the plant gained its common name.

FEATURES

The slender, arching stems of this highly desirable South African plant carry numerous bell-shaped, pendulous flowers and rise out of stiff, evergreen, sword-shaped leaves. Flowers are a rich silvery-pink in the species but there are a number of named cultivars in shades of pink, lilac, and even white.

Dense clumps of established plants produce many flowering stems, which sway in the slightest breeze to give a delightful effect. A mass planting creates a striking feature in the garden and it is often placed near water where the reflections increase its impact. Foliage grows 20in or so high but the flowering stems may be almost 6ft long in the right conditions.

DIERAMA AT A GLANCE

A perennial with graceful, slender, arching stems carrying dainty pink blooms in summer. Needs moist soil to thrive.

		Recommended Varieties
Jan	/	
Feb	/	"Blackbird"
Mar	/	"Peregrine"
Apr	/	"Slieve Donard Hybrids"
May	/	
Jun	/	
July	flowering	
Aug	flowering	
Sept	flowering	
Oct	plant	
Nov	plant	
Dec	/	

CONDITIONS

Aspect Needs full sun all day.
Site Dierama fits well in the herbaceous border. This plant needs well-drained but moisture-retentive, fertile soil containing plenty of well-rotted organic matter such as garden compost or animal manure.

GROWING METHOD

Planting Plant in mid to late fall, 3in deep and 12in apart.
Feeding A balanced fertilizer can be applied annually in early spring or after flowering. Water during late spring and summer if conditions are dry; the soil should remain moist throughout the growing season.
Problems There are no specific pest or disease problems normally experienced with this plant.

FLOWERING

Season Dierama bears its flowers from mid to late summer.
Cutting Not suitable for cutting.

AFTER FLOWERING

Requirements When spent, flower stems can be cut off at ground level, although they can be left to set seed if required. Dierama resents root disturbance, so corms should not be lifted unless it is essential. Self-sown seedlings can often be transplanted successfully to increase your stock of this plant.

ERANTHIS
Winter aconite

THE GLOSSY, golden buttercups of winter aconites, backed by their green leafy ruffs, give a welcome show of color in early spring.

"GUINEA GOLD," a variety of Eranthis x tubergenii, *has particularly large, showy flowers.*

FEATURES

The glossy yellow flowers of this tuber are a welcome sight in early spring. They are backed by a bract that forms a green leafy ruff, giving the flowers a Jack-in-the-green appearance. The true winter aconite is *Eranthis hyemalis*, with divided, pale green leaves and buttercup-yellow blooms: it seeds itself freely and soon spreads to form a carpet. *Eranthis* x *tubergenii* is a more vigorous hybrid, with larger, slightly later flowers. Both types grow to about 4in. Another type is sometimes sold as the Cilicica form of *E. hyemalis*, sometimes as a separate species, *E. cilicica*. It has deep yellow flowers, carried in March, backed by bronzy green, very finely cut foliage, and it grows to 2–3in tall.

ERANTHIS AT A GLANCE

A low-growing plant, welcome for its bright golden-yellow flowers in late winter and early spring.

Jan	/	Recommended Varieties
Feb	flowering	"Guinea Gold"
Mar	flowering	
Apr	plant / flowering	
May	/	
Jun	/	
July	/	
Aug	/	
Sept	plant (tubers)	
Oct	/	
Nov	/	
Dec	/	

CONDITIONS

Aspect	Full sun or light shade are acceptable.
Site	Winter aconites are perfect for rock gardens, the fronts of borders, or beneath deciduous trees, which allow sufficient light to the plants during their spring growing period. They prefer a free-draining but moisture-retentive soil.

GROWING METHOD

Planting	Plant the tubers in September, as soon as they are obtained—if they dry out before planting they are difficult to establish. They should be planted 1–2in deep and 3–4in apart. Eranthis are also available freshly lifted, like snowdrops, in spring, when they establish more readily.
Feeding	Ensure the soil is kept moist during the spring, especially where the plants are growing under trees or shrubs. Supplementary feeding is not normally necessary.
Problems	Plants can become invasive where conditions suit them as they seed freely; otherwise no specific problems are generally experienced.

FLOWERING

Season	Flowers from early February to mid-March or into April.
Cutting	Flowers can be cut just as the buds are opening.

AFTER FLOWERING

Requirements	Divide crowded clumps after flowering, replanting the tubers immediately.

EREMURUS
Foxtail lily

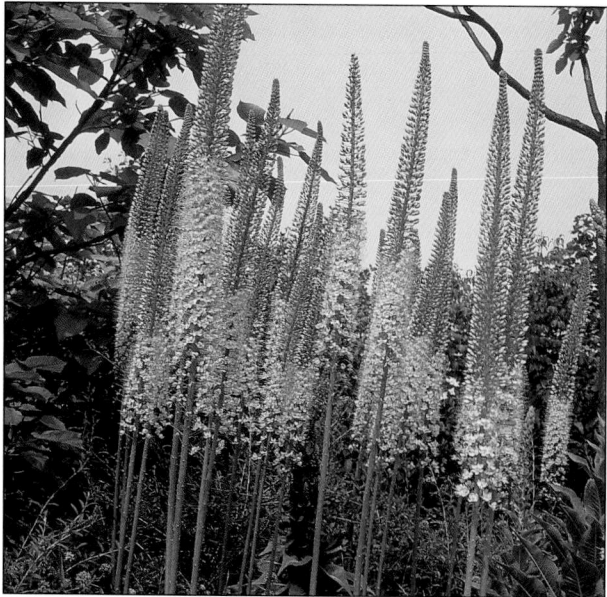

THE STATELY yellow spikes of bloom of Eremurus stenophyllus *make this border plant certain to attract attention.*

THE TALLEST member of the group is Eremurus robustus, *its salmon-pink flower spikes towering up to 10ft.*

FEATURES

These stately plants produce tall spires of numerous, star-shaped flowers, giving a very impressive display and making good focal points in the garden. Their foliage is pale green and strap shaped; the flowering spikes tower above the leaves, reaching as much as 10ft or more in some species.

Eremurus robustus is among the tallest, with 8–10ft spikes of salmon-pink blooms: *E. stenophyllus (E. bungei)* grows to about 4ft with orange-yellow flowers. Probably most popular are some of the hybrid varieties at about 6ft, which bear flowers in a range of yellow, orange, and pink shades. Because of their height, plants need a position sheltered from wind.

EREMURUS AT A GLANCE

Tall, stately plants with large, showy flower spikes made up of masses of individual starry flowers.

		Recommended Varieties
Jan	/	
Feb	/	"Shelford Hybrids"
Mar	/	"Ruiter Hybrids"
Apr	/	"Moneymaker"
May	/	
Jun	flowering	
July	flowering	
Aug	/	
Sept	plant	
Oct	plant	
Nov	/	
Dec	/	

CONDITIONS

Aspect   Eremurus are reasonably hardy but demand a sheltered position in full sun.

Site   These are excellent plants for a place at the back of a border, or plant a foxtail lily at the end of a path for a dramatic focal point. Taller varieties usually need staking. Soil must be rich and fertile but free-draining; dig some sharp sand into the site at planting time to improve drainage if necessary.

GROWING METHOD

Planting   In early to mid-fall, set the roots 4–6in deep and 2–3ft apart.

Feeding   Keep the soil moist at all times. A dressing of balanced granular fertilizer can be made over the site in early spring, or high potash liquid feed can be given occasionally during the growing season.

Problems   Usually, no problems are experienced. The young foliage is vulnerable to frost damage and may need protection in early spring when shoots first appear through the soil.

FLOWERING

Season   Flowers in early to mid summer.

Cutting   Flower spikes may be cut as the first flowers are opening. They last well in water.

AFTER FLOWERING

Requirements   Cut down flower stems when the flowers fade. Protect the crowns from frost with a mulch of sand or dry leaves over winter. When overcrowded, divide the clumps in fall.

ERYTHRONIUM
Dog's tooth violet

"PAGODA" IS DESERVEDLY one of the most popular erythronium hybrids, with its tall stems of graceful, nodding, yellow flowers.

THE DOG'S TOOTH VIOLET, E. dens-canis, has beautifully mottled foliage as well as attractive little rose-pink flowers.

FEATURES

Plants of the dappled shade of woodlands, erythroniums have attractive spring flowers, star-shaped and generally nodding, with swept-back petals.

The dog's tooth violet (named after the shape of its tuber) is *E. dens-canis*, with pinkish-purple flowers carried about 6in above the attractively mottled leaves. Slightly taller is *Erythronium californicum*, with lush, mid-green, lightly mottled leaves and creamy flowers with bronze backs to the petals. *Erythronium revolutum* grows to 12in, with white, pink, or purple mottled flowers, and has given rise to the popular hybrid "Pagoda," with 6–10 pendent, graceful yellow flowers on a slender, 16in flower stalk.

CONDITIONS

ERYTHRONIUM AT A GLANCE

Spring-flowering tubers with appealing, pendulous flowers in a range of heights and colors. Many also have attractive foliage.

Jan	/	Recommended Varieties
Feb	/	"Pagoda"
Mar	/	"Citronella"
Apr	flowering 🌸	
May	flowering 🌸	*Erythronium californicum:*
Jun	/	"White Beauty"
July	/	
Aug	plant ✋	*Erythronium dens-canis*
Sept	plant ✋	"Lilac Wonder"
Oct	/	"Rose Queen"
Nov	/	
Dec	/	

Aspect	As a woodland plant, erythronium thrives in cool conditions and light shade.
Site	Excellent under trees or among shrubs in beds and borders or on rock gardens. Fertile, moisture-retentive soil with plenty of organic matter will ensure good growth.

GROWING METHOD

Planting	Plant the tubers in groups, 3–6in deep and 4–6in apart in late summer or early fall. Do not let the tubers dry out before planting or you will find it difficult to get the plants established: plant them as soon as possible after purchase.
Feeding	Feeding is not usually necessary. Moist soil is essential during the growing season, but the tubers must never become waterlogged. Water carefully during dry spells.
Problems	No specific pest or disease problems are usually experienced with this plant. Plants resent disturbance and may be difficult to re-establish if lifted and replanted.

FLOWERING

Season	Flowers in mid-spring.
Cutting	The taller species can be cut successfully when the buds have opened.

AFTER FLOWERING

Requirements	Disturb the roots as little as possible. If clumps become so overcrowded that flowering is adversely affected, they can be lifted and divided in late summer, replanting the tubers immediately.

EUCOMIS COMOSA
Pineapple lily

THE TUFT on top of the flower spike does resemble a pineapple, but the pretty individual flowers below give a softer impression.

THE ROBUST GROWTH of this clump of pineapple lilies shows that the growing conditions in this spot are ideal.

FEATURES

This South African plant gets its common name from the pineapple-like flower spike with its topknot of tufted leaves. The greenish-white or white flowers, sometimes tinged with pink, are scented and packed tightly onto the spike; their weight can sometimes cause the stem to flop over. The broad, sword-shaped leaves are light green and attractively spotted with purple on the underside. This flower is always of interest, whether in the yard or as a potted plant: blooms are extremely long-lasting when cut. Another species in cultivation is *E. bicolor,* with attractive green and purple flowers. Both species grow to about 24in. Pineapple lily grows from a fleshy bulbous rootstock and is dormant in winter.

EUCOMIS AT A GLANCE

A tall, striking bulb with a pineapple-like flower stem. A sunny, sheltered spot is required.

Jan	/	Recommended Varieties
Feb	/	
Mar	plant 🌱	
Apr	plant 🌱	*Eucomis bicolor*
May	/	*E. b.* "Alba"
Jun	/	*E. comosa*
July	flowering 🌸	*E. pole-evansii*
Aug	flowering 🌸	*E. zambesiaca*
Sept	/	
Oct	/	
Nov	/	
Dec	/	

CONDITIONS

Aspect   Prefers full sun but tolerates light shade. Grows best in warm, sheltered areas, but can also be grown in colder gardens if the rootstock is protected or lifted for winter.

Site   Eucomis is good for the middle or back of the flower border. Needs well-drained soil enriched with decayed organic matter before planting time.

GROWING METHOD

Planting   Plant in spring, 2–4in deep and 8–12in apart.

Feeding   Apply complete plant food as new growth begins. Mulch around plants in summer with well-decayed compost or manure. Keep the soil moist while the plant is actively growing.

Problems   No specific problems are known.

FLOWERING

Season   Flowers during midsummer.

Cutting   The pineapple lily is usually enjoyed as a specimen garden plant, but if there are enough blooms, or if the stems are broken by wind, the cut flowers may last for several weeks if the vase water is changed regularly.

AFTER FLOWERING

Requirements   Cut down the flowering stem when the flowers have passed their best. Either dig up the bulb and overwinter in a frost-free place, or in mild districts, mulch the planting area with peat or dry leaves to protect the bulb over winter.

FREESIA
Freesia species and hybrids

THE SPECIES Freesia alba (also known as F. refracta) is the most heavily scented of all freesias, but can be difficult to find.

THERE ARE MANY hybrid varieties of freesia, some with strikingly bicolored flowers like these. Most, but not all, are sweetly scented.

FEATURES

Freesias are loved for their strong perfume as well as their appearance. The wild species have yellow or white flowers and may grow about 12in high: modern hybrids grow 18in or more high and are available in a wide range of colors which includes blue, mauve, pink, red, and purple. However, some of these large-flowered hybrids have no scent. The white-flowered *F. alba* (*F. refracta*) is generally considered to have the best perfume.

For growing outdoors, buy specially prepared freesias and plant them in a sheltered position; they will flower in summer. Other freesias should be planted in containers that are brought into the house and greenhouse in fall for winter flowering.

FREESIA AT A GLANCE

Fragrant, tubular flowers in a wide range of colors are held on delicate spikes. Grow indoors or outside in a sheltered position.

		Recommended Varieties
Jan	flowering** 🌿	
Feb	flowering** 🌿	"Diana"
Mar	flowering** 🌿	"Fantasy"
Apr	plant 🌿*	"Oberon"
May	/	"Romany"
Jun	/	"White Swan"
July	plant 🤚**	"Yellow River"
Aug	plant 🤚**/flowering 🌿*	
Sept	flowering* 🌿	
Oct	flowering* 🌿	
Nov	/	
Dec	/	

** indoors   *outdoors

CONDITIONS

Aspect Freesias prefer full sun but tolerate very light shade for part of the day.

Site Grow outdoors in a sheltered border. For winter flowers, plant in pots in summer, standing the pots in a sheltered position outside until fall, then bring them into a cool greenhouse or conservatory to flower. Use free-draining, John Innes, or soilless potting compost.

GROWING METHOD

Planting Outdoors, plant 2in deep and the same distance apart in mid-spring. For pot culture, plant 2in deep, six to a 5in pot in July.

Feeding Apply a high potash liquid fertilizer every 14 days through the growing season. Keep the compost just moist at all times.

Problems Aphids may attack the flower stems. Control with a contact insecticide when necessary.

FLOWERING

Season From middle to late winter through to mid-spring indoors, late summer outside.

Cutting Cut when the lowest flower on the spike is fully open and other buds are well-developed.

AFTER FLOWERING

Requirements Remove spent flower stems. When the foliage dies down, lift corms and store them in dry peat until it is time for replanting.

FRITILLARIA
Crown imperial, snake's head fritillary

THE FLOWERS of snake's head fritillary bear a distinctive, intricately checkered pattern that looks a bit like a game board.

SNAKE'S HEAD FRITILLARY is probably the easiest fritillary to grow and is ideal for damp meadows or woodlands.

FEATURES

The name fritillary comes from the Latin word *fritillus*, meaning "dice-box," as the checkered patterns on the flowers of some of the species resemble the checkerboards associated with many games played with dice. There are about 100 species of this striking bulbous plant, which is related to the lilies, but only a relatively small number are in general cultivation. The form and color of the flowers varies considerably from one species to another, and some are fascinating rather than beautiful. The flowers are generally pendent and bell-shaped, carried on leafy stems; their height varies considerably, from low-growing rock garden plants such as the 4–6in *Fritillaria michailovskyi*, to the stately and imposing crown imperials (*F. imperialis*), which can reach well over 3ft tall. Many fritillaries, especially crown imperial, have a strong "foxy" scent to them which some people find unpleasant. All parts of the plant, including the bulbs, possess this scent, which can be quite penetrating.

Uses These plants, especially crown imperial, deserve a prominent place in the spring garden. They are sometimes seen taking pride of place in a bulb garden but are more often included in a mixed border planting with other bulbs and perennials. To show them to their best advantage, plant several of the same type together as individual plants will not have the same impact. Those that multiply readily, such as the snake's head fritillary, can be naturalized in dappled shade. All species can be grown in containers but most are easier to grow in the open ground.

Availability Crown imperials and snake's head fritillaries are readily available from garden centers, but some of the other species may have to be obtained from mail order bulb specialists.

TYPES

F. imperialis The best known fritillary is the majestic crown imperial, *F. imperialis*, which has a cluster of orange, yellow, or red bell-shaped flowers hanging below a crown of green leaves on a stem 20–39in high.

F. meleagris The snake's head fritillary or checkered lily, *F. meleagris*, occurs in the wild in meadows throughout Europe and is one of the easiest to cultivate. The checkered flowers occur in shades of green, purple, magenta, or white.

Others Among the many other species worth growing are *F. acmopetala*, with bell-shaped green and brown flowers; *F. biflora* "Martha Roderick," with brown-streaked cream flowers, *F. camschatcensis*, with very deep purple, almost black flowers; *F. michailovskyi*, with yellow-tipped purple bells, *F. pallidiflora*, with soft yellow flowers veined lime-green or burgundy; *F. persica* with deep purple flowers; *F. pontica* with greenish bells; and *F. pyrenaica*, a deep burgundy purple, spotted green outside while the inside is purple-checked green.

CROWN IMPERIAL (Fritillaria imperialis) is an exciting fritillary that takes pride of place in many keen bulb growers' yards. The "crown" referred to in the common name is the topknot of leaves from which the bell-shaped flowers are suspended.

CONDITIONS

Aspect   Fritillary grows best in light shade or with morning sun and afternoon shade. Some species take full sun. All are best with protection from strong wind.

Site   Fritillaries can be grown in beds and borders, on rockeries, or in containers, according to species. *F. meleagris* can be naturalized in grass. Soil for fritillaries must be well-drained but should contain plenty of well-rotted compost or manure. The area around the plants should be well-mulched, too. *F. meleagris* prefers a more moisture-retentive soil than some of the other species.

FRITILLARIA AT A GLANCE

Unusual bulbs in a wide range of sizes and flower forms, with striking, pendent, bell-shaped blooms.

		Recommended Varieties
Jan	/	
Feb	/	*Fritillaria biflora:*
Mar	/	"Martha Roderick"
Apr	flowering	
May	flowering	*Fritillaria imperialis:*
Jun	/	"Lutea"
July	/	"Rubra Maxima"
Aug	/	"Prolifera"
Sept	plant	"The Premier"
Oct	plant	
Nov	plant	*Fritillaria persica:*
Dec	/	"Adiyaman"

GROWING METHOD

Planting   The lily-like bulbs can dry out quickly and should be planted as soon as they are available. Planting depth varies between 2–8in depending on species. Plant the large bulbs of crown imperials on their sides on a layer of sand so that water does not collect in the hollow center.

Feeding   Apply a general fertilizer after flowering or a high potash fertilizer in early spring as growth starts. Water in dry spells during the growing season, especially before flowering.

Problems   Bulbs may rot in badly drained soil.

FLOWERING

Season   Flowers appear from mid-spring to early summer.

Cutting   Despite being quite long-lasting as a cut flower, blooms are rarely used this way because of the unpleasant smell of some flowers. Unfortunately crown imperial is one of these. However, they are so striking in the garden that they are best enjoyed there.

AFTER FLOWERING

Requirements When flowers have faded, flowering stems can be cut down, but leave the flowerheads on snake's head fritillaries to set seed. Bulbs are best left undisturbed, but if necessary clumps can be divided in summer and replanted immediately.

GALANTHUS
Snowdrop

TRUE HARBINGERS of spring, snowdrops are among the first bulbs to appear in late winter, often pushing up through the snow.

THE DOUBLE SNOWDROP, Galanthus nivalis "Flore Pleno," is an easily grown, vigorous, and reliable variety.

FEATURES

The snowdrop (*G. nivalis*) is well-loved for flowering in late winter while conditions are still very bleak. Most of the dozen or so species flower in late winter to early spring although there is one fall-flowering species (*G. reginae-olgae*). *G. elwesii* and *G. caucasicus* are also very early bloomers. There are named varieties of several species available. *G. nivalis* grows only 4–5in high, but taller varieties such as *G. elwesii* can grow up to 10in. The nodding flowers have three long, pure white petals and three shorter ones marked with a bright green horseshoe shape. The dark green foliage may be matt or glossy but is usually shorter than the flowers.

GALANTHUS AT A GLANCE

A small, dainty bulb popular for its late winter and early spring flowers. Very hardy.

		Recommended Varieties
Jan	flowering	"Atkinsii"
Feb	flowering	"Cordelia"
Mar	flowering / plant "in the green"	"Sam Arnott"
Apr	/	*Galanthus lutescens:*
May	/	"Magnet"
Jun	/	*Galanthus nivalis:*
July	/	"Flore Pleno"
Aug	/	"Lady Elphinstone"
Sept	plant	"Lutescens"
Oct	plant	"Pusey Green Tip"
Nov	/	"Scharlockii"
Dec	flowering	"Viridapicis"

CONDITIONS

Aspect   Grows best in shade or dappled sunlight.

Site   Ideal for rockeries, the fronts of beds, and borders or naturalizing under deciduous trees. Soil must contain plenty of decayed organic matter to prevent excessive drying out in summer. Mulching in fall with old manure, compost, or leafmold is beneficial.

GROWING METHOD

Planting   Plant bulbs in fall 3–4in deep (deeper in light soils) and about the same apart. Do not allow the bulbs to dry out before planting. Snowdrops are much more reliable when transplanted while in growth, after flowering—known as planting "in the green." Plants are available from specialist suppliers in late winter or early spring.

Feeding   Mulch during fall with decayed organic matter. Watering is not usually necessary.

Problems   No specific problems are known.

FLOWERING

Season   Flowering is from winter through to spring, depending on species.

Cutting   Flowers can be cut for indoor decoration.

AFTER FLOWERING

Requirements   Existing clumps can be lifted, divided, and replanted as soon as the flowers have faded. Do not leave the plants out of the soil any longer than necessary.

GLADIOLUS CALLIANTHUS
Acidanthera

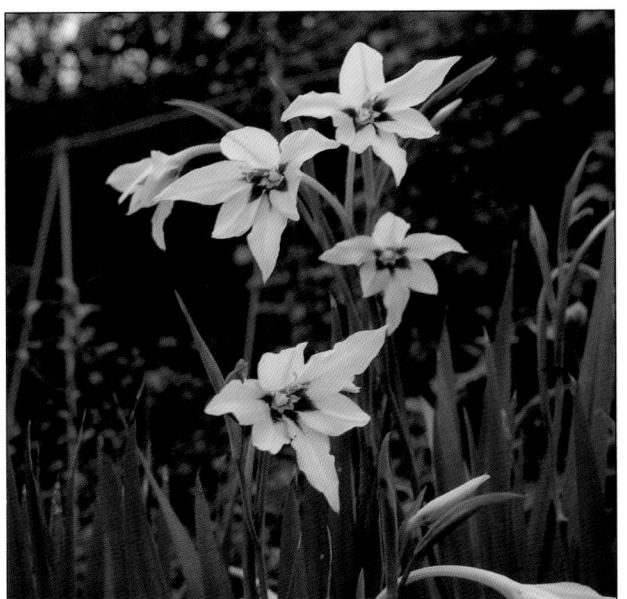

EACH BLOOM carries an attractive central, deep purple blotch, and has a slightly uneven, star-like shape.

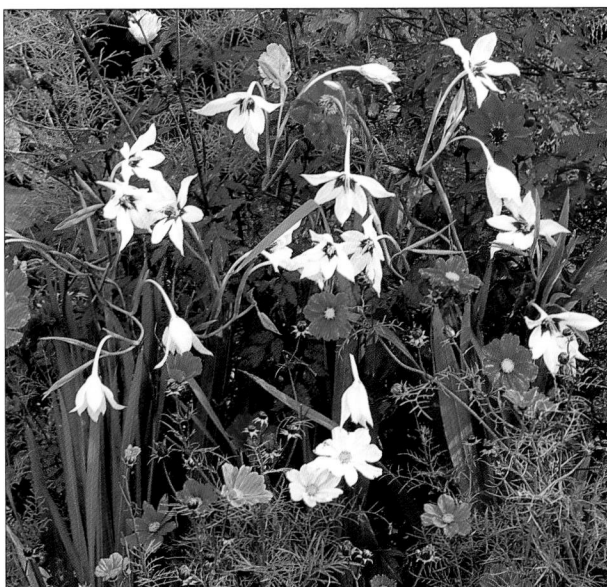

THE SWEETLY-SCENTED white blooms of acidanthera appear late in the summer, when many other bulbs are over.

FEATURES

Although this plant is now classified as a species of gladiolus, many gardeners still know it better under its previous botanical name of *Acidanthera murielae*. The pure white, slightly drooping blooms have a dark purple central blotch, and are sweetly scented; their similarity to a gladiolus flower is obvious, but they are more delicate and graceful. The leaves are erect and sword shaped, growing to about 2ft. The flowers—up to a dozen per corm—are held on slender stems above the tips of the leaves, and appear in late summer.

This is not a plant for cold, exposed yards, requiring a warm, sunny position to do well. In cold regions it can be grown successfully as a conservatory or cool greenhouse plant.

G. CALLIANTHUS AT A GLANCE

A late summer flowering plant with attractive, white, scented blooms. Suitable for growing outdoors in mild areas only.

Jan	/	Recommended Varieties
Feb	/	"Murieliae"
Mar	plant (indoors)	
Apr	plant (outdoors)	
May	/	
Jun	/	
July	/	
Aug	flowering	
Sept	flowering	
Oct	/	
Nov	/	
Dec	/	

CONDITIONS

Aspect   These plants require full sun.

Site   Acidantheras can be grown in a sheltered, sunny spot outside in mild areas: otherwise grow the corms in pots in a greenhouse or conservatory, moving the pots onto a sheltered patio or similar position in midsummer. Light, free-draining soil is required. In pots, use soiless or John Innes potting compost.

GROWING METHOD

Planting   Plant in late spring, 4in deep and 8–10in apart.

Feeding   Give an occasional application of high potash liquid fertilizer (such as rose or tomato feed) during the growing season. Pot-grown plants should be fed every 10–14 days. Watering is not necessary for plants in the open ground except in very dry conditions; water pot-grown plants sufficiently to keep the compost just moist.

Problems   Plants may fail to flower in cold, exposed yards. Corms may rot in heavy, clay soils.

FLOWERING

Season   Flowers in late summer; mid-August through September.

Cutting   Pick the stems when the buds are showing white at their tips.

AFTER FLOWERING

Requirements   Allow the foliage to die down, then lift the corms before the first frosts. Allow them to dry, brush off soil and store in dry, cool, frost-free conditions until the following spring.

GLADIOLUS HYBRIDS
Gladiolus, sword lily

THE STRIKING red and yellow flowers of Gladiolus dalenii ensure this species will always stand out in a crowd.

A POPULAR hybrid gladiolus, "Green Woodpecker" is much sought after by flower arrangers because of its unusual coloring.

FEATURES

The gladiolus with which we are most familiar comes from South Africa as do many other species, but other species originated in the Mediterranean regions and western Asia. There are about 300 species of gladiolus, many of them well worth seeking out for your garden, but the modern garden gladiolus is a hybrid. The stiff, sword-shaped leaves surround a flower spike that appears in spring and may be 39in or more high, but there are dwarf forms less than half this height. Flower spikes carry numerous individual blooms, usually densely packed on the stem and of a characteristic, irregular trumpet shape. The color range is extensive, including various shades of pink, red, yellow, orange, mauve, maroon, white, and green: flowers are often bicolored.

Special types A great range of species and cultivars is now available to add to the familiar hybrids. Baby gladiolus or painted ladies, G. x *colvillei*, (sometimes wrongly known as G. *nanus*) grows 12–16in high and comes in a range of colors, including many with contrasting markings. Green and white "The Bride" is perhaps the best known. Other species worth seeking out include G. *tristis*, with pale creamy yellow flowers; G. *dalenii* (syn. G. *natalensis*) with red to yellow flowers; G. *carneus*, with pink flowers; G. *cardinalis*, with rich red flowers marked in white; and G. *communis byzantinus*,

hardy in warmer parts of the country and producing spikes of purple-pink flowers in early summer.

Uses Gladiolus makes a great garden display and cut flower. Dwarf forms make good pot plants.

CONDITIONS

Aspect Grows best in full sun with some shelter from strong wind.

Site Gladiolus can be difficult to place, as their stiff, upright form, which usually requires staking, is very formal. They are often grown in the vegetable garden and used as cut flowers, but with care they can be grown in beds and borders. Soil should be well-drained with a high organic content. Dig in well-rotted manure or compost a month or more before planting.

GROWING METHOD

Planting Corms should be planted 3–4in deep and about 6in apart. Plant hybrid varieties in spring; stagger planting between March and May to give a succession of blooms. Spring-flowering species should be planted in fall; in colder areas of the country they are best overwintered in a cool greenhouse.

Feeding In soils enriched with organic matter

THE GLOWING red blooms of "Victor Borge" make a brilliant splash of color in any garden setting.

THE PURE WHITE of these gladiolus appears even whiter against the blue forget-me-nots. The blooms will last longer in cool areas.

supplementary feeding should not be necessary. In poor soils apply a balanced fertilizer to the soil before planting. In dry weather, water regularly throughout the growing season.

Problems Thrips, which rasp and suck sap from foliage and flowers, are a perennial problem in some areas. Deep colored flowers, such as reds and maroons, show their damage more readily than paler ones, with light-colored flecks spoiling their appearance. The summer months are the worst time for attacks, but the pest may overwinter on corms in store. Dust the corms

with a suitable insecticide before storing and again before planting. At planting time, discard corms with dark or soft spots, which may be infected with various fungal rots.

FLOWERING

Season Hybrids planted in spring will produce flowers through summer into early fall. Fall-planted species will flower in early summer.

Cutting Cut spikes for indoor decoration when the second flower on the spike is opening. Cut the flower stem without removing the leaves if that is possible. Change the water in the vase daily and remove lower blooms from the spike as they fade.

AFTER FLOWERING

Requirements Lift corms carefully as soon as foliage begins to yellow. Cut off old leaves close to the corm. Dry corms in a warm, airy place for 2–3 weeks and clean them by removing old roots and the outer sheath of corm. To increase your stock of gladiolus, remove the small cormlets from the parent bulb and store them separately. These cormlets should produce full flowering size corms in the second year. If you have had problems with thrips in previous seasons, treat corms with insecticide dust before storing.

GLADIOLUS AT A GLANCE

Popular hybrid varieties have tall, stiff spikes, packed with large, colorful flowers; more delicate species flower in spring.

		Recommended Varieties
Jan	/	
Feb	/	*Hybrids:*
Mar	plant 🌱	"Amsterdam"
Apr	plant 🌱	"Christabel"
May	flowering 🌸*/plant 🌱	"Esta Bonita"
Jun	flowering 🌸*	"Green Woodpecker"
July	flowering 🌸	"Hunting Song"
Aug	flowering 🌸	"Lady Godiva"
Sept	flowering 🌸 plant 🌱*	"Victor Borge"
Oct	/	
Nov	/	*G.* x *colvillei:*
Dec	/	"Amanda Mahy"
		"The Bride"

*fall planted species

GLORIOSA
Glory lily

FLUTED RECURVED PETALS give these flowers an airy, floating effect. Plants grow rapidly in warm, humid conditions.

THESE GLORIOSA LILIES at various stages of development display a fascinating range of colors and shapes.

FEATURES

This climber is always sure to attract attention. It grows from elongated, finger-like tubers, and needs greenhouse or conservatory conditions. A plant will grow up to 8ft in the right conditions, its long, slender stems twining their way through netting or wooden trellis supports by means of tendrils at the tips of the lance-shaped leaves. The unusual lily-like flowers are crimson and yellow, with their wavy-edged petals strongly recurved to show the prominent, curving stamens.

Gloriosa has a long flowering period through summer and fall and usually gives a spectacular display. It is worth growing in a prominent position where it can be admired, but it is not hardy enough to grow outdoors.

GLORIOSA AT A GLANCE

A greenhouse climber with spectacular summer flowers.
Minimum temperature 50°F (zone 11).

Jan	plant	
Feb	plant	
Mar	plant	
Apr	/	
May	/	
Jun	/	
July	flowering	
Aug	flowering	
Sept	flowering	
Oct	/	
Nov	/	
Dec	/	

Recommended Varieties

Gloriosa superba:
  "Rothschildiana"
  "Lutea"

CONDITIONS

Aspect   Grow in a greenhouse or conservatory, in bright light but shaded from direct summer sun.

Site   Use either soiless or John Innes potting compost.

GROWING METHOD

Planting   The tubers are planted out in late winter or early spring about 2in deep, placing one tuber in a 6in pot of moist compost. Take care not to injure the tips of the tubers.

Feeding   Apply high potash liquid fertilizer every 14 days during the growing season. Water sparingly until growth commences, more freely during active growth but never allow the soil to become waterlogged.

Problems   Slugs may attack the tubers, and poor drainage or overwatering will rot them.

FLOWERING

Season   Flowers throughout the summer.
Cutting   Flowers last well when picked.

AFTER FLOWERING

Requirements Snap off flowers as they fade. Reduce watering when flowering has finished and allow the tubers to dry out for the winter. Store them dry in their pots or in dry peat in a minimum temperature of 50°F and replant in spring.

HEDYCHIUM
Ginger lily

LONG RED STAMENS contrast nicely with the clear yellow flowers on this kahili ginger. The flowers have a strong perfume.

THIS GINGER LILY needs room to spread out and show off its strong lines. It is a useful landscaping plant.

FEATURES

There are over 40 species of ginger lily although not many species are in cultivation. These plants are strong growers, mostly to about 6ft, their growth originating from sturdy rhizomes. They can be bedded out in borders for the summer, or grown in tubs as a patio or greenhouse and conservatory plant. Mid-green leaves are lance shaped.

The tall, showy heads of flowers are carried in late summer. White ginger or garland flower, *H. coronarium*, has white and yellow, very fragrant flowers while scarlet or red ginger lily, *H. coccineum*, has faintly scented but most attractive blooms in various shades of red, pink, or salmon. Also heavily scented is kahili ginger, *H. gardnerianum*, with large, clear yellow flowers and prominent red stamens.

HEDYCHIUM AT A GLANCE

Large, showy leaves are topped by striking heads of many flowers, often scented. Needs a minimum temperature of 45°F (zone 11).

Jan	/	Recommended Varieties
Feb	/	
Mar	plant ✏	*Hedychium coccineum*
Apr	plant ✏	*aurantiacum*
May	/	*Hedychium coccineum:*
Jun	/	"Tara"
July	flowering ❀	*H. coronarium*
Aug	flowering ❀	*H. densiflorum:*
Sept	flowering ❀	"Assam Orange"
Oct	/	*H. gardnerianum*
Nov	/	
Dec	/	

CONDITIONS

Aspect Needs a bright, sunny spot.
Site In cold areas, grow in a greenhouse or conservatory; otherwise grow in a sheltered border outside. Rich, moisture-retentive soil is necessary; add well-rotted organic matter before planting time.

GROWING METHOD

Planting Plant in spring, with the tip of the rhizome just buried below the soil surface. Space rhizomes about 24in apart.
Feeding A balanced fertilizer can be applied as growth begins in spring. Keep the soil moist throughout the growing season.
Problems There are generally no particular problems experienced.

FLOWERING

Season Flowers in mid to late summer and early fall.
Cutting Flowers can be cut for indoor decoration but they will last very much longer on the plant.

AFTER FLOWERING

Requirements Cut flower stems down to the ground when the flowers have faded. Lift the rhizomes when the foliage has died down and overwinter in dry peat in a frost-free place, replanting the following spring. Pot plants can be left in their pots over winter. Rhizomes may be divided in spring to increase your stock.

HIPPEASTRUM
Hippeastrum, amaryllis

"APPLE BLOSSOM" is a cultivar with unusual soft, pastel flowers. Most hippeastrums have very strongly colored flowers in the red range.

BIG, SHOWY TRUMPET FLOWERS on stout stems are a feature of hippeastrums.

FEATURES

There are many species of hippeastrum but the most familiar plants, with their very large, trumpet-shaped flowers, are cultivars or hybrids of a number of species. They are popular winter-flowering house plants; between two and six large flowers are carried on thick stems that are generally over 20in high. Blooms appear all the more spectacular because they appear ahead of the leaves or just as the leaves are emerging. There are many cultivars available but most flowers are in various shades of red, pink, or white, separately or in combination. Because of the very large size of the bulb it is normal to use only one bulb per 7in pot. The bulbs should be allowed to rest during summer if they are to be brought into bloom again.

HIPPEASTRUM AT A GLANCE

A windowsill plant with very showy, large, trumpet-shaped flowers on tall stems in winter and spring. Minimum 56°F (zone 11).

		Recommended Varieties
Jan	flowering	
Feb	flowering	"Apple Blossom"
Mar	flowering	"Bouquet"
Apr	flowering	"Lady Jane"
May	/	"Lucky Strike"
Jun	/	"Mont Blanc"
July	/	"Flower Record"
Aug	/	"Oscar"
Sept	/	"Picotee"
Oct	plant	"Star of Holland"
Nov	plant	
Dec	plant	

CONDITIONS

Aspect Needs full sun and bright conditions.
Site Grow as a pot plant in the home or greenhouse. Use soiless potting compost.

GROWING METHOD

Planting Plant with about half to one-third of the bulb above soil level in a pot just large enough to hold the bulb comfortably. Bulbs can be planted any time between October and March. Use "prepared" bulbs for Christmas and early winter flowers.

Feeding Apply a high potash liquid feed every 10–14 days when the bulb starts into growth. Water sparingly until the bud appears, then more freely until the foliage begins to die down.

Problems No problems usually, but overwatering can cause the bulb to rot.

FLOWERING

Season Showy flowers appear in about eight weeks after planting, between late December and late spring.

Cutting With frequent water changes flowers can last well, but are usually best left on the plant.

AFTER FLOWERING

Requirements Remove spent flower stems, continue to water and feed until foliage starts to yellow and die down. Allow the bulbs to dry off in a cool place, repot in fresh compost and resume watering in fall to start them into growth.

HYACINTHOIDES
Bluebell

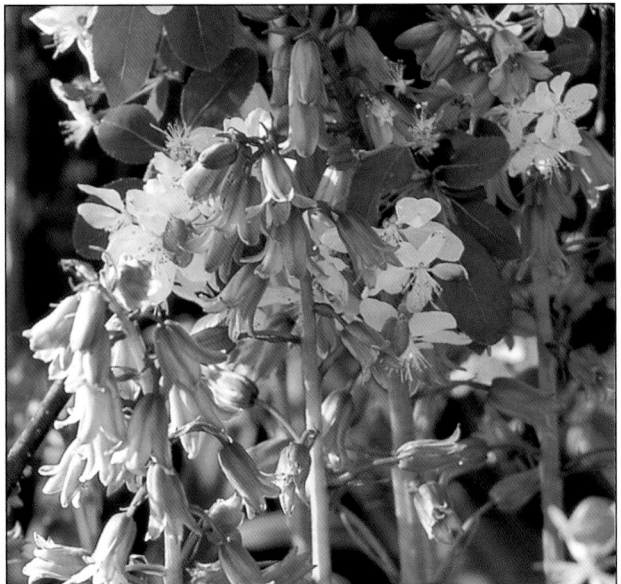

AN ALL-TIME FAVORITE, clear sky-blue bluebells don't need a lot of attention to produce a beautiful display year after year.

NATURALIZED UNDER TREES, these Spanish bluebells revel in the moist soil formed from the decaying leaf litter.

FEATURES

This is the ideal bulb for naturalizing under deciduous trees or for planting in large drifts in the yard. The delicately scented blue flowers are a great foil for many spring-flowering shrubs which have pink or white flowers: there is a white and a pink form but the blue is undoubtedly the most popular. The botanical names of these plants have undergone several changes in recent years, and they are sometimes listed under endymion and scilla as well as hyacinthoides. The Spanish bluebell (*H. hispanica*) is a little larger, up to 12in high, and more upright in growth than the English bluebell (*H. non-scripta*). Bluebells multiply rapidly and can be very invasive. They can also be grown in containers.

HYACINTHOIDES AT A GLANCE

Well-known and loved blue flowers in mid to late spring, ideal for naturalizing under deciduous trees.

Jan	/	Recommended Varieties
Feb	/	
Mar	/	*Hyacinthoides hispanica:*
Apr	flowering ❁	"Danube"
May	flowering ❁	"Queen of the Pinks"
		"White City"
Jun	/	
July	/	*Hyacinthoides non-scripta:*
Aug	plant ✎	"Pink Form"
Sept	plant ✎	"White Form"
Oct	plant ✎	
Nov	/	
Dec	/	

CONDITIONS

Aspect   These woodland plants prefer dappled sunlight or places where they receive some morning sun with shade later in the day.

Site   Perfect when naturalized under deciduous trees; bluebells also grow well in borders but don't let them smother delicate plants. A moisture-retentive soil with plenty of organic matter suits them best.

GROWING METHOD

Planting   Plant bulbs 2in deep and about 3–4in apart in late summer or early fall. The white bulbs are fleshy and brittle; take care not to damage them when planting.

Feeding   Not usually required.

Problems   No specific problems are usually experienced.

FLOWERING

Season   Flowers from middle to late spring, with a long display in cool seasons. Flowers do not last as well if sudden high spring temperatures are experienced.

Cutting   Not suitable for cutting.

AFTER FLOWERING

Requirements Remove spent flower stems unless you require plants to seed themselves. Keep the soil moist until the foliage dies down. The bulbs are best left undisturbed, but overcrowded clumps can be lifted and divided in late summer and replanted immediately.

HYACINTHUS ORIENTALIS
Hyacinth

WELL-ROUNDED FLOWER SPIKES are characteristic of the fine hyacinth cultivars available today. They make excellent pot plants.

HYACINTHS, with cool white flowers and dark green foliage, combine with a silvery groundcover to make a pretty garden picture.

FEATURES

Sweet-scented hyacinths are favorites in the garden or as potted plants. In the garden they look their best mass-planted in blocks of one color. They are widely grown commercially both for cut flowers and as potted flowering plants. Flower stems may be from 6–12in high and the color range includes various shades of blue, pink, and rose, and white, cream and yellow. Individual flowers are densely crowded onto the stem, making a solid-looking flowerhead. Bulbs usually flower best in their first year, the second and subsequent years producing fewer, looser blooms. Some people with sensitive skin can get a reaction from handling hyacinth bulbs, so wear gloves if you think you may be affected.

Types The most popular hyacinths are the so-called Dutch hybrids; many varieties are available from garden centers and mail order bulb suppliers. Blues range from deep violet to pale china blue: the rose range includes deep rosy red, salmon, and light pink. As well as white varieties, there are those with cream and clear yellow flowers. Some varieties have flowers with a lighter eye or a deeper colored stripe on the petals, giving a two-tone effect.
Roman hyacinths—*H. orientalis albulus*—have smaller flowers loosely arranged on the stems: Multiflora varieties have been treated so that they produce several loosely packed flower spikes from each bulb, and have a delicate appearance that makes them ideal for growing in pots.
Cynthella hyacinths are miniatures growing to about 6in, usually sold in color mixtures.

CONDITIONS

Aspect Does well in sun or partial shade but does not like heavy shade.
Site Grow hyacinths in pots and bowls indoors; pots and tubs outside and in flower borders. Soil must be well-drained.

GROWING METHOD

Planting Plant bulbs 6in deep and 8in apart in early to mid-fall. Apply compost or rotted manure as a mulch after planting.
Feeding Apply a balanced general fertilizer after flowering. Watering is not usually necessary in beds and borders, but bulbs in containers must be kept just moist during the growing season.
Problems Hyacinths are not generally susceptible to pest and disease problems, though bulbs will rot if soil conditions are too wet. Forced bulbs indoors often fail to flower if they have not had the correct cold, dark period after planting.

FLOWERING

Season Flowers appear from late winter to mid-spring. "Prepared" bulbs should be used for Christmas flowering, and must be planted in September.
Cutting Blooms may be cut for the vase where they will last about a week if the water is changed daily.

AFTER FLOWERING

Requirements Remove spent flower stems and continue to water and feed the plants until the foliage starts to yellow and die down.

BLUE AND WHITE are always an effective combination, a proposition amply demonstrated by this formal garden in which deep violet-blue hyacinths stud a bed of white pansies. Although they are often grown in pots, hyacinths are at their most beautiful in a setting such as this.

POTTED HYACINTHS

Features   Potted hyacinths in bloom make a lovely cut flower substitute and are ideal as gifts. They can be grown to flower in midwinter when their color and fragrance are most welcome.

Outdoors   If growing hyacinths outdoors choose a container at least 6in deep so that you can place a layer of potting compost in the base of the pot before planting. Bury the bulbs 4in below the surface of the compost. Water to moisten the compost thoroughly after planting and place the pot where it will receive sun for at least half a day. Don't water again until the compost is feeling dry or until the shoots appear. When the flower buds are showing color, move the pots indoors. When blooms have faded, cut off spent stems and water as needed until the foliage dies down.

Indoors   If growing hyacinths indoors, choose a container 4–6in deep but plant the bulbs just below the surface of the compost. (In pots without drainage holes, bulb fiber can be used intead of compost.) Water after planting, allow to drain and then transfer the pot to a cool, dark position. The pots can be placed inside a black plastic bag and put into a shed, cold frame or similar place with a temperature of about 40°F. Check from time to time to see if shoots have emerged. When shoots emerge (this usually takes about 10–12 weeks) and reach 1–2in in height, bring the pot into the light, gradually increasing the amount of light as the shoots green up. As buds appear, give them as much sunlight as possible.

In glass   Hyacinths can also be grown in a glass or ceramic container that has a narrow neck. Sometimes you can buy a purpose-built container, usually plastic, that has the top cut into segments so that the bulb sits neatly on it. Fill the container with water to just below the rim. Choose a good-sized bulb, then rest it on top of the rim of the container so that the base of the bulb is in water. Place the container in a cool, dark place and leave it there until large numbers of roots have formed and the flower bud is starting to emerge, when they can be brought into the light. These bulbs are unlikely to regrow and may be discarded after flowering.

HYACINTHUS AT A GLANCE

Sweetly scented, densely packed flower spikes, ideal for growing indoors or outside. Frost hardy.

		Recommended Varieties
Jan	flowering	"Amsterdam"
Feb	flowering	"Anna Marie"
Mar	flowering	"Blue Giant"
Apr	flowering	"City of Haarlem"
May	/	"Delft Blue"
Jun	/	"Gipsy Queen"
July	/	"Jan Bos"
Aug	/	"L'Innocence"
Sept	plant	"Lord Balfour"
Oct	plant	"Mont Blanc"
Nov	/	"Queen of the Pinks"
Dec	flowering	

1.

2.

4.

5.

HYACINTH
(HYACINTHUS ORIENTALIS)

The dense clusters of flowers on hyacinth spikes come in a wonderful range of clear colors.

1. "L'Innocence" is a pure white hyacinth first raised in 1863 and still very popular today.

2. Pale rose-pink "Lady Derby" blooms reliably in the garden or in containers.

3. The subtle stripes on the petals of the violet-blue "Ostara" make this a very attractive hyacinth.

4. "Amsterdam" is an unusually deep pink color. For a real crimson hyacinth select "Jan Bos."

5. Clear primrose yellow "City of Haarlem" breaks away from the traditional pink or blue.

6. This soft mauve-blue hyacinth is still pretty as the flower fades.

3.

6.

HYMENOCALLIS
Spider lily, Peruvian daffodil

THE WHITE or cream flowers of spider lilies are something like an exotic daffodil, with an attractive fragrance.

HYMENOCALLIS CAN be grown outside in reasonably sheltered yards, but the bulbs should be lifted in fall to ensure survival.

FEATURES

Spider lilies are native to various parts of North and South America. They produce broad, strap-shaped, deep green leaves and fascinating, lightly fragrant flowers that are carried on a stout stem. The flower has a trumpet-shaped central cup with long, narrow, petal-like segments surrounding it; flowers are usually white but can be yellow or cream. Hymenocallis can be grown in a sheltered, sunny position outside, but is often treated as a greenhouse or conservatory plant. All spider lilies can be container grown. *H.* x *festalis, H. narcissiflora* and the cultivar "Sulfur Queen" are the deciduous varieties most often grown, while the more difficult to find *H. littoralis* and *H. speciosa* are the most popular of the evergreen species. Hymenocallis is sometimes also listed as ismene.

HYMENOCALLIS AT A GLANCE

A rather tender bulb bearing unusual fragrant blooms like exotic daffodils. Can also be grown as a conservatory plant.

Jan	/	
Feb	/	**Recommended Varieties**
Mar	plant (indoors)	"Advance"
Apr	/	"Sulfur Queen"
May	(outdoors)/flowering	*Hymenocallis* x *festalis:*
Jun	flowering	"Zwanenburg"
July	/	
Aug	flowering	
Sept	/	
Oct	/	
Nov	/	
Dec	/	

CONDITIONS

Aspect   Grows in full sun or light shade with shelter from strong wind.

Site   In sheltered yards hymenocallis can be grown outside in beds and borders or containers. In cold areas, it is best grown as a greenhouse or conservatory plant. Soil must be free-draining. Use soil-less potting compost for pots.

GROWING METHOD

Planting   For growing in containers, plant bulbs in spring with the neck of the bulb just below the soil surface, using one of the large bulbs per 6in pot. Outdoors, plant in May, burying the bulbs 5in deep.

Feeding   High potash liquid fertilizer can be applied as buds form. Mulching around plants with well-rotted organic matter also supplies nutrients. Water sparingly until the shoots show, then water regularly through the growing season.

Problems   No specific problems are usually experienced.

FLOWERING

Season   The fragrant spider lilies are produced in early summer indoors, mid to late summer outside.

Cutting   Makes a delightful and unusual cut flower.

AFTER FLOWERING

Requirements   Allow the foliage to die down after flowering; lift outdoor bulbs and store in dry peat in a frost-free place over winter. Leave potted plants dry in their containers over winter and repot the following spring.

IPHEION UNIFLORUM
Spring star flower

SPRING STAR FLOWER is an ideal edging plant for a sunny yard and it can be left undisturbed for several years.

THE SOFT LILAC of the flowers makes spring star flower very versatile as it blends into most garden color schemes.

FEATURES

This low-growing plant makes an ideal edging but should be planted in large drifts wherever it is grown to produce its best effect. Tolerant of rather tough growing conditions, it is most suitable for filling pockets in a rockery or growing toward the front of a herbaceous border. It also makes a good container plant. It has grey-green, narrow, strappy leaves that smell strongly of onions when crushed; the pale blue, starry, lightly scented flowers are carried on stems 6in or so high.

There are several varieties available with flowers ranging in color from white to deep violet-blue.

IPHEION AT A GLANCE

A low-growing bulb with a profusion of starry blue or white flowers in spring.

Jan	/	
Feb	/	**Recommended Varieties**
Mar	flowering 🌱	"Album"
Apr	flowering 🌱	"Alberto Castello"
May	flowering 🌱	"Froyle Mill"
Jun	/	"Rolf Fiedler"
July	/	"Wisley Blue"
Aug	/	
Sept	plant 🖐	
Oct	plant 🖐	
Nov	/	
Dec	/	

CONDITIONS

Aspect Grows best in full sun but tolerates light shade for part of the day.

Site Good for a rockery, border, or container. Ipheion needs well-drained soil. It will grow on quite poor soils but growth will be better on soils enriched with organic matter.

GROWING METHOD

Planting Plant bulbs 2in deep and the same distance apart in fall.

Feeding Apply some balanced fertilizer after flowers have finished. Water regularly during dry spells while plants are in leaf and bloom.

Problems No specific problems are usually experienced with this bulb.

FLOWERING

Season The starry flowers appear from early spring to mid-spring.

Cutting Flowers are too short to cut for all but a miniature vase but they may last a few days in water.

AFTER FLOWERING

Requirements Shear off spent flower stems and remove the old foliage when it has died down. If clumps become overcrowded and fail to flower well, they can be lifted in fall, divided, and replanted immediately.

IRIS—BULBOUS TYPES
Irises

THE LOW-GROWING flowers of Iris danfordiae *appear very early in the year—usually February or March.*

SEVERAL DIFFERENT cultivars of Iris reticulata *are available, in varying shades of blue with yellow markings.*

FEATURES

There are many species of these irises, which have true bulbs as storage organs, unlike the creeping rhizomes of their larger cousins. The leaves are not arranged in the typical fan of sword shapes like rhizomatous irises, but are usually narrow and lance shaped, or rolled. The flowers have the typical iris form with six petals, three inner ones (standards), and three outer ones (falls). The falls are often brightly marked or veined. Many species and varieties are blue with yellow markings on the falls; some types are yellow with brown or green speckling on the falls and others are white with yellow markings. The blue varieties come in many shades, from deep violet and purple through to pale China blue.

Many bulbous irises are early-flowering dwarf forms suitable for growing on rockeries or at the front of beds: they are also excellent for shallow pots ("pans") in the greenhouse or alpine house. Other types are taller and flower in summer; they are valuable for herbaceous and mixed borders, and are particularly good for cutting for flower arrangements. There are also some spring-flowering irises that are far less commonly grown than the other groups.

POPULAR SPECIES

Bulbous irises can be split into three main groups: Reticulata irises, Xiphium irises and Juno irises.

Reticulata These irises have bulbs with a netted tunic around them which gives them their group name. They are dwarf, growing to about 6in high, and the flowers appear early in the year, usually in February and March. *I. danfordiae* has lightly fragrant flowers whose yellow petals are speckled with greenish brown. *I. reticulata* also has fragrant flowers: the petals are thinner than those of *I. danfordiae* and are blue or purple with yellow markings. Several different cultivars are available. The flowers of *I. histriodes* and its cultivars are larger and have short stems; they are deep to light blue, with dark blue, white, and yellow markings. The flowers open before the leaves reach their full height.

Xiphium This group of summer-flowering irises is popular and easily grown. It consists of Dutch irises, flowering in early summer, in white, yellow, or blue with contrasting markings; English irises, flowering in early to mid-summer in shades of white, blue, or purple; and Spanish irises, flowering in midsummer in various shades of white, blue, purple, and yellow.

Juno The Juno irises are not as well-known as the other bulbous types, probably because they are more difficult to grow well. The group includes *I. bucharica*, bearing yellow or white flowers with yellow falls, and *I. graeberiana*, which has lavender flowers with a white crest on the falls. These two are among the easiest Juno irises to grow: others include *I. fosteriana*, *I. magnifica*, and *I. rosenbachiana*, which do best in an alpine house.

WHEN EXAMINED closely, the lightly fragrant flowers of Iris danfordiae *can be seen to have attractive freckling in the throat.*

"KATHERINE HODGKIN," a cultivar of Iris histrioides*, is perhaps the most sought-after of all the dwarf irises.*

CONDITIONS

Aspect
Site   All bulbous irises like open, sunny, positions. Reticulatas are good for rock gardens, raised beds, or containers: Xiphiums and Junos for sunny, sheltered borders. Soil needs to be well-drained; Juno irises require a soil containing plenty of well-rotted organic matter.

GROWING METHOD

Planting   Plant Reticulatas 3in deep and 4in apart. Xiphiums are planted 4-6in

BULBOUS IRIS AT A GLANCE

A varied group of plants with colorful flowers in early spring or in summer. Good for a range of situations.

		Recommended Varieties
Jan	flowering	
Feb	flowering	Reticulata group:
Mar	flowering	*I. danfordiae*
Apr	flowering	*I. reticulata* "Katharine
May	flowering	Hodgkin"
		I. histrioides "Major"
Jun	flowering	Xiphium group:
July	flowering	"Bronze Queen"
Aug	/	"Excelsior"
		"Ideal"
Sept	plant	Juno group:
Oct	plant	*I. bucharica*
Nov	/	*I. graeberiana*
Dec	/	

deep and 6in apart, and Juno irises are planted 2in deep and 8in apart, taking care not to damage the brittle, fleshy roots. They are all planted in fall, in September or October.

Feeding   Supplementary feeding is not usually necessary.

Problems   Bulbs may rot in overwet soil. Bulbous irises in warmer areas of the country may be affected by iris ink disease, causing black streaks on the bulb and yellow blotches on the leaves. Destroy affected bulbs.

FLOWERING

Season   Reticulata irises flower in February and March, Junos in April and May, and Xiphiums in June and July.

Cutting   The Xiphiums make excellent, long-lasting cut flowers.

AFTER FLOWERING

Requirements   Remove faded flowers. Most bulbous irises are best left undisturbed for as long as possible; they can be increased by lifting and dividing the bulbs after flowering when necessary. Juno irises should not be divided until the foliage has died down, and must be handled very carefully. Spanish irises of the Xiphium group benefit from being lifted when the foliage has died down and replanted in September; this helps the bulbs to ripen.

IRIS—RHIZOMATOUS TYPES

Iris

IRIS WAS THE Greek god of the the rainbow, and this plant is aptly named as there are irises in every color of the spectrum.

WATER IRIS (Iris pseudoacorus) is a tall grower that needs to be planted in water or permanently wet soil.

FEATURES

Irises comprise a very large plant group of more than 200 species. Some grow from bulbs (see the previous two pages): those covered here grow from rhizomes. They have stiff, sword-shaped leaves and carry their colorful flowers on tall, stiff stems in spring and early summer. Iris flowers have six petals; three inner, vertical ones, (standards), and three outer ones, which curve outward (falls). The color range is very varied, covering blue, purple, lavender, yellow, rose, and white; many of the flowers are bicolored, and attractively marked. Rhizomatous irises contain several different groups, the most popular of which are bearded, Japanese and Siberian irises. **Bearded irises** have large, very showy flowers with a short, bristly "beard" on the falls; dwarf cultivars are also available. **Japanese irises** have unusual flat-faced flowers, and **Siberian irises** have delicate flowers with finer petals.

CONDITIONS

Aspect	Rhizomatous irises like a position in full sun, but with protection from strong winds.
Site	Excellent plants for the middle to back of a mixed or herbaceous border. Bearded irises like a slightly alkaline, well-drained soil: Japanese and Siberian irises need moisture-retentive, humus-rich loam.

GROWING METHOD

Planting	Usually sold as container-grown plants in growth. Plant shallowly, with the rhizome barely covered, in late summer.
Feeding	Supplementary feeding is rarely necessary. Ensure moisture-loving types are never allowed to dry out during the growing season.
Problems	Slugs and snails can be troublesome. Use covered slug bait where necessary, or hand pick the pests after dark.

FLOWERING

Season	Flowers are carried in early summer.
Cutting	Make beautiful cut flowers.

AFTER FLOWERING

Requirements	Cut off spent flower stems. Every few years, lift the rhizomes after flowering, cut them into sections each containing a strong, healthy fan of leaves, and replant, discarding the old, woody, worn out portions of rhizome.

RHIZOMATOUS IRIS AT A GLANCE

Stately border plants with fans of sword-shaped leaves and tall, attractively marked flowers in summer.

Month		Recommended Varieties
Jan	/	
Feb	/	*Bearded irises:*
Mar	/	"Black Swan"
Apr	/	"Rocket"
May	flowering	"White City"
Jun	flowering	*Siberian irises:*
July	flowering	"Sparkling Rose"
Aug	/	"Caesar"
Sept	plant	"Perry's Blue"
Oct	/	*Japanese irises:*
Nov	/	"Rose Queen"
Dec	/	"Moonlight Waves"

IRIS UNGUICULARIS
Winter iris, Algerian iris

THE FULL BEAUTY *of this iris can be seen in close up. Many iris have fine veining or feathering on their petals.*

A LARGE PATCH *of Algerian iris gives a great lift to the garden in winter. Even if flowers come singly their appearance is still a joy.*

FEATURES

This beardless, rhizomatous iris is different to all others in its group because it flowers throughout the winter. The beautiful little fragrant flowers rarely exceed 8in in height and may be hidden by the stiff, grassy foliage. They are ideal for cutting and taking indoors, where their sweet scent may be almost overpowering at times.

The flowers of the species are deep lavender with creamy yellow centers deeply veined in violet. There are some cultivars available, including a white form, one or two varieties in particularly deep shades of blue, one in a pale silvery lilac, and a dwarf form. A large single clump of this iris is effective but in the right position it could be mass-planted to good effect.

I. UNGUICULARIS AT A GLANCE

A low-growing iris valuable for its sweetly scented flowers which appear throughout the winter.

		Recommended Varieties
Jan	flowering	
Feb	flowering	"Abington Purple"
Mar	plant	"Alba"
Apr	/	"Bob Thompson"
May	/	"Mary Barnard"
Jun	/	"Oxford Dwarf"
July	/	"Walter Butt"
Aug	/	
Sept	/	
Oct	/	
Nov	flowering	
Dec	flowering	

CONDITIONS

Aspect Needs a reasonably sheltered position because of its flowering time. The rhizomes must be exposed to a summer baking if plants are to flower well, so a position in full sun is essential.

Site Grow in beds or borders where it will be able to spread—plants can be invasive. Soil must be well-drained. If it is very poor, dig in quantities of well-decayed manure or compost ahead of planting time.

GROWING METHOD

Planting Plant rhizomes in spring with the top at or just below soil level. Container-grown plants in growth can also be bought and planted virtually year-round in suitable weather.

Feeding Supplementary feeding is generally unnecessary. Water the plants in spring and fall if conditions are dry, but do not water in summer.

Problems Slugs and snails will often attack the flowers. Use slug pellets if necessary.

FLOWERING

Season Flowers are produced any time from late fall through winter.

Cutting The flowers make a lovely indoor decoration.

AFTER FLOWERING

Requirements Cut off spent flowers and tidy up foliage when necessary. Little other attention is required. Crowded plants can be divided in spring.

IXIA
Corn lily

EACH TALL SPIKE of corn lily produces dozens of flowers. These are still producing blooms despite the many fading and falling ones.

PALEST TURQUOISE FLOWERS make this lovely corn lily (Ixia viridiflora) a favorite although its corms are not always easy to buy.

FEATURES

This plant produces starry flowers in a stunning range of colors including white, cream, yellow, orange, red, cerise, and magenta. Hybrid varieties are the most popular, but the sought-after *I. viridiflora* has duck-egg blue flowers with a dark center. The narrow, grass-like foliage may be 12–20in high while the wiry-stemmed flower spikes stand clear of the leaves. Corn lilies are a great addition to the garden. Being quite tall they should be planted toward the back of a bed or among other bulbs and perennials. Although colors can be mixed, a better effect is obtained by planting blocks of one color.

IXIA AT A GLANCE

A rather tender plant with masses of colorful, starry flowers on slender stems.

Jan	/	
Feb	/	Recommended Varieties
Mar	plant 🖐	"Blue Bird"
Apr	plant 🖐	"Mabel"
May	flowering 🌸	"Rose Emperor"
Jun	flowering 🌸	"Venus"
July	flowering 🌸	
Aug	/	
Sept	/	
Oct	plant (indoors) 🖐	
Nov	/	
Dec	/	

CONDITIONS

Aspect Prefers full sun all day but with shelter from strong wind.
Site A good border plant in reasonably mild districts. In colder areas it can be grown in containers on a sheltered patio or in a conservatory. Needs well-drained soil.

GROWING METHOD

Planting Plant corms in the open garden in spring, about 2in deep and 3–4in apart. Plant in pots for the conservatory in fall.
Fertilizing Apply balanced liquid fertilizer in early spring to increase the size of the blooms. In dry conditions, water if necessary in spring when the shoots are growing strong.
Problems No specific pest or disease problems are usually experienced, though corms may rot in overwet soil.

FLOWERING

Season Flowers from late spring to mid-summer.
Cutting Flowers can be cut for the vase but will probably give better value in the garden.

AFTER FLOWERING

Requirements In all but the mildest gardens, lift the corms when the foliage has died down and store them in a dry place for replanting in spring.

LACHENALIA ALOIDES
Cape cowslip

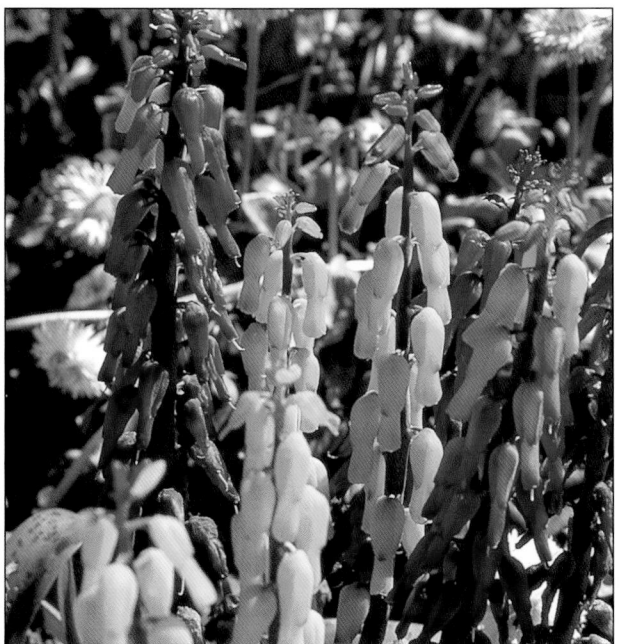

STIFF FLOWER SPIKES of yellow and red tubular bells are the feature of Lachenalia aloides.

CAPE COWSLIPS need a cool room to grow well. In the right conditions they make excellent winter-flowering house plants.

FEATURES

Also known as "soldier boys" because of their upright, neat and orderly habit, this bulb is grown as a house plant to produce its colorful bell-like flowers in midwinter. The rather stiff leaves grow to about 6in high and are dark green, often spotted with purple. The 8–12in spikes of 20 or so tubular flowers stand well above the foliage and remain colorful for several weeks. Individual blooms are yellow or orange-red, marked with red, green, or purple; they are often a deeper color in bud, becoming paler as the flowers open. There are several different varieties with subtly varying shades to the flowers.

LACHENALIA AT A GLANCE

A tender bulb grown as a house or greenhouse plant for its spikes of yellow or orange tubular flowers in winter.

Jan	flowering ❀	Recommended Varieties
Feb	flowering ❀	
Mar	flowering ❀	*Lachenalia aloides:*
Apr	/	"Aurea"
May	/	"Lutea"
Jun	/	"Nelsonii"
July	/	"Quadricolor"
Aug	plant ✍	
Sept	plant ✍	*Lachenalia bulbifera:*
Oct	/	"George"
Nov	/	
Dec	/	

CONDITIONS

Aspect   Needs a very brightly lit spot; will stand direct sun for part of the day.

Site   Grow on a bright windowsill in a cool room, or in a cool greenhouse or conservatory. Lachenalia does not like dry heat.

GROWING METHOD

Planting   Plant bulbs in late summer or early fall, growing six to a 5in pot. Set them just below the surface of the compost.

Feeding   Apply high potash liquid fertilizer every 14 days or so from when the buds appear. Water regularly while plants are in flower.

Problems   Overwatering or poorly drained compost will cause the bulbs to rot.

FLOWERING

Season   Flowers appear between midwinter and early spring.

Cutting   Not suitable for cutting.

AFTER FLOWERING

Requirements Cut off spent lachenalia flower stems. Continue to water until early summer, then gradually stop watering and allow the pot to dry out until the following fall, when the bulbs can be shaken out and repotted in fresh compost.

LEUCOJUM
Snowflake

THE WHITE BELLS *with their fresh green dots at the end of each petal make* Leucojum vernum *particularly evocative of spring.*

PREFERING SHADE *and moist soil, spring snowflake is one of the easiest bulbs to grow. This plant is typical of an established clump.*

FEATURES

Easily grown snowflakes have clusters of white, bell-shaped flowers, each petal bearing a bright green spot on its tip. Foliage is a rich, deep green and bulbs multiply readily to form good sized clumps in a few years.

There are three types of snowflake; spring snowflake (*Leucojum vernum*), summer snowflake (*L. aestivum*), and fall snowflake (*L. autumnale*). The spring snowflake flowers in February or March, while the summer snowflake, despite its name, usually flowers in late spring. Spring snowflake reaches a height of about 8in; summer snowflake up to 24in, and fall snowflake 6in, with very fine, narrow foliage. The flowers have a passing resemblance to snowdrops, but are easily distinguished by their rounded, bell shape and taller growth.

LEUCOJUM AT A GLANCE

Delicate looking plants with white bells tipped with green, appearing in spring or early fall. Hardy.

Jan	/	Recommended Varieties
Feb	flowering	
Mar	flowering	*Leucojum aestivum:*
Apr	flowering	"Gravetye Giant"
May	flowering	
Jun	/	*Leucojum autumnale:*
July	/	"Cobb's Variety"
Aug	/	"Pulchellum"
Sept	plant / flower	
Oct	plant	*Leucojum vernum:*
Nov	/	"Carpathicum"
Dec	/	"Vagneri"

CONDITIONS

Aspect Grows well in sun but also happy in shade or in dappled sunlight. Fall snowflakes prefer an open, sunny position.

Site Low-growing species are excellent for rock gardens or the front of borders; taller summer snowflakes toward the middle of a border. Spring and summer snowflakes prefer a moisture-retentive soil enriched with organic matter: fall snowflake needs light, free-draining soil.

GROWING METHOD

Planting Plant bulbs 3in deep and 4–8in apart in late summer or early fall.

Feeding An annual mulching with decayed manure or compost after bulbs have died down should provide adequate nutrients. Keep the soil for spring and summer snowflakes moist throughout the growing season.

Problems No specific problems are known.

FLOWERING

Season Spring snowflake flowers between midwinter and early spring; summer snowflake mid to late spring; and fall snowflake in September.

Cutting Best enjoyed in the garden.

AFTER FLOWERING

Requirements Remove spent flower stems. Divide crowded clumps when the foliage dies down, and replant immediately.

LILIUM
Lily

THIS BURNED ORANGE HYBRID shows the characteristic dark spotting in its throat. Lilies make excellent cut flowers.

WHITE LILIES are traditionally symbols of purity. Lilium regale is one of the most popular species, and its flowers are very strongly scented.

FEATURES

Lilies are tall, stately plants that carry a number of large, trumpet-shaped blooms on each flowering stem. Flowering stems may be anywhere from about 2ft to over 6ft high. There are 80–90 species of lily and many hundreds of cultivars, so it is difficult to outline their requirements concisely. Lily flowers are often fragrant and the main color range includes white, yellow, pink, red, and orange—many have spotted or streaked petals. A quite small range of lily bulbs is usually available in garden centers in fall and these should be planted as soon as possible after their arrival: lily bulbs have no tunic or outer covering and so can dry out unless they are carefully handled. For a greater range of species and hybrids you will need to contact specialist growers and mail order suppliers. Many lily enthusiasts belong to societies devoted to learning more about the enormous range of types available and their cultivation.

Types Some of the more popular species grown are *L. auratum*, golden-rayed lily, which has white petals with gold bands; *L. candidum*, Madonna lily, which is pure white; *L. martagon*, Turk's cap lily, with fully recurved, dark red petals with dark spots; *L. regale,* the regal lily, with white flowers that have purple backs to the petals and a yellow base; *L. speciosum* which has white petals with a deep pink center and reddish spots; and *L. tigrinum*, tiger lily, dark orange with black spots and revurving petals. As well as the species, many hybrid varieties are grown, which are classified into a number of groups. Among the most popular are the Asiatic hybrids, short to medium height, with upward-facing flowers produced early in the season; and the Oriental hybrids, which are taller and more refined, with nodding, strongly scented blooms. Asiatic hybrids are ideal for pots and are available pot-grown throughout the summer.

CONDITIONS

Aspect The ideal situation is a sunny position with a little dappled shade during part of the day. They need protection from strong wind.

Site Lilies grow well when mixed with other plants that will shade their roots, in a bed or border, or in containers. Plant them where their perfume can be appreciated. Soil must be well-drained with a high organic content. Dig in copious amounts of well-rotted manure or compost a month or so before planting.

GROWING METHOD

Planting Plant 4–9in deep and 9–15in or so apart in fall or early spring. Bulbs must not be bruised or allowed to dry out, and they should be planted as soon as possible after purchase. Apply a layer of compost or manure to the soil surface as a mulch after planting. Your stock of lilies can be increased by bulb scales, bulbils or offsets, according to type: see page 11 for more details on propagation.

THE GOLDEN-RAYED lily of Japan, Lilium auratum, *carries its attractively speckled, reflexing flowers late in the summer.*

MASSES OF BLOOMS, with buds still to open, make this yellow lily a great asset for the summer garden.

Feeding   If the soil contains plenty of organic matter these plants should not need a lot of feeding. Apply a slow-release granular fertilizer as growth starts and after flowering. Water regularly during dry spells but avoid overwatering which may rot the bulbs.

Problems   Most problems with lilies result from poor cultivation or unsuitable growing conditions. Gray mold (botrytis) can be a problem in cool, humid conditions, especially if plants are overwatered or if air circulation is poor. The small, bright red lily beetle and their larvae can cause a lot of damage in some areas:

control them with a contact insecticide and clear away plant debris in which the adults overwinter.

FLOWERING

Season   Lilies flower some time between early summer and fall with many flowering in middle to late summer. Flowering time depends on the species and, to some extent, the conditions.

Cutting   Lilies make wonderful and very long-lasting cut flowers. Cut them when flowers are just open or all buds are rounded and fully colored. Don't cut right to the bottom of the stem—retain some leaves on the lower part. Change water frequently and cut off spent flowers from the cluster to allow the other buds to develop fully.

AFTER FLOWERING

Requirements   Remove spent flower stems as they finish blooming. Remove only the flowering stem and leave as much foliage as possible. Don't be in a hurry to cut back yellowing growth too soon: allow the plant to die back naturally and mulch with chipped bark for the winter. Bulbs are best left in the ground for several years. When they are lifted they must be divided and replanted at once, as having no tunic on the bulb means they dry out very quickly. If they can't be planted at once, store them in damp sphagnum moss or peat.

LILIUM AT A GLANCE

Stately plants with trumpet-shaped, usually intensely fragrant flowers on tall spikes.

		Recommended Varieties
Jan	/	
Feb	/	"Apollo"
Mar	/	"Barcelona"
Apr	/	"Casa Blanca"
May	/	"Corsage"
Jun	flowering	"Enchantment"
July	flowering	"Green Dragon"
Aug	flowering /plant	"Mrs R. O. Backhouse"
Sept	flowering /plant	"Orange Triumph"
Oct	plant	"Shuksan"
Nov	plant	"Tamara"
Dec	/	

MORAEA
Peacock iris, butterfly iris

IT IS EASY to see how this pretty bulb got its common name of peacock iris. Iridescent blue spots are sharply defined against the white petals.

THE FOLIAGE of peacock iris looks unpromising, as it is sparse and grass-like, but the "floating" flowers are worth waiting for.

FEATURES

Of the 120 species of *Moraea*, most come from South Africa with others native to tropical Africa and Madagascar. Few are in cultivation but it is worth seeking out this unusual plant from specialist bulb growers. All grow from corms and some, such as *M. spathulata*, grow only a single leaf, which may be 8–20in high. Flowers are like those of irises, with three showy outer petals and three smaller, rather insignificant inner ones. The commonest species is *M. spathulata*, with bright yellow, summer flowers on 2ft stems. *Moraea aristata* has white flowers with a large blue blotch at the base of the outer petals, while *M. villosa* bears flowers in a range of colors with a blue blotch on the petals. Plant peacock iris in groups for the best effect.

MORAEA AT A GLANCE

An uncommon bulb with iris-like flowers, often strikingly marked. Needs a warm, sunny position.

Jan	/	Recommended Species
Feb	/	
Mar	/	*Moraea aristata*
Apr	plant 🖐	*M. bellendenii*
May	/	*M. gawleri*
Jun	flowering ❀	*M. spathulata*
July	flowering ❀	
Aug	flowering ❀	
Sept	/	
Oct	/	
Nov	/	
Dec	/	

CONDITIONS

Aspect   Moraea needs full sun all day.
Site   A warm, sunny, and sheltered position is necessary. This corm needs well-drained soil with plenty of decayed organic matter incorporated into it before planting. Moraea also makes an attractive plant for the conservatory or home when grown in containers. Use John Innes or soiless potting compost.

GROWING METHOD

Planting   Plant corms 2in deep and 8in apart in spring.
Feeding   Performance is improved by applying a balanced fertilizer as flower buds appear. Container-grown plants should be liquid-fed every three weeks or so through the growing season. Water in dry conditions, but take care not to make the soil too wet or the corms will be liable to rot.
Problems   No specific pest or disease problems are known for this plant.

FLOWERING

Season   Flowers throughout the summer.
Cutting   Not suitable for cutting.

AFTER FLOWERING

Requirements   Cut off spent flower stems unless you want to obtain seed from them. In fall, lift the corms and store them in a dry place over winter, ready for replanting the following spring.

MUSCARI
Grape hyacinth

THE FEATHERY *violet heads of* Muscari comosum *"Plumosum"* *make this showy variety quite different from other grape hyacinths.*

ROYAL BLUE *grape hyacinths here border a garden of daffodils and pop up from among the groundcover of snow-in-summer.*

FEATURES

Vigorous and easy to grow, grape hyacinths have blue flowers of varying intensity. There are several species and named varieties available, including the double "Blue Spike" and the feathery "Plumosum." *Muscari aucheri* (*M. tubergenianum*) is known as "Oxford and Cambridge" because it has pale blue flowers at the top of the spike and is dark blue at the base, reminiscent of the English universities' uniform colors. Grape hyacinths are a great foil for other bright spring-flowering bulbs such as tulips or ranunculus. Flowers are lightly scented and are carried on a stem about 4–8in tall. This plant gives the most impact when planted in drifts: in large yards where there is space it can easily be naturalized in grass or under deciduous trees.

MUSCARI AT A GLANCE

Pretty, easy-to-grow, little bulbs with short spikes of intense blue bells in spring.

Jan	/	Recommended Varieties
Feb	/	
Mar	flowering	*Muscari armeniacum:*
Apr	flowering	"Blue Spike"
May	flowering	"Early Giant"
Jun	/	
July	/	*Muscari azureum:*
Aug	/	"Album"
Sept	plant	
Oct	plant	*Muscari comosum:*
Nov	/	"Plumosum"
Dec	/	

CONDITIONS

Aspect　　Best in full sun or dappled sunlight such as is found under deciduous trees.

Site　　Useful on rockeries, in the front of borders, and for naturalizing under trees, but the plants can be invasive. Muscari needs well-drained soil, preferably with plenty of organic matter incorporated before planting.

GROWING METHOD

Planting　　Plant the bulbs about 3in deep and 4in apart in late summer or early fall.

Feeding　　Supplementary feeding is not usually necessary, but a light sprinkling of general fertilizer after flowering helps to ensure good growth. Watering is not normally necessary unless the weather is exceptionally dry.

Problems　　No specific problems are known.

FLOWERING

Season　　Flowers appear in early to mid-spring.

Cutting　　Although not often used as a cut flower, it lasts in water quite well if picked when half the flowers on the stem are open.

AFTER FLOWERING

Requirements　　Remove spent flower stems if required. Bulbs can be divided every 3–4 years in fall, replanting immediately. The foliage appears in the winter, long before the flowers.

NARCISSUS
Daffodil and narcissus

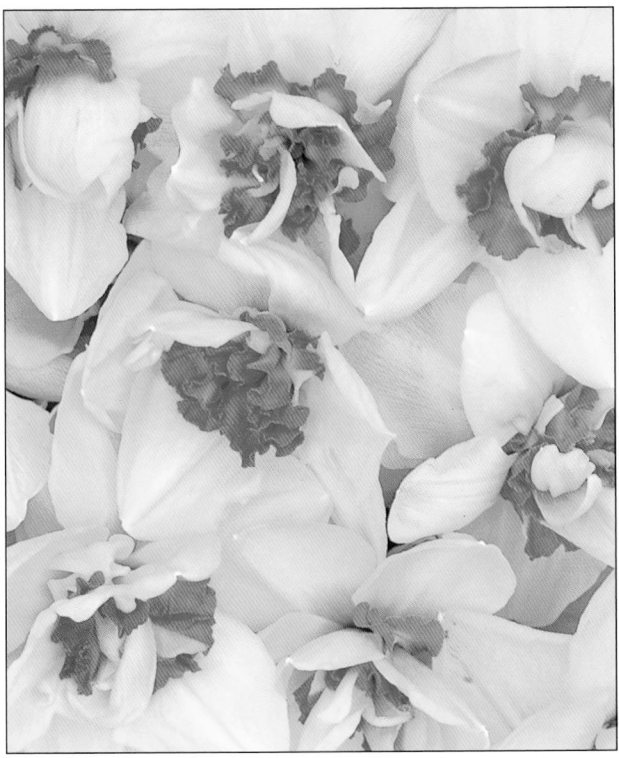

MODER *HYBRID DAFFODILS come in a wide range of forms,
including double-flowered varieties and varieties with split coronas.*

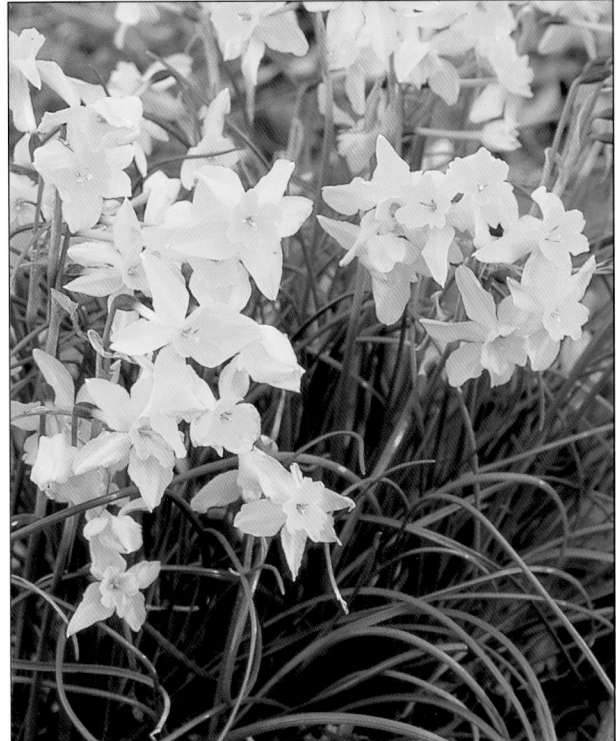

*SUNSHINE YELLOW, this group of smaller growing daffodil
cultivars lights up the late winter garden.*

FEATURES

Daffodils are probably the best known and most widely grown of all bulbs and to many they are the true indicator of spring. They look wonderful mass-planted in the garden or naturalized in grass, but they also make great pot plants and excellent cut flowers. The best-known color is yellow, but there are also flowers in shades of white, cream, orange, and pink. The trumpet, or cup, is often a different color to the petals and may be bicolored. There are many species and cultivars and the genus *Narcissus* has been divided into 12 different groups, depending on the form and size of the flowers. The height varies from 3–20in, depending on variety.

Trumpet   The trumpet (cup) is at least as long as the petals, and there is one flower per stem.

Large cupped   Cup is shorter than, but at least one-third of, the length of the petals. One flower per stem.

Small cupped   The cup is less than one-third of the length of the petals; flowers usually carried singly.

Double   Double or semi-double flowers carried single or in small groups. The whole flower may be double, or just the cup.

Triandrus   Two to six pendant flowers with reflexed petals per stem.

Cyclamineus   Slightly pendant flowers with long trumpets and strongly reflexed petals, usually one per stem.

Jonquilla   Several flowers per stem, with short cups. Sweetly scented.

Tazetta   Half hardy. Very fragrant flowers in clusters of 10 or more per stem. Early flowering.

Poeticus   Small red or orange cup and broad white petals, usually one or two per stem. Often strongly fragrant. Late flowering.

Wild   A varied group containing the species and natural varieties found in the wild.

Split cupped   The cup is split to varying degrees for at least one-third to half its length.

Miscellaneous   Hybrids that do not fit into any of the other divisions.

CONDITIONS

Aspect   These bulbs grow best in a sunny spot or under deciduous trees where they will receive sun in the early spring.

Site   Grow narcissi in beds and borders, on rockeries, or in containers for the patio or in the home. Soil must be well-drained, ideally with some well-rotted organic matter dug in a month or so before planting.

GROWING METHOD

Planting   Planting depth will vary greatly according to the size of the bulb. Plant so that the nose is covered to twice the height of the bulb, in September or October. Plant as early as possible for the best results.
Continued on page 298

1.

2.

5.

6.

7.

DAFFODILS

There are many daffodil cultivars with wonderful variety in form and color. Yellow is most common color but some have white or pinkish petals or cups.

1. "Flower Record" displays the characteristics of N. poeticus, *which is in its breeding.*

2. Bright, clear yellow "Meeting" is a fine example of modern double daffodils.

3. "E. E. Morbey," dating from the 1930s, has a particularly pretty center to its orange cup.

4. "Ice Follies" has white petals. The flared lemon cup fades as it ages.

5. Simplicity of form and white purity make "Mount Hood" a classic variety.

6. Reddish-orange inner petals on double-flowered "Tahiti" make it a very showy addition to the garden.

7. The yellow and white center of "White Lion" demonstrates another style of double daffodil.

8. Soft, pretty "Mrs Oscar Ronalds" has a long pink cup and white petals.

9. "King Alfred," raised about 1890, is possibly the most widely grown of all yellow daffodils.

1.

2.

4.

3.

JONQUILS
(NARCISSUS)

Black text Jonquils, with their multiple flowers on each stem, are lovely flowers. These pages show just some of the cultivars available.

1. "Erlicheer" is a beautiful, double jonquil with a rich creamy color and heavy perfume.

2. "Soleil d'Or," with bright yellow petals and orange cups, often flowers during midwinter.

3. "Cheerfulness," dating from 1923, is an aptly named late bloomer.

4. The subtle cream on white coloring of "Pearl" gives a delicate appearance.

5. Sturdy growth and reliable flowering make "Grand Monarque" a good choice for warm areas.

6. "Cragford" has a flattened orange cup with red rim, typical of N. poeticus *cultivars.*

5.

6.

THE ESSENCE OF SPRING BEAUTY is captured in this drift of mixed daffodils and delicate white blossom. As the planting has been kept to the edge of the lawn, the grass can be mown while still allowing the bulb foliage to die down naturally.

Continued from page 293

Feeding Feed with a balanced fertilizer in early spring. Plants can be given a liquid feed after the flowers have faded. Watering may be necessary in very dry spells, particularly once flowering has finished.

Problems Basal rot can occur in storage; destroy bulbs with any sign of softening or rot at planting time. Similar symptoms can be caused by stem eelworm; these bulbs should also be destroyed by burning. Narcissus fly lays eggs near the necks of the bulbs; these hatch into larvae that tunnel into the bulb and weaken or destroy it. Bulbs in light shade are less susceptible to attack. Pull soil up round the necks of the bulbs after flowering to discourage egg laying.

FLOWERING

Season Depending on area and variety, flowers may be carried anywhere from midwinter to early summer. Bulbs indoors may be brought into flower for Christmas or earlier; specially treated bulbs are available to ensure early flowering.

Cutting This excellent cut flower should last a week with frequent water changes, or with the use of proprietary cut flower additives. For longest vase life pick daffodils when the buds are about to burst open or as soon as they are fully open. Cut, don't pull, the stems as low as possible. Cut off any white section at the base of the stem. Don't mix daffodils with other flowers until they have spent a day in a vase on their own as their slimy sap may reduce the vase life of other blooms.

AFTER FLOWERING

Requirements Spent flowers should be removed before they set seed. Allow foliage to die down naturally; do not tie the leaves in clumps. Where bulbs are naturalised in grass, do not mow the grass until at least six weeks after the flowers have faded. Premature removal of leaves will have a detrimental effect on growth and flowering the following season.

If drainage is good, bulbs may be left in the ground and clumps can be divided after flowering every three years or so. Bulbs grown indoors in pots can be planted out in the garden after flowering, where they should recover in a season or two.

NARCISSUS AT A GLANCE

Well-known spring-flowering bulbs in a wide variety of flower forms and sizes. Most types are very hardy.

		Recommended Varieties
Jan	flowering	
Feb	flowering	"Carlton"
Mar	flowering	"Cheerfulness"
Apr	flowering	"February Gold"
May	flowering	"Irene Copeland"
Jun	/	"King Alfred"
July	/	"Minnow"
Aug	plant	"Peeping Tom"
Sept	plant	"Pipit"
Oct	plant	"Thalia"
Nov	/	*N. bulbocodium*
Dec	/	*N. canaliculatus*

NERINE
Nerine, Guernsey lily

THE GUERNSEY LILY, Nerine sarniensis, *needs to be grown in a conservatory or greenhouse except in very mild areas.*

TALL AND ELEGANT, *these bright pink nerines appear as the summer garden fades away in fall.*

FEATURES

Nerine bowdenii brightens the fall garden, producing its heads of bright pink flowers before the leaves appear. It is easy to grow and flowers last well when cut. Bulbs should be planted where they can be left undisturbed for several years; they flower best when crowded and after a dry summer. They can also be grown in containers. Flower stems grow 12–18in high and the deep green, strappy leaves from 8–12in long.

The Guernsey lily (*N. sarniensis*) has bright red flowers, and other species and cultivars of nerines may be red, white, pink or apricot, but only *N. bowdenii* is hardy enough to grow outdoors in this country.

NERINE AT A GLANCE

Heads of funnel-shaped pink flowers appear on leafless stalks in fall. Needs a warm, sheltered position.

Jan	/		Recommended Varieties
Feb	sow		*Nerine bowdenii alba*
Mar	sow		*Nerine bowdenii:*
Apr	plant		"Mark Fenwick"
May	/		"Pink Triumph"
Jun	/		"Wellsii"
July	/		
Aug	plant		N. "Corusca Major"
Sept	flowering		N. "Fothergillii Major"
Oct	flowering		*N. undulata*
Nov	flowering		
Dec	/		

CONDITIONS

Aspect Nerines require full sun and a warm, sheltered spot.

Site A useful plant for borders, especially under the shelter of a south-facing wall. The soil should be free-draining and moderately fertile. In cold areas and with the more tender species, grow bulbs in pots of John Innes potting compost.

GROWING METHOD

Planting Plant in middle to late summer or in mid-spring, 4in deep and 6in apart. In containers, plant with the neck of the bulb at or just below soil level.

Feeding Can be grown successfully without supplementary fertilizer. However, if you wish, you can give weak liquid fertilizer every couple of weeks once flower buds appear until growth slows down. Water regularly while in active growth but keep the bulbs dry during the dormant period.

Problems No specific problems are known.

FLOWERING

Season Flowers appear during early fall.

Cutting Nerines last well as cut flowers with frequent water changes.

AFTER FLOWERING

Requirements Cut off spent flower stems. Outdoors, mulch the planting site for winter protection.

ORNITHOGALUM
Chincherinchee, star of Bethlehem

CHINCHERINCHEE *gives a long and pretty floral display, as the flowers open slowly from the bottom up to the top of the cone.*

A BILLOWING CLOUD *of white flowers makes this mass planting a striking feature. Close inspection reveals the pretty green centers.*

FEATURES

There are around 100 species of *Ornithogalum* originating in Africa, Asia and parts of Europe, but the chincherinchee, *O. thyrsoides*, is perhaps the best known, with its imposing spikes of white summer flowers growing up to 18in. The leaves are narrow and sword-shaped. Other commonly grown species are *O.arabicum*, whose scented white flowers have a striking black eye, *O. nutans*, with delicate spikes of dangling white flowers, and *O. umbellatum*, or star of Bethlehem, which forms clumps of grassy foliage studded with pure white, upward-facing white blooms: these are all spring flowering. Chincherinchee and *O. arabicum* are frost tender.

ORNITHOGALUM AT A GLANCE

Half-hardy and hardy bulbs producing attractive white flowers in spring or early summer.

		Recommended Species
Jan	/	
Feb	/	*Ornithogalum arabicum*
Mar	/	*O. longibracteatum*
Apr	plant ✣/ flower ✣	*O. montanum*
May	flowering ✣	*O. nutans*
Jun	flowering ✣	*O. oligophyllum*
July	flowering ✣	*O. thyrsoides*
Aug	/	*O. umbellatum*
Sept	/	
Oct	plant ✣	
Nov	/	
Dec	/	

CONDITIONS

Aspect Prefers an open position in full sun but will grow in light shade. *O. thyrsoides* can be grown outside in summer though it will not survive the winter; in cold areas it can be grown as a pot plant in the home or greenhouse.

Site Good for mixed borders, rockeries or naturalising in grass. The bulbs need well-drained but not very rich soil.

GROWING METHOD

Planting Plant bulbs in spring or fall, 2in deep and about 8–12in apart.

Feeding Not usually essential, but an application of balanced or high potash fertilizer given as the plants start into growth may improve flowering. Watering is not necessary unless the season is exceptionally dry; for container-grown plants, keep the compost just moist.

Problems This bulb is generally trouble-free.

FLOWERING

Season Flowers will appear spring and early summer.

Cutting This is a first class cut flower.

AFTER FLOWERING

Requirements Cut spent flower stems at ground level. Non-hardy species should be lifted in fall and stored in a dry, cool place for replanting the following spring. Hardy species can be divided after flowering and replanted immediately.

OXALIS
Wood sorrel

THE SATINY WHITE FLOWERS on Oxalis purpurea *"Alba" are a far cry from the weedy forms of oxalis that invade our yards.*

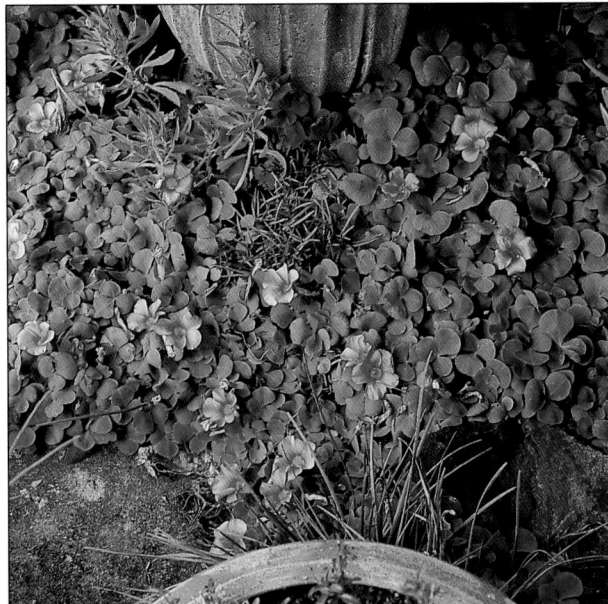

THIS PRETTY PINK OXALIS makes a charming groundcover here on the edge of a paved area.

FEATURES

A number of species of oxalis are very invasive, but others are very decorative and well worth growing. Most have clover-like leaves and five-petalled, satiny flowers which are furled in bud. The usual color is pink or white; there are also purple, yellow, orange, or red varieties. Some species need greenhouse cultivation in this country. Height varies from 2–8in.
O. adenophylla is the most popular species, with grayish leaves and silvery flowers; *O. enneaphylla* has white flowers and attractive, folded, silvery leaves. *O. laciniata* has narrow leaflets and purple, veined flowers. Once known as *O. deppei, O. tetraphylla* has brown-marked leaves and pink flowers.

OXALIS AT A GLANCE

A low-growing, clump-forming plant with clover-like leaves and attractive, satiny flowers. Can be invasive.

Jan	/	Recommended Varieties
Feb	/	"Beatrice Anderson"
Mar	/	"Bowles' White"
Apr	/	"Ione Hecker"
May	/	"Royal Velvet"
Jun	flowering 🌼	
July	flowering 🌼	*O. enneaphylla:*
Aug	/	"Alba"
		"Minutifolia"
Sept	planting ✍	"Rosea"
Oct	planting ✍	
Nov	/	*O. tetraphylla:*
Dec	/	"Iron Cross"

CONDITIONS

Aspect   Grow in full sun for good flowering and compact leaf growth.

Site   Grow on a rockery or near the front of a border, preferably in a confined bed where growth can be controlled. The more invasive varieties are best grown in pots. Free-draining soil is preferred.

GROWING METHOD

Planting   Plant in early fall, 3in deep and 4in apart. It is usual to plant clumps in growth rather than the tiny tubers or rhizomes.

Feeding   Supplementary fertilizer is rarely needed.

Problems   Few problems are usually encountered although some oxalis do suffer from the fungal leaf disease rust. Pick off the worst affected leaves and avoid overhead watering.

FLOWERING

Season   Most species flower through early and mid-summer.

Cutting   Flowers are unsuitable for cutting.

AFTER FLOWERING

Requirements Plants can be divided after flowering in summer. Clear away dead foliage once the leaves have died down; beware of putting plant debris from invasive varieties on the compost heap.

POLIANTHES TUBEROSA

Tuberose

"THE PEARL," a double-flowered cultivar, is the variety most often available to home gardeners.

PINK-TINGED BUDS open to the heavy-textured cream flowers, so prized for their characteristic strong perfume.

FEATURES

Tuberose is known for its heavily perfumed flowers—tuberose oil is used in perfume production. A double form known as "The Pearl" is the most widely grown. It can be grown in a sunny, sheltered border, but is often more reliable when grown as a conservatory or house plant, especially in cooler areas. The scent can more easily be appreciated under cover.

A flower spike 2ft or more high appears from the basal leaves in summer and early fall. The waxy flowers have a heavy texture and are white with a pinkish tinge at the base. Tubers that have bloomed once will not reflower the following season—new tubers must be planted each year.

POLIANTHES AT A GLANCE

Valued for its intensely fragrant, creamy white flowers that are carried on tall spikes in late summer.

Jan	/	Recommended Varieties
Feb	/	
Mar	plant 🖑	*Polianthes tuberosa:*
Apr	/	"The Pearl"
May	/	
Jun	/	
July	/	
Aug	flowering 🌸	
Sept	flowering 🌸	
Oct	flowering 🌸	
Nov	/	
Dec	/	

CONDITIONS

Aspect Prefers full sun and shelter from strong wind.
Site Grow in a warm, sheltered border, or in containers for the conservatory, house, or greenhouse. Use either John Innes or soil-less potting compost.

GROWING METHOD

Planting Plant 2in deep, or 1in deep in containers.
Feeding When growth appears, liquid feed with a balanced fertiliser every 14 days through the growing season. Water sparingly to start with, but keep the plant moist at all times when in growth.
Problems No particular problems are known.

FLOWERING

Season Flowers should appear during late summer or in early fall.
Cutting Makes an excellent cut flower. Cut spikes for the vase when two or three of the lower blooms are fully open. Removing spent flowers from the spike as they fade will help to prolong the vase life.

AFTER FLOWERING

Requirements Tubers are usually discarded at the end of the season. Offsets are produced, and these may sometimes be grown on to flower in two years or so, but they are often disappointing.

RANUNCULUS ASIATICUS
Ranunculus, Persian buttercup

TAFFETA-LIKE PETALS are ruffled and folded closely together around the dark eye of this vibrant scarlet ranunculus.

RANUNCULUS FLOWERS last well in a sheltered, sunny yard and close planting will produce a wonderfully colorful display.

FEATURES

One of the brightest and most colorful of all spring-flowering bulbs, ranunculus can be massed in mixed colors or blocks of single color in the yard or in containers. Left in the ground they may give several seasons, although they are often treated as annuals. However, the woody, oddly shaped tubers can be lifted and stored like other bulbs.

The many-petalled flowers of ranunculus come in bright yellow, cream, white, reds, and pinks, and stems of some strains may reach 18in in height. Although there are single flowered varieties, double or semi-double types are by far the most popular. They are usually sold as color mixtures, but separate red and yellow forms are sometimes available from specialist suppliers.

Ranunculus blooms make very good cut flowers, lasting well in the vase.

RANUNCULUS AT A GLANCE

Brightly colored, many-petalled, poppy-like flowers are carried above attractive ferny foliage in summer.

Jan	/	
Feb	/	**Recommended Varieties**
Mar	planting	"Red form"
Apr	planting	"Yellow form"
May	/	"Accolade"
Jun	flowering	
July	flowering	
Aug	flowering	
Sept	/	
Oct	/	
Nov	/	
Dec	/	

CONDITIONS

Aspect   Prefers full sun all day with shelter from very strong wind.

Site   Ideal for beds, borders, and containers, where they will make a colorful display. The soil should be well-drained, ideally with plenty of compost or manure dug in a month or so before planting.

GROWING METHOD

Planting   Plant the woody, tuberous roots 1–2in deep and about 6in apart, with the claws pointing down, in early spring. Soaking the tubers in water for a few hours before planting gets them off to a good start.

Feeding   Liquid feed with a balanced fertilizer every two weeks from when the flower buds start to appear. Keep the soil moist when the ferny leaves appear, particularly during bud formation and flowering.

Problems   Usually trouble free, though powdery mildew may occur in hot, dry seasons. Spray with a general fungicide if necessary.

FLOWERING

Season   Flowers throughout the summer.

Cutting   Cut flowers early in the morning and change the water frequently to prolong vase life.

AFTER FLOWERING

Requirements   Cut off spent flower stems. When the foliage has died down completely, tubers can be lifted, cleaned and stored in dry peat in a frost-free place until the following spring. After three seasons tubers are best replaced.

RHODOHYPOXIS BAURII
Rose grass

TINY MAGENTA CENTERS emphasise the stark white of this pretty rose grass. The unusual flower form is clearly seen here.

DEEP ROSE-PINK in color, this form of rose grass is sometimes sold as "Rosy Posy." It gives a long flowering display.

FEATURES

This enchanting little plant, which comes from high altitude areas of South Africa, is ideally suited to growing in a rock garden, on the edge of a border or in pots. The slightly hairy leaves, similar to those of a broad-leaf grass, grow to around 4in high. The flowers, which are white or pink through to deep rosy crimson, are about the same height. As they have become better known several varieties with deeper color or larger flowers have become available. They have six petals with one set of three appearing to be set on top of the other, so the flower has no visible eye. The floral display is long lasting, from late spring through to late summer.

If grown in the garden the positions of these plants should be marked in some way as they are completely dormant during winter.

RHODOHYPOXIS AT A GLANCE

A tuberous alpine with mounds of attractive pink or white flowers carried for a very long season.

Month	Activity	Recommended Varieties
Jan	/	
Feb	/	"Alba"
Mar	plant	"Dulcie"
Apr	plant	"Dawn"
May	flowering	"Douglas"
Jun	flowering	"Eva-Kate"
July	flowering	"Fred Broome"
Aug	flowering	"Garnett"
Sept	flowering	"Harlequin"
Oct	/	"Picta"
Nov	/	"Ruth"
Dec	/	"Stella"

CONDITIONS

Aspect Grows best in full sun in a sheltered spot.
Site Suitable for rockeries, scree gardens, or containers. The soil must be well drained but enriched with decayed organic matter. It needs to be lime free, as rose grass is not tolerant of alkaline soils. Good quality potting compost mixed with a little extra sharp sand should be adequate for containers.

GROWING METHOD

Planting Tubers should be planted in late spring about 2in deep and 4in apart. Lift and divide offsets in the fall.
Feeding Mulch garden plants with decayed manure or compost in late winter or early spring. Potted plants that have not been repotted will benefit from slow-release fertilizer in early spring. Water regularly during the growing period in dry spells, but keep dry through winter.
Problems No specific problems are known.

FLOWERING

Season The long flowering period runs from late spring through to late summer.
Cutting Flowers are unsuitable for picking.

AFTER FLOWERING

Requirements Spent blooms can be snipped off or ignored. Protect plants from excess winter rainfall; a sheet of glass supported horizontally over the plants on four wooden stakes should prevent the crowns rotting off in wet weather.

ROMULEA
Romulea

THE CHARMING FLOWERS of little Romulea rosea *may be best appreciated when it is grown in a container.*

PALE LAVENDER PETALS and a recessed deep gold throat make Romulea bulbocodium *worth growing. It tolerates cool conditions.*

FEATURES

These small plants have grassy leaves and brightly colored, crocus-like flowers. There are 75 species native to parts of Africa, the Mediterranean and Europe, most in cultivation being South African.

Growing 3–6in high, depending on species, they are ideal for rock gardens and pots where their neat growth can be admired. The color range includes cream and yellow, many shades of blue and violet, and also pinks and reds: many flowers have a very attractive "eye" of contrasting color in the center of the flower. The most popular type, *R. bulbocodium*, has pale lavender flowers with a yellow throat, and is hardier than some of the other species. Flowers remain closed in dull weather.

ROMULEA AT A GLANCE

A low-growing plant with crocus-like flowers which open wide in full sun. Needs a protected position.

Jan	/	Recommended Species
Feb	/	*Romulea bulbocodium clusiana*
Mar	flowering	*Romulea flava*
Apr	flowering	*Romulea sabulosa*
May	flowering	
Jun	/	
July	/	
Aug	/	
Sept	plant	
Oct	plant	
Nov	/	
Dec	/	

CONDITIONS

Aspect Needs full sun all day. The flowers will not open in shady conditions.

Site Grows best when grown in a sharply draining, rather sandy soil. Good for scree beds, rockeries and containers.

GROWING METHOD

Planting The small corms should be planted some 2in deep and 2–3in apart in the fall.

Feeding Feeding is not normally necessary for this plant, but in poor soils some balanced fertilizer may be applied as growth begins. Water freely to keep the soil moist through the growing season but keep plants dry during the summer, when they die down.

Problems No specific pest or disease problems are known for romulea.

FLOWERING

Season Flowers are carried throughout the spring months.

Cutting None of the species has flowers that are suitable for cutting.

AFTER FLOWERING

Requirements Protect the crowns with a mulch of peat or similar material for the winter months. Overcrowded clumps can be lifted and divided when the flowers have faded.

SCHIZOSTYLIS COCCINEA
Kaffir lily

THE EXTENDED FLOWER spikes give the appearance of a small gladiolus, though the individual flowers are more delicate.

THE RICH ROSE flowers of Schizostylis "Tambara" are displayed to great effect against evergreen shrubs in the late fall garden.

FEATURES

The beautiful, scarlet or pink, gladiolus-like flowers of schizostylis add a very welcome splash of color to fall borders, coming as they do right at the end of the season. The tall, grassy leaves form a clump from which 2–3ft spikes of flowers rise, bearing some 8–10 open, star-shaped blooms. There are several named varieties in a range of pink and red shades: "Major" has large, deep red flowers, "Viscountess Byng" is a delicate pink, and "Tambara" is a rich, rosy pink. "November Cheer" is one of the latest-flowering varieties. Schizostylis is not suitable for cold, exposed yards, but grows and spreads rapidly where conditions suit it.

SCHIZOSTYLIS AT A GLANCE

A valuable late fall-flowering plant for the border, with colorful scarlet or pink, gladiolus-like flower spikes.

		Recommended Varieties
Jan	/	
Feb	/	"Jennifer"
Mar	plant	"Mrs Hegarty"
Apr	plant	"November Cheer"
May	/	"Sunrise"
Jun	/	"Tambara"
July	/	"Viscountess Byng"
Aug	/	
Sept	flowering	
Oct	flowering	
Nov	flowering	
Dec	/	

CONDITIONS

Aspect A sheltered spot in full sun or light shade suits this plant.

Site Suitable for the middle of the flower border; in cold districts they do well as pot plants in a conservatory or greenhouse. Moisture-retentive, fertile soil is required.

GROWING METHOD

Planting Plant in spring, 2in deep and 12in apart. Pot-grown plants are available for planting in summer and fall. Rhizomes can also be planted in 8in pots of soil-less or John Innes compost in a sheltered position outdoors, being brought into a cool conservatory or greenhouse before the first frosts for flowering inside.

Feeding Keep the soil moist at all times. Feed pot-grown plants with high potash liquid fertiliszer every 14 days from early summer until flower buds form.

Problems No specific problems are generally experienced.

FLOWERING

Season Flowers from late September into November.

Cutting The flower spikes are excellent for cutting, lasting well in water. Pick them when the buds start to show color.

AFTER FLOWERING

Requirements Cut down faded flower stems. Protect the crowns with a mulch of chipped bark, straw, or dry leaves over winter. Overcrowded plants can be divided in fall.

SCILLA
Squill

A STARBURST of bright blue flowers topped with golden stamens makes up the pretty inflorescence of Scilla peruviana, *the Cuban lily.*

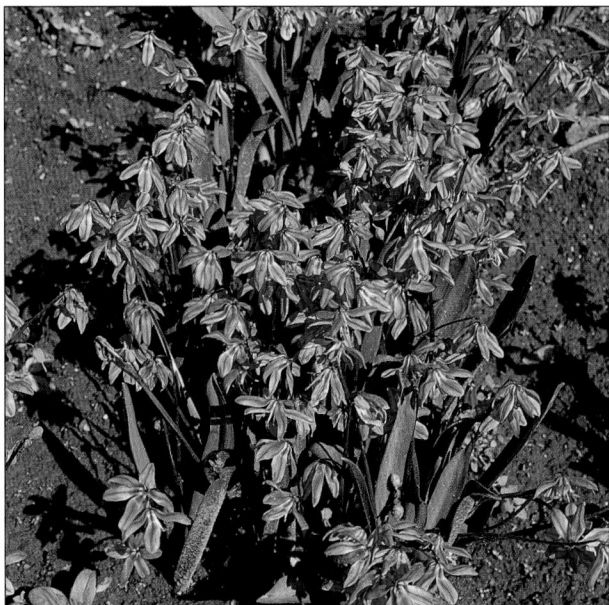

THE SIBERIAN SQUILL, Scilla siberica, *makes its appearance in early spring. "Atrocoerulea" has particularly rich blue flowers.*

FEATURES

The most familiar scillas are the dwarf varieties that flower in early spring. They include *Scilla siberica* (Siberian squill), which has clusters of nodding blue bells about 6in high, and *Scilla mischtschenkoana* (*S. tubergeniana*), which has starry, pale blue flowers with a deeper blue stripe on the petals. This species grows only 2–4in high. *S. bifolia* grows to 2–6in, with a spike of 15 or more star-shaped flowers in blue, pink, or white. Leaves of all these species are elongated and strap shaped. *Scilla peruviana*, the Cuban lily, is quite different—a tall, early summer-flowering bulb with densely packed, conical heads of purple-blue flowers.

SCILLA AT A GLANCE

Mainly dwarf bulbs with starry or bell-shaped blue or white flowers in early spring.

Jan	/	Recommended Varieties
Feb	flowering 🌱	
Mar	flowering 🌱	*Scilla bifolia:*
Apr	flowering 🌱	"Rosea"
May	flowering 🌱	*Scilla siberica:*
Jun	flowering 🌱	"Alba"
July	/	"Spring Beauty"
Aug	plant 🌿	*Scilla peruviana:*
Sept	plant 🌿	"Alba"
Oct	plant 🌿	*Scilla peruviana elegans*
Nov	/	*S. p. venusta*
Dec	/	

CONDITIONS

Aspect   Tolerates full sun but the flowers will have better, longer lasting color if they are grown in semi-shade.

Site   Grow in beds and borders, in almost any kind of soil as long as it drains well. Soils enriched with organic matter will give better results.

GROWING METHOD

Planting   Plant the bulbs about 2–4in deep and 6–8in apart in late summer or early fall.

Feeding   Apply a balanced fertiliser after flowering in early summer. Water during dry spells before and during the flowering season.

Problems   No specific pest or disease problems are known for this plant.

FLOWERING

Season   The flower spikes appear during late spring and early summer.

Cutting   Flowers can be cut successfully for indoor decoration.

AFTER FLOWERING

Requirements   Faded flower spikes should be cut off just above ground level. Clumps will usually need to be lifted only every 4–5 years unless they are very congested. Divide crowded clumps in late summer, replanting immediately to avoid drying out of the bulbs.

SINNINGIA
Gloxinia

THE VELVETY texture of trumpet-shaped gloxinia flowers shows up well here on the variety "Blanche de Meru".

"GREGOR MENDEL" is one of several fully double-flowered varieties. The heavy heads of bloom may need supporting with thin canes.

FEATURES

Gloxinias are tender plants suitable for growing in the home, greenhouse or conservatory, where they will make an impressive, colorful display. The large, showy, brilliantly colored flowers are trumpet shaped, often with speckled throats. Both flowers and leaves have a velvety feel and appearance: the large leaves are mid-green and oval.
Flowers are produced in abundance on well-grown plants, and are available in many colors, from white through pink and red to deepest blue and violet. The edges of the petals may be ruffled, or frilled with a contrasting color; there are several double-flowered varieties.

SINNINGIA AT A GLANCE

A showy house plant with colorful, velvety-textured flowers. Minimum temperature 60°F (zone 11).

Jan	plant ✋	
Feb	plant ✋	
Mar	plant ✋	Recommended Varieties
Apr	/	
May	/	"Blanche de Meru"
Jun	flowering ❁	"Mont Blanc"
July	flowering ❁	"Princess Elizabeth"
Aug	flowering ❁	"Gregor Mendel"
Sept	/	
Oct	/	
Nov	/	
Dec	/	

CONDITIONS

Aspect Choose a bright position, but not one which is in direct sun or the foliage will be scorched.

Site Gloxinias are house plants requiring average warmth; they dislike hot, dry air and benefit from standing on a dish of moist pebbles for increased humidity. Moisture-retentive soilless potting compost should be used.

GROWING METHOD

Planting Start the tubers off in moist peat or compost in a frost-free position in spring, potting them up individually once the shoots start to grow. Tubers must be planted with the dished side up, level with the surface of the compost—not buried.

Feeding Apply high potash liquid fertilizer every 14 days during the growing season. Keep the compost only just moist until growth has started, then water more freely. Take care to keep water splashes off the leaves and flowers, and never waterlog the compost.

Problems Hot, dry air causes the leaves to shrivel and flower buds to fall before opening. Overwatering leads to rotting of the roots.

FLOWERING

Season Flowers throughout the summer.
Cutting Not suitable for cutting

AFTER FLOWERING

Requirements Gradually reduce watering until the leaves have died back, then store the tubers in dry compost in a cool but frost-free place. Repot in fresh potting compost in spring.

SPARAXIS TRICOLOR
Harlequin flower

HARLEQUIN FLOWERS come in a veritable kaleidoscope of colors, with the patterned throat revealing yet more colors and patterns.

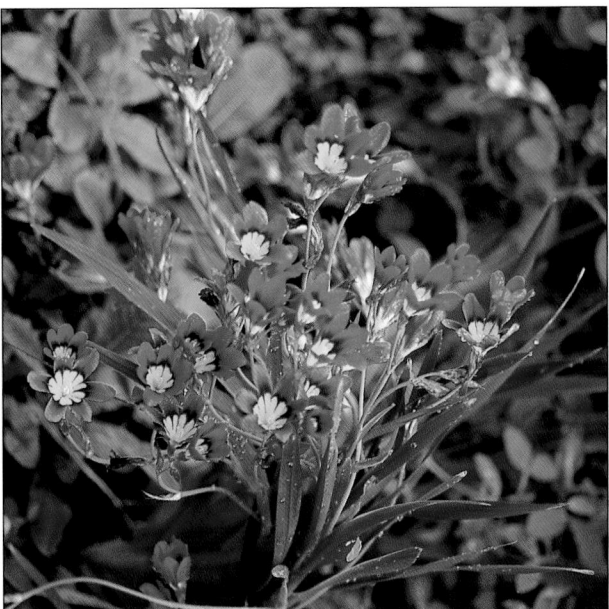

THE STRONG, BRIGHT COLORS of harlequin flowers are shown to best advantage when they are planted in an open, sunny spot.

FEATURES

This showy, easy-care plant has bright flowers of yellow, red, pink, orange, or purple carried on stems that can be anywhere from 6–18in high. Many of the brightly colored flowers have a darker purple or deep red area in the center and a yellow throat. Harlequin flowers hybridise readily, often producing seedlings that have interesting color variations. These are bulbs that thrive in dry, warm areas of the yard. They look their best when mass-planted but can also be grown in containers, where they should be crowded together for best effect. The flowers cut well for indoor decoration. Harlequin flower bulbs increase rapidly by offsets.

SPARAXIS AT A GLANCE

Very brightly colored, star-shaped flowers are carried on slender stems in early summer. Not suitable for cold, exposed yards.

		Recommended Varieties
Jan	/	
Feb	/	Usually supplied as a
Mar	/	color mixture
Apr	/	
May	flowering	
Jun	flowering	
July	/	
Aug	/	
Sept	/	
Oct	/	
Nov	plant	
Dec	/	

CONDITIONS

Aspect Needs full sun all day for best results.
Site Sparaxis needs a sheltered spot in a reasonably mild area to do well; in cold gardens it is best grown in containers under cover. Soil must be well-drained and moderately fertile.

GROWING METHOD

Planting Corms should be planted 3in deep and 3–4in apart in mid-fall. Mulch the planting area with chipped bark or leafmold for winter protection.
Feeding In very poor soil apply a balanced fertiliser in early summer after flowering. Mulch the soil in late winter with well-rotted organic matter. In dry seasons, water when the foliage emerges and as buds and flowers develop if necessary.
Problems No specific problems are known.

FLOWERING

Season Flowering should be abundant in late spring and early summer.
Cutting Sparaxis makes a good cut flower for the home and should last well in water.

AFTER FLOWERING

Requirements Allow foliage to die down naturally, then lift the corms and dry them off until it is time to replant in fall. Any cormlets that have formed can be removed when the corms are lifted and replanted separately.

SPREKELIA FORMOSISSIMA
Jacobean lily

THE SCULPTURED LINES of Jacobean lilies need to be appreciated at close quarters. Growing them in containers is a perfect solution.

THE DARK CRIMSON of the flowers tends to recede into the deep green foliage but still gives a lovely rich glow.

FEATURES

The rich crimson flowers of Jacobean lily are carried singly on stems 12–18in high and the foliage, which is about the same height, appears with or just before the flowers. This plant is sometimes called the Aztec lily and is in fact native to Mexico where it occurs in open, sunny places, often in poor soil. The unusual shape of the flower gives rise to another common name, orchid amaryllis, and the exotic-looking flower could easily be mistaken for an orchid. Unfortunately it is suitable for gardens in mild areas only; in less favored climates it must be grown as a greenhouse or conservatory plant. Formerly much more widely grown than it is today, it deserves to become more popular.

SPREKELIA AT A GLANCE

An exotic-looking, rather tender plant that needs greenhouse conditions in cooler areas. Minimum temperature 45°F (zone 11).

Jan	/	**Recommended Varieties**
Feb	/	
Mar	/	Only the straight species is grown—no cultivars or varieties of this plant are available.
Apr	plant	
May	/	
Jun	flowering	
July	/	
Aug	/	
Sept	/	
Oct	/	
Nov	/	
Dec	/	

CONDITIONS

Aspect Grows best in full sun with wind protection. Indoors it likes a bright position.

Site Suitable for a sheltered border in mild areas, or containers in a greenhouse or conservatory. Outdoors, soil must be well-drained and enriched with compost or manure. Use John Innes potting compost for containers.

GROWING METHOD

Planting Plant bulbs in spring, 2in deep and 8in apart. In containers, plant with the neck of the bulb just above the compost surface.

Feeding Give a high potash liquid feed every two or three weeks throughout the growing season. Water container plants regularly until the foliage starts to die down.

Problems No specific problems are known.

FLOWERING

Season The showy flowers appear in early summer.

Cutting Can be cut for the vase but usually better enjoyed on the plant.

AFTER FLOWERING

Requirements When the leaves die down, lift outdoor bulbs and keep them in a cool, dry place. For container-grown plants, allow the compost to dry out when the leaves die down, then keep the bulb dry in its pot until spring when watering will start it into growth again.

STERNBERGIA LUTEA

Fall daffodil, lily-of-the-field

MOST SCHOLARS today believe Sternbergia lutea is the plant referred to in the Bible as "the lily of the field."

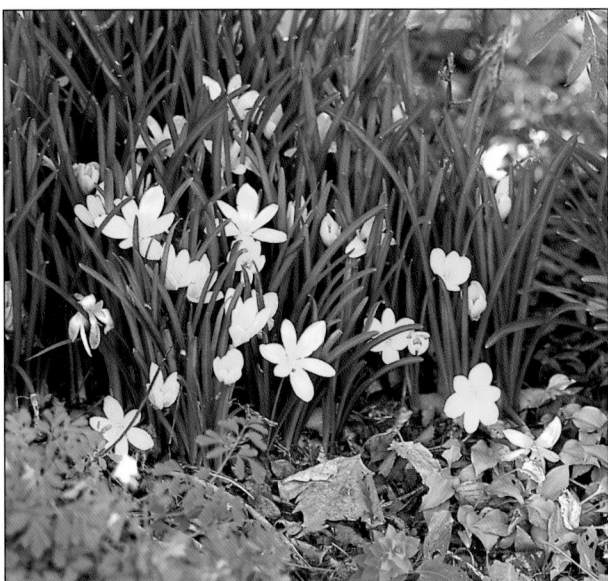

SHORT IN STATURE but big on impact, lily-of-the-field is one of the most delightful of bulbs, especially as it blooms in fall.

FEATURES

Clear, bright yellow flowers, rather like crocuses, appear on 6in stems from their surround of shorter, dark green, strappy leaves. The foliage persists until spring when it dies down to remain dormant until the following fall. Ideal for the rock garden, these plants also show to advantage when planted in the yard in good-sized groups where they can be left to multiply. This is a bulb that could be naturalized in turf but the area would have to be well-marked to avoid cutting off the emerging growth in fall, and the grass could not be mown for several months. Lily-of-the-field can be grown in containers but they are more successful in the open ground.

STERNBERGIA AT A GLANCE

A crocus-like bulb with flowers appearing in late summer and fall. Needs very well-drained soil to thrive.

		Recommended Varieties
Jan	/	
Feb	/	*Sternbergia lutea:*
Mar	/	Angustifolia Group
Apr	/	
May	/	*Sternbergia clusiana*
Jun	/	
July	plant	*Sternbergia sicula*
Aug	plant	
Sept	flowering	
Oct	flowering	
Nov	/	
Dec	/	

CONDITIONS

Aspect Prefers full sun: a summer baking of the dormant bulbs is necessary for good flowering in the fall.

Site Suitable for a rockery, raised bed, or a sunny, reasonably sheltered border. Very well-drained soil is essential for this plant. Well-rotted organic matter can be dug into the bed ahead of planting.

GROWING METHOD

Planting Plant bulbs in summer about 5in deep and the same distance apart.

Feeding Supplementary fertiliser is generally not needed.

Problems The main problem encountered is rotting of bulbs due to heavy or poorly drained soil. Improve drainage by incorporating sharp sand into the planting area.

FLOWERING

Season The small, bright golden flowers appear in fall.

Cutting These flowers are not suitable for cutting.

AFTER FLOWERING

Requirements Ensure the plants are allowed to remain dry once the foliage has died down in early summer. The site may need protection from excessive summer rain with a cloche or similar. Do not disturb established plants unless it is essential.

TIGRIDIA PAVONIA
Tiger flower, peacock flower

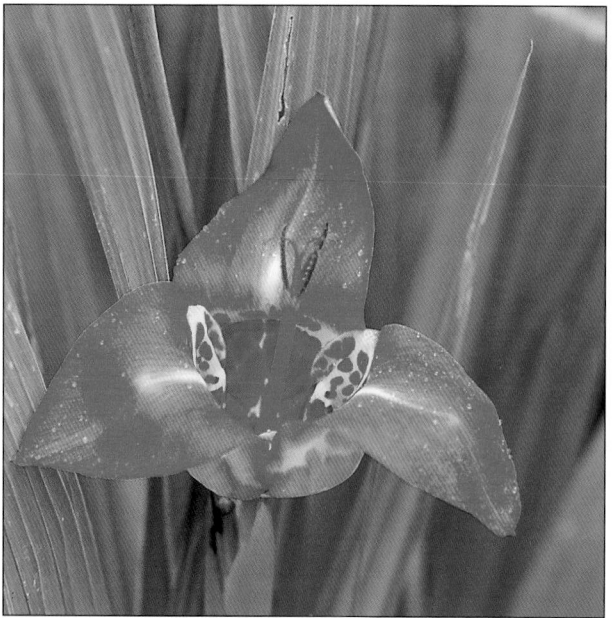

THE SHOWY FLOWERS of Tigridia pavonia *often have colorful spotting in the center, making it worth studying them closely.*

EACH EXOTIC *bloom lasts only a day, but is swiftly followed by others to give a succession of flowers over several weeks.*

FEATURES

Although each flower of the tiger or peacock flower lasts only a day, there is a succession of spectacular blooms over a long period. Flowers have six petals; the outer petals are large and broad, the inner ones smaller and thinner, usually spotted with a contrasting color. The species is red with a spotted yellow and purple center but there is a large range of colors available, in combinations of white, cream, yellow, orange, pink, mauve, and red, with contrasting spotting around the center of each flower. The tiger flower is also called jockey's cap lily in some parts of the world. Plants usually grow to around 18in. They are often included in mixed borders of summer-flowering shrubs and perennials.

TIGRIDIA AT A GLANCE

Spectacularly colorful but short-lived flowers are produced in succession from mid to late summer. Best in warmer areas.

		Recommended Varieties
Jan	/	Generally available only as color mixtures.
Feb	/	
Mar	/	
Apr	plant	
May	plant	
Jun	/	
July	/	
Aug	flowering	
Sept	flowering	
Oct	/	
Nov	/	
Dec	/	

CONDITIONS

Aspect   Prefers full sun with some wind protection. Grows best in warm, sheltered gardens.

Site   Grow the plants towards the front of beds and borders, where their flamoyant flowers can be appreciated close at hand. They need well-drained but not particularly rich soil.

GROWING METHOD

Planting   Plant in mid to late spring 4in deep and about 6–8in apart.

Feeding   Growth is usually improved by the application of a balanced fertilizer in spring. Occasional liquid feeds of a high potash fertilizer can be given through the growing season. Water during spring and summer in dry spells.

Problems   No specific problems are usually experienced with this plant.

FLOWERING

Season   Blooms appear from middle to late summer into the early fall.

Cutting   Flowers are not suitable for cutting.

AFTER FLOWERING

Requirements   Remove spent flower stems. In sheltered, mild areas and in free-draining soil the bulbs can be left in the ground over winter, but more reliable results are obtained by lifting before the first frosts, and storing bulbs in a frost-free place until the following spring.

TRILLIUM
Wake robin, wood lily

THE LATIN NAME Trillium *refers to "three" and wake robin has everything in threes: three petals, three sepals, and a ring of three leaves.*

THE LITTLE FLOWERS *of wake robin will make a delightful sight as they light up a shaded part of the garden.*

FEATURES

Trillium grandiflorum is a charming woodland plant which hails from North America. With its three pure white petals and dark foliage, it is a most arresting sight when naturalized in groups under trees to simulate its native habitat. It is not a difficult plant to grow and is well worth seeking out—it can be vigorous and long lived in the right conditions. The white flowers slowly age to pink and there is an attractive double form available called *T. grandiflorum flore pleno*. Plants grow to 15in or so high.

Other species worth growing include *T. sessile*, with dark red flowers springing from bronze blotched foliage; *T. erectum*, with maroon flowers and lighter green foliage, and *T. undulatum*, which has white or pinkish flowers streaked with red.

TRILLIUM AT A GLANCE

Attractive plants for lightly shaded or woodland conditions, with white, three-petalled flowers in early summer.

		Recommended Varieties
Jan	/	
Feb	/	*Trillium grandiflorum*
Mar	/	"Flore Pleno"
Apr	flowering	
May	flowering	*Trillium erectum albiflorum*
Jun	flowering	
July	/	*Trillium erectum luteum*
Aug	plant	
Sept	plant	*Trillium sessile luteum*
Oct	plant	
Nov	/	
Dec	/	

CONDITIONS

Aspect Needs light shade at all times or the dappled sunlight provided by overhead trees or shrubs.

Site An ideal plant for a woodland garden or a shady border. Does best in very rich, moist, but free-draining soil. Copious quantities of well-rotted cow manure or leafmould should be dug into the soil before planting. Mulch well in late winter, too.

GROWING METHOD

Planting Plant rhizomes 3in deep in late summer or early fall. Plant in groups at 12in or so intervals.

Feeding An annual dressing of leafmould or well-rotted manure should provide sufficient nutrients, but an application of general fertilizer can be given in spring. The soil must not dry out in spring and summer and so give careful attention to watering in dry weather.

Problems Slugs and snails may damage newly emerging leaves or flowers; otherwise it is generally trouble-free.

FLOWERING

Season Flowers will appear somewhere between mid-spring and early summer.

Cutting Flowers are not suitable for picking.

AFTER FLOWERING

Requirements No special attention is needed after flowering apart from tidying dead foliage. Crowded clumps can be divided and replanted immediately in the fall.

TRITELEIA
syn. *Brodiaea laxa*

"QUEEN FABIOLA" is probably the most widely planted of the triteleias. The paler center gives definition to the flower form.

BLUE FLOWERS are always a favorite, and the violet-blue, starry flowers of these triteleias fill a sheltered pocket in the garden.

FEATURES

These pretty bulbous plants are native to Oregon and California. There is some confusion over their correct name; they are often listed as brodiaea, with some species as dichelostemma. *T. laxa* is the most popular form. Flower stems may be 18–24in or so high with the strappy leaves growing to about 12in. The starry flowers are carried in loose clusters and are pale or violet blue with the most popular cultivar, "Queen Fabiola," producing deeper violet-blue blooms with a pale center. The foliage dies back in spring while the plant is in bloom, and the corm remains dormant from midsummer until winter.

TRITELEIA AT A GLANCE

Dainty clusters of tubular blue blooms are carried on slender stems in midsummer. Well-drained soil is essential.

Month		Recommended Varieties
Jan	/	
Feb	/	*Triteleia hyacinthina*
Mar	/	
Apr	/	*Triteleia ixioides*
May	flowering	
Jun	flowering	*Triteleia laxa:*
July	flowering	"Queen Fabiola"
Aug	/	
Sept	plant	*Triteleia peduncularis*
Oct	/	
Nov	/	
Dec	/	

CONDITIONS

Aspect
Site   An open, sunny but sheltered site is necessary. Grow this plant in the flower border or in containers. The soil must be light and very well-drained; triteleia cannot stand waterlogging. It can be grown in containers of sandy potting compost where the garden soil is heavy.

GROWING METHOD

Planting   Plant corms 3–4in deep and 4–6in apart in fall.

Feeding   A balanced or high potash fertiliser can be given when the flower buds appear, but normally no feeding is necessary. Plants in containers can be liquid-fed every two weeks. Watering is not normally necessary; the soil should be allowed to dry out while the corm is dormant during the summer.

Problems   There are no specific pest or disease problems known for this plant.

FLOWERING

Season   Flowers appear from early to mid-summer.
Cutting   Blooms last particularly well as a cut flower.

AFTER FLOWERING

Requirements   Flowering stems can be cut off when they are past their peak, or left to set seed. Plants resent disturbance, so should be left alone once planted.

TRITONIA
Tritonia

*THIS ORANGE TRITONIA (*Tritonia crocata*) is planted beside a path where it revels in the reflected heat and somewhat dry conditions. Like most tritonias, it will increase rapidly if it is happy with the growing conditions.*

FEATURES

This is a most undemanding little plant that will give great value in containers or as a cut flower. Tritonias are not fully hardy and in colder areas need to be grown indoors, but in sheltered gardens in milder parts of the country they can be grown outside successfully as long as they have full sun and a well-drained soil.

Most species flower from middle to late spring or in early summer on spikes that are around 12in high. *T. crocata* usually has bright orange flowers with darker markings in the throat but there are other forms with bright pink, salmon, or scarlet flowers. *T. disticha rubrolucens* has rose pink flowers and is hardier; it is often listed as *T. rosea*.

TRITONIA AT A GLANCE

Colorful, freesia-like flowers in late spring and early summer. Not suitable for growing outdoors in colder areas.

Month		Recommended Varieties
Jan	/	Usually available only as color mixtures.
Feb	/	
Mar	/	
Apr	/	
May	flowering	
Jun	flowering	
July	/	
Aug	/	
Sept	plant	
Oct	/	
Nov	/	
Dec	/	

CONDITIONS

Aspect Grows best in full sun, preferably with shelter from strong wind.

Site In mild areas, tritonias do well in pockets of a rockery or planted in generous clumps in a garden bed. Soil must be well drained but it need not be very rich. In cold gardens, grow the corms in pots of John Innes or soil-less potting compost.

GROWING METHOD

Planting Plant the corms about 2in deep and 4–6in apart in autumn. Five corms can be grown in a 6in pot.

Feeding A light application of balanced fertilizer can be given as growth starts. In containers, liquid feed every 14–21 days. Begin watering container plants when the leaves appear but allow the compost to dry out once the leaves start to turn yellow.

Problems No specific problems are known.

FLOWERING

Season Flowers are carried from mid-spring to early summer.

Cutting Flowers will last in the vase for up to a week.

AFTER FLOWERING

Requirements Cut off spent flower stems. Mulch plants growing outdoors for winter protection: allow container plants to remain dry in their pots until planting time.

TULBAGHIA VIOLACEA
Wild garlic

THE PALE PURPLE flowers of wild garlic are pleasantly fragrant, though the crushed foliage has a distinctive onion smell.

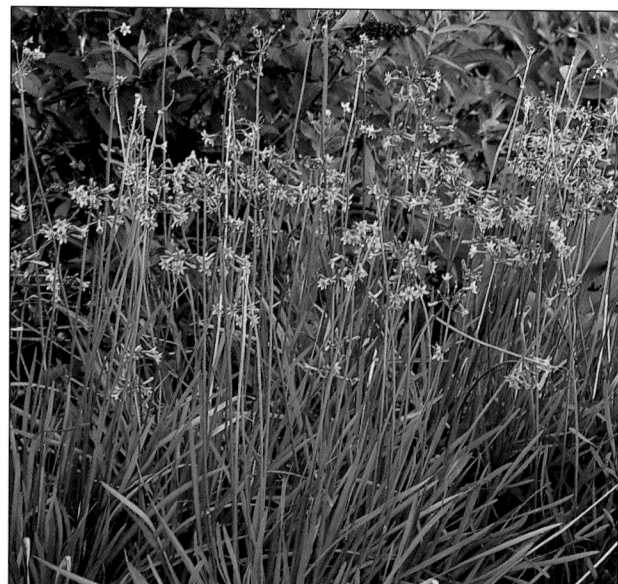

THE FLOWERS APPEAR throughout the summer above the clumps of vigorous, gray-green foliage.

FEATURES

This is another plant which needs warm, sheltered gardens to do well when left outdoors, though it can be grown as a container plant very successfully in cooler areas. The strappy leaves grow to about 12in with the flowering stems standing 4in or more above the foliage. The individual rosy-violet flowers form a rounded head of bloom. Society garlic flowers through the summer, and stems can be cut for the vase.

Tulbaghia natalensis grows to 6in high and has fragrant white flowers with a yellow center that gives them a narcissus-like appearance. This is a hardier species which is usually more successful in colder gardens, though it is not as common as *T. violacea*.

TULBAGHIA AT A GLANCE

A slightly tender plant with mounds of grassy foliage and heads of pretty pink summer flowers.

Jan	/	
Feb	/	Recommended Varieties
Mar	/	
Apr	plant 👈	*Tulbaghia violacea pallida*
May	/	
Jun	flowering 🌿	*Tulbaghia violacea:*
July	flowering 🌿	"Silver Lace"
Aug	flowering 🌿	
Sept	/	
Oct	/	
Nov	/	
Dec	/	

CONDITIONS

Aspect   Prefers a position in full sun.
Site   Tulbaghia is a good plant for seaside gardens, and can be included in a mixed border of annuals and perennials or grown in containers. Soil should be well drained and contain plenty of well-rotted organic matter.

GROWING METHOD

Planting   Plant in spring about 1in deep and 8in or so apart. Congested clumps can be lifted and divided in spring.
Feeding   If the organic content of the soil is high little extra feeding is needed. However, a light dressing of balanced fertilizer may be given as growth becomes active. Keep the soil moist during the growing season, watering in dry spells as necessary.
Problems   No specific problems are known.

FLOWERING

Season   Flowers are carried all through summer.
Cutting   Flowers are very decorative when cut for the vase, although the smell of the foliage may discourage some people.

AFTER FLOWERING

Requirements   Tidy up the foliage and apply a mulch of chipped bark, leafmould or dry leaves for winter protection. Container plants should be allowed to dry out and moved under cover for the winter.

TULIPA
Tulip

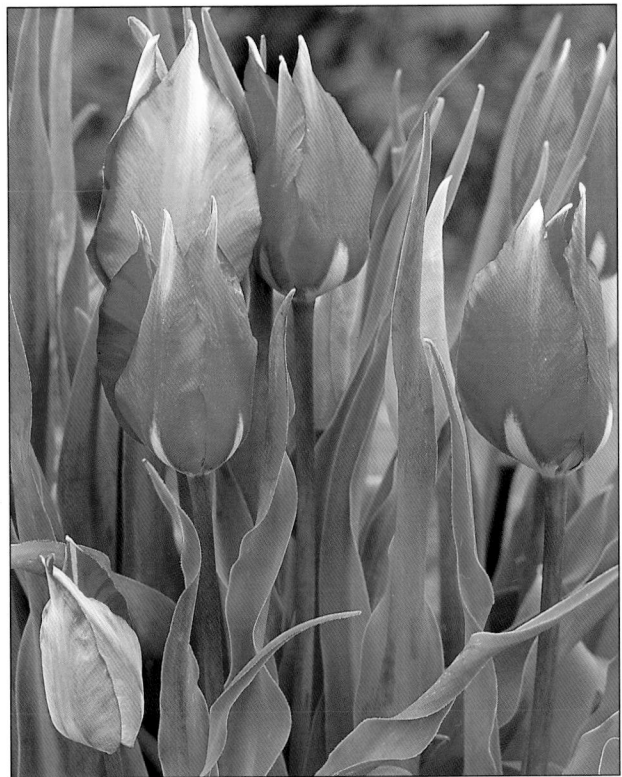

THE POINTED PETALS of these goblet-shaped, bright lipstick-pink tulips will open to form a starry shape.

A NATIVE of Crete, pale pink Tulipa saxatilis *needs a sunny, warm position with perfectly drained soil in which to grow.*

FEATURES

There are over 100 species of tulips and many hundreds of hybrids. Most modern garden tulips are the result of extensive breeding programmes that began in the late sixteenth century in Europe and are continuing to this day. Tulips were all the rage at that time as more and more species were introduced to Europe from Turkey, Iran, and central Asia. Tulip species range in height from about 6–24in but the greatest number of hybrids are probably in the range of 12–16in. Tulips look their best in mass plantings of one color but they can, of course, be mixed. They make very good container plants and are delightful cut flowers. Some of the most charming are the dwarf types which do particularly well in rock gardens and are also very suitable for containers.

Tulip bulbs are widely available in garden centers in late summer and early fall, but to get a wider choice it is often best to obtain catalogues from specialist bulb growers who run mail-order businesses. Many of the species tulips are only available from specialist growers. With careful selection it is possible to have a tulip in flower from early to very late spring.

Like daffodils, tulips are split into a number of divisions according to their flower form and time of flowering.

Single early	Cup-shaped single flowers, up to 16in in early to mid-spring.
Double early	Fully double flowers up to 16in in early to mid-spring.
Triumph	Conical then rounded, single flowers up to 20in in mid to late spring.
Darwin hybrid	Large, single flowers of varying shape, up to 24in in mid to late spring.
Single late	Single, blocky or square shaped flowers up to 30in in late spring and early summer.
Lily-flowered	Single, waisted flowers with pointed petals, up to 24in in late spring.
Fringed	Single flowers with very finely cut petal edges, up to 24in in late spring.
Viridiflora	Single flowers with green bands or streaks on the outside, up to 20in in late spring.
Rembrandt	Single flowers with a broken pattern of feathering or streaking caused by a virus. Up to 30in in late spring.
Parrot	Single flowers with very strongly frilled and curled petals, up to 24in in late spring.
Double late	Large, fully double flowers up to 24in in late spring.
Kaufmanniana	Single, often bi-colored flowers of a waterlily shape, up to 10in in late spring. Leaves may be mottled.
Fosteriana	Large, single, wide-opening flowers up to 20in in early to mid-spring.
Greigii	Large, single flowers up to 14in in mid to late spring. Leaves streaked and mottled.
Miscellaneous	Any other species, varieties, and hybrids.

1.

2.

3.

6.

7.

TULIPS
(*TULIPA*)

Tulips, with their wide range of forms and colors, are divided into fifteen horticultural groups.

1. From a crimson bud "Leen van der Mark" opens to reveal a crystalline white center.

2. A fully opened "Bokassa Red" shows its deep scarlet petals tipped with gold.

3. "Judith Lyster," a single late tulip, is rich cream merging to watermelon pink.

4. Goblet-shaped "Bokassa Rose" is deep rose pink with a yellow center.

5. "Kees Nelis" is a bright, two-tone tulip in primary red and yellow.

6. No two parrot tulip flowers are identical as this flamboyant "Flaming Parrot" proves.

7. "Princess Victoria" is a heavy-textured tulip that is more weather resistant than some other varieties.

8. "Angélique," a pale pink ruffled beauty, is best grown in pots so it can be protected from weather.

9. "Monte Carlo" is a bright gold, fully double tulip with a light scent.

4.

5.

8.

9.

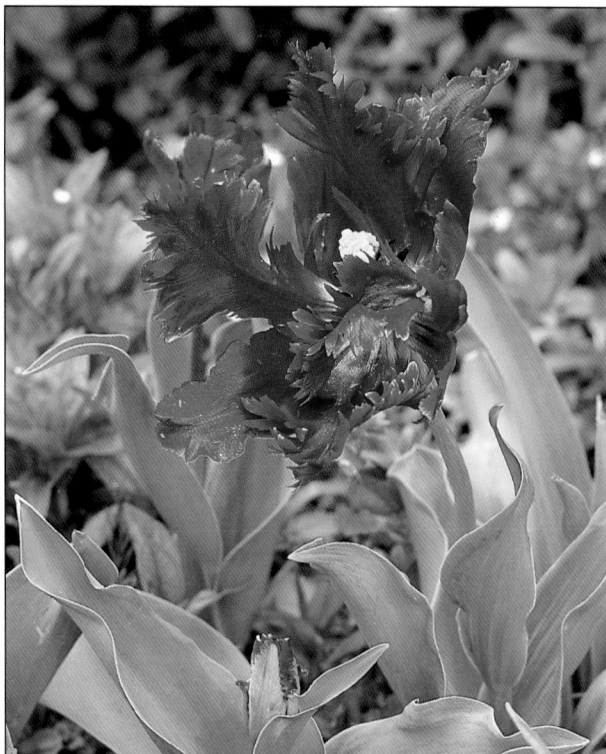

THE BIZARRE FORM of parrot tulips is exemplified by this dark crimson flower. People either love these forms or hate them.

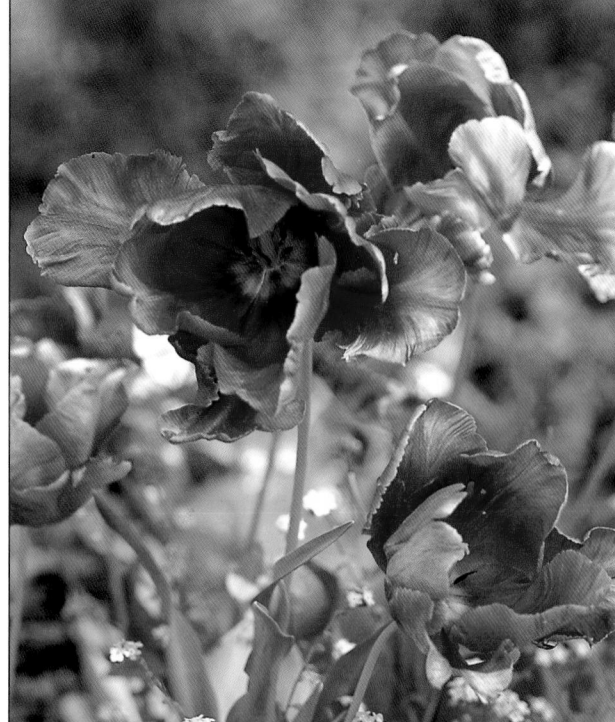

THE BURGUNDY of these full-blown tulips will appeal to lovers of the unusual but they may be hard to incorporate into the garden scheme.

CONDITIONS

Aspect Tulips need full sun for at least half the day, with some wind protection.

Site Grow tulips in beds and borders, on rockeries or in containers. Soil should be well drained with a high organic content. Add lime to acid soils.

GROWING METHOD

Planting Bulbs should be planted in late fall. Planting depth varies according to the size of the bulbs; usually 6–8in for the larger types and 4in for the smaller species. Space them 4–8in apart.

Feeding Apply liquid fertilizer as soon as buds appear and again after flowers have faded. Water regularly in dry spells, especially once the buds have appeared.

Problems Tulip breaking virus, causing streaking of the flowers, is carried by aphids. Remove affected plants and keep aphids under control. Tulip fire disease is a type of botrytis or gray mould. It causes small brown spots on flowers and leaves; stems may rot and gray furry growth may develop on the damaged areas. Destroy plants infected with this disease and avoid planting tulips in the same spot for a couple of years. Spraying with a general fungicide may control early infection.

FLOWERING

Season Tulips flower somewhere between late winter and late spring, depending on variety.

Cutting If cutting blooms for the house, choose those that are not fully open and cut them early in the morning. Change vase water frequently.

AFTER FLOWERING

Requirements Remove spent flower stems and dead foliage. Tulips may be left in the ground for two or three years, or the bulbs can be lifted once the foliage has died down, cleaned and stored in a cool, dry, airy place. Dwarf tulips tend to be left in the ground, but other varieties usually perform better if they are lifted and replanted every year. If you do not want to lift them annually, make sure the bulbs are planted deeply.

TULIPA AT A GLANCE

Well-known flowers in a very wide range of colors, sizes, and forms, flowering between late winter and late spring.

		Recommended Varieties
Jan	/	
Feb	flowering	"Peach Blossom"
Mar	flowering	"Apeldoorn"
Apr	flowering	"Clara Butt"
May	flowering	"China Pink"
Jun	/	"Burgundy Lace"
July	/	"Spring Green"
Aug	/	"Texas Gold"
Sept	/	"Angelique"
Oct	/	"Ancilla"
Nov	plant	*Tulipa fosteriana*
Dec	plant	*Tulipa greigii*
		Tulipa tarda

WATSONIA
Watsonia

THE VIVID PINK FLOWERS of watsonia make it a most desirable plant, but it is not commonly grown in gardens.

WATSONIA FLOWERS are displayed well clear of the upright foliage and so are ideal for planting at the back of a border.

FEATURES

Although there are many species of watsonias in the wild, they are not commonly cultivated plants. The stiff, sword-shaped leaves are similar to those of a gladiolus: the flower spike, growing to over 39in carries tubular flowers in various shades of pink and red, violet, magenta and orange. Watsonia is ideally placed towards the back of a mixed border. In all but very warm districts the corms should be lifted in fall and stored in a dry place until it is time to replant them the following spring. The usual species offered is *W. pillansii* (also known as *W. beatricis*), which has orange-red flowers. The slightly more tender *W. borbonica* (*W. pyrimidata*) has rich pink blooms.

WATSONIA AT A GLANCE

An unusual bulb with tall, stately spikes of pink or red flowers, good for the back of the border.

		Recommended Varieties
Jan	/	
Feb	/	
Mar	/	"Stanford Scarlet"
Apr	plant	"Tresco Dwarf Pink"
May	plant	
Jun	flowering	*Watsonia borbonica ardernei*
July	flowering	
Aug	flowering	
Sept	plant (warm areas)	
Oct	/	
Nov	/	
Dec	/	

CONDITIONS

Aspect Watsonia needs full sun and a warm, sheltered position.

Site These tall plants are good for the back of a border. They can also be grown in pots in a greenhouse. Any well-drained soil is acceptable, but growth will be better if well-rotted organic matter is dug in before planting.

GROWING METHOD

Planting Plant corms in mid to late spring, 4in deep and 12in apart. In warm, sheltered areas, corms can be planted in fall 6in deep and mulched with chipped bark or dry leaves.

Feeding Apply a long-acting fertilizer such as general fertilizer in early summer. Watering is necessary only in prolonged dry spells.

Problems Generally free from pest or disease problems when grown in an open, sunny position.

FLOWERING

Season Watsonias flower in mid-summer.

Cutting Stems can be cut for the vase. They should last well with frequent water changes.

AFTER FLOWERING

Requirements Except in very warm areas, lift the corms after flowering, when the foliage starts to die down. Clean them, allow them to dry, and store in a cool, airy place until the following spring.

ZANTEDESCHIA
Arum lily, calla lily

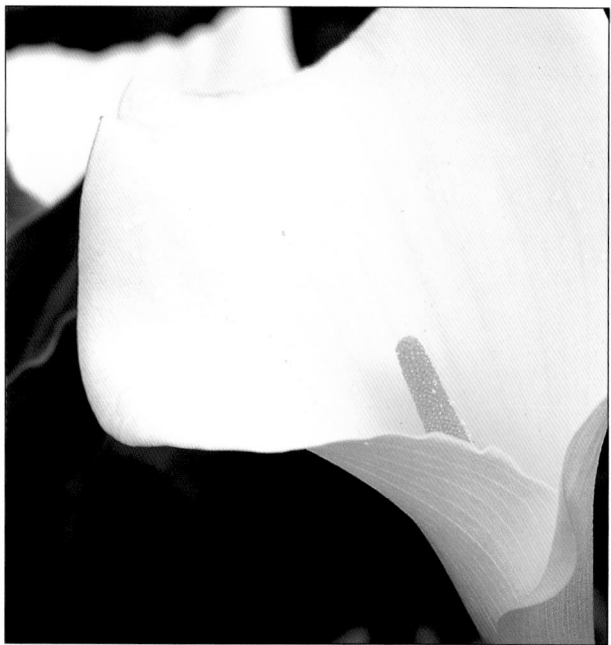

ARUM LILIES have long been favorites with flower arrangers for their texture and sculptural shape which adds form to an arrangement.

PURE WHITE FLOWERS and decorative leaves are features of arum, which are quite easy to grow in a variety of conditions.

FEATURES

Arum lilies are greatly prized for their beautiful waxy flowers, pure white with a golden central spadix. The arrow-shaped leaves are deep green, and the whole plant can grow up to 39in high. Several species are suitable for growing only in a greenhouse or conservatory, but *Z. aethiopica* can be grown outside in reasonably sheltered gardens. It likes moist, boggy conditions, and often grows best beside a pond or water feature: it can be grown as a marginal plant in up to 12in of water. *Z. elliottiana*, the golden arum, and *Z. rehmannii*, the pink arum, are good greenhouse or conservatory plants.

ZANTEDESCHIA AT A GLANCE

A rhizomatous plant grown for its beautiful waxy white flower spathes. Needs greenhouse conditions in some areas.

Jan	/	
Feb	/	Recommended Varieties
Mar	/	*Zantedeschia aethiopica:*
Apr	plant	"Crowborough"
May	/	"Green Goddess"
Jun	flowering	
July	flowering	
Aug	/	
Sept	/	
Oct	/	
Nov	/	
Dec	/	

CONDITIONS

Aspect Can be grown in full sun or light shade. It should be sheltered from strong wind.

Site *Z. aethiopica* can be grown on the fringe of a pool or in a border in moist, humus-rich soil. Other arum species need rich but free-draining soil and are grown in a greenhouse or conservatory in containers.

GROWING METHOD

Planting Plant rhizomes 6in deep and 18in apart in spring.

Feeding Apply liquid fertilizer as buds appear and continue to feed every 14–21 days while plants are in bloom. Keep the soil moist at all times while the plants are in active growth during spring and summer.

Problems Leaf spot can cause dark blotches on all parts of the plant and may cause premature leaf drop. It often occurs where conditions are too cool and damp. Destroy affected parts and spray with a suitable fungicide.

FLOWERING

Season Flowers in early summer.

Cutting Flowers are excellent for cutting.

AFTER FLOWERING

Requirements Remove flower stems as they fade. Mulch outdoor plants with dry leaves for winter.

ZEPHYRANTHES
Zephyr lily, rainflower

ZEPHYR LILY shows how even the simplest of flowers can be very beautiful. The green throat and yellow stamens emphasise the purity.

A BROAD BORDER of zephyr lily gives a star-studded performance in the fall garden.

FEATURES

With its starry white flowers and shiny green, grass-like foliage, zephyr lily is a bulb for mass planting in sheltered gardens. It is quite easy to grow and can remain undisturbed for years where conditions suit it. It can be planted in borders or on a rockery, and it can also be grown very successfully in containers. The crocus-like flowers are carried in late summer or fall, especially after showers of rain, which accounts for its common name of rainflower. *Zephyranthes candida* is the species suitable for growing outdoors in Britain; it generally reaches a height of 8–10in. *Z. grandiflora* (also called *Z. rosea*) has lovely rosy pink flowers but is only suitable for cultivation in a greenhouse or conservatory, as is the yellow flowered *Z. citrina*.

ZEPHYRANTHES AT A GLANCE

An attractive, low-growing plant with crocus-like flowers in the fall.

		Recommended Species
Jan	/	
Feb	/	*Zephyranthes candida*
Mar	/	
Apr	plant 🖙	*Z. citrina*
May	/	
Jun	flowering 🌱 *	*Z. flavissima*
July	flowering 🌱 *	
Aug	/	*Z. grandiflora*
Sept	flowering 🌱	
Oct	flowering 🌱	
Nov	/	
Dec	/	

CONDITIONS

Aspect   Grows best in full sun.
Site   Grow in beds or borders or in pockets in a rockery. Needs a well-drained but moisture-retentive soil. Growth will be improved if soils contain some humus.

GROWING METHOD

Planting   Plant in spring, 2in deep and 4in apart. For greenhouse cultivation, plant 5 bulbs in a 5in pot in loam-based potting compost.
Feeding   Supplementary fertilizer is generally not needed. Spread a mulch of well-decayed manure or compost around the bulbs in spring. Water in dry spells during spring, but stop watering when the foliage starts to die down.
Problems   No specific problems are usually experienced with this plant.

FLOWERING

Season   Flowers appear from late summer into fall, or in mid-summer in the greenhouse.
Cutting   Flowers are not suitable for cutting.

AFTER FLOWERING

Requirements   Spent flower stems may be cut off but this is not essential. No special treatment is needed as the bulbs are best left undisturbed for several years. If you wish to lift and divide a clump this is best done in spring. Greenhouse plants should be allowed to dry out when the leaves die down, and started into growth again by plentiful watering the following spring.

Growing Clematis

GROWING CLEMATIS

Swagging walls, fences and pergolas or scrambling over trees and shrubs, clematis is the queen of climbers. It ascends by wrapping leaf stalks around a support and blooms strikingly for most of the year.

FEATURES

Starry or flared bell flowers, in a kaleidoscope of dashing hues, flourish on new or one-year-old shoots. Many, such as *C. tangutica* are followed by spheres of feathery seed heads, which look dramatic when sparkling with frost.

There are species and hybrids to suit every situation and most are frost hardy. In tiny gardens or on patios or terraces, you can grow smaller varieties so that they cascade over the side. Although most shed their leaves, a small group of sculptural evergreens have a special charm.

There are six fascinating types:

Early-flowering species (Group 1)
Choice spring varieties include blue *C. alpina* 'Pamela Jackman', *C. macropetala* 'Markham's Pink,' and white *C. montana* f. *grandiflora*.

Early-flowering hybrids (Group 2)
Resulting from a cross between two or more species and cheering early summer, double-flowered, silver-mauve 'Belle of Woking' and purple-blue "The President" will glorify a west-facing wall or fence.

Late-flowering species (Group 3)
Clouds of tiny, fragrant, starry white blooms billowing from *C. flammula* and flared tulip-like red blooms peeping from *C. texensis* 'Princes of Wales', make July to October special.

Late-flowering hybrids (Group 3)
Rich purple "Jackmanii" and any of plants of the *C. viticella* clan, such as white and green 'Alba Luxurians', flourish from July to September.

Evergreens (Group 1)
Skeined with scented pink-budded, white-flowered blooms in spring, leathery scimitar-leaved "Apple Blossom" enjoys a warm, sunny aspect. In winter, reddish-spotted, cream- and fern-leaved *C. cirrhosa* "Freckles" prefer to be in a sheltered spot.

Herbaceous varieties (Group 3)
A small non-climbing group of clematis that complements border perennials. An enchanting combination is the deep blue and hyacinth-flowered *C. heracleifolia* "Wyevale," which grows to 3ft and the scented, white- and bronze-leaved *C. recta* 'Purpurea', which grows to 2–4ft. Both flower from late summer to fall.

LEFT: Many people grow clematis because of their attractive and often scented flowers: they come in a wide variety of different colors, shapes and sizes. They also have long-flowering periods so, if you select the varieties carefully, you can have year-round blooms.

CONDITIONS

Aspect
Site
There are species and varieties to suit every spot. Soil should be free-draining and fortified with well-rotted organic matter. Ideally, you should grow plants where the roots are shaded but the stems can climb into bright sunlight.

GROWING METHOD

Planting
Take out a generous hole 18in across and 15in deep, and fork old manure or rotted garden compost into the base. Fill in with a mix of fertile top soil and add two very well worked-in gloved handfuls of bone meal.
Tap the plant from its pot, tease out coiled roots at the base and set the root ball 6in deeper than it was in its pot to encourage a multi-stemmed branching system to form. Water in copiously. Finish by mulching with old manure or pulverized bark to keep roots cool. Fan-train shoots over trellis or plastic-coated wires spaced 1ft apart.

Feeding
Clematis are voracious feeders, so top dress them with 4oz per square yard of blood, fish and bone meal in spring, mid and late summer. Water it in.

Pruning
Group 1 (early-flowering species and evergreens): Don't cut them back unless they outgrow their allotted space. Shorten flowered shoots when blooms fade to just above a joint.
Group 2 (early-flowering hybrids): Cut out dead shoots in February. Shorten stems when blooms fade to encourage a second flush of blossom in late summer. Dead-head regularly.
Group 3 (late-flowering hybrids, species and herbaceous varieties): Shorten all stems to fat buds 12in from the base in February or March.

Problems
Slugs and snails rasp bark and devour new buds and shoots. Control with blue slug pellets. Wilt disease causes shoots to collapse suddenly and die back to ground level. Thankfully, new stems appear from the base. There are no effective fungicides, so instead cut back affected shoots. Plant deeply so that if stems die back to soil level, underground buds are triggered into growth and replace them.

FLOWERING

Season
By selecting varieties carefully, you can have blossom from late winter to late fall.

Cutting
Although blooms last for only for a few days, they look captivating floating in a shallow bowl of water. Gather seed heads when fluffy, spray them with hair lacquer to stop seeds from loosening and add them to dried winter displays.

AFTER FLOWERING

Requirements
Nourish spring and summer performers with fertilizer over root area when blooms fade. Water in. Feed summer to fall bloomers with bone meal in October or November.

NELLY MOSER

MONTANA "TETRAROSE"

"Nelly Moser," which blooms twice (in May and again in September), flaunts 7–9in carmine-striped, pale mauve-pink blooms. It colors well if trained against an east-, north- or west-facing wall or fence, but objects to direct sunlight, which causes its magnificent flowers to fade. Growing only to around 10ft, it is ideal for clothing an arch or a trellis around a patio.

It flowers on shoots made the previous year, so remove dead or weak stems in late June and tie in the strongest new growth to flower the following season. Devise a riveting focus by planting it next to lavender-blue "Lasurstern," which is similar in height and should be treated in the same way.

Transforming May and June with a foam of large, 3–4in, lilac-rose flowers amid bronzy-green foliage, Clematis montana "Tetrarose" grows to 20ft on a large wall, fence or sizeable pergola.

Though happy facing north, east, south or west, it is sensible to capitalise on its hardiness by planting it to cloak a cold, shaded wall or fence seared by icy winds. Alternatively, set it to climb and drape a conifer or umbrella over an old apple tree. No pruning is necessary. If it outgrows its allotted space, trim it when flowers fade in early summer.

NELLY MOSER AT A GLANCE

Flowers well when positioned against an east-, west- or north-facing wall or fence. Fully hardy to frost hardy.

Jan	rest	Nov	rest
Feb	rest	Dec	rest
Mar	planting		
Apr	feeding, mulching	OTHER EARLY-FLOWERING FORMS:	
May	flowering		
Jun	flowering	'Royalty'	
July	pruning, propagation	'Proteus'	
		'Guernsey Cream'	
Aug	tie in shoots		
Sept	flowering		
Oct	planting		

MONTANA AT A GLANCE

This variety is especially good for covering a north-facing wall. Fully hardy to frost hardy.

Jan	rest	Sept	planting
Feb	rest	Oct	planting
Mar	planting, feeding	Nov	rest
		Dec	rest
Apr	planting, mulching		
May	flowering	OTHER MONTANA FORMS:	
Jun	flowering	'Elizabeth'	
July	pruning	'Alexander'	
Aug	propagation, feeding	'Pink Perfection'	

SILVER MOON

LIBERATION

"Silver Moon" is a large-flowered variety that will enliven a dull north-facing wall or fence, but will be equally happy elsewhere. Cloaked with pearly-pink blooms, which will grow to 5–7in across, on stems up to 8–10ft high, it brightens May, June and August. It is suitable, too, for planting in a large patio pot from which blossom-clad shoots will spill appealingly.

Create a feature that all will admire by combining it with a contrasting-hued climbing rose, such as "Royal Gold," scarlet "Sympathie," yellow and red "Night Light," or rose-pink "Parade." No pruning is necessary unless it outgrows its allotted space. Then, in a mild spell in February or early March, shorten all stems to within a pair of fat buds, 12–18in from the ground.

Introduced in 1995 to commemorate the Channel Islands' 50th year of freedom from oppression by occupying forces, "Liberation" is a joy. Flaunting deep pinkish-red blooms with cerise-barred petals, up to 6in in diameter, on robust stems up to 10ft, it flourishes in late spring and early summer and again in early fall. It needs tempering with white-flowered plants because of its vibrant colours. Ideally, twin it with Solanum jasminoides "Album," a scrambler whose clusters of starry flowers stud shoots from July to October. It performs on one-year-old stems, so no regular pruning is required— merely shorten dead or weak growth to stocky buds from February to early March. Prune again, cutting back flowered stems by half their length in midsummer in order to trigger new shoots and a dazzling bonus of fall blossom.

SILVER MOON AT A GLANCE

Thrives when grown against a west-facing wall. Fully hardy to frost hardy.

Jan	rest	Nov	rest
Feb	pruning	Dec	rest
Mar	planting, feeding		
Apr	planting, mulching		
May	flowering		
Jun	flowering		
July	propagation		
Aug	flowering, feeding		
Sept	planting		
Oct	planting		

LIBERATION AT A GLANCE

Flourishes against an east or west-facing wall. Fully hardy to frost hardy.

Jan	rest	Nov	rest
Feb	rest	Dec	rest
Mar	planting, feeding		
Apr	planting, mulching		
May	flowering		
Jun	flowering		
July	propagation		
Aug	feeding		
Sept	planting		
Oct	planting		

Growing
Shrubs

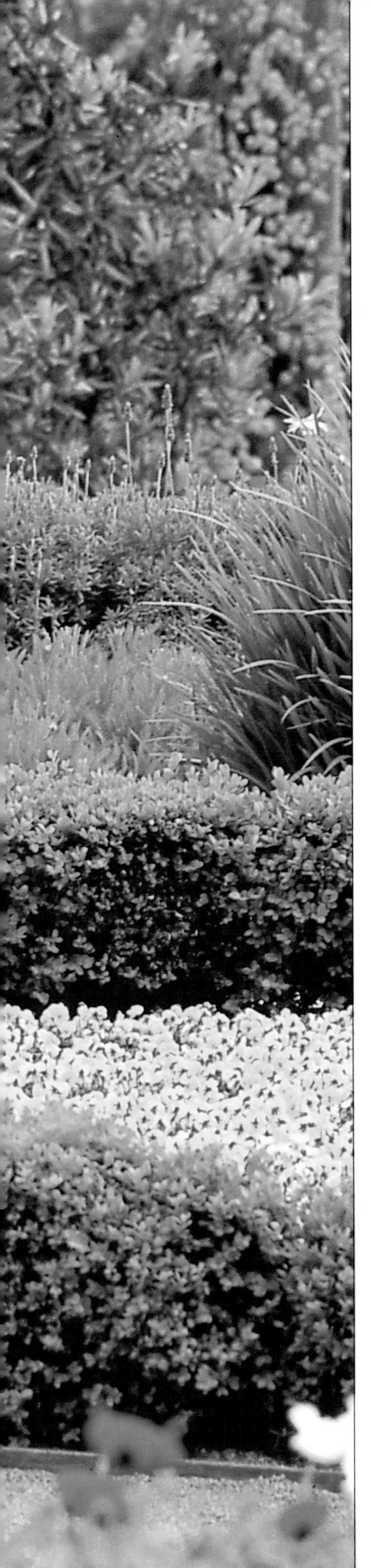

GROWING FLOWERING SHRUBS

Beautiful borders can be created almost entirely from shrubs—the bones of a garden. They impart form and character and complement trees and herbaceous perennials. All shrubs flower— and many that have small, modest flowers produce bright berries that ornament the late summer, fall, and winter garden.

Shrubs are usually defined as perennial woody plants. They are frequently multi-stemmed, but not always, and the line between tall shrubs and small trees is rather vague. Indeed, gardeners and professional horticulturists do not always agree. Shrubs may be evergreen or deciduous, leaves are small or large, glossy or matt, and come in a huge range of shapes. Some shrubs, such as hibiscus, have showy flowers. Others, such as box, have tiny, insignificant ones. Cotton lavender (*santolina*) and rosemary, among others, have aromatic foliage. A few— such as syringa, mock orange, and choisya—are prized for their sweetly perfumed blooms.

Shrubs come in every shape and size. There is a species or variety to suit virtually every situation. When you are planning a garden, select kinds that favour a particular position. Will the shrub thrive in full sun, or does it prefer shade? Consider how high and wide it will grow. Some shrubs can take up to 5–10 years to mature, become well established, and assume their final shape. Never buy a large-growing shrub for a small space, thinking you can prune it to keep it small. Repeated cutting back will spoil its natural symmetry and you will eventually come to hate it and thus remove it.

ABOVE: Brilliant red "Royal William"—a bounteous large-flowered rose.

LEFT: A sculpturally appealing symphony of golden pansies, box hedging, and green bottlebrush blooms of Euphorbia wulfenii.

PROPAGATION

Most shrubs are raised from stem cuttings. They may be grown from soft-tip cuttings (of, for example, hydrangea or fuchsia) taken in late spring and early summer; semi-ripe nodal cuttings of side shoots, or heel cuttings of shoots tugged from the main stem in midsummer—most shrubs being propagated this way; or from dormant hardwood cuttings of deciduous shrubs.

Soft-tip, semi-ripe nodal, and heel cuttings should be 2–4in long and taken from strong, healthy plants, preferably from stems that have not flowered. Hardwood cuttings of mature, dormant shoots, 10–12in long, are rooted in the fall, in a slit trench in the garden. Layering, that is, pegging down young, flexible stems close to the soil any time between spring and fall, is another easy way to multiply shrubs.

Soft-tip and semi-ripe nodal cuttings

Take these early in the day, when plump and dew-fresh. If you are not able to insert them into pots of compost immediately, enclose them in a plastic bag and keep them in a cool, shady place.

Use a very sharp knife or razor blade to remove all but the topmost two or three leaves. If the leaves are large, as in hydrangeas, it is best to shorten them by half their length. At the base of the cutting make a clean, horizontal cut, just below a node (joint) from which leaves appear. Encourage rapid rooting by dipping the cutting in hormone rooting compound. Prepare a rooting mix of three parts, by volume, of coarse, washed sand or Perlite and one part of peat or loam-based seed compost. Alternatively, use proprietary, peat-based cutting compost. Place the compost mix in a small, 4in pot and gently firm it. Make holes with a pencil where the cuttings are to go and insert them to a third of their length, about 2in apart.

Firm compost around the stems. You can place several cuttings in one pot. Water them in, allow compost to drain, then transfer them to a propagator or garden frame, or enclose them in an inflated plastic bag and place them on a windowsill. In warm conditions, soft-tip cuttings will root within 2–4 weeks. You can tell if a cutting has rooted if new leaves have formed and a gentle pull on the stem meets with resistance. A few weeks later, move the plant into a small pot of potting compost.

HARDWOOD CUTTINGS

They usually take many weeks or months to root. Leaves may form long before roots develop. They should be about 12in long and ¼–½in thick. Take them from the middle of well-ripened, current-year shoots. Prepare them by making a gently sloping cut just above the topmost bud and a horizontal cut immediately below the bottom node (joint). Next, in a sunny, well-drained area of deeply dug and friable soil, use a spade to take out a 6–8in deep trench with one vertical wall. Trickle a 1inch layer of sharp sand into it.

Insert cuttings to two-thirds their depth, 6in apart, pressing them into the sand. Tread soil firmly around them, hoe out footprints and water copiously.

Refirm cuttings in winter when hard frost lifts them. Roots will form in spring. By fall, plants will be ready for moving to where you wish to display them.

Some roses will grow quite readily from cuttings, but others will not grow vigorously on their own roots. Commercial nurseries "bud" rose varieties on to rootstocks of wild or species roses. (Budding is a form of grafting using dormant leaf buds.)

LAYERING

Take out a 6in hole next to the plant and remove any leaves that might be buried, from the selected shoot. Make a sloping, 1½in cut through a joint in the middle of the shoot and wedge open the cut with a matchstick. Half fill the hole with a mix of equal parts sharp sand and soil and then peg the cut part of the shoot into it. Cover the shoot with more of the same mix and tie the exposed end to a cane to keep it upright. Water the layer to settle the soil around it and place a large, flat stone over it to keep the soil damp.

About a year later, when roots have formed, sever the new shrub, or layer, from its parent by cutting the stem of the parent shrub where it enters the ground. Then leave your new shrub *in situ* or transplant it to a new position in the garden.

Some shrubs may be grown from seed, but only the species will produce plants that match their parent.

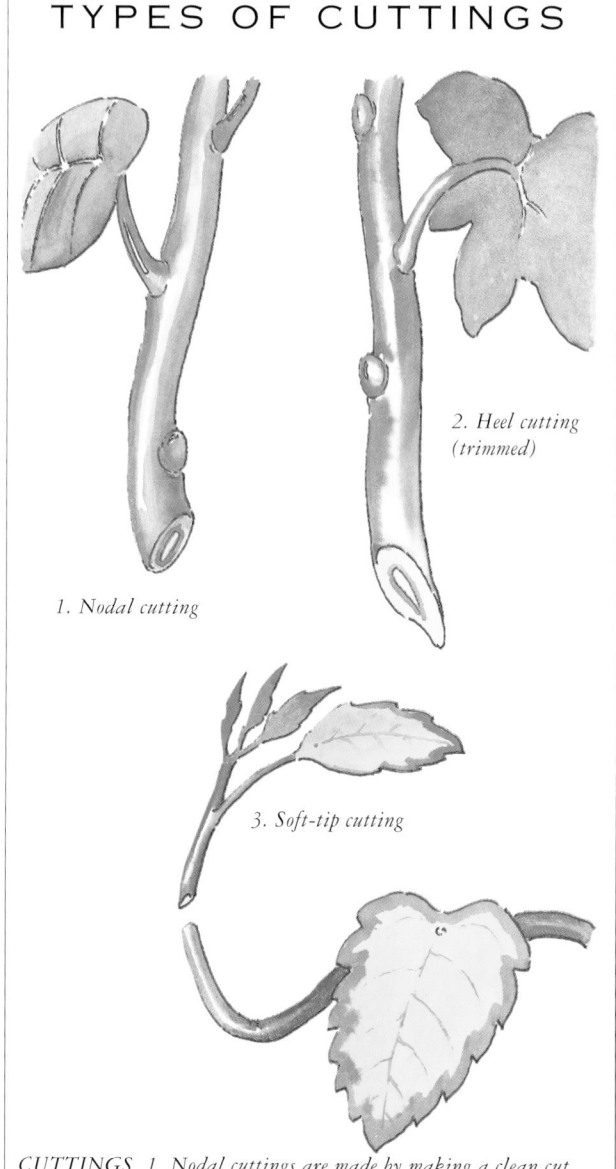

TYPES OF CUTTINGS

1. Nodal cutting

2. Heel cutting (trimmed)

3. Soft-tip cutting

CUTTINGS. 1. Nodal cuttings are made by making a clean cut ⅛in below a node (joint). 2. Heel cuttings are tugged from the main stem, to leave a tag of bark, which is trimmed back close to the base of the shoot. 3. Soft-tip cuttings are made from young, green shoot tips. Remove lower leaves (as here) before inserting in compost.

CHOOSING A PLANT

When choosing plants at a garden center, the biggest is not always the best. Look for those that are well shaped and have a good cover of healthy leaves. Avoid plants that have woody roots protruding from drainage holes, those that are excessively tall for the pot and those that have knobbly, thickened stem bases. All these features show that the plant is pot-bound and that it should have been moved into a larger container some time ago. All plants suffer from some degree of transplanting shock, but the smaller the plant the less traumatic the move. Ideally, select plants in bloom to ensure that you are getting the color and variety you want.

SOIL PREPARATION

Because most shrubs are fairly long-lived and form a garden's permanent framework, it is worth putting in a bit of time and effort into preparing a good home for them and thus protect your investment. Shrubs planted in suitable conditions will become established more quickly, and their healthy growth will be less vulnerable to attack by pests and disease than plants that are treated more hastily.

Few shrubs tolerate heavy, waterlogged soil. If drainage is poor, you may need to consider raising the planting area or installing subsoil drains. Heavy, clay soils can be improved by adding gypsum at the rate of 7–11oz per sq yd and by working in large quantities of well-rotted, organic material. Organic matter should be dug in several weeks ahead of planting. Sandy soils, in which water and nutrients are quickly lost, benefit greatly from the addition of large amounts of organic matter before planting. All plants and soils are better for being mulched with humus-forming, well-rotted animal manure, compost, leaf mould, straw, or decayed grass clippings, as these not only retain moisture in the soil but also keep the soil and plants well nourished. Mulches should only be laid on moist soil.

STRIKING SOFT-TIP CUTTINGS

1. TO TAKE A CUTTING, gather shoots when dew-fresh and place in a plastic bag. Prepare stems by trimming to length and cutting just below a node (joint). Keep cuttings cool and shaded. Remove lower leaves, which will rot if buried.

2. FILL A SMALL POT, which has plenty of drainage holes, with gritty cutting compost. Use a pencil to make holes for inserting cuttings to half their length. Firm compost around them.

3. WATER IN CUTTINGS well, but gently, taking care not to dislodge them. They should not need watering again until new growth indicates that roots have formed. If you are unsure of how dry the compost is, and the pot feels light, add just a little water.

4. MAKE A WIRE OR BAMBOO FRAME that fits inside the pot and is tall enough to clear cuttings. Place a plastic bag over the frame and secure it to the pot. The bag will keep air and soil moist. Root cuttings in good light but not direct sunlight.

FRAMED BY STATUESQUE CONIFERS and a fiery, fall-hued tree, crimson-flowered Hebe *"Great Orme" makes a fine focal point beside this gravel path. Usefully, this evergreen shrub starts blooming in July but seldom finishes before late October.*

PLANTING

With good soil preparation and correct planting techniques your shrubs should flourish. Most container-grown shrubs are transplanted throughout the year, provided the soil is crumbly and workable and frost is not forecast. In winter, in gardens prone to hard frost, it is best to transplant only dormant, deciduous plants.

Bare-rooted shrubs, usually deciduous, are planted when leaves have fallen—from fall to early spring.
• Check that the position chosen for your shrub will allow it to develop full height and spread without your having to cut it back. You should also cater for its other needs: soil type—heavy or light, warm and free-draining—and sun or shade.
• Dig a hole at least twice as wide as the plant's root system and about the same depth. Loosen soil in the bottom of the hole and around the sides. If it is clayey, work in grit or gravel to avoid creating a sump in which roots may drown.
• Do not put fresh manure into the hole. Instead, mix a balanced fertilizer, such as fish, blood, and bone meal, Growmore, or a slow-release brand, with soil you firm around the roots. Roots must not come into direct contact with fertilizer, which may burn them.
• If you are planting a container-grown shrub bought in a stiff plastic pot, thoroughly water the compost to loosen any roots clinging to the pot sides. Invert the plant and gently tap its pot rim on a hard surface so that the rootball slides out. Carefully tease out compacted, encircling roots from the rootball.
• Trim away any roots that are damaged.
• Place the plant in its hole, at the same depth that it was previously growing. Lay a cane over the hole, next to the plant, to check this. Backfill the hole with soil that you have dug out and tread the soil firmly around the rootball. Do not tread on the rootball itself.
• Water in thoroughly to remove any air pockets and settle the soil around the feeding root hairs.
• Mulch the root area, but keep mulch well clear of the stem, because its bark could rot. Organic mulches, such as manures and composts, help to condition soil and feed plants. They break down and disappear after a year or so, so replace them annually.

MAINTENANCE

Water newly planted shrubs regularly and copiously, specially in droughty weather until they are well established.

Re-feed fall-planted shrubs in spring, and spring- planted in summer, by topdressing (sprinkling) the root area with a complete plant food. Fish, blood, and bone meal or pelleted poultry manure is ideal for most shrubs, but avoid using poultry manure on lime-hating rhododendrons and summer-flowering heathers, among others.

PRUNING

Many shrubs will never need shoots removing unless you wish to rejuvenate very old plants or take out wayward stems. If you wish to cut back a spring-flowering plant, prune it when its blooms fade. The only exception to this is plants, such as firethorn and cotoneaster, that are grown for their berries. Shrubs, such as *Buddleja davidii*, that flower from mid- to late summer are best pruned the following spring.

To train a single-stemmed standard, select a young shrub with a straight stem and shorten laterals (side shoots) to within 1in of the trunk. These leafy stumps help to conduct sap to the head of the standard. If the main stem is slender—it usually is—you may need to tie it to a cane. As the stem lengthens, shorten further side shoots to an inch or so until the stem is as high as required—normally 4–6ft. Then, when the head is developing well, trim it to a ball shape and cut off side shoots flush with the stem.

HARDINESS

All plants mentioned flourish outdoors, apart from frost-tender ardisia, echium, oleander, plumbago, pomegranate, and heliotrope, which are normally overwintered in a greenhouse or conservatory and moved to a sheltered, sunny place for summer. Of the relatively hardy kinds, some in very cold, windswept, or frost-pocket gardens may need tucking up for winter. The best way to protect them is to cover them with an open-topped wigwam of bubble plastic or several layers of fiber fleece. Make sure the material does not touch the leaves or stems, or, if moist, it might rot them.

WHAT CAN GO WRONG?

Yellow leaves
• Plants have been overwatered or are too dry.
• Plants may need feeding: fertilize the plant with a high-nitrogen tonic if this has not been done for two or three months and see if there is any improvement within the next two or three weeks.
• Older leaves may turn bright yellow before dropping. Do not worry; they have finished their useful life.
• When new leaves on azaleas are pale yellow yet the veins are green, they probably require a dose of iron chelates, which aids chlorophyll production. Apply this in spring and early summer, carefully following the manufacturer's directions on the label.

Curled or distorted leaves
• Look for aphids (greenfly)—tiny, sticky, reddish-brown, gray, or green, sap-sucking insects clustering on new growth. Control them with an insecticide containing pirimicarb, permethrin, biollethrin, horticultural soap, rotenone, or pyrethrins. Spray at dusk when bees and other beneficial insects have retired for the night. Avoid spraying when it is hot, too, because foliage may be scorched by high temperatures.
• Some viruses manifest themselves this way and there is no cure. Consult reference books or experts to see if your plant has succumbed to one of these diseases. If affected, dig it up and burn it.
• Check that there has been no drift of any herbicide from nearby spraying. Even very small amounts of spray drift, especially from selective lawn weedkillers, can distort leaves of very sensitive plants, such as tomatoes and roses.

Black spots on leaves
• These may be fungal leaf spots. On roses, they are probably caused by black spot, a common disease that badly blotches leaves. Control it by spraying with bupirimate with triforine, penconazole, or myclobutanil. Ideally, improve air circulation around plants and avoid wetting leaves when watering, which should not be done late in the day. Large, brownish-black spots on camellias probably resulted from sunburn.

Gray-white powder on leaf surfaces
• This deposit is probably powdery mildew, which affects a wide range of plants. Roses, azaleas, hydrangeas, and many other shrubs are prone to this disease. Avoid watering late in the day and spray plants with bupirimate with triforine, myclobutanil, sulfur or penconazole. It is worse on wall shrubs in dry areas where air does not freely circulate.

Mottled leaves
• This is usually associated with sap-sucking insects such as scale, thrip, lace bug, and red spider mite, which is not a true insect. Stressed, rather than healthy, plants are more liable to be attacked by these insects. Plants may be stressed by drought or overwatering, or by simply growing them away from their favored aspect.
• Limpet-like scale insects come in various sizes and colors. Control small infestations by using a damp cloth to wipe them off leaves and stems. Eradicate severe infestations by spraying plants with malathion
• Thrips and lace bugs may be reduced by hosing the underside of leaves or by spraying with pyrethrins, malathion, pirimiphos-methyl, permethrin or insecticidal soap.
• In hot, dry weather, red spider mite can be a problem on shrubs growing in rain-sheltered spots, such as under the house eaves. Hosing the foliage helps to keep them down and obviate the need for spraying. If you have to resort to insecticides, malathion, bifenthrin, and pirimiphos-methyl are effective.

Holes in leaves or on leaf margins
• This may be snail or slug damage. Snails often lurk high up on the foliage. Baiting is not effective in this instance, so pick off and kill pests. Eradicate the ground-hugging tribe by sprinkling blue-dyed molluscicide pellets containing metaldehyde or methiocarb, thinly around susceptible, soft-stemmed plants. Alternatively, ring them with grit.
• Caterpillars also chew leaves. Tackle them by hand

picking or biologically controlling them with *Bacillus thuringiensis*. Effective insecticides include permethrin, bifenthrin, and pirimiphos-methyl.

Stems and leaves webbed or matted together
• Webbing caterpillars, such as those of the lackey moth, can cover buds and new shoots and extensively defoliate trees and shrubs. Pull out the webbing with a gloved hand or cut out the damaged section. Spray with permethrin, bifenthrin or pirimiphos-methyl, or control the pest biologically with *Bacillus thuringiensis*. Inspect shrubs several times a year to control this pest in its early stages.

Sooty mould (a dry, black coating on leaf surfaces)
• A fungus, sooty mould feeds on sticky honeydew secreted by sap-sucking insects, such as aphids and scales. Once the pest is controlled, the mould will gradually disappear. Hosing helps. Wipe large-leaved plants with a damp cloth.

Sudden death of plant
• If leaves turn brown but remain attached to the plant, the plant has probably died from root rot. Root systems may have been damaged by excessive watering—from rain or irrigation—quite some time before the plant expires, especially in cool weather. When plants are stressed by extreme heat or wind, damaged root systems cannot cope and death follows quickly.
• If a plant is suffering from drought, its leaves may be brown and rapidly drop when watered.

Pomegranate fruits may appear in a warm garden.

ABELIA
Abelia

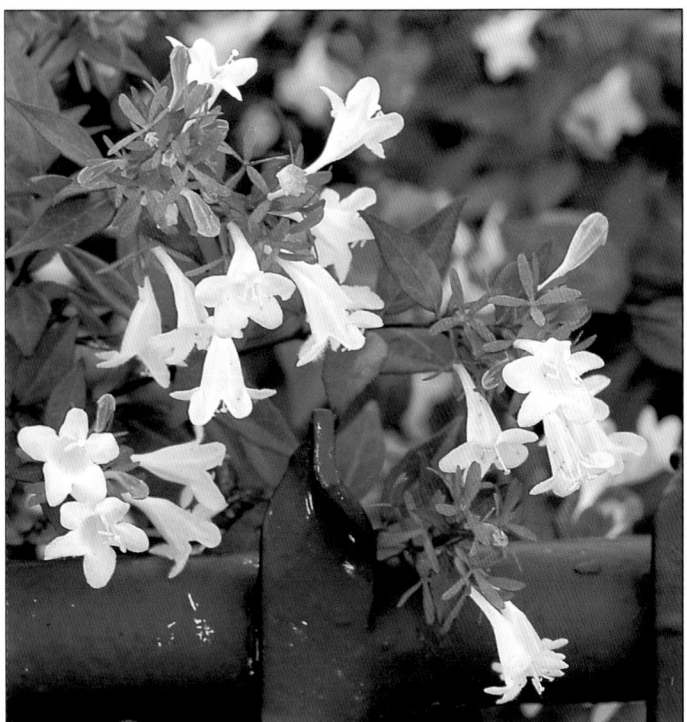

Abelia's pretty pink flowers appear at the end of summer. Striking, red calyces prolong the display.

An informal abelia hedge adds a little magic to a sunny and sheltered garden. Trim it lightly in spring.

FEATURES

Semi-evergreen and vigorous in mild districts, *Abelia* × *grandiflora* makes a dashing statement and a fine flowering hedge. From July to September, its arching shoots, clad with small, oval, pointed leaves, 4–5ft long, are sleeved with showy heads of tubular, pale pink flowers with reddish calyces. The decorative calyx persists into late fall.
"Francis Mason" is a stunning variety with golden-variegated leaves that complement a wealth of pink blossom. Other prized kinds are lilac-pink *A. chinensis* "Edward Goucher" and rosy-lilac *A. schumannii*.

ABELIA AT A GLANCE

Sporting clusters of pink or lilac flowers from late summer to fall, it needs a sheltered position. Hardy to 14°F (zone 8).

Jan	/	
Feb	/	Recommended Varieties
Mar	prune	*A. chinensis* "Edward Goucher"
Apr	plant, prune	*A.* × *grandiflora*
May	plant	*A.* × *grandiflora* "Francis Mason"
June	plant	*A. schumannii*
July	plant, flower	
Aug	plant, flower	
Sept	plant, flower	
Oct	/	
Nov	/	
Dec	/	

CONDITIONS

Aspect　Thriving in full sun and tolerating very light shade, abelia is best planted against a sheltered, south- or west-facing wall.

Site　Abelia prospers in a wide range of well-drained soils, from clay-loam to sand. Enrich rapid-draining, chalky, and sandy soils with well-rotted and moisture-conserving, bulky organic materials.

GROWING METHOD

Feeding　Topdress the root area with bone meal in spring and fall to encourage sturdy growth and profuse blooms.
Water freely after planting and mulch thickly with old manure, bark, cocoa shell, or rotted garden compost to keep roots cool and active.

Propagation　Take soft-tip cuttings in late spring and semi-ripe cuttings from mid- to late summer.

Problems　Shoots are brittle and easily snapped, so be careful when pruning and planting.

PRUNING

Flowers form on current-year shoots. Once mature, keep it youthful by cutting out a third of its oldest branches in spring.

ABUTILON VITIFOLIUM
Abutilon

In a sheltered, sunny spot, Abutilon vitifolium *becomes a glowing sentinel of saucer-shaped, pale to deep mauve blooms in early summer.*

Plant award-winning "Canary Bird" in a fertile, sun-soaked spot and enjoy a summer-long succession of pendent blooms.

FEATURES

There are few more exhilarating, summer sights than a mature shrub of *Abutilon vitifolium* festooned with white to purple-blue, saucer-shaped blooms. Studding stems clothed with three- to five-lobed, soft,gray, hairy leaves are flowers that have you looking closely at them. Making an upright "obelisk" to around 15ft, this shrub is worth a little cosseting—as are its eye-catching varieties, mauve-flowered "Veronica Tennant" and "Tennant's White".
Closely related *A. × suntense*, a fast-growing hybrid to 12ft, rewards us with pendent, white to violet-blue "saucers".
Choice forms of this hybrid are purple-blue "Geoffrey Gorer," white "Gorer's White," deep mauve "Jermyns," and dark violet-blue "Violetta". Look out, too, for "Canary Bird," whose radiant lemon-yellow blooms illuminate a border.

ABUTILON AT A GLANCE

Loosely branched, deciduous shrub sleeved with saucer-shaped, white, blue, or purple blooms in summer. Hardy to 32°F (zone 10)

Jan	/	Recommended Varieties
Feb	/	
Mar	/	*A. × suntense*
Apr	plant, prune	"Geoffrey Gorer"
May	plant	"Gorer's White"
		"Jermyns"
June	flower, plant	"Ralph Gould"
July	flower, prune	"Violetta"
Aug	plant	*A. vitifolium* "Tennant's
Sept	plant	White"
Oct	/	*A. vitifolium* "Veronica
Nov	/	Tennant"
Dec	/	

CONDITIONS

Aspect Position all varieties in full sun where shoots grow stocky and are massed with bloom. Make sure abutilon is sheltered from shoot-killing, icy winds.

Site This shrub tolerates a wide range of well-drained soils, but for the best results enrich the planting area with plenty of crumbly organic matter.

GROWING METHOD

Feeding For the strongest shoots and bounteous blossom, topdress the root area with fish, blood, and bone meal or Growmore in spring and midsummer.
Water young plants regularly and mulch them with bulky organics to keep soil cool.
In long, dry spells, take out a moat around the plant and fill it repeatedly with water. When subsoil is soaked, replace excavated soil and cover with moisture-conserving mulch.

Propagation Increase favoured varieties from semi-ripe cuttings from mid- to late summer.
A. vitifolium produces masses of fertile seed.

Problems Control aphids colonizing soft stems by spraying with pirmicarb, pyrethrins, or insecticidal soap. Leaves may be damaged by caterpillars and other chewing insects. If damage is slight, ignore it. If severe, control these pests biologically with *Bacillus thuringiensis*, or apply rotenone or pirimiphos-methyl.

PRUNING

Keep bushes compact and packed with flowering shoots by cutting back dead or dying stems to healthy growth in mid-spring. In early summer, shorten flowered stems to two-thirds their length.

SILVER WATTLE
Acacia dealbata

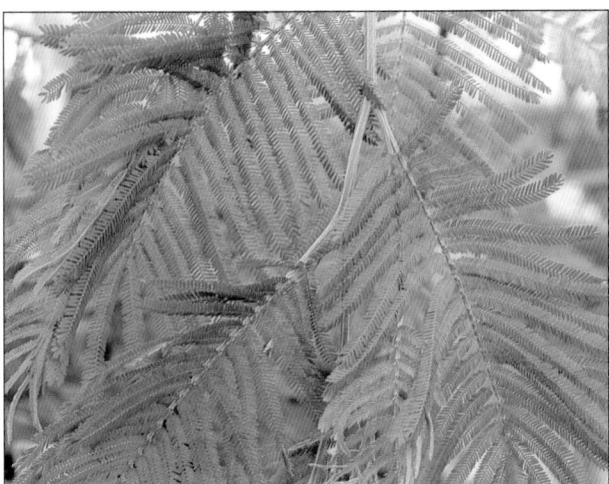

Silver wattle's ferny, silvery-green leaves are appealing all year round, specially if shoots are fan-trained against a warm wall.

There are few more riveting sights in a sheltered garden in early spring than Acacia dealbata *in full flower.*

FEATURES

There are around 900 species of wattle but only *Acacia dealbata* is sufficiently hardy for planting outdoors in mild districts. Rapidly growing to around 12ft, its soft shoots are richly and appealingly clothed with ferny and silvery-sheened, evergreen leaves.

In April, year-old shoots are thickly clustered with small, double pompoms of fragrant, bright yellow blossom.

Ideally, because several days of temperatures hovering around freezing point may kill shoots, it is best fan-trained against a warm, south-facing wall.

Only in relatively frost-free districts can you successfully grow it as a free-standing shrub in the open garden. Elsewhere, set it in a large pot or tub and grow it in a conservatory, moving it outdoors into the open garden only for summer.

SILVER WATTLE AT A GLANCE

An evergreen, tender tree with silvery, ferny leaves and bobbles of yellow flowers in spring. Hardy to 32°F (zone 10).

Jan	/	Recommended Varieties
Feb	flower	
Mar	flower	*A. dealbata*
Apr	plant, flower	
May	prune, plant	
June	plant	
July	plant	
Aug	plant	
Sept	plant	
Oct	/	
Nov	/	
Dec	/	

CONDITIONS

Aspect Choose a warm, sunny site, ideally very sheltered and facing south or south-west, where it will not be exposed to leaf-blackening easterly or northerly winds.

Site Any well-drained, lime-free soil suits it. Fortify thin, sandy, or gravelly soils with bulky, humus-enriching manure, or well-rotted garden compost. Aerate heavy clay by working in plenty of grit or shingle. Alternatively, if puddles lie, dig a 18in drainage trench, leading to a soakaway, and fill it with gravel or rubble to within 8in of the soil surface.

GROWING METHOD

Feeding Encourage robust growth by annually sprinkling fish, blood, and bone meal, or Growmore over the rooting area in April and July. Water young plants regularly, especially in droughty spells, to help them develop a good, questing root system. Acacia appreciates occasional deep watering.

Propagation Increase acacia from semi-ripe cuttings in midsummer. Also grow from seed. Speed germination by soaking seeds overnight in hot water to soften the seed coat. Sow directly.

Problems Fortunately, it is seldom attacked by sap-sucking pests or caterpillars. If aphids cluster on shoots and cripple them, control them with pirimicarb, horticultural soap, or permethrin.

PRUNING

No regular pruning is necessary. In spring, shorten any stems killed by frost back to healthy side shoots. If acacia outgrows its situation, reduce wayward stems by up to two-thirds in late spring.

CORAL BERRY
Ardisia crenata

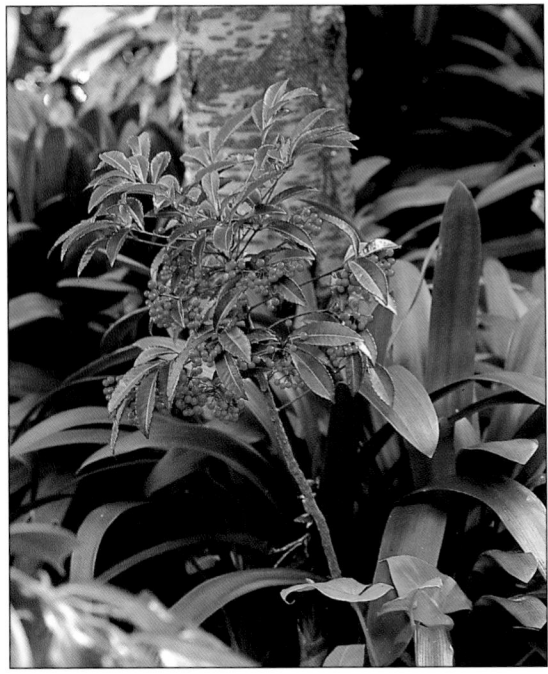

Fetching when enhancing a patio in summer, or conservatory in winter, ardisia is famed for its large clusters of scarlet berries.

A choice, compact evergreen, ardisia's panoply of white flowers in summer prelude a bounteous display of fruits.

FEATURES

Frost-sensitive, this evergreen shrub, clothed with attractive, rounded, toothed, and glossy, leathery leaves, has much to commend it. Coveted for its sprays of small, white, summer flowers, followed by a fetching and long-lasting display of bright red berries, it is easy to manage. Seldom more than 3ft high and across, it is normally grown in a large pot and confined to a frost-free conservatory in which temperatures are at least 20°F above freezing. In early summer when frosts finish, ardisia can be moved to highlight a lightly shaded patio.

CORAL BERRY AT A GLANCE

Sculptural evergreen with glossy leaves. White, summer flowers are followed by bright scarlet berries. Hardy to 50°F (zone 11).

		Recommended Varieties
Jan	/	
Feb	/	*A. crenata*
Mar	/	
Apr	plant, prune	
May	plant	
Jun	plant	
July	flower	
Aug	flower	
Sept	flower	
Oct	/	
Nov	/	
Dec	/	

CONDITIONS

Aspect Outdoors, ardisia prefers a shaded to semi-shaded position sheltered from strong winds. Indoors, from early fall to late spring, display it in a lightly shaded conservatory.

Site Help it excel by setting it in a large pot of John Innes potting compost No. 3. Based on moisture-retentive loam, it reduces the need for watering and encourages robust growth.

GROWING METHOD

Feeding Encourage lustrous leaves and bounteous flowers and fruits by feeding weekly with a high-potash liquid fertilizer from spring to late summer. Alternatively, add a slow-release fertilizer to the compost in spring and replace it a year later. Water regularly from spring to fall to keep the compost nicely moist, but ease up from fall to winter when growth is slower. Cease feeding too.

Propagation Take soft-tip cuttings in spring or summer.
Problems Plants are occasionally attacked by sap-sucking scale insects, which cling like limpets to stems and leaves. Control them by spraying with malathion. Well-grown plants are seldom troubled by pests.

PRUNING

Ardisia is neat and symmetrical and cutting back is not normally necessary. If it grows too large, shorten stems to side shoots in spring.

BARBERRY
Berberis thunbergii

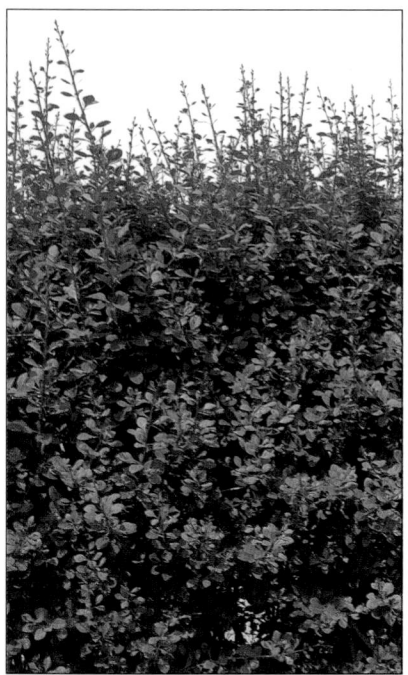

Berberis thunbergii *"Atropurpurea" glows with sunset hues in fall.*

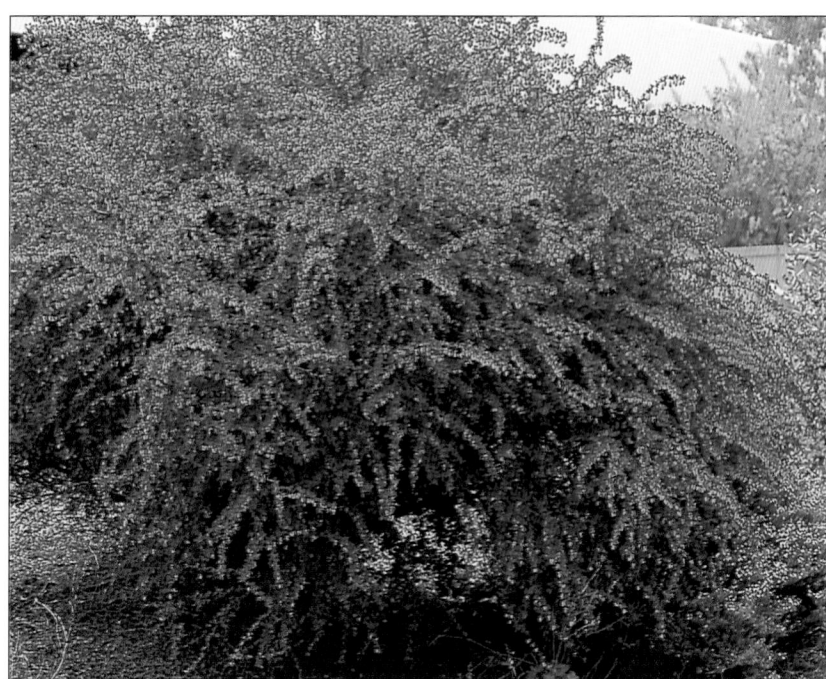

Berberis stenophylla *brightens spring with a globe of yellow blossom. Keep it youthful by shearing off faded blooms in late spring.*

FEATURES

A huge, easy family of evergreen and deciduous species and varieties, berberis will grow almost anywhere. Small bushes enhance a rock garden; larger kinds light up a border or form a burglar-proof hedge. The most popular leaf-shedding kind is *Berberis thunbergii*. A dense, rounded shrub to about 5ft high and across, it is armed with long, sharp spines. Long-lived, with small, bright yellow flowers that sleeve slender, whippy stems and cheer spring, its leaves turn scarlet in fall. Bright red berries are a winter feature. Reddish-purple-leaved *B. thunbergii* "Atropurpurea"

becomes a firebrand in October. Other choice varieties of *B. thunbergii* ideal for small gardens are golden-leaved "Aurea," purple-blackish-leaved "Dart's Red Lady" and "Harlequin". Fetching, evergreen kinds are *B. × stenophylla* and *B. candidula*.

CONDITIONS

Aspect	Very hardy. Deciduous kinds especially resist icy winds. Berberis needs full sun to flower and fruit freely, but will tolerate light shade.
Site	Berberis prospers on a wide range of soils, from sand to heavy, often waterlogged clay.

GROWING METHOD

Feeding	Work bone meal into the root area in the fall. Water copiously and regularly in the first year after planting, to encourage good growth. Thereafter, little watering is necessary.
Propagation	Layer shoots from spring to fall, or take semi-ripe cuttings from early to mid-fall.
Problems	Control rust disease by spraying with a proprietary spray.

PRUNING

Bushes:	Apart from cutting back frost-damaged shoots in May, no regular pruning is needed. Renew old gaunt bushes by cutting back a third of the older stems to near ground level in April.
Hedges:	Trim when blooms fade in spring.

BARBERRY AT A GLANCE

Undemanding shrubs—many have fiery fall leaf tints—bearing yellow or orange spring flowers. Hardy to -13ºF (zone 5).

Jan	/	Recommended Varieties
Feb	/	
Mar	plant	Deciduous
Apr	flower, prune	*B. thunbergii*
May	flower, plant	*B. thunbergii* "Atropurpurea"
June	plant	*B. thunbergii* "Dart's Red Lady"
July	plant	
Aug	plant	*B. thunbergii* "Aurea"
Sept	plant	*B. thunbergii* "Harlequin"
Oct	plant	Evergreen
Nov	plant	*B. candidula*
Dec	/	*B. × stenophylla*

BUTTERFLY BUSH
Buddleja davidii

Irresistible to butterflies that cluster on its nectar-rich flowers, varieties of Buddleja davidii *make summer special.*

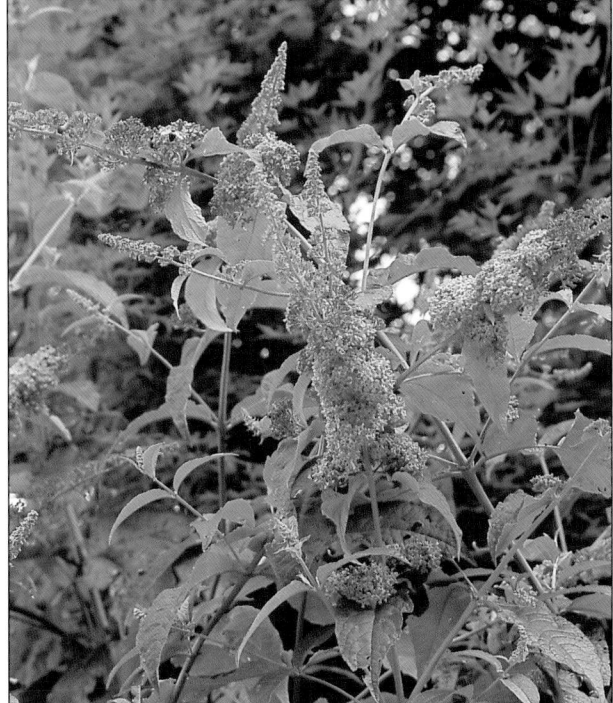

Spectacular blooms, large handsome leaves and an ability to grow almost anywhere sunny, buddleja is a good choice for beginners.

FEATURES

There are three distinctive, hardy species: deciduous *Buddleja davidii*, whose cone-shaped flowers are dark purple, purplish red, pink, white, or blue; *B. alternifolia*, yielding a waterfall of shoots sleeved with soft purple flowers; and evergreen *B. globosa*, with its clusters of small orange balls.

CONDITIONS

Aspect   These plants perform best in full sun, but tolerate slight shade; *B. davidii* resists chilly winds.

Site   Thriving in most soils, they prefer a well-drained position enriched with organic matter.

GROWING METHOD

Feeding   Boost growth by sprinkling bone meal around the shrub in April and October and hoeing it in. Take care not to damage roots. Water new plants regularly in spring and summer to encourage robust growth and bounteous blossom. Mulching helps to retain soil moisture in droughty spells.

Propagation   All kinds are easily increased from soft-tip cuttings in early summer and hardwood cuttings in the fall.

Problems   Control leaf-crippling aphids with pirimicarb, rotenone, permethrin, or pyrethrins. *B. alternifolia*, grown as a standard, needs staking throughout its life.

PRUNING

B. davidii: Cut back the previous year's flowering shoots to within 2in of the base in March.

B. alternifolia and globosa: Unlike *B. davidii*, which flowers on its current-year shoots, both *B. alternifolia* and *B. globosa* bloom on wood produced the previous year. Keep them youthful and flowering freely by shortening to the base a third of the oldest stems when the flowers fade.

BUTTERFLY BUSH AT A GLANCE

Hardy, deciduous, and evergreen or semi-evergreen shrubs. Cones or globes of blossom light up summer. Hardy to 14°F (zone 8).

		Recommended Varieties
Jan	/	
Feb	/	*B. alternifolia*
Mar	plant, prune	*B. davidii* "Black Knight"
Apr	plant	*B. davidii* "Dartmoor"
May	plant	*B. davidii* "Empire Blue"
June	flower, plant	*B. davidii* "Peace"
July	flower, plant	*B. davidii* "Pink Delight"
Aug	flower, plant	*B. davidii* "Santana"
Sept	plant	*B. fallowiana* "Alba"
Oct	plant	*B. globosa*
Nov	plant	*B. × weyeriana*
Dec	/	

Butterfly bush varieties

LEFT: Buddleja globosa, also known as the orange ball tree, bears a wealth of blossom on new shoots in June.

RIGHT: Deep purple Buddleja "Black Knight" associates strikingly with ferny and silvery-leaved Artemisia "Powis Castle".

ABOVE: Plant "Peace," a large white-flowered form of Buddleja davidii, to contrast with a deep green conifer.

BELOW: "Pink Delight" is famed for its immense and long-lasting blooms, which complement large and gray-green leaves.

ABOVE: Dramatic from spring to fall, "Harlequin's glowing red flowers tip elegant, wand-like shoots sleeved with cream or yellow-margined leaves.

ABOVE: "Nanho Purple" is a small variety in all its parts and is good for narrow borders or small yards.

BOX
Buxus

Drought-resisting common box makes a tight, neat plant in full sun. Tiny, yellow flowers stud shoots in spring.

Here, box clipped to create serpentine hedges focuses attention on the beauty of the brick paving, raised lily pond and garden bench.

FEATURES

Both common box (*Buxus sempervirens*), to around 15ft, and lower-growing, small-leaved (Japanese) box (*B. microphylla japonica*) are favored for planting in tubs and large pots and clipping into drumsticks, spirals, balls, pyramids, and other forms of topiary. *B. sempervirens* "Suffruticosa" makes the best low hedge. Box is long-lived and slow growing. If unclipped, it attains little more than 3ft within 4–5 years.

Common box has darker, more pointed foliage than the Japanese form, where leaves are shinier and lighter green. In spring, tiny, starry, and delicately perfumed, yellowish-green flowers appear in leaf axils.

BOX AT A GLANCE

A hardy evergreen for topiary or low hedges. Variegated forms must be positioned in full sun. Hardy to -13°F (zone 5).

JAN	/	RECOMMENDED VARIETIES
FEB	/	*B. microphylla* "Winter Gem"
MAR	/	
APR	flower, prune	*B. microphylla* "Faulkner"
MAY	plant, prune	*B. sempervirens*
JUNE	flower, plant	*B. sempervirens* "Handsworthensis"
JULY	plant, prune	
AUG	plant, prune	*B. sempervirens* "Suffruticosa"
SEPT	plant	*B. sempervirens* "Elegantissima"
OCT	/	
NOV	/	
DEC	/	

CONDITIONS

Aspect Plants are more compact in full sun than shade, in which the foliage has less appeal. Creamy-mottled forms must be grown in good light or the variegation will fade to green.

Soil Box thrives on chalk but also prospers on a wide range of other soils. Good drainage is vital. Enrich impoverished areas with bulky organic manure several weeks before planting.

GROWING METHOD

Feeding Encourage lusterous leaves by fortifying planting holes with fish, blood and bone meal or Growmore, and topdressing the root area with bone meal in spring and fall. These plants are not heavy feeders and normally flourish if you do forget to fertilize them. Established box tolerate fairly dry conditions.

Propagation Box species can be grown from seed but varieties must be increased from semi-ripe cuttings from early to mid-fall. Plants may also be divided in mid-spring.

Problems If not fed regularly, box is rather slow to establish on poor, sandy soil.

PRUNING

After planting, use hedging shears to shorten shoots by a third to encourage a bushy habit. Trim hedges and topiary from April to August. If a bush is old and gaunt and needs revitalizing, cut it hard back in April or May. Keep stumps moist to help them sprout. Cut out any all-green shoots on variegated plants.

BOTTLEBRUSH
Callistemon

Bottlebrush flowers are most commonly bright red but they can also be mauve, cream, and gold. It is obvious how this evergreen shrub gained its name.

A handsome shrub, callistemon thrives in a sheltered, sunny spot.

FEATURES

Commonly called bottlebrush because its flower—principally stamens—reminds you of a bottle cleaner, the blooms enclasp slender stems clad with narrow, deep green leaves. There are several choice kinds. Hardiest is reckoned to be *Callistemon sieberi*, whose spikes of creamy-yellow flowers appear from late spring to summer. Also appealing are willow-leaved *C. salignus*, a species that glows with red, pink, or mauve flowers; *C. rigidus*, another hardyish, red-flowered kind for "borderline" gardens; and rich matt-red *C. linearis*, the narrow-leaved bottlebrush. Lemon-scented *C. citrinus* "Splendens" treats us to a memorable display of soft, pinkish-red, new shoots and vivid crimson flowers. All grow to around 7ft. Create a focus by underplanting a wall-trained shrub with white petunias.

BOTTLEBRUSH AT A GLANCE

An evergreen, frost-tender shrub with scarlet or creamy-yellow, bottlebrush flowers in June and July. Hardy to 23°F (zone 9).

Jan	/	Recommended Varieties
Feb	/	
Mar	/	*C. citrinus* "Splendens"
Apr	plant, prune	*C. linearis*
May	plant	*C. rigidus*
Jun	flower, plant	*C. salignus*
July	flower, prune	*C. sieberi*
Aug	plant	
Sept	plant	
Oct	/	
Nov	/	
Dec	/	

CONDITIONS

Aspect Callistemon flowers best if fan-trained against a sheltered, sunny wall that is never shaded. This showy Australian is not for chilly gardens whipped by icy winds. If in doubt, consign it to a conservatory.

Soil Preferring organically rich, light, loamy soil that drains freely, it thrives in clay if you add grit and bulky organics to improve aeration.

GROWING METHOD

Feeding Callistemon copes reasonably well without added fertilizer but performs better if fed with fish, blood, and bone meal in spring and midsummer.
Water new plantings regularly to encourage robust growth and rapid establishment. Mature plants tolerate long, dry periods but flower more profusely if the soil is moist.

Propagation The species are easily grown from seed, but named varieties must be raised from semi-ripe cuttings, ideally with a heel of wood, in late summer.

Problems Avoid alkaline soils in which leaves may turn pale yellow and die, and north- or east-facing sites, where cold winds may shrivel new shoots.

PRUNING

Trimming is not normally required, but occasional cutting back when blooms fade helps to keep growth compact and branches furnished with fresh green shoots.
Old shrubs can be rejuvenated if you prune them back quite hard in spring, but remove only a third of the bush in any one year. Keep stumps moist to encourage new growth.

CAMELLIA
Camellia

The exquisite beauty of delicately tinted camellia blooms—so effective in a vase—makes spring memorable.

Lime hating and thriving on deep, cool, leafy soil, flamboyant and long-flowering camellias associate stunningly with azaleas.

FEATURES

Glossy-leaved and showered with blossom, evergreen camellias are a great asset. Some species and varieties flower successively from late fall through to spring. Blooms are white, pink, deep rose, or crimson, and suffusions of these colors. Ranging in size from 4–15ft, most varieties flower when 2–3 years old and mature within ten years. They grow to a great age. Plant them to form a statement in a lawn or mixed shrub border, or set them in a large pot or tub and clip them to form a loose obelisk, pyramid or drumstick. They also make a dashing flowering hedge.

CAMELLIA AT A GLANCE

Evergreen, frost-tender, or hardy shrub with single, semi-double, or fully double blooms. Hardiness according to species.

Jan	flower	Recommended Varieties
Feb	flower	
Mar	flower	*C. japonica* "Adolphe Audusson"
Apr	plant	
May	plant, prune	*C. japonica* "Berenice Boddy"
June	plant, prune	*C. reticulata* "Captain Rawes"
July	plant	
Aug	plant	*C. sasanqua* "Fuji-No-Mine"
Sept	plant	*C. sasanqua* "Nodami-Ushiro"
Oct	flower	
Nov	flower	*C.* × *williamsii* "Donation"
Dec	flower	"Jury's Yellow"

Selection

Most camellias species come from China and Japan; some from N. India and the Himalayas. They have now been extensively hybridised to yield a wide range of varieties. Specialist camellia nurseries and garden centers display flowering plants in spring. Choose a variety suited to the position you have in mind.

Types

There are four main types of camellia.
Camellia japonica: Large and glossy leaved, hardier varieties will prosper in sheltered spots. Its varieties brighten fall to spring.
C. sasanqua: Fall-flowered, from October to December, it thrives outdoors in the south. In cooler areas, varieties are better planted in pots, displayed outdoors for summer and transferred to a cool conservatory, porch or greenhouse for flowering in fall.
C. reticulata: Flowering from February to April, varieties can be grown outside in warm, sheltered, gardens. Elsewhere, display them under glass.
C. × *williamsii*: Producing tough, weather-resistant foliage, and flowering from November to April, its varieties bloom freely despite low light intensity. Each group is discussed in more detail on pages 348–349.

CONDITIONS

Aspect

Camellias grow best in sheltered, dappled shade. In cooler climates, set them in full sun or very light shade to ensure that blossom buds develop from July to October. Protect them from hot, drying, or frosty winds.

CAMELLIA

ABOVE: Vigorous and compact, Camellia japonica "Nuccio's Gem" is a formal, double variety with spirally arranged petals. Just a whiff of frost can result in brown-speckled petals.

BELOW: "Scentuous" is a small, informal, double hybrid of Camellia japonica "Tiffany" and the species C. lutchuensis. Its creamy-white flowers have pale pink outer petals and the perfume of C. lutchuensis. It blooms profusely.

RIGHT: Dense, upright, and slow growing, "Wilamina" is a small, double, incurved variety of Camellia japonica. Blooms last well when cut and hold for a long time on the bush.

BELOW: Prized for its deep pink, outer petals that shade into a creamy-white center, "Buttons and Bows," is a medium-sized, formal, double hybrid of Camellia saluenensis. It flowers over a long period.

RIGHT: "Wynne Rayner" is a saluenensis seedling. From early to mid-spring, a profusion of blooms is borne on freely branching stems clad with smallish, glossy green leaves

Camellia sasanqua

Sasanquas start the camellia season by producing flowers, depending on variety, from fall to mid-winter. They make a wonderful show in a sheltered border or cool conservatory.

The smaller, more compact varieties, such as single, rose-pink "Tanya" and double, bright rose-red "Shishigashira," make good container plants.

Others worth a little cosseting are fast-growing "Fuji-No-Mine," whose pure white, double blooms are borne on slender shoots; and bushy, upright "Nodami-Ushiro," a sumptuous, semi-double, deep pink that pleases for weeks.

Camellia reticulata

This species presents us with the largest and most spectacular of all camellia blooms, but the shrubs themselves have a sparse, open-branching habit. Many of the more recently developed hybrids are crosses between C. japonica and C. reticulata. The result is a more leafy shrub that blooms longer with flowers that are more impressive.

To perform well, C. reticulata needs lighter, more free-draining soil than other camellias. Choice varieties are rose-pink "Arbutus Gum" and carmine-rose "Captain Rawes".

Camellia japonica

This is the species that most people think of when camellias are mentioned. There is a wide range of varieties in white to pale or dark pink or red. There are picotee and bicolors. They are usually classified by flower type: that is, single, semi-double, and formal double. There are also peony and anemone forms.

VARIETIES

ABOVE: *A rapturous but seldom seen white, flushed-pink, and semi-double variety of* Camellia vernalis, *"Star Upon Star" is usually grouped with* C. sasanqua *because of similarities in habit and uses. Blooming late in spring, it is an upright grower and ideal for small gardens and patio pots.*

BELOW: *"Betty Ridley," a rarely seen, sumptuous, and profusely blooming, formal, double variety of* Camellia japonica, *is worth seeking from a specialist grower. Here it is compared with the tiny pink flower of the species,* C. rosiflora.

BELOW: *"Desire," a large, formal, double variety of* Camellia japonica, *bears arresting, mainly white petals, with rims delicately flushed with cerise pink.*

ABOVE: *A collector's piece you may have to search for, "Lois Shinault" is a large-flowered variety of* Camellia reticulata, *whose semi-double, orchid-pink flowers of fluted petals display a showy boss of golden stamens.*

Some varieties produce sports—flowers of a different color to the parent's. These "sports" are a source of new varieties. Varieties of *C. japonica*—they flower from late fall to spring—may be grown in patio tubs or planted as border specimens. They also provide a fabulous backcloth to smaller shrubs and herbaceous perennials. Varieties include: White—"Mary Costa": Unusual anemone form with incurving petals; upright growth. "Lily Pons": Single to semi-double with long, narrow petals around a barrel of stamens.

Pink—"Berenice Boddy": Semi-double; light pink with deeper pink under petals. Vigorous, spreading. Red—"Adolphe Audusson": Semi-double; good glossy leaves, open upright growth. "C. M. Hovey": Formal double rose red; freely produced blooms. Bicolor—"Lavinia Maggi": Formal double; carmine-red and pink stripes on a white background. Picotee—"Margaret Davis" Informal double to loose peony; white petals rimmed with red; upright.

Camellia × williamsii

This is a very fine group of camellias bred by crossing *C. japonica* with *C. saluenensis*. The original crosses were made in Cornwall by J.C. Williams, who gave them their name. Available in the same color range as other camellias, most are semi-double. Eagerly sought are: semi-double, orchid-pink "Donation;" anemone-centered, creamy-white "Jury's Yellow;" deep rose-pink "Elegant Beauty," also with an anemone center; and formal, vibrant, double, pink "Water Lily."

CAMELLIA

Some Camellia reticulata *varieties reward you with a breathtaking display of large, ruffled blooms from mid-winter to spring.*

Rare Camellia lutchuensis *treats you to a bounty of small and deliciously scented blooms from fall to spring.*

Site Ideally, position plants where early morning sunlight does not heat up frosted blossom buds and cause frozen tissues to rupture. Sasanqua varieties tolerate more sun than most other camellias and reticulatas need full sun for part of the day. Some varieties of *Camellia japonica*, such as "The Czar" and "Emperor of Russia," happily take full sun. They need very acid, well-drained soil rich in decomposed organic matter. Heavy, badly drained soils cause root rot and plants often die. Fortify thin, sandy soils with well-rotted leaf mould or bulky manure, before planting.

GROWING METHOD

Feeding Encourage lustrous leaves and a wealth of blossom by applying a balanced ericaceous fertilizer in April and July. It is vital that border soil or container compost is always moist, so water daily, if necessary, during prolonged hot spells. Mulch with crumbly, bulky organic manure to conserve moisture, but keep it well away from the stem, lest it causes bark to rot.

Propagation Increase plants from semi-ripe cuttings in late summer, removing a thin strip of bark from the base to reveal wood and stimulate rooting. Leaf-bud cuttings, 1in or so long, again "wounding" the base of the shoot, are also taken then. Alternatively, layer low, flexible shoots from mid-spring to late summer. Some varieties, which are very hard to grow from cuttings, are grafted on to understocks of *C. sasanqua*.

Problems You may encounter the following:
*Bud drop: This can be caused by overwet or overdry soils, root rot, or root disturbance. Some very late-flowering varieties may have buds literally pushed off the stem by new spring growth.
*Brown petals and balled blooms: This usually occurs when buds or flowers are lit by early morning sunshine while still wet with dew. Petals may be scorched and some buds "ball" and fail to open. Some varieties with clusters of big buds are prone to this. Gently breaking off some of the buds when they first form helps to reduce balling.
*Oedema: If plants are overwet and conditions overcast, small, brown, corky swellings may develop on leaves. Reduce watering and try to improve air circulation.
*Scale insects: These may be found on the upper or lower leaf surface. Limpet-like scales suck sap and debilitate plants. Spraying with malathion controls them, but spray only in cool or cloudy weather so that it does not scorch leaves.
*Leaf gall: This causes abnormal thickening and discoloration of new growth. It occurs in spring and is caused by a fungus. Pick off and destroy affected leaves before spores disperse.
*Viruses: May be responsible for variable, bright yellow patterns on leaves, or ring spot. Rings develop on leaves. As the leaf ages it becomes yellowish; the center of the ring becomes bright green. There is no cure for viruses, but plants rarely lose much vigor or have their blooming affected. Pick off the worst-looking leaves if they are spoiling your plant's appearance.

PRUNING

Little pruning is needed. Cutting blooms for the vase is usually enough to keep plants compact. However, any thin, spindly, unproductive growth should be removed from the center of the shrub after flowering. Ageing, overgrown camellias can be rejuvenated by quite heavy pruning, provided cuts are made directly above a leaf bud. If severe pruning is necessary, do it in stages, over two years, to avoid stressing the plant.

CALIFORNIAN LILAC
Ceanothus

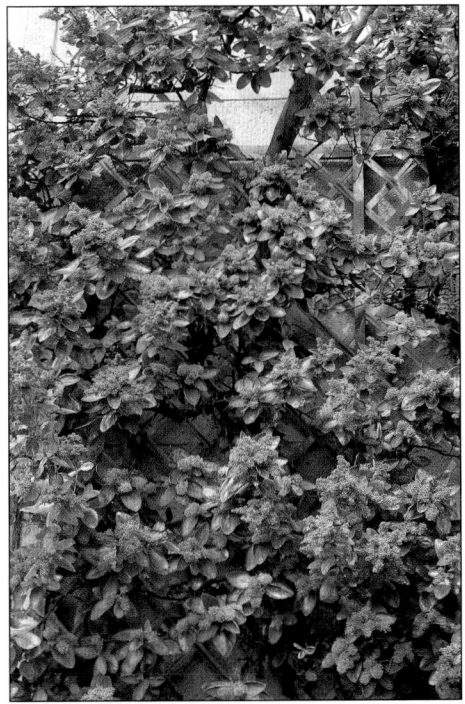

Evergreen ceanothus, such as "Puget Blue," are best fan-trained against a warm wall.

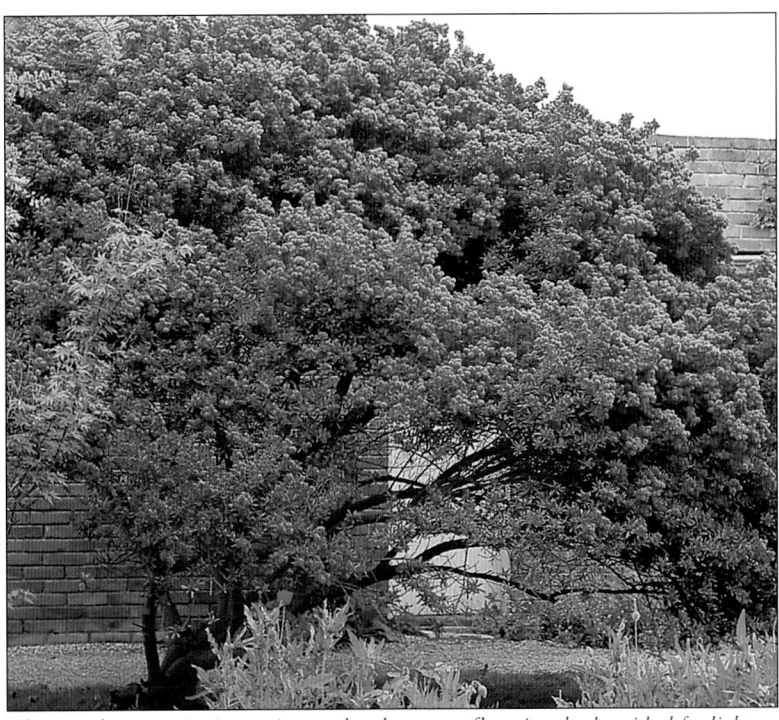

There are few more riveting, spring- and early summer-flowering shrubs—ideal for light soils that dry out quickly—than evergreen members of the Californian lilac family.

FEATURES

Prized for their massed clusters of principally pale blue to deep violet-blue, powderpuff blooms, there are evergreen and deciduous varieties. They range from carpeters to imposing bushes of around 15ft high. Most evergreens, such as "Blue Mound" and *Ceanothus thyrsiflorus* "Edinensis," bloom from May to June. Two exceptions, "Fallal Blue" and "Burkwoodii," perform from July to September. The best of the deciduous group—pink "Marie Simon" and blue "Gloire de Versailles"—flower from July to October.

CALIFORNIAN LILAC AT A GLANCE

Evergreen or deciduous shrubs with blue or pink blooms from spring to early fall. Hardy to 14°F (zone 8).

Month		Recommended Varieties
Jan	/	
Feb	/	**Evergreen**
Mar	plant, prune	"Blue Mound"
Apr	plant, prune	"Cascade"
May	flower, plant	"Concha"
Jun	flower, plant	"Puget Blue"
July	flower, plant	*C. thyrsiflorus* "Repens"
Aug	flower, plant	"Zanzibar" (variegated)
Sept	flower, plant	**Deciduous**
Oct	flower, plant	"Gloire de Versailles"
Nov	/	"Marie Simon"
Dec	/	"Perle Rose"

CONDITIONS

Aspect   All kinds, especially evergreen varieties which are best grown against a south-facing wall, need a sunny, sheltered spot where air circulates freely.

Site   Ceanothus prospers on well-drained clay loam, sandy or humus-rich, gravelly soils. It will not thrive on heavy clay that waterlogs in winter, where roots are liable to rot.

GROWING METHOD

Feeding   Keep plants lustrous and flowering freely by applying bone meal in spring and fall. Breaking down slowly, it is rich in phosphates, which encourage robust root growth. In its native habitat, this plant receives rain only in winter and has adapted to very dry summers.

Propagation   Most varieties are grown from semi-ripe cuttings taken from mid- to late summer.

Problems   Ceanothus is susceptible to root rot, caused by wet soil. It is seldom troubled by pests.

PRUNING

Evergreen varieties: Trim spring-flowering kinds when blooms fade in early summer, and cut late summer performers in April.

Deciduous varieties: In early spring, shorten the previous year's flowered shoots to within 2–3in of the older wood.

CALIFORNIAN LILAC VARIETIES

ABOVE: "Concha" forms a dense, arching, evergreen bush to 5ft high and 6ft across and enriches spring with a profusion of red-budded, deep blue flowers. Find it a warm, sunny spot and it will handsomely reward you.

ABOVE: A sumptuous, evergreen variety, "Dark Star" is prized for its spicy perfumed, purplish-blue blossoms borne in showy bunches on shoot tips in late spring. Small, oval, toothed leaves clad an umbrella of branches.

ABOVE: Glorifying May and June, Ceanothus dentatus floribundus, *as its name implies, is so massed with terminal or lateral clusters of glowing ultramarine-blue flowers that its small, evergreen leaves tend to "disappear."*

ABOVE: From mid- to late spring, the rounded to oval, deeply veined, evergreen leaves of Santa Barbara ceanothus (Ceanothus impressus) complement a dashing display of clustered, dark blue flowers on shoot tips.

BELOW: A robust form of evergreen Ceanothus arboreus *soaring to 20ft, "Trewithen Blue" drips with scented, mid-blue flowers in late spring and early summer. Plant it to make a spectacular focal point for a large, sunny, sheltered lawn.*

BELOW: Plant evergreen "Puget Blue," a zestful variety of Ceanothus impressus, *to clothe a sunny wall or fence. In spring, every shoot is thickly sleeved with rich indigo-blue flowers. Never prune it hard, for older growth seldom regenerates.*

JAPONICA
Chaenomeles

Eye-catching when grown as an espalier against a north- or east-facing wall, chaenomeles yields clusters of bloom from late winter to late spring.

Midwinter splendor: flowering quince is sleeved with blossom when many shrubs are resting.

FEATURES

Also known as japonica or flowering quince, this spiny, deciduous shrub makes a colorful bush to 7ft high or, if espalier-trained against a wall or fence, a striking drape to 9ft. Long-lived, it flowers early in life and reaches maturity in 3–5 years. It is valued for its thickly clustered blooms that transform bare branches from mid-winter to early spring. Flowers are followed by small, fragrant, quince-like fruits that ripen to bright yellow. Fruits are edible and make delicious jams and preserves. Showy varieties include apricot "Geisha Girl," pink "Moerloesii," white "Nivalis," and large, bright crimson "Rowallane". In borders, it makes a showy, rounded background plant for smaller shrubs, perennials, bulbs, and annuals.

JAPONICA AT A GLANCE

A hardy deciduous shrub, its clusters of white, pink, or red, saucer-shaped flowers brighten spring. Hardy to -13°F (zone 5).

		Recommended Varieties
Jan	/	
Feb	/	For walls
Mar	flower, plant	"Geisha Girl"
Apr	flower, prune	"Moerloesii"
May	flower, prune	"Nivalis"
June	plant	"Simonii"
July	prune	For bushes
Aug	plant	"Lemon and Lime"
Sept	plant	"Pink Lady"
Oct	plant	"Knaphill Scarlet"
Nov	plant	"Rowallane"
Dec	/	

CONDITIONS

Aspect Usefully adaptable, chaenomeles thrives in full sun or light shade, does not mind cold winds and colors cold, north- or east-facing walls.

Site Though it prefers well-drained soil, it tolerates heavy, waterlogged clay. Help sandy soils stay cool and moist by working in plenty of bulky manure or well-rotted garden compost.

GROWING METHOD

Feeding Unlike many other shrubs, chaenomeles thrives in poorish soil. For best results, build fertility by topdressing the root area with pelleted chicken manure, fish, blood, and bone meal, or Growmore in spring and midsummer. Water plants regularly in their first year.

Propagation Take semi-ripe cuttings in late summer or detach and replant rooted suckers in fall.

Problems If coral spot appears—shoots are pimpled with coral-pink or orange pustules—cut back to healthy, white wood and burn prunings. Paint stumps with fungicidal pruning compound.

PRUNING

Bushes: Apart from removing crowded shoots when flowers fade in spring, no regular cutting back is required.

Wall trained: Young plants: Tie espaliered shoots to a wire frame. In July, cut back to five leaves shoots growing away from the wall. Reduce to two buds further growth from shortened shoots. Established plants: Shorten the previous year's side shoots to two or three leaves when flowers fade in spring.

MEXICAN ORANGE BLOSSOM
Choisya ternata

Wafting citrus scent on a warm breeze, starry-flowered, evergreen Mexican orange blooms in spring and fall.

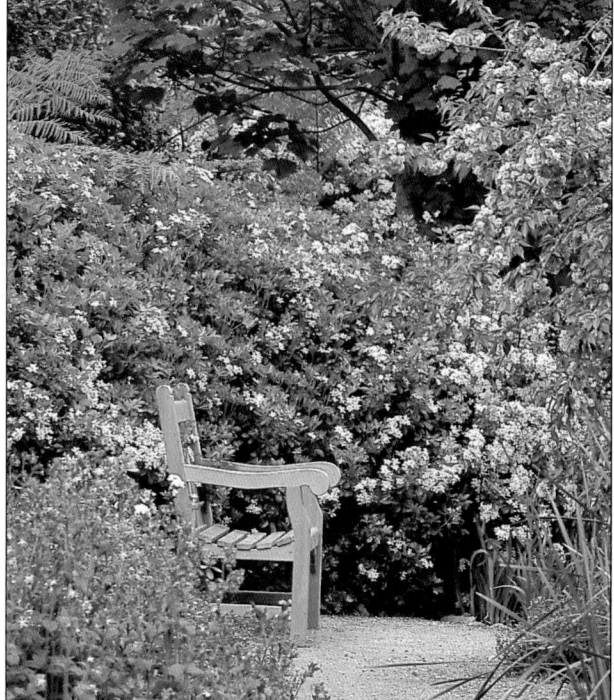

Harmonising beautifully with a pink-flowering Japanese cherry, Mexican orange blossom performs best in a sheltered, sunny spot.

FEATURES

A spring prince, evergreen *Choisya ternata*, to 6ft or more high, is regaled with orange-fragrant, starry, white flowers in April and May and again in October. Its glossy, trefoil leaves spill citrus scent when you brush against them.

"Sundance," a smaller, golden-leaved form, is particularly striking in winter when its foliage assumes orange-yellow tints. Intriguingly different—leaves are long and narrow—"Aztec Pearl" bears pink-budded, white blossoms.

CHOISYA AT A GLANCE

Hardy evergreen shrubs—"Sundance" has yellow leaves—with orange-scented, white flowers in spring. Hardy to 14°F (zone 8).

Jan	/	Recommended Varieties
Feb	/	
Mar	/	*C. ternata*
Apr	flower, plant	*C. ternata* "Sundance"
May	flower, prune	*C. ternata* "Aztec Pearl"
June	flower, prune	
July	plant	
Aug	plant	
Sept	flower, plant	
Oct	/	
Nov	/	
Dec	/	

CONDITIONS

Aspect Full sun or light shade, but "Sundance" needs more light than *C. ternata* or "Aztec Pearl," otherwise its leaves will pale to green and lose their appeal. In northern gardens, position all three kinds against a warm, sunny wall.

Site Choisya thrives in fertile, acid, neutral, or alkaline soil. Enrich nutrient-starved, quick-draining, sandy loam, or stony patches with bulky organic manure.

GROWING METHOD

Feeding Apply a complete plant food, such as Growmore or fish, blood, and bone meal in early spring and midsummer. Water regularly and copiously in long, dry periods.

Propagation Increase choisya from semi-ripe cuttings from mid- to late summer, or layer stems from early to late summer.

Problems No specific pests or diseases but flowering diminishes if shrubs are not pruned regularly and left to become woody.

PRUNING

In cold areas, cut back frost-damaged shoots to healthy, white wood in spring. Keep mature bushes—over five years old—flowering freely by removing from the base a third of the older branches when blooms fade in May or June.

ROCK ROSE
Cistus

A rapid succession of crumpled, silky, often-blotched blooms in white, pink and cerise are your reward for planting cistus.

A Mediterranean drought resister, free-flowering rock roses are also coveted for their aromatic leaves, which distil "honey" on a warm day.

FEATURES

A dandyish Mediterranean native, evergreen cistus delights us from June to August with a daily succession of saucer-shaped, crumpled, silky blooms. Bushes range in size from carpeting, white and maroon-blotched *Cistus lusitanicus* "Decumbens," to 2ft high, to white and yellow-centered *C. laurifolius*, an imposing sentinel that rises to 5ft. There are pink-, crimson- and lilac-flowered varieties, too. All varieties perform early in life and taller kinds make stunning, informal flowering hedges. Small, pot or tub-grown species and varieties, such as neat and bushy "Silver Pink" with its grayish-silvery leaves, illuminate a sun-baked patio.

ROCK ROSE AT A GLANCE

Drought-resisting evergreen for light soil, it is smothered with white, pink, or red blooms in summer. Hardy to 23°F (zone 9).

Jan	/	Recommended Varieties
Feb	/	
Mar	/	Small—up to 3ft
		C. × corbariensis
Apr	plant, prune	"Silver Pink"
May	flower, plant	*C. × skanbergii*
June	flower, plant	"Sunset"
July	flower, plant	Tall—over 3ft
Aug	plant, prune	"Alan Fradd"
		C. laurifolius
Sept	plant	*C. × purpureus*
Oct	/	
Nov	/	
Dec	/	

CONDITIONS

Aspect   Rock roses must have full sun all day to make compact, free-flowering plants. They do not mind exposed sites or salt-laden breezes, but may be damaged by frosty winds. Avoid growing them in areas of high rainfall as blooms are spoilt by prolonged, wet weather.

Site   Plants make the strongest growth on humus-rich, sandy, or gravelly loam, which drains quickly; they are less spirited on heavy, badly drained soils. In nature, rock roses flourish on porous limestone. If your soil is acid, boost growth by adding lime before planting.

GROWING METHOD

Feeding   These plants need little or no fertilizer. Apply a light dressing of bone meal in spring and fall.
Once plants are growing strongly, water is seldom needed, even during weeks of drought.

Propagation   Take semi-ripe cuttings in summer. Species can be grown from seeds or cuttings. Varieties must be raised from cuttings.

Problems   No particular pest or disease afflicts cistus, but hard pruning into older wood can inhibit stumps from re-growing.

PRUNING

Encourage newly planted shrubs to branch freely and make dense bushes by pinching out shoot tips several times throughout the first two summers. Cut back frost-damaged stems to healthy growth in spring.

SHRUBBY BINDWEED
Convolvulus cneorum

Canopied with dazzling white blossom from June to August, Convolvulus cneorum, *with red campion, flourishes in full sun.*

No garden? Plant silky-leaved, shrubby convolvulus to emblazon a patio pot or tub with a massed display of funnel-shaped flowers.

FEATURES

A coveted, silvery, silky-leaved evergreen whose pink buds open to flared, white and yellow-eyed, trumpet blooms from June to August, *Convolvulus cneorum* makes a low hummock to 18in high and 2.5ft across and has many uses.

Create a feature all will admire by associating it with *Ceanothus* "Zanzibar," prized for its powder-blue flowers and golden-variegated leaves.

Plant shrubby bindweed to highlight a rock garden or star in a patio pot or deep windowbox.

It is not fully hardy, so consign it to a very sheltered border and cover it in late fall with several layers of bubble plastic draped over an open-topped wigwam of canes. Make sure the plastic does not touch its foliage. If you plant it in a patio pot for summer, move it to a cold greenhouse for winter.

SHRUBBY BINDWEED AT A GLANCE

A borderline hardy evergreen with soft, silvery leaves; trumpet-shaped flowers appear from June to August. Hardy to 14°F (zone 8).

Jan	shield from frost	Recommended Varieties
Feb	shield from frost	
Mar	/	(only the species
Apr	plant, prune	*C. cneorum* is grown)
May	plant	
June	flower, plant	
July	flower, plant	
Aug	plant	
Sept	plant	
Oct	/	
Nov	/	
Dec	/	

CONDITIONS

Aspect   Find it a sheltered, sunny spot—it revels against a south- or west-facing wall—where it will not be damaged by chilly winds.

Site   Not fussy, it thrives in well-drained, acid to neutral soil. If your garden has badly drained clay, work in plenty of grit or sharp sand or set the plant on a raised bed. It is vital that roots are not "treading" water.

GROWING METHOD

Feeding   Boost growth by working fish, blood, and bone meal or Growmore into the root area in April and July. Add a slow-release fertilizer to patio tub compost. If planting coincides with a droughty spell, foliar feed weekly to help the plant absorb nutrients more quickly.

Water copiously after planting to settle soil around the roots. Follow by mulching with a 2 in layer of well-rotted organic material to conserve moisture.

Propagation   Increase shrubby bindweed from semi-ripe "heeled" cuttings of new side shoots from late summer to early fall.

Problems   If hard frost causes shoot tips to die back, prune them to just above a healthy bud in late spring.

PRUNING

Pruning is unnecessary unless the plant is ageing. Then, in early spring, reduce gaunt and woody stems by half their length, cutting to just above a joint or to new shoots. Keep stumps moist to help them sprout. The best way to do this, apart from sprinkling them with water, is to coat them with a plastic-based anti-transpirant, normally used for helping Christmas trees retain their needles.

FLOWERING DOGWOOD
Cornus

In mid-spring, white or pink-tinted flowers (bracts) transform the Pacific dogwood (Cornus nuttallii) *into a fascinating talking point.*

Late winter sees the bare branches of Cornelian cherry (Cornus mas) *studded with a multitude of tiny, primrose-yellow blossoms.*

FEATURES

Suddenly, in late winter—from February to March—sulfur-yellow, powderpuff blooms light up bare, slender stems. *Cornus mas* has few rivals.

In spring, when flowers fade, oval, pointed, vivid green leaves unfold. Small, edible, cherry-shaped, red fruits, good for jam, form in fall when leaves assume reddish-purple tints before falling.

A coveted, leaf-shedding native of Europe and Western Asia, it slowly forms a handsome globe to around 15ft high and across. It can also be planted to create a stocky, dense flowering hedge.

Dramatically different, the Pacific dogwood (*C. nuttallii*) bears a plethora of saucer-shaped white, pink-tinged bracts (flowers), which light up late spring. When its flowers fade, they are fetchingly replaced by orbs of multi-seeded fruits.

FLOWERING DOGWOOD AT A GLANCE

Cornus mas has sulfur-yellow flowers in February; *C. nuttallii* bears whitish-pink blooms in June. Hardy to 4°F (zone 7).

Jan	/	Recommended Varieties
Feb	flower	
Mar	flower, prune	*C. mas* "Aurea"
Apr	plant	*C. mas* "Aureoelegantissima"
May	flower, plant	*C. mas* "Hillier's Upright"
June	flower, plant	*C. mas* "Variegata"
July	plant	*C. nuttallii* "Colrigo Giant"
Aug	plant	
Sept	plant	
Oct	plant	
Nov	plant	
Dec	/	

CONDITIONS

Aspect   Though performing better in full sun, both species are good contenders for lightly shaded spots. In deep shade, they form a looser, less symmetrical branching system. They are not harmed by cold winds.

Site   *C. mas* thrives on virtually any soil, from light sand to heavy clay and chalk, provided it is not waterlogged. *C nuttallii* needs acid, fertile conditions. Enrich impoverished sand and chalk with bulky organic manure or well-rotted garden compost.

GROWING METHOD

Propagation   *C. mas:* Take semi-ripe cuttings of maturing side shoots—ready when the bark at the base of the stem turns brown and firms up—in late summer.
C. nuttallii: Best increased from soft-tip cuttings from early to midsummer.

Feeding   Boost growth by topdressing the root area with a granular form of complete plant food, or fish, blood, and bone meal in spring and midsummer. Water in if the soil is dry.
In droughty spells, keep shoots vigorous by soaking the root area or digging a moat around the shrub and repeatedly filling it with water. Follow by mulching thickly with moisture-retaining, well-rotted garden compost, bark, or cocoa shell.

Problems   *C. mas* and *C. nuttallii* have a rugged constitution and are seldom troubled by pests and diseases.

PRUNING

Pruning is not needed, apart from removing awkwardly placed shoots after flowering. Use pruning shears and cut to just above a shoot.

SMOKE BUSH
Cotinus coggygria

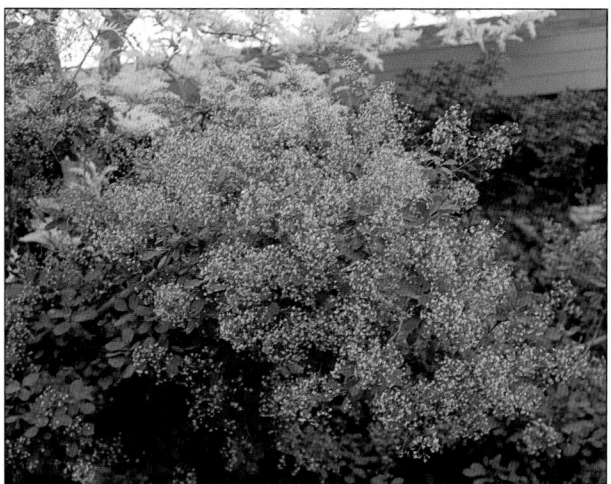

In early summer, Cotinus *"Notcutt's Variety" treats us to a fabulous display of amber, pink, and purple "smoke-like" inflorescences.*

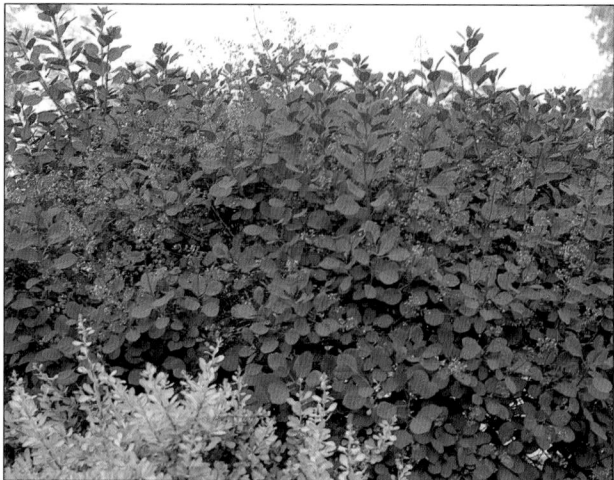

Prized for its richly hued leaves, Cotinus *"Royal Purple" contrasts fetchingly with green-leaved berberis.*

FEATURES

Remarkably drought-resistant shrub, *Cotinus coggygria*, from central and southern Europe, is appealing twice a year: in June and July when its plumy, 6–8in flowers are reminiscent of pink smoke; and in fall when leaves are suffused with vibrant, fiery, or sunset hues. Growing slowly to form an obelisk 9ft by 6ft, purple-leaved varieties associate beautifully with lemon-yellow-leaved mock orange (*Philadelphus coronarius* "Aureus"). Purple-leaved kinds also make a fetching host for scrambling *Lathyrus grandiflorus*, an exuberant, pink-flowered perennial pea.

If you do not have sufficient border space for a smoke bush, set it in a large tub of tree and shrub compost and position it to form a statement on your patio or at the end of a path. Plant a pair of shrubs to frame the entrance to a wide driveway.

SMOKE BUSH AT A GLANCE

Green or purple leaves assume sunset fall tints. "Smoky" flowering plumes make summer special. Hardy to 4°F (zone 7).

Jan	/	
Feb	/	Recommended Varieties
Mar	plant, prune	"Atropurpurea"
Apr	plant, prune	"Grace"
May	plant	"Notcutt's Variety"
June	flower, plant	"Royal Purple"
July	flower, plant	
Aug	plant	
Sept	plant	
Oct	plant	
Nov	plant	
Dec	/	

CONDITIONS

Aspect Stalwarts both, green- and purple-leaved varieties are very hardy and unaffected by cold winds.

Site The green-leaved family excels in full sun or light shade, but purple-liveried varieties must have bright sunshine or their foliage will pale to insipid green. All prefer humus-rich soil enriched with bulky organic manure or well-rotted garden compost, but they will survive without stress on thin, sandy loam.

GROWING METHOD

Feeding Fortify the root area with fish, blood, and bone meal, or Growmore, twice a year: in spring and midsummer. Water it in if the soil is dry.

Propagation Increase plants from semi-ripe cuttings of new shoots from mid- to late summer. Root them in a lightly shaded garden frame or on a brightly lit windowsill.

Problems If shoot tips die after a very hard winter, shorten them to live buds in early spring. Should mildew attack purple-leaved varieties, control it by spraying with fungicide containing carbendazim.

PRUNING

Choose one of three methods:
For a mass of flowers on a large shrub, prune only to remove dead wood.
To achieve a balance of foliage and flowers, take out a third of the oldest shoots each spring.
For dashing foliage, spectacular fall color and no flowers—ideal for purple-leaved varieties—cut back all shoots to 6in from the base in early spring. Keep cuts moist to encourage regrowth.

COTONEASTER
Cotoneaster

Herringbone cotoneaster (Cotoneaster horizontalis) *is splendid for covering walls. Pinkish-white flowers are followed by scarlet berries.*

Cotoneaster conspicuus *"Decorus's froth of white summer blossom preludes a feast of bright red fall fruits.*

FEATURES

This versatile, evergreen, semi-evergreen, or deciduous family ranges in height from carpeters of 12in to towering bushes more than 10ft high.

Choice kinds are dense and weed-suppressing, evergreen "Coral Beauty," whose glowing orange berries light up fall; semi-evergreen *Cotoneaster horizontalis*, ideal for clothing a bank or wall beneath a ground floor window; and semi-evergreen "Cornubia," an imposing, arching bush to 10ft.

Evergreen *C. lacteus* and semi-evergreen *C. simonsii* make splendid, low, flowering, and berrying hedges.

Sprays of small, white spring flowers are followed by a glowing fall to winter display of red or yellow fruits. Cotoneasters take 5–10 years to mature, depending on species and conditions, and are long-lived. Fruits are nutritious food for garden birds and winter migrants.

COTONEASTER AT A GLANCE

Deciduous, semi- or fully evergreen shrub; white blossom heralds an fall display of vibrant fruits. Hardy to -13°F (zone 5).

Jan	/	Recommended Varieties
Feb	/	
Mar	plant	Ground covering to 12in
Apr	plant	"Coral Beauty"
May	flower, prune	"Oakwood"
June	flower	"Skogholm"
July	plant	Small bushes (12–32in)
Aug	plant	*C. conspicuus* "Decorus"
Sept	plant	*C. horizontalis*
Oct	plant, prune	Taller kinds
Nov	plant, prune	"Cornubia"
Dec	/	

CONDITIONS

Aspect All kinds grow best and flower and fruit more freely in full sun. They will tolerate partial shade, but shoots are looser and berries sparse.

Site Cotoneasters prefer well-drained, medium to heavyish loam, but any reasonably fertile soil encourages stocky growth. Improve thin, sandy, or gravelly areas by digging in bulky, humus-forming, well-rotted manure, decayed garden compost, or leaf mould.

GROWING METHOD

Feeding Not essential, but an application of Growmore or fish, blood, and bone meal, carefully pricked into the root area in spring and midsummer, encourages lustrous leaves. If you are growing a small-leafed, bushy variety such as *C. simonsii* as a close-planted hedge, apply fertilizer in spring and summer. Water newly planted cotoneasters regularly in spring and summer to help them grow away quickly. Once established, they will tolerate long periods without supplementary watering.

Propagation Take semi-ripe cuttings from mid- to late summer; layer shoots from spring to summer.

Problems Fireblight: Causing flowers to wilt and wither—they appear scorched—it is controlled by cutting back affected shoots to healthy, white wood. Burn prunings.

PRUNING

Keep plants flowering and fruiting well by removing one stem in three. Tackle evergreens in mid-spring and deciduous kinds in mid-fall.

HAWTHORN
Crataegus

Hawthorn's abundant, milky-scented, white flowers in early summer are followed by clusters of scarlet or orange berries in fall and winter.

A traditional English hedgerow shrub, hawthorn (Crataegus monogyna) also makes an elegant, small flowering tree.

FEATURES

Architectural, deciduous hawthorns—ideal for focal points or screening—can be shrubby or grow into small trees to 15ft. Clad with lobed or toothed leaves, suffused with fiery scarlet tints in fall, blossom mantles shoots in May and June. Bright orange or red berries—birds adore them—persist into winter. Stems are usually spiny and native may or quickthorn (*Crataegus monogyna*) makes a formidable barrier. Others, such as glossy-leaved *C. × lavallei*, whose large clusters of white blossom are followed by orange berries coupled with richly autumn-hued leaves, and deep red-flowered *C. laevigata* "Paul's Scarlet," make fetching sentinels.

HAWTHORN AT A GLANCE

Large, deciduous bushes or small trees, their summer blossom is followed by orange or scarlet fruits. Hardy to -13°F (zone 5).

Jan	/	Recommended Varieties
Feb	prune	
Mar	plant	"Crimson Cloud"
Apr	plant	*C. × grignonensis*
May	flower, plant	*C. × lavallei*
June	flower	"Paul's Scarlet"
July	prune	"Rosea Flore Pleno"
Aug	prune	
Sept	/	
Oct	plant	
Nov	plant, prune	
Dec	prune	

CONDITIONS

Aspect   Stalwarts for exposed upland gardens raked by wind, or those fringing the sea, where leaves are powdered with salt, hawthorn flowers best in full sun. In light shade, bushes have a more open habit and fewer blooms.

Site   Though hawthorn prefers deep and heavyish but well-drained soils, it will tolerate light, sandy, or gravelly ground. Improve thin soils by working in plenty of bulky organic matter.

GROWING METHOD

Feeding   Work bone meal into the soil in spring and fall to ensure a continuous supply of root-promoting phosphates.
Water copiously in the first year after planting. Thereafter, when hawthorn is established, it is seldom stressed by drought.

Propagation   Raise species from seed, from berries mixed with damp sand and placed in a flower pot. Break dormancy by positioning the pot in the coldest part of the garden. In spring, remove seeds and sow them in an outdoor seed bed. Seedlings quickly appear.

Problems   Powdery mildew can whiten leaves. Control it by spraying with carbendazim, mancozeb, or triforine with bupirimate.

PRUNING

Bushes: Encourage a profusion of blossom by shortening the previous year's shoots by two-thirds in late winter.

Hedges: Clip in mid-July and in winter.

BROOM
Cytisus

From May to June, Cytisus scoparius *illuminates a sunny border with golden-yellow blossom. Contrast it with a purple-leaved cotinus.*

Bearing cone-shaped, richly pineapple-scented blooms in early summer, Cytisus battandieri *is best fan-trained against a sunny wall.*

FEATURES

Treating us to whippy stemmed and thickly clustered cascades of fragrant, pea flowers, deciduous and butter-yellow-flowered *Cytisus scoparius* and its kaleidoscope-hued hybrids make May and June special.

Plant them singly to punctuate a border, or group several of one color or in harmonizing shades to create an unforgettable statement. Its fetching, leaf-shedding relation Moroccan (pineapple) broom (*C. battandieri*) is famed for its June display of pineapple-scented cones of bright yellow blooms amid silvery, tri-lobed leaves. It has a lax, floppy habit so train it to embrace a sunny wall or frame a patio door. Alternatively, plant it to entwine a tall, metal obelisk in a border or at the end of a path. When in flower, a warm, breezy day wafts crushed pineapple scent around the garden.

BROOM AT A GLANCE

Massed, tiny, pea blooms or chunky, golden flower cones brighten borders from late spring to early summer. Hardy to 14°F (zone 8).

Jan	/	Recommended Varieties
Feb	/	*C. battandieri*
Mar	plant	*C. scoparius* "Andreanus"
Apr	plant	*C. scoparius* "Burkwoodii"
May	flower, plant	*C. scoparius* "Goldfinch"
June	flower, prune	*C. scoparius* "Killeney Red"
July	plant	
Aug	plant	*C. scoparius* "Killeney Salmon"
Sept	plant	*C. scoparius* "Lena"
Oct	plant	*C. scoparius* "Zeelandia"
Nov	/	
Dec	/	

CONDITIONS

Aspect *C. scoparius* and its varieties are hardier than *C. battandieri*, which needs to be sheltered from cold winds. Both flower at their best in full sun.

Site Encourage robust growth by setting plants in free-draining and well-manured, neutral, or acid, sandy soil. Lime tends to cause weak, pale green leaves.

Feeding After adding balanced fertilizer to planting holes, encourage sturdy growth by topdressing the root area with fish, blood, and bone meal in spring and again in midsummer. If your soil is chalky and hybrids are suffering from iron deficiency, help them recover by applying a soil-acidifying fertilizer.

Propagation Increase *C. scoparius* and *C. battandieri* from semi-ripe cuttings taken from mid- to late summer.

Problems When *C. scoparius* and its hybrids become woody and flower less—after ten or so years— they cannot be refurbished by hard pruning, so it is best to replace them with young, potted plants.

Occasionally, in summer, leaf buds develop into cauliflower-like growths covered with silvery hairs. Gall mites cause them. There is no chemical control, so remove affected plants and replace them with healthy stock.

PRUNING

Keep *C. scoparius* and its hybrids youthful and ablaze with flowers in spring by shearing flowered stems to just above older growth when pods form. *C. battandieri* isn't normally pruned, but cut out badly placed and weak stems after flowering If you are growing it against a wall, tie in new shoots then.

DAPHNE
Daphne

Sweetly scented Daphne odora *"Aureomarginata" rewards us with clusters of pinkish-white flowers in late winter.*

Lime-tolerant daphnes—this is Daphne odora—*have an unfounded reputation for being difficult. Find them a cool, moist and sunny spot.*

FEATURES

Grown primarily for their sweetly fragrant blooms, daphnes are best planted close to a living room where, on a warm day with a window open, scent wafts indoors. Alternatively, set bushes in pots or tubs beside a garden seat. Herald spring with deciduous *Daphne mezereum*, to 3ft, with upright stems sleeved with starry, purplish-red flowers. Slightly taller but spreading and evergreen *D. odora* "Aureomarginata," with its cream-edged, green leaves that complement clusters of pinkish-white blooms, also flowers then. From May to June, evergreen *D. burkwoodii* "Somerset," wondrous when filling a large pedestal urn and forming a focal point, exudes vanilla perfume from pale pink blooms.

DAPHNE AT A GLANCE

Deciduous or evergreen shrubs with purple-red to pink flowers from late winter to early summer. Hardy to 19°F (zone 8).

Jan	/	Recommended Varieties
Feb	flower	
Mar	flower, plant	*D. bholua*
Apr	flower, plant	*D. burkwoodii* "Somerset"
May	flower, prune	*D. cneorum*
June	flower, prune	*D. mezereum*
July	plant	*D. odora*
Aug	plant	"Aureomarginata"
Sept	plant	*D. retusa*
Oct	plant	
Nov	plant	
Dec	/	

CONDITIONS

Aspect   Daphne prospers in full sun or very light shade. Shelter it from strong, drying winds.

Site   It must have perfectly drained soil with a high organic content. Keep roots cool by mulching plants with well-decayed manure.

GROWING METHOD

Feeding   Sustain strong flowering shoots by feeding with bone meal in spring and fall. Encourage newly planted shrubs by liquid feeding with a high-potash fertilizer at weekly intervals from spring to summer.
Deep, regular watering is necessary for young plants in long, dry spells. Make sure the soil does not become soggy, for roots may rot.

Propagation   Multiply plants by layering shoots from mid-spring to late summer or by taking semi-ripe cuttings from mid- to late summer.

Problems   Sudden death is usually caused by root rot triggered by bad drainage. Daphne may also be attacked by blackening, leaf-spot fungi that speckle foliage. Control leaf spot by spraying with carbendazim or mancozeb. Viruses are also liable to attack daphne. Characterised by twisted and puckered leaves, there is no control, so dig up and burn affected plants.

PRUNING

No regular cutting back needed, apart from shortening young, straggly stems in spring to keep bushes tidy. Do not prune into older, black-barked wood, for stumps may not regenerate.

DEUTZIA
Deutzia

Flowering from spring to early summer, single, white-flowered Deutzia gracilis *makes a charming background to these late yellow primroses.*

Soaring to around 7ft, Deutzia scabra *flaunts sprays of double, white, or pink-tinged blooms from July to August.*

FEATURES

Profusely blooming, deciduous, upright or rounded deutzias are easy to grow and best displayed in a mixed border. All, apart from late-flowering *Deutzia monbeigii* with its small leaves, appealingly white beneath and complementing dense clusters of starry, white flowers from July to August, perform from May to July. An elegant, upright shrub, deutzia varies in height from deep carmine-pink-flowered *D. × rosea*, 32in by 24in, to *D. scabra* "Pride of Rochester," a handsome

leviathan that soars to 7ft. From June to July, its double, white blooms smother pleasingly, peeling-barked branches.

CONDITIONS

Aspect   Deutzia prefers full sun but will tolerate light shade. Plants should be sheltered from strong, northerly or easterly winds.

Site   This shrub flourishes on most well-drained soils, especially if fortified with organic matter.

GROWING METHOD

Feeding   Undemanding, deutzia does not need regular feeding. If growth is poor, topdress the root area with Growmore or fish, blood, and bone meal in spring and summer.

Propagation   Multiply deutzia from hardwood cuttings from mid-fall to early winter.

Problems   Late spring frosts may damage blossom buds of May-flowering varieties, so position plants carefully if you garden in a frost pocket.

PRUNING

Encourage a wealth of blossom by cutting back to near ground level a third of the older branches when flowers fade. If stems bearing flower buds are killed by frost, shorten them to healthy wood.

DEUTZIA AT A GLANCE

Deciduous shrub with shoots clothed in single or double, pink or white blooms in spring and summer. Hardy to -13°F (zone 5).

Month	Activity	Recommended Varieties
Jan	/	
Feb	/	*D. × elegantissima* "Rosealind"
Mar	plant	
Apr	plant	*D. × hybrida* "Magician" "Montrose"
May	flower, plant	
June	flower	*D. monbeigii*
July	flower, prune	*D. × rosea* "Campanulata"
Aug	plant, prune	*D. scabra* "Pride of Rochester"
Sept	plant	
Oct	plant	
Nov	plant	
Dec	plant	

PRIDE OF MADEIRA
Echium candicans (fastuosum)

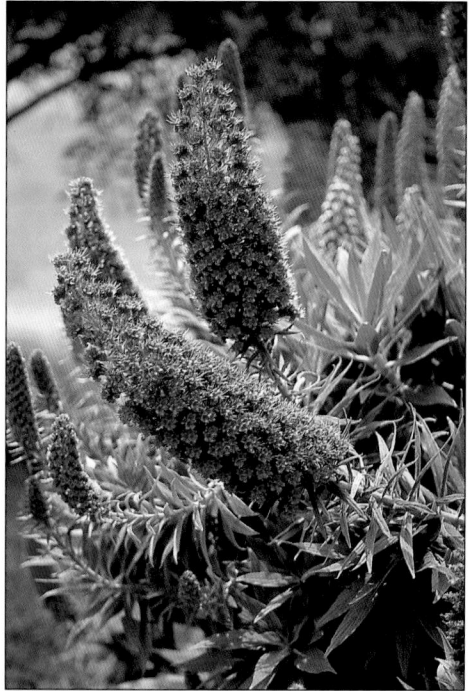

Tower of jewels is another evocative name for Echium candicans, *a remarkable, Canary Islands native.*

In a sheltered, frost-free garden, this amazing shrub will spread to 6ft across. Elsewhere, it should be grown in a container and overwintered under glass.

FEATURES

A somewhat sprawling shrub with gray-green leaves, Pride of Madeira is an exciting challenge. Growing to about 5ft high and spreading to 7ft or more, it produces long, fat spikes of sapphire to violet-blue flowers in late spring and early summer. Being frost tender, it is best grown in a pot and consigned to a high conservatory or large greenhouse. Move it to a sheltered, sunny patio or terrace in June and bring it indoors when nights turn chilly in September. It matures in 3–5 years and flowers early in life.

PRIDE OF MADEIRA AT A GLANCE

Frost tender, with blue flowers in summer. In chilly areas, it must be overwintered under glass. Hardy to 30°F (zone 9).

Jan	shield from frost	Recommended Varieties
Feb	shield from frost	*E. candicans*
Mar	shield from frost	
Apr	plant	
May	plant	
June	flower, plant	
July	flower, prune	
Aug	flower, prune	
Sept	flower, plant	
Oct	/	
Nov	/	
Dec	/	

CONDITIONS

Aspect   Echium needs full sun all day. Under glass, air must freely circulate.

Site   Set this plant in a large pot of multipurpose compost augmented with a quarter part Perlite to ensure good drainage. Pot it on in early spring when roots fill the container and mat the compost as the need for watering increases.

GROWING METHOD

Feeding   Boost growth by liquid feeding with a high-potash fertilizer, weekly from spring to late summer. Alternatively, insert aggregates of slow-release fertilizer granules into the compost in spring.

Watering: Echium tolerates very dry conditions and needs only an occasional soaking in prolonged droughty weather.

Propagation   Echium is raised from seed in spring or early summer. Alternatively, take semi-ripe heeled cuttings tugged from older stems, in midsummer. Root cuttings in a propagator heated to around 70°F.

Problems   No particular pest or disease troubles this plant. If aphids colonize shoot tips, tackle them with pirimicarb or natural pyrethrins.

PRUNING

Remove spent flower heads and shorten shoots outgrowing their allotted space.

HEATH
Erica

Plant a selection of lime-hating Erica cinerea *varieties and enjoy a succession of blossom from June to November.*

Performing from November to May, Erica carnea, *here complementing a golden-flowered berberis, is prized for its white, pink, red, lavender, or mauve display.*

FEATURES

A large, vibrant-flowered group of bushy and carpeting, evergreen shrubs, 9in–5ft high, their thickly clustered, tubular or bell-shaped blooms in white and a confection of pink, purple, coral, and crimson hues illuminate the year. Color winter with varieties of *Erica* x *darleyensis* and *E. carnea*; cheer spring by grouping *E. arborea*, and *E. erigena*; glorify summer and fall with *E. cinerea*, *E. tetralix*, and *E. vagans*.

Use them to brighten borders and rock gardens and suppress weeds. Ideally, associate them with dwarf conifers.

Create a tapestry of blossom by combining ericas with closely related varieties of ling (*Calluna vulgaris*), which flower from July to November, and Irish heath (*Daboecia cantabrica*). Some callunas, such as "Beoley Gold," yield radiant golden foliage.

CONDITIONS

Aspect Most are very hardy, tolerate chilly winds and are ideal for exposed, upland gardens. Heathers must have full sun and good air circulation. Do not crowd plants.

Site While all varieties prefer acid soil, winter-flowering *Erica carnea* tolerates slightly alkaline conditions. Good drainage is vital. Mulch plants annually, in spring, with leaf mould or well-rotted garden compost.

GROWING METHOD

Feeding Established plants need little or no fertilizer. If the soil is very poor, fortify the root area with a balanced, acidifying fertilizer in spring.

Propagation Take semi-ripe heeled cuttings from early to late summer; layer shoots in mid-spring.

Problems Heathers quickly succumb to root rot in heavy or overwet soils.

PRUNING

Lightly shear flowered shoots when blooms fade. Never cut back into older wood. Tackle fall- and winter-flowering varieties when new shoots appear in spring.

HEATH AT A GLANCE

Carpeting evergreens whose succession of blossom or foliage enchants us every month of the year. Hardy to 4°F (zone 7).

Jan	flower	Recommended Varieties
Feb	flower	
Mar	flower	Spring flowering
		"Albert's Gold"
Apr	plant, prune	"Viking"
May	flower, plant	Summer flowering
June	flower, prune	"C.D. Eason"
July	flower, prune	"Pink Ice"
Aug	flower, plant	Fall flowering
Sept	flower, plant	"Andrew Proudley"
		"Stefanie"
Oct	flower	Winter flowering
Nov	flower	"Ann Sparkes"
Dec	flower	

Heath varieties

ABOVE: A fetching variety of ling, Calluna "Kerstin," makes a dense mound to 12in high and across and treats us to a profusion of single, mauve flowers from August to September. In full sun, its shoot tips are bright yellow—a bonus in winter.

RIGHT: A newish, golden-leaved hybrid to around 4ft, Erica "Valerie Griffiths" makes a glowing, year-round focal point for a heather garden. Alternatively, it can be planted in a large pot to decorate a patio or terrace. Pale pink flowers appear from August to October.

ABOVE: Also called Irish or Mediterranean heath, Erica erigena has honey-scented sprays of deep lilac-pink flowers in spring, thickly borne on 8ft stems. An imposing sentinel, it can be planted to form a good, dense hedge which is trimmed when flowers fade.

BELOW: Colorful throughout the seasons, Calluna "Red Carpet," just 6in high, is a good choice for small gardens. Studded with spires of mauve blossom from August to September, its leaves, golden in summer, assume orange-red tints in winter.

ABOVE: There are few more wondrous heathery sights than a mature bush of Erica x veitchii "Gold Tips". Massed cones of white blossom appear from March to June and new spring foliage is tipped with gold.

LEFT: A golden-leaved beacon to 10in high, lime-tolerant Erica x darleyensis "Mary Helen" unfolds a wealth of single, pink flowers from February to April. Group it in full sunshine where its leaves will not lose their radiance, or plant it to color a deep windowbox.

ESCALLONIA
Escallonia

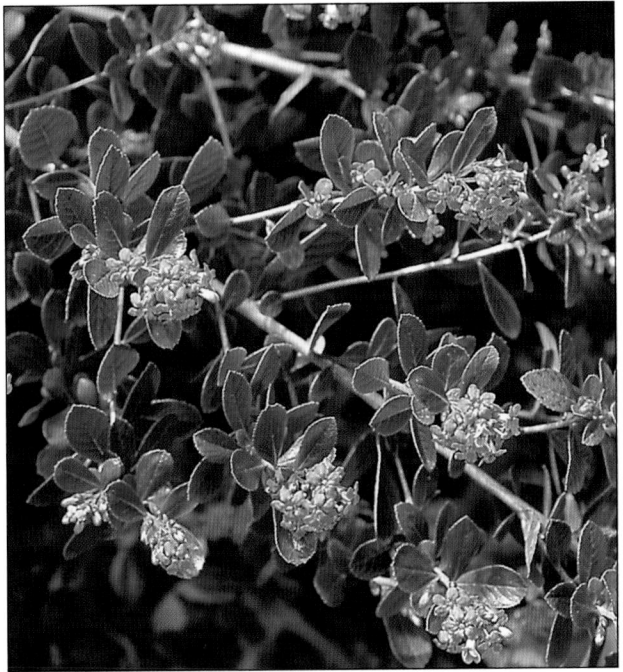

A prized and colorful shrub, especially for windy gardens, Escallonia "Pride of Donard" rewards us with sprays of pink blossom.

Semi-evergreen and summer-blossoming escallonia can be trained to form a fetching, flowering hedge in mild districts.

FEATURES

Escallonia is evergreen in mild districts but semi-evergreen elsewhere. Its arching shoots, festooned with sprays of clustered, tubular, white, pink, or red flowers amid small, glossy leaves, highlight the summer months. Long-lived, it makes a stunning sentinel to around 6ft and as a flowering hedge. The hardiest species—ideal for windswept, seaside gardens—*Escallonia rubra macrantha* delights us with many rose-crimson flowers. Other choice kinds are rich pink "Donard Radiance," rose-pink "Donard Star" and golden-leaved and rosy-red-flowered "Gold Brian."

ESCALLONIA AT A GLANCE

Evergreen or semi-evergreen, its arching shoots are sleeved with white, pink or red flowers in summer. Hardy to 14°F (zone 8).

Month	Activity	Recommended Varieties
Jan	/	"Donard Radiance"
Feb	/	"Donard Seedling"
Mar	/	"Glory of Donard"
Apr	plant, prune	"Gold Brian"
May	plant, prune	"Iveyi"
June	flower, plant	*E. rubra macrantha*
July	flower, plant	"Slieve Donard"
Aug	flower, plant	
Sept	flower, plant	
Oct	/	
Nov	/	
Dec	/	

CONDITIONS

Aspect   Though escallonia needs full sun to flower best, it does not object to light shade. Most hybrids tolerate buffeting wind. In chilly or northern gardens, it should be planted against a sheltered, south-facing wall.

Site   This splendid shrub thrives in any well-drained soil. Aerate heavy clay by working in grit or gravel; fortify light and nutrient-starved, sandy soils by working in plenty of bulky, moisture-conserving organic materials.

GROWING METHOD

Feeding   Ensure a steady release of plant foods by applying bone meal in spring and fall. After planting, water freely and regularly in dry spells to encourage strong new growth. Keep roots cool and questing freely by mulching with shredded bark, cocoa shell, crumbly manure, or rotted garden compost.

Propagation   Multiply choice varieties from semi-ripe cuttings from the middle of summer to the middle of fall.

Problems   Cut darkly stained shoots infected with silver leaf back to healthy, white wood 6in beyond the point of infection.

PRUNING

Shorten a third of the oldest stems to near ground level when blooms fade. In cold gardens, cut back frost-damaged growth to strong, new shoots in late spring.

SPURGE
Euphorbia species

The showiest part of a euphorbia 'flower' is a pair of lime-green bracts (modified leaves). The true flower is a small, yellow 'button'.

Perfect for tempering hot orange and yellow flowers, Euphorbia characias wulfenii *performs best in full sun.*

FEATURES

Pleasing us with a spring to early summer display of yellowish-green, bottlebrush blooms on stems clad with whorls of evergreen leaves, *Euphorbia characias wulfenii* is architecturally magnificent. Forming a dense bush to 1.2m (4ft), it is ideal for interplanting and tempering vibrant orange, yellow and red-flowered border perennials. This euphorbia lives for around ten or more years and matures within 2–3 years. Use it in a shrub border or as a background for annuals and perennials. A related sculptural gem, for sheltered gardens only, is Madeiran honey spurge (*E. mellifera*).

SPURGE AT A GLANCE

Evergreen shrub, *E. characias wulfenii* produces huge, bottlebrush blooms from spring to early summer. Hardy to -12ºC (10ºF).

		Recommended Varieties
JAN	/	
FEB	/	
MAR	/	*E. characias:*
APR	flower, plant	'John Tomlinson'
MAY	flower, plant	'Lambrook Gold'
JUNE	flower, prune	'Margery Fish Group'
JULY	prune, plant	'Purple and Gold'
AUG	plant	*E. characias wulfenii*
SEPT	plant	*E. mellifera*
OCT	/	
NOV	/	
DEC	/	

Seducing us with large and exotic, lance-shaped leaves, its honey-scented, brownish flower clusters form on shoot tips in spring.

CONDITIONS

Aspect	Hardy *E. characias* needs full sun; more tender *E. mellifera* requires a sheltered spot.
Site	These sub-shrubs thrive almost anywhere, even in heavy soils, provided drainage is good. Boost growth in light, sandy soil by incorporating bulky organic manure.

GROWING METHOD

Feeding	Feeding is not essential but apply fish, blood and bone meal, Growmore or pelleted chicken manure in spring.
Propagation	Take soft-tip cuttings from mid-spring to early summer.
Problems	When crowded, euphorbia may become infected with grey mould, a disease that coats leaves and stems with furry, brownish-grey mould. Control it by cutting infected shoots back to healthy tissue and spraying with carbendazim.

PRUNING

Wear gloves and safety glasses to cut back flowered stems to ground level in early summer. Strong, new shoots replace them and bloom the following year.

SPURGE VARIETIES

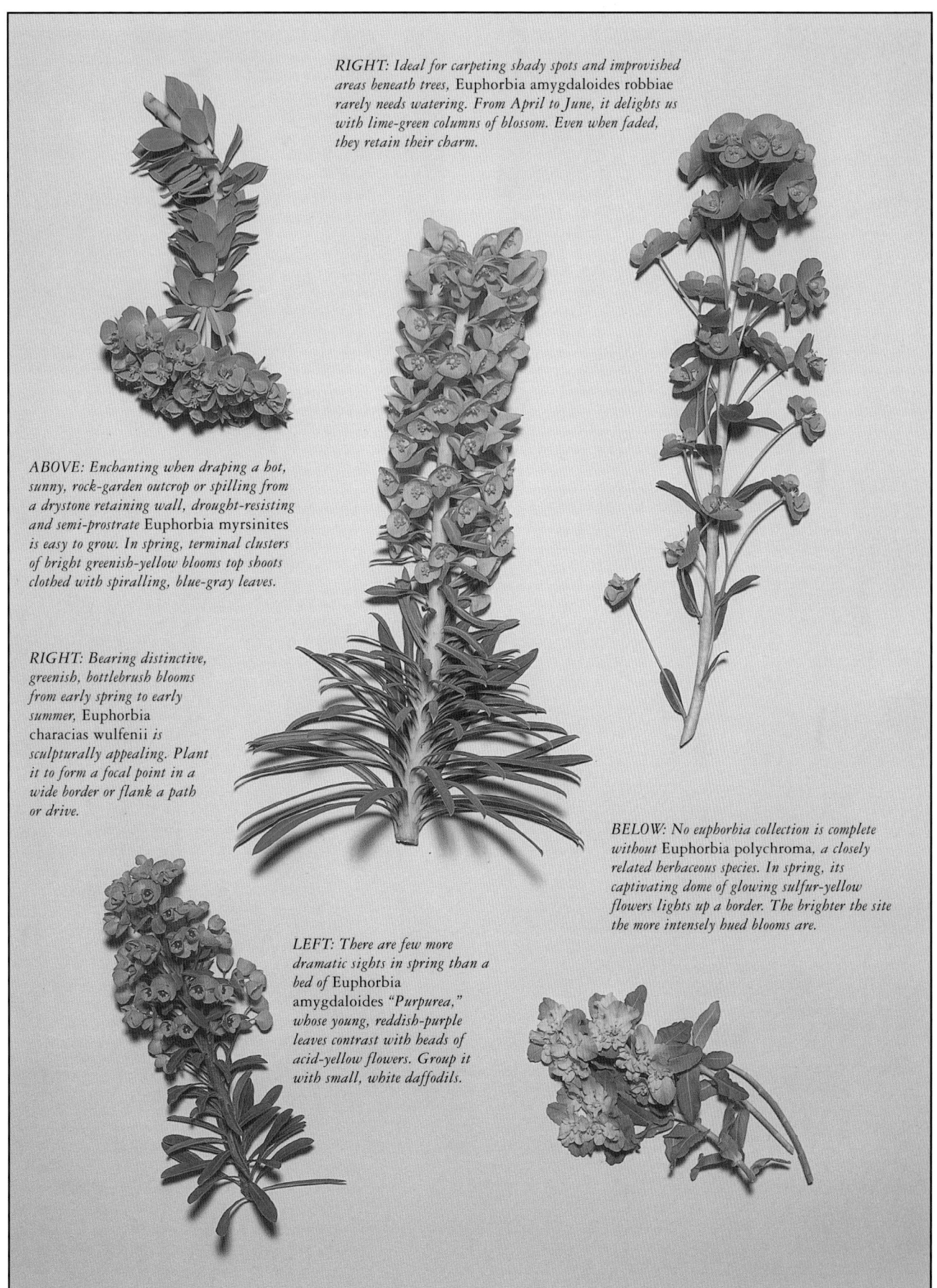

RIGHT: Ideal for carpeting shady spots and improvised areas beneath trees, Euphorbia amygdaloides robbiae *rarely needs watering. From April to June, it delights us with lime-green columns of blossom. Even when faded, they retain their charm.*

ABOVE: Enchanting when draping a hot, sunny, rock-garden outcrop or spilling from a drystone retaining wall, drought-resisting and semi-prostrate Euphorbia myrsinites *is easy to grow. In spring, terminal clusters of bright greenish-yellow blooms top shoots clothed with spiralling, blue-gray leaves.*

RIGHT: Bearing distinctive, greenish, bottlebrush blooms from early spring to early summer, Euphorbia characias wulfenii *is sculpturally appealing. Plant it to form a focal point in a wide border or flank a path or drive.*

BELOW: No euphorbia collection is complete without Euphorbia polychroma, *a closely related herbaceous species. In spring, its captivating dome of glowing sulfur-yellow flowers lights up a border. The brighter the site the more intensely hued blooms are.*

LEFT: There are few more dramatic sights in spring than a bed of Euphorbia amygdaloides *"Purpurea," whose young, reddish-purple leaves contrast with heads of acid-yellow flowers. Group it with small, white daffodils.*

FIG-LEAVED PALM
Fatsia japonica

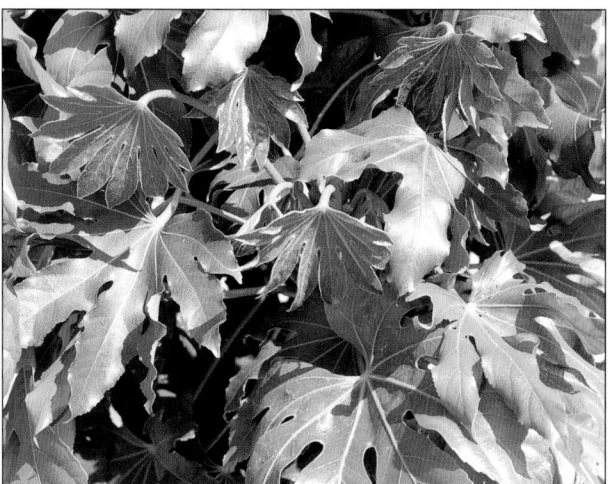

Exotic-fingered leaves are your reward for growing evergreen Fatsia japonica. *Plant it in a tub to light up a shady patio or terrace.*

Delighting us with its large heads of creamy, bobble-like blooms in fall, when most other shrubs are resting, fatsia tolerates dry soil.

FEATURES

Stunningly architectural, the large, glossy, palmate leaves of *Fatsia japonica* have an appealing leathery texture. In fall, it delights us with an exotic candelabrum of golf-ball-sized, white flower heads. Each comprises many tiny, five-petalled flowers. Large, handsome, black berries follow them. A native of South Korea and Japan, it has a spreading, suckering habit and makes a dome to 6ft high and 8ft across. Plant it to enhance a large patio tub. It tolerates air pollution, so is a good shrub for towns or cities. It resists salty sea breezes, too. Dramatise a sunny border by grouping it with golden-leaved yuccas.

If you plant fatsia in a border, create a striking feature by embracing it with tussock-forming and ground-covering *Liriope muscari*, whose spikes of bell-shaped, violet flowers complement the fatsia's white bobbles.

FIG-LEAVED PALM AT A GLANCE

Dashing focal point for a lightly shaded spot. Intriguing bobbles of white blossom appear in fall. Hardy to 4°F (zone 7).

Month	Activity	Recommended Varieties
Jan	/	
Feb	/	"Variegata"
Mar	/	
Apr	prune, plant	
May	plant	
June	plant	
July	plant	
Aug	plant	
Sept	plant, flower	
Oct	flower	
Nov	flower	
Dec	/	

CONDITIONS

Aspect Ideal for brightening sheltered and lightly shaded spots, it objects to hot sunshine, which may scorch its leaves. Protect from icy winds, which also brown its foliage.

Site It is not fussy about soil but prefers deep, rich loam, which encourages the largest, most sculpturally appealing leaves. Add grit or gravel to soggy clay to improve drainage. Apply an acidifying fertilizer, such as sequestered iron, to chalky soil to reduce risk of chlorosis. When iron is "locked up" by calcium, roots cannot absorb it and leaves turn yellow and die.

GROWING METHOD

Feeding Boost lustrous foliage by topdressing the root area in spring, and again in summer, with fish, blood, and bone meal, which enriches the soil's humus content and encourages beneficial micro-organisms. Alternatively, use quick-acting but short-lived Growmore to accelerate shoot development.
Water freely after planting to settle soil around roots. Follow with a 2in mulch of old manure, bark, or cocoa shell.

Propagation Take semi-ripe cuttings in summer and strike them in a closed cold frame or on a sunny windowsill.

Problems Control aphids, which colonize and cripple shoot tips, by spraying with a systemic insecticide.

PRUNING

Apart from maintaining its symmetry by shortening long branches or frost-damaged shoots in spring, cutting to a joint or lower shoot, no regular attention is necessary.

GOLDEN BELL BUSH
Forsythia

Forming a bushy shrub to around 6ft, generous flowering and sun-loving Forsythia "Lynwood" is draped with blossom in spring.

Create a vibrant March marriage of yellow blossom and scarlet bark by associating forsythia with a coppiced clumps of **Cornus alba** "Sibirica".

FEATURES

Heartening indeed is the spring sight of a bush thickly laden with starry, sulfur-yellow, or deep golden blooms. Flowers open naturally from March to April. Enjoy an earlier show by cutting fat-budded stems in February and forcing them into bloom in a warm room. There are two principal kinds: border forsythia (*Forsythia × intermedia*), which makes a rounded shrub to 8ft high and across, and *F. suspensa*, a snaking, weeping, or trailing form, enchanting when cascading over a wall or over the lower branches of pink, weeping cherry. Border forsythia can be also grown as a flowering hedge or trained to frame a window or doorway. Neat and compact "Golden Curls," just 2ft high and 3ft across, is ideal for a small yard.

GOLDEN BELL BUSH AT A GLANCE

Deciduous, bush and trailing/weeping varieties have flowers clothing year-old shoots in spring. Hardy to -13°F (zone 5).

Jan	/	Recommended Varieties
Feb	/	"Fiesta"
Mar	flower, plant	"Gold Cluster"
Apr	flower, plant	"Golden Curls"
May	plant, prune	"Gold Tide"
June	plant	"Lynwood"
July	plant	"Spring Glory"
Aug	plant	"Suspensa"
Sept	plant	"Weekend"
Oct	plant	
Nov	plant	
Dec	plant	

CONDITIONS

Aspect A sunny position is vital. In shade a multitude of shoots form but many will refuse to flower. Growth also becomes loose and weak. Forsythia braves cold wind.

Site This plant grows strongly in most well-drained soils, from heavy clay to light sand and chalk. Fortify impoverished borders, especially where roots from nearby trees invade, with humus-forming, old, crumbly, or proprietary composted manure, well-rotted garden compost, shredded bark, or leaf mould.

GROWING METHOD

Feeding If the soil was initially enriched with plant foods, forsythia seldom needs further feeding. If growth is slow, boost it by topdressing with a balanced granular fertilizer. Alternatively, liquid feed weekly with a high-nitrogen fertilizer from spring to midsummer. Water newly planted shrubs copiously and frequently to help them recover quickly.

Propagation Layer low flexible shoots from spring to late summer or take hardwood cuttings in the fall.

Problems Occasionally—the cause is not known—warty galls distort stems. Overcome them by cutting back affected shoots to healthy wood and burning them.

PRUNING

Once established, keep plants youthful and flowering freely by removing from the base a third of the oldest shoots when flowers fade. Clip hedges at the same time of year, so that flower buds form for the following year.

GENISTA
Genista

Swagged with golden flowers in midsummer, the Mount Etna broom makes a striking shrubby tree and revels in a warm, dry spot.

Here Genista lydia*, a hummock of blossom in June, looks good with silvery-leaved and yellow-flowered* Brachyglottis *"Sunshine".*

FEATURES

Small or rushy leaved and wiry stemmed, this accommodating deciduous family, related to broom, embraces showy, prostrate carpeters and small or large bushes to several yards high. All sport pea-like flowers in various shades of yellow.

From May to June, cushion-like Spanish gorse (*Genista hispanica*), hummocky and cascading *G. lydia* and dazzling, carpeting *G. pilosa* "Vancouver Gold" treat us to a display so radiant that it deceives you into thinking it is sunny when it is not.

Come July and August, the spring brigade is eclipsed by bushy *G. tinctoria* "Royal Gold" and the imposing and fragrant Mount Etna broom (*G. aetnensis*), with its pendulous, rush-like shoots that shower from branches 9ft high.

CONDITIONS

Aspect Hardy and tolerating exposed positions, all genistas perform best in full sun. Drought resisting, they are ideal for hot spots that cannot easily be watered.

Site Happiest in humus-rich and light, free-draining sand and loam, they also prosper in clay if you work in gravel and crumbly organic materials to improve drainage.
Usefully, *G. tinctoria* excels in chalky soil.

GROWING METHOD

Feeding Encourage robust growth by topdressing the root area with a slow-release organic fertilizer, such as bone meal, in spring and fall. Water freely in droughty periods and keep roots cool and active by mulching with old manure, well-rotted garden compost, or bark.

Propagation Increase genista from semi-ripe cuttings of side shoots from mid- to late summer. Root them in pots on a bright windowsill or in a lightly shaded cold frame.

Problems Normally trouble free.

PRUNING

Avoid cutting back *G. aetnensis*, *G. lydia*, and *G. tinctoria*, whose stumps may not regrow. You can, however, rejuvenate ageing *G. hispanica* by shortening old woody stems by two-thirds their length in spring. Keep large stumps moist in dry, windy weather to help them regenerate.

GENISTA AT A GLANCE		
Deciduous spring- or summer-flowering bushes, they need full sunshine to flower bounteously. Hardy to 14°F (zone 8).		
Jan	/	Recommended Varieties
Feb	/	
Mar	plant	*G. aetnensis*
Apr	plant, prune	*G. hispanica*
May	flower, prune	*G. pilosa* "Vancouver Gold"
June	flower, plant	
July	flower, plant	*G. tinctoria* "Flore Pleno"
Aug	flower, plant	*G. tinctoria* "Royal Gold"
Sept	plant	
Oct	plant	
Nov	plant	
Dec	/	

WITCH HAZEL
Hamamelis

A heartening winter vision is spidery, sulfur-yellow-flowered Hamamelis x *intermedia "Pallida" underplanted with snowdrops.*

A bonus of orange, scarlet and red fall tints prelude Hamamelis vernalis, Sandra's late winter display of cadmium-yellow "spiders."

FEATURES

Shining like a beacon on a winter's day, witch hazel's twisted, spidery perfumed flowers thickly clothe bare, spreading branches. Hardy and bushy, 8–10ft high and across, this deciduous shrub is a slow but worthwhile grower that rewards patience. Ideally, set it in a lawn with snowdrops and daffodils.

Choice kinds among several undemanding species and varieties are large, golden-flowered Chinese witch hazel (*Hamamelis mollis*), which blooms from December to March. *H.* x *intermedia* is a hybrid that flowers from February to March and has given us upright and primrose-hued "Westerstede," sulfur-yellow "Pallida," orange and yellow "Diane," and coppery orange "Jelena."

The large, soft-hairy leaves of *H. mollis* turn butter-yellow in the fall. The foliage of "Diane" and "Jelena" is suffused with orange-red before falling. Equally fascinating is the less fragrant Japanese witch hazel (*H. japonica* "Zuccariniana"), which from January to March produces a multitude of pale lemon "spiders."

CONDITIONS

Aspect Hamamelis flowers more freely in full sun and makes a shapelier, more compact bush than in light shade, in which branches are thinner and further apart and leaves larger. Position coppery red-flowered varieties where the sun shines at an angle through their petals and renders them fetchingly translucent.

Site Preferring well-drained, fertile, neutral to acid soil, hamamelis dislikes alkaline, chalky conditions, which causes leaves to become chlorotic. Enrich sandy soils with old manure.

GROWING METHOD

Feeding Water freely after planting to encourage rapid recovery. Each spring, mulch with crumbly manure, bark or well-rotted garden compost to keep roots cool and active. In April, topdress the root area with fish, blood and bone meal or Growmore, repeating in July.

Propagation Layer shoots from mid-spring to late summer. Alternatively, take soft-tip cuttings in late spring and root them in a mist propagating unit in a temperature of 70°F.

Problems When buying plants, opt for those more than four years old, which, unlike younger ones, have a greater chance of succeeding.

PRUNING

Not necessary, but if badly placed stems need removing or shortening, to improve symmetry, use sharp secateurs or loppers when flowers fade, in early spring.

WITCH HAZEL AT A GLANCE

Deciduous and forming a chalice of spreading branches, yellow or orange blooms sleeve stems in winter. Hardy to -13°F (zone 5).

JAN	flower	RECOMMENDED VARIETIES
FEB	flower	
MAR	plant, prune	*H. japonica* "Zuccariniana"
APR	plant	*H.* x *intermedia* "Diane"
MAY	plant	*H.* x *intermedia* "Jelena"
JUN	plant	*H.* x *intermedia* "Pallida"
JULY	plant	*H.* x *intermedia* "Westerstede"
AUG	plant	*H. mollis*
SEPT	plant	
OCT	plant	
NOV	plant	
DEC	flower	

SHRUBBY VERONICA
Hebe

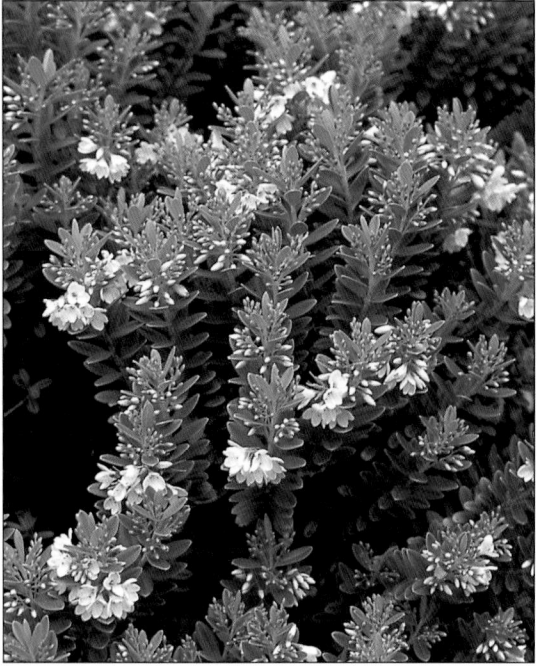

Salt-spray resistant, hebes are ideal for brightening coastal gardens in mild districts. They also tolerate air pollution.

Hebe "Great Orme," here contrasting effectively with an upright cypress, is studded with shapely spikes of blossom from July to October.

FEATURES

An immense and handsome family of small, rounded-leaved or larger, willow-leaved, evergreen New Zealanders, hebes' clustered or cone-shaped spikes of massed, tiny flowers illuminate May to late October. Resisting air pollution, these shrubs are ideal for seaside gardens in mild districts. There are three main, easy and reliable groups:

Carpeters: Forming a dense mat of weed-suppressing foliage to around 12in high, choice kinds include silvery gray-leaved and white-flowered *Hebe pinguifolia* "Pagei".

Bushes: Making bushy globes to 4ft, stunning varieties

are "Fall Glory," whose violet-blue blossoms color June to November, and "Great Orme," smothered with bright pink flowers from July to October.

Taller kinds : Imposing sentinels to 6–10ft, lilac-white *H. salicifolia* is a prince among them.

CONDITIONS

Aspect Hebes need an open position in full sun to make robust and free-flowering growth.

Site Most well-drained soils suit these plants, but they perform best in humus-rich, sandy loam.

GROWING METHOD

Feeding Boost growth by sprinkling fish, blood, and bone meal, Growmore or pelleted chicken manure over the root area in April and July. Water copiously to establish new plants. Once growing strongly, little water is needed.

Propagation Take soft-tip cuttings in early summer and semi-ripe cuttings in midsummer.

Problems Control leaf spot disease by spraying with carbendazim or mancozeb.

PRUNING

Cut back late-flowering varieties to within 6in of the base, every two years in spring, to encourage bounteous blossom. Remove any reverted, green-leaved stems from variegated varieties as soon as they appear.

SHRUBBY VERONICA AT A GLANCE

Evergreen carpeters or bushes clothed with clustered, cone-shaped flowers in white and many other colors. Hardy to 23°F (zone 9).

Month		Recommended Varieties
Jan	/	
Feb	/	"Carl Teschner"
Mar	/	*H.* x *franciscana* "Blue Gem"
Apr	plant, prune	"Great Orme"
May	flower, prune	*H. hulkeana*
June	flower, plant	"Midsummer Beauty"
July	flower, plant	*H. pinguifolia* "Pagei"
Aug	flower, plant	*H. speciosa* "Gauntlettii"
Sept	flower, plant	"Wiri Charm"
Oct	flower	
Nov	/	
Dec	/	

SUN ROSE
Helianthemum

Deep red and yellow-eyed blooms and silvery leaves make "Supreme" a prized variety.

Enjoy a tapestry of blossom by growing sun roses to cascade from a retaining wall. Here plants are camouflaging gaunt, leggy, rose stems.

FEATURES

Varieties of evergreen *Helianthemem nummularium*, commonly called rock or sun rose, make a spreading 4–12in mound to 36in across. From May to July, a network of wiry stems clothed with small, oval leaves are almost hidden beneath a daily succession of single or double flowers in glowing shades of yellow, pink, red, orange, white, or terracotta. Flowers tend to close up on dull days. Sun roses are perfect for draping rock garden pockets, cascading from retaining walls and aproning roses and other bushes flanking a path. They are not long-lived but easily raised from cuttings of maturing, current-year shoots.

CONDITIONS

Aspect Sun rose performs best in an open, brightly lit and airy position where it has room to spread and is not crowded by other plants. Avoid even a hint of shade in which growth is looser, less comely and flowering is inhibited.

Site This shrub needs well-drained and slightly alkaline conditions. Add garden lime to raise the pH of acid soil.

GROWING METHOD

Feeding Boost lustrous foliage and a wealth of blossom by applying a high-potash rose fertilizer in spring and the middle of summer.
Water newly planted shrubs regularly and copiously to help them recover quickly and make good root growth in their first year. Thereafter, they will need watering only in droughty weather. Mulch plants generously with spent mushroom compost.

Propagation Take semi-ripe heeled cuttings in midsummer. These should make flowering-sized plants by the following spring.

Problems Poor drainage or overwatering may kill plants. Powdery mildew can be a problem in crowded borders where air circulates sluggishly. Control this disease by thinning growth and spraying with carbendazim or bupirimate with triforine.

PRUNING

From early to midsummer, when blooms fade, shear back shoots to two-thirds their length. This not only keeps bushes trim and flowering well in spring, but often results in a second, smaller, flush of blossom in fall.

SUN ROSE AT A GLANCE		
A carpeting evergreen so thickly clothed with flowers from May to July that leaves are concealed by them. Hardy to 14°F (zone 8).		
Jan	/	Recommended Varieties
Feb	/	
Mar	/	"Golden Queen"
Apr	plant	"Henfield Brilliant"
May	flower, plant	"Raspberry Ripple"
Jun	flower, plant	"Red Orient"
July	flower, plant	"Supreme"
Aug	plant, prune	"The Bride"
Sept	plant	"Wisley Pink"
Oct	/	"Wisley Primrose"
Nov	/	
Dec	/	

HELIOTROPE
Heliotropium

Old-fashioned heliotrope or cherry pie is festooned with spicy-perfumed blooms from early summer until the fall, when chilly nights halt the display.

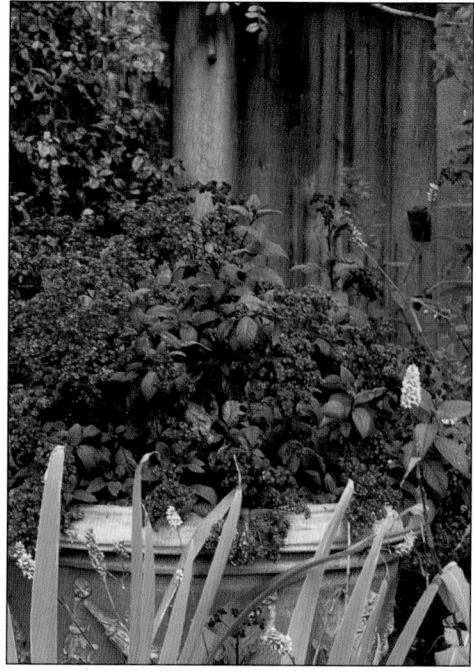

"Marine" is captivating if planted to cascade its deep violet flowers from a patio or terrace tub.

FEATURES

Heliotropium arborescens, also known as cherry pie, is a half-hardy, soft-stemmed, evergreen Peruvian shrub. Growing to 4ft high and across, it is usually bedded out for summer and overwintered in a frost-free greenhouse. A succession of vanilla-fragrant, mauve to purple flowers are borne from summer to the middle of fall, or even longer under glass.

Plant it to spill from a border and on to paving, waterfall from a raised bed or beautify a patio tub. "Lord Roberts," with very dark purple-green leaves and deep violet flowers, is probably the most popular variety.

HELIOTROPIUM AT A GLANCE

Frost-sensitive evergreen with richly fragrant, pink, purple, violet, or white flowers, bedded out for summer. Hardy to 40°F (zone 10).

Month	Activity	Recommended Varieties
Jan	/	
Feb	/	"Dame Alice de Hales"
Mar	/	"Chatsworth"
Apr	plant, prune	"Lord Roberts"
May	plant, prune	"White Lady"
June	flower, plant	"Netherhall White"
July	flower	"Princess Marina"
Aug	flower	
Sept	flower	
Oct	flower	
Nov	flower	
Dec	/	

CONDITIONS

Aspect Outdoors: Heliotrope needs a warm position sheltered from chilly winds. It flowers best in full sunshine.
Under glass: Provide full sun but reduce risk of leaf scorch by shading plants when the temperature rises above 75°F.

Site Outdoors: The soil should be crumbly and well drained. Enrich thin, sandy patches with humus-forming, well-decayed manure.

GROWING METHOD

Feeding Outdoors and under glass: liquid feed weekly with a high-potash fertilizer from spring to late summer.
In late summer or early fall, lift and pot up plants bedded out in borders and patio tub plants. Move them to a frost-free greenhouse or conservatory and keep the compost dry until late winter or early spring.

Propagation Heliotrope is easily increased from soft-tip cuttings taken in spring, and semi-ripe cuttings struck in late summer.

Problems Being half-hardy, this shrub must not be moved outdoors until frosts have finished in late May or early June.

PRUNING

Encourage new flowering stems by shortening a third of older, woody branches by half their length in early spring.

HIBISCUS
Hibiscus

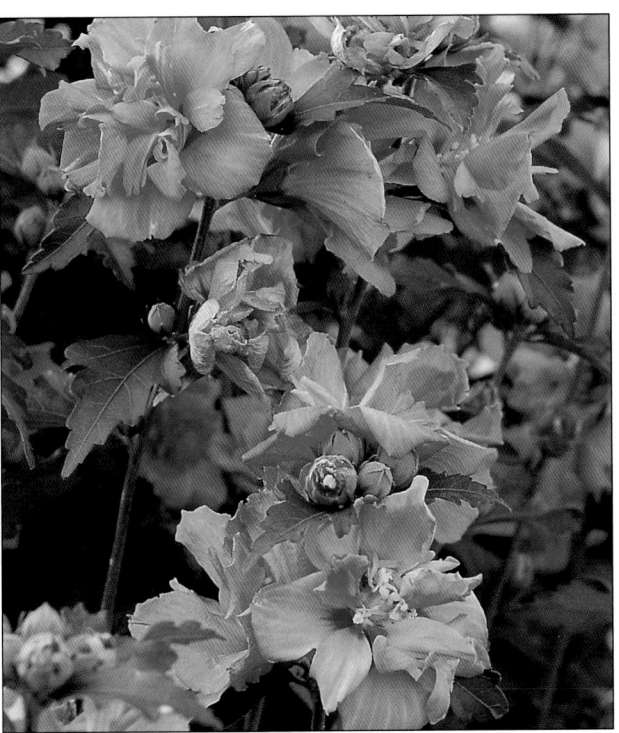

A late-summer bonus of exotic, single, or double, saucer-shaped blooms are your reward for growing a hardy hibiscus.

Healthy and seldom attracting pests and diseases, hibiscus is best planted in a sunny position so shoots ripen and flower well.

FEATURES

Also known as shrubby mallow, this deciduous, late summer statement is festooned with saucer-shaped blooms from July to September. Flowers are single or double and range in color from white, pink and blue, to purple. Several are bicolored. Most popular varieties are violet-blue and white-eyed "Blue Bird," white and crimson-eyed "Hamabo" and rose-pink and dark-centerd "Woodbridge." Long-lived, it makes an upright bush to 8ft high and across and flowers early in its life. It is very hardy.

CONDITIONS

Aspect Hibiscus grows best and flowers prolifically in full sun. Shield it from icy winds. Avoid even light shade, for shoots will not ripen well and so flowering is impaired.

Site This shrub thrives on well-drained, fertile, sandy loam but tolerates poorer soils. Enjoy good results by enriching the planting area with plenty of well-rotted organic matter.

GROWING METHOD

Feeding Apply all-purpose plant food, such as fish, blood, and bone meal, or Growmore, in spring and again in midsummer.
Water regularly in spring and summer to help newly planted hibiscus recover quickly.

Propagation Layer whippy shoots from mid-spring to late summer, and take semi-ripe heeled cuttings from late summer to early fall.

Problems Control aphids with pirimicarb, horticultural soap, or natural pyrethrins.

PRUNING

Rejuvenate ageing shrubs by shortening them to half their height in spring. This is also the best time to cut back frost-damaged shoots.

HIBISCUS AT A GLANCE		
Deciduous and slow growing, large, saucer-shaped, pink, blue, or white blooms appear in late summer. Hardy to 4°F (zone 7).		
Jan	/	Recommended Varieties
Feb	/	"Blue Bird"
Mar	plant	"Bredon Springs"
Apr	plant, prune	"Hamabo"
May	plant	"Lady Stanley"
June	plant	"Lenny"
July	flower, plant	"Meehanii"
Aug	flower, plant	"Woodbridge"
Sept	flower, plant	"William R. Smith"
Oct	plant	
Nov	plant	
Dec	/	

HYDRANGEA
Hydrangea

Ever popular hydrangea is a native of China and Japan. Ensure pink blossom by adding lime to the soil in spring. For ultramarine-blue flowers, feed with aluminium sulphate.

Position mophead and other hydrangeas in a sheltered spot in dappled shade.

FEATURES

Brightly studded with large, globular, mushroom-headed, or broadly conical flowers, hydrangeas richly color borders from July to September. Blooms come in white and shades of pink, blue, or red. Long-lived, this deciduous shrub grows 20in–8ft high and across.

Most widely grown are aptly named mophead and lacecap varieties of *Hydrangea macrophylla*. Yielding pink, mauve, or red blooms on alkaline soils and blue heads in acid conditions, they thrive in fertile ground. Characteristically, lacecaps have an outer ring of large, sterile flowers enclosing tiny, pink, or blue, fertile ones.

Other choice kinds are white, football-headed *H. arborescens* "Annabelle" and light pink, cone-flowered *H. paniculata* "Pink Diamond." *H. quercifolia* has oak-leaved foliage which complement trusses of rich creamy flowers and *H. villosa* is a gem with porcelain-blue mushrooms poised above stems clad with huge, velvety leaves.

A self-clinging climber, white, disc-flowered *H. petiolaris* beautifully transforms a cold, north-facing wall.

CONDITIONS

Aspect Dappled sunlight or morning sun and afternoon shade suit hydrangeas. Make sure they are sheltered from frosty winds, which will damage embryo blossoms.
H. macrophylla varieties are reliable seaside plants for relatively frost-free areas.

Site These shrubs need damp soil high in organic matter, so improve poor areas by digging in plenty of well-decayed manure or compost a few months ahead of planting. Also mulch plants with well-rotted organic matter.

GROWING METHOD

Feeding Apply acidifying fertilizer like sulphate of ammonia in spring and midsummer to ensure a steady release of plant foods and encourage blue flowers.

Propagation Multiply favoured varieties by layering flexible shoots from mid-spring to late summer. Take soft-tip cuttings from late spring to early summer and semi-ripe cuttings from mid- to late summer.

Problems Excessive lime prevents chlorophyll from forming and causes leaves to yellow and die. Overcome it by applying iron chelates.

PRUNING

H. macrophylla: Cut off spent flowers in spring and remove crowding shoots.

H. paniculata: Prune stems to within two buds of the base in late March.

H. petiolaris: Cut out unwanted shoots when flowers fade.

H. villosa: Remove a third of older stems in spring.

HYDRANGEA AT A GLANCE

Deciduous shrubs bearing large heads of white, pink, red, or blue flowers from mid- to late summer. Hardy to 4°F (zone 7).

Month	Activity	Recommended Varieties
Jan	/	
Feb	/	Mopheads
Mar	plant, prune	"Hamburgh"
Apr	plant, prune	"Madame E. Moullière"
May	plant	Lacecaps
June	plant	"Blue Wave"
July	flower, plant	"White Wave"
Aug	flower, plant	*H. arborescens* "Annabelle"
Sept	flower, plant	*H. paniculata* "Kyushu"
Oct	plant	*H. quercifolia*
Nov	plant	*H. villosa*
Dec	/	

HYDRANGEA VARIETIES

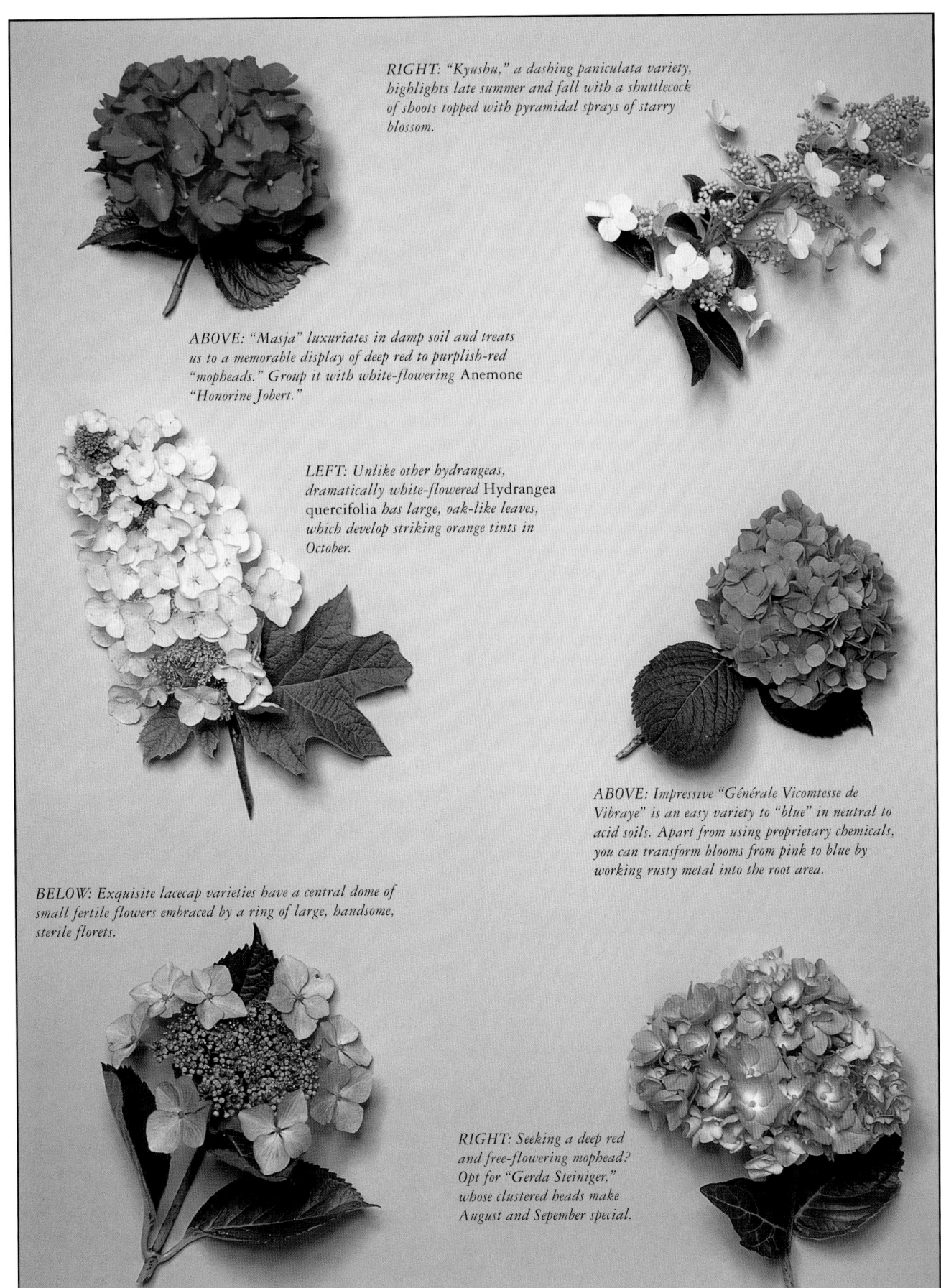

RIGHT: "Kyushu," a dashing paniculata variety, highlights late summer and fall with a shuttlecock of shoots topped with pyramidal sprays of starry blossom.

ABOVE: "Masja" luxuriates in damp soil and treats us to a memorable display of deep red to purplish-red "mopheads." Group it with white-flowering Anemone "Honorine Jobert."

LEFT: Unlike other hydrangeas, dramatically white-flowered Hydrangea quercifolia has large, oak-like leaves, which develop striking orange tints in October.

ABOVE: Impressive "Générale Vicomtesse de Vibraye" is an easy variety to "blue" in neutral to acid soils. Apart from using proprietary chemicals, you can transform blooms from pink to blue by working rusty metal into the root area.

BELOW: Exquisite lacecap varieties have a central dome of small fertile flowers embraced by a ring of large, handsome, sterile florets.

RIGHT: Seeking a deep red and free-flowering mophead? Opt for "Gerda Steiniger," whose clustered heads make August and Sepember special.

JASMINE
Jasminum

Illuminating a north or east-facing wall from November to March, Jasminum nudiflorum *flowers very freely on cascading shoots.*

Ideal for clothing a pergola or trellis work, twining Jasminum officinale affine *is swathed with scented flowers in summer.*

FEATURES

There are two forms of jasmine—climbing and bushy—both of which flower generously. Choice and reliable twining climbers—ideal for screening—are *Jasminum affine*, to 25ft, whose pink buds open to sweetly scented, white flowers from July to September; and *J. × stephanense*, to 15ft, which from early to midsummer pleases with a profusion of perfumed, pale pink blooms amid colorful, cream-flushed, green leaves.

Among bushy kinds, the popular, yellow-flowered winter jasmine (*J. nudiflorum*) is usually trained to transform a wall or fence from November to late February. After establishing a main framework, leave it to flower freely on cascading shoots. Aspiring to half that height, semi-evergreen *J. humile* "Revolutum" is dashingly clad with larger, fragrant, yellow blossoms from late spring to fall. Even smaller is yellow-flowered, mound forming *J. parkeri*, which when planted on a rock garden brightens it in early summer.

CONDITIONS

Aspect While climbing kinds need a sheltered spot and full sunshine for most of the day, the most popular bushy member—*G. nudiflorum*—thrives on a shaded, north wall lashed by frosty winds.

Site Undemanding, all flourish on most well-drained soils. Enrich and improve the water retention of thin, sandy areas by digging in bulky organics several months before planting. Help clay drain better by forking in grit.

GROWING METHOD

Feeding Give young plants a good start by consigning them to generous planting holes fortified with bone meal or Growmore fertilizer. Soak the soil after planting to settle it around roots and remove air pockets. Encourage robust growth by working bone meal into the root area in spring and the fall.

Propagation Layer whippy shoots from spring to late summer or take semi-ripe cuttings from mid- to late summer.

Problems Gray mold, a fungus covering leaves with a grayish, furry patina, may occur if shoots are crowded. Control it by removing affected parts and spraying with carbendazim.

PRUNING

Climbing kinds are not normally cut back. If they outgrow their situation, shorten shoots after flowering. Keep *J. nudiflorum* youthful and massed with bloom by removing a third of the older flowered stems when flowers fade in early spring.

JASMINE AT A GLANCE

Semi-evergreen or deciduous, twining or bush forms color walls and fences in winter and summer. Hardy to 4°F (zone 7).

Jan	flower	Recommended Varieties
Feb	flower	
Mar	prune	*J. affine*
Apr	plant	*J. humile* "Revolutum"
May	flower, plant	*J. nudiflorum*
Jun	flower, plant	*J. parkeri*
July	flower, plant	*J. × stephanense*
Aug	flower, prune	
Sept	flower, plant	
Oct	plant	
Nov	plant	
Dec	/	

KERRIA

Kerria japonica

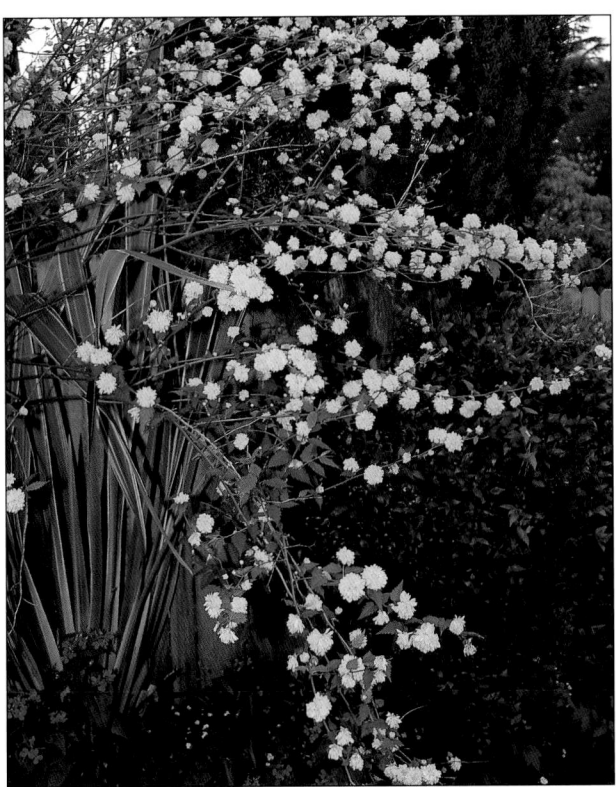

A charmingly tangled mass of bright yellow flowers in spring makes kerria an attractive screening plant, even at dusk.

Kerria has single or double flowers and leaves that develop radiant yellow tints in fall. This is the double "Pleniflora" version.

FEATURES

Graceful and arching, deciduous *Kerria japonica* makes a fascinating focus to about 6ft high. From April to May, its radiant orange-yellow blooms clothe a profusion of suckering, cane-like, green stems.

Coveted forms are "Pleniflora," magnificent with its double, golden pompons; "Golden Guinea," with beautiful, single, buttercup-yellow flowers; and smaller "Picta"—just 3ft high—whose single, yellow blossoms complement cream-edged, green leaves. Very hardy and happy almost anywhere, taller kinds making dense and colorful hedges.

KERRIA AT A GLANCE

Deciduous shrub with green stems dotted with single or double, yellow blooms in spring. Hardy to -13°F (zone 5).

Jan	/	Recommended Varieties
Feb	/	"Albescens"
Mar	plant	"Golden Guinea"
Apr	flower, plant	"Picta"
May	flower, plant	"Pleniflora"
June	plant, prune	"Simplex"
July	plant	
Aug	plant	
Sept	plant	
Oct	plant	
Nov	plant	
Dec	/	

CONDITIONS

Aspect	This shrub flowers best in full sun and performs passably well in shade.
Site	Kerria will thrive almost anywhere.

GROWING METHOD

Feeding	Keep growth vigorous and packed with blossom in spring by applying bone meal in March and October. Water new plants frequently to help them establish quickly.
Propagation	Probably the easiest shrub to multiply, it can be increased from semi-ripe cuttings in midsummer; layered shoots from mid-spring to late summer; hardwood cuttings in late fall; and suckers in early spring.
Problems	No particular pests or diseases.

PRUNING

Cut out from the base a third of older shoots when blooms fade in early summer. Remove green-leaved stems on variegated bushes.

LAVENDER
Lavendula

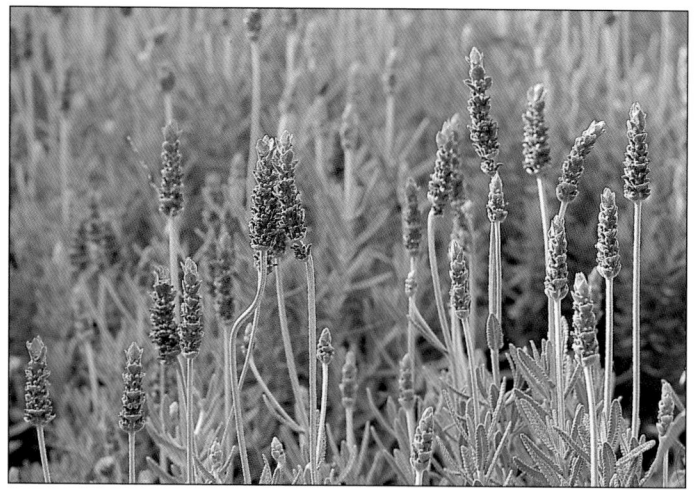

Blooming from July to September, evergreen lavender excels in free-draining "hot spots". Make sure you get the plant you want by buying it in flower.

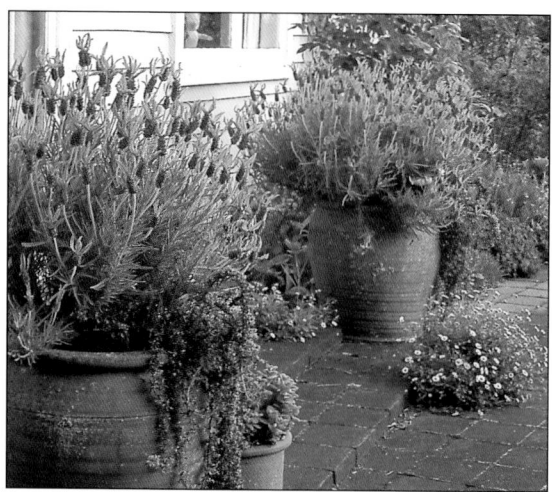

Aromatic French lavender is a delightful cottage-garden plant. Brush against it and citrus scent fills the air.

FEATURES

Never out of fashion, hardy, evergreen lavender forms a rounded shrub 12–30in high. From July to September, its aromatic, gray-green foliage complements spikes of tightly clustered, pale blue, purple, pink, or white flowers. Interplant it with other shrubs or border perennials or set it to form a fetching divide between open-plan gardens.

Choice varieties are: dwarf, compact and rich purple-blue "Hidcote"; equally neat, lavender-blue "Munstead"; and taller French lavender (*Lavandula stoechas* "Papillon"), the dark purple flowers of which are borne in dense, lozenge-shaped heads. Flowers are used fresh in posies and dried for pot-pourri or cosmetics.

Lavender is an archetypal cottage-garden plant. Its common names of French, English, or Italian lavender apply to different species, but even experts find it hard to agree upon which is which.

LAVENDER AT A GLANCE

Aromatic, grayish-leaved evergreen with scented, lavender, purple, pink, or white flowers in summer. Hardy to 14°F (zone8).

		Recommended Varieties
Jan	/	
Feb	/	"Hidcote"
Mar	/	"Loddon Pink"
Apr	plant, prune	"Munstead"
May	plant	"Nana Alba"
June	plant	"Twickel Purple"
July	flower, plant	*L. vera*
Aug	flower, plant	*L. stoechas* "Papillon"
Sept	flower, plant	
Oct	/	
Nov	/	
Dec	/	

CONDITIONS

Aspect   Lavender needs an open situation in full sun with good air circulation. Do not crowd it with other plantings.

Site   Thriving on most well-drained soils, it prefers coarse, sandy, or gravelly loam. Lime acid soils before planting.

GROWING METHOD

Feeding   Boost growth of young plants by topdressing the root area with fish, blood, and bone meal in spring and midsummer. When established, after two years, no regular fertilizing is necessary.

Water new plantings copiously to help them recover quickly. When well established, lavender is seldom stressed by droughty spells.

Propagation   Take semi-ripe cuttings from early to mid-fall. Alternatively, work sharp sand into the crown in spring, watering it well, so lower branches are buried. Detach rooted layers in fall and move them to their new positions.

Problems   Lavender is seldom troubled by pests or diseases but may succumb to root rot in heavy or overwet soils. If crowded, in sheltered gardens, the foliage may die back. Remove dead growth and thin out stems to improve air circulation.

PRUNING

Use shears to trim dead blooms from bushes and hedges after flowering.

Rejuvenate older, "tired" plants and help them bloom freely by shortening the previous year's flowered stems to new shoots within 2–4in of the base. Do this from early to mid-spring. Never cut back into older wood, for it seldom regenerates and plants may die.

LAVENDER VARIETIES

RIGHT: Create a feature by interplanting "Sawyers," a robust and deep purple-flowered variety, with Perovskia *"Blue Spire," a Russian sage with grayish-white-stemmed spikes of rich blue flowers.*

ABOVE: Thriving in a warm, sunny border, French lavender (Lavandula stoechas) *forms an appealing globe to 2ft high and across. A wealth of lozenge-shaped flower heads in summer, and leaves, emit a strong citrus scent.*

LEFT: Seeking a small, white variety for a patio pot? Opt for "Nana Alba." Just 8in high, it associates stunningly with a fringe of trailing, purple Surfinia petunias.

BELOW: An archetypal cottage-garden plant, old English lavender (Lavandula angustifolia) *makes a handsome fountain of blossom to 3ft high.*

BELOW: Keen to plant a low lavender hedge to flank a path or driveway? Plump for "Munstead," whose thickly clustered shoots are topped with dark lavender-blue flowers.

NEW ZEALAND TEA TREE
Leptospermum scoparium

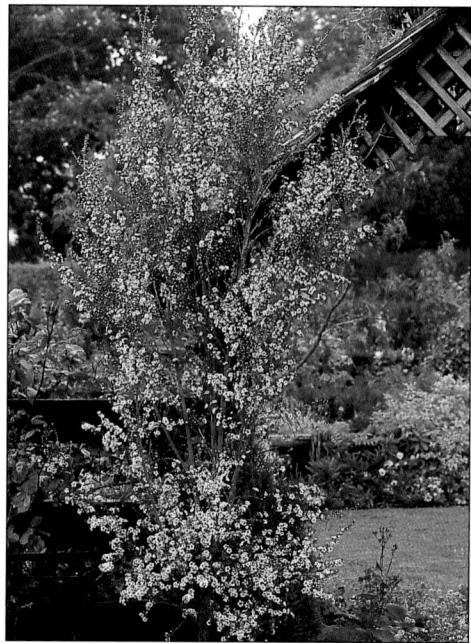

Smothered with tiny, disc-like blooms from May to June, Leptospermum *"Red Damask" is best fan-trained against a warm, sunny wall in all but very mild areas.*

Keep tea tree youthful and glowing with blossom by removing a third of the older shoots when flowers fade.

FEATURES

Bejewelled from May to June with stalkless, disc-like blooms amid small, narrow leaves, twiggy and slender, purplish-stemmed *Leptospermum scoparium* is an evergreen worth caring for. Forming a rounded bush, 6–8ft high, it is usually grown against a sheltered wall. Alternatively, set it among other shrubs that shield it from biting winds.

Trained as a mini-standard, it makes a fetching feature for a sun-soaked patio.

Favoured varieties are double "Red Damask," single, clear pink "Huia," and double, white "Snow Flurry". Be warned: tea trees may be short-lived unless conditions are ideal.

TEA TREE AT A GLANCE

A slightly frost-tender evergreen, it is studded with tiny, red, pink, or white blooms from May to June. Hardy to 23°F (zone 9).

Jan	/	
Feb	/	**Recommended Varieties**
Mar	/	
Apr	plant	"Huia"
May	flower, plant	"Kiwi"
June	flower, plant	"Red Damask"
July	plant, prune	"Snow Flurry"
Aug	plant	
Sept	plant	
Oct	/	
Nov	/	
Dec	/	

CONDITIONS

Aspect Leptospermum needs full sun and protection from cold, north or east winds. Ideally fan-train it against a south- or west-facing wall. Make sure air freely circulates to reduce risk of mildew felting and crippling leaves.

Site The planting area must be well drained. Improve light, sandy soils by digging in old manure or well-rotted garden compost.

GROWING METHOD

Feeding Encourage robust flowering growth by applying an acidifying fertilizer in spring and midsummer. Water young plants regularly in their first year after planting. Thereafter, soak the root area periodically in dry periods and mulch with shredded bark.

Propagation Multiply plants from soft-tip cuttings in June or semi-ripe cuttings in late summer.

Problems Plants are susceptible to root rot in clay soils. Avoid it by forking in grit or gravel before planting. Webbing caterpillars, such as lackey moth, can cause leaves to drop. Cut off and destroy egg bands or webbed shoots and spray with permethrin, bifenthrin, or fenitrothion.

PRUNING

If leptospermum outgrows its allotted space, remove one shoot in three from the base, when flowers fade in midsummer. Do not cut back into older wood as it seldom re-grows. Remove straggly shoots in spring.

HONEYSUCKLE
Lonicera

Small and bushy Lonicera fragrantissima *treats us to a massed display of vanilla-perfumed, creamy flowers from mid- to late winter.*

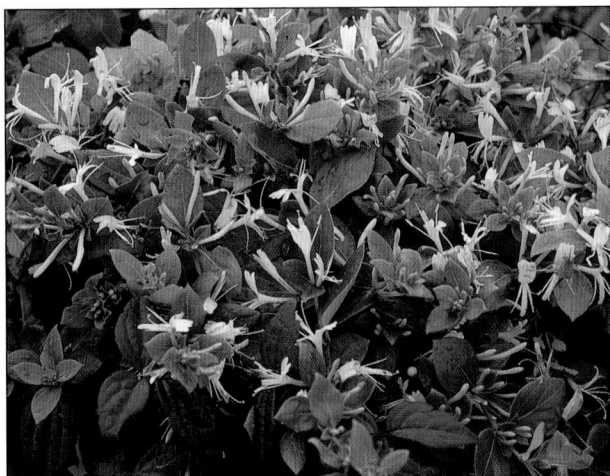

Clothed with sweetly scented blooms from June to October, Lonicera japonica *"Halliana" makes a fetching screen for a sunny patio.*

FEATURES

A trio of sweetly scented, bushy honeysuckles worth cultivating are: *Lonicera fragrantissima*, with its vanilla-perfumed, creamy-white, bell-shaped blooms, which are freely borne on twiggy shoots to 6ft from January to March; slightly smaller *L. × purpusii*, which treats us to a similar display from November to March; and *L. syringantha*, with its profusion of clustered, lilac flowers on 3ft stems from late spring to early summer.

Twining varieties, trained to frame a door or clothe a wall, fence, arbour, pergola, or arch or to scramble through a tree, enhance a garden. Color spring by planting yellow and red *L. periclymenum* "Belgica" and continue the show—from June to October—with white and red *L.p.* "Serotina."

CONDITIONS

Aspect   Plant lonicera in full or lightly dappled shade to grow strongly and flower freely.

Site   These shrubs and climbers prefer well-drained and humus-rich, sandy loam, or clay loam but also tolerate chalky soil. Improve light soils, which dry out quickly, by working in bulky organic materials well before planting.

GROWING METHOD

Feeding   Speed robust growth and a panoply of blossom by enriching the root area with bone meal in spring and fall.

Water liberally to encourage young plants to establish quickly. Once growing strongly, all varieties are unstressed by droughty periods.

In spring, mulch thickly with humus-forming organics to keep roots cool and questing and encourage a fine display of blossom.

Propagation Take hardwood cuttings in late fall or
Shrubs: early winter, or layer whippy stems from mid-spring to late summer.

Climbers: Take semi-ripe cuttings from early to midsummer.

Problems   Blackfly are attracted to new shoots, which they quickly smother. Control them with pirimicarb, natural pyrethrins, bifenthrin, or horticultural soap.

PRUNING

Keep winter-flowering *L. fragrantissima* and *L. × purpusii* shapely and full of young shoots, which flower freely, by removing one stem in three in mid-spring. Help spring- and early summer-blooming *L. syringantha* prosper by cutting back flowered shoots to new growth when blooms fade.

Prune *L. periclymenum* varieties and *L. japonica* "Halliana" by shortening flowered stems to new shoots when blooms fade.

HONEYSUCKLE AT A GLANCE		
Semi-evergreen bushes and deciduous and evergreen climbers light up spring, summer and winter. Hardy to -13°F (zone 5).		
Jan	flower	Recommended Varieties
Feb	flower	
Mar	plant	Bushes
Apr	flower, prune	*L. fragrantissima*
May	flower, prune	*L. × purpusii*
June	flower, prune	*L. syringantha*
July	flower, plant	*L. tartarica*
Aug	flower, prune	Climbers
Sept	flower, prune	"Belgica"
Oct	plant	*L. heckrottii* "Goldflame"
Nov	plant	"Serotina"
Dec	/	*L. japonica* "Halliana"
		L. tragophylla

MAGNOLIA
Magnolia

Unfolding in March and April, before leaves appear, starry-flowered Magnolia stellata *lights up dappled shade.*

Planted to contrast with a dark green-leaved shrub, the star magnolia makes a statement. Underplant it with blue-flowered grape hyacinths.

FEATURES

Heralding spring, *Magnolia stellata*, a deciduous, bushy shrub to around 7ft, illuminates borders with a multitude of fragrant, strap-petalled, starry, white flowers from March to April. Also called star magnolia, it is ideal for small gardens. Fetching varieties are pink-budded, white-flowered "Royal Star," white-flowered "Centennial," whose blooms are 5½in across, and "Waterlily," another handsome, white variety with flared, double chalices that command close attention.

Most other magnolias, such as evergreen *M. grandiflora*, which flowers best if fan-trained on a sunny, sheltered wall, and varieties of *M. soulangeana*, soar to around 15ft.

CONDITIONS

Aspect	No matter how large or small the variety, magnolias should be sheltered from strong winds. To flower well, they must receive at least half a day's sunshine.
Site	*M. stellata* and *M. grandiflora* prosper in well-drained, acid, neutral, or alkaline soil. *M. soulangeana* abhors chalk. Dig in plenty of organic matter well ahead of planting.

GROWING METHOD

Feeding	Encourage bountiful blooms by applying an acidifying fertilizer—brands for azaleas and camellias are ideal—in April and July.
Propagation	Take soft-tip cuttings from late spring to early summer. Increase *M. grandiflora* from semi-ripe cuttings in midsummer. Layering is more reliable but takes longer. Peg down shoots from spring to late summer and detach rooted stems a year later in fall.
Problems	Soft, unfolding leaves can be scorched by hot, dry, or salty winds, so position plants carefully.

PRUNING

Seldom necessary. If a shrub requires shaping or crowded branches need removing, tackle it when flowers fade in mid-spring. Never prune in winter, as corky tissues are liable to rot.

MAGNOLIA AT A GLANCE

White or pink flowers are thickly borne on leafless branches in early spring. *M. stellata* is hardy to -13° (zone 5).

Jan	/	
Feb	/	Recommended Varieties
Mar	flower, plant	*M. grandiflora**
Apr	flower, plant	*M. grandiflora* "Heaven Scent"*
May	flower, prune	*M. grandiflora* "Little Gem"*
Jun	plant, prune	
July	plant, flower*	*M. soulangeana* "Lennei"
Aug	plant, flower*	*M. soulangeana* "Picture"
Sept	plant, flower*	*M. stellata*
Oct	/	*M. stellata* "Centennial"
Nov	/	*M. stellata* "Royal Star"
Dec	/	* summer flowering

Magnolia varieties

RIGHT: A glorious sight in May, a mature bush of Magnolia soulangeana "Alba Superba" is massed with upright, tulip-like, snow-white blossoms, purple at the base. Site it carefully—in a sheltered, sunny spot free from frost, which reduces blooms to soggy mops.

ABOVE: Showered in spring with goblet-shaped blooms, rosy purple outside, suffused cream and purple within, Magnolia soulangeana "Lennei" treats us to a further, smaller display in fall.

LEFT: A Japanese gem, Magnolia liliiflora "Nigra" rewards us with a multitude of long, slender, candle-like buds that open to deep purple blooms stained creamy white and purple within. When mature, petals reflex and become starry. As well as planting it in the garden, set it in a large, well-drained patio tub in which it will grow slowly and flower bounteously.

BELOW: A good choice for a small garden, Magnolia stellata makes a neat globe to around 5ft high after ten years or so. It is very accommodating, does not need pruning and is seldom attacked by pests or diseases.

RIGHT: A hybrid raised at the US National Arboretum, Washington, Magnolia liliiflora x stellata "Judy" is one of several hybrids superior to their parents in flower size, profusion of blossom, color, and scent.

MAHONIA
Mahonia

Tall, bushy mahonias display shuttlecocks of citrus-scented, pale lemon to golden flowers from early winter to early spring. Decorative, blue berries follow in the fall.

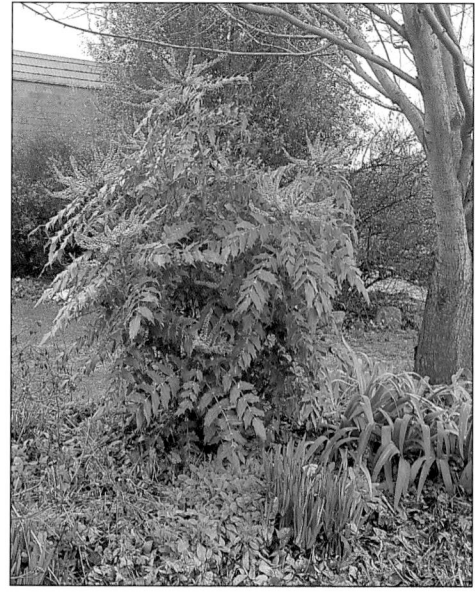

Mahonia × media *"Charity" illuminates a dry, shady spot from mid- to late winter.*

FEATURES

Ground-hugging, weed-suppressing, and good for stabilizing steep banks, tall and sculptural, evergreen mahonias have shiny, spiky, holly-like leaves that develop burnished coppery or reddish tints in winter. Flamboyant, citrus-scented heads of yellow or golden-clustered, slender, cone-like flowers appear from November to May. Blooms are followed by decorative, bluish-black berries. From 2ft to 8ft high, depending on the species, taller kinds make fetching focal points, dense screens or dashing background plants.

Varieties of suckering, ground-covering *Mahonia aquifolium*, which thrives in light shade, effectively carpet rooty areas around trees and shrubs. Position orb-shaped and free-flowering *M.* × *media* "Charity" and more upright "Lionel Fortescue" to light up winter.

CONDITIONS

Aspect   Thriving in sun or dappled shade, mahonias resist cold winds.

Site   These shrubs flourish in all but very chalky conditions. Improve poor soils by adding bulky organic matter several weeks before planting.

GROWING METHOD

Feeding   Boost growth by working fish, blood, and bone meal or Growmore into the root area in mid-spring and midsummer. If they are growing where there is root competition, mulch thickly to help conserve moisture.

Propagation   Raise species from seeds in early to mid-spring, in a garden frame.
Take leaf-bud cuttings in mid-fall or mid-spring and root in a heated propagator.
Divide *M. aquifolium* into well-rooted portions in mid-spring.

Problems   Control mahonia rust by spraying with penconazole, mancozeb, or bupirimate with triforine. *M. aquifolium* and *M. bealei* have some resistance to this disease.

PRUNING

M. aquifolium: Prevent plants from becoming leggy by removing one stem in three after flowering.

Tall, bushy hybrids: Remove flower heads when blooms fade; rejuvenate old, gaunt plants by shortening stems by half their height in May.

MAHONIA AT A GLANCE

Carpeting or upright evergreens, with holly-like leaves, color borders from November to March. Hardy to -13°F (zone 5).

Jan	flower	Recommended Varieties
Feb	flower	*M. aquifolium* "Apollo"
Mar	flower	*M. aquifolium*
Apr	flower, plant	"Atropurpurea"
May	prune, flower	*M. aquifolium* "Smaragd"
June	plant	*M. japonica*
July	feed	*M. lomariifolia*
Aug	plant	*M.* × *media* "Charity"
Sept	plant	"Lionel Fortescue"
Oct	plant	"Winter Sun"
Nov	flower	
Dec	flower	

SACRED BAMBOO
Nandina domestica

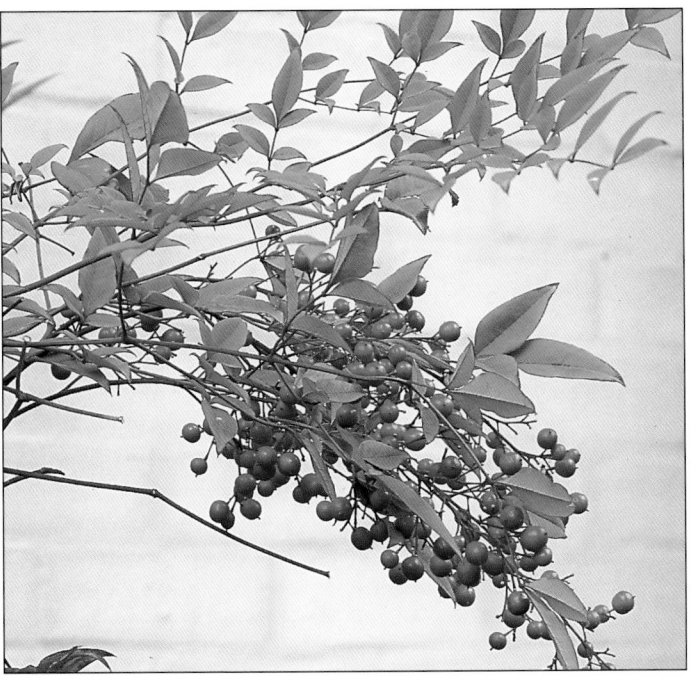

Nandina's fall bounty of bright red berries follows a summer display of white flowers. Leaves are greenish but tinted cream, pink, orange, and red.

Unlike true bamboo, the sacred version is light, airy, and not invasive and is ideal for colonising a restricted space.

FEATURES

Reminiscent of bamboo, nandina is a slender-stemmed evergreen that slowly spreads by suckers to make a fascinating focal point. Grown for its brightly hued, cream, orange, pink, and red leaves, its "airy" shoots create an impression of "lightness". Nandina, much prized for Japanese-style gardens, may also be sited elsewhere to contrast effectively with darker-toned and heavier-textured plants. Small, white flowers from June to July are followed by attractive, red berries, which linger into fall. Makes a handsome bush to 4ft high by 3ft across.

SACRED BAMBOO AT A GLANCE

Bamboo-like evergreen whose cream-, orange-, and pink-tinted leaves complement white flowers. Hardy to 14°F (zone 8).

		Recommended Varieties
Jan	/	
Feb	/	"Firepower"
Mar		"Nana Purpurea"
Apr	plant	"Richmond"
May	prune	
June	plant, flower	
July	plant, flower	
Aug	plant, flower	
Sept	plant	
Oct	/	
Nov	/	
Dec	/	

CONDITIONS

Aspect Thriving in full sun or semi-shade, it needs shielding from cold winds, which can blacken leaves. Ideally, plant it at the foot of a south- or west-facing wall.

Soil Nandina prefers well-drained and humus rich, sandy loam. Augment chalk or heavy clay soils with bulky organic materials a month or two before planting.

GROWING METHOD

Feeding Encourage luxuriant foliage and large clusters of fruit by working bone meal into the root area in spring and the fall.
Once established, nandina is fairly drought resistant. Mulch with well-rotted garden compost, manure, shredded bark, or cocoa shell in spring to insulate roots from moisture-extracting sunshine.

Propagation In the fall, extract seeds from ripe berries, sow in pots and raise in a garden frame. Take semi-ripe cuttings from mid- to late summer. Use a spade to split up large clumps in mid-spring.

Problems Severe winter weather may kill shoots to ground level and new growth from roots may be slow in appearing.

PRUNING

No regular cutting back is necessary. Rejuvenate old clumps in May by removing a third of the older stems at ground level.

OLEANDER
Nerium oleander

Delighting us with white, yellow, apricot, pink, or crimson blooms from spring to fall, evergreen but poisonous oleander is easy to grow.

Create a Mediterranean tapestry by grouping a pot-grown oleander next to a spiky-leaved yucca and scarlet pelargonium.

FEATURES

Frost-tender and principally a conservatory plant, evergreen oleander enjoys a summer airing on a sunny, sheltered patio or terrace. Depending on variety, it makes a handsome shrub, 4–6ft high. Sumptuous heads of white, yellow, pink, apricot, cerise, or scarlet, single or double blooms appear from June to November. Thrusting, upright stems are clad with slender, leathery leaves. Oleanders are long-lived and flower early in life. Choice varieties include: semi-double, light pink "Clare"; single, apricot "Madame Leon Blum"; double, white "Soeur Agnes"; and single, deep red "Hardy's Red." Double, pink-flowered "Variegatum," with cream or yellow-rimmed leaves, is very popular with flower arrangers. The plant is poisonous if eaten.

OLEANDER AT A GLANCE

Studded with showy blooms in many colors, frost-tender oleander is usually grown in a conservatory. Hardy to 45°F (zone 11).

Jan	/	
Feb	/	Recommended Varieties
Mar	plant	"Clare"
Apr	plant, prune	"Emile"
May	flower, plant	"Géant des Batailles"
June	flower, plant	"Luteum Plenum"
July	flower, plant	"Professor Granel"
Aug	flower, plant	"Soeur Agnes"
Sept	flower, plant	"Soleil Levant"
Oct	flower	"Variegatum"
Nov	flower	
Dec	/	

CONDITIONS

Aspect   Oleander needs full sun and shelter from cold winds to prosper and flower freely. Only in frost-free gardens can it be grown outdoors all year round. Elsewhere, grow it in a pot indoors—in a lounge or conservatory—and move it outside when frosts finish in late May.

Site   This shrub thrives in most free-draining soil types but abhors heavy, waterlogged clay. If growing it in a large pot or tub, set it in proprietary tub or hanging basket compost.

GROWING METHOD

Feeding   Border plants: Encourage large clusters of blossom by sprinkling bone meal over the root area in spring and fall and hoeing it in.
Tub grown (indoors in winter): Insert slow-release fertilizer granules into the compost in spring. Repot root-bound plants in spring. Though oleander tolerates long, dry periods, soak roots occasionally in hot, dry weather.

Propagation   Raise plants from seeds sown in a heated propagator in spring or take semi-ripe cuttings in midsummer.

Problems   If plants are attacked by limpet-like scale insects, control them by spraying two or three times, fortnightly, with malathion or horticultural soap.

PRUNING

Keep oleander youthful and blooming freely by shortening flowered shoots by half their length when blossoms fade. Ensure plants stay neat and bushy by shortening side shoots to 4in in spring.

OSMANTHUS
Osmanthus

Forming an umbrella of small, evergreen shoots, Osmanthus delavayi's *thickly clustered, tubular flowers sleeve shoots in spring.*

A beacon of bright, cream-rimmed, evergreen leaves from Osmanthus heterophyllus *"Variegatus" illuminates dull, winter days.*

FEATURES

An easy, enchanting, and small, glossy, leathery-leaved evergreen from western China and Japan, osmanthus forms an orb of shoots and colors spring and fall.

Light up April and May with *Osmanthus × burkwoodii*. Growing to around 6ft high by 4ft across, its toothed, pointed leaves foil slender stems massed with clusters of small, white, vanilla-fragrant, tubular blooms. Create a riveting feature by grouping it with orange or yellow deciduous azaleas. It also makes a dense, wind-proof hedge.

Closely related *O. delavayi* is another spring-flowering treasure. Arching to 5ft high, it too is smothered with bunches of small, white blooms that spill jasmine perfume on to the air. Small, black fruits follow them.

Later, from September to October, comes taller *O. heterophyllus*, to 10ft high and across, the soft leaves of which deceive you into thinking it is a form of holly. It does a sterling job in coloring the closing year with a profusion of tiny, white blossoms.

Its colored-leaved varieties—purple "Purpureus" and creamy "Aureomarginatus"—are stunning throughout the year.

CONDITIONS

Aspect   All, apart from *O. delavayi* which is best grown again against a sheltering, warm wall in cold districts, thrive in the open.

Site   If possible, set plants in free-draining, humus-rich soil that does not dry out or become waterlogged. Fortify sandy or chalky soils with bulky organic manure.

GROWING METHOD

Feeding   Boost growth by sprinkling Growmore or some other balanced fertilizer over the root area in spring, repeating in midsummer. Water it in if the soil is dry. Foliar feed in droughty spells, when roots have difficulty absorbing plant foods, to speed uptake of nutrients. Water new plants copiously and follow with a mulch of bark, cocoa shell, or well-rotted garden compost.

Propagation   Increase varieties by layering flexible shoots from late spring to late summer or take semi-ripe cuttings from mid- to late summer.

Problems   Seldom attacked by pests or diseases.

PRUNING

No regular cutting back is necessary. If awkward shoots need removing, do it in spring when flowers have finished. Shorten stems to just above a joint or to new shoots. Trim a hedge of *O. × burkwoodii* when flowers fade in May.

OSMANTHUS AT A GLANCE

Spring- or fall-flowering evergreens for sun or light shade, *O. × burkwoodii* makes a stocky hedge. Hardy to 23°F (zone 9).

		Recommended Varieties
Jan	/	
Feb	/	*O. × burkwoodii*
Mar		*O. delavayi*
Apr	flower, plant	*O. heterophyllus*
May	flower, plant	*O. heterophyllus*
June	prune	"Aureomarginatus"
July	/	*O. heterophyllus*
Aug	/	"Purpureus"
Sept	flower, plant	*O. heterophyllus*
Oct	flower	"Variegatus"
Nov	/	
Dec	/	

MOCK ORANGE
Philadelphus

Semi-arching "Belle Etoile" is thickly clothed with richly vanilla-scented, single, large, white and flushed-yellow blooms from June to July.

Plant soaring Philadelphus lemoinei *"Erectus" to brighten a sunny spot with a myriad perfumed blooms sleeving upright shoots.*

FEATURES

Often but erroneously called syringa—the correct name for lilac—its sumptuous, creamy white, single, or double and richly citrus-vanilla-scented blooms fill and brighten the high-summer gap, when the spring display of shrubs is fading and fall contenders have yet to form flower buds. Ranging in height from 2ft to over 10ft, there are candidates for most situations.

Coveted tall varieties, 6–10ft, are: large, single, and pink-centerd "Beauclerk"; semi-double and yellowish-white *Philadelphus coronarius*; and double or semi-double, pure white "Virginal". Couple flowers with striking foliage by planting semi-double, creamy white *P. coronarius* "Aureus," the leaves of which open lemon-yellow and mature to greenish yellow. This plant is perfect for lighting up a sunny or dappled shady border.

Set the smallest member, "Manteau

d'Hermine," just 2–3ft high, on a rock garden and enjoy its massed, double, creamy white blossoms. Taller kinds are good for hedging.

CONDITIONS

Aspect Ideal for windswept, hillside gardens and for tolerating salty breezes, mock orange thrives almost anywhere. All flower best in full sun and lemon-leaved *P. coronarius* "Aureus" keeps its radiant leaf color in light shade.

Site Thriving in most soils—acid sand, chalk, or heavy clay—it is best to enrich poor patches with bulky organic matter dug in several months before planting.

GROWING METHOD

Feeding Encourage bounteous blossom on sandy soil by applying annually sulfate of potash in late winter and late summer. Regardless of soil, topdress the root area with a balanced fertilizer in April and July.

In a dry spring, water regularly to encourage strong, new shoots, which will flower the following year.

Propagation Strike cuttings of semi-ripe shoots from mid- to late summer. Root them in a cold frame or on a sunny windowsill.

Problems Blackfly can colonize and cripple soft shoot tips. Control them by spraying with pirimicarb, which does not harm beneficial insects.

PRUNING

When blooms fade, cut back flowered shoots to current-year stems, which will perform the following year.

MOCK ORANGE AT A GLANCE

A deciduous shrub whose single or fully double, creamy white flowers appear from June to July. Hardy to -13°F (zone 5).

Jan	/	Recommended Varieties
Feb	/	
Mar	plant	Under 1.8m (6ft)
Apr	plant	"Belle Etoile"
May	plant	*Coronarius* "Aureus"
June	flower	"Manteau d'Hermine"
July	flower	"Sybille"
Aug	prune	Over 1.8m (6ft)
Sept	/	"Beauclerk"
Oct	plant	*Coronarius*
Nov	plant	"Virginal"
Dec	/	

PHOTINIA
Photinia

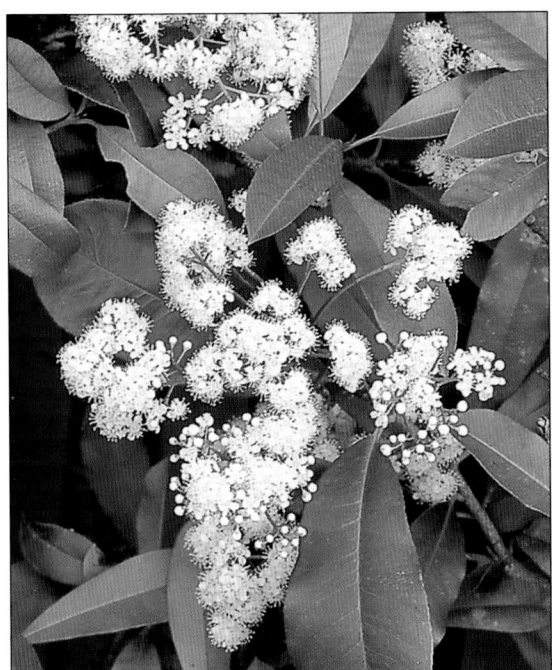

The awakening year sees Photinia fraseri *draped with clusters of tiny, white flowers, occasionally followed by red berries.*

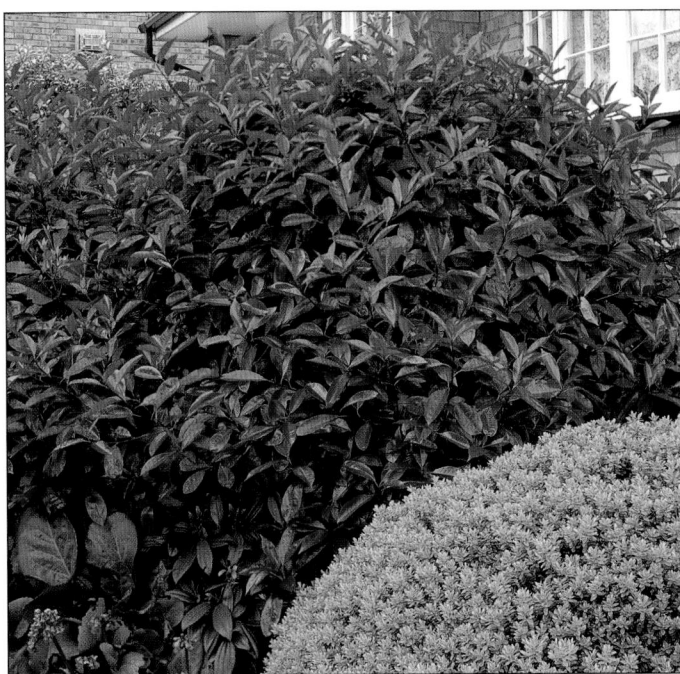

In spring and early summer, Photinia *"Red Robin" is a beacon of shining maroon-scarlet leaves. Here it is contrasting with an apple-green hebe.*

FEATURES

A valued New Zealand evergreen to around 6ft high by 5ft across, *Photinia* × *fraseri* "Red Robin" is a visual delight. From mid- to late spring, a foam of fluffy, white flowers, sometimes followed by scarlet berries, complements brilliant red, shiny leaves that mature to green. Riveting in a winter-color border, it is also appealing when fan-trained against a sunny, sheltered wall or fence. Alternatively, plant it in a large pot or tub and train it as a globe, pyramid, or drumstick. Clip trained forms in spring and summer. Photinia also makes a dense, low hedge.

PHOTINIA AT A GLANCE

The most popular kind, *P.* × *fraseri* "Red Robin," enchants us with a wealth of scarlet, new leaves. Hardy to 4°F (zone 7).

Jan	/	Recommended Varieties
Feb	/	
Mar	/	"Birmingham"
Apr	flower, plant	"Red Robin"
May	flower, prune	"Robusta"
June	flower, plant	"Rubens"
July	plant	
Aug	plant	
Sept	plant	
Oct	/	
Nov	/	
Dec	/	

CONDITIONS

Aspect   Not the hardiest of shrubs, photinia prefers a sheltered, sunny situation in which its foliage colors magnificently. It tolerates light shade.

Site   This shrub thrives on most well-drained soils but hates heavy clay and chalk. Improve sandy patches by incorporating bulky organic manures several weeks before planting.

GROWING METHOD

Feeding   Encourage stocky shoots and lusterous leaves by topdressing the root area with fish, blood, and bone meal, or some other balanced fertilizer, in spring and midsummer.
Water young plants copiously in dry spells in their first year to initiate strong, new shoots.

Propagation   Layer young stems from spring to late summer; take semi-ripe cuttings in late summer.

Problems   Photinia is susceptible to apple scab, a fungus that causes leaves to develop grayish-green spots and fall early. Control it by raking up diseased leaves, pruning out and burning scabby shoots and spraying with carbendazim, mancozeb, or bupirimate with triforine.

PRUNING

Rejuvenate old, leggy bushes by shortening stems by a third of their length in mid-spring. Remove shoot tips periodically throughout spring and summer, to encourage flushes of new, red leaves.

PIERIS
Pieris

Young pieris leaves open a vivid shade of pink or scarlet before turning yellow and ultimately green.

Some varieties, such as "Wakehurst," not only produce scarlet, flower-bright leaves but also combine them with an unstinting display of lily-of-the-valley-like blossom.

FEATURES

A captivating, evergreen shrub, 16in–9ft high and across, its bell-shaped, white, pink, or red flowers glorify spring. Its other, equally prized asset is its glowing pink or reddish shuttlecocks of new leaves.

There are many varieties. Aptly named "Flaming Silver"—2ft high, ideal for a narrow border—has fiery, new leaves which when mature are suffused with silver.

PIERIS AT A GLANCE

New, red, evergreen leaves complement sprays of white, pink, or red, bell-shaped flowers in spring. Hardy to 14°F (zone 8).

		Recommended Varieties
Jan	/	
Feb	/	"Debutante"
Mar	flower	"Firecrest"
Apr	flower, plant	"Flaming Silver"
May	flower, prune	"Forest Flame"
June	plant, prune	"Mountain Fire"
July	plant	"Pink Delight"
Aug	plant	"Valley Valentine"
Sept	plant	
Oct	/	
Nov	/	
Dec	/	

CONDITIONS

Aspect Not a candidate for exposed gardens, pieris needs shielding from strong, cold winds and hot, leaf-scorching sunshine.

Site Abhorring any degree of lime, this shrub needs deep, rich, well-drained soil. Create a good home for it by digging in generous amounts of organic material well ahead of planting time.

GROWING METHOD

Feeding Boost robust growth by applying an acidifying fertilizer in spring and midsummer. Help young plants recover quickly from transplanting by watering regularly in droughty spells and mulching with moisture-conserving organics.

Propagation Multiply plants by pegging down low shoots from mid-spring to late summer or take semi-ripe cuttings from mid- to late summer.

Problems New leaves may be damaged by wind frost.

PRUNING

Cut off faded blooms and dead or damaged shoots in early summer. Rejuvenate old bushes by shortening gaunt shoots to half their height in mid-spring. Keep cuts moist in dry spells to encourage rapid regrowth.

SHRUBBY CINQUEFOIL
Potentilla fruticosa

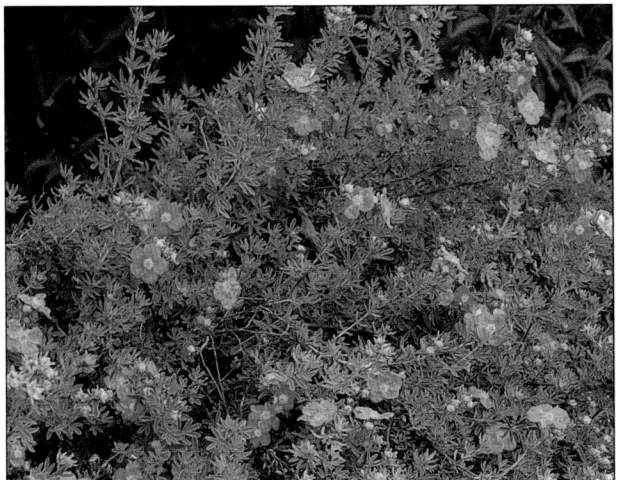

Forming a spreading clump, "Red Ace"—riveting when interplanted with Artemisia *"Powis Castle"—fires a border from May to October.*

Prized for its display of butter-yellow flowers, "Dart's Golddigger" contrasts stunningly with rosy-pink bedding geraniums.

FEATURES

Potentilla fruticosa flowers continuously from late May to September, its small, saucer-shaped blossoms clustering on dense, wiry stems.

Carpeting or bushy, to 5ft—taller kinds making colorful hedges—it is hardy and a good choice for cold gardens.

Easy, eye-catching varieties are: grayish-green-leaved and white-flowered "Abbotswood"; creamy-yellow "Tilford Cream"; ground-covering "Dart's Golddigger"; chrome-yellow "Goldstar"; salmon-pink "Pretty Polly"; vermilion-flame "Red Ace"; and deep orange to brick-red "Sunset".

All are good contenders for patio and terrace tubs and pots or deep, generous windowboxes. Arrange a potted group in several harmonizing colors to flank a doorway or form a focal point at the end of a path. Shrubby cinquefoil can also be grown to embrace pergola posts.

SHRUBBY CINQUEFOIL AT A GLANCE

Deciduous, bushy plants, which also make good hedges, they flower from May to September. Hardy to -13°F (zone 5).

		Recommended Varieties
Jan	/	
Feb	/	Carpeting
Mar	plant	"Dart's Golddigger"
Apr	plant, prune	"Pretty Polly"
May	plant, flower	"Red Ace"
June	plant, flower	"Sunset"
July	plant, flower	Bushy
Aug	plant, flower	"Goldfinger"
Sept	plant, flower	"Goldstar"
Oct	plant, flower	"Red Robin"
Nov	plant	"Tilford Cream"
Dec	/	

CONDITIONS

Aspect A good choice for borders exposed to cold winds, shrubby cinquefoil flowers profusely in an open, sunny position or very light shade. If possible, plant it facing south or west where trees will not overshadow it.

Site A very adaptable plant, it thrives in most soils, from heavy, often waterlogged clay to light, sandy areas that become parched in summer. It does not mind a little lime but on very chalky soils it is liable to become stressed and suffer from chlorosis, when leaves turn creamy or yellowish and die.

GROWING METHOD

Feeding Encourage robust flowering shoots by working fish, blood, and bone meal or some other balanced fertilizer into the root area in spring and midsummer. Apply bone meal in the fall to release plant foods in spring. If, in sandy soil, leaf margins turn brown, indicating potash deficiency, rectify by applying sulfate of potash in February and watering it in.

Once the plant is established, watering is seldom needed, but soak newly planted shrubs to settle the soil around the roots.

Propagation Increase plants from cuttings of semi-ripe shoots in midsummer. Root them in a garden frame or on a sunny windowsill.

Problems Shoots produce their leaves very late in spring, deceiving us into thinking them dead.

PRUNING

Keep bushes youthful and flowering freely year after year by removing a third of the older shoots in spring. Rejuvenate very old, woody plants at the same time by cutting them back to within 4in of the base. Trim hedges in spring.

CAPE LEADWORT
Plumbago

Commonly called Cape leadwort, plumbago rewards us with a succession of silvery-blue flowers from mid- to late summer.

Encourage plumbago to flower bounteously every year by shortening the previous year's flowered stems in February.

FEATURES

Usually grown to color a conservatory, greenhouse, or windowsill with a mist of starry, sky-blue flowers from midsummer to fall, *Plumbago auriculata* is a rambling, evergreen climber. Ideally, grow it in a large pot or tub to allow you to move it on to a patio when frosts finish in late May or early June. Growing to 15ft or so, in cultivation it is best pruned regularly to keep it neat, compact, and floriferous. In very sheltered, frost-free gardens, create a sensation in summer by training it over an arch, arbour, obelisk or trellis.

CAPE LEADWORT AT A GLANCE

Scrambling, frost-tender climber studded with pale blue flowers from midsummer to early fall. Hardy to 46°F (zone 11).

Jan	/	Recommended Varieties
Feb	prune	
Mar	/	*P. auriculata*
Apr	plant	*P. auriculata alba*
May	plant	"Royal Cape"
June	plant	
July	flower	
Aug	flower	
Sept	flower	
Oct	flower	
Nov	/	
Dec	/	

CONDITIONS

Aspect   Though plumbago flowers best in full sun, it tolerates very light shade.

Site   Set this shrub in a large, well-drained pot or small tub of multi-purpose compost.

GROWING METHOD

Feeding   Insert clusters of slow-release fertilizer granules into the compost in spring. From late spring to summer, apply a high-potash tomato feed.
When potting plants, add moisture-storage granules to help keep the compost damp during long, dry spells.
In late summer, when nights turn cold, return plumbago to a frost-free spot in good light. Keep the compost dryish from fall to spring.

Propagation   Take semi-ripe cuttings from early to midsummer.

Problems   Under glass, fluffy, waxy, white mealy bugs may colonize leaf joints and cripple growth. Control them biologically with *Aphidius colemani*, a parasitic wasp, or spray with horticultural soap.

PRUNING

Shorten the previous year's flowering shoots to within 2in of the older wood in February.

ORNAMENTAL CHERRY
Prunus

From early to mid-spring, a wealth of disc-shaped, double pink blooms transform Prunus × blireana*'s bare, twiggy branches.*

Heralding spring and suitable for all sizes of garden, white-, pink-, or red-flowering cherries associate beautifully with magnolias.

FEATURES

Deciduous or evergreen shrubs or trees 4–14ft tall, the prunus family embraces a wide range of forms. Flowers are single or double, in white, pink, and red shades. Neat dwarf Russian almond (*Prunus tenella* "Firehill") has semi-double, rosy-crimson flowers, which sleeve 4ft stems in April. Also useful for small gardens is *P. × cistena* "Crimson Dwarf," whose white flowers appear just before coppery-red leaves. White-flowering and low-growing evergreen kinds—*P.* "Otto Luyken" among them—are excellent for carpeting shady spots. Taller laurel (*P. laurocerasus* "Rotundifolia") makes a dense evergreen hedge to 6ft.

CONDITIONS

Aspect Deciduous flowering cherries, needing full sun to perform well, should be sheltered from strong winds. Evergreens thrive in light shade.

Site All prunus prosper on any well-drained soil enriched with organic matter. Evergreen varieties also thrive on thin, sandy soils.

GROWING METHOD

Feeding Work bone meal into the root area in spring and fall. Water freely in dry spells, especially when flower buds are forming.

Propagation Increase evergreen, carpeting and hedging varieties from semi-ripe cuttings from mid- to late summer. Flowering cherry trees, however, are normally grafted on to *P. avium* rootstock.

Problems Control silver leaf disease by cutting back and burning affected shoots to 6in beyond infected, purple-stained tissue, in midsummer.

PRUNING

Evergreens: Shear laurel hedges in spring and late summer.

Deciduous varieties: No regular pruning is necessary. Cut out crowding shoots from mid- to late summer.

ORNAMENTAL CHERRY AT A GLANCE

A huge family of deciduous, spring-flowering cherries and carpeting or hedging evergreens. Hardiness rating, according to species.

Month	Activity	Recommended Varieties
Jan	/	
Feb	/	**Evergreen**
Mar	plant, flower	"Otto Luyken"
Apr	prune, flower	*P. laurocerasus*
May	flower, plant	"Rotundifolia"
June	plant, flower	"Zabeliana"
July	plant, prune	**Deciduous**
Aug	plant, prune	"Amanogawa"
Sept	plant	*P. × blireana*
Oct	plant	"Cheal's Weeping"
Nov	plant	*P. mume*
Dec	/	*P. tenella* "Firehill"

CHERRY VARIETIES

ABOVE: *Pale pink blooms that open white and contrast with dark reddish-purple leaves make Pissard's purple plum (Prunus cerasifera "Pissardii") a desirable garden tree. Red fruits follow in summer.*

ABOVE: *Prunus and malus flowers are very similar. This* Malus *"John Downie" could be mistaken for a flowering cherry.*

LEFT: *Enchanting in a small border,* Prunus triloba *treats us to massed rosettes of pale pink blooms that cluster on year-old shoots in April. Keep it youthful and blooming freely by pruning out one stem in three in early summer.*

BELOW: *A snowfall of single, white blooms smothers* Prunus *"Taihaku" in May. Position it in full sun, in a large lawn, where it can develop fully without having to be cut back. Alternatively, set it near a contrasting, deep green hedge to accentuate the whiteness of its flowers.*

ABOVE: *Famed for its profusion of white, candle-like blooms in spring and again in fall,* Prunus *"Otto Luyken" is also prized for its ground-hugging, evergreen, and weed-suppressing leaves. It flourishes in sun or shade.*

POMEGRANATE
Punica

Showy, bell-shaped, orange-scarlet flowers are your reward for growing a pomegranate in a warm garden or conservatory.

Delicious fruits appear on outdoor or patio pot plants after a long, warm summer. Under glass, in a higher temperature, fruits swell to a greater size.

FEATURES

Deciduous and bearing carnation-like, single or double, brilliant orange-red flowers for most of the summer, *Punica granatum* makes a bushy shrub to 7ft high and across. Only single-flowered varieties bear fruits. Grow them as specimen plants in very sheltered borders in frost-free gardens. Elsewhere, treat this shrub as a pot plant and confine it to a conservatory from fall to late spring. Move it on to a sunny patio or terrace when frosts finish in late May or early June.

POMEGRANATE AT A GLANCE

Deciduous and bearing orange flowers in summer, it can be grown outside only in very sheltered areas. Hardy to 39°F (zone 10).

Jan	/	Recommended Varieties
Feb	/	
Mar	/	"Flore Pleno Luteo"
		"Flore Pleno Rubro"
Apr	plant, prune	*P. granatum nana*
May	plant, prune	"Striata"
June	flower, plant	
July	flower, plant	
Aug	flower, plant	
Sept	plant	
Oct	/	
Nov	/	
Dec	/	

CONDITIONS

Aspect If you are growing pomegranate outdoors, it must be in full sunshine and protected from cold winds.

Site To excel, this shrub needs well-drained loam or clay-loam soil enriched with humus-forming organics.

GROWING METHOD

Feeding Boost growth and stimulate plenty of blossom-bearing shoots by applying bone meal in spring and the fall.
Encourage young plants to establish quickly by watering liberally in the first spring and summer after planting.
In September, return potted plants that have decorated a patio for summer to a frost-free conservatory or greenhouse.

Propagation Increase this plant from semi-ripe cuttings taken from mid- to late summer.

Problems New shoots on outdoor plants can be damaged by late spring frosts, so site the shrubs carefully.

PRUNING

Remove badly placed shoots from late spring to early summer. Keep wall-trained specimens shapely by shortening flowered shoots to within four leaves of the main framework when blooms fade.

FIRETHORN
Pyracantha

A spectacular fall display of orange, red, or yellow berries, following a foam of creamy blossom, makes firethorn popular for transforming cold walls.

Planted to screen out ugly objects, firethorn's late-season bonanza of berries is a welcome winter feast for garden birds.

FEATURES

Planted mainly for screening, hedging, and training as an espalier, evergreen and hardy firethorn's spiky stems are clad with small, glossy green leaves. In early summer, showy clusters of white flowers, appearing early in the plant's life, are followed by a dramatic cloak of bright orange, yellow, or red berries from fall to winter. Garden birds feast on them. There are many long-lived varieties. Choice kinds include a trio of recently bred fireblight-resistant forms: orange-berried "Saphyr Orange"; red-berried "Saphyr Red"; and yellow-berried "Saphyr Yellow". These shrubs grow 6–10ft high, which they reach after 5–10 years.

FIRETHORN AT A GLANCE

An evergreen shrub coveted for its white flowers and display of red, orange, or yellow berries. Hardy to -13°F (zone 5).

		Recommended Varieties
Jan	/	
Feb	/	"Alexander Pendula"
Mar	/	"Dart's Red"
Apr	plant, prune	"Golden Charmer"
May	plant	*P. rogersiana*
June	flower, plant	"Saphyr Orange"
July	plant	"Saphyr Red"
Aug	plant	"Saphyr Yellow"
Sept	plant	
Oct	/	
Nov	/	
Dec	/	

CONDITIONS

Aspect Needing full sun for healthy, compact growth, firethorn flowers less and is more loosely branched in light shade. It tolerates strong gusts and is often grown as a windbreak.

Site Tolerating a wide range of soil types including chalk, it prefers well-drained loam or clay-loam enriched with organic matter. It also prospers on humus-rich, gravelly patches.

GROWING METHOD

Feeding Keep firethorn lustrous and flowering and berrying freely by working bone meal into the root area in spring and fall.
Help newly planted shrubs establish quickly by watering copiously in dry spells during their first spring and summer. Mulch thickly.

Propagation Take semi-ripe cuttings from mid- to late summer.

Problems Disfiguring leaves and berries with patches, pyracantha scab is a debilitating disease. Control it by pruning out and burning infected shoots and spraying fortnightly with carbendazim from March to July. Grow orange-red berried "Mohave," which is resistant to it.

PRUNING

Free-standing shrubs: Cut back overgrown plants in April to keep them flowering and berrying profusely.

Wall-trained espaliers: In spring, shorten non-blossoming side shoots to 4in from the base. In midsummer, reduce current-year shoots to three leaves.

RHODODENDRON
Rhododendron

Few shrubs can equal rhododendrons for a spectacular display of blossom from late winter to summer. This skillfully planned garden features a bold planting of white and rosy-red hardy hybrids framed by dark foliage that enhances rather than competes with the flowers.

FEATURES

Enriching gardens with spectacular trusses of vibrant or delicate pastel-hued blooms from December to August, there is an enormous range of evergreen and deciduous varieties. Without doubt, they are the key to creating fetching features on acid soil.

Yielding thickly or sparsely clustered, bell- or trumpet-shaped blooms, rhododendrons are long-lived and mature within 5–10 years. Plant them to enhance woodland glades, borders, rock gardens, patio pots, and conservatories. Associate them with other lime-hating plants, such as azaleas, Japanese maples, lilies, camellias, conifers, eucryphia, pieris, and embothrium.

TYPES

Hardy hybrids: Valued for their resistance to severe weather and ability to prosper in windy gardens, hardy hybrids flower from April to June. Most grow 5–8ft high and across.

They are easy to manage and the blooms, in white and shades of red, pink, lavender, purple, and yellow, are borne in large, showy trusses amid broad, pointed leaves.

Red hues: Outstanding are: ruby red "Bagshot Ruby"; bright brick-red "Vulcan"; bright red, black-speckled "Windlesham Scarlet"; dark red "Doncaster", black-veined within; and medium-red "Cynthia".

Pink hues: A trio no garden should be without is: dark green-leaved and rose-pink "Alice"; "Pink Pearl", whose rosy buds open to flesh-pink blooms; and "Furnivall's Daughter", a gem with rose-pink and dark-spotted flowers.

Purple, blue and mauve hues: Stunning among these are: violet-blue "Blue Boy"; semi-double and bluish-mauve "Fastuosum Flore Pleno"; and rosy-purple "Variegatum", whose white-rimmed leaves illuminate shady places.

White hues: White and pale yellow-eyed "Cunningham's White" and lavender-budded and white-flowered "Loder's White" light up mid-spring.

RHODODENDRON AT A GLANCE

Evergreen shrubs mantled with blooms from late winter to midsummer. All need acid soil. Hardiness ratings vary.

		Recommended Varieties
Jan	/	
Feb	flower	Hardy hybrids
Mar	flower	"Doncaster"
Apr	flower, plant	"Furnivall's Daughter"
May	flower, prune	"Pink Pearl"
Jun	flower, prune	"Fastuosum Flore-Pleno"
July	plant	"Cunningham's White"
Aug	plant	"Praecox"
Sept	/	Yakushimanum hybrids
Oct	/	"Astrid"
Nov	/	"Chelsea Seventy"
Dec	/	"Grumpy"

TOP: *Sun-loving, hardy hybrid "Blue Peter."*
ABOVE: *An exquisite-flowered Vireya rhododendron.*

A 19th-century Malaysian variety used for breeding, "Pink Delight" is spectacular for a shaded conservatory or very mild, frost-free garden, but it needs cosseting.

Low-growing varieties: Equally hardy, low-growing varieties make dense bushes 18–48in high.

Heralding spring, "Praecox" opens its rosy-lilac-to-mauve blooms in February and March; "Snow Lady" bears lovely, white flowers from March to April; and "Princess Anne" is smothered with clear yellow blooms from April to May.

Stunning, too, are drought-resisting hybrids of *Rhododendron yakushimanum*. Making dense bushes to 3ft, alluring varieties are: cerise-pink "Astrid"; salmon and carmine-rose "Chelsea Seventy"; and yellowish-white and shell-pink "Grumpy".

The sumptuous and very colorful Malaysian (Vireya) rhododendrons make exciting focal points for a frost-free greenhouse or lightly shaded and very sheltered patio or terrace in summer.

CONDITIONS

Aspect Hardy hybrids and species grow and flower best in a dappled, shady spot shielded from strong wind.

Site Soil must be acid and well-drained, cool and moist throughout the year and fortified with moisture-conserving organic matter. Dig in plenty of well-rotted manure, garden compost, or leaf mould before planting. Set greenhouse varieties in large pots of orchid-bark, mixed with ericaceous compost.

GROWING METHOD

Feeding Nourish plants with an acidifying fertilizer in spring and midsummer and mulch thickly with bulky organic materials to keep roots active and leaves lustrous in long, dry spells.

Use lime-free rain water to moisten dry soil or compost.

Propagation Take softwood cuttings from mid-spring to early summer and semi-ripe cuttings in early fall; layer stems from mid-spring to late summer.

Problems *Bud blast: This fungus turns flower buds brown and is characterised by bristly black outgrowths, is spread by rhododendron leaf hopper. This is also a pest, which lays its eggs in the bud scales. Control bud blast by picking off and burning affected buds and spraying with pirimiphos-methyl to eradicate hoppers.

*Leaf spot disease: Speckling leaves with brownish-purple spots containing raised, black, fungal fruiting bodies, it is best eradicated by spraying with mancozeb when symptoms appear.

If aphids colonize soft shoot tips, control them with pirimicarb, which is selective to this pest and does not harm beneficial insects.

*Lime-induced chlorosis: Caused by a deficiency of iron and manganese in alkaline soils, which inhibits chlorophyll production, leaves develop brown rims and yellow patches between bright green veins. Rectify it by applying a chelated compound based on iron, manganese, and other trace elements.

PRUNING

Snap off spent blooms when petals fall, to channel energy away from seed production and into strong new growth. Take care not to damage new leaves.

Keep mature bushes youthful and packed with blossom in spring by removing one in three of older, black-barked stems when flowers fade. Dwarf and low-growing varieties and species are best left unpruned.

AZALEA
Rhododendron

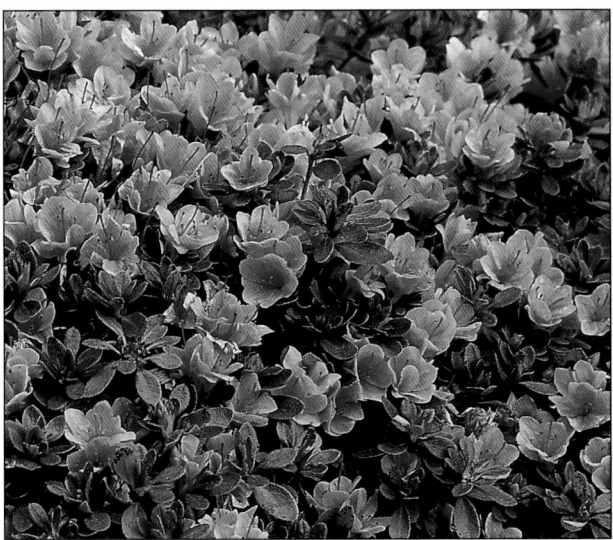

Planted to light up a woodland glade, evergreen Kurume azalea "Kirin" treats us to a massed display of small blooms in May.

Leaf-shedding Mollis azaleas yield an unforgettable display of large clusters of vibrantly hued, trumpet blooms before leaves fully unfold.

FEATURES

Enchanting us from April to June, deciduous and evergreen azaleas come in a kaleidoscope of colors and range in height, 2–8ft. They are derived from various species of rhododendron and are among the world's most widely hybridized plants. Long-lived, azaleas mature within 3–5 years and flower from the first year of planting. Grouped in mixed shrub borders, taller varieties make a stunning backcloth for annuals or small perennials. It is best to buy plants in flower so that you can be sure of getting exactly what you want. Azaleas are often planted with acid-soil-loving camellias and purple- and green-leaved Japanese maples, where the foliage tempers the more vibrant-hued varieties.

Deciduous groups: Cherished for their May to June performance of clustered, trumpet blooms in glowing pastel and strident hues and vivid fall leaf tints, there are four deciduous types:

Mollis hybrids: Making stocky bushes to about 6ft high, their large heads of scentless, bright yellow, orange, red, cream, and salmon blooms open before leaves appear. Choice among them are orange-scarlet "Spek's Brilliant" and "Koster's Brilliant Red."

Knaphill and Exbury hybrids: Also unperfumed, their May blooms can be as large as a hardy hybrid rhododendron's. Dramatic varieties are: light yellow "April Showers"; salmon-pink "Coronation Lady"; and deep carmine "Homebush."

Ghent hybrids: Making neat, twiggy bushes clothed in long-tubed, sweet-smelling, honeysuckle-like flowers with showy stamens, blossoms peak in late May and June. Fine forms are soft yellow "Narcissiflorum" and rose-pink "Norma".

Occidentalis hybrids: Flowering from mid- to late May, they reward us with trusses of sumptuous, fragrant, pastel-hued blooms. Pure white and yellow-eyed "Bridesmaid" is a good example.

Evergreen and semi-evergreen groups: There are four widely grown divisions. Largest flowering are the prolific Vuyk and Glendale hybrids, whose blooms can be 3in in diameter. The Kaempferi hybrids, such as violet "Blue Danube," have slightly smaller flowers.
Smallest of all are the very popular and bounteous-performing Kurume hybrids. These have slightly greater tolerance to low temperatures than other evergreen varieties and blooms are single or hose-in-hose—when one flower appears inside another.

CONDITIONS

Aspect Most azaleas prefer semi-shade and shelter from strong winds and hot afternoon sunshine. A new race of "sun-loving" varieties is being

---

AZALEA AT A GLANCE

A form of deciduous or evergreen rhododendron bearing trumpet blooms, it colors lightly shaded spots. Hardy to 4°F (zone 7).

Month	Activity	Recommended Varieties
Jan	/	
Feb	/	Deciduous
Mar	plant, prune	"Bridesmaid"
Apr	flower, prune	"Coronation Lady"
May	flower, prune	"Firefly"
Jun	flower, prune	"Gibraltar"
July	plant	"Koster's Brilliant Red"
Aug	plant	Evergreen
Sept	plant	"Addy Wery"
Oct	plant	"Blue Danube"
Nov	plant	"Driven Snow"
Dec	/	"Hinode-giri"

RIGHT: Too tender for planting in the garden, though they benefit from spending June to September in a cool, shaded spot outdoors, Indica azaleas are massed with blossom from December to February.

BELOW: Complementing the hardy varieties' spring display, this glowing, half-hardy Indica azalea is unusual in that it has a clearly defined, white center.

RIGHT: Deciduous Mollis azaleas come in vivid shades of orange yellow. This beautiful variety, flowering from early to mid-May, associates dramatically with pieris while it is displaying its scarlet, new leaves.

VARIETIES

LEFT: Few azaleas can surpass the brilliance of "Happy Days," a prized but rare Nuccio hybrid, the double flowers of which illuminate spring. Shield young plants from frost.

BELOW: Lighting up May and June, deciduous azaleas—this is a Mollis variety—reward us with clusters of flared-petal blooms and elegant thrusting stamens.

LEFT: This free-flowering Glenn Dale hybrid is one of many varieties bred to improve the frost-hardiness and color range of evergreen azaleas.

A riot of spring blossom in yellow, orange, and other sunny shades makes it worthwhile finding a choice site for a Mollis azalea.

bred for more open situations.

Site The soil should be acid, well-drained, and humus-rich and fortified with plenty of well-decayed organic matter several weeks before planting. In even slightly alkaline conditions, when the pH hovers just above 7.0, azaleas will suffer from iron deficiency and creamy-green, chlorophyll-deficient leaves will die. Keep plants perky in hot spells by mulching with a thick layer of organic material, such as well-rotted manure, leaf mould, compost, or decayed grass clippings.

GROWING METHOD

Feeding Nourish plants by applying an acidifying fertilizer in spring and summer and watering it in if the soil is dry.
Water new plants regularly in droughty periods to help them establish quickly. In prolonged dry weather, gently dig a moat around a bush and fill it with water. Refill it several times when the water has soaked away. Finish by replacing the soil.

Propagation Azaleas are easily increased from soft-tip cuttings taken from mid-spring to early summer; semi-ripe cuttings from mid- to late summer; and layers pegged down from mid-spring to late summer.

Problems Unfortunately azaleas suffer from a number of pests and diseases.
*Powdery mildew: Causing yellow patches to blemish upper leaf surfaces it can, occasionally, trouble heavily shaded plants in areas of high rainfall. It can also be aggravated by sluggish air flow, so remove crowded plants and set them elsewhere. Pick off and burn badly affected leaves and avoid wetting the foliage. Do not grow *Rhododendron cinnabarinum* or its hybrids, which are prone to this fungus. Control the disease chemically by spraying

with bupirimate with triforine or mancozeb the moment symptoms appear.
*Azalea gall: Blame the fungus *Exobasidium vaccinii*, which causes leaves to become swollen, fleshy, and pinkish red. Later, ripe, white spores powder the surface. In the fall, galls wither and turn brown. Fortunately, the plant does not appear to suffer from its presence. Some varieties are more susceptible than others to azalea gall. Remove and destroy affected leaves. There are no chemical controls.
*Rhododendron lace bug damages azalea and rhododendron leaves in spring, summer and into the fall in mild seasons. Affected foliage is heavily mottled grayish white. Black or brown, shiny spots, the insect's excreta, are seen on the underside of leaves. When damage first appears, it may be possible to reduce the outbreak by hosing up under the foliage; otherwise, spray with horticultural soap, pyrethrins, pirimiphos-methyl, or permethrin as soon as the symptoms are seen.
*Thrips—brownish black and ⅛in long—suck sap from the leaves. The damage is similar to that of lace bug but the leaves may have a more silvery appearance. Control these pests by spraying with pirimiphos-methyl, malathion, or dimethoate. If the infestation is severe, in dry, warm weather when thrips multiply rapidly, you may need to repeat the dosage every three weeks.
*Two-spotted mite, commonly known as red spider mite, also sucks sap from the underside of leaves. Using a magnifying glass, it is possible to see the mites. Almost colorless, with two black spots on their backs, they are usually carrying clear, round eggs.
An attack is first noticed when leaves turn bronzy, tiny webs can be seen and minute creatures, with the aid of a hand lens, can be seen on the backs of leaves. Mites are more prevalent in hot, dry weather and more inclined to infest plants in sheltered spots, such as under eaves, than in open, airy situations. If the plants are not in flower when red spider mite invades, direct a hose up into the bush every couple of days to help reduce their numbers. Alternatively, spray with bifenthrin or horticultural soap.

PRUNING

Cutting flowers for a vase is usually all the pruning these plants need. But deadhead, too, to channel energy into new growth, by nipping out faded blooms when petals fall. Rejuvenate overgrown deciduous varieties by cutting back branches to within 2ft of the ground in March, before buds burst. Try and keep cuts moist to keep alive invisible buds around the stump edge. An easy way to achieve this, apart from splashing them with water, is to coat them with Christmas tree needle spray, which covers them with a plastic film that seals in moisture. If the bush is very old, prune back half the branches in the first year and the remainder the following year. Wayward stems may be cut back at any time.

FLOWERING CURRANT
Ribes

Blooming generously from April to May, sun-loving Ribes *"Pulborough Scarlet," a flowering currant, also performs in light shade.*

Trained against a warm wall and almost evergreen, the fuchsia-flowered currant (Ribes speciosum) *makes a fascinating feature.*

FEATURES

A deciduous family that heralds spring, the most popular kind—*Ribes sanguineum* "Pulborough Scarlet"—is very hardy. Growing to around 8ft high and 6ft across, its upright shoots are thickly sleeved with pendent clusters of deep red, tubular flowers. "White Icicle," another choice form of *R. sanguineum*, has drooping, creamy-white candelabra blooms, dramatic when embraced with purple-red *Bergenia* "Evening Glow." *Ribes sanguineum* "Brocklebankii," to 4ft, is illuminatingly different, rewarding us with a heartening display of golden leaves and pink flowers. All varieties of *R. sanguineum* can be planted to form a stocky, flowering boundary hedge.
Starry, yellow-flowered *R. odoratum*, to 6ft, has leaves that assume purple tints in fall, and less hardy *R. speciosum*, prized for its scarlet, fuchsia-like flowers on upright spiny shoots and best grown against a warm wall, are also generous performers.

CONDITIONS

Aspect
Ribes is ideal for brightening a lightly shaded spot, but *R.* "Brocklebankii" must be shielded from hot sunlight otherwise its leaves will scorch. All, apart from slightly tender *R. speciosum*, prosper in exposed gardens. Make a statement by espalier training *R. speciosum* against a warm, sunny wall or set it to cascade from a pedestal pot.

Site
Undemanding ribes thrives almost anywhere. Fortify sandy spots, which parch in summer, with bulky, moisture-conserving organics. If you plant this shrub on heavy clay, add gravel to improve drainage. Chalky soils can cause leaves to become chlorotic (yellowish green). Avoid this by adding acidifying fertilizer to lower the pH level.

GROWING METHOD

Feeding
Provided the soil is reasonably fertile, a single application of bone meal in the fall is all that is necessary. After planting, no matter how damp the ground, water well to settle soil around the roots.

Propagation
Take hardwood cuttings in late fall.

Problems
This genus is prone to coral spot fungus. Causing a rash of coral-pink or orange pustules that kills shoots, it should be controlled by cutting out and burning infected plant tissue. Remove crowded shoots to improve air flow.

PRUNING

Keep ribes youthful, shapely and flowering freely by shortening a third of older shoots to new growth or near ground level when blooms fade. Remove crowding branches and cut back diseased stems to healthy wood in spring.

FLOWERING CURRANT AT A GLANCE

Deciduous bush festooned with clusters of flowers from late March to mid-May. Hardiness rating according to species.

Month	Activity	Recommended Varieties
Jan	/	
Feb	/	*R. odoratum*
Mar	flower, plant	*R. sanguineum* "Brocklebankii"
Apr	flower, plant	
May	flower, plant	*R. sanguineum* "Icicle"
Jun	plant, prune	*R. sanguineum* "Porky Pink"
July	plant	
Aug	plant	*R. sanguineum* "Pulborough Scarlet"
Sept	plant	*R. speciosum*
Oct	/	
Nov	/	
Dec	/	

ROSE
Rosa

A sport of the famous "Peace" rose, "Chicago Peace" is a vibrant Large Flowered variety that forms a stocky bush to 4ft high.

For sheltered, frost-free gardens, there are few more wonderful sights than the Cherokee rose (Rosa laevigata) draping a sunny wall.

FEATURES

For over two millennia, roses have played an important role in garden design. However, it was not until the 19th century, from an amalgam of new developments—Hybrid Musk, Hybrid Perpetual, and Large Flowered (Hybrid Tea) roses—that modern varieties evolved. Since the late 1960s, there has been great interest in what are known as "English" roses. Bred by David Austin, they are varieties that combine the many-petalled form, lovely fragrance and full vigour of an old-fashioned rose with the wide color range and repeat-flowering qualities of a modern rose.

Roses are cherished for their form and colorful blooms, and many are very fragrant. They can be evergreen or deciduous, and most varieties have prickles.

The Old Roses—varieties of *Rosa gallica*, beloved by the Greeks and Romans; Damasks, alleged to have been introduced from the Middle East by the Crusaders; Albas, grown by gardeners in the Middle Ages; and Centifolias, first seen in Britain around 1550, which flower just once, in early summer.

Modern roses—Cluster Flowered (Floribunda), Large Flowered (Hybrid Tea) produce successive flushes of bloom. Flowers may be single, semi-double, or fully double, in a wide range of colors: white, cream, yellow, apricot, orange, every shade of pink, and red. There are bicolors, too, but a true blue rose has yet to be borne.

Weed-suppressing and ideal for covering banks too steep to mow, the County Series of ground-hugging roses, such as blush-pink "Avon," gold, cerise, pink, and scarlet "Cambridgeshire" and pure white "Kent," color summer with repeat pulses of bloom. Ramblers, including coppery pink and richly scented "Albertine" flower only in midsummer. Climbers particularly modern varieties, such as "Golden Showers," salmon-pink "Compassion"

and honey-champagne "Penny Lane," have Hybrid Tea-like flowers and bloom repeatedly from June to October.

Some species, such as *R. moyesii*, produce brilliant red hips in fall and are planted specially for these, although the flowers are good too!

Uses Roses may be mass-planted in beds and borders or planted singly as sentinels. Large Flowered, Cluster Flowered and some other bush varieties are also grown as round-headed or weeping standards to flank a path or add height to a bed of roses. Thrusting through an obelisk strategically positioned in a shrub border, "Handel," a short, creamy-white and rose-pink climber, makes a riveting focal point.

Climbers and ramblers also associate strikingly with pink, red, blue, and white varieties of *Clematis viticella*, which are pruned to within 12in of the base in spring. Create a sensation by planting violet-blue C. "Etoile Violette" to entwine the climbing rose "Compassion," whose fragrant, double, light salmon-shaded, orange blooms stud strong, healthy shoots all summer.

Miniature and patio roses are ideal for planting in pots or tubs to decorate a patio or terrace. Very hardy varieties of *Rosa rugosa* are often used as hedges. Set a Large Flowered or Cluster Flowered variety *en masse* to illuminate a bed or border, or embrace a single bush with annuals, perennials, or bulbs.

CONDITIONS

Aspect The hardiness of roses is variable. Many tolerate extreme cold while others can be singed by frost.

To form stocky shoots and flower bounteously, roses need full sun all day. Good air circulation is important, too, but some shelter from strong wind is desirable to avoid flower damage.

Site These shrubs prefer heavy but well-drained,

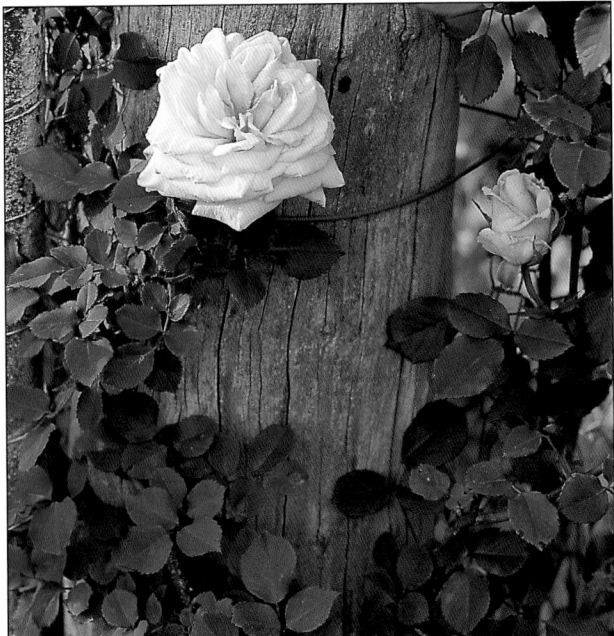

Flowering profusely in early summer and sporadically thereafter, leggy "Felicia," a Hybrid Musk, is ideal for screening eyesores.

humus-rich loam. Improve light, sandy, gravelly, or chalky soils by adding large amounts of well-rotted manure or decomposed garden compost several few weeks before planting. Add garden lime to very acid soil.

GROWING METHOD

Feeding   Encourage lustrous leaves and fine, large blooms by feeding with a proprietary rose fertilizer, containing magnesium, in mid-April and early July.

Propagation   Vigorous Cluster Flowered varieties, most shrub roses and ramblers and climbers are easily increased from hardwood cuttings in September. The only way to multiply Large Flowered varieties is to implant a bud of the variety, in July, on to a rootstock.

Problems   *Aphids, which are sap suckers, may cover new growth quite thickly. Spray with pirimicarb, horticultural soap, permethrin, pirimiphos-methyl, or derris.
*Leaf-rolling sawfly damages roses from late spring to early summer. When females lay eggs on leaves, they inject a chemical into the leaf, which causes it to roll up and protect the eggs. Affected leaflets hang down. When caterpillars emerge, they feed on the leaves. Control with heptenophos with permethrin or pirimiphos-methyl.
*Black spot causes large black blotches to disfigure leaves. Collect and burn fallen leaves and avoid overhead watering. Some roses are less prone to this disease than others. Resistant Large Flowered varieties: "Alec's Red," "Alexander," "Blessings," "Champs Elysees," "Chicago Peace," "Honey Favorite." Resistant Cluster Flowered varieties: "Allgold," "Arthur Bell," "City of Belfast," "City of Leeds," "Manx Queen," "The Queen Elizabeth," "Tip Top."
*Powdery mildew, worse in dry spots and where air circulates sluggishly, distorts leaves,

stems, and flower buds and felts them with grayish-white patches.
Control it by opening up crowded areas, watering and liquid feeding every ten days, from spring to late summer, with a high-potash fertilizer to encourage robust growth. Also guard against infection by spraying fortnightly from spring to late summer, with triforine with bupirimate, penconazole, mancozeb, or copper with ammonium hydroxide.
*Rust is another fungus that is worse in areas of high rainfall. In early summer, bright orange spots appear on the upper leaf surface and corresponding, orange spore clusters disfigure the lower surface. In late summer, dark brown winter spore masses replace summer pustules. Badly infected leaves are shed prematurely. Control rust by pruning out and burning affected stems and spraying regularly with myclobutanil, penconazole, bupirimate with triforine or mancozeb.

PRUNING

After planting: Tackle pruning in early spring before buds burst. In fall, shorten extra long stems on bush roses to avoid them catching the wind and loosening the stem. Always cut to just above a bud.
Large Flowered and Cluster Flowered bush varieties: Shorten stems to within 6in of the base.
Shrub roses: No pruning necessary.
Ramblers: Cut back shoots to 12in from the ground.
Climbers: Shorten withered tips to healthy buds.

When established: Large Flowered and Cluster Flowered: Shorten main stems by half their length; side shoots to two buds.
Shrub roses: Cut back dead and dying shoots to healthy buds.
Ramblers: Most varieties are pruned in fall; cut out flowered stems and replace with current-year shoots.
Climbers: Shorten flowered side shoots to two or three buds.
Deadhead all roses weekly to channel energy into new shoots and more flowers.

ROSE AT A GLANCE

Bushes, standards, weepers, carpeters, and climbers flower from spring to fall. Most roses are hardy to 3°F (zone 7).

		Recommended Varieties
Jan	/	
Feb	/	Large Flowered
Mar	plant, prune	"Alec's Red"
Apr	plant, prune	"Elizabeth Harkness"
May	flower, plant	English roses
Jun	flower, plant	"Graham Thomas"
July	flower, plant	Cluster Flowered
Aug	flower, plant	"English Miss"
Sept	flower, plant	Patio roses
Oct	flower, plant	"Sweet Dream"
Nov	plant	Climbers
Dec	/	"Breath of life"

LEFT: A Large Flowered and upright grower to 4ft, richly scented "Double Delight" was introduced from America around 20 years ago. Its popularity has never waned.

RIGHT: Associating roses with other plants is an exciting challenge. Here this sumptuous Cluster Flowered variety is harmonising with Crambe cordifolia *blossom.*

BELOW: Because they absorb light, it is vital to plant scarlet and other deeply hued roses in a bright, sunny spot. In even, light shade, blooms tend to disappear on dull days.

RIGHT: Vigorous and healthy bush to 3ft, "Sunblest" is a profuse Large Flowered variety, the strong stems of which are topped with tightly formed buds that open to reveal unfading, bright yellow blooms.

VARIETIES

LEFT: Though lacking the impact of semi- and fully double Large Flowered roses, single-flowered Polyantha varieties have innate charm and flower for months.

ABOVE: "Bernina," a Cluster Flowered rose yet to come to Britain, was developed for and named after the Swiss sewing machine company. It bears a multitude of scented and perfectly formed flowers.

LEFT: Appealing to flower arrangers, Cluster Flowered "Purple Tiger" is an extraordinary variety best grouped with silver-leaved Artemisia "Powis Castle".

RIGHT: Bicolored roses have special appeal. When cutting these and other varieties, plunge them to their necks in a bucket of water for a day, before arranging them.

ROSEMARY
Rosmarinus

An aromatic shrub and herb, rosemary embellishes a bed, border or patio tub with spires of blue, pink, or white flowers in mid-spring.

Exploit the beauty of prostrate varieties by planting them to soften a hard corner or spill over a retaining wall.

FEATURES

Grown for its aromatic, evergreen foliage, *Rosmarinus officinalis*—there is only one species—embraces varieties with hooded, blue, pale violet, pink, or white flowers in April and May. There are upright kinds to 6ft and compact, ground-covering forms to 2ft across. Rosemary also makes a fetching, informal hedge. Plant it to enhance a mixed shrub and perennial border, or in patio pots. If possible, position it where you will brush against it and detect its pleasing aroma. It is long-lived, matures within 3–5 years and flowers early in life. Rosemary, also a culinary herb, symbolises remembrance, love, and fidelity.

CONDITIONS

Aspect	Rosemary, which must have full sun to develop stocky, free-flowering shoots, prospers in exposed inland and coastal gardens.
Site	Preferring well-drained, poor, sandy, or gravelly soils, it abhors heavy clay.

GROWING METHOD

Feeding	Apart from working bone meal into the planting hole, no further fertilizer is usually necessary to ensure that rosemary flourishes.
Propagation	This shrub is easily increased from semi-ripe cuttings taken from mid- to late summer.
Problems	It is seldom attacked by pests and diseases, but its roots are liable to rot in soggy clay.

PRUNING

Upright varieties and hedges:	Keep plants compact and full of young growth by trimming them fairly hard with shears when flowers fade in late spring.
Carpeters:	Prune unwanted shoots in spring.

ROSEMARY AT A GLANCE

A hardy, small-leaved, aromatic, upright, or carpeting evergreen, with usually blue, spring flowers. Hardy to 14°F (zone 8).

Jan	/	Recommended Varieties
Feb	/	
Mar	/	"Aureus"
Apr	flower, plant	"Benenden Blue"
May	flower, plant	"Corsicus Prostratus"
Jun	prune, plant	"Miss Jessopp's Upright"
July	plant	Prostratus Group
Aug	plant	"Tuscan Blue"
Sept	plant	
Oct	/	
Nov	/	
Dec	/	

COTTON LAVENDER
Santolina

Effectively mantling and silvering this border edge, the dwarf form of cotton lavender, Santolina chamaecyparissus nana, *is a hardy evergreen.*

An arresting succession of lemon-yellow flowers clothe Santolina rosmarinifolia's *feathery, deep green stems from June to August.*

FEATURES

Mound forming, evergreen and ideal for making a low hedge to divide a lawn from a path or to segregate open-plan gardens, cotton lavender is prized for its aromatic, feathery, silvery-white, or gray foliage. There is also a green-leaved form.

If cotton lavender is left to mature, a wealth of button-like, yellow flowers appear from June to August. Flowers, however, tend to spoil its symmetry and give it a ragged look. If you prefer foliage to blooms, prune bushes hard each year.

It is a tough shrub and unaffected by salty winds, so makes a good seaside plant. It also has few enemies.

Widely planted *Santolina chamecyparissus*, grows to around 18in high and 30in across and is favoured for hedging or punctuating a border. Its dwarf form, *nana*, just 12in high, is fetching for edging a border or highlighting a rock garden.

Even whiter and more feathery is S. *pinnata neopolitana*, to 32in high.

Equally decorative but with thread-like, green leaves, S. *rosmarinifolia* (*virens*) is massed with long-stemmed, yellow flowers in summer.

CONDITIONS

Aspect
Santolina is very hardy and braves low temperatures. Provided you set plants in full sun, where silvery-white-leaved varieties develop full radiance, they will excel for you. The green-leaved species tolerates light shade.

Site
This shrub performs zestfully on sandy loam but abhors heavy clay, which becomes soggy and airless in winter. If you are stuck with heavy clay, drain it by working in grit and channelling a gravel-lined drainage trench to a soakaway.

GROWING METHOD

Feeding
There is little need to be diligent with feeding, for cotton lavender prospers on thin and nutrient-sparse soils. However, lush growth will please you if in spring and fall you work a dressing of bone meal into the root area.

Propagation
Increase your favorites from semi-ripe cuttings taken from early to mid-fall and rooted in a garden frame or multiply plants from hardwood cuttings in late fall.

Problems
Normally trouble free.

PRUNING

Shear off faded blooms in late August. Periodically—every 3 years or so when lower shoots are becoming woody—shorten stems to 6in from the base to stimulate new basal growth.

COTTON LAVENDER AT A GLANCE		
Evergreen bush with ferny or thread-like leaves and yellow, "button" flowers from June to August. Hardy to 14°F (zone 8).		
Jan	/	
Feb	/	Recommended Varieties
Mar	/	S. *chamaecyparissus*
Apr	plant, prune	S. *chamaecyparissus nana*
May	plant, prune	S. *pinnata neopolitana*
Jun	flower, plant	S. *virens*
July	flower, plant	
Aug	flower, plant	
Sept	flower, plant	
Oct	/	
Nov	/	
Dec	/	

CHRISTMAS BOX
Sarcococca

Vanilla scent from the tiny flowers of Sarcococca hookeriana *"Digyna," a suckering evergreen to 6ft, can waft for yards.*

Glossy leaved and smothered with scented, white blooms in winter, undemanding Sarcococca confusa *thrives in light shade.*

FEATURES

An easy, suckering, lance- or oval-leaved evergreen, sarcococca is a delight in February when tufted flowers of white or creamy male petals and smaller female blooms sleeve stems and release rich vanilla fragrance.

On a warm, breezy day, scent is detectable many yards from the bush. If you plant a group of it beneath a living-room window, the perfume will waft indoors. Cut blooms will scent a room.

Carpeting thickly and suppressing weeds, *Sarcococca hookeriana* forms a 12in high thicket, 3ft across. *Digyna*, a form of *S. hookeriana*, has purple-tinged leaves and thrusts to 4ft. Its flowers are followed by black berries. Resembling privet, *S. confusa* is a neater version, to 2.5ft. Appealingly different, *S. ruscifolia* forms a rugged bush of broader leaves, to 3ft high and across, and blooms are followed by red berries.

CONDITIONS

Aspect Ideal for clothing dappled shady areas beneath trees or borders on the north side of a wall or fence and between houses, it prospers in full sun, too. Avoid deeply shaded sites where growth is less compact and flowering inhibited.

Site Sarcococca favours deep, humus- and nutrient-rich, acid or alkaline soils that drain freely. Improve poor, sandy patches by working in bulky organic manure. Lighten and aerate heavy clay by digging in some grit or pea shingle.

Plant it in a large tub or pot to perfume a patio or terrace in mild spells during winter. Alternatively, set it to flank a path or driveway where you will brush against it and enjoy its "clean," rich scent.

GROWING METHOD

Feeding Encourage robust growth by working bone meal into the planting hole and pricking it into the root area in spring and fall. Help young plants establish quickly by watering copiously after planting and in dry spells in their first year.

Propagation Increase your stock by using a spade to slice off rooted suckers in spring or take semi-ripe cuttings of new shoots in midsummer.

Problems Small, young plants may take several months to settle down and grow enthusiastically. Encourage them to develop quickly by liquid feeding fortnightly with a high-nitrogen fertilizer in spring and summer.

PRUNING

No regular cutting back is necessary. Remove dead or damaged shoots in spring.

CHRISTMAS BOX AT A GLANCE

White-flowered and sweetly scented, bushy or carpeting evergreen for sunny or lightly shaded places. Hardy to 4°F (zone 7).

Month	Activity	Recommended Varieties
Jan	/	
Feb	flower	*S. confusa*
Mar	plant	*S. hookeriana digyna*
Apr	plant, prune	*S. hookeriana humilis*
May	plant	*S. ruscifolia*
Jun	/	
July	/	
Aug	plant	
Sept	plant	
Oct	/	
Nov	/	
Dec	/	

SPIRAEA
Spiraea

Transforming mid-spring with a fountain of snowy blossom on arching stems to 6ft, bridal wreath (Spiraea arguta) is magnificent.

Unusually, late summer-flowering Spiraea "Shirobana" yields a mix of mushroom-headed, white and rose-purple flowers.

FEATURES

An easy and floriferous family of deciduous shrubs, 18in–8ft high, spiraea rewards us with cone- or dome-shaped blooms on upright shoots or on pendulous or arching stems. There are two groups: spring flowering and summer flowering.

The finest early performers, from March to May, are epitomised by the aptly named bridal wreath (*Spiraea arguta*). Its arching stems, to 6ft, are so thickly enveloped with snowy blossom that its leaves are concealed.

Most popular summer-flowering members are forms of *S. japonica*: "Anthony Waterer," aglow with domes of carmine-pink flowers amid pink or cream-tinged leaves; and "Goldflame," prized for its dark pink flowers and radiant golden-orange leaves in spring. Another kind, *S. billiardii* "Triumphans," is ablaze with rose-purple flower cones in July and August.

Plant spiraea to punctuate a border, carpet a rock garden pocket, adorn a patio tub, or screen out an ugly view.

CONDITIONS

Aspect   Very hardy, these shrubs prefer full sun in which stocky shoots flower well and colored-leaved varieties develop vivid hues.

Site   They also thrive in a wide range of well-drained soils but dislike dry or very alkaline conditions. Improve sandy patches by digging in plenty of rotted organic matter.

GROWING METHOD

Feeding   Encourage robust growth by gently working bone meal into the root area in spring and fall. Help new plants recover quickly from transplanting by watering liberally and

mulching in dry spells in spring and summer.

Propagation   Take soft-tip cuttings in early summer; semi-ripe cuttings from mid- to late summer; or hardwood cuttings in fall. Some varieties can be divided or increased from suckers in early spring.

Problems   Control sap-sucking aphids, which colonize soft shoot tips, by spraying with pirimicarb, derris, or horticultural soap.

PRUNING

Spring- and summer-flowering kinds that flower on older shoots: Cut out from the base one older stem in three when blooms fade. Summer-flowering varieties that bloom on the current-year shoots: Shorten all stems to 4in from the base from early to mid-spring. Rejuvenate tall, old, woody varieties making little new growth by cutting all shoots to within 12in of the base in early spring.

SPIRAEA AT A GLANCE		
Spring- or summer-flowering shrubs with white, pink, or purple-rose blooms. Some have orange foliage. Hardy to -13°F (zone 8).		
Jan	/	Recommended Varieties
Feb	/	
Mar	plant, flower	Spring flowering
Apr	plant, flower	*S. arguta*
May	flower, prune	*S. thunbergii*
Jun	flower, prune	"Snowmound"
July	flower, prune	Summer flowering
Aug	flower, prune	"Anthony Waterer"
Sept	flower, prune	*S.* × *billiardii*
Oct	plant	"Gold Mound"
Nov	plant	"Little Princess"
Dec	/	"Triumphans"

LILAC
Syringa

Fragrant trusses of lilac blossom are a spring highlight. Syringa vulgaris *varieties bloom best in an open, sunny position.*

Cottage-garden pleasure: this white "Mme Lemoine" lilac has been skillfully pruned to form a globe of blossom in mid-May.

FEATURES

A vast and fragrant, deciduous family from S.E. Europe to E. Asia, its cone or plume-like flowers light up May and June. Most popular are varieties of *Syringa vulgaris*. Enchanting, double-flowered forms are mauve-pink "Belle de Nancy," dark purple "Charles Joly," and violet-red "Paul Hariot". Captivating singles include white "Maud Notcutt" and creamy-yellow "Primrose". All make upright focal points to 8–10ft.

The Canadian Hybrids—rose-hued "Bellicent" and pale lilac "Elinor"—tolerate shade better than *S. vulgaris* and bear plumy blossom. Accommodating dwarf varieties, to 4ft, for small gardens or rockeries, are lilac-pink *S. meyeri* "Palibin" and *S. pubescens* "Superba".

LILAC AT A GLANCE

Perfumed, cone- or plume-shaped blooms in many shades appear in spring. Hardiness rating according to species.

		Recommended Varieties
Jan	/	
Feb	/	*S. pubescens* "Miss Kim"
Mar	plant	*S. pubescens* "Superba"
Apr	plant	*S. vulgaris* "Belle de Nancy"
May	flower, plant	
Jun	flower, plant	*S. vulgaris* "Charles Joly"
July	plant	*S. vulgaris* "Mme Lemoine"
Aug	plant	
Sept	plant	*S. vulgaris* "Mrs Edward Harding"
Oct	plant	
Nov	plant, prune	*S. vulgaris* "Primrose"
Dec	prune	*S. × prestoniae* "Elinor"

CONDITIONS

Aspect Lilac flowers best in full sun but tolerates light shade. Choose an open site, protected from strong, drying winds, where air circulates freely, to reduce risk of leaves becoming mildewed.

Site These shrubs need well-drained, organically rich soil. Avoid chalky spots, which may cause lime-induced chlorosis, when leaves turn creamy yellow and die.

GROWING METHOD

Feeding Apply a complete plant food, such as Growmore or fish, blood, and bone meal in spring and midsummer.

Propagation Commercially, varieties are usually budded or grafted on to privet rootstock. Alternatively, take soft-tip cuttings in early summer or semi-ripe cuttings from mid- to late summer.

Problems Lilac blight, characterised by angular, brown spots, destroys leaves and buds. There are no chemical controls, so cut back affected shoots to healthy, white tissue and burn prunings. When mildew strikes, leaves are felted with powdery-white mold. Improve air flow by thinning crowded shoots and spraying with carbendazim, mancozeb, or sulfur when symptoms appear.

PRUNING

Cut out spent flowers when petals fade. Keep bushes youthful and blooming freely by pruning out a quarter of the older shoots each year in winter. Remove basal suckers.

VIBURNUM
Viburnum

Horizontally-tiered Viburnum plicatum *"Mariesii" displays its large, lacy, sterile blossoms embracing small, fertile flowers in spring.*

A spring star is Viburnum x burkwoodii, *whose multitude of orb-shaped, pinkish-white blooms spill rich vanilla scent into the air.*

FEATURES

Coveted for their blossom, berries, foliage and architectural habit, deciduous and evergreen viburnums have year-round appeal. Flowers—clusters, globes, and sprays—in pink or white, thickly clothe shoots. Most varieties are sweetly perfumed. Growing 30in–10ft or more, most species and varieties bloom within three years of planting. All make fetching statements: such as evergreen *Viburnum tinu*s, which also makes a dense, winter-flowering hedge; carpeting *V. davidii*, whose female plants are studded with turquoise-blue berries; *V carlesii*, studded with vanilla-scented, whitish-pink orbs in spring; and *V. x bodnantense* "Dawn," clustered with rose-pink flowers from October to March.

VIBURNUM AT A GLANCE

Light up winter to summer with showy flowers and fall with spectacular, scarlet berries. Hardiness according to species.

		Recommended Varieties
Jan	flower	
Feb	flower	Winter flowering
Mar	plant, flower	"Dawn"
Apr	flower, prune	"Deben"
May	flower, plant	*V. x bodnantense*
Jun	flower, plant	Spring flowering
July	plant, prune	*V. carlesii* "Aurora"
Aug	plant	*V. x carlcephalum*
Sept	plant	*V. x opulus* "Roseum"
Oct	plant	Fall berrying
Nov	plant	*V. betulifolium*
Dec	/	*V. davidii*

CONDITIONS

Aspect Viburnums need at least half a day's full sunshine to prosper. Shield large-flowering varieties from cold wind.

Site These shrubs prefer well-drained soil enriched with well-rotted organic matter several weeks before planting.
In light soils that parch quickly, mulch in spring with moisture-conserving, bulky organics to keep roots cool and active.

GROWING METHOD

Feeding Nourish growth by applying a balanced fertilizer, such as Growmore, chicken pellets, or fish, blood, and bone meal, in spring and midsummer. In a cold spring, boost growth of young plants by foliar feeding fortnightly with a high-potash fertilizer.
Water frequently newly planted viburnums in warm, dry weather.

Propagation Take soft-tip cuttings in spring; semi-ripe cuttings from mid- to late summer; and hardwood cuttings in late fall. Layer shoots from mid-spring to late summer.

Problems Tackle viburnum beetle, which shreds leaves in summer, by spraying in late spring with permethrin, bifenthrin, or pyrethrum.

PRUNING

V. tinus: Trim shoots lightly in early spring. Deciduous, winter-flowering species: Remove one stem in three every 2–3 years in spring. Evergreens: Cut out one stem in three, in midsummer, every four years.

WEIGELA
Weigela

Weigela florida *"Variegata" brightens late spring with a generous confection of pinkish blossom on year-old shoots.*

Compact and low growing, so ideal for small gardens, *Weigela 'Rumba's shoots are thickly sleeved with radiant blooms.*

FEATURES

Flowering unstintingly from May to June, weigela is a reliable, hardy, deciduous shrub. Growing 4–6ft high and across, there are two main divisions: varieties of *Weigela florida* and a range of hybrids.

Two of the showiest forms of *W. florida* are dark purple-leaved and rose-pink-flowered "Foliis Purpureis" and widely grown "Variegata," whose green-and-yellow foliage complements pale pink blooms.

Appealing hybrids include "Briant Rubidor," where golden-yellow to green leaves combine pleasingly with a wealth of vibrant, ruby-red flowers. Very different is *W.* "Looymansii Aurea," which must be grown in light shade or its leaves, bright gold in spring, will scorch.

CONDITIONS

Aspect	Most varieties flower best if planted in full sun. Shield them from strong wind, too, which can damage flowers and "burn" soft, new leaves.
Site	Encourage vigorous growth by setting plants in well-drained soil, including chalk, enriched with plenty of well-decayed manure.

GROWING METHOD

Feeding	Boost sturdy shoots sleeved with blossom by topdressing the root area with bone meal in spring and fall and mulching in spring.
Propagation	Take soft-tip cuttings in early summer; semi-ripe cuttings from mid- to late summer; and hardwood cuttings in the fall.
Problems	Pale green capsid bugs, about ¼in long, suck sap from shoot tips and secrete a toxin that kills cells. When leaves unfold, damaged areas become ragged holes. Control by spraying with pirimiphos-methyl or fenitrothion when symptoms seen.

PRUNING

Keep bushes young and packed with blossom by removing from the base one in three of the oldest flowering stems when blooms turn fade.

WEIGELA AT A GLANCE

Bushy shrubs bearing trumpet-shaped, white, pink, red, or purple-red blooms from May to June. Hardy to -13°F (zone 5).

Jan	/	Recommended Varieties
Feb	/	"Abel Carriere"
Mar	plant	"Briant Rubidor"
Apr	plant	"Carnival"
May	flower, plant	"Foliis Purpureis"
Jun	flower, plant	*W. middendorffiana*
July	prune, plant	"Newport Red"
Aug	plant	"Rumba"
Sept	plant	"Variegata"
Oct	plant	
Nov	plant	
Dec	/	

WISTERIA
Wisteria

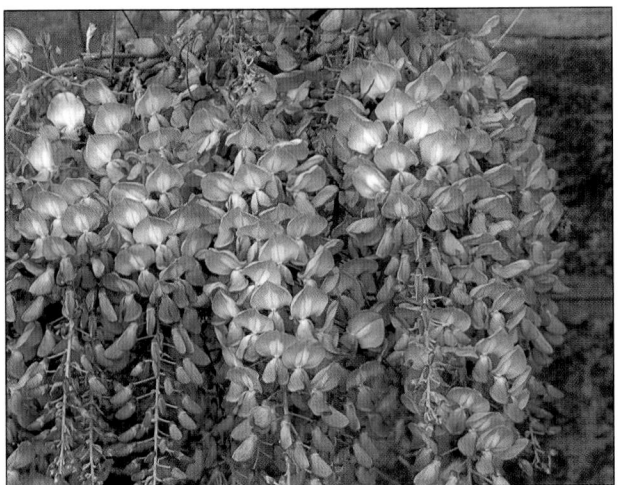

Trained to cover a warm, sunny wall, Chinese wisteria (Wisteria sinensis) yields fragrant, lilac-blue to white flowers in May and June.

Festooned with chunky blooms in late spring, Wisteria brachybotrys is also called silky wisteria because of its softly hairy leaves.

FEATURES

Wisteria takes the accolade for cloaking beautifully in May and June a wall, fence, pergola, arch, or tree. Taking 3–4 years to establish and flowering freely, its long chains of pea-like blooms cascade from woody spurs. Blossoms on some varieties are followed by attractive, runner bean-like seed pods.

Buy only grafted plants—look for a bulge where scion and stock unite—because seedlings can take many years to flower and often they do not do so at all.

If space is limited, this handsome, twining, deciduous climber can be planted in a large patio tub and trained as a standard, to around 8ft high.

Choice kinds are sweetly scented Chinese wisteria (*Wisteria sinensis*), which displays lilac-blue to white flowers. Its varieties—white "Alba" and deep violet-blue "Caroline"—are spectacular. The silky wisteria (*W. brachybotrys*) has softly hairy, pinnate leaves, which complement shortish, yellow-blotched, violet to white blooms. The stunning Japanese wisteria (*W. floribunda* "Alba") treats us to clusters of white blossom, which extend impressively to 2ft long.

CONDITIONS

Aspect A sheltered, sunny, or very lightly shaded, south- or west-facing position is essential for flowering. For unless new shoots are exposed daily to many hours of sunlight or to bright incidental light, they may not ripen sufficiently for flowers to form.

Site Virtually any well-drained soil—the more fertile the better—suits this rampant climber. Chalky, alkaline soil may inhibit the uptake of iron vital for chlorophyll formation and cause leaves to become weak and creamy green.

GROWING METHOD

Feeding A spring and fall application of bone meal encourages robust growth. Mulch with bulky organic materials to conserve moisture.
If, despite regular pruning, flowers fail to form, topdress the root area with 1oz per sq yd of shoot-ripening sulfate of potash in February.

Propagation Layer shoots from mid-spring to late summer or root soft-tip cuttings in a mist propagation unit in midsummer.

Problems Reluctance to flower can be due to planting a seedling, insufficient light or not pruning.

PRUNING

In July, shorten to five compound leaves new shoots springing from the main branches. In November, reduce shortened shoots to two buds to encourage flowering spurs to form.

WISTERIA AT A GLANCE

Spring-flowering climber laden with chains of pea flowers, for warm, sunny walls, fences and trees. Hardy to 4°F (zone 7).

Month	Activity	Recommended Varieties
Jan	/	
Feb	/	*W. brachybotrys*
Mar	plant	*W. floribunda* "Alba"
Apr	plant	*W. sinensis*
May	plant, flower	*W. sinensis* "Alba"
Jun	plant, flower	*W. sinensis* "Caroline"
July	prune	
Aug	plant	
Sept	plant	
Oct	/	
Nov	prune	
Dec	/	

Growing
Herbs

GROWING HERBS

No garden is complete without a few herbs, which are mainly used to add flavour and delight to food, but which have many other uses too: in cosmetics, craft arrangements, herbal remedies, and as good companions and edging plants in the garden. You can buy them, of course, but you will feel extra pride when using herbs you have grown yourself. And herbs are almost all very easy to grow.

To a botanist a herb is a plant that does not have a permanent woody stem: that is, one that is not a tree or shrub. Its edibility is irrelevant. Gardeners have a different definition. To them, a herb is a plant that can be added to food or used for medicinal purposes, even if the plant in question is actually a shrub, such as rosemary, or even a tree, such as the bay tree. Herbs are (or may be) used fresh, unlike spices, which are almost always dried or prepared in some other way first. (Spices, such as pepper or nutmeg, are the seeds, flowers, bark, or roots of tropical trees or shrubs.)

LEFT: A pink and gray border of pinks, lavender, and thyme harmonizes in this herb garden with old-fashioned roses, although they are not yet in bloom.

THE RICH GREEN COLOR and the soft texture of parsley makes as elegant a garnish for flowers as it does for a dinner plate. In this stunning garden it is used as contrast with miniature blue violas and white sweet alyssum.

USING HERBS

Today we use herbs most often when preparing food. Any cook knows how useful it is to have some herbs on hand. Even a pinch of dried herbs from a supermarket packet can make a great difference to a mediocre dish, but the same herbs fresh from the garden can add the savour and scent that makes the dish something special. Restraint, however, should be the order of the day. The recipe will be your guide, but remember that dried herbs are often sharper in flavour than fresh ones and fresh herbs vary in strength with the season. Add a little at a time, tasting as you go: you don't want to taste the herb before you taste the food. Go easy, too, in planning the menu. One herbed item on the plate is usually sufficient.

Herbs are used extensively in flower arrangements and crafts, where they add fragrance and different textures. Herbal pot-pourris and wall hangings are especially effective and herbs can be used in home-made cosmetics for those who want an alternative to commercial preparations.

Herbs are also credited with all sorts of medicinal qualities. In the past it was an essential part of a doctor's education to learn to distinguish beneficial herbs from useless and harmful ones, and these studies laid the foundation of the modern science of botany. Some of the old prescriptions have been verified by science and many modern drugs are still extracted from plants, although other old remedies were apparently based on nothing more than wishful thinking and superstition. (Sometimes the patient may have been merely suffering from a shortage of vitamins which a salad of green herbs made good.) The folklore attached to herbs is part of their charm, but don't dabble in herbal cures without seeking advice from your doctor or a reputable herbalist first.

HARVESTING HERBS

The traditional way to gather herbs is to pick them just as they are coming into flower (when the flavour is strongest) and use them immediately. This way you use them at their best and most attractive.

Many herbs can also be used after they have been dried. You can spread them out on a table to dry in the shade for a couple of days or, these days, the microwave oven provides a more than acceptable alternative. Gather the herbs, spread them on a paper towel, cover them with another paper towel, and zap them with the full power of the microwave for a minute or two. Check them, and if they aren't quite dry, give them some more time with the top towel off. The precise timing depends on what sort of herb it is and how dry the leaves were to start with.

Alternatively, you can freeze the fresh herbs. Just put them in a freezer bag, pop them in the freezer and take what you want when you need them.

CHOOSING HERBS TO GROW

Whether you plan to plant an extensive collection of herbs or just a few, your first choices will obviously include the ones you like best, those that feature in your favorite recipes or craft activities. (Chances are you'll probably already have them, dried, in your kitchen.) It is probably a good idea to grow several plants of these herbs to avoid harvesting them to death. However, don't let unfamiliarity stop you from trying out a plant or two of a herb with looks or fragrance that appeal to you.

PLANTING HERBS

It is a time-honored tradition to grow herbs in gardens of their own, and if you have the enthusiasm and the space, a small formal herb garden with its beds divided by paths arranged around a central feature such as a statue or a sundial can be very pretty. Most herbs are low growing, and few are all that distinguished in appearance—indeed, some are rather nondescript. Marshalling them into formal beds flatters them, and you can play their subtle foliage colors and textures off against one another. You might, for instance, contrast the gray leaves of sage with the lush green ones of parsley, or the featheriness of dill with the solidity of rosemary; and the variegated and fancy-leaved versions of such herbs as sage, balm or mint will enrich your palette.

If a formal garden is not for you, don't despair. There will be a place for herbs in any garden, for they really are very adaptable. Try one of the following ideas.
• Plant herbs in your flower beds. Being mostly low growing, they are best planted at the front, where their subtle greens and grays will set off the bright flowers behind.
• Plant them along the edges of your paths, where they will release their scent on the air as you brush past.
• They can look especially good in front of roses—and they will hide the rose bushes' thorny legs—but be careful if you have to spray the roses. You won't want the spray drifting onto the herbs and rendering them dangerous to eat.
• Be strictly utilitarian and plant them to edge the beds in the vegetable garden. Here they will give you something to look at when the beds are bare between crops.
• Most varieties grow very well in pots, which means that even if all the garden you have is an apartment balcony you can still have the pleasure of fresh herbs.
• Give your herbs a windowbox on the kitchen windowsill so that you can just reach out and harvest as you need them— but only if the window gets the sun, and make sure they are outside in the fresh air. Magazines are full of pictures of pots of herbs growing in the kitchen itself, but herbs are not indoor plants. They survive inside for a few weeks, but they get straggly and leggy and you won't get much of a harvest.
• However you choose to grow herbs in your garden, don't plant them too far from the kitchen door. Nothing is more frustrating than to find you need a sprig or two for some dish and have to make an expedition to the bottom of the garden while a pot boils over.

PROPAGATION

Most herbs can be grown from seed, but it can be a slow process and most gardeners start with purchased seedlings or by taking cuttings or dividing plants. The appropriate method for each plant is discussed under its entry.

MAINTENANCE

Growing herbs is easy. As a general rule, they love sunshine and don't need much watering: indeed the flavour is richest if they aren't encouraged to grow too lush. They don't, however, appreciate being starved so give them good, well-drained soil and some fertilizer occasionally. The main exceptions to the rule are basil and chives, which do best with generous feeding and regular watering, and bergamot and the various mints, which are lovers of damp soil. Most herbs have few specific pest or disease problems. You'll find more detail about requirements and problems in the description of each species.

STRIKING A CUTTING

If you are going to strike a herb from a cutting, take the cutting from a strong, healthy plant early in the morning. The cutting should be 2–4in long. If you are not able to plant it at once, stand it in water so that it does not wilt.

Remove the lower leaves and prepare a small pot with a mix of two-thirds coarse sand and one-third potting compost. Make a hole with your finger or a pencil where the cutting is to go, insert the cutting to about one-third of its length and firm the mix around it. Water well and then cover the pot with a plastic bag to create a mini-greenhouse.

Keep the mix damp but not wet. Once roots have formed, the plant can be planted out in the garden.

1. TO TAKE A STEM CUTTING, cut just below a leaf (node or joint). Do not bruise the stem, and trim the end of the cutting with a razor blade if need be. Prepare a pot, filling it with compost then tapping it to settle the compost.

2. INSERT ALL THE CUTTINGS into a pot (or several pots), first making a hole in the compost with your finger for each cutting and then firming the compost gently around the cuttings. Space the cuttings around the edge of the pot.

3. THEN WATER THE CUTTINGS in well but gently, taking care not to dislodge them. Make sure the container has adequate drainage holes so that excess water will drain away. If the soil remains too wet, the cuttings will rot.

4. MAKE A WIRE OR BAMBOO FRAME that fits around the pot and is tall enough to clear the cuttings. Place a polythene bag over the frame and pot: the bag will keep the air and soil moist. Place the pot in a position that is out of direct sunlight.

ALCHEMILLA
Alchemilla vulgaris

FEATURES

Alchemilla vulgaris (A. xanthochlora), the wild lady's mantle, is a hardy perennial native to the mountains of Europe, Asia, and America. It grows to 9–18in and has rounded pale green leaves, with lobed and toothed edges that collect the dew or raindrops. The water thus collected once was reputed to have healing and magical powers. Feathery heads of yellow-green flowers are produced in early summer and can continue into fall. More popular, and very widely grown as a garden plant, is *Alchemilla mollis* which is very similar in both appearance and properties. The alpine lady's mantle, *Alchemilla alpina*, a smaller plant growing to 6in, is also said to have similar, but more effective, properties.

CONDITIONS

Aspect Lady's mantle will grow in sun or moderate shade.

Site It is tolerant of most soils except waterlogged conditions.

GROWING METHOD

Sowing and planting Lady's mantle self-seeds freely and removing and replanting self-sown seedlings is an easy way to get new plants. Seed can be sown in early spring or fall. Germination takes about two or three weeks but can be erratic. Fall-sown seedlings will need to be overwintered under glass. Plant them out in spring 18in apart. Established plants can be propagated by division either in spring or fall.

Feeding The lady's mantles are tolerant plants, but be careful to avoid overwatering. Mulch alchemillas lightly in the spring and the fall and apply a balanced general fertilizer in spring.

Problems None.

ALCHEMILLA AT A GLANCE

A pretty perennial with rounded leaves and feathery flowerheads, it was traditionally a woman's herb. Hardy to 4°F (zone 7).

Jan	/		
Feb	/		*PARTS USED*
Mar	plant		Leaves
Apr	plant		Flowers
May	plant	harvest	
Jun		harvest	*USES*
July		harvest	Culinary
Aug		harvest	Medicinal
Sept	plant	harvest	Cosmetic
Oct	/		Gardening
Nov	/		
Dec	/		

THE "LADY" to whom the name lady's mantle refers, was the Virgin Mary, to whom the herb was dedicated during medieval times.

Pruning Cut back flowerheads as they start to fade to prevent self-seeding. Cut back dead foliage in late fall.

HARVESTING

Picking Young leaves can be picked as required throughout the summer, after the morning dew has dried.

Storage Leaves can be dried and stored in airtight dark glass jars.

Freezing Not suitable for freezing.

USES

Culinary Young leaves can be added to salads in small amounts. They have a mild, but somewhat bitter taste.

Medicinal In medieval times the lady's mantle was dedicated to the Virgin Mary, and was considered to be particularly a woman's herb, as it was used to treat a wide range of womens' problems, including menstrual problems, menopause, breastfeeding, and inflammations. It was also used as a wound healer for external use, and to make a mouth rinse for use after tooth extraction.

Cosmetic Lady's mantle can be used to make a soothing and healing rinse that is good for skin complaints.

Gardening Alchemilla is widely used as an edging plant as well as being grown in flower borders, and the attractive feathery heads of yellow-green flowers are particularly popular with flower arrangers.

ANISE HYSSOP

Agastache foeniculum

FEATURES

Anise hyssop, or agastache, is a perennial herb, similar to mint in appearance, but with a somewhat neater, clump-forming habit, and growing to about 2–3ft. The mid-green, nettle-shaped leaves have an aniseed scent. Long spikes of purple flowers, attractive to bees and butterflies, are produced from mid summer onward. A native of North America, it is not quite as hardy as the better known European members of the mint family. Although perennial, it tends to be short-lived and is best propagated every year, or at least every three years.

CONDITIONS

Aspect   Anise hyssop needs full sun (although it may tolerate a little light shade in mild areas) and shelter from cold winds. It may need winter protection if the temperature drops below about 23°F.

Site   It grows best in a rich, moisture-retentive soil, although it will grow in most garden soils if given a sunny position.

GROWING METHOD

Sowing and planting   Anise hyssop can easily be propagated by division in spring and also by seed and cuttings. The seeds need warmth to germinate and are best sown under glass in spring. Germination takes approximately 10–20 days. Prick out the seedlings when they are large enough to handle and plant out in mid spring at about 18in apart. Seed can also be sown outdoors in fall when the soil is warm, but the young plants will need winter protection. Cuttings can be taken in mid to late summer, and the rooted cuttings can be overwintered in a greenhouse or cold frame and then planted

BEES AND BUTTERFLIES are attracted to the tall purple-blue flower spikes of anise hyssop, borne from mid summer onward.

out in spring.

Feeding   Do not allow to dry out. Keep well watered in summer. Mulch lightly in spring and fall and apply a balanced general fertilizer in spring.

Problems   Anise hyssop rarely suffers from pests or disease, except that seedlings may damp off and the plants may suffer from mildew in hot summers.

Pruning   Cut back old flowerheads and woody growth in fall to keep plants compact and to prevent them becoming straggly.

HARVESTING

Picking   Pick the young leaves just before the plant flowers. Cut flowers just as they are beginning to open.

Storage   Dry leaves in a cool, airy space and store in dark, airtight, glass jars.

Freezing   Put leaves in a freezer bag; freeze for up to 6 months.

USES

Culinary   The leaves can be used to make a refreshing aniseed-flavoured tea. They can also be used, like borage, in summer fruit cups, and can be added to salads and used as a seasoning, particularly in savoury pork and rice dishes. The flowers will add color to salads and fruit cups.

Craft   The scented leaves of anise hyssop can be used in pot-pourri.

Gardening   Anise hyssop is an excellent bee herb. Attractive white-flowered varieties, "Alabaster" and "Alba," are also available.

AGASTACHE AT A GLANCE

A perennial herb, very similar to mint in appearance, and with a refreshing aniseed flavour. Hardy to 14°F (zones 8-9).

Month	Activity		PARTS USED
Jan	/		Leaves
Feb	/		Flowers
Mar	plant		
Apr	plant		USES
May	plant harvest		Culinary
Jun	harvest		Craft
July	plant harvest		Gardening
Aug	plant harvest		
Sept	plant		
Oct	/		
Nov	/		
Dec	/		

BERGAMOT
Monarda didyma

FEATURES

A member of the mint family with a pungent citrus-like flavour, bergamot can reach 2–3ft in height. The wild bergamot, *Monarda didyma*, also known as bee balm, is a hardy herbaceous perennial, but there are annual, biennial, and perennial varieties with brilliant scarlet red, purple, pink, or white flowers in summer. Bergamot is semi-dormant during winter, sending up squarish stems in spring bearing dark green, ovate leaves with toothed margins. The flowers attract bees.

CONDITIONS

Aspect   Prefers a sunny location; tolerates partial shade.

Site   An excellent border plant for moist soil. Grow in a humus-rich soil containing a lot of organic matter. Mulch well with leaves, straw, or compost to retain moisture and keep down weeds around this shallow-rooting herb.

GROWING METHOD

Sowing and planting   Can be grown from seed, but seeds are very fine and often unreliable—this herb is easily cross-pollinated and plants may not be true to the parent in color or form. Sow seeds in spring in trays of seed compost, covering the tray with glass. Seeds germinate within 2 weeks. Transplant seedlings to the garden when they are 3in high. More reliable is root division in spring: take sections of runners or sucker shoots from the outside of the clump, which will have roots throughout the bed. Discard the center of the clump and pot the other sections. Plant out in the garden when they are growing strongly, 32in apart.

Feeding   Water well—like all members of the mint family, bergamot requires water at all times. Add general fertilizer to the backfill when planting. Give another application of fertilizer each spring.

Problems   Powdery mildew and rust can affect bergamot. Cut back and remove diseased parts.

Pruning   In late fall prune the plant back close to ground level. It will regenerate in spring. To increase the strength of the plant, cut flowerheads before they bloom in the first year. After flowering, the plant may be cut back to within 1¼in of the soil surface as this can promote a second flowering in fall.

HARVESTING

Picking   Leaves for making tea are stripped from stems both just before and just after flowering. The colorful flower petals can also be harvested.

Storage   Leaves can be part dried in a shady place for 2 or 3 days and then drying can be completed in a very low oven. Flowers do not store well

MOST COLORFUL OF HERBS, bergamot is indigenous to the Americas. Native Americans brewed Oswego tea from its leaves.

and so should only be picked as required.

Freezing   Put sprigs in a freezer bag. They can be frozen for up to 6 months.

USES

Culinary   Fresh leaves can be used in summer fruit drinks or punches, and fresh flower petals are good for decorating salads. Leaves are also used for making tea.

Medicinal   The herb tea can be used to relieve nausea, flatulence, vomiting, colds, etc.

Craft   Dried leaves can be used in pot-pourris. The oil is used in perfumery, to scent candles etc.

Garden   The colorful flowers attract bees and this herb is therefore a good companion for plants that need insect pollination.

BERGAMOT AT A GLANCE

Attractive perennial border plant, with aromatic leaves that can be used to make a refreshing tea. Hardy to 4°F (zone 6).

			PARTS USED
Jan	/		Leaves
Feb	/		Flowers
Mar	plant		
Apr	plant		
May	plant	harvest	USES
Jun	plant	harvest	Culinary
July		harvest	Medicinal
Aug		harvest	Craft
Sept	plant	harvest	Gardening
Oct	plant		
Nov	/		
Dec	/		

BORAGE
Borago officinalis

FEATURES

A fast-growing annual or biennial growing 2–3ft tall, borage bears star-shaped flowers with protruding black anthers in summer. They are usually bright sky-blue, although they can sometimes be pink or white. The bush bears many sprawling, leafy branches with hollow stems, which can be quite fragile. The stems are covered with stiff white hairs and the grayish-green leaves are also hairy.

CONDITIONS

Aspect   Prefers sunny locations but grows in most positions, including partial shade. It needs plenty of space. The brittle stems may need staking to prevent wind damage.

Site   Grows well in most soils that are aerated, moist and mulched to keep weeds down.

GROWING METHOD

Sowing and planting   Sow seed directly into the garden and thin out the seedlings later, leaving 24in between plants. Seedlings do not transplant well once established. Successive sowings every 3 to 4 weeks will extend the harvesting period. It self-sows readily and its spread may need to be controlled.

Feeding   During spells of hot, dry weather borage plants should be kept well watered. Apply a balanced general fertilizer once each spring or use controlled-release granules.

Problems   Blackfly can be a problem. Treat with liquid horticultural soap. Mildew may also be a problem late in the year. If so, plants are best dug up and removed.

HARVESTING

Picking   Pick the leaves as required while they are fresh and young. *Caution:* handling fresh leaves may cause contact dermatitis. Use gloves. Harvest the open flowers during the summer months.

Storage   The leaves must be used fresh; they cannot be dried and stored. The flowers can be crystallized and then stored in airtight jars.

Freezing   The leaves cannot be frozen. The flowers may be frozen in ice cubes.

USES

Culinary   Borage has a faintly cucumberish taste and leaves can be added to salads, and drinks such as Pimms. Flowers may be frozen in ice cubes for cold drinks, used raw on salads, or to decorate cakes and desserts if crystallised. *Caution:* it may be a danger to health. It is now under study because of the presence of alkaloids.

IN THIS GARDEN blue borage and white garlic grow side by side. In the old days, soldiers ate the flowers of borage to give them courage.

Medicinal   Borage tea was used for colds and flu. The leaves and flowers are rich in potassium and calcium. Borage has been found to contain gamma linoleic acid (GLA) and is now being more widely grown as a commercial crop.

Cosmetic   The leaves can be used to make a cleansing facial steam.

Craft   The flowers can be added to pot-pourri.

Gardening   Borage is regarded as an excellent companion plant in the garden, especially when it is planted near strawberries.

BORAGE AT A GLANCE

A tall, fast-growing annual with bristly leaves and small bright blue star-shaped flowers. Hardy to 4°F (zone 6).

Jan	/		
Feb	/		
Mar	plant		
Apr	plant		
May	plant	harvest	
Jun	plant	harvest	
July		harvest	
Aug		harvest	
Sept		harvest	
Oct	/		
Nov	/		
Dec	/		

PARTS USED
   Flowers
   Leaves

USES
   Culinary
   Medicinal
   Cosmetic
   Craft
   Gardening

CATMINT
Nepeta cataria

FEATURES

Nepeta cataria, catmint or catnip, is a perennial, native to Europe and Asia. There are several varieties of catmint grown in gardens, all with slightly different growing habits, including *N. mussinii* and *N. x faassenii*, which have similar properties. In general they are low-growing perennials reaching 1–3ft in height. Fine white hairs cover both the stem, which is square as in all members of the mint family, and the gray-green leaves. These are coarse-toothed and ovate, although the base leaves are heart-shaped. The tubular summer flowers are massed in spikes or whorls. White, pale pink, or purplish blue in color, they produce very fine seeds. Cats find some catmints very attractive.

CONDITIONS

Aspect Prefers an open, sunny position but tolerates partial shade. Most fragrant in good sunlight.

Site Catmint does best in fertile sandy loams.

GROWING METHOD

Sowing and planting Catmint self-sows readily by seeding, once it is established, and can also be grown from cuttings taken in spring. To do this, cut a 4in piece from the parent plant, remove the tip and lower leaves, and place the cutting in a moist soil medium. Cuttings take root in 2 to 3 weeks. Divide mature plants into three or four clumps in spring or fall.

Feeding As members of the mint family have a high water requirement, keep this plant moist at all times. Do not stand pots in water, however, as this can drown the plant. Mulch lightly in spring and fall, and give a balanced general fertilizer in spring. Feed with nitrogen-rich fertilizer such as poultry manure in spring for more leaf growth.

Problems Catmint is basically pest free.

Pruning Prune back each year to keep bushes in shape.

HARVESTING

Picking Pick fresh leaves as required. Cut leafy stems in late summer when the plant is in bloom. Hang them to dry in a cool, shady place.

Storage Strip leaves and flowers from dried stems and store in airtight jars.

Freezing Leaves can be put in a freezer bag and frozen for up to 6 months.

USES

Culinary Fresh young leaves were once a popular salad ingredient and were used for herbal teas, although they are less popular now.

THE POWDER BLUE FLOWERS and softly aromatic leaves of Nepeta x faassenii are most attractive to human eyes and noses.

Medicinal Catmint was once used as a cold remedy. (The leaves have a high vitamin C content.)

Craft Dried flowers and leaves are used in pot-pourri mixtures, and in toys for cats.

Gardening Plant it near vegetables to deter flea beetles. The scent is also said to deter rats.

CATMINT AT A GLANCE

A spreading perennial with aromatic gray-green leaves, it is particularly attractive to cats. Hardy to 4°F (zone 6).

Jan	/	
Feb	/	**PARTS USED**
Mar	plant 🌿	Leaves
Apr	plant 🌿	Flowers
May	plant 🌿 harvest 🌾	
Jun	plant 🌿 harvest 🌾	**USES**
July	harvest 🌾	Culinary
Aug	harvest 🌾	Medicinal
Sept	plant 🌿 harvest 🌾	Craft
Oct	plant 🌿	Gardening
Nov	/	
Dec	/	

CHICORY
Cichorium intybus

FEATURES

This is a large perennial plant, often grown as an annual. It reaches 3–5ft or more in height. The intense sky-blue, fine-petalled flowers, borne in summer, open in the morning but close up in the hot midday sun. The broad, oblong leaves with ragged edges, reminiscent of dandelions, form a rosette around the bottom of the tall, straggly stems. The upper leaves are much smaller, giving a bare look to the top of the plant. Some varieties can be cultivated by forcing and blanching, when the lettuce-like heart of the chicory plant turns into chicons.

CONDITIONS

Aspect   Prefers full sun. May need support.
Site   These plants require deep, rich, friable soil for best growth.

GROWING METHOD

Sowing and planting   Sow seeds in spring, into drills or trenches 1.25in deep, and thin the seedlings to 12in apart when they are established. Seeds may also be germinated in seed trays and seedlings transplanted into the garden during the months of spring.

Feeding   Keep chicory well watered during spells of hot weather. Add compost to the garden bed in mid summer, but do not provide too much nitrogen or the leaves will grow rapidly at the expense of root growth.

Problems   No particular pests or diseases affect this plant.

HARVESTING

Picking   Pick young green leaves of chicory when they are required. Pick newly opened flowers in summer. Dig up roots in fall.

Storage   The leaves cannot be stored either fresh or dried. The root can be dried and then rendered into a powder.

Freezing   Not suitable for freezing.

Forcing   Lift roots in fall or winter, trim off the leaves to about 1inch from the root, and keep in the dark in a bucket of dry sand to force sweet, new growth which can be harvested in a few weeks.

USES

Culinary   Use young leaves as soon as they are picked, either in salads or in cooking, and forced leaves as winter salad. The strong, bitterish flavour is similar to dandelion. Flowers can be crystallised and used to decorate cakes and puddings. Roasted chicory root is widely used as a coffee substitute.

CHICORY is thought to have been one of the "bitter herbs" the Israelites ate with the Passover lamb. Christians thought it was an aphrodisiac.

Medicinal   A bitter tonic and digestive can be made from the leaves, and a laxative from the roots. *Caution:* Excessive continued use may cause eye problems.

CHICORY AT A GLANCE

A tall, straggly perennial with intense bright blue flowers, often grown as annual for forcing. Hardy to 4°F (zone 6).

Month	Activity		PARTS USED
Jan	/		Leaves
Feb	/		Flowers
Mar	plant		Roots
Apr	plant		Shoots
May	plant	harvest	
Jun	plant	harvest	
July	plant	harvest	USES
Aug		harvest	Culinary
Sept		harvest	Medicinal
Oct	force		
Nov	force		
Dec	force		

CHIVES
Allium schoenoprasum, a. tuberosum

GARLIC CHIVES are taller than regular chives and have pretty white flowers.

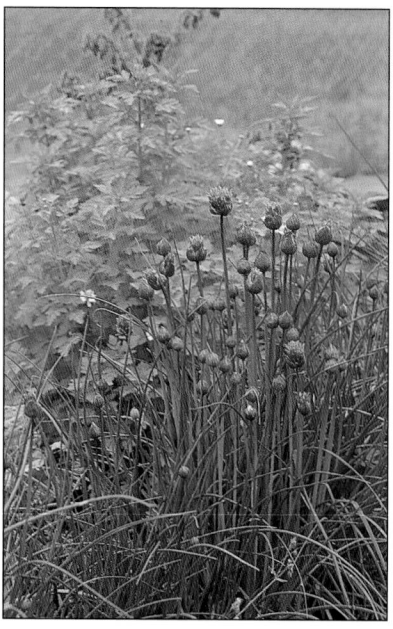

DAINTY CLUSTERS of mauve flowers and tubular leaves characterize common chives.

CHINESE CHIVES are eaten as a vegetable in China; here we substitute spring onions.

FEATURES

Chives are perennial herbs that make an attractive edging for a herb garden or bed of mixed annuals and perennials. They grow in clumps from very small bulbs that send up 12in tall grass-like, hollow, tubular, green leaves, tapering to a point at the top. The plants produce flower stems in summer. The flowers of the common chive, *A. schoenoprasum,* take the form of a dense, globular head of pinkish to pale purple blossoms. Chinese or garlic chives (*A. tuberosum*) have a flowerhead composed of star-like, white flowers and flat, narrow, light to dark green leaves. Chives can be grown successfully in small containers and clumps can even be potted up and brought indoors to keep in the kitchen.

CHIVES AT A GLANCE

This hardy perennial herb is highly valued for its tasty green leaves. Ideal for salads. Hardy to 4°F (zone 6).

Jan	/			
Feb	/			PARTS USED
Mar	plant 🌱			Leaves
Apr	plant 🌱	harvest 🌿		Flowers
May	plant 🌱	harvest 🌿		Buds
Jun	plant 🌱	harvest 🌿		
July	plant 🌱	harvest 🌿		USES
Aug		harvest 🌿		Culinary
Sept		harvest 🌿		Medicinal
Oct		harvest 🌿		Gardening
Nov	/			
Dec	/			

CONDITIONS

Aspect
Chives tolerate a wide range of conditions but grow best in a sunny position.

Site
Chives do best in rich, moist, but well-drained soil, but will tolerate a wide range of conditions.

GROWING METHOD

Sowing and planting
The simplest way to propagate chives is by division. Lift a clump in spring, separate into smaller clumps and replant into fertile ground. Chives can also be grown easily from seed, but need warm conditions to germinate, so are best sown indoors in early spring, with bottom heat. Alternatively, wait until late spring or summer to sow outdoors. Plant clumps 8in apart, in rows 1–2ft apart.

Feeding
Water chives well, especially during hot months. At planting time dig in compost or well-rotted manure and a balanced general fertilizer.

Problems
Chives can suffer from rust. Cut back and burn diseased growth, or, if bad, remove the plant completely. Mildew may also be a problem, and greenfly may attack pot-grown plants.

HARVESTING

Picking
Pick leaves as available. Do not snip off just the tips or the chive will become tough and fibrous. Clip the leaves or blades close to the ground, leaving about 2in still intact. Harvest chives regularly to keep the crop growing. Pick flowers when fully open, but before the color fades.

BORNE IN LATE SPRING, the flowers make chives one of the most decorative of herbs and a first-rate plant for edging a bed, either in a herb garden or in an old-fashioned cottage garden. Choose plants in flower if possible; some strains are much more richly colored than others.

Storage   Chives do not store very well.

Freezing   Leaves can be frozen for about 6 months. Chop them, put them in a freezer bag, and freeze them for use when needed at a later date.

USES

Culinary   Leaves of the chive, *A. schoenoprasum,* have a delicate, mild onion flavour and are added to soups or casseroles during the last moments of cooking. Chopped leaves are also used in salads, in herb butter, as a garnish over other vegetables and in the French *fines herbes*. The flowers can be eaten fresh, tossed in salads, or made into spectacular herb vinegars or butters. All parts of the Chinese chive, *A. tuberosum*, have a mild garlic flavour and the unopened flower bud has a special place in Asian cuisines.

Medicinal   The leaves are mildly antiseptic and also promote digestion.

Gardening   Chives are recommended companions for roses, carrots, grapes, tomatoes, and fruit trees. They are said to prevent scab on apples and blackspot on roses.

COMFREY
Symphytum officinale

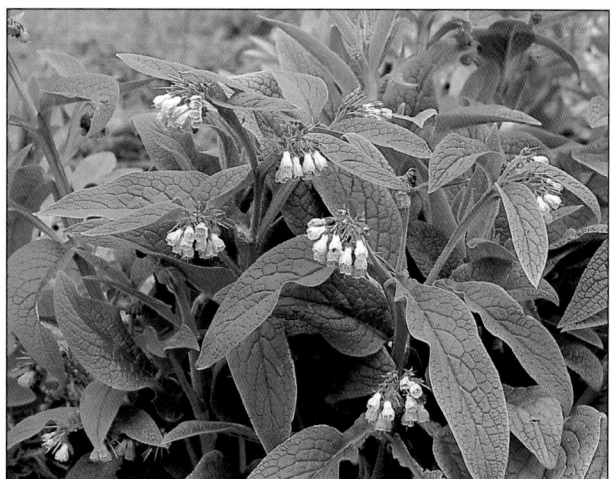

COMFREY LEAVES are handsome but you cannot eat them fresh—they are as rough as sandpaper.

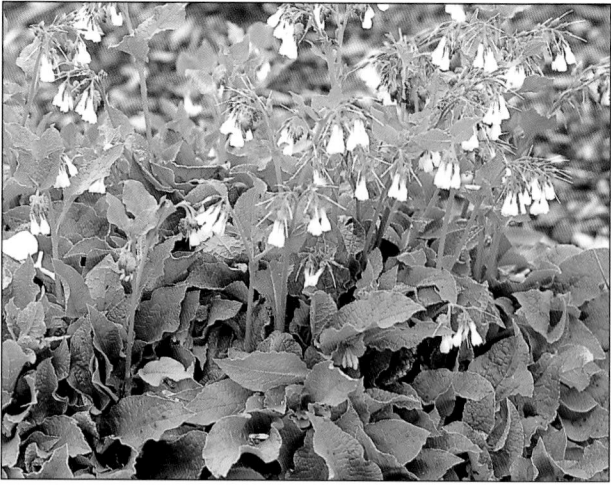

ATTRACTIVE IN GROWTH and in foliage, comfrey makes an unusual tall groundcover. Other species have blue or white flowers.

FEATURES

This large, coarse, hairy perennial grows to 39in or more high. It has dark green, lanceolate leaves, which reach 10–12in long, and clusters of bell-shaped flowers in pink-purple or white in summer. The sticky qualities of its rhizome, which is black outside and has juicy white flesh within, gave rise to its nickname of slippery root; its other name, knit-bone, comes from its use in healing. The plant dies down over winter but makes a strong recovery in spring and can be quite invasive in the garden. Confine it to distant parts of the garden where it forms a backdrop.

CONDITIONS

Aspect   Prefers sun or semi-shade, but tolerates most conditions.
Site   Prefers moist, rich soils. Prepare beds with plenty of compost and farmyard manures.

GROWING METHOD

Sowing and planting   Comfrey can be propagated from spring plantings of seed, by root cuttings at any stage of its life cycle or by root division in fall.
Feeding   Comfrey requires a great deal of water. For best growth mulch in spring and fall and apply a balanced general fertilizer in spring.
Problems   May suffer from rust or powdery mildew from late summer. Destroy affected parts.
Pruning   Cutting flowers encourages more leaf growth.

HARVESTING

Picking   Leaves can be picked from early summer to the fall. Up to 4 cuttings a year can be taken. Dig up roots in fall.

Storage   The leaves can be dried and then stored in airtight containers.
Freezing   Can be frozen for 6 months.

USES

Culinary   Not recommended as controversy surrounds the use of young leaves in salads. Dried leaves are sometimes used to make a herbal tea.
Medicinal   The plant contains high concentrations of vitamin B_{12} but a great deal would need to be eaten daily to have any beneficial effect, and some studies suggest that certain alkaloids in the plant can cause chronic liver problems. Roots and leaves are used as a poultice for inflammations, bruises, etc.
Cosmetic   An infusion of leaves makes a cosmetic wash.
Gardening   Comfrey is best used as a liquid manure: steep fresh leaves in water for several weeks. Leaves can also be used to promote decomposition in the compost heap, and so plant it close by.

COMFREY AT A GLANCE

A coarse, hairy, spreading perennial, which can be used to make an excellent organic fertilizer. Hardy to 4°F (zone 6).

Jan	/	PARTS USED	
Feb	/	Leaves	
Mar	plant 🖐	Roots	
Apr	plant 🖐		
May	plant 🖐 harvest 🌿	USES	
Jun	plant 🖐 harvest 🌿	(Culinary)	
July	plant 🖐 harvest 🌿	Medicinal	
Aug	plant 🖐 harvest 🌿	Cosmetic	
Sept	plant 🖐 harvest 🌿	Gardening	
Oct	plant 🖐 harvest 🌿		
Nov	/		
Dec	/		

DANDELION
Taraxacum officinale

FEATURES

A perennial flower often seen as a weed in lawns or neglected places, dandelion produces a flat rosette of deeply lobed, bright green leaves from a big, fleshy taproot. Bright yellow flowers are produced in spring and summer on hollow, leafless stems and develop into puffy, spherical seedheads—dandelion clocks—the individual seeds of which float away on the breeze when ripe. Dandelion has a milky sap and its hollow flower stems differentiate it from other similar weeds, such as hieraciums.

CONDITIONS

Aspect	Grows best in full sun.
Site	Not fussy as to soil but you will get the biggest and best roots and less bitter leaves by growing it in good quality, friable soil.

GROWING METHOD

Sowing and planting	Considered a weed in most yards, the problem is usually restricting or removing it rather than growing it. Remove flowerheads before it sets seed. It is difficult to dig out as any bit of root left will regrow. It is best grown in a bottomless container to confine the roots. Although it is perennial, for the best crops dig out the mature plants each spring or two and replant from small pieces of root.
Feeding	Keep the soil evenly moist. Avoid excessive fertilizing. If the bed had well-rotted manure dug into it, no further fertilizing is required. For container growth, incorporate controlled-release fertilizer into the potting mix at planting time and feed the growing plants monthly with liquid fertilizer.
Problems	No particular problems.
Pruning	Remove flower stems as they rise or, if the pretty flowers are wanted, deadhead as they

DANDELIONS are often considered a weed, but the yellow flowers are very pretty and the leaves are full of vitamins.

fade to stop unwanted seed formation. If seedheads are allowed to ripen, dandelion becomes an invasive weed.

HARVESTING

Picking	Fresh spring leaves can be picked while small and sweet. Bigger, older leaves are very bitter. Bitterness can be reduced by blanching, that is, excluding light. Do this by covering the plant with an upturned tin or flower pot, being sure that all holes are covered. The leaves are ready for picking when they have lost all or most of their green color. Harvest roots only in late fall or winter or they will lack flavour and body. Pick flowers as they open for use fresh.
Storage	Leaves and flowers must be used fresh but roots are stored by first roasting and grinding them and storing in an airtight jar.
Freezing	Roasted, ground roots will stay fresher and more flavoursome if stored in the freezer.

USES

Culinary	Young, sweet leaves are highly nutritious and can be used in salads, stir frys, or to make teas. The ground roots are used as a coffee substitute. The flowers are used to make wine.
Medicinal	The sticky, white sap of the dandelion is used to treat warts and verrucas. Dandelion coffee is sleep inducing and a detoxicant said to be good for the kidneys and liver. The leaves are a powerful diuretic.
Cosmetic	Eating the leaves is said to be good for the skin.
Craft	A yellow-brown dye is made from the roots.

DANDELION AT A GLANCE

This familiar "weed" with its yellow flowers and "dandelion clock" seedheads has many herbal uses. Hardy to 4°F (zone 6).

Jan	/		PARTS USED
Feb	/		Leaves
Mar	plant 🌱		Flowers
Apr	plant 🌱	harvest 🌿	Roots
May	plant 🌱	harvest 🌿	
Jun		harvest 🌿	
July		harvest 🌿	USES
Aug		harvest 🌿	Culinary
Sept	plant 🌱	harvest 🌿	Medicinal
Oct		harvest 🌿	Cosmetic
Nov	/		Craft
Dec	/		

DILL
Anethum graveolens

FEATURES

A hardy annual herb growing to 2–3ft, dill looks very like fennel, with its threadlike, feathery, aromatic, blue-green leaves. It has a single, thin taproot rising above the ground to form a long, hollow stalk. This stalk branches at the top to support a 6in wide mass of small, yellow flowers, appearing in clusters, in summer. Flat, oval seeds, brown in color, are produced quickly and in great quantities.

CONDITIONS

Aspect   Prefers full sun. May need support and protection from strong winds.

Site   Light, free-draining but fertile soils. Will not do well in cold, wet conditions.

GROWING METHOD

Sowing and planting   Sow seed from spring to fall. Successive planting every fortnight is recommended to ensure that there is continuous cropping. Sow the seeds in shallow furrows, with at least 2ft between the rows, and then thin the seedlings out to 1ft apart when they have reached approximately 2in in height. Dill will quite often self-sow, so choose a permanent position for the initial plantings.

Feeding   Keep well watered, especially in hot weather. Mulch well throughout spring and summer with well-rotted organic matter such as compost or farmyard manure.

Problems   No particular problems.

HARVESTING

Picking   Dill leaves can be picked within 2 months of planting. Clip close to the stem in the cooler parts of the day. Several weeks after the plant

THE FEATHERY LEAVES and greenish-yellow flowers of dill make a graceful summer picture. The flowers are used in making spiced olives.

blossoms, pick the flowerheads and place them in a paper bag—store in a cool, dry place until seeds ripen—or stems can be cut and hung upside down until seeds ripen and fall.

Storage   Leaves and stems do not keep for more than a couple of days in the refrigerator before drooping and losing flavor. Dry leaves by spreading them thinly over a firm, non-metallic surface in a warm, dark place. After drying, place them in an airtight container. Seeds are dried in a similar manner.

Freezing   Leaves and stems can be frozen for up to six months, and pieces broken off as required.

USES

Culinary   Dill has a pronounced tang which is stronger in seed than leaf. Fresh leaves are used in many dishes, and as a garnish. The seeds are used ground or whole in cooked dishes, as well as in the making of vinegars, pickles, and herb butters. Dried leaves are often added to soups or sauces. Dill is a great favorite in fish dishes. Tea can be made from the seeds.

Medicinal   Dill was traditionally an important medicinal herb for coughs, headaches, digestive problems etc, and dill water or "gripe water" is still used.

Gardening   Dill is considered an ideal companion plant for lettuce, cabbage, and onions.

DILL AT A GLANCE

A hardy annual with feathery blue-green leaves. Leaves and seeds are popular in cooking. Fairly hardy to about 14°F (zone 8).

Jan	/	
Feb	/	
Mar	plant 🌿	
Apr	plant 🌿	
May	plant 🌿	harvest 🌾
Jun	plant 🌿	harvest 🌾
July	plant 🌿	harvest 🌾
Aug	plant 🌿	harvest 🌾
Sept	plant 🌿	harvest 🌾
Oct		harvest 🌾
Nov	/	
Dec	/	

PARTS USED
Leaves
Seeds
Stems

USES
Culinary
Medicinal
Gardening

ELDER

Sambucus nigra

FEATURES

A deciduous shrub or small tree, elder or elderberry grows up to 20–28ft tall and has rough, corky bark and compound leaves composed of five or so toothed, dark green leaflets. Heads of creamy white, scented flowers appear in summer leading to shiny, blue-black berries in fall. The flowers attract bees while the berries are eaten by birds.

CONDITIONS

Aspect A sunny position is best although the plant will tolerate bright, dappled shade or a few hours of full shade each day.

Site Friable, fertile soil that drains well yet stays moist is best, but elder accepts a wide range of soil types. Grows well on chalky soils.

GROWING METHOD

Sowing and planting Plants can be grown from seed sown in spring, or suckers, with their own roots, can be dug and detached from the parent plant. This can be done at any time but spring is best. Elders can also be propagated by cuttings. Take hardwood cuttings in late summer or tip cuttings in spring. Root in containers of very sandy potting mix. Pot up and overwinter under glass before planting out into their permanent position. If you are planting a group or row, leave at least 10ft between plants to allow room for the suckers to develop.

Feeding Elders like moisture at their roots at all times, especially in hot, dry weather in summer. If rainfall is reliable and reasonably regular, mature plants usually need little extra water. In average garden soils no special fertilizing is required, especially if you mulch beneath the plants with well-rotted organic matter. If soil is not particularly fertile, a ration of a complete

THE CREAMY-WHITE FLOWERS of the elder are strongly scented. They appear in clusters during early summer.

plant food once in early spring is sufficient.

Problems No particular problems.

Pruning Elder grows rapidly and in smaller gardens may need to be cut hard back in late fall or early spring to prevent it growing too large.

HARVESTING

Picking Flowerheads are picked in the morning but only when all the flowers on each head have bloomed. Dry spread out on a fine net in a cool, dark, airy place. Berries are picked when ripe.

Storage Dried flowers can be removed from their stems and stored in airtight containers. Ripe berries can also be dried and similarly stored.

Freezing Berries that have been cooked for a few minutes may be frozen for later use.

USES

Culinary Fresh flowers are made into elderflower wine and cordials, and jams and jellies. The berries can also be made into jams or jellies and the juice can be fermented into elderberry wine. Berries should not be eaten raw.

Cosmetic Cold elderflower tea splashed onto the face daily tones and soothes the skin and is good for the complexion generally. Leaves can also be used to make a soothing, healing wash.

Medicinal An infusion of flowers is a remedy for respiratory problems, fevers, colds, and sore throats and has a mild laxative effect. Berries are a mild laxative and are also used to treat coughs, colds, bronchitis, etc.

Gardening Elderberries, with their dense growth and suckering habit, make a good privacy screen and reasonable windbreak.

ELDER AT A GLANCE

Deciduous tree with aromatic white flowers and purple berries, with many different uses. Hardy to 4°F (zone 6).

Jan	/		
Feb	/		PARTS USED
Mar	/		Flowers
Apr	plant 🐾		Berries
May	plant 🐾	harvest 🌾	Leaves
Jun		harvest 🌾	
July	/		USES
Aug	/		Culinary
Sept	plant 🐾	harvest 🌾	Medicinal
Oct	plant 🐾	harvest 🌾	Cosmetic
Nov	/		Gardening
Dec	/		

FEVERFEW

Tanacetum parthenium, syn. Chrysanthemum parthenium

FEATURES

A perennial flower, feverfew has aromatic, finely cut leaves and clusters of long-lasting small, white daisy-like flowers in summer. The plant is densely foliaged and grows about 2ft tall. Leaves are usually a fresh, light green but a golden foliaged form, "Aureum," is also sold. Pretty double-flowered forms are also available.

CONDITIONS

Aspect
Prefers full sun or light shade. Plants may grow lax and flower poorly in areas that are too shady. The golden form may scorch in full sun.

Site
Average, well-drained garden soil is all that is needed. In over-rich soils plants produce too much soft, leafy growth.

GROWING METHOD

Sowing and planting
Easily grown from seed sown in early spring. Press seeds just beneath the surface where the plants are to grow. Established plants can be dug up in fall and divided into several new plants. Each division should have its own roots and the divisions should be replanted immediately. Soft-tip cuttings taken in early summer will also root easily. Make cuttings about 3in long and insert them into small pots of very sandy potting mix. Place in a warm but shady and sheltered spot and keep them moist. Roots should form in about 3 weeks.

Feeding
Do not overwater. Feverfew does not thrive on neglect but does not need frequent watering. Overwet conditions will cause the plant to rot.
Mulch lightly in spring and fall and apply a balanced general fertilizer in spring.

Problems
No major problems.

Pruning
Can be cut back after flowering to keep a compact shape and to minimise self-seeding.

HARVESTING

Picking
All the upper parts of the plant are useful medicinally and whole plants may be harvested any time they are in full bloom. Fresh, young leaves can be harvested any time, but are best before the plant flowers. Do remember that plants need their leaves to live and you should grow enough plants so that picking is not concentrated on just one or two. Pick flowers just as they open.

Storage
Dry upper parts, including leaves, stems, and flowers, in a cool, dark, airy place. (Hang flowers upside down to dry.) When dry, coarsely chop and store in an airtight jar.

Freezing
Freshly picked leaves can be wrapped in foil and frozen, for up to 6 months, for later use.

FOR THE HERB GARDEN, most people prefer this single, daisy-like feverfew but there is also a very pretty double white one.

USES

Medicinal
Tea made from the dried upper parts is drunk to relieve indigestion and period pain. It has gained a reputation for the treatment of migraines. Eating one or two fresh leaves every day may help prevent the onset of migraines in sufferers but in some people this causes mouth ulcers.

Cosmetic
Feverfew makes a useful moisturiser.

Craft
Flower stems placed in linen closets will discourage moths. An infusion of the leaves makes a mild disinfectant.

Gardening
Feverfew is attractive and gives a good display when plants are massed together or used to border paths. It is attractive to bees and is often planted near fruit trees to assist pollination.

FEVERFEW AT A GLANCE

Perennial herb with aromatic leaves and daisy-like flowers that has a reputation for treating migraines. Hardy to 4°F (zone 6).

Month	Activity		PARTS USED
Jan	/		Flowers
Feb	/		Leaves
Mar	plant		Stems
Apr	plant		
May	plant	harvest	
Jun	plant	harvest	USES
July		harvest	Medicinal
Aug		harvest	Cosmetic
Sept	plant	harvest	Craft
Oct	/		Gardening
Nov	/		
Dec	/		

HERB ROBERT
Geranium robertianum

FEATURES

A biennial herb, often grown as an annual, herb Robert may reach a height of 12–18in. It has deeply lobed, toothed leaves which sometimes develop a reddish cast. Pinkish flowers appear in spring in airy clusters. In the wild, the plant is widely distributed in temperate parts of the northern hemisphere. Explosive seed capsules make the plant potentially invasive where the conditions suit it.

CONDITIONS

Aspect   Full sun or part shade are equally suitable.
Site   Not particularly fussy about soil types as long as they drain freely. Average garden soil is quite satisfactory.

GROWING METHOD

Sowing and planting   Herb Robert can be grown from seed saved from last year and sown shallowly in spring or from cuttings of basal shoots taken in middle to late spring. Make cuttings about 3in long and insert them into small pots of very sandy potting mix. Keep lightly moist in a warm, bright, but shaded place. Roots should form within a month and the new plants can either be placed in the garden or potted up to grow bigger. Herb Robert will self-seed freely and is considered to be a weed by many gardeners.

Feeding   Herb Robert does not need a lot of water and in places where summers are mild regular rainfall can be sufficient. If watering is necessary, water deeply once a week rather than giving more frequent light sprinklings. In garden beds that are mulched regularly with well-rotted organic matter, no further fertilizer is needed.

Problems   The fungus disease rust, which attacks all

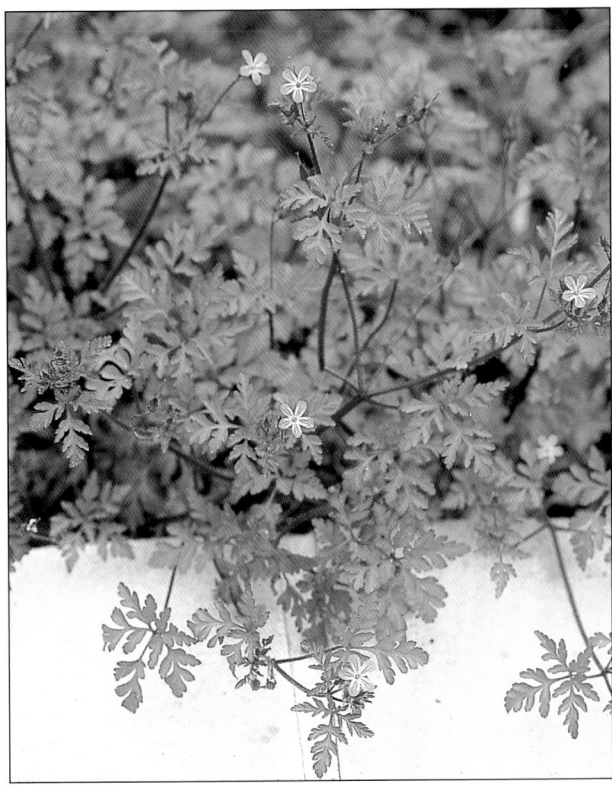

HERB ROBERT has one of those scents you either like or loathe. It is said to be named after St Robert who discovered its medicinal qualities.

plants of the *Geranium* and *Pelargonium* genera, can disfigure the foliage and weaken the plant. It appears as yellow spots on the upper surface of the leaf with raised lumps of "rust" underneath. Rust occurs mainly during warm, humid weather. To control it, either pick off affected leaves at the first sign of infection or spray the plant with a fungicide suitable for the condition (the label will tell you). Don't drop or compost any of the affected leaves. They should be burnt or placed into the rubbish bin.

HARVESTING

Picking   Leaves are used fresh and may be picked at any time as required.
Storage   Not usually stored.
Freezing   Not suitable for freezing.

USES

Medicinal   Traditionally, herb Robert has been used to treat a range of complaints as varied as toothache and conjunctivitis. *Caution:* do not use without expert supervision.
Gardening   Herb Robert plant is pretty enough in its own right and makes a good addition to a wild garden.

HERB ROBERT AT A GLANCE

Traditionally used as a medicinal herb, herb Robert is now often considered a weed. Hardy to 4°F (zone 6).

Jan	/	
Feb	plant 🖐	**PARTS USED**
Mar	plant 🖐	Leaves
Apr	plant 🖐	
May	plant 🖐 harvest 🌿	**USES**
Jun	harvest 🌿	Medicinal
July	harvest 🌿	Gardening
Aug	harvest 🌿	
Sept	harvest 🌿	
Oct	/	
Nov	/	
Dec	/	

HYSSOP
Hyssopus officinalis

FEATURES

A semi-evergreen sub-shrub growing 24–32in tall, hyssop has many erect stems clothed in narrow, lanceolate, sage green leaves. Spikes of small flowers appear on top of each stem in summer. Usually these flowers are blue-violet but they may also be pink or white. The whole plant exudes a pungent aroma and the leaves have a bitter taste.

CONDITIONS

Aspect
Full sun produces compact growth and the strongest flavour but hyssop tolerates shade for part of the day.

Site
Likes light, fertile, well-drained soils but will grow in any reasonably fertile soil as long as it drains freely.

GROWING METHOD

Sowing and planting
Hyssop can be grown from seed, softwood cuttings or division of the roots. Sow seeds in spring in trays of seed compost. Cover lightly, keep moist, and when seedlings are big enough to handle, prick out into small, individual pots to grow on. Plant out about 12in apart when plants are about 8in tall. Take 3in cuttings in early summer and insert into pots of sandy potting mix. Keep moist and in bright, sheltered shade and roots will form within a month. To divide, lift an established plant in late fall or early spring. Cut the root mass into several smaller sections, each with its own roots. Replant immediately.

Feeding
Keep soil moist, especially during the warmer months but do not overwater. Hyssop is a resilient plant that can often get by on rain. A ration of balanced general fertilizer in spring when new growth appears is enough.

Problems
No particular problems.

Pruning
When new growth begins in spring, pinching

THE RICH BLUE FLOWERS of hyssop adorn the garden in spring, and they are much loved by bees who make superb honey from them.

out the tips of young stems will encourage the plant to become more bushy and thus produce more flowers. Trim after flowering to maintain shape.

HARVESTING

Picking
Flowers for using fresh or for drying are picked when in full bloom and individual stems can be harvested as needed.

Storage
Cut bunches of flowering stems, tie them together and hang them upside down in a dim, airy place. When they are dry, crumble them into airtight jars.

Freezing
Not suitable for freezing.

USES

Culinary
One or two fresh leaves, finely chopped and added late, give an appealing piquancy to soups and casseroles while fresh flowers can be used to add flavour and color to salads.

Medicinal
Tea, made by infusing the dried stems, leaves, and flowers in boiling water, is taken to relieve the symptoms of colds; hyssop leaves are often a component in mixed herbal tonics and teas. *Caution:* do not use during pregnancy or for nervous people. Avoid strong doses and do not use continuously for long periods.

Cosmetic
Oil distilled from hyssop is used in perfumes and other commercial cosmetics. At home, it may be added to bath water, and cooled hyssop leaf tea is a cleansing, refreshing facial rinse.

Gardening
Hyssop is a decorative plant and very attractive to bees and butterflies. Use it in a border of mixed flowers or grow it as an edging to paths.

HYSSOP AT A GLANCE

A decorative semi-evergreen shrub with narrow green leaves and spikes of blue flowers. Hardy to 4°F (zone 6).

Month	Activity		
Jan	/		
Feb	/		
Mar	plant 🖐		PARTS USED
Apr	plant 🖐		Leaves
May	plant 🖐	harvest �_	Stems
Jun	plant 🖐	harvest 🌿	Flowers
July		harvest 🌿	
Aug		harvest 🌿	USES
Sept	plant 🖐	harvest 🌿	Culinary
Oct	plant 🖐		Medicinal
Nov	/		Cosmetic
Dec	/		Gardening

LAVENDER
Lavandula

FEATURES

Lavender is a traditional herb and cottage garden plant. An evergreen, bushy shrub with aromatic, narrow, gray-green leaves, it bears spikes of blue-mauve (and in some varieties pink or white) fragrant flowers in summer. There are many species and varieties to choose from, most hardy but some only half hardy, and the fragrance and herbal properties will vary with the different types. Heights vary from 12in to 32in or more. "Common" or "English" lavender is *Lavandula angustifolia* (favorite varieties include "Alba," "Hidcote," and "Munstead"). Popular half hardy lavenders include *L. dentata* and *L. stoechas.*

CONDITIONS

Aspect   Best grown in an open, sunny position, but will tolerate some shade. Lavender will not do well in cold, wet conditions.

Site   Prefers well-drained soil, but it need not be rich. If it is acid, add lime.

GROWING METHOD

Sowing and planting   Some lavenders will flower the first year from an early sowing, but taking cuttings is the easiest way to get the lavender you want. Take 2in cuttings with a heel or base of old wood in summer. Trim off lower leaves and insert into pots of a sandy potting mix. Keep on the dry side until the cutting has taken root and new leaf shoots appear. Pot on into a good quality potting mix. Plant in the garden in spring 18–24in apart. Layering is easily done in the fall with most hardy lavenders.

Feeding   Water only in dry weather as lavenders do not require a great deal of water. Applications of a balanced general fertilizer will improve fragrance. Less cold-resistant varieties may need winter mulching.

Problems   In wet conditions lavender may suffer from gray mould or botrytis. Remove and burn affected parts.

Pruning   Trim in spring and again after flowering to keep a compact shape and prevent the bush from becoming straggly. The final trim of the year should be well before the last frosts as frost will damage soft new growth. Do not cut back into old wood as this is unlikely to re-shoot.

HARVESTING

Picking   Flowers can be cut just as they open. Leaves can be picked at any time.

Storage   Dry by hanging in bunches in a dry, airy, hot place. Store dried leaves and flowers in airtight jars.

Freezing   Not suitable for freezing.

ENGLISH LAVENDER is distinguished from the dumpier French, Italian and Spanish types by its slender flower spikes.

USES

Culinary   Fresh or dried flowers and leaves are used to flavour sugars, jellies, ice creams, and cheeses. Flowers can also be crystallized and used as decoration on cakes.

Medicinal   Lavender has traditionally had many medicinal uses, including soothing and sedating and healing burns, cuts, and stings. The oil has a strong anti-bacterial action. It is also used to treat headaches.

Cosmetic   Lavender is used to make skin and hair washes.

Craft   Dried lavender spikes are used in pot-pourris, perfumed sachets, and dried arrangements. Lavender is used to make essential oil and floral waters. It is also an insect repellent.

Gardening   Popular, widely grown cottage garden plants.

LAVENDER AT A GLANCE

Popular fragrant garden plants with narrow silvery leaves and strongly scented flowers. Hardiness varies: 4 to 23°F (zones 7–9).

Jan	/	**PARTS USED**	
Feb	/	Flowers	
Mar	plant 🌿	Leaves	
Apr	plant 🌿		
May	plant 🌿 harvest 🌾		
Jun	plant 🌿 harvest 🌾	**USES**	
July	plant 🌿 harvest 🌾	Culinary	
Aug	plant 🌿 harvest 🌾	Medicinal	
Sept	plant 🌿 harvest 🌾	Cosmetic	
Oct	/	Craft	
Nov	/	Gardening	
Dec	/		

LEMON VERBENA
Aloysia triphylla, syn. Lippia citriodora

FEATURES

A large, bushy, deciduous shrub that grows 3–10ft in height, lemon verbena has long, lemony-scented, narrow leaves. Spikes or sprays of small white to mauve flowers appear in the axils of the leaves in summer. The leaves give this plant its herby quality, and their fragrance can be released simply by brushing against them in the garden. It can be grown in containers and in cooler areas brought indoors over winter, although container plants do not reach the same height as garden plants.

CONDITIONS

Aspect   Requires a sheltered, sunny position with winter protection. Against a sunny wall is ideal.
Site   Likes rich soils. Needs mulching against frosts.

GROWING METHOD

Sowing and planting   Grow from softwood cuttings in late spring or hardwood cuttings in the fall. Trim a 5in piece from the parent bush, removing a third of the upper leaves and a few of the lower leaves. Place in a sandy potting mix. Moisten the mix and cover the pot with a plastic bag to create a mini-greenhouse. Pot on into good quality potting compost when the cutting has taken root and shows renewed leaf growth. Plant in the garden when the plant is growing strongly.
Feeding   The plant is tolerant of dry conditions and will rarely require watering except when grown in a pot. Mulch with straw in the fall to protect from frost. Give an application of a balanced general fertilizer in spring.
Problems   Spider mite and whitefly can be a problem. Hose leaves frequently to remove the pests or use organic soap and pyrethrum or recommended chemicals.
Pruning   Prune each season to contain its straggly

THIS HERB was introduced to European gardens from Chile in 1746. The name Aloysia honours Queen Maria Louisa of Spain.

growth habit, and cut out frost-damaged shoots in spring. It can be trained into a formal standard.

HARVESTING

Picking   Sprigs of leaves can be harvested at any time.
Storage   Hang the branches in a cool, airy place and strip off the leaves when they are dry. Store dried leaves in airtight jars. Fragrance remains for some years.
Freezing   Put in a freezer bag and freeze for up to 6 months.

USES

Culinary   Fresh or dried leaves can be used for herbal tea or in cooking where a lemony flavour is required, as with fish, poultry, marinades, salad dressings, and puddings, and to flavour oils and vinegars.
Medicinal   Lemon verbena tea has a mild sedative effect and is good for nasal congestion and indigestion. *Caution:* long-term use may cause stomach irritation.
Cosmetic   The leaves can be used in skin creams and the essential oil is used in perfumery.
Craft   The strong long-lasting fragrance makes dried leaves a popular component of pot-pourris and sachet fillings.
Gardening   Lemon verbena is an attractive border and container plant.

LEMON VERBENA AT A GLANCE

A deciduous shrub with lemon-scented leaves which are popular ingredients in pot-pourris and sachets. Hardy to 23°F (zone 9).

Month	Activity	
Jan	/	
Feb	/	
Mar	/	
Apr	/	
May	plant 🌱	harvest 🌿
Jun		harvest 🌿
July		harvest 🌿
Aug	plant 🌱	harvest 🌿
Sept	plant 🌱	harvest 🌿
Oct	/	
Nov	/	
Dec	/	

PARTS USED
Leaves

USES
Culinary
Medicinal
Cosmetic
Craft
Gardening

NASTURTIUM
Tropaeolum majus

FEATURES

A popular trailing garden plant. Compact varieties grow to about 24in while large varieties can spread up to 10ft. The wide leaves are roundish and dark green to variegated in color and have a peppery taste. The funnel-shaped, five-petalled, and spurred flowers appear in late spring and summer and range from creamy white through yellow to salmon, brilliant orange, and red. Some varieties have double flowers and all have a slight perfume. Each bud produces a cluster of seeds. (Double forms do not produce seed.) This plant grows well in containers.

CONDITIONS

Aspect Prefers full sun although it will grow in semi-shade. Leaf growth is more pronounced in shady situations and may hide the blooms.

Site Nasturtiums do not like an over-rich soil but good drainage is necessary. Too rich a soil will encourage leaves at the expense of flowers.

GROWING METHOD

Sowing and planting For early flowers sow the large seeds under glass in spring. Plugs or small pots are ideal. Plant out 8in apart when all danger of frost has passed. Seeds can be sown outdoors in May directly where they are to grow, but the plants will not flower until a few weeks later than the early sowings.

Feeding Do not water excessively, especially when plants are well established. Nitrogen encourages the growth of leaves. More flowers and seeds will be produced if you hold back on the fertilizer and compost.

Problems Sap-sucking blackfly (aphids) love nasturtiums. Vigorously hose the pest off or treat the plant with an appropriate spray.

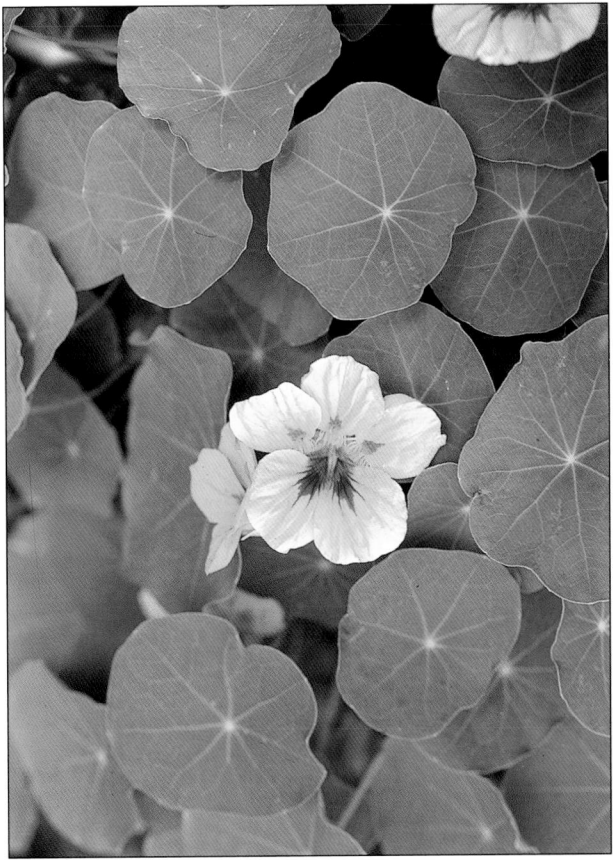

TROPAEOLUM means "a little trophy," so named because the shield-shaped leaves and golden, helmet-like flowers suggested piles of armour.

Caterpillars, particularly those of the cabbage white butterfly, can also be a problem.

HARVESTING

Picking Pick fresh leaves, buds, and flowers as required. Harvest seeds just before they lose their green color.

Storage Leaves and flowers do not store well and should be used immediately. Buds and seeds can be pickled in vinegar, stored in airtight jars and used at a later date.

Freezing Put in a freezer bag; freeze for up to 6 months.

USES

Culinary All parts of this herb are edible and have a spicy, peppery flavour. Fresh leaves and flowers are used in salads or the flowers can be used alone as a garnish. Buds and seeds are used as a substitute for capers. *Caution:* do not eat large quantities at one time.

Gardening Because they are so attractive to aphids, nasturtiums are excellent companion plants for vegetables such as cabbages, broccoli, and other brassicas. The aphids will flock to the nasturtiums and leave the vegetables alone.

NASTURTIUM AT A GLANCE

Attractive trailing annuals with brightly colored flowers, grown for decoration and for the kitchen. Hardy to 23°F (zone 9).

Month	Activity		PARTS USED
Jan	/		Leaves
Feb	/		Flowers
Mar	plant 🖐		Buds
Apr	plant 🖐		Seeds
May	plant 🖐	harvest 🌿	
Jun	plant 🖐	harvest 🌿	
July		harvest 🌿	USES
Aug		harvest 🌿	Culinary
Sept		harvest 🌿	Gardening
Oct		harvest 🌿	
Nov	/		
Dec	/		

OENOTHERA
Oenothera biennis

FEATURES

Oenothera, the evening primrose, is a hardy biennial with many upright, leafy stems. In summer each of these stems is topped with a cluster of golden yellow, sweetly fragrant flowers which open towards the end of the day. The scent is strongest in the evening. The foliage, which is bright green, forms a rosette around the base of the plant. Evening primrose should be planted with caution as it self-seeds prolifically and spreads fast in favoured locations.

CONDITIONS

Aspect   Full sun is preferred.
Site   Not very fussy about soil and grows in most places so long as the drainage is good. This plant thrives in average garden soils.

GROWING METHOD

Sowing and planting   Grows from seed sown in fall or early spring directly where it is to grow. Thin seedlings out so that there is at least 1ft between them.

Feeding   Do not overwater. Once established, plants are fairly drought tolerant. Feeding is not necessary. Rich soils can lead to excessive foliage growth and weak or deformed stems.

Problems   No particular problems.

Pruning   Pruning is not necessary. Snap off flower stems after the blooms have faded but before seeds ripen. This plant self-seeds freely and can create a major weed problem. Allow one plant to seed in order to regenerate the plants but collect the seed before it falls.

HARVESTING

Picking   Leaves may be picked at any time, while seeds

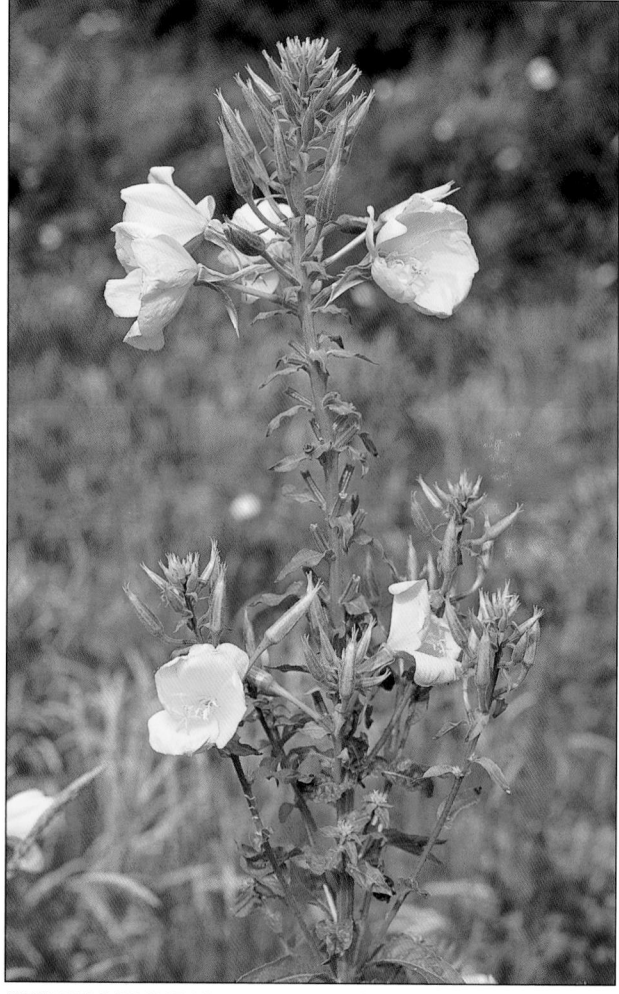

EVENING PRIMROSE earns its name by blooming at dusk. There are perennial species that keep their blooms open all day.

are harvested when ripe in fall. Pick flowers in bud or when just open. The small roots may also be dug in spring or fall.

Storage   Seeds are stored in airtight containers. Other parts of the plant are used fresh.

Freezing   Not suitable for freezing.

USES

Culinary   All parts of the plant are edible. Fresh leaves are used in salads or can be lightly steamed or stir fried. Seeds can be eaten raw or used in cooking.

Medicinal   Tea made from the leaves is good for coughs and colds and is a tonic for the liver, kidneys, and intestines. An oil (GLA, gamma linoleic acid) contained in the seeds has been credited with amazing therapeutic powers, and evening primrose is now being grown commercially on a large scale.

Gardening   Evening primrose is a pretty plant and a good partner for other meadow flowers such as Californian poppies.

OENOTHERA AT A GLANCE

The evening primrose is a pretty, fragrant, yellow-flowered biennial, now much grown commercially. Hardy to 4°F (zone 7).

Month	Activity		PARTS USED
Jan	/		
Feb	/		Leaves
Mar	plant		Stems
Apr	plant		Flowers
May	plant	harvest	Buds
Jun	plant	harvest	Seeds
July		harvest	Roots
Aug		harvest	
Sept	plant	harvest	USES
Oct		harvest	Culinary
Nov	/		Medicinal
Dec	/		Gardening

PARSLEY
Petroselinum

NO NEED TO DESPAIR *when parsley flowers as the flowers are edible too. This Italian parsley can also be used in flower arrangements.*

HERE GROWING *with lettuces, sage, and nasturtiums, curly parsley makes a very attractive addition to any bed of herbs and vegetables.*

CURLY PARSLEY *is the prettiest of garnishes and the essential ingredient in a bouquet garni. Here it grows with white alyssum.*

FEATURES

Parsley grows from a strong tap root with erect, 12in tall stems bearing divided, feather-like, small leaves which may be flattish or curly depending on variety. Tiny, yellowish-green flower clusters are borne on tall stalks in summer, and produce small, brown, oval and ribbed seeds. Common varieties of this biennial or short-lived perennial plant include curly parsley, *P. crispum*, plain-leaved or Italian parsley, *P. crispum* var. *neapolitanum*, and Hamburg or turnip-rooted parsley, *P. crispum* var. *tuberosum*.

CONDITIONS

Aspect   Grow in full sun or light shade.
Site   Parsley plants like a rich, deep, well-drained soil.

GROWING METHOD

Sowing and planting   Sow seed under cover in spring in pots or plug trays rather than seed trays as parsley dislikes being transplanted. The seed can be difficult to germinate so help to create optimum conditions by soaking the seeds in warm water for 24 hours and then pouring boiling water over the soil to raise the temperature. Plant the young seedlings out, 6in apart, after they have grown several true leaves. If parsley is grown in containers, the pots should be at least 8in deep, and the longer tap root of Hamburg parsley will require a pot that is even deeper. Once parsley plants are established in the garden, the mature plants can be left to self-sow when they go to seed during the summer months in their second year of growth.

Feeding   Keep the soil moist and do not let it dry out in dry weather. Occasional feeds of a nitrogen-rich liquid fertilizer will promote more leaf growth.

Problems   Carrot fly and root aphids can be particular problems. Destroy affected plants. Slugs also love young plants.

Pruning   Parsley can be kept productive by frequent pruning and by nipping out the flower stalks whenever they appear.

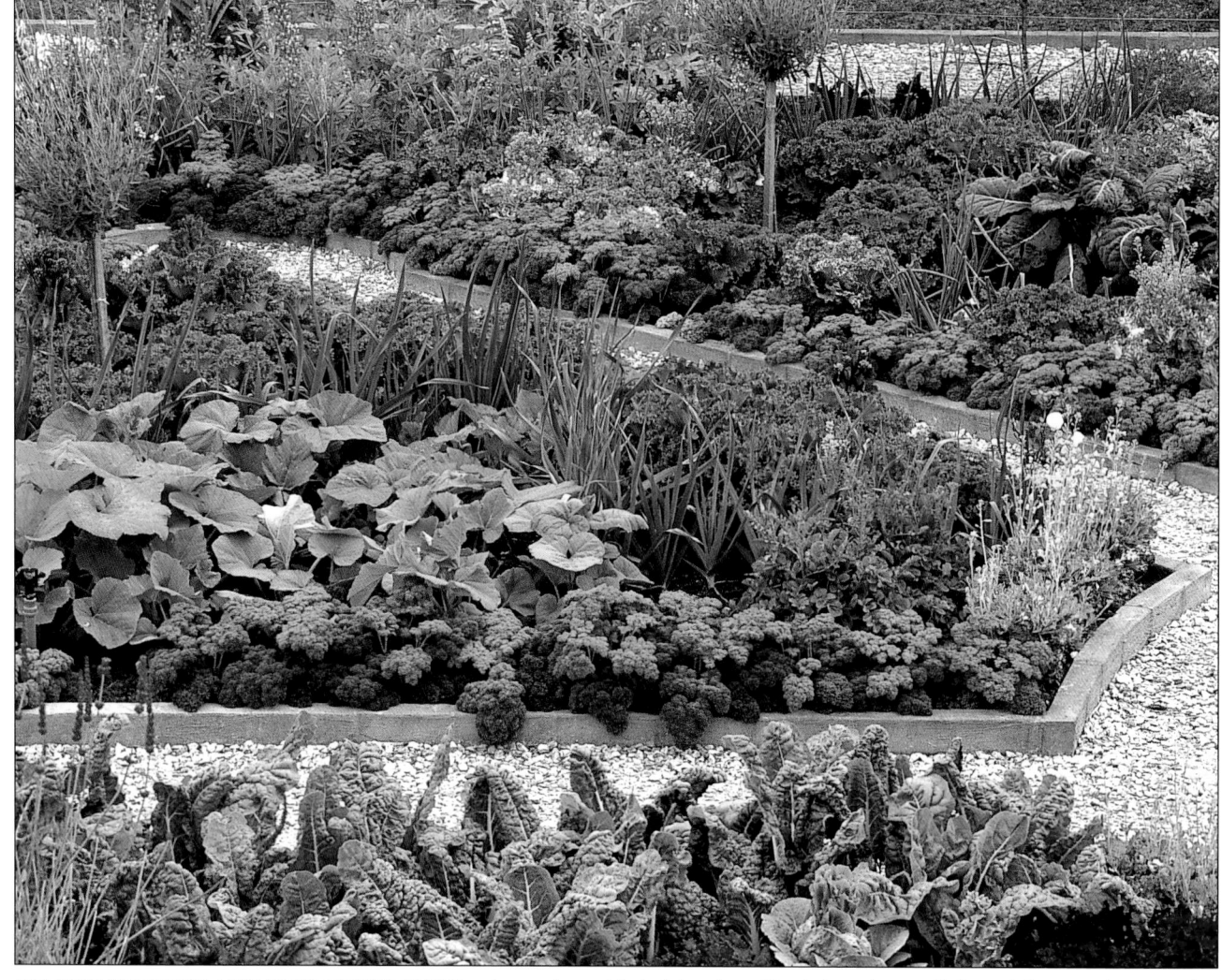

ITS FINE TEXTURE AND RICH GREEN COLOR makes parsley an ideal edging plant. Here it is used to set off the varied tones and textures of a formal vegetable garden, but it would look equally fine as a foil for brightly colored flowers.

HARVESTING

Picking New growth comes from the center of the stem, and so always pick parsley from the outside of the plant. Pick this vitamin-rich, nutritious herb as needed. Dig up young roots of Hamburg parsley in fall.

Storage Broad-leaved Italian parsley, with its stronger taste, gives a better result when dried than the other varieties.

Freezing Curly parsley freezes well. Put sprigs in freezer bags and freeze for up to 6 months.

USES

Culinary Parsley is used in salads, as a garnish, and in cooking. Hamburg parsley is used as a root vegetable.

Cosmetic An infusion can be used as a hair rinse. Chew raw parsley to promote a healthy skin.

Medicinal Parsley is very nutritious and it is a strong diuretic. Fresh parsley is a breath freshener, and is recommended for taking away the smell of garlic on the breath. It has been used in poultices and to make an antiseptic dressing for wounds and bites. *Caution:* Do not use medicinally during pregnancy.

Gardening Parsley makes an attractive edging plant.

PARSLEY AT A GLANCE

Parsley, with its tasty green leaves, is one of the best known of all the culinary herbs. Frost hardy to 4°F or below (zone 7).

Jan	/		PARTS USED
Feb	/		Leaves
Mar	plant 🌱		Flowers
Apr	plant 🌱	harvest 🍃	Roots
May	plant 🌱	harvest 🍃	
Jun	plant 🌱	harvest 🍃	USES
July		harvest 🍃	Culinary
Aug		harvest 🍃	Medicinal
Sept		harvest 🍃	Cosmetic
Oct	/		Gardening
Nov	/		
Dec	/		

PINKS
Dianthus

FEATURES

Popular garden plants, pinks are very pretty, short-lived, hardy perennials. A wide range of species and varieties is available, which vary in height from about 6in to 24in or more. One of those with the longest herbal tradition is *Dianthus caryophyllus*, the clove carnation. The rich, sweet, clove scent of the flowers has made it popular in perfumery for more than 2000 years. Generally pinks have narrow, gray-green, lance-shaped leaves. The flowers appear in spring or summer, in shades of pink or white, and are usually highly fragrant. Plants can become straggly after a few years, and are best discarded and replaced with young plants that have been grown from cuttings.

CONDITIONS

Aspect   Pinks prefer a sunny, sheltered site.
Site   Grow them in a very well-drained soil that is not too rich, and preferably alkaline.

GROWING METHOD

Sowing and Planting   Pinks can be grown from seed, but the resulting plants can be very variable. Sow the seed under glass in trays of gritty seed compost in spring or fall. Take care not to overwater and be sure to ventilate well. Plant out in spring, after hardening off, at about 1ft apart. Named forms can be propagated by cuttings, division, or layering. Take cuttings in late summer. Plants can also be layered at this time of year. The plants can also be dug up after they have finished flowering, and any rooted stems can be severed and replanted.

Feeding   Pinks tolerate relatively dry conditions. Be careful not to overwater. Pinks need little feeding. A light dressing of a balanced general fertilizer may be given in early spring. Do not

DIVINE FLOWERS: The name Dianthus comes from the words "dios," meaning divine, and "anthos," meaning flower.

mulch as this can cause the stems to rot.

Problems   The main pest is red spider mite. Also virus, leaf spots, and leaf-attacking insects may cause problems.

Pruning   Remove dead flowerheads to prolong flowering.

HARVESTING

Picking   Pick flowers when newly open. If the petals are to be used in cooking, remove the white heel from each of the petals as this has a very bitter flavour.

Storage   Dry on racks in a cool, airy place. Petals can also be crystallized.

Freezing   Not suitable for freezing.

USES

Culinary   Fresh petals can be used in salads, and also puddings and savoury dishes. They can also be used to flavour oils, vinegar, syrup, or white wine. Crystallized petals can be used to decorate cakes and puddings.

Medicinal   The petals can be used to make a tonic cordial, or can be infused in white wine to make a nerve tonic.

Craft   Dried petals can be used to add color and scent to pot-pourri mixes, and used to make scented sachets etc.

Cosmetic   Fresh petals can be used to scent a variety of cosmetic products.

Gardening   Pinks are amongst the most decorative of all the garden herbs.

PINKS AT A GLANCE

Attractive perennials with highly fragrant flowers, which have a long tradition of use in perfumery. Hardy to 4°F (zone 7).

Month	Activity		PARTS USED
Jan	/		Petals
Feb	/		
Mar	plant 🖐		USES
Apr	plant 🖐		
May	plant 🖐	harvest 🌸	Culinary
Jun	plant 🖐	harvest 🌸	Medicinal
July	plant 🖐	harvest 🌸	Craft
Aug	plant 🖐		Cosmetic
Sept	plant 🖐		Gardening
Oct	/		
Nov	/		
Dec	/		

POT MARIGOLD
Calendula officinalis

FEATURES

A bushy hardy annual with light green leaves and brightly colored flowers in shades of orange from spring to fall. The traditional cottage garden pot marigolds have single, bright orange flowers, but many more decorative double and semi-double varieties are readily available. However, if these are allowed to self-seed, which they will do freely, the single form will eventually come to dominate again.

CONDITIONS

Aspect Pot marigolds grow best in full sun or light shade. They can become leggy if grown in deeper shade.

Site Pot marigolds are very tolerant plants, growing in most soils that do not get waterlogged, but they do best in well-drained, not too rich soils.

GROWING METHOD

Sowing and Propagate from seed sown in spring or fall.

planting Plant out 12–18in apart. Pot marigolds will self-sow freely.

Feeding Do not allow the soil to become waterlogged. No special feeding required.

Problems Slugs may eat the young leaves. Blackfly may be a problem late in the season. Cut out infested areas and spray with horticultural soap. Mildew may also be a problem, but generally this does not occur until flowering is over. Remove and burn affected parts to prevent it from spreading.

Pruning No special requirements. Pinch out growing tips to prevent the plant becoming leggy. Deadhead regularly to encourage continuous flowering.

POT MARIGOLD AT A GLANCE

A popular annual herb with brightly coloured flowers that have a wide range of herbal uses. Hardy to 5°F or below (zone 7).

JAN	/	
FEB	/	
MAR	plant	
APR	plant	
MAY	plant	harvest
JUN		harvest
JULY		harvest
AUG		harvest
SEPT	plant	
OCT	/	
NOV	/	
DEC	/	

Parts used
Flowers
Leaves

Uses
Culinary
Medicinal
Cosmetic
Craft
Gardening

IN THE AMERICAN CIVIL WAR doctors on the battlefield used marigold flowers to treat the soldiers' wounds.

HARVESTING

Picking Pick the flowers just as they open for use fresh or dry. Pick leaves when they are young for fresh use.

Storage Dry pot marigold flowers slowly at low temperatures, on a non-metal rack in a cool airy place.

Freezing The petals can be frozen in ice cubes and used as required to decorate drinks.

USES

Culinary Petals can be used fresh in salads, butters, and cheeses, and also in cooked dishes including omelettes, soups, etc. They can also be used to add color to rice dishes. Young leaves can also be added to salads.

Medicinal Pot marigold flowers have antiseptic, anti-fungal, and anti-bacterial properties and have traditionally been used medicinally for a wide range of conditions, including the treatment of wounds, burns, stings and bites, chilblains, and varicose veins. An infusion was also used as an eyewash. The sap from the stem is said to remove warts.

Cosmetic Pot marigold can be used to make a range of cosmetic preparations. For example, infused flowers can be used to make skin and hair care preparations. Used in a skin lotion, they are said to help clear up spots.

Craft The dried petals can be used to add color to pot-pourri. The fresh petals produce a yellow dye.

Gardening A traditional and popular cottage garden flower. Being sensitive to temperature, they give an indication of the weather. Open flowers are said to forecast a fine day.

ROSA GALLICA
Rosa gallica var. officinalis

FEATURES

A prickly shrub that can reach a height of 4ft, the apothecary's rose, *Rosa gallica*, is a dense bush that spreads by suckers, often forming impenetrable thickets. The fragrant, semi-double, deep pink-red flowers appear in summer, followed in fall by dull red hips. Leaves are elliptical in shape and leathery.

CONDITIONS

Aspect   From south-east Europe and western Asia, apothecary's rose is best grown in full sun. An open site with good air movement helps reduce fungal diseases.

Site   Grows in a wide range of soil types but drainage must be good, especially in areas of high summer rainfall. Deep, friable clay-loam with plenty of well-rotted organic matter is best.

GROWING METHOD

Sowing and planting   Can be grown from seed collected from ripe hips in fall but sown in spring, or from suckers detached from the parent plant in late winter. Each sucker must have its own roots; replant at once. Take hardwood cuttings about 8in long in late fall; insert them into potting compost or vacant garden beds and keep moist. Rooted cuttings can be potted up or planted into the garden a year later.

Feeding   Established plants can survive on rain alone in areas of regular rainfall but the plant will look and flower better if given an occasional deep soaking during dry spells in summer. Give a balanced general rose fertilizer in spring. Mulch in spring with well-rotted organic matter to improve the soil, feed the plant and conserve moisture.

Problems   Suffers from the usual rose problems: aphids, caterpillars, scale insects, and fungus diseases,

THE "RED ROSES" in old recipes always meant the apothecary's rose, but you can substitute any sweetly scented red rose from your garden.

especially in humid conditions. Combined insecticide/fungicide, usually sold as "rose spray," controls aphids, caterpillars, and fungus diseases, and may also include a foliar feed.

Pruning   Does not need annual pruning and can be left alone for years. To rejuvenate an old bush, cut stems to the ground in winter.

HARVESTING

Picking   Hips are harvested in fall when fully ripe; flowers can be picked for immediate use as they appear.

Storage   Both hips and flowers may be stored for a few days in sealed containers in the refrigerator. The petals can be dried for use in pot-pourris, herbal sachets, etc.

Freezing   Rose hips and flowers are best used fresh.

USES

Culinary   Rosehips are made into jellies, syrups, and liqueurs (all have a very high proportion of vitamin C). Petals are used to flavor vinegar or are crystallized and eaten as a sweet.

Medicinal   Infusions made from the hips and/or petals are said to be good for headaches and a range of other common complaints such as diarrhoea, fever, mouth ulcers, and toothache.

Craft   Hips and petals are used in crafts. Dried petals are added to pot-pourris. Attar of roses, an essence extracted from the flowers, is a perfuming agent.

Cosmetic   Petals can be used to perfume creams, etc.

Gardening   This makes a good large-scale groundcover, barrier planting or hedge.

ROSA GALLICA AT A GLANCE

The apothecary's rose is a prickly shrub, grown for its vivid, highly perfumed flowers and its hips. Hardy to 4°F (zone 7).

Month	Activity		Parts used
Jan	/		**Parts used**
Feb	plant		Flowers
Mar	plant		Hips
Apr	/		
May	/		
Jun		harvest	**Uses**
July		harvest	Culinary
Aug	/		Medicinal
Sept		harvest	Craft
Oct	plant	harvest	Cosmetic
Nov	plant		Gardening
Dec	/		

ROSEMARY
Rosmarinus officinalis

THIS STANDARD ROSEMARY grows in a pot with Mexican daisies providing a dash of color around its base.

TRADITIONALLY a bringer of good fortune, rosemary is often grown by a path or steps, where its fragrance can also be enjoyed as you pass.

FEATURES

A perennial, evergreen, woody shrub, rosemary has thin, needle-like leaves, which are glossy green above and are whitish to gray-green and hairy below. They have a fragrance reminiscent of pine needles. In spring, small-lobed flowers appear among the leaves. They are pale blue to pinkish or white, depending on the variety. There are several varieties of rosemary, ranging in habit from the upright (*R. officinalis*) to the dwarf (*R. officinalis* "Nana") and the prostrate (*R. officinalis* "Prostratus"). Among the many very popular varieties are "Miss Jessop's Upright" (which is very good for hedges) and pink rosemary (*R. officinalis* "Roseus"). Rosemary bushes can be between 20in and 6ft 6in in height, depending on variety. This is a good herb to grow in containers, and it also grows well in seaside positions where not much else will grow, as it will withstand salt.

CONDITIONS

Aspect
Rosemary likes a sunny, sheltered and reasonably dry position. Although hardy in most areas, protection is advised in severe weather and in colder areas, particularly for young plants.

Site
Rosemary needs to be grown in a well-drained soil in order to lessen the risk of root rot, and the plant is more fragrant when it is grown in alkaline soils.

GROWING METHOD

Sowing and planting
Propagate mainly from cuttings and layering. Seeds are not often used because they have long germination times and tend not to come true to type. Take 4in long cuttings in late spring or early fall, trim off the upper and lower leaves and place the cuttings in small pots containing a moist mixture of two-thirds coarse sand and one-third compost. Cover with a plastic dome and set aside in a semi-shaded position until roots and new leaves form. Or layer by scarifying the underside of a lower branch and firmly securing it to the soil with a wire peg. Cover with sand and keep moist until roots form. Cut off and replant.

Feeding
Prefers soil to be on the drier side; give average garden watering. Mulch in spring and also give an application of a balanced general fertilizer at this time.

Problems
No particular problems.

Pruning
Prune if compact bushes are desired. Trim after flowering to prevent plants becoming straggly. Do not cut back in the fall or when there is a danger of frosts as the plants could be damaged.

HARVESTING

Picking
Fresh leaves or sprigs 2–4in long can be picked as required. Pick flowers in spring.

Storage
Dry sprigs in a cool, dry place, strip leaves from the stems and store in airtight jars.

Freezing
Store sprigs in plastic bags and freeze for up to 6 months. To use, crumble before they thaw.

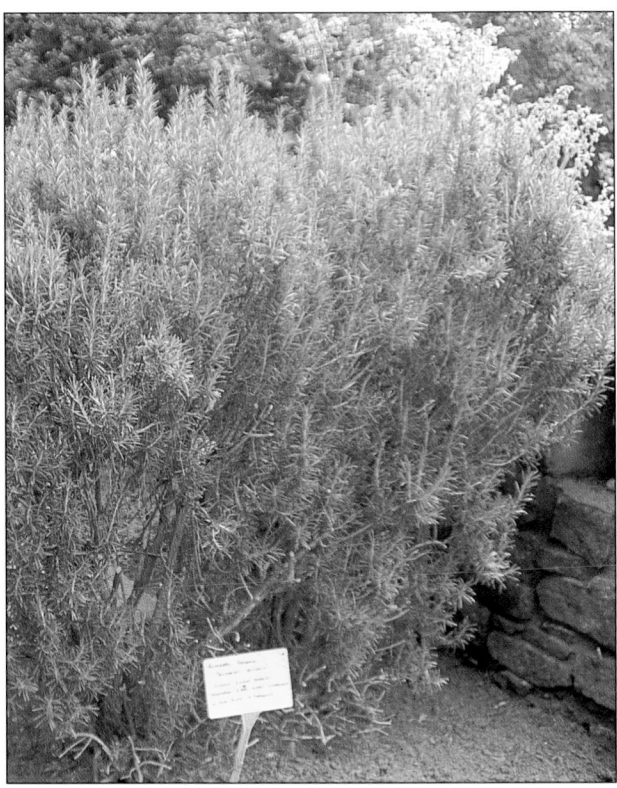

ROSEMARY BUSHES will take hard pruning but don't cut into leafless wood, which will not sprout. That's what has happened here.

ROSEMARY FLOWERS have a subtle scent, sweeter than the leaves. They are usually blue, but can be pink or white.

USES

Culinary   Fresh, dried, or frozen leaves are used in cooking, marinades, and salad dressings. Fresh leaves are used in vinegars, oils, teas, and butters. Fresh flowers are good in salads or as decorations for puddings and desserts.

Medicinal   Rosemary has many uses, including treatment for headaches, digestive problems, and poor circulation. It has anti-bacterial and anti-fungal properties, and can also be used as an insect repellant. *Caution:* do not use in large doses.

Craft   It is used in pot-pourris and herb wreaths.

Cosmetic   Rosemary hair rinses help control greasy hair.

ROSEMARY AT A GLANCE

Evergreen shrub with fragrant leaves and flowers, much used in cooking and crafts. Hardiness varies: 4 to 23°F (zones 7–9).

Month	Plant	Harvest
Jan		harvest
Feb		harvest
Mar	plant	harvest
Apr	plant	harvest
May	plant	harvest
Jun	plant	harvest
July	plant	harvest
Aug	plant	harvest
Sept		harvest
Oct		harvest
Nov		harvest
Dec		harvest

PARTS USED
  Leaves
  Flowers

USES
  Culinary
  Medicinal
  Craft
  Cosmetic
  Gardening

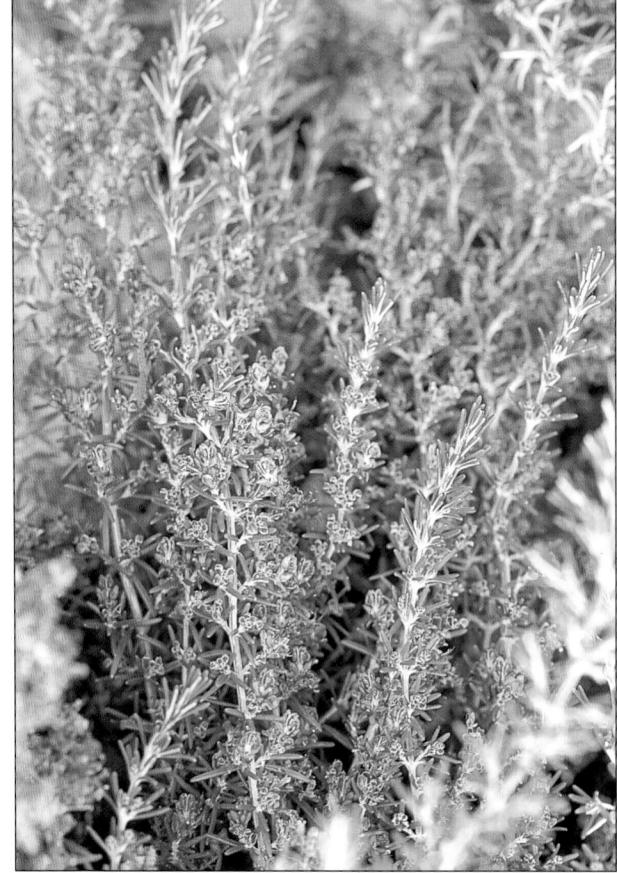

"SEVEN SEAS" has the richest blue flowers of any rosemary cultivar. Its growth is upright, but less dense and compact than most rosemaries.

SAGE
Salvia

PURPLE SAGE grows here in this wonderfully exuberant herb and vegetable garden, contributing to the subtle harmony of colors. It has cotton lavender growing on its left and a fancy-leaved lettuce on its right.

FEATURES

Sage is an evergreen sub-shrub growing to about 30in. The long, oval, gray-green leaves, velvety in texture, have a slightly bitter, camphor-like taste, while the flowers, borne on spikes in spring, are colored from pink to red, purple, blue, or white, depending on variety. There are many varieties of this beautiful herb. The most common hardy edible types are common or garden sage (*S. officinalis*), purple sage (*S. o.* "Purpurascens"), and golden or variegated sage (*S. officinalis* "Icterina"); and the more tender tricolor sage (*S. o.* "Tricolor"), and pineapple sage (*S. elegans*, syn. *S. rutilans*) are also popular. Sage needs to be replaced every four years or so as the plant becomes woody. Many ornamental sages are also grown in gardens.

CONDITIONS

Aspect Most varieties prefer a sunny, sheltered, well-drained position.

Site Garden beds in which sage is to be grown should have a rich, non-clayish soil. Add lime to acid soils, followed by plenty of organic matter. Good drainage is absolutely essential for sage plants, and so you may find it

necessary to raise the beds to at least 8in above the surrounding level.

GROWING METHOD

Sowing and planting Common sage can be grown from seed. Germination takes 2–3 weeks. Plant out when

SAGE AT A GLANCE

Evergreen shrub with silver-gray leaves used in the kitchen for stuffing, herb teas, etc. Hardiness varies: 4 to 23°F (zones 7–9).

Jan	/		
Feb	/		
Mar	plant 🌱	harvest 🌿	
Apr	plant 🌱	harvest 🌿	
May	plant 🌱	harvest 🌿	
Jun	plant 🌱	harvest 🌿	
July		harvest 🌿	
Aug		harvest 🌿	
Sept	plant 🌱	harvest 🌿	
Oct		harvest 🌿	
Nov	/		
Dec	/		

PARTS USED
Leaves
Flowers

USES
Culinary
Medicinal
Cosmetic
Craft
Gardening

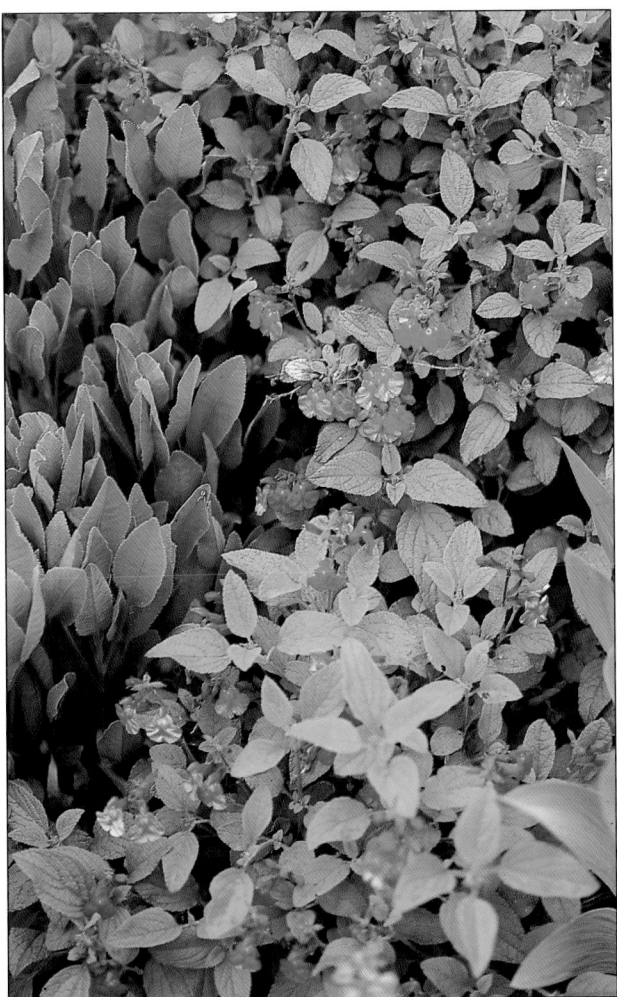

SALVIA GRAHAMII, very strong in flavour, is a metre-tall shrub from Mexico, usually grown for its long display of bright flowers.

THE PURPLE-BLUE FLOWERS of common sage go very well with its gray leaves. Trim them off when they fade to keep the garden neat.

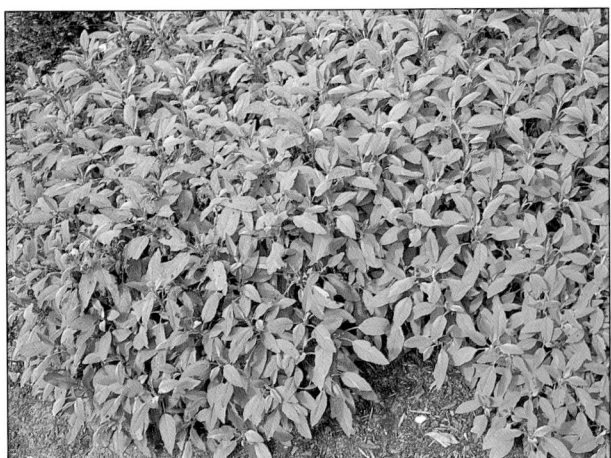

THE LEAVES of purple sage fade as they mature, but new shoots continue to add touches of color all summer. Flowers are purple-blue.

all danger of frost is passed, spacing plants 18–24in apart. Cuttings 4in long can be taken in spring or fall. Remove the upper and lower leaves and plant the cuttings in small pots containing a mix of two-thirds coarse sand to one-third compost. Water, then cover plants with a plastic bag to create a mini-greenhouse. Plant out when the cutting has developed roots and new leaves. Sage may also be layered; scarify the lower side of a branch and peg it into the soil to take root.

Feeding   Give a deep soaking once a week in dry spells. Apply a balanced general fertilizer in spring.

Problems   Spider mites can be a problem and will need to be sprayed with an insecticide. If the plant suddenly flops over for no apparent reason this is probably due to bacterial wilt affecting the vascular system. Remove affected plants. Root rot can be avoided by providing good drainage.

Pruning   Prune in spring to keep a compact, bushy shape. Cut off flowerheads as the flowers fade to stop plants from setting seed.

HARVESTING

Picking   Leaves or flowers can be picked at any time as

required. For drying purposes, harvest leaves before flowering begins.

Storage   Dry leaves on racks in a cool, airy place and then store them in airtight jars.

Freezing   Leaves can be chopped, packed in freezer bags and then frozen for up to 6 months.

USES

Culinary   Fresh or dried leaves are used extensively as a flavoring in stuffings, marinades, and cooking. The individual fruity flavour of pineapple sage complements citrus fruits and the edible flowers look decorative in salads or as a garnish. Sage leaves of many varieties can be used in herbal teas, vinegars, and herb butters.

Medicinal   Sage has long been highly regarded for its healing properties. Uses include treating colds, sore throats, and mouth ulcers. *Caution:* do not take in large quantities or for extended periods.

Cosmetic   Sage hair rinses, used regularly, will darken gray hair.

Craft   Dried leaves, especially those of purple sage can be added to pot-pourri.

Gardening   It is said that sage can be planted with cabbages to deter cabbage white butterflies.

SAVORY
Satureja

BOTH SAVORIES, winter and summer, are alike in their four-petalled, white flowers. This is the perennial winter savory.

SUMMER SAVORY, being an annual, has to be sown afresh each spring. Many cooks consider it superior in flavour to winter savory.

FEATURES

Summer savory (*S. hortensis*) is an annual plant growing to about 1ft and with small, narrow, grayish leaves that turn slightly purple during summer and early fall. The leaves are attached directly to a pinkish stem, and small white flowers appear on the plant in summer. The winter savories, both the upright (*S. montana*) and the prostrate (*S. montana* "Repens") varieties, are perennial forms and have low-growing (they may reach 1ft) or sprawling habits. Glossy, dark green, lanceolate leaves grow from woody stems in summer and white to lilac flowers are grouped in terminal spikes.

CONDITIONS

Aspect
Both varieties of savory prefer to be grown in full sun. They do not like very cold, wet conditions, and winter savory may require some winter protection.

Site
Savories like well-drained, alkaline soils. Use a soil testing kit to see how much lime to add to an acid soil. Summer savory prefers a richer soil and is ideal for container growing; winter savory favours a less rich, rather sandy soil.

GROWING METHOD

Sowing and planting
Sow seeds of summer savory directly into their final garden position in spring, after the weather has warmed up. Lightly cover them with soil and keep the soil around them damp. When the seedlings are established, thin them out to 6in apart and give the plants support by mounding soil round the base. Although it can be grown from seed, winter savory is best propagated by cuttings and root division done during either the spring or the fall. Remove the upper and lower leaves of 4–5in long cuttings and insert the trimmed stems into a mixture of two-thirds coarse sand and one-third compost. Water the container and cover it with plastic supported on a wire or bamboo frame to make a mini-greenhouse effect. Plant the seedlings out when new leaves appear and a root structure has developed. Pieces of the divided root of the parent plant can be potted up and grown on and later these can be transplanted into the open garden.

Feeding
Water these plants regularly although both summer and winter savories are able to tolerate dry conditions. Mulch winter savory in winter and spring and give a dressing of a balanced general fertilizer in spring.

Problems
Savories are not worried by pests or diseases to

THE ANCIENT ROMANS considered savory to be the most delightfully fragrant of all herbs: the poet Virgil sang its praises.

WINTER SAVORY is so called because it is available in winter when summer savory dies off—but you can, of course, eat it in summer too.

any great extent with the exception of root rot, which sometimes can affect the winter varieties. Good drainage is essential for these plants.

Pruning   Winter savory can be pruned in fall after it has finished flowering, but leaving it unpruned will leave top growth to protect the shoots below. It can be pruned in early spring—this will also provide cuttings from which you can grow new plants.

HARVESTING

Picking   Fresh leaves of both summer and winter varieties can be picked at any time for immediate use or for drying.

Storage   Dry leaves in a cool, airy space and then store them in airtight jars.

Freezing   Pack sprigs in freezer bags and freeze for up to 6 months.

USES

Culinary   Summer savory has a peppery flavour and is called the "bean herb" as it complements beans and other vegetables. It is also used in herb vinegars and butters. Winter savory is

stronger and coarser and has a more piney taste: use it with game meats and terrines. Either summer or winter savory can be used to make savory tea.

Medicinal   Summer savory is said to be good for the digestion, for the treatment of stings, and as a stimulant.

SAVORY AT A GLANCE

Both summer and winter savory have strong flavors and are used in cooking. Hardy to 4 to14°F (zones 7–8).

Jan		harvest	PARTS USED
Feb		harvest	Leaves
Mar	plant	harvest	
Apr	plant	harvest	
May	plant	harvest	USES
Jun		harvest	Culinary
July		harvest	Medicinal
Aug		harvest	
Sept	plant	harvest	
Oct		harvest	
Nov		harvest	
Dec		harvest	

THYME
Thymus

*A GARDEN SEAT surrounded by a collection of thymes makes a fragrant resting place. Position the creeping thyme (*Thymus serpyllum*) in front of the seat as it can be trodden on. Thyme has several cultivars, with white, pink, or magenta flowers in spring.*

FEATURES

Thyme is one of the most common of garden herbs, and very many varieties are grown. Most thymes are low, creeping plants although some will grow to 10–12in. The shape of the bush and the color and aroma of the leaves depends on the variety. The leaves are evergreen in shades of green, silver, and gold, and small pink or sometimes white flowers are produced in early summer. Not all thymes are used in cooking, the most commonly used varieties including lemon-scented thyme (*T. x citriodorus*), caraway thyme (*T. herba-barona*), common garden thyme (*T. vulgaris*), orange thyme (*T. vulgaris* "Fragrantissimus"), and silver posie thyme (*T. vulgaris* "Silver Posie"). Thyme plants are perennials but usually need replacing every two or three years.

CONDITIONS

Aspect   Prefers full sun or partial shade.
Site   Prefers a light, well-drained, not too rich soil,

ideally neutral or slightly alkaline, and kept on the dry side. Adding compost will help keep the soil friable. The soil should not be too acid, if necessary add lime.

THYME AT A GLANCE

Common garden herbs, thymes are popular not only for cooking but also as garden plants. Hardy to 4°F or below (zone 7).

Jan		harvest	PARTS USED
Feb		harvest	Leaves
Mar	plant	harvest	Flowers
Apr	plant	harvest	Sprigs
May	plant	harvest	
Jun	plant	harvest	
July		harvest	USES
Aug		harvest	Culinary
Sept	plant	harvest	Medicinal
Oct		harvest	Craft
Nov		harvest	Gardening
Dec		harvest	

GROWING METHOD

Sowing and planting
Thymes can be propagated from seed, but this tends to give inferior plants, and named varieties should be propagated by cuttings, division, or layering. If seed is used, sow in spring and take care not to overwater as the seedlings are prone to damping off. Dividing mature plants is the most successful method of propagation. During spring or summer, gently lift the parent plant, cut it into two or three sections, each with good roots, and replant elsewhere in the garden. Cuttings taken in spring or summer and layering are also satisfactory methods of propagation.

Feeding
Do not overwater. Thymes prefer a dryish soil. Water adequately in dry spells. No fertilizer needed.

Problems
Spider mites or aphids can affect this herb. Treat with a recommended insecticidal spray. Root rot will set in if the soil is waterlogged.

Pruning
Prune or clip to prevent woodiness. Trim after flowering to prevent plants becoming straggly.

HARVESTING

Picking
Fresh leaves and flowers can be picked as required or the whole plant can be cut back to within 2in of the ground in summer.

Storage
Leaves are dried on the stem by hanging branches in a warm, airy place. Branches are then stripped and stored in airtight jars.

Freezing
Pack in small airtight containers or freezer bags; can be frozen for up to 6 months.

USES

Culinary
Thyme is a classic component of the French bouquet garni. Varieties of thyme add special, individual flavors to many dishes. Both leaves and flowers can be eaten fresh in salads or used as garnishes or as a flavoring to honey, vinegars, stuffings, butters, or teas.

Medicinal
Thyme has strong antiseptic properties and is used to treat sore throats and as a mouthwash. *Caution:* avoid during pregnancy.

Craft
Can be added to pot-pourris and herb sachets.

Gardening
Thymes can be grown for their decorative effect as their low, matting habit makes them excellent edging or rockery plants.

WOOLLY THYME is almost prostrate in habit, its leaves covered in gray fur. The flowers are pale pink but not very abundant.

"SILVER POSIE," a small, sprawling shrub with white variegated leaves and abundant pale flowers in spring, here offers scent to the passer-by.

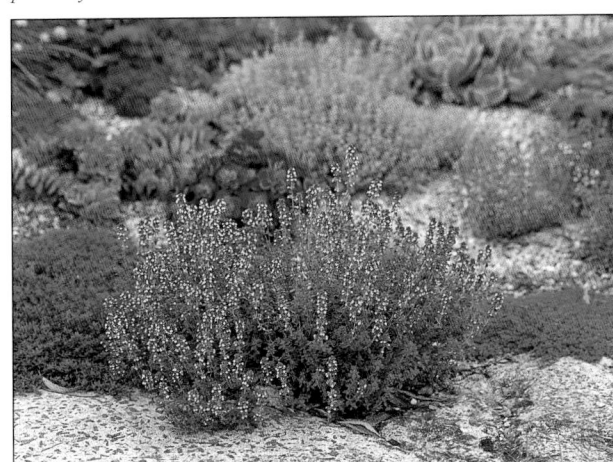

ANCIENT GREEKS AND ROMANS considered thyme honey the finest of all, and many modern connoisseurs of honey agree with them.

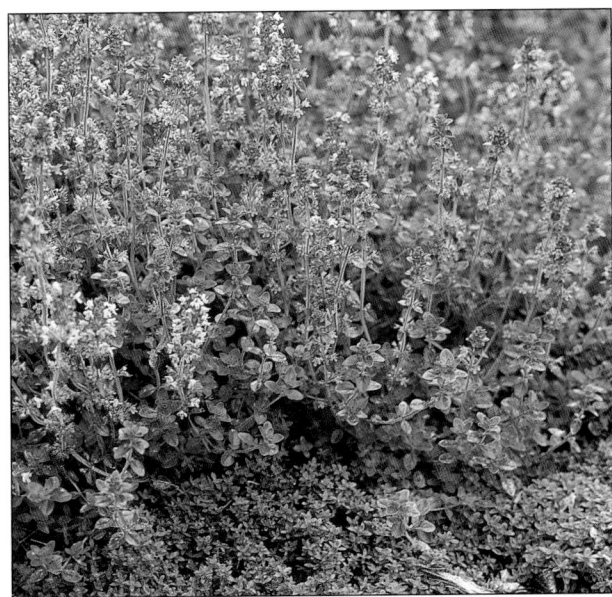

COMMON THYME, Thymus vulgaris, here sprawls over a carpet of creeping thyme, sometimes called "Shakespeare's thyme".

VALERIAN
Valeriana officinalis

FEATURES

Valerian is a tall, spreading hardy perennial, growing to about 3–5ft in height. It is native to Europe and Asia where it is found in grassland and damp meadows, close to streams. It has finely divided mid-green leaves and heads of small white or pale pink flowers that are produced in early summer. Both cats and rats are said to find the smell of valerian attractive, and it is said that the Pied Piper of Hamelin carried the root in order to charm the rats away!

CONDITIONS

Aspect   Valerian will grow in full sun or deep shade, as long as the roots are cool. The plants may need to be staked if they are grown in exposed positions.

Site   Valerian is tolerant of most soils, but prefers moist conditions.

GROWING METHOD

Sowing and planting   Valerian can be propagated by division in spring or fall, replanting the divisions immediately into well prepared ground. The seed can be sown in spring, directly where it is to grow. But for more reliable results sow the seed under glass in trays of seed compost. Do not cover the seeds as this will delay germination. When the young plants are large enough to handle they should be planted out in the garden approximately 2–3ft apart. When grown in good conditions, valerian will self-seed.

Feeding   Keep well watered as valerian prefers moist conditions. Mulch lightly in spring and also apply a dressing of a balanced general fertilizer in spring.

VALERIAN AT A GLANCE

A tall but undistinguished, strong-smelling herb, with powerful healing properties. Fully hardy to 4°F or below (zone 7).

Jan	/	
Feb	/	**PARTS USED**
Mar	plant ✎	Roots
Apr	plant ✎	
May	plant ✎	**USES**
Jun	/	Medicinal
July	/	Cosmetic
Aug	/	Gardening
Sept	plant ✎ harvest ✲	
Oct	plant ✎ harvest ✲	
Nov	/	
Dec	/	

IN THE TWO WORLD WARS an infusion made from valerian was used to treat shell-shock and nervous disorders.

Problems   Generally free from pests and diseases.

Pruning   Cut valerian back after flowering to prevent self-seeding. The top growth can be cut down in fall.

HARVESTING

Picking   Dig up the roots in late fall, when the plants are in their second or third year of growth.

Storage   To dry, cut the roots into thin slices and dry in an oven at 120–40°F, turning frequently.

Freezing   Not suitable for freezing

USES

Medicinal   Valerian has been used for many centuries for its healing properties. Traditionally, the root has been used for its sedative and anti-spasmodic effects, and for the treatment of a wide range of conditions, including nervous conditions, insomnia, headaches, and exhaustion. *Caution:* Do not take valerian in large doses or for extended periods of time. This herb is best taken only under expert supervision.

Cosmetic   Despite its rather unpleasant aroma, valerian has been used in perfumery.

Gardening   Nowadays, valerian is used more in the garden than for its medicinal properties. Although not the most decorative of herbs, it is useful to add height at the back of the border. It is also said to be a good companion plant, encouraging the growth of nearby vegetables and other plants by stimulating earthworm activity and increasing phosphorus availability.

VIOLET
Viola odorata

FEATURES

Viola odorata, the sweet violet, is a low-growing perennial just 6in tall with a wider spread. The dark green leaves are roundish or kidney-shaped with scalloped edges. Small, very sweetly fragrant flowers appear on short stalks in late winter and early spring. They are usually violet in color but there are also mauve, blue, and white forms. Violets spread rapidly by creeping roots.

CONDITIONS

Aspect Sun in winter and bright dappled shade in summer are ideal. Flowering is disappointing in too much shade.

Site Violets tolerate most soils but do best in deep soil rich in well-rotted organic matter, preferably from composted fallen leaves. Soil must drain freely but it must also remain moist between showers or watering.

GROWING METHOD

Sowing and planting Violets are easily established by division. Lift immediately after flowering and separate the cylindrical runners. Each division should have its own roots but roots usually form later if they are absent. Plant so that the runners are firmly in contact with the soil but not buried. Scatter seed, collected from ripe but unopened seed pods, where it is to grow or, for better germination, onto trays of seed compost. Cover lightly, keep moist, and place trays in a bright but shady and cool place. The seedlings can be transplanted when they are big enough to handle.

Feeding Once established, violets can usually get by on rain where it falls regularly, as long as the soil conditions suit them. If they never go dry for long periods, violets will flourish. Place a mulch of well-rotted manure around plants, but not over the root crown, each spring (this can be hard to do in a densely planted area), or sprinkle a ration of a balanced general fertilizer over the plants in spring. Once or twice during summer, water over the plants with a liquid, organic fertilizer or seaweed-based soil conditioner.

Problems Lay bait for slugs and snails, which chew holes in the leaves and destroy flowers. Spider mites and aphids can also damage plants by sucking sap. Spider mites should be treated with an insecticide as soon as they are seen. Aphids are easily controlled with low toxicity pyrethrum, garlic, or fatty acid sprays. If the plants fail to flower, the cause may be too much or too heavy shade or too much high nitrogen fertilizer.

Pruning No pruning is necessary, but if flowers fail to form cut all the leaves off in early winter to encourage spring bloom.

VIOLETS are notoriously shy: if your flowers hide, cut plants back in winter so the flowers are displayed against fresh, not-too-tall growth.

HARVESTING

Picking Pick flowers as they open and leaves as needed.
Storage Flowers may be crystallized for later use.
Freezing Not suitable for freezing.

USES

Culinary Crystallized flowers are used to decorate cakes or eaten as a sweet treat. A sweet syrup and a honey can be made with fresh flowers.
Medicinal An infusion of the leaves and flowers can be taken to relieve the symptoms of colds, etc.
Craft Flowers are used in pot-pourris, floral waters.
Gardening Violets are a very desirable groundcover in partly shaded areas. Posies of cut flowers will fill a room with fragrance.

VIOLET AT A GLANCE

Pretty, low-growing perennial with very sweetly fragrant flowers in late winter. Hardy to 4°F or below (zone 7).

Jan	/		PARTS USED	
Feb		harvest	Flowers	
Mar		harvest	Leaves	
Apr	plant	harvest		
May	plant	harvest		
Jun		harvest	USES	
July		harvest	Culinary	
Aug		harvest	Medicinal	
Sept	plant		Craft	
Oct	/		Gardening	
Nov	/			
Dec	/			

WORMWOOD
Artemisia

FEATURES

There are many species of artemisia, all with aromatic foliage and pleasant, but not particularly showy, yellow flowers. Wormwood, *A. absinthium*, is an extremely bitter plant with finely divided leaves. The related *A. abrotanum*, is also known as southernwood, or lad's love. There are many ornamental garden artemisias. Sizes and habits, however, vary enormously between species, some being ground-huggers, others being medium-sized, upright shrubs. Leaf shape and color varies, too, and combinations of different artemisias can make very attractive plantings with a silver and gray theme.

CONDITIONS

Aspect Full sun is essential, as is an open position to ensure good air movement around the plant.
Site Grows best in moderately fertile, very well-drained soil that contains a small proportion of well-rotted organic matter.

GROWING METHOD

Sowing and planting Wormwood can be started from cuttings taken in late spring and rooted in small pots of moist, sandy potting mix kept in a bright but not fully sunny spot. It may also be grown from seed sown in spring just beneath the surface, either where plants are to grow or in pots or trays of seed compost.
Feeding Very little water is needed except in very dry summers. A mulch of well-rotted manure or compost laid under and beyond the plant's foliage canopy (but not right up against the trunk) is usually all the feeding required. Otherwise, sprinkle a handful of general fertilizer under the outer edge of the foliage canopy in early spring.

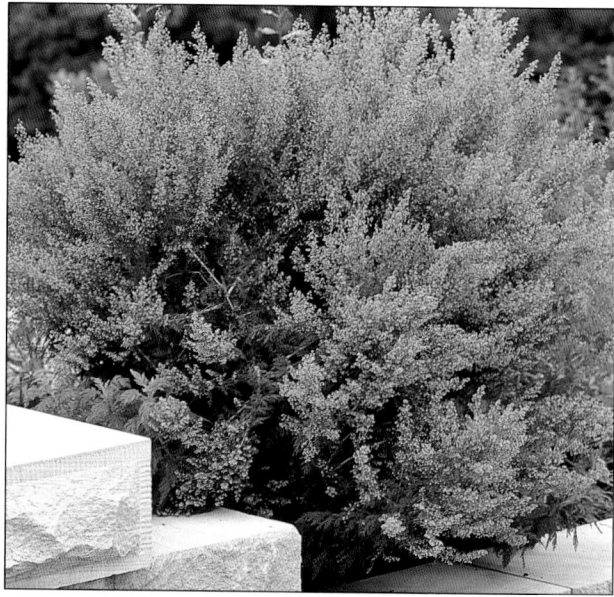

DESPITE ITS BITTERNESS, some artemisias were thought be be a potent aphrodisiac—hence the other name of "lad's love"

Problems Artemisias may sometimes suffer from blackfly. This can be treated with a liquid horticultural soap.
Pruning Cut herbaceous species of artemisia back to ground level in middle to late fall or after frosts have started. Shrubby types may be sheared all over in early spring to make them more compact. Cut back hard in spring if the shrub has become too big and/or untidy.

HARVESTING

Picking Leaves are harvested by picking whole stems on a hot, dry morning in summer.
Storage Tie stems together and hang them upside down in a dim, airy place to dry. Dried leaves may be stored in airtight jars.
Freezing Not suitable for freezing.

USES

Culinary Although it is extremely bitter, wormwood was traditionally used to flavor wines and aperitifs such as absinthe and vermouth.
Medicinal *Caution:* different parts of different types of artemisia have various medicinal uses but do not take any of these herbs without the supervision of a trained herbalist.
Craft Wormwood has insect repellent properties and it can be used to make "moth-repellent" sachets.
Gardening Wormwood, as all artemisias, has beautiful foliage and a pleasant aroma. A strong infusion of the leaves sprayed onto vegetables or ornamental plants repels caterpillars and snails; just having the plants nearby will drive some pests away.

WORMWOOD AT A GLANCE

Perennial herb with decorative, finely divided silvery foliage, traditionally used to flavour absinthe. Hardy to 4ºF (zone 7).

Jan	/	
Feb	/	
Mar	/	
Apr	plant 🌱	
May	plant 🌱	
Jun	plant 🌱 harvest 🍃	
July	harvest 🍃	
Aug	plant 🌱 harvest 🍃	
Sept	plant 🌱	
Oct	/	
Nov	/	
Dec	/	

PARTS USED
Leaves

USES
(Culinary)
(Medicinal)
Craft
Gardening

YARROW
Achillea millefolium

FEATURES

Yarrow is a low, mat-forming perennial that has dense, dark green, fern-like foliage. Flat heads of small flowers appear on top of tall, mostly leafless stems during the later summer months and in fall. They may be white, pink, or yellow. This vigorous grower is well suited to growing in rockeries or on banks. Depending on the soil and situation in which it grows it can vary in height from 2in to 24in.

CONDITIONS

Aspect Grow in full sun or light shade.
Site Well-drained, not-too-rich soil is ideal. Plants grow lax, flower poorly and die young in over-rich soil. They will rot if soil stays wet for long periods after rain or watering.

GROWING METHOD

Sowing and planting Establish yarrow in new areas by dividing the roots of mature plants in early spring or fall. It may also be started from seed sown in spring in trays of moist seed compost. Just cover the seed and place the containers in a warm, bright but shaded spot until germination is complete. Gradually expose containers to more and more sun, and then transplant seedlings into their final site when they are big enough.

Feeding Water deeply but only occasionally. Yarrow does not require constant moisture as it has deep roots that will find water at lower levels in the soil. No feeding is necessary.

Problems No particular problems.

Pruning Cut plants to the ground in middle to late fall or after frosts have started. New growth will appear in spring.

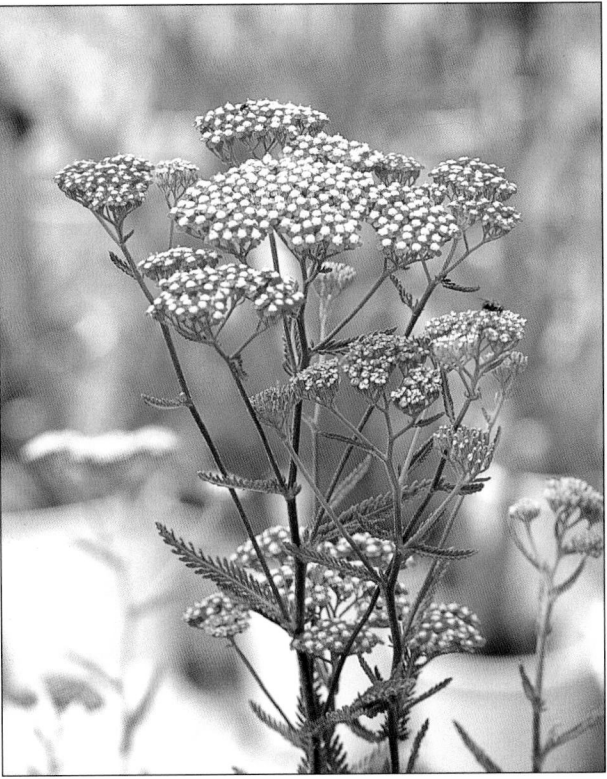

YARROW used to be grown in English churchyards to mock the dead, who supposedly were there because they hadn't eaten their yarrow broth.

HARVESTING

Picking Harvest leafy stems and flowers on a dry morning when plants are in the early stages of full bloom. Tie them together and hang them upside down in a dry, dim, airy place. If they are to be used to make dried arrangements, hang each flower stem separately.

Storage When the stems are dry, remove the flowers and leaves and break the leaves and stems into small pieces. Store these in airtight jars.

Freezing Not suitable for freezing.

USES

Culinary Young, small leaves have a slightly bitter flavor. Add a few chopped young leaves to salads or sandwiches for a piquant taste.

Medicinal Herbal tea made from the dried stems, leaves, and flowers is a good general pick-me-up, blood cleanser, tonic for the kidneys, fever treatment and, reputedly, a slimming aid. Also used externally as wound healer.

Cosmetic An infusion can be used as a herbal skin cleanser.

Craft Flowers can be used in dried floral arrangements.

Gardening Although considered a weed in lawns, yarrow is an excellent companion plant, increasing the disease resistance of nearby plants and increasing their flavour and fragrance. It has been called the "plant doctor." Add it to the compost heap to speed rotting.

YARROW AT A GLANCE

Although considered a weed by many, yarrow is an excellent companion plant and herbal tonic. Hardy to 4°F or below (zone 7).

Jan	/		
Feb	/	PARTS USED	
Mar	plant 🌱	Leaves	
Apr	plant 🌱	Stems	
May	plant 🌱 harvest ❀	Flowers	
Jun	harvest ❀		
July	harvest ❀	USES	
Aug	harvest ❀	Culinary	
Sept	plant 🌱	Medicinal	
Oct	/	Cosmetic	
Nov	/	Craft	
Dec	/	Gardening	

Growing
Cacti

GROWING CACTI

Although they are part of the large family of succulents, cacti are unlike any other group of plants. With distinguishing features such as ribbed surfaces, waxy coating and, of course, their spines, cacti deserve a special place in any creative display, invariably being grown in pots and used as focal points that are easily admired.

Cacti are magnificent plants giving architectural shapes of all kinds from tiny round balls to enormous tree-like growths, the kind of thing you see in cowboy films, and often superb flowers. In many cases the flowers only open at night, and can be wonderfully scented. Cacti need to be grown in pots, at least in winter, when the amount of drinking water they are given is strictly controlled. Too much is inevitably fatal. If they are not too heavy, pot-grown plants can be moved outside in summer, making the focal point in a bed of architectural plants. They can even be taken out of their pots, and placed in, for example, a special gravel bed, where there is excellent drainage. Alternatively, they can be grown in a special display bed in a large conservatory or greenhouse. Take care though not to confuse epiphytic cacti with the desert kind. The former tend to grow high up in trees, under the leafy canopy, in shady conditions. The latter demand day-long bright light.

KEY TO AT A GLANCE TABLES

PLANTING

FLOWERING

At a glance charts are your quick guide.
For full information, consult the accompanying text.

LEFT: A fine collection of well-grown cacti shows some of the extensive range of these fascinating plants. Variations in shapes and heights of the rounded barrel types with the vertical column cactus adds interest to the display.

GROWING CACTI

What is a cactus? What is a succulent?

A cactus is a succulent plant—but not all succulent plants are cacti. Succulent plants are xerophytes, plants able to escape or endure prolonged drought conditions. Succulents have the capacity to store water in swollen stems and roots, while some withdraw into the soil or shed their foliage in times of stress. Although succulent plants and cacti do share some characteristics, cacti have certain features that distinguish them from other plant families, including other forms of succulent plants.

FEATURES OF CACTI

Plant structure

Cacti are mainly round or cylindrical in shape, with a ribbed surface that allows for shrinkage as water is lost from the plant. The ribbed edges of cactus plants expose less surface area to the sun, which helps to reduce moisture loss. Waxy coatings on their outer surfaces also cut down moisture loss in extreme heat. Cacti have sharp, sometimes horny spines that deter animals from grazing and also provide some shade for the body of the plant. Cactus spines are in fact modified

GOLDEN BARREL CACTI dominate this carefully planned landscape of cactuses and succulents. These plants are growing in raised beds to ensure that they have perfect drainage.

leaves that have evolved to cut down moisture loss in the usually dry conditions of their native environment. There is a considerable range of spine types and sizes.

In cacti the breathing pores (stomates) enabling gas exchange between the plant and the atmosphere are located deep inside the plant walls and tend to be less numerous than those of many other plants. These stomates generally open only at night, avoiding water evaporation in the heat of the day. All cacti possess areoles, which are small woolly cushions from which emerge the spines and flower buds. These are found on top of warty protrusions known as tubercles. Many cacti have jointed parts that can be shed from the plant; these strike roots as they touch the ground and so aid in the distribution and continuity of the species.

Flowers

Cactus flowers are like jewels, glorious and showy, but they are also very short lived. Many last only one or two days while others are nocturnal, opening in the middle of the night and fading before dawn. The flowers have a silky or satiny texture and come in all colors except a true blue, although violet and purple are well represented. Many cacti have flowers in shades of pink, red, or yellow. After the flowers have been pollinated, brightly colored fruits form—these are usually red and very long lasting. In their native habitats, many cacti are pollinated by birds, especially humming-birds, while the night-flowering types are pollinated by moths, bats, or other nocturnal creatures.

Types of cacti

Cacti are roughly grouped into three types: round or barrel cacti such as the golden barrel (*Echinocactus* species) and *Mammillaria* species; elongated cacti such as column cactus (*Cereus* species) and silver torch (*Cleistocactus* species); and jointed cacti such as *Opuntia* species and crab cactus (*Schlumbergera* species).

The cristate or crested cacti are the result of mutations that cause the growing tip of a shoot to broaden out into a band, forming strange, tortuous shapes. These mutations may be due to genetic changes or they may be due to the plant suffering unusual stress.

Native habitat

True cacti, almost without exception, are native to the Americas. Although not all cacti have their origins in real deserts, the greatest number of species occur in the low rainfall areas of the south-western United States and Mexico.

Cacti in these regions of desert plains endure scorching heat by day and often freezing nights. Sporadic rainfall of generally less than 10in per annum allows the plants to store just enough water to survive. Heavy dews and the occasional snowfall augment the water supply. Snow insulates plants against cold and, when it melts, the water is directed to the plant roots.

The next largest group of species originates in the dry areas of central and eastern Brazil. Some cacti come from quite high elevations where conditions are still very harsh, but where the daytime temperatures do not reach the extremes of the true deserts.

On rocky slopes of mountains and high plateaux, the soil is often poor and the water drains away rapidly. Plants are exposed to intense sunlight and freezing night temperatures, high wind and often snow. Small cacti find a foothold among rocks and crevices that hold just enough water for survival while affording some shelter from wind. Many cacti from these habitats have dense woolly spines that provide protection from both searing sun and intense cold. Lower down the slope, large column cacti branching from heavy bases start to be seen. These and the large barrel types are able to withstand exposure to very strong winds.

A few species of cactus such as *Epiphyllum* and *Schlumbergera* are native to humid jungle environments where they grow as epiphytes on trees and sometimes on rocks. Although adapted to low light, they can also tolerate dry seasons. Some remain high in the tree canopy where there is more light while others start lower down, scrambling up as they grow towards the light.

Human use

A number of cacti have long been used by humans as food and in medicines. The fruit of some species is eaten fresh, cooked, or dried. Indian fig (*Opuntia ficus-indica*) is probably the best known of these edible cacti, but the fruits of some of the hedgehog cacti (*Echinocereus* species) and the tiny fruits of some *Mammillaria* species are also considered delicacies. In Mexico, the aromatic fruits of *Ferocactus wislizenii* are stewed, candied, and made into sweets, giving this species the common name of candy cactus. However, it is not recommended that you taste any part of a cactus unless you are certain that it is an Indian fig or another known edible variety. Many cacti contain alkaloids, which can be extremely damaging to health. On the other hand, heart-stimulant drugs are made from species of the cactus *Selenicereus*, which is widely cultivated both in the United States and Europe for this purpose.

Growing cacti under glass

It is very hard trying to group cacti with other plants; somehow they never look right. They are generally best arranged together, possibly with some excellent succulents. Fortunately, cacti come in such a wide range of shapes, from tiny quirky balls to grand theatrical vertical pillars, that you can always create a lively, contrasting mix.

The best displays of cacti are invariably in a large glasshouse where you can create a small scene from say South America. This gives you the space to plant the cacti reasonably well apart so that they can be seen from all angles, and with space to the front so that you are not endangered when they have got sharp, vicious spines. The cactus' shape is often so striking that its poor flowers seem unimportant.

Generally speaking, a dry environment must be provided, especially in winter, with bright light and excellent drainage. But when buying a cactus do try and find out where it comes from, so that you can provide the correct growing conditions. Unless you are very lucky, that almost certainly means growing them under glass, indoors or in a conservatory, where you can manufacture their special needs. And these needs mean either replicating desert or jungle conditions.

Established desert cacti grown in pots need three parts John Innes No. 2 with one part grit, well mixed together giving an open, free-draining soil. In summer they need watering (letting them dry out between each drink) and feeding as much as any thriving plant. Use special cactus feed or tomato fertilizer to encourage flowering. Over winter keep the plants dormant at about 45°F, only occasionally watering to prevent them from completely drying out and shrivelling. In fact over-watering is the commonest cause of death. When in doubt, do not water. Good light does though remain essential.

Strangely enough, some cacti prefer steamy, jungle-like conditions, which are harder to provide. Such cacti tend to be epiphytes which grow high in the branches of trees, not exposed in the open ground. You can still grow them in pots but you must provide a winter temperature nearly 50°F higher than that for the desert kind, with year-round

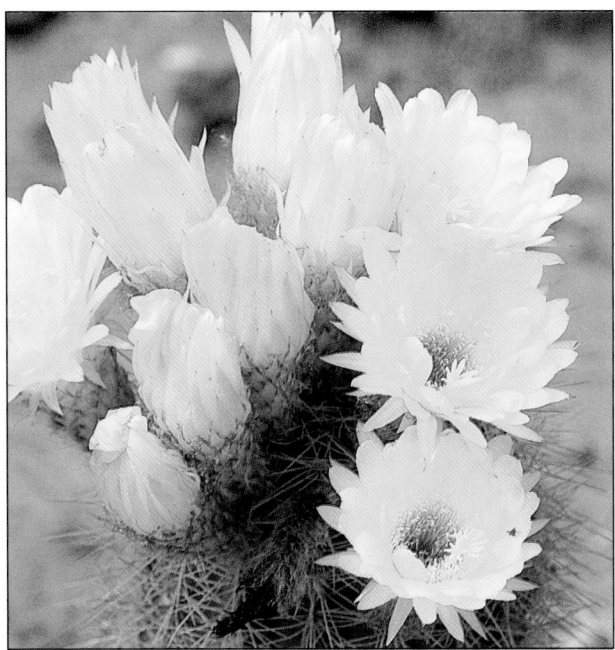

A PROFUSION of clear yellow flowers conceals the whole top of this Trichocereus huascha *(previously called* Echinopsis).

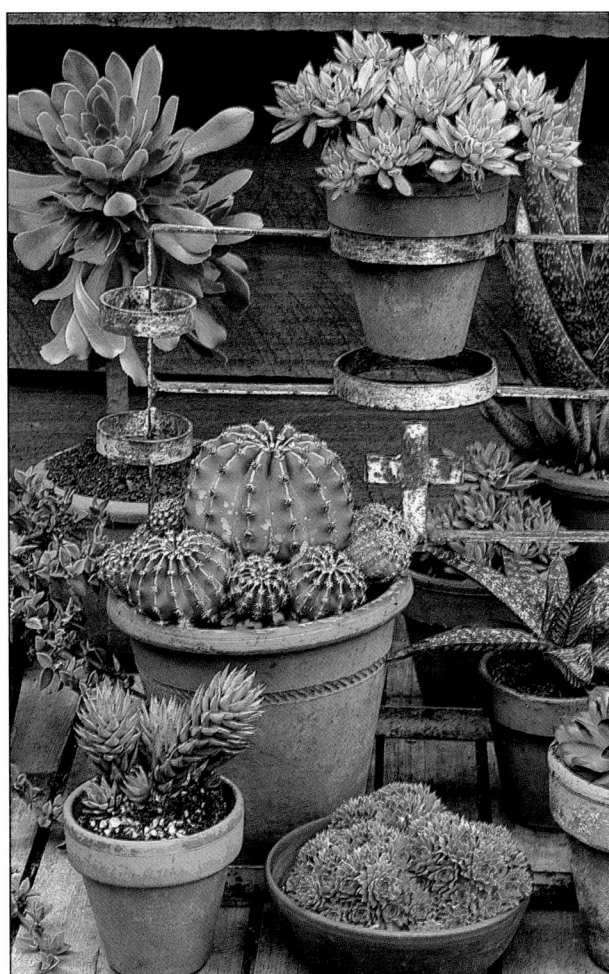

TERRACOTTA POTS make ideal containers for growing cacti and succulents. Displayed at different levels, all plants can be easily seen.

humidity. The key to success remains open, free-draining compost, and in summer constant shade from strong sunlight (in the wild they would grow well protected by the tree canopy). A summer feed will boost the show of flowers.

Growing high up, these cacti tend to send out tumbling, trailing stems and they make good ingredients for a hanging basket. The Christmas cactus (see page 484) is an astonishing sight in full flower, especially when it is a flashy scarlet. Most people grow it as a pot plant on a table, and though fine, it is never as good a spectacle as when seen from below.

GROWING CACTI IN CONTAINERS

Cacti are easy-care potted plants and can be grown as single specimens or combined in shallow bowls to make a miniature cactus garden. Miniature cactus gardens can be of great interest. You could feature a mixture of several small-growing species or you may want to display a single fine, clustering plant that has been increasing over the years. Cacti are ideal for growing on balconies or patios as they do not mind drying out and appreciate shelter from the rain.

Cactus plants definitely look most attractive when grown in terracotta pots or glazed ceramic pots; in the glazed pot range, the ones decorated in blues and greens seem to suit the cactus best. When you are choosing a pot for an individual specimen, try to find one that is not much larger than the plant's rootball.

HANDLING A CACTUS USING FOLDED PAPER

WHEN HANDLING CACTI, use a band of cardboard or folded paper held firmly around the cactus to avoid the spines.

Cacti grown in containers must be potted into a very sharp-draining mix. For a small number of pots, it may be best to purchase a cactus mix from your local nursery. If you are potting a large number of plants or filling large pots, it will probably be more economical to buy the mix in bulk (if possible), or to buy the ingredients for making your own mix: this should include bags of special horticultural sand or grit (avoid builder's sand) and John Innes No. 2. Though you may think that desert cacti in particular grow in sand alone, that is not true. They need rather more soil than added drainage material. A ratio of three parts of soil to one of grit is fine.

Pots can be displayed on purpose-built stands, on pedestals, or on the ground. Pots to be put on the ground should not be in direct contact with the soil and must be elevated very slightly to allow air to circulate under the pot base. You can purchase "pot feet" or simply use pieces of broken terracotta or stone to elevate your pot.

Potted cacti team well with Mexican and Mediterranean style decor, for example, black wrought-iron furniture or rustic unpainted timber pieces. You could extend this decorating idea by adding some feature wall tiles.

Growing cacti outdoors in summer
Like most pot plants, cacti like to stand outside during the summer. Alternatively, they can be tapped out of the pot and planted in a special bed which is very free draining. This guarantees them excellent light levels while they are in full growth and ensures that they have plenty of fresh air. It also avoids the danger of baking in an inadequately ventilated or poorly shaded glasshouse. The chances of being attacked by greenhouse pests is also reduced. Overall, a spell outside gives healthier, sturdier plants.

What is more, creating a special group of cacti in a gravel garden which sets off their shapes, or on a rockery, adds style and interest to your garden. If you are growing the taller, column cacti try moving them outside before they become too big and then experiment with uplighting them at night. In a bare, minimalist garden they make quite an impact. It is absolutely essential to keep all spiny cacti well away from sites where children play.

HANDLING CACTI

To avoid injury from the spines when handling a cactus, use a band made of cardboard or folded newspaper. Place the band around the plant to steady it and hold firmly where the two pieces come together. This should prevent your hands from coming into contact with the spines and should not damage the cactus. You should, of course, also wear sturdy gloves. When handling larger specimens of cactus plants, you may need another person to help you. In this case, you should each use a paper band, or wooden or plastic tongs such as kitchen tongs, to lift and move the cactus. It is a difficult, heavy job to move large cactus plants but careful planning before planting—deciding on the new, permanent location of your cactus and preparing the planting hole—should help you to avoid problems in the future.

WATERING

It is important to remember that at any time of the year, cacti should only be watered when the soil or potting mix has dried out completely. Withholding water from plants may result in slower growth, but this is better than killing the plants through

RICHLY COLORED SILKY FLOWERS on a cactus can look greatly at odds with the spines. In fact the flowers are often short-lived, though flowering reliably occurs each year. Two of the most reliable flowering kind are Rebutia and Mammillaria species.

watering too much or too often. Plants watered too often while they are dormant and unable to use or store water will rot and die. Large plants, because of their greater ability to store water, will need watering much less often than smaller plants. Potted plants will need watering more often than plants in the ground, especially during warmer weather, and the larger the container the less often it will need watering.

Until you feel confident about the frequency of watering needed, it is a good idea to dig into the soil or growing mix with a stick, a pencil or a thin bamboo stake to check the degree of dryness. In small pots, up to 4in diameter, the top 1–2in must be dry before more water is applied. In a 8in pot, the soil should be dry at a depth of 3in or more. Plants that have just been repotted should not be watered for at least a week afterwards. With any cactus, enough water should be applied at any one watering to thoroughly saturate the soil or mix. The frequency of watering will, of course, depend on the weather. If it is very hot and windy, plants will dry out much faster than they would in either warm, calm weather or cold conditions. In cold weather, plants may need watering only every 4–6 weeks or even less often, while in very hot weather they may need watering every few days.

Overhead watering will not hurt the cacti as it also washes dust off their surfaces, but do not do this late in the day, especially in humid districts, as water remaining on the plant overnight may predispose it to rotting. (You should note that some succulents should not be watered this way because of the waxy bloom on their foliage.) Alternatively, you should simply water the soil surface using a watering can or sit the whole pot in a container of water and allow the moisture to be drawn up from below. If available, rainwater is ideal for cacti. Cacti do not like alkaline water, so if your water supply is known to be alkaline, it may be worth collecting rainwater.

FERTILIZING

The most convenient method of fertilizing cacti is to use granular, slow-release fertilizers. A formulation containing trace elements, but low in nitrogen, is ideal. These fertilizers should be applied in spring to feed the plants slowly throughout their growing season. Follow the label directions and do not exceed the recommended amount. Feeding when plants are dormant may damage them and is a waste of fertilizer, which only starts to be released once soil temperatures rise. In the garden, you can use pelleted poultry manure as an alternative, but do not be too heavy handed.

PROPAGATION

Growing from seed

Seed is best sown in spring. Cactus seed should be sprinkled or placed on the surface of a seed-raising mix and lightly covered with the mix. You can mix very small seeds with fine sand for a more even sowing or put the seeds in a cone of paper from which you can gently shake them. Seed may germinate in a few days or a few weeks depending on the species. Keep the growing mix damp, but not soggy, by standing the pot in a container of water to draw up moisture, and then drain off any excess water from the seed-raising pot. Overhead watering will dislodge the seed. Once the seed has germinated, it may be several months before the seedlings are large enough to handle and pot up individually.

Although many home-grown cactus will not set viable seed because of the lack of suitable pollinators, it is possible to hand pollinate sometimes with good results. Use a small paintbrush to collect the pollen from one flower then gently

PROPAGATING BY CUTTINGS

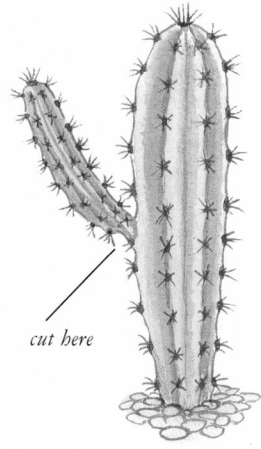

1. TAKE CACTUS cuttings by cleanly removing an offshoot from the parent plant.

cut here

2. THE BASE of the cutting should be slanted towards the central core of the stem. Dry the cutting for a few days before planting.

3. ROOTS are formed at the center stem core. The amount of time taken to form roots varies with the species of cactus and the season of the year.

dust this into the center of another flower. Pollen should go on to the stigma which is the organ in the center of the flower surrounded by numerous pollen-bearing stamens.

It is fairly easy to collect seed from cacti with fleshy fruits. Once the fruit is fully colored and ripe, pick off the fruit, slit open and squeeze out the seeds which should be cleaned and dried before sowing. It is more difficult to obtain the seed of cacti which normally shed their seed as the fruits dry and split. As the fruit is nearing maturity, a paper or mesh bag can be tied around the fruit to catch the seeds as they are dispersed from the maturing fruit.

Growing from cuttings

Some cacti form numerous offsets, which you can remove and pot up separately to start a new plant. Cut away any offsets from the parent plant by pushing a sharp knife down into the soil to sever any underground joints.

Some cacti can be propagated from cuttings of the plant, which must be taken with a very sharp, clean knife or pruning shears. You should take cactus cuttings in spring, as the new growth begins. The cuttings or offsets with wounds must be allowed to dry for a few days, or a few weeks if necessary, until the cut area is completely dry and callused over. Cuttings can be taken from side shoots or even the head of the main stem. Slant the cut towards the core of the stem and allow the cutting to dry; this should encourage roots to develop from the stem core. When the cuttings have dried, insert them into very coarse sand. Plants should not be watered until roots start to form. The time that it takes for this to happen varies from one to six months.

Propagating by grafting

Grafting of cacti is usually done simply to produce unusual effects. Different colored cacti may be joined together, or a barrel-shaped cactus may be grafted on the top of a column type. A flat graft is the easiest technique to use. Simply cut both the understock and the scion (the piece to be grafted on to the top of the understock) straight across, join the two sections neatly, and hold them in place with rubber bands or fine, strong cactus spines. At the optimum time of year— mid-spring to early fall—the graft may "take" within two weeks. Cleft and side grafts are also used, but these are not so easy for beginners.

BUYING A CACTUS

Many of the larger garden centers and nurseries will sell good-quality cactus plants that have been obtained from specialist growers. These are often small, reasonably priced plants, which will introduce you to the amazing range of cactus forms and become the beginning of a collection. Some specialist cactus nurseries sell direct to the public or by mail order. Garden centers and specialist growers are generally able to give you the right advice about the care and culture of your new plants. Novelty cactus are also on sale from florists or department stores, but the sales staff in these places are not, as a rule, qualified to give correct advice on cultivation.

Any cactus you buy must look clean and firm, and there must be no soft or decaying areas anywhere on the plant. It should not look pale or elongated, which would indicate that the cactus may have been kept for too long in poor light. The cactus must also be free of insect pests such as mealybugs, which resemble small, white, sticky patches of cotton wool and are often found between the spines.

WHAT CAN GO WRONG?

Cacti can be attacked by a range of sap-sucking insects such as aphids, mealybugs, scale insects, thrips, and two-spotted mites. Healthy, vigorous plants grown in good conditions are much less likely to succumb to an attack of these pests.

If your plants are attacked—and if you cannot manually remove the pests—you may need to spray with a registered insecticide. You will sometimes be able to dislodge mealybugs and scale insects with a cotton bud dipped in methylated spirit. Overhead watering will often discourage mites and aphids.

Soft rots and root decay are almost impossible to treat if they have become well established. If this is the case, cut away the rotted section with a sharp, clean knife to expose any healthy tissue, remove a healthy section of the plant, and then dry it and treat it as a cutting. Dusting the exposed clean tissue of the cactus with sulfur is sometimes also helpful. Most rots are caused by overwatering, especially when plants are not in active growth. If you are unsure whether or not to water, do not! When you do water, soak the cactus thoroughly and then allow the soil to dry out before you water again.

GLASSHOUSE COLLECTIONS offer a variety of shapes, like this magnificent vertical Euphorbia and Pandanus with pendulous leaves.

PROPAGATING BY GRAFTING

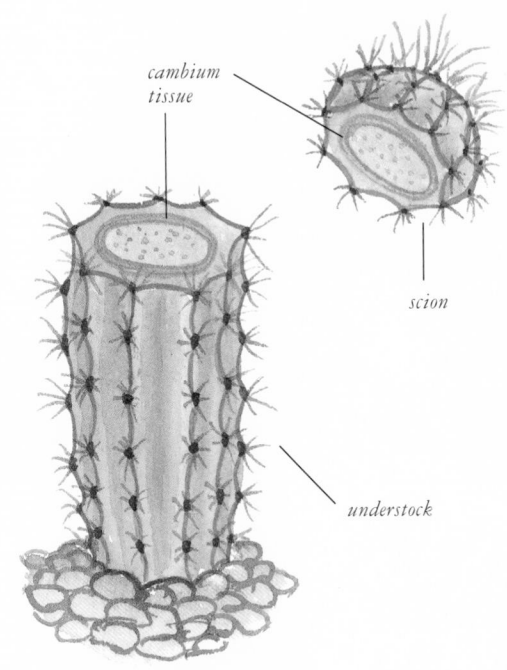

cambium tissue

scion

understock

1. WHEN GRAFTING, is most important to line up the cambium tissue of both the understock and scion to ensure a good graft union.

2. ONCE ALIGNED, firm pressure must be maintained. Rubber bands can be used to go right around the graft and the pot, or use fine pins, cactus spines, or toothpicks to hold the graft in place.

APOROCACTUS
Rat's Tail Cactus

APOROCACTUS FLAGELLI *IS ONE of the most common types to be found and is quite easy to grow, it's colorful purple-red blooms adding a touch of vibrant color to the garden in summer.*

FEATURES

Partial Shade

A good group of cacti with its botanical name in dispute; this is now classified as *Aporocactus*. These lovely, epiphytic plants are native to rainforests or damp mountainous areas of tropical and subtropical regions of the Americas where they grow from the branches of trees. Their stems are mainly jointed and flattened, tending to be long and narrow with few if any spines. They are pendulous and branching, bearing scarlet or pink flowers on the tips of the branches in late spring or early summer. These plants are delightful when grown in pots or hanging baskets which can be used for indoor decoration while the cactus is in flower. Where temperatures fall below 50°F they should be grown in a glasshouse.

APOROCACTUS AT A GLANCE

Dramatic cactuses for a hanging basket, with long trailing stems and bright showy flowers. 43°F min (zone 11).

Jan	/	Recommended Varieties
Feb	/	*Aporocactus flagelliformis*
Mar	transplant ✎	*A. martianus*
Apr	repotting ✎	
May	flowering ✿	COMPANION PLANTS
Jun	flowering ✿	Epiphyllum
July	/	Hatiora
Aug	/	Schlumbergera
Sept	/	Selenicereus
Oct	/	
Nov	sow ✎	
Dec	/	

Varieties The two most commonly found plants are *Aporocactus flagelliformis* and *A. martianus*. The latter has larger flowers than the former. Appearing in early summer, they are vivid red on gray-green stems. The plant only grows to 5in high, but can spread up to 3ft. *A. flagelliformis* is easier to grow. Its hanging growth may reach 5ft. Its purple-red blooms appear in spring when it makes a terrific sight with its snake-like stems topped by the colorful flowers.

CONDITIONS

Aspect Being epiphytic, the plants need to be grown with some degree of shade during the day. It is particularly important during the hottest, brightest part of the day. A morning of sun, and afternoon of shade is fine.

Site Grow in special epiphytic compost. Make sure that it is extremely free-draining.

GROWING METHOD

Propagation Plants can be grown from seed sown in spring, but are easier to grow from stem cuttings taken in spring or summer.

Feeding From late spring until late summer, provide a high potash or tomato feed once a month. Exceeding this dose is counter productive.

Problems Will not thrive in full sun or if overwatered.

FLOWERING

Season Rat's tail cactuses will flower either in late spring or early summer.

Fruits Flowers are followed by papery fruits.

ASTROPHYTUM
Bishop's Cap

FASTEST GROWING of all species of bishop's cap, Astrophytum ornatum *bears many yellow flowers annually after about five years.*

DEEPLY DEFINED RIBS and white scales around the upper body characterise Astrophytum ornatum, *also known as star cactus.*

FEATURES

Sun

This very small genus originates in Texas and Mexico. The two most sought-after species are virtually spineless and covered in white scales instead. The bishop's cap or bishop's mitre, *Astrophytum myriostigma*, has an unusual dull purple, bluish, or green body that is speckled all over with white scales. In the wild it may be 2ft high and 8in across, but in cultivation it is unlikely to reach melon size—and then only after many years. Its flowers are bright yellow, with the outer petals black tipped. *A. asterias*, known as the sea urchin or sand dollar cactus, is gray-green, slow growing and rarely more than 2–3in high, eventually growing to a width of about 4in. It has spectacular bright yellow flowers with deep red centers.

Varieties

A. ornatum has pronounced spines on its very well-defined ribs. It is a cylindrical shape and it grows to about 1ft. During the summer it produces yellow flower. There are many different varieties and hybrids of these popular and attractive species. If you are just starting a collection of astrophytum, it is well worth growing *A. capricorne*, known as the goat's horn cactus. It is quite a small cactus, reaching a height of only about 8in. Its common name was inspired by the bizarre form of its twisted spines which wrap themselves around the cactus instead of sticking up vertically in the usual way. This makes handling the plant quite a problem as its spines tend to get snapped off very easily.

CONDITIONS

Aspect Plants grow best in full sun, but may need a little shading if grown under glass.
Site Soil must be very free draining and should contain very little organic matter.

GROWING METHOD

Propagation Easy to raise from seed sown in spring.
Feeding Give low-nitrogen liquid plant food in spring and mid-summer or use slow-release granules.
Problems Overwatering causes them to rot and die.

FLOWERING

Season Warm spring or summer flowering.
Fruits Flowers followed by fleshy, ovoid green or red berries with long seeds within.

ASTROPHYTUM AT A GLANCE

There are four species of these slow growing, attractive roundish cactuses that like arid conditions. 50°F min (zone 11).

Jan	/	Recommended Varieties
Feb	/	*Astrophytum asterias*
Mar	/	*A. capricorne*
Apr	sow 🖐	*A. myriostigma*
May	transplant 🖐	*A. ornatum*
Jun	flowering ❀	
July	flowering ❀	COMPANION PLANTS
Aug	flowering ❀	Echinocactus
Sept	/	Epostoa
Oct	/	Gymnocalycium
Nov	/	Mammillaria
Dec	/	Rebutia

CEREUS
Column Cactus

THE LARGE AND VERY BEAUTIFUL flowers of Cereus uruguayanus *appear after dark and are worth waiting up for.*

THE BLUE-GREEN STEMS of Cereus *species are distinctly notched where the areoles and spines emerge.*

FEATURES

Sun

With a diverse range of origins from the West Indies to eastern South America, many of these cactuses are almost tree-like, while most form upright sturdy columns. The best-known species, *Cereus uruguayanus* (syn. *C. peruvianus*), is tree-like and can grow to 10ft or more with a stout, blue-green body notched where spines emerge. The "Monstrose" form makes a jumble of oddly shaped, blue-gray stems. Another tree-like species, *C. validus*, can also reach about 10ft high. Once established, it has pink-tinged white flowers in summer.
C. chalybaeus is a column cactus, often tinged blue or purple, with well-defined ribs bearing spines that mature to black. Its flowers are also white with the outer petals magenta or red.

CEREUS AT A GLANCE

A good choice if you like tall, quick growing vertical cacti, many with night-opening flowers. 45°F min (zone 11).

		Recommended Varieties
Jan	/	
Feb	/	*Cereus aethiops*
Mar	sow	*C. chalybaeus*
Apr	transplant ✽	*C. hildmannianus*
May	repotting	*C. uruguayanus*
Jun	flowering ✽	*C. validus*
July	flowering ✽	
Aug	/	Companion Plants
Sept	flowering ✽	Astrophytum
Oct	/	Echinocactus
Nov	/	Gymnocalycium
Dec	/	Mammillaria

CONDITIONS

Aspect These cactuses prefer to be grown in an open situation in full sun. Keep them well away from even the lightest shade.

Site The soil must be free draining, but need not be rich. Column cactuses come from areas with poor rocky soil. Although the size and proportion of these plants make them easiest to accommodate in a desert garden, column cactuses can also be grown in containers, which may need some extra weight such as stones or gravel in the base to stop them tipping over. Note however that some, such as the columnar *C. validus* and *C. hildmannianus monstrose*, have the potential to reach 20ft and 15ft. Of the two, the latter makes the most interesting shape with a contorted vertical stem.

GROWING METHOD

Propagation Grow plants from seed sown in spring or from cuttings of side branches.

Feeding Feed container-grown plants low-nitrogen liquid fertilizer monthly in summer. Ground-grown plants do not need feeding.

Problems No pest or disease problems are known.

FLOWERING

Season The large and lovely nocturnal flowers appear during spring and summer. The flowers usually appear after dark and fade before dawn.

Fruits Flowers are followed by round or oval fleshy fruits that ripen to yellow or red or purple.

CLEISTOCACTUS
Cleistocactus

TUBULAR FLOWERS grow directly from the stem of the silver torch cactus. A single flower near the crown creates a bird-like appearance.

BACK-LIT BY LOW SUN, the fine silvery spines of this cactus become a real feature as the silhouette of the narrow column is defined.

FEATURES

Sun

Although there are 45 species of *Cleistocactus*, all native to South America, very few are in general cultivation. Mostly branching from the base, these are upright column cactuses densely covered with fine spines that give them a silvery, woolly look. Although they look interesting as single stems, these cactuses are most spectacular when they are mass-planted. Their heights vary from 3–10ft but they are all fairly slender. The flowers, which emerge almost at right angles from the sides of the column, are mostly in shades of red and are pollinated by humming-birds in their natural habitats. The flowers never open very wide. These cactuses are fairly slow growing, making them ideal for pot culture, but they also can be grown in the open ground in conservatories. For plants in containers, regular potting on seems to produce the best growth.

CLEISTOCACTUS AT A GLANCE

These are generally quick-growing, spreading plants requiring plenty of space. Dramatic at full size. 45°F min (zone 11).

Jan	/	**Recommended Varieties**
Feb	/	*Cleistocactus brookei*
Mar	sow	*C. hyalacanthus*
Apr	/	*C. jujuyensis*
May	transplant	*C. straussii*
Jun	flowering	*C. winteri*
July	flowering	
Aug	flowering	**Companion Plants**
Sept	/	Aeonium
Oct	/	Espostoa
Nov	/	*Kalanchoe tomentosa*
Dec	/	Ferocactus
		Sansevieria trifasciata
		Yucca

Varieties The most commonly cultivated species is *C. straussii*. It grows about 6½ft high and forms clumps almost as wide. It is the species most often known by the name silver torch, and has cerise-red flowers in summer. *C. hyalacanthus* (syn. *C. jujuyensis*) is usually less than 3ft high, with columns covered in hairy, brownish to cream spines and flowers that may be bright scarlet to orange-red. *C. brookei* has one of the biggest growth potentials. Its height and spread are indefinite. In the wild it forms a superb show of red or orange flowers.

CONDITIONS

Aspect The plants need a position with continuous bright light and frequent watering during the growing season when the summer is hot. Over winter they must be kept bone dry, with a severe reduction in water from late fall.

Site Must have free-draining soil or cactus mix.

GROWING METHOD

Propagation Can be grown from seed or from stem cuttings or offsets during the warmer months.

Feeding Apply granular slow-release fertilizer in spring or feed the plants with weak solutions of liquid plant food through the growing season.

Problems Very susceptible to overwatering. If plants are indoors, mealybugs may be a problem.

FLOWERING

Season Flowers are red or pink, but also yellow, orange, or green. Most flower in summer.

Fruits Small, rounded, yellow, green, or red.

ECHINOCEREUS
Hedgehog Cactus

CYCLAMEN-PINK flowers stand like coronets to envelop the entire crown of this hedgehog cactus.

PRETTY LAVENDER-PINK flowers on Echinocereus pectinatus may be followed by edible fruits in ideal growing conditions.

FEATURES

Sun

Hailing from the south-west of North America, all 47 species in this group are in cultivation. It is a very variable genus: some types are globular, while others form short columns, some of which are pencil thin. The group is also split when it comes to their spines. Some species are heavily spined, while others are relatively smooth. Most are clump-forming or clustering, and in ideal conditions clumps of up to 3ft wide are found. Some species have edible fruits reputed to taste like strawberries. The best known of these are *Echinocereus pectinatus, E. engelmannii, E.reichenbachii,* and *E. subinermis.* The range of flower color in this group extends from white to yellow, orange, bright red, pale pink, magenta, and violet.

ECHINOCEREUS AT A GLANCE

Dramatic small cactuses, with flowers bursting through the skin. Many attractive species. 50°F min (zone 11).

		Recommended Varieties
Jan	/	*Echinocereus chloranthus*
Feb	/	*E. cinerascens*
Mar	sow 🖐	*E. engelmannii*
Apr	transplant 🖐	*E. knippelianus*
May	flowering ✽	*E. pectinatus*
Jun	flowering ✽	*E. reichenbachii*
July	/	*E. scheeri*
Aug	/	*E. subinermis*
Sept	/	*E. triglochidiatus*
Oct	/	
Nov	/	
Dec	/	

Varieties *E. knippelianus* is a striking cactus, with a dark green, almost smooth body, few spines, and pink to purple spring flowers. *E. subinermis* is one of the few yellow-flowered species, while *E. triglochidiatus* has brilliant scarlet flowers and a great range of forms. The "must have" hedgehog cactus for any collector is *E. reichenbachii* with purple-pink flowers; it makes a tidy smallish shape being 1ft high and 8in wide.

CONDITIONS

Aspect Prefers full sun with good air circulation.
Site Use a well-drained standard cactus mix. If being planted outside over summer, dig plenty of grit into the soil.

GROWING METHOD

Propagation Can be grown from seed sown in spring or from offsets taken in spring or summer.
Feeding Apply slow-release granules in spring or use weak liquid plant food in the growing season.
Problems Outdoors, few problems are encountered. If plants are grown under glasss, mealybugs or scales may be troublesome.

FLOWERING

Season Flowers appear some time during spring or summer. The flower buds form inside the plant body and then burst through the skin near the stem tips, often leaving scars.
Fruits Flowers are followed by fleshy fruits, most of which ripen to red although some fruits are green or purple.

EPIPHYLLUM
Orchid Cactus

THE CENTER of a lovely orchid cactus is dominated by a branched, star-like stigma surrounded by pollen-bearing stems.

EMERGING FROM the edge of the flattened stems, the rich red flowers of a hybrid orchid cactus cascade down from a basket.

FEATURES

Shade

Partial Shade

This group of epiphytic tropical American cactuses is known as orchid cactus because of the gorgeous, large flowers. Few of the true species are available, but the many spectacular named varieties have huge flowers 4–8in across, in shades of cream, yellow, salmon, various pinks, and reds. Some of these cultivars have a tendency to change color according to light levels and temperatures. Stems of the orchid cactus are almost spineless, broad, flattened, and leaf-like with flowers emerging from buds that are formed on the edges of these stems. These cactuses are natural epiphytes growing in tree canopies in tropical forests. As a result, they do well growing in hanging baskets or against a wall or tree that they can use for support as they scramble up.

EPIPHYLLUM AT A GLANCE	
Stunning, beautiful, often scented flowers on cactuses that look highly impressive in hanging baskets. 50°F min (zone 11).	
Jan /	Recommended Varieties
Feb /	*Epiphyllum crenatum*
Mar sow	"Fantasy"
Apr transplant	"Hollywood"
May flowering ❀	"Jennifer Anne"
Jun flowering ❀	*E. oxypetalum*
July flowering ❀	*E. pumilum*
Aug /	"Reward"
Sept /	
Oct /	
Nov /	
Dec /	

Varieties Some of the large-flowered types are slow to produce their first blooms and must be very mature before they flower regularly. However, the lovely species *Epiphyllum oxypetalum*, known as "Belle de Nuit," is nocturnal with huge white, scented flowers unfolding on warm nights to close again by daybreak. If you only have room for one small orchid, *E. laui* is an excellent choice. It grows 1ft high by 1½ft wide, and produces scented white flowers about 6in long.

CONDITIONS

Aspect Unlike many cactuses, they prefer dappled, filtered shade out of direct sunlight.

Site The soil mix must be relatively fertile, but above all open and free draining.

GROWING METHOD

Propagation Can be grown from seed sown in spring, but hybrids must be increased from stem cuttings taken during summer to early fall.

Feeding Apply granular slow-release fertilizer in spring or regular liquid feeds in the growing season.

Problems Usually trouble free in the right conditions.

FLOWERING

Season Flowers are produced on mature plants from late spring through summer. Some flowers are quite long lasting. The original species are mostly night blooming, but the majority of those available today are day flowering.

Fruits Red fruits may form on some plants.

HATIORA SALICORNIOIDES
Drunkard's dream

UNOPENED BUDS FORMING *on the tips of each slender segment of this plant are like small, glowing torches.*

A LOVELY MATURE *specimen of drunkard's dream in a hanging basket allows its fine shape to be appreciated in or out of flower.*

FEATURES

Partial
Shade

These plants bear no apparent likeness to the spiny plants so readily recognised as cactuses. They tend to be upright in early stages, but become pendulous under their own weight and so are ideal for hanging baskets. A large potted plant may need heavy stones in the container base to counterbalance the cactus's weight. The stem segments are mid-green to bronze and are topped by small, yellow to orange tubular, or funnel-shaped flowers in spring. This Brazilian group of plants includes ground growers and epiphytes and it is easy to imagine them growing from the fork or branch of a tree. *Hatiora salicornioides* is called drunkard's dream because the dense growth of tiny jointed stems resembles hundreds of tiny bottles. In Australia it is also called dancing bones.

HATIORA AT A GLANCE

Genus with many excellent species, well worth including in any collection of first-rate cactuses. 50°F min (zone 11).

Jan	/	Recommended Varieties
Feb	/	*Hatiora ephiphylloides*
Mar	sow	*H. gaertneri*
Apr	transplant	*H. rosea*
May	flowering	*H. salicornioides*
Jun	flowering	
July	/	Companion Plants
Aug	/	Astrophyllum
Sept	/	Epiphyllum
Oct	/	Rebutia
Nov	/	Schlumbergera
Dec	/	Selenicereus

CONDITIONS

Aspect   Drunkard's dream grows best in filtered sunlight or in a position that has morning sun and afternoon shade.

Site   The epiphytic kind need some shade to replicate their natural growing conditions, just under the tree canopy. Either provide filtered sunlight, or a position with morning sun and reasonable afternoon shade. Spray regularly to provide high levels of humidity, especially on hot days, when in full growth from spring to fall.

GROWING METHOD

Propagation   These plants can be grown from seed sown in spring, but it is much easier to strike cuttings from the jointed stems in spring through to early fall.

Feeding   Apply a low-level nitrogen liquid feed once a month during the growing season.

Problems   This is generally a very easy plant to grow and it has no specific pest or disease problems.

FLOWERING

Season   Small, orange to yellow tubular flowers appear from the lower half of the plant in spring. Although the flowers are not spectacular, they give the impression of tiny lights on the ends of the stems. The most impressive thing about most of these plants, is their distinctive, unusual, non-cactus like dangling growth. From a distance *H. salicornioides* looks a bit like the jangled stems of a mistletoe.

Fruits   The flowers of drunkard's dream are followed by tiny white fruits.

MAMMILLARIA
Mammillaria

THE MATURING RED FRUITS of Mammillaria prolifera *surround each rounded stem. This species readily forms large colonies which makes it a satisfying plant to cultivate, both for the novice and more experienced growers.*

FEATURES

Sun

This is probably the most popular group of cactus among growers and collectors and there are about 150 species in the genus. The largest number of these cactuses are native to Mexico, but their habitat also extends through the south-western United States south to Colombia and Venezuela. Instead of ribs, these cactuses all have tubercles which vary greatly in shape. These plants are sometimes also known as pincushion cactuses.

MAMMILLARIA AT A GLANCE

Some Mammillaria should be in every collection, for their flowers and shape, especially the terrific white snowballs. 45°F min (zone 11).

Jan	/	Recommended Varieties
Feb	/	*Mammillaria baumii*
Mar	sow	*M. bocasana*
Apr	transplant	*M. bombycina*
May	flowering	*M. candida*
Jun	flowering	*M. carmenae*
July	flowering	*M. elongata*
Aug	flowering	*M. geminispina*
Sept	flowering	*M. hahniana*
Oct	/	*M. plumosa*
Nov	/	*M. zeilmanniana*
Dec	/	

Varieties

While it is impossible to cater for all tastes, the following few species indicate the variety within the group. *Mammillaria carmenae* has feathery, white or cream spines fanning out from the woolly body, and rich creamy flowers. It rarely grows more than 4in high, forming pretty clusters. *M. bombycina* has red, brown, or yellow spines pushing through the woolly surface of the plant. This species is quick to make offsets to form a good-looking specimen, especially when topped with a ring of pretty cerise-pink flowers. *M. longimamma*, called the finger mound cactus, has fat, stubby tubercles like smooth, dark green fingers with tufts of yellow spines on each tip. Flowers borne in late spring are quite large and rich yellow, while fruits that follow are fleshy and green, not unlike the cactus itself. *M. geminispina* is another excellent cactus with small rounded shapes, and is distinguished by a covering of white spines, white areoles, and white flowers. Even better, after a few years it will start to produce plenty of young plants, eventually creating an eye-catching mound. Old lady or birthday cake cactus, *M. hahniana*, is named for the almost perfect ring of cerise flowers on the crown of the plant, which is followed by another ring of red candle-like fruits.

Snowballs

M. plumosa, M. bocasana, and *M. sempervivi* are so densely covered in white wool below the spines that they resemble snowballs or powder puffs—they are sometimes referred to by these common names.

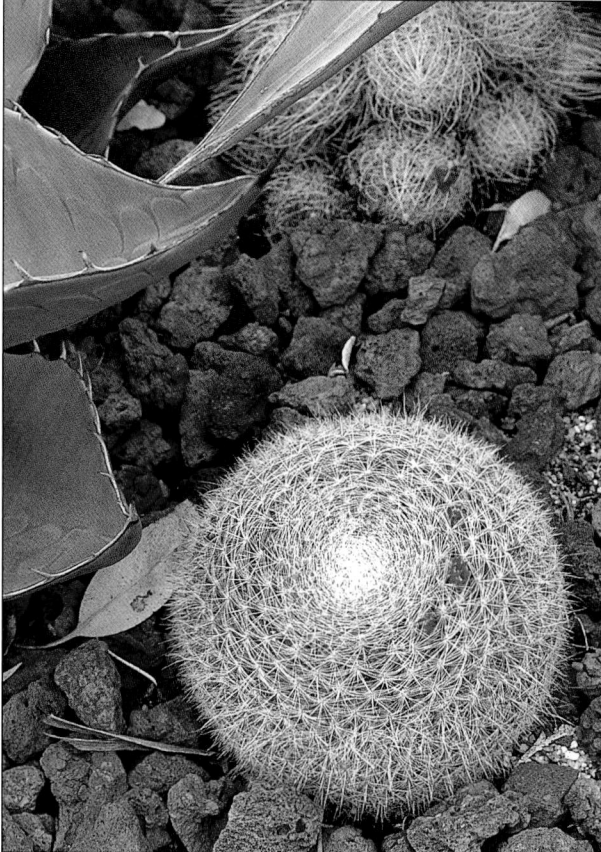

THE SMALL CERISE FLOWERS of Mammillaria hahniana *encircle the crown of the plant when fully developed.*

THIS COLUMNAR SPECIES of Mammillaria *has its crown covered with buds and flowers in spring. It is very rewarding to grow.*

Growth habit Most of these cactuses are small and rounded and thickly covered with spines, but some have finger-like stems. Most produce offsets freely, making a good show in pots or in a bed, but a few, however, are solitary growers. These cactuses are popular and satisfying to grow not only because of their easy cultivation, but because they produce rings of beautiful flowers around the crown of the plant in spring to early summer even when quite young. Spines vary from straight to curved, soft and feathery to almost rigid, and come in variable colors.

Size There is a great variation in height and size, and although a few of these cactuses may reach 12–16in in height, by far the greatest number will never exceed 6in. The ultimate spread of these species is harder to determine, but where there is space and where growing conditions are suitable, some may keep on spreading indefinitely. However, as it is easy to remove the offsets, their vigour need never be a problem.

CONDITIONS

Aspect Grow plants outdoors in full sun, but if they are under glass provide shading at the hottest time of day.

Site These cactuses are easy to grow. In pots, provide the standard cactus compost which will be free draining. When growing them in outdoor beds over summer, or in conservatory beds, make sure that the soil is on the poor side.

GROWING METHOD

Propagation These plants can be grown from seed sown in spring or by division of offsets in spring and summer. When the cactuses become quite prolific, as in the case of *M. geminispina*, it is worth removing smaller plantlets as they appear, not so much to create new plants as to maintain an aesthetically pleasing shape. It is also worth ensuring that one particularly good plant is always kept alone, without offspring, so its shape can be fully appreciated.

Feeding Apply small quantities of granular slow-release fertilizer in spring. You can also use low-nitrogen soluble liquid fertilizer at weak concentrations every month through the growing season.

Problems Some species form a thick tuberous root and these will rot if overwatered. *M. longimamma* is one of these, but all species must be considered vulnerable to overwatering.

FLOWERING

Season This cactus group produces its flowers during spring or summer, sometimes giving a second flush later in the season. They also tend to flower reliably year after year. The range of flower colors includes white, yellow, and orange with a wide range of shades of pink, red, and purple.

Fruits The berry-like fruits that follow the flowers are often bright red, but may also be green.

OPUNTIA
Opuntia

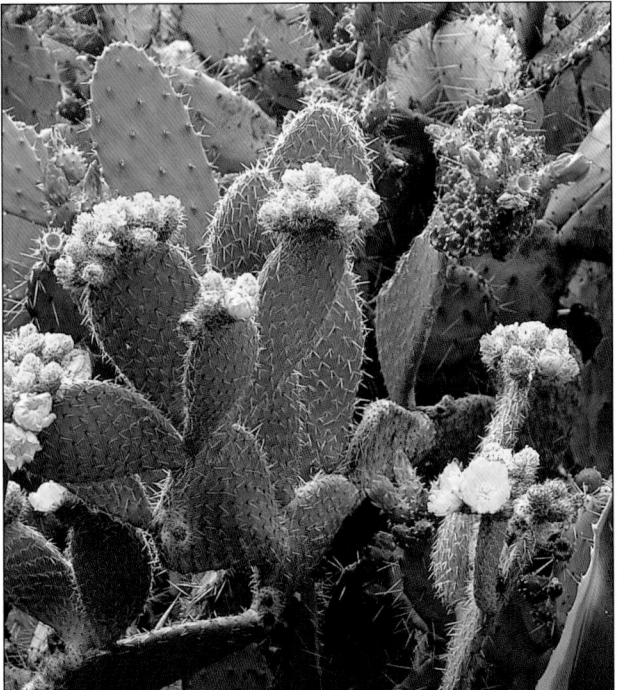

AN IMPENETRABLE BARRIER has been formed where two species of Opuntia *have become intermingled.*

FLAT, PADDLE-SHAPED segments and the sizeable growth of the edible Opuntia ficus-indica *make an impact in the landscape.*

FEATURES

Sun

Variously known as prickly pear, Indian fig, and cholla, with many more local common names, this is a very large genus of cactus with a vast geographical range. Opuntia are jointed or segmented cactuses with mainly padded and flattened joints, although sometimes these are cylindrical or rounded. Species occur naturally from southern Canada and throughout the Americas, continuing to Patagonia on the tip of South America. Long grown as living fences in their native areas, many prickly pears were introduced to other countries for this purpose, with disastrous results.

<table>
<tr><td colspan="2">OPUNTIA AT A GLANCE</td></tr>
<tr><td colspan="2">The largest group of cactus with some outstanding plants; excellent shapes and dangerous spines. 41°F min (zone 11).</td></tr>
<tr><td>Jan</td><td>/</td><td>Recommended Varieties</td></tr>
<tr><td>Feb</td><td>/</td><td>*Opuntia basiliaris*</td></tr>
<tr><td>Mar</td><td>sow ✎</td><td>*O. clavarioides*</td></tr>
<tr><td>Apr</td><td>transplant ✎</td><td>*O. ficus-indica*</td></tr>
<tr><td>May</td><td>flowering ✿</td><td>*O. microdasys*</td></tr>
<tr><td>Jun</td><td>flowering ✿</td><td>*O. imbricata*</td></tr>
<tr><td>July</td><td>flowering ✿</td><td>*O. tunicata*</td></tr>
<tr><td>Aug</td><td>flowering ✿</td><td>*O. verschaffeltii*</td></tr>
<tr><td>Sept</td><td>flowering ✿</td><td>*O. vestica*</td></tr>
<tr><td>Oct</td><td>/</td><td></td></tr>
<tr><td>Nov</td><td>/</td><td></td></tr>
<tr><td>Dec</td><td>/</td><td></td></tr>
</table>

Prickly pear *O. aurantiaca, O. stricta,* and *O. vulgaris* and a number of other species have become quite appalling weeds in Australia, Africa, and India. By 1925, there was estimated to be above 10 million acres (25 million hectares) of land infested by prickly pear in Australia. A huge program of biological control was initiated, involving the introduction of the *Cactoblastis* moth and cochineal insects.

Indian fig The Indian fig, *O. ficus-indica,* is widely grown in many parts of the world for its fruit. It is a tree-like cactus up to 17ft high and wide.

Other types Although many species of opuntia are too large to place anywhere except in a large desert garden, there are numerous other shapes and sizes, with some that are suitable for pot culture. Bunny ears, *O. microdasys,* has dark green pads dotted with white areoles, and white, yellow, or brown bristles. The brown-bristled form is known as teddy bear ears. These plants rarely grow more than 16–24in high and wide, and suit both containers or the yard. *O. tunicata* is a small, spreading bush about 24in high and up to 3ft wide. Its thick, creamy spines take on a satin sheen in sunlight. Beaver tail, *O. basilaris,* has purple-gray flat pads with few spines and spreads by branching from the base, so is rarely more than 16in high. *O. erinacea* is clump-forming with flattened blue-green pads, but it is the variety *ursina* with masses of fine hair-like spines—known as grizzly bear cactus—that attracts many growers. In the wild it grows in California and Arizona, has 4in long pinky orange flowers, and grows about 18in high.

THE VIVID RED FLOWERS are tightly ridged across the top of the young leaves of this Opuntia. *The flowers of most species are usually produced in spring or summer, and are followed by succulent fruits later in the season.*

Chollas
It is well worth knowing something about this rare group, which are rarely seen outside specialist botanical collections. The chollas (pronounced "choyas") are enormously variable in their habit of growth. They include the very spiny, almost furry-looking *O. bigelovii*, which grows to about 3–6½ft high, and the more open, tree-like *O. versicolor*, which may reach almost 13ft in height. Most of this group have easily detached segments, in particular the jumping cholla, *O. fulgida*, which hooks on to anything that passes, usually taking root and growing where it falls.

CONDITIONS

Aspect
Site
Best grown in an open, sunny situation. Provide container-grown plants with sharply drained, standard cactus mix. In the garden, they tolerate a wide range of soils as long as they drain well. All opuntias dislike having their roots cramped in a small space. The larger plants should eventually be moved to a border in the glasshouse. If you opt for a regime of constant potting up, note that the spines are vicious.

GROWING METHOD

Propagation
Easily grown from stem segments which should be separated from the parent plant from spring to fall. They can also be grown successfully from seed sown in spring.

Feeding
In spring and mid-summer, plants in the ground can be given pelletted poultry manure or granular slow-release fertilizer. Potted plants should have a dose of slow-release fertilizer in the spring or an occasional liquid feed during the growing season.

Problems
Few problems are encountered if growing conditions are suitable. The two worst offenders to look out for are scale insects and mealybugs. You will invariably need to spray to remove them, since the dangerous spines prevent you from getting in close to carry out treatment with a swab.

FLOWERING

Season
The flowers of opuntia are produced sometime during spring or summer, depending on species. The majority of species has yellow flowers, but these may also be orange, purple, or white. For example, the bright yellow flowers of *O. tunicata* appear from spring to summer, while *O. basilaris* bears its bright rose-pink flowers in summer.

Fruits
Berry-like fruits form after the flowers fade, and in some species these are edible. The Indian fig has bright yellow flowers that are followed by deep red to purple fruit. It is widely cultivated around the world for its fruit. Prepare the fruit for eating by washing and using a brush to remove the spines. Slice off the top and bottom, slit the skin, and peel. Serve in slices with a squeeze of lemon or lime juice. You can also use the pulp to make jam. *O. cochenillifera* is a source of cochineal—although today this dye is mainly synthesized.

PARODIA
Ball Cactus

DENSELY COVERED with fine yellow spines, the species Parodia claviceps *can be slow to form colonies.*

BRIGHT YELLOW FLOWERS are a feature of Parodia magnifica, *a deeply furrowed species which is not heavily spined.*

FEATURES

Sun

Partial
Shade

While the species is now known as parodia, you will find that many ball cactuses are still under the old name of notocactus. These superb cactuses are native to Brazil, Paraguay, Uruguay, and Argentina. Mostly rounded in form, although a few are column shaped, they are easy to grow and flower profusely. Many ball cactuses have deeply furrowed surfaces, but the coverage of spines varies greatly; some forms are thickly covered and others have quite sparse spines. *P. concinnus* is a small tubby shape with primrose-yellow flowers, while *P. leninghausii* can form a thick column up to 3ft high and has large yellow flowers. *P. herteri*, prized for its hot pink-purple flowers, is squat-shaped and blooms when it reaches tennis-ball size. *N. uebelmannianus* is another squat grower, with large purple or yellow flowers.

CONDITIONS

Aspect	Ball cactuses will grow in full sun or in very light shade. When standing pots outdoors in summer, make sure that the plants receive some shade around midday.
Site	When growing in pots, use a standard well-drained compost. In the ground, ball cactuses like equally well-drained soil with some well-rotted compost that slightly increases fertility.

GROWING METHOD

Propagation	Grow from seed in spring or from offsets taken in summer. None of the species will produce offsets until quite mature. Increase watering in the spring and allow the soil to dry out between waterings during the summer.
Feeding	Apply slow-release fertilizer in spring, or feed the plants with some low-nitrogen liquid fertilizer every 6–8 weeks throughout the growing season.
Problems	This is generally a trouble-free type of cactus that is easy to grow.

FLOWERING

Season	The flowers appear on the crown of ball cactuses during the spring or summer months. The central stigma of the flower is nearly always a deep reddish-purple to pink color. While the majority of the ball cactuses have yellow flowers, it is possible to obtain other species that have attractive flowers in red, pink, purple, or even orange colors. Contact a cactus nursery which specialises in parodia.
Fruits	In ideal growing conditions, as in the wild, you may find that after the flowers fade fleshy fruits ripen to red.

PARODIA AT A GLANCE

Generally globular or spherical, ribbed spiny cactuses from South America. Funnel-shaped blooms. 45°F min (zone 11).

Jan	/	Recommended Varieties
Feb	/	*Parodia chrysacanthion*
Mar	transplant	*P. concinna*
Apr	flowering	*P. herteri*
May	flowering	*P. horstii*
Jun	flowering	*P. leninghausii*
July	flowering	*P. magnifica*
Aug	sow	*P. mammulosa*
Sept	/	*P. nivosa*
Oct	/	*P. rutilans*
Nov	/	*P. schwebsiana*
Dec	/	

SCHLUMBERGERA
Christmas Cactus

A VIVID SCARLET HYBRID of Schlumbergera truncata *makes a desirable potted plant to brighten winter days.*

FLOURISHING IN LIGHT SHADE, this Christmas cactus is the cerise-pink color that most people associate with the species.

FEATURES

Partial
Shade

This group of easily grown cacti originated from only about six species, and now features almost 200 cultivars of popular flowering pot plants which are more familiar to some as *Zygocactus. Schlumbergera* species, or Christmas cacti, are epiphytic and grow on trees or sometimes rocks in their native Brazilian habitat where their flowers are pollinated by humming-birds. Their popularity as pot plants is assured because most of them flower in fall or winter, hence their common name. They have flat, jointed stems arching into small bushes, making them ideal for hanging baskets as well as pots. They come into vigorous growth in summer, and start flowering once the day length is less than 12 hours. Christmas cacti make excellent gifts.

SCHLUMBERGERA AT A GLANCE

High performance pot plants which give a big show of bright color around Christmas. Easily grown. 45°F min (zone 11).

Jan	flowering ✿		Recommended Varieties
Feb	flowering ✿		*Schlumbergera* "Bristol Beauty"
Mar	/		*S.* x *buckleyi*
Apr	sow ✍		"Gold Charm"
May	flowering ✿		"Joanne"
Jun	transplant ✍		"Lilac Beauty"
July	/		*S. opuntioides*
Aug	/		*S. truncata*
Sept	/		
Oct	/		
Nov	flowering ✿		
Dec	flowering ✿		

Varieties The silky, irregularly-shaped flowers are mainly in shades of pink or red, but hybrids can be almost pure white to cream, salmon, apricot, cerise, violet, and scarlet. Some display yellow tones that revert to pink as temperatures fall. *S. truncata*, the crab cactus, and *S.* x *buckleyi*, the Christmas cactus, provide the origins of many of the modern hybrids.

CONDITIONS

Aspect Best in partial shade or with morning sun and afternoon shade in a sheltered situation.

Site For an established pot plant, John Innes No. 2 with added grit for good drainage is ideal. Repot every three years in the spring. It is too tender to be grown outdoors.

GROWING METHOD

Propagation These plants are easy to grow from cuttings of stem sections taken in spring or summer.

Feeding A light, regular summer feed will promote plenty of new growth and guarantee an excellent display of flowers.

Problems Generally easy to grow, these plants will suffer if grown in full sun and may not flower. Overwatering causes root rot and subsequent collapse of stems.

FLOWERING

Season Masses of flowers appear in fall or winter. Once flower buds have formed, do not move the plants until buds begin to open. Flowers in spring if kept at 36–39°F over winter. Gradually increase the temperature in spring.

SELENICEREUS
Selenicereus

THESE PLANTS ARE CULTIVATED for their beautiful white, cream, or pale pink fragrant flowers, which open at night. It is amazing to see such a glorious flower emerge at dusk from a fairly ugly-looking stem but, of course, it will have faded by the following morning.

FEATURES

Partial
Shade

There are about 20 species in this group of very long-stemmed climbing epiphytic cactuses. They are native to the forests of the south-western United States, central America, the West Indies, and Colombia, where they live on trees or rocks. *Selenicereus* species have long been cultivated in Mexico for a drug used in the treatment of rheumatism and in Costa Rica for a heart-stimulant drug. They are now being cultivated in Germany and elsewhere for use in medicine, especially in the treatment of heart disorders. These plants have long, angled, or tubular stems bearing small spines on the ribs, but it is their aerial roots that enable them to climb and cling on to their host plants. They will continue to grow up-wards and spread as long as they find support.

SELENICEREUS AT A GLANCE

Strange, thin climbing stems with outstanding scented flowers, from South American forests. 59°F min (zone 11).

Jan	/	Recommended Varieties
Feb	/	*Selenicereus grandiflorus*
Mar	sow 🖐	*S. hamatus*
Apr	/	*S. innesii*
May	transplant 🖐	*S. pteranthus*
Jun	flowering ✽	*S. spinulosus*
July	flowering ✽	
Aug	flowering ✽	
Sept	/	Companion Plants
Oct	sow 🖐	Epiphyllum
Nov	/	Hatiora
Dec	/	Schlumbergera
		Selenicereus

Varieties *S. grandiflorus* is the species most often grown. Its flowers have outer petals that are yellow to brown, but the inner flower is pure white. Two other species found in cultivation are *S. pteranthus* and *S. spinulosus*. Both have cream, white, or pale pink flowers. These plants can be grown in the ground, or rooted in large pots set against some strong support.

CONDITIONS

Aspect Being epiphytic, these extraordinary cactuses need to be kept out of direct sunlight. They like filtered, dappled light, or as second best, light for half the day, shade for the rest.

Site Plants need well-drained compost with added decayed organic matter. An orchid mix would suit them.

GROWING METHOD

Propagation Plants are easily grown from stem segments taken from spring to early fall. They can also be grown from seed sown in spring.

Feeding Apply slow-release fertilizer in spring, or liquid feed occasionally in the growing season.

Problems No specific pests or diseases are known, but keep an eye out in the summer for scale insects and mealybugs.

FLOWERING

Season The spectacular, scented flowers do not appear until the plants have become quite mature. They open on summer evenings.

Fruits The fleshy fruits are hairy or spiny.

Growing
Succulents

GROWING SUCCULENT PLANTS

These unique plants vary greatly in size, shape, and leaf color, and they originate from a wide variety of habitats. One thing all succulents have in common, they are show-stoppers in the garden. They look striking against other plants, as contrasts or accents in the landscape, or when grown as individual eye-catchers.

A collection of succulents of different sizes and colors can make an attractive garden display without the need to add any other type of plant. They can also be used to vary and complement a display of cactuses to great effect. The other great advantage of succulents is that many of them can be teamed with a wide range of non-succulents without looking out of place. They can be used as feature plants, as groundcovers, in mixed borders, or as container specimens.

KEY TO AT A GLANCE TABLES

PLANTING   FLOWERING

At a glance charts are your quick guide.
For full information, consult the accompanying text.

LEFT: A perfect specimen of Agave *species dominates the planting in this well-planned succulent garden. The distinctive foliage of* Kalanchoe beharensis *fills the foreground while* K. fedtschenkoi *blooms in the background.*

FEATURES OF SUCCULENTS

Succulents are xerophytes, plants that store water in their stems, leaves, or roots to withstand harsh, dry conditions. Their thick, fleshy leaves are often covered with a waxy coating or fine hairs to reduce loss of moisture through transpiration. Although some succulents have spines on their stems or foliage, these are carried singly and do not arise from areoles, the little "cushions" that bear cactus spines. Succulents originate from a wide range of climatic regions.

Succulents come from a variety of habitats and while many are sensitive to cold, there are others that tolerate temperatures well below freezing. While all cactuses are in the one botanical family *Cactaceae*, succulents belong to a wide range of families that includes both the daisy family *Asteraceae* and the lily family *Liliaceae*.

SUCCULENTS IN THE GARDEN

Succulents are easy to incorporate into the garden as they mix very well with both cactuses and non-succulents, and they are particularly useful in the garden when planted to provide foliage contrast. Here, their distinctive forms and colors can be shown to great advantage. All that they require is to be associated with plants that enjoy the same aspect and have similar soil and water requirements.

The vast majority of succulents like to be grown in an open, sunny situation. The soil must drain well and if there is any chance of waterlogging, garden beds should be raised above the existing soil level as described in the introduction to cactus growing. The addition of some well-decayed compost or manure will improve soil aeration and drainage, as well as giving the plants a good start in life.

A SURVIVOR of harsh conditions, this tender carpobrutus produces flowers on and off throughout the year in the wild.

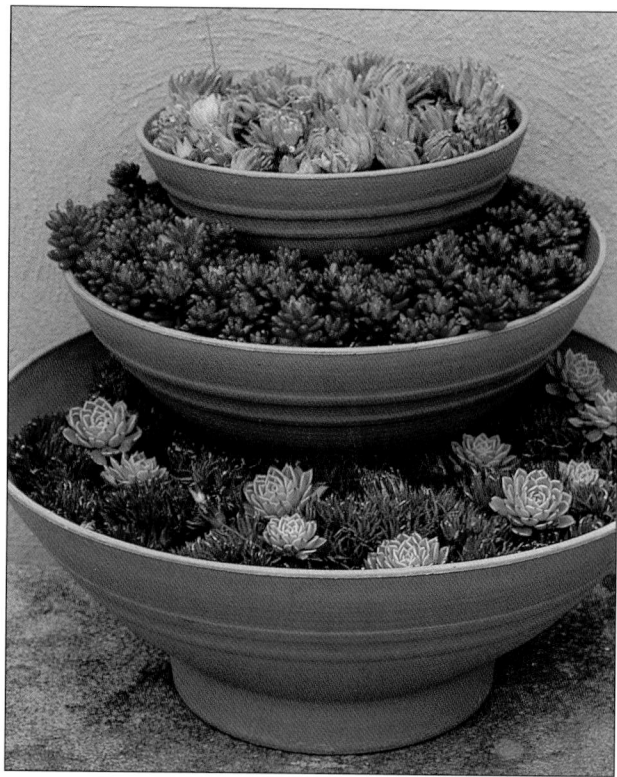

GRADED SIZES of terracotta bowls are used to display succulents. The top bowl contains Haworthia *species, the center bowl has sedums and the lowest bowl is planted with echeverias.*

GROWING SUCCULENTS IN CONTAINERS

Succulents can be grown in almost any type of container as long as there is adequate drainage. They can be grown in standard pots or hanging baskets, troughs, and window boxes, or turned into amusing novelties by planting them in old teapots or kettles, hiking boots, pottery ornaments, or anything else that takes your fancy—as long as the container allows excess water to drain away.

Some succulents have enormous appeal for children, the most popular being *Kalanchoe tomentosa* and sedums. As long as the children do not kill these plants with kindness— usually by overwatering—succulents will survive with the minimum degree of attention.

The great range of color in leaves alone can make for interesting groupings of pots of either single or mixed succulent species. A few succulents are also ideal for growing in hanging baskets. These include lampranthus and *Kalanchoe brossfeldiana*, while burro's tail must be grown this way. Mother-in-law's tongue, too, is most often grown as a container plant able to survive most conditions, both indoors and out. Large specimens of succulents can be used as feature or specimen plants in the garden or on a terrace. These include the Madagascar palm, silver jade plant, agaves, and aloes. Those succulents that have sharp spines are best positioned away from regularly used paths and entrances. Succulents that rely on finely detailed foliage patterns to make their mark, such as *Agave victoriae-reginae*, make lovely potted plants positioned where their form and markings can be seen to best advantage. Slow growers such as this agave can remain happily in the one pot for many years.

WATERING AND FERTILIZING

Most succulent plants prefer to be watered fairly regularly during the growing season, being kept drier during their dormant phase. Living in a very mild area with high winter rainfall need not rule you out of growing succulents, as long as the soil drainage is rapid. If your soil is sandy and quick draining, it will, of course, need watering much more frequently than a heavier and more moisture-retentive soil. As with all plants, you will need to become familiar with your own soil to gauge the frequency of watering required by succulents. However, succulents will generally not die rapidly if they run out of water, and it is better to water them too little than too much.

Most succulents can be grown without supplementary fertilizer unless the soil is extremely poor. Organic matter added to the soil before planting will often supply all the necessary nutrients, but low-nitrogen fertilizers can also be used during the growing season. Excess fertilizer, and especially excess nitrogen, will result in soft growth that may not stand up to tough growing conditions. If you feel that feeding is necessary, use granular slow-release fertilizers or half-strength soluble liquid plant foods. Small amounts of low-nitrogen fertilizers formulated to encourage flowering and fruiting, such as some tomato or rose foods, may also be suitable for some succulents.

PROPAGATION

Propagation from cuttings

Most succulents are very easy to grow from stem cuttings. If the stems are fairly slim, you can pot cuttings into coarse sand with a little added coir peat. Thick fleshy stems are best cut from the plant, dusted with sulfur and then allowed to dry for a few days before potting up. You can take cuttings from tips or from further down the stem—it does not seem to matter where the cutting comes from. The cuttings are best taken in the spring or mid-summer, when new roots will quickly appear. Most succulents will also grow readily from leaf cuttings. Simply break off a firm mature leaf cleanly, leave it

PROPAGATING BY LEAF CUTTINGS

1. CLEANLY snap off a healthy, mature leaf from the stock plant and put it aside to dry.

2. INSERT only the leaf base into a mix of equal parts coarse sand and perlite, or coarse sand with a little coir peat.

3. NEW GROWTH emerges from the base of the old leaf. This may take a few weeks depending on the species and time of year.

4. WHEN NEW plants are growing strongly and have good root systems, pot them on individually.

THE YELLOW-GREEN FOLIAGE of stonecrop Sedum nussbaumeranum *flushes pink in the sun. This is one of the 280 species of plants in the genus* Sedum, *many of which are good ornamentals. Their wide range of habitats varies from the tropics to cold regions.*

to dry for a few days and then insert just the base of the leaf into the growing mix. One species which will root easily this way but never make a plant is senecio. The single leaves of this plant readily form roots, but never develop further. Some species will strike even if cuttings are left sitting on top of the mix, producing roots and tiny new leaves from the base of the old leaf. A few species develop bulbils on their flowering stems and can be detached and treated like cuttings to form separate plants.

Propagation by division

Some succulents form clumps in which individual plants have their own roots. In this case, simply dig up the whole clump and pull it apart, making sure each division has some roots and shoots. If, however, you have broken off a piece without roots, you should simply treat it as a cutting. Sometimes you will need to cut through the clump with a knife, which may result in the severing of sections of the plant. If you have cut through the entire plant, or even cut through half the plant, either discard that piece or dust it with sulfur before replanting it.

Clump-forming plants like echeverias or houseleeks are best propagated by division, but sometimes you may want to remove single rosettes to give to friends or, with the latter, grow them elsewhere in the garden. If you use a narrow-bladed knife or spatula, you can usually insert this carefully between rosettes to lever out individual plants.

Layering

Many succulents will produce roots wherever they come into contact with the soil. Once you know that a section has its own roots, it can be dug up and replanted. You can encourage this layering by pegging down a section of stem with a small stone, a hairpin, or an opened paper clip. Good examples of these self-layering plants are lampranthus and London pride, or *Crassula*.

Growing from seed

Although seedling plants may be slow growing and take a number of years to flower, many growers prefer this method of propagation as they find it very satisfying. If you want to try growing from seed, use a ready-made seed-raising mix or make your own from three parts of horticultural sand and one part of coir peat. Firm the mix into a container and water well. Sow fine seed on top of the mix and leave the container uncovered. Larger seeds can be covered to a depth of between equal to and twice the seed diameter. Use a spray mister to lightly water the seeds, cover the container with a sheet of glass or plastic and keep in a bright warm place, protecting it from direct sunlight. Check every few days to see whether the seed mix needs watering; if it does, use a spray mister or set the container in a larger one of water and allow the mix to slowly draw up the water from below. Do not water heavily from above as the water may dislodge the seeds that you have sown.

The time taken for seeds to germinate will vary enormously, ranging from a few days to several weeks. Once seed has germinated, leave the cover partially off the pot to reduce humidity without sending the tiny plants into shock. Increase this exposure to the atmosphere gradually until the seedlings are looking strong and the cover is entirely off. Once they are large enough to handle, they can be potted up into small, individual pots.

Unfortunately it is all too easy for seedlings to fail because of excess moisture in the potting mix and the atmosphere. Despite the high failure rate, it can be fun to grow succulents from seed. As the majority of succulents grow so easily from cuttings or division, not many growers bother to raise seeds. There are some species, however, that can only be propagated from seed. As with any other group of plants, there is always the chance that a seedling plant will exhibit some interesting variation in color or form.These chance seedlings often give rise to new cultivars.

WHAT CAN GO WRONG?

Soil and watering

• Succulents are generally a very trouble-free group of plants. Their greatest enemy is heavy, poorly drained soil and an excess of water especially during the cooler months of the year. Most will take plenty of water during the growing season as long as the soil or potting mix drains well, but while the plants are dormant in cold weather, they will rot if the soil is kept wet all the time. A monthly watering would be adequate in a dry winter.

Pests

• Snails will sometimes eat some types of succulents leaving ugly scars that can ruin the appearance of the plant. Search for snails and destroy them or use a proprietary snail bait, taking care not to put pets or children at risk.
• Mealybugs can be a problem with any type of plant grown under shelter where conditions are dry and warm. These sap suckers, which resemble little sticky patches of cotton wool, can be wiped off with a cotton bud dipped in methylated spirits; if the infestation is severe, the plant may need spraying.

Weeds

• Weeds can spoil the appearance of a lovely patch of succulents but as many of these plants grow into clumps of rosettes or as low groundcovers, weeding can be difficult. It is hard to extract weeds without breaking these often brittle plants. Before you set your plants in the garden, turn the soil over well, water it and wait for weeds to appear. Remove the weeds by hand or spray with glyphosate. It is worth repeating the process if you have weed problems elsewhere in the garden. Make sure you dig out the bulbs of persistent perennial weeds, such as oxalis, prior to planting succulents. These stubborn weeds are almost impossible to remove completely if they appear amid a dense-growing cluster of succulents. Act before it is too late.

CLEAR YELLOW is one of the newer but quite stable colors among the hybrids of flaming Katy.

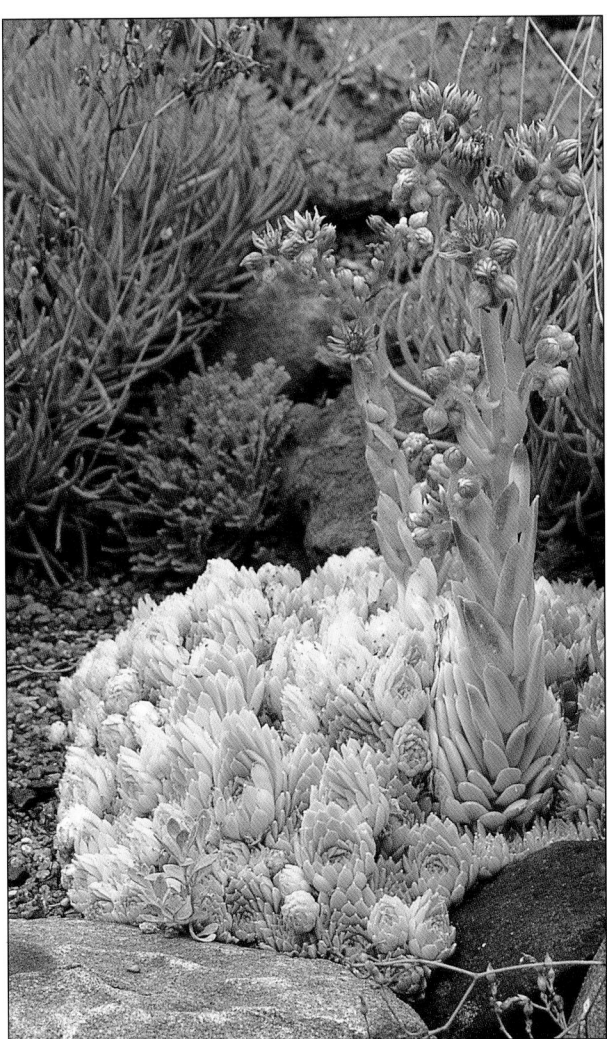

A STURDY COLUMN of fleshy leaves supports the pink flowers of this houseleek. This stem will slowly die off after the flowers fall.

CRASSULA
London Pride

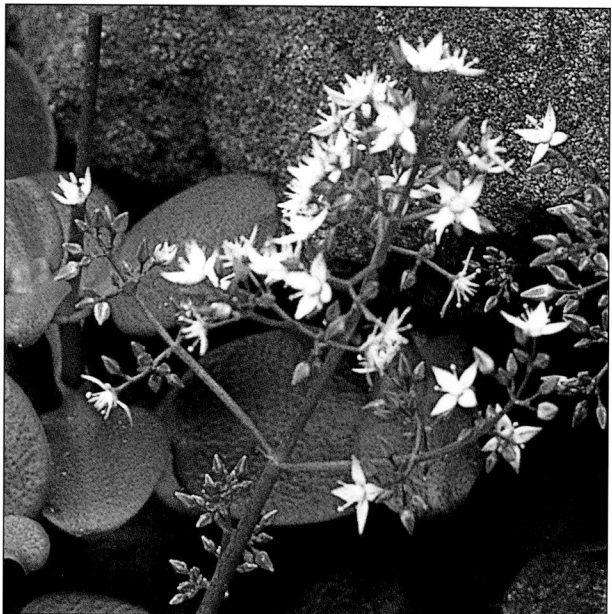

PRETTY, STARRY FLOWERS lift the leathery looking foliage. Tiny plantlets often develop after the flowers have fallen.

ADAPTABLE AND TROUBLE-FREE, London pride can survive among rocks in tiny amounts of soil.

FEATURES

Sun

Partial Shade

In warm climates, this semi-prostrate plant is a very vigorous grower, but it can be useful and decorative as a groundcover or as a filler plant in a rockery. In any event, crassula is very easy to control if it ever exceeds its allotted space. It can be upright or somewhat sprawling in habit, and when sprawling it roots itself into the ground as it spreads. It can alternatively be grown in pots or hanging baskets. Plants grow about 6–10in high, but can be taller. In warm, humid areas, one plant may spread 20in or more in a season. The fleshy leaves may be rounded, oblong, or spoon shaped, and the small pink and white starry flowers are carried on slender stems high above the foliage.

CRASSULA AT A GLANCE

Superb succulents with fleshy leaves ranging from the tiny to 15ft high in the wild. (41°F min (zone 11).

Jan	flowering ❀	Recommended Varieties
Feb	/	*Crassula falcata*
Mar	sow ✍	C. *galanthea*
Apr	transplant ✍	C. *helmsii*
May	flowering ❀	C. *milfordiae*
Jun	flowering ❀	C. *ovata*
July	flowering ❀	C. *rupestris*
Aug	/	C. *sarcocaulis*
Sept	flowering ❀	C. *schmidtii*
Oct	/	
Nov	/	
Dec	flowering ❀	

CONDITIONS

Aspect Crassula is suited to growing in sun or partial shade. Growth is more compact when the plant is situated in full sun. It benefits from being stood outside over summer, or it could be planted out in a special raised bed with excellent drainage.

Site Almost any kind of well-drained soil will suit this plant. Plants in containers prefer a mix that drains well, but also contains plenty of organic matter.

GROWING METHOD

Propagation This plant is very easily grown from stem cuttings taken any time during the warmer seasons. Tiny plantlets emerging from bulbils may sometimes form on the tips of flowered stems. These plantlets may be pegged down on a pot of coarse sandy mix to grow on and form roots.

Feeding Potted plants may need some slow-release fertilizer applied in spring. Plants grown in beds rarely need supplementary feeding.

Problems Crassula is generally an easily-grown, tough, trouble-free plant. The only problems occur in the glasshouse over summer, when you should keep an eye out for mealybugs and aphids and spray accordingly.

FLOWERING

Season Small pink and white starry flowers appear in spring. These are sometimes followed by bulbils, which grow into new plants.

CRASSULA ARBORESCENS
Silver Jade Plant

ROUNDED SILVERY LEAVES edged in red make this shrubby succulent an asset in the mild garden, in or out of flower.

RUSTY RED-BROWN CALYCES remain on the bush long after the pale starry flowers have fallen.

FEATURES

Sun

Partial Shade

Growing to over 8½ft in its native South Africa, this plant is more often seen at about 5ft when container-grown, or somewhat taller in the ground. It blends well with a range of plant types, including evergreens that enjoy the same conditions, and can be used most successfully to add height to a desert garden or a succulent display. It develops a sturdy trunk and numerous branches which carry leathery, gray-green oblong leaves with a fine red margin, sometimes dotted with tiny red spots. Plants sold as *Crassula ovata* are probably the same as or very similar to this species.

CRASSULA AT A GLANCE

C. arborescens is a highly attractive South African succulent with pink fall flowers and thick waxy leaves. 41°F min (zone 11).

		Recommended Varieties
Jan	/	*Crassula arborescens*
Feb	/	*C. falcata*
Mar	/	*C. galanthea*
Apr	sow	*C. helmsii*
May	/	*C. milfordiae*
Jun	transplant	*C. ovata*
July	/	*C. rupestris*
Aug	/	*C. sarcocaulis*
Sept	/	*C. schmidtii*
Oct	flowering ❋	
Nov	flowering ❋	
Dec	flowering ❋	

CONDITIONS

Aspect   Full sun is preferred, but this plant will tolerate shade for part of the day if necessary. However, the more light it receives the better it does.

Site   This plant can be grown in any type of well-drained soil. Container-grown plants will benefit from annual repotting, or from having the top third of the compost replaced.

GROWING METHOD

Propagation   This plant is most easily grown from leaf cuttings, which must be removed with the stem attached. It can also be grown from stem cuttings or seed. All methods of propagation are best carried out in warm weather.

Feeding   Fertilizing is generally unnecessary, but a small amount of slow-release fertilizer can be given to container-grown plants in spring.

Problems   This is a tough, trouble-free plant that is quite easily grown. The only possible irritation is that the plant may repeatedly get too big for its container. Eventually, the best solution is to replace the oversize plant with a vigorous cutting. This will mean that you can start all over again with a small pot.

FLOWERING

Season   Flowering is profuse. Masses of small, pink, starry flowers adorn the shrub in late fall to winter.

EUPHORBIA CAPUT-MEDUSAE
Medusa's Head

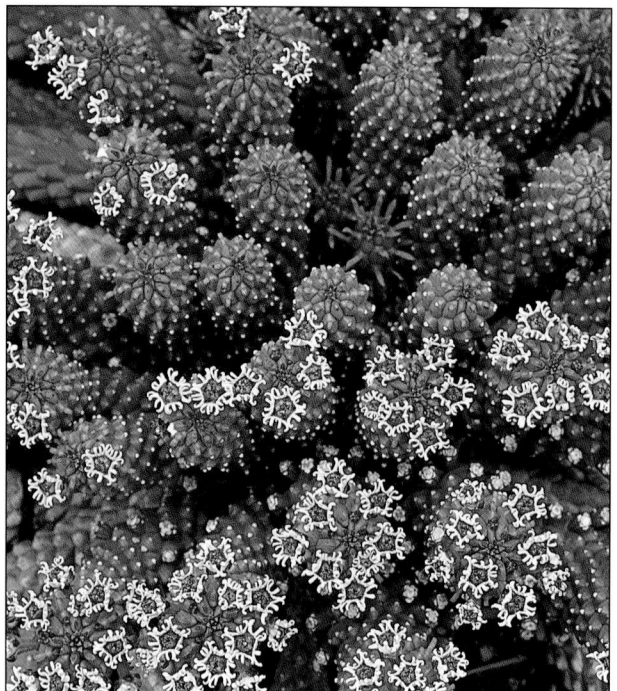

CORONETS OF SMALL FLOWERS *on the mature stems of Medusa's head lighten the appearance of the heavy stems.*

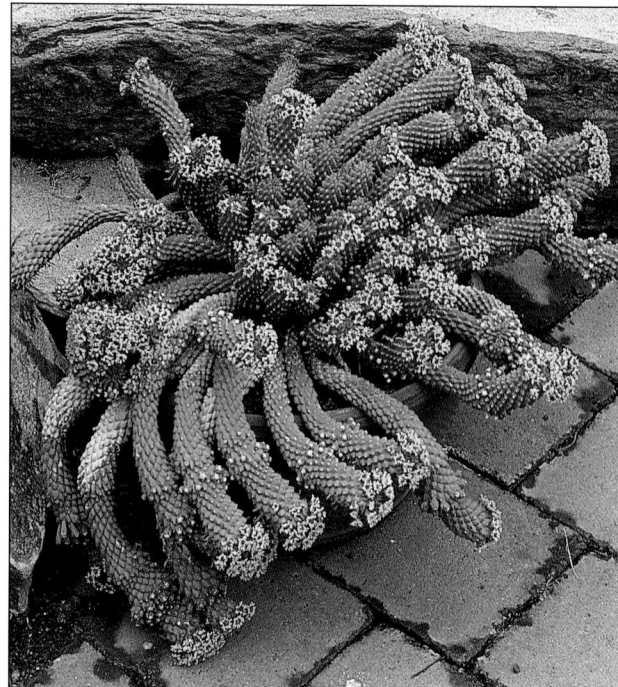

MEDUSA'S HEAD CAN BE PLANTED OUT *over summer in a gap between paving, producing a dramatic eye-catching effect.*

FEATURES

Sun

Although growing only 1ft high, this multi-branched succulent makes an impact. The rounded, thickened stem may grow partly underground, but from this stout stem a mass of gray-green knobbly branches emerge.
A well-grown plant may have a diameter of up to 3ft. Small green leaves sprout from the tips of the warty branches. Ideal as a feature for a desert or succulent garden, this plant can also be container grown. Like all the plants in this group, the milky latex in the stems is caustic and may cause severe skin problems; wear gloves and protect eyes when handling it.

EUPHORBIA AT A GLANCE

E. caput-medusae is a fine architectural South African plant with branching stems and whitish flowers. 55°F min (zone 11).

Jan	/	Recommended Varieties
Feb	/	*Euphorbia amygdaloides* var.
Mar	sow ✍	*robbiae*
Apr	transplant ✍	*E. characias* subsp. *characias*
May	flowering ✿	*E. c.* subsp. *wulfenii*
Jun	flowering ✿	*E. griffithii* "Dixter"
July	flowering ✿	*E.* x *martinii*
Aug	/	*E. myrsinites*
Sept	/	*E. palustris*
Oct	/	*E. polychroma*
Nov	/	*E. schillingii*
Dec	/	

CONDITIONS

Aspect   These plants should be grown in full sun with good air circulation around them.

Site   The soil must be well drained, but does not need to be rich. Whether growing in pots, or in the open ground over summer, make sure that plenty of grit is added to the compost or soil.

GROWING METHOD

Propagation   Medusa's head can be grown from stem cuttings taken during the warmer months, or from seed sown in spring.

Feeding   Plants grown in containers can be given a small amount of slow-release fertilizer in spring. Plants grown in the garden should not need supplementary feeding. If the soil is particularly poor though, a regular liquid feed will give the plant a decent boost.

Problems   Medusa's head is generally not prone to problems unless overwatered.

FLOWERING

Season   The cream or green flowers of this plant appear in spring or summer. The true flower is small, but it is fringed with attractive creamy white, bract-like surrounds. In a poor summer it may be best to move it back under glass where it will flower better in the higher temperatures.

EUPHORBIA MILII
Crown of Thorns

THE FLORAL DISPLAY of crown of thorns lasts many months but is more prolific in spring and summer.

THE WHITE-BRACTED FORM of crown of thorns is less vigorous than the species. It can be shaped into a neat and pretty pot plant.

FEATURES

Sun

This extremely spiny, semi-succulent plant sprawls over the ground. In warm-climate gardens it provides groundcover for places where people or animals are to be excluded, over walls or under windows, and is virtually maintenance-free. Heights vary from 3–4½ft the latter in ideal conditions. It is valued for its almost year-round display of bright red bracts which surround the insignificant flowers. In a big pot it makes a very striking feature. The leaves are a soft mid-green and can be plentiful or sparse depending on conditions, warm and wet is best.

EUPHORBIA AT A GLANCE

An excellent if spiny plant, with good bright colors, demanding a warm, humid conservatory. 54°F min (zone 11).

		Recommended Varieties
Jan	/	*Euophorbia characias* subsp.
Feb	/	*wulfenii*
Mar	repotting 🖐	*E. dulcis* "Chameleon"
Apr	sow 🖐	*E. griffithii* "Dixter"
May	flowering ❀	*E. g.* "Fireglow"
Jun	transplant 🖐	*E.* x *martinii*
July	flowering ❀	*E. myrsinites*
Aug	/	*E. polychroma*
Sept	/	*E. schillingii*
Oct	/	
Nov	/	
Dec	/	

CONDITIONS

Aspect This has to be grown in a pot or border in the conservatory. Sun or light shade is fine. Note that the more you adhere to its ideal conditions, also keeping it warm and wet, the taller and bushier it grows, and the more frequently the flowers appear on new growth. In its native Madagascar it makes a highly effective hedging plant which keeps out all intruders. With limited room it may be best to keep it healthy without encouraging too much spiny growth.

Site Grow in any type of soil that is free draining.

GROWING METHOD

Propagation Propagate from stem cuttings taken in late spring or early summer. This is also a good time to prune the plant if you need to control its spread, and the prunings can be then used as a batch of cuttings.

Feeding Slow-release fertilizer can be applied in spring, but this is unnecessary unless the soil is extremely poor.

Problems This plant is generally quite trouble-free.

FLOWERING

Season The long flowering period of this plant is technically from spring through to late summer. However, there are likely to be some flowers on it at almost any time of year in very warm conditions.

KALANCHOE BLOSSFELDIANA
Flaming Katy

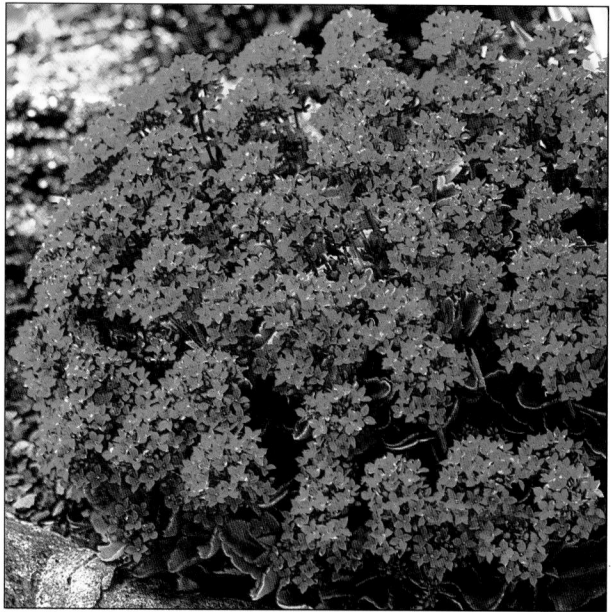

A MOUND OF BRIGHT RED FLOWERS all but obscures the foliage on this well-grown specimen of flaming Katy.

THREE VARIETIES of flaming Katy, bright pink, yellow, and red, are used here as bedding plants with white alyssum.

FEATURES

Partial Shade

This is familiar to most people as a potted flowering plant. It has scalloped, fleshy dark green leaves, often edged with red, and the original species has bright scarlet flowers. It has been extensively hybridized and there are now forms with flowers in white, yellow, and various shades of pink. There may be some color change or variation depending on aspect and climatic conditions, especially as flowers start to fade. Some of the bright pinks tend to revert to the species scarlet. A very easy-care pot plant for use indoors or out, this is also a fine summer plant for the garden. In ideal warm conditions in the glasshouse border where there is plenty of space, the stems will sprawl and take root, creating new plants.

KALANCHOE AT A GLANCE

K. blossfeldiana is a superb, reliable pot plant with heads of flowers to brighten up the glasshouse. 50°F min (zone 11).

Jan	/	Recommended Varieties	
Feb	flowering ✽	*K. beharensis*	
Mar	flowering ✽	*K. eriophylla*	
Apr	flowering ✽	*K. grandiflora*	
May	sow 🖐	*K. marmorata*	
Jun	/	*K. pubescens*	
July	transplant 🖐	*K. pumila*	
Aug	/	"Tessa"	
Sept	/	*K. tomentosa*	
Oct	/	"Wendy"	
Nov	/		
Dec	/		

CONDITIONS

Aspect In the garden, flaming Katy prefers morning sun and afternoon shade or light shade all day. Indoors, these plants should be given plenty of bright light.

Site Flaming Katy grows best in a well-drained soil that also contains plenty of decayed organic matter. In the open garden make sure that the soil has plenty of added drainage material so that the roots are not kept too wet for too long.

GROWING METHOD

Propagation Very easily grown from either leaf or stem cuttings, taken during the warmer months. The cuttings should be dried out for a few days before planting.

Feeding In spring, apply slow-release fertilizer or a small amount of pelletted poultry manure in the open garden. It does not respond well to soil that is too fertile.

Problems Flaming Katy is generally free of pests and disease.

FLOWERING

Season The true flowering time is late winter to spring, but commercial growers now force plants so that they are available in flower almost all year round. In the home yard, in the ground or in pots, they should bloom at the proper time. Flowers will generally give several weeks of bright color. After flowering, trim off spent flower heads.

LAMPRANTHUS
Lampranthus

THE PROLIFIC FLOWERING lampranthus makes great seasonal impact. It is ideal as groundcover or for a border planting in dry areas.

A BRILLIANT TAPESTRY of color is created in this mixed planting which highlights the use of lampranthus.

FEATURES

Sun

This group of plants is native to South Africa and is ideal for low-maintenance gardens in areas with low rainfall. Lampranthus is best known as a creeping or trailing plant used as a groundcover, but some species are bushier and more like shrubs. Stems of many species root as they spread, making them ideal for soil binding on banks or simply for stopping blowing sand or soil. The fleshy gray-green leaves are angled or cylindrical, and growing stems may reach 20in or so, but are more often around 12in. Individual plants may spread 12in or more in a growing season. The daisy-like flowers, which only open in sun, are shiny, brilliantly colored, and borne in such profusion that the foliage and stems are all but obscured.

LAMPRANTHUS AT A GLANCE

Prime ingredients for a dry seaside summer garden, offering big bright clusters of flowers. 5°F min (zone 7).

		Recommended Varieties
Jan	/	
Feb	flowering ✽	*Lampranthus aurantiacus*
Mar	sow ☞	*L. aureus*
Apr	/	*L. brownii*
May	/	*L. haworthii*
Jun	transplant ✎	*L. spectabilis*
July	flowering ✽	*L. s. "Tresco Brilliant"*
Aug	flowering ✽	
Sept	flowering ✽	
Oct	/	
Nov	/	
Dec	/	

Varieties

Species commonly grown include *Lampranthus aurantiacus*, with orange flowers; *L. roseus*, with pink flowers; and *L. spectabilis*, with purple to magenta flowers. Many lampranthus sold in nurseries are cultivars or hybrids bred for garden use.

CONDITIONS

Aspect These plants must be grown in full sun or flowers will not open.

Site Can be grown in almost any type of soil as long as it is well drained. Try to replicate its natural habitat which is mainly coastal South African near-desert conditions; dry and arid.

GROWING METHOD

Propagation Lampranthus are easily grown from stem cuttings taken from spring to fall. Species can be grown from seed sown in spring.

Feeding Fertilizing is generally unnecessary as plants grown "hard" usually flower better.

Problems Snails sometimes graze on foliage causing damage. Plants will not survive in heavy, poorly drained soil.

FLOWERING

Season Flowers appear through late winter and spring or during summer depending on the conditions and the species grown. Flowers may be orange, red, yellow, purple, cream, and many shades in between. In good conditions they will provide excellent, striking colors, especially the bright orange *L. aurantiacus*.

LEWESIA
Lewesia

LEWESIAS ARE SMALL, highly attractive plants that thrive, and really stand out, in a gravel garden or on a sunny slope. They should always be grouped together for maximum impact. The result is a good show of flowers in the spring and early summer.

FEATURES

Sun

The genus has 19 or 20 hardy species, and is exclusively American. The best place to grow them is on a well-drained south-facing slope, in a rock garden or even on a wall. They are low growing, often with bright flowers which are funnel shaped. The color range is mainly on the pink-magenta side, with some that are yellow and white. There are many excellent kinds to choose from, the best being *L. bracyhcalyx* which flowers in late spring and early summer, *L. cotyledon* which flowers from spring to summer in purple-pink, and *L. tweedyi* which flowers at the same time in a peachy-pink color. The best thing about lewesias is that they hybridize easily, and a collection of different plants should soon yield interesting offspring. The excellent Cotyledon Hybrids come in all colors from yellow-orange to magenta.

LEWISIAS AT A GLANCE

Marvelous small early season flowers in a wide range of colors. Excellent in small pots. Hardy to 5°F (zone 7).

Jan	/	Recommended Varieties
Feb	/	*Lewesia brachycalyx*
Mar	repotting 🖐	*L. cotyledon*
Apr	/	*L. c. Sunset Group*
May	flowering ✿	*L. Cotyledon Hybrids*
Jun	flowering ✿	"De Pauley"
July	/	"George Henley"
Aug	/	"Guido"
Sept	sow 🖐	*L. pygmaea*
Oct	/	*L. tweedyi*
Nov	transplant 🖐	
Dec	/	

CONDITIONS

Aspect These plants need full sun to thrive and if their position, the base of a wall perhaps, also reduces winter wet, all the better.

Site The soil must be fast draining, and to that end you must dig in plenty of horticultural sand or grit to provide the kind of conditions that the plant receives in its native California. Lewesias also enjoy reasonable fertility, with some added compost.

GROWING METHOD

Propagation Since lewesias freely hybridize, you do not have to do too much propagating. But you can propagate favorite colors by seed (except for the Cotyledon Hybrids) in the fall, or pot up offsets in the summer.

Feeding Plants grown outside in the border might benefit from an early-spring application of a standard plant feed. Pot-grown lewesias, perhaps on a show bench in an alpine house, benefit from a mild liquid feed in the early spring.

Problems A fatal problem for lewesias is excessive moisture during the winter, otherwise watch out for slugs and snails. Remove them by hand each night to prevent the plants from becoming an instant salad.

FLOWERING

Season Lewesias are highly valued for their smallish tubular flowers, generally about 1inch across. They are most highly visible when the plant is growing in a crack in a wall. In the garden they would be rather lost.

LITHOPS
Living Stones

THIS CLUSTER of intricately patterned Lithops turbiniformis *is livened by a bright yellow flower.*

LOOKING JUST LIKE A MOUND OF PEBBLES, a large number of living stones fills this shallow bowl.

FEATURES

Sun

Living stones, stone plants, pebble plants and flowering stone are just a few of the common names assigned to these curious succulents. They are so completely camouflaged that it would be very easy to miss them entirely unless they were in flower. In their native south-west and South Africa, they generally grow buried in sand with only the tips of their leaves exposed. Their bodies are composed of a pair of very swollen, fleshy leaves on top of a fused double column with a gap or fissure along their length. The upper surfaces of the leaves are variously patterned and textured according to species and conditions. These plants are best grown in small pots where their curious shapes and markings can be observed. They make an excellent display.

LITHOPS AT A GLANCE

Astonishing tiny succulents in a wide range of colors and patterns. Highly collectible. 41°F min (zone 11).

		Recommended Varieties
Jan	/	
Feb	/	*Lithops aucampiae*
Mar	sow ✍	*L. dorothea*
Apr	transplant ✍	*L. julii*
May	flowering ✽	*L. mormorata*
Jun	flowering ✽	*L. karasmontana*
July	flowering ✽	*L. salicola*
Aug	flowering ✽	*L. schwantesii*
Sept	flowering ✽	*L. turbiniformis*
Oct	/	
Nov	/	
Dec	/	

CONDITIONS

Aspect These plants should be grown in a position where there is full sun all day. They are best grown in pots on show benches in a glasshouse. They can cope with extreme heat, and attempts to shade them during the hottest part of the day are quite unnecessary.

Site The soil provided for living stones should drain very rapidly and small gravel or pebbles should be used as a mulch. Only use very fine pieces of gravel to set off the plants, though with some varieties it is tempting to camouflage them. It is amusing to let visitors see if they can distinguish between the real stones and the plants.

GROWING METHOD

Propagation These plants can be grown from divisions of offsets or from seed in spring to early summer. As living stones are not rapid growers, the clumps are best left undivided until they are about 4in across.

Feeding Half-strength soluble liquid plant food can be given every 4–6 weeks through the active growth period.

Problems Most problems arise from overwatering or a poorly drained growing medium. Look out for aphids when in flower.

FLOWERING

Season Flowers that emerge from the fissure of the living stone are daisy-like and yellow or white.

PELARGONIUM OBLONGATUM
Pelargonium

A SURPRISE ADDITION to a collection of succulents is Pelargonium obligatum. *It is a marvellous plant with a good display of flowers in late spring and early summer. It is also an excellent plant for maintaining a continuous show of flowers in a collection of succulents.*

FEATURES

Sun

It might sound odd to include a pelargonium in a group of succulents, but about 220 of the 280-odd species are just that. (Do not confuse them with the hardy outdoor geraniums.) *Pelargonium oblongatum* comes from South Africa, in particular the northern region of Namaqualand. It was not actually collected until the early 19th century, making it quite a recent pelargonium since most of the others were collected well before this. It has a 6in long oblong tuber (hence the Latin name), leaves with coarse hairs, and pale yellow flowers delicately feathered with maroon markings. It is definitely a collector's item, and could be the start of a collection with the orange-red *P. boranense* discovered in 1972 in Ethiopia, and *P. carnosum*, also from Namaqualand.

PELARGONIUM AT A GLANCE

P. oblongatum is a pelargonium with a difference. Try this species with delicate pale flowers. 36°F min (zone 10).

		Recommended Varieties
Jan	/	
Feb	/	*Pelargonium abrotanifolium*
Mar	/	*P. cucullatum*
Apr	repotting	*P. fruticosum*
May	flowering	*P. graveolens*
Jun	flowering	*P. papilionaceum*
July	/	*P. peltatum*
Aug	/	*P. radens*
Sept	sow	*P. tomentosum*
Oct	/	
Nov	transplant	
Dec	/	

CONDITIONS

Aspect The key requirement is bright sun; the more heat the better. In its native landscape it completely avoids any shade.

Site It needs to be grown in a pot where it can be properly cared for. Provide an open, free-draining compost. It is surprisingly easy to keep provided it is kept on the dry side while dormant in the summer. Active growth is, as in the southern hemisphere, from fall onward. Leaf drop is in the spring.

GROWING METHOD

Propagation While it can be raised from seed, as with all pelargoniums stem cuttings give an extremely high success rate. Take them in mid-fall, as new growth begins, and keep warm over winter avoiding a chilly windowsill. When mature, water well in the winter-spring period, with a reduction over summer.

Feeding Provide a mild fortnightly liquid feed when in full growth to boost the flowering show in the spring.

Problems Keep a check for aphids. They form tight packed clusters on the tasty young stems; spray accordingly. Once they take hold they can become quite a nuisance.

FLOWERING

Season There is a show of star-shaped flowers in the spring. After the bright blowsy colors with sharp reds and lipstick pinks of the more traditional pelargoniums like "Happy Thought" they come as a quieter, interesting surprise.

SEDUM
Stonecrop

A POPULAR CONTAINER or rockery plant, the rarely seen stonecrop Sedum adolphii *takes on pink to red colors in cold weather.*

STARRY FLOWERS with intricate centers are a feature of stonecrop species. Colors include white, pink, red, and yellow.

FEATURES

Sun

Partial Shade

Most plants in this large and diverse group of succulents are ideal for growing in pots, as well as in the garden where they can be used as edging, in rockeries, or tucked into walls. *Sedum spectabile* is often planted in perennial borders where other succulents may look out of place. *S. sieboldii* has spreading stems and rarely exceeds 6in in height. It has very attractive, almost round, blue-green leaves arranged in threes. It has a variegated green and gold form. *S. spathulifolium* forms a dense, low mat of small rosettes. Its variety "Cape Blanco" has a white bloom on gray-green or purplish rosettes. *S. adolphii* has yellowish green, star-like rosettes with reddish hues at times. Although capable of growing to 1ft, it is more usually 8in in height.

SEDUM AT A GLANCE

About 400 species, from annuals to shrubs, with a terrific range of shapes and strong colors. Most hardy to 5°F (zone 7).

		Recommended Varieties
Jan	/	*Sedum cauticola*
Feb	/	"Herbstfreude"
Mar	/	*S. kamtschaticum*
Apr	transplant 🌱	*S. morganianum*
May	/	"Ruby Glow"
Jun	/	*S. rubrotinctum*
July	flowering ❀	*S. spectabile*
Aug	flowering ❀	*S. s.* "Brilliant"
Sept	flowering ❀	*S. spurium* "Schorbuser Blut"
Oct	sow 🌱	"Vera Jameson"
Nov	/	
Dec	/	

CONDITIONS

Aspect Full sun is best for most species, but some will tolerate light shade.

Site The soil or potting mix must be very well drained for these plants, and the addition of organic matter for garden plants will give them a decent boost, but only moderate levels are required.

GROWING METHOD

Propagation Division of plants is best done in the early spring. Cuttings can be taken at any time during the warm summer months.

Feeding Slow-release fertilizer or a little pelletted poultry manure given in the spring. In the main, they are best left alone with only a little cutting away of dead stems. Keep a watch at night for attacks by slugs and snails, especially when new spring growth is appearing.

Problems These plants are usually trouble-free.

FLOWERING

Season Flowering time depends on species, but many flower in summer to fall. Flowers of several species are attractive to butterflies and bees, such as *S. spectabile* which has large flower heads of mauve-pink, rosy red, or brick red on stems 16–24in high in fall. *S. sieboldii* has starry pink flowers that appear in masses in late summer or fall. *S. adolphii* has starry flowers that are white. "Ruby Glow" is a low-spreader with dark ruby red flowers appearing from mid-summer into the fall, and "Herbstfreude" produces marvellous pink fall flowers that eventually turn copper-red.

Growing Orchids

GROWING ORCHIDS

Orchids make up one of the largest families of all the world's flowering plants. They occur on every continent except Antarctica and have a most remarkable diversity of habitat, form, and color. While the greatest number of orchids is found in tropical and subtropical regions, they can also be found in near-desert conditions, tundra, and in mountain country.

Orchid flowers vary in size from large, showy blooms the size of saucers to tiny treasures a fraction of an inch across. Some types of orchid are truly breathtaking in their beauty while others may be quite strange and almost ugly to some eyes, but all are simply fascinating. All orchids should have the spent flowers cut off once they are past their best. Due to the vast diversity of the orchid family, there can be orchids flowering in any season of the year. Some will adhere strictly to their season whereas others may bloom intermittently throughout the year.

LEFT: The fantastically flamboyant flowers of this Laeliocattleya Quo Vadis *"Floralia" are sure to brighten up any display.*

TYPES OF ORCHIDS

The vast majority of orchids in cultivation are epiphytes that grow on trees, but they use the tree as support only—they are not parasites. Other orchids are lithophytes that grow on rocks, or terrestrial types that grow in the ground. Orchids are further distinguished by the way they grow: monopodial orchids, mainly epiphytes, grow with a single stem and produce aerial roots, while sympodial orchids have a rhizome (running root) that produces a pseudobulb from which growth emerges. Many sympodial orchids are terrestrial. Orchids from cooler and more temperate regions are terrestrials but they can occur in warm regions too. Epiphytic orchids are found only in warmer areas.

HYBRIDS

Orchids in the wild hybridize occasionally, and so natural hybrids arise. In their natural situations orchids are pollinated by a range of creatures, including bees, wasps, birds, bats, and beetles. Today, commercial growers and enthusiasts making deliberate cross-pollinations are responsible for introducing many new orchid cultivars and varieties each year. There are now at least 100,000 registered orchid hybrids. Since the 1890s all orchid hybrids have been registered in what is now called the Orchid Hybrid Register run by the Royal Horticultural Society in London. This was previously known as Sanders' Orchid Hybrid Lists, named after the orchid enthusiast who began the daunting task of documenting the whole range of orchids and their parentage.

ORCHID CULTURE

For many years orchid culture was strictly the province of the rich and powerful, not only because of the cost of actually acquiring the plants but also because of the cost of building and heating structures for their successful cultivation. Nowadays special prize-winning plants are still expensive but the advent of plant tissue culture, which allows large numbers of plants to be propagated from very little material, has meant that plants are generally more affordable. There is now a huge number of enthusiasts growing orchids all over the world.

Today many orchids are cultivated commercially for the cut-flower trade. Apart from that, only the vanilla orchid, *Vanilla planifolia*, has commercial value. Its flowers grow on a vine and it is cultivated in tropical regions for its aromatic bean, used widely to flavour food.

BUYING ORCHIDS

For a long time the main source of orchids was plants collected in the wild. Now, with loss of habitat and deforestation of many of the world's tropical forests, it is important to conserve and protect what remains. Plants have been collected to the point of extinction in many regions and trade in endangered species is monitored by an international body, CITES or the Convention on International Trade in Endangered Species.

Orchids for sale in specialist or other nurseries are largely cultivars that have been multiplied and grown by commercial growers. If you are starting an orchid collection, you would be better off keeping to the hybrids. These are more plentiful, usually with bigger blooms, and are replaceable if accidentally killed. The species should only be grown by the skilled specialist.

Specialist nurseries have staff who are generally very knowledgeable and eager to help beginner growers, as well as catalogues to help with your choice of plants. Buy your plants while in bloom or choose ones you have seen in other people's collections or in catalogues. Choose the orchid that will give you the greatest pleasure.

Some orchid groups come in a wide range of colors and have an extended flowering season, and you may want to stay with certain color tones or concentrate on plants that flower at different times of the year. Do not let other people influence your choice.

Once you are "hooked" on orchids consider joining an orchid society as you will learn a large amount about the plants from other members. You will also have the chance to buy or exchange plants at the society's meetings.

GROWING CONDITIONS

Shade and ventilation
Orchids are not necessarily more difficult to grow than other plants if you give them the right climatic and cultural conditions. Many cool-growing orchids come from high mountain regions with frequent cloud and mist and they will not thrive in the tropics. Likewise, tropical

ANATOMY OF AN ORCHID

Flowers

Leaves

Backbulb

Pseudobulb

Root

orchids will die quite quickly if not given adequate heat and humidity. Some varieties can be grown in the open in summer. Often the dappled shade from taller trees is enough to provide good growing conditions, or you can build a shadehouse for protection from sun and wind.

Keeping orchids indoors

Orchids are becoming increasingly popular as houseplants, partly due to their high profile but also as modern hybrids, with greater tolerance and color ranges, are developed.

Modern homes often have a dry atmosphere, but as orchids prefer a humid environment, some moisture should be provided for them. By grouping orchids together or by growing them with other plants that like the same conditions, such as bromeliads and ferns, you can create a suitable microclimate for the plants. You can also stand your plants on humidity trays containing gravel or porous clay pellets. These retain moisture when plants are watered and gradually release it through evaporation, increasing the humidity. However, you should not just rely on the humidity trays to water your orchids—if roots take up too much water through the bottom of the pot they can rot. Instead, take the plants to a sink and water there, letting it flow through the pot and then leave to stand until fully drained before returning to the trays. Another way of creating the right atmosphere is to mist the foliage of the plants regularly with water, especially in warm conditions; this also helps to keep leaves dust-free.

Although orchids do not enjoy direct summer sunshine, good light must be provided if growing indoors. Place the plants near a window where they will get good light but not bright sun, which could scorch their leaves. If the plants are not getting enough light the leaves may become elongated and dark green in color, and they may even grow towards the light, becoming top heavy. Provide shade on a south-facing windowsill with a net curtain or a piece of greenhouse shade cloth to protect the plants.

Orchids enjoy a variety of room temperatures—some cool, some warm, some in between—so the correct room should be chosen for your plants. If the room is heated most of the time, the temperature not dropping below 60°F, then this is a warm climate. Although warm loving orchids will like this, do not place the plants too close to the heat source or else there is a danger of them overheating. Cooler growing orchids would prefer an unheated room indoors where the temperature drops to 50°F—if kept too warm flowering can be restricted.

Conservatories

A conservatory can make a good environment in which to keep orchids. Grow them together with other plants to create the right humid, shaded conditions.

Spraying water and misting is easier in a conservatory than indoors, providing a higher level of humidity and a better environment to grow the more challenging types. If possible, spray the floor with water daily, especially in warm weather. This will evaporate throughout the day, saturating the air. You could also make a water feature, such as a pool or waterfall, around which you can grow orchids and other moisture-loving plants.

Some heat may be required in the conservatory during the winter, as well as extra shading and ventilation in the summer. The same rules apply as with growing indoors regarding the temperature ranges; cool 50–68°F, intermediate 52–77°F, warm 60–77°F. Try not to mix orchids that need different temperatures.

The blooms of this Vanda x Ascocentrum *hybrid are perfectly shaped and finely speckled in red with rose pink margins.*

Shadehouses

If you have more than a few pots of cool orchids you may decide to house them in a shadehouse for the summer. You can make a simple structure of treated timber or galvanized piping covered with wooden or metal laths. Synthetic shadecloth providing 50 per cent shade is good, although a higher degree of shading may be required for some orchids. Laths or shadecloth will cut down the force of strong winds without making the atmosphere stagnant.

Greenhouses

Greenhouses should have roof vents that can be opened to allow hot air to escape and side vents to draw in cooler air. In very warm conditions wall or ceiling fans can keep the air moving if the humidity and heat become too high. In summer you will also need to provide shading.

Bringing orchids indoors

Many orchids can be brought into the house when in flower. For those with a short flowering period this is fine, but if the flowers last six to eight weeks it is best to cut off the flowers and enjoy them in a vase after about four weeks indoors, to avoid a setback in the plant's growth.

GROWING METHOD

Containers

Orchids can be grown in most types of containers, including terracotta and plastic pots, and baskets of wooden slats or wire. Most like to be grown in pots just

PROPAGATING A CYMBIDIUM ORCHID

1. Gently ease the plant out of its pot. Run a knife blade around the inside rim if necessary.

2. Use a sharp knife to sever the old leafless backbulbs from the younger growths.

3. Remove the old roots and leaf bases from the backbulb and pot it up. Label it clearly.

4. After several weeks or months a leaf shoot appears. It should flower in three years.

large enough to contain their roots. Many epiphytes will have aerial roots that will grow outside the container.
• Plastic pots are the most commonly used because of their relatively low cost, light weight, and ease of cleaning.
• Terracotta pots look attractive and have the advantage of "breathing," that is, allowing better aeration of the mix inside the pot. They are, however, more expensive, are heavy even before planting, dry out more quickly, and their porous surface can allow the growth of algae and slimes and the build-up of fertilizer salts.
• Hanging baskets are essential for some orchids, such as stanhopeas, as their flower spikes grow downwards. The baskets must be lined with soft material, such as coconut fibre, so that the flower spikes can penetrate it.

It is a good idea to have all your orchids in the same type of container, either plastic or terracotta. This will help you to settle on a watering programme and looks more professional.

Mounting an orchid on bark
Some orchids are happiest attached to slabs of cork or tree fern fibre. To grow on bark, either choose an orchid already established on a piece of cork, or transfer one from a pot, picking a plant that has a suitable habit. If the plant has a long, creeping rhizome between the pseudobulbs and is already climbing out of its pot then it is ideal. Plants with tightly packed pseudobulbs do not grow easily on bark.

Potting mixes
There are many types of mix for the cultivation of orchids, but they all have one thing in common: they are fast draining and provide good aeration for plant roots. Bark is the basis of most orchid composts, usually pine bark in various sizes and grades. It is used alone for some orchids or it may be mixed with charcoal, gravel, perlite, peanut shells, spent mushroom compost, coarse river sand, coir peat, and sometimes blood-and-bone or slow release fertilizer. Sometimes a mix of only two items, such as pine bark and charcoal, is used. In most cases the potting mix or growing medium is simply there to anchor the roots of the plant. Nutrients and water have to be applied regularly throughout the plant's growing season.

Watering
The amount of watering needed depends on the time of year, the weather, the growing mix and the type of orchid.

In hot weather, while plants are in active growth, most need daily watering or at least spray misting to maintain moisture around their roots. In conditions where humidity is low and the temperature high, plants may need spraying with water three or four times a day rather than watering around the roots. Damping down the floor of a glasshouse can lower the temperature and increase the humidity when needed.

In cool weather and when plants are completely or fairly dormant, some types are seldom watered. Many originate from regions with well-defined wet and dry seasons. In the wet season they make new leaves and pseudobulbs, in the dry season they rest from growth but produce flowers just before their new growing season begins. In most cases allow them to dry out between waterings. Other types may need watering about once a week during their rest period. Plants constantly watered while they are dormant are likely to collapse and die from root rots. No one can tell you exactly when to water: you have to learn by observation and experience. More orchids are killed through overwatering than anything else. Just remember orchids have growth periods and rest periods.

Feeding

As with water, apply fertilizer only to orchids in active growth. Plants can absorb nutrients only in solution and so regular watering helps orchids absorb the fertilizer. Never apply fertilizer to plants that are bone dry. Always water them first, apply the fertilizer, then water again. It is better to underfeed rather than overfeed: too much can burn and cause problems while giving less simply means that plants grow more slowly.

Garden centers stock fertilizers specially formulated for orchids, some to promote vegetative growth and others to promote flowering, the idea being that you switch from one to the other at a certain stage in the growing season. Other fertilizers are sold as complete plant foods. Soluble plant foods can be applied through the growing season or slow release granular fertilizers applied as new growth begins and again after three or four months. Fertilizers high in nitrogen are best used to promote growth while those high in potassium and phosphorus will help promote flowering. Details of fertilizer ratios are listed on the sides of packets or bottles.

Orchids growing on slabs should be fertilized by spraying with dilute soluble fertilizer. Spray when damp and the weather overcast so that no burning occurs.

PROPAGATION

Many orchids are propagated in nurseries by tissue culture, allowing a huge number of plants to be grown from a small amount of the parent plant. Plants grown from seed are also cultured in flasks. This is useful for sending plants to other countries as the plants have been grown in sterile conditions and will therefore pass quarantine regulations. They are transferred from flasks to individual pots when large enough to survive.

At home, most orchids are propagated by division of existing plants, by removing offsets that have some developed roots or by growing new plants from dormant pseudobulbs. Methods vary and the technique best suited to each group is outlined in the plant entries. Division is best done straight after flowering, as new growth appears.

WHAT CAN GO WRONG?

Orchids are remarkably trouble free. Adequate spacing of plants, good ventilation and good cultural practice should minimize problems. Remove dead or decaying material to keep plants clean and looking good. Isolate any sick plants from the rest and wash your hands and disinfect any tools before handling healthy plants. If you have to use chemicals for pest or disease control, do not spray buds or flowers as they may be distorted. It is usually the newest, most tender parts that are affected.

Pests

• Snails can chew holes in buds and flowers. Remove them by hand or place a few pellets on top of the pots to catch them before they reach the flowers.
• Vine weevils also chew holes in buds and flowers. They are hard to control but some insecticidal dusts may be able to help.
• Several types of scale insect may attack a range of orchids. Small infestations can be gently washed or wiped off with a damp cloth. For heavy infestations spray with an insecticide.
• Red spider mites may be prevalent in warm, dry weather. They can make the foliage mottled and dull looking. Overhead watering and misting the undersides of the leaves helps to discourage them. However, you may actually need to dust or spray the plant with a registered miticide.

Diseases

• Fungal leaf disease. There is a large range of fungal leaf diseases that may attack various orchids, especially in overcrowded or very humid conditions. It may be quite difficult to control them without resorting to a fungicide. Improving ventilation and spacing out the pots should help. Avoid overhead watering and try not to water late in the day if you are plagued with fungal problems.
• Virus disease. There are a number of virus diseases that may attack orchids and there is no cure. Symptoms are variable and may include pale greenish-yellow spots, streaks or patterns of brown, black concentric rings, or other patterns along the leaf blade. Serious orchid growers will generally destroy plants affected by virus disease. If you do not want to do this you must isolate the affected plant. Virus diseases may be transmitted through sap-sucking insects such as aphids, which must be controlled, and you must wash your hands and disinfect tools after working on a plant suspected of being diseased.
• Bulb or root rots are caused by organisms found in the potting medium. The organisms flourish when conditions are overwet. Rotted pseudobulbs or roots must be cut away cleanly from the healthy ones and all the old mix washed off. Scrub and disinfect the pot before refilling it with fresh potting mix and replacing the plants. Make sure the mix is very well drained; do not overwater. Some fungicides, used as drenches, can help control the problem.

MOUNTING ORCHIDS ON BARK

WHY GROW ON BARK?

Many of the orchids grown in cultivation are in nature tree-dwelling, or epiphytic. They use the trees in the rainforests as a perch on which to grow, enabling them to grow nearer to the light. Orchids that grow in this way often have a creeping habit and produce a lot of aerial roots. These are two characteristics that make them difficult to grow in a pot. They are better mounted on a piece of cork bark and allowed to grow across its surface.

PREPARING YOUR PLANT

First you will need to select the plant that you are going to mount. It must have quite a creeping habit of growth with an elongated rhizome between the pseudobulbs. A plant that has a tight cluster of pseudobulbs will not fit well and will have to be regularly remounted. The advantage of growing orchids on bark is that they can remain there for many years without having to be disturbed. If the plant outgrows the first piece, it can be trained on to another piece attached to the original.

The plant should have a healthy active root system to make it easier for it to quickly establish itself in its new position. When moving any plant, wait until it is just starting its new growth as this is when new roots are formed and the plant will suffer the least disturbance.

Choose a piece of cork bark or even a tree branch on which to mount your orchid that will give it enough room to grow for at least a few years. You may even want to mount several plants on the same large piece of wood, to make an interesting feature in your greenhouse.

Other equipment that you will need includes some sphagnum moss and coconut fiber, which will combine to form a moist area around the roots. If you cannot find these particular items then a mixture of similar moist but fibrous substances will do. Some plastic coated wire or fishing line should be used to attach the plant to the bark. After a period of time, once the plant has become established and rooted itself on to the bark, the wire will become obsolete and can be removed if wanted.

MOUNTING THE ORCHID

Take the plant out of its pot, clean away the old compost and trim any dead roots—it will produce new ones once established. Carefully wrap the moss and fiber mixture around the base of the plant, where the roots will weave their way into it, and position the plant on the bark. Secure it with some wire and, while holding it in place, tighten the wire or fasten the fishing line. Take care not to let the wire cut into any part of the plant. It is best to pass the wire in between the pseudobulbs, across the rhizome and away from the new shoots to avoid damage. Attach a wire hook to the top of the bark so you can hang it up in your greenhouse. Make sure it is sprayed or dunked in water daily to prevent drying out.

Remove the orchid from its pot, clean the compost from the roots and trim back a little. Mix moss and fiber together to form a pad on which to place the plant to provide a moist surface for the roots.

It is important to choose a type of plant, preferably with a healthy root system, that will lend itself to being mounted on bark. You will also need plastic-coated wire, pliers, a piece of cork bark and some sphagnum moss or coconut fiber.

Wrap the base of the plant with the moss mixture and position on the bark. Tie a piece of plastic-coated wire around the base of the plant, avoiding shoots or roots, and tighten just enough to keep the plant in place. Attach a hook and hang where it can be regularly sprayed.

CONVERTING A FISH TANK

AN INDOOR GROWING ENVIRONMENT

A house can be too dry an atmosphere to keep orchids successfully. This is especially true for the small growing ones that tend to dry out more quickly than the plants in larger pots. An interesting and fun way of growing them in the home is to convert an old, disused aquarium into a miniature orchid house. A humid atmosphere will be created inside the glass tank, preventing the plants from becoming too dry. The orchids can be mixed with companion plants that enjoy the same conditions as long as they stay small so the tank is not outgrown quickly.

TOP RIGHT An old, disused fish tank makes an ideal growing environment for miniature orchids. Choose some plants which will stay small and not quickly outgrow the space. Companion plants that will also remain small are helpful to the overall environment.

MIDDLE Making sure that the tank will not leak, fill the base with a layer of expanded clay pellets. These absorb the moisture sprayed on them which then gradually evaporates around the plants creating a humid atmosphere. Add some decorative pieces of wood, bark, or rock to create an interesting feature of your indoor garden.

BELOW Lastly, include the finishing touches of the plants including maybe some miniature ferns and foliage plants to complement the orchids. Regularly spray the plants and pellets in the tank to create humidity and remove the plants when you are actually watering them to prevent a build up of too much water in the base. Place near a window and use some shade cloth to cover the tank if too much bright sun is available. A lid is not essential but can be used.

GREENHOUSE CULTIVATION

WHY USE A GREENHOUSE?

To get the best out of your orchids it is advisable to set up a greenhouse especially for them. This means that you can get the growing conditions exactly right. Within this greenhouse you can regulate the temperature and humidity of the air throughout the year and determine how much light, water, and ventilation the plants receive. A better environment can be created and so a wider range of orchids can be grown in a greenhouse than in the home.

POINTS TO CONSIDER

You may wish to convert an existing greenhouse or start afresh with a newly built structure. Whatever you decide, it is important that the greenhouse is positioned in the right place. As orchids prefer a shady environment, it is best to position your greenhouse in a shaded part of the garden, near to deciduous trees as these will provide shade in the summer and let in the light in winter when they have lost their leaves. Some extra shade may be needed during summer though, when the sun is at its brightest, as orchid leaves can be easily scorched. Use paint shading on the glass or netting, which can be removed for the winter, or a combination of the two depending on your own greenhouse's situation. The orchids should be kept in dappled sunlight to gain the right amount of light; if too dark then their growth and flowering will be inhibited.

Most traditional greenhouses have glass in their roofs but there are more modern materials available now that need less maintenance, including twin or triple thickness polycarbonate sheeting. This is a rigid plastic sheeting that is very strong and acts as an extremely good insulator, cutting down on the heating requirements for the winter months. It does not matter what type of roofing material you decide to use, but it is important that you make sure that the greenhouse is well ventilated. On hot days, the temperature can rise dramatically and will quickly suffocate the plants inside if there is not enough ventilation available in the greenhouse. Side panels that open in the walls and roof ventilators should be incorporated into your greenhouse so that they can be opened on hot days to give plenty of air movement.

PREPARING YOUR GREENHOUSE

Heating is very important for orchids during the colder months of the year. Cooler growing orchids enjoy a drop in temperature but even they will not tolerate temperatures much below 50°F. Warmer varieties need a few more degrees, a minimum of 60°F, so need an extra heat supply. This can be supplied by an electric, gas, or oil fuelled greenhouse heater. Take the advice of a good supplier to choose the right equipment for your particular set up. A maximum/minimum thermometer is also a very useful piece of equipment as it allows you to keep a check on what the temperature is dropping to at night.

Benches and shelving are ideal ways to arrange your plants at the height that is comfortable for you and your plants. Large plants can be stood lower down, or even on the floor, while smaller pots can be placed on the benches or shelves. If space is at a premium then use the area above the shelves to hang plants up too. This is ideal for orchids that like a bit of extra light and they, in turn, will give a little extra shade to the plants growing below them. If your orchid collection is just beginning then they may have to share their space with other plants already living in your greenhouse. This is fine as long as they all need the same conditions. If the orchids are not compatible with your other plants then it may be necessary to partition the greenhouse with transparent, UV-treated polythene to form two or more separate growing environments. This is also a good idea if you plant to grow a mixed collection of some warm and some cool growing orchids.

CREATING THE RIGHT ATMOSPHERE

One of the best things about growing orchids in a greenhouse is that you can create a humid atmosphere in there for them. Spray the floor of the greenhouse regularly with water, especially in warm weather to keep the temperature down and the air moist. Another way of creating humidity is by growing other types of shade loving plants underneath the benches, such as ferns. This all adds to the overall atmosphere and the orchids will grow better because of it.

Spraying and watering can be done with a watering can, but as your orchid collection grows it may take many trips to fill up the can. A more convenient alternative is to install a hose pipe system that can then reach all parts of the greenhouse, maybe even with a watering lance attached to the end of it. This will allow you to regulate the amount of water that you give to each individual plant; as well as giving the choice of a variety of spraying and misting head attachments.

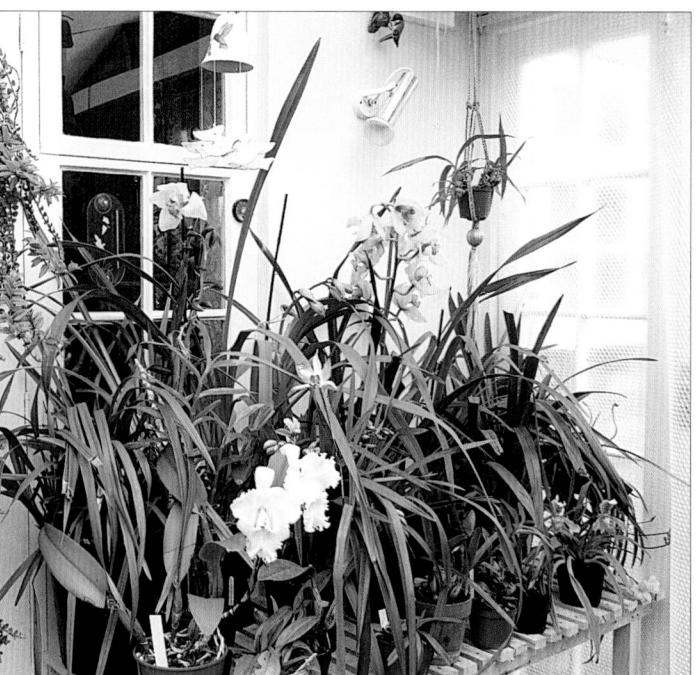

Brighten up an ordinary conservatory with a few orchids. They will enjoy the light, airy environment as well as added moisture from daily misting. Some winter insulation may be necessary as seen here with the bubble polythene covering the door.

ABOVE If you have the space then why not create your very own walk-through tropical paradise with impressive foliage plants accompanying the orchids which can live happily in this habitat. Climbing plants can create shade but be careful that they do not harbor pests.

RIGHT Make the best use of your greenhouse by creating maximum bench space and also using the space above the plants to hang some orchids in baskets and hanging pots. Foliage plants placed underneath the benching help with the humidity as well as the use of a humidifier, seen here on the floor.

ANGULOA
Tulip orchid

The Anguloa clowesii *is known as the "Tulip Orchid" because of its amazing cup-shaped flower which has a rocking lip inside it.*

A strong scent and incredibly waxy blooms are typical of this family as is seen in this Anguloa virginalis.

FEATURES

Terrestrial

This fascinating orchid—known as the tulip orchid due to its tulip-shaped flower—has another common name, cradle orchid. This names describes the lip inside the cup-shaped flower which rocks back and forth when the bloom is tipped. The genus *Anguloa* is closely related to the lycastes with which they can interbreed, making an *Angulocaste*. The species originate from Colombia, Venezuela, and Peru and are mainly terrestrial plants. Large, broad leaves are produced in the summer months from the new growth, but in the fall these die off as the plant goes into its deciduous rest for winter. Its dark green pseudobulbs will then lie dormant until the following spring.

Another feature of this genus is that the long-lasting flowers are strongly scented, often similar to a liniment fragrance.

CONDITIONS

Climate	The anguloas need cool conditions with a winter minimum of 50°F, and summer maximum of 86°F.
Aspect	Due to the soft, annual leaves, shade is required in the summer.
Potting Mix	A medium grade bark is ideal with some finer grade bark or peat mixed in.

GROWING METHOD

Propagation	It is quite a slow growing orchid, often making just one pseudobulb a year, so will not increase in size enough to divide easily. Back bulbs will sometimes re-grow if removed and potted up separately.
Watering	While the plant is in its winter rest, and is leafless, the compost should be kept dry. Watering can be resumed at the start of the new growth in spring. While it has leaves the plant should not dry out. In the fall the new pseudobulb will have been completed and the leaves will turn brown and drop off. Stop watering the plant at this point.
Feeding	Plants will benefit from regular feeding while in growth so that the new pseudobulb can develop in the short growing season.
Problems	As long as the compost is kept dry during winter then no problems should occur. Avoid water collecting inside new growth.

FLOWERING SEASON

Late spring to early summer.

ANGULOA AT A GLANCE

Better for the experienced grower. The flowers last a long time and are hightly scented. Will reach 24in.

Jan	rest	Recommended Varieties
Feb	rest	*A. cliftonii* (yellow with red markings)
Mar	water and feed	
Apr	water and feed	*A. clowesii*
May	flowering, water and feed	*A. uniflora* (white)
Jun	flowering, water and feed	*A. virginalis*
July	water and feed	
Aug	water and feed	
Sept	water and feed	
Oct	rest	
Nov	rest	
Dec	rest	

ASPASIA
Aspasia species

This charming, compact plant is easy to grow and will re-bloom very easily, even as a houseplant in a room with a little warmth.

The pretty, star-shaped flowers of Aspasia lunata *nestle around the base of the attractive, leafy plant. Several single flowers are produced.*

FEATURES

Epiphytic

This is a compact and flowering orchid perfect for the beginner. *Aspasias* are a small group of orchids, the genus containing only about ten different species. These originate from the tropical Americas, and are found growing from Nicaragua to Brazil over quite a widespread area. Although not a common orchid, it is actually quite easy to grow, increasing freely in size and producing flowers regularly and easily. Its habit is fairly compact, the height of the soft-leafed pseudobulbs reaching only around 6in, making it ideal for a small collection. Due to its naturally epiphytic nature, the plant has a creeping habit with an elongated rhizome connecting the pseudobulbs. This means that it quickly outgrows pots and is in need of annual re-potting. However, with orchids that have a tendency to do this, the plant is often happier out of the pot than in it.

CONDITIONS

Climate	Slightly cold sensitive so prefers a minimum temperature of 54°F in winter, up to 86°F in summer.
Aspect	Has pale, soft leaves so a little shade in summer will prevent paling or scorching.
Potting Mix	A medium grade general bark potting mix.

GROWING METHOD

Propagation	This orchid readily produces new growths and so multiplies quite quickly. Therefore, the plant can be divided every few years if required but will do well to be left alone to grow into a specimen plant, which will produce many flowers at once.
Watering	The plant does not always follow a strict seasonal pattern so keep it simple by watering more frequently only when in active growth and reducing this to a minimum when not.
Feeding	Use a higher nitrogen feed when applying in the growing season, a weak solution every two to three waterings.
Problems	If cultural conditions are suitable then it should have no specific problems.

FLOWERING SEASON

Varies but mostly spring and summer. Flower buds emerge from the base of the new growth and stay around plant's base.

ASPASIA AT A GLANCE

Easy to grow. Compact, attractive plant up to 5in high. Flowers, often in succession, 1¼in across.

Jan	rest		Sept	water and feed
Feb	rest		Oct	rest
Mar	flowering, water and feed		Nov	rest
Apr	flowering, water and feed		Dec	rest
May	flowering, water and feed			
Jun	flowering, water and feed		**Recommended Varieties**	
July	flowering, water and feed		*A. epidendroides* (brown petals with a purple and white lip)	
Aug	flowering, water and feed		*A. lunata*	

BIFRENARIA
Bifrenaria species

Bifrenaria tyrianthina is an unusual species to grow and is stunning with its large pink blooms on upright stems.

The more commonly seen B. harrisoniae *has a curiously furry texture and a contrasting purple lip. It is a popular and easy orchid to grow.*

FEATURES

Epiphytic

The charming and popular bifrenarias were once classified as cymbidiums, and show a resemblance to them in their flower shape. These orchids, however, mostly come from Brazil but can also be found widely distributed throughout Panama, Trinidad, northern South America, and Peru. *Bifrenaria* has always been a popular orchid for beginners and proves easy to grow and flower in the amateur's cool mixed collection. It is a compact growing plant with long-lasting, heavily textured flowers sitting around the base of the plant. As a bonus the flowers are sweetly scented. They are epiphytic orchids in nature, growing on the higher branches of trees in the South

American rain forests. It is possible to grow these orchids quite successfully in a cool to intermediate greenhouse, conservatory, or even on a windowsill with other companion plants. If in a greenhouse, the plants could be grown in a hanging basket near the light coming through the roof.

CONDITIONS

Climate	A temperature range of 50–77°F, with ventilation in the summer months.
Aspect	Good light all the year round but provide some shade in the hottest months.
Potting Mix	A general medium grade bark compost is ideal with good drainage qualities.

GROWING METHOD

Propagation	This orchid is a fairly slow grower so it could be a few years before it is ready to be divided. Best to leave as a specimen plant for as long as possible. May propagate from back bulbs that are removed and are potted up separately at potting time.
Watering	Keep compost on the dry side during the winter months when the plant is not growing. With the onset of the new growth in the spring resume watering to get the new pseudobulb plumped up by the fall.
Feeding	The plant responds to a light feeding during the growing season. Use a higher nitrogen plant food every two or three waterings.
Problems	No specific problems known if the cultural conditions are suitable.

FLOWERING SEASON

Long-lasting through spring and summer.

BIFRENARIA AT A GLANCE

Dark green broad foliage reaches 8in from pseudobulb. Single flowers with bearded lip low at base.

Jan	rest	Nov	rest
Feb	rest	Dec	rest
Mar	flowering		
Apr	flowering, water and feed	Recommended Varieties
May	flowering, water and feed	*B. atropurpurea* (dark purple-brown)
Jun	water and feed	*B. harrisoniae*
July	water and feed	*B. tyrianthina*
Aug	water and feed		
Sept	rest		
Oct	rest		

BLETILLA
Chinese ground orchid

The slightly ridged pattern on the lip of this Chinese ground orchid is very pretty when viewed at close quarters.

Reliable and easy-care, clumps of Bletilla striata multiply readily. They enjoy filtered sun in most conditions.

FEATURES

Terrestrial

Bletilla is one of a small group of terrestrial orchids from China, Japan, and Taiwan. This is a very easy orchid to cultivate. It is deciduous, dying back to ground level in the fall or early winter. It grows from a pseudobulb that looks like a corm, each producing about three bright green pleated or folded leaves up to 16in long. Flowers are slightly bell shaped, cerise-purple to magenta, and carried on one slender stem—there may be 10–12 blooms on a stem. The lip of the flower is beautifully patterned in white and cerise. There is a white form, "Alba," but it is not as vigorous. The blooms usually last a few weeks if conditions are good.

BLETILLA AT A GLANCE

Easy to grow for cool conditions similar to an alpine house. Bright purple flowers give a good winter show.

Jan	flowering, rest	Oct	rest
Feb	flowering, rest, re-pot	Nov	rest
		Dec	rest
Mar	flowering, water and feed, re-pot		
Apr	flowering, water and feed, re-pot	Recommended Varieties	
May	water and feed	*B. striata*	
Jun	water and feed		
July	water and feed		
Aug	water and feed		
Sept	water and feed		

CONDITIONS

Climate This is a very cool growing orchid and will thrive in a greenhouse if it is kept frost-free, at a minimum temperature of 41°F. Can be placed outside in summer and even planted in the ground in frost-free areas.

Aspect This orchid needs to be planted in a sheltered spot with dappled shade. It must have protection from hot sun in the middle of the day.

Potting mix Needs well-drained mix or soil with plenty of humus so that it can retain moisture during dry periods.

GROWING METHOD

Propagation Congested clumps of plants can be divided in late winter to early spring. Replant the pseudobulbs at the same depth as they were previously and remove dead leaves.

Watering Needs plenty of regular watering during hot weather through spring and summer. When the leaves begin to yellow off, decrease watering and then stop as the plant dies down.

Feeding Apply slow release fertilizer in spring or give liquid plant food at half strength every two or three weeks during the growing season to help increase growth.

Problems No specific problems are known. Foliage burns if exposed to too much hot sun in summer and plants will rot in a poorly drained medium. Keep the plant dry when not in leaf.

FLOWERING SEASON

Flowers between late winter and spring.

BRASSIA
Spider orchid

The spider orchids are fascinating with their long, thin petals and unusual green coloring, seen in this species, Brassia verrucosa.

This larger flowered hybrid, Brassia Rex has the characteristic sweet fragrance that these orchids are known for.

FEATURES

Epiphytic

This group of epiphytic orchids are extremely popular. The attractive leafy plants are easy to keep and flower well when given plenty of light. They are known for their spidery flowers, which give them their common name. The blooms are long lasting, staying on the plant for many weeks and giving off a very pleasant fragrance. There have been many hybrids developed between the species, giving extra size and quality to the flowers, for example *B*. Edvah Loo. Brassias have also been used to make hybrids with other genera such as miltonias and odontoglossums, to produce miltassias and odontobrassias, which inherit the star-shaped flowers and showy appearance of the parent. Grow the brassias in hanging baskets near the light to achieve maximum flowering potential. In this environment they also produce prolific aerial root growth.

CONDITIONS

Climate	They thrive in a cool or intermediate temperature; 50–54°F at night in winter to 68–77°F in summer.
Aspect	Brassias need light to encourage flowering, so place in a south facing aspect with a little shade from the brightest sun.
Potting Mix	Medium or coarse mixture of bark chippings.

GROWING METHOD

Propagation	The plant should produce several growths from one pseudobulb when it reaches a mature size, which will increase the size of the plant quickly. It can then be divided. Make sure divisions are not too small otherwise they will not flower well. Keep a minimum of four to six pseudobulbs.
Watering	Keep the compost moist all the year round. Watering can be reduced in winter months to prevent compost waterlogging. Regular watering while in growth and spraying of leaves and aerial roots will benefit the plant.
Feeding	Only apply fertilizer when the plant is in growth. Use a water-soluble feed and pour through the compost as well as adding it to the water used for misting leaves and roots.
Problems	Brassias may not flower well if not enough light is provided, especially in winter.

FLOWERING SEASON

Generally late spring and summer.

BRASSIA AT A GLANCE

Easy to grow. Fragrant flowers on long spike, up to 20in. Compact plant, 6–8in high.

Jan	rest	Oct	rest
Feb	rest	Nov	rest
Mar	rest	Dec	rest
Apr	rest		
May	flowering, water and feed	Recommended Varieties	
Jun	flowering, water and feed	*B. giroudiana*	
July	flowering, water and feed	*B. maculata*	
		B. verrucosa	
Aug	flowering, water and feed	*B.* Edvah Loo	
		B. New Start	
Sept	rest	*B.* Rex	
		(all green/yellow)	

BULBOPHYLLUM
Bulbophyllum species and hybrids

Bulbophyllum *Jersey has a wonderful rich red coloring and an unusual shaped flower inherited from its parents.*

This is B. lobbii, *an orchid that is well known for its lip that rocks back and forth when the flower is moved.*

FEATURES

Epiphytic

The genus *Bulbophyllum* is one of the largest in the orchid family and includes some of the most extraordinary looking flowers in the orchid kingdom. It is closely related to, and often classified with, the genus *Cirrhopetalum*. They are extremely widespread, being found in South East Asia, Africa, Australia, and the tropical Americas. The habit and appearance of the plants and flowers are as variable as their place of origin. Some have tiny flowers that you need a magnifying glass to see; others have large, unusually shaped, showy blooms. A characteristic of many of these orchids is a curiously rocking lip, which attracts certain pollinating insects to the flowers. Some are also fragrant, however this is not always pleasant. The orchids try to attract carrion flies, so they send out the scent of rotting meat. They make good specimen plants, growing well in, and over the edge of, hanging baskets, in which they can stay for years.

CONDITIONS

Climate	Due to the widespread nature of these orchids, there are both cool and warm growing species available, so check with your supplier when making a purchase. Most of the Asian types are cool, whereas the African species tend to be warmer.
Aspect	They can take a lot of light so grow well in a hanging basket near the greenhouse roof.
Potting Mix	Need an open medium or coarse grade bark with even some perlite or larger perlag mixed in to make it free draining.

GROWING METHOD

Propagation	Most will grow quickly into large clumps with multiple growths so can be divided after only a few years. Alternatively leave growing in a basket for many years until the orchid completely envelops the basket.
Watering	Let bulbophyllums dry out in between waterings and take care not to overwater them when in growth. If the pseudobulbs start to shrivel then they are too dry. By growing them in a coarse bark in open baskets they should not stay too wet.
Feeding	Give feed only when in growth, and apply this as a foliar feed by spraying it on the leaves as well as pouring through the compost. A weak dilution every two or three waterings is ideal.
Problems	No specific problems are known if the cultural conditions are suitable.

FLOWERING SEASON

Depends on the species or hybrid grown.

BULBOPHYLLUM AT A GLANCE

Strange appearance, with a variety of shapes and sizes, from 1¼–12in high. Flowers ⅛–3in across.

Jan	rest	Recommended Varieties
Feb	rest	B. careyanum "Fir Cone Orchid"
Mar	rest, re-pot	
Apr	rest, re-pot	B. graveolans (cluster of green and red flowers at the base)
May	water and feed, re-pot	
Jun	water and feed	B. lobbii
July	water and feed	B. macranthum (purple)
Aug	water and feed	B. purpureorachis (brown flowers creeping up a spiral stem)
Sept	water and feed	
Oct	rest	
Nov	rest	B. vitiense (small pink)
Dec	rest	

CYMBIDIUM
Cymbidium species and hybrids

Masses of small blooms clustered on a flower stem are a feature of many of the miniature cymbidium hybrids.

Potted cymbidiums are at home outdoors in the summer. Plants in flower should be displayed indoors in a cool position.

FEATURES

Terrestrial

Epiphytic

Cymbidiums are probably the most widely cultivated of all orchids. They originate in temperate or tropical parts of north-western India, China, Japan, through south-east Asia, and Australia. There are now thousands of cultivated varieties. These hybrids have flowers classed as standard size (4–6in across), miniature (about 2in across) or intermediate. The leaves are strap-like, upright, or pendulous, and 20in or more in length in standard growers. The foliage of the miniature plants is narrower and shorter, in keeping with the overall dimensions of the plant. Cymbidiums have a wide appeal as the flowers are decorative and long lasting.

CYMBIDIUM AT A GLANCE

Popular and widely grown. Flowers vary from 1½–4in. Easy to grow in light, cool conditions.

Jan	rest, flowering	Nov	rest, flowering
Feb	rest, flowering, repot	Dec	rest, flowering
Mar	flowering, water and feed, re-pot		Recommended Varieties
Apr	flowering, water and feed, re-pot		*C. erythrostylum* (white)
			C. lowianum (green)
May	water and feed		*C. traceyanum* (brown)
Jun	water and feed		*C.* Amesbury (green)
July	water and feed		*C.* Bouley Bay (yellow)
Aug	water and feed		*C.* Gymer (yellow/red)
Sept	rest, flowering, water and feed		*C.* Ivy Fung (red)
			C. Pontac (burgundy)
Oct	rest, flowering		

Flowers The range of flower colors covers every shade and tone of white and cream, yellow and orange, pink and red, brown and green, all with patterned or contrasting colors on the lip. Flowers are carried on quite sturdy stems standing well clear of the foliage. As many are in bloom in winter they can give a special lift to the season. Many have flowers that will last six to eight weeks.

Choosing Choose plants both by flower color and time of blooming. With careful selection you can have a *Cymbidium* in bloom every month from early fall through to late spring. Selecting plants in flower will tell you exactly what you are getting. Some orchid nurseries sell tissue cultured mericlones of these orchids as young plants: these are much cheaper but you will have to wait three to four years for them to reach flowering size. Backbulbs, if available, are also an option although these too take up to four years to flower. Buying seedlings is also cheaper and you will have the thrill of their first flowering, not knowing in advance what the flowers will be like. The parent plants may be displayed or the nursery should be able to give you an idea of the likely color range, which extends through the spectrum.

CONDITIONS

Climate Ideal conditions are humid year round, with winter temperatures not reaching much below 46–50°F and summer temperatures that are generally below 86°F. It is advisable to place the plants outside in summer. To initiate flowering many, but not all, require a distinct drop between their day and night temperatures.

Pink-flushed white flowers are popular with many Cymbidium *growers. Note the lovely spotting on the lip.*

Aspect
These plants will not flower if they do not get sufficient light. They will grow in the open with dappled shade from trees or with only morning sun in summer, but they can actually take full sun almost all day during the winter. A shadehouse with 50 per cent shade is suitable in summer. If you can see that your plants have very dark green leaves then they aren't getting enough light and are very unlikely to flower. These plants need good ventilation and protection from strong winds and rain when placed outside. In winter, place them in the lightest position available within a cool greenhouse, conservatory, or in an unheated, light room.

Potting mix
Mix or soil must be very free draining. Many species in their habitat grow in hollow branches of trees, in decayed bark and leaf litter. Hybrids can be grown in aged, medium-grade pine bark, or in pine bark plus coir peat, bracken fibre, charcoal, or even pieces of foam. Plants need to be anchored and supported but must have free drainage and good aeration around the roots. Prepared, special orchid composts are satisfactory, especially if you only have a few plants. Cymbidiums must always be potted with the base of the pseudobulb either at, or preferably just above, the level of the compost.

Containers
Make sure that there are enough drain holes in the container and, if not, punch in more. Cymbidiums are quite vigorous growers and if placed in 8in pots they will probably need potting and maybe dividing every two or three years. It is best to pot plants into containers that will just comfortably accommodate their roots. They can then be potted on into the next size when necessary. Plants that have filled their containers and need dividing are best left until spring, and then divided into sections with no fewer than three pseudobulbs per division. If divided soon after flowering in spring the plants will then have a full six months growing season ahead of them to settle into their new pot.

GROWING METHOD

Propagation
Grow new plants from backbulbs (older, leafless bulbs). These may look dead but will regrow if they are detached from the younger growths when you are dividing plants after flowering. Clean old leaf bases and trim off any old roots. Plant the bulbs into small individual or large communal pots, about one-third of their depth into a mixture of coir peat and bark. Keep damp but not wet. Once good leaf and root growth are evident, pot up into normal mix. Plants grown this way generally flower after about three years.

Watering
Frequency of watering is determined by the time of year. The mix should be moist but not wet. Always give enough at one watering for water to pour through the mix. Plants may need watering daily in summer or only every few days if conditions are wet. Water about once every one to two weeks in winter.

Feeding
Feeding can be as easy or as complicated as you like. You can simply give slow release granular fertilizers during the growing season. Or, alternatively, you can use soluble liquid feeds regularly through spring and summer. Some growers like to use high nitrogen fertilizers during spring, switching to special orchid foods or complete fertilizers that are high in phosphorus and potassium in summer. Some of these are applied monthly, others in half strength more often. It is important to follow label recommendations and not to overdo it.

Problems
Unfortunately cymbidiums are prone to some diseases, quite apart from the normal range of pests. Virus disease can be a problem and so maintain strict hygiene by disinfecting hands and tools to avoid it spreading. Bulb rots can also be a problem if potting mixes contain too much fine material, which impedes drainage. Fungal leaf spots can occur in crowded or very wet conditions. Keep an eye out for snails, slugs and aphids as your plants come into bud because they can quickly ruin your long-awaited flowers. They will attack both buds and long spikes.

Support
Light cane or metal stakes should be used to support the flower spikes as they develop. Carefully insert the support beside the developing spike and use plastic coated tie-wire or string to tie the spike as often as needed to train it into position.

FLOWERING SEASON

In bloom through fall, winter and spring with just a few summer varieties. Plants in flower can be brought into the house for decoration. Moving a plant in bud from a cool greenhouse to a warm room can make the buds drop so wait until the flowers are open and set until you move it. The cooler the plant is kept, the longer the flowers last, which is on average six to eight weeks.

Cut flowers
Professional growers cut the flower spikes a week after all flowers on the spike are open to prevent any check in the plant's growth.

5.

4.

1.

3.

CYMBIDIUMS

1 Cymbidium *Red Beauty* x *Gorey is a standard variety of the* Cymbidium, *which can reach 3¼ft in height, with tall sprays of rich pinkish-red flowers.*

2 A compact type of Cymbidium, *this beautifully colored* C. *Mini Dream "Gold Sovereign," has an unusual shade of butter yellow with yellow markings on the lip too, making a striking combination.*

3 Large flowered standard variety Cymbidium *Sleeping Nymph "Perfection" is sought after for its striking combination of apple-green petals and sepals and yellow marked lip, which is lacking the usual red pigment.*

4 These orchids can reach a fair size if they are left undivided and are of the larger growing type, as this C. Havre des Pas shows. They will produce a better show if they are allowed to grow into a larger specimen.

5 For the more modest space available, a compact variety such as C. Red Valley "Brilliant" will give a marvellous show, while taking up less space.

2.

DENDROBIUM
Dendrobium species and hybrids (Asian)

A dark blotch of color in the throat is a feature of many types of dendrobium, including this Dendrobium nobile.

One of the finest yellow orchids is Dendrobium fimbriatum. The beautiful, finely fringed lip is greatly admired.

FEATURES

Epiphytic

By far the largest number of *Dendrobium* species come from sub-tropical and warm regions of Burma, the Himalayas, Thailand, China, and Malaysia. Some of the most commonly cultivated are the varieties of species such as *D. nobile*. These are known as soft-cane dendrobiums. Many Asian species have long, cane-like growth which can grow up to 3¼ft tall, although many others are within the 12–18in range. Some are very upright while others have pendulous growth so they must be grown in hanging baskets. The species described here can be grown in a cool glasshouse where night temperatures do not fall much below 50°F.

DENDROBIUM AT A GLANCE

Popular as houseplants and flowers as cut blooms. Hybrid varieties good for beginners. Various sizes and types.

Jan	rest	Recommended Varieties
Feb	rest, flowering	*D. aphyllum* (pink/cream)
Mar	water and feed, flowering	*D. chrysanthum* (yellow)
Apr	water and feed, flowering	*D. densiflorum* (golden)
May	water and feed	*D. fimbriatum* (yellow, dark center)
Jun	water and feed	*D. nobile* (dark pink)
July	water and feed	*D.* Christmas Chimes (white, dark center)
Sept	water and feed	*D.* Red Comet (dark pink)
Oct	rest	
Nov	rest	*D.* Stardust (pink/white)
Dec	rest	

Types Some species of *Dendrobium* are evergreen while others are deciduous. The latter lose their leaves during their dormant period, which coincides with their dry season. Both types are epiphytic and are found growing on branches of trees or sometimes on mossy rocks in their habitat. The plants will easily grow into large clumps over years, producing a very spectacular show.

Flowers A few dendrobium varieties produce single flowers but most produce large, showy sprays containing numerous flowers. The color range is vast. White, cream, yellow, pale green, pink, red, maroon, purple, and magenta are all represented in this colorful group. Some have flowers of one single tone while many have contrasting blotches of color in the throat or on the lip of the flower. Many are strongly fragrant.

D. nobile *D. nobile* is a soft-cane stemmed type that can grow from 12–30in high. The species is pink with deeper cerise tips on the petals and a dark maroon blotch on the lip. The numerous cultivars of this species include many with similar tonings of lavender, purple, and red, but some have pure white petals with yellow or dark red markings on the lip.

D. chrysanthum This is an evergreen orchid with canes that often grow over 3¼ft long. It has a pendulous habit and so is best grown where its stems can hang naturally. Simulating its natural growth this way seems to promote more consistent flowering. Flowers are deep golden yellow with deep red blotches in the lip on a graceful, arching stem.

D. aphyllum *D. aphyllum* (syn. *D. pierardii*) is a deciduous species that prefers to grow in a hanging basket. Its canes can grow to over

The deep gold throat of this softly colored pink and white hybrid of Dendrobium nobile *provides an exciting contrast.*

In cool, humid conditions Dendrobium nobile *and its cultivars will produce a profusion of flowers.*

3¼ft and its delicate, pale flowers can best be enjoyed at eye height. The flowers are pale mauve to pink with the palest creamy yellow lip.

D. fimbriatum Another yellow-flowered species of *Dendrobium* that grows with tall, upright canes sometimes reaching over 3¼ft. It is evergreen and the flowers are produced on the tops of canes one year or more old. Flowers may appear even on older canes that no longer bear leaves. This flower is golden yellow and the lip is delicately fringed. The variety *oculatum* is a richer, deeper gold with a deep maroon blotch in the center of the lip. These dendrobiums can be grown either in heavy pots that have pebbles added in the base to balance the top weight of the canes, or in a hanging basket.

CONDITIONS

Climate The preferred conditions depend on the species. Cool types grow in glasshouses or conservatories, whereas warm types will live on a windowsill indoors.

Aspect These dendrobiums tolerate partial shade to full sun depending on the species. Those with red, bright pink, and yellow flowers tolerate much more sun than those with white or pale green flowers.

Potting mix Free-draining mixes must always be used. These may contain coarse bark, tree-fern fibre, sphagnum moss, perlite, and even pebbles if extra weight is needed to stabilise the containers. These plants should never be overpotted. Use a container that will comfortably hold the plant roots with a little room to spare.

GROWING METHOD

Propagation All grow from divisions of the existing plants once they have filled their pots. Divide after flowering. Some species produce offsets or aerial growths which can be removed from the parent plant once roots are well developed. Older stems of deciduous species containing dormant buds can be laid on damp sphagnum moss and kept moist until roots develop. This may take several months.

Watering During active growth in warm weather mist or water regularly, two or three times a week. Give only occasional watering in winter; keep those from monsoonal areas dry at this time.

Feeding Feed only during the growing season and not during fall or winter. Use regular applications of soluble orchid fertilizer.

Pruning Restrict pruning to removal of spent flowering stems. Do not cut out old canes of species such as *D. fimbriatum* which flower on older stems unless they have shrivelled, turned brown or died off.

Problems Chewing and grazing insects, such as snails, slugs, caterpillars, and weevils, can all damage these plants but they are a particular nuisance on the flowers. Plants grown in glasshouses may be troubled by mealybugs and mites, as well as fungal diseases if there is poor ventilation.

FLOWERING SEASON

Most flower in spring but the range may be from late winter to early summer depending on growing conditions and the species.

DENDROBIUM
Dendrobium species and hybrids (Australian)

This pretty cultivar of Dendrobium speciosum *has been given the name "Aussie Sunshine." Individual flowers are finely shaped.*

Lighting up this garden in late winter to spring are the long cream to yellow trusses of Dendrobium speciosum.

FEATURES

Epiphytic

There are about seventy Australian species of *Dendrobium* but only a few are cultivated outside Australasia. These epiphytic and lithophytic orchids can have cane-like or thick swollen pseudobulbs, but sometimes the pseudobulbs are not visible at all, as in *D. linguiforme*, which creeps over rocks producing small, fleshy, ribbed foliage. Most of these orchids have rather leathery, sometimes very rigid, leaves, and plants not in flower excite little interest. These dendrobiums are extensively grown by amateurs and professionals alike and most people recognise the "rock lily," *D. speciosum*.

DENDROBIUM AT A GLANCE

Normally three years old before flowering. Flowers last up to six weeks. Strap-like leaves vary from green to silver.

Jan	grow on, reduce watering	Sept	reduce watering
Feb	grow on, reduce watering	Oct	flowering; keep frost free
Mar	re-pot, feed	Nov	flowering, reduce watering
Apr	remove and pot on offsets	Dec	flowering, reduce watering
May	remove offsets, mist foliage		
Jun	flowering, mist and water		Recommended Varieties
July	flowering, mist and water		*D. kingianum* (pink)
Aug	reduce watering		*D. speciosum* (yellow)
			D. Delicatum (white)

Flowers The majority of the Australian *Dendrobium* species have small individual flowers, although these may be clustered on long sprays. An exception to this is the Cooktown orchid, *D. bigibbum*, floral emblem of the state of Queensland, which has larger flowers in rosy pink to purple.

Cut flowers Most Australian species do not make good cut flowers and blooms may last only three weeks or so on the plant. The flowers of *D. bigibbum*, however, are long lasting and cut well. They are often included in mixed bunches sold as Singapore orchids.

D. speciosum The rock lily or king orchid, *D. speciosum*, is possibly the species most often grown. It has very thick, fairly long, slightly curved pseudobulbs and large, stiff, dark green leaves. It grows on rocks, logs or in hanging baskets, and clumps may spread in time to over 3¼ft across. In its habitat it sometimes forms large clumps high up in trees. It is very easy to grow and its long, arching sprays of cream to yellow flowers have a light honey scent. Flowering, which usually occurs from late winter through to early spring, can vary from year to year.

D. kingianum The pink rock orchid, *D. kingianum*, is the species of *Dendrobium* most extensively hybridized. Numerous named cultivars are available from specialist growers and some amazing colors are being produced. The true species has short, thickish pseudobulbs topped with leathery leaves and produces little rounded, pink, or mauve flowers. There are also forms that have white or almost purple flowers. This is another easy-care orchid which is very appealing.

The Cooktown orchid, Dendrobium bigibbum, *is at home in the tropics, thriving in constant warmth and humidity.*

Rosy purple is one of the naturally occurring color variations in the species Dendrobium bigibbum.

D. Delicatum Probably one of the most attractive of all these orchids is the hybrid *D.* Delicatum which is a cross between *D. kingianum* and *D. speciosum*. It has long, slender pseudobulbs and produces an abundant display of upright flower spikes that may be white or palest pink, sometimes with a darker lip.

D. gracilicaule A vigorous grower often found naturally on trees that don't shed their bark. It has long, narrow, cane-like pseudobulbs and produces cream to golden yellow flowers in early spring. This is a good orchid to establish in a basket. A natural hybrid of this species and *D. speciosum* is D. *x gracillimum*, which is among the most prolific and free flowering of all these orchids, producing masses of creamy flowers each year.

D. falcorostrum Not so easy to cultivate but well worth the effort is the beech orchid, *D. falcorostrum*, which is becoming very scarce in the wild. Its preferred natural host is the Antarctic beech, *Nothofagus moorei*, which has been overcleared. This beautiful orchid has creamy white, scented flowers in short sprays that develop on top of thickish pseudobulbs that may be 6–10in long.

D. linguiforme The pseudobulbs are not visible in the tongue orchid, *D. linguiforme*, which creeps over rocks. It produces small, fleshy, ribbed foliage and abundant sprays of feathery, cream flowers appear in spring.

CONDITIONS

Climate Preferred climate depends on the species. Some grow best in the warm, others prefer cool to intermediate conditions.

Aspect Most prefer dappled sunlight, although some tolerate full sun.

Potting mix Many dendrobiums are best grown on slabs, logs, old stumps, or rocks. In containers the mix should be very coarse bark, crushed rock and tree-fern fiber.

GROWING METHOD

Propagation Most are best propagated by dividing clumps straight after flowering. Those that produce offsets from the tops of canes can have the offsets gently detached and replanted once they have developed a good root system of their own.

Watering Most of these dendrobiums prefer regular, abundant watering during spring and summer. In the cooler months water very occasionally. Dendrobiums from tropical areas with defined wet and dry seasons should be kept quite dry in their dormant stage to prevent early growth starting.

Feeding Feed with complete soluble fertilizers during spring to early summer or with slow release granules or water-soluble feed. Do not feed at all during fall or winter.

Pruning Restrict pruning to the removal of spent flower stems.

Problems Most of these plants are fairly trouble-free, although damage can be caused by slugs, snails, caterpillars, and weevils chewing flowers and new leaves. Fungal leaf diseases may attack plants that are grown in conditions where humidity is high. This is a real problem in glasshouses, especially if the ventilation is poor.

FLOWERING SEASON

Flowering time depends on species and regional growing conditions. Most flower in late winter to spring.

DISA
Disa species and hybrids

The pale flower of this lovely Disa *cultivar clearly shows the nectar-bearing spur. Red-flowered cultivars dominate most collections.*

Buds and flowers at various stages of development ensure a long flowering season for this Disa *hybrid.*

FEATURES

Terrestrial

Only one species of *Disa* is common in cultivation: *D. uniflora*, which has generally bright scarlet flowers. Flowers are mainly scarlet with red and gold venation but some golden yellow ones are found in their natural habitat. This terrestrial genus can be difficult to cultivate successfully as many species come from habitats that have soil that is permanently damp but never waterlogged. These conditions are not very easy for the orchid grower to duplicate. Disas produce a rosette of basal leaves from which a flowering stem over 24in high will emerge. Flowers are large, 3–5in across and borne in groups of mostly three or more blooms.

DISA AT A GLANCE

Unusual and challenging orchid preferring moist conditions. Bright flowers are 2–3in across.

Jan	water	Oct	water
Feb	water	Nov	water
Mar	water	Dec	water
Apr	flowering, water		
May	flowering, water	Recommended Varieties
Jun	flowering,water and feed	*D. uniflora*
July	flowering,water and feed	*D.* Inca Princess
Aug	flowering,water and feed	
Sept	water	

Origin

This group of orchids is mainly native to tropical and southern Africa and is also found in Madagascar.

CONDITIONS

Climate *Disa* needs a frost-free climate. Most are cool growers and tolerate temperatures down to about 41°F; 77°F is the preferred upper limit.

Aspect Grows best in partial shade with some sun early in the morning. In total shade plants will grow but not flower.

Potting mix The mix or soil should be moisture retentive but never soggy. A suitable mix might contain perlite, coconut fiber peat, chopped sphagnum moss, and medium-fine bark.

GROWING METHOD

Propagation Divide plants when re-potting. This should be about every two years after flowering, never more than three years apart.

Watering Avoid watering the foliage if possible. Allow water to soak up from below by standing pots in a container of water. Never allow the pots to dry out but greatly decrease water in cool weather.

Feeding Apply soluble liquid fertilizer, at a quarter to half the recommended dilution rate, while plants are actively growing.

Problems No specific problems are known if cultural conditions are met.

FLOWERING SEASON

Generally from early summer to fall, but this can vary.

ENCYCLIA
Encyclia species

Commonly known as the cockleshell orchid, the shape of the lip that gives Encyclia cochleata *its name can be seen clearly here.*

The scarlet encyclia is E. vitellina, *well known and sought after for its vibrant orange coloring.*

FEATURES

Epiphytic

Another very easy and popular group of orchids. The genus of *Encyclia* was originally classified with the epidendrums so are closely related and require very similar growing conditions. Most of the encyclias are found in Central and South America, but some inhabit Florida and the West Indies, as in the case of *E. cochleata*. This orchid was the first tropical epiphytic orchid to flower in the United Kingdom. Originally discovered in the Americas, it was brought back by the plant hunters to the Royal Botanic Gardens at Kew in London. It has the common name of cockleshell orchid, due to the shape of its upturned, almost black, lip, and is the national flower of the Central American country of Belize. The orchid will flower for months on large specimen plants. Most of the *Encyclia* species are green in color but *E. vitellina* is bright orange. Many of the green-flowered species are also sweetly scented.

ENCYCLIA AT A GLANCE

Very easy to grow; ideal in most situations. Compact plant, 8–10in high, flowers 1¼–2¼in across.

Jan	rest	Oct	rest
Feb	rest	Nov	rest
Mar	rest	Dec	rest
Apr	flowering, water and feed		
May	flowering, water and feed	Recommended Varieties
Jun	flowering, water and feed	*E. cochleata*
July	flowering, water and feed	*E. lancifolia* (cream)
Aug	flowering, water and feed	*E. mariae* (green/white)
Sept	water and feed	*E. pentotis* (cream/green)
		E. radiata (pale green)
		E. vitellina (orange)

CONDITIONS

Climate	The most popular are cool growing needing a temperature range of 50–77°F.
Aspect	A light position is required, out of direct sunshine in summer to avoid scorching. Grow well in hanging baskets in a shaded greenhouse, or as windowsill plants.
Potting Mix	An open and free-draining bark mix is good; aerial roots are often made outside the pot.

GROWING METHOD

Propagation	Can be divided and propagated after growing into a large plant over a number of years. To ensure flowering the next year, do not make individual plants too small.
Watering	Frequently water during summer—its main growing season. When not in growth it should be partially rested; just a little water is required to keep the pseudobulbs plump.
Feeding	Feed only when the plant is in active growth when it can gain full benefit from the added nutrients. Apply both in the water poured into the pot and also in the spray given to the leaves and aerial roots.
Problems	No specific problems are known if cultural conditions are suitable.

FLOWERING SEASON

Can vary but mainly the summer months.

EPIDENDRUM
Crucifix orchid

A bright pink cultivar of Epidendrum ibaguense *flowers well each year but is not as prolific as the orange-flowered species.*

Tough, reliable and flowering over many months, the crucifix orchid makes a fine garden plant in tropical countries.

FEATURES

Epiphytic

Terrestrial

This genus and its species is a large and varied group that originated in tropical America. Growth can be rampant and needs thinning out every couple of years. Plants in pots may need support. This orchid will grow without almost any attention but rewards good culture. The species *E. ibaguense* flower is orange and yellow but there are many cultivars with flowers in shades of red, pink, mauve, yellow, or white. Individual flowers are fairly small but they are carried in groups on top of reedy canes that can be 6½ft or more tall. The fleshy leaves are leathery in texture and yellowish green, especially in full sun.
E. ibaguense is one of the most familiar of the *Epidendrum* species, also known as *E. radicans* or its common name of crucifix orchid, so called because of the cross shape of the lip, when turned upside down.

Habit The crucifix orchid has a tall, reed-like habit of growth so requires some space to grow to its full potential.

CONDITIONS

Climate Grows best in an intermediate greenhouse, with a minimum of 54°F in winter.
Aspect Tolerates full sun to dappled shade. Where this orchid is grown in more tropical climates, as a bedding plant in garden borders, it is very tolerant of changing conditions and rough treatment.
Potting mix The mix or soil must be able to drain rapidly but any mixture of coarse bark, crushed rock, gravel, compost, or commercial potting mix is suitable.

GROWING METHOD

Propagation Is very easy to propagate as it produces plantlets with aerial roots on the older canes. Detach them and pot up when they are sufficiently developed during the warmer months. Large clumps can also be divided.
Watering Thrives if given regular watering during the warm months of the year and less frequent waterings in winter.
Feeding Give soluble liquid fertilizer every three or four weeks during warm weather or dress the roots with aged cow manure. In warm conditions feed year round.
Problems Trouble-free but fungal leaf diseases can occur if the weather is too cool and wet. Succulent new leaves are often eaten by slugs.

EPIDENDRUM AT A GLANCE

Easy to grow. Repeat flowers all year round. Can reach 5ft in height but flowers are only 1¼ in across.

Jan	rest, little water	**Recommended Varieties**
Feb	rest, little water	
Mar	increase water, re-pot	*E. cristatum* (brown spotted)
Apr	water and feed	*E. ibaguense* (red/yellow)
May	water and feed	*E. ilense* (pale cream)
Jun	water and feed	*E. pseudepidendrum* (green/orange)
July	water and feed	
Aug	water and feed	*E. wallissii* (lilac/brown)
Sept	water and feed	*E.* Pink Cascade (pink)
Oct	reduce water	*E.* Plastic Doll (green/yellow)
Nov	reduce water	
Dec	rest, little water	

The hybrid E. Plastic Doll flowers easily on a very young plant and continues to bloom prolifically over the years.

Epidendrum Pink Cascade is almost never out of flower; don't cut off the old flower stem as this will produce buds over and over again.

FLOWERING SEASON

Can flower almost all the year round.

OTHER EPIDENDRUMS TO GROW

This is a very large group of orchids with many varied species and hybrids available. They are easy to keep and are very rewarding. The plants have long flowering seasons, and some are sequential flowerers, producing more and more buds time after time throughout the year. All need similar cultural requirements to those of the crucifix orchid.

E. ilense This is a very tall growing species from the Tropical Americas, reaching up to 6½ft in height. The leafy cane-like pseudobulbs are semi-deciduous, losing their leaves after a year or so. The curious flowers come in bunches from the top of the newest and oldest pseudobulb, the old ones reflowering for many years. The blooms are creamy yellow and around ¾in across; the lip, which hangs down, is strangely frilled into lots of tiny threads giving a bearded effect. Flowers can appear on very young plants only 6in high.

E. pseudepidendrum Perhaps a confusing name but this is yet another different *Epidendrum*. This species will grow with a similar habit to the *E. ilense* and they grow well when positioned together. This one has a very hard, waxy flower with bright green petals and sepals, swept back from the brilliant orange lip, making a striking combination.

E. Plastic Doll This is a primary hybrid between the two species mentioned previously and it inherits qualities from both. It flowers on very young plants, and has a waxy yellow flower with a frilled lip. When larger, the plant should re-flower continually to give a perpetual show. The plant can grow tall in time as well but generally it is a very easy and rewarding orchid to keep.

E. Pink Cascade Another primary hybrid of *E. ilense* but this time it has been crossed with another species, *E. revolutum*. The Pink Cascade orchid tends to hold more flowers on the stem at one time. As the name suggests, its flowers are bright pink in color. Do not cut the flower stems on this orchid, as they will flower again and again from the top of the leafy cane.

Epidendrum cristatum grows very tall and in a large clump. Each stem produces a head of highly patterned flowers.

ERIA
Eria species

A larger growing member of the Eria *family is* E. sessiflora *with its tall spike of dainty cream flowers that are sweetly scented.*

For more of a challenge try growing erias in a cool to intermediate greenhouse or conservatory, among other similar orchids.

FEATURES

Epiphytic

This is quite a large genus, containing about 500 species, but not many species are grown in cultivation or in amateur collections. They are quite variable in their plant size and habit, but the flowers tend to be of a similar size and shape. *E. sessiflora* is quite a large growing species with a very tall spike of many creamy white flowers; *E. coronaria* in contrast has a short habit with a short swollen stem in place of a pseudobulb but has very similar cream blooms. Many of the erias are scented as well. The family of erias are originally found growing as epiphytes on the trees in the rain forests of the Malaysian Peninsula, the islands of New Guinea and Polynesia as well as some parts of Australia. The plants often have to undergo a wet and dry season in the high altitude monsoon areas so their regime of watering and resting follows this pattern.

CONDITIONS

Climate	These plants enjoy a cool to intermediate temperature range of 54–83°F from winter to summer.
Aspect	Protect the plants from the bright sun with some shading during summer to prevent the foliage from getting too red or even burnt.
Potting Mix	A medium grade of bark will be adequate and you may want to mix in some general potting compost to help keep them moist during the main growing season.

GROWING METHOD

Propagation	These orchids are not easily propagated by division as they grow and multiply slowly.
Watering	Take care not to over water during the winter when the plant is at rest. Give water once a week during the growing season, keeping the compost moist at all times.
Feeding	The plant will respond to added fertilizer during the growing season. Use a soluble fertilizer every two weeks, spraying on the leaves and pouring into the pot.
Problems	No specific problems are known if cultural conditions are suitable.

FLOWERING SEASON

Quite short-lived. Blooms for three to four weeks in mainly winter and spring seasons.

ERIA AT A GLANCE

An unusual genus and mostly for the more experienced grower. Charming, small flowers and variable plant size.

Jan	flowering, rest	
Feb	flowering, rest	**Recommended Varieties**
Mar	flowering, rest	*E. coronaria* (cream)
Apr	flowering, rest	*E. javanica* (yellow)
May	flowering, water and feed	*E. pubescens* (yellow with hairy stems)
Jun	water and feed	*E. rosea* (pink flush)
July	water and feed	*E. sessiflora* (white)
Aug	water and feed	
Sept	water and feed	
Oct	rest	
Nov	flowering, rest	
Dec	flowering, rest	

GONGORA
Gongora species

The Gongora's pendant spikes of curious shaped flowers are a constant source of amazement, as seen in this G. bufonia.

These are easy orchids to grow and are an ideal addition to any cool collection. This G. truncata *is a fragranced example.*

FEATURES

Epiphytic

This fascinating and simple to grow group of orchids originate from the American tropics. They are epiphytic, growing into large clumps over the years. The distinctive ridged pseudobulbs produce pendant flower spikes of varying lengths. The flowers that are held along the length of the thin stem are curiously shaped; the column is elongated and the sepals swept back from it almost like the wings of an insect. This is designed to attract a particular flying insect for pollination. Gongoras are relatively easy to grow in the mixed collection as well as being free flowering and usually scented.

GONGORA AT A GLANCE

Ideal for beginners and growing indoors. Plants are 4–8in in height and flower spikes reach 1ft 4in.

Jan	rest	Oct	rest
Feb	rest	Nov	rest
Mar	water and feed	Dec	rest
Apr	water and feed		
May	flowering, water and feed	Recommended Varieties
Jun	flowering, water and feed	*G. bufonia* (cream/red)
July	flowering, water and feed	*G. galeata* (orange/ brown)
		G.maculata (yellow/red)
Aug	water and feed	*G. quinquinervis* (brown/cream)
Sept	water and feed	*G. truncata* (pink/cream)

Although flowers only last a few weeks, a mature plant will often produce many flower spikes in succession over the summer months. These orchids are best grown in a basket or net pot.

CONDITIONS

Climate	The gongoras are cool growing, needing a drop to 50°F in winter. Around 60°F in summer is acceptable.
Aspect	These orchids have broad, soft green leaves so can easily burn in the sun. Good light in winter and dappled shade in summer.
Potting Mix	Needs an open free-draining potting material such as plain bark chippings.

GROWING METHOD

Propagation	Once grown into a substantial specimen can be divided up into smaller plants. Only three pseudobulbs are needed for re-flowering.
Watering	As the plants grow in open baskets, they will dry out quickly so regular watering is necessary. Immerse the whole plant in water if need be, particularly in summer.
Feeding	Only feed when the plant is in active growth, during spring or summer. You can put fertilizer into the water that the plant is being dunked into and leave it for several minutes to let the plant benefit.
Problems	No specific problems are known if cultural conditions are suitable.

FLOWERING SEASON

Usually summertime—very free flowering.

LAELIA
Laelia species

The queen of laelias is Laelia purpurata *and this variety,* carnea, *is especially beautiful with its subtle salmon-colored lip.*

A cooler growing species is L. gouldiana, *which has long-lasting large pinkish purple flowers on a long, upright stem.*

FEATURES

Epiphytic

There are many different *Laelia* species, coming mostly from Central and the more northern parts of South America. The showy blooms and relative ease of culture make it popular with beginners. It is a varied genus; the size of the plant can vary from 2in high, up to 28in high, and the flower sizes for these species are similarly different. Colors range from pure white, yellow, lavenders, and pinks to deep purples. They are very closely related to the *Cattleya* family and have been extensively interbred to produce the beautiful *Laeliocattleyas*. *L. purpurata* is perhaps the most well known, being called the queen of laelias. It is the national flower of Brazil and has more cultivated varieties than any other orchid. The laelias have thick, leathery leaves on the top of usually elongated pseudobulbs. Flowers come from inside a sheath at the apex of the newest pseudobulb.

CONDITIONS

Climate	There are both cool and intermediate growing laelias so check the label. The cooler ones need to drop to 50°F in winter, while others need a slightly warmer temperature of 54°F minimum.
Aspect	Give good light all year round, this is important to encourage flowering. Avoid direct summer sun, which can scorch leaves.
Potting Mix	Use a very open, coarse bark mix to make sure the roots are never too wet.

GROWING METHOD

Propagation	Although a little slow growing, some laelias will readily propagate after a few years of growing into a larger sized mature plant. Some will shoot from old back bulbs that can be removed at potting time and grown on in a warm, humid place.
Watering	Make sure the compost dries out in between waterings. In winter keep dry unless the pseudobulbs start to shrivel.
Feeding	Only apply a liquid feed and mist foliage when the plant is actually in growth.
Problems	No specific problems are known if cultural conditions are suitable.

FLOWERING SEASON

Most of the laelias are summer flowering, or produce from new pseudobulb in fall.

LAELIA AT A GLANCE

Long-lasting, bright flowers, some fragranced. Plants come in a variety of sizes, from 2–18in.

Jan	rest
Feb	rest
Mar	rest
Apr	rest, re-pot
May	flowering, water and feed
Jun	flowering, water and feed
July	flowering, water and feed
Aug	flowering, water and feed
Sept	water and feed
Oct	rest
Nov	rest
Dec	rest

Recommended Varieties

L. anceps (lavender)
L. fallalis (lavender)
L. briegeri (yellow)
L. harpophylla (orange)
L. pumila (purple)
L. purpurata (various: white to purple)

LEPANTHOPSIS
Lepanthopsis species

A truly miniature orchid, Lepanthopsis astrophorea *"Stalky," has flowers only a few millimetres across but is seldom out of bloom.*

Although small in stature, a mature specimen will grow into a larger plant measuring 3–4in across if left undivided for years.

FEATURES

Epiphytic

This is one of several orchid genera, including *Pleurothallis* and *Dryadella*, that is truly miniature. The plant size reaches only 1¼in at the most and the flower stem is about the same again. The plant produces a tiny spray of these exquisite little flowers, which measure only ⅛in across. The flowers are a vivid deep purple and star-shaped, which makes them a little easier to pick out, however you may still need a magnifying glass. The unusual orchid, *L. astrophorea* "Stalky," is just one of a genus of around 25 different species widely found in Central America. This genus was originally classified with the *Pleurothallis* until it was proclaimed to be different enough to be given its own name. It grows well with other members of the "Pleurothallid Alliance" including masdevallias. It can be grown for many years in the same small pot, as it will not outgrow it very easily and will stay almost perpetually in flower.

CONDITIONS

Climate	This orchid is mostly cool growing but will tolerate slightly warmer intermediate conditions if necessary.
Aspect	Provide good shade for this little plant so it does not dehydrate too much.
Potting Mix	As it is growing in a tiny pot and has a very fine root system, use a fine grade of bark with a little perlite and sphagnum moss.

GROWING METHOD

Propagation	Will propagate quite easily once you have let the plant grow on for several years to fill the pot. For best results, though, keep as one plant; it won't take up that much room.
Watering	Small pots tend to dry out more quickly than large ones so water regularly to keep from drying out. Mist the foliage also.
Feeding	Give the plant a little weak orchid feed during the summer when it is in its more active growth.
Problems	No specific problems are known if cultural conditions are suitable.

FLOWERING SEASON

Can be all the year round on a mature plant; generally does not have a strict flowering season. Long lasting for such tiny flowers.

LEPANTHOPSIS AT A GLANCE

Miniature, only 1¼in high but small flowers bloom continually. Best in sheltered, controlled environment.

Jan	water	Recommended Varieties
Feb	water	*L. astrophorea* "Stalky"
Mar	water, re-pot	
Apr	water, re-pot	
May	water	
Jun	water and feed	
July	water and feed	
Aug	water and feed	
Sept	water	
Oct	water	
Nov	water	
Dec	water	

LYCASTE
Lycaste species and hybrids

This orchid, with its delicate pink and white flowers, is derived from Lycaste skinneri, *known to some as the queen of lycastes.*

Large leaves and flowers on single stems are features of the Lycaste *species. This orchid shades prettily from dusky rose to white.*

FEATURES

Epiphytic

Terrestrial

This group of mostly epiphytic orchids originate in cloud forests in Central America and northern parts of South America. Most are found in the forks of trees but some grow in pockets of leaf litter on rocks. Lycastes can grow into clumps with large leaves and they need space to show to advantage. They produce robust pseudobulbs from which the leaves emerge in the spring. In fall the leaves will die off. Flowers are borne singly on leafless stems but each pseudobulb may produce several stems. In the most commonly grown species *Lycaste skinneri* (syn. *L. virginalis*) the flowers may vary from pure white to rose pink. There are other species and numerous hybrids with green, yellow, or even deep red flowers. Some beautifully shaded or mottled.

For beginners A good species to try is *L. deppei* from Mexico and Guatemala. This is a green flower flecked with red and with a red-spotted yellow lip. It is also fragrant.

CONDITIONS

Climate All are frost sensitive and not ideal for the tropics. Many are happy in a 50–86°F range. Some species may drop lower during their dry rest.

Aspect Plants require good shade in summer. Early morning sun with shade for the rest of the day is suitable. Ensure good air circulation.

Potting mix Use a mix of crushed fine to medium bark. Do not overpot. Select a pot large enough to take the root ball with a little extra space.

GROWING METHOD

Propagation Divide plants after flowering if they are very crowded. Leafless pseudobulbs can be detached from the clump and potted up.

Watering Give ample water during hot weather and when in active growth but avoid overhead watering. Keep compost dry when dormant.

Feeding Plants respond well to regular fertilizing during the growing season. Use soluble liquids or granular fertilizers. Those formulated for cymbidiums are suitable.

Problems No specific problems are known if cultural conditions are suitable.

FLOWERING SEASON

Mainly winter to early spring.

LYCASTE AT A GLANCE

Relatively easy to grow but best in greenhouse. Deciduous, with flowers in spring with the new growth.

Jan	rest	Oct	rest
Feb	rest	Nov	rest
Mar	flowering, water and feed	Dec	rest
Apr	flowering, water and feed		Recommended Varieties
May	flowering, water and feed		*L. aromatica* (yellow)
Jun	flowering, water and feed		*L. cruenta* (yellow)
			L. deppei (green/red)
July	flowering, water and feed, re-pot		*L. skinneri* (white/pink)
			L. Auburn (pink)
Aug	water and feed		*L.* Always (pink/red)
Sept	water and feed		

MASDEVALLIA
Kite orchid

This spotted hybrid Masdevallia *has a pattern of deep magenta markings on a white ground.*

Emerging from a base of heavy leaves, this clear yellow Masdevallia *hybrid has long, very fine tails on its flower.*

FEATURES

Epiphytic

Terrestrial

These unusual flowers are not obviously divided into petals and sepals but appear as solid, sometimes triangular shapes, often with long tails. Flowers may come singly or in small sprays above or within the foliage. The color range includes white, pink, red, yellow, orange, and greenish brown. Some flowers have contrasting venation that looks like stripes. Masdevallias are native to tropical America where they occur from warm lowlands to high altitudes. Plants may be epiphytes, lithophytes, or terrestrial and most are found in high elevations in cloud forests. They lack pseudobulbs, growing from a root system that produces short, upright stems, each with a single fleshy leaf.

MASDEVALLIA AT A GLANCE

Miniature orchids, 1¼– 6in high. Best in cool greenhouse. Flowers ¼–1¼ in across with long tails.

Jan	rest	Nov	rest
Feb	rest	Dec	rest
Mar	water and feed,		
Apr	water and feed, re-pot		Recommended Varieties
May	water and feed, re-pot		*M. barlaeana* (red)
			M. coccinea (varies)
Jun	water and feed, re-pot		*M. tovarensis* (white)
			M. Angel Frost (yellow)
July	water and feed		*M.* Marguerite (orange)
Aug	water and feed		*M.* Whiskers (orange/
Sept	water and feed		purple)
Oct	water and feed, rest		

CONDITIONS

Climate   This orchid is frost sensitive but classed as cool growing; it prefers a range of about 50–75°F.

Aspect   Needs about 70 per cent shade in the summer months; less in winter. Maintain high humidity but keep air moving with fans as good ventilation is needed to grow these little plants well.

Potting mix   Use a small pot just large enough for the roots. Use a compost of fine-grade bark mixed with charcoal, perlite, and pea gravel.

GROWING METHOD

Propagation   This is not easy. Large clumps may be divided after some years. Each division should be made up of at least four stems to make sure they continue to grow well.

Watering   Keep the compost moist at all times, especially in warm weather. Growing in small pots, with fine compost, they tend to dry out easily.

Feeding   Use soluble liquid plant foods, which can be applied during normal watering in the growing season diluted to half strength.

Problems   No specific pest or disease problems are known if the exacting growing conditions are met. If the long flower tails shrivel in warm weather the humidity is too low or the temperature is too high.

FLOWERING SEASON

Flowering depends on species but most flower through spring or summer. When grown to a large plant, masdevallias will provide a lovely show of dainty blooms.

ODONTOGLOSSUM
Tiger orchid

Brilliant colors and intricate patterns are now appearing in many of the newer Odontoglossum *hybrids.*

The darker pattern cleverly mimics the flower shape on this pretty tiger orchid, which makes a good houseplant for a cool room.

FEATURES

Epiphytic

This large group of evergreen orchids comes from Central and South America. They are epiphytes or lithophytes and most occur at high altitudes. They grow from pseudobulbs from which one or two leaves emerge. The flower spikes are very variable and may be short or tall, upright or arching in habit, but all originate from the base of the pseudobulb. Some species are grown but it is the hybrids that are widely cultivated. Hybrids occur in almost every color of the rainbow and are marked in an extraordinary range of patterns. The odontoglossums will readily breed with other closely related genera to give an ever increasing range of flower types. This interbreeding can also often make the plants much more tolerant to warmer or cooler conditions. Some examples are crossed with *Oncidium* to make *Odontocidium*, with *Miltonia* to create *Odontonia* and with *Cochlioda* to make *Odontioda*. When a third genus is involved then the names change again—for example *Odontoglossum* x *Oncidium* x *Cochlioda* makes a *Wilsonara*.

CONDITIONS

Climate	Needs a frost-free, but generally not hot, climate and prefers a temperature range from 50–77°F. High humidity is essential for this orchid.
Aspect	Needs shade, especially in summer when shadecloth of about 70 per cent should be used. Reduce in winter to provide maximum light to encourage flowering.
Potting mix	Needs very open and free-draining soil. A suitable mix would contain medium grade bark, charcoal, pea gravel, or very coarse, washed sand. A little chopped sphagnum moss can be added. Do not overpot. Use pots just large enough to confine the roots.

GROWING METHOD

Propagation	Divide plants after flowering but only when the container is overflowing. Plants resent frequent disturbance.
Watering	Never allow plants to become bone dry but roots should never be sodden. Frequency of watering depends on the mix used and the weather. Mist plants in hot, dry weather.
Feeding	Use soluble liquid plant foods at half the recommended strength every couple of weeks through the warmer months.

ODONTOGLOSSUM AT A GLANCE

Popular and easy to grow houseplants. Different varieties with attractive dark green foliage and sprays of flowers.

Jan	less water	Recommended Varieties
Feb	less water	*O.crispum* (white)
Mar	water and feed	*O. cordatum*
Apr	water and feed	(yellow/brown)
May	water and feed	*O. hallii* (yellow)
Jun	water and feed	*O. laeve* (brown/white)
July	water and feed	*Odontocidium* Purbeck
Aug	water and feed	Gold (yellow/brown)
Sept	water and feed	*Odontonia* Boussole
Oct	less water	"Blanche" (white)
Nov	less water	*Vuylstekeara* Cambria
Dec	less water	"Plush" (red/white)

This beautiful Odontoglossum *hybrid has been bred from the white species* O. crispum *giving it its clear color and arching spray.*

Bright, golden yellow is a very popular color in this easy to grow group of orchids which are often chosen as ideal beginner's plants.

Problems   No specific pest or disease problems are known for this orchid.

FLOWERING SEASON

The flowering season is very variable, depending on the species or hybrid.

OTHER ODONTOGLOSSUMS TO GROW

O. crispum   This species, with pure white flowers, was imported into Britain in large quantities at the beginning of the 20th century, when it commanded enormous prices. Still sought after, it is not found in such abundance as it used to be. Hybrids that have been made with it still retain the beautiful white coloring but tend to be easier to grow, making them good for beginners.

O. cordatum   A more compact species which is relatively easy to grow and flower for the amateur enthusiast. Star-shaped golden yellow and chestnut brown flowers are approximately 2½in across and between three and six are held on a short arching spray.

O. hallii   Larger growing, the plant height being around 12in with a spray of large yellow flowers, spotted in brown which have the added bonus of being scented and usually summer flowering.

O. laeve   Although this species has small flowers, colored in dark green and brown with a contrasting white and magenta lip, there are a lot of them held on a very tall, branching flower spike which can be up to 3¼ft high.

The flowers have a strong, sweet fragrance, which will fill your greenhouse. The plant is strong and vigorous growing which makes it good for ease of culture. There are literally thousands of *Odontoglossum* hybrids available with new ones being produced all the time; here are some examples to choose from.

Vuylstekeara Cambria "Plush"   This is a complex hybrid between three different genera, which make up part of the "*Odontoglossum* Alliance" of related genera. It is one of the all time classic hybrids and has been around since the 1930s and is still very popular today. Its ease of culture and free-flowering habit make it an ideal beginners' orchid as well as being very showy with its large bright red flowers, the lip white with red spotting.

Odontocidium Purbeck Gold   This is another classic variety, this time in a brilliant golden yellow, the petals and sepals with just a touch of chocolate brown. Flowers are 3in across on a spray reaching 12–20in, depending on the maturity of the plant. These orchids are very easy to grow and flower.

Beallara Tahama Glacier "Green"   The addition of *Brassia* into the breeding of this hybrid gives the flower a stunning, star-shaped appearance. The large blooms can measure up to 2½in across. The translucent green of the flower is contrasted with the dark red in its center. Produces tall sprays with between six and a dozen of these showy, long-lasting flowers. Tolerant of varying temperatures, this orchid will flower well in cool or warm environments. A vigorous grower, it makes an excellent specimen plant in just a few years.

2.

4.

8.

6.

7.

1.

3.

5.

ODONTOGLOSSUM

1 Sanderara *Rippon Tor "Burnham" is a very reliable bloomer, always in the late spring and rewards the grower with an attractive arching spray of patterned flowers.*

2 Odontioda *Grenadier is just one of the many red hybrids that include the bright red species* Cochlioda noetzliana *in its family tree giving the striking color that we see here and in many other red hybrids.*

3 Odontocidium *Purbeck Gold shows the introduction of the genus* Oncidium *into the breeding so giving us the bright yellow influence which also makes the plants very tolerant and easy to grow as houseplants.*

4 A more unusual type is this Colmanara *Wild Cat, which is certainly wild with its leopard spotting and readily branching spikes giving lots of long-lasting flowers. Also cool growing.*

5 Most colors are represented in this widely hybridized family and purple is no exception as seen here in the beautiful Vuylstekeara *Monica "Burnham".*

6 The Brassia *influence is clear here with the large star-shaped flowers of the* Beallara *Tahoma Glacier "Green" which is a robust and free-flowering ideal pot-plant.*

7 Odontioda *Moliere "Polka" has amazing, frilled edges to the flowers and an extremely intricate patterning in pinks and purples covering the whole flower.*

8 Odontioda *Marie Noel "Burgogne" is another highly frilled flower which makes a particularly attractive arching flower spike on a mature plant.*

PLEIONE
Pleione species and hybrids

The small treasures that make up the Pleione *species are often best grown as container plants where they can be enjoyed at close range. Among the features to watch out for is the contrasting lip of the flower, which is delicately fringed.*

FEATURES

Epiphytic

Terrestrial

Extremely cold tolerant, these orchids are native to cool areas of northern India, and to southern China and Taiwan where they are usually found in damp woodland. They are deciduous and may be terrestrial, epiphytic, or lithophytic. They die down completely in winter and renew the small pseudobulbs in spring. Plants are rarely more than 6in high and may spread to about 12in. They grow in very shallow pots. Flowers appear before the leaves and are most often white, pink, mauve, purple, or even yellow. The lip may be fringed and spotted. Individual blooms are not long lasting but make a fine display when planted en masse. Each small pseudobulb flowers only once and then

produces a folded, elliptical leaf. Pleiones make very easy orchids for beginners and especially for enthusiast children. Their compact habit and ease of culture make them ideal house plants for a very cool windowsill or greenhouse. Some alpine growers even include them in their collections. The pots can be placed out of doors for the summer months.

CONDITIONS

Climate	Some are frost hardy, others frost tender but all prefer cool to cold conditions. A minimum temperature in winter of 10°F is acceptable to these plants as long as they are in their leafless, dormant phase.
Aspect	Needs a sheltered spot in filtered sunlight with shade during the hottest part of the day. Glasshouse-grown plants will need heavy shading and cooling in summer.
Potting mix	The mix of bark, pea gravel, small pebbles, and chopped sphagnum moss or fibre peat must be perfectly drained.

GROWING METHOD

Propagation	Plants need re-potting annually at the end of winter when old pseudobulbs can be discarded. It is then, in the early spring, that the new shoots are just starting to grow, with the flower buds inside. As well as removing last year's dead pseudobulb, trim back the dead roots when re-potting. Some varieties are likely to break double each year so the number of pseudobulbs multiply easily over the years. Occasionally, small extra pseudobulbs can be formed at the top of the old, shrivelled bulb. These can be

PLEIONE AT A GLANCE

Very easy to grow and ideal for greenhouse. Can reach 6in high and flowers average 2in across.

Jan	rest	**Recommended Varieties**
Feb	repot, flowering	*P. formosana* (lilac pink)
Mar	flowering, water and feed	*P. formosana* var. *alba* (white)
Apr	flowering, water and feed	*P. maculata* (white/red)
May	water and feed	*P. praecox* (pink)
Jun	water and feed	*P. speciosa* (cerise)
July	water and feed	*P.* Eiger (lavender)
Aug	water and feed	*P.* Piton (lilac)
Sept	flowering, rest	*P.* Shantung (yellow)
Oct	flowering, rest	*P.* Stromboli (pink)
Nov	rest	*P.* Versailles (pink)
Dec	rest	

There are many hybrid pleiones which add to the range of shades of pink, white, and yellow including this striking Pleione Soufriere.

Hybrid Pleione *Shantung is just one of the easy growing orchids that are ideal beginner's plants for the cool greenhouse or conservatory.*

Watering Keep soil moist once growth has started in spring. Water regularly during flowering and the development of the pseudobulbs. These orchids make fine root systems which can dry out easily if not regularly watered. When pseudobulbs are fully matured, reduce the frequency of watering. Keep plants dry in winter while dormant and leafless. To avoid resting pseudobulbs from becoming too wet during winter remove from their pots after their leaves have fallen and leave to dry out in an empty tray or pot. You can also see clearly when the new growth starts and can then pot them up again.

Feeding Give regular, weak liquid fertilizer once growth commences and continue until pseudobulbs are well matured.

Problems Slugs and snails are a constant problem but there are no other specific pest problems. Plants can die from root rot if they are constantly wet while dormant or if they dry out completely during the growing season when they can dehydrate.

FLOWERING SEASON

Most species flower in spring but some flower in the fall.

OTHER PLEIONES TO GROW

P. formosana Probably the most popular *Pleione* species to grow, the number of bulbs multiplies up quickly over the years so a superb show can be achieved in quite a short time. Soft lavender pink petals and sepals with dark pink and brown spotting on the white lip.

P. formosana var. alba A pure white, albino form of the above species which has only a touch of yellow in the center of the lip. The pseudobulbs are also devoid of any purple coloring and are a clear apple green. Grows slightly smaller than the pink variety.

P. speciosa Known for its very vibrant cerise colored flowers which will brighten up the early spring months when it is in flower.

P. maculata An unusual species as this one flowers in the fall, one of only two species that does. White blooms, with dark red patterning in the lip, are also unusual in a mostly pink dominated genus.

P. praecox The second fall flowering species, this time in traditional pink. These two grow in just the same conditions as the spring flowering types but are perhaps a little more of a challenge.

A few hybrid pleiones have been bred between the species; the following are a few examples which are easy to grow:

P. Eiger One of the first to flower in the spring season, short stem with a pale lavender flower, very pretty and easy to keep.

P. Piton A very large sized flower in comparison to the others, 2½in across, on a taller stem, 4in high, a lovely subtle purple shade with bold spotting on the lip.

P. Shantung One of the most well known of the hybrid pleiones due to it being a yellow hybrid, the darkest form being *P.* Shantung "Ducat". Grows well but may not multiply as quickly as some of the others. The most commonly seen variety is P. Shantung "Ridgeway" AM/RHS, a soft yellow with a pink blush.

ROSSIOGLOSSUM
Clown orchid

This bright yellow and red flower is nicknamed the clown orchid after the distinctive character of the bloom.

The flowers of the Rossioglossum are showy and lasting, especially this easy-to-grow hybrid R. Rawdon Jester.

FEATURES

Epiphytic

This incredibly showy and fascinating orchid was originally part of the *Odontoglossum* family. Probably the best known of the species is *R. grande*, commonly known as the clown orchid. A little man in a colorful yellow and red outfit can be seen at the top of the lip. A few hybrids have been made between some of the species such as R. Jakob Jenny (*grande* x *insleayi*) and R. Rawdon Jester (*grande* x *williamsianum*). The pseudobulbs are oval-shaped and a handsome green with a pair of large, broad leaves in the same color. The flowers tend to be very long lasting with quite a waxy texture and reaching an amazing 6in across from petal tip to petal tip.

ROSSIOGLOSSUM AT A GLANCE

Good for beginners in the home or conservatory. Flowers reach 6in across and spike 12in above foliage.

Jan	rest	Oct	flowering, rest
Feb	rest	Nov	rest
Mar	rest	Dec	rest
Apr	rest		
May	flowering, water and feed		Recommended Varieties
Jun	flowering, water and feed		*R. grande*
			R. insleayi
July	water and feed		*R. williamsianum*
Aug	water and feed		R. Jakob Jenny
Sept	flowering, water and feed		R. Rawdon Jester (all yellow/brown)

CONDITIONS

Climate   Traditionally a popular orchid to grow in a cool greenhouse or conservatory, with a minimum temperature of 50°F throughout the year.

Aspect   The leaves prefer a shady position so protect from bright sun. Dappled shade is preferred; a north facing aspect in summer is ideal and south facing in winter.

Potting Mix   A fairly open mix is ideal, bark based with some peat or similar mixed in.

GROWING METHOD

Propagation   Rossioglossums are quite slow to grow and take many years to reach an easily dividable plant. Therefore, leave the plant until the pot is full before moving to a larger size and only split when necessary and possible.

Watering   Likes a well-defined resting period in winter, which goes on well into spring. Water regularly from the point when the new growth starts increasing over the growing season and decrease to a stop in the fall. Allow compost to dry out a little in winter.

Feeding   Use a half strength general plant food every two or three waterings in the growing season.

Problems   If a dry rest period is not observed then the plant can suffer from over-watering in the winter which can lead to root rot. Avoid spraying the foliage in winter as this can lead to spotting which can cause fungal infection.

FLOWERING SEASON

R. grande traditionally flowers in fall but some hybrids, such as *R*. Rawdon Jester will bloom easily in late spring and summer.

STANHOPEA
Stanhopea species and hybrids

Native to Nicaragua, Colombia, and Venezuela, Stanhopea wardii has a more pleasant smell than some species of this genus.

The weird and sinister-looking flowers of Stanhopea tigrina are a botanical curiosity enjoyed by many growers.

FEATURES

Epiphytic

Sometimes known as upside-down orchids, stanhopeas must be grown in hanging containers as the flowers emerge from the base of the pseudobulbs and will otherwise be squashed. They push straight through the bottom of the basket and hang down below the foliage. Stanhopeas are evergreen epiphytes from Central and South America. They grow from a fairly large, ribbed pseudobulb and produce large, solitary, dark green leaves. The strange-looking flowers are large, heavy and strongly perfumed. Not everyone finds the perfume pleasant. Flowers are not long lasting but appear in succession. Plants grow rapidly and are very easy to grow into large specimens.

STANHOPEA AT A GLANCE

Easy to grow but can reach 16in high. Flowers are large and strongly scented but short lived.

Jan	occasional water	Sept	water and feed
Feb	water and feed	Oct	water and feed
Mar	flowering, water and feed	Nov	occasional water
		Dec	occasional water
Apr	flowering, water and feed		
May	flowering, water and feed		Recommended Varieties
Jun	flowering, water and feed		*S. graveolans* (yellow)
			S. oculata (cream)
July	flowering, water and feed		*S. tigrina*
			S. wardii
Aug	flowering, water and feed		*S.* Assidensis (yellow and red)

Species

Stanhopea tigrina, with its fleshy yellow flowers blotched dark maroon-red, is the species most often cultivated, although *S. wardii* is also seen. It also has yellow flowers but with plum to purple spots.

CONDITIONS

Climate   Prefers a cool, humid climate with a minimum of 50°F and tolerates warmer temperatures in summer with shade and high humidity.

Aspect   Grows in dappled sunlight in a well-ventilated glasshouse.

Potting mix   Line the container with soft coconut fiber or other material so that the stems can push through easily. The mix of coarse bark, alone or with charcoal, must be free draining.

GROWING METHOD

Propagation   Divide the pseudobulbs after flowering, but not until the container is full to overflowing. Large specimens are the most rewarding, producing many spikes.

Watering   Water freely during warm weather and mist plants if humidity drops. Water only occasionally in winter.

Feeding   During the growing season apply weak liquid fertilizer every two weeks.

Problems   Can be prone to red-spider-mite or scale insect if not enough humidity is provided. Mist foliage regularly to prevent this.

FLOWERING SEASON

Summer or fall, depending on species. Remove spent flowers once they have faded.

Growing Bromeliads

GROWING BROMELIADS

Bromeliads are attractive plants that are easy to cultivate, both in the greenhouse, as conservatory specimens or as lush, exotic house plants. Their showy but unusual blooms are quite unlike any other flowers, while their foliage, colors, and shape hint at their tropical native habitats.

Today many species of bromeliad are threatened in the wild because the forests and woodlands of their natural habitats are rapidly vanishing. There has also been over-collection, and as many species grow very slowly from seed they are not regenerating fast enough to keep up with demand. However, many species are now being cultivated and preserved in botanic gardens and in the collections of both amateur and professional growers, so that home gardeners can continue to grow these interesting plants. Many exciting plants are sold through garden centers, nurseries, and supermarkets—all are well worth buying for the enjoyment they will provide.

LEFT: Exotic foliage and an epiphytic habit make bromeliads rewarding and sometimes challenging to grow. Larger displays for the conservatory or greenhouse can be created by attaching individual plants to old tree branches.

ORIGINAL HABITAT

Most of this large, very diverse group of plants originated in tropical America, with a few species from subtropical America and one species of *Pitcairnia* native to West Africa. Probably the best known of all bromeliads is the pineapple. Its distribution extends from the state of Virginia in the United States south to Chile and Argentina. Bromeliads are most common in rainforests but a few occur naturally in deserts, often dropping their leaves during the driest seasons.

INTRODUCTION TO HORTICULTURE

The first bromeliad introduced to horticulture outside its native habitat was the pineapple, brought to Spain from Guadaloupe in the West Indies by Christopher Columbus on his second voyage to the New World at the end of the fifteenth century. Although it had long been cultivated in the West Indies it caused quite a sensation in Europe.

By the seventeenth century a number of wealthy people were building heated glasshouses in order to be able to cultivate exotic tropical plants such as pineapples, although it was not until the late eighteenth and early nineteenth centuries that heated glasshouse culture became more commonplace. Glasshouses were still, however, the province of the wealthy.

During this period large numbers of bromeliads were introduced into Europe. In the early nineteenth century most went to France and Belgium, where there were the greatest number of enthusiasts and authorities on the subject. By the end of the century, however, collectors from many other European countries were growing and writing about this fascinating group of plants.

This century, with a few notable exceptions, collecting and interest has been most common in the United States, where the Bromeliad Society was established in Florida in the 1950s. Today, however, the cultivation of bromeliads is popular worldwide.

WHERE TO GROW BROMELIADS

In their native habitats, bromeliads thrive in tropical and sub-tropical environments, favoured with heavy rainfall, filtered sunlight, and mild or warmish temperatures.

There are a few species that will tolerate cooler conditions although frost, wind, and rain during the winter months has an adverse effect on plants—damaging leaves and disfiguring growth. Other desert species will tolerate extreme heat and full sunshine, but generally bromeliads prefer warmth, filtered sunlight and shelter from strong winds. Occasionally plants may be stood outdoors during the summer months in a partially shaded position, but in general they should be confined to the

Vibrant red bracts remain even after the flowering of Guzmania *"Luna" has finished, thus extending the period when this plant is of particular interest.*

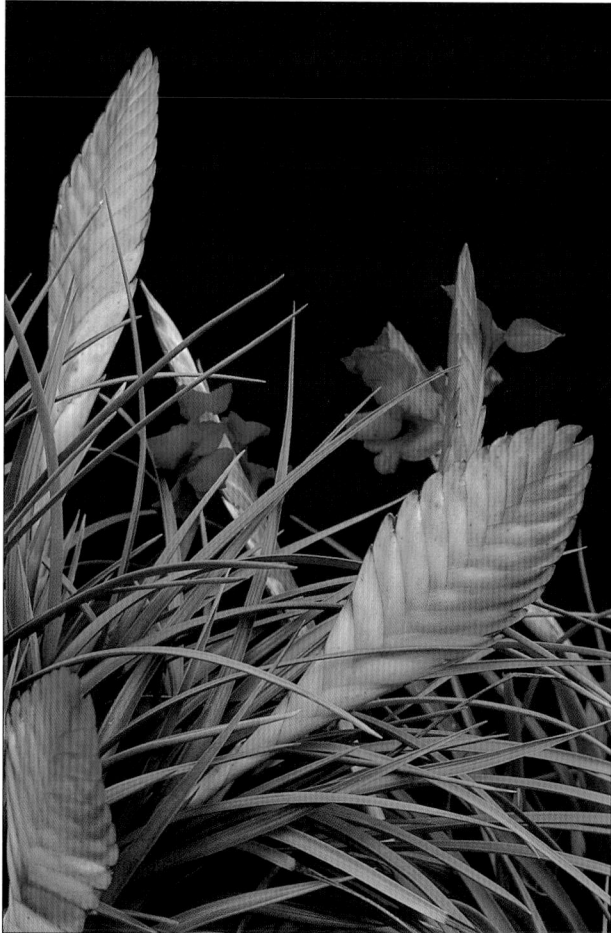

"Blue-flowered torch" is the name sometimes applied to Tillandsia lindenii. *It does, in fact, bear deep purple flowers that appear from the pink-flushed floral bracts.*

greenhouse or conservatory and for indoor culture. The occasional trip outside for a shower to remove dust and grime will pay dividends. The wide leaves accumulate dust even in the cleanest of homes, which reduces their ability to absorb sunlight and inhibits healthy growth.

Light is important if you are to enjoy a good show of bracts and flower spikes, and indoors specimen plants can be reluctant to flower. However, the lack of a flower is a small price to pay as the foliage shapes and colors of most bromeliads more than compensate.

Potted plants can be moved around at will, brought into the house or conservatory when they are looking their best, and returned to the greenhouse when they need additional care and attention. In a mixed grouping it is also possible to bring those plants that have flower spikes or are looking particularly attractive to the front of a display, moving less spectacular specimens back for a rest.

One method of display is to make a bromeliad "tree" so that the plants are seen as epiphytes, looking as they would in their natural environment (see page 554).

FEATURES

In their native habitats some bromeliads are ground dwellers while others grow on rocks or cliff faces, but many are epiphytes using other plants, especially trees, for support although they are not parasites. Most have spirally arranged leaves that channel water into the center of a rosette, which acts as a water storage tank. In their habitats these "tanks" provide a home for insects with aquatic larval stages and a breeding place for many species of tree frogs. The leaves also have fine water-absorbing scales although these are rarely obvious.

Leaves may be in various shades of plain green but many have foliage that is attractively patterned in stripes, transverse bands, or spots. Silvery gray, deep maroon, and bright crimson leaves are also found, along with a range of two-toned or multi-colored leaves. Some have leaves with smooth edges while others are very spiny or serrated.

One group that displays a vast range of foliage types is *Tillandsia*, which includes many species with a recognizable rosette of leaves as well as the fine, gray, web-like Spanish moss (*T. usneoides*) which grows in long swags draped from tree branches. The leaves are thread-like on stems covered with silver scales.

Bromeliad flowers may be spectacular and showy, held on upright or arching stems, or they may be short, blooming low down in the center of the rosettes. Some flowers last only a few days while others can remain fresh and attractive over several weeks. The color range is as extensive as the range of forms. Although some cut well and last a week or two in a vase, they are generally unsuitable as cut flowers. Whole plants in flower are often used instead to create unusual floral arrangements.

CONDITIONS

Containers

When growing bromeliads in pots, it is often necessary to crock the base of the pot with stones or terracotta chips. This provides weight in the base so that the often top-heavy plants do not constantly tip over. Terracotta pots are useful in this regard, as they are heavy enough to provide stability. Many plants are themselves so decorative with their patterned leaves and bright flowers that a simple plain container is the best choice.

Sharing a need for warmth and humidity, greenhouse displays of several different species create an exotic, almost tropical feel. Plants will appreciate shading from strong summer sun and regular misting with rainwater to maintain humid conditions.

Compost

For plants that are happiest clinging to the cleft in a tree or nestled in the leaf litter on a tropical forest floor, the compost used will dictate whether the plants are going to survive or die. The compost must imitate the natural tendency for free drainage coupled with good moisture retention. Nutrients in the wild would come from rotting leaves and dead insects that become trapped in the watery reservoir of the plants. However it is not advisable to feed your plants this way. A compost that contains a controlled release fertilizer can be used, but so long as it is coarse and free draining they will be happy.

Orchid and African violet composts are sold in garden centers and these are ideal—combining the water holding properties of peat or composted bark chips, with the free draining properties of grit or sharp sand. Leafmould would be equally suitable if you can get hold of it.

Planting

Bromeliads are very prone to rotting off if the base of the plant is kept consistently moist. A free draining compost will help, as will plenty of crocks in the bottom of the pot.

When potting it is also important to not plant too deep. The base of the plant should be level with the surface of the compost. Too deep and excess water will not be able to drain away from the central reservoir.

House plants

Light is important for good flowering and foliage color but even some of the most decorative bromeliads, like the urn plant (*Aechmea fasciata*), will thrive in the home. Bromeliads can be rather large for the average home, although a good range of smaller species and varieties are available. They look particularly striking in simple surroundings, more like a piece of art or sculpture than the traditional potted house plant.

Greenhouse growing

Those with greenhouses have the perfect environment to experiment with a wide range of bromeliads. The warm conditions and bright light will also encourage flowering. Shading in full summer is advisable, as is damping the floor to maintain high levels of humidity. Epiphytic species can be grown on pads of sphagnum moss or old logs and hung from the greenhouse glazing bars for a decorative display. Regular misting will be essential.

Conservatory culture

For the conservatory that is used for plants rather than soft furnishings, bromeliads offer a wide range of colors and forms to play with. They are quite unlike any other house plants but are easy and rewarding to grow. Larger specimens will relish the space a conservatory has to offer, and hanging specimens like Spanish moss (*Tillandsia usneoides*) will add a decorative, almost magical touch. For the more adventurous, a way of displaying a wide range of bromeliad habits is to plant up a "tree."

Many bromeliads do well in conditions that suit cymbidium orchids and growers enjoy cultivating these contrasting plant groups together. Both enjoy a free flow of air around them and a degree of humidity at all times.

A bromeliad tree

Tree stumps, especially old tree-fern stumps, make ideal hosts for bromeliads, as do pieces of weathered driftwood. Pieces of driftwood of various sizes make more or less portable "trees," which can be moved around to suit seasonal conditions or to provide striking decorative effects in different places around the house, greenhouse or conservatory, perhaps for a special event.

To attach plants to the tree, wrap the roots in sphagnum moss or peat and fix them on firmly with upholstery webbing, nylon fishing line, or old stockings. Small specimens may be attached using a little PVA glue, although you should not let the glue smother the roots.

The roots of small plants may be passed through the holes in rounds or squares of ¹/₂–1in plastic mesh and a pad of sphagnum moss placed underneath them before the mesh is stapled or tied to the tree. The type of plastic mesh sold to keep leaves out of guttering is ideal. An artificial log can also be made from this mesh by forming a cylinder and packing it with chopped bark and moss. Push the plant roots through into the growing medium and tie them on with plastic-coated wire or fishing line. Once plants are established the ties can be removed. These cylinders are light and can be suspended from greenhouse staging, glazing bars, conservatory support bars or hung in partially-shaded windows.

To grow bromeliads successfully indoors there must be plenty of light or the rich color of the foliage will not be maintained. Plants should be positioned near a sunny window but not close to the glass where the leaves may be scorched. If there is not enough light it will be obvious after a time that leaves are becoming pale and drawn. Extra light may need to be provided artificially.

Plants also need a fairly humid atmosphere, so if you have central heating or the room gets warm, sit plant pots on a bed of pebbles or gravel in a saucer of water. The pot base must be above the water level so that the potting mix is not constantly sodden. Spray-misting the plants with water is also beneficial. This can be done daily in summer but much less often in winter. Foliage should be wiped down with a damp cloth from time to time to remove dust or taken into a gently running shower for a good rinse. If possible take plants outside and gently hose them down.

GROWING METHOD

Watering

Bromeliads growing on logs or moss pads are best watered by spray misting. If you only have a few plants this can be done with a hand sprayer but larger collections will need hosing with a fine spray. Those with a vase form are best

BROMELIAD TREE

Bromeliad plant attached to plant

Tree stump

watered from above, allowing the water to fill the central cup or reservoir. As this overflows it will give roots the moisture they need. In the warmer months when plants are in active growth they may need watering two or three times a week, with misting on the other days. In winter watering once a week should be enough. If the water in your area is "hard" (has a high mineral concentration) you should collect rain water to use on your bromeliads.

Feeding

Opinions vary on the value of feeding these plants. In nature leaves and other debris fall into the vases of plants, slowly decaying and providing nutrients to the plant. If you do fertilize, make sure that it is in very weak concentrations, not too often and never in winter. Some professional growers prefer to use a little slow release fertilizer around the root zone of the plant while others use well-diluted water soluble fertilizers as a spray. If using a spray, use only a quarter to half the recommended dilution rate given for other foliage or indoor plants, and apply it only after the plant has been watered and when it is not in the sun or on very hot days. It is best not to pour even dilute fertilizer into the vase of the plant as this may scorch the foliage.

PROPAGATION

Plants that have bloomed will slowly die off over the next year or two. However, they will replace themselves by producing offsets, often called "pups," generally from the side of the base of the plant. It is best to wait until the offset has a firm base and is at least one-third the size of the parent plant before removing it. Cut off the offset as close as possible to the mother plant using a sharp knife or pruning shears. This is best done some time between spring and mid-fall. A few plants produce pups higher up on the plant and these are easily detached by hand.

Any discolored or brown leaves should be removed before potting up, and long, woody running stems (stolons) should be shortened. Offsets should be potted up into small pots containing a coarse seed and cutting compost or two parts sharp sand to one part peat or

The striking cream and green striped foliage of this Guzmania *cultivar makes this bromeliad showy and decorative all year round. The red floral display is an added bonus.*

composted bark. Some growers like to dust the base of the offset with a fungicide as a disease preventive. Don't push the offsets in too deep or they may rot. Spray mist daily, unless there is a cold spell, and roots should form on the offset in a matter of weeks. The best time to propagate by division of offsets is during the growing season, which is from spring through to mid-fall.

WHAT CAN GO WRONG?

Adequate spacing of plants, good ventilation and good cultural practice should minimize problems. Remove any dead or decaying material to keep plants clean and looking good. If you have a sick plant, isolate it from the rest of the collection and wash your hands and disinfect any tools used before handling healthy plants. If you have to use chemicals for pest or disease control, do not spray the buds or flowers as they may become distorted. Fungicidal powders may also be used.

Pests
• Scale insects. These small sap suckers appear as soft brown spots that can be easily pushed off with a finger nail. Wipe off scales with a damp cloth or spray with a suitable insecticide at half the recommended strength. Never use oil-based formulations on bromeliads as this smothers the natural breathing pores and the plant will die of suffocation.
• Mealybugs. These soft white insects resemble small

sticky pieces of cotton wool. They are usually found clustered in the leaf axils and so may be difficult to reach. Wipe them off if possible or use a suitable insecticide. They are usually only a problem if the bromeliads are grown in crowded or badly ventilated conditions.

General disorders
• Lowest leaves brown at the base. This may be caused by heavy, poorly drained mix, overwatering or deep planting.
• Inner leaves rolled or stuck together. The air may be too dry, the plant may need misting or the central vase may have completely dried out.
• Brown leaf tips. These may result from poor drainage or from overwatering, or indicate that the atmosphere is dry.
• Brown patches on leaves. These may be caused by strong sun or very high light intensity, overwatering or poor drainage.
• Bottom leaves straw to light brown in color. This is usually a sign of natural ageing as the older leaves die off.

AECHMEA
Aechmea species and cultivars

The floral bracts of "Ensign," a cultivar of Aechmea orlandia, *are made up of tightly overlapping, scarlet segments.*

Long flowering and adaptable, Aechmea weilbachii *makes a good choice of plant for fairly warm conditions.*

FEATURES

Epiphytic

These are possibly the most widely grown and best known of all the bromeliads. Generally very easy to cultivate, they can be container grown or attached to a log "tree". Although aechmeas originate from Central and South America, most tolerate temperatures down to about 41°F making them suitable for cooler conservatories. Species vary in size from a petite 6in to over 24in, although this size would be rare in cultivation. Larger plants can become top heavy so a terracotta or earthenware pot is

advisable for extra stability.

Foliage There is an amazing diversity of form and foliage color in these bromeliads. Leaves are in a rosette, forming a vase shape with an open cup in the center. They may be completely shiny green, or green above and burgundy beneath, deep burgundy on both sides or streaked, banded, or spotted with silver, or entirely silvery black. There are also variegated forms with either yellow-gold or pink variegations on a green background. Many are sharply spined along the leaf margins (needing careful handling) while others are almost smooth edged.

Flowers Many aechmeas have long-lasting flowers that make them popular for indoor decoration. Although the true flowers are often quite small they are enclosed within showy bracts that come in a great range of colors. The inflorescence or flowering spike may be red, blue, yellow, purple, pink, orange, or white and lasts for months.

Fruits Berry-like fruits follow the flowers and often persist on the plant over a long period.

A. fasciata One of the most popular species is *Aechmea fasciata* or "Urn" plant, which has gray-silver spined leaves cross-banded in silver. The whole leaf surface is densely covered with silvery scales, giving a powdery effect. The flower spike is a large, showy pyramid of pink bracts enclosing the blue flowers, which age to red.

Foster's Favorite An attractive dwarf variety is *A.* "Foster's Favorite," which has deep burgundy foliage and a pendulous flowering spike of deep

AECHMEA AT A GLANCE

A tolerant plant. Leaves are strap-like and vary in color. Plants produce floral bracts after three years.

Jan	grow on, reduce watering	Sept	/
Feb	grow on, reduce watering	Oct	flowers, fruit; keep frost free
Mar	re-pot, feed	Nov	flowers, reduce watering
Apr	remove and pot on offsets	Dec	flowers, reduce watering
May	remove offsets, mist foliage		
Jun	bracts, flowers, mist and water		Recommended Varieties
July	flowers, mist and water		*A. chantinii*
			A. fasciata
Aug	/		*A. fulgens discolor*

Aechmea fasciata *is one of the easiest bromeliads to grow and produces a magnificent pink flowerspike that will last for months.*

With purple undersides to the leaves, Aechmea fulgens discolor *also produces a stunning coral red flowerspike that is covered in berries.*

blue flowers. These may be followed by red berries. Both these forms are tolerant of a wide range of conditions.

A. chantinii   *A. chantinii* is variable both in size and foliage color. It is sometimes called Amazonian zebra plant because of its green to almost black foliage, which is heavily barred. The long-branched flowering spike is generally red or orange with flowers being red or yellow. Tends to be more cold sensitive than some.

Other species   *A. fulgens discolor* has attractive foliage and is commonly called the "Coral berry" aechmea. This species is hard to beat with its green strap-shaped leaves that are a deep purple beneath. A spike of purple flowers will turn into decorative coral red berries.

CONDITIONS

Position   Needs a frost-free climate. The plants do best in warm to hot, humid conditions with a cooler spell in winter. Morning sun, filtered sunlight or shade seems to suit this plant group. Most aechmeas like sheltered situations, preferably with overhead shading. Although some species have origins in harsh environments it is best to give them all some shelter in non-extreme conditions.

Potting mix   Plants will thrive in a very coarse, open, soilless compost. Water must be able to drain straight through. Take care not to plant too

deep to avoid rotting.

GROWING METHOD

Propagation   Start new plants by removing the offsets or pups from the parent plant once the offsets have reached about one-third of the size of the parent. Cut off and pot separately.

Watering   The cup at the center of the rosette must be kept filled with water. Plants probably need watering twice weekly or more in summer and every week or two in cold weather. Be guided by the weather and feel how moist the compost is. Mounted plants need spray watering daily in summer but much less often in winter.

Feeding   Apply slow release granules to the compost in spring. Mounted specimens may be given a foliar spray of liquid plant food at about one-third the recommended strength. Over feeding will not encourage more vigourous growth—it will scorch the leaves and roots.

Problems   There are no specific problems for this group if given reasonably good cultural and environmental conditions.

FLOWERING SEASON

Flowering times are variable but many bloom in late summer and fall, and many of them continue into winter.

ANANAS

Ananas species

The pineapple with its familiar crown of stiff leaves develops in the center of the plant. This one is almost mature.

The forms of Ananas *with variegated leaves are very attractive year round, even without the flowers.*

FEATURES

Terrestrial

Pineapple, *Ananas comosus*, is one of several species that make up this terrestrial bromeliad genus. All originate in tropical America. They have a rosette of very stiff, spiny leaves and produce purple-blue flowers with red bracts on a stem rising from the center of the plant. After the flowers fade the fruit is formed. *A. bracteatus* is grown for its showy flowers, which are followed by bright red mini pineapples. The variety *striatus* has leaves edged and striped cream to white. Unfortunately, to produce pineapples *A. comosus* must be grown in the right conditions. The form with cream striped leaves is the most popular. In bright

light variegations may turn pinkish. Take care when siting these plants as the foliage spines are sharp.

CONDITIONS

Position Needs a frost-free climate with a winter temperature above 50°F. Needs full sun or very bright light to flower and fruit. Very bright light also brings out the best color of variegated forms.

Potting mix All growing media must be well drained. Use coarse bark or peat-based mix and a heavy pot for additional stability.

GROWING METHOD

Propagation Grows from suckers or offsets from the base of the plant or from the tuft of leaves on top of the fruit. Peel off the lower basal leaves to reveal a stub and leave the stub in a dry, airy place to dry before planting it sometime from spring to fall.

Watering In summer water two or three times a week. In winter check before watering, which may be needed only every week or two.

Feeding Give slow release fertilizer in spring and early summer if desired.

Problems No specific problems are known for home growers but base and stem will rot if plants are too wet.

FLOWERING SEASON

Flowers appear from late spring to summer, depending on the season.

Fruit Fruit may take two years or more to mature, especially in cooler conditions, but the foliage makes up for this.

ANANAS AT A GLANCE

To produce pineapples grow in a hot conservatory. Flowers are purple-blue with red bracts; fruit forms after flowers.

Jan	reduce water, move to 50°F	Sept	water every two weeks
Feb	water every two weeks	Oct	water every two weeks, keep frost free
Mar	remove and pot on offsets	Nov	water every two weeks
Apr	remove and pot on offsets	Dec	water every two weeks
May	feed and light		
Jun	flowering, water three times weekly		Recommended Varieties
July	flowering		*A. comosus*
Aug	water three times weekly		*A. comosus striatus*

BILLBERGIA
Billbergia species

Bright red, overlapping bracts almost conceal the small flowers of this showy Billbergia *hybrid.*

This pendulous inflorescence reveals a mass of small blue-green flowers emerging from pink bracts.

FEATURES

Epiphytic

Terrestrial

One of the most easily grown of all bromeliads, billbergias are widely grown as house plants and are suitable for colder rooms in the house. They adapt to a wide variety of conditions, making them a good choice for the beginner. Leaves are rather stiff and form tall, tubular rosettes. Foliage is spiny and may be mottled, banded or variegated in colors from mid-green to blue-, or gray-green. Flower spikes often arch or droop. Flowers are generally not long lasting but some species flower on and off all year. Bracts are often pink or red with green or blue flower petals. Queen's tears, *Billbergia nutans*, is probably the most common. It has narrow, gray-green

leaves to 12in with blue and green flowers and pink bracts. It has been widely used in hybridizing.

Other species	*B.* x *windii* is a much larger leaved species producing 18in flower spikes over the gray-green leaves. Also, look out for *B. zebrina* and *B. pyramidalis*—both larger, more exotic species.

CONDITIONS

Position	Needs frost-free conditions with a minimum temperature above 41°F. Most species do best in fully sunny locations but need shade from the hottest summer sun, which tends to scorch leaf tips.
Potting mix	Any open, free-draining mix is suitable. Many experienced growers consider this plant does best without enriched soil conditions.

GROWING METHOD

Propagation	Grows fairly easily from divisions or offsets of older plants taken during the winter months.
Watering	Don't water too frequently but keep the cup filled with water. Spray misting to maintain a humid atmosphere around the plant is an ideal way to maintain good growth.
Feeding	Some growers advocate regular liquid feeding through the growing season, others prefer not to give supplementary feeding.
Problems	There are generally no problems.

FLOWERING SEASON

Flowering times vary according to species and growing conditions.

BILLBERGIA AT A GLANCE

Suitable for mounting on a log or in a pot. Flowers on and off all year but not long lasting. Pink bracts are spectacular.

		Recommended Varieties
Jan	flowering, water	
Feb	water	*B. decora*
Mar	/	*B. nutans*
Apr	feed	*B. nutans* "Variegata"
May	flowering, mist, repot	*B. pyramidalis*
Jun	water and mist	*B.* x *windii*
July	water and mist	
Aug	buy plant	
Sept	water	
Oct	/	
Nov	remove offsets	
Dec	flowering	

GUZMANIA
Guzmania species

Shining foliage in pink and green forms a most decorative rosette in this variegated Guzmania.

Gorgeous red flower bracts tucked into green leaves make this G. lingulata "Empire" look like a decorated Christmas tree.

FEATURES

Epiphytic

This is a large group of mainly epiphytic bromeliads with a few terrestrial species. They are grown for their lovely spreading rosettes of satiny, smooth-edged foliage, as well as for their striking flowering stems. They have been widely hybridized with *vrieseas* to produce stunning cultivars. Mature plants may be from up to 3¼ft wide when fully mature. *Guzmania lingulata* is a handsome species with shiny, mid-green leaves, and a rich, bright red inflorescence. Leaves can be up to 18in long. *G lingulata minor*, the scarlet star, is much smaller with leaves just 5in long. Named varieties include "Exodus," "Empire," "Cherry" and "Gran Prix."

Leaves   Leaves may be plain glossy green, cross-banded in contrasting colors or finely patterned with stripes. At flowering time the central leaves may color, adding to the brilliant color display.

CONDITIONS

Position   Grows happily in a warm, frost-free greenhouse or conservatory or on a bright windowsill in the home. Prefers bright filtered light away from draughts.

Potting mix   Needs a free-draining mix able to retain some moisture or use ready-made orchid compost. Use a pot that is just slightly larger than the root ball. Terracotta pots will give larger plants more stability.

GROWING METHOD

Propagation   Grows from offsets or suckers that develop around the stem of the parent plant. Plant out from spring to fall.

Watering   Mist daily in summer. Keep water in the cup at all times and water the potting mix twice weekly in summer and just occasionally in winter as necessary.

Feeding   Use weak liquid plant foods during periods of rapid growth. Do not feed too early in spring as it can scorch the leaves and roots.

Problems   No specific problems provided suitable cultural conditions are given.

FLOWERING SEASON

The showy flowers are long lasting on the plant—perhaps up to two months. Most species and varieties flower during summer and last well into fall.

GUZMANIA AT A GLANCE

Ideal for conservatory as pot plant or mounted. Grown for rosettes of spineless foliage and bright red flowering stem.

Jan	water	Dec	keep frost free
Feb	keep warm		
Mar	keep warm		**Recommended Varieties**
Apr	repot		*G. dissitiflora*
May	remove suckers and offsets		*G. lindenii*
Jun	flowering, mist, feed		*G. lingulata*
			G. monostachya
July	flowering, mist, water		*G.* "Amaranth"
			G. "Cherry"
Aug	mist		*G. lingulata* "Empire"
Sept	reduce misting		*G.* "Exodus"
Oct	keep frost free		*G.* "Gran Prix"
Nov	keep frost free		

NEOREGELIA
Neoregelia species

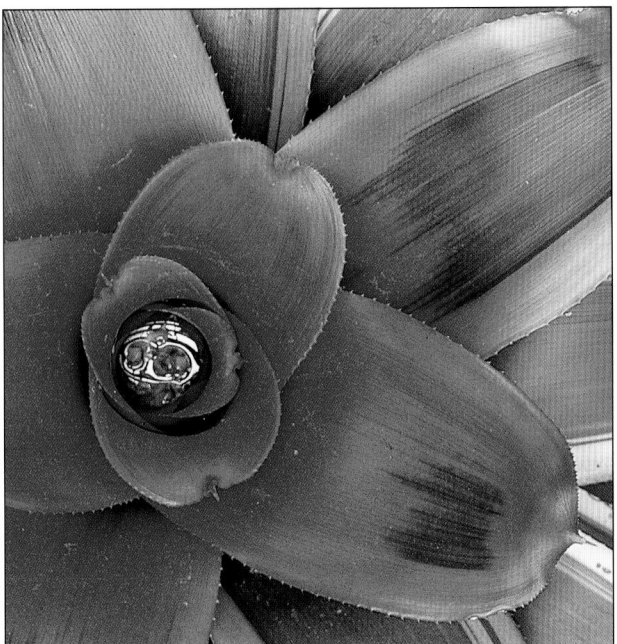

This bromeliad with its fiery red center is aptly named "Inferno." It is an outstanding example of Neoregelia.

The leaves of this variegated Neoregelia *are outlined in cream, giving it prominence among darker Aechmea hybrids.*

FEATURES

Epiphytic

Terrestrial

Often called heart of flame or blushing bromeliads, neoregelias are very popular for their ease of culture and their dazzling variety. In nature they grow as epiphytes on trees or as terrestrials. Species vary from tiny plants not more than 2in wide to those spreading to over 3¼ft. They can be grown as houseplants or as epiphytes attached to logs in the conservatory (see page 554). However, to enjoy them at their best they should be sited low where their beauty can best be appreciated. The group has been widely hybridized, resulting in some truly outstanding cultivars.

NEOREGELIA AT A GLANCE

Varieties vary in size and flowers do not last long. Similar to guzmanias but broader leaves. Keep frost free.

Jan	water	Recommended Varieties
Feb	water	
Mar	re-pot if needs it	N. carolinae
Apr	remove offset	N. carolinae marechalii
May	move away from sunlight	N. carolinae tricolor
		N. spectabilis
Jun	mist and water	
July	flowering, water	
Aug	buy plant	
Sept	reduce water	
Oct	water crown	
Nov	keep frost free	
Dec	keep frost free	

Flowering Most varieties produce a startling color change in the center of the plant at flowering time, the color remaining long after flowering has ceased. This color is mostly red, hence the common name "Blushing Bromeliad". This group lacks the tall, showy flowering spikes of other genera as the flowers—purple, blue, or white—form in the center of the leaf rosette.

Foliage Leaf rosettes are wide and spreading, the foliage shiny with serrated margins. Leaves may be plain green, red, burgundy, or patterned with stripes, bands, or spots, or even marbled.

N. carolinae *Neoregelia carolinae* is undoubtedly the most commonly grown and numerous lovely hybrids have originated from this species. The straight species forms a compact rosette with leaves about 10in long. The color of the center at flowering varies through shades of crimson to cerise and the flowers are deep violet. *N.c. tricolor* has foliage that is cream and green striped. This takes on a pinky red flush as flowering begins and the center of the plant turns crimson. Other varieties of this species include those with cream or white margined leaves. *N. carolinae marechalii* is another fine species but without the cream stripes. Leaves are plain olive green but flushed with crimson at the base during flowering.

N. spectabilis The fingernail plant, *N. spectabilis*, has red-tipped olive green leaves banded gray on the undersides. A hardy species, it is best grown in bright light, where the undersides of the leaves take on a rosy pink color. Place high

Small flowers are forming in the vase of leaves on this Neoregelia. *The orange-red shading on the leaves is an added bonus.*

This bromeliad with dark foliage is named "Hot Gossip." Speckled bronze-green leaves are margined in deep pinky red.

Other species up on a shelf so that the gray-barred, pink foliage is seen to advantage. Another species used in hybridizing is *N. fosteriana* which features burgundy foliage. *N. marmorata* has wide leaves growing about 12in long. They are marbled in red on both sides and have red tips. *N. eleutheropetala* has sharply spined mid-green leaves that turn purple-brown at the center. The inflorescence mixes white flowers and purple-tipped bracts.

CONDITIONS

Position These plants must be grown in frost-free conditions with a minimum temperature of 50°F. A cool greenhouse, conservatory, or light room are perfect. Most neoregelias grow well in filtered or dappled sunlight. Where summers are very hot with long hours of sunshine, greenhouse shading may be needed. Indoors these plants will thrive in bright light but not direct sun through a window. For shady spots with no direct sun, the plain green leaved varieties will do best.

Potting mix The compost must be free draining and coarse to allow air to the roots. A mix of bark and gravel or coarse sand is suitable, with added charcoal if this is available. Don't overpot as roots may not utilize all the mix and watering becomes a problem. A pot large enough for a year's growth is ideal—stones or large pebbles can be put in the base to prevent the plant toppling over. Keep the leaf bases just above soil level.

GROWING METHOD

Propagation Detach offsets from the parent plant once they are a good size. New roots form more rapidly if the offset is potted into a seed-raising compost mix or a mix of sand and peat or peat substitute, whichever you prefer.

Watering Water should be kept in the cup at all times. Water about twice a week in summer, with daily misting unless the atmosphere is extremely humid. In winter water only occasionally. When watering, flood the central cup so that stagnant water is changed to avoid problems of rot.

Feeding In the house, greenhouse or conservatory, plants can be given slow release fertilizer when active growth resumes in mid-spring and again in early to midsummer. Many growers believe plants grown without fertilizer produce more vibrant colors. Feed once a month in summer or when the plant is actively growing.

Problems There are no specific problems if cultural conditions are suitable. Apart from rots, usually caused by overwatering in cool weather, dying leaf tips are a sign of trouble. This symptom could be caused by cold, by dry, hot conditions, by drought or by frequent overwatering.

FLOWERING SEASON

Flowers are short lived. They do not usually rise above the rim of the cup. Most flower during late spring or summer.

PUYA
Puya species

The gray leaves with their spiny edges and the whole shape of this Puya *species make it look like a giant starfish.*

A heavy pink stem supports the large inflorescence of Puya venusta, *which here is part of a large collection of the species.*

FEATURES

Terrestrial

This group of terrestrial bromeliads contains the largest species known, *Puya raimondii* from Peru and Bolivia, which is capable of growing to 9–12ft high. This very slow-growing plant takes up to 100 years to produce its first flower spike, which contains thousands of individual flowers. Puyas are mostly terrestrial, although some are rock dwellers, and most come from inhospitable habitats in the Andes. In nature most are pollinated by humming birds or starlings. Some come from cold, damp, windswept regions, others from dry grasslands where intense sunlight, heat, and drought are balanced by heavy winter frosts. Many team well with succulents that require similar conditions.

PUYA AT A GLANCE

Varieties vary in size. Flowers any time of year and last for a long time. Can go outside in summer. Keep frost free.

Jan	keep dry	Nov	keep dry
Feb	keep dry	Dec	keep dry
Mar	water		
Apr	remove offsets	Recommended Varieties	
May	repot	*P. alpestris*	
Jun	water	*P. berteroniana*	
July	water, take outside	*P. chilensis*	
Aug	/	*P. coerulea*	
Sept	bring in	*P. mirabilis*	
Oct	reduce water and remove offsets	*P. venusta*	

Appearance	Most are large, from 3¼ft upwards, and grow in clumps so that ample space is needed. The heavily spined leaves may be green or gray and silver and are a decorative feature. They form dense rosettes from which tall spikes of flowers appear. Flowers are green, violet, blue, or white, often with colorful contrasting bracts.
Species	*P. venusta* grows to about 4¼ft, producing eye-catching purple flowers on a tall, rose-pink stem and bracts. *P. berteroniana*, over 3¼ft high, has metallic greenish blue flowers.

CONDITIONS

Position	Many tolerate cold winters if kept dry. Most endure extremes of climate with very high daytime temperatures and freezing nights. Grows best in the large conservatory or greenhouse border.
Potting mix	The growing medium must be coarse and well drained. A mix of coarse sand and crushed rock with added peat or a peat substitute would be suitable.

GROWING METHOD

Propagation	Remove offsets from spring to fall.
Watering	Water regularly to establish plants but once established they need only occasional deep watering while in active growth.
Feeding	Little or no fertilizer is needed.
Problems	Generally trouble-free and easy to grow.

FLOWERING SEASON

Flowering times vary with species and district. Most have long-lasting blooms.

TILLANDSIA
Tillandsia species

Fairly common in cultivation, the attractive Tillandsia fasciculata *features an unusual inflorescence of three or four stems.*

Starbursts of silver gray seemingly suspended in mid-air, these tillandsias are growing in baskets along with Spanish moss.

FEATURES

Epiphytic

Tillandsias are mostly epiphytes with very poorly developed root systems, and some absorb water and nutrients through their foliage. Habitats vary from sea level to high altitudes and even the desert. One of the best known is Spanish moss, *Tillandsia usneoides,* with thread-like leaves on long silvery stems. Most species form rosettes of green, gray, or reddish foliage, and those from arid regions have silver scales. Soft green-leaved species are generally native to humid forests and adapt well to pot culture, while many from arid regions are more easily grown on bromeliad "trees" or moss pads. Flowers are tubular and may be violet, white, pink, red, yellow, blue, or green.

TILLANDSIA AT A GLANCE

Easy to look after; grow on a log. Flowers are varied and can appear in almost any month of the year.

Jan	mist twice weekly	Dec	mist twice weekly
Feb	mist twice weekly		
Mar	mist twice weekly, remove offsets	Recommended Varieties	
Apr	keep at 61°F; mist twice daily	T. abdita	
May	flowering, mist	T. argentea	
Jun	flowering, mist	T. bulbosa	
July	flowering, mist	T. butzii	
Aug	flowering, mist	T. cyanea	
Sept	mist	T. usneoides	
Oct	mist twice weekly, remove offsets		
Nov	mist twice weekly		

CONDITIONS

Position   Most species need frost-free conditions—a cool greenhouse or conservatory is ideal. Green-leaved species need filtered sunlight year round while the gray- or silver-leaved varieties can be grown in full or partial sun. With a mixed collection it may be advisable to provide filtered sunlight, especially if the humidity is low.

Potting mix   The mix must be very open and well drained. Use fairly coarse composted bark or a special orchid mix, sold at garden centers or nurseries. Driftwood, logs, or cork slabs are ideal for mounting plants.

GROWING METHOD

Propagation   Grows from offsets produced sometime during spring to fall. (A few species produce offsets between the leaf axils: these may be difficult to remove without damage.) When they have been cut from the parent plant, allow the bases to dry for a few days before fixing them in their permanent positions with a little PVA glue.

Watering   Water or mist plants daily during hot weather. Mounted specimens can suffer if not moistened daily. In cool weather mist several mornings a week.

Feeding   Not necessary although a very weak liquid feed during the warmest months of the year may encourage better growth.

Problems   No specific problems are known.

FLOWERING SEASON

Flower form and color are variable. Most flower in late spring or summer.

VRIESEA
Vriesea species

The leaves of Vriesea gigantea *are finely checkered or tessellated. This broad, spreading species can grow to 3¼ft across.*

Parrot feather *is a name sometimes given to* Vriesea psittacina*. This variable species may grow 16–24in wide.*

FEATURES

Epiphytic

Terrestrial

Vrieseas are very adaptable, tolerating conditions in the home, conservatory, or greenhouse. Most are epiphytes growing on trees in forests but some larger species are terrestrials. Some species in the wild are pollinated by nocturnal insects attracted to the scented flowers. Few of these larger terrestrials are grown outside specialist collections. Leaves are spineless and may be plain glossy green or attractively banded, spotted or variegated. They form neat rosettes. Many species have striking bracts. The true flowers are usually yellow, green, or white but the bracts may be red or purple, yellow or green. Plants may be 6–8in high or reach over 13ft. Some are very wide spreading.

VRIESEA AT A GLANCE

Ideal for mounting or in a pot inside. The scented flowers are long lasting and appear any time of year.

Jan	keep air moist	Oct	remove offsets
Feb	water center of plant	Nov	keep frost free and water center of plant
Mar	feed	Dec	/
Apr	remove offsets, repot		
May	water and mist		**Recommended Varieties**
Jun	mist; keep humid		*V. hieroglyphica*
July	mist, needs high temperatures		*V. carinata*
			V. x *poelmanii*
Aug	mist, water center of plant		*V.* x *polonia*
			V. saundersii
Sept	mist		

CONDITIONS

Climate   Copes with very high temperatures if not direct sun; does best in humid conditions. Many species tolerate low, frost-free temperatures. Most prefer bright, filtered light and good air circulation, again similar to the conditions favoured by orchids. A group of these plants will create a more humid microclimate.

Potting mix   Need good drainage and aeration. Use coarse bark, sand, gravel, and charcoal as the base, with leaf mold, well-decayed compost, or even polystyrene granules added.

GROWING METHOD

Propagation   Grow from offsets produced at the base of the plant during spring to fall. In spreading species they will be under the foliage: once they are sufficiently advanced remove them before they distort the foliage.

Watering   Keep the cup in the center of the rosette filled. In summer, water two or three times a week, spray misting on the other days or if humidity is low. In the conservatory or greenhouse, damp down the floor on hot days. In winter, water only every couple of weeks but maintain atmospheric humidity.

Feeding   Apply slow release granular fertilizer in spring and midsummer, or use soluble liquid foods monthly at half the recommended strength. Ensure fertilizer does not touch foliage. Feed only in the warmer months.

Problem   No specific problems are encountered.

FLOWERING SEASON

Species flower at different times of the year. Most have long-lasting flowers.

Growing Hedges

GROWING HEDGES

Hedges have many uses, especially as screens, fences and windbreaks. In suburban areas they are most often used to screen out ugly views, create a sense of privacy or divide off a utility area from the rest of the garden. In formal garden designs, low, clipped hedges are very popular as edgings or they can be used to create a parterre.

In rural districts, dense prickly hedges of hawthorn (*Crataegus* species), wild rose (*Rosa* species), firethorn (*Pyracantha* species) and barberry (*Berberis* species) have traditionally been used instead of fences as they keep animals in and also provide shelter from wind. Hedges are sometimes planted as noise barriers, but their effectiveness varies considerably. However, even blocking out the sight of the noise source can be helpful.

LEFT: The strong rectangular form of this clipped Camellia sasanqua *hedge contrasts strongly with the mounded shapes of weeping Japanese maples in front, and the fiery sugar maples in the background.*

NEATLY CLIPPED HEDGES and shaped plants, especially standards and topiary, are the essence of formal gardens. In the very stylish setting of this country garden, tightly pruned dwarf box hedges are planted in circles around rows of standard bay trees.

PLANT SELECTION

When selecting plants for screens and hedges, make sure the chosen species suits your local climate, as well as the aspect and soil of your garden. Consider, too, the height and spread of the plant. A vigorous, tall-growing shrub for a 6½ft high hedge can mean a lot of time and work are spent on training and pruning the hedge to shape.

Most hedges are long-term plantings—don't just opt for the fastest growing species. If quick screening is essential, consider planting fast-growing "nurse" trees, such as wattle, behind your slower growing, long-term plants. They can be removed once the main hedge has developed some fullness.

Evergreen shrubs are best for screening, but do not rule out deciduous shrubs. They may be appropriate if you want winter sun in the screened part of the garden, and the mass of bare branches will still give some privacy.

Selection of plant species will also depend to a great extent on your primary reason for establishing a hedge. In suburban gardens you may want to create an outdoor living space by screening off neighboring properties, or to conceal an ugly view, unsightly structure or utility area from the rest of the garden. Don't use a particularly prickly or thorny plant in these areas as children or adults could hurt themselves if they fell against them.

HEDGE PLANTS

FORMAL HEDGES

- box
- cherry laurel
- cypress
- dwarf honeysuckle
- firethorn
- holly
- lavender
- photinia
- privet
- *Camellia sasanqua*
- spindle bush

INFORMAL HEDGES

- abelia
- **cotoneaster**
- elaeagnus
- escallonia
- fuchsia
- laurustinus
- **rose**
- rosemary
- spindle tree
- wattle

If you grow a hedge to delineate the boundary of your property, make sure you know exactly where the boundary lies before you start, and whether you want a real barrier or just an indication of the fenceline.

A hedge may be grown as a windbreak, taking into account the fact that it filters the wind but doesn't increase wind speed on the lee side as can happen with solid structures. A hedge that is not too dense is best. There are plenty of variegated evergreens that look good in winter sun.

ESTABLISHING A HEDGE

Soil preparation

Before digging trenches or holes for planting, use a string line and pegs to mark the planting positions. This is essential for formal hedges to ensure straight lines and even spacing. It is less important for informal hedges but, even so, it will give a better finished appearance. Dig the planting trench, or holes for individual plants, and check the drainage by filling them with water. If there is water still lying in the base after about twenty-four hours, you may need to put in subsoil drains.

Because hedges are close-planted, root competition is intense and you must therefore dig in plenty of well-decayed manure or compost a month before planting. When it is time to plant, add scatterings of fish, blood and bone, which is a slow-release fertilizer, to the soil. It adds nitrogen (promoting vigorous plant growth) and phosphates (encouraging healthy root growth). It gives the hedge a head-start and helps it quickly to become established and happy in its position. Clay soil needs breaking up with horticultural grit.

A VARIEGATED PIERIS hedge borders this path, softening the effect of the dry-stone wall that runs along the other side.

Planting

Most hedge plants are placed from 20in–3½ft apart, depending on their growth habit and the hedge style. Very close planting tends to make plants grow taller as they compete for sunlight. Water the plants in their pots the night before, or at least a couple of hours before planting.

Having removed the plants from their pots, loosen the root ball, and plant so that the soil level is the same as it was in the pots. Give them a thorough watering, and then mulch the area with old manure or compost. Regular watering and mulching is essential. You can also plant bare root specimens between the months of November and March.

TYPES OF HEDGES

Formal or informal

Hedges may be formal or informal. Formal hedges can be used to good effect in gardens of any size and may cover a large or small area. They are usually made from plants with small leaves, as large leaves would be cut in half when the hedge is trimmed and result in an untidy appearance. Well-kept formal hedges can be very labor intensive when it comes to clipping. Unless you grow miles of hedge this should not be a problem. Tall clipped hedges can be a problem though, requiring ladders and boards to cut the uppermost parts.

Informal hedges, which do not have neat outlines, don't need as much attention as formal hedges and can usually be maintained with only one or two clippings a year. In fact, they may not need any clipping at all. Some informal hedges simply need the occasional removal of a wayward stem or branch. Informal hedges probably have a greater impact if they span a reasonably long distance. But remember that without clipping, hedges will grow quite wide and take up quite a bit of space.

SHRUBS FOR A MIXED HEDGE

SCREENING HEDGES

- box
- cotoneaster
- escallonia
- holly
- leyland cypress
- privet
- spindle bush
- yew

FLOWERING HEDGES

- fuchsia
- hebe
- honeysuckle
- lavender
- quickthorn
- rhododendron
- rose
- vibernum

HEDGES FOR BERRIES AND "CATKINS"

- barberry
- cotoneaster
- holly
- itea
- ivy
- privet
- firethorn
- rose

Mixed hedges

For variety in a hedge you can use plants of a species that has flowers of different shades, for example camellias. However, the most striking effects come when you have continuity of both foliage and flower color. Hedges or screens of mixed shrubs only look their best when they are quite long. They also look more harmonious if they grow to the same height.

For a mixed hedge you can choose plants that have a similar leaf texture and shape, or you can go for a complete contrast, although this is usually only an option for hedges of considerable length. Over a short distance the hedge may look spotty if you use more than two species.

Low-clipped hedges for garden borders are sometimes made up of two species such as lavender and box, or lavender and small-leaved honeysuckle, giving contrast of both color and texture. This can be very effective as the small scale allows you to see the repeated pattern.

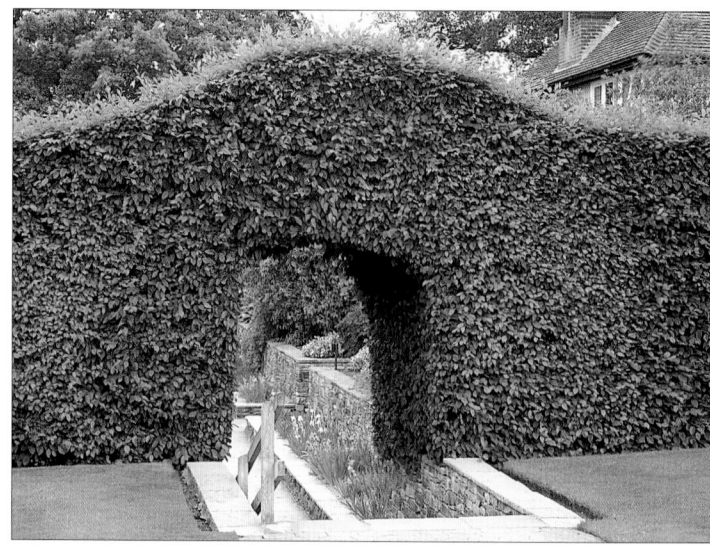

RIGHT: This hedge achieves an architectural quality as it divides the garden. It needs to be accurately sheared to maintain its form.

BELOW: This formal hedge of Japanese box encloses a rose garden. Striking primary colors always stand out best, like this bold red rose.

BELOW: The sinuous curves of this formal photinia hedge give an illusion of distance.

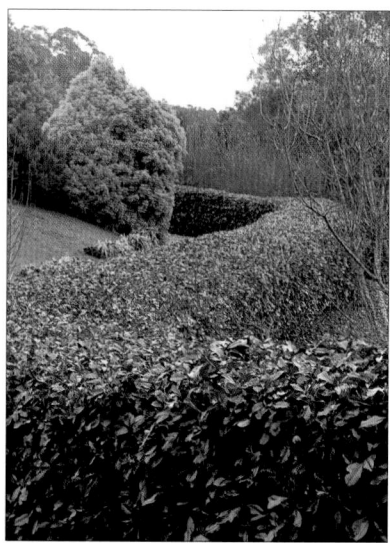

BELOW: In this elegant, formal garden, an urn planted with echeveria and surrounded by a circle of trimmed box forms a neat focal point.

ABOVE: Starkly contrasting colors are here used to great effect to create a sculptural feature and a backdrop for a seating area.

ABOVE: The dark, glossy foliage on this cherry laurel provides a foil for the brilliant fall color of deciduous trees.

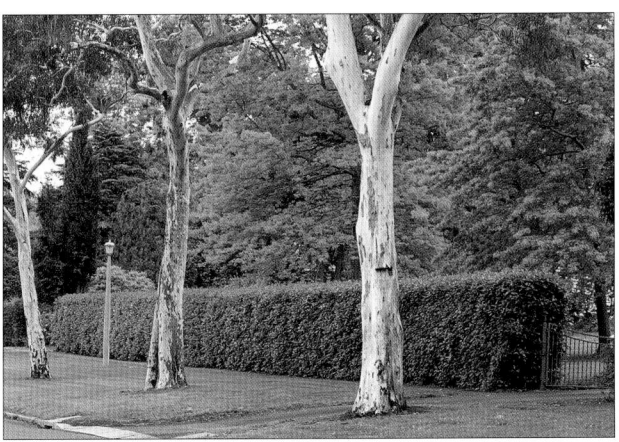

ABOVE: A photinia hedge with pinky-red new growth is here used in place of a fence.

BELOW: A tightly clipped spindle bush hedge divides a utility area from the garden.

ABOVE: Bamboo has been used here to make temporary screens while slow-growing hedges mature. It is decorative in its own right.

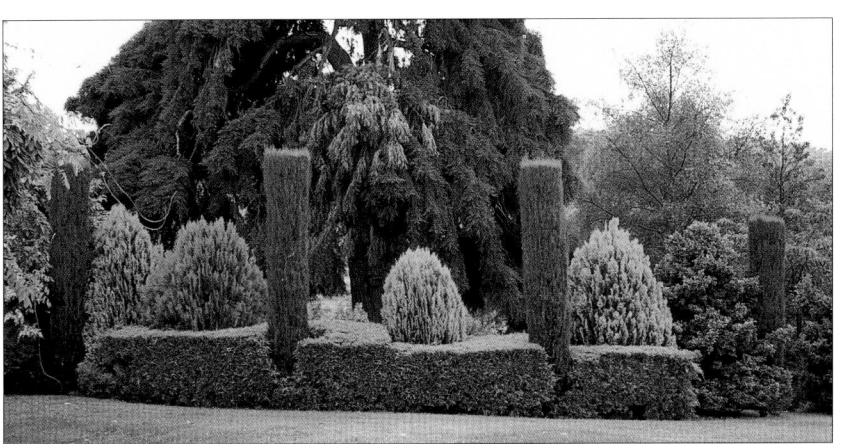

ABOVE: This pretty, informal hedge of Camellia sasanqua *perfectly matches the relaxed sub-tropical style of the house and garden.*

ABOVE: Vertical pillars of cypress punctuate the squared blocks of a clipped conifer hedge in this very formal arrangement. The rounded shapes of the cypresses soften the geometric style.

PRUNING

Shaping

Opinions differ on how to go about training and pruning a hedge. Some gardeners believe the plants should be allowed to grow to the desired height before the leading growth is cut off. Tip pruning of the lateral branches is carried out as seems necessary. Once the leading shoots are taken out, lateral growth should increase. This method suits informal hedges.

To develop a dense formal hedge, it is better to severely cut the vertical growth as soon as the plants are established, to encourage low branching, and then to continue cutting all upward growing shoots until the base has filled in well.

Always prune your hedge so that the top is just slightly narrower than the bottom, to prevent the lower growth dying back through lack of sunlight (see the diagrams opposite). This is especially important with conifers such as cypresses because once the lower growth dies, it does not usually regenerate. Conifers should be pruned little and often, and never into older wood, as many of them have no dormant buds on their stems capable of reshooting from bare wood.

The right equipment

Most domestic hedges can be managed with hedging shears. If, however, you have very extensive hedges to maintain, it may be worth investing in power-driven mechanical shears. With electric sheers use a special circuit-breaker device that cuts out if the lead is cut or severed, and always wear goggles to prevent shards of wood flying in your eyes. If you have to mount a ladder to trim the top parts of a hedge, be certain that the ladder is firm and steady.

ELECTRIC HAND SHEARS make trimming this small-leaved honeysuckle hedge both quick and easy.

HAND CLIPPERS are used to shape, not shear this variegated pittosporum.

THIS LAURUSTINUS HEDGE is being trimmed with the aid of a string line. It ensures that the hedge is perfectly straight, something difficult to achieve by eye.

SHAPING A HEDGE

THE SLIGHTLY NARROWER top of this hedge prevents the lower growth from dying out and ensures fullness of foliage all over.

A PYRAMIDAL SHAPE is easiest to achieve if you start with a plant that has a natural taper to the top. Cypress and juniper are ideal.

A ROUNDED or bun shaped hedge may be difficult to maintain if it is too high or wide. You need to be able to prune across the top.

WHAT CAN GO WRONG?

Yellow leaves
• Plants may have been overwatered or they may be too dry.
• Plants may need feeding: fertilize them if this has not been done for two or three months and see if there is any improvement within the next two or three weeks.
• Older leaves on shrubs may turn bright yellow before dropping off. Don't worry, they have finished their useful life.

Curled or distorted leaves
• Look for aphids, small sticky insects clustering on the new growth. You can wash them off with a hose, spray them with soapy water or use an insecticidal soap or chemical spray.
• Some virus diseases manifest themselves this way and there is no cure for viruses in plants. Consult reference books or a nursery to see whether your plant is likely to have this problem.
• Check that there has been no drift of any herbicide from nearby spraying. Even very small amounts of spray drift can distort the leaves on those plants that are very sensitive to chemicals.

Black spots on leaves
• These may be fungal leaf spots. Avoid wetting the leaves when hosing and avoid watering plants late in the day.

Gray/white powder on leaf surfaces
• This deposit is probably powdery mildew, which affects a wide range of plants. Avoid watering gardens late in the day and spray plants with a chemical treatment if necessary.

Mottled leaves
• Mottling on leaves is usually associated with sap-sucking insects such as scales and thrips, and mites (which are not true insects). Plants that are under stress are more frequently attacked by these insects. Stress may be induced in plants by drought or overwatering, or simply by trying to grow a plant outside its preferred climate or aspect.
• Scales may be flat or rounded in various sizes and colors. Small infestations may be wiped off with a damp cloth. Control severe infestations by giving plants a chemical spray such as Malathion or insecticidal soap.
• Mites can be a particular problem in hot, dry weather. Hosing the foliage helps to reduce the numbers and may avoid the need for spraying. Note though that many mites are predators of insects or other mites, and are beneficial.

Holes in leaves or on leaf margins
• This may be snail or slug damage. Search for snails as they are often quite high up in the foliage and so do not take baits. Pick them off by hand. Keep a special watch at night. Baits can be used at the base of plants if you don't have pets.
• Caterpillars, weevil beetles, and snails also eat leaves. You may need to dust your plants on several consecutive nights with derris dust, or spray the plants with carbaryl if damage persists. This is only likely in rare, extreme cases.

Sooty mould
• This dry, black coating on the leaf surface grows and feeds on sticky honeydew secreted by sap-sucking insects such as aphids and scales. The honeydew looks like tiny beads of sticky sweat. Once the insect pest is controlled, the sooty mould will gradually weather off. Hosing helps; large-leaved plants can be wiped with a damp cloth.

Sudden death of plant
• If the leaves have turned brown but remain attached to the plant, the plant has probably died of root rot. The root systems may have been damaged by excessive watering, from rain or irrigation, quite some time before the plant dies, especially in cold, wet winters. Make sure the soil is lightened for new, hardier plants. When stress such as an extremely hot or windy day is experienced, the damaged root system cannot cope and the plant appears to have died almost overnight.
• If a plant is suffering from drought the leaves may be brown and rapidly drop off when the plant is given a good watering. These plants may recover if they have not been water-stressed for too long.

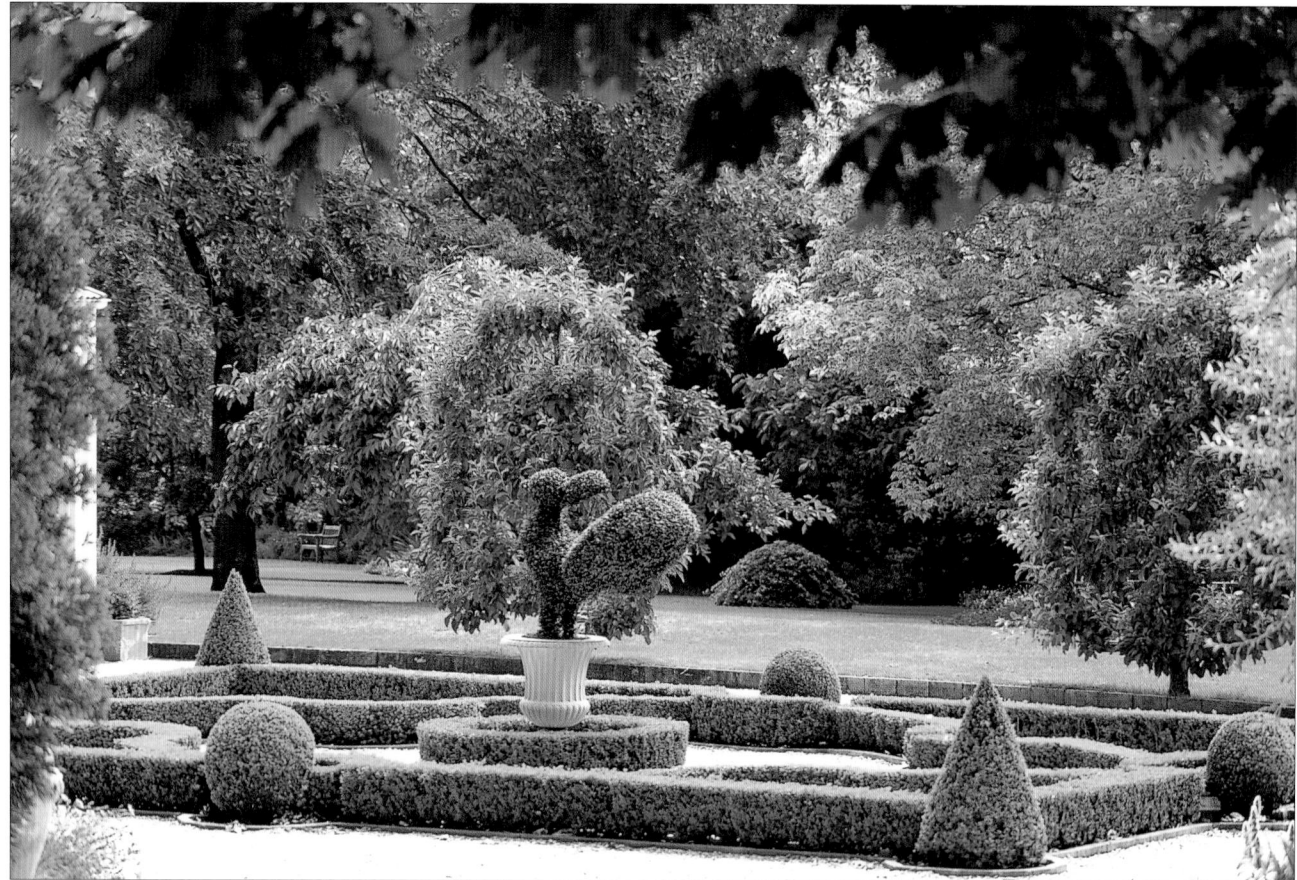

CLIPPED BOX was used to create this wonderful modern version of a parterre garden. A topiary peacock has pride of place in the center, while the low hedges are interrupted by the formal pyramid and ball shapes. A parterre garden need not be large: the effect is achieved by the intricate shapes.

PARTERRE GARDENS

Parterre means "on or over the ground" but it has come to mean a level space containing ornamental garden beds. Early parterre gardens were arranged in geometric patterns within an outer square. Flowers were not used as they distracted the viewer from the design, which was more important than the plants. A very limited range of plants was used.

In the later medieval period knot gardens were developed, and they evolved further during the early Renaissance period in Europe. The gardens were designed to be looked on from above, either from an upper floor of a building or from a garden terrace. Sometimes the pattern was punctuated with tightly clipped, formally shaped conifers. Often the ordered, formal parterre was used to offer a distinct contrast with the wider, natural landscape viewed in the distance. Gravel and brick dust were used on the ground between the clipped plants to further emphasize the design.

The formal parterre layout was incorporated into the grand gardens of Rome and Tuscany during the 15th and 16th centuries, and persisted in Italy until the end of the 18th century. These Italian gardens maintained a strict economy of plant material, with no distracting color. By the middle of the 17th century in France, broderies or parterres were all the rage. Broderies were made using the elaborate patterns, colors and designs of the embroidered silks which were imported from India and China. The French fashion spread throughout Europe. Armies of gardeners were employed to maintain these floral artworks in perfect condition. Although many of these famous gardens have been destroyed and are known only from engravings and paintings, some have been restored and can still be seen.

Modern parterre gardens

Today there is a revival of interest in parterre gardens. Modern interpretations are more flexible than their historical ancestors and may have informal plantings inside a formal shape that is defined by small hedges. These hedges are often planted with English or Japanese box. The dwarf edging box, *Buxus sempervirens* 'Suffruticosa', is most commonly used and while there are other forms of box this is the one for small topiary. Other modern parterre gardens are created with strict geometric designs and use a limited range of plants with contrasting color and foliage characteristics. Plants commonly used include box, cotton lavender, true lavender, and small-leaved honeysuckle (*Lonicera nitida*).

If you want to have informal plantings inside a formal hedge, consider how much attention the plantings will need and whether they will look attractive for many months without intense management. Also, when planning the garden, remember that if the area is close-planted you will need to be able to reach into the center of the planting from the side as there will be nowhere to step. And give some thought to whether a parterre garden suits the style of your house and whether you have the time or interest to devote to its maintenance. Such schemes invariably look best where the buildings can provide architectural formality and where they have loving owners willing to put in the hours.

TOPIARY

Topiary is the art of training and pruning plants into specific shapes. Many topiary shapes are geometric, with triangles or pyramids, cones and squares being widely used. Balls and cylinders are other very popular shapes, but plants can also be trained to resemble animals and birds or even architectural features. Peacocks and wrens have always been popular.

Topiary is an ancient art. It was practised by the Romans and spread throughout the Roman Empire as far as Spain and Turkey. Topiary was widely used in Italian and French gardens during the Renaissance and has been used in a great many gardens in Britain. Levens Hall in Cumbria is judged to be the finest surviving topiary garden in the world. It was originally developed in the 17th century, the hard-clipped shapes being composed of yew and box. Some of these shapes have become massive with time despite the regular shearing.

Topiary today

Topiary is once again becoming popular, one of the most commonly seen forms being a clipped, rounded ball. Plants are also trained into spirals, juniper being one of the most widely used plants for this form, and into layers of foliage with bare stem or trunk in between. These formally shaped plants are often used as large potted specimens to flank an entrance way. They have a place as accent plants to highlight a section of a garden or to draw the eye to a specific point.

A wider variety of plants is used today but still the most popular are the plants with fine, dense foliage such as juniper and cypress, and small-leaved evergreens such as box, privet, and small-leaved honeysuckle.

Creating topiary

The creation of good topiary effects requires a great deal of time, patience, and skill. Careful, painstaking clipping has to be done throughout the growing season. This input of time and skill is reflected in the high price charged for a good specimen at the nursery.

If you decide to try creating topiary for yourself, choose a young plant that is in vigorous growth. When you need to remove foliage right back to the trunk or stem, young plants will heal their scars less noticeably than older plants. Sometimes unwanted foliage can be rubbed off with the fingers, especially if it is young regrowth from a previous cut. And don't aim too high at your first attempt—start with a simple shape such as a ball, cube or pyramid.

First you will need to shape with pruning shears, but once the plant begins to take on the form you want, growth can be shorn off quickly, little and often, using a pair of shears.

For your first efforts in topiary, it is best to select a plant that is vaguely the shape you want to achieve. If you would like a triangular or pyramidal shape, look for a plant that is wide at the base and has a natural taper towards its top. For rounded or ball shapes, choose a multi-stemmed shrub that has a good overall cover of foliage.

Don't make your first shaping too severe as you need to see how quickly new growth emerges from the pruned stems. If you are adventurous enough to try a layered look straight away you will need to select a tree or shrub specimen that has foliage almost to soil level, and one that is at least 3½ft high. Otherwise you won't have enough to work with.

Quick "topiary"

Sometimes small-leaved plants and climbers are trained over wire shapes to create a particular form, and while this is a much quicker way to produce a finished specimen, it is not strictly speaking topiary. However, they do create a pleasing effect and are relatively maintenance-free. Some public parks, zoos and even railway stations have emblems and animals created this way—the finished product always creates interest with children and adults alike.

IN THIS LOVELY GARDEN a formal hedge of Japanese box encloses an informal planting of azalea, roses, and lilac.

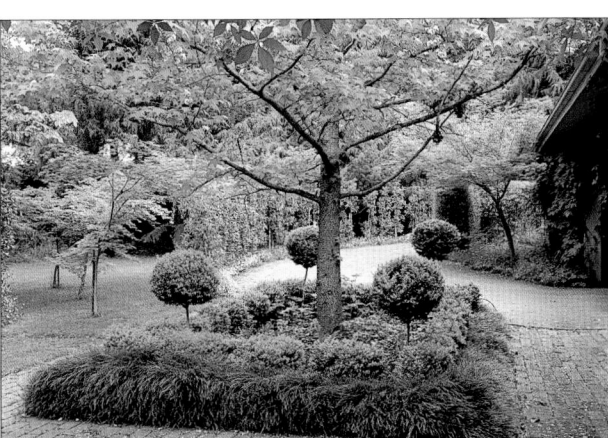

STANDARD BOX TREES on short stems accent the corners of this bed, with its tiny box hedges and massed mondo grass.

A YOUNG PLANTING of dwarf box is here laid out to complement the tall standard box trees. Some people call them "lollipop" trees.

ABELIA X GRANDIFLORA
Abelia

SPLASHED WITH pale gold, the leaves of Abelia *"Francis Mason" can light up your garden. Plant it near darker plants for contrast.*

IF NOT TRIMMED too severely, abelia makes a dense and pretty hedging or screening plant. It is very easy to care for.

FEATURES

Informal

This evergreen shrub with slightly arching canes makes an easy-care informal hedge or screen. Growing to about 6½ft high and wide, it has glossy green leaves and produces masses of pink flowers throughout summer and into early fall. Its decorative effect is prolonged by the persistent pinky-red calyces (flower bases) which remain on the bush until fall. This is a long-lived plant. There is a variegated leaf form known as "Francis Mason," which is generally less vigorous in growth.

CONDITIONS

Aspect   Grows best in full sun but tolerates some shade for part of the day. Since it isn't fully

hardy, provide a warm, protected spot. These plants are best grown in city gardens that do not get blitzed by frosts.

Site   Needs well-drained soil, preferably enriched with organic matter, although it will grow in poorer soils.

GROWING METHOD

Propagation   Grow abelia from semi-hardwood cuttings taken in late summer to early fall, or from hardwood cuttings of leafless canes taken during the winter months. This is a remarkably unfussy plant.

Spacing   Set plants at about 3½ft intervals.

Feeding   Apply complete plant food in spring and again in midsummer.

Problems   No problems are known.

FLOWERING

Season   There is a long flowering period through summer and sometimes into fall. Afterwards, the red calyces of the flower will often remain on the shrub, giving color until the fall.

PRUNING

General   The main pruning should be done in early spring. As an informal hedge it does not need shearing, which would spoil the arching habit of the growth. *Abelia triflora* is the tallest, reaching about 10ft high. It can be rather gaunt though. The best looking hedge plant is *Abelia* x *grandiflora* which is slightly shorter.

ABELIA AT A GLANCE

Abelia x *grandiflora* is a fine evergreen shrub with dark glossy leaves and scented white flowers. Hardy to 23°F (zone 9).

Jan	foliage 🌿	Recommended Varieties
Feb	foliage 🌿	*Abelia chinensis*
Mar	foliage 🌿	A. "Edward Goucher"
April	foliage 🌿	A. *floribunda*
May	foliage 🌿	A. x *grandiflora*
June	foliage 🌿	A. x *g.* "Francis Mason"
July	flowering ❀	A. x *g.* "Goldsport"
Aug	flowering ❀	*Abelia triflora*
Sept	flowering ❀	
Oct	foliage 🌿	
Nov	foliage 🌿	
Dec	foliage 🌿	

ACACIA
Wattle

A CREAMY YELLOW WATTLE in full bloom is a magnificent sight, and many have the added advantage that they bloom in winter.

ACACIA BINERVIA is one wattle that makes a fine hedge: it responds well to pruning, although it may never bloom.

FEATURES

Informal

Acacias are quite tender, best grown in sheltered gardens in the warm south-west, where they escape the frosts. They can be used as novel, mainly evergreen hedges about 7ft high. They provide marvellous soft delicate foliage and fluffy flowers, usually yellow, in early spring. The flowers appear on last year's wood. The best kinds for a hedge are *Acacia cultriformis*, and *A. verticillata*, known as prickly Moses. Both are natives of Australia. They need to be well pruned after flowering to promote an abundance of short stems creating a thick, bushy effect. In colder regions acacias are best grown against warm sheltered walls where they will not get blitzed by icy winds.

ACACIA AT A GLANCE

Acacias make a highly attractive, unusual, yellow-flowering hedge in warm-climate gardens. Hardy to 32°F (zone 10).

		Companion Plants
Jan	foliage	Crocus
Feb	foliage	Daffodil
Mar	flowering	Erythronium
April	foliage	Fritillaria
May	foliage	Iris
June	foliage	Scilla
July	foliage	Tulip
Aug	foliage	
Sept	foliage	
Oct	foliage	
Nov	foliage	
Dec	foliage	

CONDITIONS

Aspect   Most acacias prefer full sun for best results. Some, such as *Acacia binervia* and *A. longifolia* will tolerate exposed coastal conditions.

Site   The soil must be well drained, but need not be particularly rich. Acacias will tolerate sites with slightly acid soils.

GROWING METHOD

Propagation   Grow from seed removed from ripe pods. Pour almost boiling water over the seed and allow it to soak overnight before planting. Alternatively take semi-ripe cuttings in the summer.

Spacing   Plant at 3½–5ft intervals.

Feeding   Fertilizing is not essential. A light application of blood and bone may be given in spring.

Problems   In the open acacias are remarkably trouble-free, assuming that frosts do not get them. Under glass, however, they are prone to red spider mites.

FLOWERING

Season   Depends on the species chosen. Most flower in early spring. The milder the winter has been the better the flowers.

PRUNING

General   For a formal shape, pruning may be necessary two or three times during the growing season but then you may get little or no flowering.

BERBERIS THUNBERGII
Barberry

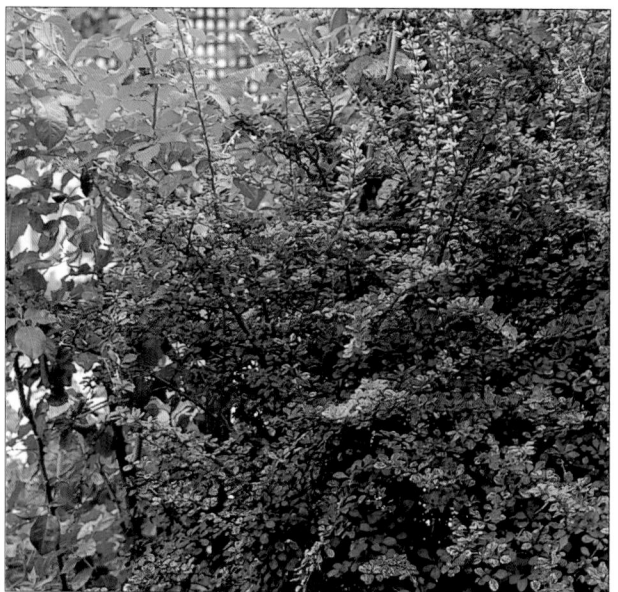

AN UNPRUNED BARBERRY has a loose, open habit. Full sun is needed to maintain the color of the burgundy and pink forms.

CLOSELY CUT barberry forms a living fence on this property. The trees behind provide lovely contrasts in foliage, shape and texture.

FEATURES

Formal or Informal

Growing about 3ft high and wide, this is a very spiny plant that makes a useful hedge where a real barrier is wanted. Although it is deciduous, growth is very dense. In the species, leaves are deep green but there are cultivars with foliage that is burgundy or burgundy splashed with pink. This shrub gives year-round value, producing small, bright yellow flowers in spring, followed in fall by bright red berries that persist through winter. The foliage colors well before falling.

CONDITIONS

Aspect   Prefers full sun all day, though many happily tolerate part shade, or shade for some of the day.

BERBERIS AT A GLANCE

Deciduous *Berberis thunbergii* has good fall orange-red colors, and makes an ornamental hedge. Hardy to 0°F (zone 7).

		Recommended Varieties
Jan	/	
Feb	/	*Berberis darwinii*
Mar	/	*B. d.* "Flame"
Apr	flowering ✿	*B. dictyophylla*
May	flowering ✿	*B.* "Goldilocks"
Jun	foliage 🍃	*B.* "Red Jewel"
July	foliage 🍃	*B.* x *stenophylla*
Aug	foliage 🍃	*B. thunbergii atropurpurea*
Sep	foliage 🍃	*B. wilsoniae*
Oct	foliage 🍃	
Nov	/	
Dec	/	

Site   Although barberry is tolerant of a range of soil types, this shrub will give its best growth in well-drained soils that contain plenty of organic matter.

GROWING METHOD

Propagation   The species can be grown from seed that is taken from ripe berries, cleaned and planted. Cultivars are best grown from semi-ripe cuttings taken in the summer.

Spacing   Barberry needs planting at about 20in intervals for hedging.

Feeding   Apply complete plant food as soon as growth begins in spring. A thick spring layer of well-rotted organic matter will act as a mulch, keeping in moisture and feeding the soil.

Problems   Barberry is sometimes attacked by scale insects, which are readily controlled by spraying with insecticidal soap. In general though, these plants suffer from few problems, and they tend to look after themselves.

FLOWERING

Season   Bright yellow flowers appear in spring.

Berries   Flowers are followed by berries that ripen to bright red by fall. They may persist during the early winter months.

PRUNING

General   The main pruning should be done in late winter but tip pruning can be done at almost any time. Thin each year by removing some growth down near the base.

BUXUS
Box

NEAT, GLOSSY FOLIAGE characterizes common box, which is probably the most widely used of all hedging plants.

THE PALE NEW GROWTH on this Japanese box will darken as it ages. The compact rosettes of echeveria emphasise the formal hedge shape.

FEATURES

Formal

Formal box hedges have been used for many centuries in Europe and are still used in many parts of the world. Box plants are very long lived. If left untrimmed, they can grow quite tall but for hedging are usually kept under 3ft high. There are several varieties in use for hedges. Common box (*B. sempervirens*) has very dark green, pointed leaves, while Japanese box (*B. microphylla* var. *japonica*) has lighter green, more rounded leaves. There is also a dwarf edging box (*B. sempervirens* "Suffruticosa") with very small leaves and a compact habit which can be planted at 6in intervals. Box plants need clipping only once or twice a year. Start gently pruning box at a young age to make sure that the plants bush out from low down and create a dense solid shape. Otherwise they can take on a sparse look.

BUXUS AT A GLANCE

A first-rate hedging plant, giving well-defined, evergreen, topiarized shapes. Clip regularly. Hardy to 5°F (zone 7).

Jan	foliage	Recommended Varieties
Feb	foliage	*Buxus sempervirens*
Mar	foliage	*B. s.* "Elegantissima"
April	flowering	*B. s.* "Handsworthensis"
May	flowering	*B. s.* "Latifolia Maculata"
June	foliage	*B. s.* "Suffruticosa"
July	foliage	*B. microphylla* var. *japonica*
Aug	foliage	
Sept	foliage	
Oct	foliage	
Nov	foliage	
Dec	foliage	

CONDITIONS

Aspect For dense compact growth, plants should be grown in full sun. They will tolerate partial even total shade.

Site Tolerant of poor soils, box does best in well-drained soil with plenty of decayed organic matter. Thrives on lime and chalk soils.

GROWING METHOD

Propagation From semi-ripe cuttings taken in summer.

Spacing For hedging box can be planted at 12–20in spacings. While more informal hedges can be planted in zigzags, using two parallel lines, formal box hedges should be planted in straight lines.

Feeding Apply complete plant food in spring and again in midsummer. Give a February feed with nitrate of soda. It'll grow fuller and quicker.

Problems A virulent fungal box blight can affect *B. sempervirens* and its cultivars. Infected leaves turn brown and fall. Try to be sure to buy unifected plants. Prune and destroy any infected leaves.

FLOWERING

Season The tiny but lightly perfumed flowers appear during spring. They are very attractive to bees. Frequently pruned box may not flower.

PRUNING

General Formal box hedging should be pruned as often as needed to maintain its shape.

CAMELLIA SASANQUA
Camellia

THE CLEAR PINK FLOWERS of Camellia sasanqua *"Plantation Pink"* are shown off to perfection by the rich glossy foliage.

PRUNING to a formal shape may reduce the quantity of blooms on this camellia hedge, but it will still look good throughout the year.

FEATURES

 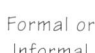

Formal or Informal

Although other species of camellia can be grown as screening plants, *C. sasanqua* is the most suitable for use as hedges, whether formal or informal. Like all camellias, it is long lived. The growth habit of the cultivars varies and for hedging it is best to choose an upright grower such as "Narumigata," "Navajo," and "Nodami-ushiro." You can choose the height of your hedge but camellias are usually topped off somewhere between 6½–10ft. Blooming in mid- to late fall, the flowers may be single or double, and they come in a color range of white, pale pink, rose, cerise and red.

CONDITIONS

Aspect These camellias tolerate sun or shade but are probably best in shade for part of the day. They

Site only withstand wall-to-wall sun when fully established, and even then their roots must be kept on the cool side. As a general rule, keep them sheltered from harsh cold winds which can quickly send them into a major sulk. Needs well-drained, slightly acid soil that has been heavily enriched with organic matter. Plants also need mulching with decayed manure or compost.

GROWING METHOD

Propagation From semi-ripe cuttings taken in late summer.
Spacing Plant at about 20in intervals.
Feeding Apply blood and bone fertilizer, or camellia and azalea food, when growth starts in spring and again in midsummer.
Problems Root rot caused by overwatering or poorly drained soil will kill these plants, but otherwise they are fairly trouble free. In some years a fungal leaf gall has been known to occur on selected varieties, causing abnormal thickening and discoloration of new growth. Pick off and destroy any leaves that are affected by this pest.

FLOWERING

Season There is a late flowering period which begins in the fall.
Cutting Flowers dismantle easily and so are not suitable for picking.

PRUNING

General The main pruning should be done in late winter just before new growth begins. Trimming can be done at any time of the year.

CAMELLIA AT A GLANCE

Camellia sasanqua is a terrific late-season flowering hedge, but is not suitable for the cold north. Hardy to 5°F (zone 7).

		Recommended Varieties
Jan	foliage	*Camellia japonica* "Bob Hope"
Feb	foliage	
Mar	foliage	
April	foliage	*C. j.* "Guilio Nuccio"
May	foliage	*C. j.* "Kumasaka"
June	foliage	*C. j.* "Miss Universe"
July	foliage	*C.* "Leonard Messel"
Aug	foliage	*C. sasanqua* "Narumigata"
Sept	foliage	*C. s.* "Navajo"
Oct	flowering	*C. s.* "Nodami-ushiro"
Nov	flowering	*C.* x *williamsii* "Elsie Jury"
Dec	foliage	

CARPINUS BETULUS
Hornbeam

LINES OF DIFFERENT color help this Carpinus betulus *to look quite at home, as well as creating a graceful corridor effect.*

ALTHOUGH IT DOES produce flowers in the spring, the vibrant leaves of C. betulus *make a wonderfully lush display of their own.*

FEATURES

Formal

The common hornbeam, *Carpinus betulus*, grows wild in many areas. An extremely strong wood, it is used for butchers' chopping blocks. If left to grow it can form a massive tree, 60ft high. But it is also the mainstay of wild hedges, withstanding severe pruning, and is grown for its spring catkins and fall color when the leaves turn yellowish-orange. It is particularly useful on heavy ground, and is worth using if you have thick clay soil. It also makes a quick growing, traditional formal hedge, and is a good alternative to hawthorn, beech, holly, privet, laurel and yew. The form "Aspleniifolia" has more shapely, toothed leaves. For a long hedge, seek a specialist supplier who sells inexpensive young plants in bulk.

CARPINUS AT A GLANCE

Ever-reliable deciduous hedging plant, looks best in a cottage garden. Hardy to 0°F (zone 7).

		Companion Plants
Jan	/	
Feb	/	Bluebell
Mar	/	Crocus
April	foliage	Cyclamen
May	foliage	Erythronium
June	foliage	Fritillaria
July	foliage	Poppy
Aug	foliage	Primrose
Sept	foliage	Rose
Oct	foliage	
Nov	/	
Dec	/	

CONDITIONS

Aspect Hornbeam thrives in full sun and partial shade. The lighter the position the more quickly and densely it grows.

Site Gardeners on heavy clay soil need not worry too much. Extreme cases should be lightened, but it is not necessary to spend hours trying to provide impeccable drainage by adding copious amounts of horticultural sand and grit.

GROWING METHOD

Propagation Take fresh cuttings in early summer.

Spacing Set plants about 3ft apart, depending on the density required.

Feeding Hornbeam does not require over-rich, well-worked soil. Moderate fertility is quite acceptable. On planting add plenty of well-rotted organic matter, and mulch to keep in moisture. It should get off to a very good start.

Problems Highly robust trees that take care of themselves. Need little fussing.

FLOWERING

Season The big decorative feature is a massed display of catkins (yellow when male, and greenish when female) in the spring. Useful in cut-flower displays.

PRUNING

General One of the principle advantages of growing hornbeam is that you can cut it back quite severely and it will always re-shoot, putting on plenty of new growth.

CHAENOMELES SPECIOSA
Japonica

THE DELICATE APPEARANCE of the flowers belies the tough nature of japonica. Flowers can be apricot, white, pink or crimson.

DENSE, TWIGGY GROWTH and ease of cultivation make japonica a practical and secure choice for boundary planting.

FEATURES

Informal

Also known as flowering quince, japonica is a deciduous, multi-stemmed shrub that grows 6–8ft high. The stems are thorny, making it good for barrier planting. Fairly quick growing, it is also long lived. Japonica is a great asset to the garden in winter, producing its flowers on the bare branches in the spring. There are several lovely cultivars with flowers in scarlet, apricot, crimson, pink, or white. Examples can be closely planted and trimmed, but japonica looks unnatural when cut into a box shape. It is usually best to let japonicas grow naturally.

CONDITIONS

Aspect   Prefers full sun but can get by with just half a day of sun. Not happy in shaded areas.

CHAENOMELES AT A GLANCE

An excellent large deciduous shrub with scarlet flowers in the spring. Makes a good tapestry hedge. Hardy to 0°F (zone 7).

		Recommended Varieties
Jan	/	
Feb	/	*Chaenomeles* x *californica*
Mar	/	"Enchantress"
April	flowering ✿	*C. japonica*
May	flowering ✿	*C. speciosa*
June	foliage	*C. s.* "Moerloosei"
July	foliage	*C. s.* "Simonii"
Aug	foliage	*C. s.* "Umbilicata"
Sept	foliage	*C.* x *superba* "Crimson and
Oct	foliage	Gold"
Nov	/	*C.* x *superba* "Knap Hill
Dec	/	Scarlet"

Site   Tolerates a wide range of soils as long as the drainage is good.

GROWING METHOD

Propagation   Japonica is most easily grown from cuttings of dormant hardwood, but can also be grown from semi-ripe cuttings taken in the summer.

Spacing   For an informal hedge, japonicas will need 3ft spacings between them.

Feeding   Japonica can be grown without supplementary feeding, but if the soil is poor give complete plant food in the spring. In dryish areas a spring mulch of well-rotted manure will both keep moisture in, and improve the soil quality.

Problems   The shrub itself has no major problems but do keep a look out for possible canker, scale insects, and aphids. Canker is the most troublesome. The bark becomes raised and splits, and it tends to ring right round the affected stem, and everything above starts to die. Cut back to healthy wood, and spray with an appropriate fungicide. Ready-made sprays are available at garden centers.

FLOWERING

Season   Flowers are produced on the bare branches in spring to early summer.

Cutting   Stems of japonica can be cut to make a lovely indoor decoration.

PRUNING

General   The main pruning should be done straight after flowering. As the plant becomes very congested, saw out some of the older canes at ground level to make way for younger wood.

COTONEASTER SIMONSII
Cotoneaster

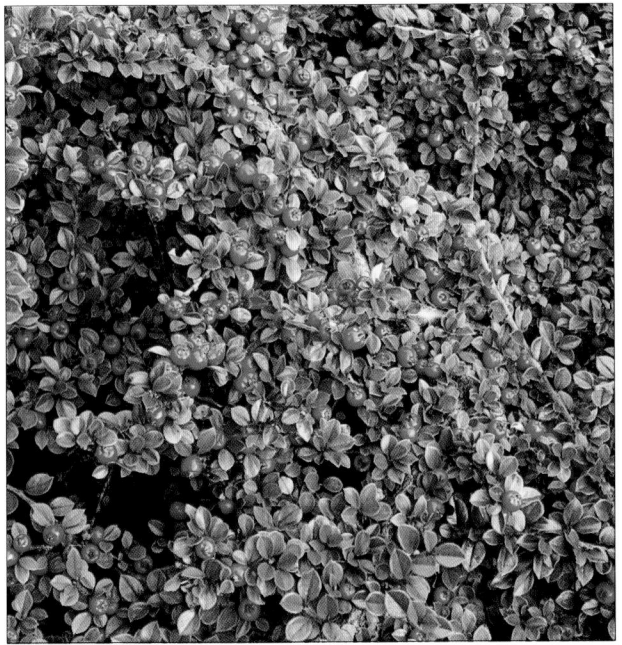

THE INTENSE COLORS of cotoneaster berries make these useful plants true stars of the garden in the fall and early winter.

THE THICK, TWISTING habit of cotoneasters provides a dense mass of foliage and stem, making for an effective barrier.

FEATURES

Informal

Cotoneasters are highly underrated. Few people think past *Cotoneaster horizontalis* but there are about 320 kinds that you can buy from specialist nurseries. They range from tight, hard mounds as big as a large pumpkin, to giants. *C. simonsii* is an award-winning semi-evergreen (in warm areas) or deciduous shrub, upright in growth. The leaves redden in the fall, and the berries are bright orange-red. It can get quite big, about 6ft high and wide, but can be pruned and kept shorter. As a hedge it is definitely for the wilder part of the garden. Like most cotoneasters, the big selling point is the major show of bright berries, some hanging on well in winter.

COTONEASTER AT A GLANCE

Cotoneaster simonsii is a high-performance shrub with white summer flowers and orange-red berries. Hardy to 0°F (zone 7).

		Recommended Varieties
Jan	/	*Cotoneaster acutifolius*
Feb	/	C. *conspicuus*
Mar	/	C. *franchetii*
April	/	C. "Herbstfeuer"
May	/	C. *hupehensis*
June	foliage 🌿	C. *marquandi*
July	flowering ❀	C. *nitidus*
Aug	foliage 🌿	C. *simonsii*
Sept	foliage 🌿	C. *splendens*
Oct	foliage 🌿	C. *divaricatus* "Valkenburg"
Nov	/	
Dec	/	

CONDITIONS

Aspect   Provide full sun, though partial shade is acceptable. The more sun, the more growth, the more berries.

Site   Cotoneasters tolerate most soils, except for the extremes of dry and wet. As a general rule though, do not overfeed, and make sure that there is good drainage.

GROWING METHOD

Propagation   The easiest method is by seed. Sow fresh seed and cover the soil surface with grit. Keep warm indoors, and then put in the refrigerator for six weeks, followed by more warmth. Or take cuttings in mid- and late summer.

Spacing   Set *C. simonsii* about 3ft apart.

Feeding   Unless the soil was remarkably poor in quality to begin with, extra feeding will not be necessary. If feeding is needed, a slow-release spring fertilizer, such as blood, fish and bone mixture, will then suffice.

Problems   One drawback of these plants is that they can be afflicted by a wide range of problems. Look out for the cotoneaster webber moth which makes the foliage darken and dry up, and for signs of silk webbing. Cut away affected areas and spray with permethrin.

PRUNING

General   Most tolerate regular pruning. They also survive hard pruning, but it takes several years for the shrub to perform well again.

ELAEAGNUS PUNGENS
Elaeagnus

WITH ITS ATTRACTIVE *variegated yellow and green foliage*, Elaeagnus pungens *"Maculata" makes a stylish hedge for any garden.*

THE PLANT THAT *has it all.* Elaeagnus pungens *provides year-round variegated foliage, sweetly scented fall flowers and berries.*

FEATURES

Informal

For a foolproof, hardy, evergreen hedge, with a decent show of berries, elaeagnus comes in the very top league. *Elaeagnus pungens* grows about 6ft high and wide, and has small, white, sweetly scented fall flowers hidden amongst the foliage, followed by fruit that quickly reddens. The shrub only requires minimal pruning to keep it in shape. There are other excellent forms. "Dicksonii" is less vigorous but more upright, and has bright yellow-edged leaves, and "Maculata" is a quick-growing, branching plant that has a big yellow patch in each leaf center. The sunnier and hotter the summer, the better the show of berries. If you need an even bigger, denser hedge of elaeagnus, try *E. macrophylla*. The fall flowers have a strong, sweet scent.

ELAEAGNUS AT A GLANCE

Elaeagnus pungens makes a terrific all-purpose hedge, offering shelter, color and berries. Hardy to 0°F (zone 7).

Jan	foliage	Recommended Varieties
Feb	foliage	*Elaeagnus pungens*
Mar	foliage	E. p. "Dicksonii"
April	foliage	E. p. "Frederici"
May	foliage	E. p. "Goldrim"
June	foliage	E. p. "Maculata"
July	foliage	E. p. " Variegata"
Aug	foliage	
Sept	foliage	
Oct	flowering	
Nov	flowering	
Dec	foliage	

CONDITIONS

Aspect   Though elaeagnus will grow in shade, they then tend to produce a disappointing show of fall berries. The sunnier and hotter the conditions, the better.

Site   Not particularly fussy, any well-tended ground, avoiding extremes, is fine. Provide rich soil and good drainage.

GROWING METHOD

Propagation   Take semi-ripe cuttings in the summer. They quickly take. It is quite possible to raise elaeagnus from seed, but is hardly worth the bother given how relatively quick and successful are the cuttings.

Spacing   Set plants about 2½ft apart.

Feeding   It is tempting with reliable performers like elaeagnus to plant them and leave them alone, but a regular spring mulch of well-rotted manure, or a feed of slow-release fertilizer, will ensure that the bold leaved variegated forms really develop well and stand out.

Problems   None of any note.

FLOWERING

Season   Though *E. pungens* does flower in the fall, the display is not anything to get excited about. The eyecatching variegated foliage scores more points.

GENERAL

Pruning   Prune to maintain shape in the spring.

ESCALLONIA "EDINENSIS"
Escallonia

BURSTING INTO BLOOM in late spring, Escallonia "Edinensis" will keep producing interest through the summer and into the fall.

THE OVERALL distribution of flowers on this E. "Edinensis" makes for a pleasing mixture of color with the glossy green of the leaves.

FEATURES

Informal

Escallonia are underrated evergreen shrubs, with glossy leaves that in hot weather give off a gentle, sweet smell. The best kind to use for a hedge are the bushy ones that can be well clipped. "Peach Blossom," growing 6ft high with pink flowers, and *Escallonia rubra* "Crimson Spire" which is slightly taller with red flowers, are both impressive. The latter is traditionally grown in seaside gardens as a hedge windbreak, since the plants can withstand both wind and salt. "Edinensis," with pinkish-red flowers in the first half of summer, grows about 6ft high. New flowering shoots keep appearing up until the fall. Other forms of escallonia, like the white-flowering "Iveyi," can be slightly more tender, and may need to be grown against warm sheltering walls in cold regions.

ESCALLONIA AT A GLANCE

Escallonia "Edinensis" is a versatile shrub for a windbreak and gives a good show of flowers. Hardy to 5°F (zone 7).

Jan	foliage ❄	Recommended Varieties
Feb	foliage ❄	*Escallonia* "Edinensis"
Mar	foliage ❄	E. "Peach Blossom"
April	foliage ❄	E. *rubra* "Crimson Spire"
May	flowering ✽	
June	flowering ✽	
July	flowering ✽	Companion Plants
Aug	flowering ✽	Bluebell
Sept	flowering ✽	Daffodil
Oct	foliage ❄	Fritillaria
Nov	foliage ❄	Hyacinth
Dec	foliage ❄	Tulip

CONDITIONS

Aspect　Keep out of the shade and give as much wall-to-wall sun as you can.

Site　Good drainage and decent, fertile soil are the key requirements. A well-tended garden, without extremes of soil type, will be fine.

GROWING METHOD

Propagation　The best method of propagation is to take cuttings during the summer. You can also do this over winter, but you will get quicker results with the former.

Spacing　*Escallonia* "Edinensis" can eventually grow to about 8ft wide, but with pruning allow for a gap of 3ft.

Feeding　It is useful to keep up the soil fertility. Either mulch in the spring with well-rotted manure, or add spring helpings of slow-release fertilizer such as blood and bone.

Problems　Remarkably free of pests and diseases.

FLOWERING

Season　The main flowering burst lasts from late spring to midsummer, but extra flowers usually keep appearing through late summer and into the start of the fall.

PRUNING

General　Either prune after the main burst of flowering in midsummer, or if you want extra flowers leave it until the following spring. Overgrown, misshapen, tangled shrubs can be cut back hard without inflicting serious damage.

EUONYMUS FORTUNEI
Spindle tree

LOOKING AS IF it has been covered with a fine coating of snow, Euonymus fortunei *"Silver Queen" makes for a very elegant hedge.*

THE OVERALL IMPRESSION of the E. fortunei *is light and frothy, offering a pleasant contrast to shrubs with darker green foliage.*

FEATURES

Informal

The species most usually grown as a hedge is *Euonymus japonicus*, but *E. fortunei* provides plenty of extra possibilities. It is usually regarded as semi-prostrate, but it is quite capable of bulking and mounding up, creating a substantial evergreen division. It is a slow grower, but eventually will look hugely impressive. It can be pruned and smartened up. Many gardeners grow it against walls or fences, where it actually starts to climb. "Silver Queen" is the best known form, and it develops distinctive green leaves with a flashy white margin; in the cold it has a pinkish tinge. Other good forms include "Emerald Gaiety" and the eyecatching "Emerald'n'Gold," which turns reddish in winter. The more the shrub does mound up, the better it flowers and fruits, the latter being white.

EUONYMUS AT A GLANCE

Euonymus fortunei makes a fine division in large borders, or a sprawling divider. Exceptional foliage. Hardy to 5°F (zone 7).

		Companion Plants
Jan	foliage	*Euonymus alatus*
Feb	foliage	*E. cornutus* var.
Mar	foliage	*quinquecornutus*
April	foliage	*E. europaeus* "Red Cascade"
May	flowering	*E. japonicus*
June	foliage	*E. latifolius*
July	foliage	*E. lucidus*
Aug	foliage	*E. planipes*
Sept	foliage	
Oct	foliage	
Nov	foliage	
Dec	foliage	

CONDITIONS

Aspect   Full sun gives the best results. Light shade is acceptable, but otherwise keep away from the dark. Some wind protection helps. Cold and exposed positions do not often work well.

Site   Average fertile soil is fine, with good drainage. A thick mulch of well-rotted organic matter in the spring, especially in hot dry sites, will work wonders.

GROWING METHOD

Propagation   Take semi-ripe cuttings in the summer. For seed see *E. japonicus*.

Spacing   Reckon on 3ft apart or more, but it depends what size shrubs you buy. If small, remember that they grow quite slowly. These shrubs do not sprint away.

Feeding   Over-rich soil is not necessary. Average garden fertility is fine. A spring slow-release fertilizer is quite adequate.

Problems   In general, euonymus is remarkably trouble free. In some locations powdery mildew may strike. Take appropriate chemical action and improve the growing conditions.

FLOWERING

Season   A hot spring will produce greater flower growth, but you should get 10 days in May when it is thick with whiteish blossom.

PRUNING

General   Gently prune in the spring, taking care not to try and create too formal a shape.

EUONYMUS JAPONICUS
Spindle bush

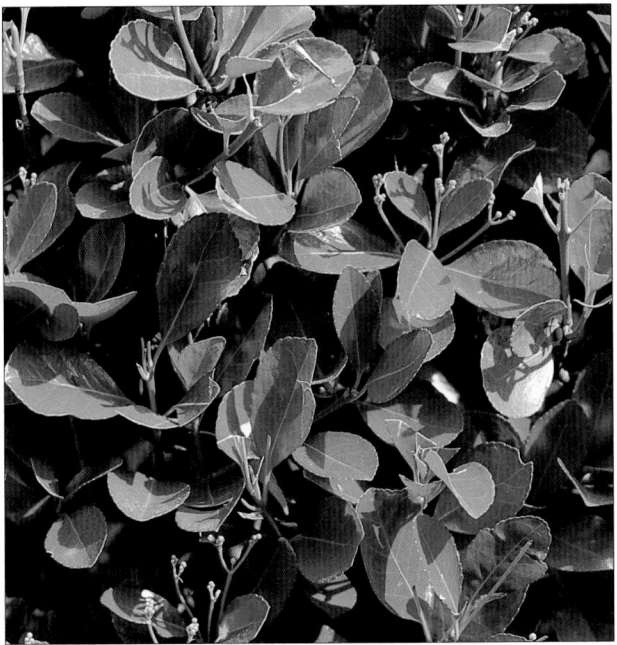

THE DENSE GROWTH and neat, rounded leaves of Euonymus japonicus *make for a compact habit that is ideal for hedging.*

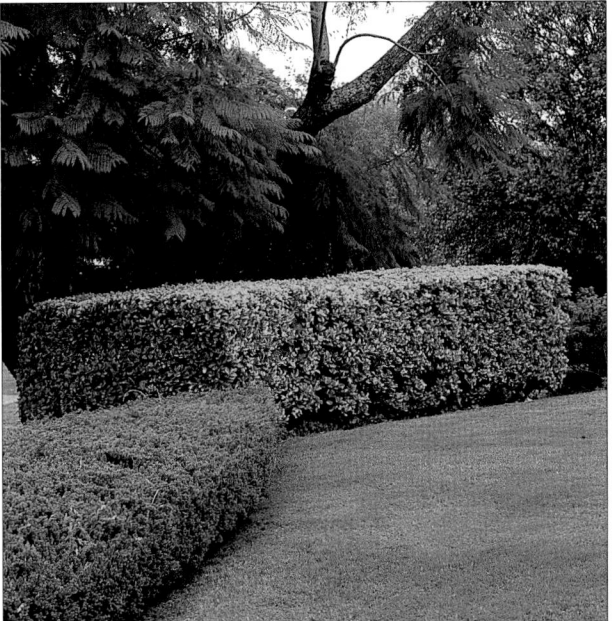

A HEDGE of golden spindle bush, here pruned into a formal, compact block, forms a bright contrast to a low juniper hedge.

FEATURES

Formal

An evergreen shrub growing 10–13ft high and 6½ft or more wide in very old age, *Euonymus japonicus* can be hedged at any height over 3ft. The species has glossy green leaves, but the many variegated cultivars with margins or splashes of cream or yellow are more common. A neat plant, *E. japonicus* is a moderate grower and long lived. It is a low-maintenance and adaptable shrub.

CONDITIONS

Aspect   · Needs full sun for good, compact growth. Avoid the shade at all costs.

EUONYMUS AT A GLANCE

A good choice for a more traditional, well-shaped hedge with berries and bright leaves. Hardy to 23°F (zone 9).

Jan	foliage ❀	Recommended Varieties
Feb	foliage ❀	*Euonymus japonicus*
Mar	foliage ❀	E. j. "Albomarginatus"
April	foliage ❀	E. j. "Aureus"
May	flowering ❀	E. j. "Macrophyllus"
June	foliage ❀	E. j. "Macrophyllus
July	foliage ❀	Aureovariegatus"
Aug	foliage ❀	E. j. "Ovatus Aureus"
Sept	foliage ❀	
Oct	foliage ❀	
Nov	foliage ❀	
Dec	foliage ❀	

Site   Soil should be well drained and preferably enriched with organic matter.

GROWING METHOD

Propagation   The species can be raised from cleaned seed extracted from berries in fall and stored in the refrigerator to be sown in spring. Alternatively, cultivars can be grown from semi-ripe cuttings taken in the summer.

Spacing   Plant at about 3ft, depending on how quickly you want the hedge to be established.

Feeding   Apply complete plant food in spring.

Problems   There are no known problems.

FLOWERING

Season   Greenish white flowers are produced in late spring but they are not a key feature of this plant in terms of its appearance.

Berries   Deep red berries follow the flowers in fall. They score more points than the flowers.

PRUNING

General   Prune in the spring. The plant can also be trimmed at other times of the year to control any wayward growth. *E. japonicus* does not generally need a great deal of pruning. As with *E. fortunei*, make sure that you take care not to ruin the attractive leaves, one of the main reasons for growing this plant, especially the variegated forms like "Ovatus Aureus." It is therefore best to use pruning shears.

ILEX AQUIFOLIUM
Holly

VARIEGATED HOLLY *with a cream leaf margin provides a fine contrasting backdrop for this little garden statue.*

DECORATIVE AND SECURE, *this holly hedge makes a great wall substitute. The tall, pink-flowered shrub is English hawthorn.*

FEATURES

Formal or Informal

Evergreen holly makes a hardy, long-lived hedge. The glossy green leaves are spiny in most varieties and there are many cultivars available, some with cream or gold variegated foliage. Male and female flowers are usually borne on separate plants, and a brilliant display of scarlet or orange berries follows on the female plants. Left unpruned, holly grows into a fairly large tree but it is often hedged at about 10ft high or less. It makes an extremely good windbreak hedge, and also tolerates air pollution.

CONDITIONS

Aspect   Prefers a sunny spot. Variegated kinds look best in sun, where the colors really stand out.

ILEX AT A GLANCE

Ilex aquifolium has many excellent forms making marvellous, dense, free-berrying hedges. Hardy to 0°F (zone 7).

Jan	foliage ❄	Recommended Varieties
Feb	foliage ❄	*Ilex aquifolium*
Mar	foliage ❄	*I. aquifolium* "Argentea
April	foliage ❄	Marginata"
May	flowering ✽	*I. aquifolium* "Ferox"
June	flowering ✽	*I. aquifolium* "Golden Queen"
July	foliage ❄	*I. aquifolium* "Handsworth
Aug	foliage ❄	New Silver"
Sept	foliage ❄	*I. aquifolium* "Silver Queen"
Oct	foliage ❄	*I. cornuta* "Burfordii"
Nov	foliage ❄	*I. crenata*
Dec	foliage ❄	

Site   These plants will need well-drained soil enriched with plenty of organic matter. Heavy clay soil must be broken up and lightened with horticultural sand and grit.

GROWING METHOD

Propagation   To grow large numbers of plants, clean and sow the ripened berries, but to maintain the purity of cultivars grow them from semi-ripe cuttings taken in the summer. Use a hormone rooting powder to increase the success rate.

Spacing   Plant at 3ft intervals for hedging.

Feeding   Apply complete plant food in early spring.

Problems   Holly has few problems but keep an eye out for aphids which can attack young shoots.

FLOWERING

Season   The small, creamy flowers are borne in late spring and early summer.

Berries   The flowers are followed by berries which ripen through fall, hanging on through winter. Note that the form called "Silver Queen" and "Golden Queen" are actually male, and that the otherwise excellent, self-pollinating "J. C. van Tol" does not actually make the best hedge.

PRUNING

General   Main pruning is done in late winter but wayward growth can be trimmed off at other times as well. To make a formal holly hedge you may need to prune two or three times during the growing season, depending on the vigor of the growth.

LAVANDULA
Lavender

THE UPRIGHT SPIKES *of French lavender provide interesting vertical lines above the rounded form of a mature lavender bush.*

UNCLIPPED LAVENDER BUSHES *make informal hedges beside a path, where fragrance will be released as passers-by brush against them.*

FEATURES

Formal or Informal

Most lavenders grow into rounded bushes about 3ft high and wide, but some dwarf forms grow only 12–16in high. All lavenders are suitable for hedging as they respond well to regular clipping. The highly aromatic foliage is gray-green and flower spikes may be pale lavender to rich purple. Plant a lavender hedge to define a path or to outline a terrace—these are the places where passers-by will brush against them and release the fragrance. Lavender can also be planted to provide color contrast in a formal garden.

CONDITIONS

Aspect Needs full sun for good dense growth. Keep them well away from the shade.

Site Needs an open, well-drained soil that need not be rich. Add lime to very acid soil before planting lavender. Heavy wet soil needs to be vigorously broken up with plenty of horticultural sand and grit.

GROWING METHOD

Propagation Grow from tip cuttings taken from spring until fall, or from lateral cuttings with a heel of older wood in fall or early winter. The success rate is usually quite high.

Spacing For hedging, plant lavenders at 18–24in intervals, dwarf forms at 12–16in intervals.

Feeding Needs little fertilizer. Apply pelleted poultry manure in spring as growth begins.

Problems Overwatering or poorly drained soils will induce the rotting of roots. Also beware attacks of honey fungus. The stems die back, and the attack can either be swift and sudden or quite gradual, lasting a number of years. The only solution is to dig up the affected plants entirely, dig over the area, and replant with shrubs that better resist such attacks. They include choisya, pieris, and pittosporum.

FLOWERING

Season The main flowering season is in the height of the summer, adding fresh gray-green foliage and blue flowers to planting schemes.

Cutting The flowers make wonderful posies and can also be dried. Regular clipping may reduce the flowering display.

PRUNING

General Clip the shrub little and often to maintain dense growth. If necessary, hard prune in late winter, but not into old wood.

LAVANDULA AT A GLANCE

Free-flowering, aromatic shrubs that quickly make impressive hedges; a good alternative to box. Hardy to 23°F (zone 9).

Month	Status	Recommended Varieties
Jan	foliage	*Lavandula angustifolia*
Feb	foliage	*L. a.* "Hidcote"
Mar	foliage	*L. a.* "Munstead"
April	foliage	*L. a.* "Twickel Purple"
May	foliage	*L.* x *intermedia*
June	flowering	*L. lanata*
July	flowering	*L. latifolia*
Aug	flowering	*L. stoechas*
Sept	foliage	
Oct	foliage	
Nov	foliage	
Dec	foliage	

LIGUSTRUM OVALIFOLIUM
Golden privet

A FAVORITE PLANT for hedging since Victorian times, golden privet needs very little care indeed.

PATCHES of the plain green species are starting to appear in this golden privet hedge. They may take over unless they are cut out early.

FEATURES

Formal

Many of the 50 species of privet have been grown in the past as hedges. This variety, *Ligustrum ovalifolium* "Aureum," or golden privet, can grow to 12ft but is usually seen hedged to 3–6½ft. Its foliage may be variegated dark green and gold but is often almost entirely yellow. This is a quick growing, hardy and easy-care plant, able to tolerate a wide range of conditions. It can be grown as a solid dividing hedge, or can be clipped and pruned to give all kinds of different shapes. The form "Argenteum" has leaves with a white margin if the yellow seems a bit too brash.

LIGUSTRUM AT A GLANCE

Excellent, all-purpose, robust hedge with summer flowers that can be shaped and pruned. Hardy to 0°F (zone 7).

Jan	foliage ❀	Recommended Varieties
Feb	foliage ❀	*Ligustrum japonicum*
Mar	foliage ❀	*L. lucidum*
April	foliage ❀	*L. lucidum* "Excelsum
May	foliage ❀	Superbum"
June	flowering ❀	*L. obtusifolium*
July	foliage ❀	*L. ovalifolium* "Argenteum"
Aug	foliage ❀	*L. ovalifolium* "Aureum"
Sept	foliage ❀	*L. vulgare*
Oct	foliage ❀	
Nov	foliage ❀	
Dec	foliage ❀	

CONDITIONS

Aspect   Must have full sun all day for dense growth and to retain the golden color.

Site   Should be well drained but it does not need to be rich. Giving privet a spring feed of slow-release fertilizer, and/or a spring mulch, helps keep it in good condition.

GROWING METHOD

Propagation   Grow from semi-ripe tip cuttings taken in the summer. Alternatively use hardwood cuttings taken in the winter.

Spacing   Plants can be spaced at 16–20in intervals to achieve a good, thick hedge.

Feeding   Can be grown without supplementary fertilizer. If the soil is very poor, apply all-purpose plant food in spring.

Problems   There are no known problems.

FLOWERING

Season   Flowers appear in midsummer. Many people find the scent unpleasant and overpowering.

PRUNING

General   As the growth of this plant is particularly rapid, privet needs to be trimmed frequently. Cut out any growths that you can see are reverting to plain green. As flowers appear, shear or tip prune to avoid fruit setting.

LONICERA NITIDA
Honeysuckle

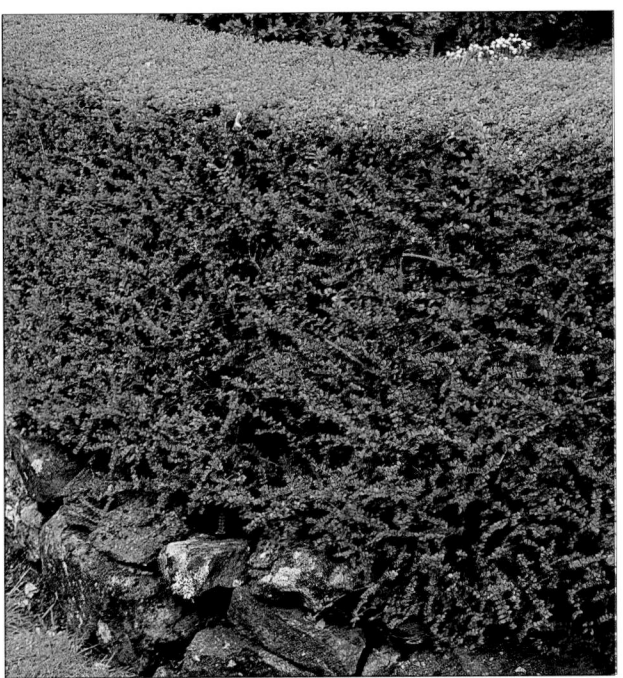

TINY, CLOSE-GROWING LEAVES make this an ideal choice for hedging where a tight formal shape is wanted.

A GAP in this honeysuckle hedge allows access to an enclosed garden and frames a young crab-apple tree.

FEATURES

Formal

This small-leaved, dense evergreen plant is sometimes known as box-leaf honeysuckle. It is quick growing but also long lived. While plants can reach almost 8ft in height, they are most often seen hedged at about 20in or even less. Honeysuckle is an ideal shrub for formal hedges around garden beds or, when it is allowed to grow taller, for dividing sections of a garden or accenting a path or drive. It can also be clipped to various shapes for topiary. Honeysuckle bears strongly perfumed cream flowers during the late spring and early summer, although few blooms appear if the plants are kept close clipped.

LONICERA AT A GLANCE

Lonicera nitida is a highly valued, quick growing, scented evergreen shrub with blue berries. Hardy to 0°F (zone 7).

Jan	foliage	**Companion Plants**
Feb	foliage	*Campsis radicans*
Mar	foliage	Clematis
April	foliage	Climbing rose
May	flowering ❀	*Cobaea scandens*
June	flowering ❀	Ipomoea
July	foliage	Jasmine
Aug	foliage	*Lonicera similis* var. *delavayi*
Sept	foliage	Tropaeolum
Oct	foliage	
Nov	foliage	
Dec	foliage	

CONDITIONS

Aspect Prefers an open, sunny position but will also tolerate some partial shade.

Site The soil should be well drained but need not be rich, although soil that is high in organic content will give more vigorous growth and a better display of white flowers.

GROWING METHOD

Propagation Can be grown from firm tip cuttings taken in early or midsummer.

Spacing For a quick effect, honeysuckle can be planted at 10in spacings, but 18in might be more sensible.

Feeding Apply complete plant food in early spring.

Problems There are no known problems, but keep an eye out for aphid attacks.

FLOWERING

Season Small, perfumed, creamy flowers appear in late spring and early summer. However, if the plants are clipped regularly through the growing season flowers may not develop.

PRUNING

General To maintain low, dense growth honeysuckle needs regular clipping throughout the growing season; up to three cuttings in a season is quite typical.

OLEARIA X HAASTII
Daisy bush

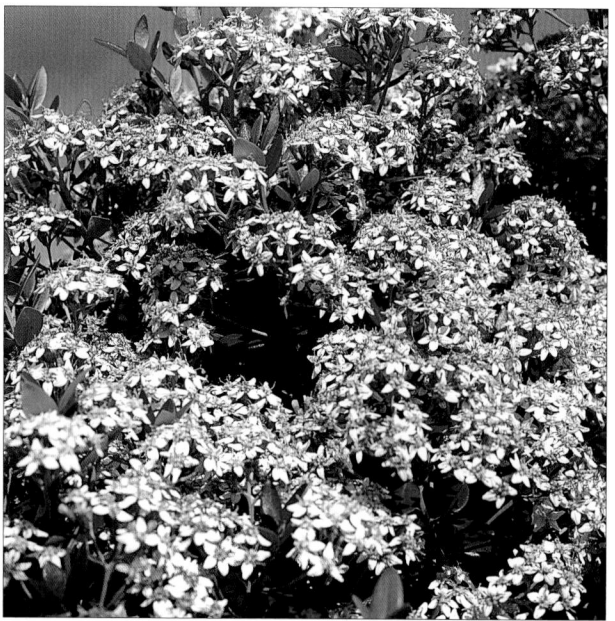

MIDSUMMER IS that much brighter when you have an Olearia x haastii's *blinding white blooms glinting under the blue sky.*

THE FLOWERS of O. x haastii *develop through the season, before giving way to the fluffy, brown seedheads, providing interesting texture.*

FEATURES

Informal

If you need a highly unusual idea for a flowering hedge, this is it. A New Zealand bushy shrub with small, dark green leaves in the spring, and a white felt-like covering beneath. It is grown for its big show of white starry flowers in mid- and late summer, and the scent is a bit like that of hawthorn. The flowers are followed by brown fluffy seedheads. It grows at least 4ft high, and easily as wide, so just five plants would create an impressive summer windbreak hedge. It can be livened up with climbers like clematis and honeysuckle. A nearby purple *Buddleja davidii*, flowering at the same time, gives a strong contrast of colors. Despite its southern origins, this olearia is perfectly hardy.

OLEARIA AT A GLANCE

Olearia x *haastii* is a bushy shrub with a big summer show of daisy-like white flowers. Thrives in coastal areas. Hardy to 5°F (zone 7).

Jan	foliage ✿	Companion Plants
Feb	foliage ✿	Clematis
Mar	foliage ✿	*Cobaea scandens*
April	foliage ✿	Ipomoea
May	foliage ✿	Lapageria
June	foliage ✿	Passion flower
July	flowering ✽	Rose
Aug	flowering ✽	Tropaeolum
Sept	foliage ✿	
Oct	foliage ✿	
Nov	foliage ✿	
Dec	foliage ✿	

CONDITIONS

Aspect   Full sun gives the best display of flowers. Do not hide theses shrubs away in the shade.
Site   The more sun the better.

GROWING METHOD

Propagation   The best results are from summer cuttings, which are semi-ripe, in pots of cuttings compost. They should take quite quickly. Give frost-protection the first winter, for planting out the following spring.
Spacing   Set plants from 2–3ft apart.
Feeding   A spring application of a slow-release fertilizer should suffice. The ground should have been well prepared before planting, with generous quantities of well-rotted organic matter. Make sure there is good drainage.
Problems   Olearia is virtually trouble-free. An easy grow, low-maintenance shrub.

FLOWERING

Season   *Olearia* x *haastii* flowers at the height of summer, and makes an incredible sight when, as an enormous hedge, it is in full flower. Contrasting colored climbers can easily be grown through it.

PRUNING

General   Only needed to keep the plant in shape, or remove frost damage. If cutting to restrict size, prune up to one-third of last year's growth.

PHOTINIA
Photinia

FLUFFY, CREAMY-WHITE FLOWERS can be profuse on unpruned photinia. Few, if any, are seen on a formally trained hedge.

THE BRIGHT CRIMSON-PINK new growth on this photinia hedge makes a magnificent contribution to the garden.

FEATURES

Formal or Informal

Evergreen and deciduous photinias, with their dense foliage, are among the most popular of hedging plants. The dark green, slightly leathery foliage is highlighted by bright pinky-red new growth. If the plant is trimmed regularly, this new growth is evident throughout the growing season. In spring and summer clusters of small white flowers appear. If unpruned, most bushes will grow to 10–15ft high but they can be hedged at around 6ft. Photinias do, however, make very fine tall hedges and windbreaks. These plants are moderate growers and will be long lived if grown in suitable conditions.

PHOTINIA AT A GLANCE

Under-used shrubs giving fresh new growth, often vividly colored, and early season white flowers. Hardy to 5°F (zone 7).

		Companion Plants
Jan	foliage	Anemone
Feb	foliage	Bluebell
Mar	foliage	Crocus
April	flowering	Daffodil
May	flowering	Erythronium
June	flowering	Fritillaria
July	flowering	Hyacinth
Aug	foliage	Iris
Sept	foliage	Scilla
Oct	foliage	Tulip
Nov	foliage	
Dec	foliage	

CONDITIONS

Aspect Needs to be grown in full sun. Will also tolerate some degree of partial shade.
Site Soil must be well drained and ideally should contain plenty of organic matter.

GROWING METHOD

Propagation Can be grown from semi-ripe cuttings taken during the summer.
Spacing Plant at about 3ft spacings.
Feeding Apply complete plant food during the spring and summer growing season.
Problems Photinias have no specific pest problems but will quickly succumb to root rot in heavy, poorly drained soil. It is therfore essential that you do not grow them in cold wet clay.

FLOWERING

Season Clusters of white flowers appear during spring. One of the earliest is *Photinia* x *fraseri*, *P. glabra* flowers in early summer, and *P. nussia* in mid-summer.
Cutting Flowers are not suitable for cutting.

PRUNING

General Carry out the main pruning in late winter but lighter pruning can be done at other times of the year. Light summer pruning promotes plenty of attractive young foliage.

POTENTILLA FRUTICOSA
Cinquefoil

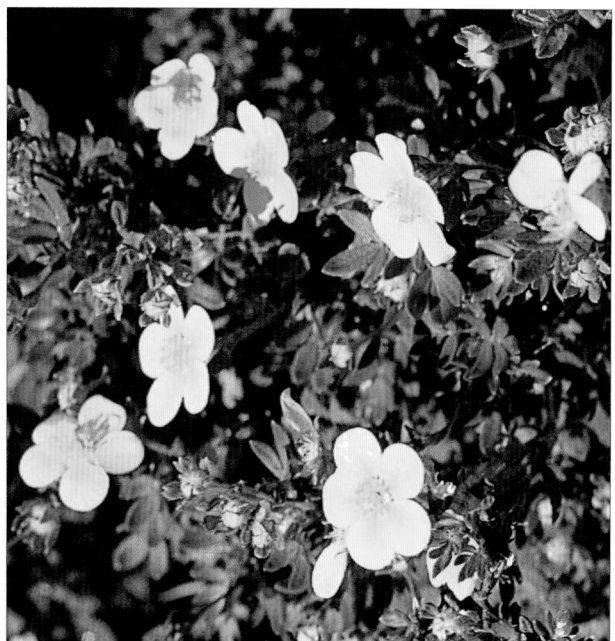

CATCHING THE LATE afternoon sun, these flowers of Potentilla fruticosa *make bright yellow highlights among the dark green foliage.*

THERE ARE MANY colors of P. fruticosa *varieties to choose from. This one,* P. f. *"Tangerine" has rich yellow/orange flowers.*

FEATURES

Informal

This is a small, easy-care, informal flowering shrub. It grows about 3ft high and has masses of yellow flowers from late spring right through to mid-fall. It can be grown in one long yellow hedge, but looks best in a sequence of different potentillas. Look for those flowering in contrasting red, pink, white and orange, but make sure that they all grow to, or can be pruned to, the same height. All you need do is give them the gentlest late winter prune all over to stimulate plenty of new growth. The flowers appear on the current season's growth. When buying a potentilla look at the label carefully since some only grow 4in high.

POTENTILLA AT A GLANCE

Potentilla fruticosa makes the perfect small, informal, flowery hedge. It has many excellent forms. Hardy to 5°F (zone 7).

Jan	/	Recommended Varieties
Feb	/	*Potentilla fruticosa*
Mar	/	"Daydawn"
Apr	/	*P. f.* "Friedrichsenii"
May	flowering ❀	*P. f.* "Goldfinger"
Jun	flowering ❀	*P. f.* "Katherine Dykes"
July	flowering ❀	*P. f.* "Maanelys"
Aug	flowering ❀	
Sep	flowering ❀	Companion Plants
Oct	flowering ❀	Box
Nov	/	Fuchsia
Dec	/	Lavender

CONDITIONS

Aspect   The plants generally prefer full sun, but will tolerate partial shade.

Site   Over-rich soil is not necessary. Potentillas prefer the ground to be slightly on the poor side, with excellent drainage. Clay soil must be well broken up with plenty of added horticultural sand and grit.

GROWING METHOD

Propagation   The quickest methods are either by division in the spring or fall, or taking cuttings in the first part of summer. They strike very quickly.

Spacing   Plant at 2ft intervals, allowing each plant to grow about 4ft wide.

Feeding   They benefit from a feed in the spring of a slow-release fertilizer.

Problems   There are no known problems.

FLOWERING

Season   An exceptional flowering period, with the yellow flowers in bloom from the spring, through summer, into the fall. The flowers, which resemble small wild roses, have five petals—hence the name cinquefoil.

PRUNING

General   In the fall, after flowering, prune for shape and to take out any old, dead, or twiggy wood. Give a light late winter prune if necessary.

PRUNUS LAUROCERASUS
Cherry laurel

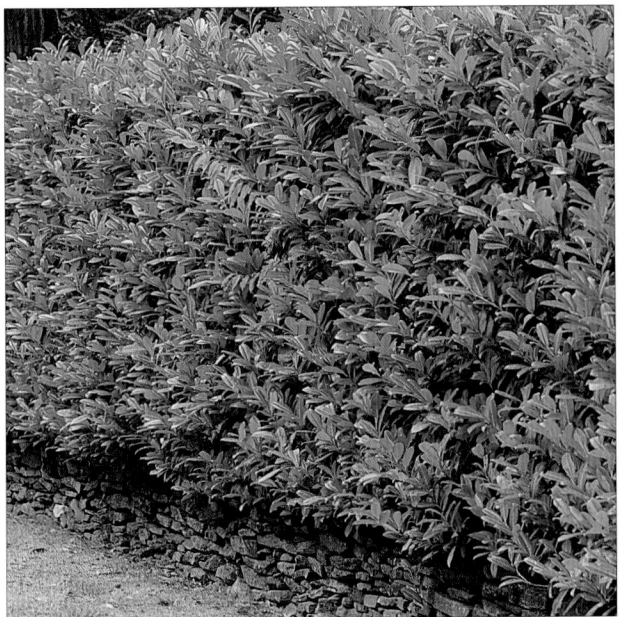

CHERRY LAUREL *makes a rather massive hedge, providing good shelter for an exposed garden. The dry-stone wall adds a rustic touch.*

KEPT AT FENCE HEIGHT, *this cherry laurel hedge will allow tantalising glimpses into the lovely garden behind.*

FEATURES

Formal

If left unpruned, cherry laurel grows into a tree-like shape, but pruned it makes an imposing hedge for a larger garden, most often to about 10ft, thus providing privacy and a windbreak. The evergreen foliage is dark green and glossy; perfumed white flowers are followed by red, cherry-like fruits. This is a very long-lived plant. There are a number of excellent cultivars available.

CONDITIONS

Aspect Grows in sun or partial shade.
Site This plant prefers to root into well-drained soil that is heavily enriched with decayed organic matter. Therefore, avoid the two extremes of nutritionless, free-draining chalk soil and a heavy, wet, boggy ground.

GROWING METHOD

Propagation Grow from semi-ripe tip cuttings that are taken in midsummer. It can also be grown from seed if the ripe berries are picked, cleaned of the pulp and then stored in damp sand or damp sphagnum moss in the refrigerator for about three months before they are sown.
Spacing It should be planted at about 3ft spacings. Do not be tempted to plant any closer together because crowding them is counter-productive—give them space to grow.
Feeding Apply plant food after spring flowering.
Problems No specific problems are known.

FLOWERING

Season The small, white, scented flowers appear in spring. However, flowers will not appear if the plant is pruned in late winter.
Berries The flowers are followed by red berries that ripen to black. Birds love them. A good alternative to holly, box, and yew.

PRUNING

General If you want flowers, do your main pruning immediately after flowering has finished; otherwise it can be done in late winter. Other trimming can be done throughout the growing season if necessary.

PRUNUS AT A GLANCE

Prunus laurocerasus can make a 6m (20ft) high tree, but pruned is a fine, sturdy, thick hedge. Hardy to 0°F (zone 7).

Jan	foliage	Companion Plants
Feb	foliage	Anemone
Mar	foliage	Bluebell
Apr	flowering ❀	Crocus
May	flowering ❀	Daffodil
Jun	foliage	Erythronium
July	foliage	Fritillaria
Aug	foliage	Hyacinth
Sep	foliage	Iris
Oct	foliage	Scilla
Nov	foliage	Tulip
Dec	foliage	

PYRACANTHA
Firethorn

THE ABUNDANT CLUSTERS of bright fruits on this firethorn provide a wonderful bounty during the fall months.

OCCASIONAL PRUNING is enough to keep this firethorn hedge dense and attractive, easily fulfilling its role as boundary and screen.

FEATURES

Formal or
Informal

These evergreen shrubs with thorny stems are often planted as hedges in rural areas, but they are just as much at home in suburban districts. Unpruned, they will be 6½–10ft high but are often pruned to less than that. Firethorns are fairly fast growing but are also long lived. The leaves are glossy and clusters of small, white flowers appear in spring or early summer. These are soon followed by bright red or orange berries (the "fire" of the firethorn) which are very decorative and most attractive to birds. Branches of the bright red or orange berries can be cut for indoor decoration once they are fully colored. Be careful where you plant it though because the sharp pointed spines are dangerous.

PYRACANTHA AT A GLANCE

High quality berrying plants that make an eye-catching hedge. Beware of the spines though. Hardy to 5°F (zone 7).

Jan	foliage ❀	Recommended Varieties
Feb	foliage ❀	*Pyracantha coccinea* "Red
Mar	foliage ❀	Column"
Apr	flowering ❀	P. "Golden Charmer"
May	flowering ❀	P. "Mohave"
Jun	flowering ❀	P. "Orange Glow"
July	flowering ❀	*P. rogersiana*
Aug	foliage ❀	*P. rogersiana* "Flava"
Sep	foliage ❀	P. "Soleil d'Or"
Oct	foliage ❀	P. "Watereri"
Nov	foliage ❀	
Dec	foliage ❀	

CONDITIONS

Aspect Needs full sun and tolerates exposure to wind. Will tolerate some partial shade.

Site Grows on a wide range of soils, including poor soils, but best growth will be in those enriched with organic matter. For a good show of bright colored berries, rich soil is best.

GROWING METHOD

Propagation Grow from seed removed from ripe berries and planted fresh. Plants can also be grown from semi-ripe cuttings taken in summer.

Spacing Plant at intervals of 28in–3ft.

Feeding Feeding is not essential, but on poor soils give complete plant food in early spring.

Problems They suffer from a range of pests and diseases like caterpillars, scale, canker, and fireblight.

FLOWERING

Season The white flowers appear in the spring (*Pyracantha rogersiana*), early summer (*P.* "Orange Charmer"), and mid-summer (*P. angustifolia*). Although they provide a good show, they are outdone by the brilliant berries.

Berries The flowers are followed by clusters of berries that will ripen to a blazing red, orange, or yellow, depending on the species.

PRUNING

General Best pruned in spring. Start training and pruning in the first couple of years of growth.

RHODODENDRON
"Loder's White"

THE FLOWERS of the rhododendron are among the most sumptuous to be found. And this Rhododendron "Loder's White" is no exception to the rule. The frilly petals are set off by delicate stamen to create a delightful texture. The blooms time their appearance to perfection, enjoying the midsummer sun.

FEATURES

Informal

Rhododendrons come in all shapes and sizes, from 3ft high to tree-like giants growing 20ft or so. They are traditionally grown as individual eyecatchers, with a big show of flowers anytime from late fall to late summer, though the bulk perform in the spring and early summer. They can also make thick hedges or windbreaks, in the case of *Rhododendron* "Loder's White" about 8ft high and wide. You need a big garden, and one with acid soil. The plants also need dappled shade, and protection from cold winds. With adequate space, grow different colored rhododendrons to make a patchwork effect. It is worth visiting a specialist collection to see the full range now available.

RHODODENDRON AT A GLANCE

Rhododendron "Loder's White" gives an excellent display packed with scented white flowers. Hardy to 5°F (zone 7).

		Recommended Varieties
Jan	foliage	*Rhododendron* "Anna Rose
Feb	foliage	Whitney"
Mar	foliage	*R.* "Blue Peter"
Apr	foliage	*R.* "Cynthia"
May	foliage	*R.* "Gomer Waterer"
Jun	flowering ✿	*R.* "Hydon Dawn"
July	flowering ✿	*R.* "Kilimanjaro"
Aug	foliage	*R.* "Loderi King George"
Sep	foliage	*R.* "Mrs Furnival"
Oct	foliage	*R.* "Razorbill"
Nov	foliage	
Dec	foliage	

CONDITIONS

Aspect   Sun with dappled shade is ideal, approaching a light woodland setting. Avoid both full sun and constant shade.

Site   Acid soil is absolutely essential. Individual plants can be grown in tubs with ericaceous compost. Trying to turn an alkaline garden area acid by adding replacement acid soil might work for one season, but thereafter the surrounding alkaline soil will gradually seep back in, and the rhododendrons will falter.

GROWING METHOD

Propagation   Take semi-ripe cuttings from midsummer.

Spacing   *R.* "Loder's White" should be spaced about 4ft apart. Do not try and plant them any closer together. Each shrub needs to be able to show off all its flowers.

Feeding   Give an annual mulch using leaf mold.

FLOWERING

Season   It flowers right in the middle of summer, at the height of the season. After flowering, attempt to deadhead as much as possible to preserve energy for next year's display. Adding other rhododendrons that flower in early and late summer will extend the show.

PRUNING

General   Leave to realize its full potential. It will automatically thicken up and get quite bushy.

ROSA RUGOSA
Rose

THE DELICATE PURPLE hues of this plant's flowers belie the tough nature of Rosa rugosa, *able to survive in exposed positions.*

WITH THEIR ORANGE centers, R. rugosa *flowers are a pleasant feature of the garden from early summer right through to the fall.*

FEATURES

Informal

Flowering hedges are making a comeback, and one of the best involves *Rosa rugosa*. It grows about 7ft high and wide, and makes a good, tough barrier. Extremely hardy, bushy, and tolerant of coastal winds and sandy soils (it dislikes clay instead), this rose scores high marks. It also has a long purple-rose flowering season from early summer, large cherry-red hips, and even fall color. Two excellent forms of this useful species are "Alba," with single white flowers against dark green leaves, and the crimson-wine "Rubra." The cross between *R. rugosa* and *R. wichurana* led to "Max Graf," which is quite different and makes a good weed-obscuring groundcover, about 2ft high. It does not make a hedge. Other crosses involving *R. rugosa* have produced many excellent shrub roses, especially the white "Blanc Double de Coubert," which grows 6ft high.

ROSA AT A GLANCE

Rosa rugosa is an excellent multi-purpose shrub, giving great flowers and scent through summer. Hardy to –18°C (0°F).

		Companion Plants
Jan	/	Clematis
Feb	/	Crocus
Mar	/	Cyclamen
April	foliage 🌿	Erythronium
May	foliage 🌿	Ipomoea
June	flowering ✿	Primrose
July	flowering ✿	Winter jasmine
Aug	flowering ✿	
Sept	flowering ✿	
Oct	flowering ✿	
Nov	/	
Dec	/	

CONDITIONS

Aspect   Provide full sun, or at the very least dappled shade. The sunnier the garden, the better.

Site   Famed for growing in sandy soils, average garden conditions are fine. So too are beds with deep rich soil and plenty of humus, though sound drainage is always required. The plant does not like heavy clay soils, and these will need to be broken up and lightened so that water drains away more freely.

GROWING METHOD

Propagation   In the fall take 8in long hardwood cuttings, and set in trenches with the top quarter showing above soil level. They make roots slowly and will be ready to plant out the following fall.

Spacing   Set *R. rugosa* about 4ft apart.

Feeding   Feeding twice a summer with a proprietary rose feed will be fine. Also, mulch with well-rotted organic matter.

Problems   No serious problems that should alarm potential growers.

FLOWERING

Season   An excellent extended season, with long, pointed buds. Though the flowers can be short-lived in hot weather, there is no let-up in the development of more buds.

PRUNING

General   Not necessary beyond giving a light trim in February to promote plenty of fresh new shoots. At the same time remove old, unproductive stems or those that have died.

ROSMARINUS
Rosemary

THE INTENSE LIGHT blue of this Rosmarinus officinalis *"Miss Jessopp's Upright" seems to explode from a plain, red brick wall.*

FRESH NEW SHOOTS of rosemary respond to a light pruning. A few plants should keep a whole household supplied with the delicious herb.

FEATURES

Informal

Rosemary makes an excellent edging-cum-hedging plant. The big problem is that it is quite slow growing, so do not count on a sudden, big thick hedge packed with scented leaves. It will gradually give a 4ft high tangle of stems, and marvelous pale blue flowers from early spring. Since there are about 20 kinds of *Rosmarinus officinalis* you could create a long stretch with as many tall kinds as you can collect. "Tuscan Blue" has strong, dark blue flowers, "Roseus" pink flowers, *R. o.* var. *albiflorus* is white, and "Sissinghurst Blue" is extremely free-flowering. Note that some like "Benenden Blue" grow just 3ft high, and others ("Majorca Pink") are even shorter at 18in.

ROSMARINUS AT A GLANCE

Rosmarinus officinalis "Miss Jessopp's Upright" is a "must" for the edible garden. Hardy to 14°F (zone 8).

		Recommended Varieties
Jan	foliage	*Rosmarinus officinalis*
Feb	foliage	*R. o.* var. *albiflorus*
Mar	foliage	*R. o.* "Aureus"
April	flowering	*R. o.* "Fota Blue"
May	flowering	*R. o.* "McConnell's Blue"
June	flowering	*R. o.* "Miss Jessopp's
July	foliage	Upright"
Aug	foliage	*R. o.* "Prostratus Group"
Sept	foliage	*R. o.* "Severn Sea"
Oct	foliage	*R. o.* "Sissinghurst Blue"
Nov	foliage	*R. o.* "Tuscan Blue"
Dec	foliage	

Aspect — Full sun is required. These Mediterranean plants need as much light as they can get.

Site — Anything from quite poor, stony ground to average fertility. The most important point is that they receive good drainage. They will not enjoy heavy, cold, wet clay.

GROWING METHOD

Propagation — Take semi-ripe cuttings through the summer season. It is an inexpensive, if slow way of creating new plants. If you can afford it, buy large-sized specimens giving an instant effect.

Spacing — "Miss Jessopp's Upright" is one of the tallest rosemarys at 5ft. Space individual plants at half that distance.

Feeding — Not necessary except on the poorest of soils.

Problems — Rosemary is a remarkably easy-care plant, and suffers from very few setbacks.

FLOWERING

Season — The show of pale blue flowers from early spring, near adjacent daffodils, gives the garden an excellent boost.

PRUNING

General — The only form of pruning required is to snip back lanky stems in the spring. Regular summer snippings for the kitchen will see to the rest. Old overgrown plants can be cut back by half, and will reshoot. If you need rosemary for cooking the more plants you grow the better, or young ones quickly get massacred.

TAXUS BACCATA
Yew

MATURE YEW PLANTS *have somber, dark green foliage but new spring growth, such as that shown here, is much brighter.*

YEW IS *the ideal hedging plant for cool climates. Formal shapes can be achieved and maintained over a long time.*

FEATURES

Formal

The English yew is extremely long lived and fairly slow growing, but it makes a dense hedge that can be closely clipped. It is also widely used in topiary, and there are specimens that have been clipped for several hundred years. In Britain and Europe yew hedges have been traditionally used to shelter herbaceous borders or as a background for statuary and garden ornaments. Foliage is dark and evergreen, and it produces a red fleshy fruit that is quite poisonous. Unpruned trees may grow to 50ft or more but yew is generally hedged at about 8ft. There are a number of cultivars of yew, providing many variations in form and foliage color.

TAXUS AT A GLANCE

Taxus baccata provides a traditional, formal hedge that can be topiarized to give geometric shapes. Hardy to 0°F (zone 7).

Jan	foliage	Recommended Varieties
Feb	foliage	*Taxus baccata*
Mar	foliage	*T. b.* "Adpressa"
April	flowering	*T. b.* "Fastigiata"
May	flowering	*T. b.* "Fastigiata Aurea"
June	foliage	*T. b.* "Fastigiata
July	foliage	Aureomarginata"
Aug	foliage	*T.* x *media*
Sept	foliage	*T.* x *media* "Brownii"
Oct	foliage	
Nov	foliage	
Dec	foliage	

CONDITIONS

Aspect   Prefers an open, sunny position. This plant is tolerant of windy sites.

Site   Soil should be well drained and enriched with organic matter. Mulch around plants with decayed manure or compost. It is tempting to plant yew and then completely forget about it, but good care yields fine, dense growth.

GROWING METHOD

Propagation   Take firm cuttings with a heel of older wood in fall. These may not be well rooted until the following summer. Use a hormone rooting gel or powder to increase the strike rate.

Spacing   Yew can be planted at 20in–3ft spacings, depending on the density required.

Feeding   Apply complete plant food or slow-release fertilizer in spring.

Problems   There are no specific problems. Yew is an easy-care, reliable shrub or small tree.

FLOWERING

Products   Yew is a conifer, not a flowering plant. It produces very small cones in season as well as bright red, poisonous fruits.

PRUNING

General   To create your hedge, prune little and often. However, yew can be cut back severely and still regenerate well.

VIBURNUM TINUS
Laurustinus

LAURUSTINUS is not often seen grown as a standard but, in fact, it responds well to this form of training.

THIS FORMAL HEDGE of laurustinus is healthy and flourishing. It needs little pruning apart from trimming to shape.

FEATURES

Formal or Informal

This is a dense, evergreen shrub that needs little training to make a good hedge. It is reasonably fast growing and long lived in good conditions. Laurustinus bears masses of small white flowers with a pink base during late winter and spring. The flowers are followed by berries, which ripen to blue-black. This shrub can grow to 10ft high but can be kept at about 6ft. It is generally easy to care for.

CONDITIONS

Aspect   *Viburnum tinus* prefers sites with full sun.

VIBURNUM AT A GLANCE

Viburnum tinus is a fine evergreen shrub, with white, late winter flowers. Makes excellent topiary. Hardy to 0°F (zone 7).

		Recommended Varieties
Jan	foliage	*V.* x *bodnantense* "Dawn"
Feb	flowering	*Viburnum* x *burkwoodii*
Mar	flowering	*V.* x *burkwoodii* "Anne
April	flowering	Russell"
May	foliage	*V.* x *burkwoodii* "Fullbrook"
June	foliage	*V. davidii*
July	foliage	*V. japonicum*
Aug	foliage	*V. odoratissimum*
Sept	foliage	*V. plicatum* "Grandiflorum"
Oct	foliage	
Nov	foliage	
Dec	foliage	

Site   Needs well-drained soil that has been enriched with organic matter.

GROWING METHOD

Propagation   Grow from semi-ripe cuttings taken in the summer. Plants can also be grown from cleaned seed collected in the fall and stored in damp sphagnum moss in the refrigerator until spring.

Spacing   Planting should be at about 3ft intervals, but can be closer if cover is needed quickly.

Feeding   Apply all-purpose plant food in spring.

Problems   The main problems to look out for are viburnum beetles, aphids, whiteflies, and honey fungus. The first damage leaves mainly from late spring to early summer. Treat with a proprietary spray. The second and third are easily tackled, again with chemical measures. The fourth is a big problem. It involves discarding the entire plant, with stump. Fortify the soil with organic matter, and replant with box, bamboo, or chaenomeles.

FLOWERING

Season   Small flowers appear in late winter and spring.

Berries   The flowers are followed by berries that ripen in fall to a blue-black color.

PRUNING

General   Best done after spring flowering.

Growing
Groundcover

GROWING GROUND-COVER

Groundcover gives the finishing touches to the garden—it could be described as a living carpet. By covering the ground between shrubs and other plantings, groundcover creates a soft, natural look. In nature there is always something growing on the ground under trees and shrubs except where there is very deep leaf litter or very low light levels.

Groundcover has practical aspects, too. Once it is established it can suppress weeds and has a natural mulching effect on the soil, helping to maintain a fairly even temperature and moisture level around the roots of larger plants. It is ideal in low-maintenance gardens and as grass substitutes in heavy shade under trees or on sloping ground that is too difficult to mow. Groundcover can also be used to hold soil on steep sites, thus helping to prevent erosion, and as cover on landfill or very poor soil.

LEFT: In full flower, snow-in-summer is as pretty a groundcover as you could wish for. Flowers almost obscure the foliage and give added height to the planting during the blooming period. When blooming is over, a quick shear reveals the neat, silvery leaves. The pretty tree on the right is a standard weeping mulberry.

A PLEASANT EFFECT is produced by this Vinca major*, growing at the base of a tree. Groundcover plants can frequently be used to add color and texture to an area where other plants could not grow.* V. major *in particular will grow well in shaded areas.*

CHOOSING A GROUNDCOVER

Groundcover comes in a variety of different forms. There are plants that spread by runners, such as blue bugle flower, and trailing plants. Mat-forming plants such as baby's tears and thrift are excellent groundcovers, as are those that spread by horizontal growth. Climbing plants such as ivy can also be used successfully as groundcovers.

As with any other type of plant, it is important to choose the right groundcover for the aspect, climate, soil, and space available. Some groundcover plants are suitable for sunny spots but some prefer shade. Growing a plant in the wrong place will lead to disappointment. Some

WHAT CAN GO WRONG?

The different kinds of groundcover described in the following entries are all remarkably free of pest and disease problems. Any specific problems related to each plant are discussed under the plant entry. Groundcover plants tend to take care of themselves, as long as they are given favorable aspects and soil conditions.

groundcover plants, such as *Viola hederacea*, can be very vigorous, and need constant control if planted for a small space. Other mat-forming plants, such as *Armeria maritima* (sea thrift), are more sedate and easy to confine.

PLANTING

Most groundcovers are long-term plantings and so it is worth putting some effort into good soil preparation and weeding. Since the new plantings may have to compete against established trees or shrubs, it is a good idea to give them plenty of food by digging in some well-decayed manure or compost a few weeks before planting.

Weed eradication is important as it is frustrating to find weeds coming up through groundcover. Most weeds will not be eliminated in one go. Dig out any you can see or spot-spray them with glyphosate. Once they have gone or are dead, fork over the soil again, water it and wait for the next crop of weeds to emerge. This reduces the bank of weed seeds lying dormant in the ground. Perennial weeds such as oxalis will need a determined effort to get rid of.

Spacing plants
When you are planting groundcover, space the individual plants out carefully to achieve the desired result. If you need to cover an area quickly, space the plants closer together, but remember to make allowance for the final size of the plants. A large grower such as rosemary may be spaced at 3ft intervals or for quicker cover at 18in spacings. A smaller, clumping plant such as lamb's ears

could be planted at spacings of 9in for quick cover or as far apart as 3ft. If covering a large area of ground, zigzag the plantings to ensure good final cover. Mulch the areas of bare soil between the plants while you wait for them to grow.

MAINTENANCE

The ultimate spread of a groundcover will depend on the type of plant, the soil conditions and the care it receives. Most groundcovering plants need regular feeding during the growing season because of the intense root competition that will occur if they are planted under trees and shrubs. Regular watering is also needed, especially in the early stages of establishment. And remember to keep any bare areas between plants mulched to prevent weeds establishing themselves.

Controlling growth

Once the plants have become established, they need little maintenance beyond shearing off spent flower stems or trimming to confine them to a specific area. They are often quite hardy plants whose rambling habit of growth makes them tough and resistant to extremes of weather.

Some plants need time and trouble spent to get them established, but thereafter they will virtually look after themselves. They may still need occasional trimming along the edges to keep them under control.

Plants such as blue bugle flower can become very dense and congested. This ultimately means that the growth may end up not looking very attractive. If this happens, it is usually easy to pull out some of the excess growth throughout the area, or to lift and divide whole sections of the planting. Replant younger looking growths and discard the old ones.

If any sections of your groundcover have died out altogether, dig them out and replace them with fresh plants from the edges of the planting or lift and divide healthy, vigorous growths. If it is not the kind of plant that can be lifted and divided, look for any pieces that have rooted down or take fresh cuttings.

It is very tempting to plant up an area with groundcover and then forget about it and leave it alone. But it is well worth the occasional check. Growth might be more rampant in one spot than another and need to be evened out, or there might be the odd bare patch. Groundcover invariably spills out of its allotted space and heads toward an area with ornamental plantings. Without a regular look you may suddenly find that your ornamental bed is losing its shape and being taken over. Be ruthless. Cut back the groundcover with a spade.

USING GROUNDCOVERS IN ROCKERIES

Many groundcover plants are also suitable for use as rockery plants, but as always it is essential to choose the right plant for the particular situation. For a small rockery, you should try to choose plants that will not outgrow their allotted space too soon, but for very large rockeries you may have enough room for more spreading or trailing groundcover. Plants used in rockeries should not need a constantly moist soil, as the soil in rockeries tends to dry out fairly quickly.

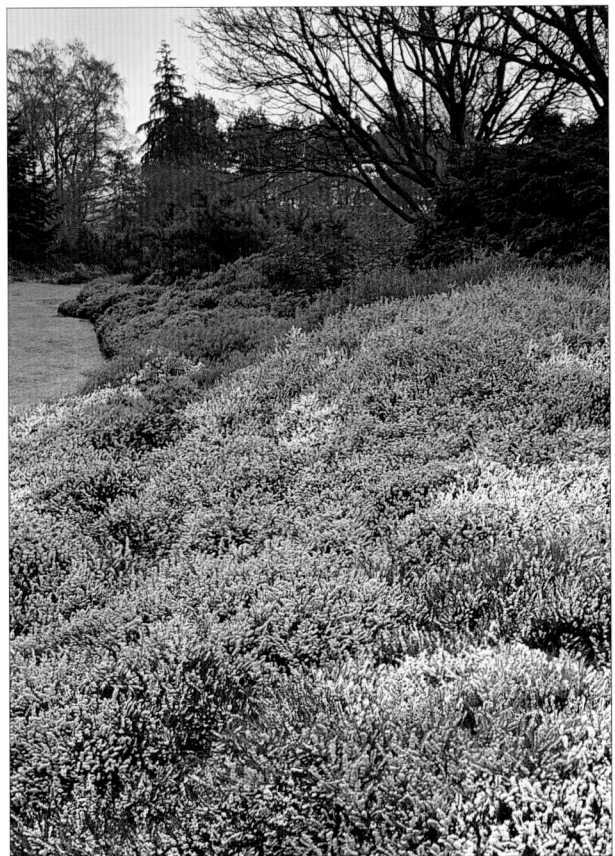

THESE DIFFERENT-COLORED ericas have formed a sea of color on this slope. Their tiny flowers create a pleasing texture.

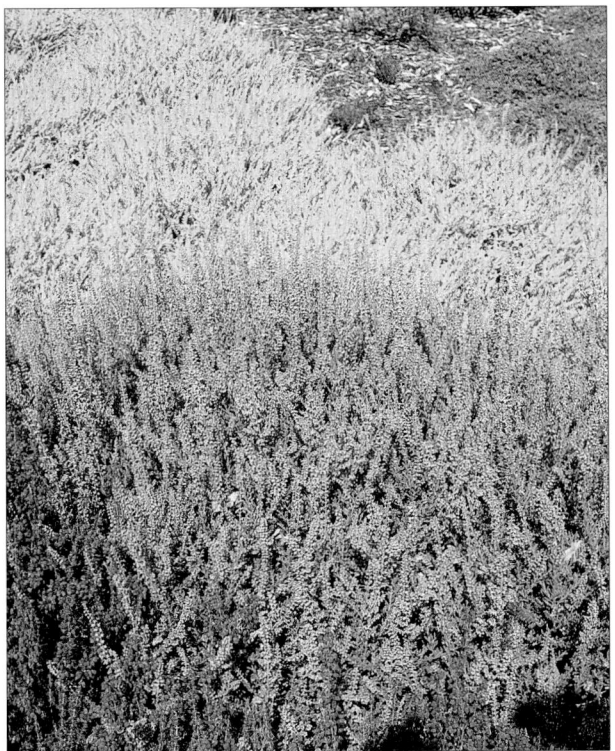

CREATING A PATCHWORK effect, these rosemarys are not just groundcover, but also plants that add color and scent to the garden.

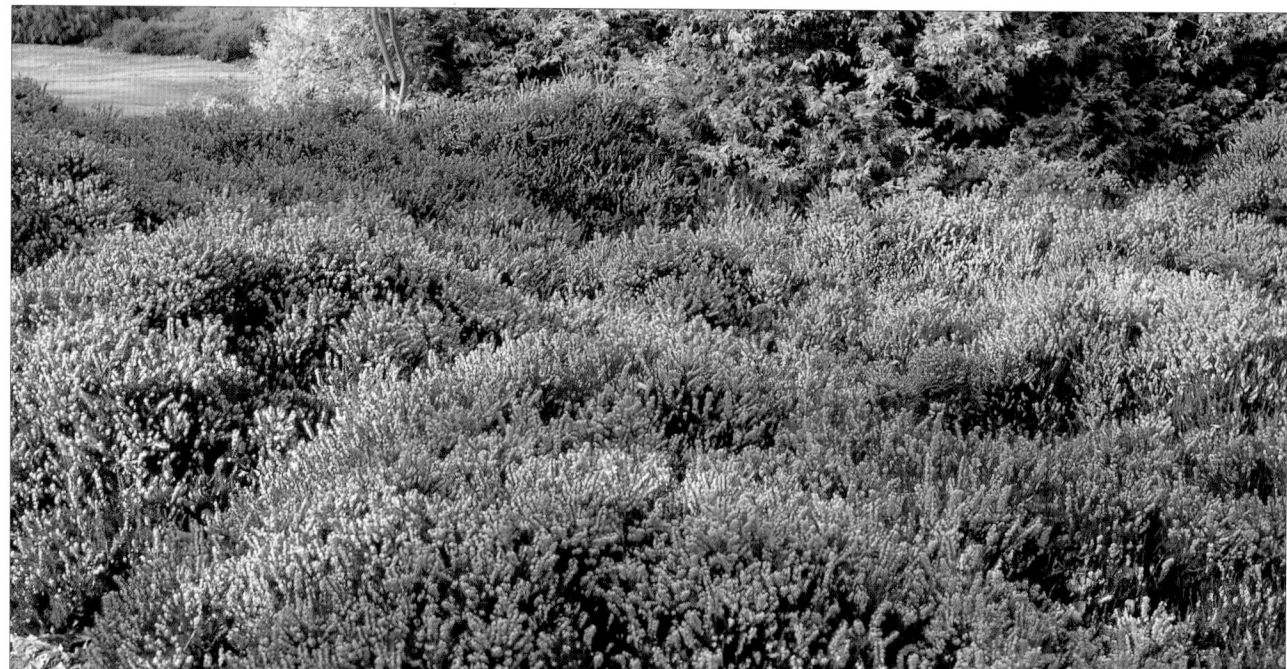

A ROLLING CARPET of purple erica transforms what would otherwise be a rather plain area. Taking up large areas of the garden, groundcover suppresses weeds and requires very little in the way of maintentance. The fact that erica is pleasing to the eye is an added bonus.

Establishing a rockery

A rockery is usually best sited on sloping ground where it looks natural and rocks can be partly bedded securely into the ground. This also means that drainage is fairly rapid, therefore suiting plants that like dry conditions.

Choose rock that occurs naturally in the area as this will blend in better with the site, but never remove rocks from the countryside. This is very destructive to the environment as the rock, once removed, cannot be replaced. In most areas rock should be available from building excavations. If the rock looks too raw, mix some cow manure and water to a thin slurry and paint it over the rock—this will hasten the weathered look and encourage the growth of lichens and mosses.

Rock gardens are fairly high maintenance areas, at least in their early years, and so it is important to remove perennial weeds and grasses from the area before planting. Once the rockery has been planted it is extremely difficult to get rid of more persistent weeds with long, deep tap roots. Any pieces of root not removed can produce new plants. Roots of trees adjacent to the area may also invade the rockery once the soil has been loosened and new plants are being watered and fed regularly.

Selecting plants

A rockery doesn't have to have a different kind of plant in every available pocket—in fact, that could result in a very "spotty" effect. Aim for harmony of color or repeat the same plant in different parts of the rockery. For instance, if you are using a gray-foliaged plant, it may look better to place two or three together in different parts of the planting. A very attractive display may even be made using only one type of plant in many colors. An exception to this would be a rockery planted with a collection of true alpine plants, many of which are miniature treasures grown by an avid collector who wishes to try as many different types as possible.

NATIVE VIOLETS can become a little invasive but they make a top groundcover for their ease of culture and long flowering.

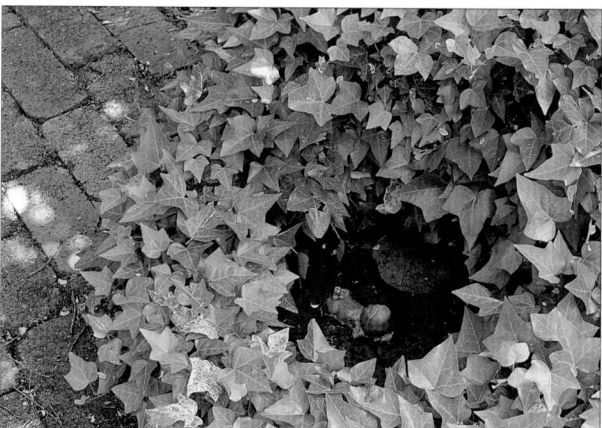

AN EYE-CATCHING FEATURE has been made of this Common ivy encircling a tiny pond. Ivy is a good groundcover under trees.

AJUGA REPTANS
Blue bugle flower

THE FLOWER SPIKES of Ajuga reptans *sit up above the rosettes of foliage. Their color varies with the variety and exposure to the sun.*

SOME VARIETIES of A. reptans *produce pink and cream tones. To retain their color, they need more sun than the plain species.*

FEATURES

Partial Shade

A lovely groundcover for shady, slightly moist sites, *Ajuga reptans* grows as a neat rosette of leaves but spreads by stolons (running stems). Leaves are shiny and may be dark green or bronzed green. The cultivars "Burgundy Lace" and "Multicolor" are mottled cream, pink, or burgundy. This long-lived plant rarely grows more than 6in high, although the deep blue flower spikes may be taller. It is an ideal groundcover under trees and is a good soil binder. It is also used as a border plant and can be grown in troughs or pots. Once the plant is established, growth is dense so that it suppresses weeds very well.

CONDITIONS

Aspect   A woodland and hedgerow plant, *A. reptans* prefers shade or dappled sunlight.

AJUGA AT A GLANCE		
Ajuga reptans is a quality groundcover plant, with excellent colored forms for the late spring garden. Hardy to 5°F (zone 7).		

		Recommended Varieties
Jan	foliage 🌿	
Feb	foliage 🌿	*Ajuga reptans*
Mar	foliage 🌿	A. r. "Braunherz"
April	foliage 🌿	A. r. "Burgundy Glow"
May	flowering ✿	A. r. "Catlin's Giant"
June	flowering ✿	A. r. "Multicolor"
July	foliage 🌿	A. r. "Tricolor"
Aug	foliage 🌿	A. r. "Variegata"
Sept	foliage 🌿	
Oct	foliage 🌿	
Nov	foliage 🌿	
Dec	foliage 🌿	

Site   This plant does best in well-drained, but somewhat moisture-retentive soil that has been enriched with plenty of organic matter prior to planting. It can also sometimes occur in surprisingly boggy places.

GROWING METHOD

Propagation   Best grown from divisions of existing clumps, *A. reptans* roots easily from stem nodes and any small sections that are dug up will rapidly re-establish.

Feeding   Feed with an application of blood and bone, pellets of poultry manure or any complete plant food after flowering.

Problems   *A. reptans* can be badly affected by powdery mildew if air circulation is poor or the soil is badly drained. If the weather is not too hot, sulphur dust or spray can suppress this mildew. Otherwise use a fungicide registered for powdery mildew.

FLOWERING

Season   The attractive bright blue flower spikes are produced in spring, or in the early summer in cool areas. They make a lovely garden display. "Variegata" is probably the best form with its highly-decorative white edged leaves. It is not that reliable though and needs close attention. "Braunherz" has a remarkably rich bronze color.

Cutting   The flowers of *A. reptans* are good as cut flowers.

PRUNING

General   Pruning should be restricted to the removal of the spent flower stems.

ALCHEMILLA MOLLIS
Lady's mantle

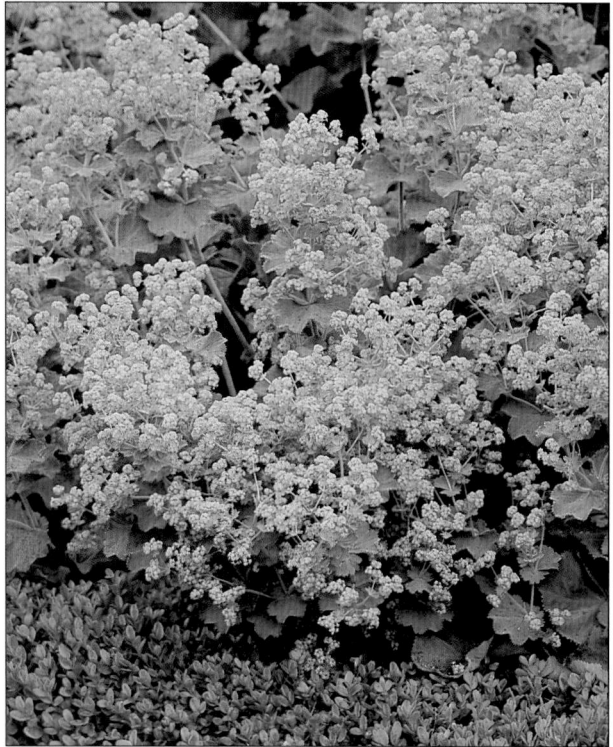

LIME-GREEN FLOWERS light up Alchemilla mollis. *Although it is not a particularly bright color, it lifts the whole area.*

THIS MASSED PLANTING of A. mollis *behind a dwarf box hedge will defy any competition from weeds or other plants.*

FEATURES

Sun or
Part Shade

Alchemilla mollis is a quick-growing, herbaceous perennial that is mostly used along the edges of paths or borders. It is effective for suppressing weeds and sows itself freely, often popping up in cracks in paths or paving. Growing to anything up to 2ft high, one plant may spread to 30in. The rounded, slightly hairy leaves overlap one another and it produces trusses of bright lime-green flowers through summer. It provides a lovely contrast with other strong colors.

ALCHEMILLA AT A GLANCE

A. mollis is a self-seeding perennial for cottage gardens that can form incredible groundcover. Hardy to 0°F (zone 7).

		Companion Plants
Jan	/	Cotoneaster
Feb	/	Elaeagnus
Mar	/	Fuchsia
April	foliage 🌿	Hebe
May	foliage 🌿	Holly
June	flowering ❀	Lavender
July	flowering ❀	Pittosporum
Aug	flowering ❀	Rose
Sept	flowering ❀	
Oct	foliage 🌿	
Nov	foliage 🌿	
Dec	foliage 🌿	

CONDITIONS

Aspect The more sun it receives the better. It is a willing performer, a sure spreader, and also grows well in light shade.

Site Needs to be grown in well-drained soil with a high organic content.

GROWING METHOD

Propagation Self-sown seedlings can easily be transplanted to other positions. Clumps can be divided in either fall or spring.

Feeding Apply blood and bone or complete plant food in spring as new growth begins.

Problems No specific problems are known.

FLOWERING

Season Masses of lime-green flowers appear throughout summer.

Cutting Flowers are popular with flower arrangers.

PRUNING

General Shear the whole plant back hard in midsummer and you get a fresh surge of new lime green foliage and flowers. Otherwise it takes care of itself.

ANEMONE
Windflower

BETWEEN THEM, the anemones have just about all the colors of the rainbow, with various shades of red, pink, mauve, blue, and yellow. There are species, such as Anemone ranunculoides, *that enjoy a partially shaded position and are therefore perfect for woodland areas of the garden.*

FEATURES

Shade or
Part Shade

Anemones are a large genus with lots of excellent woodland plants like *Anemone ranunculoides*. It is a spreading perennial growing about 4in high, and 18in wide, with yellow flowers in spring. Other good woodland-type anenomes include the white *A. nemorosa*, slightly shorter and it does not spread quite as far. Most of the other anenomes are more strikingly obvious, like the dark pink *A. hupehensis* which grows 2ft high or more. The Japanese anemone, *A. hupehensis japonica*, has striking white flowers. It lasts well into the fall.

ANEMONE AT A GLANCE

Anemone ranunculoides is a spring-flowering woodland plant with agood spread. There is a double form. Hardy to 5°F (zone 7).

		Recommended Varieties
Jan	/	*Anemone blanda*
Feb	/	*A. blanda* "Radar"
Mar	/	*A. blanda* "White Star"
April	foliage 🌿	*A. hupehensis*
May	flowering ❀	*A. hupehensis* "Hadspen
June	foliage 🌿	Abundance"
July	foliage 🌿	*A. hupehensis* "Bressingham
Aug	foliage 🌿	Glow"
Sept	foliage 🌿	*A.* x *hybrida* "Honorine
Oct	/	Jobert"
Nov	/	*A. ranunculoides*
Dec	/	

CONDITIONS

Aspect   *Anemone ranunculoides* needs a rather shady position, as if growing in an open woodland. Some shade during the day is necessary.

Site   The soil should be dampish, and definitely not hot, dry, and free-draining. Adding well-rotted organic matter should aid moisture retention, and improve and feed the soil.

GROWING METHOD

Propagation   Divide the rhizomes in the spring, or in the fall when the leaves have dropped. One mature plant should yield plenty of new vigorous plants.

Feeding   Apply a slow-release fertilizer in the spring. This should ensure a spectacular flower display through the season.

Problems   The most typical problem comes from hungry slugs. They can ruin the foliage and new shoots. Spreading sharp sand or gravel round the plants keeps slugs away.

FLOWERING

Season   *A. ranunculoides* flowers in the spring.

Cutting   It makes good cut flowers.

PRUNING

General   No pruning is necessary.

ANTHEMIS TINCTORIA
Ox-eye chamomile

THE YELLOW FLOWERS of Anthemis tinctoria *light up the garden on the grayest day, contrasting well with the dark foliage.*

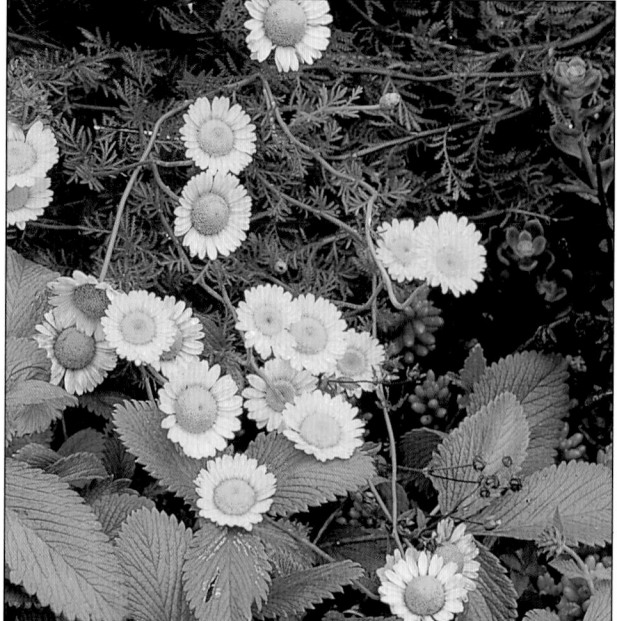

THE LONG FLOWERING PERIOD, pretty foliage and ease of maintenance make A. tinctoria *a good choice for busy gardeners.*

FEATURES

Full Sun

With ferny foliage and bright yellow daisy flowers, *Anthemis tinctoria* makes a striking and easy-care groundcover. The plant may grow up to 3ft high and spread by the same amount. The floral display is long lasting: it should be around through late spring and summer. There are a number of named cultivars available. This is a vigorous plant that may sometimes need restraining, although it never gets totally out of hand. Ox-eye chamomile plants need renewing every two or three years but they are easy to propagate. An alternative common name for this plant is dyer's chamomile, because the flowers yield a distinctive yellow dye.

ANTHEMIS AT A GLANCE

Anthemis tinctoria gives both decent cover and a fine array of yellow flowers at the height of summer. Hardy to 0°F (zone 7).

		Recommended Varieties
Jan	/	*Anthemis* "Grallagh Gold"
Feb	/	*A. punctata cupaniana*
Mar	/	*A. tinctoria*
April	/	*A. tinctoria* "Alba"
May	foliage 🌱	*A tinctoria* "E. C. Buxton"
June	flowering ❀	*A. tinctoria* "Kelwayi"
July	flowering ❀	*A. tinctoria* "Sauce
Aug	flowering ❀	Hollandaise"
Sept	foliage 🌱	*A. tinctoria* "Wargrave
Oct	foliage 🌱	Variety"
Nov	/	
Dec	/	

CONDITIONS

Aspect Must have full sun all day for best flowering. Keep it well out of the shade.

Site Soil should be well drained but need not be rich. *A. tinctoria* will tolerate quite poor soil.

GROWING CONDITIONS

Propagation The one big problem with *A. tinctoria* is that it has quite a short shelf-life. Either prune (see below) or regularly grow new young plants from divisions. Divide plants in the spring or the fall, making sure each section has good roots. You can also increase your stock by taking cuttings in the spring.

Feeding Fertilize lightly with blood and bone, poultry manure or complete plant food in early spring.

Problems No specific problems are known.

FLOWERING

Season Flowering right through the summer.

Cutting Flowers can be picked for posies.

PRUNING

General Prune flowers as they fade to prolong blooming. This also forces plants to develop new strong growths which prolong their lifespan. Also note that plants can be cut back at any time during the growing season if they need restricting.

ARABIS CAUCASICA
Rock cress

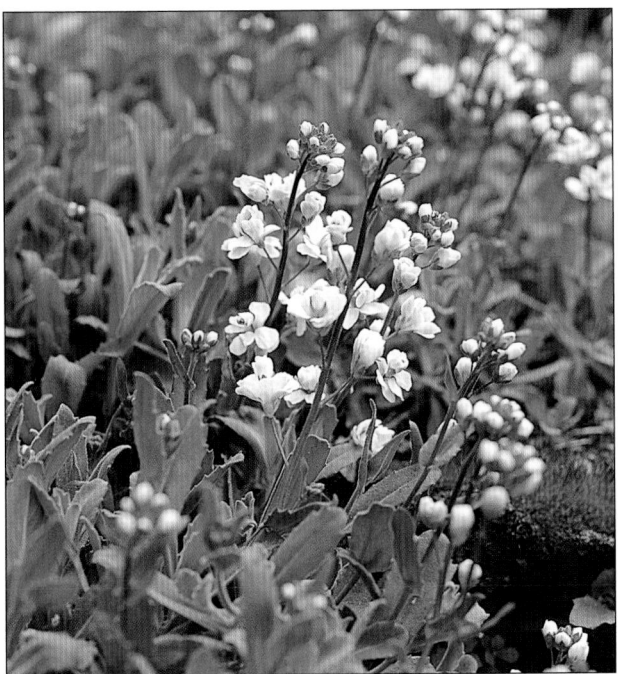

THIS DOUBLE WHITE FORM of rock cress closely resembles its relative, the stock. The light fragrance is reminiscent of stock too.

A GENEROUS DRIFT of rock cress fills a section of this perennial border, which is edged with low-growing, pink alpine phlox.

FEATURES

Full Sun

Of the many species of rock cress, this is probably the most commonly grown. It spreads to form mats of leafy rosettes and will grow to around 6in high. This vigorous plant may spread to 1ft. It can be grown in rockeries, between paving stones or as a border plant. Flowers are produced over a long season from late winter into summer. They are white in the species but there is a pink form and also a double white variety, "Flore Pleno." There are a number of other named cultivars. *Arabis caucasica* is related to stock as is obvious from the flowers, and it has the fragrance associated with stocks.

ARABIS AT A GLANCE

Arabis caucasica is a white-flowering evergreen perennial best grown in walls. It can be quite invasive. Hardy to 0°F (zone 7).

		Recommended Varieties
Jan	foliage	*Arabis* x *arendsii* "Rosabella"
Feb	foliage	*A. blepharophylla*
Mar	foliage	"Fruhlingszauber"
April	foliage	*A. bryoides*
May	flowering ❀	*A. caucasica* "Flore Pleno"
June	foliage	*A. caucasica* "Variegata"
July	foliage	*A. procurrens* "Variegata"
Aug	foliage	
Sept	foliage	
Oct	foliage	
Nov	foliage	
Dec	foliage	

CONDITIONS

Aspect Needs full sun.

Site Soil must be very well drained but need not be rich. Add lime or dolomite to very acid soils before planting. Heavy soils must be broken up with sharp grit and sand.

GROWING METHOD

Propagation Make divisions of an existing clump in the fall or spring. Generally, though, it is often easier to leave plants where they are and then to propagate from cuttings taken in the summer.

Feeding Apply a light dressing of complete plant food in spring.

Problems Avoid overwatering and make sure these plants are situated where air circulation is good. Plants can collapse in warm, moist conditions but this is extremely unlikely to occur in our climate.

FLOWERING

Season The brief but eyecatching display happens in spring with the warm weather.

Cutting Flowers can be picked for posies if the stems are long enough.

PRUNING

General Can be cut back hard once after blooming.

ARMERIA MARITIMA
Sea thrift

ARMERIA MARITIMA *IS known as "sea pink" in its natural habitat where it forms dense mounds on exposed sea cliffs.*

A GENEROUS PLANTING of A. maritima *fills a sunny corner by an old wall. Dainty little erigeron creeps out from under the thrift.*

FEATURES

Full Sun

Also known as "sea pink," this small, tufted plant makes mounded cushions of foliage. Established growth is very dense. Flowers, which may be pink, white or nearly red, stand above the foliage on stems that reach up to 8in or more. There are a number of named cultivars available. *Armeria maritima* has a long flowering period provided spent flowers are removed regularly. It is mostly used as an edging plant or grown in rockeries but it can be grown in containers too.

CONDITIONS

Aspect Needs an open, sunny position; tolerates exposed, windy coastal conditions extremely

ARMERIA AT A GLANCE

Armeria maritima is the indispensable perennial for seaside gardens. Hardy to 0°F (zone 7).

Month	Activity	Recommended Varieties
Jan	/	Armeria alliacea
Feb	/	"Bees Ruby"
Mar	/	A. juniperifolia
April	foliage	A. juniperifolia "Bevan's
May	foliage	Variety"
June	flowering	A. maritima
July	foliage	A. maritima "Bloodstone"
Aug	foliage	A. maritima "Vindictive"
Sept	foliage	A. pseudarmeria
Oct	/	
Nov	/	
Dec	/	

well, hence its name, though it is also found growing in mountains.

Site Soil must be very well drained but it need not be rich. Do not risk growing it on heavy wet soils, where its roots will rot the first winter and die.

GROWING METHOD

Propagation Grows best from divisions of an existing clump, which should be broken up and replanted during the first part of spring.

Feeding Apply little or no fertilizer as this may stimulate lush foliage growth, which is prone to problems. If the soil is very poor, feed lightly with some complete plant food during early spring. A slow-release fertilizer is best, rather than a sudden quick-fix application.

Problems Rust, a fungal disease, can be a problem in very humid conditions—spray with a registered fungicide. Overwatering and poor drainage will cause plants to collapse.

FLOWERING

Season The pink, white or red flowers will appear from spring through summer if spent flowers are removed regularly.

Cutting Flowers can be cut for the vase or spent blooms simply cut off.

PRUNING

General Remove spent flowers. Deadheading prolongs flowering.

BALLOTA
Ballota

THE PLEASANT SCALLOPED foliage of Ballota pseudodictamnus *creates a variegated effect as the lighter-colored undersides of the leaves curls up and catch the sunlight. The downy texture of these plants also provides an attractive contrast of texture with glossier, darker green foliage.*

FEATURES

Full Sun

Ballota pseudodictamnus is a mound-forming evergreen sub-shrub, growing about 18in high, and spreading to about 2ft. It has an abundance of rounded leaves covered with silvery gray wool. It needs very little care beyond a spring prune, and its whitish flowers appear from spring into early summer. It thrives best in full sun and, like the other ballotas commonly available, is not quite fully hardy. *B. acetabulosa* is slightly bushier and taller, making a more dominant plant. Neither belong to the first division of shrubs, but they are good at covering bare patches of soil. They can be pruned giving a shorter height, emphasizing the spread.

BALLOTA AT A GLANCE

Ballota pseudodictamnus has all-year woolly leaves, and white flowers with a pink tinge. Hardy to 23°F (zone 7).

Jan	foliage	Recommended VArieties
Feb	foliage	*Ballota* "All Hallows Green"
Mar	foliage	*B. nigra*
April	flowering	*B. n.* "Archer's Variegated"
May	flowering	*B. acetabulosa*
June	flowering	*B. pseudodictamnus*
July	foliage	
Aug	foliage	
Sept	foliage	
Oct	foliage	
Nov	foliage	
Dec	foliage	

CONDITIONS

Aspect Full sun or sun for most of the day is the key to success with these plants. Keep them away from the shade.

Site Completely avoid any soil that has been enriched. Ballotas will flourish in soils other plants would consider poor. It should also be quite light and free draining.

GROWING METHOD

Propagation The best and cheapest method for propagation is to take dozens of cuttings in the early part of summer. They quickly take but do need protection through the cold winter months. Plant out the following spring when they are well hardened off.

Feeding This is one occasion when feeding of any description is really not necessary.

Problems Ballotas are remarkably trouble free. The plants take care of themselves.

FLOWERING

Season The small white flowers with a pink tinge appear through late spring, and the first part of summer. In the case of *B. acetabulosa* they appear in the middle and end part of summer.

PRUNING

General A spring prune produces plenty of fresh new growth and keeps it in good shape.

BERGENIA CILIATA
Elephant's ears

THE LARGE LEAVES *of bergenias lead to their popular name of elephant's ears. This foliage makes them prime groundcover plants.*

PROVIDING A WELCOME *lift to the garden in the winter, the blooms of* Bergenia ciliata *bob amid a sea of lush green foliage.*

FEATURES

Shade or
Part Shade

Bergenias make excellent evergreen groundcover plants. They are also known as elephant's ears because of the large, rounded leaves about 8–12in long. They are often leathery and glossy, generally green, many turning reddish in the fall. The flowers are held on short stems from mid-spring to early summer. *Bergenia ciliata* has pink flowers and tends to lose its foliage in cold winters. It should survive most winters but in very bad freezing spells it may succumb, and should be protected. It grows about 1ft high, and 18in wide. Like all bergenias it is generally long living and easy to propagate. It is a useful plant, able to colonize areas other plants can't reach, such as beneath trees. It can also be used at the front of a border, or even to line the edge of paths.

BERGENIA AT A GLANCE

Bergenia ciliata is a large-leaved, pink flowering perennial that thrives in a wide range of conditions. Hardy to 5°F (zone 7).

		Recommended Varieties
Jan	/	
Feb	/	*Bergenia* "Adenglut"
Mar	flowering ❀	B. "Baby Doll"
April	flowering ❀	B. "Bressingham Salmon"
May	foliage	B. "Bressingham White"
June	foliage	B. *ciliata*
July	foliage	B. *cordifolia* "Purpurea"
Aug	foliage	B. *c.* "Morgenrote"
Sept	foliage	B. *purpurascens*
Oct	/	B. *p.* "Silberlicht"
Nov	/	
Dec	/	

CONDITIONS

Aspect It grows in either full sun or shady areas, but avoid extremes of the latter.

Site Likes well composted, moist soil with good drainage. It will tolerate much poorer conditions that bring out a richer leaf color in winter.

GROWING METHOD

Propagation Grow from seeds sown in the spring to produce hybrids, or divide in the spring or fall every five years or so. This will rejuvenate a declining plant. Place up to 2ft apart, depending on the variety, or closer for immediate coverage.

Feeding Feed generously in early spring with a complete plant food, especially on poorer ground, and give a generous layer of mulch both in the spring, and again in the fall.

Problems Slugs and snails can be a major problem to the young foliage, ruining its shapely appearance. Pick off, or attack with chemicals. Spray with a fungicide if leaf spot occurs.

FLOWERING

Season The flowers appear from late winter or early spring, depending on variety, for a few weeks.

Cutting Though the flowers are useful in cut flower arrangements, the foliage, especially when red in winter, makes a particularly attractive foil.

PRUNING

General Remove the spent flower stem and foliage.

CALLUNA VULGARIS
Heather

A MASSED PLANTING of Culluna vulgaris "Firefly" creates a rippling sea of magenta, as the blooms emerge.

HEATHER CAN BE a spectacular display plant, as this group demonstrates. The variety of colors creates a stunning patchwork effect.

FEATURES

Full Sun

The heathers are evergreen shrubs that demand acid soil. There is just one species with scores of excellent cultivars. The best way to choose between them is to visit special heather gardens and nurseries, buying forms that make a fun "patchwork quilt." Many have colored foliage with red, purple, bronze, gray, and gold, and many green-leaved ones change color come the fall. The key difference between heathers and ericas is that the latter include varieties that flower in late winter/spring, while heathers peak from midsummer to fall. Most heathers spread about 18in. Some have flowers that contrast with and stand out against the foliage. One such is the cultivar "Firefly," with magenta flowers and beige leaves.

CALLUNA AT A GLANCE

Heathers are vital components of the winter garden, valued for their range of colored foliage. Hardy to 0°F (zone 7).

		Recommended Varieties
Jan	foliage	*Calluna vulgaris*
Feb	foliage	
Mar	foliage	C. v. "Allegro"
April	foliage	C. v. "Beoley Gold"
May	foliage	C. v. "Blazeaway"
June	foliage	C. v. "Elsie Purnell"
July	flowering	C. v. "Firefly"
Aug	flowering	C. v. "Johnson's Variety"
Sept	flowering	C. v. "Mair's Variety"
Oct	foliage	C. v. "Peter Sparkes"
Nov	foliage	C. v. "Wickwar Flame"
Dec	foliage	

CONDITIONS

Aspect   Full bright sun is vital. The sun also emphasizes the color of the foliage, its chief virtue in the winter garden.

Site   These plants will only flourish in acid soil that is free draining. It should also be rich in well-rotted organic matter.

GROWING METHOD

Propagation   Increase your number of plants by taking semi-ripe cuttings in the first part of summer. They root quickly.

Feeding   Make sure that the soil has plenty of organic matter added to keep it rich and fertile.

Problems   Only in extremely persistent humid conditions might heathers develop gray mold or disease. Otherwise, once planted, these are remarkably problem free.

FLOWERING

Season   The flowers appear after midsummer, and continue their display right through into the fall. There is a wide range of colors with dark red "Allegro," white "Beoley Gold," mauve "Blazeaway," pink "Elsie Purnell," and purple-pink "Johnson's Variety." The white "Mair's Variety" makes good cut flowers.

PRUNING

General   Give the plants a light prune in the spring if required, or for shape. Other than these cases, pruning is not necessary.

CAMPANULA
Bellflower

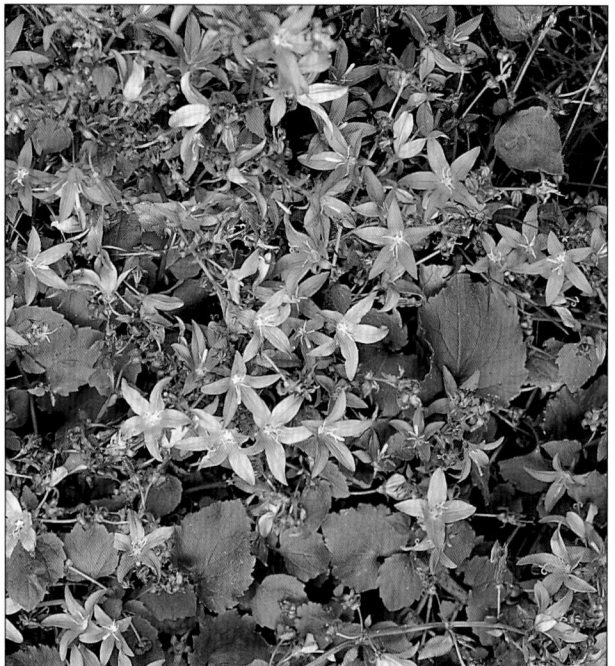

AS THE STARRY mauve-blue flowers appear, the bellflower plant seem to expand. It is a pretty plant that never fails to delight.

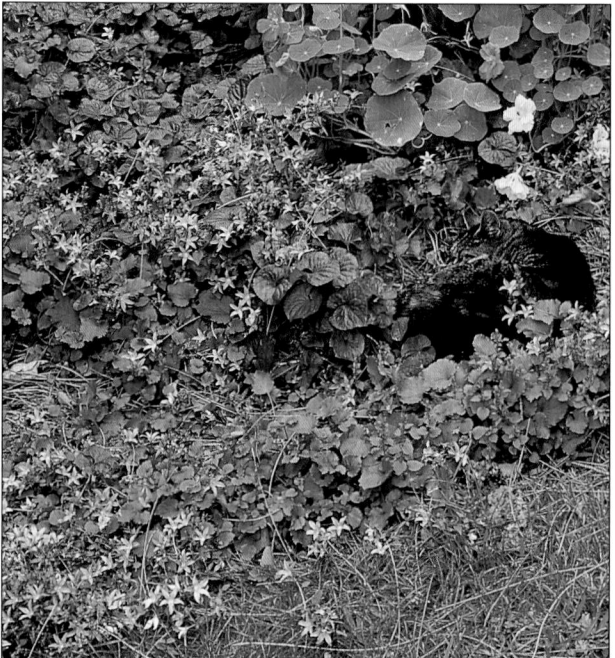

SCRAMBLING ALONG on its own or among other plants, the bell-flower is undemanding and gives the gardener great rewards.

FEATURES

Partial Shade

Bellflowers are a large group of 300 species, varying from mat-like or rosette-forming plants to tall, upright species. These evergreen, groundcovering species are generally easy to grow, vigorous without being troublesome, good weed suppressors, and delightful in flower. Flowers, appearing from midsummer, are mostly mauve-blue, although white forms are available. Plants are low growing, rarely exceeding 6in in height but they can spread a good distance. Bellflowers can be grown as groundcover, in walls, or in pots and troughs. They sometimes self-seed, appearing in cracks in paths or walls.

CAMPANULA AT A GLANCE

Campanula portenschlagiana is a moderate spreading bellflower with purple flowers in the summer. Hardy to 5°F (zone 7).

Jan	foliage ❀	Recommended Varieties
Feb	foliage ❀	*Campanula* "Birch Hybrid"
Mar	foliage ❀	*C. cochleariifolia*
April	foliage ❀	*C. garganica*
May	foliage ❀	*C. glomerata*
June	foliage ❀	*C. poscharskyana*
July	flowering ❀	*C. pulla*
Aug	flowering ❀	*C. takesimana*
Sept	foliage ❀	*C. portenschlagiana*
Oct	foliage ❀	
Nov	foliage ❀	
Dec	foliage ❀	

CONDITIONS

Aspect   Grows best in semi-shade or morning sun with afternoon shade.

Site   Soil must be well drained. *Campanula portenschlagiana* comes from the mountainous parts of Croatia. It is tolerant of a range of soil types but grows best in soil enriched with organic matter.

GROWING METHOD

Propagation   Increase stock by dividing clumps of rooted stems. The minute seed will also self-seed.

Feeding   Can be grown without supplementary fertilizer, but benefits from an application of complete plant food as growth commences in spring.

Problems   No specific problems are known.

FLOWERING

Season   Flowers profusely from mid-spring through to early summer. The flowers are a gorgeous rich purple, nearly 1in long.

Cutting   Attractive though they are, the flowers are not suitable for cut-flower arrangements.

PRUNING

General   Remove spent flower stems. Once blooms have finished the entire flowering stem is easily and lightly pulled off.

CERASTIUM TOMENTOSUM
Snow-in-summer

THE FLOWER STEMS of snow-in-summer rise high above the silvery foliage. This plant likes dry conditions and flourishes on a steep slope.

FROM A DISTANCE this flowering mass truly looks like snow as it carpets the ground beneath a weeping mulberry.

FEATURES

Full Sun

Cerastium tomentosum is an attractive plant with small, silver-gray leaves and sprays of white flowers that appear in late spring and summer. The silvery foliage provides a good color contrast with brighter colors in the garden. It has a low, creeping habit with stems that root down as they travel along. Ideal for sunny rockeries and dry areas, it is quite quick growing and long lived in the right conditions. Position the plants at about 1ft intervals for quick cover. Once it is established, *C. tomentosum* suppresses weeds well but it may also invade areas where it is not wanted. It is, however, a simple matter to dig out any offending sections.

CERASTIUM AT A GLANCE

Cerastium tomentosum is a sun-loving, white-flowering spreader, excellent on any spare piece of ground. Hardy to 5°F (zone 7).

		Companion Plants
Jan	/	Berberis
Feb	/	Cotoneaster
Mar	flowering ✿	Elaeagnus
April	flowering ✿	Ilex
May	flowering ✿	Prunus
June	flowering ✿	Pyracantha
July	foliage	Rosa
Aug	foliage	Viburnum
Sept	foliage	
Oct	/	
Nov	/	
Dec	/	

CONDITIONS

Aspect This plant must be grown in full sun to achieve its potential.

Site Soil must be well drained.

GROWING METHOD

Propagation The easiest method of propagation is by division of a rooted clump, but tip cuttings may be taken in late spring and summer. Given the rate at which it spreads, it is unlikely you will need more plants.

Feeding Apply complete plant food or pelleted poultry manure in early spring. However, feeding is unnecessary, and snow-in-summer is almost as vigorous on quite poor soil.

Problems This plant has no specific pest or disease problems, but overwatering or poorly drained soil will cause plants to rot and die.

FLOWERING

Season Pretty white flowers are produced through spring and into early summer in cool areas.

PRUNING

General No pruning is needed beyond shearing off spent flower stems or trimming growth to control its spread. You can be as ruthless as you want. *C. tomentosum* is quite tough, and keeps coming back even when you thought you'd pruned it excessively hard.

DIANTHUS DELTOIDES
Maiden pink

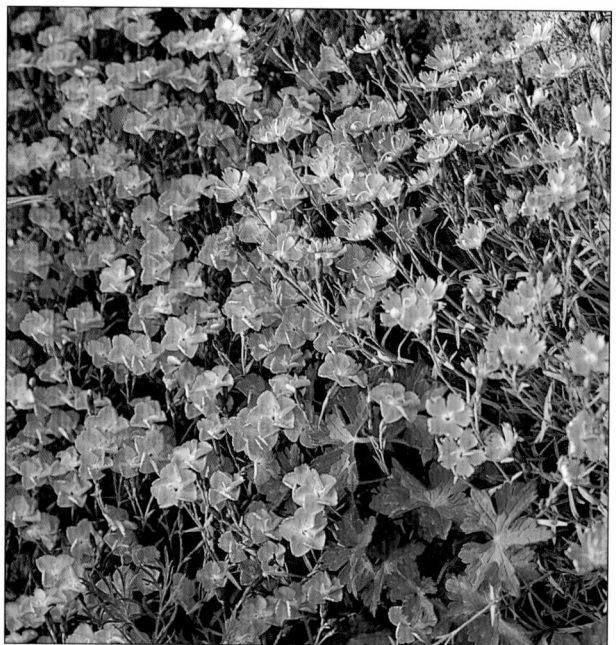

A PROLIFIC SHOW of flowers can always be expected from this pretty dianthus, one of the many known as pinks.

SPILLING OVER a gravel path, this pink dianthus revels in the full sun and sharp drainage afforded by the small stones.

FEATURES

Full Sun

There are about 300 species of dianthus, including annual and perennial growers, and several of the alpine dianthus make low mounded growth suitable for groundcover. This species, *Dianthus deltoides*, makes a delightful groundcover with its thick, spreading mat-like growth. Foliage height rarely reaches more than 4¾in, while the pretty, fringed flowers stand about 8in high. Flowers in the species, which appear in the summer, are deep rose pink but there are cultivars with flowers in various colors, including white, red, and other shades of pink. In good conditions one plant can spread to 18in.

DIANTHUS AT A GLANCE

Dianthus deltoides is a low spreading perennial producing white, pink, or red summer flowers. Hardy to 5°F (zone 7).

Jan	foliage	Recommended Varieties
Feb	foliage	*Dianthus armeria*
Mar	foliage	"Doris"
April	foliage	*D. erinaceus*
May	foliage	*D.* "Haytor White"
June	flowering	*D.* "Joe Vernon"
July	flowering	*D.* "Mrs Sinkins"
Aug	flowering	*D. pavonius*
Sept	foliage	*D. scardicus*
Oct	foliage	*D. superbus*
Nov	foliage	
Dec	foliage	

CONDITIONS

Aspect   Prefers full sun all day. Keep away from anywhere remotely shady.

Site   Soil must be well drained, and decayed organic matter added well ahead of planting time is beneficial. Very acid soils should be dressed with lime. Heavy clay soils need to be thoroughly broken up before planting with plenty of sand and horticultural grit.

GROWING METHOD

Propagation   Grow from division of rooted sections of an existing plant, or from cuttings taken in late summer. Make sure that the cutting is a non-flowering one.

Feeding   Give complete plant food in spring.

Problems   No specific problems are known, but keep an eye out for aphids and slugs. Tackle the latter either with slug pellets or, if you don't want to use chemicals, instigate a nightly patrol, picking them off when seen.

FLOWERING

Season   Flowers appear in the summer.

Cutting   The flowers may be cut for posies but the stems are rather short.

PRUNING

General   Shear off flowers once they have faded. No other pruning is needed.

ERICA CARNEA
Erica

A WHOLE SECTION of hillside is blanketed in color. Flowering at the end of winter, ericas herald the coming of spring.

THE SMALL FLOWERS and dark green foliage of this erica create a frothy white mass. Ericas are at their best in full sunshine.

FEATURES

Full Sun

Otherwise known as winter or alpine heath, this is a small evergreen shrub growing about 10in high at most, and spreading twice that distance. At its best on acid soil it will, however, tolerate some lime. The great virtue of ericas is that they provide indispensable winter foliage color. *Erica carnea* has dark green leaves and dark pink flowers that last from winter well into early spring. Other excellent forms of erica include "Adrienne Duncan" with bronze tinged foliage, "Ann Sparkes" with lime green leaves, and "Challenger" with rich red flowers. "Golden Starlet" has white flowers and pale green foliage, and "Vivellii" bronze leaves with pink flowers. The best way to grow ericas is in "patchwork quilts," with great sheets of merging and contrasting colors.

ERICA AT A GLANCE

Erica carnea is a fine shrub with a wide range of excellent forms. A "must" on acid soil. Hardy to 0°F (zone 7).

Jan	flowering ❁	Recommended varieties
Feb	flowering ❁	*Erica carnea*
Mar	flowering ❁	E. c. "Adrienne Duncan"
April	flowering ❁	E. c. "Ann Sparkes"
May	foliage	E. c. "Challenger"
June	foliage	E. c. "December Red"
July	foliage	E. c. "King George"
Aug	foliage	E. c. "March Seedling"
Sept	foliage	E. c. "Myretoun Ruby"
Oct	foliage	E. c. "Springwood White"
Nov	foliage	E. c. "Vivellii"
Dec	foliage	

CONDITIONS

Aspect   Ericas need as much sun as they can get. They not only thrive in it, but you can really appreciate the full range of hues and tones. In darker parts of the garden their virtues will not stand out.

Site   Moist, acid soil is the key. *Erica carnea* is unusual because it can tolerate slightly more alkaline conditions.

GROWING METHOD

Propagation   The simplest method involves taking semi-ripe cuttings during the first part of summer.

Feeding   This is not necessary. You can scatter ericaceous compost round new plants to give them a head start.

Problems   They can suffer from fungal attacks in very humid conditions, but this is extremely unlikely. Otherwise, quite indestructible.

FLOWERING

Season   *E. carnea* and its various excellent forms flower from around Christmas well into spring. There is a wide range of colors, many showing up well against the foliage which ranges from yellow lime green to bronze.

PRUNING

General   This certainly is not necessary to keep plants in check since growth is very slow. You can prune to shape though, and this is best done after flowering in the spring before new growth appears.

GERANIUM
Cranesbill

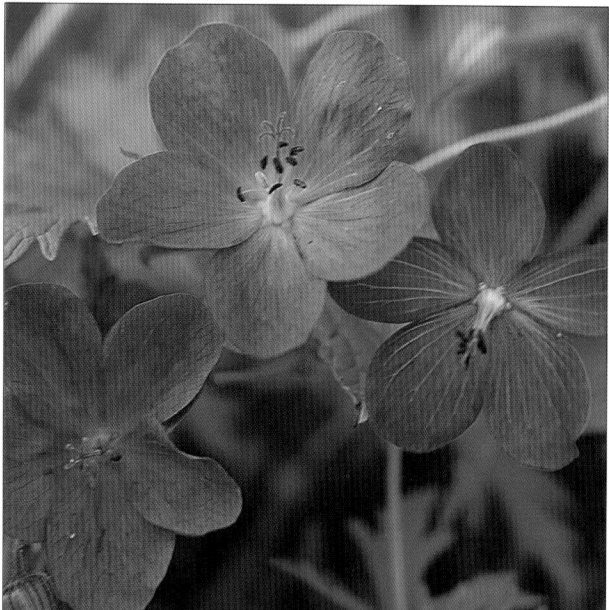

THESE BLOOMS OF Geranium *"Johnson's Blue"* appear in the summer, and contrast well with the light green foliage.

THE ROUNDED FORMS of the G. *"Johnson's Blue"* flowers are set off perfectly by the intricate shapes of this sun-loving plant's leaves.

FEATURES

Sun or Part Shade

There is a terrific choice of excellent geraniums, and one that always makes it to the top of the list is "Johnson's Blue." It grows about 16in high and double that in width. Right through the summer it is covered in rich blue flowers. It can be grown in the border, under apple trees, and to cover a spare patch of ground. It is easy to get hooked and start collecting more. "Ann Folkard" has magenta flowers, grows 2ft high, and flops 3ft wide or more. And *G. psilostemon* stands up 4ft high, extends 2ft wide, giving more rich, magenta flowers. Most geraniums are in the soft pink, lavender-blue, or white range. Easy to grow, they quickly make decent-sized perennials.

GERANIUM AT A GLANCE

Geranium "Johnson's Blue" is one of the best hardy geraniums, giving a summer of rich blue flowers. Hardy to 5°F (zone 7).

Jan	/	Recommended Varieties
Feb	/	*Geranium* "Ann Folkard"
Mar	/	*G. endressii*
April	/	*G. himalayense* "Gravetye"
May	foliage ❀	*G.* "Johnson's Blue"
June	flowering ❀	*G.* x *oxonianum* "Wargrave
July	flowering ❀	Pink"
Aug	flowering ❀	*G. pratense* "Mrs Kendall
Sept	foliage ❀	Clark"
Oct	foliage ❀	*G. psilostemon*
Nov	/	*G. sylvaticum* "Mayflower"
Dec	/	

CONDITIONS

Aspect   The more sun the better. Note that when deciding where to grow "Johnson's Blue," the color blue always appears much more intense in early evening as the light fades. That's the time of day when it really stands out.

Site   Typical garden soil is fine, with average fertility and decent drainage. Avoid extreme conditions of wet and over-dry soil.

GROWING METHOD

Propagation   The easiest way to give yourself more "Johnson's Blue" is to take a spade and slice vertically through the plant in the spring. Make sure each section has a good root system. You can still do this in the fall.

Feeding   If the soil is on the poor side, bump up the fertility with a slow-release fertilizer in the spring. Or mulch around the plant with well-rotted organic matter.

Problems   Geraniums tend to dislike having cold wet roots all through the winter. Some of the species need very good winter drainage. Add horticultural sand or grit to the soil to improve drainage if required.

FLOWERING

Season   Right through the summer.

PRUNING

General   This really is not necessary.

HEDERA HELIX
Common ivy

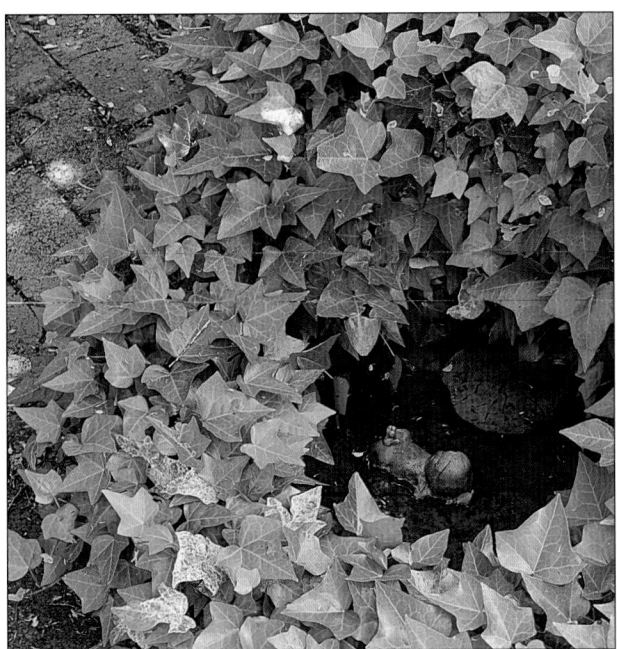

THE RICH GREEN LEAVES *of ivy can be trimmed and trained into a variety of shapes, including this striking circle.*

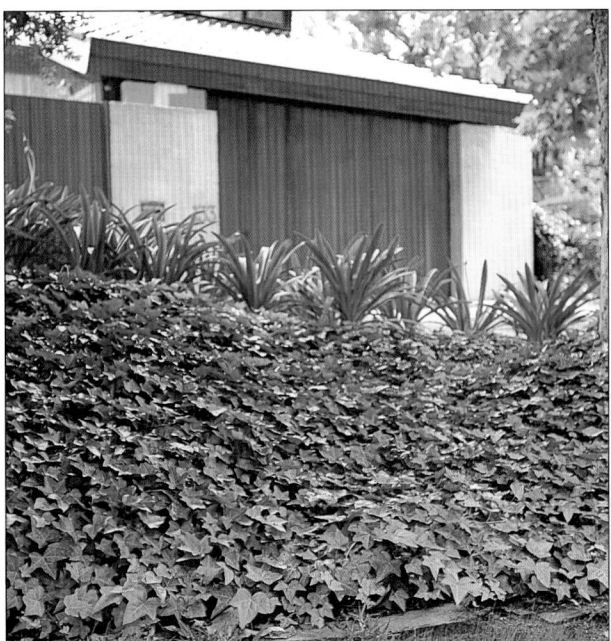

COMMON IVY *is used here to spill over a retaining wall. In such a situation it will need very little trimming.*

FEATURES

Sun, Shade
or Part
Shade

Hedera helix is generally thought of as a climbing plant but it can also make an excellent, low-maintenance groundcover, with a dense mass of foliage. It is especially good in shady areas under trees and will readily climb up them, but keep ivy away from ornamental trees or they will quickly be obscured. *H. helix* may also be used in place of a lawn in formal areas where it is kept well clipped, and it is also suitable for planting where it can spill over a wall or bank. The straight species has very dark green, lobed leaves, but there are many dozens of cultivars with leaves edged, spotted, or streaked with cream or gold, as well as great variation in leaf shape and size.

HEDERA AT A GLANCE

Hedera helix is a first-rate climber that also can be used as groundcover, and to romp over sheds. Hardy to 0°F (zone 7).

Jan	foliage 🌿	Recommended Varieties
Feb	foliage 🌿	*Hedera helix*
Mar	foliage 🌿	*H. h.* "Angularis Aurea"
April	foliage 🌿	*H. h.* "Atropurpurea"
May	foliage 🌿	*H. h.* "Buttercup"
June	foliage 🌿	*H. h.* "Glacier"
July	foliage 🌿	*H. h.* "Ivalace"
Aug	foliage 🌿	*H. h.* "Pedita"
Sept	foliage 🌿	*H. h.* "Shamrock"
Oct	flowering ✽	*H. h.* "Spetchley"
Nov	foliage 🌿	
Dec	foliage 🌿	

CONDITIONS

Aspect Tolerates full sun but is at its best in dappled sunlight or shade. A wonderfully adaptable plant for which a place can generally be found in the garden.

Site Grows in poor soil, but best in moisture-retentive soil enriched with organic matter.

GROWING METHOD

Propagation It is easy to strike from semi-ripe tip cuttings taken through summer and early fall. It roots easily from layers, too. You can even take spring cuttings and stick them straight back in the soil.

Feeding Apply complete plant food in early spring. Unless the soil is in a very poor state though, ivy can be left to get on with it.

Problems No special problems are known.

FLOWERING

Season Tiny, inconspicuous flowers are produced only on very mature, adult foliage and are never seen on plants that are kept clipped.

Berries Blue-black berries follow the flowers.

PRUNING

General Restrict pruning to cutting off wayward stems or keeping the plant within bounds. Trim in any season, but severe cutting is best in late winter, just before new growth.

HOSTA "FRANCEE"
Plantain lily

THIS FINE SPECIMEN of a Hosta "Francee" demonstrates how the plant forms dense mounds of foliage. An excellent groundcover plant.

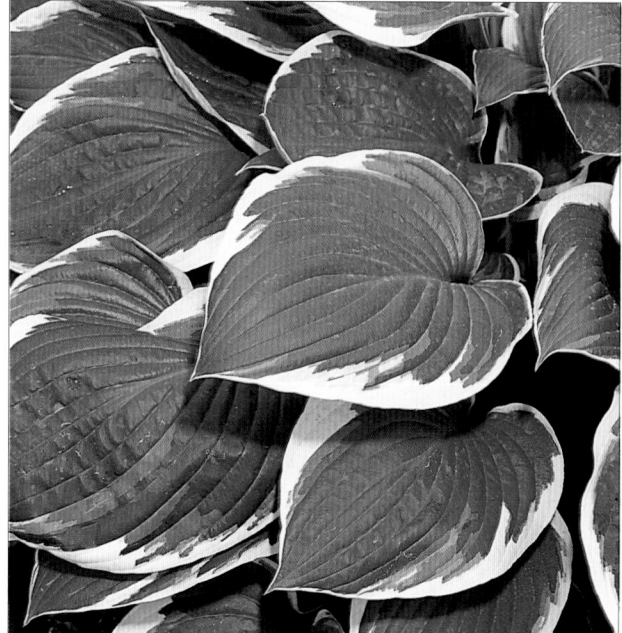

THE MAIN ATTRACTION of the hostas in general are their variegated foliage, especially this H. "Francee" with its white edges.

FEATURES

Sun, Shade or Part Shade

Every garden has room for a hosta. They are grown for their marvelous, decorative foliage which provides shade for the frogs and keeps down the weeds. "Francee" stands out with its white margined leaves. Grow it with different colored hostas like the bluish-leaved "Hadspen Blue," which makes a neat, dense clump. "Frances Williams" is blue-green with a yellowish margin. And "Patriot" is another excellent white-edged hosta if you cannot get hold of "Francee." They can also be mass planted near water features, or just allowed to multiply in the shade under trees. With room for one only, try growing it in a pot, topping the soil with pebbles to set it off.

HOSTA AT A GLANCE

Hosta "Francee" is a vigorous, clump-forming perennial that provides marvellous groundcover. Hardy to 0°F (zone 7).

Jan	/	Recommended Varieties
Feb	/	*Hosta* "Aureomarginata"
Mar	/	*H.* "Blue Angel"
April	foliage ✿	*H.* "Francee"
May	foliage ✿	*H.* "Frances Williams"
June	foliage ✿	*H.* "Golden Tiara"
July	flowering ✿	*H.* "Love Pat"
Aug	foliage ✿	*H.* "Patriot"
Sept	foliage ✿	*H.* "Shade Fanfare"
Oct	foliage ✿	*H.* "Wide Brim"
Nov	/	
Dec	/	

CONDITIONS

Aspect Most hostas grow in full sun if well watered. They also thrive in shade or dappled light. The blue-leaved kind are the hardest to place because they turn green with too much or too little shade. The yellow forms are best with direct sun either early or late in the day.

Site Provide rich, moisture-retentive soil. Add well-decayed manure to the ground before planting, and mulch afterwards. Avoid dry, free-draining, infertile ground.

GROWING METHOD

Propagation Divide the fleshy rhizomes in early spring. Most hostas perform best if they are divided every four to five years.

Feeding Apply scatterings of pelleted poultry manure in the spring.

Problems The chief enemies of these plants are slugs and snails which can devastate the incredibly attractive foliage. Spread sharp sand around the plants to deter intruders and use traps or bait.

FLOWERING

Season The white or pale violet flower spikes are interesting and usually appear in the summer, but the chief attraction has to be the foliage.

PRUNING

General Not necessary.

HOUTTUYNIA CORDATA
Houttuynia

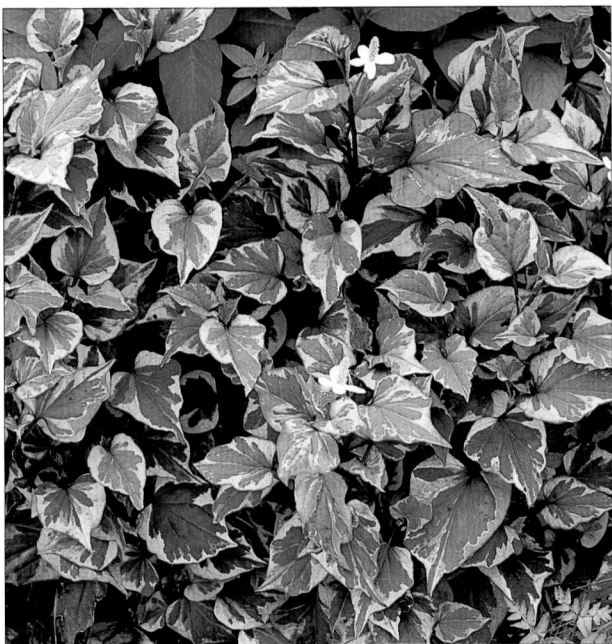

THIS WELL-ESTABLISHED Houttuynia cordata is flourishing in a moist soil, although it would also provide good cover in a dry site.

DECORATIVE VARIEGATED LEAVES splashed with cream and brilliant red are the most striking feature of the cultivar "Chameleon".

FEATURES

Sun or Part Shade

This is a groundcover plant for marshy, damp, cool parts of the garden, and can even grow in shallow water. In the right conditions the species makes a decent spreader, and can in fact become quite invasive. Its two most distinguishing features are that it has marvelously scented leaves, with the aroma of citrus fruit, and these turn reddish in the fall. There are two good forms, slightly less invasive than the species, "Chameleon" and "Flore Pleno." The first has fantastically eyecatching foliage. It has four colors, bronze, red, yellow, and dark green. The second, which is much harder to find, has white cones of petals. A highly useful plant.

HOUTTUYNIA AT A GLANCE

Houttuynia cordata is an excellent stream-side plant that spreads well and provides fresh white spring flowers.

		Companion Plants
Jan	/	Camassia
Feb	/	Euphorbia
Mar	/	Francoa
April	foliage ❀	Gentiana
May	flowering ❀	Gunnera
June	foliage ❀	Heuchera
July	foliage ❀	Hosta
Aug	foliage ❀	Iris
Sept	foliage ❀	Ligularia
Oct	foliage ❀	Lychnis
Nov	foliage ❀	
Dec	/	

CONDITIONS

Aspect Houttuynia grows in both full sun and light shade. "Chameleon" gets better colored leaves in the sun, where its colors look much more marked. Do not waste it in the shade.

Site The soil needs to be on the damp side, and rich with plenty of well-rotted organic matter.

GROWING METHOD

Propagation It is unlikely that you will ever need to propagate *H. cordata*, given how well it spreads, but you can easily make extra plants. Divide the plant in the spring, or take cuttings at the same time of year. The new growth quickly takes.

Feeding It is unlikely to need extra nutrients if grown in the right conditions.

Problems Apart from being attacked by slugs and snails, the only problem you might encounter is when trying to grow it in a basket in the water. It will need regular potting up to stop it bursting out of the container.

FLOWERING

Season The flowers appear in the spring, and show up well against the foliage.

PRUNING

General This is rarely necessary. Use a spade to slice off any unwanted, excess spread.

LAMIUM
Dead nettle

SOFT PINK FLOWERS and foliage boldly striped in silver make dead nettle a very desirable groundcover for any garden.

THE FOLIAGE of this dead nettle is almost entirely silver. It reflects any available light and will certainly give a lift to a shady corner.

FEATURES

Shade or
Part Shade

Despite its rather unattractive common name, *Lamium* is quite a pretty, soft-leaved groundcover that spreads by running stems (stolons) which root down as they spread. Some are very vigorous and may be invasive, and although individual plants are generally only 6–18 in high, they can spread to cover 6 ft in warm, humid climates. There are many variegated forms with leaves splashed, speckled, or spotted with silver or cream. Different species or cultivars produce flowers that may be pink, purple, cream or yellow. Dead nettle also makes a good basket plant. In the garden it is easy to grow and maintain, and is long lived.

LAMIUM AT A GLANCE

Lamium is a useful groundcover with small pretty leaves, but can be highly invasive. Hardy to 0°F (zone 7).

Jan	/	Recommended Varieties
Feb	/	*Lamium galeobdolon*
Mar	/	*L. galeobdolon* "Hermann's
April	/	Pride"
May	foliage	*L. garganicum*
June	flowering	*L. garganicum* "Golden
July	flowering	Carpet"
Aug	flowering	*L. maculatum*
Sept	foliage	*L. m.* "Aureum"
Oct	foliage	*L. m.* "Beacon Silver"
Nov	/	*L. m.* "Cannon's Gold"
Dec	/	*L. m.* "White Nancy"

CONDITIONS

Aspect   *Lamium* does best in shade or semi-shade and when sheltered from strong wind.

Site   Tolerates a wide range of soils but is best in well-drained soils rich in organic matter. The ground should also be fairly moist.

GROWING METHOD

Propagation   Easily grown by dividing rooted plants. Alternatively you can grow from seed sown in the spring or the fall.

Feeding   Fertilizing is not necessary unless the soil is extremely poor, in which case complete plant food can be applied in early spring. An annual mulch with well-rotted organic matter also helps in this case.

Problems   There are no known problems.

FLOWERING

Season   Flowering spikes appear in the summer months, depending on species.

PRUNING

General   Pruning of plants is unnecessary but if they become too vigorous you may need to remove whole sections with a spade. If growing *L. galeobdolon*, you may need to insert a barrier into the soil to confine it. Use several thicknesses of builders' waterproofing plastic or metal sheeting, up to 1ft deep.

LITHODORA DIFFUSA
Lithospermum

INTENSE ROYAL BLUE FLOWERS are the highlight of this lithospermum planting, which trails over a low retaining wall. The color is intensified by the contrast with the chalk-white sweet Alice growing beside it.

FEATURES

Full Sun

This small, prostrate groundcover shrub is highly popular because of its brilliant blue flowers which cover the plant in late spring and early summer. It looks well and flourishes if grown in rockeries or on the edges of raised beds where it has perfect drainage. *Lithodora diffusa* can also be grown as a wall plant or between pavers or stepping stones. It does, however, need to be mass planted to get the best effect. There are a couple of cultivars available that have flowers either slightly larger than those of the species or in a different shade of blue, but it is, in fact, hard to beat the straight species for attractiveness.

LITHODORA AT A GLANCE

Lithodora diffusa is a shortish evergreen, 6in high, with good forms making fine cover in acid soil. Hardy to 0°F (zone 7).

Jan	foliage	Companion Plants
Feb	foliage	Azalea
Mar	foliage	Calluna
April	foliage	Erica
May	flowering	Gaultheria
June	flowering	Hydrangea
July	foliage	Kalmia
Aug	foliage	Pieris
Sept	foliage	Vaccinum
Oct	foliage	
Nov	foliage	
Dec	foliage	

CONDITIONS

Aspect Needs full sun exposure. Do not attempt to hide it away in the shade. The consequent damp soil will also be a major problem.

Site This plant needs an acid soil. If you do not have acid soil in the garden it can be grown in tubs surrounding a feature plant.

GROWING METHOD

Propagation Grows from cuttings taken in late summer or from seed sown in the fall.

Feeding Apply complete plant food in spring as new growth commences.

Problems No pest or disease problems are known, but permanently wet and poorly drained soil will kill these plants.

FLOWERING

Season This evergreen shrub has a decent flowering period from late spring to early summer. To make sure that it is well seen, also try growing it on rockeries where it thrives with the excellent drainage. The forms "Grace Ward" and "Heavenly Blue" are the best and easiest to get.

Cutting Flowers are unsuitable for cutting.

PRUNING

General Lightly prune these plants after flowering to remove spent stems.

LYSIMACHIA NUMMULARIA
Creeping Jenny

THE SPECIES of creeping Jenny produces pretty yellow flowers and deep green foliage. Flowers are rarely seen on the golden form.

"AUREA," the golden cultivar of creeping Jenny, can be truly eye-catching when the sun strikes the yellow leaves.

FEATURES

Sun or
Part Shade

Usually seen in its golden-leaved form, "Aurea," this groundcover has small, rounded leaves on stems that spread and root down as they go. The bright yellow leaves seem to light up the area where it is growing and it is often grown as a basket plant. Small, bright yellow flowers are produced in good conditions, and are more common on the plain species. Growth is flat, rarely more than 2in above the ground and one plant will cover 20in or so within a growing season, if conditions are good. *Lysimachia nummularia* can be long lived.

CONDITIONS

Aspect Grow *L. nummularia* in either sun or semi-shade but always give it some protection from the hottest summer sun. The golden form will lose its bright color unless it gets enough sun or bright light.

Site Prefers a well-drained but moist soil rich in organic matter. It is well worth forking in plenty of compost before planting so that it gets off to an excellent start.

GROWING METHOD

Propagation This plant is easily grown from division of the rooted sections of the parent plant. However, it also grows well from firm-tip cuttings that are taken during the summer months. They quickly start to root.

Feeding Complete plant food may be applied in early spring, but unless soil is very poor this will not be necessary.

Problems No specific problems are known but these plants will die if they are short of water during the summer months. If one group of plants is going to get watered during a drought, make sure *L. nummularia* is included.

FLOWERING

Season Small, yellow flowers are produced right through the summer.

PRUNING

General No general pruning is necessary but *L. nummularia* may need occasional trimming to confine its growth to the desired area. If the central growth starts to become thin, cut back some of the trailing stems to promote more growth from the center.

LYSIMACHIA AT A GLANCE

L. nummularia is a reliable ground-hugging spreader with a spread of yellow flowers in summer. Hardy to 0°F (zone 7).

Month		Recommended Varieties
Jan	/	
Feb	/	*Lysimachia atropurpurea*
Mar	/	*L. ciliata*
April	/	*L. clethroides*
May	foliage ❧	*L. minoricensis*
June	flowering ❀	*L. nummularia* "Aurea"
July	flowering ❀	*L. thyrsiflora*
Aug	foliage ❧	*L. vulgaris*
Sept	foliage ❧	
Oct	foliage ❧	
Nov	/	
Dec	/	

NEPETA X FAASSENII
Catmint

THE SPIKES of mauve-blue catmint flowers persist over a long period and the bush, when grown in full sun, becomes quite dense.

WILD CATMINT or catnip, N. cataria, is the species most attractive to cats. Rubbing or bruising the foliage releases the unusual scent.

FEATURES

Sun or
Part Shade

The gray-green leaves of *Nepeta* x *faassenii* are a lovely foil for other, brighter colors in the garden. Its mauve-blue flowers are produced over a long period too, making this is a useful plant for a sunny spot in the garden. It is quite quick to establish and is fairly long lived. The height is rarely more than 1ft and one plant may cover 18in or so, making roots as it goes. The foliage is aromatic when bruised and can then be attractive to cats. *N.* x *faassenii* is sometimes used as a cover planting between roses, especially old roses, as it provides a pleasing contrast in texture and color. It is a great favorite for garden edgings and cottage garden plantings and can be grown in a hanging basket or container. There is a cultivar known as "Six Hills Giant," which has taller growth and larger flowers.

NEPETA AT A GLANCE

N. x *faassenii* is a good plant for cottage gardens, with sprays of lavender flowers and grayish leaves. Hardy to 5°F (zone 7).

Jan	/	Recommended Varieties
Feb	/	*Nepeta* x *faassenii*
Mar	/	*N. govaniana*
April	/	*N. grandiflora*
May	foliage	*N. nervosa*
June	flowering	*N. racemosa*
July	flowering	*N.* "Six Hills Giant"
Aug	flowering	
Sept	flowering	
Oct	foliage	
Nov	/	
Dec	/	

CONDITIONS

Aspect This plant grows best in full sun but tolerates shade for part of the day.

Site Needs well-drained soil and tolerates poor soils, but growth is best if some organic matter is dug in well ahead of planting time.

GROWING METHOD

Propagation *N.* x *faassenii* is easy to grow from rooted suckers, which are produced freely. It may also be grown from cuttings taken through summer. Alternatively, lift and divide established plants in the spring as active growth begins.

Feeding Does not generally need fertilizer, but if the soil is very poor, complete plant food may be applied in early spring. In good conditions extra feeding is not necessary.

Problems No specific problems are known but overwatering or heavy, poorly drained soil can eventually kill this plant.

FLOWERING

Season *N.* x *faassenii* has a long flowering period from early summer into early fall. The colors are generally on the soft side being pale blue, or lilac-pink. The best display is in early summer, but by cutting it back you promote fresh new growth and another good display.

PRUNING

General Cut back old growth in spring to promote young, fresh growth.

PACHYSANDRA TERMINALIS
Pachysandra

A LOVELY SHEEN is a feature of the foliage on this variegated form of pachysandra, while the cream leaf margins brighten the leaves and add interest to what is already a handsome plant. This is a long-term planting and is an ideal groundcover under trees.

FEATURES

Shade or
Part Shade

Sometimes also known as Japanese spurge, this is an ideal groundcover under trees as it is happy in shade and tolerates dry soil. It has glossy, toothed leaves in a rosette form. Quite fast growing but long lived, it rarely grows more than 8in high. It spreads with runners and makes a dense, weed-suppressing cover once established. Plant at about 1ft intervals for quick cover. *Pachysandra terminalis* produces greenish white flower spikes in spring. There is a cultivar with white variegated leaves known as "Variegata."

PACHYSANDRA AT A GLANCE

Pachysandra terminalis is an evergreen with shiny dark leaves. White flowers appear in early summer . Hardy to 0°F (zone 7).

		Companion Plants
Jan	foliage	
Feb	foliage	Euonymus
Mar	foliage	Hydrangea
April	foliage	Mahonia
May	foliage	Phillyrea
June	flowering ❀	Rubus
July	foliage	Sambucus
Aug	foliage	Skimmia
Sept	foliage	Vaccinium
Oct	foliage	Viburnum
Nov	foliage	
Dec	foliage	

CONDITIONS

Aspect   Although tolerant of sun or shade, this plant is best in shaded and fairly sheltered positions.

Site   Tolerates damp or dry soil but not heavy, waterlogged clays.

GROWING METHOD

Propagation   Grows from divisions of older clumps lifted in the spring. Make sure that each section looks healthy, and has buds and roots, before replanting it in the garden.

Feeding   Apply complete plant food in early spring.

Problems   No specific problems are known.

FLOWERING

Season   Greenish white flower spikes are produced in the first part of summer but they are not very showy. Note that there are two other forms but that they do not offer a choice of flowers. "Green Carpet" has finer, smaller leaves, and "Variegata" has foliage with a white edge.

PRUNING

General   Pruning is not necessary. If growth becomes too dense and congested, it is a simple matter to thin it out—pull up unwanted plants, or lift clumps and replant the younger growths.

PERSICARIA AFFINIS
Persicaria

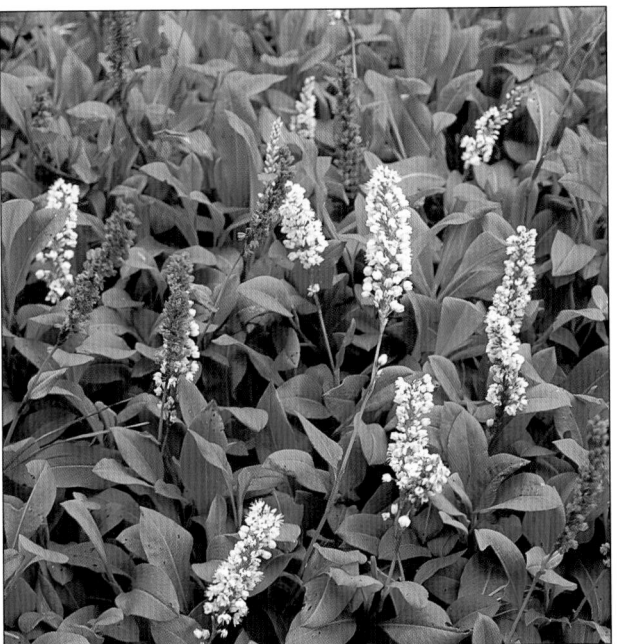

A STUNNING PLANTING of Persicaria affinis makes a thick evergreen cover, enlivened by the long-lasting show of flowers.

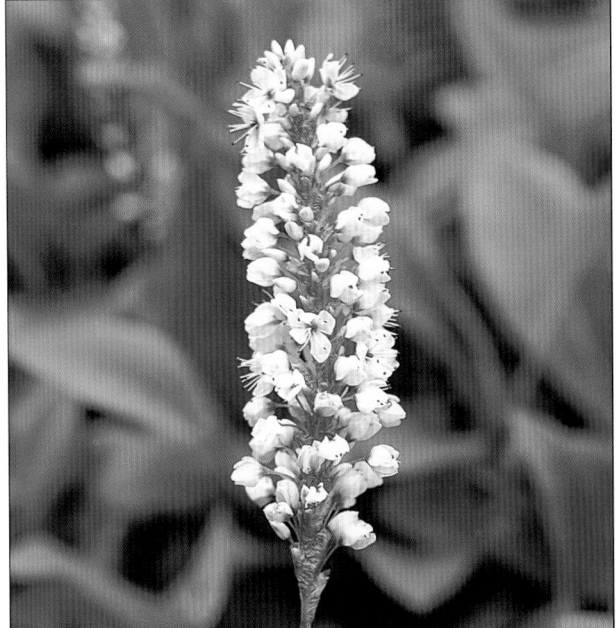

DENSE PINK SPIKES appear from midsummer, later highlighted against striking red-bronze fall leaves.

FEATURES

Full Sun

Persicaria affinis is a very useful evergreen groundcover plant. It forms an extensive carpet of dark green foliage that turns brown-bronze in the fall. The eyecatching 3in long spikes of bright red flowers are held on stems well clear of the foliage. Individual plants grow about 1ft high, and twice as wide. There are several excellent forms which many consider superior to the species. "Darjeeling Red" has larger, 4in long leaves, some even bigger, and two-tone flowers that start pink and darken to red. "Donald Lowndes" has more pointy leaves, and pale then dark pink flowers. "Superba" is pink tinged red, with bronze leaves in fall.

PERSICARIA AT A GLANCE

Persicaria affinis is a remarkably reliable evergreen groundcover plant, with a long flowering season. Hardy to 5°F (zone 7).

		Companion Plants
Jan	foliage	Francoa
Feb	foliage	Geum
Mar	foliage	Gunnera
April	foliage	Hellebore
May	foliage	Hosta
June	foliage	Iris
July	flowering	Lychnis
Aug	flowering	Primula
Sept	flowering	Rheum
Oct	flowering	
Nov	foliage	
Dec	foliage	

CONDITIONS

Aspect It needs either bright sun or light shade. It should perform equally well in both.

Site Provided the soil is on the moist side and does not dry out, which is the key requirement, it should thrive. An excellent plant for growing near streams where the soil remains quite damp. In the right conditions it forms very good groundcover, and can even be invasive.

GROWING METHOD

Propagation The quickest method involves digging up plants in the spring or fall, and dividing them into strong healthy sections. Make sure each has good roots.

Feeding This is rarely necessary.

Problems *P. affinis* and its forms are generally problem free, though slugs can attack fresh new growth. However, the forms which are most prone to slug and snail damage are *P. campanulata* and *P. virginiana*.

FLOWERING

Season Given plenty of sun, these plants should have a long flowering season. It begins about the middle of summer and graces the garden well into the fall.

PRUNING

General Pruning is not necessary.

PHLOX SUBULATA
Alpine phlox

THE DAINTY FLOWERS on alpine phlox create a tremendous impact when they are massed in full bloom.

GROWN AS A BORDER around beds of bulbs and perennials, this planting of alpine phlox is so full of flowers, the foliage is hidden.

FEATURES

Full Sun

Phlox subulata grows about 6in high and spreads into a mat about 20in across. In bloom it is a mass of small, flattish flowers in white, pink, rose, mauve or blue. There are many named cultivars available and they can flower for several weeks. *P. subulata* grows ideally in rockeries, trailing over walls or on slightly sloping ground where excellent drainage is assured. Although plants last well over several years, the best blooming comes from younger plants. Start new plants every few years to maintain vigor.

PHLOX AT A GLANCE

Phlox subulata makes an evergreen mat of fresh green leaves with bright late spring flowers. Hardy to 5°F (zone 7).

		Recommended Varieties
Jan	foliage	*Phlox adsurgens*
Feb	foliage	*P. a.* "Chattahoochee"
Mar	foliage	*P. a.* "Emerald Cushion"
April	foliage	*P. a.* "Kelly's Eye"
May	flowering	*P.* x *procumbens*
June	flowering	*P. subulata*
July	foliage	*P. s.* "Amazing Grace"
Aug	foliage	*P. s.* "G. F. Wilson"
Sept	foliage	*P. s.* "Marjorie"
Oct	foliage	*P. s.* "McDaniel's Cushion"
Nov	foliage	*P. s.* "Scarlet Flame"
Dec	foliage	

CONDITIONS

Aspect Grow this plant in full sun.
Site Must have very well-drained soil (if it is at all on the heavy side, make sure that it is well broken up with plenty of horticultural sand and grit), but the soil need not be very rich.

GROWING METHOD

Propagation Detach rooted sections from the parent plant in early spring, or take tip cuttings during summer and early fall.
Feeding Apply complete plant food as new growth begins in the spring.
Problems No specific problems are known but poor drainage will rot the plants.

FLOWERING

Season Flowers should be produced from mid-spring to early summer. For a color contrast also grow "Amazing Grace" which has pale pink flowers, "Scarlet Flame" in scarlet, and "Temiskaming" in magenta.
Cutting Flowers are not suitable for cutting.

PRUNING

General No pruning is needed beyond shearing off the spent flower heads.

PULMONARIA
Lungwort

A SHADY GARDEN AREA is enlivened by the mass of dark blue flowers that decorate Pulmonaria "Lewis Palmer" during spring.

THE FUNNEL-SHAPED BLOOMS of Pulmonaria species are a prized feature, and some forms also have attractively variegated leaves.

FEATURES

Partial
Shade

Pulmonaria is well suited to planting under trees, between shrubs or at the front of a shady border. The abundant flowers appear before the leaves have fully developed, and are mostly in shades of blue, pink, and white. The foliage is very handsome, often silver spotted, and if given a shearing after flowering produces a second, fresh mound of leaves. The whole plant rarely grows more than 10–12in high, and when established is very decorative, even out of flower.

PULMONARIA AT A GLANCE

A genus of 14 species with deciduous and evergreen perennials. A flowering spreader for damp shade. Hardy to 0°F (zone 7).

Jan	foliage 🌿	Recommended Varieties
Feb	foliage 🌿	*Pulmonaria angustifolia*
Mar	flowering ✿	*P. a.* "Munstead Blue"
April	flowering ✿	*P.* "Lewis Palmer"
May	flowering ✿	*P. longifolia* "Bertram
June	foliage 🌿	Anderson"
July	foliage 🌿	*P. officinalis* Cambridge Blue
Aug	foliage 🌿	Group
Sept	foliage 🌿	*P. officinalis* "Sissinghurst
Oct	foliage 🌿	White"
Nov	foliage 🌿	*P. rubra*
Dec	foliage 🌿	*P. saccharata* Argentea Group

CONDITIONS

Aspect Grows best in light shade, or in the borders that are shady during the hottest part of the day. The leaves quickly wilt under a hot sun.

Site The soil should be heavily enriched with decayed organic matter, but it also needs to drain quite well.

GROWING METHOD

Propagation Grows from ripe seed, or by division of clumps either after flowering or in the fall. Re-plant divisions about 6in apart. Better still, let plants freely hybridize. Young and established plants need moist soil during the growing season.

Feeding Apply a little complete fertilizer in early spring, and mulch well.

Problems No specific problems to worry about.

FLOWERING

Season *Pulmonaria* flowers in the spring.

Cutting The flowers last quite well in a vase.

PRUNING

General Only necessary when shearing over the plant to get a second flush of flowers.

ROSA HYBRIDS
Rose

"SNOW CARPET" is a lovely miniature rose that produces masses of flowers and very healthy foliage. It makes a beautiful groundcover.

THIS CARPET ROSE bears prolific bright pink flowers and looks spectacular when it is used as a groundcover.

FEATURES

Full Sun

Most people think of roses as shrubs, standards or climbers but there are a number of roses that can be used for groundcover. The "Noatraum" rose, with its bright pink blooms, was introduced within the last few years and is deservedly popular for its long flowering period and disease resistance. There is also "Snow Carpet," with masses of small white blooms, while the excellent Japanese "Nozomi" has pink-white flowers. Look at rose catalogs for others that can be used this way.

CONDITIONS

Aspect   Must have full sun and good air circulation. and plenty of room to spread in all directions.

ROSA AT A GLANCE

Some roses make excellent flowering groundcover, adding an extra layer of interest. Hardy to 0°F (zone 7).

		Recommended Varieties
Jan	/	
Feb	/	*Rosa* "Grouse"
Mar	/	R. "Hertfordshire"
April	foliage	R. "Magic Carpet"
May	foliage	R. "Max Graf"
June	flowering	R. "Nozomi"
July	flowering	R. "Raubritter"
Aug	foliage	R. "Snow Carpet"
Sept	foliage	R. "Suffolk"
Oct	foliage	
Nov	/	
Dec	/	

Site   Soil should be well drained and well prepared by the addition of large amounts of organic matter. Add lime to acid soils.

GROWING METHOD

Propagation   Many of these roses strike fairly easily from cuttings of dormant wood taken in the fall. Some roses must be budded on to species understocks.

Feeding   Apply complete plant food in spring and again in midsummer. Spreading an organic matter mulch round the plant in the spring will help to feed the soil.

Problems   Roses are vulnerable to attack by a number of garden pests and diseases. Aphids clustering on new growth can simply be hosed off or sprayed with pyrethrum. Black spot and powdery mildew can be troublesome in humid weather, you may have to resort to chemical spraying of the plants. Many groundcover roses have good resistance to these diseases.

FLOWERING

Season   A succession of blooms appear from summer to fall, depending on the variety.

Cutting   Usually short stemmed, groundcover roses add to most cut flower displays.

PRUNING

General   Cut off spent flower stems throughout the season. The main rose pruning is done in early spring. At other times remove any dead, diseased or damaged wood.

ROSMARINUS OFFICINALIS
Rosemary

ROSEMARY IS *typically seen as a herb but it also gives marvelous blue color in the spring garden, when yellow tends to dominate.*

THIS VERY HEALTHY *prostrate rosemary is enjoying the sharp drainage provided by the raised garden bed.*

FEATURES

Full Sun

The evergreen, prostrate-growing *Rosmarinus officinalis* "Prostratus" has all the features of the shrubby rosemary, including highly aromatic, needle-like foliage and small-lobed blue flowers that appear among the leaves in spring. It looks lovely planted on top of a wall or raised garden bed where it can spill over, or it can be grown beside a path where it will be brushed by passers-by to release the strong fragrance. It is a very hardy plant and tolerant of a wide range of growing conditions. Rosemary is the herb of remembrance and fidelity and has many culinary and herbal uses.

ROSMARINUS AT A GLANCE

Rosemary can be trained into all kinds of shapes, but left alone, in time, makes a great scented bush. Hardy to 0°F (zone 7).

		Recommended Varieties
Jan	foliage	*Rosmarinus officinalis*
Feb	foliage	*R. o.* var. *albiflorus*
Mar	flowering	*R. o.* "Benenden Blue"
April	flowering	*R. o.* "Fota Blue"
May	flowering	*R. o.* "Majorca Pink"
June	flowering	*R. o.* "Miss Jessopp's
July	foliage	Upright"
Aug	foliage	*R. o.* Prostratus Group
Sept	foliage	*R. o.* "Severn Sea"
Oct	foliage	*R. o.* "Tuscan Blue"
Nov	foliage	
Dec	foliage	

CONDITIONS

Aspect Needs full sun and tolerates windy, exposed coastal conditions. Do not attempt to hide it away in the shade. Rosemary is naturally very slow growing so do not slow it down any more.

Site Soil must be well drained but this plant grows well in poor soils. Add lime or dolomite to very acid soils before planting.

GROWING METHOD

Propagation Grow from semi-ripe cuttings taken in the summer. If you need a quick effect it is worth buying well-established plants. However, if growing a rosemary hedge, one good-sized plant can yield hundreds of cuttings.

Feeding Little or no fertilizer is needed.

Problems No specific problems are known.

FLOWERING

Season The blue flowers are produced in spring. They generally last into early summer.

PRUNING

General Pruning is not necessary unless it is to trim a wayward upward branch or to train the plant to shape. However, by taking regular cuttings for cooking you will automatically keep pruning the plant.

SAPONARIA
Soapwort

THE STEMLESS PINK FLOWERS OF Saponaria "Bressingham" seem to smother the foliage, making a strong and colorful impact.

DELICATE ROCK-GARDEN PLANTS are often grown singly, but S. "Bressingham" is best densely planted as a filler or edging plant.

FEATURES

Full Sun

Saponaria includes plants for the border and wild garden, and for rock gardens. *S. officinalis* is the one for the former, making a brightly colored invader—the form "Rubra Plena" spreads more than most. *S.* "Bressingham" provides good cover for a rock garden. It grows 3in high, spreading 12in wide, and has gorgeous, dark pink flowers. It is sometimes called "Bressingham Hybrid." The common name arises because the leaves of *S. officinalis* can be used as a kind of soap.

SAPONARIA AT A GLANCE

S. "Bressingham" gives good cover in the rock garden and produces pink flowers in summer. Hardy to 0°F (zone 7).

		Recommended Varieties
Jan	/	
Feb	/	*Saponaria* "Bressingham"
Mar	/	*S. caespitosa*
April	/	*S. ocymoides*
May	foliage ❀	*S. officinalis*
June	flowering ❀	*S. o.* "Alba Plena"
July	flowering ❀	*S. o.* "Rosea Plena"
Aug	foliage ❀	*S. o.* "Rubra Plena"
Sept	foliage ❀	*S. x olivana*
Oct	foliage ❀	
Nov	/	
Dec	/	

CONDITIONS

Aspect   This plant is exclusively for a place in full sun. Do not try to grow it anywhere else.

Site   The soil needs to be reasonably fertile, but the main requirement is excellent drainage and plenty of added grit.

GROWING METHOD

Propagation   You can either take cuttings in the first part of summer, or increase your stock and cover by sowing seed in the spring or the fall. Note that each plant has a good spread though. You are unlikely to need many cuttings.

Feeding   Do not attempt to over-feed, which is counter-productive. Average fertility is fine.

Problems   The border plants can be shredded in extreme cases by slugs and snails, but because "Bressingham" grows in the rockery, which contains gritty sharp stone in the soil, slugs will keep well away.

FLOWERING

Season   A decent summer show of dark pink flowers.

PRUNING

General   Not necessary.

SAXIFRAGA X URBIUM
London pride

SAXIFRAGA X URBIUM *is an easy plant to grow, and makes a graceful plant to flank a shady pathway through the garden.*

LEATHERY LEAVES WITH unusual serrated edges contrast beautifully with the airy blooms that are held high above them.

FEATURES

Full Shade

Saxifraga x *urbium* is a useful, quick-spreading, attractive plant producing scores of leathery, fresh green leaves. In summer whiteish-pink flowers appear on tall stems. It grows 1ft high and is quite invasive. There are several other first-rate groundcover saxifrages. One is "Bob Hawkins." It forms a carpet of rosettes with variegated leaves, and white flowers tinged green in summer. It grows 8in high, and spreads about 1ft. *S. exarata moschata* makes a cushion with cream or yellow star-like flowers. It is much shorter at 4in, and spreads about 1ft. The form "Cloth of Gold" is even better and has gold colored foliage that stands out.

◆ SAXIFRAGA AT A GLANCE

Saxifraga x *urbium* is an extremely useful plant growing well in the shade. It is also a prodigious spreader. Hardy to 0°F (zone 7).

		Recommended Varieties
Jan	foliage	*Saxifraga* "Bob Hawkins"
Feb	foliage	*S. cuneifolia*
Mar	foliage	*S. exarata moschata*
April	foliage	*S. marginata*
May	foliage	*S. paniculata*
June	flowering	*S. sempervivum*
July	flowering	*S.* x *urbium*
Aug	foliage	
Sept	foliage	
Oct	foliage	
Nov	foliage	
Dec	foliage	

CONDITIONS

Aspect *S.* x *urbium* thrives in the shade, both light and deep. Keep it out of the sun.

Site The best soil for *S.* x *urbium* is moist and rich, with plenty of well-rotted organic matter added before planting. An annual spring mulch around the base should boost its performance, with extra rosettes.

GROWING METHOD

Propagation *S.* x *urbium* can easily be increased by taking off a rosette in the spring, and treating it as a cutting. It will quickly root. You can also sow by seed in the fall.

Feeding Given rich, moist soil, this plant should not need extra nutrients. It only requires a boost on poor soil.

Problems The biggest problem comes from slugs and snails. Both can devastate the young foliage. Use slug pellets as required, or keep a look out at night by torchlight.

FLOWERING

Season The flowers appear in the summer. They are held high above the foliage.

PRUNING

General The only pruning necessary is to slice off unwanted spreading growth to keep London pride in a particular area.

SOLEIROLIA SOLEIROLII
Baby's tears

THE TINY LEAVES of baby's tears grow very thickly, making it a good weed suppressor. It looks good even in shaded and moist conditions.

BABY'S TEARS will grow over any surface. Although considered a problem by some people, it will flourish where other plants struggle.

FEATURES

Shade or
Part Shade

Although native to the western Mediterranean and Italy, this flat, mat-forming, creeping groundcover with tiny leaves flourishes in shady, damp conditions. It is known by many other common names, including mind-your-own-business, Irish moss, Japanese moss, Corsican curse, and Corsican carpet plant. It is often used as a surface cover around the base of potted plants and as a groundcover under shrubs in shady areas. It can become rather weedy as it grows from seeds shed from its inconspicuous flowers, and from small pieces detached from the main growth. In its preferred damp, shady habitat, it is both long lived and persistent.

SOLEIROLIA AT A GLANCE

Soleirolia soleirolii is a fantastically invasive spreader with tiny white flowers in summer. Hardy to 5°F (zone 7).

Jan	foliage	Recommended Varieties
Feb	foliage	*Soleirolia soleirolii* "Aurea"
Mar	foliage	*S. s.* "Variegata"
April	foliage	
May	foliage	
June	flowering	Companion Plants
July	flowering	Gunnera
Aug	foliage	Lysichiton
Sept	foliage	Lysimachia
Oct	foliage	Primrose
Nov	foliage	
Dec	foliage	

CONDITIONS

Aspect Grows best in shady, damp areas or where it receives dappled sunlight. So do not plant in direct sun as this may cause burning, especially during the height of summer.

Site *Soleirolia soleirolii* will grow in a range of soil types but it prefers well-drained soils that are rich in organic matter. It makes good cover near a stream where the conditions are often ideal, but note that it is a rapid spreader. Check that it will not throttle nearby ornamental plants.

GROWING METHOD

Propagation *S. soleirolii* will usually propagate itself, sometimes where it is not wanted, but new plants can be started easily from small sections of rooted stems.

Feeding Fertilizing is not generally necessary.

Problems No specific problems are known.

FLOWERING

Season Flowers can be very tiny and very difficult to see fully without a magnifying glass.

PRUNING

General As *S. soleirolii* is a flat-growing plant, pruning is not necessary. However, you may find that it is necessary to cut back sections of the mat if it becomes too invasive.

STACHYS BYZANTINA
Lamb's ears

THE LEAVES OF Stachys byzantina *have the texture of soft velvet, making them one of the most inviting plants in the garden.*

THESE INVALUABLE lush, green carpeters are commonly grown as edging in flower borders and rock gardens.

FEATURES

Full Sun

Stachys byzantina is a low-growing, evergreen perennial often used as an edging plant. It is good in rose beds, but wherever it is planted it must have excellent drainage and full sun. The leaves are densely covered with hairs, giving them a white or pale gray woolly appearance, hence its common name. It produces pink-purple flowers on spikes that stand above the foliage, but they are not especially attractive; it is usually grown for its foliage, and not the flowers. The exceptions are *Stachys macrantha* "Robusta" and *S. officinalis*. "Cotton Ball" has woolly flowers good for dried arrangements. Plants grow 6–8in high, but spread a good distance.

STACHYS AT A GLANCE

Stachys byzantina is a silver-leaved plant that is well worth growing in every garden. Hardy to 0°F (zone 7).

		Recommended Varieties
Jan	/	*Stachys byzantina*
Feb	/	*S. b.* "Cotton Ball"
Mar	/	*S. b.* "Primrose Heron"
April	foliage	*S. coccinea*
May	foliage	*S. macrantha*
June	flowering	*S. m.* "Robusta"
July	flowering	*S. officinalis*
Aug	flowering	
Sept	foliage	
Oct	foliage	
Nov	/	
Dec	/	

CONDITIONS

Aspect   Full sun is essential all day for the plants to thrive and perform well.

Site   Needs very fast-draining soil. It grows well in poor sandy or gravelly soil. Avoid thick, wet, heavy clay at all costs.

GROWING METHOD

Propagation   *S. byzantina* grows readily from cuttings that are taken in the spring or fall. The new divisions must be planted out about 8in apart. Water new plants regularly. Once they are established, they need to be watered very occasionally.

Feeding   Grows without supplementary fertilizer, but a little complete plant food can be applied in the early spring.

Problems   There are no specific problems but container plants will quickly fail if they are over-watered, and border plants will rot if they become waterlogged.

FLOWERING

Season   The flowers are produced in the summer, sometimes into fall. But the tactile gray foliage is by far the chief attraction.

PRUNING

General   Pruning is rarely necessary. If any cutting back is needed do it in early spring.

SYMPHYTUM OFFICINALE
Comfrey

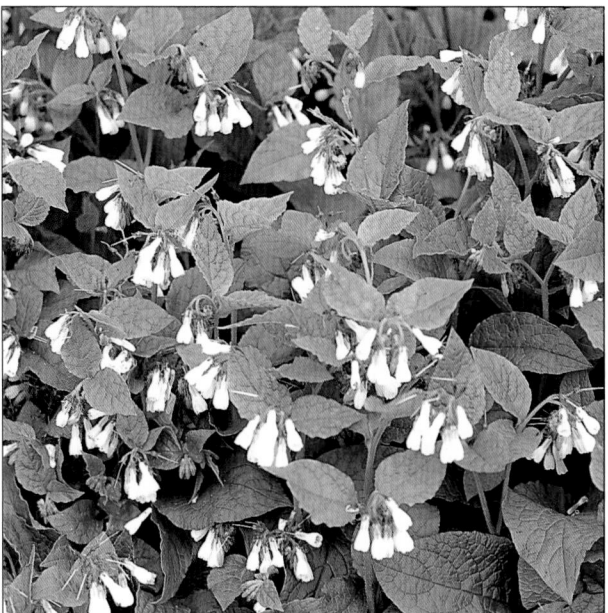

SYMPHYTUM CAUCASICUM *is a vigorous and tolerant plant that is often used as groundcover in wilder parts of the garden.*

THE BELL-SHAPED FLOWERS *of* Symphytum *are held in clusters above the foliage, and festoon the plant in spring and summer.*

FEATURES

Sun or
Part Shade

Symphytum officinale is one of the best groundcovering plants. In the right conditions, just one plant can spread 6ft, even climbing over low walls. *S. officinale* has a mass of violet, pink or yellow flowers. Experts prefer other forms like *S. x uplandicum* "Variegatum," which has superb gray-green leaves with a creamy-white edge. The flowers are lilac-pink. The only problem is that it can revert to a dark green leaf, especially in the wrong conditions. It is much less invasive than *S. officinale*, with one plant spreading 2ft. "Goldsmith" also has attractive foliage, dark green leaves with cream markings around the outside, but spreads about half as much as "Variegatum," which has leaves edged in white.

SYMPHYTUM AT A GLANCE

Symphytum officinale is a free-spreading, spring-flowering perennial. The leaves are tough. Hardy to 0°F (zone 7).

		Recommended Varieties
Jan	/	
Feb	/	*Symphytum caucasicum*
Mar	/	*S.* "Goldsmith"
April	/	*S.* "Hidcote Blue"
May	flowering ❀	*S. ibericum*
June	flowering ❀	*S. officinale*
July	foliage 🌱	*S. tuberosum*
Aug	foliage 🌱	*S. x uplandicum* "Variegatum"
Sept	foliage 🌱	
Oct	foliage 🌱	
Nov	foliage 🌱	
Dec	foliage 🌱	

CONDITIONS

Aspect   This plant thrives in either full sun or partial, dappled shade, such as woodland areas.

Site   The soil needs to be on the damp side and quite fertile. Clay soil that has been reasonably broken up and lightened is ideal. *S. officinale* should spread quite quickly.

GROWING METHOD

Propagation   With a fast spreader like *S. officinale*, there is no need to propagate. But when you need more plants to colonize another area, divide plants in the spring. They quickly settle. Close planting gives more immediate cover but just a few plants will give good cover over 8ft or so.

Feeding   Assuming that the plant is growing in clay soil which is perfectly fertile, additional feeding is not necessary. Otherwise, give a little slow-release fertilizer in spring.

Problems   *S. officinale* is a remarkably tough and resourceful plant, which is easy to grow and attracts very few problems.

FLOWERING

Season   The flowers appear in the spring and early summer. The species which produces the most distinctive colored flowers is *S. caucasicum*, which has bright blue blooms .

Pruning   Only prune if it is necessary to confine the plant's growth. Slice off any unwanted growth with a spade. Otherwise, let the plant spread wherever it wants.

THYMUS
Thyme

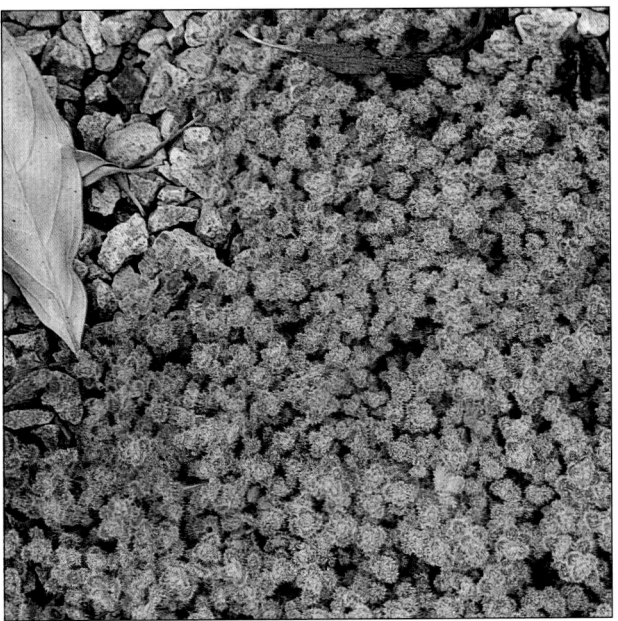

WOOLLY THYME is a carpeting plant often grown in gaps between pavers and paths. The tiny leaves are covered in dense hairs.

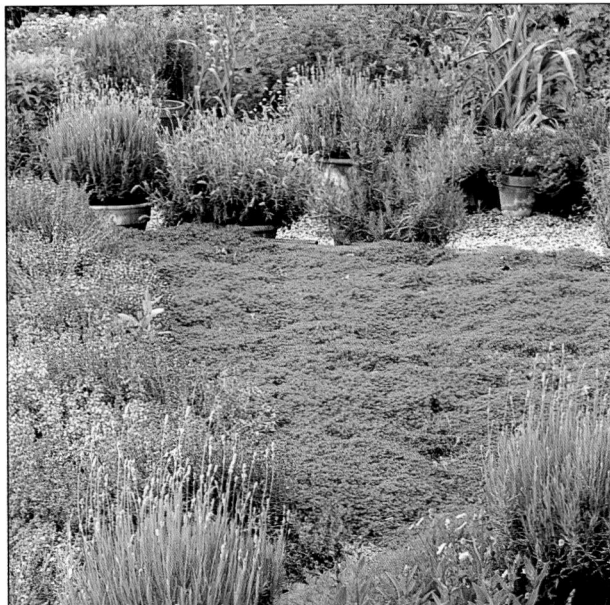

A SMALL THYME LAWN here forms a neat green triangle. In this open, sunny spot it thrives and needs little maintenance.

FEATURES

Full Sun

There are over 300 species of thyme, many of which are suitable for use as groundcovers. *Thymus serpyllum*, which reaches 10in in height, is commonly grown this way, as is *T. polytrichus* which grows 2in high and 2ft wide. These and others thymes have a creeping, mat-like habit, rooting down at the nodes as they grow. They are tough, low-maintenance groundcovers for hot, dry spots between paving stones, in rockeries, or along the edges of garden or raised beds. All have aromatic foliage that releases its scent when bruised or crushed—you can step on them occasionally. The leaves can also be used in cooking. The small pink or mauve flowers are very attractive to bees.

THYMUS AT A GLANCE

Thymes give three plants in one. Good groundcover, pretty flowers, and excellent herbs for cooking. Hardy to 5°F (zone 7).

Jan	foliage	Recommended Varieties
Feb	foliage	*Thymus* x *citriodorus*
Mar	foliage	*T.* x *c.* "Aureus"
April	foliage	*T.* x *c.* "Bertram Anderson"
May	foliage	*T.* "Coccineus"
June	flowering	*T.* "Doone Valley"
July	flowering	*T. herba-barona*
Aug	foliage	*T. serphyllum coccineus*
Sept	foliage	*T. vulgaris*
Oct	foliage	
Nov	foliage	
Dec	foliage	

CONDITIONS

Aspect Needs full sun all day. These are mainly Mediterranean plants used to long hot summers, with the minimum amount of shade.

Site Soil must be well drained but it need not be rich. Add lime to very acid soils before planting. Heavy wet ground needs to be thoroughly broken up, with large handfuls of horticultural sand and grit around the plant. If the roots stay cold and wet over winter, the plants will not survive.

GROWING METHOD

Propagation Firm-tip cuttings can be taken at any time through the spring and summer. Rooted sections of plants can be dug up and transplanted during early spring.

Feeding Fertilizing is generally not needed.

Problems No problems are known.

FLOWERING

Season The small pink or mauve flowers are profuse during the summer.

PRUNING

General Regular pruning is not needed. Plants may need occasional trimming. By taking regular cuttings for cooking and salads, you automatically prune the plant. Growing two or three thymes mean you can safely take plenty of leaves without massacring one plant.

TIARELLA WHERRYI
Foam flower

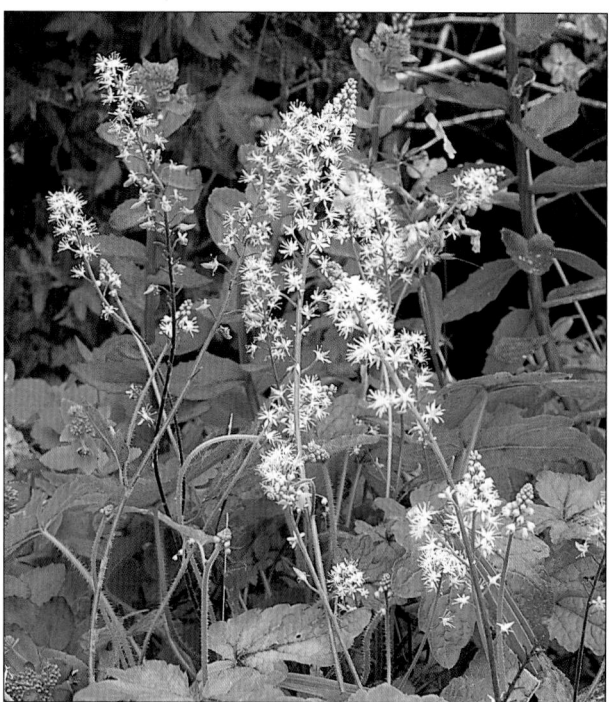

DELICATE TIARELLA WHERRYI *thrives here in a woodland. Its compact growth pattern also makes it ideal edging for a rock garden.*

FROTHY SPRAYS *of white flowers give* Tiarella wherryi *its pretty common name. They make a charming addition to the garden in spring.*

FEATURES

Shade or
Part Shade

Tiarella wherryi is an American clump-forming perennial, ideal for small, shady areas. Its natural habitat is shady ravines and rocky woods. The white flowers are tinged pink. The form "Bronze Beauty" is a popular choice, with contrasting white flowers and bronze-red foliage. Good alternatives are *T. trifoliata* which makes excellent groundcover in light shade. From late spring to early summer it produces light, airy sprays of white flowers on 1ft long panicles, held above the foliage. More invasive still is *T. cordifolia* which spreads by underground stolons.

TIARELLA AT A GLANCE

Tiarella wherryi is a North American perennial for moist, shady areas. Good show of early season flowers. Hardy to 5°F (zone 7).

Jan	/	Recommended Varieties
Feb	/	*Tiarella cordifolia*
Mar	/	*T. c.* "Mint Chocolate"
April	/	*T. c.* "Ninja"
May	flowering ✽	*T.* "Elizabeth Oliver"
June	flowering ✽	*T. polyphylla*
July	foliage ❧	*T.* "Tiger Stripe"
Aug	foliage ❧	*T. wherryi*
Sept	foliage ❧	*T. wherryi* "Bronze Beauty"
Oct	foliage ❧	
Nov	/	
Dec	/	

CONDITIONS

Aspect   Thrives in both dappled and darkish shade, which is its natural habitat.

Site   It tolerates a wide range of soils but naturally prefers rich, fertile ground, damp but definitely not boggy.

GROWING METHOD

Propagation   Division is the simplest method, though ripe seed can also be sown. Sow in pots in the fall in a cold frame. And keep young plants well watered. Do not let them dry out.

Feeding   The ground needs to be quite rich. Fork in leafmold and well-rotted organic matter in the early spring, and again in the fall.

Problems   Slugs can strike, and where this becomes a major problem treat with slug pellets. Alternatively keep patrol at night, picking them off by hand. Discard as you will.

FLOWERING

Season   The flowers appear in late spring, and at the beginning of the summer.

PRUNING

General   Not necessary, but with more invasive kinds prune in the growing season when growth threatens to get out of control.

VERONICA
Speedwell

GENEROUS VERONICAS *bear masses of rather stately spires in summer, making them invaluable plants for the front of a border.*

THE GENTLE POWDER-BLUE blooms of Veronica gentianoides *can be used effectively to offset the brighter colors of other flowers.*

FEATURES

Full Sun

Veronicas are sun-loving plants, and include annuals, perennials and sub-shrubs. *Veronica gentianoides* comes from the Caucasus and is a mat-forming perennial with shiny leaves and spires of pale blue flowers that open in early summer. Growing 18in high and wide, it is good in a border. "Variegata" has creamier leaves than the species, *V. spicata* "Icicle" has white flowers and *V. peduncularis* "Georgia Blue" dark blue flowers. If you need a low-growing plant that spreads well, try *V. prostrata*. It grows 6in high, and has a spread of 16in.

VERONICA AT A GLANCE

Veronica gentianoides provides a fine array of pale blue flowers in early summer, cooling down hotter adjacent colors. Hardy to 5°F (zone 7).

Jan	/	Recommended Varieties
Feb	/	*Veronica austriaca* "Shirley
Mar	/	Blue"
April	foliage	*V. cinerea*
May	foliage	*V. gentianoides*
June	flowering	*V. g.* "Variegata"
July	foliage	*V. peduncularis* "Georgia
Aug	foliage	Blue"
Sept	foliage	*V. prostrata*
Oct	foliage	*V. spicata* "Icicle"
Nov	/	*V. s.* "Rotfuchs"
Dec	/	*V. s.* "Wendy"

CONDITIONS

Aspect   Only grow in full sunlight. *V. gentianoides* needs wall-to-wall sun and will not tolerate anything less than this.

Site   The key to success is very good drainage. The soil need not be that fertile, and in fact can be quite poor. South-facing banks or slopes often make a very good site.

GROWING METHOD

Propagation   Since veronica does not provide the fastest kind of groundcover, it is well worth propagating several more plants. Either divide them in the spring or in the fall, or sow plenty of seed in the fall.

Feeding   Not necessary, but in poor, unpampered soil add a slow-release fertilizer in the spring.

Problems   The main problem is usually downy mildew, which is best tackled by quickly removing all affected leaves, thus providing better air circulation around the plant. Powdery mildew needs to be tackled with a chemical spray.

FLOWERING

Season   *V. gentianoides* gives a good but brief show of flowers in early summer.

PRUNING

General   Pruning is not necessary.

VINCA MINOR
Periwinkle

NEATLY EDGED in cream, the foliage of this variegated periwinkle is very decorative. The plant has a dense growth habit.

PERIWINKLE CARPETS an extensive area in this garden and contrasts well with the dwarf sacred bamboo and dark laurustinus.

FEATURES

Sun or Part Shade

Vinca minor comes in a plain green-leaved form and several variegated forms, including "Argenteovariegata," although the blue flowers are, as a rule, more profuse on the plain form. They appear during the spring. The plant has a creeping growth habit, rooting down at the nodes, and one plant will eventually cover 6ft. *V. minor* is an excellent carpeting plant for shaded areas under trees, on banks or in large rockeries. Its growth can be rather vigorous, even invasive in warm climates, but it is not as invasive as its close relative
V. major, which can also be grown in gardens.
V. minor is very easy to care for and will withstand poor conditions, although growth will be more attractive if it is given some care.

VINCA AT A GLANCE

V. minor never fails. Masses of groundcover and a long season of blue flowers. Other colors are available. Hardy to 0°F (zone 7).

Jan	foliage	Recommended Varieties
Feb	foliage	*Vinca major*
Mar	foliage	*V. m.* "Maculata"
April	foliage	*V. m.* "Variegata"
May	flowering	*V. minor*
June	flowering	*V. m.* "Argenteovariegata"
July	flowering	*V. m* "Azurea Flore Pleno"
Aug	flowering	*V. m* "Gertrude Jekyll"
Sept	flowering	*V. m* "Le Grave"
Oct	foliage	
Nov	foliage	
Dec	foliage	

CONDITIONS

Aspect *V. minor* grows best in shade, in filtered sunlight or with morning sun and afternoon shade. However, the greater the amount of sunshine received, the more the plant will flower over a longer period.

Site Tolerates any kind of soil but prefers a well-drained soil enriched with organic matter.

GROWING METHOD

Propagation Layering is the easiest way to produce more plants. Rooted sections can also be dug up, or semi-ripe cuttings can be taken in the summer. Given the rate at which it produces, you are unlikely to need to propagate more plants once the earmarked site has been well planted with *V. minor*.

Feeding Apply complete plant food once new growth begins in spring.

Problems No specific problems are known.

FLOWERING

Season The mauve-blue flowers of *V. minor* appear in spring. Note that there are also many different forms which have plum or purple, pale blue and white flowers.

Cutting Flowers are not suitable for cutting.

PRUNING

General May need occasional pruning to control its shape and spread. If it gets out of hand you can be as ruthless as you like.

VIOLA HEDERACEA
Ivy-leaved violet

THE DELICATE FLOWERS of ivy-leaved violet have great appeal as they push their way up through the mass of bright leaves.

IVY-LEAVED VIOLET forms a thick, soft border for this pebble path and looks entirely natural as it creeps out between the stones.

FEATURES

Shade or
Part Shade

Viola hederacea is an excellent groundcover plant that is suitable for shaded and semi-shaded positions. It is easy to maintain, but can be rather invasive where the conditions are suitable. *V. hederacea* is best kept out of rockeries as it can be almost impossible to confine it to its allotted space. The small, rounded leaves grow from 2–4in high, and the pretty white and mauve violets are carried on stems above the foliage. New plantings should be spaced about 1ft apart. This well-loved plant makes a good groundcover under trees where grass will not grow, as it will tolerate occasional foot traffic. *V. hederacea* also makes a very attractive plant for troughs and hanging baskets.

VIOLA AT A GLANCE

Viola hederacea is an evergreen violet that can cover big sweeps of ground, providing late summer flowers. Hardy to 0°F (zone 7).

		Recommended Varieties
Jan	foliage	
Feb	foliage	*Viola cornuta*
Mar	foliage	*V. gracilis*
April	foliage	*V. hederacea*
May	foliage	"Huntercombe Purple"
June	foliage	*V. obliqua*
July	foliage	*V. odorata*
Aug	flowering	*V. sororia*
Sept	flowering	*V. x wittrockiana* cultivars
Oct	foliage	
Nov	foliage	
Dec	foliage	

CONDITIONS

Aspect   Dappled sunlight or shade is suitable but the flowering is better if grown in some sun.

Site   Tolerates a wide range of soils, but try to avoid any extremes, either of a damp or dry kind.

GROWING METHOD

Propagation   Can be readily increased from runners or by division of clumps. This is best carried out in either the spring or the fall. Replant each section, making sure that it has got a good root system.

Feeding   Feeding is generally not necessary. If the soil is extremely poor, give a light dressing of blood and bone in early spring.

Problems   On the whole, *V. hederacea* is unlikely to suffer from major problems, but keep a close look out for marauding snails and slugs.

FLOWERING

Season   The main flowering period is late summer. The flowers come in a wide color range, and are either violet (light to dark) or creamy-white. If you get very close you might just be able to detect some scent.

Cutting   The flowers can be cut for a miniature posy.

PRUNING

General   Actual pruning is not necessary but sections may need to be pulled up or cut out if the plant is spreading where it is not wanted.

Growing Palms

GROWING PALMS

Palms conjure up images of the tropics, and indeed the vast majority of species are native to tropical or sub-tropical regions of the world. There are a few species that occur in warm and cool climates but they are rare in arid areas and cannot survive in very cold regions.

Palms are grown mainly for their evergreen foliage and are popular garden plants in the warmer parts of the world, but even in areas prone to frosts in winter they can still be used for garden display in summer by growing them in pots or tubs and taking them under cover for the winter. Palms are used extensively for indoor decoration in warm and cold climates.

Palms vary widely in their habits and preferences. Most have tall trunks, either single or several forming a clump. The large compound leaves are popularly known as fronds. These may be fan shaped or very feathery. Palms are long lived and while some reach sufficient maturity to flower within five years or so, others may take about 40 years to start flowering.

LEFT: The pleated fronds of a fan palm radiate outward and make a dazzling geometric display.

USES IN GARDENS

A palm has a woody trunk that grows with age but it does not start developing that trunk until it has reached a certain size. This accounts for the slow development of some palms. The leaves or fronds arch out from the top of the stem like a crown. Therefore the palm is a very distinctive plant, quite unlike others, capable of providing exotic effects and bringing lushness to the garden. Palms have the advantage that their shape and ultimate size are very predictable, unlike some other trees and shrubs, so there is no excuse for them outgrowing their allotted space. Nevertheless palms have to be used carefully in gardens in cool temperate climates or they will look out of place. There are two ways to use them in these gardens: permanently plant hardy palms to create focal points, or move tender pot-grown palms outside for the summer.

Hardy palms

One of the hardiest palms is *Trachycarpus fortunei*, the Chusan palm, which is frost hardy, taking temperatures down to 23°F. It is often seen in mild seaside gardens and parks and other favored areas inland. *Jubaea chilensis*, the Chilean wine palm, is also frost hardy and suitable for growing outside, particularly in mild coastal areas. These two species are also suitable for gardens in towns and cities, which tend to be a few degrees warmer than more open and exposed areas.

These palms can be used as specimen trees, for example in lawns, to create focal points. Or a group of perhaps three can serve the same purpose on a larger scale. They probably look best in formal settings, with good expanses of well-manicured green lawn and formal flower beds containing Large-flowered and Cluster-flowered roses or brightly colored summer bedding. They also look good beside formal water features such as pools and canals.

Hardy palms are ideal for creating an exotic atmosphere in a courtyard garden. Here they can be used with other "architectural" or distinctive plants, such as *Fatsia japonica* (Japanese fatsia) with its large evergreen hand-shaped leaves, hostas, or plantain lilies, bamboos, the palm-like *Cordyline australis* (New Zealand cabbage palm), ferns of various kinds, and perhaps a hardy grape vine trained to the wall. If the courtyard garden is completely paved, these palms and other plants could be grown in large ornamental tubs and pots. Very fashionable today are blue glazed pots, which make ideal containers for many of these plants.

Hardy palms can also look good in an "exotic" woodland garden and are sometimes used for this purpose in milder areas. An exotic woodland garden is one on acid or lime-free soil that is planted with rhododendrons, camellias, pieris, magnolias, and other choice woodland shrubs and perennials and is a familiar site in many of the large gardens open to the public. This is quite natural for *Trachycarpus fortunei*, for instance, as it is a native of

THIS BUSY, EXOTIC garden in the Scilly Isles takes full advantage of the local climate. The palms in this border are a pleasing jumble of sizes, each one given the space to fulfil its potential but kept in order by the brick wall backdrop.

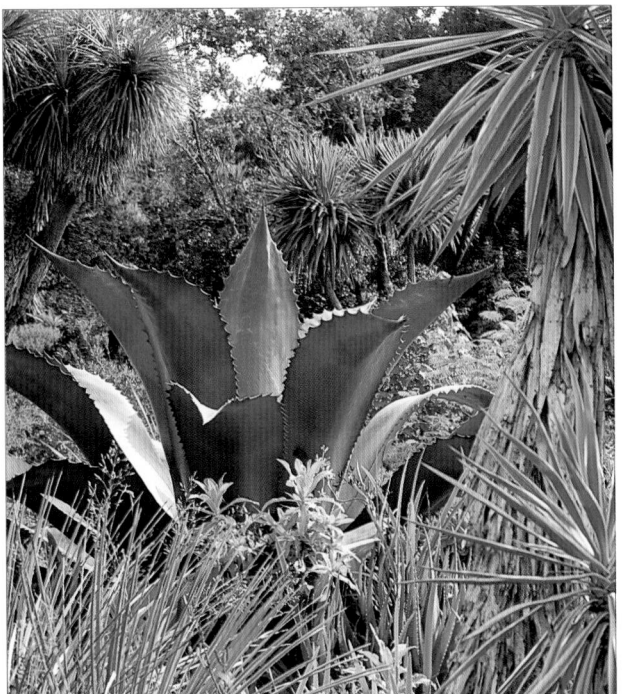

SUBTROPICAL SUMMER displays are coming back into fashion. Palms can be used to great effect in these exotic plantings.

A FANTASTIC HILLSIDE scene is decked with palms to effect an otherworldly landscape, again created in the Scilly Isles.

forests, particular mountain forests, in sub-tropical regions of Asia. Of course, there is no reason why owners of smaller gardens should not have a woodland garden. All you need is a minimum of one small tree, such as a birch, to create the dappled shade that is loved by these plants. A small group of trees would be even better, if space permits). Hardy palms, if used, should be sited in a more sunny part of the woodland garden, but make sure they are well sheltered from wind.

Tender palms

Tender palms grown in pots and wintered under glass or indoors can be used for summer display out of doors. But place them in shade as sun will scorch the fronds. One way to use them is in formal summer bedding schemes, especially in light shade. The pots can be plunged to their rims in the soil. This prevents root disturbance that would occur if planting them, and also prevents the compost from drying out rapidly. Known as plunge bedding, this method was very popular in Victorian times.

In summer bedding schemes palms can be used as dot plants (specimen plants) in the main carpet of plants, which may be fibrous-rooted begonias, impatiens, fuchsias, and the like. In a small bed, perhaps a single palm could be used in the center, or in a larger bed maybe a palm could be plunged in each corner with another in the center.

Plunging is also a technique that can be used to create subtropical summer displays, which are coming back into fashion, having had their heyday in the Victorian period. Again palms can be used, together with other large pot-grown tropical and subtropical plants such as bananas, brugmansias (Angel's trumpets), and cordylines to form the "framework." Then smaller subjects, which can be planted normally, are used to fill in, such as cannas (Indian shot), solenostemons (Coleus), fuchsias, and so on. Remember that plunged pots will need regular watering as they will still dry out, albeit not so quickly.

Potted palms can also be brought out for the summer to decorate a patio. Leave them in their pots or tubs and just stand them around, perhaps in combination with tubs of colorful summer bedding plants.

CULTIVATION OUTDOORS

Aspect

The hardy palm *Trachycarpus fortunei* (Chusan palm) can be grown in either full sun or light dappled shade, such as provided by deciduous trees, but *Jubaea chilensis* (Chilean wine palm) needs a position in full sun. Provide shelter from strong winds to avoid the fronds from being torn or scorched. *Trachycarpus fortunei* is more tolerant of winds than other palms but nevertheless it is best to provide it with wind protection. Shelter is best provided by trees and shrubs nearby that filter and slow down the wind. The alternative is to erect, on the windward side, an artificial windbreak made of windbreak netting, but this is unsightly and should only be considered as a temporary measure until trees and shrubs are established.

When standing potted palms outside for the summer, you will need to take their requirements into account in respect of sun and shade. For information on individual species see the descriptive lists on pages 658–669.

THE VARIOUS SHADES of green created by palm fronds make an interesting texture on their own. However, the careful placing of brightly colored flowers can also be added to create spectacular highlights. It is important not to overwhelm the garden—single colors are far more effective.

Soil

Palms will thrive in various types of soil and although many will take quite poor conditions, generally the better the soil the better the growth will be.

The ideal soil would be slightly acid to neutral but alkaline conditions are acceptable provided the soil is not a very thin chalky type. Soil should be moisture-retentive but well drained. Avoid sites that become waterlogged in winter as this may result in the death of the palm due to root rot. There should be a good depth of soil so that the palm can root deeply and it should be reasonably fertile.

Before planting, all soils can be improved by digging, to open them up and aerate them, and to provide the opportunity of adding bulky organic matter such as garden compost, very well-rotted manure, or composted shredded or chipped bark. Add a generous amount of organic matter to each trench during digging. It provides humus and helps light sandy soils to retain moisture. Organic matter will also open up heavy clay soils, thus helping excess water to quickly drain away.

Planting

Palms are generally bought in containers and come in various sizes, but large ones that are used to create an immediate effect are proportionately more expensive than small specimens, and a deep pocket will be needed to purchase them.

Although container-grown plants can in theory be planted at any time of year, provided the ground is not frozen or very wet, palms are best planted in mid- to late spring when the soil is warming up and drying out. Then they will quickly root into the soil and become established. If they are planted into cold soil they will just sit still and not make new roots, and may then even die, especially if the soil is also wet.

Occasionally large palms may be available rootballed, with the roots enclosed in a ball of soil tightly wrapped in netting or hessian. These are usually plants that have been grown in a nursery field. The same planting time is recommended for rootballed palms in order to get them established quickly.

When preparing the planting hole make sure it is slightly wider than the rootball. The palm should be planted to the same depth as before so make the hole of suitable depth to allow this. The rootball must be moist at the time of planting so if necessary water the plant thoroughly several hours beforehand. When removing the palm from a container aim for as little root disturbance as possible. If planting a rootballed palm, remove the hessian or netting only when the plant is in the hole, to minimize the risk of soil falling away. Return fine soil around the rootball, firming it well with your heels as you proceed. Then water thoroughly to settle the soil around the plant.

Care

During warm dry weather make sure the palms do not dry out. Water them thoroughly whenever the soil starts to become dry. They will also appreciate a mulch of organic matter, such as composted chipped or shredded bark. This will prevent the soil from rapidly drying out during hot dry weather. A layer about 2in deep can be applied in spring. The soil should be moist when laying a mulch.

As with trees and shrubs, the best and easiest way to feed palms is to give them an annual application of slow-release organic fertilizer such as blood, fish, and bone. This feed is best given in the spring.

For the first few years young palms need to be given additional protection from wind and frost in the winter. A screen made of hessian or windbreak netting can be erected on the windward side. It should be taller than the palm. Alternatively small palms can be surrounded by a cylinder of the same material. To protect roots from severe frosts, young palms can be given a deep mulch of straw for the winter.

Potted palms placed or plunged out of doors for the summer will need to be checked daily for watering— remember that pots can dry out rapidly during hot weather. For watering and feeding of potted palms see Cultivation Indoors, pages 655–657.

Palms do not need pruning, only the removal of dead leaves, which should be cut back to the main stem. This often leaves a pleasant criss-cross pattern on the stem.

CULTIVATION INDOORS

Where to grow

Palms make a delightful addition to an interior and are widely used in homes, offices, hotels, public buildings and the like. However, it should be borne in mind that high light levels are needed plus a humid atmosphere if they are to flourish. The ideal conditions are most easily provided in a conservatory or glasshouse, as long as suitable temperature levels are maintained.

Among the most popular indoor palms are *Howea forsteriana* (Kentia palm), which is slow growing, often an advantage indoors as it does not outgrow its allotted space for years, but it makes good-sized specimens expensive; *Chamaedorea elegans* (Parlour palm) and its relatives; and *Rhapis excelsa* (Miniature fan palm). Many other palms are suitable, too, if you can provide the conditions they require, and have the space, as some grow very large.

Palms generally appreciate a spell outdoors when the weather warms up, so they can be taken outside for the summer and used for garden display (see Uses in Gardens, pages 652–653). Do not move them outside until all danger of frost is over. It should be safe by early summer. And remember to move them back inside before frosts commence in the fall. The plants should certainly be indoors again by early fall. Outdoors make sure they are placed in shade, no matter how much light they have been receiving inside, as sun will scorch the fronds.

BACK LIT by the sinking afternoon sun, this row of palms gives the impression of an entire jungle beginning at the foot of this Scilly Isles garden. Palms can be used to make fine, architectural boundary markers, providing a striking backdrop for the rest of the garden.

A WINDING PATH in this Scilly Isles garden takes the observer through a theme park of amazing palm forms and colors. Dense groundcover plants produce a rich carpet from which the striking shapes of the palms can erupt, heightening their dramatic impact on the eye.

Conditions

When growing palms indoors provide bright light but not direct sun that can scorch the foliage. Make sure there are facilities for shading them if necessary during sunny weather. It is essential that a conservatory or glasshouse is fitted with shading blinds, to protect not only palms but also other plants from direct sun. Choose palms suited to the temperatures that you can provide—there are species suitable for cool and warm conditions.

Palms detest dry air that can cause browning of leaf tips, so you will have to provide them with moderate to high humidity according to species. In a conservatory or glasshouse a humid atmosphere is easily provided by damping down the floor and benches and by mist spraying the leaves with plain water. This will need to be done daily in warm conditions, less often in cool conditions.

In the house it is more difficult to provide a humid atmosphere. You may be able to mist spray the leaves if you are careful, but a better method is so stand the pots in trays filled with pebbles or gravel. Keep water under the pebbles but not high enough to reach the pot base. This will ensure the plants are surrounded by humid air.

Care

Water palms moderately when they are in growth, which is from late spring to the end of summer. Moderate watering means providing water when the compost is becoming dry on the surface. For the rest of the year, when the plants are resting or making slower growth, water more sparingly, keeping the compost only just moist. If in doubt, push your finger down into the compost to feel how moist or dry it is. If you can feel moisture then the compost is probably damp enough. Water thoroughly each time, to ensure that the entire depth of compost is moistened. Fill the space between the compost surface and the rim of the pot with water.

Feed palms once a month from late spring to late summer with a balanced liquid fertilizer to keep them growing steadily. A proprietary houseplant fertilizer is suitable, but the compost must be moist.

Palms grown inside are prone to attack by several pests. Scale insects, red spider mites, and thrips are the main ones to watch out for. Scale insects are scale-like, motionless insects that you may be able to wipe off with soapy water, or you may need to spray with malathion insecticide. Red spider mites are microscopic creatures whose feeding results in fine pale mottling on the leaves. A humid atmosphere keeps them at bay but if they do attack then spray with malathion or pirimiphos-methyl, or under glass use biological control (the predatory mite *Phytoseiulus persimilis*). Banded palm thrips are tiny insects that cause silvery brown discoloration of the foliage. To control them, spray plants with pyrethrum of permethrin.

Before palms outgrow their pots and become pot-bound (pots densely packed with roots) they should be potted on, using a pot two sizes larger. Once in final-size pots or tubs they need to be repotted into the same size container every two years to provide fresh compost. Tease away some of the old compost from around the roots to make room for the new compost. These operations are best carried out in spring. Soil-based potting compost is suitable, especially for large specimens as it holds them

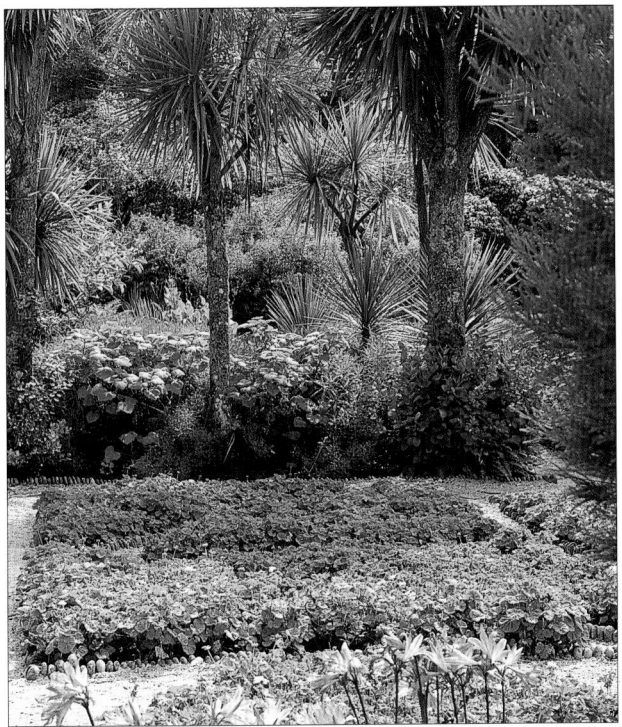

PALMS ARE USED here for a specific function: to act as elegant features to carry the eye across the formal area in the foreground.

more firmly than soil-less compost. In the years between repotting, topdress with fresh compost in the spring, first scraping away about 2in of the old compost from the surface.

PROPAGATION

Palms can be raised from seeds, but best results are obtained with fresh seeds, sown as soon as ripe. This is impossible for most people, who will buy seeds rather than collect their own. Purchased seed is best soaked in warm water for at least 24 hours then sown immediately. Also file the hard coats of woody seeds in one or two places to allow moisture to penetrate. Sow seeds singly in deep 3½in clay pots, using soil-less seed compost. Cover with a layer of compost that equals the seed's own diameter. Big seeds like coconuts are usually half buried.

Germinate seeds in a closed propagating case, as high humidity is needed, at 77–82°F for tropical species, and 55–64°F for temperate palms. Seeds of some species may germinate in a few days or several months; others may take a couple of years. Protect seedlings and young plants from direct sun.

Palms such as *Rhapis*, *Phoenix* and some *Chamaedorea* species produce offsets that can be used for propagation. Remove offsets in spring by taking the plant from its pot, scraping soil away to expose the base of the offset, then carefully cutting it off. Pot it in a deep clay pot.

TALL PALMS AND SIMILAR PLANTS WITH spiny fronds act as framing devices for this semi-ruined archway. Palms in general work well with architectural elements in a garden, as their upright forms and starbursts of foliage accentuate the curves and straight lines of buildings.

BUTIA CAPITATA
Jelly palm

THE SPECTACULAR Butia capitata is a highly effective feature palm, with its gently arching branches and sprays of spiny gray-green fronds creating a stunning display. This plant is suitable for growth in a container, but indoor specimens are unlikely to achieve these proportions.

FEATURES

Shade

A native of the cooler parts of South America, this plant is popularly known as the Jelly palm because of its edible but rather tough fruits, which can be boiled to make a jelly. The distinctive gray-green arching fronds consisting of numerous leaflets contrast well with many other palms. This species makes a sturdy trunk from 18–20ft in height and the fronds spread to 10–15ft. It is a very long-lived palm but slow growing and ideally suited to cultivation in a container. Suitable for a cool conservatory or glasshouse, it also makes a good houseplant.

BUTIA CAPITATA AT A GLANCE

A slow growing half-hardy palm with gray-green feathery foliage. Provide a minimum temperature of 41–50°F (zone 11).

Jan	/	Companion Plants
Feb	/	Because of the distinctive
Mar	planting 🌱	color of its fronds, *Butia*
Apr	planting 🌱	*capitata* contrasts well with
	foliage 🍃	many other palms.
May	foliage 🍃	
Jun	flowering ✿	
July	flowering ✿	
Aug	flowering ✿	
Sep	/	
Oct	/	
Nov	/	
Dec	/	

CONDITIONS

Aspect   Although the Jelly palm needs very bright light it should not be subjected to direct sun or the fronds may become scorched. Provide moderate humidity. If placed outdoors ensure it is sheltered from cold winds to prevent frond damage.

Site   In containers grow in soil-based potting compost.

GROWING METHOD

Propagation   Raise from seeds sown as soon as available and germinate at 77–82°F.

Watering   Moderate watering in growing season from late spring to late summer, then for the rest of the year water sparingly.

Feeding   Apply a balanced liquid fertilizer monthly during the growing season from late spring to late summer.

Problems   Under glass this palm is prone to attacks by red spider mites and scale insects.

FOLIAGE/FLOWERING

Foliage   Looks good all the year round but at its best in the growing season—spring and summer.

Flowers   Trusses of yellow flowers in summer are followed by purple fruits.

GENERAL CARE

Requirements   Remove dead fronds when necessary by cutting them off close to the trunk.

CHAMAEDOREA ELEGANS
Parlour palm

NEAT FOLIAGE and tolerance of low light levels make the parlour palm most useful. This one shows an immature flower stem.

PARLOUR PALMS are ideal for container growing, indoors or out. A handsome terracotta pot shows this one to advantage.

FEATURES

Shade

A native of Mexico and Guatemala, it is called the Parlour palm because of its widespread popularity as a houseplant. Hailing from a jungle environment, they are quite happy in poorly lit rooms. A smallish palm, it produces a clump of slender stems topped with deep green pinnate fronds about 2ft in length. Eventually it reaches a height of 6–10ft, with a spread 3–6ft. The Parlour palm flowers more freely than many other palms, even indoors, but does not usually set fruits when grown as a houseplant and in any case male and female plants would be needed. A long-lived palm, it is ideal for growing in containers and is a suitable subject for a warm conservatory or glasshouse.

CHAMAEDOREA AT A GLANCE

A smallish palm producing thin stems with rich green feathery fronds. Provide a minimum temperature of 61°F (zone 11).

Jan	/	Recommended Varieties
Feb	/	The variety "Bella" is more
Mar	planting ✎	compact in habit and flowers
Apr	planting ✎	more freely than the species.
	flowering ✿	
May	flowering ✿	
Jun	flowering ✿	
July	flowering ✿	
Aug	flowering ✿	
Sep	flowering ✿	
Oct	/	
Nov	/	
Dec	/	

CONDITIONS

Aspect Grow the Parlour palm in bright light but do not subject it to direct sun that may scorch the foliage. Provide high humidity. Outdoors avoid windy situations that may result in damage to the fronds.

Site In containers grow this palm in soil-less potting compost.

GROWING METHOD

Propagation Sow seeds as soon as available and germinate at a minimum temperature of 77°F.

Watering Plenty of water in growing season from late spring to late summer, then for the rest of the year water sparingly.

Feeding Apply a balanced liquid fertilizer monthly during the growing season from late spring to late summer.

Problems Under glass the Parlour palm is liable to be attacked by scale insects, red spider mites, and thrips.

FOLIAGE/FLOWERING

Foliage Being evergreen the foliage looks good all the year round. At its best in spring and summer.

Flowers Yellow flowers are produced from spring to fall and are followed by tiny black fruits.

GENERAL CARE

Requirements Remove dead fronds when necessary by cutting them off close to the trunk.

CHAMAEROPS HUMILIS
Dwarf fan palm

THE EXPLOSIVE DISPLAY of Chamaerops humilis *fronds, reminiscent of a fireworks display, makes it a useful feature plant.*

C. HUMILIS *FRONDS radiate outward from the stem. These serve to direct much-needed water to the base of the plant.*

FEATURES

Shade

A native of the Mediterranean region, this is a moderate sized, very bushy, suckering palm with somewhat variable, fan-shaped, pinnate, gray-green or blue-green leaves, up to 39in in length. These leaves have a very feathery appearance and are highly attractive. The Dwarf fan palm eventually reaches a height of 6–10ft, with a spread of 3–6ft. It has a moderate rate of growth (it is fully grown after 10 years) and is long lived, making it ideal for growing in containers. This palm rarely grows a full trunk—except in perfect conditions. Suitable for a cool conservatory or greenhouse, it is ideal, too, for growing as a houseplant and it fares especially well outside in the summer.

CHAMAEROPS AT A GLANCE

A bushy suckering palm with fan-shaped, very feathery leaves. Half-hardy, it can take temperatures down to 32°F (zone 10).

Jan	/	Companion Plants
Feb	/	Looks good with other cool-growing palms and is an
Mar	planting ✥	ideal subject for combining
Apr	planting ✥	with brightly colored
	flowering ✿	summer bedding plants
May	flowering ✿	outdoors. Under glass could
Jun	flowering ✿	combine with
July	flowering ✿	bougainvilleas.
Aug	flowering ✿	
Sep	/	
Oct	/	
Nov	/	
Dec	/	

CONDITIONS

Aspect   Grow the Dwarf fan palm in bright light but do not subject it to direct sun that may scorch the foliage. Provide moderate humidity. Outdoors place in a sheltered position.

Site   In containers grow this palm in soil-based potting compost.

GROWING METHOD

Propagation   Sow seeds as soon as available and germinate them in a minimum temperature of 72°F. Remove rooted suckers in spring and pot up individually.

Watering   Moderate watering in growing season from late spring to late summer, then for the rest of the year water sparingly.

Feeding   Apply a balanced liquid fertilizer monthly during the growing season from late spring to late summer.

Problems   Under glass this palm may be attacked by red spider mites.

FOLIAGE/FLOWERING

Foliage   This evergreen palm looks good all year round but is especially useful for summer displays.

Flowers   Yellow flowers are produced in spring and summer followed by brown to yellow fruits.

GENERAL CARE

Requirements   Remove dead fronds when necessary by cutting them off close to the trunk.

HOWEA FORSTERIANA
Kentia palm, Thatch leaf palm

THE SLOW GROWTH of Howea forsteriana makes it a suitable candidate for indoor cultivation. It makes an elegant feature.

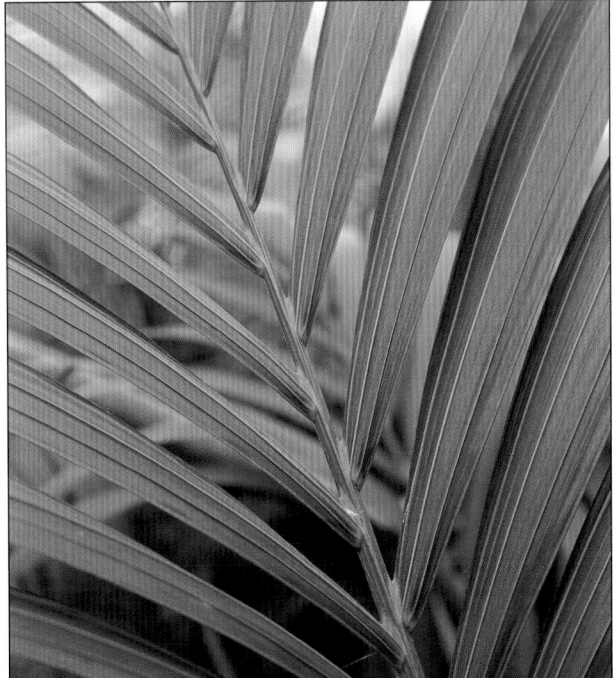

THE FINE LINES running along the length of H. forsteriana's leaves contribute to the general appearance of this graceful palm.

FEATURES

Shade

A native of Australia—Lord Howe Island—this is a particularly graceful palm with feathery, gently arching leaves. The slender trunk supports pinnate mid- to deep green leaves that are carried on long stalks and reach 6–10ft in length. This palm will eventually attain a height of up to 60ft, with a spread of 20ft. However, it is fairly slow growing and is therefore good for a container. Potting on or repotting is needed only infrequently. It is suited to a warm greenhouse or conservatory and small specimens are suitable for use as houseplants.

HOWEA AT A GLANCE

A very slender stem supports almost horizontal feathery leaves. Provide a minimum temperature of 59°F (zone 11).

Jan	/	**Companion Plants**
Feb	/	Under glass it associates well
Mar	planting 🌱	with other palms requiring
Apr	planting 🌱	the same conditions. Also
	foliage 🍃	try combining this palm
May	foliage 🍃	with tropical foliage plants
Jun	flowering ❀	such as philodendrons and
July	flowering ❀	*Monstera deliciosa*.
Aug	flowering ❀	
Sep	/	
Oct	/	
Nov	/	
Dec	/	

CONDITIONS

Aspect   Provide bright light, but direct sun may scorch the foliage. Provide moderate humidity. Outdoors place in a sheltered position.

Site   In containers grow in soil-based potting compost with leafmould and shredded bark.

GROWING METHOD

Propagation   Sow seeds as soon as available and germinate them at a temperature of 79°F.

Watering   Moderate watering in growing season from late spring to late summer, for the rest of the year water sparingly.

Feeding   Apply a balanced liquid fertilizer monthly during the growing season.

Problems   Under glass may be attacked by red spider mites and scale insects.

FOLIAGE/FLOWERING

Foliage   This evergreen palm looks good all year but is especially attractive in spring and summer.

Flowers   Clusters of star-shaped flowers are produced in summer, the females green, the males light brown, followed by orange-red fruits.

GENERAL CARE

Requirements Remove dead fronds when necessary by cutting them off close to the trunk.

JUBAEA CHILENSIS
Chilean wine palm

THE SPACING BETWEEN the fine leaves of Jubaea chilensis give this palm its overall feathery appearance.

ALTHOUGH SMALL in its younger years and suitable for indoor settings, J. chilensis eventually grows into a mighty palm.

FEATURES

Sun

A native of the warm temperate coastal regions of Chile, the Wine palm is a truly massive tree that dominates the landscape. It eventually forms a huge, fat gray trunk topped with a crown of light to deep green pinnate fronds that can grow to 15ft in length. The trunk contains a lot of sugar, which the Chileans use to make an alcoholic beverage—thus the name. Mature height up to 80ft with a spread of 28ft. It is slow growing when young but when a trunk has formed it develops more rapidly. When young this is an attractive feathery palm that makes a good houseplant and is ideal too for the cool glasshouse or conservatory. Place it outside for the summer. In favored areas it can be grown permanently out of doors.

JUBAEA AT A GLANCE

A feathery palm when young with pale to dark green leaves. Frost hardy, taking a minimum temperature of 23°F (zone 9).

Jan	/	Companion Plants
Feb	/	Outdoors combine with
Mar	planting 🌱	colorful summer bedding
Apr	planting 🌱	plants, or plants in a sub-
May	foliage 🌿	tropical scheme. Under glass
Jun	flowering ❀	grow with *Strelitzia reginae*
July	flowering ❀	(Bird of paradise) or *Musa*
Aug	flowering ❀	(banana) species.
Sep	/	
Oct	/	
Nov	/	
Dec	/	

CONDITIONS

Aspect Outdoors grow in a sheltered position in full sun. Indoors provide bright light but do not subject it to direct sun that may scorch the foliage. Provide low to moderate humidity.

Site Outdoors grow in well-drained but moisture-retentive soil. In containers grow in soil-based potting compost.

GROWING METHOD

Propagation Sow seeds as soon as available and germinate them at a temperature of 77°F. Very slow to germinate.

Watering In containers, moderate watering in growing season from late spring to late summer, then for the rest of the year water sparingly.

Feeding In containers apply a balanced liquid fertilizer monthly during the growing season from late spring to late summer.

Problems Under glass may be attacked by scale insects and red spider mites.

FOLIAGE/FLOWERING

Foliage Being evergreen this palm looks good all year round but is especially attractive in spring and summer.

Flowers Long trusses of small purple and yellow flowers in summer followed by yellow fruits.

GENERAL CARE

Requirements Remove dead fronds when necessary by cutting them off close to the trunk.

LIVISTONA CHINENSIS
Chinese fan palm

THE MODERATE-SIZED Livistona chinensis *(Chinese fan palm) has long stems before the eruption of leaves at the top of the plant.*

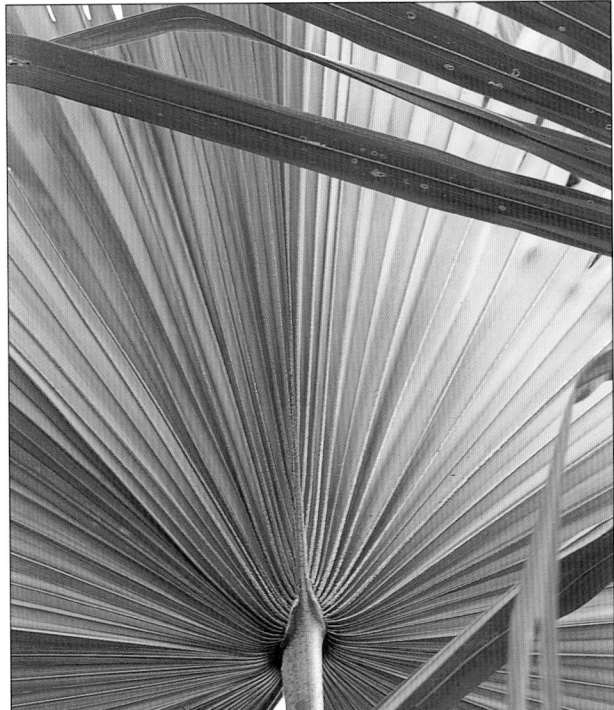

A BEAUTIFUL PEACOCK'S tail of leaves makes L. chinensis *a striking houseplant or conservatory specimen.*

FEATURES

Shade

The Chinese fan palm is a native of Japan and Taiwan. Of moderate size when mature, the trunk has a distinctive swollen base. The pinnate, shiny, dark green leaves grow up to 6ft in length and are carried on spiny stalks. The eventual height is up to 40ft, with a spread up to 15ft. This palm, suitable as a houseplant when young, is also recommended for a cool glasshouse or conservatory and is happy to be placed out of doors for the summer. It can be grown in a container for many years.

LIVISTONA AT A GLANCE

The trunk has a swollen base and supports dark green leaves. Provide a minimum temperature of 37–41°F (zones 10–11).

Jan	/	Companion Plants
Feb	/	Under glass grow with other
Mar	planting ✎	palms such as *Jubaea chilensis*
Apr	planting ✎	and with other bold foliage
May	foliage ✿	plants such as *Musa* species
Jun	flowering ✿	(banana), and *Citrus* species.
July	flowering ✿	Outdoors combine with
Aug	flowering ✿	colorful summer bedding
Sep	/	plants or include in a
Oct	/	subtropical scheme.
Nov	/	
Dec	/	

CONDITIONS

Aspect Provide bright light but do not subject it to direct sun. Provide moderate humidity. Outdoors place in a sheltered position.

Site In containers grow this palm in soil-based potting compost.

GROWING METHOD

Propagation Sow seeds as soon as available and germinate them at a temperature of 73°F.

Watering Water well in growing season from late spring to late summer, then for the rest of the year water sparingly.

Feeding Apply a balanced liquid fertilizer monthly during the growing season.

Problems Under glass may be attacked by scale insects and red spider mites.

FOLIAGE/FLOWERING

Foliage This palm looks good all year round but is especially attractive in spring and summer.

Flowers Trusses of cream-colored flowers are produced in summer followed by grayish or bluish fruits.

GENERAL CARE

Requirements Remove dead fronds when necessary by cutting them off close to the trunk.

PHOENIX CANARIENSIS
Canary Island date palm

CLASSIC PALM FRONDS, as produced by Phoenix canariensis. *They are particularly pleasing when they sway in light breezes.*

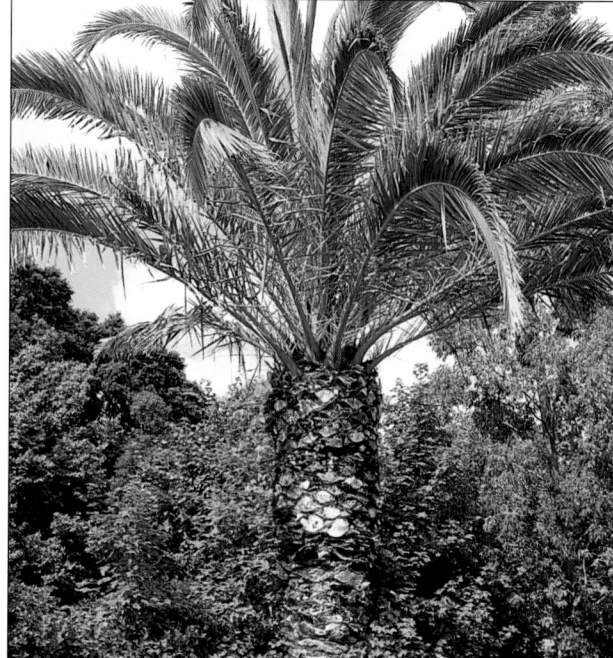

RISING MAJESTICALLY above the lower shrubs, P. canariensis *stocky trunk finishes in a triumphant display of arching fronds.*

FEATURES

Shade

This well-known and widely grown palm is a native of the Canary Islands. Of medium size, it eventually forms a fat heavy trunk. Wide arching fronds, which are very spiny at the base, grow up to 20ft in length on mature plants, and carry many bright or deep green leaflets. The mature height is up to 50ft with a spread of 40ft. As a young specimen this palm makes an ideal houseplant and it can also be recommended for an intermediate to warm conservatory or glasshouse. Place it out of doors for the summer. This palm will produce flowers and fruits in warm climates.

PHOENIX AT A GLANCE

The bright or deep green leaves, consist of many leaflets. Provide a minimum temperature of 50–61°F (zone 11).

Jan	/	Companion Plants
Feb	/	Under glass grow with other
Mar	planting 🌱	palms such as *Howea*
Apr	planting 🌱	*forsteriana*, and with other
May	foliage 🍃	foliage plants like *Monstera*
Jun	flowering ✽	*deliciosa*. Outdoors combine
July	flowering ✽	with brightly colored
Aug	flowering ✽	summer bedding or
Sep	/	subtropical plants.
Oct	/	
Nov	/	
Dec	/	

CONDITIONS

Aspect   Provide bright light but do not subject it to direct sun. Provide moderate humidity. Outdoors place in a sheltered position.

Site   In containers grow this palm in soil-based potting compost.

GROWING METHOD

Propagation   Sow seeds as soon as available and germinate them at a temperature of 66–75°F.

Watering   Water freely in growing season from late spring to late summer, then for the rest of the year water sparingly.

Feeding   Apply a balanced liquid fertilizer monthly during the growing season from late spring to late summer.

Problems   Under glass may be attacked by red spider mites and scale insects.

FOLIAGE/FLOWERING

Foliage   Being evergreen this palm looks good all year round but is especially attractive during the spring and summer.

Flowers   In summer trusses of yellow or cream flowers are produced, followed by yellow fruits.

GENERAL CARE

Requirements   Remove dead fronds when necessary by cutting them off close to the trunk.

PHOENIX ROEBELENII
Pygmy date palm

THE DELICATE LEAVES of Phoenix roebelenii *sprout from equally delicate stems, creating a subtle and elegant palm that can be grown indoors, and outdoors in warm areas. The plant's white flowers are rarely seen in Britain, as it needs warmer conditions for them to set seed.*

FEATURES

Shade

A native of Laos in south-east Asia, this is a small, slender, elegant-looking palm of feathery appearance that may be multi- or single stemmed. The leaves, which grow up to 4ft in length, have many shiny dark green leaflets which are somewhat spiky, so be careful where you place it. The eventual height is at least 6ft with a spread of 8ft. Widely grown as an indoor plant, it can also be recommended for an intermediate to warm conservatory or glasshouse. It will be happy out of doors for the summer.

PHOENIX AT A GLANCE

An elegant slender palm with long, feathery, dark green shiny leaves. Provide a minimum temperature of 50–61°F (zone 11).

Jan	/	Companion Plants
Feb	/	Under glass grow with other
Mar	planting 🌱	palms such as *Howea*
Apr	planting 🌱	*forsteriana*, and with other
May	foliage 🍃	foliage plants like *Monstera*
Jun	flowering ❀	*deliciosa*. Outdoors combine
July	flowering ❀	with brightly colored
Aug	flowering ❀	summer bedding or
Sep	/	subtropical plants.
Oct	/	
Nov	/	
Dec	/	

CONDITIONS

Aspect Provide bright light but do not subject it to direct sun. Provide moderate humidity. Outdoors place in a sheltered position.

Site In containers grow this palm in soil-based potting compost.

GROWING METHOD

Propagation Sow seeds as soon as available and germinate them at a temperature of 66–75°F. If produced, remove and pot up rooted offsets.

Watering Water freely in growing season from late spring to late summer, then water sparingly.

Feeding Balanced liquid fertilizer monthly during the growing period.

Problems Under glass may be attacked by red spider mites and scale insects.

FOLIAGE/FLOWERING

Foliage Looks good all year round but is especially attractive in spring and summer.

Flowers Cream flowers in summer, followed, if male and female plants are grown, by black fruits.

GENERAL CARE

Requirements Remove dead fronds when necessary by cutting them off close to the trunk.

RHAPIS EXCELSA
Miniature fan palm

THIS INDOOR Rhapis excelsa, *with its dense foliage of widely spaced leaves, adds a lush air to this trellised corner of a conservatory.*

AN EIGHT-LEAVED R. excelsa *frond with distinctive veins running along the length, creating interesting light and dark patterns.*

FEATURES

Shade

A native of southern China, this small palm forms clumps of thin, almost bamboo-like stems. The fan-shaped leaves have long stalks and are divided virtually to their bases, giving the impression of leaflets. This palm was imported to 17th century Japan and became popular among aristocratic circles. A number of cultivars were bred by the Japanese. The leaves of this versatile and undemanding plant are deep green and glossy and can grow up to 12in in length. The eventual height and spread of the plant is 5–15ft, but it is slow growing. Very suitable as a container plant, it makes a good houseplant and is also recommended for the intermediate conservatory or glasshouse. It will also be happy placed out of doors for the summer.

RHAPIS AT A GLANCE

Forms clumps of thin stems topped with fan-shaped, glossy leaves. Provide a minimum temperature of 50–55°F (zone 11).

Jan	/	Companion Plants
Feb	/	Under glass grow with other
Mar	planting 🌱	palms such as *Phoenix* species
Apr	planting 🌱	and with other foliage plants
May	foliage 🍃	like *Monstera deliciosa*.
Jun	flowering ❀	Outdoors combine this palm
July	flowering ❀	with brightly colored
Aug	flowering ❀	summer bedding or
Sep	/	subtropical plants.
Oct	/	
Nov	/	
Dec	/	

CONDITIONS

Aspect Provide bright light but do not subject it to direct sun. Provide moderate humidity. Outdoors place in a sheltered position.

Site In containers grow this palm in soil-less potting compost.

GROWING METHOD

Propagation Sow seeds as soon as available and germinate them at a temperature of 81°F. Alternatively remove and pot rooted offsets in spring, or divide an entire clump.

Watering Water freely in growing season from late spring to late summer, then for the rest of the year water moderately.

Feeding Apply a balanced liquid fertilizer monthly during the growing season from late spring to late summer.

Problems Under glass may be attacked by red spider mites.

FOLIAGE/FLOWERING

Foliage Being evergreen this palm looks good all year round but is especially attractive in spring and summer.

Flowers Clusters of cream flowers are produced in summer followed by white, waxy fruits if fertilization has taken place.

GENERAL CARE

Requirements Remove dead fronds when necessary by cutting them off close to the trunk.

SABAL PALMETTO
Blue palmetto, Cabbage palmetto

THE TRUNK of the Sabal palmetto develops a criss-cross pattern as the dead fronds are cut back at consistent lengths.

THE DEAD FRONDS of this S. palmetto have been trimmed to allow neat, healthy growth to appear at the top of the plant.

FEATURES

Shade

A native of southern USA (it is the state tree of both Florida and South Carolina), this large palm has a fat, rough-textured trunk and tends to dominate the landscape in the wild. The feathery, fan-shaped leaves are deep green and deeply divided. They attain a length of 6ft and are carried in a somewhat rounded crown. The mature height of this palm is 100ft, with a spread of up to 22ft. As a young plant it makes a good houseplant and is also recommended for the cool conservatory or glasshouse. It likes to be placed out of doors in a bright spot for the summer.

SABAL PALMETTO AT A GLANCE

The dark green, deeply divided, fan-shaped leaves are feathery. Provide a minimum temperature of 41–45°F (zone 11).

Jan	/	Companion Plants
Feb	/	Looks good with other cool-growing palms and is an
Mar	planting 🌱	ideal subject for combining
Apr	planting 🌱	with brightly colored
May	foliage 🌿	summer bedding plants
Jun	flowering ❀	outdoors. Under glass could
July	flowering ❀	combine with bougainvillea.
Aug	flowering ❀	
Sep	/	
Oct	/	
Nov	/	
Dec	/	

CONDITIONS

Aspect Provide bright light but do not subject it to direct sun. Provide high humidity in summer. Outdoors place in a sheltered position.

Site In containers grow this palm in soil-based potting compost.

GROWING METHOD

Propagation Sow seeds as soon as available and germinate them at a temperature of 66–75°F.

Watering Moderate watering in growing season from late spring to late summer, then water sparingly.

Feeding Apply a balanced liquid fertilizer monthly during the growing season from late spring to late summer.

Problems Under glass may be attacked by scale insects and red spider mites.

FOLIAGE/FLOWERING

Foliage Being evergreen this palm looks good all year round, but it is especially attractive during the spring and summer.

Flowers Long trusses of cream flowers are produced in summer, followed by small black fruits.

GENERAL CARE

Requirements Remove dead fronds when necessary by cutting them off close to the trunk.

TRACHYCARPUS FORTUNEI
Chusan palm

THE FOLIAGE of Trachycarpus fortunei *is arranged in neat layers, with the rather stiff fan fronds standing out from the trunk.*

MATURE EXAMPLES of T. fortunei, *with their characteristic covering of dark fibres, here flank a young one.*

FEATURES

Sun

It is not known for certain where this palm originates from but it is probably a native of Burma and China. It gets its common name from the island of Chusan on the east coast of China, where it grows abundantly. It forms a single fibrous trunk topped with fan-shaped, deeply lobed, deep green fronds, which grow up to 30in in length. The eventual height is 70ft, with a spread of 8ft. The Chusan palm has a reputation as one of the hardiest of all palms, and survives snowy winters. It is therefore hardy enough to be grown out of doors, but in regions subject to very hard winters grow the plant in a tub in a cool conservatory or glasshouse and place it outside for the summer.

TRACHYCARPUS AT A GLANCE

Forms a tall fibrous trunk topped with fan-shaped leaves. Frost-hardy, taking a minimum temperature of 23°F (zone 9).

Jan	/	Companion Plants
Feb	/	Generally grown as a
Mar	planting 🌿	specimen tree in gardens.
Apr	planting 🌿	Looks good with formal
May	foliage 🌱	beds of roses as well as
Jun	flowering ✿	brightly colored summer
July	flowering ✿	bedding plants.
Aug	flowering ✿	
Sep	/	
Oct	/	
Nov	/	
Dec	/	

CONDITIONS

Aspect   Outdoors grow in a sheltered position in full sun or light dappled shade. Indoors provide bright light but do not subject it to direct sun. Provide low humidity.

Site   Outdoors grow in deep, well-drained but moisture-retentive soil. In containers grow in soil-based potting compost.

GROWING METHOD

Propagation   Sow seeds as soon as available and germinate them at a temperature of 75°F.

Watering   In containers, moderate watering in growing season from late spring to late summer, then for the rest of the year water sparingly.

Feeding   In containers apply a balanced liquid fertilizer monthly during the growing season.

Problems   Under glass may be attacked by red spider mites and scale insects.

FOLIAGE/FLOWERING

Foliage   Being evergreen this palm looks good all year round but is especially attractive during the spring and summer months.

Flowers   Dangling clusters of small yellow flowers are produced in summer, followed, on female plants, by blue-black fruits.

GENERAL CARE

Requirements   Remove dead fronds when necessary by cutting them off close to the trunk.

WASHINGTONIA
Cotton palm

WASHINGTONIA (COTTON PALMS) *are named for their fine, curled cotton-like threads. These palms are most imposing in maturity.*

THE SHAPELY FRONDS *of this young* Washingtonia *are shown to advantage against this white-painted brick wall.*

FEATURES

Shade

The two species of *Washingtonia* are native to the south-western USA and northern Mexico. They form a single trunk topped with large, fan-shaped, deeply lobed fronds. *Washingtonia filifera* (Desert fan palm, Northern washingtonia), has 6–10ft long gray-green leaves with cotton-like threads and an eventual height of 50–70ft, with a spread up to 20ft. *W. robusta* (Thread palm, Southern washingtonia) has a tapered trunk topped with 3ft long bright green fronds. Its eventual height is 80ft, and its spread reaches 15ft. Young specimens make good houseplants, or grow them in an intermediate glasshouse or conservatory. Place outside for the summer.

WASHINGTONIA AT A GLANCE

Single-stemmed palms noted for their large fan-shaped, lobed leaves. Provide a minimum temperature of 45–50°F (zone 11).

Jan	/	Companion Plants
Feb	/	Good specimen plants for
Mar	planting ✎	use with summer bedding.
Apr	planting ✎	Under glass grow with
May	foliage ✿	bougainvilleas and
Jun	flowering ✸	*Citrus* species.
July	flowering ✸	
Aug	flowering ✸	
Sep	/	
Oct	/	
Nov	/	
Dec	/	

CONDITIONS

Aspect Provide bright light but do not subject to direct sun. Provide moderate humidity. Outdoors place in a sheltered position.

Site In containers grow in soil-based potting compost with some leafmold and coarse sand added to the mixture.

GROWING METHOD

Propagation Sow seeds as soon as available and germinate them at a temperature of 75°F.

Watering Moderate watering in growing season from late spring to late summer, then for the rest of the year water sparingly. In winter, keep the soil almost dry.

Feeding Apply a balanced liquid fertilizer monthly during the growing season.

Problems Under glass may be attacked by scale insects and red spider mites.

FOLIAGE/FLOWERING

Foliage Being evergreen these palms look good all year round but are especially attractive in spring and summer.

Flowers Long arching trusses of cream-white flowers are produced in summer, followed by purple or brown fruits.

GENERAL CARE

Requirements Remove dead fronds when necessary by cutting them off close to the trunk.

Growing Climbers

GROWING CLIMBERS

Climbers are among the most useful of garden plants. They provide color and interest on a higher level without taking up much space near the ground. They are very versatile and can be used in many ways, primarily for covering fences, walls, and outbuildings. They can be grown up trellis screens in the garden, and when trained over pergolas will provide shade for a patio or terrace. Suitable climbers can be trained up trees and over large shrubs, and some can be used as groundcover. They can also be grown on free-standing supports in borders.

Climbers can also be used as focal points in a garden by training them over an ornamental arch, say at the end of a pathway. Although few people think of them when planning balcony gardens, they are ideal for this purpose as they take up little horizontal space while decorating an otherwise blank wall.

LEFT: This glorious display of wisteria is at its peak, and it perfectly complements the iron lacework on this long verandah.

WISTERIA SINENSIS *and a white climbing rose have been trained to grow up opposing ends of this metallic arch. With a few more years' growth these plants should tangle together delightfully. The shape of the structure will create a pleasant flowering window between two areas of the garden.*

HABITS OF GROWTH

Unlike the other groups of woody plants, the trees and shrubs, climbing plants do not have self-supporting trunks or stems and therefore use various modifications to lift themselves up toward the light. In their natural habitats there may not always be a convenient support for the plant and so it may trail over the ground or over a rock. We can make use of this method of growth in gardens by using some climbers are groundcover, just allowing them to sprawl over the soil surface. It is a good way of quickly covering large areas, especially banks.

Climbers are grouped into four broad groups according to the mechanism they use to climb: tendril climbers, twiners, scramblers, and self-clinging climbers.

Tendril climbers
Tendril climbers have thin, curling tendrils that coil around their supports, whether it's wire, netting, or trellis. Tendrils are modified organs; in the case of climbers they are generally modified leaves. The grape vine, *Vitis vinifera*, is a good example of a tendril climber. Some tendril climbers, such as *Parthenocissus tricuspidata* (Boston ivy) have adhesive suckers or disks on the tips of their tendrils that stick to smooth surfaces such as walls.

Twiners
Twiners are climbing plants that twine their new shoots entirely around a support. *Wisteria*, which is among our best-loved climbers, is a twiner, and a vigorous one at that. This group of climbers will twine either clockwise or anticlockwise according to species.

Scramblers
Scramblers often climb and support themselves by means of thorns that usually curve downwards, acting as hooks. Climber and Rambler roses come in this group, as do the brambles or *Rubus* species, such as *Rubus henryi* var. *bambusarum*. Scramblers attach themselves to other plants or supports to pull themselves up. Some scrambling plants

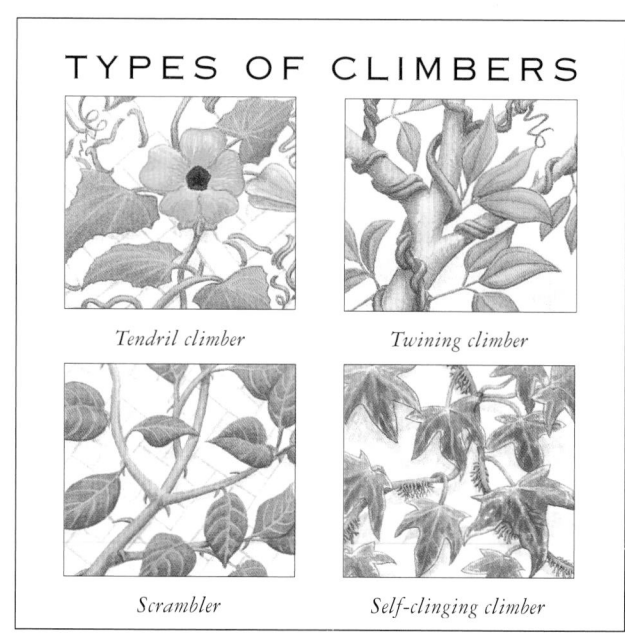

TYPES OF CLIMBERS

Tendril climber

Twining climber

Scrambler

Self-clinging climber

are described as lax, having very long thin thornless stems, an example being *Jasminum nudiflorum* (Winter jasmine). In the wild these just sprawl over other plants or rocks but when grown in gardens they need to have their stems tied in to supports to help them climb.

Self-clinging climbers

Self-clinging climbers are not as common as the other kinds. They produce short roots from their stems, known as aerial roots, that attach themselves firmly to supports. Self-clinging climbers are capable of attaching to completely flat, relatively smooth surfaces such as walls. In the wild they would attach themselves to tree trunks or rock faces. These adventurous roots make their way into any tiny crack or rough patch in the surface of the support. The best-known examples of self-clinging climbers are *Hedera* species (Ivy), *Hydrangea anomala* subsp. *petiolaris* (Climbing hydrangea) and *Schizophragma hydrangeoides*, a relation of the hydrangea.

Matching climbers to supports

Now that we know the methods that climbers use to climb and to support themselves, we can choose suitable plants for the existing supports. On the other hand, if you want to grow a particular climber, you could provide a custom-made support if necessary. Climbers vary tremendously in height and this is an important consideration when choosing plants for the garden.

Some are capable of reaching to the tops of the tallest walls or trees, while others are much less vigorous and will not grow any taller than an ordinary garden fence.

Flamboyant flowers

Apart from their methods of supporting themselves, climbers are diverse in other respects, too. Many are noted for their colorful flower displays. Many hardy climbers have quite flamboyant flowers and are capable of providing an exotic effect in gardens. *Wisteria* is a good example, with its long trusses of pea-flowers, but there are many others such as *Abutilon megapotamicum* (Flowering maple) with red and yellow bells, *Campsis radicans* (Common trumpet creeper) with large orange trumpet-shaped flowers, *Clianthus puniceus* (Glory pea, Lobster claw) with bright red claw-like flowers, *Fremontodendron californicum* with large saucer-shaped yellow flowers, and *Passiflora caerulea* (Blue passion flower), which looks as though it should be grown under glass but which is in fact hardy enough to survive outdoors in many areas.

For sheer quantity of flowers over a long period in summer there is nothing to beat the Climbing and Rambler roses. Some have only one flush of flowers in summer, but if you choose the right cultivars you will get several flushes throughout summer.

Many roses have fragrant flowers, and this is a characteristic of numerous other climbers. For many people the first choice for fragrance, apart from roses,

THIS FINE Clematis *"Etoile Violette" has large, violet flowers with contrasting yellow stamens. The Viticella Group of clematis of which this is one, contains a host of vigorous, free-flowering varieties. These clematis bloom from the midsummer to late fall.*

is honeysuckle such as *Lonicera caprifolium* (Italian honeysuckle), *L. japonica* "Halliana" (Japanese honeysuckle), and *L. periclymenum* cultivars (Common honeysuckle, Woodbine). Some jasmines also have highly fragrant blooms, especially *Jasminum beesianum*, *J. humile* "Revolutum" and, the most fragrant of all, *J. officinale* (Common jasmine). Not related to jasmine, but still with very fragrant flowers, is *Trachelospermum jasminoides* (Star jasmine). And don't forget the reliable *Wisteria* when it comes to fragrance, particularly *W. floribunda* and *W. sinensis* and their various cultivars.

Attractive foliage

Climbers may be deciduous, in other words they lose their leaves in the fall, or evergreen—retaining their leaves all the year round. The latter are particularly valuable where an object such as a wall needs to be covered all the time. Many climbers are, in fact, grown for their attractive foliage, some of which can be quite exotic-looking, especially the large leaves of the deciduous *Actinidia kolomikta*, which are dark green, pink, and white. The evergreen *Euonymus fortunei* cultivars are often brightly variegated and make a splash of color in a shady situation. The same is true of ivies, both the small-leaved *Hedera helix* cultivars (Common ivy) and cultivars of the large-leaved kinds such as *H. canariensis* (Canary Island ivy) and *H. colchica* (Persian ivy). All have green-leaved cultivars, too. The related X *Fatshedera lizei* (Tree ivy), has large

dark green ivy-like leaves, or variegated in some of the cultivars. *Humulus lupulus* "Aureus" (Golden hop) is one of the most colorful foliage climbers with its golden-yellow, deciduous leaves.

Several deciduous climbers are grown for their fall leaf color. Supreme in this respect are species of *Parthenocissus*. Probably the best known and most widely planted is *P. quinquefolia* (Virginia creeper) whose leaves become brilliant red in fall. Also good are *P. tricuspidata* (Boston ivy) and *P. henryana* (Chinese Virginia creeper). Another superb climber for fall leaf color is *Vitis coignetiae*, an ornamental vine, one of the largest-leaved hardy climbers available, whose foliage becomes bright red before it falls.

USES IN GARDENS

Climbers are a highly versatile group of plants and can be used in many ways in the garden. Do not think only in terms of using them to cover a wall. Be more imaginative and adventurous and try using them as free-standing features in beds and borders, growing them over large shrubs, or even using them as groundcover.

It is important that climbers are matched to their supports, so bear this in mind when choosing plants for your garden. Some climbers are very vigorous and only suitable for covering the largest walls, and would therefore need a lot of pruning to keep them within

DESPITE ITS YOUTH, a young honeysuckle plant nevertheless provides a bright show of vibrant red flowers. This species, Lonicera x brownii "Fuchsioides," *is quite hardy and will make a good wall-covering climber. It flowers throughout the summer.*

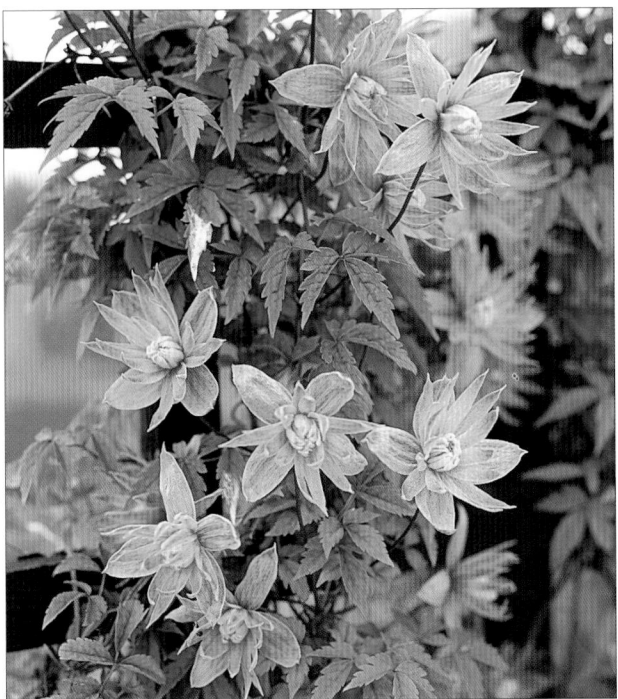

A TRELLIS makes the perfect support for this Clematis macropetala *"Markham's Pink." The plant will grow leaving decorative windows.*

THE LINES of this trellis are consumed by a mass of Parthenocissus *leaves. Climbers will help any object to blend into the garden.*

bounds. On the other hand there are many of more modest stature, suitable for even small gardens.

Walls and fences

It is safe to say that all climbers can be grown on walls. On the walls of the house it is probably best to avoid those that produce aerial roots such as ivies, and tendril climbers with adhesive suckers like *Parthenocissus*, for not only are they vigorous but once attached are very difficult to remove. These would be better for tall boundary walls. Instead, for the average house, go for more manageable climbers such as roses, *Clematis* and jasmines; or wall shrubs such as *Abutilon megapotamicum* (Flowering maple), *Chaenomeles speciosa* (Flowering quince), *Cotoneaster horizontalis* (Fishbone cotoneaster), and *Fremontodendron californicum* (Flannel bush). Wisterias are often grown on house walls but bear in mind that they are tall, vigorous climbers and need a lot of pruning. They are probably better for large houses.

For boundary fences, which are generally about 6ft high maximum, such as close-boarded or panel fences, again use the smaller, more manageable climbers as suggested above. If you have a chain-link fence you could choose from the group known as twiners. These will support themselves by twining their shoots through the mesh. Wisterias are twiners, and although very tall, they can be grown on low fences by training the stems horizontally. *Muehlenbeckia complexa* is another twiner suitable for covering chain-link fencing.

Pergolas, arches and arbours

These are excellent supports for many climbers but not for those that produce aerial roots like ivies, or adhesive suckers such as *Parthenocissus*. Favorites for pergolas are grape vines, *Vitis vinifera*, either fruiting or ornamental kinds, which quickly provide welcome shade over a patio. Climbing roses are also popular, and look especially attractive trained over an arch or arbour. Roses can be grown with *Clematis*, allowing the two to intertwine for some really stunning effects. *Wisteria*, again, is a favorite for larger pergolas, especially as the dense flower trusses hang down inside the structure.

Obelisks for borders

Few people think of growing climbers in beds and borders as free-standing specimens. Yet this is an excellent way to grow the smaller kinds such as Large-flowered climbing roses, *Clematis* (try combining the two), and *Humulus lupulus* "Aureus" (Golden hop). Obelisks make ideal supports, and are obtainable in steel or wood. Woven hazel or willow obelisks are also available and their rustic appearance makes them ideal for cottage or country gardens. DIY enthusiasts could probably save some money by making their own obelisks out of timber.

Trees and shrubs

Large mature trees make suitable supports for tall vigorous climbers such as *Rosa filipes*, particularly the cultivar "Kiftsgate." With its white flowers, this is very effective when grown through a large mature dark green conifer. Ivies, *Parthenocissus*, *Hydrangea anomala* subsp. *petiolaris* (Climbing hydrangea), and other self-clinging climbers are suitable for big deciduous trees. Thin-stemmed, light and airy climbers such as *Clematis viticella* cultivars can be grown through large mature shrubs.

THIS SOLANUM CRISPUM *hangs lush and colorful over a bed of assorted plants. The addition of a climber can lift an entire bed and completes the decorative effect. Plantings should be thought out with the use of climbers in mind—they can revolutionize your entire garden look.*

Ugly outbuildings

To quickly cover and hide ugly outbuildings such as sheds and garages choose a vigorous climber. These include plants such as *Ampelopsis glandulosa* var. *brevipedunculata* "Elegans," *Campsis radicans* (Common trumpet creeper), *Celastrus orbiculatus* (Staff vine), the extremely vigorous *Fallopia baldschuanica* (Russian vine), *Hedera colchica* (Persian ivy), or *Parthenocissus* species.

Pots and tubs

While most climbers are planted directly in the open ground, some can also be grown in tubs and pots. For example, if you have a pergola built over a paved area such as a patio, or you want to grow a climber on a patio wall, there may be no soil available in which to plant. Large containers filled with soil-based potting compost will make suitable homes for the less-vigorous climbers. The container needs to be a minimum of 12in in diameter and depth; 18in or larger would be better. A good depth is particularly important as then the compost will not dry out quickly and the climber will be able to root deeply, resulting in better growth.

Less-vigorous climbers are best suited to containers as then they will not quickly outgrow them. Many *Clematis* are ideal, particularly the summer-flowering Large-flowered hybrids and the *C. viticella* cultivars. Other suitable plants you might like to try include *Abutilon megapotamicum* (Flowering maple), *Clianthus puniceus*

(Glory pea, lobster claw), X *Fatshedera lizei* (Tree ivy), hederas (Ivies), *Humulus lupulus* "Aureus" (Golden hop), and Large-flowered climbing roses (these need a large tub). Very vigorous climbers should not be attempted, although wisterias are sometimes trained as standards (like small trees, with a single stem) in large tubs, and they make unusual features on a patio. *Vitis vinifera* (Grape vines) can be grown in the same way.

Container-grown plants will need extra maintenance in the way of regular watering and feeding through the year, but the results are certainly worthwhile.

Groundcover

Some climbers make excellent groundcover, say among shrubs, under trees, or even for covering a steep bank. *Cotoneaster horizontalis* (Fishbone cotoneaster), although a wall shrub rather than a climber, is often used for this purpose. It has a prostrate, spreading habit of growth when used for ground cover.

Euonymus fortunei cultivars make excellent evergreen groundcover and are particularly good for growing in shady areas of the garden, although the variegated cultivars develop a better color when exposed to at least some sun. The same applies to ivies. The small-leaved *Hedera helix* cultivars (Common ivy) create a marvelous flowing texture when grown as groundcover, and the large-leaved ones such as *H. colchica* (Persian ivy) create a different but still pleasing effect.

THIS CLIMBING ROSE has managed to extend itself across the entire width of this house, and is enlivening the whole of the front of the house with an amazing abundance of light pink flowers. At this height, dead-heading becomes a major effort—but as this picture shows it is well worth the trouble.

Parthenocissus can be used for covering large areas and is effective when cascading down a bank, especially in fall when the leaves turn brilliant red, giving the effect of a stream of molten lava.

PROVIDING SUPPORTS

Many climbers, apart from the self-clinging kinds, need a bit of extra help to climb their supports. For example, they will not be able to hold on to a wall or fence, or the pillars of a pergola, without some additional support. And free-standing climbers in beds and borders, for instance, will need some kind of structure to climb.

Walls and fences
The traditional method of supporting climbers on walls and fences is with a system of horizontal wires, to which the stems of the climbers can be tied as they grow. Heavy gauge galvanized or plastic-coated wire is recommended for this purpose. The wires, which can be spaced about 12–18in apart up the wall or fence, can be stretched tightly between vine eyes, which are like screws but with a ring at the top. Provide one of these at each end of the wire, and if it is a long stretch insert one or two in between to prevent the wire from sagging too much. To achieve really tight wires you may have to use stronger devices such as straining bolts instead of vine eyes.

CLIMBERS FOR GROWING AS GROUNDCOVER

- *Akebia quinata* (Chocolate vine)
- *Ampelopsis glandulosa* var. *bevipedunculata* "Elegans"
- *Clematis*, Viticella Group
- *Cotoneaster horizontalis* (Fishbone cotoneaster)
- *Decumaria barbara*
- *Euonymus fortunei*
- *Hedera canariensis* (Canary Island ivy)
- *Hedera colchica* (Persian ivy)
- *Hedera helix* (Common or English ivy)
- *Hydrangea anomala* subsp. *petiolaris* (Climbing hydrangea)
- *Lonicera periclymenum* (Common honeysuckle)
- *Parthenocissus henryana* (Chinese Virginia creeper)
- *Parthenocissus quinquefolia* (Virginia creeper)
- *Parthenocissus tricuspidata* (Boston ivy)
- *Rubus henryi* var. *bambusarum* (Bramble)
- *Schisandra chinensis*
- *Schizophragma hydrangeoides*
- *Trachelospermum jasminoides* (Star jasmine)
- *Vitis coignetiae* (Vine)
- *Vitis vinifera* "Purpurea" (Grape vine)

Vine eyes hold the wires a short distance away from the wall, and this allows free circulation of air between the wall and the plants. Good air circulation is particularly recommended for house walls to prevent the possible development of dampness. It also lessens the risk of diseases attacking the plants.

The alternative to horizontal wires is to fix trellis panels to walls and fences, to which climbers can be tied. Available in wood, metal, or plastic, they can generally be fixed to the wall with rust-proof screws, placing a wooden block between the wall and the panel wherever screws are used, to ensure a space of at least 2in for air circulation. Old cotton reels make good "buffers."

Wires or trellis panels can also be used on outbuildings to support climbers. A particularly unsightly building can be made more attractive by completely covering the walls with attractive wooden trellis.

Substantial and long-lasting materials are needed to tie in climbers to their supports. The traditional material is tarred string which has a long life. Otherwise use ordinary thick garden string or twine. Small proprietary plastic ties of various kinds are also suitable. Do not use wire, as this will cut into the stems.

Pergolas, arbours, and arches

A pergola is one of the most popular supports for climbers. It is a tall garden structure that can take various forms. Basically it consists of a series of pillars. These are generally made of timber, but pillars can be constructed with brick or natural stone, these being more suitable for large gardens as they are bulky structures. The pillars support horizontal beams.

Pergolas can be various shapes but the most popular is to have pillars along each side of a path linked by cross beams, thus creating a covered walk. Also popular is a square or rectangular pergola covering or partially covering a patio or other paved area that is used for outdoor living, the idea here being to create a pleasant shady area in which to sit, relax, and enjoy alfresco meals.

It is possible to buy pergola kits. Timber is the most popular material for construction and is available from many DIY superstores and garden centers. Metal pergolas, available from specialist suppliers, are more expensive. DIY enthusiasts may be able to construct their own timber pergola, using smooth, pressure-treated timber or, for a country or cottage garden, rustic poles.

Arches also make good supports for climbers, again available in kit form, timber, or metal. They consist of upright pillars with cross pieces at the top and are generally used to form an entrance—again, perhaps, placed over a path. These can be highly effective with a flowering climber draping itself overhead.

An arbour or bower is a traditional support for climbing plants. These are essentially intimate alcoves where one can sit and enjoy a pleasant view of the garden. An arbour is often combined with a pergola, being placed

A FETCHING ARCH over a path, seating area and lavender bed benefits from a climber. Used with architectural elements, climbers act to soften harsh lines and help to make objects such as this arch to merge into the general flow of the garden.

BIRDS LOVE the twisting branches of climbers as sites for their nests. Here a clematis provides decoration and a home.

THIS LARGE-FLOWERED Clematis cultivar has a good hold on a timber post, and provides a column of vibrant colors.

at the end of a path. There are timber or metal versions available, but the DIY enthusiast may be able to construct one from wooden trellis panels.

Most climbing plants will need some help to grow up the timber pillars used for garden structures, as well as brick or stone pergola pillars. Vertical wires can be fixed to pillars, to which the climbers can be tied, again using vine eyes or even ordinary screws which end up looking less conspicuous. Generally there is no problem tying in climbers to metal structures, and no additional support is needed to keep the plants in place.

Free-standing supports
To grow climbers, such as clematis and roses, in a bed or border you will need to provide some kind of support. Very popular are obelisks, specially designed for the purpose. Proprietary ones are available in metal or wood. If you want a more rustic kind, opt for woven willow or hazel designs. Obelisks come in various heights—make sure you choose a suitable height for your subject. For most climbers 6ft would be the minimum. Pot obelisks are also available for patio tubs. Simply tie in climbers to these supports with garden twine.

Alternative supports for climbers in beds and borders are wooden pillars. Stout fencing posts about 8ft long are ideal for the purpose, and should be sunk about 24in into the ground. Provide a vertical wire on each side of the post for tying in the climber.

Growing up trees
Climbers other than self-clinging kinds will need additional means of support on large trees until they reach the branches, which will then take over as supports. So to start with insert long bamboo canes into the ground against the trunk of the tree, one for each stem. The young stems can then be tied into these with garden twine. Self-clinging climbers generally need to be provided with just one shorter cane after planting to initially guide the young stem to the trunk.

GROWING CONDITIONS

To ensure optimum growth and flowering from your climbers you must grow them in the right conditions. It is a case of choosing exactly the right spot in your garden for the particular plant, taking into account aspect and soil conditions. Specific conditions are given for each climber in the plant section (see pages 692–723).

Aspect
The majority of climbers grow best in sites with full sun but there are some that tolerate partial shade, in other words, where the sun reaches for part of the day only. Others will take full shade, with no sun at all. Some climbers like the best of both worlds—an example being clematis, which like a cool shaded root run but their heads in the sun. To achieve this, grow them in a sunny spot but ensure their roots are shaded by shallow rooting, low growing or groundcover plants. Heavy mulching over the root area will achieve the same result.

South- and west-facing walls and fences are usually the sunniest and warmest areas of the garden, while north- and east-facing ones are the coolest and shadiest. Those facing east receive some sun in the morning while northerly aspects receive no sun at all.

Many climbers need shelter from strong winds, not only to prevent their stems being whipped around and damaged (although if tied in properly this should not happen), but also to prevent the foliage being scorched by cold drying winds. Some of the less hardy climbers in particular need a warm, sheltered spot to ensure good growth and flowering. If the garden is not naturally sheltered, wind protection can be provided in various ways, for example by planting large wind-resistant shrubs on the windward side of the garden to filter and slow down the wind. Also large shrubs planted further in the garden to form a screen can have the effect of creating a favourable microclimate for less-hardy plants. Sheltered courtyards are also ideal for the less-hardy climbers.

Soil

There are climbers to suit all types of soil, from heavy clay, through loams, to chalky types and light sandy soils, and from moisture-retentive to dry. The majority of climbers will grow well in any type of soil if it has been well prepared, and in both acid (lime-free) and alkaline (limy) soils. Some, however, prefer limy or chalky soils, such as clematis, while others must have acid conditions,

an example being *Berberidopsis corallina*, although it would survive in neutral soil. Check your soil for acidity or alkalinity (also called its pH) with a simple soil-testing kit, obtainable from many good garden centers.

Many climbers are long-lived plants and respond well to thorough soil preparation and improvement before planting. In particular it is important to ensure that the soil is adequately drained and does not become waterlogged in the winter. Soil is prepared by digging to the depth of the spade blade and at the same time any improvements can be carried out.

Loamy soils are the best, being fertile and well-drained, and need little in the way of improvement. However, even these benefit from the addition of bulky organic matter during digging, adding it to the bottom of each trench and then forking it in. You can use garden compost, well-rotted manure, or composted bark. These all break down in the soil and become humus that helps to improve the structure of all soils and also aids in the retention of moisture and nutrients.

Clay soils may be poorly drained. To improve drainage, again incorporate bulky organic matter, but also add copious amounts of horticultural grit or coarse sand if

A POPULAR CLIMBER. Wisteria floribunda "Multijuga" arranges itself in a pleasantly regular fashion over the rear of this house. Its pendulous blooms of lilac-blue make a striking textural as well as colorful display. These flowers appear in late spring and early summer.

drainage is poor. These materials open up the soil and improve both drainage and air circulation. Add sand or grit to the bottom of the trenches during digging and also mix it into the top 12in of soil.

Adding bulky organic matter to the freely drained chalky and sandy soils, which are inclined to dry out rapidly, will help them to retain moisture during dry periods. Unfortunately the humus thus created does not last long in these soils, but can be replaced by the application of a heavy mulch.

Following the initial preparation of a planting site, leave the ground to settle for a few months before planting. Then just before the plants go in fork a general-purpose fertilizer into the surface.

Planting

As with most plants these days, climbers are bought in pots, whether from a garden center or from a mail-order nursery. So they can be planted at any time of year because their roots are not disturbed when planting. However, never plant when the soil is cold and wet, or frozen, in the winter as the roots may rot before the plant has a chance to become established. It is not a good idea to plant during drought conditions as then much more water will be needed to get plants established. The ideal time to plant is in the spring, as the soil is warming up and drying out. Then the plants will quickly root into the soil and become established. Some gardeners also favor fall planting, while the soil is still warm.

To plant a pot-grown climber, make a planting hole slightly wider than the rootball, and of such a depth that after planting the top of the rootball is only just below the soil surface. Return fine soil around the rootball, firming it well with your heels or fist as you proceed.

If initial supports are needed, such as a bamboo cane to guide the stems to the main support, insert this before returning soil around the plant, to avoid pushing it through the roots, which may damage them.

It is the usual practice to set climbers at least 12in away from a wall or fence and to guide the stems to the support with bamboo canes angled in towards it. This is because the soil can be very dry immediately in front of a wall or fence, because rain is deflected, so climbers may not establish well in this "rain shadow." The same applies when planting against a large tree. After planting, mulch the plants with bulky organic matter.

When planting in pots and tubs, first put a 2in deep layer of drainage material in the bottom (broken clay flower pots or pebbles), cover this with a layer of chipped bark, then use a good soil-based potting compost to fill the container. Half fill the container, set the plant in the center, then fill up with more compost.

GENERAL CARE

Having taken care to get your new climbers off to a good start by preparing the soil well and planting them correctly and in the best positions, it is sensible to look after them well for the rest of their lives. They will repay you with healthy growth and prolific flower displays.

Mulching

A modern gardening trend is to permanently mulch the ground between plants in beds, including shrubs, climbers, and hardy perennials. This will help to prevent

STAR JASMINE is widely grown for its dark, glossy foliage and heavily scented white flowers. It will soon twine around this post.

the soil from losing moisture rapidly during dry periods and also acts to prevent weeds establishing themselves. It can also give the bed a neater appearance than bare soil.

However, the ground must first be completely free from weeds, particularly perennial kinds, before laying a mulch. Perennial weeds will force their way up through organic mulching materials, so if necessary kill them off first with glyphosate weedkiller. A modern idea is to lay a geotextile sheet mulch, such as bonded fibre fleece or woven polypropylene, around plants to suppress weeds and then cover it with a more decorative, such as an organic, mulching material. Sheet mulches allow air and water to pass through, but do make it quite difficult to apply fertilizer around plants.

Organic mulches are widely used. A particular favorite is chipped bark or wood, used both fresh and composted, and available in various grades and wood to bark ratios. Garden compost and well-rotted manure are also good but not as attractive as bark. These materials are laid about 2in deep over the entire bed or border, but not hard up against the stems of plants.

An organic mulch can initially be laid in the spring and then topped up as necessary. The soil must be moist rather than dry before laying a mulch.

Watering

All newly planted climbers, like any other plants, will need regular watering if the soil starts to dry out, until they become established. Until new roots have made their way into the soil plants are very susceptible to water stress. Check new plantings every few days during dry weather in spring, summer and fall and if the soil feels dry water heavily. When plants are established they usually need watering only during long periods of dry weather, if the soil is drying out.

Apply sufficient water for it to penetrate the soil to at least 6in. This means about (4 gal per sq/yd. This equals about 1in of rain. Use a garden sprinkler or, even better, a permanent seep hose laid among the plants, ideally under a mulch.

Pots and tubs will need checking daily in spring, summer and into fall for water requirements. Remember they can dry out rapidly in warm weather, especially when plants are well rooted in them. Fill up the space, usually about 1in, between the compost surface and the rim of the pot with water to ensure the entire depth of compost is moistened.

Feeding

Established climbers benefit from an annual application of fertilizer in the spring. Use a general purpose slow-release fertilizer. A good organic one is blood, fish, and bone. The soil should be moist, but not sodden, when the fertilizer is applied. If the soil has a mulch over it you will need to scrape this away from the plants before applying fertilizer. Ideally fertilizer should be lightly forked into the soil surface to speed up its absorption.

Climbers in pots and tubs can also be fed once a year in the spring, again using a slow-release fertilizer that will keep them going throughout the growing season.

Tying in

If necessary, the young stems of climbers should be tied in to their supports as they grow. This will prevent them being whipped around by the wind or snagged by passers-by and damaged. It is always easier to train stems when they are young and supple, because as they age they become more woody and therefore difficult to position exactly where you want them. Mature stems are also more prone to snapping. Stems should always be spaced out evenly on the support and tied in with tarred or ordinary garden twine or small plastic ties.

Winter protection

Some climbers and wall shrubs are less hardy than others and could be damaged by hard frosts. If you are tempted to grow any of these and live in a cold part of the country it would be advisable to provide some form of protection during the winter, particularly for the lower parts of the stems to prevent these being killed off. A protective screen about 6ft high can be formed from two sheets of wire netting with a layer of bracken or straw sandwiched in between them. Wire them together then form the

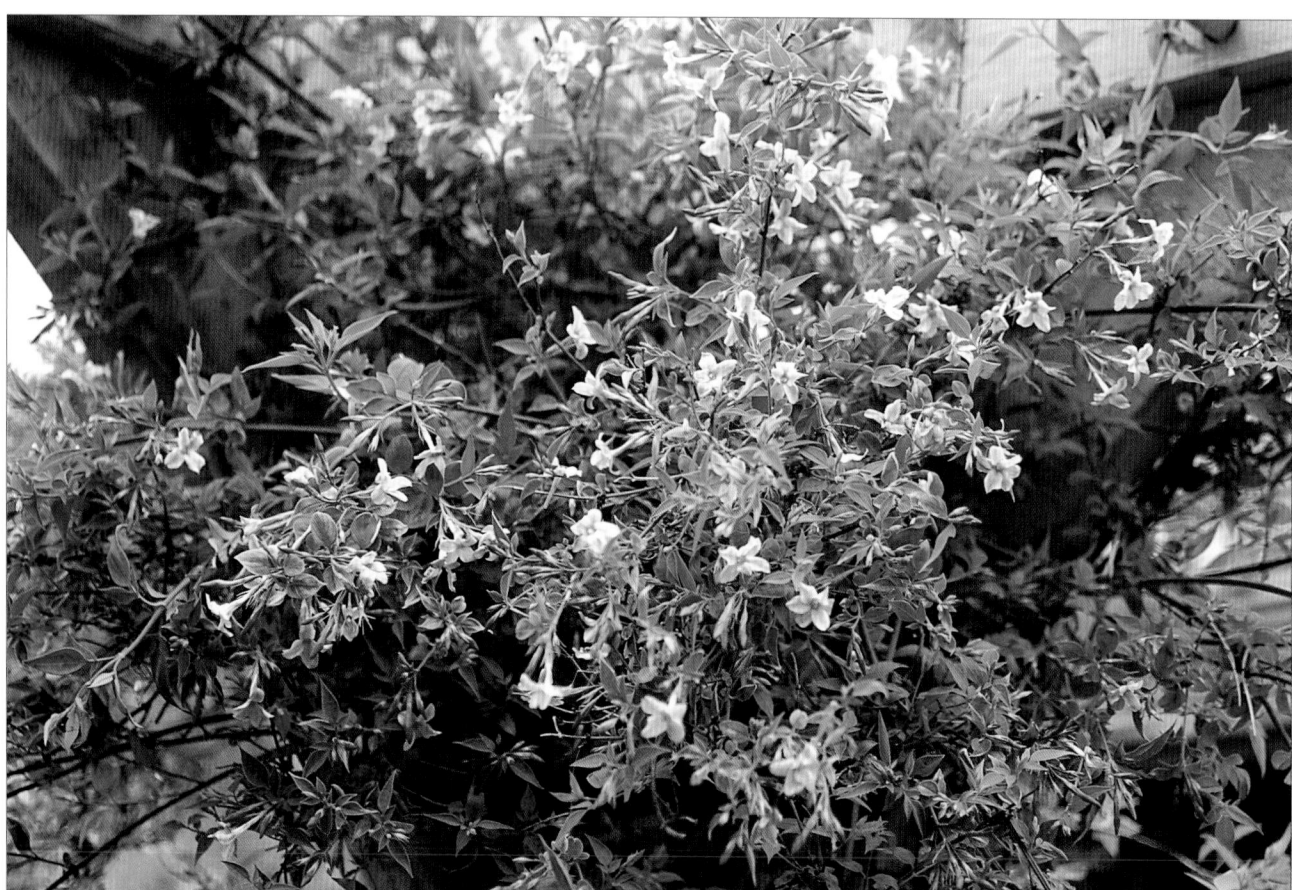

THIS PRETTY PINK jasmine, Jasminum beesianum, *has found itself a pleasant spot nestled in the corner of a large pergola. It makes a wonderfully bright highlight in what would otherwise have been a rather dull and uninteresting corner. It also provides scent to fragrance the area.*

MAKING FULL USE of each plant's habit of growth, this meeting of white foxgloves from below and white climbing roses from above makes for an upward sweeping movement.

ENJOYING PERFECT health, this clematis shines forth with an abundance of scarlet flowers, enhanced with bright yellow stamens.

"sandwich" into a half cylinder and place it in front of the climber, hard up against the wall or fence. This should provide sufficient protection from hard frosts. If the tops of the stems are killed by frost, cut them back to live tissue in the spring, and they should re-grow.

Pests and diseases
Fortunately most climbers are not troubled much by pests and diseases. Occasionally they may be attacked by aphids or greenfly but these are easily controlled by spraying with an insecticidal soap or pyrethrum. These products will also control any infestations of caterpillars. Powdery mildew may crop up occasionally, particularly on grape vines, creating a white deposit on the leaves and shoot tips. If you notice this on the plant, spray it with a fungicide such as carbendazim.

One or two climbers, however, have more than their fair share of troubles, particularly roses. These may be attacked by the diseases rose black spot (black spots on leaves), rose rust (rust-colored spots on leaves), and rose powdery mildew. Aphids (greenfly) are also very fond of roses. Wherever possible buy cultivars that are resistant to diseases, particularly black spot. If you have to resort to spraying, opt for a combined rose spray that controls pests and diseases. Very often rose diseases can be prevented by spraying regularly before they appear.

Clematis are prone to a very serious fungal disease known as clematis wilt, which causes shoots and foliage to wilt and die back. If this occurs, cut back affected stems to healthy wood. It may even be necessary to remove stems at ground level or below. If the attack is not too severe, the plant should produce new growth.

PRUNING AND TRAINING

Many climbers do not need regular pruning, only the occasional removal of old and congested growth. This is just as well as pruning these plants is a time-consuming process, much of which may have to be done from ladders or stepladders. However, some climbers do need annual pruning to keep them under control and to ensure good growth and flowering. These need to be grown where they are easily reached and not, for example, up a tall tree or very high wall. Specific pruning requirements and when to prune are given for each climber in the plant section (see pages 692–723). The various techniques for pruning climbers are discussed here.

Basic techniques
You will need a good pair of parrot-bill pruning shears for pruning thin stems, for example when you are spur pruning a wisteria. You will also need a pruning saw or heavy-duty loppers (like long-handled pruning shears) to tackle thick growth, such as when you are renovating an old climber. Shears are useful for pruning or trimming some climbers, particularly those which produce a mass of thin stems such as hederas (ivies) and loniceras (honeysuckles). It would be too time consuming to prune these stems individually with pruning shears so shears are used to considerably speed up the job.

Always use really sharp tools to ensure clean cuts that heal more rapidly than ragged cuts made with blunt implements. The latter may encourage the entry of diseases, resulting in stems dying back.

IVIES ARE among the most frequently seen climbers. Many varieties are vigorous growers and some can be invasive, smothering formal beds. Under close supervision, however, they make superb groundcover (above) as well as excellent climbers, with some species displaying variegated foliage.

Individual pruning cuts, for example when spur pruning, are made directly above a bud on the stem. Always cut to a bud that points in the direction that you want growth to occur. Never cut back to buds that face in towards the wall or other support. Do not leave a length of stem or "stub" above a bud, as it will only die back and look unsightly and may create an entry point for diseases. If stems have buds arranged alternately, make the cut slightly slanting, in the direction that the bud is pointing, to allow rainwater to run off. If there are pairs of opposite buds, as in clematis for example, make a straight cut just above them.

There is no need to seal pruning cuts, although very large wounds, such as occur when cutting out old, thick wood, could be sealed with proprietary pruning "paint" to prevent moisture and diseases from entering. If you are pruning plants that are diseased, you should regularly disinfect your tools by wiping the blades with methylated spirit or dipping them in horticultural disinfectant.

It is important to prune climbers at the right time of year. Generally deciduous climbers are pruned in the winter while they are dormant, ideally in late winter, and evergreens in the spring, when they will rapidly produce new shoots to hide the pruning cuts. Some flowering climbers are pruned in spring or summer immediately after the flower display is over.

Initial training
Before planting a new climber, remove any weak, dead or damaged stems. If it has only one or two stems and you want more, cut out the tips to encourage new shoots to be produced from lower down. Some young climbers have only a single stem when purchased, including many clematis. It is best to allow such plants to become established over a complete growing season before cutting back the stem in early spring to encourage more stems to grow. With clematis the stem can be cut back really hard, near to the soil. Other climbers can have their stem reduced by one-third to half its length.

Tie in the stems of all climbers after planting, whatever their habit of growth may be, and keep them tied in as they grow. Self-clinging climbers do not adopt this habit to start with so keep them tied in until they can support themselves.

In the first few years young climbers do not need much pruning but you should concentrate on training the stems to their supports. If the plant is neither branching enough nor making sufficient stems to cover a given area, then cut back the leading shoots to encourage the production of side shoots.

Aim to develop a basic framework of stems that covers the support well. Train the stems as evenly as possible, making sure they are well spaced out, especially on a wall or fence where they can be trained to a fan shape. Bear in mind that stems trained horizontally often flower much better than those trained vertically. The same applies to stems spiralled around the support, such as a post or pillar. Some flowering climbers, such as wisterias, can have all their stems trained horizontally, on a low fence or wall for example, which will encourage prolific flowering. Climbing and Rambler roses also respond especially well to horizontal training.

Stems are trained vertically on pillars and posts, or they can be spiralled around the support to encourage better flowering. When the stems reach the top of structures such as pergolas, arches, and arbours they are trained horizontally over the structure.

Regularly cut out any shoots that are growing in toward the wall or growing outward, or train them in a different direction. Do not allow stems to grow across each other. Any shoots that are not needed for the main framework can be cut back to at least three buds. They may then produce flowers.

Annual spur pruning

Much annual pruning of established climbers to encourage the production of flowers or fruits, and prevent congested growth, takes the form of spur pruning. It is generally deciduous climbers that produce their flowers on shoots produced in the current season, such as climbing roses, that are spur pruned. In late winter side shoots produced from the main framework are cut back to within three to six buds of their base. These spurs develop to produce flowers later in the year.

However, if the climber flowers on shoots produced in the previous year, it should be spur pruned as soon as flowering season is over, an example of this being *Jasminum nudiflorum* (Winter jasmine).

Very vigorous climbers such as wisteria are pruned twice a year, once in summer to reduce the length of the vigorous side shoots, and then in winter when they are reduced further, to within two or three buds of their base.

Trimming

Established climbers that do not need regular pruning, such as hederas (ivies), *Clematis montana* and its cultivars and *Lonicera* (honeysuckle) species and cultivars, produce a heavy mass of growth over a period of time and need cutting back with shears to reduce their bulk. They can be pruned hard back to their support in late winter or early spring, just leaving the main framework of stems which will then produce a fresh crop of new growth. To prevent ivies from becoming bulky they can, alternatively, be trimmed annually in spring.

Thinning and renovating

Established climbers that are not pruned regularly may eventually need to have their main body of growth thinned out. It is not advisable to allow plants to become too congested before pruning, as it will then involve a large amount of work and may end up spoiling the overall appearance of the plant. Thinning will help to prevent the plant from becoming too heavy and congested and allows light and air to reach the center, which is necessary for continued healthy growth.

The technique involves cutting back some of the older stems to younger shoots lower down which will then replace them. Alternatively old stems may be cut down fairly close to the ground to encourage them to produce

AN OLD WISTERIA in full bloom grows over an arch where the lovely pendulous flowers can be best appreciated.

THE FROTHY flowers of this rose are trained to poke through the trellis. Intertwined ivy is set off beautifully by the stained blue wood.

new shoots from very low down. Always cut out stems in short sections as it makes the job easier. Trying to pull out a long stem from a congested mass of growth is not only difficult but can also damage the plant. In a dense mass of growth it is not always easy trace the entire length of a stem, and you may cut out a young vigorous stem by mistake. To overcome this problem, cut back an old stem, even close to the ground, and then wait a few days for it to wilt so that it can be easily seen.

If a climber has been badly neglected and not pruned for years (perhaps in a garden that you have recently inherited from a previous owner) some drastic action may be called for to rejuvenate it. If the plant is a species that is known to respond well to severe pruning, be brave and cut it down almost to ground level—within 12–24in. This hard pruning should be carried out in the winter. In the spring the plant will produce new shoots. For plants that will not tolerate such drastic action, such as many evergreens, do the job over several years, cutting back only one or two of the oldest stems each time. During this renovation remove any dead wood and tie in young replacement stems.

Dead growth

Always cut out dead, dying, diseased and damaged stems as soon as they are noticed, regardless of time of year. Prune the shoots right back to healthy tissue. If you have the time it is always a good idea to remove dead flowers regularly, as not only does this make the plant look tidier, but also often results in more flowers following in the same season. This is certainly true of many climbing roses, for instance. It also reduces the risk of disease moving in to dead areas. However, some climbers are grown for their fruits or attractive seed heads, including various clematis species, so do not dead-head these.

Standard climbers

Some climbers can be grown as standards in large tubs to make unusual patio features. Standards are like small trees, with a single stem and a head of branches at the top. Climbers that are spur pruned, such as grape vines, *Wisteria, Solanum crispum,* and *S. jasminoides,* are ideal for training as standards, as are *Lonicera* species (honeysuckles) that do not mind regular pruning.

To create a standard, first pot and stake a single-stemmed young plant, then cut back the stem by about one-third. Lateral or side shoots are allowed to grow on this to encourage it to thicken, and are removed gradually over three years, those remaining being shortened by two-thirds in the summer. In the first winter remove the lower third of laterals, in the second winter the middle third and in the third winter the top laterals. Lightly cut back the leading shoot each year, again to help strengthen and thicken the stem. When the desired height is reached, normally about 5ft, allow laterals to develop at the top of the stem to form a head of branches.

A WONDERFUL MIXTURE of colors brings life to this classic garden scene. Note how the blooms of the climbing rose combine well with the bed in the foreground and the light brown stone of the house wall. Such roses can be dead-headed through the flowering season to prolong the display.

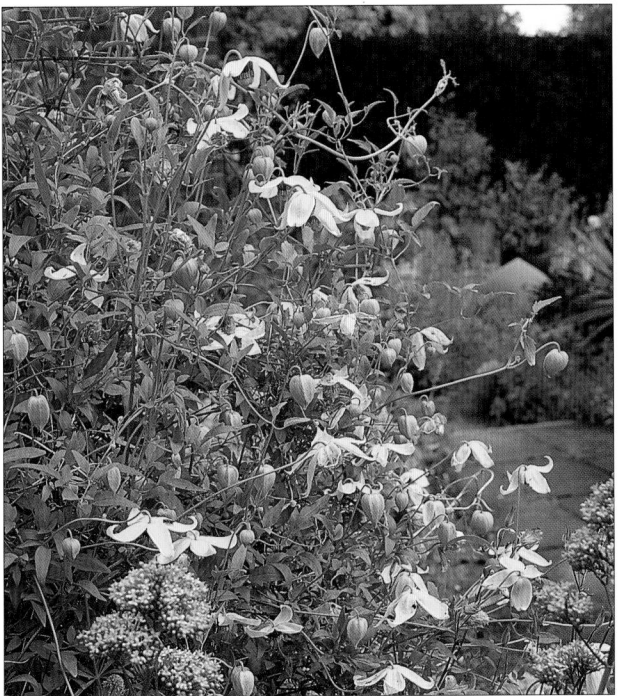

GLORIOUS YELLOW Clematis tangutica *flowers and frothy foliage merge with flowering plants in a decorative border.*

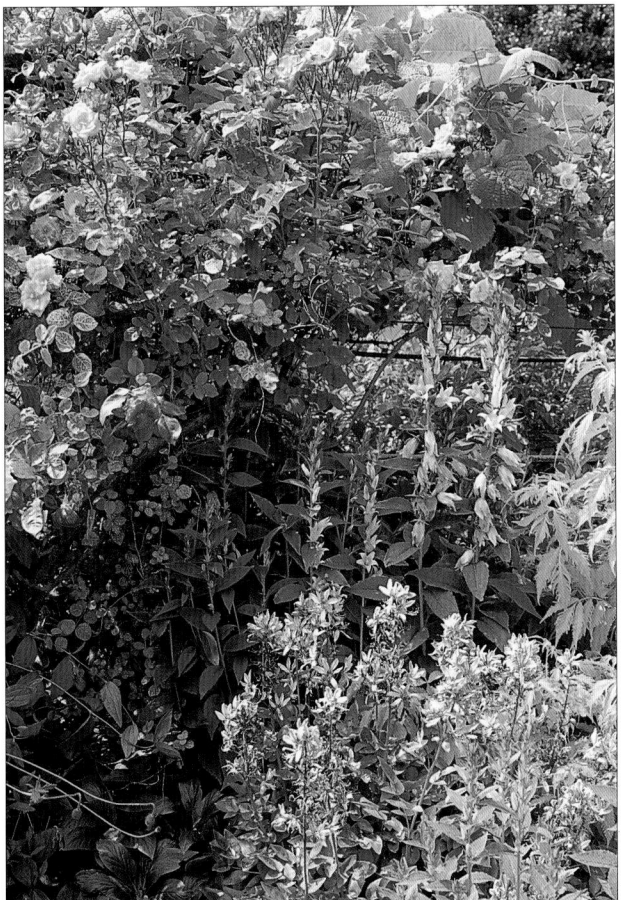

A LUSH CORNER, brimming with foliage and flowers. The climbing rose and Vitis *vine sweep in from above and complete the picture.*

The procedure for pruning the head of established standards is the same as for climbing plants, and a permanent wooden stake will be needed for support.

PROPAGATION

Propagating your own climbers is an economical way of obtaining new plants. Rooting cuttings is a widely used method, especially where many new plants are required. The same is true of raising plants from seeds, but this method is suitable only for species, not cultivars and hybrids that do not come true to type. Many climbers can be propagated by layering, which involves rooting a stem while it is still attached to the parent plant. This technique is ideal where only a few new plants are needed.

Taking cuttings
Stem cuttings are the most widely used, consisting of a portion of stem in various degrees of ripeness or maturity: one can take softwood, semi-ripe, and hardwood cuttings. You need to choose the best type of cutting for the particular plant being propagated.

Softwood cuttings taken in spring and early summer are the most challenging to root because very soft shoots are used, which wilt all too easily. They are suitable for many deciduous climbers. Select new soft shoots 1½–2in long and cut just below a node or leaf joint at the base. Remove the lower leaves (leave two or three pairs of leaves at the top) and the soft tip, and dip the base of the cutting in hormone rooting powder. Insert in pots of cuttings compost (equal parts peat and coarse sand), water in and place in a heated, humid propagating case with a temperature of 59°F. The cuttings should develop roots in a few weeks.

Semi-ripe cuttings, taken in mid- to late summer, are also prepared from current season's shoots, but are soft at the tip and hard or ripening at the base. They are suitable for a very wide range of deciduous and evergreen climbers. Cuttings vary in length from 2½–4in depending on growth. Cut the shoot immediately below a node or leaf joint at the base, remove the lower third of leaves and then

CLIMBERS FOR TRAINING AS STANDARDS

- *Actinidia kolomikta*
- *Campsis radicans* (Common trumpet creeper)
- X *Fatshedera lizei* (Tree ivy)
- *Hedera helix* (Common or English ivy)
- *Hydrangea anomala* subsp. *petiolaris* (Climbing hydrangea)
- *Lonicera japonica* (Japanese honeysuckle)
- *Lonicera periclymenum* (Common honeysuckle)
- *Schizophragma hydrangeoides*
- *Solanum crispum* (Chilean potato tree)
- *Solanum jasminoides* (Potato vine)
- *Vitis vinifera* (Grape vine)
- *Wisteria floribunda* (Japanese wisteria)
- *Wisteria sinensis* (Chinese wisteria)

dip the base of the cutting in hormone rooting powder. Insert the cuttings in pots of cuttings compost, water in and place in a cold frame to root, or in a propagating case if the subject needs heat to root. A humid atmosphere is required for rooting. Cuttings should be rooted by the following growing season.

Hardwood cuttings are prepared from late fall to mid-winter from current-season's shoots that are fully ripe or hard. They are suitable for various deciduous climbers such as *Vitis* (Grape vines) and *Fallopia baldschuanica*. Select leafless stems and cut them into lengths of 8in with pruning shears, below a bud at the base and above a bud at the top. Dip in hormone rooting powder, insert in deep pots of cuttings compost and place in a cold frame. Hardwood cuttings are slow rooting, often producing leaves in spring before they have rooted. Allow a year before lifting and planting out. Rooting can be speeded up by placing cuttings in a heated propagating case, as is usually practiced with vines.

Leaf-bud cuttings are modified versions of stem cuttings and are useful for several deciduous and evergreen climbers. They can be softwood or semi-ripe. Climbers commonly propagated from leaf-bud cuttings include clematis (softwood or semi-ripe) and ivies (semi-ripe). You get more cuttings from a length stem than with conventional stem cuttings. Each cutting consists of a 1in

length of stem, cut between nodes at the base but just above a node at the top, with a leaf or pair of leaves at the top containing a growth bud in the leaf axil. Otherwise treat leaf-bud cuttings as for softwood or semi-ripe stem cuttings.

Layering
Layering involves encouraging a stem to root while still attached to the plant. It is a suitable and easy method of propagating many deciduous and evergreen climbers such as clematis, wisterias, and akebias. Some climbers may self-layer if the stem comes into contact with the soil, such as ivies used as ground cover. Layering is carried out in the spring and stems can take up to a year to root.

Serpentine layering is used for climbers, rooting the stem in a number of places along its length. Use one of the previous year's stems. You need to wound the underside of the stem where you want it to root, by making a slanting cut about 1in long between nodes to form a tongue. Keep this cut open with a matchstick and dust it with hormone rooting powder. Using a V-shaped wire pin, peg down the stem where wounded into an 3in deep depression in the ground and cover with soil. The stem is "snaked" in and out of the soil, ensuring that at least one bud stays above soil between the wounded areas. An alternative technique is to wound through nodes or

BOSTON IVY is being trained against this brick wall, which it will eventually cover. In the meantime it still looks decorative.

A HEAVY SWATHE of star jasmine hangs across the top of this gate and down beside the steps. In full bloom the perfume is all-pervading.

A TRADITIONAL "English garden" combination of roses, delphiniums, and wisteria creates a delightful effect in early summer. Wisteria, a twining climber, is easily trained to any shape desired, on both high and low supports.

leaf joints, or just behind them, and pin the stem where wounded to the soil surface. Keep layers moist at all times. Lift the new plant when it has rooted and sever from parent plant.

Growing from seeds
Seeds of some climbers need a cold period in winter before they will germinate in the spring, examples being members of the rose family such as climbing roses and cotoneaster. Fleshy fruits and berries of other climbers generally need the same treatment. Sow these as soon as collected in late summer or fall and stand the pots in a cold place to alternately freeze and thaw throughout winter, a technique known as stratification.

Seeds of other climbers can be sown in spring. Seeds with very hard coats, such as those of the pea family, need to have their coats scarified to allow moisture to penetrate before they will germinate. Rub the seeds between two sheets of sandpaper to scratch the surface, or pour boiling water over them and let them soak for 24 hours.

Sow seeds in pots of soil-based seed compost and for spring sowings cover very lightly with compost, followed by a ½in layer of fine-grade vermiculite (a natural mineral). Seeds to be stratified over winter are also lightly covered with compost followed by a ¼in layer of grit. Spring sowings are best germinated in a heated propagating case, a temperature of 59–68°F being suitable for most subjects.

CONTRASTING COLORS are used here to great effect. Using Clematis species and a cultivar with different foliage textures and flower colors makes a lively display—rather like a vertical border.

ABUTILON MEGAPOTAMICUM
Flowering maple

IN THE RIGHT PLACE this graceful evergreen wall shrub is a fast grower, but it needs a good soil and plenty of sunshine and shelter.

A CONTINUOUS SUPPLY of red and yellow bell-like flowers is produced by this exotic climber throughout summer and into the fall.

FEATURES

Wall shrub

A native of Brazil, this thin-stemmed evergreen or semi-evergreen shrub is fairly hardy. However, it prefers to be grown and trained against a warm sheltered wall or fence for protection from severe weather. The bright green leaves are oval or spear-shaped but the plant is grown primarily for its exotic-looking, symmetrical red and yellow bell-shaped flowers, which are produced continuously throughout summer and into fall on arching shoots. Height and spread 6ft. This is an ideal plant for a sheltered courtyard garden or other enclosed area. The stems are trained out evenly on the support to form a permanent woody framework.

ABUTILON AT A GLANCE

This wall shrub creates an exotic effect with its masses of colorful bell-shaped flowers. Hardy to 23°F (zone 9).

Jan	/	Recommended Varieties
Feb	/	*Abutilon megapotamicum*
Mar	planting ✍	"Variegatum" has yellow and
Apr	planting ✍	green variegated foliage.
May	/	
Jun	flowering ✿	
July	flowering ✿	
Aug	flowering ✿	
Sep	flowering ✿	
Oct	flowering ✿	
Nov	/	
Dec	/	

CONDITIONS

Aspect It should be grown in full sun against a warm sheltered wall or fence.

Site This shrub grows best in reasonably fertile, well-drained soil.

GROWING METHOD

Propagation Sow seeds in the spring and germinate at 59–64°F. Take softwood cuttings in the spring.

Watering Apply water only if the soil starts to dry out in summer.

Feeding Feed annually in the spring with a slow-release fertilizer such as the organic blood, fish, and bone.

Problems Generally trouble free out of doors.

FLOWERING/FOLIAGE

Flowers The flowers are produced continuously in summer and fall.

Foliage This species is evergreen or semi-evergreen but the leaves are not particularly attractive, except in the cultivar "Variegatum," which has variegated foliage.

PRUNING

Requirements This shrub needs annual pruning to encourage flowering and to prevent congested growth. Cut back old flowered shoots to within two or three buds of the main stems in early spring.

AKEBIA QUINATA
Chocolate vine

THE CHOCOLATE VINE is not over-vigorous but this particular vine is producing a great show of flowers. It is hard to describe their color but it is a dark pinkish or purplish brown, and they have an unusual chocolate smell. Leaves consist of five deep green leaflets.

FEATURES

Twiner

The fascinating and unusual purple-brown flowers of the Chocolate vine, a native of China, Japan and Korea, have a light but distinctive smell of chocolate. The foliage is also decorative, and therefore this climber looks good even when not in flower. It is a long-lived twining semi-evergreen climber capable of growing up to 30ft, although it may be less in some gardens. Growth is fairly vigorous once the plant is established but it is rather open in habit and never ends up looking heavy. This climber is seen to best advantage when grown over a trellis screen, pergola or arch, and is also a suitable subject for growing into a large tree.

AKEBIA QUINATA AT A GLANCE

One of the earliest climbers to flower, with unusual chocolate-scented blooms. Hardy to 5°F (zone 7).

Jan	/	Companion Plants
Feb	planting 🖐	Strong-growing summer-
Mar	flowering ❀	flowering clematis or
Apr	flowering ❀	climbing roses will take over
May	flowering ❀	from the spring display.
Jun	/	
July	/	
Aug	/	
Sep	/	
Oct	/	
Nov	/	
Dec	/	

CONDITIONS

Aspect   Akebia will grow equally well in full sun or partial shade.

Site   The soil must be well-drained, moisture-retentive, and reasonably fertile.

GROWING METHOD

Propagation   Sow seeds in fall and place in a cold frame. Take semi-ripe cuttings in summer. Carry out serpentine layering in the spring.

Watering   Make sure the soil does not dry in the summer.

Feeding   This is necessary only once a year in spring. Apply a slow-release organic fertilizer such as blood, fish, and bone.

Problems   Not troubled by pests or diseases.

FLOWERING/FOLIAGE

Flowers   The scented flowers are produced throughout spring and followed by long fleshy fruits. Warm conditions throughout spring and summer are necessary for fruit to be produced.

Foliage   The foliage consists of five deep green leaflets. Leaves may become flushed with an attractive purple color in the winter.

PRUNING

Requirements   If necessary trim the plant after flowering to keep it within bounds. It may eventually need some of the oldest stems thinned out, or renovation pruning.

ARISTOLOCHIA
Dutchman's pipe

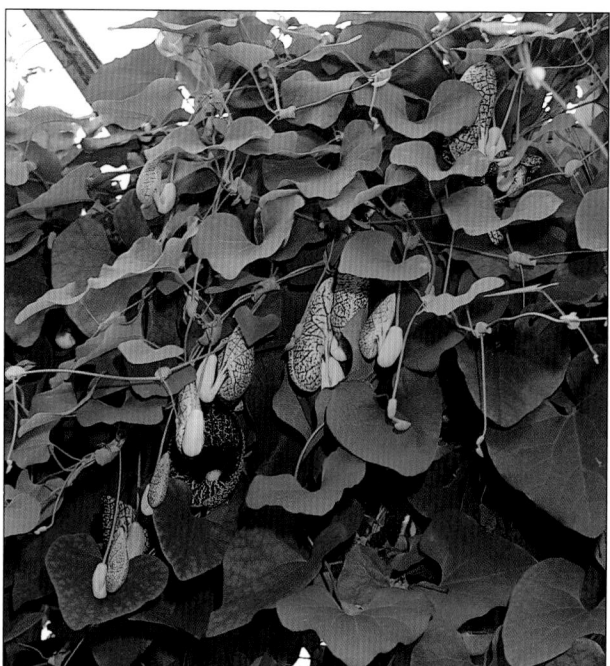

THE VIGOROUS Aristolochia littoralis *swathes itself effectively from the roof support of a conservatory, creating an exotic scene.*

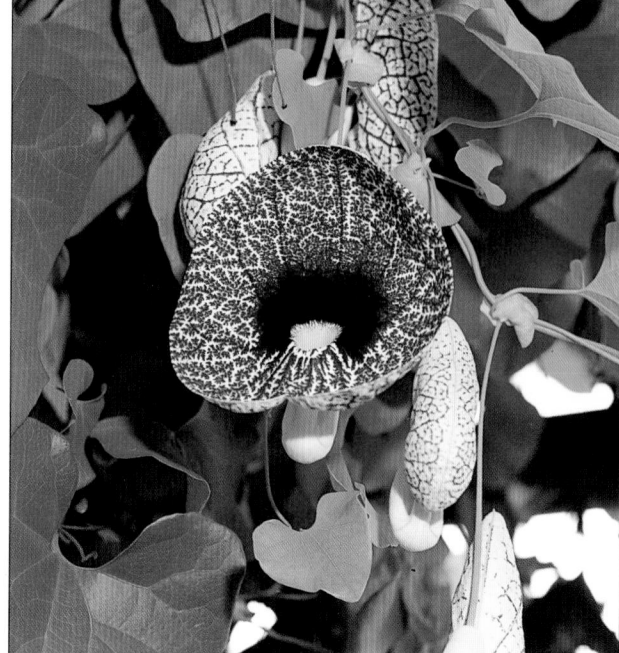

ARISTOLOCHIA FLOWERS are strangely beautiful and intriguing objects. They might need to be encouraged from under the dense foliage.

FEATURES

Twiner

Aristolochia macrophylla is a deciduous climber from the south-east USA. It has very unusual pipe- or siphon-shaped flowers in summer. These are green, strikingly marked with brown, purple and yellow. The foliage is also very attractive so the plant looks good all through spring and summer. It is a strong grower and in good conditions can reach a height of 30ft, but in some gardens it may be considerably less. Another aristolochia is *A. littoralis*, which can only be grown in a warm greenhouse or conservatory. You will need plenty of space to grow Dutchman's pipe, such as a high wall or fence.

ARISTOLOCHIA AT A GLANCE

An exotic-looking climber with bizarre flowers and attractive heart-shaped leaves. Hardy to 23°F (zone 9).

Month		
Jan	/	
Feb	/	
Mar	/	
Apr	planting ✐	**Companion Plants**
May	planting ✐	It needs an equally vigorous companion. For a long period of interest, try it with wisteria, which flowers before aristolochia, in spring.
Jun	flowering ❀	
July	flowering ❀	
Aug	flowering ❀	
Sep	/	
Oct	/	
Nov	/	
Dec	/	

CONDITIONS

Aspect   This climber will grow well in full sun or partial shade.

Site   The soil should be well-drained and reasonably rich. Even a dryish soil is suitable.

GROWING METHOD

Propagation   Sow seeds in spring and germinate at 61°F. Take softwood cuttings in summer.

Watering   Only apply water if the soil is drying out in the summer. It likes to be on the dry side throughout the winter.

Feeding   Do not over-feed, as this is a naturally vigorous climber. A slow-release organic fertilizer applied each spring will be sufficient.

Problems   Not usually troubled by pests or diseases.

FLOWERING/FOLIAGE

Flowers   Grown mainly for its flowers but unfortunately they are inclined to be obscured from view by the plant's lush foliage.

Foliage   The large, heart shaped, deep green leaves are very attractive.

PRUNING

Requirements   This climber can either be spur pruned in early spring, or simply trimmed in spring to keep it within bounds, but eventually it will need thinning or renovation pruning.

BERBERIDOPSIS CORALLINA
Coral vine

THE INTENSE SCARLET of these Berberidopsis corallina *flowers makes up for their small size, and they blaze amid the rich foliage.*

THE DEEP GREEN foliage of B. corallina *makes a marvelous background for the vibrant flowers.*

FEATURES

Twiner

A spectacular evergreen climber from Chile, valued for its exotic-looking pendulous red flowers, and ideal for a shady wall or fence. It can be especially recommended for a shady courtyard that is well protected from cold winds, but it also looks at home in a woodland garden, with suitable perennials and shrubs, as it grows in woodland in the wild. The Coral vine can also be grown through large shrubs or up mature trees. It can reach a height of up to 15ft. A severe winter may kill back the stems but it may still go on to produce new shoots from the base in the spring.

CONDITIONS

Aspect   The Coral vine needs a position in shade or partial shade, with shelter from cold winds. The soil must be acid or neutral, contain plenty of humus, and be able to retain moisture yet well drained. A deep organic mulch applied in fall will protect the roots from severe frosts. Coral vine grows best on wire or trellis but will also scramble over fences, tree stumps, and other objects.

Site

GROWING METHOD

Propagation Sow seeds in spring and germinate in a cold frame. Carry out serpentine layering in spring. Take semi-ripe cuttings toward the end of summer.
Watering   Do not allow the plant to dry out at any time. Keep the soil steadily moist.
Feeding   Once a year in spring, using a slow-release fertilizer, but avoid alkaline types.
Problems   Neither pests nor diseases are a problem.

FLOWERING/FOLIAGE

Flowers   Long-stalked pendulous flowers are carried in rows on the shoots.
Foliage   Elliptical deep green leaves have spiny edges and gray-green undersides.

PRUNING

Requirements Minimal pruning is needed for this climber. It is best not to prune unless it is considered essential. The Coral vine certainly does not like hard cutting back. Spring is the best time for pruning, removing dead growth and any very weak stems. Eventually, as the plant matures, some judicious thinning may be necessary.

BERBERIDOPSIS AT A GLANCE

Pendulous red flowers and deep green spiny foliage. Hardy to temperatures of 23°F (zone 9).

Jan	/	Companion Plants
Feb	/	Looks good with x *Fatshedera*
Mar	/	*lizei*, which will also take
Apr	planting ✾	shade. Also woodland-garden
May	planting ✾	shrubs and perennials,
Jun	flowering ✲	including ferns.
July	flowering ✲	
Aug	flowering ✲	
Sep	flowering ✲	
Oct	/	
Nov	/	
Dec	/	

CHAENOMELES SPECIOSA
Flowering quince

THERE IS A DEEP GLOSSY SHEEN to the oval leaves, which usually emerge after the flowers have bloomed on the bare branches.

THIS ADAPTABLE PLANT makes a good hedge, does well in a flower border and can be trained to grow up a sunny wall.

FEATURES

Wall shrub

This deciduous spiny shrub, a native of China, is very amenable to training flat against a wall or fence. The spines and thick growth of this plant make it a practical barrier shrub—and it can also be trained as a hedge. It flowers only from young shoots, so build up a system of permanent stems, tying them in to their support, and the flowers will be produced on the previous year's side shoots. The rich red blooms appear in spring, often very early in the season. Although of vigorous habit, growing up to 8ft high with a spread of 15ft, it is ideally suited to growing on a wall of the house, or on a fence of normal height, as it can be kept smaller if desired by pruning.

CHAENOMELES AT A GLANCE

A spiny shrub with cup-shaped flowers, often on bare stems, in the spring. Hardy to 5°F (zone 7).

		Recommended Varieties
Jan	/	"Geisha Girl," double, deep
Feb	planting 🌱	apricot
Mar	planting 🌱	"Moerloosei," white and pink
Apr	flowering ✿	"Nivalis," white
May	flowering ✿	"Simonii," double, deep red
Jun	/	
July	/	
Aug	/	
Sep	/	
Oct	/	
Nov	/	
Dec	/	

CONDITIONS

Aspect	The Flowering quince should be grown in full sun or partial shade. However, flowering is most prolific in sun.
Site	This shrub will thrive in any well-drained soil that is reasonably fertile.

GROWING METHOD

Propagation	Sow seeds in fall and stratify them over winter. Take semi-ripe cuttings in summer.
Watering	Watering is only needed if the soil starts to dry out excessively in the summer.
Feeding	In the spring apply a slow-release organic fertilizer such as blood, fish and bone.
Problems	The plant may be attacked by pests including aphids and scale insects.

FLOWERING/FOLIAGE

Flowers	Bowl-shaped flowers, which are usually red with yellow anthers, are produced in the spring. They are followed by fragrant, apple-shaped, greenish yellow edible fruits, which can be used to make jelly.
Foliage	The oval leaves are shiny and deep green.

PRUNING

Requirements	Build up a permanent framework of stems and then spur prune annually after flowering—cut back the old flowered shoots to within two to four buds of the framework.

CLEMATIS
Clematis species and cultivars

THE FIRST FLOWER *of this* C. montana *cultivar is fully open and the plump buds promise more in the near future.*

C. armandii *"Apple Blossom" is a vigorous spring-flowering evergreen that needs to be grown in a warm, sheltered position.*

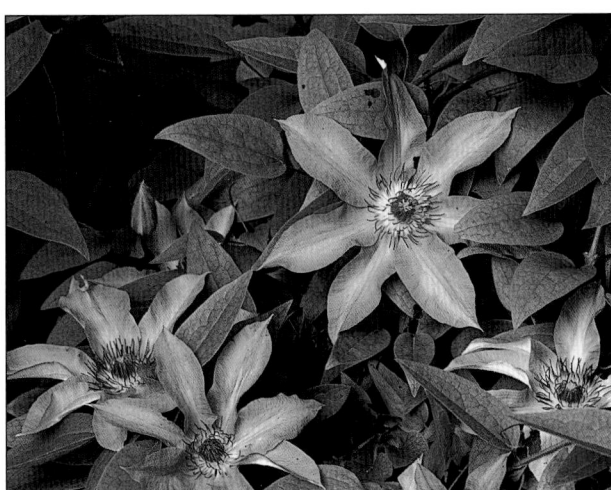

FLOWERS *of the Jackmanii hybrids are by far the largest of all cultivated clematis. These large lavender-blue ones are quite lovely.*

FEATURES

Twiner

There are at least 200 species, deciduous and evergreen, and countless cultivars and hybrids of clematis, the most popular of all climbers. They are native mostly to the northern hemisphere. *Clematis vitalba* (Traveller's joy, Old man's beard), sprawls over hedgerows and produces greeny white flowers in summer followed by silky seed heads. This is not generally grown in gardens as it is not sufficiently decorative. The many other species, cultivars and hybrids are more preferable.

The deciduous spring-flowering *C. montana* and its cultivars are especially popular, with flowers in white or in shades of pink. *C. armandii* and its cultivar "Apple Blossom" are vigorous spring-flowering evergreens, with white and pink-tinged flowers respectively.

The large-flowered hybrids are the most popular of all, flowering in the summer. They have some of the most spectacular flowers imaginable. All are deciduous and of modest growth. They come in a range of colors, including white, blue, purple, mauve, and red shades, and some are bicolored. Perhaps the best known is "Jackmanii" with deep purple flowers.

Tall clematis such as *C. montana* are often allowed to climb into mature trees where their flowers tumble out over the canopy. Less-vigorous clematis, such as the large-flowered hybrids, are excellent for walls, fences, pergolas, arches, arbors, obelisks, and tubs. Thin stemmed, light and airy clematis, such as the Viticella Group, are ideal for growing over large shrubs or for use as ground cover. They are also good for containers.

CONDITIONS

Aspect   Clematis like to have their top growth in full sun but their roots in the shade. Roots can be shaded with plantings of groundcover plants or with other low-growing subjects, with paving slabs or with even a deep mulch of organic matter.

Site   Clematis grow well in any well-drained, reasonably rich soil containing plenty of humus. They are particularly suitable for chalky soils. Keep the plants permanently mulched with organic matter.

GROWING METHOD

Propagation Sow seeds as soon as collected in the fall and stratify them over winter. They should then go on to germinate in the spring. Take softwood or semi-ripe leaf-bud cuttings in spring or summer. Carry out serpentine layering in the spring.

THIS TRANQUIL RURAL VIEW is beautifully framed by a fence covered with a rambling Clematis montana. *The delicate tracery of the stems and the scattering of white flowers would be just as attractive in a city garden.*

Watering	Clematis should not be allowed to suffer from lack of moisture, so water plants well during rainless periods if the soil starts to dry out.
Feeding	An annual application of slow-release organic fertilizer, such as blood, fish, and bone, should be applied in the spring.
Problems	Clematis wilt is the biggest problem. To help overcome this disease, plant clematis deeply, covering the top of the rootball with 3in of soil. This also ensures that new stems grow from below ground. Aphids may infest plants in the summer.

FLOWERING/FOLIAGE

Flowers	Clematis flower mainly in the spring, summer and fall, according to type. A few species bloom in the winter. Flowers come in all colors and they may be flat, bell-shaped, or cup-shaped.
Foliage	This may be deciduous or evergreen, according to the individual species. Generally the leaves have twining stalks.

PRUNING

Requirements Pruning varies according to the group that clematis are in. Group 1 contains clematis that flower early in the year on previous year's shoots, including *C. montana* and cultivars, *C. alpina*, *C. cirrhosa* var. *balearica*, *C. macropetala*, and *C. armandii*. The only pruning these plants need is thinning when they become congested. This is done after flowering. If renovation pruning is needed, cut down the complete plant to within 12in of the ground after flowering.

Group 2 contains large-flowered hybrids that produce a flush of flowers in early summer on last-year's shoots, and then another flush of blooms in late summer and fall on current year's shoots. These are pruned in late winter or early spring. Established plants can get by with very little pruning. The simplest technique is to cut them to within about 12in of the ground, every three to four years. After pruning you will lose the early summer flowers but they will bloom in late summer.

Group 3 contains clematis that flower in late summer and early fall on current season's shoots. This growth comes from the base of the plant. Included in this group are *C. viticella* and its cultivars and hybrids, *C. orientalis*, and "Jackmanii." Plants are pruned annually in late winter or early spring down to within 12in of the ground.

CLEMATIS AT A GLANCE		
Very variable climbers, suitable for many situations. Flat, bell-shaped or cup-shaped flowers. Most are hardy to 5°F (zone 7).		
Jan	/	Recommended Varieties
Feb	planting	Other clematis worth
Mar	planting	growing:
Apr	flowering	*C. alpina*, blue flowers,
May	flowering	spring
Jun	flowering	*C. cirrhosa* var. *balearica*,
July	flowering	cream, winter/spring
Aug	flowering	*C. macropetala*, blue, spring
Sep	flowering	*C. orientalis*, yellow, summer
Oct	flowering	*C. tangutica*, yellow,
Nov	/	summer/fall
Dec	/	

CLIANTHUS PUNICEUS
Glory pea

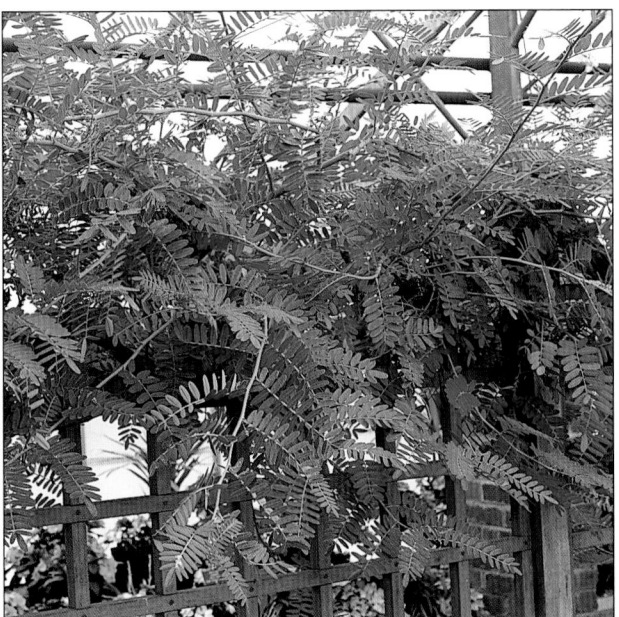

IN AREAS SUBJECT to hard frosts in winter, grow Clianthus puniceus *in a cool conservatory or greenhouse.*

AS WELL AS its eyecatching red blooms in spring, C. puniceus *is grown for the all-year interest of its attractive pinnate leaves.*

FEATURES

Scrambler

This flamboyant semi-evergreen or evergreen climber will provide a touch of the southern hemisphere, as it is a native of the north island of New Zealand. Flowering in spring and early summer, it produces clusters of unusual, scarlet, claw-like flowers, another of its popular names being Lobster claw. These flowers are the plant's principal attraction. It will grow up to 12ft tall and needs to be grown against a warm sheltered wall. When grown unsupported it tends to spread horizontally. The Glory pea is an ideal subject for a small courtyard or other enclosed area. In parts of the country that are subject to hard frosts, it would be better to grow this climber in a frost-free conservatory or glasshouse.

CLIANTHUS AT A GLANCE

Scarlet claw-like flowers and handsome pinnate foliage. Hardy to temperatures of 23°F (zone 9).

Jan	/	Recommended Varieties
Feb	/	"Albus," white flowers
Mar	/	"Roseus," deep rose-pink
Apr	planting ✍	flowers
May	flowering ✿	
Jun	flowering ✿	
July	/	
Aug	/	
Sep	/	
Oct	/	
Nov	/	
Dec	/	

CONDITIONS

Aspect   It must have a position in full sun and be well sheltered from cold winds.

Site   The soil should be very well drained. This climber will thrive in quite poor soils. A deep permanent mulch of organic matter is recommended to protect roots from frost.

GROWING METHOD

Propagation   Take softwood or semi-ripe cuttings in spring or summer. Sow seeds in spring, first soaking them in water or abrading them (see pages 690–691). Germinate at 64°F.

Watering   Fairly drought tolerant but apply water if the soil dries out excessively in the summer.

Feeding   Give an annual spring application of a general purpose slow-release organic fertilizer, such as blood, fish, and bone.

Problems   There are no problems from pests or diseases.

FLOWERING/FOLIAGE

Flowers   Valued for its early, exotic-looking flowers.

Foliage   The shiny pinnate leaves are attractive.

PRUNING

Requirements   Very little needed. This climber will not survive severe pruning. Cut out any weak or dead shoots as necessary. Stems may be killed back by hard frosts, but the plant may produce new shoots from the base in spring. Cut back dead growth to live tissue.

DECUMARIA BARBARA
Decumaria

APPEARING IN EARLY summer, the delightful puffs of cream-colored sweetly-scented flowers are the main attraction of Decumaria barbara. *This plants is a sturdy climber and can easily scale and cover large walls and substantial trees.*

FEATURES

Self-clinging climber

This deciduous climber from the south-east USA has stems that produce aerial roots, so eventually it is self-supporting. Decumaria is grown for its flat heads of fragrant, cream flowers that are produced in early summer. Attaining a height of 30ft, it is ideal for growing up a tall mature tree or high wall. Be wary about growing this climber on a house wall, as it will be impossible to remove it for house maintenance without damaging the stems. There is also the risk of damaging the wall itself. This plant makes good and unusual groundcover in a woodland garden or shrub border. It will also enjoy the partial or dappled shade of these situations.

DECUMARIA AT A GLANCE

A self-clinging climber with flat heads of cream flowers and handsome glossy foliage. Hardy to 23°F (zone 9).

Jan	/	Companion Plants
Feb	/	Looks good with climbing
Mar	planting 🖉	roses, which should flower at
Apr	planting 🖉	the same time.
May	/	
Jun	flowering ✽	
July	/	
Aug	/	
Sep	/	
Oct	/	
Nov	/	
Dec	/	

CONDITIONS

Aspect Grows well in full sun or partial shade. Provide shelter from cold drying winds as this climber is not fully hardy and may therefore be damaged in an exposed situation.

Site Any well-drained fertile soil will be suitable for this climber.

GROWING METHOD

Propagation Take semi-ripe cuttings in late summer. When grown as ground cover it will self-layer, so simply remove rooted portions of stem, complete with buds or young shoots, if new plants are required.

Watering If the soil starts to dry out in summer water the plant well. It dislikes drying out.

Feeding An annual spring application of slow-release fertilizer, such as the organic blood, fish, and bone, will be sufficient.

Problems Not troubled by pests or diseases.

FLOWERING/FOLIAGE

Flowers The cream flowers, which are produced in early summer, smell of honey.

Foliage The large deep green leaves are attractive and make a good background for the flowers.

PRUNING

Requirements No regular pruning needed. If necessary trim after flowering to keep within allotted space.

FALLOPIA BALDSCHUANICA
Russian vine

A WAVE OF the exceptionally vigorous Fallopia baldschuanica, *vibrant with white flowers, overcomes a garden wall and door.*

THE LIVELY TEXTURE of F. baldschuanica *is largely created by its stems of white flowers as they twist to point up toward the sky.*

FEATURES

Twiner

The other popular name for this deciduous climber, Mile-a-minute plant, sums up its habit of growth. It is extremely vigorous, even rampant, and grows up to 40ft tall. Grow this plant only if you have plenty of room for it to take off, otherwise you will be forever cutting it back to keep it in check. It is best suited to informal or wild gardens where it can be left to "run free." Its rampant nature also makes it ideal for filling a space or even hiding an unsightly structure in the garden. The Russian vine is originally a native of eastern Europe and Iran. From late summer and into fall it is covered in a froth of small white, pink-flushed flowers that hang in decorative swags. It is ideal for quickly covering large outbuildings, or for growing up very high walls or large mature trees.

FALLOPIA AT A GLANCE

One of the fastest-growing climbers available, it has luxuriant growth and a froth of white flowers. Hardy to 5°F (zone7).

Jan	/	**Companion Plants**
Feb	planting 🌿	As it is such a large vigorous
Mar	planting 🌿	plant, this climber is best
Apr	planting 🌿	grown alone.
May	/	
Jun	/	
July	/	
Aug	flowering ✿	
Sep	flowering ✿	
Oct	flowering ✿	
Nov	/	
Dec	/	

CONDITIONS

Aspect Suitable for full sun or partial shade.
Site Any soil, even poor conditions. However, the soil should be moisture retentive yet well drained.

GROWING METHOD

Propagation Take softwood or semi-ripe cuttings in spring and summer, or hardwood cuttings in late fall or winter. Hardwood cuttings are easier to root than other types and should be rooted in a frost-free glasshouse.
Watering If the soil starts to dry out excessively in summer, water heavily.
Feeding It does not need much encouragement to grow, but can be given a slow-release organic fertilizer in spring.
Problems Not usually troubled by pests or diseases.

FLOWERING/FOLIAGE

Flowers The plant flowers very freely and looks its best when covered in a froth of white blossom.
Foliage The deep green leaves are heart shaped.

PRUNING

Requirements It can be allowed to grow without pruning as it forms a tangled mass of stems. If you need to restrict growth, prune back stems by one-third, using shears. If the plant needs renovating, cut it down to within 3ft of the ground. This will result in vigorous new growth. The time to prune is late winter or early spring.

X FATSHEDERA LIZEI
Tree ivy

THE STUNNING LEAVES *of* X Fatshedera lizei *are evergreen, and very deply lobed. Being deep green and very shiny they create a luxuriant effect in any garden. The Tree ivy can be grown as a climber, as groundcover, or even as a standard in a tub.*

FEATURES

Scrambler

An evergreen shrub of spreading habit. It is not a true climber but can be trained against a wall, on an obelisk, or as a standard in a tub. The Tree ivy also makes good ground cover. It is a hybrid of *Fatsia* and *Hedera* (ivy) that originated under cultivation, and has the characteristics of both parents. The Tree ivy is valued for its lush foliage that looks good all the year round. Highly adaptable, it is a very good choice for shady town and city gardens, and takes atmospheric pollution in its stride. The plant is of modest stature, growing to a height of 4–6ft, or more when trained to a support.

X FATSHEDERA LIZEI AT A GLANCE

An ivy-like shrub with lustrous dark green foliage. Hardy to 23°F (zone 9).

Jan	foliage	Recommended Varieties
Feb	foliage	"Annemieke," yellow
Mar	foliage	variegated leaves
Apr	planting	"Variegata," white-edged
May	planting	leaves
Jun	foliage	These two are half-hardy and
July	foliage	should be grown in pots
Aug	foliage	under glass.
Sep	flowering	
Oct	flowering	
Nov	foliage	
Dec	foliage	

CONDITIONS

Aspect Good for partial shade but also grows well in a sunny spot.

Site Thrives in any soil. The ideal soil is reasonably rich, moisture-retentive yet well-drained.

GROWING METHOD

Propagation Take semi-ripe leaf-bud cuttings in summer. Stems can also be layered.

Watering Keep the soil moist in summer during dry spells as the plant dislikes drying out.

Feeding Give an annual spring application of slow-release organic fertilizer such as blood, fish, and bone.

Problems Generally free from pests and diseases.

FLOWERING/FOLIAGE

Flowers Heads of tiny green-white flowers are produced in fall. These are not the most showy of flowers and the plant is grown primarily for its decorative foliage.

Foliage The evergreen deeply lobed leaves are deep green and shiny, creating a luxuriant effect.

PRUNING

Requirements Does not need pruning, only the removal or cutting back of any shoots that spoil the overall shape. Pruning should be carried out in late winter or early spring.

FREMONTODENDRON
Flannel bush

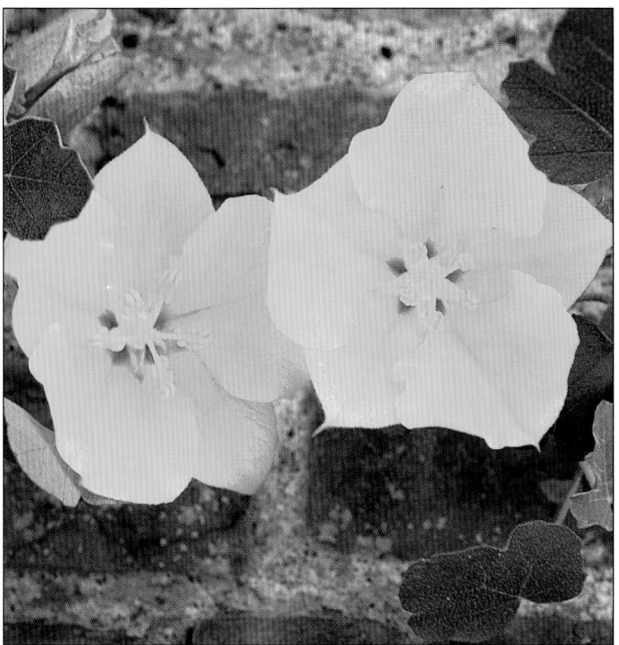

A GENEROUS DISPLAY OF yellow blooms cover this plant for months at a time, but flowering may be affected if the soil is too rich.

THE DARK GREEN leaves of Fremontodendron "California Glory" provide the perfect canvas for its vibrant yellow blooms.

FEATURES

Wall shrub

This large evergreen shrub, the full name of which is *Fremontodendron californicum*, is spectacular when laden with its large bowl-shaped bright yellow flowers in summer and fall. It grows up to 20ft tall and so needs a reasonable amount of headroom. It is a native of the USA, especially California.
Unfortunately the Flannel bush can be quite a short-lived plant so it is best to propagate it to ensure you have some young replacement plants should it suddenly expire. It is a great choice for a house or other high wall and relishes a sheltered courtyard garden or other secluded area. It looks good growing with a blue-flowered ceanothus.

FREMONTODENDRON AT A GLANCE

A large vigorous shrub with shallow bowl-shaped yellow flowers over a very long period. Hardy to 23°F (zone 9).

Jan	/	Recommended Varieties
Feb	/	*Fremontodendron* "California
Mar	/	Glory," deep yellow flowers.
Apr	planting ✿	
May	planting ✿	
Jun	flowering ❀	
July	flowering ❀	
Aug	flowering ❀	
Sep	flowering ❀	
Oct	flowering ❀	
Nov	/	
Dec	/	

CONDITIONS

Aspect Grow against a warm sunny wall. Needs to be well sheltered from wind.

Site Can be grown in a wide range of well-drained soils, from dry to moist, but prefers alkaline or neutral conditions. Ideally suited to poor soils.

GROWING METHOD

Propagation Sow seeds in spring and germinate at 59–68°F. Take semi-ripe cuttings in late summer and root in a heated propagating case. Hardwood cuttings in late fall or winter are easier. Root them in a cool glasshouse.

Watering This plant takes quite dry conditions, so it is not necessary to water unless the soil becomes excessively dry.

Feeding Give an annual application of slow-release organic fertilizer in the spring.

Problems Not generally troubled by pests or diseases.

FLOWERING/FOLIAGE

Flowers It is grown for its flamboyant yellow flowers produced over a very long period.

Foliage Dark green lobed leaves. Shoots hairy and covered in scales.

PRUNING

Requirements Minimal pruning in midsummer after the first flowers. Wear goggles: the mealy coating on the shoots and leaves can irritate the eyes.

HEBE HULKEANA
New Zealand lilac

THIS YOUNG Hebe hulkeana *needs careful training to contain its loose growth habit. It tolerates some shade, but does best in full sun.*

SHAPELY LEAVES ARE a key attraction of the hebes, and many have subtle distinguishing features, such as the thin red edging here.

FEATURES

Wall shrub

This is an evergreen shrub from New Zealand, with a slender, loose, sprawling habit of growth. It is best grown by training it to a warm sunny wall, where it will benefit from the protection afforded, as it is not one of the hardiest subjects. The New Zealand lilac is a beautiful shrub, though, and well worth growing for its spring and summer display of lavender-blue flowers. As a free-standing shrub it grows to about 3ft high, but will grow taller against a wall, up to 6ft. For those who live in areas subject to very hard winters, this hebe can be grown in a cool conservatory. It will particularly enjoy and thrive in mild seaside gardens. The *Hebe* genus as a whole is valued by gardeners for its versatility, fine flowers and neat foliage.

HEBE HULKEANA AT A GLANCE

A loose, slender evergreen shrub with heads of lavender-blue flowers. Hardy to 23°F (zone 9).

Jan	/	Companion Plants
Feb	/	Associates well with early-
Mar	/	flowering climbing roses
Apr	planting ☞	with pink or red flowers.
May	flowering ❀	
Jun	flowering ❀	
July	/	
Aug	/	
Sep	/	
Oct	/	
Nov	/	
Dec	/	

CONDITIONS

Aspect   Will grow in sun or partial shade, but needs to be well protected from cold drying winds.

Site   This plant requires well-drained yet moisture-retentive soil, ranging from alkaline to neutral and low to moderate fertility.

GROWING METHOD

Propagation   Take softwood cuttings in spring or early summer, or semi-ripe cuttings in summer. It is best to have some young plants in reserve to replace the main plant if it is killed off by hard frosts.

Watering   Do not let the plant dry out. Water if the soil starts to become dry in summer.

Feeding   Once a year, in spring, apply a slow-release organic fertilizer, such as blood, fish, and bone.

Problems   These plants may be attacked by aphids in spring or summer.

FLOWERING/FOLIAGE

Flowers   This shrub is grown primarily for its flowers, which are produced in decorative trusses on the ends of the shoots.

Foliage   The shiny evergreen elliptic leaves with red edges are attractive.

PRUNING

Requirements   No regular pruning needed. Spread out and train young stems to their supports. Cut back any frost-damaged or dead growth in spring. Remove dead flower heads.

HOLBOELLIA LATIFOLIA
Holboellia

THE GLOSSY eye-shaped leaves of Holboellia latifolia are a principal attraction of this appealing climber.

HANGING IN GENTLE cascades from a house wall, H. latifolia creates a verdure of pleasant sun-catching foliage.

FEATURES

Twiner

This unusual spring-flowering evergreen climber is originally a native of Asia, and is particularly at home in the foothills of the Himalaya mountain range. It is not one of the hardiest climbers but it will thrive in gardens in the milder parts of the country if it is provided with a warm and sheltered situation. Holboellia is grown just as much for its attractive foliage as for its decorative purple female flowers. When situated in suitable conditions it is a vigorous climber, growing up to 15ft tall. It is suitable for growing on a pergola, arbor or arch, or for growing up a mature tree. A high wall makes another suitable support, as does a trellis screen.

HOLBOELLIA AT A GLANCE

Spring-flowering evergreen climber with purple flowers and handsome deep green foliage. Hardy to 23°F (zone 9).

Jan	foliage	Companion Plants
Feb	foliage	Makes a good partner for spring-flowering clematis.
Mar	planting	
Apr	flowering	
May	flowering	
Jun	foliage	
July	foliage	
Sep	foliage	
Oct	foliage	
Nov	foliage	
Dec	foliage	

CONDITIONS

Aspect   Grows in full sun or partial shade. Must provide shelter from wind, which could result in damage to the plant.

Site   Any well-drained yet moisture-retentive soil that contains plenty of humus.

GROWING METHOD

Propagation   Sow seeds in the spring and germinate in a temperature of 61°F. Take semi-ripe cuttings in late summer. Layer stems in spring.

Watering   If the soil starts to become excessively dry in summer, water the plant well.

Feeding   In the spring each year apply a slow-release organic fertilizer, such as blood, fish, and bone.

Problems   Not troubled by pests or diseases.

FLOWERING/FOLIAGE

Flowers   Male flowers are green-white, female flowers are purple. Both are borne on the same plant. Long red or purple fruits may follow, but cannot be guaranteed.

Foliage   Deep green, consisting of elliptical leaflets.

PRUNING

Requirements   Needs no regular pruning but you can, if desired, shorten side shoots to six buds in summer, as these tend to be vigorous and spread outward. Or just trim the plant in summer to fit allotted space.

JASMINUM
Jasmine

THE GLOSSY lance-shaped leaves of jasmine are decorative enough to earn it a place in the garden even if it didn't produce its flowers.

TREASURED for their subtle fragrance, the flowers of Jasminum officinale *also make a delightful display in summer and fall.*

FEATURES

Scramblers twiners

These deciduous and evergreen climbers are among the most popular of all, many being valued for their sweetly fragrant flowers. Due to their informal habit they are great favorites for cottage and country gardens, where they combine well with old-fashioned flowers. Try grouping them with old-fashioned roses, for instance, and shrubs such as philadelphus (Mock orange), which is also highly scented. But the versatile jasmines can be used in any type of garden. They can be grown up and over various kinds of support. Use them to cover walls, fences, trellis screens, pergolas, arches and arbors. They can even be trained up large mature trees. Large mature shrubs might also make good hosts, but then pruning of the jasmines becomes more difficult.

JASMINUM AT A GLANCE	
Scrambling climbers. The species in the main text are hardy to 23°F (zone 9), *J. nudiflorum* is hardy to 5°F (zone 7).	
Jan flowering ❀	Companion Plants
Feb flowering ❀	Jasmines look lovely
Mar planting ✎	intertwining with climbing
Apr planting ✎	or rambler roses. Ivy is a
May flowering ❀	good companion for the
Jun flowering ❀	winter jasmine.
July flowering ❀	
Aug flowering ❀	
Sep flowering ❀	
Oct /	
Nov /	
Dec flowering ❀	

There are many species of jasmine but some are too tender to be grown out of doors in cold climates. These are best grown in a cool conservatory. However, there are still many good species suitable for growing in gardens, including *Jasminum beesianum*, a Chinese twiner that is evergreen in milder gardens but deciduous in colder areas. The flowers, produced in the first half of the summer, are fragrant and red-pink in color. It grows to a height of 15ft so would be suitable for training on a wall of the house.

Jasminum humile "Revolutum" (Yellow jasmine), is of garden origin, but the species is a native of China, Afghanistan and the Himalayas. This semi-evergreen scrambler has bright yellow scented flowers in late spring and early summer and reaches a height of at least 8ft. Again this is another suitable species for the walls of the house.

The ever-popular Winter jasmine, *J. nudiflorum*, is a scrambling, deciduous, Chinese shrub that is ideally suited to training to a wall. The green stems and shoots carry bright yellow flowers in winter and into spring. Height 10ft. It can also be used as groundcover to clothe a bank.

Jasminum officinale (Common jasmine), a twining, deciduous climber from China and the Himalayas, can grow up to 40ft in height, but may be kept shorter by pruning. It is an extremely popular species and an essential choice for cottage gardens. Sweetly scented white flowers appear in summer and fall. There are several good cultivars and forms including *J. o.* f. *affine* whose white flowers are tinted with pink; "Aureum" with yellow-variegated leaves; and "Argenteovariegatum" with white-edged leaves.

JASMINE MAKES a perfect plant to drape over various garden structures, and here forms a scented canopy over an arbor.

MASSES OF FLOWERS adorn Jasminum nudiflorum *from late fall to early spring, providing a wall of color.*

CONDITIONS

Aspect Ideally jasmines should be grown in full sun, where they flower most freely, but partial shade is acceptable. The Winter jasmine, especially, is suitable for partial shade.

Site Jasmines are highly adaptable plants and will grow in any well-drained and reasonably fertile soil. The soil should be capable of retaining moisture during dry weather—so add bulky organic matter before planting.

GROWING METHOD

Propagation The easiest way to propagate jasmines is to carry out serpentine layering in the spring. Alternatively take semi-ripe cuttings in summer. However, hardwood cuttings in winter are better for *J. nudiflorum* and *J. officinale*, rooting them in a cold frame or in a cool glasshouse.

Watering It is important not to allow jasmines to suffer from extended lack of moisture, try to keep the plants well watered during any prolonged dry spells if necessary.

Feeding Apply a slow-release fertilizer annually in the spring just as growth is starting. Blood, fish, and bone is a good organic choice.

Problems Jasmines may be attacked by aphids, but these pests are easily controlled by spraying with a suitable insecticide.

FLOWERING/FOLIAGE

Flowers Jasmines are grown primarily for their flowers, which are often highly fragrant.

Foliage Many jasmines have pinnate foliage. It may be evergreen or deciduous, depending on species and/or climate.

PRUNING

Requirements Jasmines vary in their pruning requirements according to species. *Jasminum humile* "Revolutum" needs thinning out regularly to prevent congested growth. When flowering is over, cut out completely no more than two of the oldest stems. Neglected and overgrown plants can be renovated by cutting them back hard in early spring.

Jasminum nudiflorum requires annual pruning. This should take place as soon as flowering is over. Carry out spur pruning by cutting back the old flowered shoots to within two or three pairs of buds of the main framework of the plant.

For established plants of *J. officinale* and *J. beesianum* thin out congested growth as soon as flowering is over by cutting back the flowered shoots. If necessary neglected plants can be hard pruned by cutting back old stems to within 3ft of the ground in late winter or early spring.

LONICERA
Honeysuckle

TOLERANT OF PARTIAL shade, Lonicera japonica *"Halliana" is also fast-growing and makes an ideal cover for pergolas.*

THE FLUTED BLOOMS of Lonicera sempervirens *hang in attractive bunches that add to their visual impact.*

FEATURES

Twiners

Honeysuckles are widely grown climbers, ranking in popularity with clematis and jasmines. Like the latter, many have highly fragrant flowers and are valued for this alone, but the blooms also make a colorful display in the summer.

They have a very informal habit of growth, making them ideally suited to cottage and country gardens, where they could be grown with old-fashioned flowers and other plants, such as old roses. Try growing them with climbing roses and let them intertwine for some really stunning effects, although bear in mind that pruning of both may then be more difficult. Owners of more modern gardens should also consider growing honeysuckles as they will not look out of place.

Honeysuckles can be grown up a variety of supports, including walls, fences, pergolas, arbors, arches, obelisks in a shrub border, and large mature trees. They look particularly at home in a woodland garden, as they often grow in woodland conditions in the wild. The Common honeysuckle or Woodbine, *Lonicera periclymenum* and its cultivars, makes good groundcover in shrub borders and woodland gardens. Some species can be grown in tubs and trained as standards, including *L. japonica* "Halliana" (Japanese honeysuckle) and *L. periclymenum* cultivars.

There are many species and cultivars to choose from but the following are probably among the best loved. *Lonicera* x *brownii* "Fuchsioides" (Scarlet trumpet honeysuckle), has clusters of slightly fragrant, tubular, orange-scarlet flowers in summer. A twiner of garden origin, it is deciduous or, in some climates, evergreen, and can attain a height of 12ft.

Lonicera caprifolium, (Italian honeysuckle), a native of Europe and western Asia, is a deciduous twiner producing, in summer, clusters of highly fragrant, tubular, cream or yellow flowers flushed with pink. It can grow to a height of 20ft.

The extremely vigorous *L. japonica* "Halliana" (Japanese honeysuckle), is a semi-evergreen or evergreen twiner with white tubular flowers which turn yellow as they age. The blooms are highly fragrant and the flowering period is from spring to the end of summer. It grows to a height of 30ft. The species is a native of eastern Asia.

The Common honeysuckle, also known as Woodbine, *L. periclymenum,* is a native of Britain where it scrambles over hedgerows.

LONICERA AT A GLANCE

Vigorous twiners with tubular flowers in summer. Hardy to temperatures of up to 5°F (zone 7).

Jan	/	Companion Plants
Feb	planting	Honeysuckles look good
Mar	planting	accompanied by climbing
Apr	planting	or rambler roses.
May	flowering	
Jun	flowering	
July	flowering	
Aug	flowering	
Sep	flowering	
Oct	/	
Nov	/	
Dec	/	

A PROFUSION of flowers smothers this Lonicera pericylmenum *"Belgica". The flowers fill the air with their powerful fragrance.*

THE DELICATE TUBULAR flowers of Lonicera pericylmenum *"Belgica" are prized for their perfume and distinctive appearance.*

It is a very vigorous twiner that produces fragrant flowers from mid- to late summer. The species is not generally grown in gardens, most gardeners preferring to use its cultivars. *L. p.* "Belgica" is popularly known as the Early Dutch honeysuckle and has white blooms that age to yellow. These are flushed with red on the outside. *L. p.* "Serotina" is the Late Dutch honeysuckle with cream flowers that are flushed with reddish-purple on the outside. Both of these decorative cultivars can grow up to 20ft tall.

Hailing from the USA, *Lonicera sempervirens*, known as Trumpet honeysuckle, is an evergreen or deciduous twiner with tubular flowers that are reddish orange on the outside but yellow-orange within. The flowers are produced throughout summer and into fall. It reaches up to 12ft in height.

CONDITIONS

Aspect	All species and their cultivars will grow in full sun or partial shade.
Site	Honeysuckles are very adaptable and will grow in any well-drained but moisture-retentive, humus-rich soil of reasonable fertility.

GROWING METHOD

Propagation	The easiest method of propagation is to carry out serpentine layering in the spring. Alternatively take softwood or semi-ripe cuttings in spring and summer. Sow seeds in fall and stratify over winter.
Watering	Do not let honeysuckles suffer from prolonged lack of moisture. Water the plants thoroughly if the soil starts to dry out during long dry periods in the summer.
Feeding	Apply a slow-release fertilizer, such as the organic blood, fish and bone, in the spring.
Problems	Plants may become infested with aphids during the summer.

FLOWERING/FOLIAGE

Flowers	Honeysuckles are grown primarily for their flowers, and the scented kinds are most popular.
Foliage	Evergreen or deciduous, the leaves being arranged in opposite pairs.

PRUNING

Requirements	The congested growth of *Lonicera japonica* can be thinned out in early spring. Prune back any very long shoots. If renovation is needed, cut back the entire plant to within 3ft of the ground in late winter or early spring. With the species *L. periclymenum*, *L. x brownii*, *L. caprifolium*, and *L. sempervirens*, you can either allow them to grow at will or reduce the flowered shoots by one-third in early spring to restrict the size of the plant. Shears may be used to trim the entire plant. Renovation pruning is the same as for *L. japonica*.

PASSIFLORA CAERULEA
Blue passion flower

THE FLOWERS of Passiflora *are famous for their intricate petals and stamens. Only* P. caerulea *is hardy enough to be grown outside.*

MILDLY FRAGRANCED and producing yellow or orange fruit in late summer and early fall, P. caerulea *provides plenty of interest.*

FEATURES

Tendril climber

The Blue passion flower is a fast-growing climber from Brazil and Argentina with evergreen or semi-evergreen foliage. The very complex flowers, basically bowl shaped, come in a striking color combination of white and green, zoned with blue, purple, and white. This species grows to at least 30ft tall. As it is not one of the hardiest climbers available the Blue passion flower is best grown against a warm, sunny, sheltered wall. This makes it an ideal subject for a courtyard garden or any similar enclosed area. Alternatively, it could be grown on the wall of the house. It really flourishes in mild parts of the country, and in colder areas this plant will need adequate protection from cold drying winds.

PASSIFLORA AT A GLANCE

A vigorous tendril climber producing exotic-looking flowers followed by orange fruits. Hardy to 23°F (zone 9).

Jan	/	Recommended Varieties
Feb	/	*P. c.* "Constance Elliot" has
Mar	/	white flowers.
Apr	planting ✤	
May	planting ✤	
Jun	flowering ✽	
July	flowering ✽	
Aug	flowering ✽	
Sep	flowering ✽	
Oct	flowering ✽	
Nov	/	
Dec	/	

CONDITIONS

Aspect   Best in full sun but can also be grown in partial shade. This plant needs to be well sheltered from cold winds.

Site   Grows in any reasonably fertile, well-drained yet moisture-retentive soil.

GROWING METHOD

Propagation   Take softwood or semi-ripe leaf-bud cuttings in spring and summer. Carry out serpentine layering in the spring. Sow seeds in spring, after soaking in hot water for 24 hours. Germinate at 64°F.

Watering   If the soil starts to dry out in the summer water the plant well.

Feeding   Apply a slow-release fertilizer in the spring, such as the organic blood, fish, and bone.

Problems   Passifloras are not usually troubled by pests and diseases out of doors.

FLOWERING/FOLIAGE

Flowers   Bowl-shaped flowers over a very long period, followed by egg-shaped light orange fruits.

Foliage   Dark green and deeply lobed.

PRUNING

Requirements   Train a framework of permanent stems on the support and in spring just before growth starts, carry out spur pruning by cutting back flowered shoots to within two or three buds of this framework.

PERIPLOCA GRAECA
Silk vine

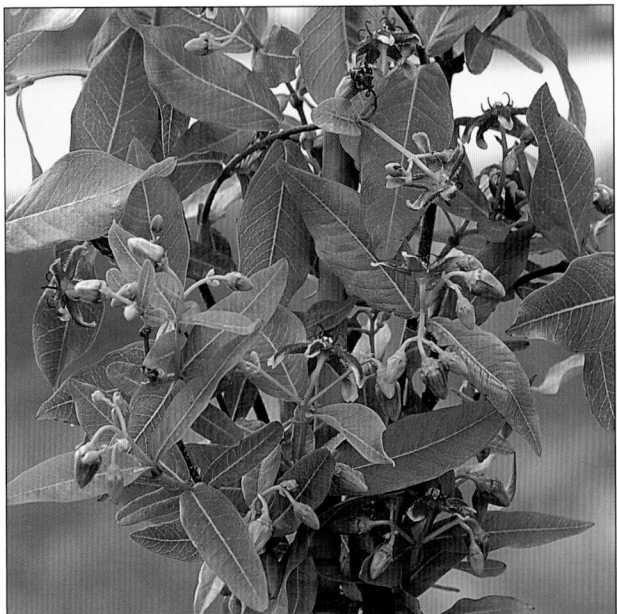

THE STAR-SHAPED flowers of Periploca graeca, *the Silk vine, are followed by silky seeds, hence the common name.*

THIS EXOTIC VARIETY, Periploca laevigata, *a native of north Africa and the Canary Islands, produces amazing star-shaped flowers.*

FEATURES

Twiner

This is a vigorous deciduous climber, a native of south-west Europe and south-west Asia. The Silk vine is grown primarily for its attractive-looking star-shaped flowers in the summer. Unfortunately these flowers also have a rather unpleasant fragrance. It is the most commonly grown species, of which there are about 11 altogether in the genus. Growing to a height of 28ft, the Silk vine is suitable for a warm sheltered wall or close-boarded fence where it will be well protected. This plant is also suitable for a pergola or trellis screen, as long as the chosen site is well sheltered from cold and drying winds. It will make an ideal climber for a courtyard garden with its own favorable microclimate.

PERIPLOCA GRAECA AT A GLANCE

A vigorous deciduous climber with star-shaped yellow-green and purple flowers in summer. Hardy to 23°F (zone 9).

Month		
Jan	/	
Feb	/	
Mar	planting ✍	**Companion Plants**
Apr	planting ✍	Grow with other climbers
May	/	and wall shrubs that need
Jun	/	similar conditions, such as
July	flowering ✿	*Abutilon megapotamicum.*
Aug	flowering ✿	
Sep	/	
Oct	/	
Nov	/	
Dec	/	

CONDITIONS

Aspect	The Silk vine requires a position in full sun that is also warm and sheltered.
Site	Any soil is suitable provided it is well drained.

GROWING METHOD

Propagation	Sow seeds in the spring and germinate them in a temperature of 61°F. Root semi-ripe cuttings during the summer.
Watering	Do not let this climber suffer from drought. Water the plant well if the soil starts to dry out excessively.
Feeding	An annual application, during the spring, of a slow-release fertilizer will keep the plant going. The organic blood, fish and bone is a suitable choice.
Problems	The Silk vine is not usually troubled by any pests or diseases.

FLOWERING/FOLIAGE

Flowers	Star shaped, yellow-green, and purple, followed by long thin seed pods that split open to reveal silky seeds, hence the common name.
Foliage	Deep green shiny leaves make a good background for the flowers.

PRUNING

Requirements	In early spring simply trim if necessary to keep the plant within its allotted space. Eventually renovation pruning may be needed by thinning out the oldest stems.

PILEOSTEGIA VIBURNOIDES
Pileostegia

PILEOSTEGIA VIBURNOIDES *shows a fetching contrast between its bold leaves and its lacy puffs of cream-white flowers.*

DRAMATIC FIREWORK *bursts of white, the flowers of* P. viburnoides *reveal their intricate beauty on close inspection.*

FEATURES

Self-clinging climber

This is a very vigorous, tall-growing evergreen climber that supports itself by means of aerial roots produced from the stems. It is related to schizophragma (see page 717). Pileostegia is a native of China, Taiwan and India. This climber is grown for its flowers, which are produced in summer and fall, and for its dense, good-looking foliage that effectively hides the support. Growing up to 20ft in height, pileostegia is suitable for growing on high walls or up large mature trees but is not a suitable subject for small gardens or where space is restricted. It is also a good shade survivor, which might make it a suitable choice for shaded areas that other climbers cannot endure.

PILEOSTEGIA AT A GLANCE

Vigorous evergreen climber with deep green foliage and cream-white flowers in late summer and fall. Hardy to 23°F (zone 9).

Jan	/	Companion Plants
Feb	/	Due to its vigour, best grown
Mar	planting 🖐	alone, but could combine
Apr	planting 🖐	with a vigorous rambler rose.
May	/	
Jun	/	
July	/	
Aug	flowering ✾	
Sep	flowering ✾	
Oct	flowering ✾	
Nov	/	
Dec	/	

CONDITIONS

Aspect	Pileostegia will endure most light conditions, from full sun to full shade.
Site	This climber will grow in any reasonably rich soil provided the drainage is good.

GROWING METHOD

Propagation	Take semi-ripe cuttings in summer and ideally root them in a cold frame.
Watering	Do not let this climber dry out excessively, so water well in prolonged dry spells in summer.
Feeding	An annual feed, in spring, of slow-release fertilizer, such as the organic blood, fish, and bone, is all that is required.
Problems	Pileostegia is not troubled by pests or diseases.

FLOWERING/FOLIAGE

Flowers	The heads of cream-white flowers are produced late in the summer.
Foliage	The deep green elliptical leaves have a leathery texture.

PRUNING

Requirements	Prune in early spring. Minimal pruning needed. Shorten any over-long or badly placed shoots as necessary. This climber produces most flowers at the top so do not prune to reduce height. Hard renovation pruning is acceptable if necessary—simply leave a main framework of stems. Ideally spread this type of pruning over several years to prevent too much loss of flower following pruning.

ROSA
Rose species and hybrids

ROSA "ALBERTINE" is a beautiful, heavily scented rambler rose, shown in this garden in its full glory. Although it produces only one long blooming each year, its lovely salmon-pink color and scent are well worth the wait. It is one of the most popular rambler roses.

FEATURES

Scramblers

The climbing roses rank among the most popular of all climbing plants. There are climbing roses suitable for walls and fences of all sizes, and vigorous ramblers and climbers that can be allowed to grow up through large mature trees and evergreen conifers. Many climbers and ramblers are ideal for pergolas, arches, arbors, and obelisks.

Modern hybrid climbers such as "Alchemist" are the most popular. They are recurrent flowering, producing several flushes of flowers in summer, and there is a large range to choose from in a wide selection of colors. Older cultivars may have only one flush of blooms.

Ramblers, both species and cultivars, are generally more vigorous than modern hybrid climbers and need plenty of space. Many have only one main flush of flowers in the summer, such as the popular old "Albertine" and "Wedding Day."

Species roses are also well worth considering, including *Rosa banksiae*, the double white Banksian rose. This climber has double, sweetly scented, white flowers in late spring and is one of the earliest roses to flower. Also recommended is the yellow Banksian

rose, *R. b.* "Lutea," with double yellow flowers. The species itself is very tall, up to 40ft, but the yellow cultivar is much shorter, about 20ft. The Banksian roses are hardy to 23°F and are best grown on a warm sunny sheltered wall or fence.

CONDITIONS

Aspect Full sun is required for best flowering.
Site Roses like a fertile, deep, moisture-retentive, yet well-drained soil. Dig in plenty of bulky organic matter before planting to provide humus, which helps to retain moisture during dry periods. Keep roses well mulched with bulky organic matter.

GROWING METHOD

Propagation It is not really feasible for home gardeners to propagate many of the climbing roses. Commercially they are propagated by budding onto suitable rootstocks. You could try ramblers and species roses from hardwood cuttings in winter. Root them in a cold frame.
Watering Keep roses well watered if the soil dries. They dislike very dry or drought conditions.

| Feeding | You could use a proprietary rose fertilizer. Alternatively apply blood, fish, and bone fertilizer. Apply in the spring as growth is starting, and after the first flush of flowers. |
| Problems | Roses have more than their fair share of problems: aphids, rose black spot, rose powdery mildew and rose rust, to name some of the most troublesome. Wherever possible buy disease-resistant roses. Carry out preventative spraying to control diseases, starting as soon as new foliage appears. Use a combined rose spray. |

FLOWERING/FOLIAGE

| Flowers | May be single, semi-double, or fully double, fragrant or without scent. Flowering may be a single flush in the summer, or repeat-flowering throughout summer. |
| Foliage | The leaves are made up of leaflets in varying shades of green, often shiny, but generally not particularly attractive. |

PRUNING

Requirements Roses flower on current or previous year's shoots, so prune annually. Wherever possible train stems horizontally as they then produce better distributed flowers, instead of blooming only at the top. Of course, this method of training is not possible when growing on pergola pillars and obelisks. There are hybrid climbing roses that are suitable for these types of supports, or spiral training could be used to give you blooms all the way up the support.

Ramblers flower best on stems produced in the previous year, but will also flower on older ones. Prune after flowering by cutting out some of the oldest flowered stems to ground level. Then space out and tie in the remaining stems.

For modern hybrid climbers train a main framework of stems to the support. This produces side shoots that in turn produce flowers. Prune in late winter or early spring by cutting back side shoots to two or three buds from the main stems. Cut back the oldest stems once they start producing fewer flowers.

R. "WEDDING DAY," a lovely single white rambler rose, bears a great profusion of blooms. Here it has a sturdy metal frame for support.

WELL-SPACED STEMS encourage the best flowering and allow all flowers to be seen. This peachy-apricot climbing rose is R. "Alchemist."

THE WEIGHT of growth from this prolific pink-flowering climbing rose may require an extra cross-bar support for the pergola.

ROSA AT A GLANCE		
Summer-flowering scramblers, with flowers in a wide range of colors, many being fragrant. Most roses are hardy to 5°F (zone		
Jan	planting 🌱	Companion Plants
Feb	planting 🌱	Summer-flowering clematis
Mar	planting 🌱	are particularly good
Apr	planting 🌱	companions. You can allow
May	flowering 🌼	the two to intertwine.
Jun	flowering 🌼	
July	flowering 🌼	
Aug	flowering 🌼	
Sep	flowering 🌼	
Oct	planting 🌱	
Nov	planting 🌱	
Dec	planting 🌱	

RUBUS HENRYI
Rubus

THE DISTINCTIVE three-fingered leaves of Rubus henryi *var.* bambusarum *are joined by pink flowers in early summer.*

MANY OF the decorative members of the Rubus *genus are grown for their glossy and pleasantly-shaped leaves.*

FEATURES

Scrambler

The genus *Rubus* is huge, containing over 250 species, some of which are well-known edible fruits such as blackberries and raspberries. There are also numerous ornamental species and one of the most decorative is *R. henryi* var. *bambusarum*. This handsome evergreen climber from China has long spiny stems with white hairs. It is grown for these attractive stems, as well as for the foliage and summer flowers. It is a vigorous plant, growing 20ft tall, and is a good subject for a shrub border or woodland garden. In these situations it can be grown either as a climber, perhaps over a large shrub, up a mature tree, or on an obelisk or as a groundcover plant.

RUBUS HENRYI AT A GLANCE

R.h. var. *bambusarum* is a handsome blackberry relation with spiny stems and pink summer flowers. Hardy to 5°F (zone 7).

Jan	/	Companion Plants
Feb	planting 🌱	This climber looks good
Mar	planting 🌱	with shrubs, particularly
Apr	planting 🌱	woodland-garden kinds.
May	/	
Jun	flowering ❀	
July	flowering ❀	
Aug	flowering ❀	
Sep	/	
Oct	/	
Nov	/	
Dec	/	

CONDITIONS

Aspect Suitable for sun or partial shade.
Site *R. h.* var. *bambusarum* will grow in any soil that is well drained and reasonably fertile.

GROWING METHOD

Propagation Take semi-ripe cuttings in summer. You can also use semi-ripe leaf-bud cuttings. Layer stems in the spring. Groundcover plants may self-layer.
Watering It likes moist conditions so do not allow the plant to dry out during prolonged dry spells in summer.
Feeding Apply a slow-release fertilizer in the spring, such as the organic blood, fish, and bone.
Problems Not generally troubled by pests or diseases.

FLOWERING/FOLIAGE

Flowers Clusters of small bowl-shaped pink flowers are followed by shiny black berries.
Foliage The shiny deep green three-lobed leaves with white undersides are very attractive.

PRUNING

Requirements Pruning aims to ensure plenty of new stems, so in late winter or early spring each year cut some of the stems that produced flowers the previous year down to ground level. New shoots will then appear from the base of the plant in the spring.

SCHISANDRA CHINENSIS
Schisandra

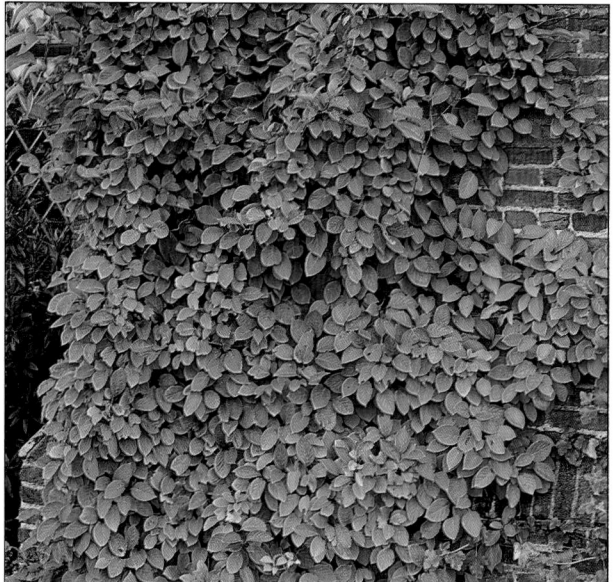

THE LUSH *deciduous foliage of the Asian climber* Schisandra chinensis *contrasts well with a red brick wall.*

NESTLING AMID *the leaves of a female* S. chinensis, *berries are just beginning to blush a light shade of red.*

FEATURES

Twiner

The genus contains about two dozen species, some of which are evergreen, others being deciduous. *Schisandra chinensis* is one of the best known and most widely grown. It is a deciduous climber from eastern Asia, specifically India and Burma, and is suitable for growing on shady walls, fences, and trellis screens. It is also an ideal subject for a woodland garden, as the species grows in woodland conditions in the wild. It looks equally at home in a shrub border. This climber can be grown up large mature trees or over large shrubs, but this technique is only recommended for gardens in mild climates. Height 30ft. Female plants produce small red berries, used in Chinese medicine to treat a wide range of ailments.

SCHISANDRA AT A GLANCE

A twining climber which has clusters of cream flowers followed by red fruits. Hardy to 5°F (zone 7).

Jan	/	Companion Plants
Feb	planting ✤	Schisandra associates well
Mar	planting ✤	with shrubs and woodland-
Apr	planting ✤	garden plants
May	flowering ✽	
Jun	flowering ✽	
July	flowering ✽	
Aug	flowering ✽	
Sep	/	
Oct	/	
Nov	/	
Dec	/	

CONDITIONS

Aspect Grows well in either full sun or partial shade.
Site Moisture-retentive but well-drained, reasonably fertile soil is recommended.

GROWING METHOD

Propagation Sow seeds as soon as collected in the fall and germinate them in a cold frame. Take semi-ripe cuttings in summer.
Watering Apply water if the soil starts to dry out excessively during the summer.
Feeding Apply a slow-release fertilizer, such as the organic blood, fish and bone, in the spring.
Problems Schisandra is not troubled by pests or diseases.

FLOWERING/FOLIAGE

Flowers Fragrant cream flowers are carried in clusters. Female plants produce red fruits in pendulous spikes. You will need to grow a male plant close by for fruit production to take place.
Foliage The elliptical leaves are deep green and shiny.

PRUNING

Requirements No regular pruning needed but cut back any overlong or badly placed shoots to within several buds of the main stems. You can also cut back shoots to keep the plant within its allotted space. Renovation may be needed after some years, cutting the oldest stems down to the ground. This is best done over a few years to prevent too much loss of flower. Pruning is carried out in late winter or early spring.

SCHIZOPHRAGMA
Schizophragma

SCHIZOPHRAGMA HYDRANGEOIDES *has plenty to shout about, with rich green leaves in season and ebullient white blooms.*

IN THE SUMMER, S. hydrangeoides *is a seething mass of pleasant white flowers, so densely packed that the foliage is hardly visible.*

FEATURES

Self-clinging climber

Schizophragma hydrangeoides is a deciduous climber from Japan and Korea. It supports itself by means of aerial roots. It is a lofty climber, growing up to 40ft tall, so it preferably needs a high wall or fence. Alternatively, grow it through a large tree, or use it as groundcover, for example in a woodland garden or shrub border. This climber is grown mainly for its unusual and conspicuous heads of flowers produced in summer, but the foliage is also attractive and covers its support well. There is one other species in the genus, *S. integrifolium*, which is not quite so hardy.

SCHIZOPHRAGMA AT A GLANCE

A self-clinging climber with large flat heads of cream flowers surrounded by conspicuous bracts. Hardy to 5°F (zone 7).

Jan	/	**Recommended Varieties**
Feb	/	*S. h.* "Moonlight" has variegated
Mar	planting 🖐	foliage.
Apr	planting 🖐	*S. h.* "Roseum" has rose-tinted
May	/	bracts.
Jun	/	
July	flowering ❀	
Aug	flowering ❀	
Sep	/	
Oct	/	
Nov	/	
Dec	/	

CONDITIONS

Aspect   A good choice of plant for partial shade but it also grows well in full sun. Must be well sheltered from cold drying winds.

Site   Well-drained yet moisture-retentive soil that contains plenty of humus.

GROWING METHOD

Propagation   Take semi-ripe cuttings in summer. Sow seeds in fall and stratify over winter.

Watering   Do not let the plant suffer from lack of moisture, so water well if the soil starts to dry out in summer.

Feeding   An annual spring application of slow-release fertilizer such as the organic blood, fish, and bone will keep the plant going all season.

Problems   This climber is not usually troubled by pests or diseases.

FLOWERING/FOLIAGE

Flowers   Flat heads of cream flowers with large oval bracts of the same color around the edge.

Foliage   The large, oval, deep green leaves are attractive in season.

PRUNING

Requirements   No regular pruning needed. If necessary, after flowering, cut back by about two-thirds any overlong shoots and trim the plant to fit the available space.

SOLANUM
Potato tree, Potato vine

THESE DAINTY FLOWERS belie the vigor of Solanum crispum. It may put forth flowers over many months of the summer.

THE POTATO VINE, S. jasminoides, here in its cultivar "Album," is a half-hardy climber, needing conservatory protection in most areas.

FEATURES

Scramblers

Two evergreen or partially evergreen species of this genus are generally grown. Both of these are very vigorous, growing to 20ft tall. *Solanum crispum* (Chilean potato tree) from Chile and Peru has fragrant blue flowers in the summer. The cultivar "Glasnevin," with purple-blue flowers, is more widely grown than the species. The Chilean potato tree can be grown on a wall or fence, or used to cover an unsightly outbuilding. *S. jasminoides* (Potato vine) is a half-hardy climber originating from the jungles of Brazil and will need the protection of a cool conservatory in most areas. In the garden it must have a very well sheltered sunny wall. It bears scented, pale blue flower in summer and fall. Both species can be grown as standards.

SOLANUM AT A GLANCE

Vigorous climbers with clusters of potato-like flowers. *S. crispum* is hardy to 23°F (zone 9), *S. jasminoides* to 32°F (zone 10).

Jan	/	Companion Plants
Feb	/	Solanums look lovely with
Mar	/	red or pink climbing or
Apr	planting ✬	rambler roses
May	planting ✬	
Jun	flowering ✿	
July	flowering ✿	
Aug	flowering ✿	
Sep	flowering ✿	
Oct	/	
Nov	/	
Dec	/	

CONDITIONS

Aspect   These plants need a warm, very sheltered position in full sun.
Site   Well-drained yet moisture-retentive, reasonably fertile soil, ideally slightly alkaline.

GROWING METHOD

Propagation   Take semi-ripe cuttings in summer.
Watering   Water only if the soil starts to dry out excessively in the summer.
Feeding   An annual application of slow-release fertilizer such as blood, fish, and bone, preferably in the spring, will be sufficient.
Problems   Plants are prone to attacks from aphids.

FLOWERING/FOLIAGE

Flowers   Produces large clusters of potato-like (star-shaped) flowers.
Foliage   The deep green oval leaves of these plants are not particularly attractive.

PRUNING

Requirements   Solanums flower on the current year's shoots. Train a permanent framework of stems and spur prune back to this in early spring each year by cutting back lateral shoots to within two or three buds of the main stems. Also prune the plant back to fit the available space. Renovation pruning is not recommended— better to replace overgrown plants. Wear gloves when pruning as the sap can cause an allergic reaction in some people.

STAUNTONIA HEXAPHYLLA
Stauntonia

JUST AS IN its natural habitat in Japan and south Korea, this Stauntonia hexaphylla *has found a tree to twine its way around.*

ALTHOUGH IT DOES produce attractive flowers, S. hexaphylla *is also grown for its pleasant, lush, evergreen foliage.*

FEATURES

Twiner

This is a vigorous, evergreen climber from Japan and south Korea, where it is largely found growing in woodland conditions. It is related and similar to *Holboellia latifolia* (see page 705). Stauntonias are grown for their attractive bell-shaped flowers, which are produced in spring, and for their lush foliage that serves to cover their support well. Grow this climber on a sheltered wall or fence, or allow it to scramble through a large mature shrub or up a tree. Although this plant is frost hardy it will not survive severe cold spells. In areas that suffer from hard frosts it is best to grow it in a cool conservatory. The eventual height of this plant is 30ft.

STAUNTONIA AT A GLANCE

A vigorous twiner with white, violet-flushed, bell-shaped flowers in spring. Hardy to 23°F (zone 9).

Jan	/	Companion Plants
Feb	/	Try growing this climber
Mar	/	with spring-flowering
Apr	planting 🖐	clematis.
May	flowering ❀	
Jun	/	
July	/	
Oct	/	
Nov	/	
Dec	/	

CONDITIONS

Aspect   Full sun or partial shade, warm and well sheltered from cold winds.

Site   Stauntonia will get by in any well-drained soil that is reasonably fertile.

GROWING METHOD

Propagation Semi-ripe cuttings taken in summer. Sow seeds in spring and germinate in a temperature of 61°F.

Watering   Water the plant well if the soil starts to dry out excessively in the summer.

Feeding   Feed annually in the spring. The slow-release organic fertilizer, blood, fish, and bone can be recommended.

Problems   There are no problems from pests or diseases.

FLOWERING/FOLIAGE

Flowers   Pendulous clusters of scented, white, bell-shaped flowers, tinted with violet may be followed by edible, purple fruits (a male and female plant are necessary to obtain fruits).

Foliage   Deep green, shiny, leathery, hand-shaped leaves make a good background for the flowers.

PRUNING

Requirements Spur pruning. To keep growth under control, shorten lateral shoots to six buds in summer, and then in early spring cut them back again, to within two or three buds of the main stems.

TRACHELOSPERMUM
Star jasmine

THE WHITE FLOWERS of Trachelospermum jasminoides *are enjoyed for their appearance as well as their strong perfume.*

THIS LUSH PLANT of T. jasminoides *has been trained and pruned most effectively to echo the angle of the steps and then curve up again.*

FEATURES

Twiner

Trachelospermum jasminoides is a handsome, evergreen, twining climber from China, Japan and Korea. It is valued for its pleasing foliage and for its clusters of strongly perfumed white flowers, which appear in mid- to late summer and age to cream through the flowering season. The blooms are reminiscent of the true jasmine (see pages 706–707). It is an ideal subject for growing on walls, fences, trellis screens, pergolas, arches and arbours. Star jasmine can also be grown as ground cover, for example in a shrub border, or used for covering a bank. Once established it grows quite quickly, and in maturity it reaches a height of 28ft. In areas subject to very hard winters this climber should be grown in a cool conservatory or glasshouse.

TRACHELOSPERMUM AT A GLANCE

A jasmine-like climber with very dense growth and sweetly fragrant white flowers. Hardy to 23°F (zone 9).

Jan	/	Companion Plants
Feb	/	A good companion for red or
Mar	planting 🖐	pink climbing roses.
Apr	planting 🖐	
May	planting 🖐	
Jun	/	
July	flowering ✿	
Aug	flowering ✿	
Sep	/	
Oct	/	
Nov	/	
Dec	/	

CONDITIONS

Aspect   Must be very well sheltered and warm. Full sun or partial shade are acceptable.

Site   This climber likes a good, reasonably rich soil that is well drained.

GROWING METHOD

Propagation   Take semi-ripe cuttings in the summer and then provide them with bottom heat—about 68°F. Carry out serpentine layering in the spring.

Watering   Do not let the star jasmine suffer from lack of moisture. Water well in summer if the soil starts to become excessively dry.

Feeding   Give an annual spring application of slow-release fertilizer, such as blood, fish, and bone.

Problems   There are no problems from pests or diseases.

FLOWERING/FOLIAGE

Flowers   Clusters of white, star-shaped, highly fragrant flowers reminiscent of jasmine.

Foliage   Deep green, shiny, oval leaves.

PRUNING

Requirements Needs little pruning. In early spring thin out some of the oldest stems if necessary. Bear in mind that this climber is naturally very dense in habit so do not attempt to thin it out too much. Prune back the plant as necessary to keep it within its allotted space, but avoid hard pruning. It is best to replace very old neglected plants rather than renovate them.

VITIS
Vine, grape vine

THE LEAVES OF Vitis vinifera *"Pupurea" are purple in summer and become darker in fall before they fall.*

GROWING UP OUT of a bed, this V. vinifera *"Pupurea" adds a vertical element to the planting, and fills the blank space of the fence.*

FEATURES

Tendril climbers

Apart from the well-known edible grape vine, cultivars of *Vitis vinifera*, there are several ornamental vines that are valued for their fall leaf color. *Vitis coignetiae* is a very vigorous species from Japan and Korea and is also one of the largest leaved. In fall the leaves turn brilliant red. It reaches 50ft in height. *V. vinifera* "Purpurea" has purple leaves in summer that become darker in fall, and reaches 22ft. These vines, whose summer foliage is also attractive, are ideal for pergolas, arches and arbours; also trellis screens, walls and fences. They can be used for groundcover, and *V. vinifera* "Purpurea" makes a good standard for the patio.

VITIS AT A GLANCE

Tendril climbers valued for their large lobed leaves. Hardy to temperatures of 5°F (zone 7).

Jan	/	Companion Plants
Feb	/	These vines look good with
Mar	planting 🪴	large-leaved ivies such as
Apr	planting 🪴	*Hedera colchica* and
May	foliage 🍃	*H. canariensis.*
Jun	foliage 🍃	
July	foliage 🍃	
Aug	foliage 🍃	
Sep	foliage 🍃	
Oct	foliage 🍃	
Nov	/	
Dec	/	

CONDITIONS

Aspect	Full sun or partial shade.
Site	Any well-drained soil, but alkaline or neutral conditions preferred. Soil should also contain plenty of humus.

GROWING METHOD

Propagation	Take hardwood cuttings in late fall or winter, rooting them in a bottom-heat temperature of 70°F. Carry out serpentine layering in spring.
Watering	Vines will tolerate fairly dry conditions but it is best to water them well if the soil starts to dry out excessively.
Feeding	Apply a slow-release organic fertilizer in the spring, such as blood, fish and bone.
Problems	Leaves may be affected by powdery mildew.

FLOWERING/FOLIAGE

Flowers	Trusses of tiny green flowers followed by purple or black grapes which, in the ornamental vines, are not palatable.
Foliage	Handsome, large lobed leaves.

PRUNING

Requirements	Build up a permanent framework of stems and spur prune annually in mid-winter. Cut back side shoots to within two or three buds of their base. During the summer any very long shoots can be shortened if desired.

WISTERIA
Wisteria

EVEN THE STEMS of this wisteria have disappeared beneath an abundance of bloom—and there is no foliage yet to distract the eye.

THIS WHITE WISTERIA has been trained along a wire frame. The cascades of flower make it a high point of the garden in spring.

FEATURES

Twiner

These very vigorous, fast-growing, long-lived deciduous climbers are desired by most garden owners for their spectacular spring display of pendulous, often fragrant flowers that generally appear just before or with the new leaves. The plants eventually develop thick stems and therefore are very weighty, needing strong supports. They are very amenable to training and can be formed into virtually any shape desired. Wisterias are often used to cover large pergolas, when the flowers "drip" down inside in a very dramatic fashion. They can also be trained vertically along veranda railings or low walls. These climbers are often seen on house walls. Wisterias are ideal, too, for growing up large mature trees.

If you do not have the wall space or other suitable support for one of these magnificent climbers, then consider growing one in a tub and training it into a standard to decorate the patio. Bear in mind that young wisteria plants can take up to seven years, or even longer, to start flowering, so patience is needed after planting. In the meantime, simply enjoy the foliage, which looks particularly lush when newly opened in the spring.

Probably the most popular wisteria is *W. floribunda* "Multijuga," a cultivar of the Japanese wisteria. The fragrant lilac-blue flowers are carried in pendulous trusses up to 4ft in length. If this cultivar is grown on a pergola it is a truly magnificent sight when in full flower and the trusses are dangling down inside. It grows to a height of at least 28ft. There are many other cultivars of *W. floribunda*. These include *W. f.* "Kuchi-beni" ("Peaches and Cream") with its pink and white flowers, and *W. f.* 'Alba' with white flowers.

Also widely grown is *W. sinensis* (Chinese wisteria), with scented, lilac-blue flowers in trusses up to 12in in length. It is a fast-growing and vigorous climber with dense trusses of flowers, growing to the same height as *W. floribunda* 'Multijuga'. Again there are numerous cultivars.

CONDITIONS

Aspect
Wisterias ideally need a warm sheltered site in full sun. Good growth and flowering are also possible in partial shade.

Site
There is every chance that young wisterias start flowering sooner in poorish or moderately fertile soil. If the soil is too rich they will tend to produce a huge amount of leaf and stem growth instead of focusing their energy on flowers. The site should also be well-drained yet at the same time moisture-retentive.

WISTERIA AT A GLANCE

Vigorous, deciduous twiner with long trusses of pea-like flowers in spring and early summer. Hardy to 5°F (zone 7).

		Recommended Varieties
Jan	/	*W. floribunda* cultivars:
Feb	/	"Alba," white
Mar	planting ✎	"Kuchi-beni," pink and white
Apr	planting ✎	"Rosea," pink
May	flowering ✿	"Royal Purple," purple-violet
Jun	flowering ✿	"Violacea Plena," double,
July	/	violet-blue
Aug	/	*W. sinensis* cultivars:
Sep	/	"Alba," white
Oct	/	'Amethyst', light rose-purple
Nov	/	'Prolific', lilac-blue
Dec	/	

THE DELICATE SHADE of this Wisteria sinensis *and the abundance of its blooms, make it a favorite in British gardens.*

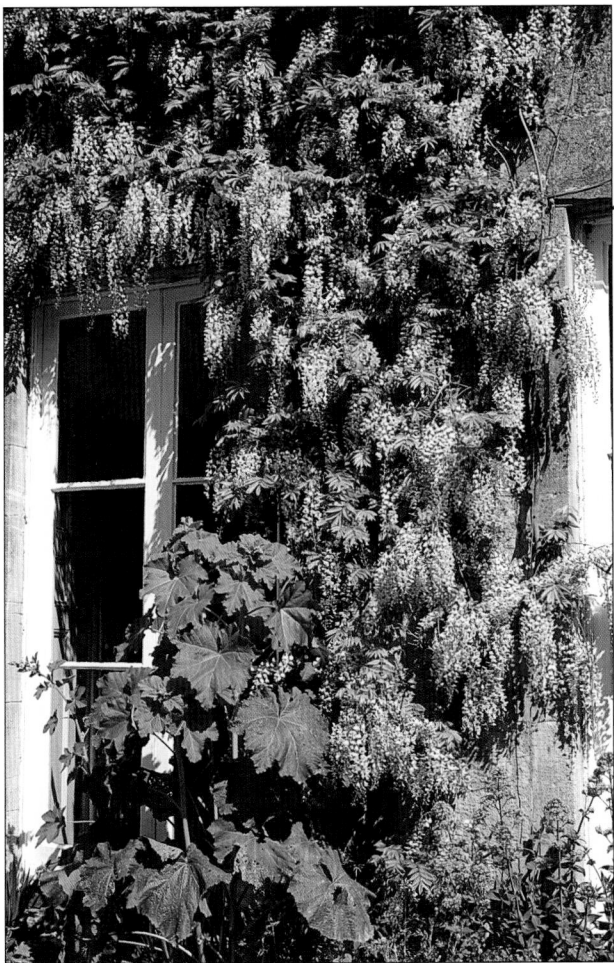

WISTERIA IS particularly effective for framing windows, doors and other architectural elements. Blooms can be trained to droop into view.

GROWING METHOD

Propagation The easiest and most reliable method of propagation for the home gardener is to carry out serpentine layering in the spring. The stems, which are pegged down in a number of places along their length, should be well rooted after a year. Hardwood cuttings of dormant wood may be taken in winter, but these may prove a little slow to root. Once established, wisterias can go on to live for hundreds of years.

Watering Keep young plants well watered. Water established plants only if the soil starts to become excessively dry in summer.

Feeding Avoid fertilizers that are very high in nitrogen as they result in vegetative growth at the expense of flowers. Instead opt for a balanced slow-release organic fertilizer such as blood, fish, and bone. One application per year, made in the spring just as growth is about to start, will be sufficient. Plants in tubs may need a further feed in the summer as plant foods are quickly leached out of containers.

Problems There are a few pests that may trouble wisterias, particularly aphids and scale insects. Also, a fungal leaf spot may appear but it is not considered to be serious. It shows itself as dark brown spots on the foliage.

FLOWERING/FOLIAGE

Flowers The flowers are similar in shape to those of garden peas, and in fact the two plants are related. Unlike peas, though, the flowers are carried in long, pendulous trusses. Blooms are generally fragrant. They appear in late spring and early summer.

Foliage Large, pinnate, mid- to deep green leaves are attractive in spring and summer.

PRUNING

Requirements Train a permanent framework of stems to the shape desired, then spur prune to this. Wisterias can be trained to virtually any shape, but on walls the espalier is a good shape as it has many horizontal branches. These flower much more freely than branches that are trained vertically. This shape also provides a stable base for heavy wisterias. The espalier is completely flat and consists of a single, upright stem with horizontal branches evenly spaced out on each side.

Routine pruning of established wisterias is carried out twice a year to keep new growth under control. In mid-summer cut back the new lateral shoots to within five or six buds of the main framework. Then in mid-winter prune them back further, to within two or three buds of the framework.

If renovation pruning ever becomes necessary, spread the task over several years, thinning out one of the oldest stems each year. Otherwise the flower display will be reduced considerably. The heads of standard wisterias are also spur pruned, in the same way as those grown as climbers.

Cottage
Gardening

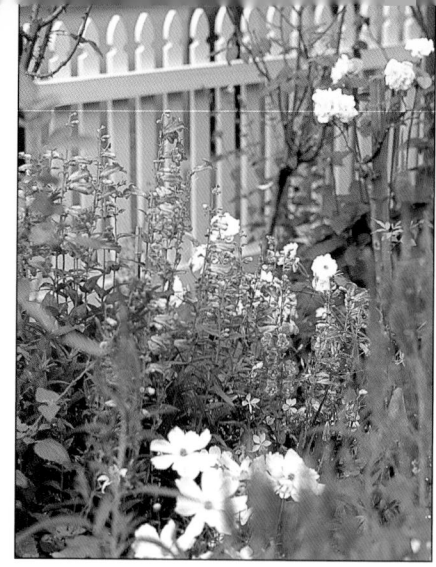

CREATING A COTTAGE GARDEN

ABOVE LEFT: A romantic color scheme in blue, lilac, pink, and white is here carried out with long-blooming summer flowers: pink petunias, blue salvias, *Gaura lindheimeri,* and roses, against a backdrop of a fine blue spruce. ABOVE CENTER: A path through a shaded corner is dressed up for spring in white honesty and sweet bluebells, with a flowering branch of white *Viburnum plicatum* in the foreground. ABOVE RIGHT: Old-fashioned picket fences suit just about any style of house, from the humblest to the grandest. The flowers grown here are deep pink penstemons, cosmos, and white roses. OPPOSITE: This richly-planted border in front of a traditional thatched cottage is packed with a variety of popular cottage garden plants, including lupins, iris, and geraniums. INSET: Yellow Californian poppies and blue iris.

Fashions change in horticulture as they do in all aspects of life. A few years ago, the cry was "Easy maintenance!," the idea being that we were all so busy doing the exciting things that the twentieth century made possible (watching television, traveling, driving fast cars, eating in gourmet restaurants, and working long hours to pay for it all) that we had no time for such old-fashioned chores as working in the garden.

But then some people realized that gardening can still be fun, and that while an easy-maintenance garden of trees, paving, and groundcover plants can indeed be very beautiful, there is great satisfaction to be gained in watching the growth of things that we have actively cultivated.

And so cottage gardens came back into fashion, and it looks as though they will be with us for a very long time to come. For this is the style of gardening that offers most scope to the enthusiastic gardener, and you can make a beautiful cottage garden on a tiny plot just as well as you can on a big one.

But just what is a cottage garden? For that matter, what is a cottage? Originally, a cottage was the dwelling of a farmer or someone who worked on the estate of one of the great landowners, and if cottage gardens had a distinctive style it grew from the way of life of their inhabitants. These were people with little money and less leisure to spend on ornamental gardens.

The plants that the cottagers of old grew on these little plots of land were mainly vegetables and fruit trees, and the herbs that could be used for home-made medicines. They were grown from cuttings and seeds that they exchanged with neighbors and friends. It may seem surprising to us today just how many of our favourite garden plants were originally grown for their usefulness rather than their beauty. Roses, lilies, hollyhocks, foxgloves, calendulas, lily-of-the-valley, and forget-me-nots, were all commonly grown plants which combined beauty with usefulness. (We might wonder

ABOVE LEFT: Bright red poppies sit in front of a generous assortment of perennials, giving the air of lush and informal planting that is characteristic of the cottage garden style.

ABOVE RIGHT: Nowadays we have more time to enjoy our gardens than the cottagers of old. So, whatever its size, make room in your garden for a table and chairs where you can entertain your guests, or simply relax and enjoy the results of your handiwork.

whether sometimes the usefulness was an excuse for the beauty. How often do we justify some small luxury on the grounds that it might be useful?)

There was no room in these early cottage gardens to segregate the plants by type the way we do now—fruit trees here, flowers there, vegetables somewhere else—and so they were all grown together. This happy blending of plants of all types is the legacy of the cottagers to modern gardens.

Not that these gardens were untidy hodgepodges: it was a matter of pride to have a neat and attractive front garden. (The back gardens tended to be filled with washing lines, sheds and chicken runs.) The plants were arranged to give pleasure to the eye—tall hollyhocks at the back, beds edged in lavender or pinks to create a neat finish, and roses trained around doors and along fences.

MODERN COTTAGE GARDENS

Times have changed and we are now wealthy and leisured to a degree that the old cottagers could only dream of. We are no longer dependent on the produce of our gardens for our dinner, and we can indulge in creating gardens for no other reason than simply for our pleasure.

Yet most of us live in smallish houses and our gardens are getting smaller all the time: not for us the splendors of massed trees and banks of shrubs or great sweeps of immaculate lawns and formal rose gardens with twenty bushes of the same variety to a bed. Like the early cottagers, our scope is limited, and like them we find our pleasure in gardening on a small scale—the small view, focusing on the scent of a rose or the graceful lines of a lily—

ABOVE: The cottage gardens of old were very much working gardens, where the cottagers would grow their vegetables and fruit. In this garden the owner has followed in the old tradition by creating a cottage garden potager.

TOP: The gravel path that winds through this cottage garden can scarcely be seen for the profusion of flowers and foliage that tumble over the edges or that have self-seeded amongst the stones and gravel.

LEFT: Their ease of cultivation and wide range of flowers and foliage make the hardy geraniums invaluable plants for the modern cottage garden border.

not massed by their hundreds but in three of this and four of that. Whenever we grow many different flowers in a relatively small space, we are indeed gardening in the cottage style.

Some gardeners feel very strongly that a modern cottage garden should be a re-creation of an old one. They choose to limit what they grow in their cottage garden to "old-fashioned" flowers, and they worry about whether it is "authentic" to have a lawn or to grow flowering shrubs.

If you live in an old cottage (or indeed in a grand old house) you might care to take this approach, it is in a sense the horticultural equivalent of restoring and furnishing a house "in period." But while it can be fun to re-create an "authentic" cottage garden there is no need to keep to such a strictly limited style if you do not feel that you want to. The cottage garden style is a manner of gardening that is as flattering to a modern house as it is to an old one.

Let your approach and your layout be simple and straightforward, and designed to suit your own personal requirements and interests, and those of your family. If you need a lawn for the children to play on, or a terrace or patio on which to sit and talk to friends, or entertain them to a meal, then make them. Adapt the style to suit you.

Plant trees and shrubs for shade and privacy; and indulge yourself in your favorite plants and flowers, whether they are old or new, mixing and matching them with each other and with herbs and edible plants. Some of the plants you choose may be modern hybrids, some may be plants that the cottagers could never afford, but many will be the old-fashioned, easy to grow favorites. For, as the saying goes, fashions may change, but beauty, never!

ABOVE LEFT: Hollyhocks are among the first plants you turn to when planting your cottage borders. Here they are planted with shrubby lavateras against a warm brick wall in front of trained fruit trees.

ABOVE RIGHT: If allowed, perfumed climbers and wall shrubs soften house walls and frame windows. That way, they'll mingle seductively with the scent from windowboxes like this one planted with stocks.

PLANNING AND PLANTING

The cottage garden embodies an idyll of rural life set against a background of bulging thatch, lichen-encrusted stone, and leaded lights. There's no doubt that it has a romantic, beguiling quality that holds many of us in its spell and it has become a style that is universally admired. Part of the charm is that it looks so effortlessly achieved, as though it hasn't actually been planned at all, but has just grown up out of the surrounding landscape. It would be misleading, though, to suggest that maintaining a cottage garden is as leisurely as the once yearly clip over with the shears that a heather garden requires. Like many things in life, it reflects the effort and imagination we put in. But exactly how is it done? Here are some ground rules for ingredients, that, when assembled, should fulfil all your most romantic yearnings, in a cottage garden at least!

HALLMARKS OF THE COTTAGE GARDEN
- A framework of paths and walls built using local materials—stone, brick, cobbles, and gravel—will echo the construction of the house.
- An element of self-seeding is essential. Plants popping up out of cracks and crevices in walls and paving will look more spontaneous than any attempt at introducing them.
- Naturalise bulbs in rough cut grass, like snowdrops, crocus, narcissus, and snakeshead fritillary. They look charming amongst wizened apple trees in flower, with speedwell running through the grass, reflecting the blue sky above.
- Encourage native species to encroach on the boundaries. Plants from hedgerows and woodland, such as nettle-leaved bellflower, red campion, bluebells, and anemones, can be

encouraged and will blur the division between country and garden. Don't raid the countryside for them, though!

• The scene is incomplete without a generous assortment of plants, including cottage perennials, climbers, shrubs, herbs, alpines, annuals, and bulbs, to give a rich profusion of flowers, foliage and perfume to clothe walls, fill borders and cheer up containers. Choose old-fashioned varieties if possible, not highly bred, often over-sized versions, that have lost the natural character of the species.

Sometimes it's easier to decide what to include in your layout by identifying "no go" areas. Here are a list of ingredients that definitely won't fit into the traditional cottage garden.

OUT OF CONTEXT
The following plants and features will strike a discordant note:
• Dwarf conifers—pass these over in favour of clipped box, holly, and yew.
• Rock gardens—plant dry stone walls and raised beds with alpines instead.
• Deep lawn edges with soil thrown back in a steep camber.
• Bamboos, hybrid tea roses, beds planted exclusively with heathers.
• Modern paving materials, classical statues and urns, balustrading.

LEARNING FROM THE PAST

If you've got your sights set on recreating a traditional cottage garden layout, it is worth looking again, briefly, at the significance attached to the gardens and specific plants they contained. During the latter part of the nineteenth century a farm laborer would have

ABOVE LEFT: Each of these three plants will perpetuate itself freely from seed. Orange Pilosella has worked its way up through our native Tutsan (*Hypericum androsaemum*). Lady's mantle provides the edging.

ABOVE RIGHT: *Smyrnium perfoliatum* is an eye-catching biennial that resembles a euphorbia, but is in fact related to cow parsley. It blends in beautifully with purple honesty rising above a haze of forget-me-nots.

ABOVE: With a rich scent of myrrh, the shrub rose "Constance Spry" is of recent origin but has the character of old-fashioned roses and looks lovely with honeysuckle growing nearby.

TOP: Lavender and cottage pinks make ideal companions for roses. Here David Austin's recent introduction "Scepter'd Isle" is further enhanced by the deep red *Astrantia* "Hadspen Blood".

ABOVE RIGHT: For hot, dry beds on the fringes of the garden, imposing Scotch thistle will soon form self-perpetuating colonies as it has among these opium poppies. The idea would also work well in gravel.

earned little for a week's work on the land, so his garden provided plenty of food, a point graphically illustrated in *Larkrise to Candleford* by Flora Thompson: "The men took great pride in their gardens... Fat green peas, broad beans as big as a halfpenny, cauliflowers a child could make an armchair of, runner beans and cabbage and kale, all in their season... A few slices of bread and home-made lard flavored with rosemary, and plenty of green food "went down good" as they used to say."

Nowadays, ornamental plants will certainly dominate the modern cottage garden, but if you want fruit and vegetables tucked in among the blooms in your garden, try gooseberries, rhubarb, red cabbage, lettuce, and curly kale—all will appeal to the eye and the tastebuds.

It is great fun to entertain your guests with a few amusing anecdotes. Include the following plants in your garden scheme and you'll have the perfect excuse to introduce a good story.

• Cottagers would take comfort in the knowledge that their tight cluster of houseleeks (*Sempervivum*) growing on the roof tiles would protect their property from being struck by lightning.

• As well as providing food for birds and looking informal enough to be planted in the cottage garden, a rowan tree was said to ward off witches.

• Colorful plants were given colorful names by country folk. Once you have heard the red valerian (*Centranthus ruber*) referred to as "Welcome home husband though never so drunk", you'll never see it in quite the same light again. It does have a habit of wandering around the garden in a rather aimless fashion!

ABOVE: Avoid the regimented parks department approach to tulips by planting them in clumps so they emerge through carpets of poached-egg flower and dainty violas.

TOP: In wilder areas of the cottage garden why not let vigorous carpeters like snow in summer and suckering spurge cypress loose among self-seeding blue alkanet, aquilegia and pot marigold.

ABOVE LEFT: To encourage a rich variety of wild flowers to grow like these you must start with a poor soil and fine grass seed mixture. A corner summerhouse made in a vernacular style makes a fine viewpoint.

ADAPTING THE STYLE

If you're lucky enough to live in a honey-colored Cotswold stone cottage then you have the perfect excuse to adopt the cottage garden look, hook line and sinker, and are probably already collecting the free range eggs and filling your hanky drawers with lavender bags. But what if you live in a relatively new house or in a town or city semi or in a row of Victorian terraces? Don't worry, because the look travels well. It's only likely to jar against the backdrop of an ultra modern steel and glass style house or a formal Georgian town house with a central door and windows arranged symmetrically either side. Elsewhere you can enjoy the rich variety of planting or those rustic eye-catchers like staddle stones, thatched bird houses and old mangles. Cottage garden practices bring with them many advantages. A mixed country style hedge, for example, is likely to attract a rich variety of birds into your garden, more even perhaps than in a country setting, especially if surrounded by prairie style, intensively managed farmland. It is certainly a more attractive proposition than a sombre wall of leylandii conifers or surrounding your plot with stark off-the-peg mass-produced fence panels. With hazel, hawthorn, holly, guelder rose, and beech in your hedge and carpets of daffodils, bluebells, and wood anemones beneath, it is not hard to imagine yourself in the very heart of the countryside.

The more we begin to think about the practical requirements our garden has to fulfil, the less realistic it becomes to live inside a chocolate box cover. Families in particular put stresses and strains on our plots, and play areas and cycle tracks for the children, parking spaces for cars and caravans and utility areas for drying clothes and storing dustbins must all be considered at the outset. Privacy and screening are also a primary concern in gardens

ABOVE: This lovers' knot has been planted with low interlocking hedges of lonicera and santolina and filled in with pansies and forget-me-nots. Wallflowers tie the garden neatly together like a yellow ribbon right outside a cottage window. The centrepiece is tulips planted in an upturned rhubarb forcing pot. Because the hedges are both evergreen they will give a permanent structure that can be bedded out around and in between them twice a year. Nasturtium "Alaska Mxd" and pot marigold "Fiesta Gitana Mxd" would make a pleasing summer scheme.

that are surrounded by houses, and strategically placed evergreens are likely to be essential. Don't worry. By breaking up the garden into a series of smaller units, it's quite possible to zone all your wants and needs so they don't conflict one with the other.

PATIOS, PATHS AND BOUNDARIES

The patio is probably the most fundamental feature in the garden nowadays and even the most hardworking "cottagers" will welcome the opportunity to sit back and relax with a drink and a biscuit and gaze out on their handiwork. Large wall-to-wall strips of buff paving slabs pointed with mortar across the back of the house are most unlikely to achieve the desired look for they will deny plants the chance to seed themselves and the garden to appear to flow right up to the house walls. Here are some tips to enable you to integrate your patio into the cottage style:

• A paved area that combines together three or four surfaces in a rich pattern adds contrast of color and texture.
• Include pockets of loose-laid materials like pebbles, gravel, and setts that can be put down on sand (or even soil if it is light and free draining). You can then plant herbs and alpines to grow through them, sow seed of hardy annuals or let nature take its course and see what seeds itself.
• Rather than have one huge patio, consider building two or three smaller ones facing different points of the compass, or follow the sun around your garden and build, for example, a west-facing patio to catch the evening sun.
• Decorate your patio with clusters of pots, stone troughs and an old watering

can or two. Go mad and lay old timber beams, fire-baskets, fossils, millstones, and even bottles (neck down) into your paved mosaic for a slightly eccentric look.

• Let the planting wrap itself around your patio in a soft embrace. You'll enjoy the proximity of scented leaves and blooms and your patio will quickly achieve a look of maturity beyond its years.

With your patio in place, the next logical step is to link it to the rest of the garden through a network of paths. Traditional cottage garden layouts were surprisingly formal with a straight path up the plot (often to the front or back door) bisected by other paths coming off at right angles. The reason they don't appear so formal is that once plants have spilled over and seeded into the paths, the hard lines are softened and disguised. These grid systems of paths will result in the most authentic layouts and if each path leads to, say, a seat in a perfumed bower, a sundial or, more practically, the tool shed or hen house, the garden will be both rewarding and easy to work in. You may like to set as an objective being able to reach all your borders from a pathway (even if it's with a hoe) to keep the soil off your boots as much as possible.

As with patios, combining materials in your paths will make them a feature in themselves.

CHOOSING MATERIALS.

Choose from old materials:

• Broken and random rectangular York stone.
• Salvaged bricks, stable pavers, and granite setts.

ABOVE LEFT: Don't be reluctant to sow varieties of annuals that are more highly bred than their wild counterparts when they're as big an improvement as these "Fiesta Gitana" strain of pot marigolds. They are a lovely contrast to *Fuchsia* "Mrs Popple".

ABOVE RIGHT: Red cabbage is handsome enough to mix with flowers from early summer right through to the fall. "Ruby Ball" acts as a foil to pansies and Sweet Williams.

RIGHT: This cast iron harrow has been used to support a handsome collection of striped marrows as their skins ripen and harden in the late summer sunshine. The cosmos, behind, seed in this garden from year to year.

ABOVE: Old clay roof tiles laid sideways on don't need to be arranged as expertly as these, though they do undeniably make a beautifully mitered corner.

ABOVE: These square concrete block pavers have been tumbled in a giant mixer to age them. Creeping thyme and chamomile provide further softening.

ABOVE: Old timber beams are used to box in salvaged bricks and make a patio that is almost a mirror image of the cottage walls.

- Quarry tiles, clay roof tiles laid on edge.
- Roof slates broken up into small pieces.

New materials:

- Paving slabs that have been cast from moulds taken from older materials such as Victorian flagstones.
- Bricks and concrete pavers that have been "tumbled" to knock off the corners and give an aged finish.
- "Antique" look concrete bricks and tiles that have been made to look like clay and terracotta.
- Pebbles, gravel, and chippings.
- Stock and brindles with several soft colors in their make up rather than raw red engineering bricks.

BOUNDARIES

As well as the country-style hedge mentioned earlier, fences made from natural materials, although more expensive than more widely available alternatives, lend an instant flavor of the countryside and an almost medieval character. Peeled, woven willow and hazel hurdles and tree heather panels look superb even without clothing plants. Low lengths of willow can be used to define the edge of beds and miniature split hazel "gates" are a delight along cottage borders or even as a support for a top-heavy plant.

Yew, quickthorn, beech, box, and field maple are all good choices for hedges; Leyland cypress is definitely not.

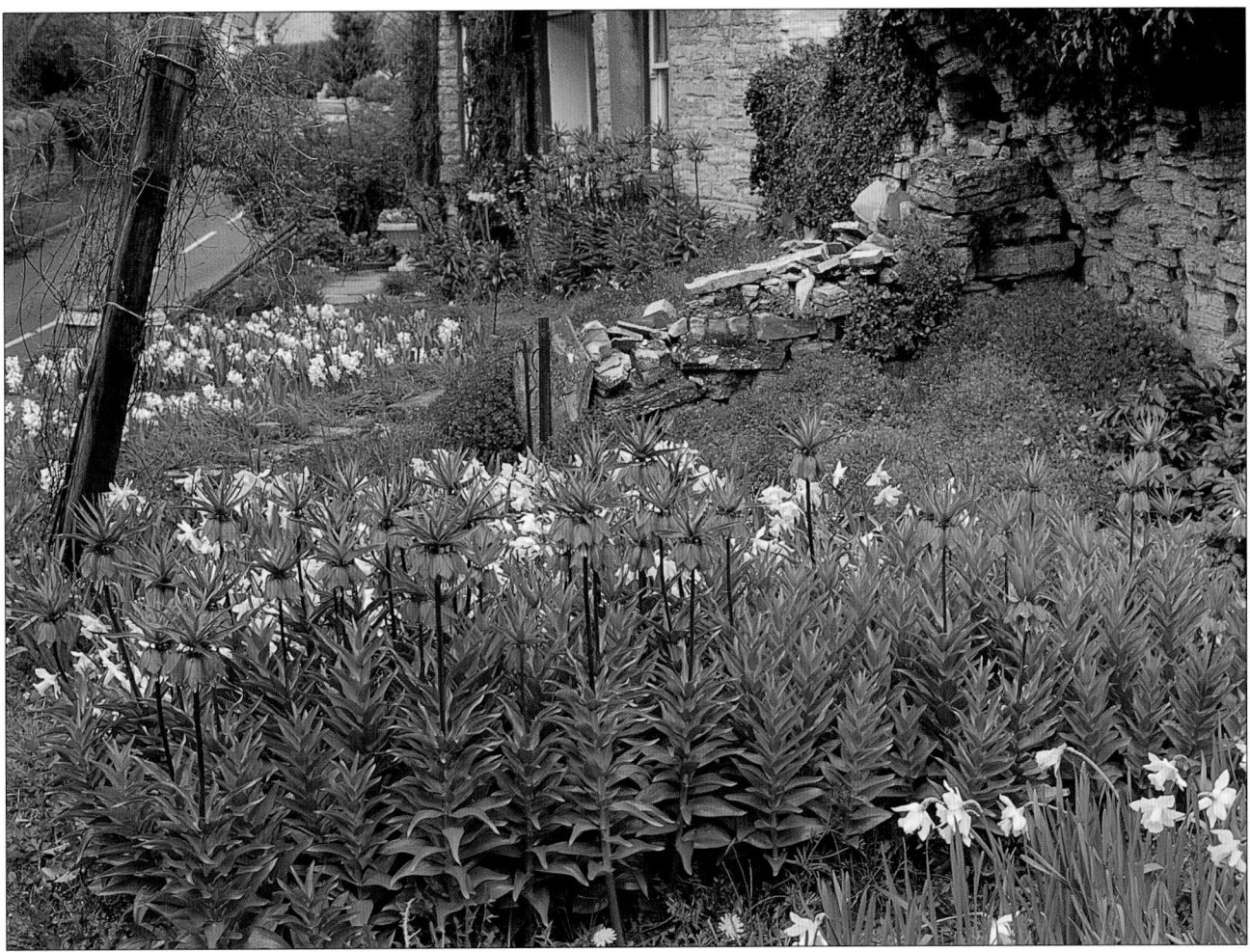

PLANTING UP YOUR GARDEN

There's no denying that we are spoilt for choice when it comes to choosing plants for our garden nowadays and cottage gardeners of old would have taken great delight in the many new and improved varieties of old favorites and even some plants that would be unknown to them. However, if a traditional style of planting is your aim, then there are species that just don't sit comfortably with all those hollyhocks, rambling roses, and Canterbury bells. Plants of exotic or contemporary appearance like phormiums and cordylines, for example. Similarly, aristocrats like tree magnolias and large-leaved rhododendrons would have represented a king's ransom to a cottage gardener. Here is a list of classic varieties that are guaranteed to exist in harmony. You will find out about many of them later in the book.

CLASSIC COTTAGE GARDEN PLANTS
Herbaceous perennials—hollyhocks, pinks, lady's mantle (alchemilla), lupins, delphiniums, Hattie's pincushion (astrantia), bleeding heart (dicentra), Michaelmas daisies, auriculas, pyrethrums, poppies, irises, bellflowers, cowslips, and primroses.
Shrubs —lavender, rosemary, flowering quince, old roses, daphne, hardy fuchsia, mock orange, buddleja, lilacs.
Annuals and biennials—wallflowers, Sweet Williams, double daisies, pansies and violas, cornflowers, love-in-a-mist, nasturtiums, candytuft, Canterbury bells, larkspur, stocks, sunflowers.
Herbs—many would have been grown for their medicinal properties: feverfew, fennel, comfrey, lemon balm, chamomile, chives, sage, thyme, rue, hyssop, marjoram, mint.

ABOVE: Who could imagine a more charming spring scene than this thriving colony of red crown imperials marching through daffodils and past stone walls encrusted with aubrieta right up to the cottage door. Of course, a garden that is too reliant on spring bulbs will lack interest later in the year, so aim to have plenty of perennials planted in between to keep up the momentum.

ABOVE LEFT: Everything except the kitchen sink is a bit of an exaggeration, but by mixing different types of paving units and even including this iron firebasket you can create an interesting patterned mosaic.

ABOVE RIGHT: Although dry stacked bricks laid like this may at first appear unstable, surprisingly, they will in fact make a sturdy wall that requires little expertise to build and has a pleasing, informal quality that makes a perfect backdrop for informal cottage garden planting.

Self-seeding plants—honesty, forget-me-not, Welsh poppy, red valerian, verbascum, fennel, columbine, foxgloves, nettle-leaved bellflower, love-in-a-mist, opium poppy, Scotch thistle. *Bulbs*—crown imperials, Madonna and martagon lilies, snowdrops, narcissus, aconites, and anemones.

CHOOSING YOUR PLANTS

Most cottage garden plants are by their very nature obliging and easy to please, but it is still important to consider your own unique conditions before rushing out and buying on impulse. Choose plants that will tolerate or even thrive in hot sun or dry shade, wet sticky soil or soil that is alkaline (limey). Exposure too is a factor. Tall delphiniums would soon be blown over in windy sites and in a low-lying spot you may find that frost collects and plants may be damaged (fruit blossom, for example) whereas further up the slope the blooms are untouched.

YEAR ROUND COLOR

As you'll see from the list of recommended plants, cottage gardens are a jostling mixture of everything from a tree to a bulb or hardy annual, but in our desire to recreate those idyllic cottage cameos typified by the watercolors of Helen Allingham it's easy to plant for summer at the expense of wintertime and those cottage borders must have reverted to a forest of sticks by November. Evergreens are needed to give backbone so aim for at least a quarter of your plants to retain their leaves by choosing the likes of box, holly, viburnum, yew, elaeagnus, spotted laurel, and mahonia; berries and bark will also add much appeal.

We don't often consider the fact that a double red peony is only at its best for a few days, but it's important to weigh up a plant's flowering period, particularly if space is limited. Compare this with *Aster* x *frikartii* or *Coreopsis verticillata* that give months of bloom. Some plants have such charisma that you accept their shortcomings; rust disease on hollyhocks, for example.

WORKING TO A BUDGET

If you're on a tight budget, here are some ideas to save money:

• Grow perennials from seed. Most seed catalogues list varieties that can be readily grown from seed. Some like achillea, coreopsis and *Lobelia cardinalis* will produce a few flowers in the first year.

• Look out for big clumps of perennials for sale in small pots. These can be split in spring and early summer into two or even three separate pieces.

• Swap plants with friends and neighbors, but identify any incomers first in case they take over the garden!

SPACING

A good rule of thumb when planting out perennials is to put in five plants per square metre but such large blocks of a single variety may not be in keeping with the spontaneous explosion of color where plants jostle and compete for space and attention. Neither will a

ABOVE RIGHT: A weathered statue of Pan sits alongside a fallen apple tree bough in this stark wintry scene. As he is a woodland creature, the chosen setting for Pan is perfect.

ABOVE LEFT: Staddle stones were used to raise wooden grain stores off the ground and secure them against rats and would inevitably find their way into cottagers' plots. This lichen-encrusted top contrasts beautifully with a carpet of aubrieta.

ABOVE LEFT: Clematis and honeysuckle are beginning to entwine in a delightful duet along an old wall where the niches have been filled with a pensioned-off teapot, houseleeks and a terracotta finial.

ABOVE RIGHT: It's hard to imagine a more apt and romantic viewpoint than this from which to look out on your garden. This willow seat has already begun to take on an air of permanence with ivy clambering up the sides and poking through the weave.

border carefully regulated for height from front to back give the desired effect. The best technique is to build a framework of permanent plants to start with by laying out key trees and evergreen and deciduous shrubs first, using their heights and spreads after ten years to guide you. Then fill in the gaps with cottage perennials and annuals. Include self-seeders and they will soon get a foothold, and in the fall underplant with bulbs. Do any fine tuning in the second year for most plants won't object to being moved about. You may wish to avoid potential color clashes, orange with pink for example, or not be too precious about color themes, and concepts. Contrast, however, is important so juxtapose tall spires with round shapes and low spreaders every now and then for a stimulating picture.

GROUND PREPARATION AND PLANTING

Here are some useful tips:
- Keep off the soil when wet and avoid planting when the ground is frozen or waterlogged.
- Dig in plenty of organic matter: garden compost, spent mushroom compost, or composted bark for example.
- Stand bare-root or container-grown plants in water for an hour before planting so they are thoroughly soaked.
- Prepare a planting hole deep and wide enough to allow the roots to spread.
- A mulch of bark chippings or cocoa shell around your plants will keep in moisture and suppress weeds.
- Keep plants well watered and staked (if necessary) and watch for pests and diseases.

ABOVE: Cats are guaranteed to find the warmest, cosiest spot and no cottage garden is really complete without one. They have a way of watching you at work as if to say, "I wouldn't do it like that."

TOP: The best place for rhubarb forcing jars is in the rhubarb patch and likewise seakale forcing jars. Seakale is a handsome vegetable with clouds of white flowers and leathery gray leaves.

ABOVE LEFT: Cast iron garden rollers have long ceased to be an essential piece of gardening equipment, but they still make an impression, abandoned, like this one, in an overgrown patch.

EYE-CATCHERS

Perhaps even more enjoyable than getting your plants into position is adding those finishing touches that catch the eye and add that little spark of magic that singles out an average garden from something really special. It's very much like positioning your favorite ornaments in a room that's just been decorated. It also requires a similar level of thought, for just plonking down your cottage props wherever there's a gap will rarely succeed. Often it's fun to come across an ornament by chance, tucked away perhaps amongst planting. A garden roller in the orchard half concealed by flowers and grasses is more romantic than one stranded on the patio. Even staddle stones look more permanent when "anchored" by carpeting plants at their base.

Here are a selection of suitable props for an authentic working cottage garden environment:
- Eye-catchers—these should be unpretentious, ideally the sort of everyday objects that would be in the garden anyway: boot scraper, besom (twig broom), wooden wheelbarrow, old watering can, garden roller, bee hive, stone water trough, seakale and rhubarb forcers, hens, well-head (beware of twee versions), pig sty, outdoor privy, sundial, cast-iron pump.
- Planters—half oak barrels, simple hand-thrown earthenware pots, stone troughs, galvanised baths, and dolly tubs.

When everything's in place, sit back in your woven armchair and admire your handiwork, but don't let the grass grow under your feet!

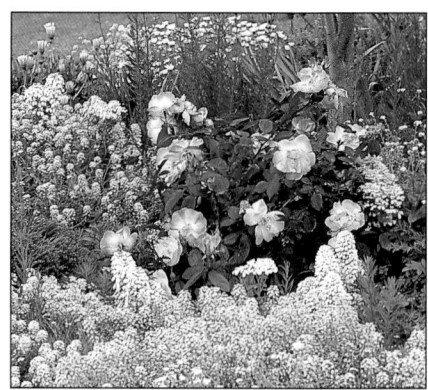

CREATING A FRAGRANT GARDEN

ABOVE LEFT: There is plenty of scent in this garden from lavender and the climbing roses; the daisies can be just eye-pleasing.
ABOVE CENTER: Plants with scented leaves are favorites for growing along paths, where you can brush against them as you pass by and release their fragrance. Here mounds of golden lemon thyme and gray lavender add tang to a kaleidoscope of early summer flowers.
ABOVE RIGHT: Everyone loves the scent of roses but not all offer much to the nose. This one, 'Escapade', is pleasantly fragrant. The white flowers are candytuft.
OPPOSITE: Cottage pinks and sweet Williams combine in an old galvanised tub to give a pot-pourri of fragrance. The edging is the dwarf form of golden feverfew.
INSET: A hedge of fragrant lavender (*Lavandula dentata*) edges this path.

Of our five senses, the sense of smell is the least developed but that doesn't prevent it being perhaps the most subtle. Any woman knows that perfume is an important part of feeling her best. While a garden composed of scentless plants can be very beautiful, it is fragrance that makes it romantic and memorable. Many old-fashioned plants are delightfully scented, and no cottage garden would be complete without a selection of fragrant flowers and foliage, not only for enjoying as you walk through the garden or linger on a well-placed seat, but also for cutting for the house or preserving as pot-pourri or fragrant sachets so that you can enjoy their perfumes for longer.

The fragrance of a garden comes from many different things. There is the scent of freshly dug earth, heavy with fertility, the soft odor of new-mown grass and the sharp tang of compost—this is the smell of decay, certainly, but it is a decay that is rich with the promise of new life. After rain, the air in the garden smells fresh and sweet. These are the scents that signal that a garden is alive. It is against this background, which is almost unnoticed, that the gardener then weaves magic with the fragrance of flowers and scented leaves.

It is easy when drawing ideas from books to forget just how powerful this magic can be—scent cannot be photographed, and there are few words to describe it. We can say that a particular flower is pink, or blue, and the reader can then form a picture of what it might look like—but scents can't really be described except by comparison. You can say a flower has a scent like wine, but that doesn't really help much.

Plants don't give off their fragrance all the time in the same way. Night-scented flowers that may be overwhelming in the evening are apt to be odorless by day, and often the fragrance of a flower changes subtly as it develops. Many roses, for instance, offer a slightly different perfume when fully blown from that they gave when they were just opening.

ABOVE: A comfortable chair invites you to sit a little while and enjoy the blended scent of lilac and white banksian roses while they are at their early summer best. It can be moved when they are finished to wherever other scented blossoms are enjoying their flowering season.

OPPOSITE: Profuse and generous planting is a hallmark of cottage garden style. A colorful assortment of perennials mingle with annuals, bulbs and shrubs, while climbers cover the walls of the cottage. Many of the old-fashioned cottage garden plants are delightfully fragrant, so place these alongside paths and next to doors and windows so that you can enjoy their perfume whenever you pass by.

Scent varies with the weather, too. The scent of flowers is best on warm, humid days, and after a shower of rain. It blows away on a windy day, and evaporates rapidly if the air is too dry and hot. This leads us to the first rule for the creation of a fragrant garden—let it be sheltered.

As any garden designer faced with a client who dislikes pink (or yellow, or blue) knows, people's perception of color varies greatly, and our perception of scent varies even more. What to one person is pleasing and refreshing, to another may be heavy and cloying. We know, too, that the sense of smell declines as you get older or if you are in the habit of smoking heavily.

Happily, the blending of scents isn't as fine a business as that of harmonising color. Place two colors side by side, and the eye sees them separately, judging whether their juxtaposition is harmonious or not. Plant two scented plants together and, provided one doesn't overwhelm the other, the first impression you get will be a blend of the two. Move in closer and sniff each in turn, and the nose will forget the first one when sensing the second.

So, as long as the scented plants you choose please your senses, you can mix and match them without fear of clashing. But don't expect that anyone will notice the subtle scent of a bearded iris if there is a jasmine in full bloom nearby.

SITING FRAGRANT PLANTS

How should you place your fragrant plants? The real garden-scenters such as the jasmines and honeysuckles can be placed almost anywhere and the nose will seek them out. But most flowers offer their delights best on close sniffing, and you don't want to have to wade through a bed of other plants to reach them. They should be placed toward the front of the bed, lining the path where you walk, next to a favorite garden chair or by the front door where a visitor can enjoy their perfume while they are waiting for you to answer the bell.

Climbing plants with a strong fragrance are perfect for surrounding an arbor or garden seating area and for growing on walls next to doors and windows. They bring their flowers up to a height where you can most enjoy the perfume, and when the doors and windows are open the fragrance will waft into the house, so it can be enjoyed both indoors and out. Don't forget to include some fragrant flowers in your windowboxes and hanging baskets too, as they can be enjoyed in much the same way.

Scented leaves demand to be put where you will encounter them closely—most of them will not release their fragrance unless they are disturbed. Plant them where you will brush against them as you walk past: a lavender hedge along a path, a clump of eau-de-cologne mint at the front gate, or scented herbs lining the edges of vegetable beds, where you will brush against them as you lean over to gather cabbages. Low-growing, creeping thymes and chamomile can be planted between the paving stones in a path or patio. They are surprisingly tolerant of being walked on and will release a delightful fragrance as you walk across them. You could position a raised tub of aromatic foliage close to where you like to sit, or even construct an old-fashioned chamomile seat.

Flowers that only bloom late in the day or at night, such as the evening primrose and night-scented stocks, are well worth growing but need special thought when it comes to placing them. Most of us don't wander very far into the garden at night, and so they should be positioned where you can light them up and see them as well as smell them, such as by a patio or the path to the front door. The same applies to those that remain open but scentless by day, such as tobacco flowers.

With all this concentration on detail, don't forget the bigger picture. Fragrant or not, any garden needs to suit the way you live—you'll need trees for shade, carefully chosen to be the right shape and size for your particular garden and cunningly placed so that they allow in the winter sun; a place for the children to play; maybe a vegetable patch; and paths (of easy gradient, with steps as needed) to lead you from one part of the garden to the other—these provide the melody, the orchestra if you like, with which your scented plants will sing.

Patio gardens

Containers are an ideal way to bring color and life to your patio. They will give you much greater flexibility in planning your design, and allow every bit of space to be exploited to the full. The dullest corner of the patio can be instantly transformed, and pots and plants can be mixed and matched to keep your patio looking good at all times. They can disguise an eyesore, fill an awkward corner, or create an instant effect. For example, just a few pots of bright annuals will bring color to a newly-constructed patio while more permanent planting is established.

Containers in all shapes and sizes are ideal for breaking the monotony of large expanses of paving, adding color, softening hard lines, and enabling you to create your own special style. Whether you prefer the look of a cottage garden, formal terrace, Mediterranean sun-trap, exotic Oriental garden or cool, green oasis, using containers will make it quick and easy to create the effect. And if you change your mind, it is just as simple to swop the containers around for a completely different style.

You can even change the apparent shape of the patio by moving containers to different positions, or you can break up a large featureless area into a linked group of smaller, more intimate spaces.

Tall pots, or climbers and other tall-growing plants, can be especially valuable in bringing height to large flat areas, dividing up the space, or creating instant screens.

There are many different ways

Bank up a wall of summer color at the edge of your patio by placing a collection of pots side by side.

Herbs like parsley and golden-leaved marjoram provide a decorative and useful foil amongst bright bedding.

to make use of patio pots. The door to the patio can be made into a feature by positioning tubs on either side of it, filled with either formal or informal planting.

Containers could be placed at intervals around the edge of the patio, either defining a boundary separating the patio from the surrounding garden, or, by careful choice of complementary plants, linking it with the general garden. Pots can also be usefully positioned to mark the corner of the patio or the edge of a path or set of steps.

As patios are so often positioned next to the house, they can be used to create a visual link between house and garden, and this can be worth considering when planning patio containers. The different colors, shapes and textures of both pots and plants can be chosen to complement the decor of the house as well as each other to make a co-ordinating display.

The junction between patio

and house wall is one of those spots that can so often look bleak and bare and a few tubs filled with colorful flowers will provide a quick and simple way of brightening this space.

Unlike a permanent border planting, the pots can easily be moved if you need to get at the house for painting or general maintenance. Adding a few pots of climbers will add height and form and will quickly give a more established air.

CHOOSING PLANTS

Carefully chosen plants can make all the difference between a dull patio and one that is full of color and interest. You can have potted flowers throughout the year if you choose plants with a variety of flowering times. The table on page 748 provides a general guide to seasonal flowers and foliage, although the precise flowering times will depend on the local conditions in your area.

While it is always a good idea to arrange your garden so that there is something of interest all year round, this is even more important when planning patios because they are nearly always sited where they can seen from the house and are therefore seen more frequently than other areas of the garden. It is therefore well worth making the effort to create a display that you can enjoy all the time, even on rainy days when you can only look out of the window.

As patio plants will be seen at closer quarters than most other plants in the garden, you will want plants that are looking their best. Container plants are ideal here as they can be moved onto the patio as they come into flower, and removed and swopped for something else as they start to fade.

Consider the aspect of your patio, and choose your container plants accordingly. A dark, north-facing patio need not be dull if you choose plants that will thrive in a shady spot, such as brightly variegated ivies and other foliage plants.

In contrast, a sunny south-facing patio will heat up surprisingly quickly and should be planted with drought-tolerant varieties if you want to keep your plants in good condition and cannot manage regular watering.

Houseplants can even be given a holiday and used to brighten dull corners of a patio when the warmer summer days arrive. Many houseplants have exotic flowers and foliage that can be used to add a new dimension to a patio arrangement.

If you use your patio a lot in the evenings, choose big and bold containers and plants with strong, architectural shapes that will show up well in poor light. Consider how colors appear in the low light at dusk too. Flowers in colors such as white and blue will show up well, while reds and purples, for example, will disappear into the background.

COLOR

Color is very much a question of personal taste, and while some may prefer a brilliant patchwork of colors, in the restricted space of small patios too many colors can sometimes look too 'busy' and can result in too many color clashes, and it is often best to keep to no more than three colors.

More subtle, single or two-tone color schemes can also work particularly well in the restricted space of a patio.

The choice of color will have a great influence on the mood you can create. Hot colors such as red, orange, or yellow are vibrant and will draw the eye and foreshorten a view, while pastel colors have a far more tranquil character.

Choose shades that will harmonise with one another for a restful effect, or those that will create a contrast for a more striking and exciting display.

Good use can be made of foliage too; the greens and grays of leaves are great harmonisers, balancing and softening the impact of the stronger colors in a display, while colorful foliage can

FALL	WINTER	SPRING	SUMMER
Asters	Bergenias	Anemone	Alyssum
Fall crocus	Box	Aubrieta	Begonia
Chrysanthemum	Christmas rose	Azalea	Busy Lizzie
Cobaea scandens	Crocus	Bergenia	(Impatiens)
Cotoneaster	Dwarf conifers	Bluebell	Calendula
Cyclamen	Euonymus	Camellia	Campanula
Dahlia	Gaultheria	Chionodoxa	Clematis
Fuchsias	Hollies	Clematis	Everlastings
Heathers	Iris histriodes	Dianthus	Felicia
Japanese anemone	Ivies	Forget-me-not	Fuchsia
Japanese maples	Mahonia	Fritillaries	Geranium
Michaelmas daisy	Pansies	Grape hyacinth	Helichrysum
Ornamental	Polyanthus	Hyacinth	Herbs
cabbage and kale	Skimmia	Lenten rose	Hosta
Sedum	Snowdrops	Magnolia	Lilies
	Topiary	Narcissus	Lobelia
	Viburnum tinus	Periwinkle	Marigolds
	Winter-flowering	Polyanthus	Nicotiana
	heathers	Primulas	Pelargonium
		Rhododendron	Petunia
		Tulip	Rock rose
		Wallflower	Rose
			Salvia
			Snapdragon
			Strawberries
			Sweet pea

often provide a longer-lasting effect than flowers.

Create new effects by planting different varieties close together and allowing the plants to mingle – the flowers of the different plants appearing to grow together, or the flowers of one emerging through the leaves of another.

SHAPE

Take structure and form into account, as well as color, when planning your patio containers. A variety of shapes and heights will add much to the design and trailing plants always look good tumbling over the edge of containers, softening the outline and linking the container with the surroundings.

When planning your containers, consider how they will look from all angles. If the containers are to stand against a house wall the design only needs to be considered from the front, but if you are creating a free-standing arrangement, it needs to appear equally attractive from all sides.

An often-quoted general rule is to put the tallest plants at the centre or back, surrounded by lower growing ones, but equally effective displays can be created with an off-center scheme. Do not be afraid to experiment. After all, a container display is so easy to change if you find you do not like the effect.

FRAGRANCE

A sunny patio can provide an ideal setting for scented plants as a warm position will encourage the release of fragrant oils which will linger longer in the sheltered air. Place a raised tub of fragrant flowers or aromatic foliage next to a favourite seat, or put pots of

scented plants near doors and windows so that their fragrance can be enjoyed from the house as

Geraniums are real sun-lovers and flower best when a little root-bound – but do not forget to water them regularly.

well as the patio. If you use the patio for evening meals and entertaining, you could also include flowers that have a stronger fragrance in the evening, such as night-scented stocks and nicotianas.

Patio plants are likely to be brushed against frequently so include some plants with aromatic foliage, such as lemon verbena and scented-leaved geraniums, so that you can enjoy their fragrance as you pass by.

A KITCHEN GARDEN

Keen cooks could group pots of herbs together close to the back door, or to a barbecue area, to

form an instant kitchen garden from which they could gather a few sprigs for cooking. Most

herbs grow well in containers and it can be an excellent way of keeping some of the more invasive herbs, such as mints, under control. A grouping of small pots makes a versatile arrangement that can easily be arranged to suite the mood – or the menu.

A FAMILY GARDEN

A note on safety should be added for those planning a display in a family garden. If there are likely to be children playing around the patio, make sure the containers are stable and secure and have no sharp edges, and avoid spiky, prickly or poisonous plants.

Balcony gardens

With a little care you can create a beautiful miniature landscape on even the tiniest balcony. Potted plants will help soften severe lines, add color to an otherwise drab area and create a welcoming spot for relaxation. Experiment with lighting effects and you can also make your balcony a truly magical place to be at night.

Ideally, to make the most of your balcony, you should leave enough room for two chairs and a small table, and adequate space for pottering. Rectangular planters that can be placed along the edges of the balcony are good space-savers, as are hanging baskets and half-circle containers that can be attached to the wall. Try to use the largest containers that will fit comfortably. Small containers dry out quickly and will not provide adequate compost for good plant growth. It is far more effective to have two large containers with flourishing plants than a lot of small pots dotted about.

In planning a balcony garden, always check the structural condition of your balcony first, and consider the weight the floor of the balcony will have to bear. Use lightweight containers, such as plastic or fibreglass, and spread the load over a wide area. Soil-less peat or peat

Decorative iron railings need only a few plants to set them off. Here succulents sit on the balcony floor and ivy geraniums are attached to the handrail.

substitute composts are the lightest, but you will need to check and water them more often, as they can be difficult to re-wet once they have dried out.

It is also important to ensure that surplus water can drain away. If your balcony does not have a drain, check that dripping water will not trouble neighbors on floors below or passers-by. Some containers come with matching saucers, but after watering you may need to drain off excess water from the saucers as many plants do not appreciate wet feet.

Strong winds and frosts can be a problem on exposed balconies, and you may find it beneficial to erect a sturdy trellis screen. This can also provide a home for climbing plants, although it could obstruct the view if not carefully positioned. Of course, this could be a benefit if there is an ugly view you want to hide.

When planning your plants,

Pansies look lovely when massed in a container on a sunny balcony.

remember that for much of the time they will be seen from inside. Choose plants to suit the amount of sunlight available. A sunny balcony is perfect for colorful annuals, succulents, herbs, miniature roses, summer bulbs and salad vegetables. If your balcony receives too much hot afternoon sun, you might need to install blinds or awnings.

A balcony that faces north or is shaded by nearby buildings is ideal for a large number of shade-loving plants. Lush foliage plants and white-flowering annuals, such as primulas and polyanthus, are good in shady spots and look wonderful lit up at night. Azaleas, fuchsias, camellias, busy lizzie (*Impatiens*), hydrangeas and daphne will flourish with some morning sun but shade for the rest of the day.

Evergreen shrubs and conifers, and climbers such as ivy, can be used to make a permanent scheme, against which background you can introduce seasonal displays. A balcony is a perfect place to

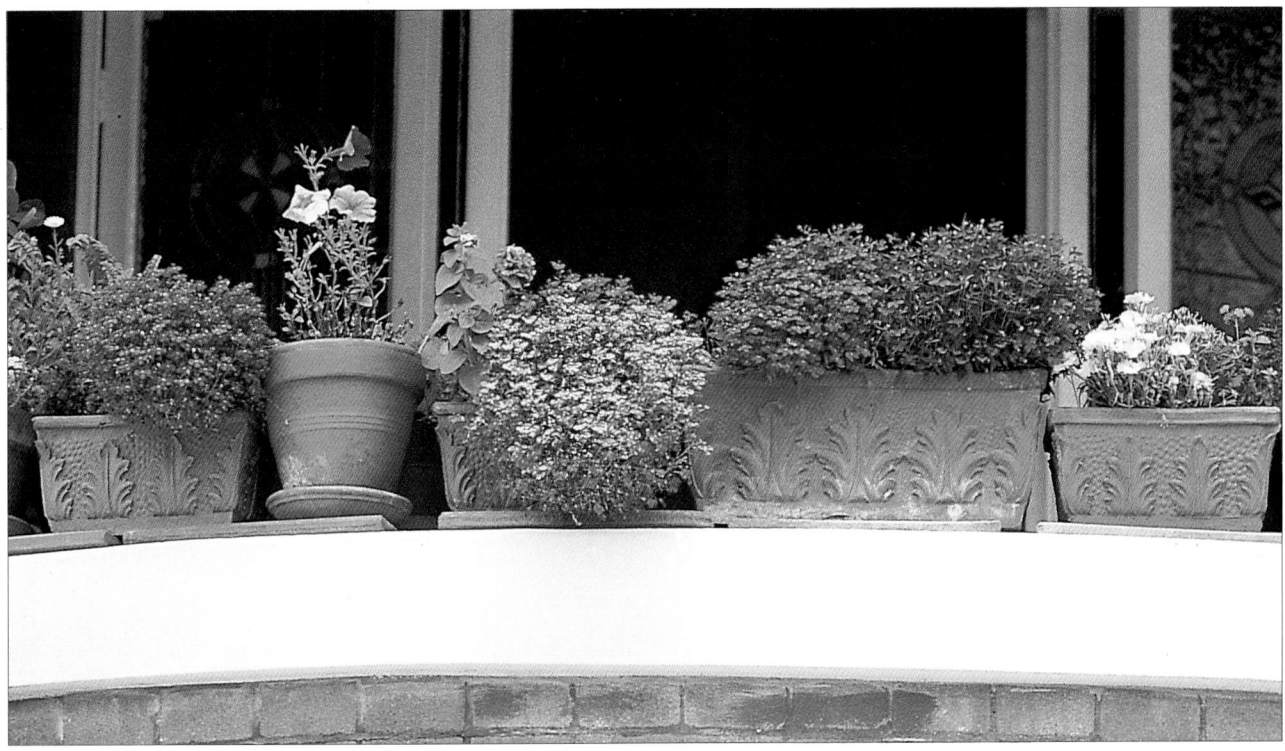

On this sunny balcony, a collection of decorative terracotta containers is used to show off petunias and lobelias.

introduce some fragrant flowers too, as their scent can also be enjoyed through open windows and doors even when you are inside. To make the most of the restricted space on a balcony, include some annual climbers which will rapidly give a backdrop of color.

CARING FOR BALCONY PLANTS

If your balcony is high rise or in a very windy area you will need to choose sturdy, compact plants and low, squat pots that are unlikely to be blown over. Choose plants such as lavender, rosemary, variegated euonymus and box that are tough enough to withstand draughts and winds. (These plants will also tolerate salt spray should your balcony be near the sea.) Do not place hanging baskets in an unprotected

Geraniums are colorful container plants for any sunny position.

position where they will dry out very rapidly.

Plants in containers exposed to wind dehydrate very quickly and plants on balconies often do not receive the full benefit of rainwater because of awnings, guttering, a roof or overhead balcony. On hot summer days you should inspect container plants frequently to check

that the potting mix has not dried out, particularly in small containers. 'Self-watering' planters that have a reservoir of water for the plants to draw on can be useful, as can automatic watering systems. If a plant becomes very dry, take it to a sink and stand the pot in water until the soil is saturated.

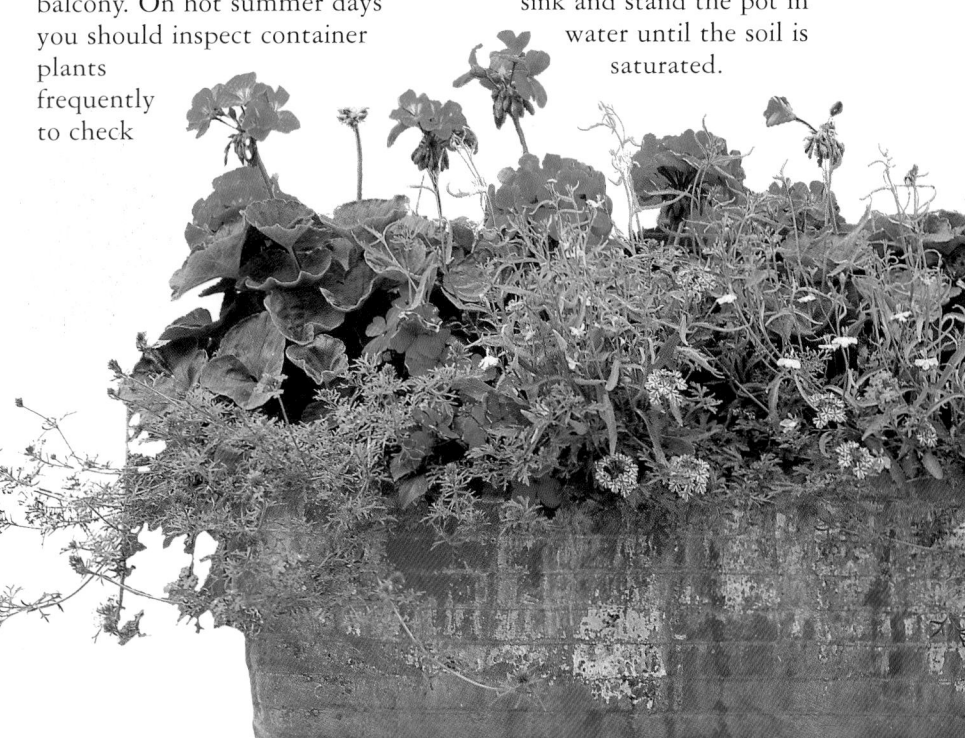

COTTAGE GARDEN CONTAINERS

OPPOSITE PAGE TOP LEFT: Crown imperials have the sort of quirky nature that makes them perfect for rambling cottage gardens. These yellow blooms have been underplanted with the ferny leaves and red pendant flowers of dicentra and the pot placed on a slab in a border to add instant height and color.

TOP RIGHT: As an alternative to a windowbox, a large hay basket can be easier to fix, will give a larger volume of soil for bedding plants and it is easier to clothe the front edge too. Line the flat back of the basket with polythene to prevent the wall getting damp.

BOTTOM RIGHT: Sizeable clumps of London pride, houseleeks, variegated lemon balm, and gray and purple-leaved *Sedum spathulifolium* "Purpureum" make lively contrasts in shape and color and will survive on a good soaking every two or three days. Stand them on a wall or a sunny window ledge.

BOTTOM LEFT: Hardy annuals (pansies) and tender perennials (*Verbena* 'Sissinghurst') a half-hardy annual (*Salvia farinacea*) and cottage pinks combine to make a lively quartet that will give weeks of color. You may need to insert some sticks and tie up the top-heavy pinks to stop them flopping down in the wind and rain.

Even if you can't aspire to the full cottage garden look, you can still sigh over a few cottage-style containers and dream of what might have been. To be sure of getting the authentic, slightly frayed effect, your pots and plants may have to dress down a bit for the occasion. Out go those classical urns, Versailles tubs, and elaborate decorated terracotta pots, and in come the oak half barrels, simple hand-thrown earthenware pots, stone troughs, galvanised baths, and dolly tubs.

Busy lizzies, cannas, begonias and space-age celosias must be shown short shift in favour of dwarf cornflowers, rudbeckias, violas, lavatera, morning glory, and pot marigolds.

There are plenty of hardy perennials that can be mingled in to add a buffer to all

those flowers. Evergreen shrubs too, such as skimmia, variegated holly, *Viburnum tinus* and pyracantha can be included as specimens in individual pots or as a backbone to seasonal spring and summer bedding plants and are very valuable in winter. Informality is the key so avoid container plants that have been clipped rigidly into spires, lollipops, or spirals. Light-hearted topiary, a fox, teddy bear, dove or fat hen will succeed however, whereas a row of clipped pyramid bay trees in classical style pots will be far too grand and ostentatious for the cottage plot.

Scaling up to trees, a small specimen grown in a roomy container like a half barrel can be invaluable to cast a little welcome shade on the patio on the hottest days and will provide a leafy canopy to soften house walls where a tree in the ground might not be practical. A variety of rowan like *Sorbus vilmorinii* will give flowers, berries and fall tints. Snowy mespilus is also a strong contender with flowers and glorious oranges and reds at leaf fall. For winter flowers, the cherry *Prunus subhirtella* "Fallalis" would be a tempting choice, while for pretty white variegated foliage flushed pink when emerging, try *Acer negundo* "Flamingo."

LEFT: A wooden wheelbarrow has become something of a cliché when filled with trailing petunias and pelargoniums. However, lined with hay and filled with a collection of pots planted for seasonal color it is easier to ring the changes. A late winter show like this can be wheeled under the house wall for extra protection.

PUTTING ON A SHOW

How you arrange your containers can add considerably to their impact. Clustered together on steps, window ledges, on the edge of wide paths, and around doors and windows they will sit comfortably, especially if you bank them up and contrast shallow pans with long tom terracotta pots. You can mix plants similarly, putting the spreading with the tall and erect. Adding some *objets trouvés* around the base of your pots; fossils, flints, fir cones, driftwood, even rusty horseshoes, will add some rustic charm and reflect a little of your own personality.

Avoid rigid set pieces, two cabbage palms (*Cordyline*), for example, flanking a front door. It may be fine for a London town house but an asymmetrical style with perhaps a stone sink to the left balanced by a cluster of terracotta pots to the right will sit far more comfortably in a cottage garden.

Think also about using plants in pots to enhance and build on another eye-catcher in the garden. A sundial surrounded by pans of sun-loving thyme, sedum, chamomile, and scented-leaved pelargoniums will have double the impact. Similarly a seat becomes immersed in perfume when you have stationed pots of tobacco plants, night-scented stock, heliotrope, and mignonette alongside it.

BELOW: If you want to grow some of the most authentic cottage garden summer annuals you'll need to raise them from seed. The double dwarf sunflower "Teddy Bear" is rarely seen for sale as a young plant but when combined with violas and pansies it more than justifies the extra work involved in raising it from seed yourself.

LEFT: Pansies and wallflowers will succeed together in almost any combination of colors. Line up your wallflowers behind the pansies in the fall for troughs and windowboxes for a show like this in April and May. Scaling down the idea, use the dwarf wallflower "Prince Mxd" with tiny violas. Pebbles are useful to cover bare soil.

TOP LEFT: If you've got plenty of space in borders then you can give Chinese lanterns (*Physalis*) their head and let them run around like mint, but containing the spreading roots in an old bucket concentrates the interest and prevents less robust plants from being swamped.

TOP RIGHT: Drawing inspiration from flowering borders, these terracotta pans fill a gap in June before summer bedding gets into its stride. Choose scented French lavender and Sweet Williams, each with a low drape of yellow-leaved Creeping Jenny and Lamium "White Nancy." The vibrant red flower is a selection from *Achillea* "Summer Pastels."

FOUR SEASON PROGRAM

Maintaining interest in your cottage containers is more of a challenge in the winter months, especially before the earliest of the bulbs like snowdrops, dwarf iris and crocus burst onto the scene. You can always rely on winter heathers though and some, like varieties of *Erica* x *darleyensis,* begin to open in the new year, and the red buds of *Skimmia* "Rubella" will look good for months alongside.

Dwarf bulbs will inject some color later as will primroses and, amongst the perennials, lungwort, elephant ears (*Bergenia*), and lenten rose can be relied on whatever the weather.

As spring progresses, taller daffodils and tulips will add impact and can be used as high spots among those classic country style bedders—wallflowers, polyanthus, double daisies, and pansies in mixed colors

that rarely seem to clash. When there is still a chance of late frost rely on hardier summer bedders like marguerites, osteospermums, and diascias amongst pansies and blowsy ranunculus. Hardy dicentras, lamiums, and euphorbias will add to the appeal.

During the summer you are spoilt for choice but don't be tempted by highly bred, over-sophisticated types as these reduce to mere blobs of color at ankle height. With regular watering, feeding and deadheading many will carry on until the frosts. There are lots of ideas on these pages to show you how to pick and mix and create a memorable show.

Finally, seek out the best color mixtures. "Antique" pansies and annual Phlox "Tapestry" are delectable while *Brachyscome* "Bravo" soothes many a color clash. With so much choice and an almost endless list of combinations, the danger is you'll run out of space all too soon!

OPPOSITE: Bring your cottage garden indoors by picking a variety of flowers such as these. Roses, daisies, tulips, cornflowers, irises and heads of viburnum are here combined into a colorful cottage-style arrangement.

CUT FLOWERS

Gardens full of flowers are a major delight, but we spend much of our time indoors, away from their beauty. Potted plants in bloom can be brought inside, or you can use vases of cut flowers to create a garden-like atmosphere in any room.

PICKING FLOWERS

Always pick flowers from the garden in the cool of the day, early in the morning or late in the afternoon, and put them in a cool place for a couple of hours to recover. (If you're picking a bunch of flowers from your garden for a friend, give them at least half an hour in water before tying them up.)

ARRANGING FLOWERS

Before arranging the flowers, cut an inch or so off the stems, under water, with sharp pruning shears. Don't crush the stems; cut them off cleanly so that they can take up water easily. Strip off any leaves that are likely to be under the water, as they will rot rapidly, polluting the water and giving off a rotting smell.

Be sure your vases and the water are perfectly clean; if necessary, wash the vases out with bleach to remove old stains. Change the water daily and top it up as necessary. You may use a purchased floral preservative, or make your own by adding sugar and bleach to the water.

On page 759 you will find details of some popular flowers suitable for cutting.

REVIVING FLOWERS

If flowers start to droop, it is often because an air lock has formed in the stem. The easiest way to revive them is to cut 1in off the stem and place the flowers upright in water with the water reaching up to the head. Let them stand for several hours. This is the best treatment for most bulb flowers—tulips, daffodils, lilies, irises. Another way of reviving wilting flowers is to stand them in a n inch of boiling water. When the water is cool, they should have revived. Then recut the stems under water, removing the boiled bits of stem, and give the flowers an hour or two in deep water.

PLACING ARRANGEMENTS

Place your arrangements out of direct sunlight and draughts, and away from fruit because the ethylene given off by ripening fruit will age the flowers rapidly.

BUYING FLOWERS

If you wish to supplement your own garden flowers, choose ones that are bright and fresh looking and just starting to open. Avoid those with yellow leaves or slimy, brown stems that have obviously been sitting around for some time. And remember that flowers exposed to sunlight or strong winds will age faster. When you get home, put them into cold water immediately.

SPECIAL HINTS

Re-cut the stems of woody stemmed flowers, such as **rhododendrons**, **lilacs**, **azaleas** and **magnolias**, under water, taking off half an inch or so, and remove all excess foliage. Some people like to split the ends of the stem for about half an inch.

   Roses are delicate and they should be cut during the cool of the day, re-cutting their stems under water. They don't like the water too cold and must be kept out of the sun. Remove all thorns to make them easier to handle—this also creates extra places where the stems can absorb water. Don't cut too many flowers on long stems or you risk weakening the bush; and in any case you will find that short-stemmed roses will last longer.

   Flowers with sticky sap, such as **dahlias**, **cosmos** and **poppies**, need their cut stems cauterised or they will bleed to death. Either plunge them into a centimetre or two of boiling water for a minute or so, or pass the ends through a flame for a few seconds.

Daffodils and **hyacinths** are an exception: they like to have their excess sap gently squeezed out.

Poppies are best if the water in the vase is only an inch or so deep – the stems are apt to rot in deep water.

Stocks and **wallflowers** foul their water very quickly and so they look awful in glass vases. Be extra careful to remove any leaves that will be under water and be sure to change the water regularly.

   The leaves of **chrysanthemums** die off faster than the flowers. When the leaves become tatty, strip them all and then rearrange the flowers.

   Camellias absorb water faster through their faces than the stems and they last best if you spray them daily. Handle them with care because they bruise easily.

   Violets absorb water similarly—the best method with them is to dunk the whole bunch in water daily.

   Each **hibiscus** flower will live only a day, dying in the evening, but you can usually keep them fresh through a dinner party if you cut them in the morning and store them in the fridge until the last moment.

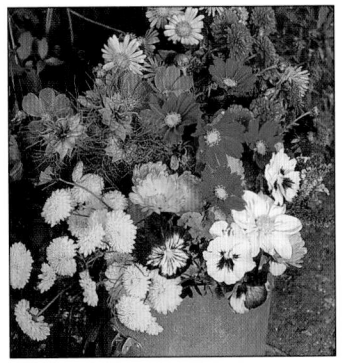

*P*LANTS FOR
CUTTING

When you've got your flowering borders up and running another urge is almost certain to take hold; the desire to decorate your porch, hall, windowsills, mantelpiece and even dressing table with blooms that encapsulate the very essence of the cottage garden style. Don't be surprised that by placing flowers in such close proximity to each other a whole stream of planting ideas present themselves. In addition, the scent from blooms confined indoors will, of course, be far less elusive than in the garden, especially on breezy days.

Both the containers for your cut flowers and the flowers themselves should suggest a breath of country air. The cottage garden style has certainly been influential in the trend towards a much more relaxed and spontaneous approach to arranging flowers. Stiff and formal, triangular and "L"-shaped designs are far too contrived for the cottage window. Even when embellished with grapes and gold cherubs they have invisible lines dictating the boundaries. The secret is to make your cut flowers look as though they haven't been "arranged" at all— though a motley selection of plants merely stuffed into a jam jar with foliage submerged under the water will neither look the part nor last long.

One of the nicest aspects of cut flower cottage garden style is that you are harvesting the fruits of your own labour. They will fit in perfectly with their

environment, blurring the dividing line between home and garden, whether glimpsed from a pathway, through an open window or framing a view from your favorite armchair. During cold spells in winter and spring, what could be more delightful than the scent from winter iris or more delicate than a small bouquet of snowdrops with the gossamer-like seed heads of old man's beard?

Planting up a selection of shrubs, perennials and bulbs that will link together to form a continuous stream of flower production for twelve months of the year is one secret of success. For foliage, variegated forms of euonymus, weigela and elaeagnus are invaluable.

TOP LEFT: Posies of primroses and grape hyacinths, dwarf daffodils and drumstick primulas will bring a breath of spring to your home.

TOP RIGHT: Pansies, love-in-a-mist, cosmos and pot marigolds will seed themselves each year. Add Michaelmas daisies, single annual asters and chrysanthemums for a real late summer festival of color.

BELOW: Teapots filled with asters, pansies, fuchsias and nasturtiums arranged on a tray of fall leaves and ripe crab apples makes an eye-catching table decoration.

FLOWER CRAFTS

 Bringing flowers indoors can increase the pleasure you get from your garden, but, unfortunately, cut flowers die quickly. Flower crafts —that is, those crafts that use fresh or, more often, dried flowers to add beauty and fragrance to your life—allow you to extend the usefulness of the flowers for a much longer period of time. Most crafts use dried flowers as the drying process prolongs their beauty and fragrance.

Bunches of dried flowers can look lovely in themselves, or the flowers can be more formally arranged in wreaths and wall hangings. Petals, sprigs, and leaves can be made into pot-pourris that will be used to perfume the house, or they can be packaged into sachets or little fragrant pillows. Tuck them away to scent drawers and cupboards, storage areas or bags, or tie them to door knobs or chair backs for a decorative effect.

Roses and lavender are among the most

popular flowers for drying as they retain their fragrance and shape well. Many of the herbs such as rosemary, lemon verbena, oregano, and thyme are useful additions.

Flowers and herbs can also be used to make perfumed waters and oils and a variety of cosmetic products, such as face cleansers, skin fresheners, moisturisers, and hair rinses. Packaged in attractive bottles and decorated with ribbon, they also make attractive gifts.

You can also press flowers and use them as pictures and to decorate any number of things, from pictures and bookmarks to cards and candles.

There are few joys in life that surpass that of making something. All craftspeople know this, but they also know how disappointing it can be if the idea fails, especially if a lot of effort has been put in. The simple projects described here have been chosen so that they can be made by everyone—try them and you too will have created something beautiful.

DRYING FLOWERS

Drying flowers for use in wreaths, hangings and pot-pourris has become increasingly popular. With only a little effort you can preserve their color and fragrance for future pleasure.

There are several ways to dry flowers, depending on the type of flower and the way you want to use it. Some methods preserve the shape of the flower better than others; some are practical only for petals or foliage. Investigate the different methods before selecting one for your flowers. The simplest of the processes is air drying and it has the added advantage that the bunches of flowers, hanging from racks, poles or the ceiling, look decorative while they are drying. Other drying processes include the silica gel, glycerine and microwave techniques.

Freeze drying is a commercial technique in which flowers are preserved by freezing the moisture in stems and blooms and then removing it, while retaining the shape and original color of the material. Freeze-dried flowers are available from dried flower outlets and florists' shops.

SILICA GEL DRYING

Silica gel drying is best for flowers with delicate petals such as daisies, roses, and pansies, and can be purchased from craft shops. The amount you need will depend on the size of the container and the number of flowers you want to dry at any one time. Always buy the blue crystals because they turn pink when moisture has been absorbed. If that happens, place them in a shallow tray inside an oven heated to 270°F to dry out (the color will return to blue).

If only the flowers are to be dried, follow the steps on the opposite page, and use a shallow plastic container.

Silica gel is ideal for drying flowers with delicate petals that might be damaged with most other drying methods. Shown here (clockwise from the top left) are pinks, Dutch iris, double narcissus, larkspurs, rosebuds, calendulas, lilac, tulips, and love-in-a-mist. As the silica gel absorbs moisture from the petals (and the air) it will turn from blue to pink, as it has here. It can then be dried out in the oven and will be ready to be used again.

Step 1 Place silica gel in a container until it is 0.5–1in deep, and then place the heads of the flowers on top of the crystals, making sure the petals do not overlap.

Step 2 Spoon more crystals under, between and finally over the flowers until they are completely covered, taking care that the petals are not damaged. After two or three days, check to see the flowers have dried, and then pour off the crystals. Use a fine paintbrush to clean any crystals from the flowers.

To dry whole flowers, including the stems, make a shelf from foil-covered cardboard to fit inside a deep container. At even intervals in the shelf pierce holes (very slightly larger than the diameter of the stems) and thread the stems through the shelf, so that the flower heads sit flat on top of the shelf and the stems hang down. Also leave holes in the shelf to pour in silica gel. Fill the container with crystals, making sure they are under, between and around the flowers, and then seal it and leave the flowers to dry in the same way as before.

MICROWAVE DRYING

There are no definite rules for microwaving flowers and much of the process is trial and error. It is best to use less mature foliage, or the flowers and leaves may fall off after microwaving. As with all drying methods, always pick flowers and foliage when they are dry, never after rain or before dew has evaporated.

Foliage is best dried by placing the leaves in a paper bag, which is then folded over at the end and placed on top of a microwave-proof bowl, or by placing them between layers of absorbent paper. Microwave them on MEDIUM for about 2 minutes, then check. It will take 2–5 minutes, depending on the type of foliage. Microwave in short bursts until the desired effect is achieved.

Flowers dry best in the microwave when placed in a microwave-proof dish with silica gel. Cover the base of the dish with about 2in of crystals and rest the flowerheads on top, poking any short stems into the crystals. Cover with more crystals and place the dish in the oven with half a cup of water in another container. Cook on MEDIUM for 2–4 minutes, checking progress during the cooking. Let flowers with delicate petals stand for at least 10 minutes after microwaving and those with large petals for 30 minutes.

AIR DRYING

Air drying is the simplest and most commonly used technique for drying flowers, since very little equipment is needed and the technique is suitable for almost all flowers. Only heavy-headed or very delicate flowers, such as spring blooms, are unsuitable.

Pick flowers for drying as early in the day as possible so that they are quite fresh. Remove excess foliage and gather the flowers into bunches. Fasten the bunches together firmly using an elastic band, and then thread florists' wire through and around the stems of the flowers, leaving a long length of wire at the end from which to hang up the bunch.

Hang the bunches upside down in a dry and airy place, leaving enough space for the air to circulate between them. Try to hang them out of direct sunlight. Always put your flowers in the place where they will dry most quickly as this will give the best results and ensure that they do not become mouldy.

The flowers can be hung from a laundry rack or from bamboo poles or branches suspended from the ceiling. In this way the flowers dry efficiently while providing a colorful display.

It will take anything from five days to three weeks for the flowers to dry, depending on the type of blooms and the weather. When completely dry the flowers should feel slightly crisp and the leaves should be dry and brittle.

Flowers with woody stems can be dried standing upright in a container but they will need to be supported. Place chicken wire over the top of the container and thread the stems through to prevent them from becoming damaged. Petals for pot-pourris or sachets can be dried spread on a wire rack or newspaper.

GLYCERINE DRYING

Glycerine, used for drying foliage, can be purchased from pharmacies or craft shops. Mix one part glycerine with two of boiling water, stir and pour into a jug.

Cut the stems of the foliage on an angle under warm water, and stand them in the solution (the stems should be covered with 4–6in of the solution). Place the container in a cool, dry, dark place until the leaves have absorbed the mixture and changed color. The drying time will be 2–3 weeks; check every so often to see if the solution needs topping up. When the stems are ready, remove them and wash them in clean water. Then dry them on blotting paper.

ABOVE: Air drying is the simplest way to dry flowers and seedheads and is suitable for many. Here are (left to right) larkspurs, wheat, roses, lavender, marguerites, and yellow calendulas. The bunches have a cottagey feel as they dry.

BATH BAGS

Nothing is more relaxing than settling back in a warm bath

scented with herbs and floral notes. Just tie a bath bag to the tap

and run the water over it to release the fragrance.

These bath sachets are made from muslin and can be tied up with raffia, string or hessian ribbon, which can in turn be tied onto the bath tap. The water runs over the bag, perfuming the bath. Bath bags can be quite small, about 4in long and 2in wide.

The herbal bags can be reused for several baths; the oatmeal recipe will leave the skin feeling soft and refreshed but can be used only once. The mixtures should be prepared following the instructions for making pot-pourri for a sachet (page 768).

ABOVE LEFT: Muslin bath bags tied with string make perfect gifts. Make six or eight and pack them in a small box for the best effect. Choose a lovely colorful box and pretty ribbons or continue the natural, cottagey look with a cardboard box and raffia.

Soothing herbal bath bags

½ cup lavender
½ cup mint or peppermint
½ cup rose petals
½ cup chamomile

Skin softening bath bag

1 cup oatmeal
1 cup mixed herbs such as
    rosemary, lemon verbena
    sage, or bay leaf

Spicy Lemon and Lavender Pot-pourri

2 cups lavender

1 cup lemon verbena

1/2 cup lemon-scented
    geranium leaves

1/4 cup crushed
    cinnamon sticks

1/4 cup dried lemon peel

2 tbsp whole cloves

1 tbsp crushed cloves

2 teaspoons allspice

1 teaspoon nutmeg

1 tablespoon orris root
    powder

10 drops lavender oil

5 drops lemon verbena oil

POT-POURRIS

Beautifully scented, colorful pot-pourris of dried leaves and flowers

have long been used to bring fragrances from the garden into the house.

 Pot-pourris can be made from any of the scented flowers or herbs in the garden. Experiment to find a mix you like, or make up any one of the lovely recipes on these pages. Your pot-pourri can be displayed in a pretty ceramic bowl or in any of your favorite containers.

MATERIALS

DRIED MATERIAL
Always use the best quality dried material in your pot-pourri as it has to be visually pleasing as well as fragrant. Choose flowerheads in full bloom and add herbs, nuts, berries, cinnamon sticks, pine needles, and citrus peels.

FIXATIVES
The dried ingredients are the base of a pot-pourri but a fixative is needed to make sure that the fragrance will be lasting. A number of different fixatives are available from herbal suppliers, shops selling natural beauty and health products, and some pharmacies and craft shops. The most commonly used is orris root powder but it must be used sparingly or the pot-pourri will have a dusty look. Other fixatives include oakmoss, gum benzoin, cloves and spices, and tonka beans.

ESSENTIAL OILS
The final ingredient in a pot-pourri is a scented oil. The amount of oil added to a pot-pourri will vary according to the quantity of dried materials and can be increased to suit personal taste. The oils help to keep the mixture fragrant and additional oil can be added whenever necessary to replenish the fragrance of an old pot-pourri.

Old-fashioned Rose Pot-pourri

3 cups mixed rose petals

½ cup lemon verbena

1 tablespoon orris root powder

¼ cup oakmoss, chopped into small pieces

10–15 drops rose oil

Mixed Floral and Herb Pot-pourri

1 cup rose petals

½ cup lavender

¼ cup violets

¼ cup cornflowers

½ cup marigold flowers

½ cup sweet mixed herbs

1 tablespoon orris root powder

2 teaspoons cinnamon powder

5 drops rose oil

3 drops lavender oil

2 drops lemon oil

Cottage Garden Pot-pourri

4 cups rose petals

2 cups rose geranium leaves

2 cups flowers such as freesias, jasmine, delphiniums

½ cup eau-de-cologne mint

½ cup marjoram

½ cup lemon verbena

6 sticks cinnamon

¼ cup cloves, coarsely ground

1 cup oakmoss

Few drops rose oil

Few drops geranium oil

Pressed pansies

MAKING A DRY POT-POURRI

MATERIALS

Dried material • Fixatives • Essential oil • Measuring cups • Glass eyedroppper
• Mixing bowls • Scoop • Wooden spoons • Clothes pegs • Brown paper bags

Step 1 Place all the dried materials in a mixing bowl and gently mix them together with a wooden spoon, being careful not to break the flower petals.

Step 2 Place the spices and fixatives in another mixing bowl and, using the eyedropper, add the essential oil. (Remember, extra oil can be added later if the scent is not strong enough.) Mix these ingredients together thoroughly.

Step 3 Add the fixative and oil mixture to the dried materials and stir with a wooden spoon. Place the mixture in a brown paper bag that is large enough for the mixture to be shaken inside. Fold the end over and hold it closed with a clothes peg. (An extra bag can be used as a lining if the mixture is quite oily.)

Step 4 Store the mixture in a cool, dark place for 2–4 weeks, shaking the bag gently every 2–3 days to blend the ingredients. When the pot-pourri is ready, scoop it out, place the mixture in a container and decorate the top with extra dried flowerheads, if desired.

BELOW: The ingredients of Cottage Garden Pot-pourri, shown here before drying. OPPOSITE: Six lovely, fragrant pot-pourris. Top to bottom: Fall Spice (pine cones, leaves, cedar wood shavings, spices, daisies and marigolds); Summer Sherbet (citrus leaves, wood shavings, dried orange, and lemon, daisies); Tudor Rose (roses); Natural Forest (ferns, acorns, chillies, berries, orange slices); Peach Daisy (peach slices, daisies, wood shavings); Strawberry Cinnamon (cinnamon, white daisies, star anise, leaves, strawberries).

Suitable plants for pots

For many years we grew only a handful of trustworthy favorites in pots and yet, if the right variety is chosen, there are very few plant groups that cannot be grown well in containers—for example, you can create a beautiful potted garden consisting only of edible plants, and some plants actually prefer the special conditions a container can provide.

Flowers galore
Annuals, perennials and bulbs

Many colorful flowers can be grown in pots and they can be easily changed from season to season to achieve varying effects and color combinations. Extensive plant breeding programs have provided a wonderful range of dwarf varieties that are ideal for small pots, baskets, and windowboxes, or can be tucked in around shrubs and trees in large tubs.

Some of the most popular flowers and bulbs are described here.

Agapanthus
Agapanthus need a sunny sheltered position. Grow them in well-drained compost, and water well in dry spells. They flower in mid to late summer or early fall, and make handsome container plants with tall stems of blue flowers and strap-like leaves. Feed with any all-purpose plant food. Cut off dead flower stems unless you want to save the seed. Divide clumps in early spring. From seed, plants take about three years to flower. Watch for

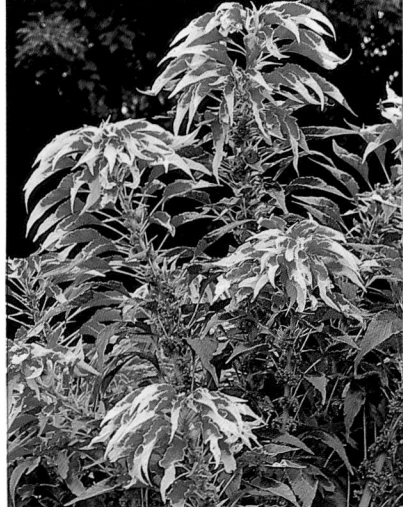

The dazzling foliage of Amaranthus "Joseph's Coat", a summer annual.

snails, which like hiding in the foliage.

Alyssum (*Lobularia maritima*)
Sweet alyssum is a fast-growing, spreading, annual plant flowering mainly in summer and early fall. Sow seed under glass in early spring, or outdoors in late spring. Alyssum is tolerant of hot positions in full sun, and

becomes thin and leggy in shade.

Amaranthus
A spectacular annual for full sun and a warm, sheltered spot. Sow seed in early spring for a long summer display. Water and feed regularly during the growing season. Aphids can be a problem.

Anemone (*Anemone* De Caen)
Plant corms of spring-flowering varieties in fall at a depth of 1–1.5in for spring flowers. Anemones need sun. After planting and initial watering do not keep the mix too moist or the corms will rot. After plants emerge, water regularly in warm weather. Remove spent flowers to prolong flowering. They make excellent cut flowers.

Arum lily (*Zantedeschia aethiopica*)
Summer-flowering, frost tender perennials producing a handsome and distinctive funnel-shaped spathes. They prefer full

The prostrate white Alyssum "Carpet of Snow" in two tiers of pots.

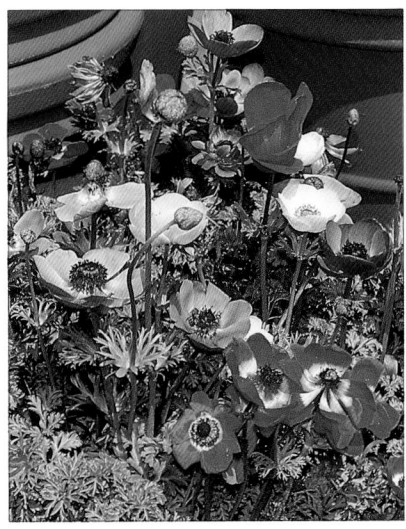

Anemones are among the longest flowering of spring bulbs.

Arum lilies like lots of water—stand the pot in a full basin.

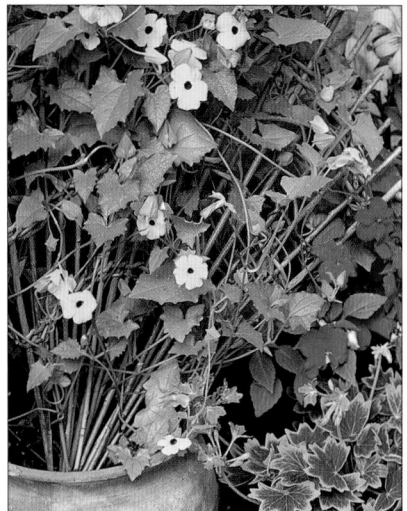

The bright yellow flowers of the twining black-eyed Susan.

Busy lizzies (Impatiens) *will flower for months, indoors or out.*

The butterfly flower is a rather delicate annual, best grown in a pot.

sun or partial shade and a well-drained potting mix and need ample water in the growing season and some all-purpose food. Propagate arum lilies from offsets in winter. Snails can be a problem. The arum lily makes an unusual cut flower. "Crowborough" is a good white variety, and "Green Goddess" produces striking green spathes that are splashed with white.

Fall crocus (*Colchicum*)
Plant corms in spring for fall flowers. They need a sunny, sheltered spot and should be left undisturbed for about three years for the clump to multiply. Feed after flowering and do not cut down the foliage. Allow it to die down naturally.

Begonia
Bedding begonias will bloom throughout the summer in semi-shade or sun, producing colorful single or double flowers. The seed is extremely fine and difficult to handle and it is much easier to buy seedlings. Begonias need good drainage and regular but not excessive watering. They can get powdery mildew if too shaded and damp.

Black-eyed Susan (*Thunbergia alata*)
This annual twining climber for full sun is a moderately fast grower and flowers from early summer to early fall. It can be grown from cuttings or seed, and needs regular water and fertilizer and a support.

Browallia
This tender perennial is generally grown as an annual, and is sown in spring for summer flowers, or in summer for winter flowers under cover. Seed should not be covered. It prefers full sun or at least a half day's sun, and a fertile, well-drained soil that should not be allowed to dry out completely. Feed regularly when flowering, and pinch out young shoots to encourage bushiness.

Bugle (*Ajuga*)
Bugle flowers in spring, but is often planted for its evergreen foliage color as much as its spikes of blue flowers. A variety of foliage colors are available from metallic bronze to variegated pink and cream. In gardens it is used as a ground-cover. Bugle can be divided in fall or winter. It grows in sun or shade and any

soil. Water regularly and give some fertilizer in warm months. Watch out for powdery mildew on leaves which can be a problem for bugle in crowded, humid conditions.

Busy lizzie (*Impatiens*)
Modern varieties produce compact plants in a wide range of vivid colors. They are ideal for pots or hanging baskets, and look best when several pots are grouped together. They are easily grown from tip cuttings taken in spring or summer. Impatiens are frost sensitive and do best in a partially shaded position. They need regular watering but will rot if too wet, and they should be fed with a liquid plant food.

Buttercup (*Ranunculus asiaticus*)
Plant the tuberous roots, claws down, 1–1.5in deep in fall for a spring display. Buttercups need good drainage (restrict watering until growth starts), full sun or part shade and wind protection. Water regularly in dry, windy weather, especially when in flower. When the foliage dies down, they can be lifted, dried and stored.

Celosias and French marigolds compete with each other for intensity of color. Both enjoy a hot spot.

Dwarf asters, like these "Comet Mxd", come with surprisingly large flowers. Cool them down with blue ageratum.

Blue spring-flowered clematis, like this C. macropetala, can be snaked over shrubs like pieris to good effect.

Butterfly flower *(Schizanthus)*
Also called poor man's orchid, this is excellent close-planted in baskets and pots. It prefers sun and protection from wind. Sow seed in spring for a summer to fall display. Water regularly and feed as necessary.

Campanula
There are many species and varieties, ranging from annual Canterbury bells to the many perennial types. The low-growing perennial varieties can be grown in pots or baskets or as ground cover at the base of larger plants. They grow in sun or shade, but the flowers keep their color better in shade. Some are propagated from seed, others from division of established clumps. Slugs can be a problem.

Celosia
Erect, bushy perennials grown as annuals, with conical feathery flowerheads in a wide range of colors. Sow seed in spring for a long summer to fall display. They grow best on a sunny, sheltered patio. In summer give the plants regular water and fertilizer.

Chamomile *(Anthemis; Chamaemelum nobile)*
There are both annual and perennial varieties, with finely-divided, often aromatic, foliage and daisy-like flowers. They need full sun and well-drained soil and do not like a lot of fertilizer.

China aster *(Callistephus)*
The China aster is a fast-growing bushy annual with daisy-like flowers in a wide color range. Tall varieties make excellent cut flowers. They need a sunny spot and wind protection. Tall cultivars may need support. Sow seeds in spring for summer flowers, feed regularly and give ample water in hot weather.

Chrysanthemum
Popular summer to fall flowers in a wide range of colors and forms, they can be grown from root divisions or cuttings in spring. Chrysanthemums need plenty of organic matter to get the best results, and full sun and wind protection. Pinch out the growing tips when the plants are 4–6in high and continue to pinch out sideshoots until the plants

are large. You can remove some smaller buds as they develop if you want fewer larger flowers. Fungal leaf spot can be a problem in showery humid conditions: water early in the day and avoid overhead watering. After flowers have faded, cut off spent blooms, repot and feed. Half-hardy types can be lifted and stored in a frost-free place over winter.

Clematis
Many clematis, especially *C. alpina* and *C. macropetala* types, make excellent container plants, as long as the container is big enough, as they make a large root system. Ideally, choose a container at least 18 x 18in and fill it with good quality compost, such as John Innes No 3. Clematis need good drainage. Keep moist at all times and feed regularly, at least once a week, with a general liquid fertilizer. Provide your clematis with support, and it will reward you with a pillar of flowers in spring or summer, depending on the variety.

If possible, provide some shade for the container, as clematis like to have cool roots.

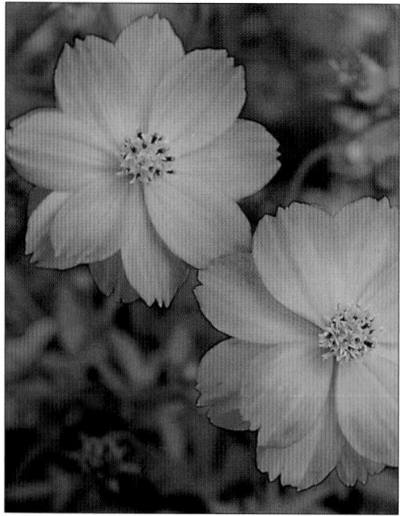

The compact Cosmos sulphureus *is also available in yellow.*

Cyclamen need perfect drainage and are valuable for fall displays.

The early-flowering "Fortune" daffodil is one of the most reliable.

Coleus

Decorative foliage plants for full sun, coleus may be grown from seed but are easy to propagate from soft tip cuttings taken in spring and summer. They need a fertile, well-drained potting mix and ample water in warm weather. Pinch out growing tips to encourage a bushy plant. Remove flowers when still small.

Cosmos

Sow seeds in fall or spring, barely covering the seed, for bright daisy-like flowers in summer and early fall. Plants need full sun and wind protection but are not fussy about fertilizer. Water well in dry weather. Pinch out tips to encourage sturdy growth.

Cyclamen

Cyclamen will bring color to the garden in fall and early winter, producing a succession of flowers, often lasting 2–3 months. Some have plain, heart-shaped leaves, while others have very attractive patterned leaves. Miniature cyclamen bloom as profusely as the larger plants. Give them a humus-rich, well-drained potting mix in sun or part shade. Water around the edge of the pot, or stand the pot in a saucer of water; do not water directly on to the corm.

Daffodil *(Narcissus)*

In fall plant bulbs about 4in deep. Restrict watering until growth starts. Plants need shelter but full to half sun. They flower from early spring to early summer, depending on variety. Feed after flowering and water regularly until foliage dies down. Plant out in a border as they are unlikely to flower as well again if kept in a container.

Dahlia

Colorful summer- and fall-flowering perennials, offering a dazzling display of blooms in a variety of colors and shapes, with many patio varieties that are ideal for pots. Tubers can be over-wintered in a frost-free place and potted up each spring. Plant 3–4in deep in a large pot, in a mix well enriched with organic matter. Unless dwarf forms are chosen, a stake should be inserted at planting time. After initial watering, water sparingly until

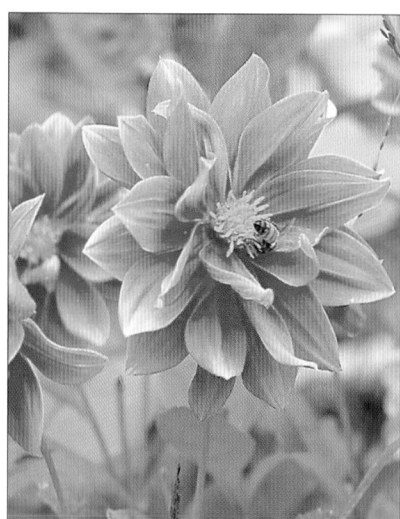

Dwarf dahlias are the best choice for containers as they do not need staking.

Daylilies flower for a long summer season and are best in large pots.

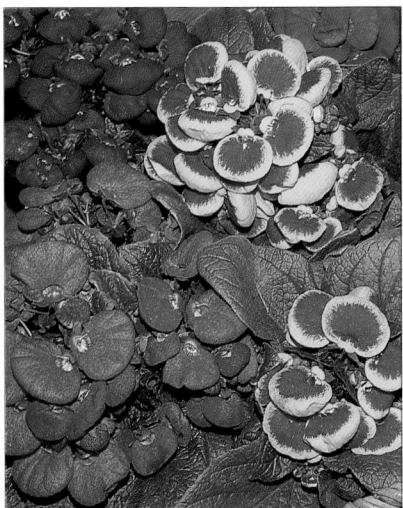

Dutchman's purse like shade and warmth. They also do well indoors.

This is Rhodanthe "Paper Cascade", a bushy perennial everlasting.

Floss flowers, felicias, and lavender – a perfect mix of blue and mauve.

plants are 4–6in high. Then they should be watered and fed regularly. Tip prune to encourage branching. Snails can be a problem. Dahlias can also be grown from seed or bought as young plug plants.

Daylily *(Hemerocallis)*
The individual, trumpet-like flowers last only a day—hence the name—but are produced in succession over a long summer season. Plants do best in full sun and moist, fertile soil. While they are surprisingly tolerant of dry conditions, they respond to water in hot weather. One clump needs a 10–12in pot. Divide clumps in winter or early spring.

Double daisy *(Bellis perennis)*
Many varieties with larger, more colorful flowers are now readily available. Sow seed in early summer, or divide after their spring flowering. Grow in sun or part shade in fertile, well-drained soil.

Dutch iris
(Iris xiphium hybrids)
Plant bulbs 1.5–2in deep in fall for spring flowers. Place in full sun and protect from wind. Be careful not to overwater in the early stages

of growth but water regularly when buds form.

Dutchman's purse *(Calceolaria)*
Compact, bushy plants with rounded, pouch-shaped flowers in shades of red, orange, and yellow in late spring or summer. Most prefer a sheltered, sunny site with a gritty, peaty soil. Keep well-watered and protect against aphids.

Everlasting daisies
There are many varieties of everlasting daisies, which although more commonly associated with dried indoor arrangements, make excellent container plants putting on a long-lasting display of flowers. *Helichrysum bracteatum* "Bright Bikini" is a good dwarf strain. It produces masses of richly-colored papery flowers from mid to late summer. Trim off flowers when they are fully expanded to encourage more to develop. Rhodanthe is an eye-catching spill-over plant, ideal for planting in hanging baskets and around the edges of pots. It bears masses of small, papery white daisies that open from purplish buds. Sow seed in a very well-drained mix and be sure not to overwater. Give them full sun to flourish.

Fan flower *(Scaevola)*
Bushy, trailing, vigorous plants ideal for pots and baskets in semi-shade. Buy young plants from retailers or by mail order for flowers all summer and well into fall. Give little or no fertilizer and water regularly in hot weather, but allow to dry out a little between waterings.

Felicia
A tender, bushy perennial, usually grown as an annual for its bright blue, yellow-centered daisy flowers, borne on long stalks from late spring to fall. Sow seed or buy young plants in spring. Give felicias a sunny position as the flowers remain closed in dull weather, and grow in a well-drained potting mix. Water moderately as they do not like wet conditions. Deadhead regularly and keep trimmed back to prevent it becoming straggly.

Floss flower *(Ageratum)*
Hummock-forming annuals with clusters of feathery flowerheads from summer to fall. Sow seed in spring and grow in fertile, well-drained soil. Deadhead regularly to maintain flowering and don't allow to dry out or flowering will be poor.

Forget-me-nots, loved for their soft blue blooms, will flower for weeks.

Short-growing foxgloves such as "Foxy" are the best for containers.

Freesias look best with as many bulbs as the pot will hold.

Forget-me-not (Myosotis)
Starry blue forget-me-nots grow very easily from seed sown in summer for spring flowering. It prefers to grow in semi-shaded positions. The plants produce masses of sticky seed that will germinate wherever it falls.

Foxglove (Digitalis)
Grow foxgloves as biennials by sowing them in summer to bloom in early summer the following year. They prefer half shade and moist, well-drained

Ivy-leaved geraniums, here trailing from a tall urn, will flower for months.

soil, but tolerate most conditions. Give water when plants are starting to grow rapidly in spring. Snails can be a problem.

Freesia
Plant bulbs 1–1.5in deep in fall for spring flowers. Provide full sun but don't feed until after flowering and don't overwater. Support the sprawling foliage with a few twiggy sticks.

Gazania
The perfect plant for a dry spot, producing jewel-bright, daisy-like flowers over a long summer season. Sow seed in spring, buy young plug plants or divide existing clumps. Plants need little care once established but summer flowers are larger if watered regularly.

Geraniums (Pelargonium)
Geraniums (zonal and ivy-leaved pelargoniums) are easy to propagate from tip cuttings taken from spring to fall. They flower best in full sun and will withstand periods of hot, dry weather. Sow seed in early spring or buy plugs or young plants in 3.5in pots. Don't overwater or use too much fertilizer as this

encourages soft, sappy growth. Their bright cheery flowers are produced mainly through the summer but they will spot flower over a longer period and some have beautifully marked foliage. They are ideal for container growing and perfect for windowboxes.

Lanky growers can be kept compact by cutting back the stems by one-third or even more. Remove faded flowers to stimulate further blooms.

Plants may be overwintered in the greenhouse, cutting them back to 5in and repotting.

Geraniums are prone to fungal disease and rust. Pick off the worst leaves, avoid overhead watering and water early in the day. You may need to spray with a fungicide. Watch for leaf-chewing caterpillars.

Grasses and sedges
Gardeners are increasingly realising the potential of ornamental grasses and sedges in the garden, and container gardening is no exception. Many varieties will grow very well in pots, and their long, arching leaves are useful for adding an extra dimension to any design.

They can also add extra elements of movement and sound as the leaves will rustle in even a gentle breeze.

Clump-forming grasses and sedges are ideal for pots, but containers also provide a way of growing some of the more spreading species which would be likely to over-run beds and borders in the open garden.

For long-lasting effect, choose varieties with colorful foliage; many silver- and gold-variegated forms are available.

Many grasses also have very decorative fluffy or feathery flower spikes that remain attractive even in the depths of winter.

Grape hyacinth (*Muscari*)
Plant bulbs 1.5in deep in fall for a spring display of dense flower spikes, usually in various shades of blue. They prefer a sunny position in well-drained soil. Restrict watering until growth starts, begin feeding after flowering and allow foliage to die down naturally.

Heart's ease (*Viola tricolor*)
Seed can be sown in summer for spring flowers (it self-seeds

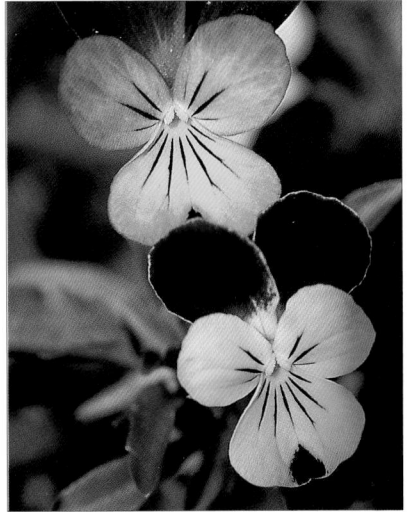

Heart's ease are tiny wild pansies. They love half shade.

freely), in sun or shade.

Hyacinth (*Hyacinthus*)
These fragrant and colorful flowers are amongst the most popular of spring-flowering bulbs. Often forced as Christmas houseplants, and excellent as spring bedding, they are also ideal for bringing color and fragrance to any spring container display.

Plant the bulbs 2in deep in fall for a spring show. They prefer an open sunny position, or part

shade. Restrict watering until growth starts and then water regularly. After flowering cut off spent blooms, feed with bulb fertilizer and water regularly until the foliage starts to yellow and die down.

Japanese anemone (*Anemone hupehensis*)
A hardy, branching perennial with cup-shaped soft pink flowers in summer and early fall. Divide plants in spring. Place in shade or half sun and provide wind protection—although these plants are known as windflowers. Plants require little fertilizer but respond to regular watering in hot weather.

Kalanchoe
Available in flower for much of the year, kalanchoes will add bright flowers to outdoor displays of succulents. The kalanchoes like a half day's to a full day's sun and prefer to dry out between waterings. No special soil, fertilizer or other requirements.

Diminutive grape hyacinths give the richest and purest of spring blues.

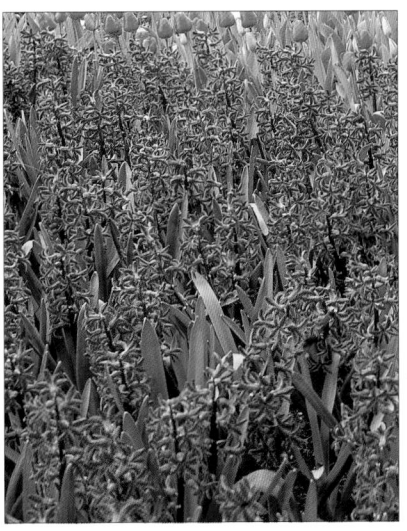

Half a dozen potted hyacinths can be just as rewarding as a bedful.

Kalanchoe blossfeldiana *is available in a variety of bright colors.*

Kangaroo paw *(Anigozanthos)*

This exotic-looking flower requires a baking hot position and must have perfect drainage, full sun and good air circulation. Allow it to dry out between waterings and give little or no fertilizer. There are several good hybrids available, in a variety of colors.

Lamb's ear *(Stachys byzantina)*

This needs full sun, good air circulation and excellent drainage. It dislikes humid conditions. It is grown for its silvery foliage, but produces spikes of flowers in early summer if not cut back.

Lenten rose *(Helleborus)*

The common names of the Lenten rose and the related Christmas rose refer to the flowering times, but these do vary according to the weather and local conditions. They need shade, shelter, and regular watering, but can live for many years in a pot. Clumps can be divided and hellebores self-seed readily. Remove spent flowers or any leaves past their prime. Snails can be a problem.

Kangaroo paws will make an exotic display in a hot spot.

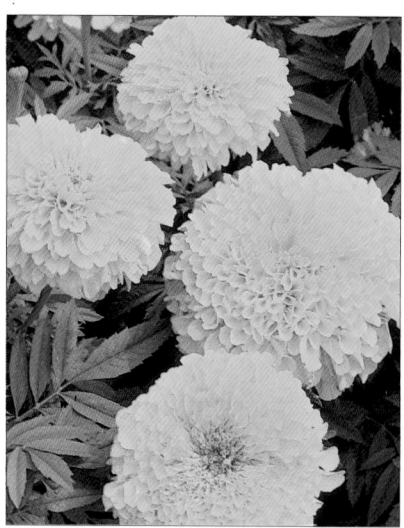

African marigolds come in tall and short varieties, in orange or gold.

Lobelia

Popular for edging pots, where the trailing varieties will cascade over the sides, these are now available in white, pink red, and mixtures as well as the traditional blue. Sow seeds in early spring for flowers through summer. Grow in full or half sun.

Marguerite daisy *(Chrysanthemum frutescens)*

Easily grown from tip cuttings taken all year except winter, marguerites bear masses of daisies in spring, summer and fall. They prefer to grow in full sun. Regularly remove the spent flowers to prolong flowering and prune the plants back hard after flowering.

Marigold, African and French *(Tagetes)*

Mostly flowering through summer and fall, both African and French marigolds are readily grown from seed sown under glass in spring. They need a well-drained, sunny position for the best results. Regular watering and feeding and constant removal of dead flowers will help to maintain a long flowering period.

Marigold, English *(Calendula officinalis)*

Sow seeds of this fast-growing, bushy annual in spring or fall for a long flowering display of daisy-like flowers in shades of orange from spring to fall. Grow them in full sun. There are single- and double-flowered forms and softer pastel shades. The dwarf varieties are most suitable for containers and are delightful with herbs and vegetables.

Nasturtium *(Tropaeolum)*

Sow the seed in spring for early summer to early fall flowers. Grow the plants in full sun and a well-drained mix but don't feed them as this will stimulate leaf production at the expense of the flowers. Keep a watch out for blackfly which love nasturtiums. Caterpillars can also be a problem.

Nemesia

Sow seed in spring to provide flowers for summer bedding. There are also good perennial varieties. For the best plants, a position in full sun with wind protection is necessary.

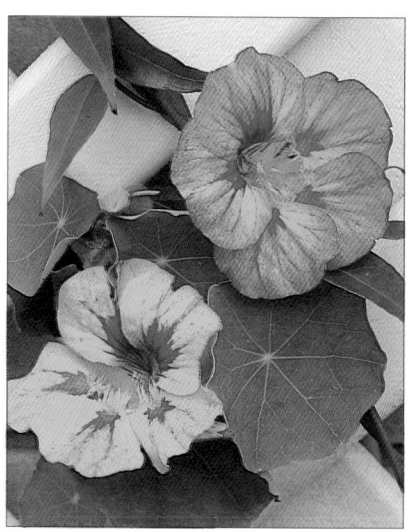

Nasturtiums flower most freely if the soil isn't too fertile.

Ornamental kale has ruffled leaves, ornamental cabbages plain ones. Both do very well in containers and give soft color for months in fall and winter.

Pansies are old favorites for containers. They like rich soil.

Ornamental kale (Brassica oleracea)

Sow outdoors in spring for a long-lasting display of ornamental foliage in fall and winter. Give plants full sun and don't let them starve in small pots. Watch out for both snails and caterpillars.

Osteospermum

The bright summer flowers of the South African daisies do not open in the shade or on dull days, so these are plants for a hot, sunny position. Sow seed under glass in spring, buy young plants or propagate from cuttings of non-flowering shoots in summer, and grow in a well-drained potting mix. Water and feed regularly, and deadhead to prolong flowering. These tender perennials can be overwintered in a coldframe or greenhouse.

Pansy (Viola x wittrockiana)

As well as the summer-flowering types, winter-flowering varieties are widely available and are ideal for adding bright color to winter containers. Pansies grow best in full sun. Regularly remove the spent blooms to ensure a long flowering season. They are easy to grow and have no special needs.

Periwinkle (Vinca)

This very hardy plant tolerates sun or shade but it flowers more freely in sun. The pretty blue or white flowers are produced from spring to late summer or early fall. Propagate periwinkles from rooted sections of older plants in summer, or by division from fall to spring. They have no special needs for water or fertilizer.

Petunia

Half-hardy perennials grown as annuals for their bright display of showy, colorful flowers through the summer. Petunias love hot, dry conditions, and hate wet, humid summers. The multiflora hybrids are more rain-resistant. For colorful, weather-resistant flowers, that are ideal for containers, little can beat the surfinia petunias. These vigorous trailing, free-flowering plants bloom from mid-June to fall. Don't overwater. Few problems but snails love them.

Petunias are naturally trailing and thus wonderful for hanging baskets.

779

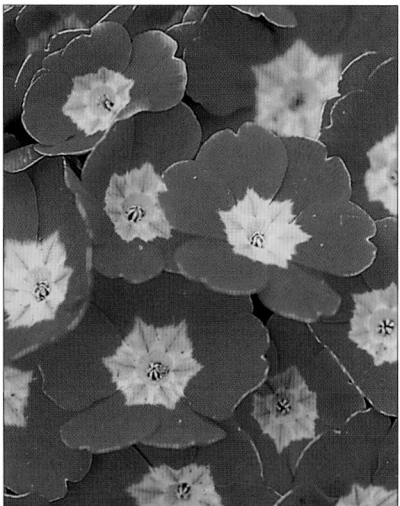

Polyanthus bear clusters of gold-centred flowers in bright colors.

Give portulacas sun; the flowers close up in shade.

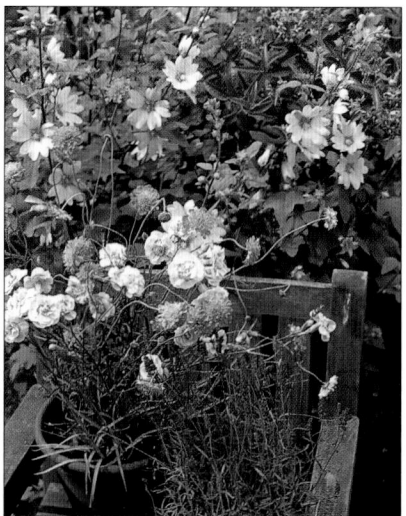

An old garden chair will raise pinks and lavender up to nose height.

Phlox

Sow the seeds of phlox in spring for summer and fall flowers. Give them a position in full sun or semi-shade. Plants must be well watered and fed during the growing season. Cut back hard after the first blooming to encourage sideshoots to flower further down the stems.

Pinks *(Dianthus)*

Annual pinks should be sown in spring, just covering the seeds, for flowers from summer to early fall. Pinks need full sun and regular fertilizer. Don't overwater. They can be cut back after flowering but regrowth is often rather unsatisfactory.

Perennial cottage pinks can be grown from cuttings in spring and summer or from division of clumps in spring.

There are many named varieties that flower in late spring or summer. Many of the newer varieties are repeat-flowering with two or three flushes of flower in summer. They need full sun and very good drainage. A little lime added to the compost can be beneficial. Plants can collapse in wet, humid summers.

Polyanthus (*Primula x polyantha*)

Growing polyanthus from seed can be a slow process, so it is easier to purchase plants in flower in winter and then keep them blooming through spring by picking off spent flowers. They prefer shade to semi-shade and to be moist but not wet. Watch for snails and give liquid feed monthly. Plants can be grown on for the following season in a shady position with occasional watering.

The long spikes of Salvia farinacea *bloom for most of the summer.*

Portulaca

Sow seed under glass in early spring and plant out in early June. The plants will flower through summer and fall but they must have a hot, sunny spot; the flowers will close in shade. Don't overwater or overfeed the plants. Aphids can be a problem.

Salvia

Many types of perennial salvia are worth considering, including variegated herbs like sage grown for their colorful foliage as well as the salvias grown for their spikes of vibrant flowers. *Salvia splendens* is usually grown as an annual and should be sown in spring for its bright scarlet summer and fall flowers. Provide a warm spot in full sun. Cut the plants back after their first flowering for a second flush of blooms.

Skimmia

Dense, bushy evergreen shrubs with glossy green leaves and clusters of red buds which make a cheery winter display. Clusters of small white flowers in spring are followed by bright red fruits on female plants. The fruits last

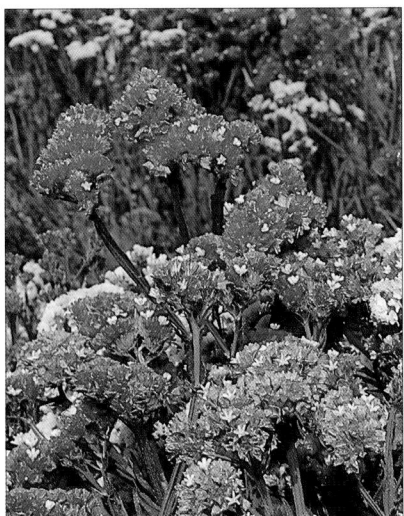

Statice is a tall grower and may need twiggy sticks for support.

Grow tall sweet peas up a tripod of light stakes, or choose a bush variety that will trail unsupported over the edge of the pot. Their scent is famous.

well, adding extra color in fall and winter containers but, except with *S. japonica* ssp. *reevsiana*, they are only produced if both male and female varieties are grown. Propagate by cuttings in late summer, and grow in shade or semi-shade in a fertile, moist mix. Too much sun or poor soil may cause yellowing of the leaves.

Snapdragon *(Antirrhinum)*

Usually grown as annuals for their spring to fall display of colorful spikes of tubular or trumpet-shaped flowers. Sow the seed indoors in spring or buy tiny plugs or young plants in bloom. The plants take four or five months from seed to flower. Provide the plants with full sun and wind protection, and feed monthly for best results. Rust can be a problem in humid conditions. Water the plants early in the day and avoid overhead watering.

Statice
(Limonium; Psylliostachys)

Statice seeds may be sown in early spring for summer and fall flowers. They need full sun and perfect drainage, and once

established will tolerate drought and salty winds. The long-lasting summer-fall blooms will dry well in the vase.

Sunflower *(Helianthus)*

Sunflowers are very easy to grow from seed sown in spring for summer or fall flowers. They can be very tall and so need wind protection and staking. They must have full sun, regular water and monthly feeding. Watch for snails which can be a problem.

Dwarf sunflowers are well below knee-height and ideal for containers.

Swan river daisy *(Brachyscome)*

This bushy annual or tender perennial, with small, daisy-like flowerheads blooms in summer and early fall and is good for pots or hanging baskets. It grows well from tip cuttings or from seed sown in spring. Provide a position in full sun, don't overwater and give little or no fertilizer. Cut back the plants after the first flowering to encourage bushy growth and continued blooming.

Sweet peas
(Lathyrus odoratus)

Sow seed of sweet peas half an inch deep in fall or spring for delightfully scented flowers from summer to early fall. Seed can be soaked overnight before sowing to aid germination. Give a good initial watering and then restrict watering until the seedlings have emerged; water regularly once the seedlings are growing strongly. Liquid feed every seven to ten days. Plant in full sun, provide support and give wind protection.

Keep picking the flowers to prolong blooming. Dwarf types such as "Bijou" are best for containers.

Verbenas are trailers and spill flowers over the lip of the container.

Clear-complexioned cousins of the pansy, violas are smaller in flower but every bit as prolific and valuable for containers. This is "Tinkerbelle."

Sweet William
(*Dianthus barbatus*)

Sow this biennial in summer for spring flowers the following year or under glass in March for flowers the same year. Grow in full sun, provide good drainage and don't overwater. Feed monthly when the plants are growing strongly. Remove spent flowers; you may get a second flush. Dwarf forms are particularly suitable for pots.

Tobacco plant (*Nicotiana*)

The flowers of the tobacco plant release a rich fragrance in the evening, and will bloom from midsummer until the first frosts. Position them near a door or window to enjoy their fragrance even when you are indoors. Sow seed in spring, and grow in sun or semi-shade in rich compost. Feed regularly or add a slow-release fertilizer to the compost. Dwarf varieties are generally best for containers, but check that the one you choose has a good fragrance as some dwarf strains have less scent.

Tulip (*Tulipa*)

Plant the bulbs 2.5in deep in fall for spring flowers. They need full sun and wind protection. Water sparingly until leaves emerge and then more regularly, but never allow the mix to be too wet. Pot-grown tulips rarely re-flower if kept in the container, but will often give a presentable display if planted out in the garden.

Verbena

Buy a collection of plug plants by mail order or buy larger plants in bloom in the spring. Clusters of small flowers on trailing stems make a bright summer display. Plant in full sun, with good drainage. Don't overwater or overfertilize. Watch for snails.

Viola

Sow seed in fall or spring for flowers in spring and summer. Pinch out the tips to encourage a

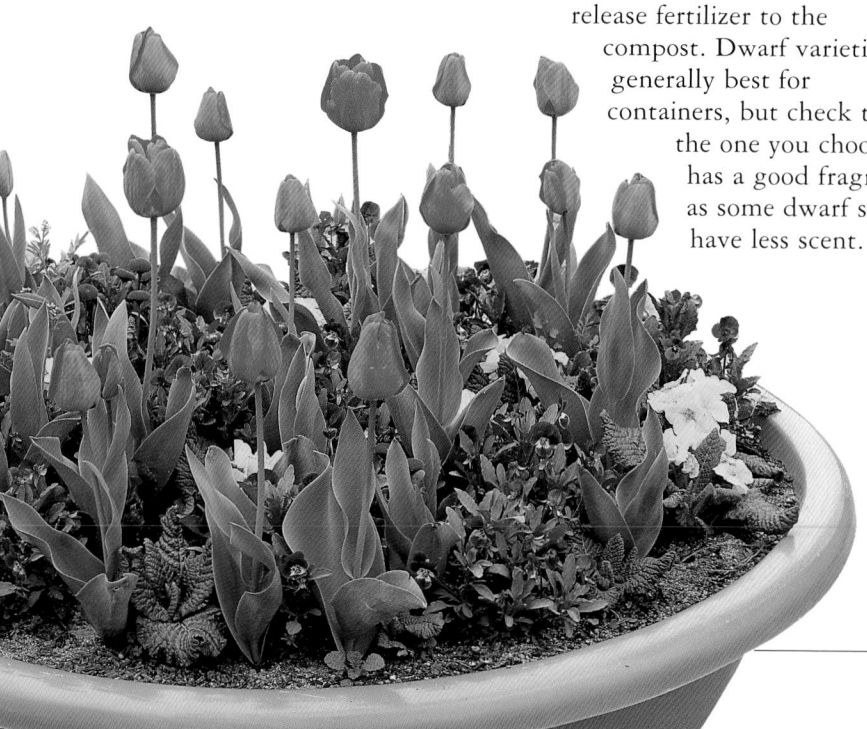

Tulips are brief in bloom; extend the season by under-planting them with annuals.

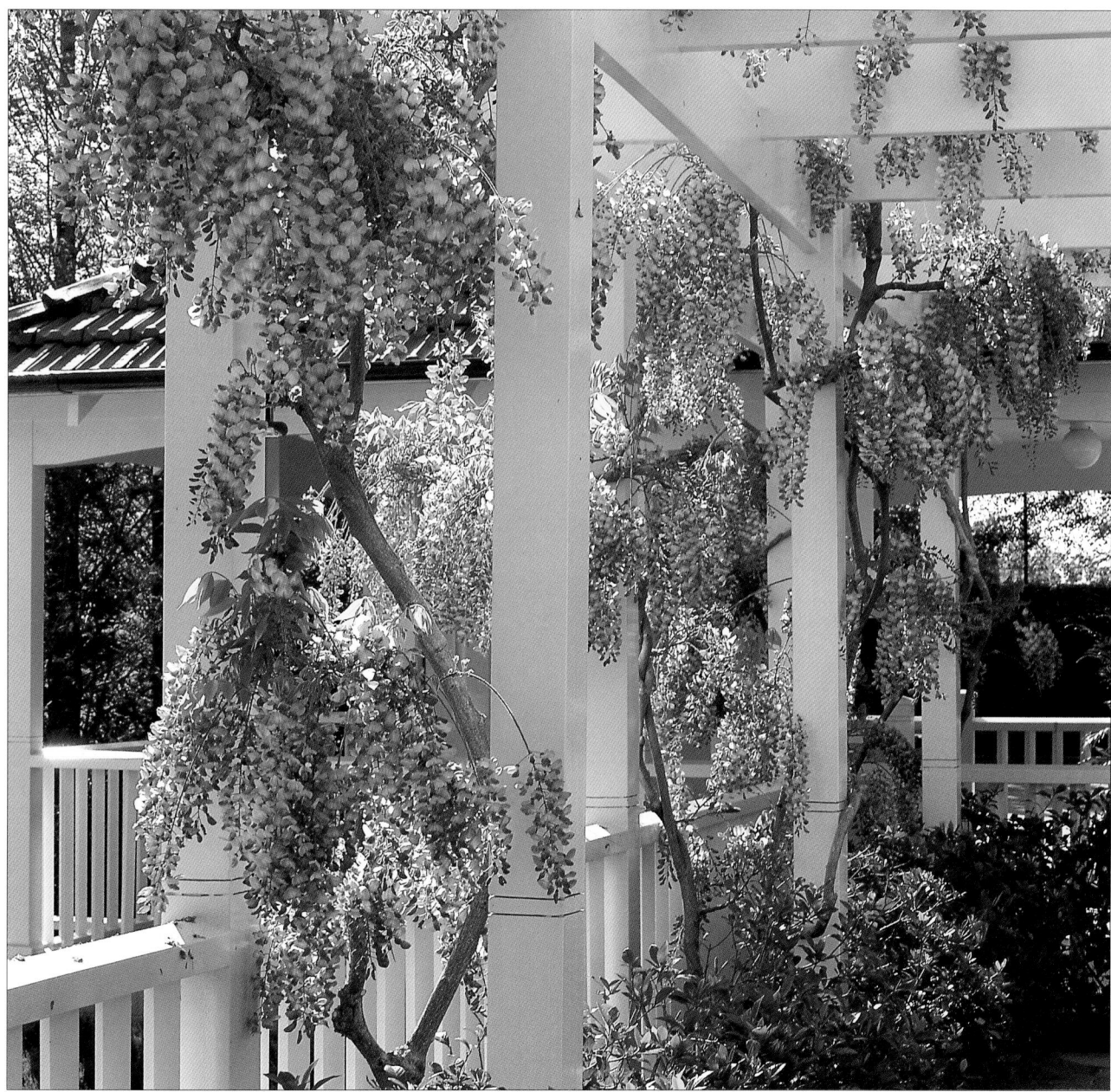

Wisteria is one of the strongest of all flowering vines, but pruning after bloom will keep it in bounds.

bushy plant. Water regularly in dry spring weather and feed regularly once established. Remove spent flowers as they fade in order to prolong the period of blooming.

Wallflower (Cheiranthus)

Propagate by seed in summer or buy plants in late summer or early fall. Wallflowers need an open, sunny spot but shelter from strong wind. The mix should be very well drained. Feed the plants about a month after setting them out. They will produce their fragrant, richly-colored flowers in the spring. The plants should be discarded after flowering.

Wisteria

A very vigorous climber with long racemes of scented, pea-like flowers in early summer, it can be trained as a standard but will otherwise need a strong support. If it is to be grown in a container wisteria will require a large tub. The plant may need cutting back several times during the growing season and careful pruning after leaf fall to encourage flowering spurs. It should be given regular summer water but it is tolerant of a wide range of conditions, although it will not flower well in shade.

Hanging baskets

Growing plants in hanging containers is a wonderful way to bring plant life to a height where it can be most appreciated. A suspended garden can also soften bare walls, hide ugly spots and provide plant interest at a number of different levels. However little space is available, there is always room for a hanging basket or two.

The traditional place to hang a basket is by a doorway where it can be seen whenever you enter or leave the house. A pair of baskets look superb either side of a front door and will create a bright welcoming effect, both for you and your visitors. They are as attractive by windows as they are by doors, and the planting can be planned to complement both windowboxes and borders.

But why stop at one or two? A row of well-filled baskets will look spectacular enough to stop passers-by in their tracks. Any bare wall or fence, shed or garage, will benefit from a display of hanging baskets, to brighten a boring area, disguise an eyesore, or create a link between different areas of the garden. Interesting effects can be achieved by hanging baskets from the branches of a tree, or, with free-standing posts and brackets, a hanging basket can be positioned anywhere you choose.

Filled with flowers, hanging baskets can be a spectacular sight in the warmer summer months and it is often assumed that hanging baskets are just for summer. There is good reason for this as the limited amount of compost the basket contains and its exposure to wind and weather from all sides makes it very vulnerable to freezing and to drying out in cold winter winds.

However, if you can give your basket a sheltered position, away from the worst of the weather, you will find that is possible to create year-round displays. While there are not as many colorful flowers readily available as there are to fill summer baskets, you will find that there are still plants that you can use in winter baskets, such as winter-flowering pansies, variegated ivies, and small shrubs, and winter heathers, and the color they provide is all the more

welcome at a time of year when there is much less color in the garden in general.

Don't forget to consider the practicalities when deciding where to hang your baskets. Don't hang them so low that you will bump your head on them, or so high that you cannot reach them. You may think they look spectacular by second-floor windows, but if you need a ladder to water and deadhead them you will soon change your mind. In any case,

You will need at least a 16-inch basket to recreate this profusion of petunias, blue scaevolas, begonias, bacopas, and fuchsias.

This ball of Begonia semperflorens matches its setting to perfection.

you can enjoy your plants more when they are placed at eye level. Although you may be tempted to hang the container in a constantly sunny position, this will probably double its water requirements. Try to position it so that it does not receive strong afternoon sun during the summer.

CHOOSING A BASKET

The look of the container used as a hanging basket is in most cases of far less importance than with other types of container as the aim with most hanging baskets is that the plants, when fully grown, should completely cover the basket.

Once all that was available were wire baskets that we lined with sphagnum moss, and later fiber or foam liners. They were followed by plastic containers with drip trays. Today we can find a wonderful range of containers in a great variety of materials, from elegant dark green metal baskets to large flower balls with interchangeable pots. You can also buy self-watering hanging pots that allow the plants to draw

A predominance of lobelia and ivy-leaved geraniums give a light, airy feel.

exactly the amount of water they need from the built-in reservoir in the base of the container.

If your basket will show through the planting, choose one in a complementary color and style. Some modern designs will even look decorative when empty and can be left in place between plantings. Unconventional baskets, from wicker baskets to old kettles and colanders, can also look very effective.

Baskets can be purchased in various sizes. Choose the largest that is practical (14-inch diameter and upwards), as larger baskets hold more compost and dry out less rapidly, making it easier to grow healthy, good-looking plants.

SUPPORTING HANGING BASKETS

When you select a hanging basket or wall container, give thought to its weight when full of plants and potting mix. Remember, too, that a container is going to take lots of water in the course of its life—think carefully about where you put it so it has adequate support, is easily accessible and will not drip on passers-by.

The most common and simplest method of supporting baskets is with wall-mounted brackets or hooks that have been designed for the purpose. Make sure that they are strong enough to take the weight of the basket when it is full of potting compost and plants and that they are securely attached. When choosing a bracket make sure that the arm is longer than half the diameter of the basket, otherwise the basket and plants will be damaged by catching against the wall.

Shop around to find brackets that are attractively designed, or at the very least will not stand out from the display like a sore thumb.

The bracket will need to take a lot of weight so make sure it is attached securely to a solid, flat surface with the correct length and gauge of screws. It is worth checking occasionally to make sure that the screws have not worked loose.

Heavy-duty hooks are also available so that baskets can be hung overhead from wooden porches or balconies. These should be strongly made with a metal plate to prevent the screws from splitting the wood.

PLANTING A HANGING GARDEN

There are potting composts available specifically for hanging baskets, although any proprietary potting compost can be used. If weight is a problem, peat or peat substitute composts are lighter, but don't forget that they are difficult to re-wet once they have dried out. Adding some vermiculite to the mix will help minimize the weight. To help retain moisture, mix some water-retaining granules with the compost before planting. A slow-release fertilizer can also be mixed in to avoid the need for weekly feeding.

To make planting easier, place the container in the mouth of a bucket or large pot to hold it steady while you are making up your arrangement. Line the basket with sphagnum moss or with a foam or fiber or other synthetic liner. If using moss, add an inner plastic lining, making holes in it for drainage. Fill the basket to about one-third full with potting compost and insert the first layer of plants. Make slits in the liner first, if necessary, then thread small plants through and anchor them firmly by packing more compost around the roots. Add more compost and more plants around the sides of the basket, planting up the top of the basket last. Add taller more upright plants in the centre of the basket, and trailing plants around the edge.

Do not skimp on the number of plants or the basket will look thin and unimpressive. In fact, it may be best to err on the side of overplanting when it comes to hanging baskets as they look most spectacular when over-flowing with flowers and foliage.

If possible, immerse the planted container in water for

PREPARING A HANGING BASKET

Stand basket in a pot and line basket.

Add a plastic lining or drip tray and some potting mix.

Remove plants from pots and place in basket, keeping root balls intact. Start at edges.

Add potting mix to fill air pockets, firming gently, and finish with taller plants in the center. Water well.

half an hour or so to ensure the new soil is completely moist. Drain well before hanging the basket in its final position.

WATERING AND FEEDING

The limited size of hanging baskets, and their greater exposure to the weather, means that they tend to demand more care and attention than other types of container, and that they cannot be left unattended for any length of time. However, planted well, and regularly fed, watered

and deadheaded, a hanging basket should look good throughout the summer months.

In the weeks after planting, water the basket regularly, particularly in dry, windy weather. Because a large number of plants are sharing a limited amount of compost, they will take up water and nutrients far more rapidly than in a larger container and daily watering may be needed on hot summer days. "Self-watering" containers, with a reservoir of water for the plants to draw on, will mean that you

White trellis cut-outs make a clever frame for this free-standing basket.

need to water less frequently. Should a hanging container completely dry out it may be difficult to re-wet the soil. Take the container down, stand it in a sink or bucket of water and allow it to soak for half an hour. It will then be well wetted and can be put back in position.

It is essential to position your basket where there is safe and easy access or you will soon tire of struggling to water it every day, and the display will suffer. Where the basket is easily accessible, you can take the basket down before watering and feeding and allow it to drain before replacing it. If a basket can be watered from a window or balcony, this will make the job easier. Various hose extensions and pump watering systems can be purchased from garden centers and shops to make reaching high baskets easier. Some baskets can be raised up and down by a pulley system which makes maintenance easier, but you should take care to choose one where the pulley

mechanism is easy to use and does not detract from the display. Perhaps the easiest system of all, if the most expensive, is to install an automatic drip watering system, linked to an outdoor tap. By adding one of the sophisticated "water computers" now available, your hanging

Thoughtful planting and regular care will give you a stunning basket like this.

baskets can even be watered while you are away.

A couple of weeks after planting, start to feed with a liquid fertilizer. A high potash feed, such as tomato fertilizer, will encourage flowering, high nitrogen feeds are good for foliage, and a balanced fertilizer is best for mixed plantings. Feed weekly, following the manufacturer's directions. Only apply fertilizer when the plants are in active growth and when the soil is moist after watering. Alternatively, insert a slow-release fertilizer into the compost before planting. Check the instructions to be sure how long each type will last. Although many will last a whole summer, others will need to be supplemented at intervals.

PLANTS FOR A HANGING BASKET

Hanging baskets hold so little compost, and are dried out so quickly by the sun and the wind, that it is worth choosing plants that are tolerant of drying out occasionally.

The most appropriate plants are either those with a neat, mounded growing habit or those that trail. Upright plants, such as fuchsias and pelargoniums, can be grown in the top of a basket, but avoid anything that grows too tall. A basket can accommodate a large number of plants for its relative size and it looks all the better for being crowded. Pick plants with a long flowering season to avoid the need to replant. There are lots of proven old favorites to choose from, including begonias, busy lizzies, creeping Jenny, fuchsias, helichrysum, ivy-leaved pelargoniums, ivies, lobelias, mimulus, nasturtiums, petunias, tradescantias, and trailing verbenas. Decide whether you will hang your basket in sun or shade and choose your plants accordingly. Busy lizzies, mimulus, begonias, pansies, and ivies, for example, are ideal for a shady basket.

It seems that most people still aim for a "riot of color" when planting their baskets, and certainly brightly colored mixed plantings look stunningly effective, but single color schemes can also look very striking, as can simple combinations of two or three complementary shades. Simple baskets of evergreen foliage such as variegated ivies can have a stylish effect and will last all year round. Consider, too, the background against which the plants will hang. For example, some colors will clash with bright red brickwork, and white flowers will stand out well against almost everything except a white wall.

Herbs also grow well in hanging gardens. Oregano, mints, thyme, and prostrate rosemary are all generous spill-over plants that will soon cover most of the container. Upright herbs such as parsley, sage, basil and sorrel can be planted in the center. Herbs can also make a very pleasing combination when planted with flowers.

BAGS, POUCHES AND SOCKS

The most recent additions to the range of hanging containers are re-usable bags, pouches, and socks. Easy to use, they add another dimension to hanging displays. In their simplest form these are long, narrow bags made of strong, plastic with slits in one side for planting and handles at the top for hanging them up.

This basket is watered daily by an automatic pipe and drip system.

Flanking baskets and tubs and an overhead trough make this a very welcoming doorway.

Other types are more elaborate, allowing planting all round and incorporating a water reservoir. Simple but effective, they are filled with compost, which can be mixed with water-retaining granules and slow-release fertilizer, and planted through the slits in the sides with young plants of all sorts of summer bedding, and even strawberries or plants for winter displays. They can be hung anywhere a basket can be hung, and look quite spectacular when covered with blooms.

Windowboxes

Wherever you may live, nothing brightens the look of a house as much as well-planted windowboxes or hanging baskets, brimming with colorful flowers or cool, fresh foliage.

Although they are particularly valuable for town and city dweller who have little or no garden, windowboxes will enhance the look of any house, brightening dull expanses of brick and stone, lighting dark corners, softening hard lines, and creating an attractive and welcoming appearance that will bring

pleasure not only to you but also to your guests and passers-by. Even if you put your windowboxes in the back garden where they will be for your eyes only, they can bring year-round pleasure for relatively little cost and effort.

To get the most enjoyment from your boxes, position them where you will see them most often, either at the front of the house where you will see them as you come and go each day, or outside a window you look out of frequently, such as that of the

kitchen or living room, so that you can enjoy the display from inside the house as well, whatever the weather.

CHOOSING A WINDOWBOX

One of the first steps is to choose an appropriate style of container. The best windowboxes are those that are not there just to hold the plants that grow in them but to enhance their appearance. Unless completely hidden by the planting, they will make their own contribution to the display, and should be chosen to complement the window and the general architecture of the house as well as the plants. Consider the style and color of the background against which they will be seen. An overly ornate formal box, or one painted in bold, brash colors would look out of place against a rustic cottage, for example. However, while many gardeners prefer boxes of simple, clean lines, in natural colors, there is lots of scope for those who prefer more individual designs.

If you are looking for inspiration, take a look at other windowboxes in your neighborhood to see which styles you think work successfully, and to discover which plants grow well in your area.

SIZE

It is important that the container should be in proportion to the window and to the plants growing in it. The best looking boxes are generally those that fill the space available, so look for a

Give your window a complete makeover with a color co-ordinated hanging basket to match the windowbox, and a climber to frame the scene.

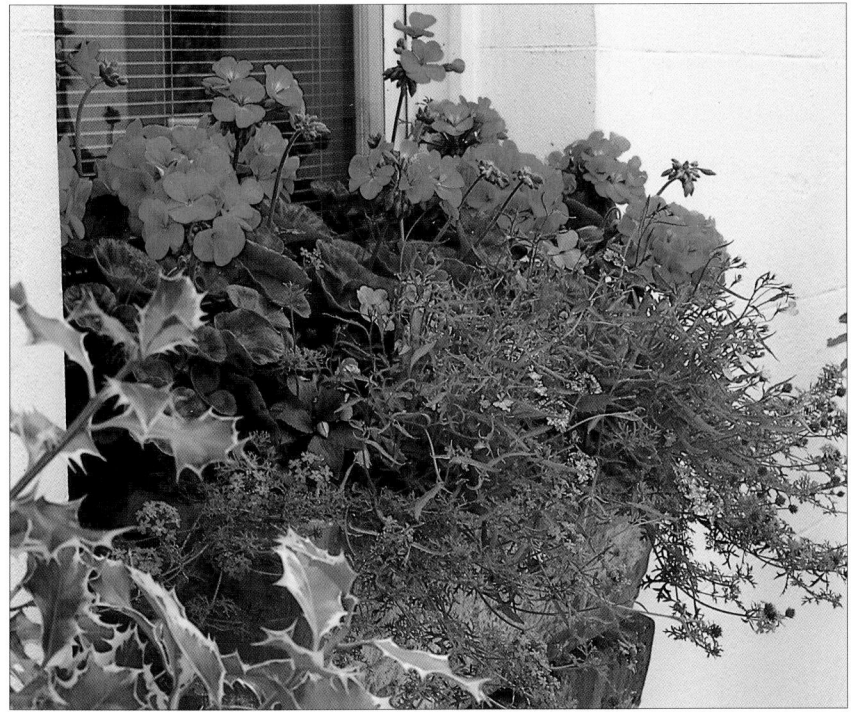

Geraniums and verbenas always look bright and fresh against a white wall.

box that is as large as the window ledge will allow. If the box is too small for the ledge it will look lost and out of place. Large boxes are also more practical than smaller ones, as they hold more compost and more plants, and will not dry out as rapidly. And where the windowbox is easily accessible from the street, large, tightly-fitting boxes are less likely to be stolen than small, more portable ones. Avoid very shallow containers too as these will dry out very fast and need more frequent watering. The larger and deeper the box, the easier it is to grow healthy and attractive plants. Ideally boxes should be at least 8in deep, and anything less than 6in is not advisable for most plants.

If your sill is very narrow, don't feel that you can only have a very narrow box. It is quite practical for the box to be a little wider than the ledge or to be attached below rather than on the ledge, as long as it is well secured. If your sill is of an unusual shape or size, you don't need to make do with a hotch-potch of odd-sized containers as it is relatively simple to make a tailor-made wooden box to fit exactly, and this will be much more effective. An alternative is to make a fake windowbox, by fixing a "front" across the sill, behind which you can stand containers of all shapes and sizes but still have a co-ordinated look from the front.

COLOR

The color of the box can be chosen to be a subdued background for the plants or to be a bold and integral part of the display. Boxes can be chosen, or painted, to blend—or contrast with—the background of the house. For a co-ordinated effect, the box can be chosen to match the paintwork of windows and doors, or to blend with the walls. This can be particularly effective where the box is fixed below the window and you want it to blend with, rather than stand out from, the background.

SUNNY POSITION	SHADY POSITION
Brachyscome	Ageratum
Calendula, dwarf	Begonia, bedding
Chives	Box
Chrysanthemum, dwarf	Busy lizzie (Impatiens)
Dianthus	Cyclamen
Felicia	Euonymus
Fuchsia	Ferns
Heliotrope	Forget-me-not
Marigold, French	Holly
Nemesia	Ivy
Pansy	Mint
Pelargoniums	Pansy
Petunia	Parsley
Rosemary	Polyanthus
Salvia	Primula
Silver foliage plants	Skimmia
Tagetes	Vinca
Thyme	
Tomatoes, cherry	
Verbena	

MATERIALS

The most widely available types of windowbox are those made of plastic. They are cheap, light and easy to handle, and they do not dry out as rapidly as other materials such as terracotta, but are perhaps the least attractive of the materials available. However, that said, modern plastics and modern designs are much improved and there is now a wide range available. If your sills will not take a lot of weight, plastic is often the best choice and requires less support.

Fiberglass is also a good choice where weight could be a limiting factor. And as well as being light in weight it is tough and long-lasting and can be made to imitate other materials such as stone and can be molded into interesting shapes.

Stone itself is far too heavy for most windowsills, as are reconstituted stone, concrete, and lead. However, if you have a position that will tolerate the weight, both stone and lead make very attractive, long-lasting, and maintenance-free containers.

Terracotta troughs make attractive windowboxes, but are fragile and must be very securely attached. Make sure you choose one that is frost-proof if you plan to leave it outdoors all year round, and remember that

A windowbox display can be designed to blend in with the planting in the border below, either by using the same plants or by using a complementary color scheme.

PLANTING BULBS IN WINDOWBOXES

BULB	DEPTHS
Anemone	1½in
Bluebells	2in
Daffodils	4in
Dutch iris	1½in
Freesia	1in
Grape hyacinth	1½in
Hyacinth	4in
Ranunculus	1in
Tulip	4in

terracotta containers dry out quickly and will need more frequent watering.

Timber is one of the most popular choices for windowboxes, either leaving the natural grain of the wood to form part of the display, or painting and decorating it to match the surroundings. It is relatively inexpensive, particularly if you make your own boxes, and is light enough for most windowsills. One drawback is that wood has to be treated with a horticultural preservative or painted every 2 or 3 years otherwise it will rot. Although you can plant directly into wooden boxes it best to use a plastic liner to protect the wood.

ATTACHING A WINDOWBOX

Make sure the sill is structurally sound and will take the weight of the box, and freshen up any paintwork before you attach the box. Check which way the window opens, and take care to position the box so that it will not prevent it from opening.

Windowboxes can be positioned not only on the sill, but also below the sill or even above the window, as long as there is easy access to the box for watering and maintenance.

Whatever style of box you choose, it must be securely attached to the wall or sill. This is particularly important on

This windowbox is given added support by Fuchsia "Thalia" rising up from a container placed below it.

upstairs windowsills, and where people will pass by beneath the box. When full, a box is very heavy and could cause serious damage or injury if it fell.

Even if the windowsill is deep enough for the box simply to sit on the sill, it is best to secure it to ensure that it cannot be knocked off accidentally. This can be done with safety chains, wires or brackets, or by a hook and eye attachment which makes it easier to remove the box for maintenance. Some sills slope, and in such cases wedges should be placed under the front of the box to ensure it is level. For a more decorative effect, ornamental "rails" can be attached across the ledge in front of the box.

If the ledge is narrow or non-existent the box should be attached to the wall below the window with sturdy brackets. When choosing brackets, bear in mind the weight as well as the size of the box. Fix the brackets to the wall by drilling holes in the wall using a power drill with a masonry bit, and using wall plugs and screws.

PLANTING UP A WINDOWBOX

Position your windowbox before filling it with soil and adding the plants. Include only those plants that require similar amounts of water, fertilizer and sun and the same soil conditions.

Drainage is important, especially if a box is exposed to the rain, so whichever type of box you choose it should have drainage holes in the base. The box should not sit directly on a flat surface but should be raised up on blocks or small "feet"

otherwise water may not be able to escape through the drainage holes. Make sure there is a good layer of crocks or other drainage material in the base.

Fill the box just over half full with compost. Soil-less, peat-based compost is best for fast-growing temporary plantings and is lighter and easy to work, but for long-term permanent plantings a good soil-based compost is better, as it retains water and nutrients longer. Position the plants and fill in with compost to about 1in from the top of the box, firm well and water.

Don't skimp on the planting if you want a luxuriant display, but do not cram the plants in so tight there is no room for root growth. As well as putting plants for long-term or permanent displays directly into the box, you can also put pots of plants inside the box, packing peat or a lightweight "plunge" material around them to disguise the inner pots and help keep the plants moist and cool. If you water the peat at the same time as the pots, it will also provide a reservoir of moisture for the plants to draw on and reduce the frequency of watering required.

Another advantage of using pots

or removable liners is that you can always have the next season's display growing on in readiness for when the present display has finished. It is then a simple matter to swap the pots or liners over, and you will have a display that always looks at its best.

CARE AND MAINTENANCE

To keep a windowbox looking good, it will require regular attention. Pick off all finished flowers and prune any plants that become leggy or straggly.

Water the plants carefully for the first few weeks until they are established. A light mulch will help to conserve moisture. Windowboxes dry out rapidly, so it is essential to remember to water: in summer this might mean every day. Aim to keep the soil just moist, but not soggy. Try to water your boxes when they are out of direct sunlight, preferably in the early morning or evening.

Windowbox plants will need regular feeding. Use a slow-release fertilizer for long-term plantings, or diluted liquid plant food for annuals and vegetables, beginning about a month after planting and continuing every 1–2 weeks. Do not apply fertilizers to dry soils.

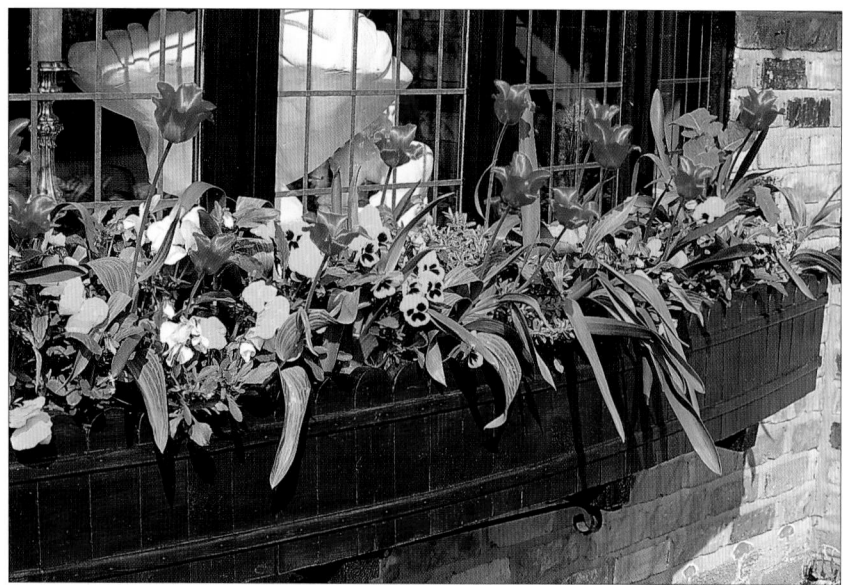

This custom-made box fits perfectly around a bay window.

Tulips and pansies are followed by non-stop begonias and surfinia petunias.

SELECTING PLANTS FOR WINDOWBOXES

The key to a beautiful and healthy windowbox display is choosing suitable plants for your particular position. It is, of course, essential to choose plants that like the same conditions of soil, climate and aspect for each box. For example, which direction does the box face? Will it be in sun or shade for most of the day? In the box on page 791 are some favorite windowbox plants, listed according to whether they prefer a sunny or shady position. When planning your display, it can be helpful to look at other boxes in your neighborhood to give you an idea of which plants are most successful in your area.

The plants chosen should be in proportion to the container and to the window, and should complement the house and the surrounding planting. If you have a border below the window, you may choose to echo the border planting in the windowbox, to choose complementary plants and colors, or perhaps to create a complete contrast.

Some gardeners like changing seasonal schemes, such as spring bulbs followed by summer bedding then winter heathers, while others prefer a fairly permanent year-round scheme based on evergreen perennials. Seasonal schemes can involve more work, planning and replanting, but will reward you with a constant succession of color through the year.

Permanent schemes require less work but tend to be rather less colorful, although a careful choice of foliage plants combined with plants that produce flowers and berries at different times of year can also make an attractive year-round display.

If you have more than one box you can compromise by having both seasonal and permanent displays, or if you have a large box, it is possible to have a background of a permanent planting of evergreens to which you can add seasonal display of colorful flowers. These can either be planted directly into the box or to make it simpler to swop them over they can be placed in small pots which can be

exchanged for new ones as soon as the flowers are over.

Unless you particularly want to screen an ugly view from the window you will need to select low-growing plants that will not obstruct either the view or the light entering the room, or prevent the window being opened. Boxes positioned on the wall under the sill offer an advantage here, allowing you to grow taller plants without causing obstruction.

For many windows, therefore, tall plants are best grown to one or both sides of the windowbox. If you want to add extra height, climbers are also useful positioned at the ends of a box where they can be trained to grow up and around the window. The design should, of course, be tailored to suit the size of the window, larger windows being able to accommodate a much wider range of plants without causing too much obstruction.

Trailers, like climbers, will add another dimension to the display. Plant them around the edges of the box where they can drape over the sides, and either allow them to tumble freely for an informal effect, or keep them lightly trimmed for a more tailored look.

Summer bedding is still the most popular choice for a windowbox display and there is an enormous range of flowers to choose from, providing long-lasting bright color, often from late spring until early fall. There are plants to suit both sunny and shady boxes, and they can be used in many ways. A box planted with a single variety can have as striking an effect in its simplicity as a mixed planting where different types of flowers and foliage intermingle.

Color, too, is an important consideration, blending or contrasting with the background of the container and the building. Depending on your personal taste you could choose a single color scheme with lots of impact, a subtle blend of harmonious tones, or a vibrant patchwork of bright colors—they can all be equally effective in the appropriate setting.

Don't just rely on flowers for color though. There are many attractive foliage plants with leaves in colors such as silver, gold, yellow, cream, white, pink, purple, or blue which will provide even longer lasting color than the flowers. Color theming with foliage plants can be especially effective in a winter windowbox when there are fewer flowers to choose from.

Foliage plants are also useful for adding that other essential, shape, to a windowbox design. Trained topiary specimens or spiky yuccas, for example, are perfect for setting off formal designs. Plants with different leaf shapes and textures can be used

For sheer flower power, line up hyacinths behind mixed winter heathers.

to create variety and interest. Low-growing foliage plants are also excellent for filling in around the base of the display, to cover the bare compost.

Even edible plants can be grown in a windowbox, from radish and baby carrots to colorful herbs such as variegated sages and thymes. A windowbox with a variety of herbs at a sunny kitchen window is beautiful to look at as well as very convenient if you want to pick a sprig or two while you are cooking.

Many herbs have a wonderful scent too, and fragrance is something that should not be ignored when considering windowbox plants, as the scent will waft into the house whenever you open the windows.

A final point to consider is that there can be a pollution problem if you have a windowbox near a busy town or city thoroughfare. Try growing plants that will

Spring miniatures in white and cream combine in a color-themed display.

tolerate some air pollution such as ivies, rhododendrons and azaleas, polyanthus, dianthus, and bulbs. You can help your plants by cleaning the grime off shiny-leaved evergreens, and making sure the potting mix does not become too acid.

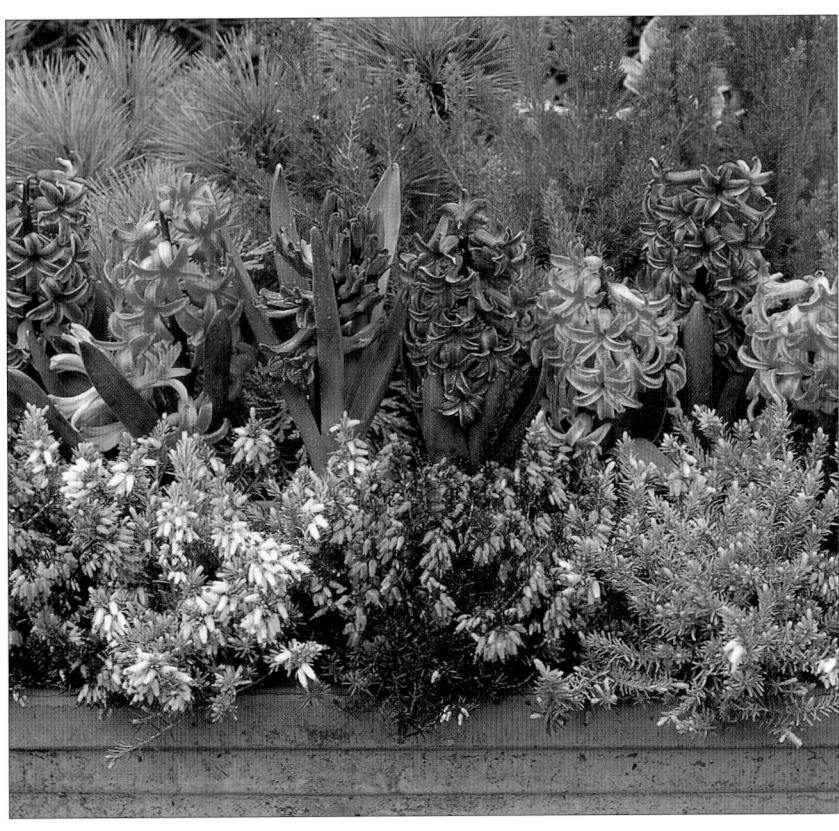

INDEX

Abelia	338	Ballota	617	Cereus	474
Abelia x grandiflora	578	Barberry	342	Chaenomeles speciosa	584, 696
Abutilon	128, 339	Begonia	135	Chamaedorea elegans	659
Abutilon megapotamicum	692	Begonia	244	Chamaerops humilis	660
Acacia	579	Bellis	136	Cheiranthus	147
Acanthus mollis	22	Berberidopsis corallina	695	Chicory	431
Achillea	23	Berberis thunbergii	580	Chionodoxa	247
Achimenes	236	Bergamot	428	Chives	432
Aechmea	556	Bergenia	34	Chrysanthemum Hybrids	37
Agapanthus	24, 237	Bergenia ciliata	618	Clematis	697
Agrostemma	130	Bifrenaria	518	Cleome	148
Ajuga reptans	611	Billbergia	559	Cleistocactus	475
Akebia quinata	693	Bletilla	519	Clianthus puniceus	699
Alcea	131	Borage	429	Clivia miniata	248
Alchemilla	426	Bottlebrush	346	Colchicum autumnale	249
Alchemilla mollis	25, 612	Brachyscome	137	Comfrey	434
Allium	238	Brassica	138	Consolida	149
Alstroemeria	26, 239	Brassia	520	Convallaria	39
Amaranthus	132	Broom	361	Convallaria majalis	250
Amaryllis belladonna	240	Browallia	139	Coral Berry	341
Ananas	558	Butia capitata	658	Coreopsis	40, 150
Anemone	241, 613	Butterfly bush	343	Corydalis	41
Anemone x hybrida	27	Buxus	581	Cosmos	151
Anguloa	516			Cotoneaster	359
Anise Hyssop	427	Calceolaria	140	Cotoneaster simonsii	585
Anthemis tinctoria	614	Calendula	141, 448	Crassula	494
Anomatheca	243	Californian Lilac	351	Crassula arborescens	495
Antirrhinum	133	Callistephus	142	Crinum	251
Aporocactus	472	Calluna vulgaris	619	Crocosmia	252
Aquilegia	28	Camassia	245	Crocus	253
Arabis caucasica	615	Camellia	347, 350	Cyclamen	255
Arctotis	134	Camellia sasanqua	582	Cymbidium	522
Aristolochia	694	Campanula	35, 143, 620	Cynara cardunculus	42
Armeria maritima	29, 616	Canna	246	Cyrtanthus elatus	257
Aspasia	517	Cape Leadwort	396		
Aster	30	Carpinus betulus	583		
Astilbe hybrids	31	Catharanthus	144	Dahlia	152, 258
Astrantia major	32	Catmint	430	Dandelion	435
Astrophytum	473	Celosia	145	Daphne	362
Aurinia saxatilis	33	Centaurea	146	Decumaria barbara	700
		Centranthus ruber	36	Delphinium	43, 153
		Cerastium tomentosum	621	Dendrobium	526, 528

Deutzia	363	Fig-leaved Palm	370	Honeysuckle	385
Dianthus barbatus	154	Firethorn	400	Hosta	63
Dianthus caryophyllus	44	Flowering Dogwood	357	Hosta "Francee"	626
Dianthus chinensis	155	Freesia	265	Houttuynia cordata	627
Dianthus Cultivars	45	Fremontodendron	703	Howea forsteriana	661
Dianthus deltoides	622	Fritillaria	266	Hyacinthoides	275
Diascia	46			Hyacinthus orientalis	276
Dicentra spectabilis	47	Galanthus	268	Hydrangea	378
Dierama pulcherrimum	260	Gazania	160	Hymenocallis	280
Digitalis	48, 156	Genista	372	Hyssop	440
Dill	436	Geranium	54, 624		
Disa	530	Geum chiloense	55	Iberis	167
Dorotheanthus	157	Gladiolus callianthus	269	Ilex aquifolium	590
		Gladiolus hybrids	270	Impatiens	168
Echinacea purpurea	49	Gloriosa	272	Ipheion uniflorum	281
Echinocereus	476	Godetia	161	Ipomoea	169
Echinops	50	Golden Bell Bush	371	Iris—bulbous types	282
Elaeagnus pungens	586	Gomphrena	162	Iris—rhizomatous types	284
Elder	437	Gongora	535	Iris unguicularis	285
Encyclia	531	Gunnera manicata	56	Ixia	286
Epidendrum	532	Guzmania	560		
Epimedium	51	Gypsophila	163	Japonica	353
Epiphyllum	477	Gypsophila paniculata	57	Jasmine	380
Eranthis	261			Jasminum	706
Eria	534	Hatiora salicornioides	478	Jubaea chilensis	662
Erica carnea	623	Hawthorn	360		
Eremurus	262	Heath	365	Kalanchoe blossfeldiana	498
Eryngium	52	Hebe hulkeana	704	Kerria	381
Erythronium	263	Hedera helix	625	Kniphofia	65
Escallonia	367	Hedychium	273	Kochia	170
Escallonia "Edinensis"	587	Helenium autumnale	58		
Eschscholzia	158	Helianthus	164	Lachenalia aloides	287
Eucomis comosa	264	Helichrysum	165	Laelia	536
Euonymus fortunei	588	Heliotrope	376	Lamium	628
Euonymus japonicus	589	Helipterum	166	Lampranthus	499
Euphorbia	53, 159	Helleborus	59	Lathyrus	171
Euphorbia caput-medusae	496	Hemerocallis	60	Lavandula	591
Euphorbia milii	497	Herb Robert	439	Lavender	382, 441
		Heuchera sanguinea	62	Lavatera	172
Fallopia baldschuanica	701	Hibiscus	377	Lemon Verbena	442
X Fatshedera lizei	702	Hippeastrum	274	Lepanthopsis	537
Feverfew	438	Holboellia latifolia	705	Leucanthemum	66

Leucojum	288	Moraea	291	Phlox paniculata	85
Lewesia	500	Muscari	292	Phlox subulata	634
Ligularia	67	Myosotis	184	Phoenix canariensis	664
Ligustrum ovalifolium	592			Phoenix roebelenii	665
Lilium	289	Narcissus	293	Photinia	393, 595
Limnanthes	173	Nasturtium	443	Physostegia virginiana	86
Limonium	174	Nemesia	185	Pieris	394
Limonium latifolium	68	Nemophila	186	Pileostegia viburnoides	712
Linaria	175	Neoregelia	561	Pinks	447
Liriope muscari	69	Nepeta x faassenii	631	Platycodon	87
Lithodora diffusa	629	Nerine	299	Pleione	544
Lithops	501	New Zealand Tea tree	384	Polianthes tuberosa	302
Livistona chinensis	663	Nicotiana	187	Polygonatum	88
Lobelia	176	Nigella	188	Pomegranate	399
Lobelia cardinalis	70			Portulaca	196
Lobularia	177	Odontoglossum	540	Potentilla	89
Lonicera	708	Oenothera	80, 444	Potentilla fruticosa	596
Lonicera nitida	593	Oleander	390	Pride of Madeira	364
Loosestrife	74	Olearia x haastii	594	Primula	197
Lunaria	178	Opuntia	481	Primula vulgaris	90
Lupinus	179	Ornamental Cherry	397	Primula Species	91
Lupinus polyphyllus	71	Ornithogalum	300	Prunus laurocerasus	597
Lycaste	538	Osmanthus	391	Pulmonaria	92, 635
Lychnis coronaria	72	Osteospermum	189	Pulsatilla vulgaris	93
Lysimachia nummularia	630	Oxalis	301	Puya	563
Lysimachia punctata	73			Pyracantha	598
		Pachysandra terminalis	632		
Magnolia	386	Paeonia	81	Ranunculus	94, 198
Mahonia	388	Papaver nudicaule	190	Ranunculus asiaticus	303
Malcolmia	180	Papaver orientale	83	Reseda	199
Mammillaria	479	Papaver rhoeas	191	Ribes	407
Masdevallia	539	Parodia	483	Ricinus	200
Matthiola	181	Parsley	445	Rhapis excelsa	666
Meconopsis	75	Passiflora caerulea	710	Rhododendron	401, 403, 599
Melianthus major	76	Pelargonium	192	Rhodohypoxis baurii	304
Mexican Orange Blossom	354	Pelargonium oblongatum	502	Rock Rose	355
Mimulus	77, 182	Penstemon	84	Rodgersia	95
Miscanthus sinensis	78	Periploca graeca	711	Romneya coulteri	96
Mock Orange	392	Persicaria affinis	633	Romulea	305
Moluccella	183	Petunia	193	Rosa	408, 713
Monarda didyma	79	Phlox	195	Rosa gallica	449

Rosa hybrids	636	Sparaxis tricolor	309	Viola cornuta	214
Rosa rugosa	600	Spiraea	415	Viola hederacea	647
Rosemary	450	Sprekelia formosissima	310	Viola odorata	111
Rosmarinus	412, 601	Spurge	368	Viola tricolor	215
Rosmarinus officinalis	637	Stachys byzantina	104, 641	Viola wittrockiana	216
Rossioglossum	546	Stanhopea	547	Violet	459
Rubus henryi	715	Stauntonia hexaphylla	719	Vitis	721
Rudbeckia	97, 201	Sternbergia lutea	311	Vriesea	565
		Stokesia laevis	105		
Sabal palmetto	667	Sun Rose	375	Washingtonia	669
Sacred Bamboo	389	Symphytum officinale	642	Watsonia	321
Sage	452	Syringa	416	Weigela	418
Salpiglossis	202			Wisteria	419, 722
Salvia	98, 203	Tagetes	208	Wormwood	460
Santolina	413	Taxus baccata	602		
Saponaria	638	Thalictrum	106	Yarrow	461
Sarcococca	414	Thunbergia	209		
Savory	454	Thyme	456	Zantedeschia	322
Saxifraga x urbium	639	Thymus	643	Zephyranthes	323
Scabiosa	100, 204	Tiarella	107	Zinnia	217
Schisandra chinensis	716	Tiarella wherryi	644		
Schizanthus	205	Tigridia pavonia	312		
Schizophragma	717	Tillandsia	564		
Schizostylis coccinea	306	Tithonia	210		
Schlumbergera	484	Torenia	211		
Scilla	307	Trachelospermum	720		
Sedum	503	Trachycarpus fortunei	668		
Sedum spectabile	101	Tradescantia	108		
Selenicereus	485	Trillium	109, 313		
Senecio	206	Tritonia	315		
Shrubby Bindweed	356	Tropaeolum	212		
Shrubby Cinquefoil	395	Tulbaghia violacea	316		
Shrubby Veronica	374	Tulipa	317		
Silver Wattle	340				
Sinningia	308	Valerian	458		
Sisyrinchium	102	Verbascum	110		
Smoke Bush	358	Verbena	213		
Solanum	718	Veronica	645		
Solidago	103	Viburnum	417		
Solenostemon	207	Viburnum tinus	603		
Soleirolia soleirolii	640	Vinca minor	646		

First published in 2001 by
Murdoch Books UK Ltd
Ferry House, 51–57 Lacy Road
Putney, London, SW15 1PR
Reprinted 2002, 2003 twice, 2004,
2006

ISBN 1-74045-922-9

All text, photographs and design
©Copyright Murdoch Books UK Ltd

Design and Editorial by
Prima Creative Services

CEO: Juliet Rogers
Publisher: Kay Scarlett

Colour separation by
Colourscan, Singapore
Printed and bound by
Sing Cheong Printing Co. Ltd.
Printed in China

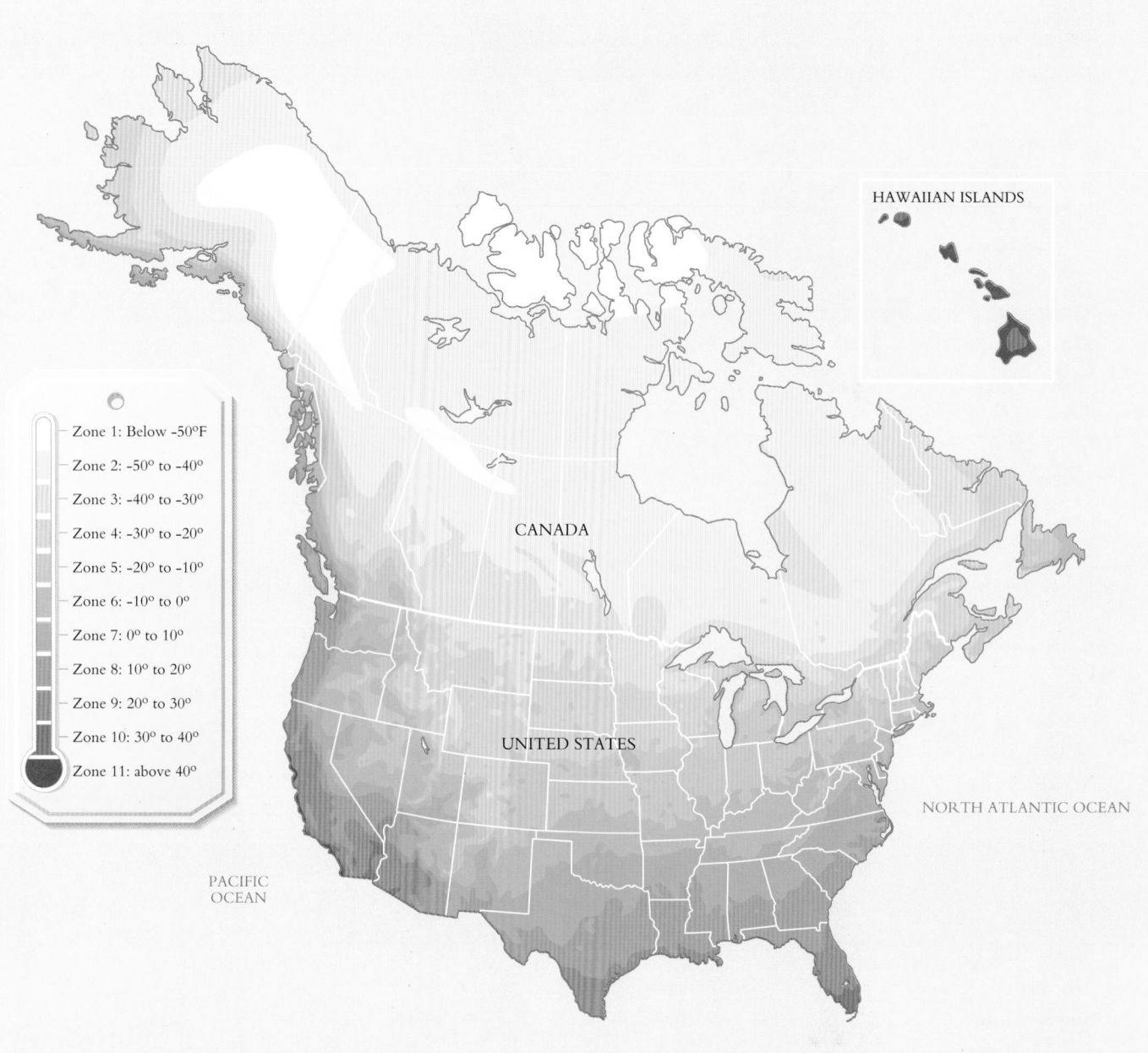

HAWAIIAN ISLANDS

Zone 1: Below -50°F
Zone 2: -50° to -40°
Zone 3: -40° to -30°
Zone 4: -30° to -20°
Zone 5: -20° to -10°
Zone 6: -10° to 0°
Zone 7: 0° to 10°
Zone 8: 10° to 20°
Zone 9: 20° to 30°
Zone 10: 30° to 40°
Zone 11: above 40°

CANADA

UNITED STATES

NORTH ATLANTIC OCEAN

PACIFIC
OCEAN